REMEDIES Cases and Materials in Australian Private Law

Remedies Cases and Materials in Australian Private Law presents a selection of cases and legislation to introduce students to the remedies available under Australian law. It offers the depth and context required to understand and analyse the application of private law remedies.

Developed to accompany the second edition of *Remedies in Australian Private Law*, and following that book's accessible and systematic structure, this casebook contains carefully curated extracts from landmark cases, legislation and secondary sources. The selected extracts offer a comprehensive yet concise guide to the application of remedies and cover topics including the *Australian Consumer Law*, torts, contract, vindicatory damages and coercive remedies.

Each chapter includes clear explanations of topics and links to material in the principles text, along with flowcharts and diagrams to summarise complex cases and concepts. Review questions throughout each chapter encourage students to analyse decisions from important cases and test their knowledge progressively.

Written by an expert author team, *Remedies Cases and Materials in Australian Private Law* is an invaluable resource which enables students to understand remedial law and identify appropriate remedial solutions.

Katy Barnett is Professor in the Melbourne Law School at the University of Melbourne.

Kenneth Yin is a Lecturer at Edith Cowan University.

Martin Allcock is a Senior Lecturer at Edith Cowan University.

Cambridge University Press acknowledges the Australian Aboriginal and Torres Strait Islander peoples of this nation. We acknowledge the traditional custodians of the lands on which our company is located and where we conduct our business. We pay our respects to ancestors and Elders, past and present. Cambridge University Press is committed to honouring Australian Aboriginal and Torres Strait Islander peoples' unique cultural and spiritual relationships to the land, waters and seas and their rich contribution to society.

REMEDIES
Cases and Materials in Australian Private Law

Katy Barnett
Kenneth Yin
Martin Allcock

CAMBRIDGE
UNIVERSITY PRESS

CAMBRIDGE
UNIVERSITY PRESS

Shaftesbury Road, Cambridge CB2 8EA, United Kingdom

One Liberty Plaza, 20th Floor, New York, NY 10006, USA

477 Williamstown Road, Port Melbourne, VIC 3207, Australia

314–321, 3rd Floor, Plot 3, Splendor Forum, Jasola District Centre, New Delhi – 110025, India

103 Penang Road, #05–06/07, Visioncrest Commercial, Singapore 238467

Cambridge University Press is part of Cambridge University Press & Assessment, a department of the University of Cambridge.

We share the University's mission to contribute to society through the pursuit of education, learning and research at the highest international levels of excellence.

www.cambridge.org
Information on this title: www.cambridge.org/highereducation/isbn/9781108811972

First published 2023

Cover designed by Fiona Byrne
Typeset by Integra Software Services Pvt. Ltd.
Printed in China by C & C Offset Printing Co., Ltd., November 2022

A catalogue record for this publication is available from the British Library

A catalogue record for this book is available from the National Library of Australia

ISBN 978-1-108-81197-2 Paperback

Additional resources for this publication at
www.cambridge.org/highereducation/isbn/9781108811972/resources

CONTENTS

Preface xxiii
Acknowledgements xxv
Table of cases xxviii
Table of statutes xl

Chapter 1 Introduction **1**

I Introduction 1

II What is a remedy? 1
Ashby v White 2
Photo Production Ltd v Securicor Transport Ltd 5
A Monism and dualism 7

III The common law and equity divide in Australia 12
Roxborough v Rothmans of Pall Mall Australia Ltd 13

IV A functional approach to remedies 18

PART 1 GENERAL PRINCIPLES OF COMPENSATION 21

Chapter 2 Assessment of compensation **22**

I Introduction 22

II The compensatory principle and the identification of the wrong 22
Butler v Egg and Egg Pulp Marketing Board 23
Gates v City Mutual Life Assurance Society Ltd 24

III Losses and benefits 26
A Non-pecuniary loss 26
B Cost of repair and diminution in value 27
C Betterment discount 27
Tyco Australia v Optus Networks Pty Ltd 27
Gagner Pty Ltd v Canturi Corporation Pty Ltd 29
Hoad v Scone Motors Pty Ltd 30
Hyder Consulting (Australia) Pty Ltd v Wilh Wilhemsen Agency Pty Ltd 30
D Benefits flowing from mitigating actions of the plaintiff 32
Haines v Bendall 32
British Westinghouse Electric and Manufacturing Co Ltd v Underground Electric Railways Co of London Ltd 33
Jenkinson v Young 34
Origin Energy LPG Ltd v BestCare Foods 35

E Other benefits arising from the wrong 37
Insurance Australia Ltd v HIH Casualty & General Insurance Ltd (in liq) 38
Monroe Schneiders Associates (Inc) v No 1 Raberem Pty Ltd 39
F The impact of tax law 41

IV Certainty of loss and recovery for the loss of a chance 42
A Overview of the current law 43
Malec v JC Hutton Pty Ltd 43
Sellars v Adelaide Petroleum NL 46
B Consequential loss 49
Glenmont Investments Pty Ltd v O'Loughlin 50
C Personal injury as initial harm 51
Tabet v Gett 52
D Pure economic loss as initial harm 54
Crown Insurance Services Pty Ltd v National Mutual Life Association of Australasia Ltd 55
Chaplin v Hicks 57
Hendriks v McGeoch 59
Badenach v Calvert 61
E Hypothetical conduct of the defendant 64
Commonwealth v Amann Aviation Pty Ltd 64
Port Macquarie-Hastings Council v Diveva Pty Ltd 67

V Temporal considerations 70
A The lump sum rule and the 'once and for all' rule 70
B Date of assessment 71
Re Dawson (Deceased) 71
O'Brien v McKean 72
Webster v Coles Myer Ltd 73
Johnson v Perez 74
Vieira v O'Shea 76
HTW Valuers (Central Qld) Pty Ltd v Astonland Pty Ltd 77
Potts v Miller 78
C Relevance of inflation 79
Egan v State Transport Authority 79
O'Brien v McKean 80
D Determining the present equivalent of future pecuniary loss 81
Todorovic v Waller 81
Competition and Consumer Act 2010 (Cth) s 87Y(1) 82
Civil Liability Act 2002 (NSW) s 14(1)–(2) 82
Transport Accident Act 1986 (Vic) s 93(13) 83
Law Reform (Miscellaneous Provisions) Act 1941 (WA) s 5(1) 83
E Interest on compensation awards and compensation for the loss of the use of money 83
Hungerfords v Walker 84

Chapter 3 Attribution of responsibility **88**

I Introduction 88

II The legal concept of causation 88

Barnett v Chelsea and Kensington Hospital Management Committee 89

Alexander v Cambridge Credit Corporation Ltd 91

March v E & MH Stramare 92

Civil Liability Act 2002 (NSW) s 5D 96

Wallace v Kam 96

III Factual causation 97

A Overview 97

B The 'but for' test and its application 98

Adeels Palace Pty Ltd v Moubarak 98

C Causal overdetermination (multiple sufficient causes) 100

1 Duplicative causation 100

Elayoubi v Zipser 101

2 Pre-emptive causation 103

Performance Cars Ltd v Abraham 103

D Evidential uncertainty 104

1 Inference of factual causation 104

Tubemakers of Australia Ltd v Fernandez 104

Amaca Pty Ltd v King 105

2 Material contribution to the harm 106

Bonnington Castings Ltd v Wardlaw 106

Amaca Pty Ltd v Booth 107

Amaca Pty Ltd v Ellis 108

3 Material increase in risk 110

McGhee v National Coal Board 110

Fairchild v Glenhaven Funeral Services Ltd 111

Civil Liability Act 1936 (SA) s 34(2)–(3) 113

IV Scope of liability 113

A Subsequent event 115

1 Distinction between basic loss and additional loss 115

2 Additional loss: intervening event 115

Chapman v Hearse 116

Alexander v Cambridge Credit Corporation Ltd 117

Scott Carver Pty Ltd v SAS Trustee Corporation Ltd 120

Hay Property Consultants Pty Ltd v Victorian Securities Corporation Ltd 121

Modbury Triangle Shopping Centre Pty Ltd v Anzil 122

Caterson v Commissioner for Railways 123

3 Basic loss: causally independent subsequent event 124

Kmart Australia Ltd v McCann 124

Calvert v William Hill Credit Ltd 126

Golden Strait Corporation v Nippon Yusen Kubishika Kaisha (The Golden Victory) 127
Turjman v Stonewall Hotel Pty Ltd 130
DNM Mining Pty Ltd v Barwick 131
Baker v Willoughby 132
4 Basic loss: causally dependent subsequent event 133
Faulkner v Keffalinos 134
B Remoteness of damage 134
C The purpose of the duty breached 135
Roads and Traffic Authority v Royal 135
Wallace v Kam 136
D The plaintiff's contribution to the loss 137
1 Contributory negligence 137
Smith v Badenoch 137
2 Mitigation 138
Burns v MAN Automotive (Aust) Pty Ltd 140
Clark v Macourt 142
Doyle v Olby (Ironmongers) Ltd 145
Simonius Vischer & Co v Holt & Thompson 146

Chapter 4 Multiple wrongdoers **148**

I Introduction 148

II Common law rules 148
Grunwald v Hughes 149
Thompson v Australian Capital Television Pty Ltd 150
The Koursk 152
Schumann v Abbott 153
Mahony v J Kruschich (Demolitions) Pty Ltd 154
Brinsmead v Harrison 156
James Hardie & Co Pty Ltd v Seltsam Pty Ltd 157
Chillingworth v Chambers 158
Albion Insurance Co Ltd v Government Insurance Office (NSW) 159

III Contribution statutes 160
Wrongs Act 1958 (Vic) s 24AA 161
De Reus v Gray 161
Wrongs Act 1958 (Vic) s 23B(1) 163
Wrongs Act 1958 (Vic) s 24(2) 163
Vinidex Tubemakers Pty Ltd v Thiess Contractors Pty Ltd 164

IV Proportionate liability statutes 165
Wrongs Act 1958 (Vic) s 24AI(1)(a) 166
Hunt & Hunt Lawyers v Mitchell Morgan Nominees Pty Ltd 166
Bathurst Regional Council v Local Government Financial Services Pty Ltd (No 5) 169

V Interplay of the three regimes 171

PART 2 COMPENSATION IN SPECIFIC CONTEXTS 173

Chapter 5 Compensation for breach of contract 174

I Introduction 174

II Assessment of compensation 174

A Protection of the plaintiff's expectation interest 176

Robinson v Harman 176

B Measure of expectation loss in particular contexts 178

Commonwealth v Amann Aviation Pty Ltd 178

1 Failure to deliver goods as promised 180

Clark v Macourt 180

Sale of Goods Act 1923 (NSW) s 54 181

2 Failure to convey land as promised 182

Bain v Fothergill 182

3 Failure to build, maintain or repair property as promised 183

Bellgrove v Eldridge 183

Tabcorp Holdings Ltd v Bowen Investments Pty Ltd 184

Ruxley Electronics and Construction Ltd v Forsyth 185

Stone v Chappel 187

4 Failure to provide other services as promised 188

GEC Marconi Systems Pty Ltd v BHP Information Technology Pty Ltd 188

Zomojo Pty Ltd v Hurd (No 4) 189

C The impact of *Clark v Macourt* 190

D Compensation of reliance loss 190

McRae v Commonwealth Disposal Commission 190

Commonwealth v Amann Aviation Pty Ltd 191

E Non-pecuniary loss 193

1 Restrictions at common law 193

Baltic Shipping Co v Dillon 193

2 Restrictions under statute 195

Civil Liability Act 2002 (NSW) ss 11A, 16, 27–28, 31 195

III Attribution of responsibility 196

A Remoteness of damage 197

Alexander v Cambridge Credit Corporation Ltd 197

1 The *Hadley v Baxendale* test 199

Hadley v Baxendale 199

2 The significance of the defendant's knowledge of the plaintiff's circumstances 200

Victoria Laundry (Windsor) Ltd v Newman Industries Ltd 200

3 Assumption of responsibility as overriding criterion? 201

Transfield Shipping Inc v Mercator Shipping Inc (The Achilleas) 202

B Contributory negligence 203

Chapter 6 Compensation in tort **205**

I Introduction 205

II Assessment of compensation 205

A General principle 207

Livingstone v Rawyards Coal Co 207

B Specific contexts 208

1 Damage to reputation: defamation 208

Carson v John Fairfax & Sons Ltd 208

2 Damage to land or fixtures 210

Evans v Balog 210

Pantalone v Alaouie 212

3 Other wrongful interference with land 213

Balanced Securities Ltd v Bianco (No 2) 214

4 Damage to goods 216

Jansen v Dewhurst 216

5 Other wrongful interference with goods 217

Butler v Egg and Egg Pulp Marketing Board 217

6 Defective premises or goods 219

Pyrenees Shire Council v Day 220

7 Damage to economic interests: reliance on a misrepresentation 221

Toteff v Antonas 221

III Attribution of responsibility 223

A Remoteness of damage 226

1 The test of natural and probable consequences 226

Palmer Bruyn & Parker Pty Ltd v Parsons 226

2 The test of reasonable foreseeability 228

Overseas Tankship (UK) Ltd v Morts Dock & Engineering Co Ltd (Wagon Mound No 1) 228

Overseas Tankship (UK) Ltd v Miller Steamship Co Pty Ltd (Wagon Mound No 2) 230

Wyong Shire Council v Shirt 232

Mt Isa Mines Ltd v Pusey 234

Sutherland Shire Council v Becker 236

Mayfair Ltd v Pears 238

3 The test of reasonable contemplation 239

National Australia Bank Ltd v Nemur Varity Pty Ltd 240

4 The 'eggshell skull' rule 241

Purkess v Crittenden 242

Nader v Urban Transport Authority NSW 243

B Contributory negligence 244

1 Common law 244

Radley v London and North Western Railway Co 245

2 Contributory negligence statutes 246

Wrongs Act 1958 (Vic) s 26(1) 247

3 Civil liability statutes 247

4 The plaintiff's conduct 247

Civil Liability Act 2002 (NSW) s 5R 248
Civil Law (Wrongs) Act 2002 (ACT) s 95 248
5 Factual causation and scope of the duty 249
Allan v Fletcher 249
6 Apportionable loss 251
Wrongs Act 1958 (Vic) s 26(1)(b) 251
7 Apportionment 251
Pennington v Norris 252

Chapter 7 Compensation for personal injury and death **254**

I Introduction 254

II The impact of legislation 254
A Statutory compensation schemes and ancillary regulation of common law damages 255
Workers' Compensation and Injury Management Act 1981 (WA) ss 3(a)(i)–(ii), 18(1)–(2) 255
B Civil liability statutes 256
Civil Liability Act 2002 (Tas) ss 3, 3B, 24 256

III Meaning of 'personal injury' 257
Civil Liability Act 2002 (NSW) ss 11, 27, 28(1), 31 257

IV Loss suffered by an injured person 258
A Pecuniary loss resulting from needs created by the injury 261
1 Medical expenses and cost of institutional care 261
Blundell v Musgrave 262
2 Domestic services provided to the injured person 263
Griffiths v Kerkemeyer 263
Civil Liability Act 2003 (Qld) s 59 265
3 Increased cost of living at home 266
4 Cost of managing a lump sum award 266
Civil Liability Act 1936 (SA) s 57 266
Gray v Richards 266
B Pecuniary loss resulting from the impairment of capacities 267
1 Loss of earning capacity 268
Graham v Baker 268
Civil Liability Act 1936 (SA) ss 3(1), 54(1)–(2) 269
2 Loss of employment-related benefits 270
Delphin v Martin 270
Civil Liability Act 2002 (Tas) s 25 272
3 Loss of social security benefits 272
4 Loss of capacity to do domestic work 272
CSR Ltd v Eddy 272
Civil Law (Wrongs) Act 2002 (ACT) s 100 274
C Non-pecuniary loss 275
1 Pain and suffering 275
Skelton v Collins 275

2 Loss of amenities 277
Lawrence v Mathison 277
3 Loss of expectation of life 278
Sharman v Evans 278
4 Statutory regulation 279
Civil Liability Act 2002 (WA) ss 9–10 279
D Overlap between different heads of loss 281

V Benefits arising from an injury 281
National Insurance Co of New Zealand v Espagne 282
Health and Other Services (Compensation) Act 1995 (Cth) ss 3, 7(1), (3), 8(1) 283

VI Claims based on injury to another person 285
A Loss of an employee's services 285
Barclay v Penberthy 285
B Loss of consortium 286
Civil Liability Act 1936 (SA) s 65(1) 286
Civil Law (Wrongs) Act 2002 (ACT) s 218 287

VII Actions on death 288
A Claim by the estate of the deceased 289
B Claim by the dependants of the deceased 289
Fatal Accidents Act 1846 (UK) 289
Wrongs Act 1958 (Vic) ss 16–17 290
Lyle v Soc 291
Compensation (Fatal Injuries) Act 1974 (NT) s 10(4)(h) 292
De Sales v Ingrilli 293
Civil Proceedings Act 2011 (Qld) s 67 295

Chapter 8 Compensation under the *Australian Consumer Law* **297**

I Introduction 297

II Assessment of compensation 298
A General principles 299
Wardley Australia Ltd v Western Australia 299
B Compensation for misleading or deceptive conduct 301
1 Reliance loss as the general measure of compensation 301
Gates v City Mutual Life Assurance Society Ltd 301
Marks v GIO Australia Holdings Pty Ltd 302
2 Compensation of expectation loss 304
Murphy v Overton Investments Pty Ltd 304
3 Compensation of reliance loss in excess of expectation loss 305
Henville v Walker 305
C Non-pecuniary loss 306
New South Wales Lotteries Corporation Pty Ltd v Kuzmanovski 306
D Certainty of loss and recovery for the loss of a chance 309

III Attribution of responsibility 309
A The common sense test of causation 311
B Factual causation 311
Henville v Walker 311
C Scope of liability 313
1 Intervening cause 313
Henville v Walker 313
Hay Property Consultants Pty Ltd v Victorian Securities Corporation Ltd 314
2 Foreseeability of the loss 315
Henville v Walker 315
3 The purpose of the provision contravened 316
Travel Compensation Fund v Tambree 316
4 The plaintiff's contribution to the loss 317
Competition and Consumer Act 2010 (Cth) s 137B 317
Henjo Investments Pty Ltd v Collins Marrickville Pty Ltd (No 2) 318
D Multiple wrongdoers 319

Chapter 9 Equitable compensation for equitable wrongs **320**

I Introduction 320

II Assessment of equitable compensation 320
A Object of equitable compensation 321
O'Halloran v RT Thomas & Family Pty Ltd 321
B Recoverability of non-pecuniary loss 323
Giller v Procopets 323
C Basic measure of equitable compensation 324
Nocton v Lord Ashburton 324
Agricultural Land Management Ltd v Jackson (No 2) 326

III Attribution of responsibility 328
A Breach of trust 330
1 Independent non-wrongful event 331
Re Dawson (Deceased) 331
Target Holdings Ltd v Redferns 332
Youyang Pty Ltd v Minter Ellison Morris Fletcher 333
Agricultural Land Management Ltd v Jackson (No 2) 335
2 Intervening acts and remoteness of loss 338
AIB Group (UK) plc v Mark Redler & Co Solicitors 338
B Breach of fiduciary duty 340
1 Construction of the hypothetical world 341
Brickenden v London Loan & Savings Co 341
Commonwealth Bank of Australia v Smith 342
2 Intervening acts and remoteness of loss 343
Hodgkinson v Simms 343
Canson Enterprises Ltd v Boughton & Co 344

3 Contributory negligence 346
Pilmer v Duke Group Ltd (in liq) 346
4 Mitigation 347
Canson Enterprises Ltd v Boughton & Co 347
C Breach of an equitable duty of care 348
1 Scope of liability 349
Permanent Building Society (in liq) v Wheeler 349
Bristol and West Building Society v Mothew 351
2 Contributory negligence 352
Youyang Pty Ltd v Minter Ellison Morris Fletcher 352

PART 3 REMEDIES COMPELLING PERFORMANCE AND RELATED REMEDIES 355

Chapter 10 Specific performance **356**

I Introduction 356
II The nature of specific performance 356
III The relationship between specific performance and injunctions 357
IV Inadequacy of damages and subject matter of contract 357
A Inadequacy of damages 358
Harnett v Yielding 358
B Subject matter of contract 359
1 Contracts involving land 359
Pianta v National Finance & Trustees Ltd 359
Loan Investment Corporation of Australasia v Bonner 360
Semelhago v Paramadevan 361
2 Contracts involving goods 362
Dougan v Ley 362
Howard Perry & Co Ltd v British Railways 363
Eastern Rolling Mill v Michlovitz 364
3 Contracts involving shares and stock 365
Georges v Wieland 365
Wight v Haberdan Pty Ltd 366
4 Contracts to loan money 367
5 Contracts for the benefit of third parties 368
Beswick v Beswick 368
Coulls v Bagot's Executor and Trustee Co Ltd 369
6 Contracts involving intellectual property 370
Cogent v Gibson 370
7 Contracts for services 371
Byrne v Australian Airlines 371
V Other requirements for specific performance 372
A Personal remedy 372

B Binding contract 372

Costin v Costin 373

Joseph v National Magazine Co 374

REW08 Projects Pty Ltd v PNC Lifestyle Investments Pty Ltd 375

VI Discretionary factors and bars to relief 377

A General equitable bars to relief 379

Patel v Ali 379

Summer v Cocks 380

Lindsay Petroleum v Hurd 381

No 68 Ltd v Eastern Services Ltd 382

B Bars to relief relevant only to specific performance 383

Price v Strange 384

Cannavo v FCD (Holdings) Pty Ltd 385

Ryan v Mutual Tontine Westminster Chambers Association 386

Posner v Scott Lewis 388

Cooperative Insurance Society Ltd v Argyll Stores (Holdings) Ltd 389

Patrick Stevedores Operations No 2 Pty Ltd v Maritime Union of Australia (No 3) 390

Diagnostic X-Ray Services Pty Ltd v Jewel Food Stores Pty Ltd 392

VII Specific performance under the *Australian Consumer Law* 394

Futuretronics International Pty Ltd v Gadzhis 394

VIII Specific restitution or specific delivery of property 395

Doulton Potteries Ltd v Bronotte 396

IX Debt as a species of specific relief? 397

Young v Queensland Trustees Ltd 398

White and Carter (Councils) Ltd v McGregor 399

Chapter 11 Injunctions **400**

I Introduction 400

II The rights protected by injunctions and inadequacy of damages 401

A Inadequacy of damages 403

Evans Marshall & Co Ltd v Bertola SA 403

B The rights protected by injunctions 404

1 Injury to property rights in land 404

Bendal Pty Ltd v Mirvac Project Pty Ltd 404

2 Injury to property rights in goods and funds of money 406

Aristoc Industries Pty Ltd v RA Wenham (Builders) Pty Ltd 406

3 Injury to intellectual property 407

Patents Act 1990 (Cth) s 122(1) 407

4 Injury to economic rights 407

Erven Warnink BV v J Townend & Sons (Hull) Ltd 407

5 Injury to bodily integrity 408

Parry v Crooks 408

6 Injury to reputation 409

Chappell v TCN Channel Nine Pty Ltd 409
7 Injury to privacy 410
McKennitt v Ash 410
8 Injunctions restraining breaches of negative covenant in a contract 411
9 Contracts for services 412
Curro v Beyond Productions Pty Ltd 412

III *Quia timet* injunctions 413

IV Discretionary factors and bars to relief 414
A General equitable bars to relief 415
1 Hardship and the public interest 415
Shelfer v City of London Electric Lighting Co 415
Lawrence v Fen Tigers Ltd 416
2 Lack of clean hands 418
Duchess of Argyll v Duke of Argyll 418
3 Laches: delay with acquiescence and delay with prejudice 419
B Bars to injunctions that are equivalent to those in specific performance 419

V Injunctions under statutes 420
Cardile v LED Builders Pty Ltd 421
A Intellectual property 421
B The *Australian Consumer Law* 422
Australian Consumer Law s 232(1)(a), (4) 422
ICI Australia Operations Pty Ltd v Trade Practices Commission 423
C The *Corporations Act 2001* (Cth) 424
Corporations Act 2001 (Cth) s 1324(1), (6)–(8) 424
Australian Securities and Investments Commission v Storm Financial Ltd (in liq) (recs and mgrs. apptd) (No 2) 425
D Other statutory injunctions 426

Chapter 12 'Equitable damages' or Lord Cairns' Act damages **427**

I Introduction 427

II History 429
Chancery Amendment Act 1858 (21 & 22 Vict c 27) s 2 429

III Advantages of Lord Cairns' Act damages for a plaintiff 429

IV Jurisdiction to award Lord Cairns' Act damages 430

V The need for a 'wrongful act' in some Australian jurisdictions 431
A Australian legislation which mentions 'wrongful act' 432
Supreme Court Act 1970 (NSW) s 68 432
B Australian legislation which does not mention 'wrongful act' 432
Supreme Court Act 1986 (Vic) s 38 432
Giller v Procopets 433
C Lord Cairns' Act damages for statutory wrongdoing 434
Wentworth v Woollahra Municipal Council 434

VI Factors influencing the exercise of the jurisdiction 436
A General principles 436
1 Where specific relief is no longer available or in addition to specific relief 436
2 To provide a 'middle ground' solution between no relief and specific relief 436
Bendal Pty Ltd v Mirvac Project Pty Ltd 437
3 To provide relief for future losses 438
4 To provide novel forms of relief 438
Giller v Procopets 438
B The *Shelfer* criteria 441
Shelfer v City of London Electric Lighting Co 441
Lawrence v Fen Tigers Ltd 442

VII The basis of assessment 446
A Timing 446
B Gain-based relief – 'reasonable fee' awards 446
Morris-Garner v One Step (Support) Ltd 447
C Loss-based relief – compensatory awards of various kinds 448

VIII Discretionary bars to relief 449

IX Part 9.5 of the *Corporations Act 2001* (Cth) 449
Corporations Act 2001 (Cth) s 1324(10) 450

X The future of Lord Cairns' Act damages 450

PART 4 REMEDIES AS VINDICATION 453

Chapter 13 Self-help remedies **454**

I Introduction 454

II Tort and self-help 454
A Eviction of trespassers 456
Cowell v Rosehill Racecourse Co Ltd 456
B Self-defence of property 456
Hackshaw v Shaw 456
C Self-defence of the person 458
Fontin v Katapodis 458
D Recaption, replevin and specific restitution 459
Toyota Finance Australia Ltd v Dennis 459
E Abatement of nuisance 462
Traian v Ware 462

III Contract and self-help 464
A Rescission 465
B Liquidated damages and penalties 465
1 Is this a clause to which the penalties doctrine applies? 466
Andrews v Australia and New Zealand Banking Group Ltd 466
2 On the facts, is this clause a penalty? 469
Paciocco v Australia and New Zealand Banking Group Ltd 469

C Debt 474
D Other stipulated contractual remedies 475

Chapter 14 Exemplary damages and aggravated damages **476**

I Introduction 476

II Exemplary damages 476
A The nature and history of exemplary damages in Australia 480
Gray v Motor Accident Commission 480
1 Need to make out the 'host' cause of action 484
Fatimi Pty Ltd v Bryant 484
2 Unavailable if criminal punishment already imposed 486
3 Calculation of exemplary damages 486
Pollack v Volpato 487
B The causes of action for which exemplary damages can be awarded in Australia 488
1 Exemplary damages available for tort 488
2 Exemplary damages available for breach of some statutes 489
Copyright Act 1968 (Cth) s 115(4) 489
3 Exemplary damages not available for breach of contract 490
4 Exemplary damages not available for equitable wrongdoing 490
Harris v Digital Pulse Pty Ltd 490
5 Exemplary damages not available for breaches of the *Australian Consumer Law* 493

III Aggravated damages 494
A The distinction between exemplary damages and aggravated damages 496
Carson v John Fairfax & Sons Ltd 496
B Availability of aggravated damages in Australian law 499
1 Aggravated damages available for tort 500
2 Aggravated damages available for some statutory causes of action 500
3 Aggravated damages not available for breach of contract 500
4 Aggravated damages not available for equitable wrongdoing 500
Giller v Procopets 500
5 Aggravated damages available for breaches of the *Australian Consumer Law* 502
New South Wales Lotteries Corporation Pty Ltd v Kuzmanovski 502

IV 'Vindicatory damages' 504
Lewis v Australian Capital Territory 504

Chapter 15 Apologies and declaratory relief **511**

I Introduction 511

II Apologies, declarations and nominal damages 511
A Apologies 512
Wrongs Act 1958 (Vic) ss 14I–14J 512
Civil Law (Wrongs) Act 2002 (ACT) ss 12–14 513

Defamation Act 2005 (NSW) s 20 514
Eatock v Bolt 514
B Declarations, nominal damages and contemptuous damages 516
1 Declarations 516
Supreme Court Act 1970 (NSW) s 75 517
Competition and Consumer Act 2010 (Cth) s 163A 517
Corporations Act 2001 (Cth) s 1317E(1)–(2) 518
Forster v Jododex Pty Ltd 518
2 Nominal damages 521
The Owners of the Steamship 'Mediana' v The Owners, Master and Crew of the Lightship 'Comet' (The 'Mediana') 521
3 Contemptuous damages 523
Grobbelaar v News Group Newspapers Ltd 523

III Other vindicatory remedies under the *Australian Consumer Law* 524
Australian Consumer Law s 246 525
Director of Consumer Affairs Victoria v Gibson (No 3) 526

PART 5 ACCOUNT OF PROFITS AND OTHER GAIN-BASED RELIEF FOR WRONGS 531

Chapter 16 Disgorgement of gains and 'reasonable fee' damages 532

I Introduction 532

II The distinction between compensation, restitution and disgorgement and the nature of gain-based remedies 533

III Disgorgement 534
A Equity and the account of profits 534
Warman International Ltd v Dwyer 535
B Election 540
Personal Representatives of Tang Man Sit v Capacious Investments Ltd 540
C Intellectual property and the account of profits 544
Copyright Act 1968 (Cth) s 115(2) 544
D Torts and 'waiver of tort' 545
Hospitality Group Pty Ltd v Australian Rugby Union Ltd 545
E Breach of contract 549
Hospitality Group Pty Ltd v Australian Rugby Union Ltd 549
Attorney-General v Blake 550
F The *Australian Consumer Law* 556

IV 'Reasonable fee' damages 558
A Introduction and history 559
B Academic and judicial accounts 559
1 Compensatory analyses 559
2 Restitutionary analyses 560
C General patterns 561

D Equity 562
E Intellectual property 562
F Tort 563
LJP Investments Pty Ltd v Howard Chia Pty Ltd 563
Strand Electric and Engineering Co Ltd v Brisford Entertainments Ltd 564
Morris-Garner v One Step (Support) Ltd 567
G Contract 570
Wrotham Park Estate Co Ltd v Parkside Homes Ltd 570
Morris-Garner v One Step (Support) Ltd 573

V Allowances, discretionary factors and bars to relief 581
A Allowances for skill and effort 581
Dart Industries Inc v Décor Corporation Pty Ltd 582
B Discretionary factors and bars to relief 584

VI The future of gain-based relief in Australia 584

PART 6 RESTITUTION AND GIVING BACK 585

Chapter 17 Personal remedies for unjust enrichment 586

I Introduction 586

II The elements of unjust enrichment 587

III Precise remedies for unjust enrichment 587
A Money claims 588
David Securities Pty Ltd v Commonwealth Bank of Australia 589
B Services claims 590
Pavey & Matthews Pty Ltd v Paul 590
C Goods claims 592

IV Defences to a claim for restitution 592

V The relationship between contract and restitution for unjust enrichment 593
Mann v Paterson Constructions Pty Ltd 594

Chapter 18 Rescission 609

I Introduction 609
A Legal rescission 611
B Equitable rescission 611
C Rescission under the *Australian Consumer Law* 611
Australian Consumer Law s 243(a)–(d) 611

II The requirement of *restitutio in integrum* 612
Clarke v Dickson 613
Alati v Kruger 614
Maguire v Makaronis 618

III Election 619
A How to make an election to rescind 620

Car & Universal Finance Co Ltd v Caldwell 620
B The consequences of an election to rescind 623
Daly v Sydney Stock Exchange Ltd 624
C The reasons behind the election requirement 626

IV 'Partial' rescission 627
Vadasz v Pioneer Concrete (SA) Pty Ltd 627

V Bars to rescission 630
A Impossibility of complete restoration 631
Quek v Beggs 631
B Affirmation 633
C Delay 633
Allcard v Skinner 633
D Intervening third party rights 636
Hartigan v International Society for Krishna Consciousness Inc 636
E Executed contracts and innocent misrepresentation 639

PART 7 PROPRIETARY REMEDIES 641

Chapter 19 Proprietary remedies **642**

I Introduction 642

II Proprietary remedies 642
A Constructive and resulting trusts 643
Muschinski v Dodds 644
B Proprietary powers 648
C Equitable liens 649

III Criteria for award of proprietary remedies 650
A Proprietary remedies and unconscionability 651
B Proprietary remedies and perfection 651
C Proprietary remedies and unjust enrichment 652
Wambo Coal Pty Ltd v Ariff 653
D Proprietary remedies and wrongdoing 657
Grimaldi v Chameleon Mining NL (No 2) 658

IV Discretionary factors and bars to relief 663

V The need for more defined criteria 664

PART 8 ENFORCEMENT OF REMEDIES 665

Chapter 20 Enforcement of remedies **666**

I Introduction 666

II Interlocutory injunctions 666
A Legal, equitable or statutory right 667
Australian Broadcasting Corporation v Lenah Game Meats Pty Ltd 667

B 'Serious question to be tried' (or a 'prima facie case') 669
Australian Broadcasting Corporation v O'Neill 670
C The balance of convenience 673
D Mandatory interlocutory injunctions 674
E *Quia timet* interlocutory injunctions 674
F Interlocutory injunctions which finally determine the matter 674
G Undertakings as to damages 676
H Interim injunctions under statute 676
Australian Consumer Law s 234 676
Corporations Act 2001 (Cth) s 1324(1), (4), (8) 677

III Other pre-judgment remedies 678
A Arrest of the person 678
Debtors Act 1870 (Tas) s 5 679
Absconding Debtors Act 1978 (NT) ss 5–6 680
B Freezing orders (Mareva orders) 681
Supreme Court (General Civil Procedure) Rules 2015 (Vic) rr 37A.02–37A.04 681
C Search orders (Anton Piller orders) 684
Uniform Civil Procedure Rules 2005 (NSW) rr 25.19–25.20 684

IV Post-judgment enforcement 685
A Enforcement of money remedies 686
Court Procedures Rules 2006 (ACT) rr 2150, 2154 686
Uniform Civil Procedure Rules 1999 (Qld) rr 828–829 688
Uniform Civil Procedure Rules 1999 (Qld) rr 855–856 689
Uniform Civil Procedure Rules 1999 (Qld) rr 875, 877 691
B Enforcement of specific remedies 692

Index *694*

PREFACE

In 2018, Katy was asked by her students when she was going to write a casebook to accompany the textbook she co-wrote with Sirko Harder, *Remedies in Australian Private Law*, now in its second edition (referred to in this book as the 'principles text'). Coincidentally, at that time she was approached by Cambridge University Press to provide them with a casebook, and hence she accepted the proposal gratefully.

As the students told Katy, a casebook is useful to students because it allows them to integrate their readings of cases and legislation with the principles text, and because it gives students resources such as diagrams and tables which may aid in their understanding of sometimes complex areas of law.

It has ended up being a much longer process than expected, as we were interrupted by the COVID-19 pandemic and various other crises. However, we're delighted to bring you this companion casebook to the second edition of *Remedies in Australian Private Law*. It includes extracts from recent cases such as *Morris-Garner v One Step (Support) Ltd* [2018] UKSC 20 and *Mann v Paterson Constructions Pty Ltd* [2019] HCA 32.

Katy was primarily responsible for Chapters 1, 3, 12, 13, 14, 15, 16, 17, 18, 19 and 20, Martin was primarily responsible for Chapters 4, 6 and 7, and Ken was primarily responsible for Chapters 2, 5, 8, 9, 10 and 11, but as with the principles text, the casebook is a joint work. We have considered material available to us before April 2022.

Katy would like to thank her family (Scott, Eloise, Josh and Hamish) for supporting her through the writing process, and Martin and Ken for joining her on the casebook journey. As with the principles text, she would also like to thank her JD and Masters students at Melbourne Law School for making her constantly think about how to present the law of remedies more clearly (a few of the diagrams in Katy's chapters have been 'road-tested' on students). Special thanks to Jared Mintz for providing research assistance for many of the chapters, to Hannah Robert for her draft of Chapter 3 upon which Katy was able to build, and to Melbourne Law School for being consistently supportive when Katy suffered from severe health issues from 2018 onwards.

Martin would like to thank his family, and his colleagues at Edith Cowan University for their unending support. Martin would also like to specifically extend his thanks to Katy and Ken, along with Emily Baxter and Lucy Russell, for inviting him to join this wonderful project. It has been a privilege and an honour.

Ken would like to thank all his colleagues on the third floor of Building 2, Edith Cowan University, for their generous support and friendship throughout the writing process. He joins with Katy and Martin in their collective gratitude to Emily and Lucy.

Katy and Ken would like to thank Martin for joining us on this project at a time when his assistance was pivotal.

We would like to thank the anonymous reviewers for their helpful comments. We would also like to thank Emily Baxter, Lucy Russell, Rose Albiston and the other staff at Cambridge University Press for their professionalism and patience. Without their faith in this project, this textbook would have faltered.

Katy Barnett
Martin Allcock
Ken Yin
May 2022

ACKNOWLEDGEMENTS

The authors and Cambridge University Press would like to acknowledge Hannah Robert for her contribution in writing early versions of Chapter 3 'Attribution of responsibility'.

The authors and Cambridge University Press would like to thank the following for permission to reproduce material in this book.

Extract from Peter Birks, 'Three Kinds of Objections to Discretionary Remedialism' (2000) 29(1) *University of Western Australia Law Review* 1: © UWA Law Review.

Extract from Andrew Burrows, 'We Do This at Common Law but That in Equity' (2002) 22(1) *Oxford Journal of Legal Studies* 1: © Andrew Burrows, reproduced by permission of Oxford University Press.

Extract from James Edelman, *Gain-Based Damages: Contract, Tort, Equity and Intellectual Property* (Hart Publishing, 2002): © James Edelman, 2002, *Gain-Based Damages: Contract, Tort, Equity and Intellectual Property*, Hart Publishing, an imprint of Bloomsbury Publishing Plc.

Extract from Leon Fuller and William Purdue, 'The Reliance Interest in Contract Damages 1' (1936) 46(1) *Yale Law Journal* 52: reproduced with permission from *Yale Law Journal*.

Extract from Grant Hammond, 'Rethinking Remedies: The Changing Nature of the Conception of the Relationship Between Legal and Equitable Remedies' in Jeff Berryman (ed), *Remedies: Issues and Perspectives* (Carswell, 1991): reproduced by permission of Thomson Reuters Canada Limited.

Extract from Harvey McGregor, 'Mitigation in the Assessment of Damages' in D Saidov and R Cunnington (eds), *Contract Damages: Domestic and International Perspectives* (Hart, 2008): © Harvey McGregor, 2008, *Contract Damages: Domestic and International Perspectives*, Hart Publishing, an imprint of Bloomsbury Publishing Plc.

Extract from Robert J Sharpe and Stephen M Waddams, 'Damages for Lost Opportunity to Bargain' (1982) 2(2) *Oxford Journal of Legal Studies* 290: reproduced by permission of Oxford University Press.

Extract from David Wright, 'Wrong and Remedy: A Sticky Relationship' (2001) (2) *Singapore Journal of Legal Studies* 300: © David Wright, 2001.

Extract from Rafal Zakrzewski, *Remedies Reclassified* (Oxford University Press, 2005): © Rafal Zakrzewski, 2005. Reproduced with permission of the Licensor through PLSclear.

Extracts from JD Heydon, MJ Leeming and PG Turner, *Meagher, Gummow and Lehane's Equity: Doctrines and Remedies* (LexisNexis, 5th ed, 2015); All England Law Reports (All ER); Australian Corporations and Securities Reports (ACSR); Butterworths Property Reports (BPR); New Zealand Law Reports (NZLR); New South Wales Reports (NSWR): originally published by LexisNexis.

Extracts from Walter Sofronoff, 'Interlocutory Injunctions Having Final Effect' (1987) 61(7) *Australian Law Journal* 341; Australian Law Journal Reports (ALJR); Commonwealth Law Reports (CLR); Federal Court Reports (FCR); Local Government and Environmental Reports of Australia (LGERA); Northern Territory Reports (NTR); Scots Law Times (SLT);

South Australia State Reports (SASR): reproduced with permission of Thomson Reuters (Professional) Australia Limited, legal.thomsonreuters.com.au.

Extracts from High Court of Australia (HCA): © Commonwealth of Australia.

Extracts from New South Wales Court of Appeal (NSWCA); New South Wales District Court (NSWDC); New South Wales Supreme Court (NSWSC): © State of New South Wales (Department of Communities and Justice). For current information go to https://www.caselaw.nsw.gov.au/policy.

Extracts from New South Wales Law Reports (NSWLR): reproduced with permission from the Council of Law Reporting for New South Wales.

Extract from South Australia Supreme Court (SASC): reproduced with permission from the Attorney-General for the State of South Australia and the South Australian Courts Administration Authority.

Extract from Supreme Court of Tasmania (TASSC): reproduced with permission from the Supreme Court of Tasmania.

Extracts from Victoria Court of Appeal (VSCA); Victorian Reports (VR); Victoria Supreme Court (VSC): the publication of these extracts in *Remedies and Cases in Australian Private Law* is made with the consent of the Council of Law Reporting in Victoria.

Extracts from Western Australian Reports (WAR): reproduced by permission of the copyright owner, the State of Western Australia.

Extract from *Costin v Costin* [1995] ANZ Conv R 289: © Australian and New Zealand Conveyancing Reports, Wolters Kluwer Asia Pacific.

Extracts from Canada Law Reports, Supreme Court (SCR): reproduced with the permission of the Supreme Court of Canada, 2022.

Extracts from Law Reports, Appeal Cases (AC) (Third Series); Law Reports, Chancery Division (Ch) (Third Series); Law Reports, Queen's Bench (QB) (Third Series); Weekly Law Reports (WLR): reproduced with permission of the Incorporated Council of Law Reporting for England and Wales.

Extracts from United Kingdom House of Lords (UKHL): © Parliamentary copyright. Contains Parliamentary information licensed under the Open Parliament Licence v3.0: https://www.parliament.uk/site-information/copyright-parliament/open-parliament-licence/.

Extracts from United Kingdom Supreme Court (UKSC): © Crown Copyright. Reproduced under the Open Government Licence: https://www.nationalarchives.gov.uk/doc/open-government-licence/version/3/.

Extracts from Commonwealth legislation: sourced from the Federal Register of Legislation and reproduced under Creative Commons Attribution 4.0 International (CC BY 4.0). For the latest information on Australian Government law please go to https://www.legislation.gov.au.

Extracts from Australian Capital Territory legislation: reproduced with permission from the ACT Parliamentary Counsel's Office.

Extracts from New South Wales legislation: sourced from the New South Wales Legislation website at April 2022. For the latest information on New South Wales Government legislation please go to https://www.legislation.nsw.gov.au. Reproduced under a CC BY 4.0 licence: https://creativecommons.org/licenses/by/4.0/.

Extracts from Queensland legislation: sourced from the Queensland legislation website at April 2022. For the latest information on Queensland Government legislation please go to https://www.legislation.qld.gov.au. Reproduced under a CC BY 4.0 licence: https://creativecommons.org/licenses/by/4.0/.

Extracts from South Australian legislation: sourced from the South Australian Legislation website at April 2022. For the latest information on South Australian Government legislation, please go to www.legislation.sa.gov.au/. Reproduced under Creative Commons Attribution 4.0 International Licence (CC BY 4.0): https://creativecommons.org/licenses/by/4.0/.

Extracts from Tasmanian legislation: sourced from the Tasmanian Legislation website at April 2022. For the latest information on Tasmanian Government legislation please go to www.legislation.tas.gov.au. Reproduced under a CC BY 4.0 licence: https://creativecommons.org/licenses/by/4.0/.

Extracts from Victorian legislation: © State of Victoria, Australia. Copyright in all legislation of the Parliament of the State of Victoria, Australia, is owned by the Crown in right of the State of Victoria, Australia. DISCLAIMER: This product or service contains an unofficial version of the legislation of the Parliament of State of Victoria. The State of Victoria accepts no responsibility for the accuracy and completeness of any legislation contained in this product or provided through this service.

Extract from Western Australian legislation: sourced from the Western Australian legislation website at April 2022. For the latest information on Western Australian legislation, visit www.legislation.wa.gov.au. Reproduced under a CC BY 4.0 licence: https://creativecommons.org/licenses/by/4.0/.

Extract from United Kingdom (UK) legislation: © Crown Copyright. Contains public sector information licensed under the Open Government Licence v3.0: https://www.nationalarchives.gov.uk/doc/open-government-licence/version/3/.

Every effort has been made to trace and acknowledge copyright. The publisher apologises for any accidental infringement and welcomes information that would redress this situation.

TABLE OF CASES

A v New South Wales (2007) 230 CLR 500, 479, 495
Abbey Forwarding Ltd v Hone (No 3) [2015] Ch 309, 683
Adams v Kennedy (2000) 49 NSWLR 78, 479
Adeels Palace Pty Ltd v Moubarak (2009) 239 CLR 420, 98–100
Admiralty Commissioners v Steamship Amerika (Owners) [1917] AC 38, 285
A-G v Blake [2001] 1 AC 268, 447, 549, 550–6, 573, 575
A-G v Observer Ltd [1990] 1 AC 109, 544
A-G (England and Wales) v The Queen [2002] 2 NZLR 91, 549
Agricultural Land Management Ltd v Jackson (No 2) (2014) 48 WAR 1, 326–7, 331, 335–8, 340
AIB Group (UK) plc v Mark Redler & Co Solicitors [2015] AC 1503, 338–40
Air Express Ltd v Ansett Transport Industries (Operations) Pty Ltd (1979) 146 CLR 249, 676
Akron Securities Ltd v Iliffe (1997) 41 NSWLR 353, 612
Alati v Kruger (1955) 94 CLR 216, 465, 614–18, 620
Albion Insurance Co Ltd v Government Insurance Office (NSW) (1969) 121 CLR 342, 159–60
Aldersea v Public Transport Corporation (2001) 3 VR 499, 495
Alexander v Cambridge Credit Corporation Ltd (1987) 9 NSWLR 310, 91–2, 117–19, 197–8
Allan v Fletcher (2001) 79 SASR 559, 249–51
Allan v Snyder [1977] 2 NSWLR 685, 652
Allcard v Skinner (1887) 36 Ch D 145, 633–5, 656, 664
Amaca Pty Ltd v Banton (2007) 7 DDCR 314, 479
Amaca Pty Ltd v Booth (2011) 246 CLR 36, 100, 107–8, 111, 112
Amaca Pty Ltd v Ellis (2010) 240 CLR 111, 108–9
Amaca Pty Ltd v King (2011) 35 VR 280, 105
American Cynamid Co v Ethicon [1975] AC 396, 669
Anderson v Liddell (1968) 117 CLR 36, 689
Andrew Shelton & Co Pty Ltd v Alpha Healthcare Ltd (2002) 5 VR 577, 592
Andrews v Australia and New Zealand Banking Group Ltd (2012) 247 CLR 205, 465, 466–9
Anton Piller KG v Manufacturing Processes Ltd [1976] Ch 55, 684
Archer v Brown [1985] QB 401, 495
Aristoc Industries Pty Ltd v RA Wenham (Builders) Pty Ltd [1965] NSWR 581, 406–7
AS v Murray [2013] NSWSC 733, 479
ASA Constructions Pty Ltd v Iwanov [1975] 1 NSWLR 512, 431
Ashby v White (1703) 92 ER 126, 2
Australian Broadcasting Corporation v Lenah Game Meats Pty Ltd (2001) 208 CLR 199, 403, 667–9
Australian Broadcasting Corporation v O'Neill (2006) 227 CLR 57, 669, 670–2
Australian Consolidated Press Ltd v Morgan (1965) 112 CLR 483, 692, 693
Australian Securities and Investments Commission v Mauer Swisse Securities Ltd (2002) 42 ACSR 605, 677
Australian Securities and Investments Commission v Parkes (2001) 38 ACSR 355, 677

Australian Securities and Investments Commission v Pegasus Leveraged Options Group Pty Ltd (2002) 41 ACSR 561, 677
Australian Securities and Investments Commission v Storm Financial Ltd (recs and mgrs. apptd) (in liq) (No 2) [2011] FCA 858, 425–6
Australian Securities and Investments Commission v Triton Underwriting Insurance Agency (2003) 48 ACSR 249, 677
AW v New South Wales [2005] NSWSC 543, 479

Babanaft International Co SA v Bassatne [1990] Ch 13, 683
Backwell v AAA [1997] 1 VR 182, 479, 495
Badenach v Calvert (2016) 257 CLR 440, 61–2
Badman v Drake [2008] NSWSC 1366, 656, 664
Bain v Fothergill (1874) LR HL 158, 182
Baker v Bolton (1808) 170 ER 1033, 285
Baker v Willoughby [1970] AC 467, 132–3
Balanced Securities Ltd v Bianco (No 2) (2010) 27 VR 599, 214–15
Baltic Shipping Co v Dillon (1993) 176 CLR 344, 193–5
Bank of New South Wales v Commonwealth (1948) 76 CLR 1, 109
Barbagallo v J & F Catelan Pty Ltd [1986] 1 Qd R 245, 438
Barclay v Penberthy (2012) 246 CLR 258, 285–6
Barlow v Neville Jeffress Advertising Pty Ltd (1994) 4 Tas R 391, 413
Barnett v Chelsea and Kensington Hospital Management Committee [1969] 1 QB 428, 89–90
Bathurst Regional Council v Local Government Financial Services Pty Ltd (No 5) [2012] FCA 1200, 169–70
Baumgartner v Baumgartner (1987) 164 CLR 137, 651, 652, 656
Bellgrove v Eldridge (1965) 90 CLR 613, 183–4
Bendal Pty Ltd v Mirvac Project Pty Ltd (1991) 23 NSWLR 464, 404–5, 437
Benedetti v Sawiris [2014] AC 938, 591
Beswick v Beswick [1968] AC 58, 368
Bilbie v Lumley (1802) 102 ER 448, 589
Birmingham v Renfrew (1937) 57 CLR 666, 652
Black v S Freedman & Co (1910) 12 CLR 105, 651, 657
Blackburn v Smith (1804) 154 ER 707, 611
Blades v Higgs (1861) 142 ER 634, 460
Blundell v Musgrave (1956) 96 CLR 73, 262–3
Boardman v Phipps [1967] 2 AC 46, 651, 657
Bofinger v Kingsway Group Ltd (2009) 239 CLR 269, 7
Bonnard v Perryman [1891] 2 Ch 269, 403
Bonnington Castings Pty Ltd v Wardlaw [1956] AC 613, 106
Bosaid v Andry [1963] VR 465, 431
Break Fast Investments Pty Ltd v Giannopoulos (No 5) [2011] NSWSC 1508, 657
Brickenden v London Loan & Savings Co [1934] 3 DLR 465, 341–2
Bride v KMG Hungerfords (1991) 109 FLR 256, 495
Bridgewater v Leahy (1998) 194 CLR 457, 630
Brinsmead v Harrison (1871) LR 7 CP 547, 156–7
Bristol & West Building Society v Mothew [1998] Ch 1, 349, 351–2

British Westinghouse Electric and Manufacturing Co Ltd v Underground Electric Railways Co of London Ltd [1912] AC 673, 33–4
Brooks v Wyatt (1994) 99 NTR 12, 431
Brown v Smitt (1924) 34 CLR 160, 618
Bunnings Group Ltd v Chep Australia Ltd (2011) 82 NSWLR 420, 567
Burke v LFOT Pty Ltd (2002) 209 CLR 282, 158
Burns v MAN Automotive (Aust) Pty Ltd (1986) 161 CLR 658, 140–2
Butler v Egg and Egg Pulp Marketing Board (1966) 114 CLR 185, 23–4, 207, 217–19
Byrne v Australian Airlines (1995) 185 CLR 410, 371

CAL No 14 Pty Ltd v Motor Vehicle Accidents Insurance Board (2009) 239 CLR 290, 455
Calvert v William Hill Credit Ltd [2009] Ch 330, 126
Cambridge v Anastopoulos [2012] NSWCA 405, 103
Cannavo v FCD (Holdings) Pty Ltd [2000] NSWSC 304, 383, 385–6
Canson Enterprises Ltd v Boughton & Co [1991] 3 SCR 534, 344–6, 347–8
Car & Universal Fiannce Co Ltd v Caldwell [1965] 1 QB 525, 620–4
Cardile v LED Builders Pty Ltd (1999) 198 CLR 380, 421, 682, 683, 691
Carson v John Fairfax & Sons Ltd (1993) 178 CLR 44, 208–9, 495, 496–8
Cassell & Co Ltd v Broome [1972] AC 1027, 479
Caterson v Commissioner for Railways (1973) 128 CLR 99, 123–4
Catton v Wyld (1863) 55 ER 105, 436, 448
Cavendish Square Holding BV v Makdessi [2015], 470
Cayzer, Irvine & Co v Carron Co (1884) 9 App Cas 873, 245
Chabot v Davies [1936] 3 All ER 211, 562
Chan v Zacharia (1984) 154 CLR 178, 651, 657
Chang v Registrar of Titles (1976) 137 CLR 177, 652
Chaplin v Hicks [1911] 2 KB 787, 57–8
Chapman v Hearse (1961) 106 CLR 112, 116–17
Chapman, Morsons & Co v Guardians of the Auckland Union (1889) 23 QBD 294, 436, 448
Chappell v TCN Channel Nine Pty Ltd (1988) 14 NSWLR 153, 409–10
Chase Manhattan NA v Israel-British Bank (London) [1981] Ch 105, 652
Chillingworth v Chambers [1896] 1 Ch 685, 158–9
City of London Brewery Co v Tennant (1873) LR 9 Ch App 212, 431
Clark v Macourt (2013) 253 CLR 1, 142–5, 180–1, 190
Clark Equipment Credit of Australia Ltd v Como Factors Pty Ltd (1988) 14 NSWLR 552, 682
Clarke v Dickson (1858) 120 ER 463, 613–14
Cogent v Gibson (1864) 55 ER 485, 370–1
Colbeam Palmer Ltd v Stock Affiliates Pty Ltd (1968) 122 CLR 25, 544–5, 584
Cole v South Tweed Heads Rugby League Football Club Ltd (2004) 217 CLR 469, 455
Colls v Home and Colonial Stores Ltd [1904] AC 179, 437
Commercial Bank of Australia Ltd v Amadio (1983) 151 CLR 447, 630
Commonwealth v Amann Aviation Pty Ltd (1991) 174 CLR 64, 64–5, 68, 178–9, 190, 191–3
Commonwealth v Murray (1988) Aust Torts Reports 80–207, 479
Commonwealth Bank of Australia v Smith (1991) 42 FCR 390, 342
Commonwealth Life Assurance Society Ltd v Brain (1935) 53 CLR 343, 495
Cook v Saroukas (1989) 97 FLR 33, 479

Cooperative Insurance Society Ltd v Argyll Stores (Holdings) Ltd [1998] AC 1, 387, 389–90, 419, 693
Corin v Patton (1990) 169 CLR 540, 652
Costin v Costin [1995] ANZ Conv R 289, 373–4
Coulls v Bagot's Executor and Trustee Co Ltd (1967) 119 CLR 460, 368, 369–70
Cowell v Rosehill Racecourse Co Ltd (1937) 56 CLR 605, 456
Coyle v New South Wales [2006] NSWCA 95, 479
Crown Insurance Services Pty Ltd v National Mutual Life Association of Australasia Ltd (2005) 13 ANZ Ins Cas 61–659, 55–7
CSR Ltd v Eddy (2005) 226 CLR 1, 272–4
Curro v Beyond Productions Pty Ltd (1993) 30 NSWLR 337, 412, 419

Dart Industries Inc v Décor Corporation Pty Ltd (1993) 179 CLR 101, 582–3
Davenport v Rylands (1865) LR 1 Eq 302, 436, 448
De Reus v Gray (2003) 9 VR 432, 161–2, 495
De Sales v Ingrilli (2002) 212 CLR 338, 293–4
Dell v Beasley [1959] NZLR 89, 431
Delphin v Martin [2012] TASSC 13, 270–1
Derby & Co Ltd v Weldon [1990] Ch 48, 683
Diagnostic X-Ray Services Pty Ltd v Jewel Food Stores Pty Ltd (2001) 4 VR 632, 392–3
Digital Pulse v Harris (2002) 166 FLR 421, 490
Director of Consumer Affairs Victoria v Gibson (No 3) [2017] FCA 1148, 526–9, 534, 556
DNM Mining Pty Ltd v Barwick [2004] NSWCA 137, 131–2
Doherty v Allman (1878) 3 App Cas 709, 403, 411
Dougan v Ley (1946) 71 CLR 142, 362–3
Doulton Potteries Ltd v Bronotte [1971] 1 NSWLR 591, 396–7, 692
Doyle v Olby (Ironmongers) Ltd [1969] 2 QB 158, 145–6
Duchess of Argyll v Duke of Argyll [1967] Ch 302, 418–19
Dunlop Pneumatic Tyre Co Ltd v New Garage and Motor Co Ltd [1915] AC 79, 470

Eastern Rolling Mill v Michlovitz, 157 Md 51 (1929), 364–5
Eatock v Bolt (2011) 197 FCR 261, 514–15
Economy Shipping Pty Ltd v ADC Building Pty Ltd [1971] 1 NSWLR 37, 693
Edward Street Properties Pty Ltd v Collins [1977] Qd R 399, 431
Edwards v Lee's Administrator, 96 SW 2d 1028 (Ky Ct App, 1936), 548
Egan v State Transport Authority [1982] 31 SASR 481, 72, 79–80
Elayoubi v Zipser [2008] NSWCA 335, 101–2
Equuscorp Pty Ltd v Haxton (2012) 246 CLR 498, 594, 595
Erven Warnick BV v J Townend & Sons (Hull) Ltd [1979] AC 731, 407–8
Essa v Laing Ltd [2004] ICR 746, 89
European Bank Ltd v Evans (2010) 240 CLR 438, 676
Evans v Balog [1976] 1 NSWLR 36, 210–11
Evans Marshall & Co Ltd v Bertola (SA) [1973] 1 WLR 349, 403–4

Fairchild v Glenhaven Funeral Services Ltd [2002] 1 AC 32, 111–12
Farah Constructions Pty Ltd v Say-Dee Pty Ltd (2007) 230 CLR 89, 7
Fatimi Pty Ltd v Bryant (2004) 59 NSWLR 678, 484–6
Faulkner v Keffalinos (1970) 45 ALJR 80, 134

Felton v Callis [1969] 1 QB 200, 680
Ferguson v Wilson (1866) LR 2 Ch App 77, 431
FHR European Ventures LLP v Mankarious [2015] AC 250, 662
Fielding v Variety Inc [1967] 2 QB 841, 495
Flamingo Park Pty Ltd v Dolly Dolly Creations Pty Ltd (1986) 6 IPR 431, 479
Fontin v Katapodis (1962) 108 CLR 177, 458–9, 479
Forster v Jododex Pty Ltd (1972) 127 CLR 421, 518–21
Frigo v Culhaci (New South Wales Court of Appeal, Mason P, Sheller JA and Sheppard AJA, 17 July 1998), 682, 683
Fritz v Hobson (1880) 14 Ch D 542, 436, 448
Futuretronics International Pty Ltd v Gadzhis [1992] 2 VR 217, 394–5

Gafford v Graham (1999) 77 P & CR 73, 437
Gagner Pty Ltd v Canturi Corporation Pty Ltd (2009) 262 ALR 691, 29
Gates v City Mutual Life Assurance Society Ltd (1986) 160 CLR 1, 24, 301–2
GEC Marconi Systems Pty Ltd v BHP Information Technology Pty Ltd (2003) 128 FCR 1, 188–9
General Tire and Rubber Co v Firestone Tyre and Rubber Co Ltd [1975] 1 WLR 819, 562
Georges v Wieland [2009] NSWSC 733, 365–6
Giller v Procopets (2008) 24 VR 1, 323–4, 430, 433–4, 438–41, 448, 500–2
Giumelli v Giumelli (1999) 196 CLR 101, 652
Glenmont Investments Pty Ltd v O'Laughlin (2000) 79 SASR 185, 49–51
Glenwood Management Group Pty Ltd v Mayo [1991] 2 VR 49, 682, 683
Glover v Walters (1950) 80 CLR 172, 680
Golden Strait Corporation v Nippon Yusen Kubishika Kaisha (The Golden Victory) [2007] 2 AC 353, 127–30
Goodwin v Duggan (1996) 41 NSWLR 158, 158
Graham v Baker (1961) 106 CLR 340, 268–9
Grant v Dawkins [1973] 1 WLR 1406, 436, 448
Gray v Motor Accident Commission (1998) 196 CLR 1, 479, 480–4, 486
Gray v Richards (2014) 253 CLR 660, 266–7
Green v Green (1989) 17 NSWLR 343, 652
Griffiths v Kerkemeyer (1977) 139 CLR 161, 263–5
Grimaldi v Chameleon Mining NL (No 2) (2012) 200 FCR 296, 658–62
Grobbelaar v News Group Newspapers Ltd [2002] 1 WLR 3024, 523–4
Grunwald v Hughes 1965 SLT 209, 149–50

Haber v Walker [1963] VR 339, 291
Hackshaw v Shaw (1984) 155 CLR 624, 456–8
Hadley v Baxendale (1854) 156 ER 145, 181, 199–200
Haines v Bendall (1991) 172 CLR 60, 32–3, 84
Haiti (Republic) v Duvalier [1990] 1 QB 202, 683
Hamer-Mathew v Gulabrai (No 2) (1995) Aust Torts Reports 81–334, 479
Hampton v BHP Billiton Minerals Pty Ltd [2012] WASC 285, 564
Harnett v Yielding [1803–1813] All ER 704, 358
Harris v Digital Pulse Pty Ltd (2003) 56 NSWLR 298, 490–3
Harriton v Stephens (2006) 226 CLR 52, 207
Hartigan v International Society for Krishna Consciousness [2002] NSWSC 810, 636–9

Hartley Poynton Ltd v Ali (2005) 11 VR 568, 480
Hawker Pacific Pty Ltd v Helicopter Charter Pty Ltd (1991) 22 NSWLR 298, 633
Hay Property Consultants Pty Ltd v Victorian Securities Corporation Ltd (2010) 29 VR 503, 121–2, 314–15
Healing (Sales) Pty Ltd v Inglis Electrix Pty Ltd (1968) 121 CLR 584, 479
Hendriks v McGeoch (2008) Aust Torts Reports 81-942, 59–61, 62–3
Henjo Investments Pty Ltd v Collins Marrickville Pty Ltd (1988) 39 FCR 546, 612
Henjo Investments Pty Ltd v Collins Marrackville (No 2) (1989) 40 FCR 76, 318–19
Henry v Thompson [1989] 2 Qd R 412, 479, 495
Henville v Walker (2001) 206 CLR 459, 305–6, 311–12, 313–14, 315
Hoad v Scone Motors Pty Ltd [1977] 1 NSWLR 88, 30
Hodgkinson v Simms [1994] 3 SCR 377, 343–4
Hobol v Hobol [1981] VR 221, 652
Holroyd v Marshall (1862) 11 ER 999, 652
Hooper v Rogers [1975] Ch 43, 431, 448
Horkin v North Melbourne Football Club Social Club [1983] 1 VR 153, 455
Hospitality Group Pty Ltd v Australian Rugby Union Ltd (2001) 110 FCR 537, 545–50
Howard Perry & Co Ltd v British Railways [1980] 1 WLR 1375, 363–4
HTW Valuers (Central Qld) Pty Ltd v Astonland Pty Ltd (2004) 217 CLR 640, 77–8
Hungerfords v Walker (1989) 171 CLR 125, 83–6
Hunt v Silk (1804) 102 ER 1142, 611
Hunt & Hunt Lawyers v Mitchell Morgan Nominees Pty Ltd (2013) 247 CLR 613, 166–9
Huntley v Thornton [1957] 1 WLR 321, 495
Husher v Husher (1999) 197 CLR 138, 207
Hyder Consulting (Australia) Pty Ltd v Wilh Wilhemsen Agency Pty Ltd [2001] NSWCA 313, 30–1

ICI Australia Operations Pty Ltd v Trade Practices Commission (1992) 38 FCR 248, 422, 423–4
Inland Revenue Commissioners v Hoogstraten [1985] QB 1077, 693
Insurance Australia Ltd v HIH Casualty & General Insurance Ltd (in liq) (2007) 18 VR 528, 38
Interstar Wholesale Finance Pty Ltd v Integral Home Loans Pty Ltd (2008) 257 ALR 292, 466
Isenberg v East India House Estate Co Ltd (1863) 46 ER 637, 431, 437, 438

Jackson v Sterling Industries Ltd (1987) 162 CLR 612, 682, 683
Jaggard v Sawyer [1995] 1 WLR 269, 437, 448
James v Faddoul [2007] NSWSC 821, 495
James Hardie & Co Pty Ltd v Seltsam Pty Ltd (1998) 196 CLR 53, 157
Janney v Steller Works Pty Ltd (2017) 53 VR 677, 445
Jansen v Dewhurst [1969] VR 421, 216–17
JC Williamson Ltd v Lukey (1931) 45 CLR 282, 403, 412, 431
Jenkinson v Young [2004] SADC 30, 34–5
Jervois Sulphates (NT) Ltd v Petrocarb Explorations NL (1974) 5 ALR 1, 495
Jira v Burcher (1960) 78 WN (NSW) 421, 680
Johnson v Agnew [1980] AC 367, 436, 446
Johnson v Perez (1988) 166 CLR 351, 74–5
Johnstone v Stewart [1968] SASR 142, 495

Jolly v Kine [1907] AC 1, 437
Jordan House v Menow [1974] 30 DLR (3d) 105, 455
Joseph v National Magazine Co [1959] Ch 14, 374
Joyce v Sengupta (1993) 1 WLR 337, 495

Kansas v Nebraska, 135 S Ct 1042 (2015), 549
Kardynal v Dodek (1977) 5 Fam LR 706, 652
Keech v Sandford (1726) 25 ER 223, 651, 657
Khodaparast v Shad [2000] 1 WLR 618, 495
Kine v Jolly [1905] 1 Ch 480, 437
Kmart Australia Ltd v McCann [2004] NSWCA 283, 124–5

Lamb v Cotogno (1987) 164 CLR 1, 479
Lamine v Dorrell (1706) 92 ER 303, 545
Latec Investments Ltd v Hotel Terrigal Pty Ltd (1965) 113 CLR 265, 624
Lawrence v Fen Tigers Ltd [2014] AC 822, 416–17, 442–5, 449
Lawrence v Mathison (1981) 11 NTR 1, 277–8
Leeds Industrial Cooperative Society Ltd v Slack [1924] AC 851, 448
Lewis v Australian Capital Territory (2020) 271 CLR 192, 504–10
Lewis Trusts v Bambers Stores [1982] FSR 281, 562
Lindsay Petroleum v Hurd (1875) LR 5 PC 221, 381–2
Livingstone v Rawyards Coal Co (1880) 5 App Cas 25, 207–8
LJP Investments Pty Ltd v Howard Chia Pty Ltd (1990) 24 NSWLR 499, 563–4
Loan Investment Corporation of Australasia v Bonner [1970] NZLR 724, 360–1, 367
London City Agency (JCD) Ltd v Lee [1970] Ch 597, 403
Lord v McMahon [2015] NSWSC 1619, 445
Louth v Diprose (1992) 175 CLR 621, 652
Lumbers v W Cook Builders Pty Ltd (in liq) (2008) 232 CLR 635, 7, 593–4
Lunn Poly Pty Ltd v Liverpool & Lancashire Properties Ltd [2007] L & TR 6, 437
Lysaght v Edwards (1876) 2 Ch D 499, 652

Mafo v Adams [1970] 1 QB 548, 479, 495
Maguire v Makaronis (1997) 188 CLR 449, 618–19, 630, 631
Mahaffy v Mahaffy [2013] NSWSC 245, 686
Mahoney v J Kruschich (Demolitions) Pty Ltd (1985) 156 CLR 522, 154–5
Malec v JC Hutton Pty Ltd (1990) 169 CLR 638, 43–4, 48, 49, 50
Mann v Paterson Constructions Pty Ltd (2019) 267 CLR 560, 587, 594–607
Marathon Asset Management LLP v Seddon [2017] EWHC 300 (Comm), 562
March v E 7 MH Stramare (1991) 171 CLR 506, 92–5
Mareva Compania Naviera SA v International Bulkcarriers SA [1975] 2 Lloyd's Rep 509, 681
Marks v GIO Australia Holdings Pty Ltd (1998) 196 CLR 494, 302–4
Martin v Ishard (1946) 48 WALR 52, 121
Matthews v ACP Publishing Pty Ltd (1998) 87 FCR 152, 435
McCracken v Phoenix Constructions (Qld) Pty Ltd [2013] 2 Qd R 27, 450
McFadzean v Construction, Forestry, Mining and Energy Union [2004] VSC 289, 479, 495
McGhee v National Coal Board [1973] 1 WLR 1, 110–11
McGroder v Maguire [2002] NSWCA 261, 121

McKenna v Richey [1950] VLR 360, 431
McKennitt v Ash [2008] QB 73, 410–11
McLoughlin v O'Brian [1983] 1 AC 410, 89
McMahon v Ambrose [1987] VR 817, 431
McNeilly v Imbree (2007) 47 MVR 536, 266
McRae v Commonwealth Disposal Commission (1951) 84 CLR 377, 190–1
Mercedes-Benz AG v Leiduck [1996] AC 284, 681
Midalco Pty Ltd v Rabenalt [1989] VR 461, 479
Mills v Ruthol Pty Ltd (2004) 61 NSWLR 1, 431
Millstream Pty Ltd v Schultz [1980] 1 NSWLR 547, 431
Modbury Triangle Shopping Centre Pty Ltd v Anzil (2000) 205 CLR 254, 122–3
Monks v Poynice Pty Ltd (1987) 11 ACLR 637, 592
Monroe Schneiders Associates (Inc) v No 1 Raberem Pty Ltd (1991) 33 FCR 1, 38, 39–40
Morris-Garner v One Step (Support) Ltd [2018] UKSC 20, 446, 447–8, 556, 559, 567–9, 573–9
Moss & Co v Johnston (1896) 22 VLR 530, 681
Mouat v Clark Boyce [1992] 2 NZLR 559, 347
Munchies Management Pty Ltd v Belperio (1988) 58 FCR 274, 612
Municipality of Peel v Canada [1992] 3 SCR 762, 592
Murphy v Overton Investments Pty Ltd (2004) 216 CLR 388, 301, 304–5
Musca v Astle Corporation Pty Ltd (1988) 80 ALR 251, 479, 480
Muschinski v Dodds (1985) 160 CLR 583, 652
My Kinda Town Ltd v Soll [1983] RPC 15, 544
Myers Stores Ltd v Soo [1991] 2 VR 597, 495

Nader v Urban Transport Authority (NSW) (1985) 2 NSWLR 501, 243–4
National Australia Bank Ltd v Dessau [1988] VR 521, 683
National Australia Bank Ltd v Nemur Varity Pty Ltd (2002) 4 VR 252, 240–1
National Insurance Co of New Zealand v Espagne (1961) 105 CLR 569, 282–3
New South Wales v Ibbett (2006) 229 CLR 638, 479
New South Wales Lotteries Corporation Pty Ltd v Kuzmanovski (2011) 195 FCR 234, 306–9, 502–3
Ninemia Maritime Corporation v Trave Schiffahrtsgesellschaft mbH & Co KG [1983] WLUK 838, aff'd [1983] 1 WLR 1412, 683
No 68 Ltd v Eastern Services Ltd [2006] 2 NZLR 43, 382–3
Nocton v Lord Ashburton [1914] AC 932, 324–6
Nominal Defendant v Gardikiotis (1996) 186 CLR 49, 207

Oakacre Ltd v Claire Cleaners (Holdings) Ltd [1982] Ch 197, 448
O'Brien v McKean (1968) 118 CLR 540, 72, 79, 80
O'Connor v Pitcairn (1901) 27 VLR 2, 681
O'Dea v Allstates Leasing System (WA) Pty Ltd (1983) 152 CLR 359, 474
Ogilvie v Ryan [1976] 2 NSWLR 504, 652
O'Halloran v RT Thomas & Family Pty Ltd (1998) 45 NSWLR 262, 321–2
Oldham v Lawson (No 1) [1976] VR 654, 495
Olins v Walters [2009] Ch 212, 652
Olwell v Nye & Nissen, 173 P 2d 652 (Wash, 1946), 548
One Step Support Pty Ltd v Morris-Garner [2018] UKSC 20, [2019], 561
Organic Marketing Australia Pty Ltd v Woolworths Ltd [2011] FCA 279, 677

Origin Energy LPC Ltd v BestCare Foods [2013] NSWCA 90, 35–7
Oughton v Seppings (1830) 109 ER 776, 545

Paciocco v Australia and New Zealand Banking Group Ltd (2016) 258 CLR 525, 469–74
Page One Records Ltd v Britton [1968] 1 WLR 157, 413, 414, 419
Pantalone v Alaouie (1989) 18 NSWLR 119, 212–13
Paramount Pictures Corporation v Hasluck (2006) 70 IPR 293, 479
Parry v Crooks (1981) 27 SASR 1, 408–9
Parsons v Burk [1971] NZLR 244, 680
Parsons v McBain (2001) 109 FCR 120, 652
Patel v Ali [1984] 1 Ch 283, 379–80
Patrick Stevedores Operations No 2 Pty Ltd v Maritime Union of Australia (No 3) (1998) 195 CLR 1, 152, 390–1, 683
Pavey & Matthews Pty Ltd v Paul (1987) 162 CLR 221, 590–1, 593, 595
Pearce v Hallett [1969] SASR 423, 479, 495
Pearson v Arcadia Store, Guyra, Ltd (No 2) (1935) 53 CLR 587, 685
Pell Frischmann Ltd v Bow Valley Iran Ltd [2011] 1 WLR 2370, 448
Pennington v Norris (1956) 96 CLR 10, 252–3
Performance Cars Ltd v Abraham [1962] 1 QB 33, 103
Permanent Building Society (in liq) v Wheeler (1994) 11 WAR 187, 349–51
Personal Representative of Tang Man Sit v Capacious Investments Ltd [1996] AC 514, 540–4
Peter Pan Manufacturing Corporation v Corsets Silhouette Ltd [1964] 1 WLR 96, 544
Photo Ptoduction Ltd v Securicor Transport Ltd [1980] AC 827, 5–6
Photographic Performance Ltd v Amusement Caterers (Peckham) Ltd [1964] Ch 195, 693
Pianta v National Finance & Trustees Ltd (1964) 180 CLR 146, 359–60
Pilmer v Duke Group Ltd (in liq) (2007) CLR 165, 346–7
Pollack v Volpato [1973] 1 NSWLR 653, 487–8
Port Macquarie-Hastings Council v Diveva Pty Ltd [2017] NSWCA 97, 64, 67–8
Posner v Scott Lewis [1997] Ch 25, 388–9
Potts v Miller (1940) 64 CLR 282, 78–9
Price v Strange [1977] 3 All ER 371, 383, 384–5
Proctor v Bayley (1889) 42 Ch D 390, 413
PT Bayan Resources TBK v BCBC Singapore Pte Ltd (2014) 320 ALR 289, 683
Purkess v Crittenden (1965) 114 CLR 164, 242–3
Pyrenees Shire Council v Day (1998) 192 CLR 330, 221

QB Investments Pty Ltd v Reed [1979] Qd R 58, 680
Quek v Beggs (1990) 5 BPR 11, 761, 631–3, 652, 656, 664

Radley v London and North Western Railway Co (1876) 1 App Cas 754, 245–6
Re Boyes (1884) 26 Ch D 531, 652
Re Dawson (Deceased) [1966] 2 NSWR 211, 71–2, 331–2, 340, 351
Re Goodchild [1997] 1 WLR 1216, 652
Re Jarvis (Deceased) [1958] 1 WLR 815, 581
Re Rose [1952] Ch 499, 652
Re Wan Ze Property Development (Aust) Pty Ltd (2012) 90 ACSR 593, 657
Redland Bricks Ltd v Morris [1970] AC 652, 693
Reid v Reid (New South Wales Supreme Court, Bryson J, 30 November 1998), 652, 656

Renard Constructions (ME) Pty Ltd v Minister of Public Works (1992) 26 NSWLR 234, 595
Renehan v Leeuwin Ocean Adventure Foundation Ltd (2006) 17 NTLR 83, 272
REW08 Projects Pty Ltd v PNC Lifestyle Investments Pty Ltd (2017) 95 NSWLR 458, 375–6
Roads and Traffic Authority v Royal (2008) 245 ALR 653, 135–6
Robinson v Harman (1848) 154 ER 363, 174, 176–7
Rookes v Barnard [1964] AC 1129, 479, 495
Rosseel NV v Oriental Commercial Shipping (UK) Ltd [1990] 1 WLR 1387, 683
Roxborough v Rothmans of Pall Mall Australia Ltd (2001) 208 CLR 516, 7, 13–14, 586, 587, 657
Rufo v Hosking (2004) 61 NSWLR, 54
Ruxley Electronics and Construction Ltd v Forsyth [1996] AC 344, 185–6
Ryan v Mutual Tontine Westminster Chambers Association [1893] 1 Ch 116, 386–7, 419, 448

Sanders v Snell (1997) 73 FCR 569, 479
Sanders v Snell (1998) 196 CLR 329, 479
Sayers v Collyer (1884) 28 Ch D 103, 431
Schumann v Abbott [1961] SASR 149, 153–4
Scott Carver Pty Ltd v SAS Trustee Corporation Ltd [2005] NSWCA 462, 120
Seager v Copydex (No 1) [1967] 1 WLR 923, 558, 562
Seager v Copydex (No 2) [1969] 1 WLR 809, 558, 562
Sellars v Adelaide Petroleum NL (1994) 179 CLR 332, 43, 46–9, 50, 54, 58, 62, 303, 309
Semelhago v Paramadevan [1996] 2 SCR 415, 361–2
Sharman v Evans (1977) 138 CLR 563, 278–9
Shelfer v City of London Electric Lighting Co [1895] 1 Ch 287, 415–16, 441–2
Shiffon Creations (S) Pte Ltd v Tong Lee Co Pte Ltd [1991] 1 Malayan LJ 65, 448
Simonius Vischer & Co v Holt & Thompson [1979] 2 NSWLR 322, 146–7
Sinclair Investments (UK) Ltd v Versailles Trade Finance Ltd [2012] Ch 453, 662–3
Skelton v Collins (1966) 115 CLR 94, 275–6
Sky Petroleum Ltd v VIP Petroleum Ltd [1974] 1 WLR 576, 431
Smith v Badenoch [1970] SASR 9, 137–8
Soames v Edge (1860) 70 ER 588, 430, 448
Sopov v Kane Constructions Pty Ltd (No 2) (2009) 246 CLR 498, 595
Stone v Chapppel (2017) 128 SASR 165, 187–8
Strand Electric and Engineering Co Ltd v Brisford Entertainments Ltd [1952] 2 QB 246, 564–7
Summer v Cocks (1927) 40 CLR 321, 380–1
Svanosio v McNamara (1956) 96 CLR 186, 639
Symons v Stacey (1922) 30 CLR 169, 245

Tabcorp Holdings Ltd v Bowen Investments Pty Ltd (2009) 236 CLR 272, 184–5
Tabet v Gett (2010) 240 CLR 537, 52–4
Tamplin v James (1880) 15 Ch D 215, 431
Target Holdings Ltd v Redferns [1996] AC 421, 325, 330, 332–3, 335, 340
TCN Channel Nine Pty Ltd v Anning (2002) 54 NSWLR 333, 495
Tenji v Henneberry & Associates Pty Ltd (2000) 98 FCR 324, 612
The Koursk [1924] P 140, 152–3
The Owners of the Steamship 'Mediana' v The Owners, Master and Crew of the Lightship 'Comet' (The 'Mediana') [1900] AC 113, 521–3

Thompson v Australian Capital Television Pty Ltd (1996) 186 CLR 574, 150–1, 156
Thorner v Major [2009] 1 WLR 776, 652
Timber Engineering Co Ltd v Anderson [1980] 2 NSWLR 488, 657
Todorovic v Waller (1981) 150 CLR 540, 81–2
Toteff v Antonas (1952) 87 CLR 647, 221–2
Toyota Finance Australia Ltd v Dennis (2002) 58 NSWLR 101, 459–61
Traian v Ware [1957] VR 200, 462–3, 495
Transfield Shipping Inc v Mercator Shipping Inc (The Achilleas) [2009] 1 AC 61, 201–3
Travel Compensation Fund v Tambree (2005) 224 CLR 627, 316–17
Tubemakers of Australia Ltd v Fibremakers (1976) 10 ALR 303, 104
Turf Club Auto Emporium Pte Ltd v Yeo Boong Hua [2018] SGCA 44, 561
Turjman v Stonewall Hotel Pty Ltd [2011] NSWCA 392, 130–1
Tyco Australia v Optus Networks Pty Ltd [2004] NSWCA 333, 27–9

University of Manitoba v Sanderson Estate (1998) 155 DLR (4th) 40, 652
Uren v John Fairfax & Sons Pty Ltd (1966) 117 CLR 118, 495

Vadasz v Pioneer Concrete (SA) Pty Ltd (1995) 184 CLR 102, 627–30
Van Son v Forestry Commission (1995) 86 LGERA 108, 495
Verrall v Great Yarmouth Borough Council [1981] QB 202, 431
Victoria Laundry (Windsor) Ltd v Newman Industries Ltd [1949] 2 KB 528, 200–1
Vieira v O'Shea [2012] NSWCA 21, 76
Vinidex Tubemakers Pty Ltd v Thiess Contractors Pty Ltd [2000] NSWCA 67, 164–5

Wakelin v London and South Western Railway Co (1887) LR 12 App Cas 41, 245
Wallace v Kam (2013) 250 CLR 375, 136–7
Wambo Coal Pty Ltd v Ariff (2007) 63 ACSR 426, 653–6, 657
Wardley Australia Ltd v Western Australia (1992) 175 CLR 514, 299–300
Warman International Ltd v Dwyer (1995) 182 CLR 544, 535–40, 581
Webster v Coles Myer Ltd [2009] NSWDC 4, 73
Wentworth v Woollahra Municipal Council (1982) 149 CLR 672, 432, 434–5
Westdeutsche Landesbank Girozentrale v Islington London Borough Council [1996] AC 669, 652
White and Carter (Councils) Ltd v McGregor [1962] AC 413, 399
Whitfield v De Lauret & Co Ltd (1920) 29 CLR 71, 479
Wight v Haberdan Pty Ltd [1984] 2 NSWLR 280, 366–7
Wilde v Gibson (1848) 9 ER 897, 639
Williams v Hursey (1959) 103 CLR 30, 479, 495
Willoughby Municipal Council v Halstead (1916) 22 CLR 352, 479, 495
Winnebago Industries Inc v Knott Investments Pty Ltd (No 4) (2015) 241 FCR 271, 562
Witham v Holloway (1995) 183 CLR 525, 692
Wotton v Queensland (No 5) (2016) 157 ALD 14, 515
Wotton v Queensland (No 6) [2017] FCA 245, 515
Wroth v Tyler [1974] 1 Ch 30, 446
Wrotham Park Estate Co Ltd v Parkside Homes Ltd [1974] 1 WLR 798, 556, 570–3

XL Petroleum (NSW) Pty Ltd v Caltex Oil (Australia) Pty Ltd (1985) 155 CLR 448, 156, 479

Yerkey v Jones (1939) 63 CLR 649, 611
York Air Conditioning & Refrigeration (A/asia) Pty Ltd v Commonwealth (1949) 80 CLR 11, 589
Young v Queensland Trustees Ltd (1956) 99 CLR 560, 398
Youyang Pty Ltd v Minter Ellison Morris Fletcher (2003) 212 CLR 484, 325, 330, 333–5, 340, 349, 352–3

Zhen v Mo [2008] VSC 300, 683
Zhou v Kousal (2012) 35 VR 419, 689
Zhu v Sydney Organising Committee for the Olympic Games [2001] NSWSC 989, 479, 495
Zhu v Treasurer (NSW) (2004) 218 CLR 530, 479, 495
Zomojo Pty Ltd v Hurd (No 4) [2014] FCA 441, 189–90
Zuecker v Bruggmann (No 3) [2017] QSC 259, 657

TABLE OF STATUTES

Commonwealth

Australian Consumer Law, 7, 135, 137, 297, 394, 422, 493, 511, 556, 676
- ch 2, 297
- ch 3, 297
- ch 4, 297
- s 18, 297, 319, 611
- s 19, 611
- ss 20–22A, 611
- s 232, 422, 426
- s 232(1)(a), 422
- s 232(4), 422
- s 234, 676–7
- s 236, 297, 306, 309
- s 236(1), 317
- s 237, 297
- s 238, 297
- s 243(a)–(d), 611–12
- s 246, 525–6
- s 246(2)(a), 526
- s 246(d), 526

Australian Securities and Investments Commission Act 2001, 298, 426
- s 12CA, 298
- s 12DA, 298

Circuit Layouts Act 1989
- s 27(2), 422, 544
- s 27(4), 480

Competition and Consumer Act 2010, 261, 274, 297, 422, 517
- pt VIA, 319
- s 87E, 495
- s 87W(2), 261, 265
- s 87Y, 82
- s 87Y(1), 82
- s 87ZB, 495
- s 131A, 298
- s 137B, 317
- s 163A, 517
- sch 2, 556, 611, 676

Copyright Act 1968, 544
- s 115(2), 421, 544
- s 115(4), 480, 489

Corporations Act 2001, 424, 450, 518, 676, 677
- pt 9.5, 449–50
- s 601ED, 425
- s 1317E(1)–(2), 518
- s 1323, 682
- s 1324, 424, 426
- s 1324(1), 424, 677
- s 1324(4), 677
- s 1324(6)–(8), 424–5
- s 1324(8), 677
- s 1324(10), 450

Designs Act 2003
- s 75(1)(a), 421
- s 75(1)(b), 544
- s 75(3), 480

Federal Court of Australia Act 1976
- s 51A(2)(d), 84
- s 52, 84

Federal Court Rules 2011
- rr 7.31–7.38, 681
- r 7.32(1), 683
- rr 7.41–7.47, 684
- r 41.06, 692
- r 42.14, 693

Health and Other Services (Compensation) Act 1995
- s 3, 283
- s 7(1), 284
- s 7(3), 284
- s 8(1), 284

High Court Rules 2004
- r 8.05, 692
- r 11.02.3, 693

Income Tax Assessment Act 1936
- s 261, 589

Law Reform (Contributory Negligence and Tortfeasors' Contribution) Act 1947
- s 7(2), 163

Military Rehabilitation and Compensation Act 2004, 255
National Consumer Credit Protection Act 2009
sch 1, 691
sch 1 ss 94–97, 691
National Disability Insurance Scheme Act 2013
s 106, 283
Naval Defence Act 1910, 262
Patents Act 1990
s 122, 421
s 122(1), 407, 544
s 122(1A), 480
Plant Breeder's Rights Act 1994
s 56(3), 422, 544
Racial Discrimination Act 1975, 514
s 18C, 514
Safety, Rehabilitation and Compensation Act 1988, 255
Seafarers Rehabilitation and Compensation Act 1992, 255
Trade Marks Act 1995
s 126(1)(a), 421
s 126(1)(b), 544
s 126(2), 480
Trade Practices Act 1974, 7, 297, 423
s 52, 121, 297, 311, 502
s 82, 311

AUSTRALIAN CAPITAL TERRITORY

Civil Law (Wrongs) Act 2002, 249, 289
ss 12–14, 513
s 16(2), 480
s 20(1), 161
s 21(1), 163
s 21(2), 163
s 23(3)(b), 163
s 23(3)(c), 163
s 24, 288, 289, 290
s 45(2), 113
s 92, 255
s 93, 255
s 100, 274
s 102, 247
s 102(1)(b), 251
s 107B(3)(a), 166
s 107F(1)(a), 166
s 139F(2), 495
s 139H, 480
s 173, 639
s 218, 287
Civil Liability Act 2002
s 11A(2), 255
Court Procedures Rules 2006
pt 2.18, 687
rr 740–745, 681
r 741(1), 683
r 741(2), 683
rr 750–755, 684
r 1617, 84
r 2001, 686
r 2150, 686
r 2154, 687
r 2157, 686
r 2201, 689
r 2202, 689
r 2216(8), 689
r 2217, 689
rr 2218–2221, 689
r 2368, 690
rr 2400–2407, 690
r 2403(1), 690
r 2403(2), 690
r 2420, 690
r 2421, 690
r 2442(1)(b), 692
r 2472, 693
r 2500, 686
r 2503, 693
r 2506, 693
rr 2550–2564, 678
Crimes (Sentence Administration) Act 2005, 504
Law Reform (Miscellaneous Provisions) Act 1965
s 9(1)(b), 251
Public Interest Disclosure Act 2012
s 41(3), 480, 495
Supreme Court Act 1933
s 34, 427, 432
Workers Compensation Act 1951, 255

NEW SOUTH WALES

Builders Licensing Act 1971
s 45, 590

Civil Liability Act 2002, 98, 193, 195
s 5D, 96, 136
s 5D(2), 99, 109
s 5R, 96
s 5R(2), 248
s 11, 257
s 11A, 195
s 14, 82
s 14(1)–(2), 82
s 15(2), 261, 265
s 15B, 261, 274
s 15B(5)(b), 261, 281
s 15C, 261, 272
s 16, 195
s 21, 480, 495
s 27, 257–8
ss 27–28, 195–6
s 28, 258
s 31, 196, 258
s 34(1)(a), 166
s 35(1)(a), 166
s 50(3), 248
s 50(5), 248
Civil Procedure Act 2005
pt 8, 687
s 85, 84
s 124, 678
s 126, 690
s 130, 686
s 131, 686
Compensation to Relatives Act 1897
s 3(1), 288, 289, 290
Conveyancing Act 1919
s 37A, 421
Defamation Act 2005
s 20, 514
s 20(3), 514
s 35(2), 495
s 37, 480
s 38, 514
Equity Act 1901
s 10, 519
Law Reform (Marital Consortium) Act 1984
s 3(1), 287
Law Reform (Miscellaneous Provisions) Act 1944
s 2(2)(a)(i), 480
Law Reform (Miscellaneous Provisions) Act 1946
s 5(1)(a), 161
s 5(1)(c), 163
s 5(2), 163
Law Reform (Miscellaneous Provisions) Act 1965
s 9, 247
Liquor Act 1982, 98
Motor Accident Injuries Act 2017
s 49, 82
Motor Accidents Act 1988
s 81A, 480
Motor Accidents Compensation Act 1999, 480
Public Lotteries Act 1996, 502
Sale of Goods Act 1923
s 4(2A)(b), 639
s 54, 181–2
Securities Industry Act 1975
s 97(1)(b), 624
Supreme Court Act 1970, 427
s 68, 432
s 75, 517
Supreme Court Rules 1970
pt 55 r 10, 693
pt 55 r 13, 693
Uniform Civil Procedure Rules 2005
pt 37, 686
r 25.3, 681
rr 25.10–25.17, 681
r 25.11(1), 683
rr 25.18–25.24, 684
rr 25.19–25.20, 684
r 36.5(2), 692
r 39.6(2)(c), 689
r 39.6(3)(b), 689
rr 39.7–39.14, 689
r 39.7(2), 689
r 39.10, 689
r 39.38(2), 690
r 39.44, 690
r 39.45, 690
r 40.6(2)(c)(ii), 693
Workers Compensation Act 1987, 255
s 151J, 82
s 151R, 480
Workplace Injury Management and Workers Compensation Act 1998, 255

NORTHERN TERRITORY

Absconding Debtors Act 1978, 678, 686
- s 4(1), 679
- ss 5–6, 680
- ss 13–15, 679, 682

Compensation (Fatal Injuries) Act 1974
- s 7(1), 288, 289, 290
- s 10(4)(h), 292

Defamation Act 2006
- s 32(2), 495
- s 34, 480

Law Reform (Miscellaneous Provisions) Act 1956
- s 12(2), 161
- s 12(4), 163
- s 13, 163
- s 16, 247
- s 16(1)(b), 251

Personal Injuries (Liabilities and Damages) Act 2003
- s 4(1), 255
- s 14, 248
- s 19, 480, 495
- s 22, 82
- s 23(1), 261, 265

Proportionate Liability Act 2005
- s 4(3)(a), 166
- s 13(1)(a), 166

Return to Work Act 2015, 255

Supreme Court Act 1979
- s 14(1)(b), 427, 432

Supreme Court Rules 1987
- ord 37A, 681
- ord 37B, 684
- ords 66–74, 687
- ord 66 r 75.08, 693
- ord 73, 690
- ord 74, 690
- r 37A.02(1), 683
- r 66.05, 692
- r 73.07, 690

QUEENSLAND

Civil Liability Act 2003
- s 23(1), 248
- s 23(2), 248
- s 28(3)(a), 166
- s 31(1)(a), 166
- s 47(1)–(3), 248
- s 50, 255
- s 52, 480, 495
- s 56, 261, 272
- s 57, 82
- s 59, 265
- ss 59A–59D, 261, 274
- s 59A(1), 281
- s 59B(1)–(2), 281
- s 59C(4)(b), 281

Civil Proceedings Act 2011
- s 8, 427, 432
- s 59(2), 84
- s 61, 82
- s 64, 288, 289, 290
- s 67, 295
- s 67(2), 292
- s 67(3), 292
- s 68(4)(a), 295
- s 68(4)(b), 295
- s 100, 678, 686

Defamation Act 2005
- s 35(2), 495
- s 37, 480

Law Reform Act 1995
- s 6(a), 161
- s 6(c), 163
- s 7, 163
- s 10, 247
- s 10(1)(b), 251
- s 13, 286

Succession Act 1981
- s 66(2)(b), 480

Uniform Civil Procedure Rules 1999
- ch 19, 687
- ch 19 pt 8, 690
- ch 19 pt 9, 690
- r 259(2)(c), 679
- rr 260–260G, 681
- r 260A(1), 683
- rr 261–261F, 685
- rr 828–829, 688
- r 829(1)(b), 689
- r 833, 689
- rr 855–856, 689–90
- r 856(3), 690
- r 875, 691
- r 877, 690, 691

Uniform Civil Procedure Rules 1999 (cont.)
r 878, 690
r 904(1)(b), 692
r 919, 693
r 927, 693
r 931, 693
r 941, 678
r 942, 681
Water Act 2000
s 788(2)(b), 480
Workers' Compensation and Rehabilitation Act 2003, 255
s 306B, 480

SOUTH AUSTRALIA

Civil Liability Act 1936, 261, 269, 272
s 3(1), 269
s 23, 288, 289, 290
s 34(2), 113
s 34(2)–(3), 113
s 44(1), 248
s 46(1), 248
s 46(2), 248
s 54(1)–(2), 269
s 57, 266
s 58(1)(a), 261, 265
s 65(1), 286–7
Debtors Act 1936
s 4, 680
Defamation Act 2005
s 33(2), 495
s 35, 480
Enforcement of Judgments Act 1991, 678, 687
s 5, 686
s 5(7), 686
s 6(2), 690
s 6(7), 690
s 8, 690
s 12, 693
s 14, 680
Family Relationships Act 1975
s 11A, 287
Law Reform (Contributory Negligence and Apportionment of Liability) Act 2001, 247
s 3(2)(a)(i), 166
s 6(1), 163
s 6(5)–(7), 163
s 7(2)(b), 251
s 8(2), 166
s 12(1), 161
Misrepresentation Act 1971
s 6, 639
Return to Work Act 2014, 255
Supreme Court Act 1935
s 30, 427, 432
s 30C(4)(e), 84
s 114(1), 84
Supreme Court Civil Rules 2006
r 225(3), 692
r 247, 681
r 247(2)(a), 683
r 248, 685
r 306, 693
r 320, 689
Survival of Causes of Action Act 1940
s 3(1)(b), 480

TASMANIA

Administration and Probate Act 1935
s 27(3)(a), 480
Civil Liability Act 2002
s 3, 256
s 3B, 256–7
s 5(1), 248
s 5(4), 248
s 23(1), 248
s 23(2), 248
s 24, 257
s 25, 272
s 28A, 82
s 28BA(3), 261, 274
s 28D, 287
s 43A(1), 166
s 43B(1)(a), 166
Debtors Act 1870
s 5, 678, 679
s 5(2), 678, 679
Debtors Act 1888, 686
Defamation Act 2005
s 35(2), 495
s 37, 480
Environmental Management and Pollution Control Act 1994
s 48(5)(g), 480

Fatal Accidents Act 1934
s 4, 288, 289, 290
Supreme Court Civil Procedure Act 1932
s 11(13), 427, 432
s 11(13)(b), 430
s 35(2), 84
s 165, 84
Supreme Court Rules 2000
pt 35, 687
pt 36 div 1, 690
r 876(3)(c)(ii), 693
r 883(1)(b), 692
r 906(3)(c), 689
r 932(2)(b), 690
rr 937A–937H, 681
r 937B(1), 683
rr 937I–937O, 685
r 941(2)(d), 693
r 942(4), 693
Workers Rehabilitation and Compensation Act 1988, 255
Wrongs Act 1954
s 3(1)(a), 161
s 3(1)(c), 163
s 3(2), 163
s 4, 247
s 4(1), 251

VICTORIA

Administration and Probate Act 1958
s 29(1), 289
s 29(2)(a), 480
Australian Consumer Law and Fair Trading Act 2012
s 24(1), 639
Defamation Act 2005
s 35(2), 495
s 37, 480
Domestic Building Contracts Act 1995, 594
s 38, 594
Imprisonment of Fraudulent Debtors Act 1958, 686
Judgment Debt Recovery Act 1984
s 7, 686
s 19, 686
Magistrates' Court Act 1989
s 111(10)–(12), 690
Marketing of Primary Products Act 1958, 217
Protected Disclosure Act 2012
s 47(3), 480, 495
Supreme Court Act 1986
s 37(3), 682
s 38, 427, 432, 500
s 60(2)(f), 84
ss 86–100, 678
s 87(a), 679
s 101(1), 84
s 119, 678
Supreme Court (General Civil Procedure) Rules 2015
ord 37A, 681
ord 52B, 685
ords 66–74, 687
ord 73, 690
rr 37A.02–37A.04, 681–2
r 37A.02(1), 683
r 66.05(2)(c)(ii), 693
r 66.10, 692
r 73.07(2), 690
r 75.08, 693
r 75.08.1, 693
r 75.11(3), 693
Transport Accident Act 1986
s 93(7), 480
s 93(13), 82, 83
Workplace Injury Rehabilitation and Compensation Act 2013, 255
s 345, 82
Wrongs Act 1958
ss 14I 14J, 512–3
s 16, 289, 290
ss 16–17, 290
s 19(2)–(4), 292
s 23B(1), 163
s 24(2), 163
s 24AA, 161
s 24AG(1), 166
s 24AI(1)(a), 166
s 26, 247
s 26(1), 247
s 26(1)(b), 251
s 28B, 255
s 28C, 255

Wrongs Act 1958 (cont.)
s 28IA(1), 261, 265
s 28ID, 261, 274
s 28ID(3)(b), 261, 281
s 28IE, 261, 274
s 28LB, 255
s 28LC, 255
s 28N, 255
s 62(1), 248
s 62(2), 248
s 281, 82

WESTERN AUSTRALIA

Civil Judgments Enforcement Act 2004, 687
s 8(1), 84
s 66, 689
Civil Judgments Enforcement Regulations 2005
r 35, 689
Civil Liability Act 2002
s 3, 255
s 5AI, 166
s 5AK(1)(a), 166
s 5K(1), 248
s 5K(2), 248
s 5L, 248
s 6, 255
ss 9–10, 279–80
s 12(3), 261, 265
s 12(4), 261, 265
s 13, 261, 265
Defamation Act 2005
s 35(2), 495
s 37, 480
Electricity Act 1945
s 50(2), 480
Fatal Accidents Act 1959, 291, 293
s 4(1), 288, 289, 290, 291
Law Reform (Contributory Negligence and Tortfeasors' Contribution) Act 1947
s 4, 247
s 4(1), 251
s 7(1)(a), 161
s 7(1)(c), 163
Law Reform (Miscellaneous Provisions) Act 1941
s 3, 287
s 5, 82
s 5(1), 83
Law Reform (Miscellaneous Provisions) Act 1955
s 4(2)(a), 480
Motor Vehicle (Third Party Insurance) Act 1943
s 16, 71
Restraint of Debtors Act 1984, 678, 686
ss 17–19, 679, 682
Rules of the Supreme Court 1971
ord 42 r 3, 692
ord 52A, 681
ord 52A r 2(1), 683
ord 52B, 685
ord 55 r 6, 693
ord 55 r 7(1), 693
Supreme Court Act 1935
s 25(10), 427, 432
s 62(2)(a), 679
ss 63–64, 678
ss 63–68, 678, 679
Workers' Compensation and Injury Management Act 1981 255
s 3a(i)–(ii), 255
s 18(1)–(2), 256

United Kingdom

Chancery Amendment Act 1858, 429
s 2, 429
Contempt of Court Act 1981
s 14(1), 693
Fatal Accidents Act 1846, 289–90
Misrepresentation Act 1967
s 1(b), 639
Official Secrets Act 1911, 550
Rules of the Supreme Court 1883
ord 25 r 5, 519

1 INTRODUCTION

I	Introduction	1
II	What is a remedy?	1
	A Monism and dualism	7
III	The common law and equity divide in Australia	12
IV	A functional approach to remedies	18

I Introduction

This chapter considers the law of civil remedies: the definition and nature of 'remedies' and the relationship between remedy and right. It provides extracts which discuss the ongoing debate about whether judges should have discretion in the remedies they grant. It considers the nature of the common law and equity divide in Australian law as expressed in case law and in academic discussion. Finally, it outlines a functional approach to remedies.

II What is a remedy?

Concept	Short explanation	Relevant authorities	Principles text
What is a remedy?	A civil remedy can be viewed as a secondary right arising from the breach of a primary right (such as the right to performance of a contract). However, it has been suggested that the definition of remedy include the rights arising from judicial enforcement of a pre-litigation grievance, usually an actual or threatened infringement of a right.	*Ashby v White* (1703) 92 ER 126 John Austin, *Lectures on Jurisprudence*, Robert Campbell and John Murray (eds), (J. Murray, 5th ed, 1885) vol 2, lecture XLV, 788–95 *Photo Production Ltd v Securicor Transport Ltd* [1980] AC 827 Rafal Zakrzewski, *Remedies Reclassified* (Oxford University Press, 2005) 1–2	Chapter 1: [1.4]–[1.16]
Monism and dualism	There is a debate as to the relationship between remedy and right, and the extent to which a judge should have discretion.	Peter Birks, 'Three Kinds of Objections to Discretionary Remedialism' (2000) 29(1) *University of Western Australia Law Review* 1	Chapter 1: [1.17]–[1.20]

Concept	Short explanation	Relevant authorities	Principles text
	The monist view asserts the remedy is simply a mirror of the plaintiff's cause of action and there is no or little discretion. The dualist view asserts that the judge should chose whatever remedy is appropriate for the case.	Grant Hammond, 'Rethinking Remedies: The Changing Nature of the Conception of the Relationship Between Legal and Equitable Remedies' in Jeff Berryman (ed), *Remedies: Issues and Perspectives* (Carswell, 1991) 85	
	The compromise position asserts there is a 'sticky' relationship between remedy and right which allows for some discretion.	David Wright, 'Wrong and Remedy: A Sticky Relationship' (2001) (2) *Singapore Journal of Legal Studies* 300	

The extracts in this section deal with the legal definition of private law remedies, and the relationship between remedies and fundamental rights. The next case explains the importance of remedies in legal systems.

Ashby v White (1703) 92 ER 126

Facts and issues

A bailiff prevented an eligible voter from casting his vote. The voter's preferred candidate was elected anyway.

Decision

Holt CJ's dissent (later upheld by the House of Lords) is relevant for his discussion of rights and remedies.

Holt CJ (nominate)

> [**953**] If the plaintiff has a right, he must of necessity have a means to vindicate and maintain it, and a remedy if he is injured in the exercise or enjoyment of it; and indeed it is a vain thing to imagine a right without a remedy; for … want of right and want of remedy are reciprocal. … [**954**] Where a man has but one remedy to come at his right, if he loses that he loses his right. It would look very strange, when the commons of England are so fond of their right of sending representatives to Parliament, that it should be in the power of a sheriff, or other officer, to deprive them of that right, and yet that they should have no remedy; it is a thing to be admired at by all mankind.

The extract which follows is taken from the writings of John Austin (1790–1859), an English legal theorist who was strongly influenced by the legal positivism of the time. His theories of rights and remedies have been influential.

John Austin, *Lectures on Jurisprudence*, Robert Campbell and John Murray (eds), (J. Murray, 5th ed, 1885) vol 2, lecture XLV, 788–95

[**788**] … There are facts or events from which rights and duties arise, which are legal causes or antecedents of rights and duties, or of which rights and duties are legal effects or consequences. There are also facts or events which extinguish rights and duties, or in which rights and duties terminate or cease. The events which are causes of rights and duties may be divided in the following manner: namely, into acts, forbearances, and omissions, which are violations of rights or duties, and events which are not violations of rights or duties.

Acts, forbearances, and omissions, which are violations of rights or duties, are styled delicts, injuries, or offences.

Rights and duties which are consequences of delicts, are sanctioning (or preventive) and remedial (or reparative). In other words the ends or purposes for which they are conferred and imposed, are two: first to prevent violations of rights and duties which are not consequences of delicts; secondly to cure the evils or repair the mischiefs which such violations engender.

…

[**789**] All the rights and duties which I style sanctioning or secondary, are undoubtedly means or instruments for making the primary available. They arise out of violations of primary rights, and are mainly intended to prevent such violations: though in the case of the rights and duties which arise out of civil injuries, the secondary rights and duties also answer the subordinate purpose of giving redress to the injured parties.

But though secondary rights and duties are merely adjective or instrumental, many of the rights and duties which I style primary are also of the same character. …

In short, rights and duties are of two classes:

1st. Those which exist in and per se: which are, as it were, the ends for which law exists: or which subserve immediately the ends or purposes of law. 2ndly. Those which imply the existence of other rights and duties, and which are merely conferred for the better protection and enforcement of those other rights and duties whose existence they so suppose.

Though secondary rights and duties (or rights and duties arising out of injuries) are of this instrumental character, many rights and duties which are primary or principal (or which do not arise out of injuries) are also of the same nature. …

[**790**] Those which I call primary do not arise from injuries, or from violations of other rights and duties. Those which I call secondary … arise from violations of other rights and duties, or from injuries, delicts, or offences.

The rights and duties which I style secondary, suppose that the obedience to the law is not perfect, and arise entirely from that imperfect obedience. If the obedience to the law were absolutely perfect, primary rights and duties are the only ones which would exist; or, at least are the only ones which would ever be exercised, or which could ever assume a practical form. If the obedience to the law were absolutely perfect, it is manifest that sanctions would be dormant: and that none of the rights and duties which sanction others, or which are mainly intended to protect others from violation, could ever exist in fact or practice, although they would be ready to start into existence on the commission of injuries or wrongs. If the disposition to obey the law were perfect, and if the law were perfectly known by all, there would be no injuries or violations of the law: and, by consequence, all the law relating to injuries, to the rights, duties, and other consequences flowing from injuries, and to procedure, would lie dormant.

...

[**791**] I do not deny that rights of the sort which I have called primary, may arise from injuries in a remote and consequential manner; as, for example, the rights arising from a judgment, or the lien of the plaintiff on the lands and goods of the defendant. But these rights do not arise so much from the injury itself, as from a peculiar title or mode of acquisition, namely the judgment and the institution of the suit. In order, however, to meet this objection, I will define primary rights and duties to be those which do not arise from violations of other rights or duties directly.

...

[**792**] It is said by Heineccius, 'actio non est *jus*, sed *medium* jus persequendi.'[1] But it is impossible to distinguish completely a *right of action* from the action or procedure which enforces it. For much of the right of action consists of rights to take those very steps by which the end of the action is accomplished.

It is perfectly true, that the scope or purpose of the right of action is distinct from the procedure resorted to when the right is enforced. Much of the procedure consists of rights which avail against the ministers of justice rather than against the defendant. And the parts of it which consist of rights against the defendant himself, are totally distinct from the end which it is the object of the process to accomplish.

But still it is impossible to extricate the right of action itself from those subsidiary rights by which it is enforced. And it is manifestly absurd to deny that the process involves *rights*, because the rights which it involves are instruments for the attainment of another right. And this is a reason for joining the law of procedure to the law of civil injuries and crimes.

...

[**793**] ... In most systems of law, a vast number of primary rights and duties are not separated from the secondary: That is to say; The primary right and duty is not described in a distinct and substantive manner; but it is created or imposed [**794**] by a declaration on the part of the legislature, that such or such an act, or such and such a forbearance or omission, shall amount to an injury: And that the party sustaining the injury shall have such or such a remedy against the party injuring; or that the party injuring shall be punished in a certain manner.

Nay, in some cases, the law which confers or imposes the primary right or duty, and which defines the nature of the injury, is contained by implication in the law which gives the remedy, or which determines the punishment.

And it is perfectly clear that the law which gives the remedy, or which determines the punishment, is the only one that is absolutely necessary. For the remedy or punishment implies a foregone injury, and a foregone injury implies that a primary right or duty has been violated. And, further, the primary right or duty owes its existence as such to the injunction or prohibition of certain acts; and to the remedy or punishment to be applied in the event of disobedience.

The essential part of every imperative law is the imperative part of it: ie the injunction or prohibition of some given act, and the menace of an evil in case of non-compliance.

1 This translates to: 'An action is not a right; but it is the means the law affords for pursuing the right'.

The reason for describing the primary right and duty apart; for describing the injury apart; and for describing the remedy or punishment apart, is the clearness and compactness which results from the separation. The cause of the greater compactness is that the same remedial process is often applicable, not merely to this particular right, but to a great variety of classes of rights; and, therefore, if it be separated from the rights to which it is applicable, it may be disposed of at once; otherwise it must be frequently repeated. But it is perfectly clear that the description of any of the separate elements, is not complete without reference to the rest. I have no right, independently of the injunction or prohibition which declares that some given act, forbearance or omission, would be a violation of my right; nor would the act or forbearance be a violation of my right, [**795**] unless my right and the corresponding duty were clothed with a sanction, criminal or civil.

In strictness, my own terms, 'primary and secondary rights and duties,' do not represent a logical distinction. For a primary right or duty is not of itself a right or duty, without the secondary right or duty by which it is sustained; and *e converso*.

So complete is the complication of the one branch of the law with the other, that some primary duties cannot be described with any approach to completeness in their own part of the law; they can only be apprehended by looking at the description of the corresponding injury. [Footnotes omitted]

The distinction between primary rights and secondary rights has been accepted by Lord Diplock in the following case.

Photo Production Ltd v Securicor Transport Ltd [1980] AC 827

Facts and issues

The primary issue was whether an exclusion clause in a contract was effective to exclude an accidental fire caused at Photo Production's factory by an employee of Securicor.

Decision

For present purposes, only Lord Diplock's discussion of the rights arising from a breach of contract is relevant.

Lord Diplock

[**848**] A basic principle of the common law of contract, to which there are no exceptions that are relevant in the instant case, is that parties to a contract are free to determine for themselves what primary obligations they will accept. They may state these in express words in the contract itself and, where they do, the statement is determinative; but in practice a commercial contract never states all the primary obligations of the parties in full; many are left to be incorporated by implication of law from the legal nature of the contract into which the parties are entering. But if the parties wish to reject or modify primary obligations which would otherwise be so incorporated, they are fully at liberty to

do so by express words. Leaving aside those comparatively rare cases in which the court is able to enforce a primary obligation by decreeing specific performance of it, breaches of primary obligations give rise to substituted or secondary obligations on the part of the party in default, and, in some cases, may entitle the other party to be relieved from further performance of his own primary obligations. These secondary obligations of the contract breaker and any concomitant relief of the other party from his own [**849**] primary obligations also arise by implication of law – generally common law, but sometimes statute … . The contract, however, is just as much the source of secondary obligations as it is of primary obligations; and like primary obligations that are implied by law, secondary obligations too can be modified by agreement between the parties, although, for reasons to be mentioned later, they cannot, in my view, be totally excluded. In the instant case, the only secondary obligations and concomitant reliefs that are applicable arise by implication of the common law as modified by the express words of the contract.

Every failure to perform a primary obligation is a breach of contract. The secondary obligation on the part of the contract breaker to which it gives rise by implication of the common law is to pay monetary compensation to the other party for the loss sustained by him in consequence of the breach; but, with two exceptions, the primary obligations of both parties so far as they have not yet been fully performed remain unchanged. This secondary obligation to pay compensation (damages) for non-performance of primary obligations I will call the 'general secondary obligation.' It applies in the cases of the two exceptions as well.

The exceptions are: (1) Where the event resulting from the failure by one party to perform a primary obligation has the effect of depriving the other party of substantially the whole benefit which it was the intention of the parties that he should obtain from the contract, the party not in default may elect to put an end to all primary obligations of both parties remaining unperformed. (If the expression 'fundamental breach' is to be retained, it should, in the interests of clarity, be confined to this exception.) (2) Where the contracting parties have agreed, whether by express words or by implication of law; that *any* failure by one party to perform a particular primary obligation … irrespective of the gravity of the event that has in fact resulted from the breach; shall entitle the other party to elect to put an end to all primary obligations of both parties remaining unperformed. …

Other theories seek to relate remedies to their judicial origin. For example, Rafal Zakzrewski sets out a theory of remedies which links remedies to their source: judicial commands and orders.

Rafal Zakrzewski, *Remedies Reclassified* (Oxford University Press, 2005) 1–2

[**1**] The word 'remedy' is constantly on lawyers' lips. Legal remedies are claimed, sought, found, had, requested, elected, chosen, pursued, used, available, refused, allowed, obtained, awarded, dispensed, granted, given, provided, fashioned, and [**2**] enforced. They are described

as common law, equitable, statutory, discretionary, as of right, *in rem, in personam*, proprietary, personal, specific, substitutional, monetary, non-monetary, coercive, non-coercive, enforceable, constitutive, declaratory, judicial, non-judicial, self-help, civil, private, public, or administrative. But, rather disturbingly, as Burrows points out '[t]he concept of a remedy has rarely been subjected to rigorous analysis.'

As a consequence, remedy is used synonymously with a wide range of different terms and, what is probably worse, by way of contrast to an equally long and diverse list. It is used synonymously with action, response, redress, and relief. It is used in contradistinction to wrong, injury, cause of action, liability, substance, institution, and doctrine. Most confusingly, it is used both as a synonym of right and in opposition to it. In short, the concept of a remedy is unstable. It comprises a number of different but insufficiently differentiated legal concepts.

...

Remedies will be broadly approximated to court orders. They will be rigorously separated from substantive rights, that is, rights which can be said to exist prior to the making of a court order. More strictly, remedies will be identified as the rights immediately arising from certain judicial commands and statements which aim to redress a pre-suit grievance, usually an actual or threatened infringement of a substantive right. [Footnotes omitted]

A Monism and dualism

There are three sources of remedies in Australian law: common law, equity and statute.

Australian law generally takes a discretionary approach to remedies, particularly in equity and statute. As Paul Finn has noted,[2] this stems from Australia's commitment to traditional equity, and from the influence of the *Trade Practices Act 1974* (Cth) (now the *Australian Consumer Law*) and the unhierarchical 'basket of remedies' available under that statute. By contrast, English legal scholarship has tended to decry discretionary remedialism. In what follows, the 'monist', 'dualist' and moderate approach to remedies will be outlined.

Peter Birks, the Regius Professor of Civil Law at the University of Oxford from 1989 until his death in 2004, expressed a monist view of remedies, saying, '[t]he secondary obligation to pay compensatory damages is ... the same thing as the right looked at from the other end'.[3] While he was very influential in England, his theories were rejected by the High Court on several occasions,[4] and thus should be treated with care in an Australian context.

2 P Finn, 'Equitable Doctrine and Discretion in Remedies' in WR Cornish, R Nolan and J O'Sullivan (eds), *Restitution Past, Present and Future* (Hart Publishing, 1998) 251.

3 P Birks, 'Definition and Division: A Meditation on Institutes 3.13' in P Birks (ed.), *The Classification of Obligations* (Clarendon Press, 1997) 24.

4 *Roxborough v Rothmans of Pall Mall Australia Ltd* (2001) 208 CLR 516; *Farah Constructions Pty Ltd v Say-Dee Pty Ltd* (2007) 230 CLR 89; *Lumbers v W Cook Builders Pty Ltd (in liq)* (2008) 232 CLR 635; *Bofinger v Kingsway Group Ltd* (2009) 239 CLR 269.

Peter Birks, 'Three Kinds of Objections to Discretionary Remedialism' (2000) 29(1) *University of Western Australia Law Review* 1

Birks defines 'discretionary remedialism' as:

> [**3**] The simplest way to sum this up might be to say that discretionary remedialism remakes the civil law into the mould of the criminal law. In the latter the judge generally has a discretion to impose the sentence which he thinks best. In some cases, not very many, the sentence will be fixed. In the rest it will usually be only rather loosely constrained. Where the criminal judge has a discretion, there will be principles of sentencing to take into account, but the discretion remains a strong discretion. The proof of that is that the law does not set itself any goal gradually to eliminate discretion as matters become better understood. The judge's sentencing discretion is a permanent feature of the criminal landscape. Attempts by politicians to fix sentences are generally greeted with howls of dismay. Meanwhile, the question whether the accused is guilty or not guilty – the equivalent of 'liability' on the civil side – remains closely defined by the law. … Once the accused is found guilty, he is at the mercy of the judge's sentencing discretion.

Birks advances three objections to discretionary remedialism. The first, 'No historical legitimacy' is outlined at 8:

> **[8]** The first and most immediate of the three families of objection is that discretionary remedialism can only be introduced by statute. It is beyond the [**9**] range of interpretative creativity. This is an argument chiefly from authority. As an interpreter a judge must limit his creativity to what can be said to be already the case, according to arguments consonant with the rules of recognition operative in the jurisdiction in question.
>
> …
>
> One might agree with the discretionary remedialists that where conduct amounts to a legal wrong … a choice does initially have to be made between a variety of responses. There is no naturally correct response to a civil wrong. Choices have to be made. However, it has not in the past been for the judges to choose. It has been for the law to make the choice and, where the law makes no final selection, for the plaintiff. For example, a question arises whether the wrongdoer shall pay punitive damages. The law makes the choice, not the judge. Again, shall the wrongdoer give up his gain? Once more, the law makes the choice. As the choice is made, the law confers on victim-plaintiffs a defined remedial right.

The second, 'Managing dispute settlement', is outlined at 14–15:

> [**14**] Uncertainty as to the sum winnable will undermine important decisions all along the line. Settlements are generally looked on as a good thing: 'interest rei publicae ut sit finis litium' (it is in the public interest that there should be an end to quarrels). They are not a good thing, but a simple engine of injustice when the uncertainty of the law leads to a despairing splitting of differences.
>
> The pleader faces special problems. … The new doctrine makes the whole basket of possible orders available to the court. Perhaps the pleader has only to ask, quite generally,

> for 'a remedy', since the basket is in the court's keeping. One suspects that the courts would not be happy [15] with that. If they are not, what would the pleader have to do? It would be pointless to list the whole contents of the basket every time. On the other hand, the strong discretion seems to mean that the plaintiff cannot be confined to those remedies which he asks for.

The third, 'Losing faith in the rule of law', is outlined at 15–16:

> [**15**] The most precious values of our civilisation can come to be taken for granted, just as the value of peace is less keenly felt as memories of war recede. The third set of objections to discretionary remedialism arise from the need to reinforce our commitment to the rule of law. The suggestion that judges should be free to apply whatever remedy they think best for the trouble in hand emanates from our taking the rule of law for granted.
>
> ...
>
> [**16**] We are learning to value the sub-cultures of its different ethnic and religious groups and its different socio-economic groups. Society is plural, and its interlocking sub-cultures are well-informed and articulate. In such a society law which is demonstrably a rational system of rules striving to reach determinate results can be acceptable to all. Reason legitimates. Reason communicates. Judicial discretion is by contrast dangerous. Discretionary remedialism requires all the very different sub-cultures to accept the judges' instinct for the just result. If discretionary remedialism will work anywhere, it will work in a monolithic society. In a plural society judges should regard it as political dynamite. The judge as expert in applying the law is entitled to respect. The judge as a fountain of intuitive justice is not. [Footnotes omitted]

Grant Hammond, a former Judge of the New Zealand Court of Appeal and former President of the New Zealand Law Commission, has expressed a dualist view of remedies law in the extract which follows.

Grant Hammond, 'Rethinking Remedies: The Changing Nature of the Conception of the Relationship Between Legal and Equitable Remedies' in Jeff Berryman (ed), *Remedies: Issues and Perspectives* (Carswell, 1991) 85

[**90**] The historically close relationship between rights and remedies has often been remarked on. Indeed some scholars have been overtly concerned as to whether there *is* such a thing as a *remedy*, which exists separate and apart from a cause of action or a *right*. Hence it is necessary to deal with this at the outset. If we cannot establish a rational basis for a separate remedies regime, then the whole intellectual and operational framework of modern remedies would need to be reassessed.

There are two possible schools of thought on this issue. It is generally claimed that a man has a 'right' to his reputation. The Monist asserts that the existence of such a right is, in general, meaningless. 'Rights are not protected interests, but the means by which interests are protected.'

Thus, unless and until, for instance, a court declares that the plaintiff has been defamed and awards monetary compensation (and, sometimes, exemplary damages) there is no 'right'. Abstract rights can be, and in practice often are, disregarded. So, the argument goes, on any realistic basis there is no such thing as a 'right to reputation' but only a particular form of relief if a person's name is unjustifiably impugned. There is thus a complete congruence of right and remedy.

The Dualist school of thought asserts that there *is* a valid distinction between an antecedent 'right' in respect of which 'relief' or a 'remedy' may be given. The late Professor Derham offered three reasons to support [**91**] this line of thought. First, 'the language of the law becomes difficult if we ignore such antecedent rights as a right to property, a right to reputation.' Second, '[l]aw does not exist only to provide constraint but also to create the conditions under which community life is possible and to increase the powers of men.' Law, in short, is larger than litigation, and rights have a meaning of their own, independent of enforcement. Third, 'the law *in fact* allows some antecedent rights to be specifically enforced.' Derham gives the example of specific performance of a contract.

…

[**92**] A sensible remedial system would provide a sufficient range of choice between remedies to allow an appropriate solution to be fashioned in the particular case.

…

[**93**] As matters stand, the remedial hierarchy is still the single greatest constraint on a more responsive system of judicial remedies. It sets up an artificial primacy. Those countries which derive their law from the [94] common law tradition have a marked preference for money awards. Equity remedies rank second. Declaratory relief is a distant third.

As long ago as 1923, Roscoe Pound criticised the development of remedial justice applied 'through money damages … [W]e hesitate to employ restitution or coercion or specific action or prevention until we are convinced that our common law remedial technique will not suffice. … This attitude colours our whole administration of justice.' …

In face of these legitimate and forcefully expressed concerns, the continued formal preference of money-based remedies over performance based remedies is puzzling. … [Footnotes omitted]

Hammond goes on to outline the factors he thinks are relevant to the exercise of discretion when judges choose remedies: at **[101]** ff. His list includes:

- the relative severity of the claimed remedies on the parties
- economic efficiency
- the 'weight' or moral value to be attached to the interest at stake
- the effect of a given remedy on third parties or the public
- the conduct of the parties
- the difficulty of calculating loss and
- the practicability of enforcement.

In between the two extremes, Australian academic Dr David Wright has suggested a middle ground between a monist approach and a dualist approach.

David Wright, 'Wrong and Remedy: A Sticky Relationship' (2001) (2) *Singapore Journal of Legal Studies* 300

[**322**] The courts should consider the legal obligation that has been breached when awarding a remedy. Some legal obligations are more important than others. There is a connection between the wrong and the remedy. It is a 'sticky' [**333**] relationship. That is, the wrong does not mechanically determine the remedy, nor are they completely separate. The legal obligation that has been breached does provide relevant information on the remedy that is awarded. Barker has stated that 'we judge the nature and power of a primary right by observing the way courts react to its violation in their selection of remedy or – which is the same thing – in their allocation of secondary rights.' In addition, Barker has alerted the legal world to the fact that the process works in reverse by observing '[r]ights bear upon remedies and remedies bear upon our understanding of rights.' The moderate position is correct. There is a limited separation between wrong and remedy.

Nor can the separation between wrong and remedy between wrong and remedy be total, as case law has clearly indicated. … The wrong and the remedy are still relevant to each other. Neither are they completely separate from each other, nor are the [sic] completely linked. There is middle or moderate position between these two extreme views. This moderate position, which recognises the 'sticky' relationship between wrong and remedy, is correct.

Once the breach of the legal obligation has been identified and examined, the court must then consider the 'appropriate' remedy. It is relatively easy to say that the court should search for the most appropriate remedy. [Footnotes omitted.]

Review Questions

(1) To what extent can a plaintiff be said to have a right if there is no remedy or secondary right attached to it?

(2) Lord Diplock in *Photo Production Ltd v Securicor Transport Ltd* [1980] AC 827 talks of two ways a court may respond to a breach of contract: either by 'enforc[ing] a primary obligation by decreeing specific performance' and 'substituted or secondary obligations'. What is the primary obligation, and what is the secondary obligation?

(3) What does the word 'remedy' mean to you? How do the definitions above differ from your definition?

(4) What are the three sources of rights and remedies in Australia? Is it easier to argue for a dualist or discretionary approach in relation to some sources as compared to others?

(5) Which approach to remedies do you find most convincing and why?

III The common law and equity divide in Australia

Common law remedies (such as damages) are preferred for common law causes of action such as tort and contract, and equitable remedies such as specific relief and injunctions are only exceptionally awarded.

Conversely, equitable remedies such as specific relief and accounts of profits are generally available for equitable breaches. Equitable compensation outside the trust accounting context only became available in the early 20th century.

There is debate as to whether the common law and equity divide should be retained.

Concept	Short explanation	Relevant authorities	Principles text
The common law and equity divide in Australia	Meagher, Gummow and Lehane argue for a strict division between law and equity which is also reflected in the remedies. Consequently, it is argued that equitable remedies should not be available for common law causes of action where this was not possible before fusion and *vice versa*. In *Roxborough*, Gummow J also rejects restitutionary scholarship.	JD Heydon, MJ Leeming and PG Turner, *Meagher, Gummow and Lehane's Equity: Doctrines and Remedies* (LexisNexis, 5th ed, 2015) [2–140], [2–330]–[2–340] *Roxborough v Rothmans of Pall Mall Australia Ltd* (2001) 208 CLR 516	Chapter 1: [1.33]–[1.47]
	Conversely, Andrew Burrows, a restitutionary scholar, argues that common law and equity should be fused to a greater degree.	Andrew Burrows, 'We Do This at Common Law but That in Equity' (2002) 22(1) *Oxford Journal of Legal Studies* 1	

The original authors of the famous Australian textbook *Meagher, Gummow and Lehane's Equity: Doctrines and Remedies*, Meagher J (formerly of the New South Wales Supreme Court of Appeal), Gummow J (formerly of the Federal Court and the High Court), and Lehane J, (formerly of the Federal Court), decried 'fusion fallacy'. The authors of the current edition take a more conciliatory approach, but still refer to the previous views.[5]

JD Heydon, MJ Leeming and PG Turner, *Meagher, Gummow and Lehane's Equity: Doctrines and Remedies* (LexisNexis, 5th ed, 2015) [2–140], [2–330]–[2–340]

[2–140] … All editions of this work have denounced the fusion fallacy in the following trenchant prose:

> The fusion fallacy involves the administration of a remedy, for example common law damages for breach of fiduciary duty, not previously available at law or in equity, or in the modification of principles in one branch of the jurisdiction by concepts that are imported from the other

5 See JD Heydon, MJ Leeming and PG Turner, *Meagher, Gummow and Lehane's Equity: Doctrines and Remedies* (LexisNexis, 5th ed, 2015) [2–140], [2–330]–[2–340].

> and thus are foreign, for example by holding that the existence of a duty in tort may be tested by asking whether the parties concerned were in fiduciary relations. Those who commit the fusion fallacy announce or assume the creation by the Judicature system of a new body of law containing elements of law and equity but in character Equity different from its components. The fallacy is committed explicitly, covertly, and on occasion with apparent indifference. But the state of mind of the culprit cannot lessen the evil of the offence.

...

[2–330] Previous editions of this work expressed a pessimism which, although apt at the time, may no longer be called for. The first and all subsequent editions included this unsanguine passage:

> But for this a price has been paid and at a higher level of expense than that of administrative inconvenience. ... The 'fusion fallacies' revealed in this chapter but otherwise embodied in the case law are depressing evidence of the damage done to equity in England since 1873. ...

...

[2–340] On occasion there can be a need for criticism to be forceful, colourful, memorable and indeed at its most extreme, pungent. ... However, the position in the twenty-first century seems much less dire than it appeared in the final quarter of the twentieth century. ... ' [Footnotes omitted]

Peter Birks, mentioned on page 8, argued for an alternative taxonomy of rights and remedies. He sought to divide remedies into four categories, derived from Roman law: (1) wrongs (which included tort and equitable wrongdoing); (2) consent (which included contract and express trusts); (3) unjust enrichment (which included personal restitutionary remedies and resulting trusts); and (4) other. This cut across the common law and equity division. In the next case, Gummow J rejected this approach.

Roxborough v Rothmans of Pall Mall Australia Ltd (2001) 208 CLR 516

Facts and issues

The case involved an excise tax which had been paid by tobacco retailers to tobacco wholesalers in the anticipation that the money would be passed on to the New South Wales government. The excise tax was declared unconstitutional, and the retailers sought to recover the tax from the wholesalers via an action for money had and received (a restitutionary remedy).

Decision

For present purposes, the important point is Gummow J's rejection of Birks's theories of restitution and taxonomy.

Gummow J

> [**543**] Writing extrajudicially, Justice Paul Finn has said of the concept of 'unjust enrichment' that '[a]t a quite visceral level it provides an important catalyst to further legal inquiry',

particularly as 'a unifying legal concept' which 'explains why the law recognises an obligation to make restitution in particular contexts'. The conventional view is that it is the unjust enrichment which gives rise to the obligations of restitution. However, Justice Finn expresses concern that the concept of unjust enrichment may 'contrive legal analysis' and continues (in a passage I would adopt):

> [T]o the extent that it directs attention to outcomes and to the character to be attributed to them, it is capable of concealing rather than revealing why the law would want to attribute a responsibility to one party to provide satisfaction to the other. This is particularly so where, as is so often the case, it is conduct in a relationship or dealing – an expectation created and relied upon; a mistake not corrected; etc. – which provides the focus of legal attention and which generates the issue of legal policy for which resolution is required. This, I suspect, provides the reason why 'unconscionable conduct' and not 'unjust enrichment' (a possible effect of that conduct) has achieved the currency it has in Australian law.

...

[**544**] Considerations such as these, together with practical experience, suggest caution in judicial acceptance of any all-embracing theory of restitutionary rights and remedies founded upon a notion of 'unjust enrichment'. To the lawyer whose mind has been moulded by civilian influences, the theory may come first, and the source of the theory may be the writing of jurists not the decisions of judges. However, that is not the way in which a system based on case law develops; over time, general principle is derived from judicial decisions upon particular instances, not the other way around. In *McGinty v Western Australia*, McHugh J referred to Judge Posner's description of 'top-down reasoning' by which a theory about an area of law is invented or adopted and then applied to existing decisions to make them conform to the theory and to dictate the outcome in new cases. Judge Posner spoke of the use of the theory by its adherents:

> to organize, criticize, accept or reject, explain or explain away, distinguish or amplify the existing decisions to make them conform to the theory and generate an outcome in each new case as it arises that will be consistent with the theory and with the canonical cases, that is, the cases accepted as authoritative within the theory.

As it happens, Lord Mansfield favoured the development of legal principle by a journey in the opposite direction. ...

Unless, as this Court indicated in *David Securities Pty Ltd v* [**545**] *Commonwealth Bank of Australia*, unjust enrichment is seen as a concept rather than a definitive legal principle, substance and dynamism may be restricted by dogma. In turn, the dogma will tend to generate new fictions in order to retain support for its thesis. It also may distort well settled principles in other fields, including those respecting equitable doctrines and remedies, so that they answer the newly mandated order of things. Then various theories will compete, each to deny the others. There is support in Australasian legal scholarship for considerable scepticism respecting any all-embracing theory in this field, with the treatment of the disparate as no more than species of the one newly discovered genus.

Andrew Burrows was a Professor of the Law of England at the University of Oxford at All Souls College, and is now a judge of the UK Supreme Court. He has written widely in the area of private law, restitution and remedies. By contrast to Gummow J, he argues for fusion of some areas of common law and equitable remedies.

Andrew Burrows, 'We Do This at Common Law but That in Equity' (2002) 22(1) *Oxford Journal of Legal Studies* 1

[**5**] For the purposes of developing the argument that we should take fusion seriously, I shall put to one side immediately ... any areas where the law has already reached the advanced position that common law and equity cannot be distinguished at all, and where there is therefore no fusion work left to be done. The rest of English private law, which is the vast bulk of it, can then be conveniently divided into three categories. As shall be seen, my main focus will be on the third of these categories.

The first category is where common law and equity co-exist coherently and where the historical labels of common law and equity remain the best or, at least, useful terminology. I particularly have in mind here that greatest invention of equity, the trust. It is very hard – albeit not impossible as is shown by the approach in some other jurisdictions – to describe the trust without at some stage relying on, and referring to, the split between legal and equitable title. Similarly, the general priority rule that a bona fide purchaser for value of a legal interest without notice takes free of a prior equitable interest in the same property is very hard to replicate without using the law and equity labels.

The second category is where common law and equity co-exist coherently but, in contrast to the first category, there is nothing to be gained by adherence to those historical labels. If we are to take fusion seriously, the labels common law and equity in the areas of the law covered by this category should be abandoned at a stroke.

...

[**6**] The third category is more complex. It comprises probably most of our civil law. In this category, in contrast to both of the first two categories, common law and equity do not co-exist coherently. If we are to take fusion seriously, what is [**7**] needed is a change in the law, albeit often only a small change, so as to produce a principled product which may combine elements of law and equity.

...

The basic picture in relation to monetary remedies for civil wrongs is of a separation of common law and equitable wrongs, with equitable wrongs generally triggering different monetary remedies than common law wrongs. An antifusionist might say that the two types of wrong do, and should, co-exist happily because they operate independently from each other. The better view is that this would be to accept superficial coherence. In reality, if one strips away the clothing of historical labels, one sees that in common law and in equity one is dealing [**8**] with the same essential facts, ideas and concepts and yet treating them differently. And in this area, as in other areas within category three, taking fusion seriously requires some adjustments, albeit minor, to the present law. The argument will be developed under six heads: (i) identification of the wrong; (ii) compensation and its restrictions; (iii) restitution for wrongs; (iv) punishment; (v) anticipated wrongs, and (vi) general defences.

In relation to 'Identification of the Wrong' at 8–9:

> **[8]** … [W]e know that there are two main types of common law wrong; breach of contract and torts. Applying the same test, of whether compensation is available for loss caused, we can say that there are four types of conduct which are treated, in equity, as wrongs: breach of fiduciary duty, breach of confidence, dishonestly procuring or assisting a breach of fiduciary duty (the wrong recognized by the Privy Council in *Royal Brunei Airlines v Tan*), and those forms of estoppel that constitute causes of action, in particular proprietary estoppel.
>
> Of these equitable wrongs, the most wide-ranging and important – and the most difficult to pin down – is breach of fiduciary duty.
>
> …
>
> **[9]** The central point for the theme of this article is that both common law and equity recognize what, at root, is exactly the same phenomenon, namely wrongs or breaches of duty triggering compensation. While, as I have argued elsewhere, there may be good sense in treating breach of contract separately from torts, there is no rational reason for having another category of wrongs, labelled equitable wrongs. All equitable wrongs should be treated as examples of breach of contract or torts.

In relation to 'Compensation and its Restrictions' at 9–11:

> **[9]** It is trite law that the primary remedy for the common law wrongs is compensatory damages. Such damages are always available for a breach of contract or tort and are measured by the claimant's loss; that is, they basically aim to put the claimant into as good a position as if no wrong had occurred. We also know that there are restrictions on compensatory damages, in particular, remoteness, intervening cause, the so-called duty to mitigate, and contributory negligence. These restrictions generally apply whether the claim is brought in contract or tort albeit that the content of the restriction may vary both as between contract and tort and in some instances as between different types of tort.
>
> In order to compare compensatory damages for common law wrongs with compensation for equitable wrongs there are two features of the restrictions on compensatory damages at common law that are particularly noteworthy.
>
> …
>
> **[10]** The first is that the courts have a wide discretion in deciding the losses to be compensated by damages for common law wrongs. Sometimes, as with intervening cause, there is no test laid down at all. … Even where there is a test, it is open-ended; reasonable foreseeability or reasonable contemplation, as regards remoteness; whether reasonable steps have been taken, as regards the duty to mitigate; and a reduction of damages 'to such extent as the court thinks just and equitable' … in relation to contributory negligence.
>
> The second feature of the restrictions on compensatory damages is that, because it involves dishonesty, the tort of deceit has been treated differently from most other torts and breach of contract. So … a wider remoteness test than reasonable foreseeability applies to the tort of deceit. And … contributory negligence of the claimant does not apply to reduce damages for the tort of deceit.

With these two features of restrictions on compensatory damages in mind, we can now switch across to compensation and its restrictions for equitable wrongs. Here we find that an important remedy … is the remedy called 'equitable compensation'. Although there has been some doubt about this, the basic aim of equitable compensation, as its name suggests, is to compensate a loss. In other words, it is concerned to put the claimant into as good a position as if no wrong had occurred. It therefore has exactly the same aim as compensatory damages. This is why the House of Lords in the much-discussed case of *Target Holdings Ltd v Redfern* was, in my view, correct to say that there could be [**11**] equitable compensation where the loss in question would have been suffered even if there had been no breach of duty by the defendant solicitors; that is, the breach of fiduciary duty had caused the claimant no loss.

Of course, and just as at common law, what is a loss, and hence what is the precise aim of the compensation, will vary according to the duty broken. … But, with respect, the suggestion in *Bristol & West Building Society v Mothew* that equitable compensation may sometimes have a special more restrictive restorative aim than compensatory damages should be resisted: it confuses the aim of the remedy – compensation – with the application of that aim to different duties broken.

When we turn to restrictions on equitable compensation, we find conflict in the cases both in England and elsewhere. Although there are shades of opinion in between, there are two main opposing views. On the one hand, there are those who consider that restrictions on compensatory damages, such as remoteness, intervening cause and contributory negligence, do not apply to equitable compensation. That was the opinion of Lord Browne-Wilkinson giving the leading speech in *Target Holdings v Redfern*. In emphasizing that a trustee would be liable for breach of trust even if the immediate cause of the loss was a third party, his Lordship said, 'Thus the common law rules of remoteness of damage and causation do not apply'.

The opposing view is that the restrictions of remoteness, intervening cause and so on apply in the same way to equitable compensation as to compensatory damages. This derives some support from the judgment of Millett LJ in the *Mothew* case.

…

This second approach should be supported.

In relation to 'Punishment' at 13:

> [**13**] [I]n … Canada and New Zealand … punitive damages can be awarded for equitable wrongs. Not surprisingly, the Law Commission has recommended legislation which would effect a principled reform. According to this, the courts would have the power to award punitive damages for torts and equitable wrongs according to the same principled basic test of whether there was an outrageous and deliberate disregard of the claimant's rights.

In relation to 'Anticipated Wrongs' at 13–14:

> [**13**] For the purposes of this article, there are two important points to make about equitable damages. First, it is clear that equitable damages can be awarded for [**14**] common law, as well as equitable, wrongs. Indeed they have most commonly been awarded in respect of

anticipated proprietary torts, such as nuisance and trespass to land. Second, in *Johnson v Agnew* the House of Lords laid down that the principles for assessing damages should not differ as between common law and equitable damages.

It follows from these two points that it would involve only a small step forward to rid ourselves of the concept of equitable damages and to recognize simply that damages may be awarded not only for accrued wrongs but also, exceptionally, for anticipated wrongs.

Finally, in relation to 'General Defences' at 14–15:

[14] ... [T]here is a tendency to exaggerate the distinctions between common law and equitable defences by comparing defences to equitable specific remedies, such as specific performance and injunctions, with those applying to common law damages.

...

[**15**] The real question is whether there are defences that would apply to rule out equitable monetary remedies that would not apply to rule out common law monetary remedies. [Footnotes omitted]

Review Questions

(1) Which approach do you prefer: Meagher, Gummow and Lehane's or Burrows'? What are the advantages and flaws of each?

(2) Do you think statutes such as the *Australian Consumer Law* have rendered debates about common law and equity pointless in modern Australia?

IV A functional approach to remedies

This casebook and the principles text follow a functional approach which divides remedies according to whether the function is compensation, compulsion, vindication, deterrence or restitution.

However, not all topics discussed fit into this general structure, including proprietary remedies (which fulfil several functions) and enforcement of remedies (the orders are procedural, and do not finally determine the parties' rights).

Some remedies perform multiple functions (eg aggravated damages, which could be said to have a compensatory and a vindicatory function) or their functions are unclear (eg 'reasonable fee' damages have been argued to be compensatory, restitutionary and to effect disgorgement). Consequently, others may place those remedies under other functions.

Figure 1.1 Functional diagram of the law of civil remedies

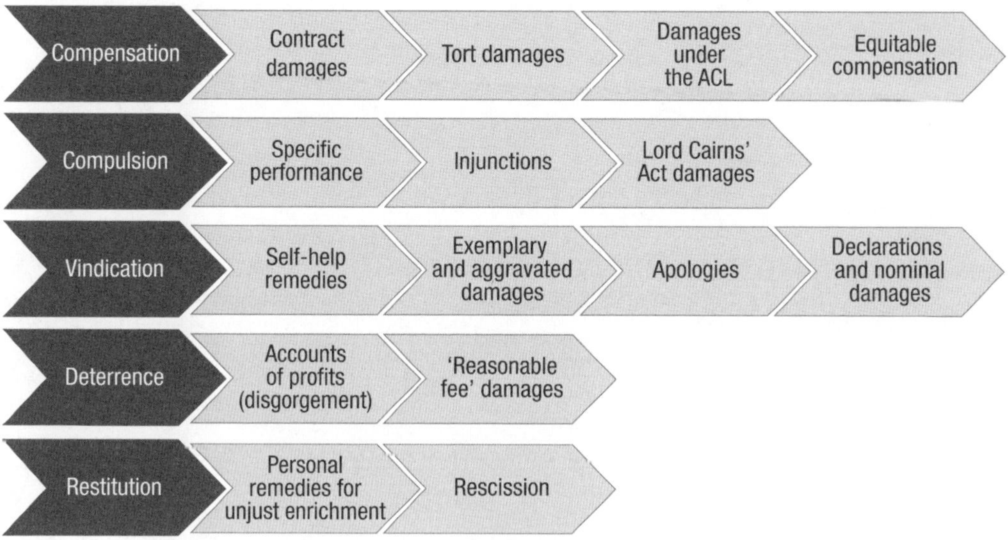

Note: Proprietary remedies and enforcement of remedies are outside the scheme.

PART 1

GENERAL PRINCIPLES OF COMPENSATION

2 ASSESSMENT OF COMPENSATION

I Introduction 22
II The compensatory principle and the identification of the wrong 22
III Losses and benefits 26
A Non-pecuniary loss 26
B Cost of repair and diminution in value 27
C Betterment discount 27
D Benefits flowing from mitigating actions of the plaintiff 32
E Other benefits arising from the wrong 37
F The impact of tax law 41
IV Certainty of loss and recovery for the loss of a chance 42
A Overview of the current law 43
B Consequential loss 49
C Personal injury as initial harm 51
D Pure economic loss as initial harm 54
E Hypothetical conduct of the defendant 64
V Temporal considerations 70
A The lump sum rule and the 'once and for all' rule 70
B Date of assessment 71
C Relevance of inflation 79
D Determining the present equivalent of future pecuniary loss 81
E Interest on compensation awards and compensation for the loss of the use of money 83

I Introduction

The overarching principle governing compensation for a civil wrong is that compensation be awarded to the plaintiff for losses suffered but must not place the plaintiff in a better position than if the wrong had not occurred – the 'compensatory principle'.

II The compensatory principle and the identification of the wrong

The 'compensatory principle' focuses on the plaintiff's position had the wrong not occurred. Where, say, a false statement is made that the plaintiff relied on, the assessment of the plaintiff's loss may depend whether a contractual warranty of the accuracy of the statement was given. If so, the plaintiff may be entitled to relief based on breach of contract but if not, relief might be calculated to put the plaintiff in the position they would be in had no representation been made, the tortuous measure.

Concept	Short explanation	Relevant authorities	Principles text
The 'compensatory principle'	The need to put the plaintiff in the same place but for the wrong	*Butler v Egg and Egg Pulp Marketing Board* (1966) 114 CLR 185 *Gates v City Mutual Life Assurance Society Ltd* (1986) 160 CLR 1	Chapter 2: [2.2]–[2.4]

Figure 2.1 The compensatory principle – breach of contract and tort

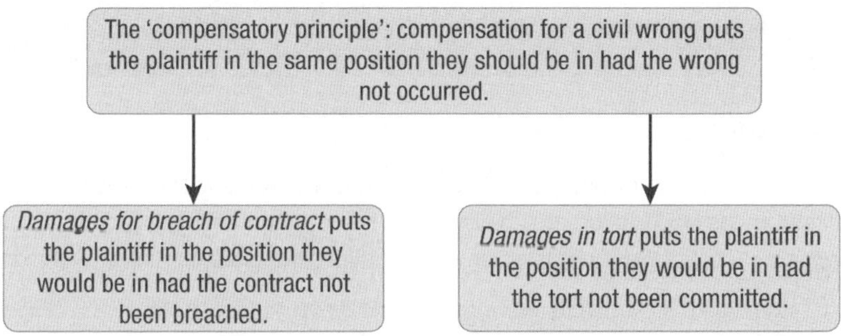

Butler v Egg and Egg Pulp Marketing Board (1966) 114 CLR 185

Facts and issues

Under Victorian legislation, property in eggs when laid vested in the Marketing Board with the producer being entitled to a share of the proceeds from their sale. Butler failed to deliver eggs to the Board and sold them, committing conversion. At trial, damages were assessed as the full value of the eggs. The issue on appeal concerned the measure of damages to be applied to compensate the Board.

Decision

The damages awarded, for conversion, were not the full value of the eggs but the difference between their value and what the Board would have had to pay Butler.

Taylor and Owen JJ

> [**191**] The injured party should receive compensation in a sum which, so far as money can do so, will put him in the same position as he would have been in if the contract had been performed or the tort had not been committed: *Livingstone v Rawyards Coal Co.* And this principle is as much applicable to actions of conversion as it is to the case of other actionable wrongs. In most cases of conversion it is, of course, obvious that its application will result in the injured plaintiff recovering the full value of the property converted since that will usually represent the loss that he has sustained by the defendant's wrongful act.
>
> …

The Board's loss must, in our opinion, be determined by considering what sum of money would be required to place it in the same position as it would have been in if the appellants had performed their statutory obligation. Had they done so, the Board would, on the figures agreed upon by the [**192**] parties have realized £4000 by selling the eggs and out of that sum would have had to pay the appellants £2900. Its loss resulting from the appellants' tortious act is therefore £1100.

Gates v City Mutual Life Assurance Society Ltd (1986) 160 CLR 1

Facts and issues

An insurer represented to a proposer for insurance that the total disability clause in a policy entitled him to benefits from his occupation as a builder. The insured suffered an injury which disabled him from occupation as a builder but not from *any* occupation; the clause entitled him to benefits only in the latter event.

Decision

Damages were awarded on the tortuous measure.

Mason, Wilson and Dawson JJ

[**11**] This passage correctly states the legal effect of Mr Rainbird's assurance. It was not contractual in character.

...

[**12**] Two established measures of damages, those applicable in contract and tort respectively, compete for acceptance. In contract, damages are awarded with the object of placing the plaintiff in the position in which he would have been had the contract been performed – he is entitled to damages for loss of bargain (expectation loss) and damage suffered, including expenditure incurred, in reliance on the contract (reliance loss). In tort, on the other hand, damages are awarded with the object of placing the plaintiff in the position in which he would have been had the tort not been committed (similar to reliance loss).

The differences and the similarities between the two approaches are best illustrated by contrasting the damages recoverable for breach of contractual warranty on a purchase of goods with those recoverable for a fraudulent misrepresentation inducing entry into a contract for the purchase of goods on the assumption that the contracts are identical except that in one case the representation amounts to a warranty and in the other it is merely a non-contractual representation. For breach of warranty the plaintiff is prima facie entitled to recover the difference between the real value of the goods and the value of the goods as warranted. In deceit the measure of damages is the difference at the time of purchase between the real value of the goods, and the price paid..

[The plaintiff recovered the difference between the difference he paid in premiums and the value of the disability clause, the tortious measure. Had the contractual measure been applied, he would have recovered the benefits available under the policy.]

NOTE

Figure 2.2 illustrates the computation of compensation for making a false statement, adopting a hypothetical example of the sale of a ring to show the differences the contractual and tortuous measures.

Figure 2.2 The fundamental difference between the assessment of compensation for tort and for breach of contract, illustrated using a simplistic example

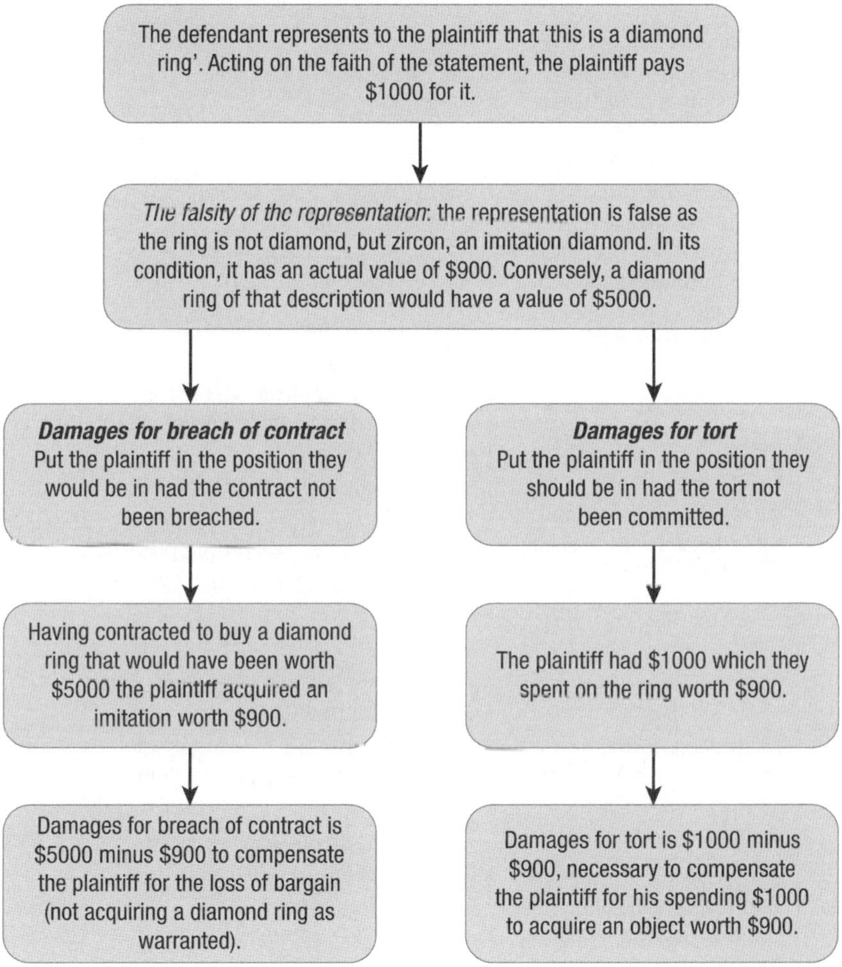

REVIEW QUESTIONS

(1) Are damages for breach of contract likely to be greater than tort?

(2) As compensation for contract often exceeds compensation for tort, is there a benefit in seeking damages on both bases?

III Losses and benefits

Concept	Short explanation	Relevant authorities	Principles text
Non-pecuniary losses	Losses other than financial, eg hurt feelings, loss of reputation, anxiety and distress.	For breach of contract, see *Baltic Shipping Co v Dillon* (1993) 176 CLR 344 (see Chapter 5, page 193 for extract) For tort, see *Giller v Procopets* (2008) 24 VR 1 (see Chapter 9, page 323, Chapter 12, pages 433 and 438 and Chapter 14, page 500 for extracts).	Chapter 2: [2.8]–[2.10]
Cost of repair and diminution in value	Whether the cost of repair or diminution in value of the destroyed or damaged property should be adopted as the basis of compensation.	*O'Brien v McKean* (1968) 118 CLR 540 (see Chapter 2, pages 72 and 80 for extracts)	Chapter 2: [2.11]–[2.16]
Betterment discount	Benefits derived from the plaintiff's being placed in a better position than they would be in without the defendant's wrong may reduce the defendant's liability.	*Tyco Australia v Optus Networks Pty Ltd* [2004] NSWCA 333 *Gagner Pty Ltd v Canturi Corporation Pty Ltd* (2009) 262 ALR 691 *Hoad v Scone Motors Pty Ltd* [1977] 1 NSWLR 88 *Hyder Consulting (Australia) Pty Ltd v Wilh Wilhemsen Agency Pty Ltd* [2001] NSWCA 313	Chapter 2: [2.17]–[2.27]
Benefits flowing from mitigating actions of plaintiff	The defendant is entitled to the benefits of mitigating action taken by the plaintiff.	*Haines v Bendall* (1991) 172 CLR 60 *British Westinghouse Electric and Manufacturing Co Ltd v Underground Electric Railways Co of London Ltd* [1912] AC 673 *Jenkinson v Young* [2004] SADC 30 *Origin Energy LPG Ltd v BestCare Foods* [2013] NSWCA 90	Chapter 2: [2.26]–[2.38]
Other benefits arising from the wrong	The wrongdoer may be entitled to a 'credit' for the benefits received by the plaintiff.	*Insurance Australia Ltd v HIH Casualty & General Insurance Ltd (in liq)* (2007) 18 VR 528 *Monroe Schneiders Associates (Inc) v No 1 Roberm Pty Ltd* (1991) 33 FCR 1	
The impact of tax law	The consideration of tax law in the assessment of compensation.		Chapter 2: [2.44]–[2.56]

The various heads of loss and benefit conventionally considered in assessing compensation for a civil wrong are summarised in Table 2.1.

A Non-pecuniary loss

Whether compensation can be recovered for non-pecuniary losses (such as anxiety or distress) varies with the cause of action.

Table 2.1 Overview of the ascertainment of losses and benefits recoverable as a result of a wrong

	Type	Explanation
Losses	Non-pecuniary loss	These are *generally* irrecoverable for breach of contract although generally compensable in tort. Such losses are also generally irrecoverable in equity save for breach of confidence, eg loss of reputation and hurt feelings.
	Cost of repair and diminution in value	The court generally will award the cost of repair but may decline to do so when unreasonable or it is excessive when compared to its diminution in value.
	The impact of tax law	Where compensation awarded to compensate the aggrieved party for a loss that has been suffered, there will likely be tax implications, particularly in relation to the question of payment of GST which will often arise in relation to the question of whether the payment is to be treated as income.
Benefits	Betterment discount	Benefits enjoyed by the plaintiff by being placed in a better position than without the defendant's breach must be deducted, except where collateral. This is a nuance of the more general rule arising from the consequences of mitigation.
	Benefits flowing from mitigating actions of the plaintiff	'Avoided loss' must be deducted from a damages award. These include loss that is set off by benefits flowing from mitigating steps, but not indirect or collateral benefits.
	Other benefits arising as a direct result of the wrong	These may reduce the defendant's liability. These do not include collateral benefits.

B Cost of repair and diminution in value

Two methods apply to compensate the plaintiff for damage or destruction to property:

(1) the difference between the value of the property with the damage and its value without the damage

(2) the money required to put it in the state it would have been but for the wrong (the cost of repair). The choice of method can vary greatly.

C Betterment discount

If as a result of the defendant's wrong the plaintiff gets a benefit putting him in a better position than without the defendant's wrong, these benefits – 'betterment discount' – might be deducted.

Tyco Australia v Optus Networks Pty Ltd [2004] NSWCA 333

Facts and issues

Following damage to Optus's data processing facilities, Optus was awarded damages for negligence against Tyco. Optus in mitigation acquired additional computer equipment. The question was whether the benefits Optus enjoyed from the acquisition of the equipment had to be deducted from the award of compensation.

Decision

Betterment discount was given as a 'credit' for those benefits.

Hodgson JA

[260] Where it appears that a plaintiff may in some respects be better off as a result of expenditure it has incurred in consequence of a defendant's wrong or breach of contract, difficult questions can arise. … The basic principle is that the plaintiff is to be compensated for its loss, and no more, and there is no more particular statement of principle that will determine the result in all cases; but in my opinion, the authorities do support a number of subsidiary propositions.

[261] First, if a plaintiff choses to acquire a more valuable asset than that which had to be replaced, where the plaintiff could for a lesser expenditure have acquired an asset that would have been as satisfactory as that replaced, the plaintiff cannot recover more than that lesser expenditure: *British Westinghouse Electric & Manufacturing Co Ltd v Underground Electric Railways Co of London Ltd* [1912].

[262] Second, even if there is no alternative available to a plaintiff other than to acquire a more valuable asset, a plaintiff may have to give credit reflecting the greater value of this asset to the plaintiff, if there is a benefit to the plaintiff which is not remote in time or speculative, and which can be quantified. In *Hoad v Scone Motors Pty Ltd*, it was accepted that the plaintiff had no reasonable alternative other than to acquire a new tractor; but since the plaintiff was shortly to sell his business including this tractor, the greater second-hand value of this tractor over that which had been destroyed would have to be deducted from the plaintiff's damages. … In *Hyder Consulting (Australia) Pty Ltd v Wilh Wilhelmsen Agency Pty Ltd*, there was no deduction where a pavement with a life expectancy of twenty years collapsed after four years, and was replaced by one with a similar life expectancy; the prospect that, about sixteen years in the future, the new pavement would probably continue for four years longer than the original pavement should have done, was considered too remote and speculative. …

[263] Third, where any benefit received by the plaintiff is considered as not truly caused by the defendant's conduct and expenditure undertaken in consequence of it (and paid for by the defendant), but rather considered as being collateral, no credit is given for it: *Monroe Schneider Associates (Inc) v No.1 Raberem Pty Ltd*. …

[264] Fourth, although the plaintiff has the general onus of proof of damages, there can be legal or at least evidentiary onuses cast on the defendant. If a defendant wishes to say that the plaintiff incurred loss or expenses that it could have avoided by taking reasonable steps in mitigation, the onus of proof is on the defendant. …

[265] Optus acquired the pool kit equipment and cleaned most of the damaged equipment. At the end of the recovery program, the pool kit equipment was left performing functions that had been performed by the damaged equipment. Although the pool kit equipment was newly purchased, it was not submitted by Tyco that damages should be reduced by reason of any superiority of this new equipment over the equipment it replaced: it did the same job, and it was not suggested that it would deliver savings by way of increased performance or longer life. Indeed, as pointed out by Handley JA at para [22] of his judgment, the primary judge held that the value of leftover equipment, which was equivalent to pool kit equipment, equated in substance with the value of that pool kit equipment.

[266] However, Optus plainly did have a benefit from the recovery program, namely the cleaned leftover equipment which was left free because of the continued use of the pool kit equipment. Optus could have sold that leftover equipment, and given credit to Tyco for the proceeds of sale. Provided Optus proved it obtained a reasonable price, Tyco could then not have claimed any greater deduction from the damages than the proceeds of sale, unless Tyco proved that the sale of the equipment was not a reasonable course of action, for example by proving that Optus would have benefited more from this equipment by putting it to some use.

...

[272] Credit should be given to Tyco for the cost of acquiring the equivalent pool kit equipment new between April and June 1998.

Gagner Pty Ltd v Canturi Corporation Pty Ltd (2009) 262 ALR 691

Facts and issues

Canturi operated a jewellery store. Gagner occupied the floor above the store. Due to Gagner's negligence, water escaped and damaged 10 per cent of Canturi's floor space. Canturi refurbished the whole floor, requiring the jewellery store to be closed for 29 days. The issue was how compensation should be awarded to place Canturi in the position it would have been had Gagner not caused the damage.

Decision

Damages were awarded in the amount needed to refurbish the premises to their original position, but not to refurbish the entire floor. An allowance for 10 days' business interruption, not 29, was granted.

Campbell JA

[**694**] The measure of damages that the judge allowed concerning rectification costs to the premises was, in broad terms, the amount it would have cost to bring the premises back as close as was possible to their undamaged condition (including goods and services tax ['GST'] on that cost), together with an allowance for 10 working days' business interruption, at a daily rate that the parties had agreed. Ten working days was the time that the premises would have been closed if the Respondent had restored the premises as exactly as possible to their pre-accident condition.

...

[**714**] In the present case, the effecting of the total refit of the premises had the effect that the Respondent no longer suffered any damage in consequence of the flooding, but the refit cost the Respondent money. To the extent that, by effecting the refit, the Respondent obtained more than a rectification of the damage caused by the flood, the compensatory principle requires that it must itself bear the cost of obtaining that extra.

Hoad v Scone Motors Pty Ltd [1977] 1 NSWLR 88

Facts and issues

Through Scone's negligence, Hoad's seven-year-old tractor and three-year-old mower were destroyed. Hoad, unable to find suitable second-hand equipment to sow crop, bought a new tractor and mower. Hoad normally replaced his tractor every five years but did not this time as he was about to surrender his lease of the farm. The issue was whether Hoad was entitled to claim compensation for the full cost of buying the replacement equipment or if Scone was entitled to a betterment discount.

Decision

Scone was entitled to a betterment discount for the benefits conferred by the better performance of the new equipment and their resale.

Moffitt P

> [**94**] As has been repeatedly said, the assessment of damage is a question of fact in each case.
>
> …
>
> Farm equipment depreciates rapidly, and it is either written off or is replaced at short intervals. Planned replacement at short intervals was in fact the business practice of the plaintiffs. If this practice would have continued, then the consequence of the fire was merely to accelerate the inevitable capital expense of acquiring a new tractor and mower.
>
> …
>
> [**95**] If the circumstances are such that it is found it is reasonable to lay out capital, and this results also in gain for the plaintiff, then the gain is causally connected with the damage otherwise and the wrong, and I find no logic in conferring on the plaintiff a benefit in excess of his true loss, when he is doing no more than is reasonable.
>
> …
>
> The measure of loss is not the gross cost of replacement of the equipment. Thus the award cannot be supported on that basis. The measure of damage … is the nett detriment arising from acquisition of the new equipment. This issue has not been determined and, it seems, not properly litigated.
>
> It was directed there be a new trial on the assessment of damages.

Hyder Consulting (Australia) Pty Ltd v Wilh Wilhemsen Agency Pty Ltd [2001] NSWCA 313

Facts and issues

Hyder negligently performed restoration works on Wilhemsen's pavement. The pavement was intended to last 20 years but failed shortly after commencement of use. After using the defective pavement for four years, Wilhemsen replaced it with new pavement. Wilhemsen could not have replaced the defective pavement with a four-year old pavement. Wilhemsen claimed the full cost of the replacement pavement, while Hyder argued that a deduction of 20 per cent should be applied as the new pavement would last four years longer. The issue was whether Hyder was entitled to betterment discount.

Decision

Hyder was not entitled to betterment discount.

Sheller JA

> **[28]** In *Halsbury's Laws of Australia,* Volume 9, 'Damages', appear the following passages. The first is:
>
>> The plaintiff must credit the defendant for the fact that the plaintiff now receives new goods in place of old (that is, for betterment) (*Hoad v Scone Motors Pty Limited*) except where the plaintiff would never have replaced the chattel in question *(Harbutt's 'Plasticine' Limited v Wayne Tank and Pump Co Limited).*
>
> **[29]** The second passage is:
>
>> Where cost of reinstatement is the appropriate measure of damages, plaintiffs must give credit for betterment where the property increases in value after reinstatement, except where reinstatement involves plaintiffs in making an investment they would never had made at all *(Harbutt's).*
>
> ...
>
> **[55]** The facts in *Hoad* and *British Westinghouse* are distinguishable from the facts in this case. The plaintiff had no choice but to replace the defective pavement with new pavement. It could not do so by paying less for a four-year old pavement. There was no evidence of any advantage to the plaintiff beyond the speculative proposition that the new pavement might last longer than the old one would have, if it had been properly laid … .On the evidence in this case, no allowance should have been made for betterment and this ground of cross-appeal fails.

Giles JA

> **[107]** The general principle of restitutio in integrum, that a plaintiff should be compensated for its loss but not over-compensated, is undoubted. Its application will vary according to the circumstances. In the present case the owner was entitled to a sound pavement, and from the time it was laid the pavement failed and the owner did not have a sound pavement. It had to be replaced, and the owner could not replace it with a sound four-year old pavement. Any benefit to the owner seems to be that, whereas it would otherwise have had to spend money repairing or replacing the pavement in (say) 2015, having reconstructed the pavement in 1999 it will now not have to spend money repairing or replacing it until (say) 2020. So the owner will have the use for five years of the money spent on the repair or replacement.

Figure 2.3 summarises the principles relating to a consideration of benefits flowing from mitigating actions of the plaintiff as usefully summarised in *Tyco Australia v Optus Networks Pty Ltd*.

Figure 2.3 Betterment discount: the fundamental principles set out in *Tyco Australia v Optus Networks Pty Ltd*

First, if a plaintiff chooses to acquire a more valuable asset than that which had to be replaced, where the plaintiff could for a lesser expenditure have acquired an asset that would have been as satisfactory as that replaced, the plaintiff cannot recover more than that lesser expenditure.

↓

Second, even if there is no alternative available to a plaintiff other than to acquire a more valuable asset, a plaintiff may have to give credit reflecting the greater value of this asset to the plaintiff, if there is a benefit to the plaintiff which is not remote in time or speculative and which can be quantified.

↓

Third, where any benefit received by the plaintiff is considered as not truly caused by the defendant's conduct and expenditure undertaken in consequence of it (and paid for by the defendant), but rather as being collateral, no credit is given for it.

↓

Fourth, although the plaintiff has the general onus of proof of damages, there can be legal or at least evidentiary onuses cast on the defendant; where a defendant says that the plaintiff incurred loss or expenses that it could have avoided by taking reasonable steps in mitigation, the onus of proof is on the defendant.

D Benefits flowing from mitigating actions of the plaintiff

Benefits from the plaintiff's taking steps to mitigate its loss (other than collateral benefits) must be taken into account in reduction of the compensation.

Haines v Bendall (1991) 172 CLR 60

Facts and issues

Bendall sustained injuries in an accident for which he received workers compensation of $49 037 for non-economic loss. He subsequently recovered common law damages of which $75 000.00 was for non-economic loss. On receipt of common law damages, the workers compensation was returned. The question was the amount on which pre-judgment interest on damages for past non-economic loss be awarded.

Decision

Pre-judgment interest on damages for past non-economic losses could only be awarded on the difference between $75000.00 and $49037.00 because the plaintiff had not lost the use of the latter.

Mason CJ, Dawson, Toohey and Gaudron JJ

> **[67]** The discretion [to award interest] must be exercised in conformity with the general principles governing the award of damages so that an award of interest on damages for personal injury should do no more than assist in the restoration of a plaintiff to the position in which he or she would have been but for the defendant's negligence.
>
> ...
>
> **[68]** The precise question for determination is whether, for the purpose of oomputing interest, the amount of the respondent's pre-judgment non-economic loss assessed at $75 000 should be reduced by the amount of the s 16 payment.
>
> ...
>
> **[69]** The injury for which compensation is payable under s 16 is an injury or loss for which common law damages are recoverable against a tortfeasor when the injury is occasioned by the wrongful conduct of the tortfeasor. It has not been, and could not be, suggested that compensation payable under the Act extends to loss or damage of a kind not compensable at common law.
>
> ...
>
> **[71]** It follows from all that we have said that compensation paid under s 16 serves the same purpose as the award of damages at common law. Having regard to our earlier conclusion that the respondent's enjoyment of the s 16 payment before judgment cannot be attributed to the respondent's economic loss to that date, it should in the circumstances of this case have been taken into account in computing the sum on which interest was calculated in respect of the respondent's non-economic loss.

British Westinghouse Electric and Manufacturing Co Ltd v Underground Electric Railways Co of London Ltd [1912] AC 673

Facts and issues

British Westinghouse ('BW') supplied turbines to Underground Electric Railways ('UER') which did not comply with the requisite specifications, being deficient in power and economy. UER used the turbines until they replaced them with more efficient turbines. BW claimed the balance of the price and UER counterclaimed damages for breach of contract. The question was how the benefits derived from the superiority of the new turbines should be treated in the assessment of UER's damages.

Decision

The benefits derived from the superiority of the new turbines must be deducted from the cost of installing them.

Viscount Haldane

> [**689**] The fundamental basis is thus compensation for pecuniary loss naturally flowing from the breach; but this first principle is qualified by a second, which imposes on a plaintiff the duty of taking all reasonable steps to mitigate the loss consequent on the breach, and debars him from claiming any part of the damage which is due to his neglect to take such steps
>
> … this second principle does not impose on the plaintiff an obligation to take any step which a reasonable and prudent man would not ordinarily take in the course of his business. But when in the course of his business he has taken action arising out of the transaction, which action has diminished his loss, the effect in actual diminution of the loss he has suffered may be taken into account even though there was no duty on him to act.
>
> …
>
> [**691**] The principle which applies here is that which makes it right for the jury or arbitrator to look at what actually happened, and to balance loss and gain. The transaction was not res inter alios acta, but one in which the person whose contract was broken took a reasonable and prudent course quite naturally arising out of the circumstances in which he was placed by the breach. Apart from the breach of contract, the lapse of time had rendered the appellants' machines obsolete, and men of business would be doing the only thing they could properly do in replacing them with new and up-to-date machines.

Jenkinson v Young [2004] SADC 30

Facts and issues

Jenkinson and Young entered into an agreement for a joint venture for the refurbishment and sale of antique furniture and jointly occupied shop premises owned by Young and adjoining premises for this purpose. Young repudiated the agreement, forcing Jenkinson to relocate to less suitable premises. Jenkinson put more time and effort into other aspects of the business and made significant profits from those sales. The question was whether the extra profits made had to be set off against the profits lost from the antique business conducted under the joint venture.

Decision

The additional profit made by Jenkinson had to be set off against the profit lost in the antique business.

Judge Herriman

[287] The defendant must show that all reasonable steps were not taken [to mitigate] and show that what the plaintiff did do was not reasonable.

...

[288] In the ordinary course of their business, the plaintiffs have, in consequence of their forced move to Glen Osmond, done 'what they ought to have done as reasonable men' and placed more focus upon aspects of their business other than retailing. These other activities have nevertheless been in the ordinary course of their business as, save for e-bay sales, they have always been parallel and associated activities to retailing.

...

[290] Further, whether bound or not to mitigate, I am satisfied the plaintiffs have in fact averted any losses (and, indeed, increased overall income) in 1999 and 2000 and have otherwise suffered a small loss in 2001.

Origin Energy LPG Ltd v BestCare Foods [2013] NSWCA 90

Facts and issues

BestCare conducted the business of manufacture and supply of pet food. Due to Origin's negligence, BestCare's factory was destroyed. Rather than repair the factory, BestCare bought another factory at Dubbo. After two years' operation, BestCare sold the factory. The question was whether the proceeds of sale reduced BestCare's loss.

Decision

The damages award did not include a component for the replacement or reinstatement of the damaged property; furthermore, the damages award compensated the plaintiff for lost profits but not for goodwill, which for accounting purposes was treated differently. Therefore, the proceeds of sale of the Dubbo property and the goodwill of the business should be *not* taken into account in assessing the plaintiff's loss.

Ward JA (MacFarlan AJ and Hoeben JA agreeing)

[197] (ii) Credit for salvage value ground of appeal ($13.6 million)
The second ground of appeal relates to the question whether the sum of $13 681 333 received as the net proceeds of the sale of the Dubbo business (including land, plant and equipment, stock and goodwill) should have been deducted from the overall amount awarded to BestCare. The sale price had been apportioned as to $2 000 000 for the land; $7 358 479 for the plant and equipment; $1 389 176 for the stock and $2 933 678 for the goodwill. There was no dispute as to the manner in which the sale price had been so apportioned.

[198] The issue as to whether such a deduction should be made was first raised in Mr Fayad's first report. There, he considered it appropriate to deduct that sum for reasons to which I will shortly return. The referee (having recommended its deduction) did not make such a deduction from the overall award and McDougall J considered that the referee was correct not to make such a deduction. Origin maintains that such a deduction should have been made.

[199] There was no dispute between the parties as to the general principle, in case of tortious damage to property, that the plaintiff is entitled to the cost of reinstatement (provided that reinstatement is reasonable) or else the diminution in value of the property (*Evans v Balog*; *Gagner Pty Ltd v Canturi Corporation Pty Ltd*). Similarly, there was no dispute that, where the plaintiff (acting reasonably) decides not to reinstate the damaged property but to acquire an alternative property, the plaintiff may recover the cost of the alternative property in lieu of recovering the cost of reinstatement of the damaged property (*Dominion Mosaics v Trafalgar Trucking*; *McGregor on Damages*, 18th ed, 34–009) and that if, having acquired an alternative property in such circumstances, the plaintiff subsequently sells the alternative property for a profit, then the plaintiff does not have to account to the defendant for that profit (Dominion Mosaics).

...

[201] The judgment sum included an award of $10 523 572 (plus interest) to compensate BestCare for the cost of buying the Dubbo factory and re-establishing its operations there (as recommended by the referee).

...

[218] Ultimately, the area of real debate on the $13.6 million issue focused on the treatment of that component of the sale proceeds that represented the goodwill of the business. That is because any residual value of the other components has already been taken into account in the overall damages award.

...

[222] [It] was accepted that the experts' reports and the referee's findings proceeded upon the basis that the goodwill was totally destroyed by the explosion. It was also accepted that there must have been some residual value since BestCare had been trading at the date of the explosion and, on its own case, had good future prospects. It was BestCare's submission that the question of any deduction for residual goodwill is answered by reference to the manner in which the referee had assessed the particular heads of loss in this case.

[223] In other words, since what the referee (and the experts) had assessed was the loss of profits (not the value of the business including an assessment of the goodwill of the business), there was no error in not making a deduction for any residual goodwill value. The distinction between loss of profits and loss of goodwill can be seen by reference to the methodologies described for the assessment of the latter in *The Commissioner of Taxation of the Commonwealth of Australia v Murry*.

[224] As noted earlier, there was some reference by the referee to evidence relating to whether the value of brand names and goodwill had been impacted by the explosion and BestCare's consequent absence from the market for some time. The referee said that:

> There was no evidence of an adverse affectation to either once those consequences of the explosion were overcome,

and noted that the submissions seemed to have treated them as continuing. On that basis it seems that no assessment was made as to diminution in the value of the goodwill nor was its value calculated.

[225] The recommended award for loss of profits was not an award for the diminution in the value (including goodwill) of the enterprise conducted by BestCare. Given the basis on which the referee approached the damages calculation it cannot be said that it was manifestly unreasonable for the primary judge to reject the recommendation that Origin was entitled to a credit for the sale of the business prior to judgment. Accordingly, Origin's appeal on this ground fails.

Table 2.2 Benefits flowing from mitigating actions of the plaintiff: the general concepts

Principle	Relevant authority
Benefits flowing from mitigation – 'avoided losses' – will reduce the plaintiff's damages save where the action is *res inter alios acta*.	*British Westinghouse Electric & Manufacturing Co Ltd v Underground Electric Railways Co of London Ltd* [1912] AC 673
Benefits flowing from the superior performance of the replacement machines were deducted from their cost.	*British Westinghouse Electric & Manufacturing Co Ltd v Underground Electric Railways Co of London Ltd* [1912] AC 673
Whether the steps taken by the plaintiff in mitigation are reasonable or not, if they result in reducing their loss, they must be set off.	*Jenkinson v Young* [2004] SADC 30
When the mitigating actions of the plaintiff entirely avoid the loss, then in truth no loss has been suffered and compensation is not recoverable.	*Haines v Bendall* (1991) 172 CLR 60
Proceeds of the sale of an item the subject of a repudiated lease were not applied in reduction of damages for breach of the lease as the sale of the item was *res inter alios acta*.	*Frankipile Pty Ltd v Acsas Pty Ltd* (New South Wales Court of Appeal, Samuels, Mahoney and McHugh JJA, 7 November 1988)
The defendant bears the onus of proving that benefits have flowed from mitigating actions.	*Tyco Australia v Optus Networks Pty Ltd* [2004] NSWCA 333
Where the award does not compensate the plaintiff for the damage or reinstatement to property or for goodwill, then the defendant is not upon the plaintiff's subsequent resale of the property or the receipt of monies representing goodwill, entitled to a credit.	*Origin Energy LPG Ltd v BestCare Foods* [2013] NSWCA 90

E Other benefits arising from the wrong

Benefits received as direct results of the wrong may be deducted unless indirect or collateral. Two subsidiary principles arise:

(1) Credit need not be given by an injured party for moneys not to be characterised as extinguishing or reducing that party's loss but received independently of that right of

redress, a principle well recognised in insurance law at least – *Insurance Australia Ltd v HIH Casualty & General Insurance Ltd (in liq)* (2007) 18 VR 528.

(2) A deduction of moneys made by a third party may be rejected even though the third party had no charitable motive – *Monroe Schneiders Associates (Inc) v No 1 Raberem Pty Ltd* (1991) 33 FCR 1.

Insurance Australia Ltd v HIH Casualty & General Insurance Ltd (in liq) [2007] VSCA 223; (2007) 18 VR 528

Facts and issues

Following the liquidation of HIH, HIH Claims Support Ltd ('HCSL') was appointed to administer a fund to assist HIH's insured. Steele, the second respondent, had offered HCSL an assignment of his rights under the HIH policy. Steele was a defendant in an action for breach of contract in which judgment was ordered against him in the sum of $1 461 045.00. HCLS satisfied the judgment against Steele. The question was whether credit should be given for the receipt of the monies paid by HCSL.

Decision

The payments by HCSL were made under a contract of indemnity and not characterised as extinguishing or reducing the injured party's loss but received independently of right of redress. Credit was not given for their receipt.

Ashley JA

> **[159]** There was an important matter which must be considered. It concerns the proper characterisation of the moneys paid by HCSL. There is a broad principle, applicable at least in insurance law and torts law, that credit need not be given by an injured party for moneys received by it which are not to be characterised as extinguishing or reducing that party's loss, but are rather to be characterised as having been received independently of right of redress. In the field of insurance, the principle is exposed in cases such as *Burnand v Rodocanachi Sons & Co*.
>
> …
>
> **[163]** There is no doubt that the principle is firmly established.
>
> …
>
> **[169]** In the present case, I consider that the circumstances, however they are considered, lead to a conclusion that what was paid was an indemnity.

Monroe Schneiders Associates (Inc) v No 1 Raberem Pty Ltd (1991) 33 FCR 1

Facts and issues

Monroe Schneiders Associates ('MSA') was a carpet retailer, and Raberem was a carpet wholesaler. Raberem delivered carpets to MSA at a low price in reliance on a false representation that MSA had already onsold the carpets to third parties. To honour the quotation, Raberem purchased carpets from a third party, Feltex, putting Raberem in financial difficulties. Feltex later contributed NZ$400 000 to Raberem for an advertising campaign jointly promoting their products. Raberem was held to be entitled to damages from MSA's fraud. The issue was whether the payment by Feltex should be taken into account to reduce the damages to Raberem.

Decision

The monies paid by Feltex to Raberem should not reduce MSA's liability to Raberem as they were not intended to reduce MSA's liability.

Burchett J

> **[21]** A key decision on the question whether a benefit received by a plaintiff must be taken into account in the calculation of his damages is *Espagne* [*National Insurance Co of New Zealand Ltd v Espagne*].
>
> …
>
> In *Espagne*, Dixon CJ said:
>
>> There are certain special services, aids, benefits, subventions and the like which in most communities are available to injured people. Simple examples are hospital and pharmaceutical benefits which lighten the monetary burden of illness. If the injured plaintiff has availed himself of these, he cannot establish or calculate his damages on the footing that he did not do so. On the other hand there may be advantages which accrue to the injured plaintiff, whether as a result of legislation or of contract or of benevolence, which have an additional characteristic. It may be true that they are conferred because he is intended to enjoy them in the events which have happened. Yet they have this distinguishing characteristic, namely, they are conferred on him not only independently of the existence in him of a right of redress against others but so that they may by enjoyed by him although he may enforce that right: they are the product of a disposition in his favour intended for his enjoyment and not provided in relief of any liability in others fully to compensate him. This is readily seen in the case of benevolence. If a fund is raised by subscription for the benefit of a badly injured neighbour, obviously this cannot operate in relief of the liability of a man who negligently caused the injury …
>
> …

[23] There is, indeed, ample authority to support the proposition that charitable donations for the relief of an injured person … will not generally be taken into account as mitigating an injured person's loss for the purposes of a claim for damages.

…

[26] In my view, the principle of *Espagne* is applicable generally, and not merely as a rule in actions for damages for personal injuries. To the extent that the payment of $NZ400 000 was a response by Feltex NZ to its understanding that Solomons were deserving … of assistance, I think the principle has direct application to the present case. In the words of Dixon CJ, the benefit has the distinguishing characteristic that it was conferred on Solomons 'independently of the existence in [Solomons] of a right of redress against others'.

…

[28] [It] may be said that the occasion of the arrangement with Feltex NZ was the situation in relation to the carpet transaction. But any direct link was denied by the refusal of Feltex NZ to amend its price in relation to that transaction. What followed was a collateral transaction, involving separate obligations in respect of advertising and promotion …

…

[29] In my opinion the appeal should be dismissed with costs.

Credit was not given for the amounts received from Feltex.

Table 2.3 Overview of the deduction of other benefits arising from the wrong.

Principle	Relevant authority
Benefits received as a direct result from a wrong may be deducted but not where they are indirect or collateral or not intended to reduce the liability of the wrongdoer.	*Johns v Prunell* [1960] VR 208 *Monroe Scheider Associates (Inc) v No 1 Raberem Pty Ltd* (1991) 33 FCR 1
Factual causation demonstrating the receipt of benefits is necessary but not sufficient for reduction of liability.	*Ruthol Pty Ltd v Tricon (Australia) Pty Ltd* (2005) 12 BPR 23, 923
The determination of whether a benefit is direct, or collateral, involves value judgements.	*Johns v Prunell* [1960] VR 208
In insurance law, credit need not be given for moneys received by an injured party which are not characterised as extinguishing or reducing that party's loss but were received independently of right of redress.	*Insurance Australia Ltd v HIH Casualty & General Insurance Ltd (in liq)* (2007) 18 VR 528
Charitable actions by a third party will not reduce the defendant's liability unless the third party intended that effect.	*Powercor Australia Ltd v Thomas* (2012) 43 VR 220 *Cusack v Heath* [1950] QWN 16
Actions by a third party not directed to reducing the defendant's liability (such as to maintain good standing with the plaintiff) will not reduce the defendant's liability.	*Monroe Schneiders Associates (Inc) v No 1 Raberem Pty Ltd* (1991) 33 FCR 1

F The impact of tax law

The assessment of loss may involve the consideration of tax law, a complex exercise. Two aspects are considered below:

(1) the income tax implications of the receipt of an award and

(2) where compensation is awarded for damage to property.

Table 2.4 Overview of the tax implications of an order for compensation

Principle	Relevant authority
Compensation for lost income is assessed by reference to the plaintiff's after-tax income.	*Cullen v Trappell* (1980) 146 CLR 1 *Gill v Australian Wheat Board* [1980] 2 NSWLR 795
Compensation which is a substitute for lost income is subject to income tax even if ordered as a lump sum.	
Compensation for personal injury impairing the plaintiff's ability to work is usually treated as loss of earning capacity, conceptualised as being of a capital nature not subject to income tax. Similarly with pre-judgment interest on compensation for personal injury.	*Groves v United Pacific Transport Pty Ltd* [1965] Qd R 62 *Whitaker v Federal Commissioner of Taxation* (1998) 82 FCR 261
If the plaintiff is liable for capital gains tax, the amount awarded is adjusted so that the deduction of the tax rate leads to the amount that would be awarded if no tax is payable.	*Provan v HCL Real Estate Ltd* (1992) 24 ATR 238
Future loss is accounted for as being the present value of future loss. The potential tax payable on the compensation must be taken into account and will vary depending on whether it is paid as a lump sum in which case the compensation is reduced to take into account the advantage of receiving it as a lump sum, but itself must be reduced to take into account the tax likely to be paid on the income from investing.	

REVIEW QUESTIONS

(1) What is the overarching principle governing the recovery of compensation for lost income as far as income tax is concerned?

(2) What are the GST considerations when compensation is assessed by reference to the price or value of goods?

IV Certainty of loss and recovery for the loss of a chance

The broad approaches concerning the treatment of the recovery of damages for the loss of a chance are:

- *To determine the likelihood of the event's occurring on the balance of probabilities*: if the probability of the event exceeds 50 per cent, the plaintiff recovers everything, but nothing if the probability less than 50 per cent. This approach is conventionally taken to establish the *existence* of an opportunity.
- *To assess loss on a sliding scale*: damages are calculated by multiplying the probability of the occurrence with the amount of loss generated by the occurrence. This approach is conventionally taken to assessing the *value* of the lost opportunity.

Concept	Short explanation	Relevant authorities	Principles text
Overview of the current law	The relevance of 'probability' in assessing the loss of a chance or opportunity.	*Malec v JC Hutton Pty Ltd* (1990) 169 CLR 638 *Sellars v Adelaide Petroleum NL* (1994) 179 CLR 332	Chapter 2: [2.62]–[2.70]
Consequential loss	Once liability for initial loss is established, the assessment of consequential loss is dependent upon hypothetical past events by evaluating the chances of each event occurring.	*Malec v JC Hutton Pty Ltd* (1990) 169 CLR 638 *Glenmont Investments Pty Ltd v O'Loughlin* (2000) 79 SASR 185	Chapter 2: [2.71]–[2.76]
Personal injury as initial harm	The uncertainty of hypothetical past events on which the initial harm depends is resolved on the balance of probabilities.	*Tabet v Gett* (2010) 240 CLR 537	Chapter 2: [2.77]–[2.87]
Pure economic loss as initial harm	Where the plaintiff has missed an opportunity for economic gain as a result of the wrong, the assessment of damage is conducted within two-steps: the *first*, whether on the balance of probabilities, the plaintiff would not have lost that opportunity but for the wrong; the *second*, the value of that lost opportunity.	*Crown Insurance Services Pty Ltd v National Mutual Life Association of Australasia Ltd* (2005) 13 ANZ Ins Cas 61-659 *Sellars v Adelaide Petroleum NL* (1994) 179 CLR 332 *Chaplin v Hicks* [1911] 2 KB 787 *Hendriks v McGeoch* [2008] NSWCA 53 *Badenach v Calvert* (2016) 257 CLR 440	Chapter 2: [2.88]–[2.107]
Hypothetical conduct of the defendant	The consideration of the course of conduct that the defendant might have taken rather than the wrong; the effects on the recovery of compensation where the defendant hypothetically might have conducted themselves in a legally compliant way.	*Commonwealth v Amann Aviation Pty Ltd* (1991) 174 CLR 64 *Port Macquarie-Hastings Council v Diveva Pty Ltd* [2017] NSWCA 97	Chapter 2: [2.108]–[2.116]

A Overview of the current law

Malec v JC Hutton Pty Ltd[1] ('*Malec*') and *Sellars v Adelaide Petroleum NL*[2] ('*Sellars*') are the two seminal cases.

The Court in *Malec* adopted a degree of probability approach to assess consequential loss arising from personal injury. The *value* of that loss is ascertained by reference to the degree of probabilities. Compensation for the loss of a commercial opportunity was treated the same way in *Sellars,* where the High Court expressly adopted the *Malec* approach.

The *balance of probabilities* approach is generally adopted to assess the *existence of an opportunity* and considers whether there is a 50 per cent or higher likelihood of the event occurring. If the chance is 50 per cent or higher the fact of the event is established, and the amount of loss generated is awarded; if the likelihood is less than 50 per cent nothing is awarded.

The *degree of probabilities* approach is generally adopted to assess the *value of a lost opportunity*. It operates on a 'sliding scale', considering the degree of probability of the event's occurrence, and awards a sum calculated by multiplying the probability of the event's occurrence with the amount of loss generated by the event's occurrence.

Malec v JC Hutton Pty Ltd (1990) 169 CLR 638

Facts and issues

Malec, while employed by Hutton, contracted brucellosis as a result of Hutton's negligence. Depression is a possible consequence of brucellosis. Malec subsequently developed a neurotic condition and was unable to work and developed a back condition rendering him unemployable. The Full Court of the Supreme Court of Queensland found that even if Malec had not contracted brucellosis, he would have developed the back condition which coupled with the resulting unemployment would have caused him to develop his neurotic condition. The Full Court denied Malec damages for the time after the onset of the back condition. The issue was in the High Court was whether Malec was entitled to damages for that period.

Decision

Malec was entitled to damages for that period on the footing that, once liability is established on the balance of probabilities, consequential loss is assessed with reference to the degree of probability of the event's causing the loss happening.

Deane, Gaudron and McHugh JJ

> **[640]** The issue in this appeal concerns the valuation of a plaintiff's damage caused by the tortuous conduct of the defendant, after it is found that it is more likely than not that the damage would have occurred in any event as the result of conditions or events for which the defendant is not legally responsible..
>
> ...

1 (1990) 169 CLR 638.

2 (1994) 179 CLR 332.

[**641**] They [the Queensland Full Court] held that the plaintiff's damages should be assessed on the basis that his neurotic condition at the time of the trial was caused by depression induced by acute brucellosis.

...

[642] Assessing damages for future or potential events

When liability has been established and a common law court has to assess damages, its approach to events that allegedly would have occurred, but cannot now occur, or that allegedly might occur, is different from its approach to events which allegedly have occurred.

...

[**643**] In the case of an event which it is alleged would or would not have occurred, or might or might not yet occur, the approach of the court is different. The future may be predicted and the hypothetical may be conjectured. But questions as to the future or hypothetical effect of physical injury or degeneration are not commonly susceptible of scientific demonstration or proof. If the law is to take account of future or hypothetical events in assessing damages, it can only do so in terms of the degree of probability of those events occurring. The probability may be very high – 99.9 per cent – or very low – 0.1 per cent. But unless the chance is so low as to be regarded as speculative – say less than I per cent – or so high as to be practically certain – say over 99 per cent – the court will take that chance into account in assessing the damages. Where proof is necessarily unattainable, it would be unfair to treat as certain a prediction which has a 51 per cent probability of occurring, but to ignore altogether a prediction which has a 49 per cent probability of occurring. Thus, the court assesses the degree of probability that an event would have occurred, or might occur, and adjusts its award of damages to reflect the degree of probability.

The assessment of damages in the present case

In the present case, the majority of the Full Court fell into error in concluding that the plaintiff was not entitled to damages for economic loss sustained after May 1982. The plaintiff proved that, at the date of the trial, as the result of the defendant's negligence, he suffered from a psychiatric condition which rendered him unemployable. On the evidence there was little, if any, chance that he would either recover or ever be employable. Subject to an allowance for the ordinary vicissitudes of life, the plaintiff was prima facie entitled to be compensated for the near certainty that, as the result [**644**] of the defendant's negligence, he will suffer from his psychiatric condition and be unemployable for the rest of his life. However, the majority in the Full Court found that it was 'likely' that, independently of the defendant's negligence, by May 1982 the plaintiff would have been unemployable and suffering from a similar neurotic condition. By the term 'likely', their Honors no doubt meant that there was more than a 50 per cent chance that this would have occurred. On that hypothesis, the damages otherwise recoverable by the plaintiff would have to be reduced to provide for that chance. On the evidence, it is impossible to conclude that it is 100 per cent certain that the plaintiff's back condition would have rendered him unemployable if he had not contracted brucellosis. So, on the majority's finding, the reduction in his damages for loss of earning capacity would be somewhere between 51 per cent and 99 per cent. But whatever the precise chance of the plaintiff's back condition totally or partially reducing his earning capacity, the majority in the Full Court erred in refusing to award him any damages for economic loss suffered after May 1982.

The Full Court of Queensland and High Court's reasoning is illustrated in Figure 2.4, showing the ultimate adoption of the degrees of probabilities approach in assessing the value of the lost opportunity.

Figure 2.4 The comparative reasoning of the Full Court of Queensland and High Court in *Malec v JC Hutton Pty Ltd*

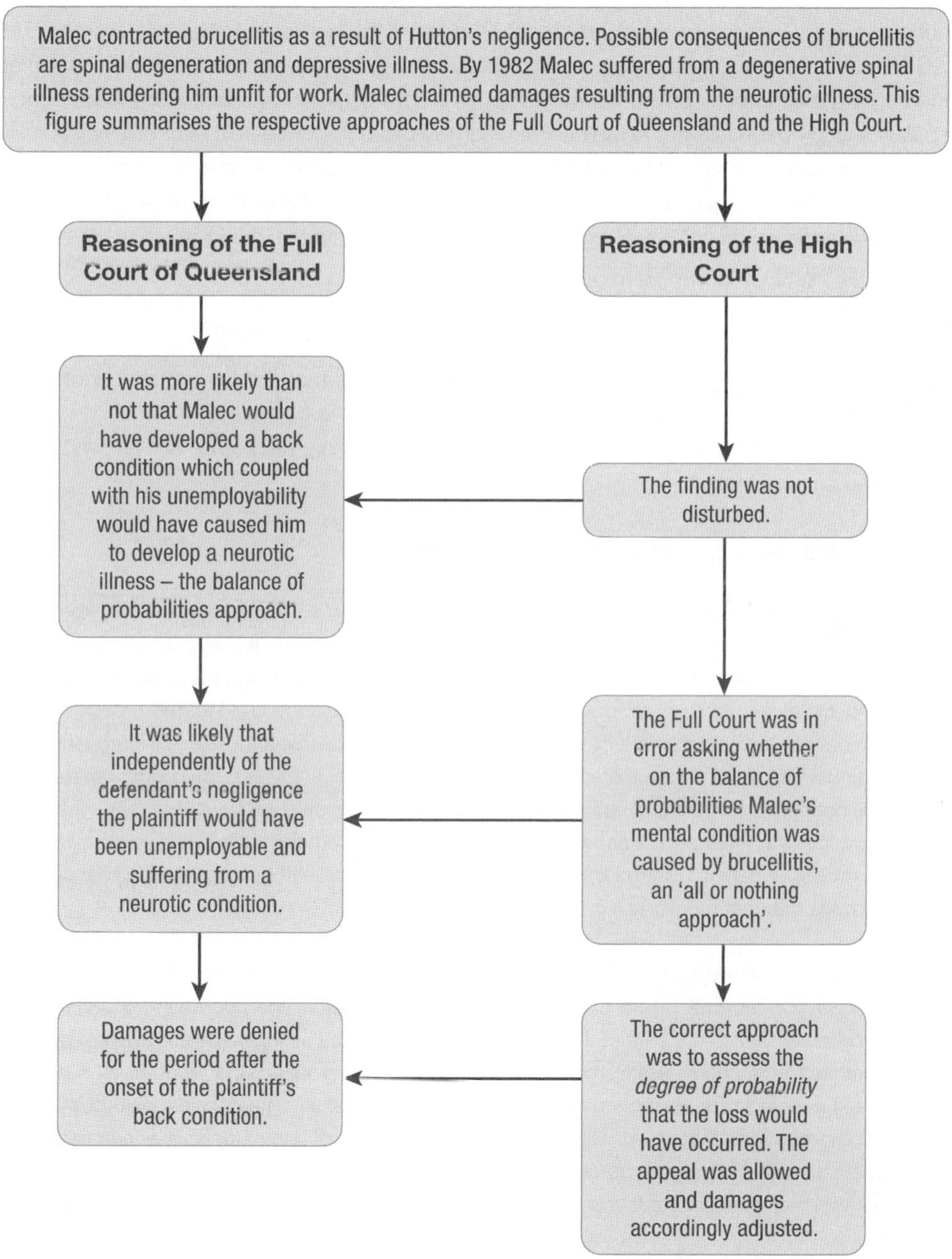

Sellars v Adelaide Petroleum NL (1994) 179 CLR 332

Facts and issues

Adelaide Petroleum entered parallel negotiations concerning the sale of its shares with Poseidon Ltd and Pagini Resources. As a result of misleading statements by Poseidon, Adelaide Petroleum discontinued negotiations with Pagini. When Adelaide Petroleum discovered the truth, it resumed negotiations with Pagini and eventually reached agreement. Adelaide Petroleum claimed that if it had continued the initial negotiations with Pagini, it would have arrived at a more favourable outcome, and claimed the difference as damages from Poseidon. The trial judge had found on the balance of probabilities that Adelaide Petroleum would but for Poseidon's wrong have entered into a contract with Paginin but that there was a less than even chance that the conditions of that contract would be satisfied and deducted 60 per cent from the damages to reflect the possibility that the conditions would not have been met. The central issue before the High Court was whether Adelaide Petroleum was entitled to that amount in damages.

Decision

Adelaide Petroleum's damages were calculated on the basis that the loss of its opportunity to negotiate a better outcome with Pagini must be proven on the *balance* of probabilities (the first step) then, if established, on the value of that lost opportunity on the *degree* of that probability of that loss (the second step).

Mason CJ, Dawson J, Toohey J and Gaudron J

> [**349**] In contract law, the loss of a chance to win a prize in a competition resulting from breach of a contract to provide the chance is compensable, notwithstanding that, on the balance of probabilities, it is more likely than not that the plaintiff would not win the competition. As the contract contained a promise to provide the chance, the breach of the contract resulted in the loss of the chance and that loss was for relevant purposes an actual loss. And, where there has been an actual loss of some sort, the common law does not permit difficulties of estimating the loss in money to defeat an award of damages. The damages will then be ascertained by reference to the degree of probabilities, or possibilities, inherent in the plaintiffs succeeding had the plaintiff been given the chance which the contract promised.
>
> ...
>
> [**355**] We consider that acceptance of the principle enunciated in Malec requires that damages for deprivation of a commercial opportunity, whether the deprivation occurred by reason of breach of contract, tort or contravention of s 52(1), should be ascertained by reference to the court's assessment of the prospects of success of that opportunity had it been pursued. The principle recognized in Malec was based on a consideration of the peculiar difficulties associated with the proof and evaluation of future possibilities and past hypothetical fact situations, as contrasted with proof of historical facts. Once that is accepted, there is no secure foundation for confining the principle to cases of any particular kind.

...

Hence the applicant must prove on the balance of probabilities that he or she has sustained some loss or damage. However, in a case such as the present, the applicant shows some loss or damage was sustained by demonstrating that the contravening conduct caused the loss of a commercial opportunity which had some value (not being a negligible value), the value being ascertained by reference to the degree of probabilities or possibilities. It is no answer to that way of viewing an applicant's case to say that the commercial opportunity was valueless on the balance of probabilities because to say that is to value the commercial opportunity by reference to a standard of proof which is inapplicable.

The conclusion which we have reached on this question finds support in other considerations. The approach results in fair compensation whereas the all or nothing outcome produced by the civil standard of proof would result in the vast majority of cases in over-compensation or under-compensation to an applicant who has been deprived of a commercial opportunity.

...

[**356**] On the findings made by the trial judge, the Pagini contract would have been entered into but for the contraventions of s 52(1). Although, on the probabilities, it would not have been completed, there was a significant chance that it would be completed.

Brennan J

[**359**] The cases where a plaintiff seeks damages only for breach of a contractual promise to afford the plaintiff an opportunity to acquire a benefit are in a different category from cases under s 82(1) and cases in tort where damage is the gist of the cause of action. In a case like *Chaplin v Hicks*, the relevant loss is identified by the contractual promise to afford the plaintiff an opportunity to acquire a benefit or to avoid a detriment.

...

But in cases arising under s 82(1) of the Act, as in cases of tort where damage is the gist of the action, a lost opportunity may or may not constitute compensable loss or damage. In such cases, the existence and causation of a compensable loss cannot be proved by reference to an antecedent promise to afford an opportunity. The plaintiff, who bears the onus of proving a loss suffered as the result of the defendant's contravening or tortious conduct must prove the existence and causation of the alleged loss in some other way. The manner of discharging the plaintiff's onus will presently be mentioned.

...

[**364**] As a matter of common experience, opportunities to acquire commercial benefits are frequently valuable in themselves, not only when they will probably fructify in a financial return but also when they offer a substantial prospect of a financial return. The volatility of the market for speculative shares testifies to both the valuable character of commercial opportunities and the difficulty of assessing the value of opportunities which are subject to serious contingencies. Provided an opportunity offers a substantial, and not merely speculative, prospect of acquiring a benefit that the plaintiff sought to acquire or of avoiding a detriment that the plaintiff sought to avoid, the opportunity can be held to be valuable. And,

if an opportunity is valuable, the loss of that opportunity is truly 'loss' or 'damage' for the purposes of s 82(1) of the Act and for the purposes of the law of torts. In a statute which is intended to govern commercial transactions, it would be pedantically inappropriate to exclude the loss of a valuable commercial opportunity from the categories of 'loss' and 'damage' in s 82(1) of the Act.

However, a causal relationship between the loss of such an opportunity and the defendant's contravening or tortious conduct must be proved before any issue of assessment of the amount of the loss arises.

...

[**368**] Where a loss is alleged to be a lost opportunity to acquire a benefit, a plaintiff who bears the onus of proving that a loss was caused by the conduct of the defendant discharges that onus by establishing a chain of causation that continues up to the point when there is a substantial prospect of acquiring the benefit sought by the plaintiff. Up to that point, the plaintiff must establish both the historical facts and any necessary hypothesis on the balance of probabilities. A constant standard of proof applies to the finding that a loss has been suffered and to the finding that that loss was caused by the defendant's conduct, whether those findings depend on evidence of historical facts or on evidence giving rise to competing hypotheses. In any event, the standard is proof on the balance of probabilities.

Although the issue of a loss caused by the defendant's conduct must be established on the balance of probabilities, hypotheses and possibilities the fulfilment of which cannot be proved must be evaluated to determine the amount or value of the loss suffered. Proof on the balance of probabilities has no part to play in the evaluation of such hypotheses or possibilities: evaluation is a matter of informed estimation.

NOTE

The High Court in *Sellars* approved *Malec* and adopted a two-step approach for the assessment of damages:

- Step 1 – the loss of the opportunity must be proven on the balance of probabilities (the first step), then
- Step 2 – the value of that lost opportunity is made by calculating the degree of probability that the loss would occur from the lost opportunity.

The assessment of damages for the loss of an opportunity for breach of contract is different to tort where damages is the gist of the cause of action. With tort, the plaintiff must prove that the loss occurred on the balance of probabilities in accordance with the *Malec* approach (as in *Sellars* at 355 per Mason CJ, Dawson J, Toohey J and Gaudron J). With contract, unlike tort, 'the relevant loss is identified by the contractual promise to afford the plaintiff an opportunity to acquire a benefit or to avoid a detriment' (*Sellars* [359], [368] per Brennan J). Once the breach of the contract has been established, the *value* of the loss as with tort is assessed in accordance with the degree, and not the balance, of probabilities (*Sellars* [355] per Mason CJ, Dawson J, Toohey J, Gaudron J and [368] per Brennan J).

Figure 2.5 The *Sellars* two-step approach to the recovery of compensation for loss of a commercial opportunity

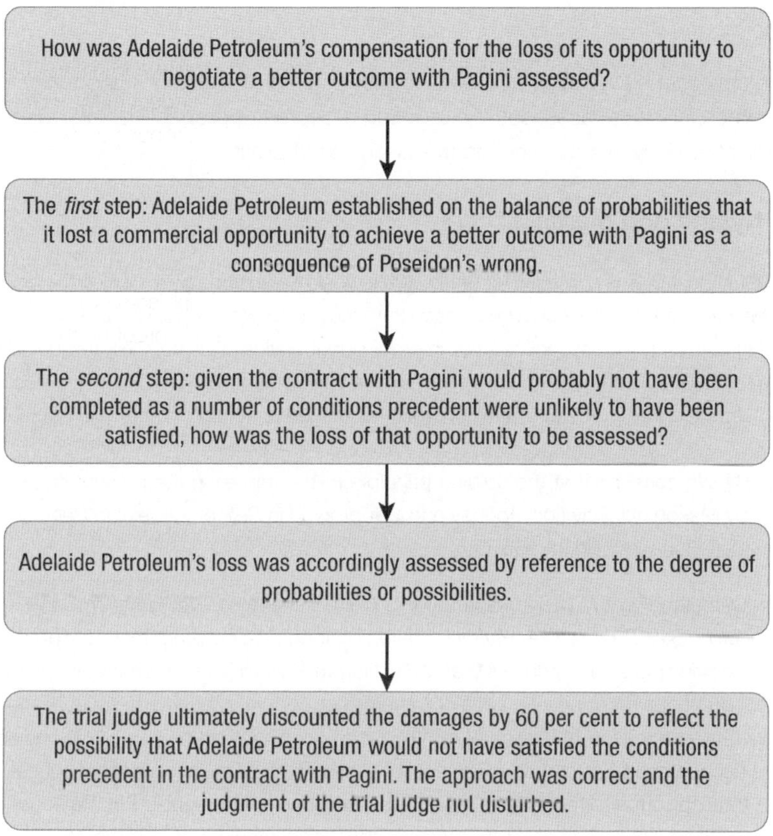

B Consequential loss

The assessment of the wrongdoer's liability for initial loss is on the balance of probabilities. Consistent with the *Malec* approach, damage caused by consequential loss is assessed by the degree of probabilities. While *Malec* was a case of personal injury, the *Malec* approach is applied also in cases of economic loss (eg *Sellars* itself) and property damage cases (see, eg, *Glenmont Investments Pty Ltd v O'Loughlin*).

Glenmont Investments Pty Ltd v O'Loughlin (2000) 79 SASR 185

Facts and issues

A large mechanical dinosaur owned by Glenmont was destroyed in a fire for which the respondents were liable. The relevant issue concerned the assessment of the loss of opportunity to exploit the dinosaur commercially.

Decision

Adopting the approaches in *Malec* and *Sellars,* damages for the loss of opportunity to exploit the dinosaur commercially were assessed by adopting a degree of probabilities approach, evaluating the probability of all likely events affecting the likelihood of profit.

Doyle CJ, Nyland and Martin JJ

> **[419]** Glenmont claims damages for profits that it would have made by exhibiting the dinosaur, together with profits that it would have made from the production and release of a film featuring the dinosaur and from associated commercial opportunities. In a nutshell, the defendants argued at trial that Glenmont would not have made any worthwhile profits from the dinosaur ... They submitted that ... the estimates of profit that the judge accepted were wildly unrealistic.
>
> ...
>
> **[421]** We consider that the guiding principle to be applied in the present case is that stated by Mason CJ, Dawson, Toohey and Gaudron JJ in *Sellars v Adelaide Petroleum NL* where their Honours said [at 355–6]:
>
>> Notwithstanding the observations of this Court in *Norwest Refrigeration Services Pty Ltd v Bain Dawes (WA) Pty Ltd* [citation omitted], we consider that acceptance of the principle enunciated in *Malec v J C Hutton Pty Ltd* [citation omitted] requires that damages for deprivation of a commercial opportunity, whether the deprivation occurred by reason of breach of contract, tort or contravention of s 52(1), should be ascertained by reference to the court's assessment of the prospects of success of that opportunity had it been pursued. The principle recognized in *Malec* was based on a consideration of the peculiar difficulties associated with the proof and evaluation of future possibilities and past hypothetical fact situations, as contrasted with proof of historical facts. Once that is accepted, there is no secure foundation for confining the principle to cases of any particular kind.
>>
>> On the other hand, the general standard of proof in civil actions will ordinarily govern the issue of causation and the issue whether the applicant has sustained loss or damage. Hence the applicant must prove on the balance of probabilities that he or she has sustained *some* loss or damage. However, in a case such as the present, the applicant shows *some* loss or damage was sustained by demonstrating that the contravening conduct caused the loss of a commercial opportunity which had *some* value (not being a negligible value), the value being ascertained by reference to the degree of probabilities or possibilities. It is no answer to that way of viewing an applicant's case to say that the commercial opportunity was value-

less on the balance of probabilities because to say that is to value the commercial opportunity by reference to a standard of proof which is inapplicable.

The conclusion which we have reached on this question finds support in other considerations. The approach results in fair compensation whereas the all or nothing outcome produced by the civil standard of proof would result in the vast majority of cases in over-compensation or under-compensation to an applicant who has been deprived of a commercial opportunity. Furthermore, it is an approach which conforms to the long-standing practice of taking into account contingencies in the assessment of damages.

…

[430] In our view, the answer to the submission advanced on appeal is that given by the majority in Malec in the passage we have cited. In essence, the submission by the defendants invites the Court 'to ignore altogether a prediction which has a 49 per cent [or less] probability of occurring'. The passages to which we have referred from Malec and from Sellars establish that the Court's assessment of the probabilities of the profit being realized, and of the probabilities of it being at one end or the other of the likely range, is to be used to adjust the amount of the award, subject of course to the Court ignoring opportunities which have negligible prospects of occurring or would be of negligible value should they occur.

…

[441] On the basis of Mr Gerlach's evidence, our view is that the share of profits from films, videos, television, merchandising and other appearances passing to Glenmont is unlikely to have exceeded $40 million. …

[442] One must then allow for a number of matters. First, the risk of Glenmont never overcoming its financial problems. Next, the impact of all the practical obstacles to the various proposals … It is not appropriate simply to take a figure of $100 million as his Honour did, or even the figure of $50 million suggested by us, and then to apply a certain percentage to that figure. The process is necessarily subjective, but it requires appropriate allowance to be made for all the relevant factors.

[443] There were many obstacles to Glenmont realising the commercial opportunities upon which it relied at trial. We take the view that the estimate of the value of those opportunities was speculative. They might have been worth a good deal less than $50 million. In our opinion his Honour's figure of at least $100 million was an unduly high starting point. We take the view that a figure of $50 million is a reasonable starting point. But then one must allow for broad contingencies to which we have referred. An award of damages of $5 million would, on the evidence before the judge, have been an adequate award for the loss of commercial opportunities.

C Personal injury as initial harm

This question often arises how hypothetical past events impact on the assessment of damages in personal injury. Fundamentally the uncertainty in respect of these hypothetical past events is resolved on the balance of probabilities. Particular complications arise with hypothetical past natural events such as the way that the hypothetical development of a medical condition is to be assessed.

Tabet v Gett (2010) 240 CLR 537

Facts and issues

On 11 January 1991, Tabet was admitted to hospital suffering from headaches, nausea and vomiting. Her doctor, Gett, negligently did not then order a CT scan which would have revealed a brain tumour. Tabet suffered a seizure on 14 January. A CT scan was then performed which revealed the brain tumour. As a result of the seizure, the tumour, the operation and the post-operative treatment, she suffered irreversible brain damage.

In the NSW Court of Appeal, it was held that as the connection between Tabet's damage and Gett's negligence could not be established in accordance with the balance of probabilities, her claim was dismissed. Tabet appealed to the High Court.

Decision

The New South Wales Court of Appeal was not in error in applying the balance of probabilities approach to the assessment of damages in cases involving an opportunity for a better medical outcome. Tabet's appeal was dismissed.

Gummow ACJ

> **[2]** The appellant pleaded her case as one in which breach by the respondent of his duty to manage her with due care and skill caused or contributed to cause her injury, loss and damage, or, in the alternative, led to 'the loss of an opportunity to avoid injury, loss and damage'. The appellant at trial failed on the first ground but succeeded on the second.
>
> ...
>
> **[31]** If the likelihood of a better outcome had been found to be greater than 50% then on the balance of probabilities the appellant would have succeeded, not failed, on the main branch of her case in negligence. The question of principle thus becomes whether the law permits recovery in negligence on proof to the balance of probabilities of the presence of something else, namely a chance, opportunity or prospect of an outcome the eventuation of which, however, was less than probable.
>
> ...
>
> **The issue of principle**
>
> **[46]** Further, and as an additional ground of decision, in personal injury cases the law of negligence as understood in the common law of Australia does not entertain an action for recovery when the damage, for which compensation is awarded consequent upon breach of duty, is characterised as the loss of a chance of a better outcome of the character found by the trial judge in this case.
>
> **[47]** It should be said immediately that the principles dealing with recovery of damages for breach of contract offer no appropriate analogy. The action for breach of contract lies upon the occurrence of breach, but that in negligence lies only if and when damage is sustained. This has significance for the application of limitation statutes. But it has the further

and relevant importance identified by Brennan J in *Sellars*. This is that in a negligence action, unlike an action in contract, the existence and causation of compensable loss cannot be established by reference to breach of an antecedent promise to afford an opportunity.

[48] In a contract case the plaintiff should be entitled at least to nominal damages for loss of the promised opportunity. …

[49] *Chaplin* [*Chaplin v Hicks* [1911] 2 KB 786] is authority for the proposition that if a plaintiff, by the breach of contract by the defendant, has been deprived of something which has a monetary value, there is to be an assessment of damages notwithstanding difficulty in calculation or impossibility of making an assessment with certainty. …

[50] But these considerations do not appear in the frame of reference for the present case. As Brennan J indicated in *Sellars* in an action in tort where damage is the gist of the action, the issue which precedes any assessment of damages recoverable is whether a lost opportunity, as a matter of law, answers the description of 'loss or damage' which is then compensable.

…

[54] In the present case, with reference to what had been said in *Sellars* when dealing with an action to recover 'loss or damage' under s 82 of the *Trade Practices Act 1974* (Cth) for contravention of s 52 of that statute, the Court of Appeal referred to the existence in commerce of a coherent notion of loss of a right of a chance of financial benefit. In that regard, the statement of principle by Brennan J in *Sellars* is significant:

> As a matter of common experience, opportunities to acquire commercial benefits are frequently valuable in themselves, not only when they will probably fructify in a financial return but also when they offer a substantial prospect of a financial return. … . Provided an opportunity offers a substantial, and not merely speculative, prospect of acquiring a benefit that the plaintiff sought to acquire or of avoiding a detriment that the plaintiff sought to avoid, the opportunity can be held to be valuable. And, if an opportunity is valuable, the loss of that opportunity is truly 'loss' or 'damage' for the purposes of s 82(1) of the Act and for the purposes of the law of torts.

[59] It may be said that the 'all or nothing' outcome on the balance of probabilities leads to 'rough justice'. But the traditional approach in personal injury cases represents the striking by the law of a balance between the competing interests of the parties, and the substitution of the loss of a chance as the actionable damage represents a shift in that balance towards claimants. Again, there may be a view that, especially with respect to medical treatment, the substitution assists in the maintenance of standards where there is a less than even chance of a cure … But any such potential benefit to the public weal has to be weighed against, for example, the prospect of 'defensive medicine' with emphasis upon costly testing procedures in preference to a sequential deductive approach to diagnosis and treatment.

…

[63] The Court of Appeal reached the correct result on the matters of which the appellant complains in this court. Further, the court should not so modify the common law as to produce a different result.

Kiefel J

[123] It was recognized in *Sellars* that a loss of the opportunity to obtain a commercial advantage or benefit is loss or damage for the purposes of s 82(1) of the Trade Practices Act 1974 (Cth), where the cause of action arose under s 52(1) of that Act. Previous decisions allowing for recovery had been based in contract, where the breach of the promise to provide the chance itself gave rise to the loss of that chance. But as Brennan J said, in cases under s 82(1), 'as in cases of tort where damage is the gist of the action, a lost opportunity may or may not constitute compensable loss or damage' and it must be proved in some other way.

[124] What cases in contract, such as *Commonwealth v Amann Aviation Pty Ltd* and *Sellars* have in common is that the commercial interest lost may readily be seen to be of value itself. The same cannot be said of a chance of a better medical outcome or a person's interest in it. Lord Hoffmann observed in *Gregg* that most cases where there has been recovery for loss of a chance have involved financial loss, where the chance itself can be regarded as an item of property. And in *Sellars* Brennan J observed that, '[a]s a matter of common experience, opportunities to acquire commercial benefits are frequently valuable in themselves'. So long as an opportunity provides a substantial and not merely a speculative prospect of acquiring a benefit, it can be regarded as of value and therefore loss or damage. A loss of a chance of a better medical outcome cannot be regarded in this way. As the assessment of damages in this case shows, the only value given to it is derived from the final, physical, damage.

NOTE

A view was previously held that, analogous to commercial loss, the loss of an opportunity for a better medical outcome was a compensable loss – *Rufo v Hosking* (2004) 61 NSWLR. The New South Wales Court of Appeal in *Tabet* expressly rejected the notion that the loss of an opportunity for a better medical outcome, unlike the loss of a commercial opportunity, was *ipso facto* a compensable loss, and dismissed Tabet's claim. Gummow ACJ's at [63] specifically confirmed the correctness of that reasoning. The High Court's reasoning differentiated between cases where the negligence allegedly led to the loss of an opportunity of a better medical outcome, and where negligence led to the loss of a commercial opportunity. *Sellars* was an example of the latter.

D Pure economic loss as initial harm

Where initial harm is pure economic loss, the hypothetical existence of a missed opportunity to benefit the plaintiff affects the assessment of the loss. The overarching principle is these cases is once it has been established that on the balance of probabilities the plaintiff would have taken a particular action but for the defendant's wrong, the assessment of the loss from being deprived of the benefits of taking that action is on the degree of probabilities, consistent, again, with the *Sellars* 'two-step approach'. The corollary is that where on the

Figure 2.6 The *Tabet v Gett* balance of probabilities approach where personal injury is the initial harm

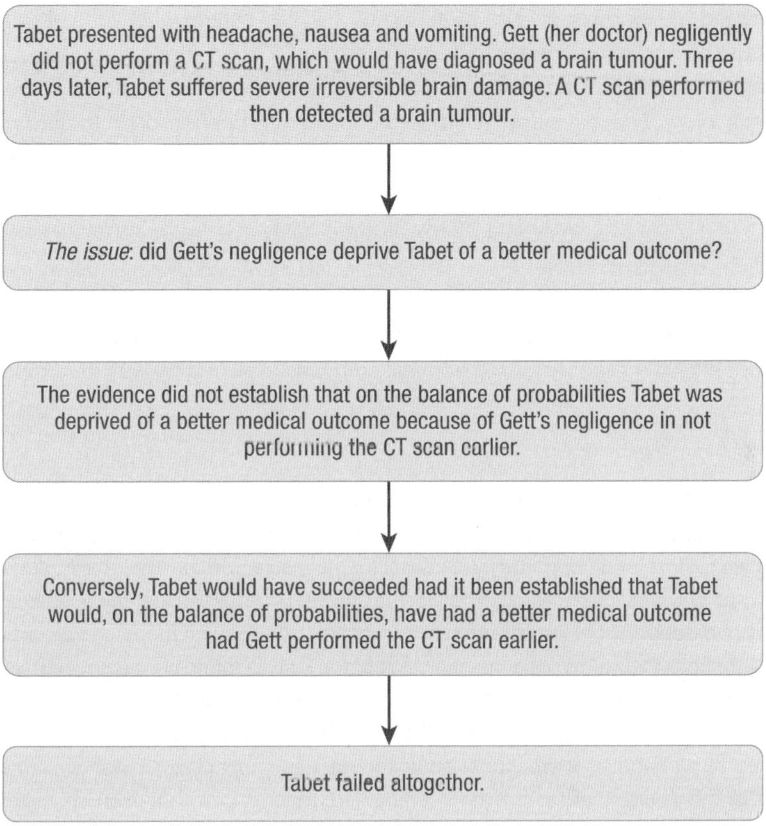

balance of probabilities it cannot be established that the plaintiff would have taken a particular action but for the defendant's wrong, no compensation is recovered.

Crown Insurance Services Pty Ltd v National Mutual Life Association of Australasia Ltd [2005] VSCA 218; (2005) 13 ANZ Ins Cas 61-659

Facts and issues

National Mutual Life Association of Australasia ('NM') issued a policy of disability insurance to the insured by which it agreed to pay the insured a lump sum if he was disabled. Unknown to NM, the insured had a CT scan and X-ray of his spine which showed normal degeneration. The insurer's agent, Crown Insurance Service ('CIS'), had failed to ask the insured about medical conditions.

The insured became disabled with spine injuries two weeks after the policy issued and claimed the insurance. The insured settled with the NM who claimed reimbursement from CIS. CIS was to have breached duties owed to NM by failing to ask the insured questions about his medical conditions. If asked, the insured would have revealed the CT scan and X-rays. However, there was an 80 per cent chance that if so revealed, NM would still have issued a policy without excluding liability for back injury. The trial judge awarded the insurer compensation in the amount of 20 per cent of the settlement sum. CIS appealed. The question concerned the how compensation should be assessed in the light of the finding that there was an 80 per cent chance that NM would still have issued a policy without excluding liability for back injury.

Decision

Having determined on the balance of probabilities that NM would still have issued a policy to the insured without excluding liability, only a nominal sum was awarded by way of compensation.

Buchanan JA

> [**8**] The agent contended that as there had been a determination of what would have occurred but for the defendant's breach of duty, there was no room for an award [**9**] of damages for loss of an opportunity. Counsel for the insurer, on the other hand, submitted that it was only required to establish on the balance of probabilities that the agent's breach of duty had deprived it of the opportunity to impose a condition on the insurance excluding liability for back injury. Provided that the value of the lost opportunity was not negligible, its value was to be determined according to the degree of probabilities or possibilities, and it was no answer to the insurer's claim that the opportunity had no value because on the balance of probabilities it would not have imposed any conditions. It was submitted on behalf of the insurer that the trial judge embarked upon an irrelevant exercise in deciding whether, on the balance of probabilities, the insurer would have imposed a condition excluding liability for back injury if the agent had fulfilled its duty. Once it had been held on the balance of probabilities that the insurer had lost the opportunity to impose the condition as a result of the agent's breach, all that needed to be determined was the value of the lost opportunity, and that question was not to be answered by applying the ordinary civil standard of proof.
>
> The insurer, like any plaintiff, was obliged to prove on the balance of probabilities that it had sustained compensable loss. Unless the insurer proved that it would have imposed a condition excluding liability for back injury if it had been informed of the scan and X-ray, it could not establish any loss caused by the agent's wrongdoing. In *Sellars v Adelaide Petroleum NL*, Mason, CJ, Dawson, Toohey and Gaudron JJ said:
>
>> The distinction between proof of causation and damages was emphasized in *Hotson v East Berkshire Area Health Authority.* There Lord Ackner stated that the first issue that fell to be determined was that of causation. This was to be determined on the balance of probabilities …
>>
>> …

[**10**] In the present case the issue of causation depended upon what the insurer would have done, and accordingly it was appropriate that that issue should be decided on the balance of probabilities. Unless the insurer proved that it would have imposed a condition excluding liability if the agent had performed its duty, it had not established any loss caused by breach of the duty.

...

[**14**] Loss in a case like the present, which was dependent upon establishing what the plaintiff would have done but for the defendant's breach, is not to be characterised as loss of an opportunity. Rather, loss of the benefit, not the opportunity to gain it, is to be established on the balance of probabilities.

...

[**15**] Accordingly, I would allow the appeal and set aside the judgment and orders made by the trial judge on 11 September 2003. In lieu thereof I would give judgment for the respondent against the appellants in a nominal sum.

Chaplin v Hicks [1911] 2 KB 787

Facts and issues

The defendant in breach of contract failed to view the plaintiff to decide whether she was one of 12 most attractive women in a group, those 12 being offered employment as actresses. The fact she was not interviewed meant that the defendant's breach deprived her of the chance of being one of the 12 winners. The question concerned how damages for breach of contract should be assessed.

Decision

The award of substantial damages was upheld.

Vaughan Williams LJ

[**791**] Now, the moment it is admitted that the contract was in effect one which gave the plaintiff a right to present herself and to take her chance of getting a prize, and the moment the jury find that she did not have a reasonable opportunity of presenting herself on the particular day, we have a breach attended by neglect of the defendant to give her a later opportunity; and when we get a breach of that sort and a claim for loss sustained in consequence of the failure to give the plaintiff an opportunity of taking part in the competition, it is impossible to say that such a result and such damages were not within the contemplation of the parties as the possible direct outcome of the breach of contract.

...

Then came the point that was more strenuously argued, that the damages were of such a nature as to be impossible of assessment. It was said that the plaintiff's chance of winning a prize turned on such a number of contingencies that it was impossible for anyone, even after arriving at the conclusion that the plaintiff had lost her opportunity by the breach, to say that there was any assessable value of that loss. It is said that in a case which involves so many contingencies it is impossible to say what was the plaintiff's pecuniary loss. I am unable to agree with that contention. I agree that the presence of all the contingencies upon which the winning of the prize might depend makes the calculation not only difficult but incapable of being carried out with certainty or precision. The proposition is that, whenever the contingencies on which the result depends are numerous and difficult to deal with, it is impossible to recover any damages for the loss of the chance or opportunity of winning the prize.

...

[**792**] In the case of a breach of a contract for the delivery of goods the damages are usually supplied by the fact of there being a market in which similar goods can be immediately bought, and the difference between the contract price and the price given for the substituted goods in the open market is the measure of damages; that rule has been always recognized. Sometimes, however, there is no market for the particular class of goods; but no one has ever suggested that, because there is no market, there are no damages. In such a case the jury must do the best they can, and it may be that the amount of their verdict will really be a matter of guesswork. But the fact that damages cannot be assessed with certainty does not relieve the wrongdoer of the necessity of paying damages for his breach of contract. I do not wish to lay down any such rule as that a judge can in every case leave it to the jury to assess damages for a breach of contract ... None of the 50 competitors could have gone into the market and sold her right; her right was a personal right and incapable of transfer. But a jury might well take the view that such a right if it could have been transferred, would have been of such a value that everyone would recognise that a good price could be obtained for it.

NOTE

The approaches to the assessment of damages for breach of contract and tort can both be analysed within the framework of the *Sellars* two-step approach. With tort, the first step is achieved only by proof of damage in showing on the balance of probabilities that the plaintiff was deprived of an opportunity to make a profit by defendant's wrong. The second step is performed by showing the quantum of that loss by reference to the degree of probabilities. With contract, if the breach results in the loss of a commercial opportunity, then it is the task of the court to value the loss of that opportunity. In other words, the fact of the breach without more represents the figurative first step in the *Sellars* two-step approach. Then, as with tort, damage is assessed by reference to the degree of probabilities.

Figure 2.7 The assessment of compensation for a contractual breach such as in *Chaplin v Hicks* analysed through the framework of the *Sellars* two-step approach

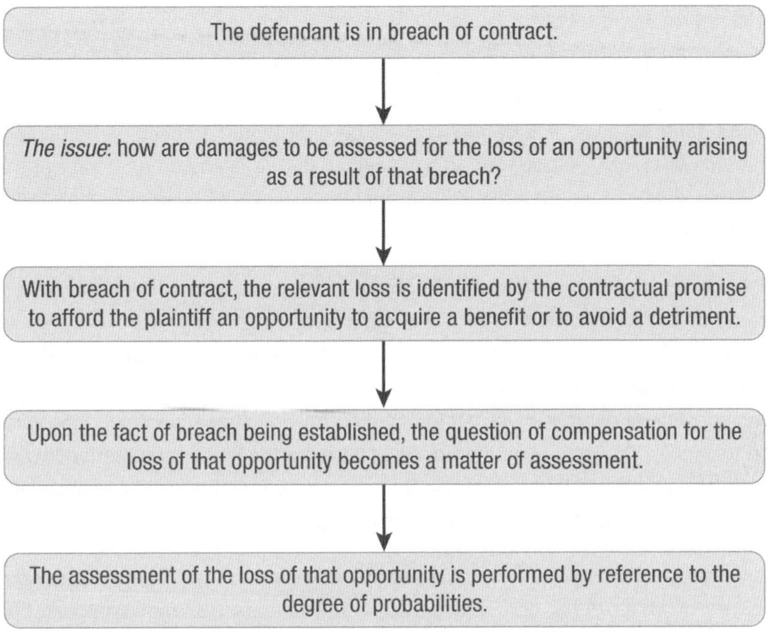

Hendriks v McGeoch [2008] NSWCA 53; (2008) Aust Torts Reports 81-942

Facts and issues

Hendriks, a solicitor, acted for a family of whom McGeoch was a member. McGeoch claimed damages from Hendriks who, in breach of a duty of care, failed to draft a will that gave effect to Hendriks' interests, resulting in the loss of his inheritance. The trial judge awarded damages based on the full value of the lost inheritance and did not take into account a 20 per cent chance that the testator would not have executed the will. The issue concerned how compensation be assessed for McGeoch's lost inheritance.

Decision

McGeoch was entitled to 80 per cent of the lost inheritance, his loss being assessed on the degree of probabilities.

Basten JA

[84] His Honor held, in considering a breach of duty under a retainer between the respondent and Mr Hendriks:

> He failed to draw up and have executed an agreement that would protect Mr Jon McGeoch's interests by binding his mother not to alter her will with respect to the devise of the Mollymook property. There is no doubt that had such an agreement been drawn, Mrs McGeoch would have signed it. She executed a transfer of the Mollymook property before the issue of the adverse effect on her pension entitlement arose.

[85] This was a finding of breach of contract and not an assessment of loss. It is not precise as to the time of the breach, although it appears to assume that at the relevant time, Mrs McGeoch's intentions would have been the same as at 22 January 1996 when she executed the transfer.

[t]he question of damages was left for a further hearing subsequent upon the finding in relation to liability. The issue was then dealt with briefly. His Honor commenced by noting that he had been referred to a passage in *Sellars v Adelaide Petroleum NL* in the joint judgment of Mason CJ, Dawson, Toohey and Gaudron JJ stating:

> Damages in tort have also been assessed by reference to the probabilities or possibilities of what will happen or what would have happened. That approach has been frequently adopted in the assessment of damages for personal injuries where a court has been called upon to assess future possibilities and past hypothetical situations. In *Malec v J C Hutton Pty Ltd* (1990) 169 CLR 638, this Court drew a distinction between, on the one hand, proof of historical facts – what has happened – and, on the other hand, proof of future possibilities and past hypothetical situations. The civil standard of proof applies to the first category but not to the second, particularly when it is necessary to determine future possibilities and past hypothetical situations for the purpose of assessing damages.'

[86] Whether his Honor adopted that approach is not entirely clear.

...

His Honor awarded the full amount of the loss as calculated by the parties.

[87] The solicitors did not contend in this Court that the assessment of the past hypothetical situation could result in a percentage chance of less than 51 per cent. A lower possibility had not been contended for below, apparently on the basis, which was not challenged, that his Honor had already found on the balance of probabilities that Mrs McGeoch would have signed such an agreement. They nevertheless contended that unless the chance of that happening were virtually certain, the award of 100 per cent of the calculated loss should not have been allowed.

...

[99] If an agreement which rendered the testamentary disposition of Mollymook to the respondent irrevocable had been presented to Mrs McGeoch on 19 December 1995, his Honor's conclusion that Mrs McGeoch would undoubtedly have signed it might be accepted. However, that was no more than part of the proposal and there was no breach of duty in not taking that step at that time.

By mid-February 1996, a degree of uncertainty must attend the assessment of Mrs McGeoch's attitude. That degree of uncertainty is neither insignificant nor considerable. I do not accept, as suggested by the solicitors, that it would warrant a discount of 40 per cent or more. As best these things can be gauged, I would assess the uncertainty at 20 per cent. Accordingly, the respondent should have received a loss of chance calculated at 80 per cent. Damages and interest prior to judgment should be assessed accordingly.

Badenach v Calvert (2016) 257 CLR 440

Facts and issues

Badenach, a solicitor, was engaged to prepare a will to leave his client's estate to Calvert. After the client's death, the client's daughter, whose existence Badenach was unaware of, brought a claim against the estate, depleting it. Calvert sued Badenach for negligence in failing to advise the testator of the possibility that his children could have a claim against the estate and of the steps that could be taken to avoid such a claim. The trial judge left open the question whether Badenach owed a duty of care to Calvert, but dismissed the action as he was not satisfied that knowledge of a possible claim by the daughter would have triggered an enquiry by the testator about ways of protecting Calvert's position. The Tasmanian Full Court held that Badenach did owe Calvert a duty of care and, overturning the trial judge, that Calvert was entitled to damages because he had lost a more then negligible chance that the testator would have taken action to protect his estate. The issue on appeal to the High Court was whether Badenach owed Calvert a duty of care and if so if he was entitled to damages.

Decision

Overturning the Tasmanian Full Court, the High Court held that Badenach did not owe a duty of care to the beneficiary of his client and if he did then it was not established on the balance of probabilities that the testator if properly advised would have taken steps to protect the estate.

French CJ, Kiefel and Keane JJ

[36] The respondent must prove, on the balance of probabilities, that but for the solicitor's failure to give the advice contended for, the respondent would have received the client's estate. The respondent has not discharged this onus of proof.

[37] The respondent seeks to overcome problems of proof by redefining the loss occasioned by the alleged breach of duty as the loss of the chance that the client may have undertaken the inter-vivos transactions. The chance could not be of a better testamentary disposition; none is identified as available.

[38] It has been explained that to speak of loss as the loss of a 'chance' distorts the question of causation. It involves the application of a lesser standard of proof than is required by the law … It confuses the issue of the loss caused with the issue of assessing damages which are said to flow from that loss. In that assessment a chance may be evaluated.

[39] The respondent's case on causation is not improved by seeking to equate the chance spoken of with an opportunity lost. It may be accepted that an opportunity which is lost may be compensable in tort. But that is because the opportunity is itself of some value. An opportunity will be of value where there is a substantial, and not a merely speculative, prospect that a benefit will be acquired or a detriment avoided.

[40] It remains necessary to prove, to the usual standard, that there was a substantial prospect of a beneficial outcome. This requires evidence of what would have been done if the opportunity had been afforded. The respondent has not established that there is a substantial prospect that the client would have chosen to undertake the inter vivos transactions. Therefore, the respondent has not proven that there was any loss of a valuable opportunity.

[41] The onus of proving causation of loss is not discharged by a finding that there was more than a negligible chance that the outcome would be favourable, or even by a finding that there was a substantial chance of such an outcome. The onus is only discharged where a plaintiff can prove that it was more probable than not that they would have received a valuable opportunity. To the extent that the majority in *Allied Maples Group Ltd v Simmons & Simmons (a Firm)* holds that proof of a substantial chance of a beneficial outcome is sufficient on the issue of causation of loss, as distinct from the assessment of damages, it is not consistent with authority in Australia.

Ultimately, causation was not established.

NOTE

Hendriks and *Badenach* concerned complaints of loss arising from a solicitor's preparation of a will. Although different approaches *appear* to have been adopted, the consistency in the underpinning reasoning is clearer when analysed within the framework of the *Sellars* two-step approach:

(1) In *Hendriks,* once established that a chance was lost, the assessment of that loss and compensation was ordered by reference to the degree of probabilities that the testatrix would have executed the will.

(2) In *Badenach,* assuming a duty of care existed, the High Court was then not satisfied on the balance of probabilities that the testator would have taken steps to protect the estate from the claim by the daughter. The plaintiff did not get to the first step of the *Sellars* two-step approach since he could not demonstrate on the balance of probabilities that the plaintiff was deprived of a beneficial outcome. Although the Court in *Badenach* expressed their reasoning in the language of causation rather than assessment, it did not disapprove the *Sellars* approach to the assessment of damages.

Figures 2.8 and 2.9 illustrate the reasoning in *Badenach* and *Hendriks* within the framework of the *Sellars* two-step approach.

Figure 2.8 *Badenach v Calvert* viewed through the framework of the *Sellars* two-step approach

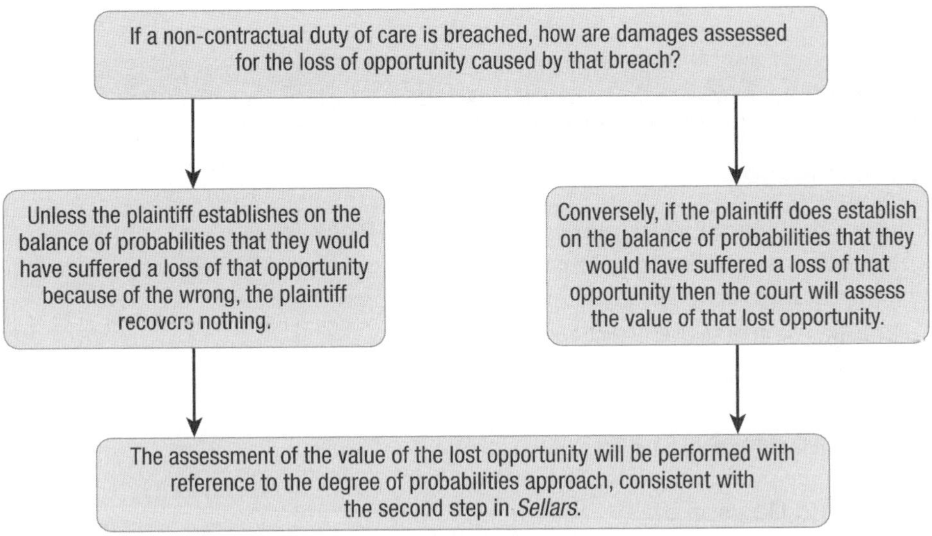

Figure 2.9 *Hendriks v McGeoch* analysed within the framework of the *Sellars* two-step approach

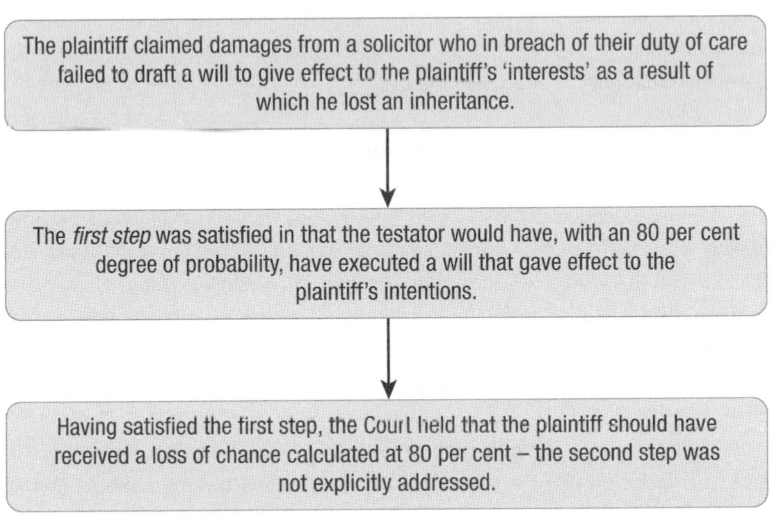

E Hypothetical conduct of the defendant

The possibility that the defendant's hypothetically acting in a lawful way could impact on the assessment of damages is also addressed within the framework of the 'balance of probabilities' and 'degree of probabilities' approaches; see *Commonwealth v Amann Aviation Pty Ltd* and *Port Macquarie-Hastings Council v Diveva Pty Ltd* below.

Commonwealth v Amann Aviation Pty Ltd (1991) 174 CLR 64

Facts and issues

Amann Aviation ('Amann') sought among other things reliance damages in consequence of the Commonwealth's repudiating its contract with Amann. There was a 20 per cent chance that the Commonwealth might have lawfully terminated the contract. The question arose how this would have affected Amann's claim for reliance damages.

Decision

Amann was entitled to all its reliance loss.

Mason CJ and Dawson J

> [**95**] The Commonwealth mounts another argument to the effect that no damages should be awarded and that, if damages are awarded, any damages should not be substantial. This argument is put on the footing that the Commonwealth would have validly terminated the contract in any event for breach pursuant to cl 2.24. The Commonwealth argues that the amount of damages awarded should have been discounted in accordance with the prospect of valid termination by the Commonwealth and that, in assessing this prospect, it should be presumed that the Commonwealth would have acted so as to minimise its liability in conformity with The Mihalis Angelos.
>
> ...
>
> [**97**] Beaumont J resolved these competing arguments by holding that there was a 50 per cent possibility of cancellation pursuant to cl 2.24. But, in arriving at this conclusion, his Honor proceeded on the footing that the Secretary in exercising the power of cancellation was free to pursue the interests of the Commonwealth without any relevant qualification. The Full Court did not agree with that interpretation of the clause. The Full Court's more restricted view of the Secretary's power of cancellation led, quite naturally, to that court assessing the possibility of cancellation at 20 per cent.
>
> We are not persuaded that this was an erroneous estimate.
>
> ...
>
> Consequently, we are not persuaded that the Full Court was wrong in either its estimate or its conclusion that the amount of damages to be awarded should [**98**] not be discounted on account of an event which was unlikely to occur.

Brennan J

[**104**] Where a contract has been rescinded for breach, the amount which a plaintiff has reasonably expended in reliance on the defendant's promise and which is wasted by reason of the defendant's breach of his promise is a proper subject of damages for breach of contract: *McRae v Commonwealth Disposals Commission*. Damages assessed for wasted expenditure incurred in reliance on the defendant's promise may be described as reliance damages to distinguish them from damages assessed for loss of the benefits which the plaintiff expected from performance of the contract. A plaintiff who seeks to recover reliance damages must ordinarily prove that the net value of the benefits to which he would have been entitled if the contract had been performed ($B – $y) would have exceeded the wasted expenditure incurred in reliance on the defendant's promise ($x) [**105**] and, to the extent that he fails to do so, his claim will fail. To discharge the onus of proof, however, the plaintiff may be able to raise and rely on an inference that a party would not incur expenditure in reliance on the other party's promise without a reasonable expectation that, on performance of the contract, the expenditure would be recouped.

...

[**107**] Where justification for reversing the onus exists, reliance [**108**] damages may be recovered; absent that justification, the plaintiff must recover expectation damages, if any, by proof of the value of benefits and the cost of performance; that is, by proof that $B – $y is greater than $x.

...

Had Amann borne the onus of proving its damages as expectation damages, the assessment would have had to allow for the possibility that the power to terminate under cl 2.24 would have been exercised. That possibility, assessed at 20% by the Full Court, would have reduced those damages. In the assessment of reliance damages, the possibility remains relevant to the value of Amann's contractual benefits. But the Commonwealth bears the onus of proving that the possibility of termination under cl 2.24 reduces the net value of Amann's benefits to an amount less than its expectation damages. Had the contract not been repudiated, the circumstances would have revealed whether or not the contract would have been terminated under cl 2.24. The repudiation leaves that possibility uncertain and the Commonwealth must bear the consequences. Even if the Commonwealth be held to have proved that there was a 20% possibility that the contract would have been terminated under cl 2.24, that finding does not enable the Commonwealth to discharge its onus. The Commonwealth remains unable to prove either that $B – $y is less than $x or that 80% of ($B – $y) is less than $x.

NOTE

While the outcome was the same, it is informative to appreciate the fundamental differences between the approaches of Mason CJ and Dawson J, and Brennan J, illustrated in Figures 2.10 and 2.11.

Figure 2.10 The 'balance of probabilities approach' per Mason CJ and Dawson J

There was a 20 per cent chance that the party in breach (the Commonwealth) might have taken a non-wrongful course of action (the lawful termination of the contract).

↓

The non-wrongful course of action (lawful termination by the Commonwealth) was considered unlikely to occur.

↓

The assessment of damages should not take into account this 'unlikely' event.

↓

Amann's claim was accordingly undiminished by the possibility that the Commonwealth *might* have taken a non-wrongful course of action (lawful termination of the contract).

↓

Amann was awarded 100 per cent of its claimed reliance damages.

Figure 2.11 The 'discharge of evidentiary onus' approach per Brennan J

There was a 20 per cent chance that the party in breach (the Commonwealth) might have taken a non-wrongful course of action (the lawful termination of the contract).

↓

A plaintiff (Amann) is entitled to reliance costs unless the defendant (the Commonwealth) is unable to discharge the onus of showing the expenditure would not have been incurred. Sometimes, the inference would be of sufficient strength to enable the plaintiff to discharge the onus; sometimes the inference would be too weak.

↓

Postulated on a 20 per cent chance that the Commonwealth might have taken a non-wrongful course (the lawful termination of the contract) such that the loss would ot have been incurred, the inference was *not* strong enough to dicharge the onus.

↓

Amann was entitled to all its claimed reliance damages.

Port Macquarie-Hastings Council v Diveva Pty Ltd [2017] NSWCA 97

Facts and issues

Diveva had an option of renewal under a contract with Port Macquarie-Hastings Council ('Council') for the supply and laying of asphalt. Council refused to recognise Diveva's exercise of the option in the erroneous belief that Diveva's work had been defective. Council invited new tenders for the work. Diveva did not participate in the new tender process. The trial judge awarded damages for the loss of profits that the plaintiff would have made in the option period as well as under two future contracts which would have been awarded under the new tender processes. Council appealed.

Decision

Adopting a degree of probabilities approach, the appeal was dismissed.

Payne JA

> **[79]** A contract to provide a commercial advantage or opportunity, if breached, enables the innocent party to bring an action for the loss of that advantage or opportunity: *Amann Aviation*.
>
> ...
>
> **[81]** Damages for deprivation of a commercial opportunity which occurred by breach of contract are ascertained by the court's assessment of the prospect of success of that opportunity had it been pursued: *Sellars v Adelaide Petroleum*.
>
> **[82]** A defendant to proceedings to recover damages for breach of contract has the right under the contract to alternate methods of performance; it should be assumed that the contract will be performed in the way most advantageous to the defendant: The Mihalis Angelos. At least one important qualification to that principle is that when the facts available to the court, up to the date of the trial, demonstrate that the defendant would not (leaving to one side the circumstances of the breach of contract which has been found) have acted so as to perform the contract in that more advantageous way, the natural inference that the defendant would be understood to do so for the purposes of the damages calculation does not arise: *TCN Channel 9 v Hayden Enterprises*. As Deane J explained in *Amann Aviation*:
>
>> The 'rule' recognized in cases such as *The Mihalis Angelos* does not require an assumption that, after full performance of a contract, the defaulting party would have acted against his own interests and obligations by, for example, declining to accept the most favourable tender for a further contract. It is no more an answer to Amann's claims to say that the Commonwealth might, at the end of the day, have arbitrarily refused to deal with Amann than was the possibility that the defendant might have arbitrarily refused to give the plaintiff a prize in answer to the claim in

> *Chaplin v Hicks* or the possibility that the defendant might have acted unreasonably in answer to the plaintiffs' claim in *Abrahams v Herbert Reiach Ltd* …
>
> …
>
> **[86]** In my view, the primary judge was correct to conclude that Diveva's lost opportunity to successfully participate in two future tender processes was compensable as a probable result of a breach of contract by the Council. But for the Council's conduct, which the Council accepted was 'wrong-headed', about the Ocean Drive works, the option would have been successfully exercised and there is every reason to think that Diveva would have had a good chance of success in at least the next two tender processes.
>
> **[87]** Diveva's long and successful incumbency meant, at least, that it had an intimate knowledge of the Council's asphalting requirements, that it had all of the appropriate plant and equipment to successfully perform its obligations under the putative Council contracts and that its business operations were suitable to successfully performing those obligations … Despite the Council's attempt to distinguish this case on its facts from *Amann Aviation*, this case is sufficiently similar to it to support the primary judge's findings that the loss of the chance of renewal of future contracts to this incumbent was compensable.
>
> **[88]** Rejection of the Council's submission that Diveva had failed to prove that there would not have been a termination by the Council during the option period did not involve a reversal of the onus of proof. The Council's reliance on the principle recognized in cases such as The *Mihalis Angelos* is here misplaced. Absent the 'wrong-headed' conduct of the Council about Ocean Drive, it would be wrong to assume that the Council would have acted against its own interests and obligations by, for example, terminating on 30 days' written notice…It would have been against Council's interests as it would have involved the loss of a valued contractor, the wasted expenditure of a further tender and the possibility that important asphalting works for which Council was responsible would be delayed. Absent the 'wrong-headed' conduct, which can be put to one side for this purpose, there is no reason to think the Council would have, in the words of Diplock LJ in *Lavarack v Woods of Colchester Ltd* 295–296 'cut off its nose to spite its face'.

Port Macquarie-Hastings Council is a clear illustration of the degree of probabilities approach – a cautionary word is advised, however, in order to avoid confusion; as pointed out at [2.114] of the principles text, in purporting to endorse *Commonwealth v Amann*, it did not explain the fact that in *Commonwealth v Amann,* the High Court in fact adopted a *balance* of probabilities approach. Figure 2.12 clarifies the reasoning in *Port Macquarie-Hastings Council.*

Figure 2.12 The degree of probabilities approach adopted in *Port Macquarie-Hastings Council v Diveva Pty Ltd*

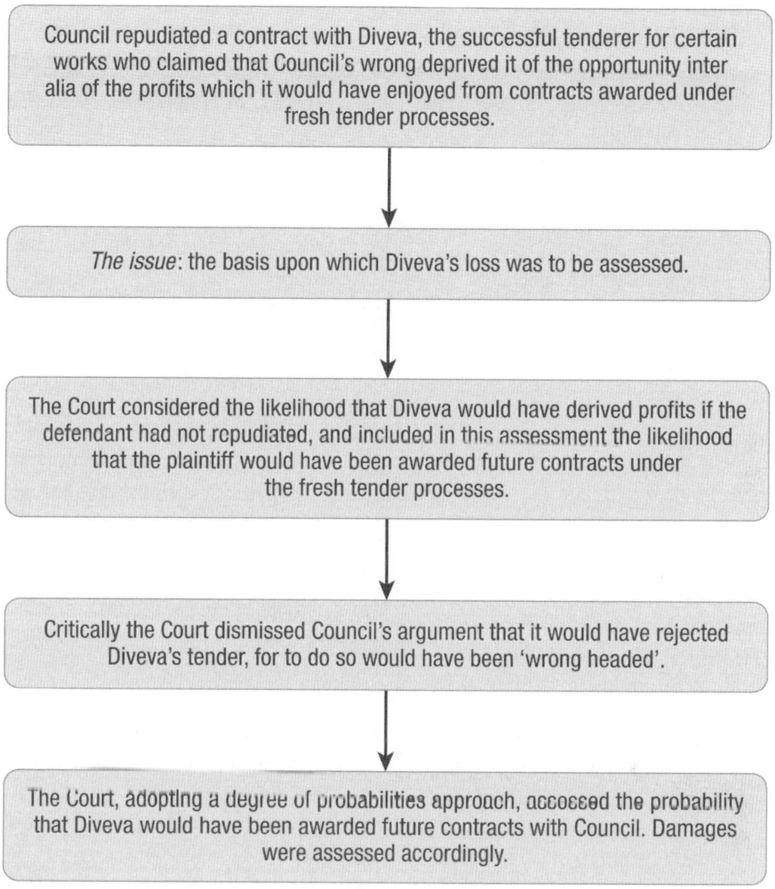

REVIEW QUESTIONS

(1) What did Brennan J consider in *Sellars v Adelaide Petroleum NL* (1994) 179 CLR 332 to be the conceptual difference between the assessment of damages for breach of contract when compared to tort?

(2) When viewed through the viewpoint of the two-step approach, how is the assessment of damages for the loss of an opportunity performed for breach of contract when contrasted to tort?

(3) What was the reasoning behind the court's rejection in *Tabet v Gett* (2010) 240 CLR 537 of the argument that the loss of an opportunity for a better medical outcome was a compensable loss?

V Temporal considerations

A matter often gets to trial long after the dispute arises, giving rise to questions concerning the time for the assessment of compensation.

Concept	Short explanation	Relevant authorities	Principles text
The lump sum rule and the 'once and for all' rule	Damages are awarded as a 'lump sum', assessed 'once and for all'.		Chapter 2: [2.120]–[2.127]
Date of assessment	The date on which compensation is assessed varies, taking into account the factors which impact on the question of how loss is to be assessed.	*Re Dawson (Deceased)* [1966] 2 NSWR 211 *O'Brien v McKean* (1968) 118 CLR 540 *Webster v Coles Myer Ltd* [2009] NSWDC 4 *Johnson v Perez* (1988) 166 CLR 351 *Vieira v O'Shea* [2012] NSWCA 21 *HTW Valuers (Central Qld) Pty Ltd v Astonland Pty Ltd* (2004) 217 CLR 640 *Potts v Miller* (1940) 64 CLR 282	Chapter 2: [2.128]–[2.144]
Relevance of inflation	The extent to which the court takes into account the diminishing purchasing power of money in an award of damages.	*Egan v State Transport Authority* (1982) 31 SASR 481 *O'Brien v McKean* (1968) 118 CLR 540	Chapter 2: [2.145]–[2.147]
Determining the present equivalent of future economic loss	Since compensation is awarded in a lump sum, the court must find a present equivalent for future loss.	*Todorovic v Waller* (1981) 150 CLR 540	Chapter 2: [2.148] – [2.153]
Interest on compensation awards and compensation for the loss of the use of money	The plaintiff until paid compensation is deprived of the use of his money and might be awarded interest on any compensation awarded.	Statutory provisions *Hungerfords v Walker* (1989) 171 CLR 125	Chapter 2: [2.156]–[2.168]

A The lump sum rule and the 'once and for all' rule

The 'once-for-all rule' is that generally damages are granted as a lump sum, and assessed once-for-all for the same wrong. The corollary is that damage from different wrongs can be claimed separately, but additional loss from the same wrong cannot be claimed. Continuing wrongs, for continuous wrongful conduct, are not covered by the rule.

The principle is sometimes modified by legislation. See, for example, s 16 of the *Motor Vehicle (Third Party Insurance) Act 1943* (WA):

> (4) On the hearing and determination of any action or proceedings a court shall, without in any way limiting its usual powers in relation thereto, have the following further powers –
> (a) to award by way of general damages either a lump sum or periodical payments or a lump sum and periodical payments, such periodical payments to be for such period and upon such terms as the court determines; and
> (b) at any time either of its own motion or on the application of any party to the action or proceedings –
> (i) to review any periodical payment and either continue, vary, reduce, increase, suspend, or determine it, or on the review to order payment to the claimant of a further lump sum; or
> (ii) to order that any such periodical payments be redeemed by payment of a lump sum.

B Date of assessment

The 'date of assessment' refers to the date the court assesses compensation to the plaintiff. Numerous factors impact on how the date is fixed, including the cause of action sued on, whether in contract or tort, or if sought in equity.

Re Dawson (Deceased) [1966] 2 NSWR 211

Facts and issues

PSD, the trustee of the New Zealand assets of a deceased estate, improperly paid away NZ£4700.00, which were lost to the estate. At the time, there was parity between the Australian and New Zealand currencies. However, at the time of the proceedings to enforce restoration, NZ£4700 was worth A$5829. The question concerned the date used for the assessment of payment to restore the monies to the estate.

Decision

The appropriate day for the assessment of compensation was the date of the proceedings to enforce restoration.

Street J

> **[216]** … the distinction between common law damages and relief against a defaulting trustee is strikingly demonstrated by reference to the actual form of relief granted in equity in respect of breaches of trust. The form of relief is couched in terms appropriate to require the defaulting trustee to restore to the estate the assets of which he deprived it. Increases in market values between the date of breach and the date of recoupment are for the trustee's account: the effect of such increases would, at common law, be excluded from the computation of

damages, but in equity a defaulting trustee must make good the loss by restoring to the estate the assets of which he deprived it notwithstanding that the market values may have increased in the meantime. The obligation to restore to the estate the assets of which he deprived it necessarily connotes that, where a monetary compensation is to be paid in lieu of restoring assets, that compensation is to be assessed by reference to the value of the assets at the date of restoration and not at the date of deprivation. In this sense the obligation is a continuing one and ordinarily if the assets are for some reason not restored in specie it will fall for quantification at the date when recoupment is to be effected and not before.

O'Brien v McKean (1968) 118 CLR 540

Facts and issues

O'Brien was awarded compensation for personal injury including for loss of earning capacity, pain, suffering, loss of enjoyment of life, and for future needs that would not have existed but for the injury. A question that arose for determination was the date which the court should assess compensation.

Decision

Compensation was assessed as of the date of the verdict.

Barwick CJ

> [**545**] In the case of such personal injuries, though there may be something to be said logically for making the assessment of damages as at the date of the receipt of the injuries, the date of the verdict is, in my opinion, the proper date as at which to make the assessment. It may be that delay on the part of the injured person in bringing or prosecuting his claim could on this basis in some circumstances advantage the plaintiff, though, except in the case of some dramatic change in purchasing power, this possible advantage would be minimal and largely theoretical. However, even if in some case it became necessary to prevent a plaintiff obtaining a substantial advantage by his own dilatory conduct, the date as at which to make the assessment would not, in my opinion, be the date of the injuries but some later date, probably related to the time as at which a diligent plaintiff would have brought his proceedings to a verdict.
>
> The assessment will therefore in general be made in relation to the purchasing power of the currency at the date of the assessment of the damages.

NOTE

The further question of whether account need be taken of the decline in the purchasing power of currency, raised in the case, is addressed in *Egan v State Transport Authority* [1982] 31 SASR 481 on page 79 and *O'Brien v McKean* above.

Webster v Coles Myer Ltd [2009] NSWDC 4

Facts and issues

In October 2004, an employee of Coles Myer described the plaintiff to police as being Lebanese in appearance and who attempted to buy gift vouchers with stolen credit cards. In proceedings for defamation, it was found that those statements imputed that the plaintiff was dishonest and had attempted to obtain gift vouchers by means of deception. An issue arose as to the time at which compensation be assessed.

Decision

Compensation should be assessed at the time of judgment.

Gibson DCJ

[343] The general principles for economic loss are set out in *Rabay v Bristow*:

> Compensation for loss of earning capacity is awarded because of the diminution in an injured plaintiff's earning capacity 'is or may be productive of financial loss': *Graham v Baker*. It is incumbent upon the plaintiff to prove the loss for which compensation is claimed: *Todorovic v Waller* but, conversely, it is not incumbent upon the injured plaintiff to prove what employment he or she 'is not incapacitated from performing'. It is for a defendant which contends that the plaintiff has a residual earning capacity to adduce evidence of what the plaintiff is capable of doing and what jobs are open to such a person: H Luntz, *Assessment of Damages for Personal Injury and Death*.

...

[344] It is for a defendant who contends that the plaintiff has a residual earning capacity to adduce evidence of what the plaintiff is capable of doing and what jobs are open to him, and the primary judge can take into account past employment history. Further economic loss tends to require the process of estimation of possibilities and is of necessity an imprecise exercise.

...

[347] Mr Thompson should be entitled to be recompensed for his past economic loss as claimed. The problem is to determine what the future holds for him. Clearly he is likely to be able to return to the workforce and in fact Dr Jacobson says he expects Mr Thompson will resume his normal social and work life within six months of 22 January 2009.

[348] In practical terms, having regard to Mr Thompson's ability to work, the most sensible approach is to award a cushion representing 1 to 2 years of his previous salary. These are difficult times to obtain employment, and his long period of time out of the work force and medical history may cause him problems. Doing the best I can, I propose to award the sum of $50 000 for future economic loss.

[349] I similarly propose to award a cushion for future out-of-pocket expenses of $5000. It may be that in the future Mr Thompson recovers quickly; it may be that he requires a considerable amount of future therapy and medical assistance. I am satisfied that his counselling relates to the problems he developed after the incident and consider a reasonable cushion to allow for such counselling expenses should be given.

Table 2.5 Considerations relevant to the date of the assessment of compensation for personal injury and death

Principle	Relevant authority
Damages for personal injuries or death are assessed at time of the verdict, taking into account any diminished loss in earning capacity and the vicissitudes of life.	*O'Brien v McKean* (1968) 118 CLR 540
Where a plaintiff has been dilatory, the date of assessment would be assessment related to the time as at which a diligent plaintiff would have brought his proceedings to a verdict.	*O'Brien v McKean* (1968) 118 CLR 540
Future depreciation in the value of money cannot be taken into account as compensation for lost earning capacity.	*O'Brien v McKean* (1968) 118 CLR 540
Where an appellate court reassesses the award, the reassessment will be made at the date of the appellate judgment.	*Monie v Commonwealth* [2017] NSWCA 230
Similar principles apply to the date of assessment of damages for other violations of personal interests such as defamation or false imprisonment.	*Webster v Coles Myer Ltd* [2009] NSWDC 4

Johnson v Perez (1988) 166 CLR 351

Facts and issues

Perez sustained injuries in the course of employment with three separate employers. He had instructed his solicitors, Johnson, to commence proceedings for damages but those actions were dismissed for want of prosecution. He successfully sued Johnson, claiming that their negligence allowed his claims to lapse. Perez also claimed he suffered a psychological reaction to the delay. At issue was the date upon which damages should be assessed.

Decision

Damages were assessed by reference to the amount appropriately awarded when his action would ordinarily have been determined but for the solicitor's negligence.

Mason CJ

> [**355**] The guiding principle in the assessment of damages is compensatory. The object is to award the plaintiff an amount of money that will, as nearly as money can, put him in the same position as if he had not been injured by the defendant: *Todorovic v Waller*, per Gibbs CJ and Wilson J. However, the time as at which damages are assessed can significantly affect the amount actually awarded. This aspect of the assessment of compensation is particularly noticeable in the present era of inflation, with its fluctuating economic values. This is because in times of inflation the amount awarded is likely to be larger if it is assessed at a later rather than an earlier date.

When a court assesses damages, it converts the value of the injury into nominal terms; it fixes or liquidates that value. That conversion into monetary terms avoids the difficult task of inquiring into the value of goods and services over time and is necessary for the stability of economic legal relationships. The theory according to which damages are awarded by the courts is that a plaintiff's loss or injury can be adequately compensated by a lump or fixed sum of money which is not subsequently revised.

...

There is a general rule that damages for torts or breach of contract are assessed as at the date of breach or when the cause of action arises. But this rule is not universal; it must give way in particular cases to solutions best adapted to giving an injured **[356]** plaintiff that amount in damages which will most fairly compensate him for the wrong he has suffered.

Wilson, Toohey, and Gaudron JJ

[367] The starting point is that 'a plaintiff who has been injured by the negligence of the defendant should be awarded such a sum of money as will, as nearly as possible, put him in the same position as if he had not sustained the injuries': *Todorovic v Waller*; see also *Livingstone v Rawyards Coal Co*. In each of the present cases the respondent would, but for the negligence of his solicitor, have recovered damages for personal injuries against his employer. It is that loss for which he is to be compensated; he is not to be compensated as if his claim against his solicitor was a claim for damages for personal injuries.

As a general rule, 'damages for tort or for breach of contract are assessed as at the date of the breach': Lord Wilberforce in *Miliangos v Frank (Textiles) Ltd* ... The rule will yield if, in the particular circumstances, some other date is necessary to provide adequate compensation: see, for example, *Wenham v Ella*; *Dodd Properties Ltd v Canterbury County Council*; *County Personnel Ltd v Alan R. Pulver & Co*. But, in the circumstances of the present appeals, there is no reason why an assessment of damages as at the date each action was dismissed for want of prosecution will not compensate the respondent adequately. Of course, the loss to which we have referred may not be the only loss for which he is to be compensated.

...

[368] the actions by the respondent against his solicitors were heard much later in time than the original actions against the respondent's employers were likely to have been heard. In those circumstances the period of time between the date when each cause of action against the employer arose and the date when the cause of action against the solicitor arose, together with the prospect of the respondent having recovered statutory interest against his employer for that period, is a matter which may be taken into account in assessing the damages due to the respondent.

NOTE

Ultimately, it was ordered that damages recoverable from the solicitor were assessed by reference to the amount appropriately awarded when his action would ordinarily have been determined but for the solicitor's negligence.

Vieira v O'Shea [2012] NSWCA 21

Facts and issues

Vieira bought an interest in a racehorse on the recommendation of O'Shea that it was free from health problems. The horse had health problems requiring surgery. Vieira sued O'Shea for breach of contract. At issue was the date damages should be assessed.

Decision

Damages for breach of contract were assessed not between the price Vieira paid for his interest and the actual value of the interest at the time he acquired the interest but between the price paid by him and the actual value of the interest at the earliest date at which the plaintiff could reasonably have been expected to sell the interest.

Basten and Meagher JJA

> [**44**] The appellant's case was that absent breach of contract, he would not have purchased Dashere. Accordingly, he was entitled to receive the sum of money which would as nearly as possible place him in the position he would have been in had he not purchased the horse. The general rule is that damages for breach of contract are assessed at the date of breach. However, that rule will yield if 'in the particular circumstances, some other date is necessary to provide adequate compensation': *Johnson v Perez*; *Smith New Court Securities Ltd v Citibank NA*.
>
> The complaint by the respondent that the time for assessment could only have been the time of breach was not, in principle, supportable: see, eg, Treitel, *The Law of Contract* (12th ed, 2007) at 20–064.
>
> [**45**] The general rule must give way if, in the interests of justice, another approach is necessary to give the plaintiff an amount of damages which will compensate for the breach of contract.
>
> That may be the case where the plaintiff has acquired an asset which would not otherwise have been acquired and the asset is not readily marketable at the time of acquisition; or if the plaintiff does not discover until sometime after acquisition, the matter which meant that the asset would not have been acquired; or if for some other reason the plaintiff is 'locked in' to holding the asset. In each of these circumstances, the plaintiff may not have acted unreasonably in retaining the asset: see *HTW Valuers*; *Smith New Court Securities v Citibank*.
>
> [**46**] … as the primary judge held, the appellant did not become aware of the horse's condition until July 2007. At that time the horse was undergoing surgery and until its condition settled down the appellant was effectively 'locked in'. The primary judge's assessment that it was unreasonable to expect the appellant to have sold before March 2009 has not been shown to be an error. By that time the appellant had also incurred expenditure in relation to the horse's condition. Accordingly, to compensate the appellant fairly it was necessary to assess damages as at March 2009 and to include in that compensation the additional expenditure incurred to that time.

HTW Valuers (Central Qld) Pty Ltd v Astonland Pty Ltd (2004) 217 CLR 640

Facts and issues

Astonland engaged HTW Valuers ('HTW') to advise it in relation to tenancy demand. HTW gave advice that retail rent levels in a particular location were maintainable despite the forthcoming opening of a new supermarket. Astonland relying on that advice bought the land, comprising an arcade, then fully tenanted. Shops in the arcade thereafter began falling vacant. In proceedings against HTW based in misleading or deceptive conduct, it was found that the principal cause of the drop in tenancy levels was the opening of the supermarket. Astonland claimed that HTW failed to qualify their advice to warn that the effect of the shopping centre was uncertain. The question concerned the basis damages for misleading or deceptive conduct should be assessed including the time of assessment.

Decision

The assessment of damages should be calculated on the difference between the price paid for the asset and its value at the time of purchase though the court can take into account events occurring after the purchase to assess the value of the asset at the time of purchase, in this case the effect of the shopping centre's opening.

Gleeson CJ, McHugh, Gummow, Kirby and Heydon JJ

> **[34]** [The plaintiff's] argument was that the correct measure of damages, apart from consequential losses, was to deduct the value of the Plaza at the date of acquisition from the purchase price, and in assessing that value to bear in mind post- acquisition events.
>
> **[35]** The approach of subtracting value from price is commonly employed where the acquisition of land, chattels, businesses or shares is induced by deceit. It has also been commonly employed under s 82 of the Act. It is sometimes described as the rule in *Potts v Miller*. Even in the areas in which that approach is often applied, and even apart from cases in which consequential losses have been recovered, the 'rule' is not universal or inflexible or rigid. …
>
> **[36]** One key qualification of the rule which prevents it from being inflexible is that the test depends not on the difference between price and 'market value', but price and 'real value' or 'fair value' or 'fair or real value' or 'intrinsic' value or 'true value' or 'actual value' or what the asset was 'truly worth' or 'really worth' or 'what would have been a fair price to be paid … in the circumstances … at the time of the purchase'. This distinction is sometimes difficult to draw, but it is old and fundamental.
>
> …
>
> **[40]** Finally, although the court is entitled to take into account events after the date of acquisition, it must distinguish among possible causes of the decline in value of what has been bought. 'If the cause is inherent in the thing itself, then its existence should be taken into account in arriving at the real value of the shares or other things at the time of the

purchase. If the cause be 'independent', 'extrinsic', 'supervening' or 'accidental', then the additional loss is not the consequence of the inducement.'

...

[42] Indeed the cause of the decline was what the defendant was found liable for not warning about. While 'unexpected competition' has been described as a 'supervening' event, expected competition is not, and competition from the Beach Road Shopping Centre was expected.

[43] The 'subsequent events' in this case arose from 'the nature' of the Plaza and its commercial and geographical environment; they were not events which arose from 'sources supervening upon or extraneous to the fraudulent inducement'. The rental levels (and therefore the value) of the Plaza were doomed from the start – 'pregnant with disaster' – because so long as the building of the Beach Road Shopping Centre continued, the loss was inevitable … … The Plaza may be compared to a horse which 'dies of some latent disease inherent in its system at the time' of its purchase, as distinct from one which dies of some disease contracted after the purchase.

Potts v Miller (1940) 64 CLR 282

Facts and issues

Potts successfully claimed damages for fraud from Miller, which induced him to buy shares in New Zealand Theatres Ltd. Potts also alleged that, in consideration of underwriting the shares, Miller stated he would pay him all calls that were made in respect of the shares in excess of the sum of 7s, 6d per shares. The issue was the time at which damages should be assessed.

Decision

Potts was entitled to damages based on the difference between the amount paid for the shares and the real value of the shares at the time of allotment and not any other period although subsequent events may throw light on the value at the time of allotment.

Starke J

[**289**] The measure of damage in cases in which a person is induced by fraud to take up shares is the difference between the amount he subscribed or paid for the shares and the real value – not the market value – of the shares on allotment:

> Although the value of the shares is not to be ascertained at the subsequent period so as to take into account for the benefit of the plaintiff events subsequent which depreciated their value, yet those events, if they show that the company was originally, with the capital which it had got, a company which was worthless, may … be taken into account as evidence of what was the value of the shares immediately after they were allotted to the plaintiff.

See *Peek v Derry*.

Dixon J

[**296**] According to the findings of the jury, the plaintiff acted upon the supposed representations. What he did was first to enter into an underwriting agreement, next to extend it, and thirdly to [**297**] accept an allotment of shares.

In an action for fraudulent misrepresentation inducing the representee to purchase bank stock and pay calls thereon, Lord *Campbell* said that the proper mode of measuring the damages was to ascertain the difference between the purchase money and what would have been a fair price to have paid for the shares in the circumstances of the company at the time of the purchase *(Davidson v Tulloch)*. The measure of damages in an action of deceit consists in the loss or expenditure incurred by the plaintiff in consequence of the inducement upon which he relied, diminished by any corresponding advantage in money or money's worth obtained by him on the other side.

C Relevance of inflation

The purchasing power of money declines over time because of inflation. The approach to assessing the effects of inflation may depend whether the loss occurs before judgment (see, eg, *Egan v State Transport Authority* (1982) 31 SASR 481) or after judgement (see, eg, *O'Brien v McKean* (1968) 118 CLR 540). Both approaches will be illustrated.

Egan v State Transport Authority (1982) 31 SASR 481

Facts and issues

It was a term of Egan's with State Transport Authority ('STA') to construct bridges that STA determined the contract upon certain events, the plant and materials used by Egan would become STA's property. STA purported to determine the contract and took possession of Egan's plant and equipment. Egan claimed that STA was not entitled to determine the contract and sought damages for the wrongful detention of his plant and materials. At issue was the assessment of his damages for conversion, including the impact of inflation.

Decision

Damages for conversion were assessed in present-day money terms.

White J

[**528**] When assessing damages in conversion as at the 1966 age and state of plant and materials I would express the award in present day money in the particular circumstances of this case. In addition, I would express Egan's dynamic/consequential losses in conversion with respect to both plant and materials, in present day money terms.

…

[529] In conclusion, the damages in conversion are to be expressed in 1982 money terms with respect to the basic/static loss of the chattels themselves; and the dynamic/consequential losses suffered year by year until useless in relation to the plant, and in a once-for-all profitable use in relation to the materials.

O'Brien v McKean (1968) 118 CLR 540

Facts and issues

As set out on page 72, the High Court determined that the O'Brien was entitled to compensation for personal injuries, the quantum of which was determined at the date of the verdict. A further question was whether the award should take into account the prospect of further depreciation in the value of money subsequently.

Decision

Further depreciation in the value of money should not be taken into account.

Barwick CJ

[547] For the loss of a present capacity, with all its inherent probabilities, the injured person is to be presently compensated by an immediate payment of money. Upon the award being made, the successful plaintiff becomes entitled to that money free to do with it what he will. He can protect himself against the possibilities of continuing or increasing inflation to the same extent as any other citizen with an investible fund. The successful plaintiff has, as it were, exchanged an earning capacity for such a capital fund. In my opinion, neither possible nor probable changes in the purchasing power can be relevant to the assessment of the capital sum so to be paid.

...

[549] This brings me to the final question, namely, whether or not a firm basis can be found for the inclusion amongst the factors to be considered in deciding the proper global sum to be awarded for personal injuries of a figure to reflect the probability of rising costs of the particular goods and services. ...

[550] Whatever the overall experience in relation to goods and services generally, nothing better in general than a speculation can be made as to the cost in the future of particular goods and services. There is no more room, in my opinion, in the determination of an award of damages, for acting upon a speculation than there is for doing so in the determination of liability. Solid proof, on the basis of probability, is required of all the elements which can properly be reflected in the award. Consequently, in my opinion, evidence which does no more than provide ground for speculation as to the future cost of the required goods and services is inadmissible.

D Determining the present equivalent of future pecuniary loss

Conventionally, compensation is awarded in a lump sum, and the court must find a present equivalent for all future pecuniary loss. Since there is an advantage in receiving an investable lump sum, the court takes account the effect of future inflation and future rises in GST, achieved by applying a discount rate to an award of damages.

Todorovic v Waller (1981) 150 CLR 540

Facts and issues

Waller successfully sued Todorovic for personal injuries that resulted in his suffering brain damage and being rendered unemployable. Damages to Waller included compensation for his loss of earning capacity. The question was whether the advantage of presently receiving a lump should be discounted for GST changes and inflation.

Decision

The advantage to Waller of receiving an investable lump sum as damages must be discounted by taking into account future inflation and rises in GST.

Gibbs CJ and Wilson J

> [424] We consider that in future the courts in Australia, in States where the question is not governed by statute, should in assessing damages arrive at the present value of a future loss by discounting at a fixed rate which will be applied in all cases and which will in itself reflect the effect of notional tax on notional income from the invested fund. To take this course may seem to involve some sacrifice of accuracy in the interests of predictability, but the whole process involves so much speculation that it is impossible to pretend to accuracy. In fixing the discount rate, the fact that for so long the rates applied by the courts in Australia have been at a level of 5 per cent and above should not be disregarded. Some downward adjustment is necessary to take account of notional tax.
>
> …
>
> We therefore concur in the view, to which we understand a majority of the Court is prepared to subscribe, that until this Court otherwise decides, a discount rate of 3 per cent should in future be applied and that no further allowance should be made for notional tax.

NOTE

The 3 per cent discount rate adopted in *Todorovic v Waller* has sometimes been modified by statute in personal injury and death by prescribing discount rates of between 5 per cent[3] and 6 per cent.[4] A sampling of these statutes is set out.

Competition and Consumer Act 2010 (Cth) s 87Y(1)

The Act prescribes a discount rate of 5 per cent.

87Y Damages for future economic loss – discount rate

(1) If an award of personal injury damages in a proceeding to which this Part applies is to include any component, assessed as a lump sum, for future economic loss of any kind, the present value of that future economic loss is to be determined by applying:

(a) a discount rate of the percentage prescribed by the regulations; or

(b) if no percentage is prescribed – a discount rate of 5%.

...

Civil Liability Act 2002 (NSW) s 14(1)–(2)

The Act prescribes a discount rate of 5 per cent.

14 Damages for future economic loss – discount rate

(1) If an award of damages is to include any component, assessed as a lump sum, for future economic loss of any kind, the present value of that future economic loss is to be determined by adopting the prescribed discount rate.

(2) The prescribed discount rate is –

(a) a discount rate of the percentage prescribed by the regulations, or

(b) if no percentage is so prescribed – a discount rate of 5%.

...

3 See, eg, *Competition and Consumer Act 2010* (Cth) s 87Y; *Civil Liability Act 2002* (NSW) s 14; *Motor Accident Injuries Act 2017* (NSW) s 49; *Workers Compensation Act 1987* (NSW) s 151J; *Personal Injuries (Liabilities and Damages) Act 2003* (NT) s 22; *Civil Liability Act 2003* (Qld) s 57; *Civil Proceedings Act 2011* (Qld) s 61; *Civil Liability Act 2002* (Tas) s 28A; *Wrongs Act 1958* (Vic) s 281.

4 See, eg, *Transport Accident Act 1986* (Vic) s 93(13); *Workplace Injury Rehabilitation and Compensation Act 2013* (Vic) s 345; *Law Reform (Miscellaneous Provisions) Act 1941* (WA) s 5.

Transport Accident Act 1986 (Vic) s 93(13)

The Act prescribes a discount rate of 6 per cent.

93 Actions for damages

...

(13) Where an award of damages in accordance with this section is to include compensation, assessed as a lump sum, in respect of damages for future loss which is referable to –

(a) deprivation or impairment of earning capacity; or

(b) loss of the expectation of financial support; or

(c) a liability to incur expenditure in the future –

the present value of the future loss must be qualified by adopting a discount rate of 6 per centum in order to make appropriate allowance for inflation, the income from investment of the sum awarded and the effect of taxation on that income.

...

Law Reform (Miscellaneous Provisions) Act 1941 (WA) s 5(1)

The Act prescribes a discount rate of 6 per cent.

5 Discount rate applicable to damages awarded for future loss

(1) Where an award of damages that relates to personal injury or the death of a person is to include compensation, awarded as a lump sum, in respect of damage for future loss that is referable to –

(a) loss or impairment of capacity to earn;

(b) loss or diminution of future probable earnings; or

(c) a liability to incur expenditure in the future,

the present value of the future loss shall be quantified by adopting –

(d) a discount rate of the percentage fixed by the Governor by Order; or

(e) where no percentage is fixed as referred to in paragraph (d), a discount rate of 6%.

...

E Interest on compensation awards and compensation for the loss of the use of money

As a plaintiff is deprived of the use of money from the time their cause of action accrued until actual payment of damages, they should be entitled to compensation for the loss of its use – see *Hungerfords v Walker*.[5]

5 (1989) 171 CLR 125.

Statutory provisions in Australian jurisdictions also enable the award of post-judgment interest (from the time of judgment until payment) and pre-judgment interest (from the time of the accrual of the cause of action until judgment). The award of interest under statute is always qualified by the compensatory principle that compensation aims to do no more than place the plaintiff in the position as if the wrong had not been committed – see *Haines v Bendall*.[6] On the other hand, the statutory rate might be inadequate; if so the principles in *Hungerfords* allow the recovery of compensation for the full loss of the use of money.

Australian statutory provisions empowering the award of interest on compensation can be summarised as follows:

- The statutory power to award interest does not prevent the award of interest pursuant to a rule of the common law or in equity (*Federal Court of Australia Act 1976* (Cth) s 51A(2)(d); *Supreme Court Act 1935* (SA) s 30C(4)(e); *Supreme Court Civil Procedure Act 1932* (Tas) s 35(2); *Supreme Court Act 1986* (Vic) s 60(2)(f).
- A court can order post-judgment interest (ie from judgment) awarded on the whole amount ordered to be paid (*Federal Court of Australia Act 1976* (Cth) s 52; *Court Procedures Rules 2006* (ACT) r 1617; *Civil Procedure Act 2005* (NSW) s 85; *Civil Proceedings Act 2011* (Qld) s 59(2); *Supreme Court Act 1935* (SA) s 114(1); *Supreme Court Civil Procedure Act 1932* (Tas) s 165; *Supreme Court Act 1986* (Vic) s 101(1); *Civil Judgments Enforcement Act 2004* (WA) s 8(1)).
- The statutory provisions to award pre-judgment interest are complex and vary from state to state (eg compound interest is prohibited in all jurisdictions apart from Tasmania). Further, they may not have the effect of awarding full compensation.

Hungerfords v Walker (1989) 171 CLR 125

Facts and issues

Hungerfords negligently prepared the Walker partnership's tax accounts. As a result the partnership overpaid tax for 1975–77. Walker sued in breach of contract and negligence to recover the overpaid tax and for compensation for the loss of the use of money.

Decision

Walker was entitled to compensation for the loss of the use of the money, including the loss of opportunities arising from money's being withheld.

Mason CJ and Wilson J

> [**132**] This appeal raises the important question whether, at common law, a court, when awarding damages for breach of contract or negligence, can include in its award damages, assessed by reference to appropriate interest rates, for the loss of the use of money which the plaintiff paid away and lost as a direct consequence of the defendant's breach of contract or negligence.

6 (1991) 172 CLR 60, 67.

...

[**143**] The requirement of foreseeability is no obstacle to the award of damages, calculated by reference to the appropriate interest rates, for loss of the use of money. Opportunity cost, more so than incurred expense, is a plainly foreseeable loss because, according to common understanding, it represents the market price of obtaining money. But, even in the case of incurred expense, it is at least strongly arguable that a plaintiff's loss or damage represented by this expense is not too remote on the score of foreseeability. In truth, it is an expense which represents loss or damage flowing naturally and directly from the defendant's wrongful act or omission, particularly when that act or omission results in the withholding of money from a plaintiff or causes the plaintiff to pay away money.

...

Incurred expense and opportunity cost arising from paying money away or the withholding of moneys due to the defendant's wrong are something more than the late payment of damages. They are pecuniary losses suffered by the plaintiff as a result of the defendant's wrong and therefore constitute an integral element of the loss for which he is entitled to be compensated by an award of damages

...

[**145**] ...The point is that the loss of the use of the money paid away is so directly related to the wrong that the loss cannot be classified simply as due to the late payment of damages: see also *General Securities Ltd v Don Ingram Ltd* (the plaintiff recovered a business loss incurred as a borrower in consequence of the lender's breach of obligation to advance the money) and *Pelletier v Pe Ben Industries Co Ltd* (damages awarded on a contract to purchase a truck in consequence of the defendant's wrongful dismissal of the plaintiff from his employment). These cases proceed on the proposition that the cost of borrowing money to avoid a loss caused by a breach of contract is recoverable and not too remote.

...

Brennan and Deane JJ

[**152**] There is, a critical distinction between an order that interest be paid upon an award of damages and an actual award of damages which represents compensation for a wrongfully caused loss of the use of money and which is assessed wholly or partly by reference to the interest which would have been earned by safe investment of the money or which was in fact paid upon borrowings which otherwise would have been unnecessary or retired. On the one hand, there is no common law power to make an order for the payment of interest to compensate for the delay in obtaining payment of what the court assesses to be the appropriate measure of damages for a wrongful act. If such interest is to be awarded at common law, it must be pursuant to statutory authority. On the other hand, there is no acceptable reason why the ordinary principles governing the recovery of common law damages should not, in an appropriate case, apply to entitle a plaintiff to an actual award of damages as compensation for a wrongfully and foreseeably caused loss of the use of money.

...

[the] breach of the duty of care which the appellants owed to the respondents caused overpayments of tax by the respondents. The direct and foreseeable effect of those overpayments was that specific sums of money (ie the amounts of the overpayments), which would otherwise have been available to avoid, repay or offset the costs of some of the

> significant borrowings of the respondents' business, were unavailable to the respondents from the time of the respective overpayments. The injury sustained by the respondents by reason of the loss of the use of the amounts of the overpayments was as foreseeably caused by the breach of the appellants' duty of care as would have been the case if the appellants had wrongfully deprived the respondents of the use of their money by locking it in a foolproof safe and withholding the key. The quantum of damages which represents appropriate compensation for that loss plainly fell to be assessed by reference to (among other things) the rates of interest paid by the respondents upon borrowings which would probably have been avoided, retired or offset but for the overpayments.

Following *Hungerfords v Walker,* the loss of the use of money, or the 'opportunity cost' of the use of money, is treated as a separate head of damage. Figure 2.13 broadly illustrates the reasoning in *Hungerford*.

Figure 2.13 The reasoning in *Hungerfords v Walker* (1989) 171 CLR 125

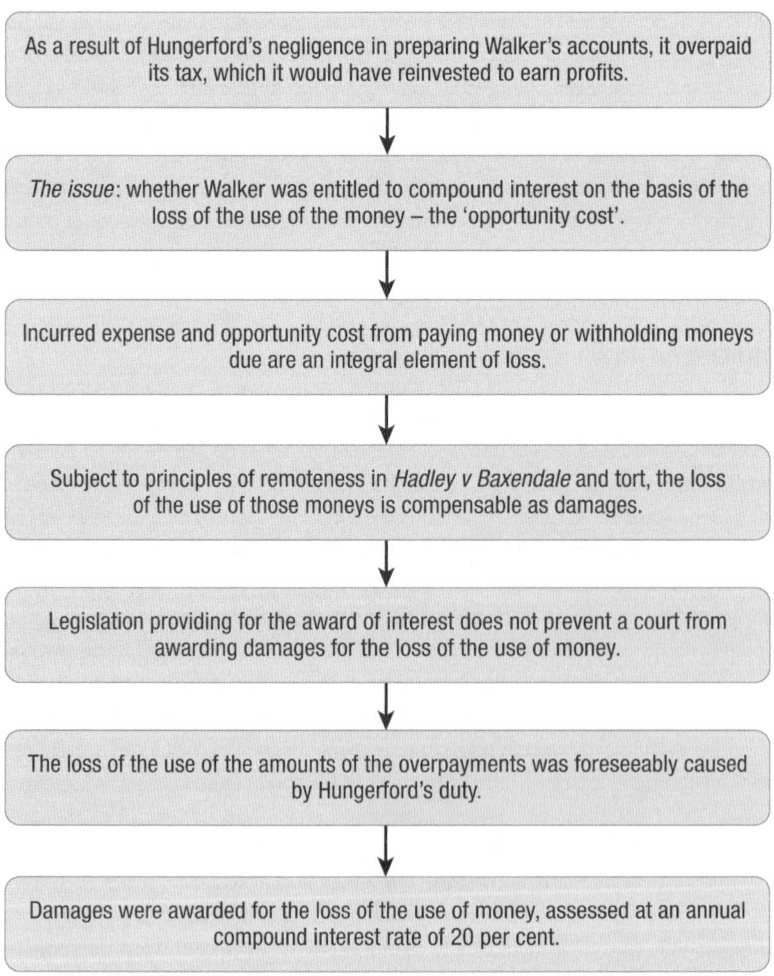

The principles contained in *Hungerfords* apply in several different situations. They are broadly illustrated in Table 2.6.

Table 2.6 Judicial consideration of *Hungerfords v Walker* (1989) 171 CLR 125

Principle	Relevant authority
Damages assessed by reference to interest is recoverable for the loss of the use of money if the loss is foreseeable.	*Hungerfords v Walker* (1989) 171 CLR 125
The plaintiff bears the onus of proving the loss of the use of money.	*Commonwealth v Chessell* (1991) 30 FCR 154
Damages is recoverable also where the wrong deprived the plaintiff of the opportunity of profitably investing more money.	*Hardie v Shadbolt* [2004] WASCA 175
A plaintiff who has not borrowed money must prove that the money would have been invested, and the rate at which it would have been invested.	*Duke Group Ltd (in liq) v Pilmer* (1999) 73 SASR 64
Damages for the loss of the use of money can be awarded where the wrong is trespass to land.	*Balanced Securities Ltd v Bianco (No 2)* (2010) 27 VR 599
Damages have been awarded for the wrongful withholding of an asset which would have been sold.	*Balanced Securities Ltd v Bianco (No 2)* (2010) 27 VR 599
The court may have regard to the interest rate under a relevant statute providing for pre-judgment interest in considering the amount of damages.	*Palasty v Parlby* (2007) 13 BPR 25,311
The discretion to award interest is still qualified by the compensatory principle that compensation be no more than put the plaintiff in the position as if the wrong had not been committed.	*Haines v Bendall* (1991) 172 CLR 60

REVIEW QUESTIONS

(1) Does the award of interest under the principles set out in *Hungerfords v Walker* (1989) 17 CLR 125 reflect the (fundamental) compensatory principle?

(2) What are the advantages of being awarded damages in a lump sum and how is this addressed in an award of compensation?

(3) What principles apply to take into account inflation in awarding damages?

3 ATTRIBUTION OF RESPONSIBILITY

I	Introduction	88
II	The legal concept of causation	88
III	Factual causation	97
	A Overview	97
	B The 'but for' test and its application	98
	C Causal overdetermination (multiple sufficient causes)	100
	D Evidential uncertainty	104
IV	Scope of liability	113
	A Subsequent event	115
	B Remoteness of damage	134
	C The purpose of the duty breached	135
	D The plaintiff's contribution to the loss	137

I Introduction

Before a plaintiff can obtain compensation for harm suffered due to any wrong, they need to attribute the harm to the defendant's wrongful conduct. Broadly, the defendant's conduct must be a cause of the harm. There is usually a double inquiry here – first, into whether there was a factual historical link between the wrong and the harm ('factual causation') and, second, a value judgment on whether liability for the harm ought to be imposed upon the defendant ('legal causation' or 'scope of liability').

Attributing responsibility is sometimes part of establishing liability (eg for wrongs actionable only on proof of damage, such as negligence), but for wrongs which are actionable per se, it is a matter of remedy.

While the rules on attribution of liability are not the same for every wrong, there are significant similarities. The cases detailed in this chapter illustrate key commonalities and differences across the various wrongs in the rules governing attribution of responsibility. More detail of the specific rules used to attribute responsibility for the individual wrongs is found in the specific chapters on those wrongs.

II The legal concept of causation

Concept	Short explanation	Relevant authorities	Principles text
Legal concept of causation	The legal concept of causation requires us to engage in a counterfactual inquiry as to whether the loss would still have occurred if the wrong had not occurred (ie the 'but for' test).	*Barnett v Chelsea and Kensington Hospital Management Committee* [1969] 1 QB 428 *Alexander v Cambridge Credit Corporation Ltd* (1987) 9 NSWLR 310	Chapter 3: [3.4]–[3.18]

Concept	Short explanation	Relevant authorities	Principles text
	However, Australian courts have historically required a 'but for' plus common sense approach (where common sense looks at whether new intervening acts 'broke the chain of causation'). This remains the test in contract law, and for some torts. Moreover, civil liability statutes have required a separation of factual causation and 'scope of liability' questions (which include common sense causation questions) in the area of negligence. This may become the general test in tort.	*March v E & MH Stramare* (1991) 171 CLR 506 *Civil Liability Act 2002* (NSW) s 5D *Wallace v Kam* (2013) 250 CLR 375	

Common law courts have developed legal concepts of causation which are distinct from ideas of causation within philosophy and science. English courts have broken down their analysis of causation into two phases sometimes described as causation in fact (factual causation) and causation in law (scope of liability or legal causation).[1]

'Factual causation' asks whether the plaintiff's harm would have occurred *but for* the defendant's wrongful conduct (the 'but for' test). If the harm would have occurred *even if* the defendant had done the right thing, then the defendant's wrong usually cannot be regarded as a factual cause of the harm. It requires courts to conduct a counterfactual enquiry into what would have transpired if the defendant had not committed the wrong. An example of how the 'but for' analysis proceeds is outlined below.

Barnett v Chelsea and Kensington Hospital Management Committee [1969] 1 QB 428

Facts and issues

Barnett was a nightwatchman on duty on New Year's Eve 1965, along with two others. They had drinks together to celebrate the New Year, then at 5 am, they drank some tea. All three started vomiting shortly after. At 8 am, they presented to the casualty department at the defendant's hospital. The nurse on duty thought their illness was alcohol-related. She rang the doctor, who advised her to tell the men to go home and go to bed and call their own doctors in the morning. The men returned home, Several hours later, Barnett died of arsenic poisoning from the tea. The medical evidence indicated that even if Barnett had been admitted to the hospital wards when he presented at casualty and treated with all care, he would nonetheless have died from the poisoning.

1 See, eg, *McLoughlin v O'Brian* [1983] 1 AC 410, 432 (Lord Bridge); *Essa v Laing Ltd* [2004] ICR 746, [92], [105].

Decision

The hospital owed Barnett a duty of care and breached that duty because the doctor did not see, examine, admit or treat him. The onus of proof to show that the breach caused Barnett's death remained with the plaintiff (his widow). She failed to show that but for the breach (ie had the hospital met the reasonable standard of care) the harm would not have occurred (ie Barnett would not have died).

Nield J

> **[434]** [T]he plaintiff, Mrs Bessie Irene Barnett, has failed to establish, on the balance of probabilities, that the death of the deceased, William Patrick Barnett, resulted from the negligence of the defendants, the Chelsea and Kensington Hospital Management Committee, my view being that had all care been taken, still the deceased must have died.
>
> **[438]** ... I find that under all four headings the defendants were negligent and in breach of their duty in that they or their servants or agents did not see and did not examine and did not admit and did not treat the deceased ... It remains to consider whether it is shown that the deceased's death was caused by that negligence or whether, as the defendants have said, the deceased must have died in any event ...
>
> The deceased attended at the casualty department at five or ten minutes past eight in the morning. If the casualty officer had got up and dressed and come to see the three men and examined them and decided to admit them, the deceased (and Dr Lockett agreed with this) could not have been in bed in a ward before 11 am. I accept Dr Goulding's evidence that an intravenous drip would not have been set up before 12 noon, and if potassium loss was suspected it could not have been discovered until 12.30 pm. Dr Lockett, dealing with this, said 'If this man had not been treated until after 12 noon the chances of survival were not good.'
>
> ... For those reasons, I find that the plaintiff has failed to establish, on the balance of probabilities, that the defendants' negligence caused the death of the deceased.

'Scope of liability' in contrast, asks whether the defendant *should* be held responsible for the harm – applying a value judgment as to how far people should be held responsible for the consequences of our actions. Sometimes a person's wrongful act sets off an unpredictable chain of events, so that it may (depending on your perspective) be unfair to hold that person responsible for harm caused as a result. Common law has therefore developed doctrines which can exonerate a defendant in situations where an intervening act broke the chain of causation between the defendant's conduct and the plaintiff's harm (*novus actus interveniens*), where the harm was too remote from the wrong (remoteness), or where the harm fell outside the scope of the duty breached by the defendant, or that the plaintiff contributed to the loss or failed to mitigate it (contributory liability, mitigation).

Australian courts have adopted these doctrines, but rather than conduct the inquiry in two distinct phases as is done in England, they have generally merged factual and legal causation into a single test, by asking whether, as a matter of common sense, the defendant's conduct constitutes a cause of the plaintiff's harm.

The Australian approach to in causation in contract uses a 'commonsense' notion of causation. The case below outlines how the 'commonsense' causation test works in contract.

Alexander v Cambridge Credit Corporation Ltd (1987) 9 NSWLR 310

Facts and issues

Cambridge Credit Corporation ('CCC') was a finance and land development company which raised funds for its enterprises from the public by issuing debentures. CCC's trust deed allowed it to issue debentures worth a maximum of five times the total amount of shareholder funds and required the trustees to appoint a receiver if provisions were breached. The 1971 accounts stated that CCC had $12 million in shareholder funds, meaning it could raise up to $60 million in debentures. In fact, however, shareholder funds were only $3 million, allowing for only $15 million in debentures. In 1971, CCC issued $56 million in debentures. CCC's auditor – Alexander – did not detect the misstatement, and wrongly certified to the trustees that the accounts for 1971 were true, that CCC had not contravened the trust deed, and the limits on issuing debentures had not been exceeded. The officers and managing director of CCC knew about this discrepancy, so they did not rely on Alexandor's report, but the trustees (who had no contractual relationship with Alexander) did.

In 1974, the land price collapsed, and because CCC had issued debentures far in excess of what the trust deed allowed, it was left with a $155 million shortfall and the trustees appointed a receiver. The receiver (in the name of CCC) sued Alexander.

The trial judge held that Alexander had breached the audit contract by issuing inaccurate certificates in 1971. He held that but for the breach the trustee would have appointed a receiver in 1971. Instead, CCC kept trading, and the shortfall increased from $10 million to $155 million. The judge awarded the difference – $145 million – as damages.

Decision

In a leading judgment by McHugh JA (who later joinod the High Court), the NSW Supreme Court set out a single 'commonsense' test for causation for breach of contract. The appcal was allowed, because the inaccurate certificates in 1971 could not be a commonsense cause of trading losses by 1974 just because they had helped the company keep trading, particularly as other events such as the collapse of the property market contributed to tho losses.

McHugh JA

> **[349]** The common law has followed the ordinary man's notion of causation instead of the theories espoused by philosophers and scientists …
>
> However, whether or not a particular act or omission attracts legal liability ultimately depends on policy and not logic. This is the basis of the 'but for' test of causation which is championed by many legal writers and applied in practice by courts and juries …
>
> It accords with ordinary habits of thought and speech. People attribute as a cause any condition or relation known to them 'but for' which the result would not have occurred.
>
> …
>
> **[351]** I am of the opinion that, leaving aside the intervention of a new act (novus actus interveniens), the issue of causation is to be resolved in general by simply applying the 'but for' test in a practical commonsense way …
>
> …

> [**358**] Accordingly, to establish a causal connection between a breach of contract and the damage which the plaintiff has suffered, he need only show that the breach was a cause of the loss. In general, the application of the 'but for' test will be sufficient to prove the necessary causal connection. But that test is only a guide. The ultimate question is whether, as a matter of commonsense, the relevant act or omission was a cause …
>
> I do not think that the certificates constituted a cause of Cambridge's loss of $145 000 000. The existence of a company cannot be a cause of its trading losses or profits. Yet that is what the case for Cambridge comes to. To assert that the issue of the certificates was a cause of the loss is to depart from the commonsense notion of causation which the common law champions.

The 'common sense' approach to causation has also been used for tort and remains in use for many torts. However, while the case below deals with the operation of 'common sense' causation in negligence, the test for negligence has since been changed by statute.

March v E & MH Stramare (1991) 171 CLR 506

Facts and issues

The defendant's truck was parked in the middle of a main CBD road at 1 am with its red taillights and orange flashing hazard lights illuminated, while the defendant was loading it with fruit and vegetables. The plaintiff, March, who was drink-driving and speeding, hit the rear of the truck and suffered serious injuries.

Decision

The trial judge apportioned responsibility 70 per cent to March and 30 per cent to Stramare, but the Full Court of the Supreme Court of South Australia held March's own negligence was the sole effective cause of the accident and quashed the original damages award. On appeal, the High Court held that the defendant's negligence was the cause of the accident because it was the 'very kind of thing' which might happen.

Mason CJ (Toohey and Gaudron JJ agreeing)

> [**508**] … I do not accept that the 'but for' (causa sine qua non) test ever was or now should become the exclusive test of causation in negligence cases.
>
> …
>
> [**515**] The common law tradition is that what was the cause of a particular occurrence is a question of fact which 'must be determined by applying common sense to the facts of each particular case', in the words of Lord Reid: Stapley … .
>
> …

Commentators subdivide the issue of causation in a given case into two questions: the question of causation in fact – to be determined by the application of the 'but for' test – and the further question whether a defendant is in law responsible for damage which his or her negligence has played some part in producing … . It is said that, in determining this second question, considerations of policy have a prominent part to play, as do accepted value judgments. However, this approach to the issue of causation (a) places rather too much weight on the 'but for' test to the exclusion of the 'common sense' approach which the common law has always favoured; and (b) implies, or seems to imply, that value judgment has, or should have, no part to play in resolving causation as an issue of fact. As Dixon CJ, Fullagar and Kitto JJ remarked in *Fitzgerald v Penn*: 'it is all ultimately a matter of common sense' …

…

[**519**] Viewed in this light, the respondents' negligence was a cause of the accident and of the appellant's injuries. The second respondent's wrongful act in parking the truck in the middle of the road created a situation of danger, the risk being that a careless driver would act in the way that the appellant acted. The purpose of imposing the common law duty on the second respondent was to protect motorists from the very risk of injury that befell the appellant. In these circumstances, the respondents' negligence was a continuing cause of the accident. The chain of causation was not broken by a novus actus. Nor was it terminated because the risk of injury was not foreseeable; on the contrary, it was plainly foreseeable.

Deane J

[**522**] … For the purposes of the law of negligence, the question of causation arises in the context of the attribution of fault or responsibility: whether an identified negligent act or omission of the defendant was so connected with the plaintiff's loss or injury that, as a matter of ordinary common sense and experience, it should be regarded as a cause of it … . The 'but for' (or 'causa sine qua non') test may well be a useful aid in determining whether something is properly to be seen as an effective cause of something else in that sense. In particular, the test will commonly exclude causation for the purposes of the law of negligence if the answer to the question it poses is that the accident which caused the injuries would have occurred in the same way and with the same consequences in any event … . There are however, in my view, convincing reasons precluding its adoption as a comprehensive definitive test of causation in the law of negligence. First [**523**] the clear weight of authority is against the substitution of such a formularized test of causation for a 'common sense idea of what is meant by saying that one fact is a cause of another' … . Secondly, unqualified acceptance of the 'but for' test as even a negative or exclusionary test of causation for the purposes of the law of negligence would lead to the absurd and unjust position that there was no 'cause' of an injury in any case where there were present two independent and sufficient causes of the accident in which the injury was sustained. Less importantly, acceptance of the 'but for' test as a comprehensive test would carry with it the need to draw somewhat artificial distinctions to avoid the type of confusion between an accident which happened and one which did not … .

McHugh J

[**530**] Whatever label is given to such a rule – 'common sense [**531**] principles', 'foreseeability', 'novus actus interveniens', 'effective cause', 'real and efficient cause', 'direct cause', 'proximate cause' and so on – the reality is that such a limiting rule is the product of a policy choice that legal liability is not to attach to an act or omission which is outside the scope of that rule even though the act or omission was a necessary precondition of the occurrence of damage to the plaintiff. That is to say, such a rule is concerned only with the question whether a person should be held responsible for an act or omission which ex hypothesi was necessarily one of the sum of conditions or relations which produced the damage.

That a policy choice is involved in the use of some rules which limit liability for wrongful acts and omissions is obvious. ... Nevertheless, the use of commonsense notions of causation ... require the application of a policy choice, for they allow the tribunal of fact to determine legal liability on broad grounds of moral responsibility for the damage which has occurred.

Despite the numerous judicial statements to the effect that being a causa sine qua non of the occurrence of damage is not enough to make an act or omission a cause of damage for legal purposes, another school of opinion asserts 'that the only genuine causal issue is that of sine qua non or 'cause in fact'': see Hart and Honore ... . Many, probably most, academic legal writers on the subject assert that, once the 'but for' or causa sine qua non test is satisfied, the issue of causation is spent. Other issues [**532**] such as 'proximate cause', 'sole cause', 'novus actus interveniens', 'real cause' and so on are the product of policy choices whose objects are to limit legal responsibility for damage resulting from acts or omissions of the kind in question. Accordingly, on this view, if a negligent act or omission materially contributed to the occurrence of damage, it will still be a cause of the damage for legal purposes even though, for policy reasons, there may be no legal liability for that act or omission. Moreover, a negligent act or omission will be held to have materially contributed to the damage if its contribution was not de minimis ... .

...

Moreover, it is doubtful whether there is any consistent commonsense notion of what constitutes a 'cause'. As Dr Lloyd-Bostock has asserted in 'The Ordinary Man, and the Psychology of Attributing Causes and Responsibility', (1979) 42 *Modern Law Review* 143, at p 167, modern psychological research:

> illustrates how judgments of causes and responsibility (by an ordinary person) are reached by an active, constructive process which goes beyond the information given and is therefore subject to various forms of error and bias: are structured by as well as expressed in language: and are influenced by the motives, values, experiences, and other characteristics of the judger, the specific context, and the anticipated consequences. These various effects are interwoven and difficult to disentangle both conceptually and empirically, but in general talking about the ordinary man, common sense, and everyday judgments appears somewhat hazardous.

[**533**] Indeed, I suspect that what commonsense would not see as a cause in a non-litigious context will frequently be seen as a cause, according to commonsense notions, in

> a litigious context. This is particularly so in many cases where expert evidence is called to explain a connection between an act or omission and the occurrence of damage. In these cases, the educative effect of the expert evidence makes an appeal to commonsense notions of causation largely meaningless or produces findings concerning causation which would often not be made by an ordinary person uninstructed by the expert evidence.
>
> ...
>
> In my opinion, now that legislation allows liability for damage to be apportioned in accordance with what the court thinks is just and [**534**] equitable having regard to the comparative responsibility of the parties, the preferable course is to use the causa sine qua non test as the exclusive test of causation. One obvious exception to this rule must be the unusual case where the damage is the result of the simultaneous operation of two or more separate and independent events each of which was sufficient to cause the damage. None of the various tests of causation suggested by courts and writers, however, is satisfactory in dealing with this exceptional case. Perhaps no more can be done in this situation than to treat each wrongful act as an independent cause for legal purposes. The terms of a statute, legal rule or legal instrument may also require a different approach from the 'but for' test. In general, however, the 'but for' test should be seen as the test of legal causation. Any other rule limiting responsibility for damage caused by a wrongful act or omission should be recognised as a policy-based rule concerned with remoteness of damage and not causation.

At odds with the common law's merged 'common sense' approach, civil liability statutes in all Australian states and the Australian Capital Territory now require separate consideration of factual causation and scope of liability, in line with the suggestion of McHugh J in *March v E & MH Stramare* (excerpted on page 92). Unfortunately, the coverage of the provisions varies wildly.

Table 3.1 Coverage of causation sections of civil liability statutes from broadest to narrowest

	State/territory	Act and provision	Coverage
Broadest	WA	*Civil Liability Act 2002* (WA) s 5A	'any claim for damages for harm caused by the fault of a person' regardless of cause of action.
	ACT, NSW, SA, Vic	*Civil Law (Wrongs) Act 2002* (ACT) s 45; *Civil Liability Act 2002* (NSW) s 5D; *Civil Liability Act 1936* (SA) s 34; *Wrongs Act 1958* (Vic) s 51	'negligence' defined as 'failure to exercise reasonable care' whether the claim is brought in tort, contract, under statute or otherwise.
Narrowest	Qld, Tas	*Civil Liability Act 2003* (Qld) s 11 and sch 2 (definition of 'duty'); *Civil Liability Act 2002* (Tas) ss 3 (definition of 'duty'), 13	Breach of tortious duty of care, a contractual duty of care that is coextensive with a tortious duty of care, and any other duty concurrent with these duties.

Civil Liability Act 2002 (NSW) s 5D

This legislation requires courts to separate out factual causation and 'scope of liability' (including common sense considerations).

5D General principles

(1) A determination that negligence caused particular harm comprises the following elements:

(a) that the negligence was a necessary condition of the occurrence of the harm ('factual causation'), and

(b) that it is appropriate for the scope of the negligent person's liability to extend to the harm so caused ('scope of liability').

(2) In determining in an exceptional case, in accordance with established principles, whether negligence that cannot be established as a necessary condition of the occurrence of harm should be accepted as establishing factual causation, the court is to consider (amongst other relevant things) whether or not and why responsibility for the harm should be imposed on the negligent party.

(3) If it is relevant to the determination of factual causation to determine what the person who suffered harm would have done if the negligent person had not been negligent–

(a) the matter is to be determined subjectively in the light of all relevant circumstances, subject to paragraph (b), and

(b) any statement made by the person after suffering the harm about what he or she would have done is inadmissible except to the extent (if any) that the statement is against his or her interest.

(4) For the purpose of determining the scope of liability, the court is to consider (amongst other relevant things) whether or not and why responsibility for the harm should be imposed on the negligent party.

In *Wallace v Kam*,[2] the High Court flagged that the statutory two-step approach to causation may eventually be adopted at common law. This would bring a welcome consistency between common law and statute and give greater clarity.

Wallace v Kam (2013) 250 CLR 375

Facts and issues

A neurosurgeon, Dr Kam, performed surgery on Wallace for a back condition. Dr Kam failed to warn Wallace of two inherent risks of the surgery – neurapraxia (temporary local nerve damage to the thighs) and permanent paralysis. Had Dr Kam only warned of the first risk, the trial judge found Wallace would have gone ahead with the surgery. It was the first risk which eventuated.

2 (2013) 250 CLR 375.

Decision

While the failure to warn about both risks may have been causally linked to the injury (factual causation), the neuropraxia fell outside the scope of Kam's liability because Wallace was prepared to accept that risk. The High Court indicated a shift towards a two-step approach to attributing responsibility might be appropriate in the common law more generally.

French CJ, Crennan, Kiefel, Gageler and Keane JJ

> [**381**] The common law of negligence requires determination of causation for the purpose of attributing legal responsibility. Such a determination inevitably involves two questions: a question of historical fact as to how particular harm occurred; and a normative question as to whether legal responsibility for that particular harm occurring in that way should be attributed to a particular person. The distinct nature of those two questions has tended, by and large, to be overlooked in the articulation of the common law. In particular, the application of the first question, and the existence of the second, have been obscured by traditional expressions of causation for the purposes of the common law of negligence in the conclusory language of 'directness', 'reality', 'effectiveness' and 'proximity'.

REVIEW QUESTIONS

(1) How would you define and apply the test of 'factual causation'?

(2) What do you think of the test of 'common sense' causation outlined in *Alexander v Cambridge Credit Corporation Ltd* (1987) 9 NSWLR 310 and *March v E & MH Stramare* (1991) 171 CLR 506? Do you think it impermissibly blends questions of policy (ie should the defendant be fairly responsible for that loss) with questions of fact?

(3) Do you think it is unsatisfactory to have 'common sense' causation in many areas of law (eg contract, most torts) and a different test in negligence or other situations where there is a failure to exercise reasonable care?

III Factual causation

A Overview

While the 'but for' test remains the primary way of determining factual causation, the common law has also developed doctrines to address multiple sufficient causes and evidentiary uncertainty.

Concept	Short explanation	Relevant authorities	Principles text
The 'but for' test and its application	The 'but for' test involves asking whether the harm would have occurred 'but for' the event that is alleged to have triggered liability.	*Civil Liability Act 2002* (NSW) s 5D (excerpted on page 96)	Chapter 3: [3.24]–[3.27]
Causal overdetermination	Where there are multiple sufficient causes, the 'but for' test may give absurd results. Factual causation may be established if the defendant's conduct was a 'necessary element of a sufficient set' of factors causing the harm ('NESS' test).	*Elayoubi v Zipser* [2008] NSWCA 335 *Performance Cars Ltd v Abraham* [1962] 1 QB 33	Chapter 3: [3.28]–[3.48]
Material contribution	Where there is evidentiary uncertainty, factual causation may be inferred if the defendant's conduct made a material contribution to the harm.	*Bonnington Castings Ltd v Wardlaw* [1956] AC 613 *Amaca Pty Ltd v King* (2011) 35 VR 280	Chapter 3: [3.50]–[3.59]
Material risk	Under SA and ACT statutes, if causation cannot be proved via the 'but for' test or material contribution, it may be enough if the defendant's conduct materially increased the risk that the harm may occur.	*McGhee v National Coal Board* [1973] 1 WLR 1 *Civil Liability Act 1936* (SA) s 34 *Civil Law (Wrongs) Act 2002* (ACT) s 45	Chapter 3: [3.60]–[3.68]

B The 'but for' test and its application

Adeels Palace Pty Ltd v Moubarak (2009) 239 CLR 420

Facts and issues

Adeels Palace was a function venue in Punchbowl, Sydney, where the plaintiffs, Bou Najem and Moubarak, attended a New Year's Eve party in December 2002. A fracas broke out, and Moubarak hit a man in the face. The man left the party and returned with a gun to take revenge on Moubarak, shooting and injuring both Moubarak and Bou Najem. Bou Najem had no connection to the fight, but was shot anyway. They brought proceedings against Adeels Palace claiming damages for personal injury, alleging that they had suffered injury as a result of Adeels Palace's negligence in not providing sufficient (or indeed any) security during the function on New Year's Eve. Was the lack of licensed security personnel a cause of the shooting of either plaintiff under the *Civil Liability Act 2002* (NSW), particularly given the responsibility of a licensee under the *Liquor Act 1982* (NSW) to turn out any patron who was quarrelsome and disorderly?

Decision

While Adeels Palace had an obligation to take reasonable care to prevent customers from being harmed by quarrelsome and disorderly patrons, it was not proven that 'but for' the absence of security personnel, the patrons would not have been shot. Nor was this an 'exceptional case' within the meaning of s 5D(2) of the *Civil Liability Act 2002* (NSW) (excerpted on page 96) where 'but for' causation did not have to be shown.

French CJ, Gummow, Hayne, Heydon and Crennan JJ

> [**441**] The evidence at trial did not show that the presence of security personnel would have deterred the re-entry of the gunman. That conclusion could have been reached only if it was assumed that the gunman would have acted rationally … The gunman's conduct at the restaurant on this night was dictated neither by reason nor by prudential considerations. He shot the man who had struck him during the mêlée that broke out after the confrontation on the dance floor. And before shooting that man, the gunman had shot a man who had done nothing to him and who, defenceless, begged for mercy.
>
> Nor did the evidence show that security personnel could or would have prevented re-entry by the gunman: a determined person armed with a gun and irrationally bent on revenge. The evidence given at trial by the plaintiffs' expert security consultant did not go beyond the assertion that a security person confronting the gunman at the entrance to the restaurant 'would have at least altered the chain of events and thereby likely altered the outcome'. The security consultant called on behalf of Adeels Palace emphasised that the overriding principle which should govern the conduct of security personnel confronted by a gunman is 'safety for all parties' and that 'once a determined gunman is targeting a victim or victims there [is] no guaranteed safe or effective option'.
>
> [**442**] Recognising that changing any of the circumstances in which the shootings occurred might have made a difference does not prove factual causation. Providing security at the entrance of the restaurant might have delayed the gunman's entry; it might have meant that, if Mr Bou Najem was a random victim, as seemed to be the case, someone else might have been shot and not him. But neither plaintiff proved factual causation by pointing to possibilities that might have eventuated if circumstances had been different.
>
> Nor was 'but for' causation established in these cases by observing that the relevant duty was to take reasonable care to prevent injury to patrons from the violent, quarrelsome or disorderly conduct of other persons. That is, the question of factual causation was not answered in these cases by pointing out that the relevant duty of care was to take reasonable steps to prevent violent assault, that each plaintiff was the victim of a violent assault, and that the damage sustained by the plaintiffs was 'the very kind of thing' which the relevant duty obliged Adeels Palace to take reasonable steps to prevent. That observation may bear upon questions about scope of liability. Describing the injury as 'the very kind of thing' which was the subject of the duty must not be permitted to obscure the need to prove factual causation … .
>
> …
>
> In the present case, in contrast, the 'but for' test of factual causation was not established. It was not shown to be more probable than not that, but for the absence of security personnel (whether at the door or even on the floor of the restaurant), the shootings would

not have taken place. That is, the absence of security personnel at Adeels Palace on the night the plaintiffs were shot was not a necessary condition of their being shot.

...

[443] ... [I]t would be contrary to established principles to hold Adeels Palace responsible in negligence if not providing security was not a necessary condition of the occurrence of the harm but providing security might have deterred or prevented its occurrence, or might have resulted in harm being suffered by someone other than, or **[444]** in addition to, the plaintiffs. ... [T]he event which caused the plaintiffs' injuries was deliberate criminal wrongdoing, and the wrongdoing occurred despite society devoting its resources to deterring and preventing it through the work of police forces and the punishment of those offenders who are caught. That being so, it should not be accepted that negligence which was not a necessary condition of the injury that resulted from a third person's criminal wrongdoing was a cause of that injury. Accordingly, the submission that the plaintiffs' injuries in these cases were caused by the failure of Adeels Palace to take steps that *might* have made their occurrence less likely, should be rejected.

C Causal overdetermination (multiple sufficient causes)

A key problem with the 'but for' test arises where there are two or more acts or events, each of which would be sufficient to bring about the plaintiff's injury. For example, A and B each negligently start a fire, the fires combine and burn down C's house. But for A's negligence, C's house would be lost, and but for B's negligence, C's house would still have been lost – leading to the absurd conclusion that neither A nor B factually caused the loss. Courts have responded in different ways depending on the type of overdetermination (duplicative or pre-emptive) and on whether the other cause was a third party's wrong or a non-wrongful event. For example, French CJ remarked in *Amaca Pty Ltd v Booth* (2011) 246 CLR 36 (extracted further on page 107) that:

> factual causation does not require that the propounded cause be one link in a chain of causative factors or events. It may be, as some commentators have suggested, a 'necessary element of a sufficient set' of causes.[3]

This is a reference to Richard Wright's argument that a defendant's conduct may be a factual cause of harm if it is one element which makes a set of conditions jointly sufficient to bring about the harm.[4]

1 Duplicative causation

Where two factors were sufficient to cause the harm, and each factor duplicated or reinforced the effects of the other (as in C's house being burnt down by fires started by A and B), this is duplicative causation. Where both events were wrongs (eg A and B each acted negligently

3 (2011) 246 CLR 36, [57].

4 R Wright, 'The NESS Account of Natural Causation: A Response to Criticisms' in R Goldberg (ed), *Perspectives on Causation* (Hart Publishing, 2011), 285.

Figure 3.1 Types of causal overdetermination

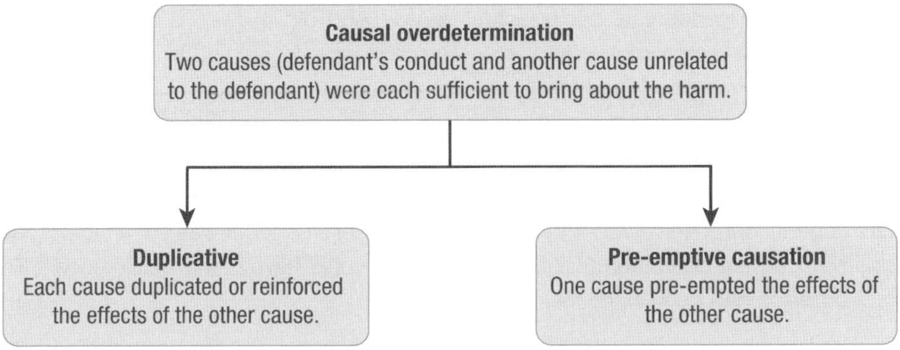

in starting their own fire), each wrong is regarded as a factual cause of the harm – either as an exception to the 'but for' test (ie under s 5D(2) of the *Civil Liability Act 2002* (NSW)), or because 'a necessary condition of the occurrence of the harm' includes a necessary element of a sufficient set to bring about the harm (ie under s 5D(1)). (Section 5D is excerpted on page 96). Case law is not as clear if one event was the defendant's wrong and the other was not a wrong (eg A acted negligently in starting their fire, but B's fire was started by lightning and could not have been prevented). Commentators have argued that factual causation is likewise established, but that the defendant should not be liable because the loss falls outside the scope of liability as the loss could have been sustained without any wrong occurring.[5]

Elayoubi v Zipser [2008] NSWCA 335

Facts and issues

Mrs Kolled had a baby by C-section in Preston Hospital in 1978. The surgeons used an incision with a higher risk of uterine rupture in subsequent pregnancies, but failed to advise Mrs Kolled of these risks. When she was pregnant again (with the plaintiff, her fourth child), her doctor, Dr Zipser, negligently failed to request Mrs Kolled's records from Preston Hospital. There was some doubt about whether Preston Hospital had recorded the information because they had been destroyed before trial (but after the birth of the second child). The trial judge found that on the balance of probabilities that they had mentioned the upper uterine incision.

Because he was unaware of the previous upper uterine incision, Dr Zipser did not take additional precautions, and during birth, the plaintiff was deprived of oxygen and suffered disabilities. To prevent the plaintiff's injuries, Preston Hospital needed to record the type of incision, and Dr Zipser

5 RW Wright, 'Causation in Tort Law' (1985) 73(6) *California Law Review* 1735, 1775–6, 1798; American Law Institute, *Restatement (Third) of Torts: Liability for Physical and Emotional Harm* (2010) §27 cmt (d).

needed to request the records (both wrongful omissions). If, but for Dr Zipser's negligence, the injury would have happened anyway (because Preston Hospital did not record the information), was Dr Zipser's negligence was not a factual cause? And did it make a difference if Preston Hospital's omission was wrongful or innocent? (The case was decided under common law rules.)

Decision

The Court of Appeal affirmed the trial judge's finding that the notes included the critical information about the incision, and there was no omission on Preston Hospital's part. However, even if Preston Hospital's conduct *had* been a wrongful omission, Dr Zipser's conduct was still a factual cause of the loss. The court left open the question of whether it would have made a difference if Preston Hospital's omission had been innocent.

Basten JA (Beazley JA and Allsop P agreeing)

> **[56]** First, in relation to the finding of a failure to advise Mrs Kolled in 1978 of the risks she faced in relation to a future pregnancy, it is clear that the risk materialised in the sense that, on the factual assumption, she did not take steps which would have avoided or reduced the harm suffered by the plaintiff. Even if it be assumed that, had Dr Zipser not been negligent, he would have discovered the true situation, with the result that the risk might not have materialised, nevertheless his failure to take that step did not break the causal link between the failure to warn and the harm suffered. Secondly, in relation to the negligence of Dr Zipser in not inquiring as to the nature of the earlier operation, any negligence of Dr Dawson in failing to record the details of the operation would itself have contributed to the materialisation of the risk, but would not have prevented Dr Zipser's negligence being a contributing cause.
>
> **[57]** … If the negligence of two tortfeasors each contributes to the indivisible harm suffered by the victim, each is liable for the harm suffered. If neither were negligent, no harm would have been caused. If either one were negligent and the other not, in each case the negligence would have caused the harm. But a conclusion that if both were negligent and the harm eventuated, neither was responsible for that harm, invites a question as to whether the reasoning process has gone awry. One basis for justifying the preferred approach is that the common law has 'substituted the test of responsibility or fault for that of causation', as explained by Professor A L Goodhart, 'Appeals on Questions of Fact' (1955) 71 *LQR* 402 at 413. As he noted, that approach is reflected in statutory amendments which occurred in similar form in England and in New South Wales, dealing with apportionment between tortfeasors and responsibility for contributory negligence. Each provision speaks of damage suffered 'as a result of' a tort, thereby avoiding 'caused by': see *Law Reform (Miscellaneous Provisions) Act* 1946 (NSW) s 5(1); *Law Reform (Miscellaneous Provisions) Act* 1965 (NSW) s 9(1). A normative element, requiring appropriate allocation of responsibility for tortious conduct should be accepted as part of the assessment of causal connection (potentially to an expansive or a restrictive effect). Although the *Civil Liability Act* 2002 (NSW) is not consistent in its terminology, it affirms the importance of the normative approach, requiring the court (in cases where it operates) to consider 'whether or not and why responsibility for the harm should be imposed on the negligent party': s 5D(4).

2 Pre-emptive causation

Pre-emptive causation involves two factors sufficient to cause the harm, but one factor pre-empted the effects of the other.

Performance Cars Ltd v Abraham [1962] 1 QB 33

Facts and issues

Performance Cars' Rolls Royce 'Silver Cloud' motor-car was damaged in two collisions, two weeks apart. Performance Cars had obtained judgment against the person responsible for the first accident, which included a sum of £75 for a respray, but it was unsatisfied, and appeared unlikely to be paid. At the time of the second accident, caused by Abraham, repairs had not yet been carried out from the first accident. Performance Cars then sued Abraham, and the trial judge awarded damages including £75 for a respray, on the basis that there were two tortfeasors, each liable to put the damage right.

Had the defendant's wrong caused the plaintiff's loss of £75 for respraying, or was it pre-empted by the third party's prior wrong?

Decision

The plaintiff's claim against the driver responsible for the second collision failed, as the collision caused no additional loss to the plaintiff.

Lord Evershed MR (Harman and Donovan LJJ agreeing)

> **[753]** In my judgment in the present case the defendant should be taken to have injured a motor-car that was already in certain respects (that is, in respect of the need for respraying) injured; with the result that to the extent of that need or injury the damage claimed did not flow from the defendant's wrongdoing. It may no doubt be unfortunate for the plaintiffs that the collisions took place in the order in which they did. Had the first collision been that brought about by the defendant and had they recovered the £75 now in question from him, they could not clearly have recovered the same sum again from the other wrongdoer. It is, however, in my view irrelevant (if unfortunate for the plaintiffs) that the judgment obtained against the other wrongdoer has turned out to be worthless.

A similar result was reached in *Cambridge v Anastopoulos*,[6] where the plaintiff's motorboat was damaged by the first and second defendants. Additional damage was suffered when the motorboat came loose from the towbar when it was being towed back to the owner by the third defendant. The third defendant was only liable for additional loss suffered, not for the initial loss caused by the first and second defendants.

6 [2012] NSWCA 405.

D Evidential uncertainty

Judges have also developed some exceptions or workarounds for the 'but for' test where there is evidential uncertainty as to whether or not the plaintiff's harm would have occurred without the defendant's conduct.

1 Inference of factual causation

Courts can infer from the facts that the defendant's wrong caused or materially contributed to the plaintiff's harm.

Tubemakers of Australia Ltd v Fernandez (1976) 10 ALR 303

Facts and issues

Fernandez was operating a bevelling machine at work when a fault in the machine caused a heavy steel tube to strike his right hand. The hand became increasingly painful. Six months later, a specialist diagnosed Dupuytren's contracture (a fibroproliferative disorder causing the fingers to contract towards the palm). After surgery, the condition recurred and disabled Fernandez from carrying out his normal duties and made him unable to find steady employment. The specialist gave evidence that Fernandez's injury 'could have' played a part in the condition of his right hand. The appellant's medical witness deposed that the condition was in no way related to the injury but suggested no alternative cause.

Could factual causation be inferred from medical evidence?

Decision

There was sufficient evidence for the jury to infer that the condition suffered by the respondent was caused by the appellant's negligence.

Mason J (Barwick CJ and Gibbs J agreeing)

> [**310**] In my opinion, this evidence left it open to the jury to infer that on the probabilities the injury caused or materially contributed to the occurrence of the condition. In drawing such an inference the jury was entitled to have regard, in addition to the matters referred to by Dr Sweeney in his evidence, to other significant circumstances: (a) that before the accident the respondent had suffered no disability in his right hand; (b) that the condition made its appearance shortly after the accident; and (c) that no alternative cause was established or indeed suggested in evidence. The combination of these circumstances, taken together with Dr Sweeney's evidence, provided in my opinion a sufficient basis from which the jury could draw an inference favourable to the respondent.

Amaca Pty Ltd v King (2011) 35 VR 280

Facts and issues

At 62, King was diagnosed with terminal mesothelioma caused by asbestos exposure. In 1972, he had been a fitter and turner with an engineering company contracted to repair a machine involved in producing asbestos sheeting for the defendant, formerly James Hardie & Coy Pty Ltd ('Hardie'). King was sent into the Hardie factory on a number of occasions to do the repairs. He gave evidence that 'everything around him was grey in colour and that the factory was gloomy and appeared to be a dusty place. He could not recall being provided with any protective equipment or mask'. Internal records indicated that Hardie management were, from at least 1966, aware of a significant risk that even minimal exposure to asbestos dust could result in asbestosis or mesothelioma.

The question was whether the respondent's exposure to asbestos fibres at the appellant's factory was a cause of him contracting mesothelioma.

Decision

It was open for the jury to infer a sufficient causal link between King's exposure to asbestos at the defendant's factory and his mesothelioma, even though the medical evidence was that it was possible rather than probable.

Nettle, Ashley and Redlich JJA

> [**301**] The question then became whether, on consideration of all the evidence, the jury was satisfied that the respondent had established causation by [his exposure at the defendant's factory] or [a combination of exposure at the defendant's factor and background exposure] – in the latter case by establishing that factory exposure in breach of duty materially contributed to the contraction of the disease. We say 'consideration of all the evidence' because the submissions for the appellant often seemed to imply [**302**] that the respondent's case required probability as adjudged by a medical witness, and that in the absence of such probability the respondent's case must fail. That is not so. Consideration of the entirety of a plaintiff's case may persuade the tribunal of fact that a sufficient causal link is established although expert medical witnesses gave evidence in the language of possibility only.
>
> ...
>
> [**303**] ... the jury was authorised, having considered all the evidence, to return a verdict for [**304**] the respondent so long as – (1) the present state of medical knowledge admitted of an affirmative answer in his favour, or (2), 'competent and trustworthy expert opinion' regarded an affirmative answer as not lacking justification as a probable inference, or at least as 'an accepted hypothesis'.

2 Material contribution to the harm

Where there are multiple factors (eg the defendant's wrong and a non-wrongful factor) which together caused one indivisible harm to the plaintiff, it is usually impossible for the plaintiff to prove causation via the 'but for' test. The common law has therefore developed the principle that a material contribution to the harm amounts to a factual cause.

Bonnington Castings Ltd v Wardlaw [1956] AC 613

Facts and issues

Wardlaw worked for the defendants, who exposed him to silica dust from a pneumatic hammer and swing grinders. There was no way to protect workers from the dust from the pneumatic hammers (and therefore no breach of duty), but the defendants failed to take available precautions to protect workers from dust created by the swing grinders. Wardlaw contracted pneumoconiosis and sued the defendants for damages.

The defendants argued that Wardlaw could not prove that he would not have contracted the disease if he had been protected against the dust from the swing grinders, because the dust from the hammers alone might have been sufficient to cause the disease.

Decision

The House of Lords held the employer liable on the ground that the dust from the swing grinders had materially contributed to the development of the disease.

Lord Reid, Viscount Simonds, Lord Somervill agreeing

> [**626**] The [plaintiff] has … in my opinion, proved enough to support the inference that the fault of the [defendants] has materially contributed to his illness. During the whole period of his employment he has been exposed to a polluted atmosphere for which the [defendants] are in part to blame. The disease is a disease of gradual incidence. Small though the contribution of pollution may be for which the [defendants] are to blame, it was continuous over a long period. In cumulo it must have been substantial, though it might remain small in proportion. It was the atmosphere inhaled by the [plaintiff] that caused his illness and it is impossible, in my opinion, to resolve the components of that atmosphere into particles caused by the fault of the [defendants] and particles not caused by the fault of the [defendants], as if they were separate and independent factors in his illness. Prima facie the particles inhaled are acting cumulatively, and I think the natural inference is that had it not been for the cumulative effect the [plaintiff] would not have developed pneumoconiosis when he did and might not have developed it at all. The inference, of course, would have been different if it could be shown that the [plaintiff] could not have inhaled any particles [**627**] given off from the swing grinding operations, or that the particles negligently released from the swing grinding operations were released at intervals so infrequent, or in quantities so insignificant, even if taken cumulatively, as to make it unreasonable to regard them as a material contributing cause of the [plaintiff's] disease. But that, in my opinion, the [defendants] are unable to show. On the whole evidence, I consider that the [plaintiff] has discharged the onus that is upon him of showing that the [defendants'] fault was a material contributing cause of his illness.

Amaca Pty Ltd v Booth (2011) 246 CLR 36

Facts and issues

Booth suffered from mesothelioma due to asbestos exposure. He worked for 27 years as a motor mechanic, regularly replacing asbestos brake linings made by the defendants (formerly, James Hardie & Coy Pty Ltd), and had three brief incidental exposures to asbestos outside of that work. From expert evidence, the trial judge found that 'all cumulative exposure to asbestos fibre must play some part in "causation" in an individual case'. Epidemiological evidence showed no statistically significant increase in risk in motor mechanics, relative to other occupational categories, and there was a chance that the incidental exposures on their own could have caused his illness. The question was whether the epidemiological evidence on risk indicated that the defendants' products could not have caused Booth's illness.

Decision

The High Court held that it was enough for the plaintiff to prove that the negligence of the defendant 'caused or materially contributed to the injury'. While evidence of risk could be relevant in establishing a causal explanation, evidence of low risk did not preclude an inference in a particular case that the defendant's negligence materially contributed to the plaintiff's injury.

French CJ

> [**53**] Causation in tort is not established merely because the allegedly tortious act or omission increased a risk of injury. The risk of an occurrence and the cause of the occurrence are quite different things.
>
> ...
>
> The existence of an association or a positive statistical correlation between the occurrence of one event and the subsequent occurrence of another may be expressed as a possibility, which may be no greater than a 'real chance' that, if the first event occurs, the second event will also occur. The mere existence of such an association or correlation does not justify a statement, relevant to factual causation in law, that the first event 'creates' or 'gives rise to' or 'increases' the probability that the second event will occur. Such a statement [**54**] contains an assumption that if the second event occurs it will have some causal connection to the first. However, if the association between two events is shown to have a causal explanation, then the conclusion may be open, if the second event should occur, that the first event has been at least a contributing cause of that occurrence. An after-the-event inference of causal connection may be reached on the civil standard of proof, namely, balance of probabilities, notwithstanding that the statistical correlation between the first event and the second event indicated, prospectively, no more than a 'mere possibility' or 'real chance' that the second event would occur given the first event. There may of course be cases in which the strength of the association, as measured by relative risk ratios, itself supports an inference of a causal connection.
>
> ...
>
> [**57**] ... [A] finding that a defendant's conduct has increased the risk of injury to the plaintiff must rest upon more than a mere statistical correlation between that kind of

conduct and that kind of injury. It requires ... a causal connection between the conduct and the injury, albeit other causative factors may be in play. As demonstrated by medical evidence in this case ... a causal connection may be inferred by somebody expert in the relevant field considering the nature and incidents of the correlation ... Where the existence of a causal connection is accepted it can support an inference, in the particular case, when injury has eventuated, that the defendant's conduct was a cause of the injury ... Where such an inference is drawn, the probability that it is correct is not to be determined only by reference to epidemiologically based ex ante probabilities.

Gummow, Hayne and Crennan JJ (agreeing with French CJ on the outcome, giving their own reasoning)

[**62**] The 'but for' criterion of causation proved to be troublesome in various situations in which multiple acts or events led to the plaintiff's injury, for example, where the development of a particular medical condition was the result of multiple conjunctive causal factors. In such cases what may be unclear is the extent to which one of these conjunctive causal factors contributed to that state of affairs. These situations have been addressed by the proposition stated by Lord Watson in *Wakelin v London and South Western Railway Co* that it is sufficient that the plaintiff prove that the negligence of the defendant 'caused or materially contributed to the injury'.

Amaca Pty Ltd v Ellis (2010) 240 CLR 111

Facts and issues

The plaintiff was the executor for the late Peter Cotton, who died of lung cancer and who had been exposed to respirable asbestos fibres due to working for two of the defendants and working with cement pipes produced by Amaca (formerly James Hardie & Coy Pty Ltd). He had also smoked 15–20 cigarettes a day for 26 years. The question was whether the smoking or the exposure to asbestos fibres had caused Cotton's lung cancer.

Decision

The High Court indicated that 'material contribution' could not apply here because asbestos exposure was one of two substances that could have caused Mr Cotton's cancer, and the expert evidence was that Mr Cotton's smoking carried a much higher risk than the asbestos exposure.

French CJ, Gummow, Hayne, Heydon, Crennan, Kiefel and Bell JJ

[126] [E]ach [medical expert] witness gave a relative risk from smoking that was many times greater than the relative risk from exposure to asbestos.

...

> **[136]** The issue in Bonnington Castings was whether one source of an injurious substance contributed to a gradual accumulation of dust that resulted in disease. The issue here is whether one substance that can cause injury did cause injury ... [W]as Mr Cotton's cancer 'intimately connected with and contributed to' by his exposure to asbestos? Questions of material contribution arise only if a connection between Mr Cotton's inhaling asbestos and his developing cancer was established. Knowing that inhaling asbestos can cause cancer does not entail that in this case it probably did. For the reasons given earlier, that inference was not to be drawn in this case.
>
> ...
>
> **[137]** [N]o scientific or medical examination can now say, with certainty, what caused Mr Cotton's cancer or lung cancer in any other particular case ... [D]espite this uncertainty, the courts must, and do, 'reduce to legal certainty [a question] to which no other conclusive answer can be given'.[7] The courts do that by asking whether it is more probable than not that X was a cause of Y. Saying only that exposure to asbestos may have been a cause of Mr Cotton's cancer is not a sufficient basis for attributing legal responsibility. Observing that a small percentage of cases of cancer were probably caused by exposure to asbestos does not identify whether an individual is one of that group. And given the small size of the percentage, the observation does not, without more, support the drawing of an inference in a particular case. The paradox, if there be one, arises from the limits of knowledge about what causes cancer.

Legislative sections such as s 5D(2) of the *Civil Liability Act 2002* (NSW) allow for factual causation to be established in an 'appropriate' or 'exceptional' case, 'in accordance with established principles' where there has been a material contribution to the harm (because material contribution to the harm is an established principle). However, the statutes of the Australian Capital Territory and South Australia only allow for 'material increase in risk' to establish factual causation. Table 3.2 outlines the variations between different state and territory jurisdictions.

Table 3.2 When 'material contribution to the harm' and 'material increase in risk' may be used to establish factual causation

	Statute	Factual causation can be satisfied by: 'Necessary condition' (BUT FOR test)	If BUT FOR test not met, in accordance with established principles (incl material contribution) in an:
NSW	*Civil Liability Act 2002* (NSW) s 5D(2)	✓	Exceptional case
QLD	*Civil Liability Act 2003* (Qld) s 11(2)	✓	Exceptional case
SA	*Civil Liability Act 1936* (SA) s 34(2)	✓	Limited to where plaintiff exposed to similar risk of harm by multiple defendants ('material risk')

7 *Bank of New South Wales v Commonwealth* (1948) 76 CLR 1, 340.

Table 3.2 *(cont.)*

	Statute	Factual causation can be satisfied by: 'Necessary condition' (BUT FOR test)	If BUT FOR test not met, in accordance with established principles (incl material contribution) in an:
Tas	*Civil Liability Act 2002* (Tas) s 13(2)	✓	Exceptional case
Vic	*Wrongs Act 1958* (Vic) s 51(2)	✓	Appropriate case
WA	*Civil Liability Act 2002* (WA) s 5C(2)	✓	Appropriate case
ACT	*Civil Law (Wrongs) Act 2002* (ACT) s 45(2)	✓	Limited to where plaintiff exposed to similar risk of harm by multiple defendants ('material risk')
NT	Common law (on duty of care and causation)	Common law	Common law

3 Material increase in risk

In the United Kingdom, a material increase in risk of the injury is treated as a material contribution to the injury.

McGhee v National Coal Board [1973] 1 WLR 1

Facts and issues

The respondent employed McGhee to do hot dusty work emptying brick kilns, but, in breach of duty, failed to provide facilities to shower after work. McGhee cycled home caked in dust and sweat. After several days after this work, he developed dermatitis.

The dermatitis was attributable to McGhee working in the brick kilns, but he could not prove that he would not have developed dermatitis had shower facilities been provided, because his exposure during work hours may have caused it anyway.

Decision

The respondent was liable because the failure to provide shower facilities materially increased the risk of dermatitis and, according to the majority, this constituted a material contribution to the injury.

Lord Reid (Lord Simon of Glaisdale and Lord Salmon substantially agreeing)

> [4] It has always been the law that a [plaintiff] succeeds if he can show that fault of the [defendant] caused or materially contributed to his injury. There may have been two separate causes but it is enough if one of the causes arose from fault of the [defendant].

The [plaintiff] does not have to prove that this cause would of itself have been enough to cause him injury.

...

[I cannot] accept the distinction drawn ... between materially increasing the risk that the disease will occur and making a material contribution to its occurrence. There may be some logical ground for such a distinction where our knowledge of all the material factors is complete. But it has often been said that the legal concept of causation is not based on logic or philosophy. It is based on the practical way in which the ordinary man's mind works in the everyday affairs of life. From a broad and practical viewpoint I can see no substantial difference between saying that what the [defendant] did materially increased the risk of injury to the [plaintiff] and saying that what the [defendant] did made a material contribution to his injury.

Lord Wilberforce

[6] [McGhee's] dermatitis resulted from a combination, or accumulation, of two causes: exposure to dust while working in hot conditions in the kiln and the subsequent omission to wash thoroughly before leaving the place of work; the second of these, but not the first, was, on the findings, attributable to the fault of the respondents. The appellant's expert was unable to attribute the injury to the second of these causes for he could not say that if the appellant had been able to wash off the dust by showers he would not have contracted the disease. He could not do more than say that the failure to provide showers materially increased the chance, or risk, that dermatitis might set in.

...

[7] [T]he employers should be liable for an injury, squarely within the risk which they created and ... they, not the [plaintiff], should suffer the consequence of the impossibility, foreseeably inherent in the nature of his injury, of segregating the precise consequence of their default.

Fairchild v Glenhaven Funeral Services Ltd [2003] 1 AC 32

Facts and issues

Three men were exposed to asbestos dust during periods of employment with several employers. Each employer breached its duty to protect the employee from the inhalation of asbestos dust.

Accepted expert evidence indicated that exposure to a single fibre of asbestos could trigger mesothelioma, so that further exposure had no impact. (Note: different expert evidence regarding cumulative asbestos exposure was accepted in *Amaca v Booth Pty Ltd* (2011) 246 CLR 36, extracted on page 107). The single-fibre theory made it impossible to prove that, but for the breach of duty by any one particular employer, the plaintiff would not have contracted mesothelioma. Had *all* the employers discharged their duty of care, however, none of the plaintiffs would have contracted mesothelioma. The question was whether this was enough for factual causation.

Decision

The House of Lords held all employers liable for the mesothelioma because each employer's breach of duty increased the risk of the employee developing mesothelioma.

Lord Bingham of Cornhill

> **[67]** … [I]f the appellants' argument is upheld … an employer may be held liable for damage he has not caused … . On the other hand, there is a strong policy argument in favour of compensating those who have suffered grave harm, at the expense of their employers who owed them a duty to protect them against that very harm and failed to do so, when the harm can only have been caused by breach of that duty and when science does not permit the victim accurately to attribute, as between several employers, the precise responsibility for the harm he has suffered … … . [S]uch injustice as may be involved in imposing liability on a duty-breaking employer in these circumstances is heavily outweighed by the injustice of denying redress to a victim.

Lord Nicholls of Birkenhead

> **[69]** In some circumstances a lesser degree of causal connection [than meeting the but for test] may suffice. This sometimes occurs where the damage flowed from one or other of two alternative causes. Take the well-known example where two hunters, acting independently of each other, fire their guns carelessly in a wood, and a pellet from one of the guns injures an innocent passer-by. No one knows, and the plaintiff is unable to prove, from which gun the pellet came. Should the law of negligence leave the plaintiff remediless, and allow both hunters to go away scot-free, even though one of them must have fired the injurious pellet?
>
> Not surprisingly, the courts have declined to reach such an unjust decision … As between the plaintiff and the two hunters, the evidential difficulty arising from the impossibility of identifying the gun which fired the crucial pellet should redound upon the negligent hunters, not the blameless plaintiff. The unattractive consequence, that one of the hunters will be held liable for an injury he did not in fact inflict, is outweighed by the even less attractive alternative, that the innocent plaintiff should receive no recompense even though one of the negligent hunters injured him … Insistence on the normal standard of causation would work an injustice. Hunting in a careless manner and thereby creating a risk of injury to others, followed by injury to another person, is regarded by the law as sufficient causal connection in the circumstances to found responsibility.

The *Fairchild* doctrine remains controversial elsewhere in Australia, including in the High Court. As the extract from French CJ's judgment in *Amaca Pty Ltd v Booth* (2011) 246 CLR 36 indicates (see [41]), the High Court has declined to accept that causation in tort is established simply because an allegedly tortious act or omission increased the risk of injury.

The Ipp Report recommended that Australia take a similar approach in appropriate cases.[8] Specific provisions within civil liability statutes in South Australia and Australian

8 *Review of the Law of Negligence: Final Report* (2002).

Capital Territory allow for material increase in risk to establish factual causation,[9] but other jurisdictions do not have equivalent provisions (see Table 3.2). Consequently, it is unclear whether material increase in risk is an 'established principle' which satisfies the 'exceptional' or 'appropriate' case in other jurisdictions.

Civil Liability Act 1936 (SA) s 34(2)–(3)

The South Australian civil liability legislation allows for a material increase in risk to establish factual causation.

> **34 General principles**
>
> ...
>
> (2) Where, however, a person (the ***plaintiff***) has been negligently exposed to a similar risk of harm by a number of different persons (the ***defendants***) and it is not possible to assign responsibility for causing the harm to any one or more of them –
>
> (a) the court may continue to apply the principle under which responsibility may be assigned to the defendants for causing the harm; but
>
> (b) the court should consider the position of each defendant individually and state the reasons for bringing the defendant within the scope of liability.
>
> (3) For the purpose of determining the scope of liability, the court is to consider (amongst other relevant things) whether or not and why responsibility for the harm should be imposed on the negligent party.
>
> ...

REVIEW QUESTIONS

(1) What is the difference between duplicative causation and pre-emptive causation?

(2) What is the difference between 'material contribution to the harm' and 'material increase in risk'?

(3) Do you think the variation in civil liability statutes dealing with multiple sufficient causes is helpful?

IV Scope of liability

Once factual causation is established, the court still needs to make a value judgment on whether the harm comes within the defendant's scope of liability – ie *should* the defendant be held responsible? Despite Australia's merged 'common sense' notion of causation, distinct doctrines persist which help decide the scope of liability: subsequent events (particularly *novus actus interveniens*), remoteness, contributory negligence and mitigation.

9 *Civil Law (Wrongs) Act 2002* (ACT) s 45(2); *Civil Liability Act 1936* (SA) s 34(2).

Concept	Short explanation	Relevant authorities	Principles text
Subsequent event	Where a subsequent event (sometimes called a *novus actus interveniens*) has caused the same harm (basic loss) or further harm (additional loss) as the harm caused by the defendant's conduct, it may be treated as breaking the chain of causation and putting the harm outside the scope of the defendant's liability.	*Chapman v Hearse* (1961) 106 CLR 112 *Alexander v Cambridge Credit Corporation Ltd* (1987) 9 NSWLR 310	Chapter 3: [3.69]–[3.114]
Remoteness	If the defendant's conduct factually caused the plaintiff's harm but the harm suffered was too remote, then it may be outside the scope of the defendant's liability.	See cases for *novus actus interveniens* in Chapters 5 and 6.	**Breach of contract** Chapter 5: [5.89]–5.104] **Tort** Chapter 6: [6.56]–[6.88] **Equitable compensation** Chapter 9: [9.54]–[9.61]
Contributory negligence	If the plaintiff's conduct contributed to the harm, then the scope of the defendant's liability may be reduced correspondingly.	See cases in Chapters 5 and 6.	**Breach of contract** Chapter 5: [5.105]–[5.114] **Tort** Chapter 6: [6.89]–[6.116] **ACL compensation** Chapter 8: [8.46]–[8.48] **Equitable compensation** Chapter 9: [9.62]–[9.66], [9.77]
Mitigation	Once the plaintiff knows (or should know of the basis of the wrong) they must mitigate their loss – ie take reasonable care of their own affairs. If they fail to do so, any harm as a result is beyond the scope of the defendant's liability.	*Burns v MAN Automotive (Aust) Pty Ltd* (1986) 161 CLR 658 *Clark v Macourt* (2013) 253 CLR 1	Chapter 3: [3.132]–[3.138]

A Subsequent event

1 Distinction between basic loss and additional loss

If the defendant's wrong factually caused the plaintiff's injury, but then a subsequent event occurs which would have caused a similar level of injury (basic loss) or causes a further level of injury (additional loss), courts must decide whether the subsequent event (sometimes called a *novus actus interveniens*) affects the scope of the defendant's liability. Many of these judgments use remoteness principles to determine whether an intervening act (including at times, an unreasonable act by the plaintiff) breaks the chain of causation.

Figure 3.2 Subsequent events

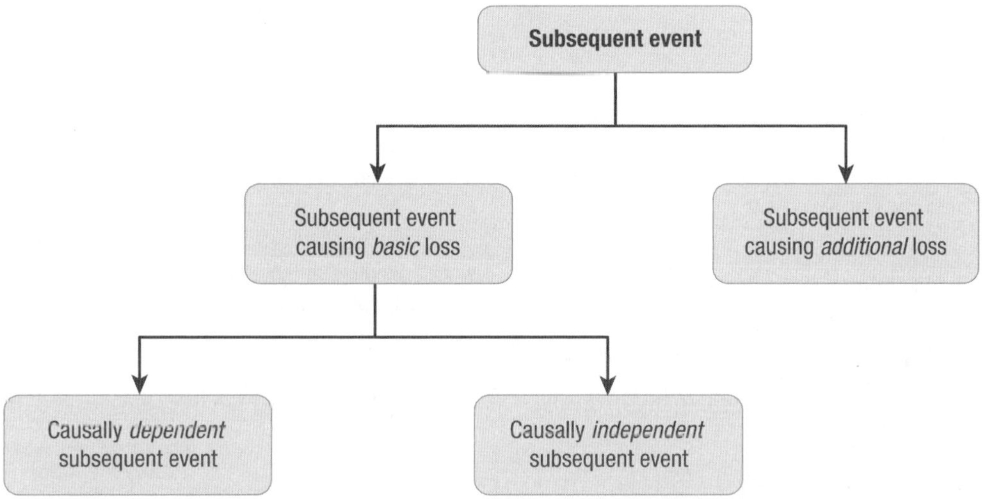

2 Additional loss: intervening event

If the additional loss would have occurred even without the defendant's wrong, the wrong is not a factual cause of the loss and the defendant is not liable. But where there is a factual causal link between the defendant's wrong and the subsequent event, the court must decide whether the basic and additional loss should still come within the *scope* of the defendant's liability. An event which 'breaks the chain of causation' between the defendant's wrong and the loss in this way is usually called an intervening event or *novus actus interveniens*.

Table 3.3 Intervening acts and qualifications to general principles

What actions might be intervening events?	Qualifications
Unforeseeable, random and uncontrollable events	• D may still be liable if D's wrong created the very risk of injury that occurred. • D might still be liable if the place was an inherently dangerous place.
Voluntary human conduct by a third party	• If third party's conduct was a normal reaction to danger, it will not be an intervening event. • If D's very duty was to guard against the risk or D's wrong generated the risk, it will not be an intervening event, unless the conduct was extremely unreasonable.
Intentional harm by a third party	• D may still be liable for intentional harm by third parties in three instances: (1) where D was under a duty to control the third party (2) where the duty breached by D aimed to prevent the very harm which occurred and (3) where D has a duty to protect P even from random, unpredictable behaviour.
Deliberate self-harm by P	• Note that there is some overlap here with *contributory negligence*.
Unreasonable conduct by P	• Again, note that there is some overlap here with *contributory negligence*.

In some negligence cases, the law regarding intervening causes has been assimilated with the question of whether the loss was too remote, as in the case below.

Chapman v Hearse (1961) 106 CLR 112

Facts and issues

On a rainy night, Chapman negligently caused a car accident which resulted in him lying unconscious on a highway. Dr Cherry, another driver, stopped to give assistance. Hearse was also driving, but failed to see Cherry or Chapman. Hearse's car hit Cherry, causing him fatal injuries. Cherry's estate sued Hearse. At trial, it was found that both Hearse and Chapman had been driving negligently, and the trial judge ordered Hearse to pay £16 584 11s 0d in damages, and Chapman to contribute a quarter of that. Hearse and Chapman appealed. The question was whether Hearse's subsequent negligent driving broke the chain of causation between Chapman's initial negligent driving and Cherry's death. Chapman argued that he should not be liable.

Decision

The High Court dismissed the appeals, holding that while it was Hearse who was 'principally responsible' for Cherry's death, it was not a *novus actus interveniens,* so Chapman was nonetheless liable to pay one-fourth of the damages.

Dixon CJ, Kitto, Taylor, Menzies and Windeyer JJ

[122] [T]he term 'reasonably foreseeable' is not, in itself, a test of 'causation'; it marks the limits beyond which a wrongdoer will not be held responsible for damage resulting from his wrongful act. This distinction is of some importance in cases such as the present where there have been successive acts of negligence and where it is sought to establish, notwithstanding the fact that the ultimate consequence might have been reasonably foreseeable at the time of the earlier act of negligence, that the later negligent act was the sole cause of the damage complained of. This … is what Chapman seeks to do … . [H]e concedes the foreseeability of some event such as that which actually happened, but asserts that as a matter of practical fact, Dr Cherry's death was caused solely by Hearse's negligent driving. It was, it is said, a case of *novus actus interveniens*, or that … Hearse's negligent driving operated to break the chain of causation between the original negligent act and Dr Cherry's death. Whether this was so or not must, we think, be very much a matter of circumstance and degree.

…

[125] There can … be no doubt that Dr Cherry's presence in the roadway was, immediately, the result of Chapman's negligent driving … . The degree of risk which his presence in the roadway entailed depended, of course, on the circumstances as they in fact existed and the circumstances were, in fact, such that the risk of injury from passing traffic was real and substantial and not, as would have been the case if the accident had happened in broad daylight, remote and fanciful. Perhaps, some confirmation for the proposition that the risk was substantial may be found in the fact that within a minute or two, or even less, Dr Cherry was run down by a driver whose vision of the roadway must have been impeded to a great extent by the prevailing conditions. In these circumstances, we have no doubt that Chapman's negligence must be regarded as a cause of Dr Cherry's death and since, for the reasons which we have given, some casualty of that character was within the realm of reasonable foreseeability the judgment against Chapman should stand.

Similarly, in some contract cases, questions of new intervening acts have also been assimilated with questions of remoteness.

Alexander v Cambridge Credit Corporation Ltd (1987) 9 NSWLR 310

Facts and issues

(See also the previous discussion on page 91.) There were two causes of the $145 million loss arising from a failed company, Cambridge Credit Corporation: the defendant's breach of contract (without which, the company would have ceased trading earlier) and a market downturn which occurred after the breach, as a result of government policy. The question was whether the market downturn was an intervening act which more closely caused the loss.

Decision

A majority of the New South Wales Court of Appeal (McHugh JA and Mahoney JA) decided that the market downturn was the true cause of the loss and either rendered the loss too remote or broke the chain of causation. Glass JA dissented on the facts, and would have held the auditors liable, but agreed with McHugh JA on the law.

McHugh JA

> [361] **Novus actus interveniens:**
> However, the common law has not been content to let liability depend only on whether the damage was reasonably foreseeable in the case of tort or within the reasonable contemplation of the parties in the case of contract. Notwithstanding that a defendant's act or omission has a causal connection with the damage of the person aggrieved, no liability arises if an independent intervening act or event in conjunction with the defendant's act or omission has brought about the plaintiff's damage and the intervening act or event can be treated in a practical sense as the sole cause of the damage. In this case the auditors contended that in a practical sense the credit squeeze was the sole cause of Cambridge's loss.
>
> Until the recent decision in *Mahony v J Kruschich (Demolitions) Pty Ltd* …, it was possible to argue in Australia that a wrongdoer was liable for all damage resulting from foreseeable intervening conduct whether it was wrongful or otherwise … . But in *Mahony's* case the High Court said (at 528):
>
>> … A line marking the boundary of the damage for which a tortfeasor is liable in negligence may be drawn either because the relevant injury is not reasonably foreseeable *or because the chain of causation is broken by a novus actus interveniens: M'Kew v Holland & Hannen & Cubbitts* … But it must be possible to draw such a line clearly before a liability for damage that would not have occurred but for the wrongful act or omission of a tortfeasor and that is reasonably foreseeable by him is treated as the result of a second tortfeasor's negligence alone: see *Chapman v Hearse* … Whether such a line can and should be drawn is very much a matter of fact and degree … . (My emphasis.)
>
> The reference to *M'Kew v Holland & Hannen & Cubbitts (Scotland) Ltd* … is instructive because that case held that a defendant had no responsibility for a second injury to which its negligence had contributed when that injury was brought about by unreasonable conduct even though the unreasonable conduct was foreseeable as likely to result from the original negligence. Moreover, *Mahony* makes it clear … that the exacerbation of an injury by negligent medical treatment though reasonably foreseeable will constitute a novus actus interveniens if the treatment is inexcusably bad or improper.
>
> It is well-established that, in contract as in tort, the intervening act, sufficient to constitute a novus actus interveniens and break the chain of causation, can be the act of a third party … . However, the intervening act of a third party will not operate as a novus actus

interveniens if the contractual duty of which the defendant is in breach was to guard against the very act of the intervener or that class of act **[362]** … . Further, an abnormal intervening event, which combines with the defendant's breach of contract to cause damage to the plaintiff, will generally break the chain of causation unless the intervening event was of a kind which was to be reasonably anticipated … .

The intervening act/s in this case

If, contrary to my view, the breach of contract by the auditors in 1971 was a cause of the loss of $145 000 000 by Cambridge the collapse of the real estate market, as the result of the policies of the then Australian government, constituted a novus actus interveniens which *in point of law* broke the causal connection.

…

… The dramatic changes in economic conditions and policies between 1972 and 1974 clearly influenced the expansion and ultimately brought about the destruction of the business of Cambridge as a real estate investor.

…

[363] Cambridge's business activities expanded dramatically while monetary policy was highly expansionary throughout the period 1972–1973. But once liquidity became very tight in the last half of the financial year 1973–1974 as the result of 'the credit squeeze engineered by the authorities', Cambridge's position became hopeless particularly as income from land sales dried up. Saddled with interest bearing debts of over $150 000 000 and, because of the policy of the then government, unable to borrow to meet its commitments and finding it difficult to sell its land in a falling market, Cambridge simply collapsed. If, contrary to my view, there was a connection between the issue of the certificates in 1971 and this collapse, it was so superseded in potency by supervening events as not to rank as a cause either in commonsense or in law. The package of economic factors together with the decisions of the directors of Cambridge to increase its borrowings and investment in real estate constituted a novus actus interveniens.

If, notwithstanding the statements in *Mahony v J Kruschich (Demolitions) Pty Ltd*, a defendant is liable for intervening events of a kind which he ought to reasonably foresee, then in my opinion the novus actus interveniens was beyond the reasonable foresight of an ordinary person or, if it matters, an auditor or businessman.

So if, contrary to my view, there was a causal connection between the breach of contract and the loss of $145 000 000, then, by reason of the novus actus interveniens, the auditors are not responsible for that loss. The package of factors, together with the investment and borrowing decisions of the directors of Cambridge after 1971, were, in a practical sense, the sole cause of the loss of $145 000 000.

However, in some cases, a defendant may be liable for the consequences of a subsequent event (even tortious conduct by a third party) where the defendant's wrong created the very risk of injury that occurred, and the injury occurred in the ordinary course of things, as in the following case.

Scott Carver Pty Ltd v SAS Trustee Corporation Ltd [2005] NSWCA 462

Facts and issues

An architecture firm, Carver, won a design competition to build a glazed pavilion. During construction, negligence by the glass installer, O'Brien, caused a waterproofing defect. Carter was negligent in designing rectifications, and Nubra and Rightway (contractors implementing the rectifications) were also negligent. SAS Trustee Corporation Ltd ('SAS') had settled with O'Brien. The question was whether O'Brien's breach was an operative cause of SAS's loss, so that damages from the defendants should be reduced. SAS argued that the subsequent conduct of Carver, Nubra and Rightway broke any causal connection between O'Brien's breach and the loss.

Decision

O'Brien was liable for the consequences of subsequent defects, because O'Brien's wrong created the very risk of injury that occurred and the injury occurred in the ordinary course of things.

Hodgson JA

> **[60]** ... [T]he question is whether the subsequent negligence of the architects and the others involved was the very kind of thing which was likely to happen when a contractor charged with installing external windows in a building which obviously would have to be water proof, did so negligently. O'Brien created a situation which would cause there to be a breakdown in the waterproofing. That may or may not be able to be rectified by some other contractors, but it clearly opened the way for there to be an ultimate problem if it was not able to be fixed or if it was sought to be fixed improperly.
>
> **[61]** It is notorious that many waterproofing problems occur in glass walled buildings .... The fact that there may be any variety of further problems when attempting to fix O'Brien's faulty workmanship indicates that this possibility is one of the very kind of things which was likely to happen. The need to fix it would obviously be very likely because the problem existed. The fact that the work to 'fix' the problem may not be appropriate is, I would have thought, something that should have been foreseen given the care that is needed in respect of waterproofing work.
>
> **[62]** In these circumstances ... the actions of Carver, Nubra and Rightway in negligently carrying out their respective tasks are not a supervening cause or nova actus interveniens severing the causal connection.
>
> ...
>
> **[65]** ... O'Brien's breach impeded the performance of works intended to waterproof the pavilion, and the fact that the efforts of others to overcome the problems created by O'Brien were, because of their negligence, not fully effective, is insufficient to destroy the causal connection between O'Brien's breach and the waterproofing problems. The negligence of persons attempting to deal with the situation created by O'Brien's negligence is not something so unusual or unforeseeable as to have that effect.

Negligent actions of a third party will not exonerate the defendant where it was the very duty of the defendant to guard against that wrong occurring or where the defendant's wrong generated the risk of injury occurring. So, for example, in *McGroder v Maguire*,[10] Maguire suffered a neck injury at work, and his employer's doctor, McGroder, negligently referred him to a chiropractor without examining him or viewing Maguire's medical records. The chiropractor negligently exacerbated the injury, making Maguire unfit for work. The chiropractor's action did not exonerate McGroder, because the doctor's very duty was to ensure Maguire was properly treated.

However, a defendant may be exonerated is if the third party was extremely unreasonable or 'inexcusably bad'.[11]

Defendants will not be liable where third parties deliberately (or even criminally) harmed the plaintiff and the defendant inadvertently provided an opportunity for this to occur, as the next case shows.

Hay Property Consultants Pty Ltd v Victorian Securities Corporation Ltd [2010] VSCA 247; (2010) 29 VR 503

Facts and issues

Victorian Securities Corporation Ltd ('VSC') engaged Hay Property Consultants Pty Ltd ('HPC') to value several properties proposed as security for a loan. HPC negligently over-valued the properties as being worth $800 000. VSC provided security for a loan of 65 per cent for $520 000. However, the real value of the properties was $575 000. The borrowers defaulted, but before VSC took possession, an unknown third party or third parties vandalised the properties, reducing the value of the properties by $215 000. VSC only realised $380 000 on the sale and had a shortfall of around $170 000. VSC sued the HPC for a breach of s 52 of the *Trade Practices Act 1974* (Cth), on the basis that the loan would not have been made 'but for' the valuation. HPC argued that if the properties had not been damaged by vandals, VSC would still have recovered the loan value, and that the true cause of the loss was the actions of the vandals.

Decision

HPC were not liable for the loss in property value resulting from the criminal damage.

Neave JA (Ashley and Hansen JA agreeing)

> **[86]** In my opinion the lender was not entitled to damages under s 82 of the TPA for the loss in value of the properties resulting from the criminal acts of third parties. The loss on resale was not an indivisible loss which was caused by the misleading representations by the valuers, but comprised two separate and distinct types of loss, one of which was attributable to the fact that the properties were damaged by third parties. I have reached that conclusion for the following reasons.

10 [2002] NSWCA 261.

11 See *Martin v Ishard* (1946) 48 WALR 52, 56 (Walker J).

> **[87]** First, although the lender would not have made the loan but for the valuers' misrepresentations, the satisfaction of the 'but for test' is not sufficient to establish that the loss was caused 'by' the negligent conduct of the valuers. …
>
> **[88]** True it is the lender would not have suffered any loss if it had not made the loan. But the misrepresentations simply initiated a train of events, commencing with the making of the loan, and did not create a legally causal relationship between the loss caused by the damage to the properties and the making of the loan. The criminal damage could have occurred regardless of the valuers' negligent misstatement.
>
> **[89]** Secondly, as I have previously said, the legal context in which the right to recover damages arises must be taken into account in resolving causation issues. The purpose and policy of the TPA does not require a negligent valuer to be held liable for loss caused by the criminal acts of third parties, except in circumstances where the original breach increased the risk that those acts would occur. …
>
> …
>
> **[91]** [A]n abnormal event intervening between the breach and the damage … breaks the chain of causation between the misleading representation and the loss suffered as the result of the subsequent criminal acts.

A difficult question arises when people are attacked at school or work by third parties when there was inadequate lighting or security measures supplied by the school or employer. Sometimes plaintiffs have recovered; however, the case below is an instance where the plaintiff did not recover.

Modbury Triangle Shopping Centre Pty Ltd v Anzil (2000) 205 CLR 254

Facts and issues

Modbury Triangle Shopping Centre Pty Ltd ('Modbury') owned a shopping centre and controlled the car park lighting. Anzil worked in a video shop at the centre. Modbury started turning off the lights before the video shop closed, and Anzil was attacked in the dark car park by three men after closing the shop. The question was whether Modbury's actions in turning off the lights had caused Anzil's injuries from the third-party attack. The Full Court of the Supreme Court of South Australia had found that Modbury was responsible for Anzil's injuries on a common sense basis.

Decision

A majority of the High Court (Kirby J dissenting) found that Modbury was not responsible for Anzil's injuries and that the true cause was the attack by the three men.

High Court, Gleeson CJ (Gaudron, Hayne and Callinan JJ agreeing)

> **[269]** The case provides an illustration of the interrelationship that sometimes exists between questions of legal responsibility and causation.

In the Full Court, it was said that common sense indicated that causation was established. However, that was against the background of a previously expressed conclusion that the appellant had a legal responsibility for the security of the first respondent.

The issue of causation in the present case arises in circumstances where the objective facts are not disputed, and there is no question about physical cause and effect. The direct and immediate cause of the injuries was the conduct of the three attackers, who were acting independently of the appellant. The conclusion that, if the car park lights had been on, the three men would not have attacked the first respondent, may or may not be dictated by common sense. Let it be supposed that it is correct, or at least not such as to warrant interference by this Court. In a case such as the present, it is difficult to see what further role common sense can play. The answer to the question whether, upon that hypothesis, the appellant's omission was a cause of the first respondent's injuries depends upon the view that is taken of the appellant's responsibilities.

... The finding on causation ... can only be justified on the basis of an erroneous view of the nature of the appellant's duties as occupier. On an accurate legal appreciation of those duties, the appellant's omission to leave the lights on might have facilitated the crime, as did its decision to provide a car park, and the first respondent's decision to park there. But it was not a cause of the first respondent's injuries.

A voluntary action undertaken in an emergency or in situations or serious inconvenience will not exonerate the defendant.

Caterson v Commissioner for Railways (1973) 128 CLR 99

Facts and issues

Caterson was assisting a friend departing on a regional train with some luggage when the train started to move off without warning, leaving Caterson's young son alone on the platform. Caterson jumped from the train and was injured. The question was whether his voluntary action (in jumping from the train) was an intervening event which exonerated the defendant.

Decision

Caterson's act did not exonerate the defendant because it was exactly the kind of thing likely to happen as a result of moving the train without warning.

High Court, Gibbs J (Barwick CJ, McTiernan, Menzies JJ agreeing in substance)

[110] [Gibbs J cited *Haynes v Harwood*].

> If what is relied upon as novus actus interveniens is the very kind of thing which is likely to happen if the want of care which is alleged takes place, the principle embodied in the maxim is no defence. The whole question is whether or not ... the accident can be said to be 'the natural and probable result' of the breach of duty.

The jury was entitled to consider that the appellant's action of jumping from the carriage was 'in the ordinary course of things' and 'the very kind of thing' likely to happen as a result of the respondent's negligence.

3 Basic loss: causally independent subsequent event

A causally independent subsequent event is one where:

- the defendant's wrong is not a factual cause of the subsequent event
- the defendant is not responsible for the subsequent event and
- the defendant's wrong pre-empted the effects of the subsequent event.

Liability depends on whether these events are actual or hypothetical, wrongful or non-wrongful.

Table 3.4 Liability of defendant for different subsequent events

Subsequent event type	Liability of defendant
Actual non-wrongful event	Not within scope
Hypothetical non-wrongful event	Not within scope
Actual wrongful event	Probably within scope
Hypothetical wrongful event	Within scope

An actual non-wrongful subsequent event features in the next case.

Kmart Australia Ltd v McCann [2004] NSWCA 283

Facts and issues

McCann was a self-employed solicitor. While in a Kmart supermarket, he was injured when a basketball set fell on his head and shoulders. He was forced to change his work practices, reducing his earnings. Fifteen months after the accident, he suffered an unrelated heart attack, which rendered him unable to work for 16 months. The trial judge awarded him damages for loss of earning capacity for that 16-month period.

Decision

The New South Wales Court of Appeal held that Kmart should not be liable for the period when he was unable to work because of the heart attack, because, even if the accident had not occurred, he would have been rendered unable to work in any case.

Pearlman AJA (Handley JA and Ipp JA agreeing)

[49] In my opinion, the trial judge erred in law in the approach that he took. It was held by the House of Lords in *Jobling v Associated Dairies Ltd* ... that the court should not disregard supervening factors in arriving at just and sufficient but not excessive compensation. That was a case where the plaintiff had suffered an accident in the course of his employment. By reason of his employers' negligence, he sustained a back injury that reduced his earning capacity by 50 per cent. He later developed a condition, unrelated to the earlier injury, that rendered him totally unfit for work. The issue was whether the liability of the employers was limited to loss of earnings up to the time when the later condition resulted in total incapacity or whether the employers were liable to pay damages for loss of earnings for the period which, in the absence of the later condition, would have represented the balance of the plaintiff's working life. It was held that the later condition had to be taken into account which had the effect of rendering the employers liable for damages only up to the emergence of the later condition. …

[50] Their Lordships were at pains to distinguish or at least question the earlier House of Lords decision of *Baker v Willoughby* … . That was a case where the plaintiff had sustained a leg injury due to the driver's negligence in a motor vehicle accident. Before his trial for damages due to that injury, he was shot in the same leg during a robbery and that necessitated the amputation of the leg. At the trial, he was awarded damages for the continued disability in his left leg, despite the fact that the disability from the first injury had been obliterated by the amputation. At least one of the bases for their Lordships in *Jobling v Associated Dairies* departing from the earlier decision was the different facts. The earlier decision concerned a supervening injury as a consequence of a later tortious act; in *Jobling v Associated Dairies,* the supervening condition was a natural event and not the consequence of a tortious act.

[51] In the present case, the facts are more analogous to those in *Jobling v Associated Dairies* than in *Baker v Willoughby* in that the respondent's stress attack was a supervening natural occurrence and not the consequence of any subsequent tortious act. To that extent at least, the decision in *Baker v Willoughby* may be put aside for present purposes. …

[52] The relevant authorities were considered at some length by Giles JA (with whom Santow JA and Windeyer J agreed) in the recent decision of *DNM Mining Pty Ltd v Barwick* … . His Honour said, at [39]:

> Since the court acts on facts rather than speculation where it can, if prior to the hearing there has been an event which would independently have caused loss in whole or part of the lost earning capacity, that event must be taken into account in determining the duration or extent of the exercise of the lost earning capacity and so in arriving at the plaintiff's damages.

[53] In the present case, the respondent's supervening stress attack had the consequence that, for a period of 16 months, his earnings were extinguished. To hold in those circumstances that the appellant should be liable to pay damages for economic loss for the second period would be to put the respondent in a better position than he would be in if he had never suffered the accident (*cf Jobling v Associated Dairies* per Lord Bridge …). That result is contrary to legal principle, and the trial judge erred in law in coming to such a result.

[54] The conclusion is that the damages assessed by the trial judge for past economic loss must be reduced insofar as they relate to the second period. That is, no damages should be awarded for economic loss in respect of the second period.

A hypothetical non-wrongful event is not within the scope of the defendant's liability, as the following case illustrates.

Calvert v William Hill Credit Ltd [2009] Ch 330

Facts and issues

The defendant bookmaker offered problem gamblers a self-exclusion option, by which the defendant would not take any bets for the next six months. Calvert requested this option, but the defendant negligently failed to implement it, and Calvert gambled away £2 million over the following six months. The trial judge found that if the self-exclusion had been properly implemented, Calvert would still have lost the same amount through betting with other bookmakers. The question was whether this limited the scope of the defendant's liability.

Decision

The scope of the defendant's liability was limited where a hypothetical event would have caused the same loss.

Lord Justice Lloyd and Lord Justice Etherton

> [**348**] The defendants did not assume responsibility to prevent the claimant from gambling. They assumed a responsibility not to allow him to place telephone bets with them. They did not assume a responsibility to prevent him from gambling in other ways – in betting shops or on the internet – nor with other bookmakers. As a matter of fact as found by the judge, he did gamble in other ways and with other bookmakers even during the time when he was betting on the telephone with the defendants. The scope of their duty was to help him to control his gambling. The harm from which their duty was intended to help protect him was gambling; it was to go some way to protect him from his gambling propensity. It follows, in our judgment, that the quantification of his loss for breach of a duty of this scope cannot as a matter of law ignore the other probable consequences of his gambling propensity. … As Mr Fenwick rightly submitted and as the judge in [**349**] substance rightly held, the defendants did not assume a responsibility to enable the claimant to gamble free from all risk.
>
> It follows, in our judgment, that the claimant's case over-concentrates on the causation element of the composite whole. … The claimant's claim does not fail, in our judgment, because his continued gambling with the defendants was his own deliberate act breaking a chain of causation; but because the scope of the defendants' duty of care did not extend to prevent him from gambling, and because the quantification of his loss cannot ignore other gambling losses which the claimant would probably have sustained but for their breach of duty. The law not only prescribes the appropriate causal connection, but also the scope of the duty and the scope of the loss which the causal connection links.

While the case above discusses hypothetical lawful conduct of the *plaintiff*, the case below discusses hypothetical lawful conduct of the defendant, where the *defendant* would have lawfully terminated the contract in any case.

Golden Strait Corporation v Nippon Yusen Kubishika Kaisha (The Golden Victory) [2007] 2 AC 353

Facts and issues

Nippon Yusen Kubishika Kaisha ('Nippon Yusen') chartered Golden Strait Corporation's ship for seven years. Clause 33 of the contract entitled Nippon Yusen to terminate if war or hostilities broke out between specified countries. Nippon Yusen repudiated the contract in December 2001, with four years of the charter still to run (until December 2005). In March 2003, the Second Gulf War broke out, involving some of the specified countries. The question was whether Golden Strait Corporation could claim damages to December 2005, given that Nippon Yusen would have been lawfully entitled to terminate the contract in March 2003 in any case.

Decision

A majority of the House of Lords found that the hypothetical lawful conduct of the defendant must be taken into account, and therefore damages were limited to the period before March 2003. Lords Bingham and Walker dissented.

Lord Bingham (Lord Walker agreeing)

Principle

[**370**] The repudiation of a contract by one party ('the repudiator'), if accepted by the other ('the injured party'), brings the contract to an end and releases both parties from their primary obligations under the contract. The injured party is thereupon entitled to recover damages against the repudiator to compensate him for such financial loss as the repudiator's breach has caused him to suffer. This is elementary law.

The damages recoverable by the injured party are such sum as will put him in the same financial position as if the contract had been performed. This is the compensatory principle which has long been recognised as the governing principle in contract. Counsel for the charterers cited certain classical authorities to make good this proposition, but it has been enunciated and applied times without number and is not in doubt. It does not, however, resolve the question whether the injured party's loss is to be assessed as of the date when he suffers the loss, or shortly thereafter, in the light of what is then known, or at a later date when the assessment happens to be made, in the light of such later events as may then be known.

An injured party such as the owners may not, generally speaking, recover damages against a repudiator such as the charterers for loss which he could reasonably have avoided by taking reasonable commercial steps to mitigate his loss. Thus where, as here, there is an available market for the chartering of vessels, the injured party's loss will be calculated on the assumption that he has, on or within a reasonable time of accepting the repudiation, taken reasonable commercial steps to obtain alternative employment for the vessel for the best consideration reasonably obtainable. This is the ordinary rule whether in fact the injured party acts in that way or, for whatever reason, does not. The actual facts are ordinarily irrelevant. The rationale of the rule is one of simple commercial fairness. The injured party owes no duty to the repudiator, but fairness requires that he should not ordinarily be permitted to rely on his own unreasonable and uncommercial conduct [**371**] to increase the loss falling on the repudiator. …

It is a general, but not an invariable, rule of English law that damages for breach of contract are assessed as at the date of breach.

…

[377] **Conclusion**

The thrust of the charterers' argument was that the owners would be unfairly over-compensated if they were to recover as damages sums which, with the benefit of hindsight, it is now known that they would not have received had there been no accepted repudiation by the charterers. There are, in my opinion, several answers to this. The first is that contracts are made to be performed, not broken. It may prove disadvantageous to break a contract instead of performing it. The second is that if, on their repudiation being accepted, the charterers had promptly honoured their secondary obligation to pay damages, the transaction would have been settled well before the Second Gulf War became a reality. The third is that the owners were … entitled to be compensated for the value of what they had lost on the date it was lost, and it could not be doubted that what the owners lost at that date was a charterparty with slightly less than four years to run. This was a clear and, in my opinion, crucial finding, but it was not mentioned in either of the judgments below, nor is it mentioned by any of my noble and learned friends in the majority. On the arbitrator's finding, it was marketable on that basis. I can readily accept that the value of a contract in the market may be reduced if terminable on an event which the market judges to be likely but not certain, but that was not what the arbitrator found to be the fact in this case. There is, with respect to those who think otherwise, nothing artificial in this approach. If a party is compensated for the value of what he has lost at the time when he loses it, and its value is at that time for any reason depressed, he is fairly compensated. That does not cease to be so because adventitious later events reveal that the market at that time was depressed by the apprehension of risks that did not eventuate. A party is not, after all, obliged to accept a repudiation: he can, if he chooses, keep the contract alive, for better or worse. …

There is, however, a further answer which I, in common with the arbitrator, consider to be of great importance. He acknowledged the force of arguments advanced by the owners based on certainty ('generally important in commercial affairs'), finality ('the alternative being a running assessment of the state of play so far as the likelihood of some interruption to the contract is concerned'), settlement ('otherwise the position will remain fluid'), consistency ('the idea that a party's accrued rights can be changed by subsequent events is objectionable in principle') and coherence ('the date of repudiation is the date on which rights and damages are assessed'). … [**378**] The importance of certainty and predictability in commercial transactions has been a constant theme of English commercial law at any rate since the judgment of Lord Mansfield CJ in *Vallejo v Wheeler* … .

Lord Scott of Foscote (Lords Carswell and Brown of Eaton-under-Heywood agreeing)

[**379**] My Lords, the answer to the question at issue must depend on principles of the law of contract. It is true that the context in this case is a charterparty, a commercial contract.

But the contractual principles of the common law relating to the assessment of damages are no different for charterparties, or for commercial contracts in general, than for contracts which do not bear that description. The fundamental principle governing the quantum of damages for breach of contract is long established and not in dispute. The damages should compensate the victim of the breach for the loss of his contractual bargain. The principle was succinctly stated by Parke B in *Robinson v Harman* ... and remains as valid now as it was then.

> The rule of the common law is, that where a party sustains a loss by reason of a breach of contract, he is, so far as money can do it, to be placed in the same situation, with respect to damages, as if the contract had been performed.

If the contract is a contract for performance over a period, whether for the performance of personal services, or for supply of goods, or, as here, a time **[380]** charter, the assessment of damages for breach must proceed on the same principle, namely, the victim of the breach should be placed, so far as damages can do it, in the position he would have been in had the contract been performed.

If a contract for performance over a period has come to an end by reason of a repudiatory breach but might, if it had remained on foot, have terminated early on the occurrence of a particular event, the chance of that event happening must, it is agreed, be taken into account in an assessment of the damages payable for the breach. And if it is certain that the event will happen, the damages must be assessed on that footing. In *The Mihalis Angelos* ..., Megaw LJ referred to events 'predestined to happen'. He said, at p. 210, that:

> ... if it can be shown that those events were, at the date of acceptance of the repudiation, predestined to happen, then ... the damages which [the claimant] can recover are not more than the true value, if any, of the rights which he has lost, having regard to those predestined events.

Another way of putting the point being made by Megaw LJ is that the claimant is entitled to the benefit, expressed in money, of the contractual rights he has lost, but not to the benefit of more valuable contractual rights than those he has lost. In *Wertheim v Chicoutimi Pulp Co.* ... Lord Atkinson referred, at 307, to:

> ... the general intention of the law that, in giving damages for breach of contract, the party complaining should, so far as it can be done by money, be placed in the same position as he would have been in if the contract had been performed

and, in relation to a claim by a purchaser for damages for late delivery of goods where the purchaser had, after the late delivery, sold the goods for a higher price than that prevailing in the market on the date of delivery, observed, at 308, that:

> ... the loss he sustains must be measured by that price, unless he is, against all justice, to be permitted to make a profit by the breach of contract, be compensated for a loss he never suffered, and be put, as far as money can do it, not in the same position in which he would have been if the contract had been performed, but in a much better position.

The result contended for by the appellant in the present case is, to my mind, similar to that contemplated by Lord Atkinson in the passage last cited. If the charterparty had not been repudiated and had remained on foot, it would have been terminated by the Charterers in or shortly after March 2003 when the Second Gulf War triggered the clause 33 termination option. But the Owners are claiming damages up to 6 December 2005 on the footing, now known to be false, that the charterparty would have continued until then. It is contended that because the Charterers' repudiation and its acceptance by the Owners preceded the March 2003 event, the rule requiring damages for breach of contract to be assessed at the date of breach requires that event to be ignored.

That contention, in my opinion, attributes to the assessment of damages at the date of breach rule an inflexibility which is inconsistent both with principle and with the authorities. The underlying principle is that the [**381**] victim of a breach of contract is entitled to damages representing the value of the contractual benefit to which he was entitled but of which he has been deprived. He is entitled to be put in the same position, so far as money can do it, as if the contract had been performed. …

…

[**383**] The arguments of the Owners offend the compensatory principle. They are seeking compensation exceeding the value of the contractual benefits of which they were deprived. Their case requires the assessor to speculate about what might happen over the period 17 December 2001 to 6 December 2005 regarding the occurrence of a clause 33 event and to shut his eyes to the actual happening of a clause 33 event in March 2003. The argued justification for thus offending the compensatory principle is that priority should be given to the so-called principle of certainty. My Lords there is, in my opinion, no such principle. Certainty is a desideratum and a very important one, particularly in commercial contracts. But it is not a principle and must give way to principle. Otherwise incoherence of principle is the likely result. The achievement of certainty in relation to commercial contracts depends, I would suggest, on firm and settled principles of the law of contract rather than on the tailoring of principle in order to frustrate tactics of delay to which many litigants in many areas of litigation are wont to resort. Be that as it may, the compensatory principle that must underlie awards of contractual damages is, in my opinion, clear …

A hypothetical wrongful event does not remove the basic loss from the scope of the defendant's liability; in other words, the defendant cannot deny liability on the basis that if he had not inflicted the loss, someone else would have wrongfully done so.

Turjman v Stonewall Hotel Pty Ltd [2011] NSWCA 392

Facts and issues

Turjman was injured when a ceiling collapsed in a nightclub run by Stonewall Hotel Pty Ltd ('Stonewall', the tenant of the building). The trial judge found that Stonewall breached the standard of care by failing to inform the structural engineer (Byatt) that the spaces were used for 'dancing/jumping', but that this breach did not cause the injuries because it was the ceiling rather than the floor which collapsed, and even if informed of the dancing activities, a competent structural engineer would not have investigated the ceiling fixings. The question was whether Stonewall's liability was reduced by the hypothetical possibility that Byatt had been negligent.

Decision

If Stonewall's duty required investigation of ceilings as well as floors, the possibility that Byatt may been negligent in assessing the ceilings would not have excused Stonewall from liability.

Giles JA (Bathurst CJ and Allsop P agreeing)

> **[82]** … [I]n the enquiry into factual causation it should be asked what a non-negligent Mr Byatt would have done had he been provided with the relevant information or, for practical purposes, what would have been required of a competent structural engineer. What would have been sufficient for a structural engineer to have done, acting reasonably in discharge of his or her retainer?
>
> …
>
> **[99]** The course reasonably taken by the structural engineer would begin from the task required of him or her, that is, certification that the hotel building was structurally sound and capable of withstanding the likely loadings arising from its use. This was concerned with structural elements, not the ceiling … [Turjman] did not establish that, had Stonewall provided the relevant information to Mr Byatt, the adequacy of the fastening of the ceiling would have been investigated by the competent structural engineer.

An actual wrongful event means that the harm is probably within the scope of the defendant's liability, as illustrated by the next case.

DNM Mining Pty Ltd v Barwick [2004] NSWCA 137

Facts and issues

Barwick sustained a back injury in DNM Mining Pty Ltd's ('DNM') mine due to negligence, and could no longer work as a miner. He instead worked as a farmworker, but after a car accident on the way home from the farm caused neck and shoulder injuries, the combination of back, neck and shoulder injuries made him unfit for any work. The car accident therefore caused basic loss (substantially similar to the loss caused by the mining accident) as well as additional loss (reducing his work capacity to zero). Although the defendant's wrong factually caused part of the loss of future earning capacity, there was a question whether the subsequent accident put any loss of future earnings beyond the scope of the defendant's liability.

Decision

The New South Wales Court of Appeal reduced the plaintiff's compensation on the basis that only loss of earning capacity from the mining accident which would not have been lost in the car accident was compensable.

Giles JA (Santow and Windeyer JJ agreeing)

[39] In recognition of the object of the award of damages, it is necessary to allow, amongst other positive and negative contingencies, for the contingency that the lost earning capacity would have been lost in whole or part from a cause independent of the defendant's tortious act. The earnings which the lost earning capacity would have brought to the plaintiff would have been more or less according to the duration and extent of its exercise, and there would be over-compensation if the lost earning capacity were valued regardless of the possibility that it would otherwise have been lost. Since the court acts on facts rather than speculation where it can, if prior to the hearing there has been an event which would independently have caused loss in whole or part of the lost earning capacity, that event must be taken into account in determining the duration or extent of the exercise of the lost earning capacity and so in arriving at the plaintiff's damages.

[41] … It would be absurd to take account of the contingency of death or illness when hypothetical but refuse to take account of it when a known fact, and similarly for the contingency of accident.

…

[47] It may be that [Barwick's] loss of earning capacity from the mining accident was not wholly overtaken by the loss of earning capacity from the car accident. But that is not an answer to [DNM's] submissions. Even if there were some ongoing effect of the back injury on earning capacity, it was necessary to consider whether the neck and shoulder injuries would have incapacitated the respondent from working as a miner. If they would have, continuing economic loss assessed on the basis that he could work as a miner should not have been awarded. The contingency of the car accident was known as a fact at the time of the hearing, and account had to be taken of it. In not doing so the judge was in error, and his award of damages for economic loss cannot stand.

…

[53] [A] broadly assessed lump sum must be struck to allow for any loss of earning capacity in the mining accident which would not have been lost in the car accident.

This can be compared with the English case below.

Baker v Willoughby [1970] AC 467

Facts and issues

Baker suffered an injury to his left leg in a car accident caused by Willoughby, with the possibility of future degeneration of his leg. Subsequently, he was shot in the injured leg in an armed robbery, and the leg had to be amputated. The question was whether the shooting had removed the effect of the accident, so that no losses after the second accident could be claimed against Willoughby.

Decision

Both the accident and the shooting contributed to Baker's disability, and therefore Willoughby was liable for Baker's losses due to having a stiff leg rather than a healthy leg, even though after the shooting the leg was amputated.

Lord Reid

> **[2]** After the accident [Baker] tried various kinds of work, finding some too heavy by reason of his partial incapacity. In November 1967 he was engaged in sorting scrap metal and while he was alone one day two men came in, demanded money, and, when they did not get it, one of them shot at him. The shot inflicted such serious injuries to his already damaged leg that it had to be amputated. Apparently he made a fairly good recovery but his disability is now rather greater than it would have been if he had not suffered this second injury. He now has an artificial limb whereas he would have had a stiff leg.
>
> [Baker] argues that the loss which he suffered from the car accident has not been diminished by his second injury. He still suffers the same kind of loss of the amenities of life and he still suffers from reduced capacity to earn though these may have been to some extent increased. And he will still suffer these losses for as long as he would have done because it is not said that the second injury curtailed his expectation of life.
>
> [Willoughby] on the other hand argues that the second injury removed the very limb from which the earlier disability had stemmed, and that therefore no loss suffered thereafter can be attributed to [his] negligence. He says that the second injury submerged or obliterated the effect of the first and that all loss thereafter must be attributed to the second injury. ...
>
> ...
>
> If it were the case that in the eye of the law an effect could only have one cause then [Willoughby] might be right. It is always necessary to prove that any loss for which damages can be given was caused by the defendant's negligent act. But it is a commonplace that the law regards many events as having two causes: that happens whenever there is contributory negligence for then the law says that the injury was caused both by the negligence of the defendant and by the negligence of the plaintiff. And generally it does not matter which negligence occurred first in point of time.
>
> I see no reason why [Baker's] present disability cannot be regarded as having two causes ... .

4 Basic loss: causally dependent subsequent event

This section deals with cases where each of the defendant's wrong and a subsequent event were sufficient to bring about the loss, and the subsequent event would not have occurred 'but for' the defendant's wrong. Whether the defendant is liable depends upon the 'scope of liability' of the defendant.

Faulkner v Keffalinos (1970) 45 ALJR 80

Facts and issues

Keffalinos was injured in two successive car accidents – but only the first was due to the wrong of Faulkner (his employers at the time). Should Faulkner's liability for loss of earning capacity be reduced to take into account the fact that further injuries had been incurred as a result of the (unrelated) second accident?

Decision

Damages for future earning capacity were reduced because such awards generally had to be discounted to allow for possible contingencies, and here, the second accident was a contingency that had actually occurred. Even though 'but for' the defendant's wrong, Keffalinos may not have been injured in the second accident, this did not mean Faulkner's wrong caused the second accident 'in any relevant sense'.

Windeyer J

> [**85**] … [I]n assessing damages for the destruction or reduction of earning capacity an allowance must ordinarily be made for the contingency—if in the particular case it is seen as a reasonable possibility—of interruptions of a man's working life by periods of unemployment, sickness or accident. If in fact any of such things occurs before the assessment has to be made, what would have been allowed for as a possibility has become an actuality: the risk of an interruption of earnings has materialised and a hypothetical deduction to be made in the computation of damages has crystallised. It is therefore a mistake to think of damages recoverable for the consequences of the first accident as diminished by the second accident. So far as the damages result from the impairment of earning capacity, the second accident merely supplies a measure of one thing that must be taken into account, namely the risk of an accident.
>
> [**86**] The consequences that flow from the second accident cannot I think be regarded as caused, in any relevant sense, by the respondents' tort. I realise that philosophers and casuists may see these as indirect consequences. But for the first accident, [Keffalinos] might still have been employed by [Faulkner], and therefore not where he was when the second accident happened: but lawyers must eschew this kind of 'but for' or sine qua non reasoning about cause and consequence.

B Remoteness of damage

There are two definitions of remoteness: a narrow and a wide definition. In the narrow sense, remoteness of damage is concerned only with the question of whether damage is foreseeable. In the wide sense, remoteness is concerned with foreseeability and intervening acts. Here, we are concerned with the former. In terms of ascertaining whether damage is foreseeable, among other things, it is relevant whether the defendant intended to cause that harm, and whether or not the damage was unusual or to be expected.

The test for remoteness varies according to the specific cause of action involved. For intentional torts, liability under the *Australian Consumer Law* and equitable compensation, the remoteness tests are more generous to plaintiffs. For contract, the remoteness test is less generous to a plaintiff, and some other torts (such as negligence) fall somewhere in between contract and intentional torts. For discussion on remoteness:

- in breach of contract, see Chapter 5
- in tort, see Chapter 6
- under the *Australian Consumer Law*, see Chapter 8
- in equitable compensation, see Chapter 9.

C The purpose of the duty breached

Where the purpose of the duty breached is to prevent one kind of harm, but the breach instead factually causes another kind of harm, the harm will generally be beyond the scope of the defendant's liability.

Roads and Traffic Authority v Royal [2008] HCA 19; (2008) 245 ALR 653

Facts and issues

Royal was injured in a car accident which was found to be one-third his fault and two-thirds the fault of the other driver. Royal claimed that the Roads and Traffic Authority ('RTA') breached its duty to prevent collisions by constructing a staggered T intersection with better visibility. The question was whether Royal's injuries fell within the scope of the RTA's liability to road users.

Decision

While the intersection had poor visibility and the RTA had a duty to prevent collisions by constructing an intersection with good visibility, this accident was not caused by visibility issues, and therefore the injuries were outside the scope of the RTA's liability.

Gummow, Hayne and Heydon JJ

> **[25]** The problem – the danger, the risk – thus discussed, however, had nothing to do with the collision in question. The problem or danger or risk was that where two vehicles were approaching in adjoining lanes, one might obscure the other. That did not happen in this case. It was clear from the evidence … that the defendant's vehicle was not obscured from the plaintiff's view by another vehicle. … [E]ven if it could be said that the appellant's breach of duty 'did materially contribute' to the occurrence of *an* accident, 'by creating a heightened risk of such an accident' due to the obscuring effect of one vehicle on another in an adjoining lane, it made no contribution to the occurrence of *this* accident.
>
> …

> **[32]** … Discussions about the effect of a novus actus interveniens necessarily assume that a breach of duty has been causative. In the majority's view, there was a potential risk of injury, depending on the position of the cars on the Pacific Highway in any given circumstances, arising from the problem of one car masking another in an adjoining lane. That risk did not exist in relation to any of the cars involved in this collision: there was no car on the defendant's left masking it from the plaintiff.

Similarly, the following case deals with a consideration of these issues in light of s 5D of the *Civil Liability Act 2002* (NSW).

Wallace v Kam (2013) 250 CLR 375

Facts and issues

Dr Kam performed a surgical procedure on Wallace which had two risks: (1) *neurapraxia* (temporary damage to nerves in the thighs) and (2) permanent, catastrophic paralysis. Dr Kam did not inform Wallace of either risk, but it was found that Wallace would have still undergone the operation if he had been informed of the first risk (which was the risk which eventuated).

Should Dr Kam's liability extend to the neurapraxia given that Wallace would have chosen to undergo surgery if Kam had warned him only about the risk of neurapraxia?

Decision

The purpose of a doctor's duty to warn of risks is to protect the patient from the occurrence of an injury the risk of which is unacceptable to the patient. The duty does not aim to protect the patient from an injury the risk of which the patient is prepared to accept.

French CJ, Crennan, Kiefel, Gageler and Keane JJ

> [**389**] Consideration of a case involving the materialisation of one of a number of distinct risks of different physical injuries makes it necessary to return to the nature of the duty and the policy that underlies its imposition. The duty of a medical practitioner to warn the patient of material risks inherent in a proposed treatment is imposed by reference to the underlying common law right of the patient to choose [**390**] whether or not to undergo a proposed treatment. However, the policy that underlies requiring the exercise of reasonable care and skill in the giving of that warning is neither to protect that right to choose nor to protect the patient from exposure to all unacceptable risks. The underlying policy is rather to protect the patient from the occurrence of physical injury the risk of which is unacceptable to the patient. It is appropriate that the scope of liability for breach of the duty reflect that underlying policy.
>
> The appropriate rule of attribution, or 'rule of responsibility' to use the language of Allsop P, is therefore one that 'seeks to hold the doctor liable for the consequence of material risks that were not warned of [and] that were unacceptable to the patient'. The

> normative judgment that is appropriate to be made is that the liability of a medical practitioner who has failed to warn the patient of material risks inherent in a proposed treatment 'should not extend to harm from risks that the patient was willing to hazard, whether through an express choice or as found had their disclosure been made'.

D The plaintiff's contribution to the loss

A plaintiff's unreasonable act may affect the scope of liability under three overlapping doctrines: intervening event (discussed above), contributory liability or mitigation.

1 Contributory negligence

Contributory negligence generally concerns the plaintiff's unreasonable conduct which contributes to the original event by which the defendant's wrong causes harm. Mitigation concerns the plaintiff's conduct once they are aware (or should be aware) of the defendant's wrong. From then on, the plaintiff has a duty to mitigate their loss, that is, to take reasonable care of their own affairs to minimise loss flowing from the defendant's wrong. Sometimes, however, courts have found contributory negligence flowing from the plaintiff's unreasonable conduct after discovering the defendant's wrong, creating some overlap with mitigation.

It should be noted at this point that contributory negligence is generally regarded as something related to torts specifically (see Chapter 6) and that, often, questions of the plaintiff's own contribution to their loss are dealt with by mitigation in contract (see Chapter 5). However, contributory negligence can also be a factor under the *Australian Consumer Law* (as described in Chapter 8). It is not generally a factor which operates in equitable compensation (as described in Chapter 9).

Smith v Badenoch [1970] SASR 9

Facts and issues

Badenoch, a farmer, started a fire in order to clear the land, and negligently allowed it to spread to Smith's adjoining land. Smith became aware of the fire just before midnight, but did not call fire services until 7:30 am the next morning. The question was whether Smith's failure to call fire services contributed to his loss.

Decision

Badenoch was liable for the damage to the plaintiff's land, but damages were reduced by 15 per cent to account for Smith's contribution to the damage.

Zelling J

> **[15]** I am … of opinion that [Smith] was negligent in not seeking assistance at or immediately after 11.45 p.m. It is obvious from [the statement of a particular witness] that had the

Emergency Fire Services been called at 11.45 p.m. or thereabouts they would have come and that they could have fought the fire effectively by night as well as by day. [Smith] gives various reasons such as the difficulty of the terrain, the fact that the police had given him certain advice in previous cases, and that because the wind was dropping he had no real fear of the fire spreading. The third of these is I think probably his true reason, and it means to my mind that he decided to take a calculated risk of doing nothing before 7.30 the following morning. In doing so, in my opinion, he showed lack of proper care for the safety of his own property and he was guilty of contributory negligence. Had he summoned the Emergency Fire Services unit at near midnight the fire could have been confined to a very small area of [Smith's] property.

2 Mitigation

Edelman in *McGregor on Damages* sums mitigation into three rules:

(1) a defendant is not liable for loss which the plaintiff incurred but could have avoided by acting reasonably ('avoidable loss')

(2) a plaintiff can recover losses incurred in reasonable attempts to mitigate loss, even if those attempts made the loss worse ('mitigation costs') and

(3) a defendant is not liable for loss which the plaintiff did not incur because they met (or went beyond) their duty to mitigate ('avoided loss' – whether the loss was incurred or not is an assessment of compensation issue – discussed in Chapter 2).[12]

The next extract explains McGregor's approach to mitigation.

Harvey McGregor, 'Mitigation in the Assessment of Damages' in D Saidov and R Cunnington (eds), *Contract Damages: Domestic and International Perspectives* (Hart, 2008) 329

[329] At the outset we must distinguish between two aspects of mitigation … the one, and the much more frequently invoked, relating to loss that should have been avoided, the other to loss that has in fact been avoided. The terms which I use here … are therefore avoidable loss and avoided loss.

[330] Avoidable loss

The rule is simple: the … party who has suffered a breach of contract … **[331]** is required to take all reasonable steps to cut down and reduce his loss consequent on the breach of contract and may not claim for any part of the loss which is due to his neglect of taking such steps. … [T]he crucial

12 J Edelman, *McGregor on Damages* (Sweet & Maxwell, 20th ed, 2018) [9–004]–[9–006].

question in each case is whether the aggrieved party has acted, or has failed to act, reasonably. Adding causation into the mix gives no assistance in answering this question.

When it comes to ascertaining whether the aggrieved party has acted reasonably, which is what he is required to do … two features of this requirement immensely favourable to the aggrieved party must be kept in mind. The first, established very early in *Roper v Johnson*, is that the burden of proof on the issue of mitigation lies on the contracting party in breach, and thus in contrast to the position with remoteness. [**332**] The second feature favourable to the complaining party is that the standard of reasonableness is not an exacting one. The rationale for this has been best put by Lord Macmillan in *Banco de Portugal v Waterlow*, where he laid down that the measures adopted by a contracting party to extricate himself from the position in which he has been placed by the breach of contract 'ought not to be weighed in nice scales at the instance of the party whose breach of contract has occasioned the difficulty'. He added that the law is satisfied if the aggrieved party has acted reasonably 'in the adoption of remedial measures and he will not be held disentitled to recover the cost of such measures merely because the party in breach can suggest that other measures less burdensome to him might have been taken' … .

In countless cases the issue of mitigation does not make an appearance. While this is commonly because the aggrieved party has in his own interests taken the necessary steps in mitigation, it can also be because, the way to mitigation being so clear, mitigation has become incorporated into the normal measure of damages. When this happens mitigation loses its identity and does not expressly appear as a separate issue. This is particularly true where the sale of goods is concerned. Thus, if a seller fails to deliver the goods contracted for, the buyer cannot sit back on a rising market, or wait till his sub-sale to a third party has fallen through, but must go into the market with all reasonable speed and buy equivalent goods there … . … [**333**] … The normal measure of damages in cases of sale of goods, or shares, not delivered or not accepted is therefore the difference between the contract price and the market price, assuming an available market. The time of assessment is generally at breach, so the market price is taken as at that date; this is the so-called breach date rule … . Mitigation therefore does not come into it and there is no need to say that the failure to replace or to resell is not a failure to mitigate.

…

[336] Avoided loss

…

[**337**] … [W]hat is the difference between avoidable loss and avoided loss when the loss is avoided by action after the breach by the aggrieved contracting party? Can it not be said that such avoided loss [**338**] simply represents the result of his carrying out his so-called duty to avoid loss? It is in fact a good deal more than that. It is where the aggrieved party has gone further than he need and, by sound action, has avoided more loss than the dictates of the law required of him.

The tricky question is: when is conduct giving rise to a benefit to be taken into account? [I]n *British Westinghouse* … Viscount Haldane formulated the basic rule … 'the subsequent transaction, if to be taken into account, must be one arising out of the consequences of the breach' and, further, that it 'formed part of a continuous dealing with the situation … and was not an independent or disconnected transaction'. For what it is worth, my own formulation, in addition to these, is that the benefit must arise out of the mitigating act itself.

The next cases involve an application of the 'avoidable loss' rule.

Burns v MAN Automotive (Aust) Pty Ltd (1986) 161 CLR 658

Facts and issues

In 1977, Burns entered into a hire-purchase contract whereby MAN Automotive (Aust) Pty Ltd ('MAN') agreed to supply him with a prime mover truck. MAN warranted that the engine of the vehicle had been fully reconditioned. The truck broke down repeatedly. One year after purchase, in 1978, Burns learned that the engine had not been reconditioned. He could not afford to have the truck reconditioned, nor to hire a new truck, and MAN refused to recondition it. He could no longer complete lucrative interstate haulage contracts because the truck was so defective, and instead he used it for less lucrative work within Queensland. In 1979, a year after Burns discovered the fault with the engine, it broke down totally, and Burns was forced to leave it by the roadside, where it was repossessed by the hire-purchase company.

The trial judge found that if the truck had complied with the warranty, it would have operated for four years (until 1981) and awarded his loss of earnings for that full four-year period. He had in fact also made actual losses by being forced to undertake less lucrative intrastate haulage.

The Queensland Court of Appeal held that Burns could not recover either his loss of potential earnings or his actual losses once he discovered the true state of the engine in 1978. Burns appealed to the High Court.

Decision

Burns's appeal was dismissed by a majority of the High Court. Wilson, Deane and Dawson JJ treated it as an issue of remoteness and held that all losses suffered after the breakdown of the truck were too remote.

Gibbs CJ considered that Burns's losses of potential earnings for four years were not too remote, but Burns had not done all that was reasonable to mitigate his damage (specifically, it was not reasonable to carry on business once he knew he was operating at a loss) and therefore his actual losses suffered during that period were unrecoverable. Brennan J wrote a strong dissent where he argued that Burns's impecuniosity was caused by MAN's breach, and thus entirely foreseeable, or, in the alternative, his decision not to mitigate was reasonable.

Gibbs CJ

> **[658]** Loss of profits for the 4 years during which the reconditioned engine could probably have been used was within the reasonable contemplation of the parties as a consequence of a breach of the warranty. Any damage from a breach of the contract, reasonably within the contemplation of the parties when the contract was made, is recoverable even though the appellant's impecuniosity contributed to it.
>
> … [T]he appellant was bound to take all reasonable steps to mitigate the loss. One course open to him was to have the engine reconditioned or to buy another to replace it. However his impecuniosity prevented him from taking that course. The question whether

the appellant is [**659**] debarred from claiming damages attributable to his failure to take steps in mitigation, when he was unable to take those steps because of his lack of means, must be answered in the negative.

A plaintiff's duty to mitigate does not require him to do what is unreasonable and it would seem unjust to prevent a plaintiff from recovering damages caused by breach of contract because he lacked means to avert the consequences of the breach. [T]he financial difficulties of the appellant were largely brought about by the respondent in supplying him with a defective engine and refusing properly to rectify the defects, although the respondent should have known that the appellant lacked resources to pay to have the engine reconditioned.

...

[**660**] For these reasons it appears to me that the appellant is entitled to recover whatever damage he suffered by loss of profits that would otherwise have been earned during the 4 years of effective life of the motor.

However, it was not reasonable for him to carry on his business with the defective prime mover, once he knew that he was operating at a loss and should have known that he had no prospect of making a profit. This was not a case of a purchaser locked into a business; the appellant was under no compulsion to go on losing money. It was not wrong to hold that the respondent should not be charged with actual losses incurred by the appellant after June 1978, although the appellant was entitled to loss of profit suffered after that date.

Brennan J (dissenting)

[**673**] When an act on the part of the person to whom a warranty is given is needed to put an end to losses resulting from breach of the warranty, foreseeability provides no different limitation on damages from the limitation which is imposed by a failure to act reasonably in mitigation of damage. A party who, when he gives a warranty, has such knowledge that he can foresee that the loss which will result from a breach of the warranty will continue until the other party acts to stop the loss, can foresee that the loss will continue until it is reasonable to expect that the injured party will act to stop it. Foreseeability extends until it would be unreasonable for the injured party to fail to act to mitigate his loss, and the onus of proving such a failure is on the party in breach.

[**674**] Unless the respondent showed that the appellant unreasonably failed to avoid the losses incurred after July 1978, those losses were as foreseeable after July 1978 as they were before. Apart from foreseeability (in the sense explained in *Victoria Laundry*), a plaintiff must show that the loss he seeks to recover results from the breach of contract relied on. If the loss results from some extraneous factor, the plaintiff fails to establish the essential causal link between the breach and the loss.

His Honour discussed *Liesbosch, Dredger v Edison, SS (Owners)*[13] ('The Liesbosch') and continued:

[**675**] The finding of fact which Lord Wright was prepared to make in *The Liesbosch* cannot be made here. The appellant's impecuniosity in this case was itself caused by or

13 [1933] AC 449.

contributed to by the breach of warranties which founded the action. The appellant's losses incurred prior to July 1978 would have diminished any capacity he might otherwise have had to outlay $7000 or $8000 to have the engine reconditioned. …

The limitation placed on the recovery of loss resulting from breach of contract when the loss would have been avoided by the injured party taking reasonable steps to mitigate the loss is not so draconian as to deny recovery to an impecunious victim who, if he were not impecunious, could have avoided the loss but who, being impecunious, has suffered it. …

…

[**676**] The choices which confronted the appellant in July 1978 were fourfold: to complain to the respondent and request it to recondition the engine, to terminate the hire-purchase agreement, to pay to repair the engine to a condition where the vehicle could be used for haulage on a reduced scale, or to pay the full cost of reconditioning. Consider each of those choices. The first was not available. Though the appellant sought redress from the respondent it was refused. … The second option would have left the appellant without any prospect of working his way out of the Esanda debt [to the hire-purchase company]. … However, it was reasonable to try to haul supplies to the central Queensland coal mines in an effort to earn sufficient to pay out the hire-purchase liability. That was the third choice and the one he took: by revising the hire-purchase agreement in July 1978, he obtained the money to pay for the needed repairs and he thus obtained a chance to use the vehicle profitably. The fourth choice would have involved an outlay of $7000 to $8000 which he did not have. He was not bound to take [**677**] it. …

It would be wrong to find that the course taken by the appellant in having some repairs done to the engine in 1978 was an unreasonable step to take in mitigating his loss unless it appeared that he was bound to suffer further losses when he went back on the road. The respondent, on whom the onus lay, did not establish that fact.

Clark v Macourt (2013) 253 CLR 1

Facts and issues

Dr Macourt sold the business of St George Fertility Centre to Dr Clark for $386 950.01. A term of the contract warranted that all relevant consents and identifying information was provided for all donor sperm – this was incorrect and 1996 of the straws of sperm could not be legally used. It was also illegal for a doctor to treat donor sperm as a commodity – by profiting from making it available to patients. It cost Clark $1.2 million to purchase and ship replacement sperm which met the applicable legal and ethical requirements. This cost was passed on to patients via a levy, but Clark made no profit on it. Clark claimed $1.2 million in damages for breach of contract. The trial judge awarded her $1 246 025.01, but this was overturned by the New South Wales Court of Appeal. On appeal to the High Court, the question was whether this was a case of 'avoided loss', that is, Clark had placed herself in a better place than if the contract had been performed.

Decision

The majority found that it was irrelevant that Clark had passed on the costs of obtaining the compliant sperm to patients, because the substitute performance was neither better nor worse in quality that the original performance. Mitigation principles did not apply, so she was able to recover the $1.2 million. Gageler J dissented on other grounds (measurement of loss).

Hayne J

> [8] **Mitigation?**
> As already noted, however, the Court of Appeal concluded that the appellant had mitigated her loss by buying replacement sperm from Xytex. In respect of 'the loss of each straw of replacement sperm actually sourced from Xytex' before the date of assessment of damages, Tobias AJA concluded that the chief component of the appellant's 'loss' would be 'the sum (if any) representing that part of the overall cost of acquisition of that straw not recouped from a patient'. And in respect of 'the residue of the 'lost' 1996 straws over and above those in fact replaced by Xytex sperm up to the date of trial', Tobias AJA concluded that 'the appropriate course would have been to assume that [the appellant] would continue to source straws of donor sperm from Xytex at a cost consistent with that which had prevailed since August 2005, and that she would continue to recoup from patients the same proportion of that cost as she had done in the past'. On this footing, Tobias AJA concluded that the appellant's damages in respect of straws not 'replaced' would be 'the aggregate of the discounted present value of the *un-recouped* balances (if any) of that cost as at the date of their assessment'. [Emphasis added.]
>
> Two points must be made about this analysis. First, the calculations described would reveal whether, and to what extent, the appellant was, or would be, worse off as a result of the breach of warranty. That is, the calculations of the net amount which the appellant had outlaid, and would thereafter have to outlay, would reveal the amount needed to put [**9**] the appellant in the position she would have been in *if the contract had not been made*. The calculations would not, and did not, identify the value of what the appellant would have received *if the contract had been performed*.
>
> Secondly, the reference to mitigation of damage was apt to mislead. In order to explain why, it is necessary to say something about what is meant by 'mitigation' of damage.
>
> For present purposes, 'mitigation' can be seen as embracing two separate ideas. First, a plaintiff cannot recover damages for a loss which he or she *ought to have* avoided, and secondly, a plaintiff cannot recover damages for a loss which he or she *did* avoid.
>
> The Court of Appeal's analysis, and the respondent's argument in this court, both depended upon engaging the second of these propositions. In this court, the respondent submitted, correctly, that it is a proposition recognised in the speech of Viscount Haldane LC in *British Westinghouse Electric & Manufacturing Co Ltd v Underground Electric Railways Co of London Ltd*. But there remains for consideration how the proposition applied in this case.
>
> The appellant's subsequent purchases and use of replacement sperm left her neither better nor worse off than she was before she undertook those transactions. In particular, unlike British Westinghouse and other cases referred to in the speech of Viscount Haldane,

the appellant obtained no relevant benefit from her subsequent purchases of sperm. The purchases replaced what the vendor had agreed to supply.

The purchase price paid for the replacement sperm revealed the value of what was lost when the vendor did not perform the contract. But the commercial consequences flowing from the appellant's subsequent use of those replacements would have been relevant to assessing the value of what should have been supplied under the contract only if she had obtained some advantage from their use, or if she had alleged that the replacement transactions had left her even worse off than she already was as a result of the vendor's breach.

If she had obtained some advantage, the value of the advantage would have mitigated the loss she otherwise suffered. If she had been left even worse off (for example by losing profit that otherwise would have been made), that additional loss may have aggravated her primary loss. But the appellant was not shown to have obtained any advantage from the later transactions and she did not claim that they had left her any worse [**10**] off. Those transactions neither mitigated nor aggravated the loss she suffered from the vendor not supplying what it had agreed to supply. The value of that loss was revealed by what the appellant paid to buy replacement sperm from Xytex.

Showing that the appellant had charged, or could charge, third parties (her patients) the amount she had paid to acquire replacement sperm from Xytex was irrelevant to deciding what was the value of what the vendor should have, but had not, supplied. If the contract had been performed according to its terms, the appellant would have had a stock of sperm having the warranted qualities which she could use as she chose. She could have stored it, given it away or used it in her practice. In particular, she could have used it in her practice and charged her patients nothing for its supply. But because the vendor breached the contract, the appellant could put herself in the position she should have been in (if the contract had been performed) only by buying replacement sperm from Xytex. Whatever transactions she then chose to make with her patients are irrelevant to determining the value of what should have been, but was not, provided under the contract.

Gageler J (dissenting)

[**22**] The primary judge found that the company's failure to deliver 3500 contractually compliant straws of frozen sperm deprived Dr Clark of the expected use in the normal course of her practice of 1996 of those straws. To what extent was Dr Clark worse off in that factual position of non-fulfilment of her contractual expectation of taking possession of frozen sperm of which she could have used 1996 straws in the normal course of her practice than she would have been in the counterfactual position of having that contractual expectation fulfilled? Dr Clark was worse off to the extent that later she was forced to incur, but was not able to recoup from her patients, the additional costs of sourcing 1996 straws of sperm from an alternative supplier.

Keane J

[**36**] To say that in the conduct of [Clark's] practice she was able to recover the cost to her of the Xytex sperm incurred in the course of her practice after acquiring the assets is

> to fail to address the claim which [she] actually made. The loss for which [Clark] claimed compensation occurred at the completion of the Deed, at which time the assets which she acquired were not as valuable as they would have been had St George's performance measured up to its warranties. … [A]t the completion of the Deed, if [Clark] had been minded to on-sell her business **[37]** (enhanced by the acquisition of the assets from St George) the value of that business would have been substantially less because much of the stock in trade could not have been profitably deployed by the purchaser. …
>
> … [Clark] suffered a real loss in terms of the benefit of her bargain at the date of completion of the acquisition of the assets [in] … another way. [She] may have been able to charge fees for her services in the conduct of her practice which were within the market range but returned her a greater profit because she was not obliged to incur the extra cost of replacement sperm. Whether or not she chose to realise the value of compliant St George sperm in this way was a matter for her. Whether or not she would have been disposed to take such a course was not explored in evidence at trial; but that is not a deficit in her claim. She was entitled to claim the measure of damages under the ruling principle without going into such matters.

While mitigation applies strictly to contract, it can apply less strictly to intentional torts involving fraud.

Doyle v Olby (Ironmongers) Ltd [1969] 2 QB 158

Facts and issues

Doyle purchased an ironmonger's business from Olby, relying on Olby's accounts for the preceding three years which showed satisfactory turnover and annual profits. Having undertaken significant liabilities, Doyle found that Olby had misrepresented the turnover and that Olby's brother had, contrary to Olby's representations, retained part of the business and was trading in competition with him. After three years' disastrous efforts to trade, Doyle sold the business but was left with liabilities of some £4000 (he had taken out loans to keep the business afloat). The question was whether the additional consequential loss was recoverable, or was too remote, and in what circumstances a plaintiff might have to mitigate.

Decision

Principles of mitigation apply in actions for fraud, but they apply in a less stringent manner. Here, Doyle's actions were reasonable, and there was nothing more he could have done to avoid consequential losses.

Lord Denning

> **[167]** The object of damages is to compensate the plaintiff for all the loss he has suffered, so far, again, as money can do it. In contract, the damages are limited to what may

reasonably be supposed to have been in contemplation of the parties. In fraud, they are not so limited. The defendant is bound to make reparation for all the actual damages directly flowing from the fraudulent inducement. The person who has been defrauded is entitled to say: 'I would not have entered into this bargain at all but for your representation. Owing to your fraud, I have not only lost all the money I paid you, but, what is more, I have been put to a large amount of extra expense as well and suffered this or that extra damages.' All such damages can be recovered: and it does not lie in the mouth of the fraudulent person to say that they could not reasonably have been foreseen. [I]n this … case Mr Doyle has not only lost the money which he paid for the business, which he would never have done if there had been no fraud … but also he has been put to expense and loss in trying to run a business which has turned out to be a disaster for him. He is entitled to damages for all of his loss, subject, of course to giving credit for any benefit that he has received. There is nothing to be taken off in mitigation: for there is nothing more that he could have done to reduce his loss. He did all that he could reasonably be expected to do.

Winn J

[168] [W]here there has been a breach of warranty of authority, and still more clearly where there has been a tortious wrong consisting of a fraudulent inducement, the proper starting point … is to compare [the plaintiff's] position before the representation was made to him with his position after it, brought about by that representation, always bearing in mind that no element in the consequential position can be regarded as attributable loss and damage if it be too remote a consequence: it will be too remote not necessarily because it was not contemplated by the representor, but in any case where the person deceived has not himself behaved with reasonable prudence, reasonable common sense or can in any true sense be said to have been the author of his own misfortune. The damage that he seeks to recover must have flowed directly from the fraud perpetrated upon him.

Simonius Vischer & Co v Holt & Thompson [1979] 2 NSWLR 322

Facts and issues

Simonius Vischer ('Vischer') was a firm of wool buyers based in Basel, Switzerland, with branch offices in Australia. Vischer engaged Holt as accountants to audit their Sydney wool futures division. Unbeknownst to Vischer's Basel office or to the auditors, staff in the Sydney office were trading speculatively on the Sydney Wool Futures Exchange beyond Vischer's authority. The auditors' accounts showed profits being earned, whereas in fact losses were being incurred as a result of the unauthorised dealings. When Vischer discovered the true position in June 1965, it closed out some, but not all, of the unauthorised contracts, believing that the market would fall, and that closing them later would minimise their losses. Instead, this decision resulted in more losses. Could it recover these additional losses incurred from holding onto the excess unauthorised contracts in an attempt to mitigate their loss?

Decision

Holt could not establish that Vischer's decision was unreasonable; therefore it was liable for the additional losses arising from Vischer's attempts to mitigate.

Samuels JA (Moffitt P and Reynolds JA agreeing)

> [**355**] The defendants next submitted that the plaintiffs had failed to act reasonably to mitigate their damage … . The defendant submitted that it was the plaintiffs' duty to close out all contracts once they had ascertained their position, and the degree to which they were at risk. Their decision to hold in anticipation of a favourable turn in the market meant that, thereafter, they retained these contracts as a speculation on their own account, so that the further losses which were incurred were not recoverable.
>
> The plaintiffs had to determine how they could best reduce the losses which had then accrued by reason of their large excess of sold contracts, and the price at which it would have been necessary to buy matching contracts. Their decision … was reasonably and bona fide made in an endeavour to restore their trading position at a time when they had not finally determined to sue the defendants, and were primarily concerned to secure their own situation … . [A]s a result of reasonable steps to mitigate their damage, the plaintiffs suffered a further loss of money.
>
> …
>
> [**356**] [O]nce the plaintiffs' conduct is found to have been reasonable, the defendants are bound to make good the loss thereby sustained.

Review Questions

(1) Are the principles for dealing with intervening acts clear or appropriate?

(2) How do you think the concepts of contributory negligence, mitigation and remoteness overlap?

4 MULTIPLE WRONGDOERS

I	Introduction	148
II	Common law rules	148
III	Contribution statutes	160
IV	Proportionate liability statutes	165
V	Interplay of the three regimes	171

I Introduction

This chapter considers the legal rules applicable to multiple wrongdoers. The common law differentiates between cases involving joint wrongdoers who cause separate harms to the plaintiff, and cases of multiple concurrent wrongdoers which involve two or more wrongdoers causing a single indivisible harm to the plaintiff. Contribution and proportionate liability legislation now exists in each state and territory in Australia, altering the common law position. This chapter considers the position with respect to multiple wrongdoers at common law, and the statutory provisions which alter the common law.

II Common law rules

Concept	Short explanation	Relevant authorities	Principles text
Solidary liability	The common law imposes solidary liability on multiple concurrent wrongdoers and on joint non-concurrent wrongdoers.	*Grunwald v Hughes* 1965 SLT 209	Chapter 4: [4.6]
Joint tortfeasors	Joint tortfeasors are wrongdoers responsible for the same tort (as opposed to the same harm – see several concurrent wrongdoers).	*Thompson v Australian Capital Television Pty Ltd* (1996) 186 CLR 574	Chapter 4: [4.8]–[4.9]
	Multiple wrongdoers will be considered joint tortfeasors when one wrongdoer is vicariously liable for the tort of another, when multiple wrongdoers are in breach of jointly held duty, or when multiple wrongdoers are acting in concert.	*The Koursk* [1924] P 140 *Schumann v Abbott* [1961] SASR 149	
Several concurrent tortfeasors	Several concurrent wrongdoers are those wrongdoers responsible for the same indivisible harm.*	*Mahony v J Kruschich (Demolitions) Pty Ltd* (1985) 156 CLR 522	Chapter 4: [4.10]

Concept	Short explanation	Relevant authorities	Principles text
Effect of distinction	At common law, a plaintiff may bring a cause of action against any or all concurrent tortfeasors, but only one action against all joint tortfeasors.	*Brinsmead v Harrison* (1871) LR 7 CP 547	Chapter 4: [4.11]–[4.14]
	Judgment against one joint tortfeasor bars the bringing of an action against any others, even if the judgment remains unsatisfied.	*James Hardie & Co Pty Ltd v Seltsam Pty Ltd* (1998) 196 CLR 53	
	Except in the case of joint contractors, the common law denies entitlement to contribution in the case of concurrent wrongdoers.	*Chillingworth v Chambers* [1896] 1 Ch 685	
	Contributions claims may be brought in equity between concurrent wrongdoers in the cases of trustees liable for breach of trust, company directors liable for breach of equitable duty towards the company, and where one wrongdoer has paid more than their share of the damages.	*Albion Insurance Co Ltd v Government Insurance Office (NSW)* (1969) 121 CLR 342	

* That is, where one is not vicariously liable for the tort of another, or where multiple wrongdoers are not in breach of a jointly held duty or acting in concert.

The extracts in this section concern the imposition of liability in circumstances where there are multiple concurrent wrongdoers. The following cases demonstrate that solidary liability will be imposed where there are multiple concurrent wrongdoers.

Grunwald v Hughes 1965 SLT 209

Facts and issues

This was a claim brought by the owners of a restaurant against an architect they had contracted to design structural renovations to their premises, and heating engineers that the restaurant owners had also contracted to install under-floor heating for the purposes of the renovations. The negligence of both the architect and the heating engineers caused a boiler to catch fire. The fire spread to the rest of the premises, causing considerable damage. The plaintiffs sued both the architect and the heating engineers for damages in contract 'jointly and severally or severally'. At issue in this case was whether an action for joint and several liability against multiple defendants could be maintained under the law of contract.

Decision

The Court held that an action for joint and several liability could be maintained against multiple defendants under the law of contract where the actions of those wrongdoers in combination contributed to produce the one wrong against the plaintiff.

Second Division (The Lord Justice-Clerk (Grant))

> [**211**] In an action based on delict it is commonplace to have a joint and several conclusion against two delinquents who have both contributed to the single wrong which the pursuer has suffered. … [H]owever, this action is based, not on delict, but on breach of contract – or, to put the matter more accurately, on the respective breaches by the two defenders of their respective and separate contracts with the pursuers. Furthermore, there is no provision in either contract which imposes on either defender a liability for a breach of contract committed by the other. That being so, it was argued, the second-named defender can be liable only for any damage flowing from a breach of his own contract but cannot be held responsible for any breach of contract by the other defender … I can find no trace of such a distinction in the cases which were cited to us. It seems to me that the test which has been, and should be, applied is the same whether the action be based on delict or on breach of contract. That test is whether the two defenders have contributed, albeit in different ways, to cause a single wrong …
>
> [**212**] **…** As Lord Adam, who gave the judgment of the Court in *Belmont Laundry* put it …, 'No doubt the ground of action against each defender is different – that against [the ex-employee] being breach of contract, and that against the [new employer] the doing of a wrongous and illegal act – but they both contributed to produce the one wrong of which the pursuers complain; and therefore, I think, they are conjunctly and severally liable in the consequences' … I agree with [this dictum].

The following extracts concern liability at common law in cases concerning joint tortfeasors. They also demonstrate that multiple tortfeasors will be considered joint tortfeasors where wrongdoers are responsible for the same tort.

Thompson v Australian Capital Television Pty Ltd (1996) 186 CLR 574

Facts and issues

A television station (Channel 9 – one of the defendants in the initial action and second respondent in this appeal) produced and broadcast a television program in New South Wales that contained allegations of a defamatory nature against Thompson (the plaintiff in the initial action and the appellant in this appeal). Another television station (Channel 7 – one of the defendants in the initial action and first respondent in this appeal) broadcast the program in the Australian Capital

Territory pursuant to a licence agreement with Channel 9. Thompson and Channel 9 executed a deed pursuant to which Channel 9 paid Thompson $50 000, simultaneously releasing Channel 9 from liability relating to the broadcast of the program. At issue was whether the Channel 7 and Channel 9 were joint tortfeasors and, if so, whether the deed between Thompson and Channel 9 also released Channel 7 from liability.

Decision

The Court found that Channel 7 and Channel 9 were joint tortfeasors. In broadcasting the program in question which contained the defamatory content, Channel 7 and Channel 9 acted together, in concert, towards a common end. As such, the deed releasing Channel 9 from liability also released the Channel 7 from liability at common law.

Brennan CJ, Dawson and Toohey JJ

> [**580**] …
>
> **Joint tortfeasors**
>
> We have no doubt that Channel 9 and Channel 7 were joint tortfeasors. The difference between joint tortfeasors and several tortfeasors is that the former are responsible for the same tort whereas the latter are responsible only for the same damage (citation omitted) … Principal and agent may be joint tortfeasors where the agent commits a tort on behalf of the principal, as master and servant may be where the servant commits a tort in the course of employment. Persons who breach a joint duty may also be joint tortfeasors. Otherwise, to [**581**] constitute joint tortfeasors two or more persons must act in concert in committing the tort. Torts of all kinds may be joint and defamation is no exception. The transmission of the television program in question was the result of concerted action on the part of Channel 9 and Channel 7 and that made them joint tortfeasors. In the same way, the journalist, printer, publisher and distributor are joint tortfeasors in respect of the ultimate publication of a libellous periodical or book (citation omitted). In the present case, PBL had licensed Channel 7 to transmit the program in question. The relevant licence agreement established the common design, namely, the transmission of the program by Channel 7 to the Australian Capital Territory and adjoining areas in pursuit of commercial gain. While Channel 7 had the right not to broadcast any particular program or part of a program, where a program was in fact broadcast it was because Channel 9 and Channel 7 acted together – in concert – to achieve a common end (citation omitted).

Multiple wrongdoers will be considered joint tortfeasors where one wrongdoer is vicariously liable for the tort of another, where multiple wrongdoers are in breach of jointly held duty, and where multiple wrongdoers are acting in concert. The following case extracts outline the legal principles relating to the determination of whether multiple wrongdoers are considered to have been acting in concert.

The Koursk [1924] P 140

Facts and issues

This case involved a claim for damages arising out of an accident involving five separate ships sailing abreast from one another in a convoy connected by cables, resulting in the sinking of the *Itria*. The claim was made by the owners of the *Itria*, who argued that the damage suffered by them was a result of the negligence of the owners of the *Koursk* and the owners of the *Clan Chisholm*, two of the ships sailing in the convoy. The issue in this case was whether the owners of the *Koursk* and the owners of the *Clan Chisholm* were joint tortfeasors with respect to the damage suffered by the *Itria*, with the result of this finding being that the owners of the *Itria* would be barred from bringing an action against the owners of the *Koursk*, having already successfully brought an action again the owners of the *Clan Chisholm.*

Decision

For multiple wrongdoers to be considered joint tortfeasors, 'there must be a concurrence in the act or acts causing damage, not merely a coincidence of separate acts which by their conjoined effect cause damage'. Joint tortfeasors are those acting in furtherance of a common design, acting in concert towards a common end. While the damage to the *Itria* was the same damage, the negligence of the *Koursk* and the negligence of the *Clan Chisholm* were two separate acts of wrongdoing, and they were therefore not joint tortfeasors.[1]

Scrutton LJ

> [**155**] The substantial question in the present case is: What is meant by 'joint tortfeasors'? and one way of answering it is: 'Is the cause of action against them the same?' ...
>
> Counsel for the *Koursk* argued at first that if the physical damage was the same all persons who contributed to it without lawful excuse were joint tortfeasors. This would cover the case of two ships which by quite independent action and separate negligence ran into a third ship, one on the starboard and one on the port side, whereby she sank; of two persons uttering independently separate and distinct slanders concerning a servant, whereby his master dismissed him; of two separate excavators who by independent excavations [**156**] brought down the house of a third party.
>
> ...
>
> I am of opinion that the definition in *Clerk and Lindsell on Torts*, 7th ed., p. 59, is much nearer the correct view: 'Persons are said to be joint tortfeasors when their respective shares in the commission of the tort are done in furtherance of a common design' ... . 'but mere similarity of design on the part of independent actors, causing independent damage, is not enough; there must be concerted action to a common end.' Still more so when there is not even similarity of design, but independent negligences accidentally resulting in one damage ...

1 Cited with approval in *Patrick Stevedores Operations No 2 Pty Ltd v Maritime Union of Australia (No 3)* (1998) 195 CLR 1, 30, [32].

> [**157**] ... In the present case the *Koursk* was guilty of negligence in proceeding out of course across the line of its convoy; the *Clan Chisholm* was guilty of quite independent negligence in not reversing when the action of the *Koursk* was observed. These two separate and independent negligences resulted in a collision, the direct consequence of which was a collision with the *Itria*. In my view, the *Koursk* and the *Clan Chisholm* were not joint tortfeasors of the same tort, but separate tortfeasors of two different torts, and therefore at common law judgment against one in respect of the cause of action against it would not be an answer to a claim against the other in respect of the different cause of action on which it was sued.

Sargant LJ

> [**159**] It would appear ... that in order to constitute joint tortfeasance in the strict sense of the word ... there must be a concurrence in the act or acts causing damage, [**160**] not merely a coincidence of separate acts which by their conjoined effect cause damage.
>
> [**161**] ...
>
> It seems to me therefore that the Itria had two separate [**162**] and distinct causes of action, the one against the *Clan Chisholm* and the other against the *Koursk*, though the resulting damage was the same in both cases.

Schumann v Abbott [1961] SASR 149

Facts and issues

Schumann sued the defendants, two inquiry agents employed by her husband, claiming damages for trespass. The husband and the two agents entered the wife's property without her authority, and proceeded to search for evidence of adultery. They remained on the property conducting the search despite the protests of the wife, only leaving once instructed to do so by police officers. At issue was whether the defendants and the husband were joint tortfeasors.

Decision

Multiple tortfeasors will be considered joint tortfeasors where wrongdoers are acting in furtherance of a common design. The Court in this case held that the defendants and the husband were joint tortfeasors, as their respective actions in the commission of the tort against the plaintiff were done in furtherance of a common design.

Reed J

> [**150**] The plaintiff's action is for damages for trespass which ... she claims should be exemplary. The defendants are licensed inquiry agents, who on the day in question were employed by ... the husband of the plaintiff.
>
> At the material time the plaintiff was the tenant and occupier of a flat forming portion of the house situated at 11 Augusta Street, Glenelg. She lived there with her three children

and a nursemaid. On 28th April, 1960, at about 8.50 a.m., Mr Schumann, together with the two defendants, entered the flat and proceeded to search it. Shortly after their entry the plaintiff communicated with the Glenelg Police Station, and some ten minutes later two police officers arrived. After Schumann and the two defendants had been in the flat for a total period of some twenty minutes they left the premises.

...

At the trial a good deal of evidence was given in relation to what appears to be a straightforward case of trespass.

...

[**154**] It was no doubt the right of Schumann to watch his wife and to secure, if possible, evidence to support his suspicion that she was misconducting herself with another man, although that person had not been a party in the action which had recently been heard. He did not, however, have any authority or justification for entering his wife's flat. Having gained admission, under circumstances that I do not regard as constituting an invitation to enter, he should have left as soon as the plaintiff objected to his presence ...

...

The question, however, is as to the liability of the defendants. They and Schumann, in my view, were joint tortfeasors, as their respective shares in the commission of the tort were done in furtherance of a [**155**] common design: cf. *The Koursk* (citation omitted). There was undoubtedly 'concerted action to a common end,' although Schumann was the principal and the two defendants were his employees, and that is so even if the plaintiff has no right of action against her husband. However that may be, there was at least a common design between the two defendants; and if there was a common design between the three, the two defendants may be sued without joining Schumann.

Several concurrent wrongdoers are those wrongdoers responsible for the same indivisible harm, in circumstances where one is not vicariously liable for the tort of another, or where multiple wrongdoers are not in breach of a jointly held duty or acting in concert. The following case demonstrates that where multiple tortfeasors are causally connected to the same indivisible harm but were not acting in concert, they will be considered several concurrent wrongdoers at common law, and each will be considered separately responsible for the harm it has caused.

Mahony v J Kruschich (Demolitions) Pty Ltd (1985) 156 CLR 522

Facts and issues

Glogovic brought an action in negligence against his employer J Kruschich (Demolitions) Pty Ltd ('Kruschich'), arguing that he had suffered injuries in the course of his employment. He subsequently sought medical treatment for his injuries from Dr Mahony. Kruschich brought a cross-claim against Dr Mahony seeking either complete indemnity or contribution from Mahony, arguing that Mahony's negligent treatment of Glogovic caused or contributed to Glogovic's ongoing injuries. At issue was whether several concurrent wrongdoers could be responsible for the same harm.

Decision

Several concurrent wrongdoers can be held responsible for the same harm where the harm is a foreseeable consequence of each wrongdoer's act of negligence, even where the negligent acts in question occurred successively.

Gibbs CJ, Mason, Wilson, Brennan and Dawson JJ

> [**527**] … In negligence, 'damage' is what the plaintiff suffers as the foreseeable consequence of the tortfeasor's act or omission. Where a tortfeasor's negligent act or omission causes personal injury, 'damage' includes both the injury itself and other foreseeable consequences suffered by the plaintiff. The distinction between 'damage' and 'damages' is significant. Damages are awarded as compensation for each item or aspect of the damage suffered by a plaintiff, so that a single sum is awarded in respect of all the foreseeable consequences of the defendant's tortious act or omission. But concurrent tortfeasors whose negligent acts or omissions occur successively rather than simultaneously may both be liable for the same damage, being a foreseeable consequence of both torts, although one is liable for some only of the damage for which the other is liable and an award of damages against the one would necessarily be less than an award of damages against the other.
>
> …
>
> [**528**] … A negligent tortfeasor does not always avoid liability for the consequences of a plaintiff's subsequent injury, even if the subsequent injury is tortiously inflicted. It depends on whether or not the subsequent tort and its consequences are themselves properly to be regarded as foreseeable consequences of the first tortfeasor's negligence. A line marking the boundary of the damage for which a tortfeasor is liable in negligence may be drawn either because the relevant injury is not reasonably foreseeable or because the chain of causation is broken by a novus actus interveniens (citation omitted). But it must be possible to draw such a line clearly before a liability for damage that would not have occurred but for the wrongful act or omission of a tortfeasor and that is reasonably foreseeable by him is treated as the result of a second tortfeasor's negligence alone (citation omitted). Whether such a line can and should be drawn is very much a matter of fact and degree (citation omitted) …
>
> Where it is not possible to draw a clear line, the first tortfeasor may [**529**] be liable in negligence for a subsequent injury and its consequences although the act or omission of another tortfeasor is the more immediate cause of that injury …
>
> … When an injury is exacerbated by medical treatment … the exacerbation may easily be regarded as a foreseeable consequence for which the first tortfeasor is liable. Provided the plaintiff acts reasonably in seeking or accepting the treatment, negligence in the administration of the treatment need not be regarded as a novus actus interveniens which relieves the first tortfeasor of liability for the plaintiff's subsequent condition. The original injury can be regarded as carrying some risk that medical treatment might be negligently given … It may be the very kind of thing which is likely to happen as a result of the first tortfeasor's negligence: cf. per Lord Reid in *Dorset Yacht Co. v Home Office* (citation omitted) …

The distinction between multiple concurrent tortfeasors and joint tortfeasors at common law is significant for a number of reasons. In the case of joint tortfeasors, judgment against one joint tortfeasor bars the bringing of an action against any others. By comparison, in the case of multiple concurrent tortfeasors, a plaintiff may bring as many causes of action as there are defendants, and judgment against one defendant does not prevent the plaintiff bringing an action against another if the judgment remains unsatisfied. The distinction between multiple concurrent tortfeasors and joint tortfeasors at common law also has a significant bearing on whether multiple wrongdoers can claim contribution from other wrongdoers both at common law and in equity.

Brinsmead v Harrison (1871) LR 7 CP 547

Facts and issues

Brinsmead sued Harrison for wrongful detention of a piano. The piano had been wrongfully detained by Harrison and another named Thompson, and judgment had previously been obtained against Thompson, although remained unsatisfied. The issue in this case was whether judgment against Thompson prevented Brinsmead from bringing an action against Harrison, even in circumstances where the judgment against Thompson remained unsatisfied.

Decision

The Court of Exchequer held that judgment against one tortfeasor is a bar to an action against other joint tortfeasors for the same cause of action, even of the judgment remained unsatisfied.[2]

Kelly CB

> [**551**] In this case a right of action has accrued to the plaintiff in respect of the wrongful detention of a pianoforte. This act was the joint act of two wrongdoers, the defendant and another. The defendant by way of plea alleges that an action was brought for the same cause against the other wrongdoer, and a judgment obtained against her, which remains in full force: and the question is whether that affords any defence to this action. That a judgment and execution, with satisfaction, would be a defence, is not disputed. A long series of authorities has so laid down: but it was doubted at one time whether judgment and execution, without satisfaction, was a bar also. It will be right, therefore, to consider whether this latter is not upon principle a good and valid defence. If it were held not to be a defence, the effect would in the first place be to encourage any number of vexatious actions wherever there happened to be several joint wrongdoers. An unprincipled attorney might be found willing enough to bring an action against each and every of them, and so accumulate a vast amount of useless costs, if judgment against one of them did not operate as a bar to proceedings against the others …
>
> [**552**] … But, independently of the mischief which would result from holding the law to be as contended for by [the defendant], let us see how the authorities stand. In the first

2 See *XL Petroleum (NSW) Pty Ltd v Caltex Oil (Australia) Pty Ltd* (1985) 155 CLR 448, 456; *Thompson v Australian Capital Television Pty Ltd* (1996) 186 CLR 574, 582.

place, there is no authority whatever, – since the reigns of the Henrys and the Edwards nothing approaching to an authority has been cited, – to shew that such a plea as this would not be a good defence. In the absence, therefore, of authority to the contrary, and upon principle, and also upon what I conceive to be binding authorities in its favour, I come to the conclusion that such a plea as this affords a good defence.

James Hardie & Co Pty Ltd v Seltsam Pty Ltd (1998) 196 CLR 53

Facts and issues

A plaintiff brought an action against three defendants in the Dust Diseases Tribunal of New South Wales, arguing that the defendants were concurrent tortfeasors. At issue in this case was whether the third defendant was a joint tortfeasor and therefore whether the first and second defendants were entitled to claim contribution from the third defendant.

Decision

Except in the case of joint contractors, the common law denies entitlement to contribution in the case of concurrent wrongdoers.

Kirby J

History of the statutory provision

[75 [60]] In order to ascertain the purpose of [the *Law Reform (Miscellaneous Provisions) Act 1946* (NSW)], it is invariably useful to define the mischief which occasioned its enactment. In the case of s 5(1) of the Act, the purpose is not difficult to find. At common law, subject to certain exceptions not presently material, there was no contribution between either joint (citation omitted) or concurrent (citation omitted) tortfeasors. The origins, and even the applicability, of the common law rules were obscure, and sometimes contested. The best explanation that could be offered for them was that they were grounded in 'the rule that wrongdoers cannot have redress or contribution against each other … where the person seeking redress must be presumed to have known that he was doing an unlawful act' (citation omitted). Whatever the explanation and history of the rule, by 1894 it was accepted as a settled principle of English law deriving its principal authority from the decision in *Merryweather v Nixan* (citation omitted). The rule had its critics. Lord Kenyon's judgment in *Merryweather* was castigated in the House of Lords in *Palmer v Wick & Pulteneytown Steam Shipping Co* as 'somewhat meagre' such that it did 'not appear to … be founded on any principle of justice or equity, or even of public policy' (citation omitted). On that footing, the Law Lords in 1894 declined to extend the rule to Scotland. However, they concluded, with obvious reluctance, that *Merryweather* 'has been so long and so universally acknowledged as part of the English law that even if one's own judgment did not concur with its principle it would be now too late to question its applicability to all cases in England' (citation omitted).

Contribution claims may be brought in equity between concurrent wrongdoers in the cases of trustees liable for breach of trust, company directors liable for breach of equitable duty towards the company, and where one wrongdoer has paid more than their share of the damages.

Chillingworth v Chambers [1896] 1 Ch 685

Facts and issues

The plaintiff (Chillingworth) and defendant (Chambers) were trustees of a will, and invested trust funds in certain securities as authorised by the will. Then Chillingworth subsequently became a beneficiary under the will. The securities invested in by Chillingworth and Chambers caused the trust to suffer losses, for which Chillingworth and Chambers were held jointly and severally liable. Chillingworth's share of the trust estate was used to make good the losses. The issue in this case was whether Chillingworth had a right of contribution from Chambers in relation to the amount paid by Chillingworth to the trust estate.

Decision

The Court of Appeal held that as Chillingworth and Chambers were equally at fault, Chillingworth possessed a right as trustee to contribution from Chambers as co-trustee to the extent of one-half the loss. However, in this case, Chillingworth's right to contribution from Chambers was neutralised by Chillingworth's obligations as beneficiary.[3]

Lindley LJ

> [**698**] … In order to determine the rights of the parties it is necessary to consider – first, the plaintiff's right in his character of trustee against the defendant; and, secondly, the defendant's right against the plaintiff in his character of cestui que trust [beneficiary]. To the extent to which the plaintiff's right as trustee is neutralized by his obligation as cestui que trust he will have no right to contribution. But except so far as it is thus neutralized his right to contribution will remain. In other words, if the plaintiff as trustee is entitled to throw half the loss on the defendant, and if, on the other hand, the defendant is protected, against any claim of the plaintiff in respect of his share of the trust estate, then, as that share exceeds half the loss, the plaintiff will not be entitled to anything from the defendant, and must bear the whole loss which he has sustained. On the other hand, if the plaintiff as cestui que trust is not precluded from recovering from the defendant so much as one-half the loss, the plaintiff's right as co-trustee to contribution from the defendant will still be enforceable for the excess. This, in my opinion, is how the conflicting rights of the two parties have to be adjusted, and it only remains to work them out.
>
> The plaintiff and the defendant being in pari delicto [equally at fault], the plaintiff's right as trustee to contribution from the defendant as co-trustee to the extent of one-half the loss is established by a long series of authorities, of which it is only necessary to

3 See *Goodwin v Duggan* (1996) 41 NSWLR 158, 166; *Burke v LFOT Pty Ltd* (2002) 209 CLR 282, [14].

> mention *Lingard v Bromley* (citation omitted) and *Bahin v Hughes*. (citation omitted) On the other hand, the right of the defendant as trustee to be indemnified out of the share of the plaintiff as cestui que trust against the consequences of a breach of trust committed at his request and for his benefit is equally indisputable. It was treated by Lord Eldon as clear law in his day that a cestui que trust who concurs in a breach of trust is not entitled to relief [**699**] against his co-trustee in respect of it: see *Walker v Symonds*. (Citation omitted)

Albion Insurance Co Ltd v Government Insurance Office (NSW) (1969) 121 CLR 342

Facts and issues

Albion Insurance Co Ltd ('Albion', the appellant in this appeal) indemnified A & V Bence Pty Ltd under an employers' insurance policy for a sum of money which the company had become liable to pay to one of their employees for negligently caused personal injury. At issue in this appeal was whether Albion was entitled to seek contribution from the Government Insurance Office (NSW) (the Respondent in this appeal), as provider of a motor vehicle third party insurance policy to A & V Bence Pty Ltd, which also covered the loss suffered by them.

Decision

The High Court held that the right of contribution arises at both common law and at equity where one of several persons have paid more than their proper share in the discharge of a common obligation.

Kitto J

> [**350**] The general doctrine of contribution, as I have said, forms part of the common law. It was applicable by Lord Mansfield in *Godin v London Assurance Co.* (citation omitted) and *Newby v Reed* (citation omitted) no less than by Lord Chief Baron Eyre when exercising the equitable jurisdiction of the Court of Exchequer in *Dering v Winchelsea (Earl)* (citation omitted). This was because the basic concept was accepted by both law and equity as one of natural justice, as indeed it had been by the law of other countries since ancient times … Lord Mansfield put the matter squarely on that ground: 'If the insured is to receive but one satisfaction, natural justice says that the several insurers shall all of them contribute pro rata, to satisfy the loss against which [**351**] they have all insured' (citation omitted); and indeed Mr Justice Park, in his work on *Marine Insurance*, had described the principle of contribution as a principle of natural justice … Lord Redesdale had observed that the principle was universal 'that the right and duty of contribution is founded in doctrines of equity' (citation omitted); and the reference was not to doctrines peculiar to chancery but to doctrines of equity in the sense of 'reason, justice and law' … The judgment in *Dering v Winchelsea* (citation omitted) itself had said that 'If we take a view of the cases both in law and equity, we shall find that

contribution is bottomed and fixed on general principles of justice' – 'founded on equality, and established by the law of all nations' ... – and it had gone on to show that law and equity were at one as to the nature of the right ... The right arises at law when 'one of several persons has paid more than his proper share towards discharging a common obligation' (citations omitted) ... and it arises in equity when a liability of one of several to pay more than his share has been ascertained (citations omitted).

REVIEW QUESTIONS

(1) Do you agree with the finding in *The Koursk* [1924] P 140 that the owners of the *Koursk* and the owners of the *Clan Chisholm* were not joint tortfeasors but instead were concurrent wrongdoers, in light of the finding in *Schumann v Abbott* [1961] SASR 149 that the defendants in that case were joint wrongdoers?

(2) The court in *Brinsmead v Harrison* (1871) LR 7 CP 547 found that the risk of vexatious actions being brought against joint tortfeasors was a sufficient reason to bar further action where judgment against one wrongdoer has been obtained. Do you think this is a sufficient justification for barring further action, even in cases where the judgment remains unsatisfied?

III Contribution statutes

Concept	Short explanation	Relevant authorities	Principles text
Contribution statutes alter the common law rules regarding multiple wrongdoers	Contribution statutes alter the common law rules that only one action for one amount of damages can be brought against joint tortfeasors, and that concurrent tortfeasors are precluded from making claim for contribution between each other.	*Wrongs Act 1958* (Vic) s 24AA *De Reus v Gray* (2003) 9 VR 432 *Wrongs Act 1958* (Vic) s 23B(1)	Chapter 4: [4.16]–[4.24]
	Each wrongdoer's respective contribution towards the plaintiff's damage is determined by the proportion of each wrongdoer's responsibility for the damage.	*Wrongs Act 1958* (Vic) s 24(2) *Vinidex Tubemakers Pty Ltd v Thiess Contractors Pty Ltd* [2000] NSWCA 67	

Wrongs Act 1958 (Vic) s 24AA[4]

Section 24AA of the *Wrongs Act 1958* (Vic) (and its equivalents in other jurisdictions) abolishes the common law rule that judgment against one tortfeasor precludes an action being brought against any others.

> **24AA Proceedings against persons jointly liable for the same debt or damage**
> Judgment recovered against any person liable in respect of any debt or damage shall not be a bar to an action, or to the continuance of an action, against any other person who is (apart from any such bar) jointly liable with the first-mentioned person in respect of the same debt or damage.

The following case extract demonstrates the effect of the *Wrongs Act 1958* (Vic) s 24AA in a case involving joint tortfeasors.

De Reus v Gray (2003) 9 VR 432

Facts and issues

This was a claim for mental distress by Gray (the respondent in this appeal) arising from a non-lawful strip search of Gray by the appellant police officers. The originating claim was brought in trespass and negligence against the appellants. The appellants who conducted the unlawful strip search were police officers H and P, whose actions were ordered by the officer in charge at the time, De R. One of the issues in this appeal was whether a court could assess aggravated compensatory damages differentially against two or more joint tortfeasors who were liable in respect of the same damage.

Decision

Section 24AA of the *Wrongs Act 1958* (Vic) abolishes the common law rule that only one action for one amount damages can be maintained against joint tortfeasors.

Winneke P[5]

> [**449 [24]**] The primary point in issue is whether a court can, and in what circumstances, assess aggravated compensatory damages differentially against two or more joint tortfeasors who are liable in respect of the same damage. The substantive common law rule was that where two or more tortfeasors were sued for damages for a joint tort, there was only one

4 Equivalent provisions in the other jurisdictions are: *Civil Law (Wrongs) Act 2002* (ACT) s 20(1); *Law Reform (Miscellaneous Provisions) Act 1946* (NSW) s 5(1)(a); *Law Reform (Miscellaneous Provisions) Act 1956* (NT) s 12(2); *Law Reform Act 1995* (Qld) s 6(a); *Law Reform (Contributory Negligence and Apportionment of Liability) Act 2001* (SA) s 12(1); *Wrongs Act 1954* (Tas) s 3(1)(a); *Law Reform (Contributory Negligence and Tortfeasors' Contribution) Act 1947* (WA) s 7(1)(a).

5 Ormiston and Charles JJA in agreement (Ormiston JA, 457, [40]), (Charles JA, 458, [41]).

wrong and one cause of action and that, therefore, there could only be one judgment for one sum of damages. The parallel common law rule was that a judgment obtained against one joint tortfeasor was a bar to an action against the others for the same cause of action even though the judgment remained unsatisfied (citation omitted). However, as the High Court made clear in the [450, [24]] *XL Petroleum case*, (citation omitted) this latter rule (that is, the 'merger doctrine') was effectively abolished in New South Wales by s 5(1) of the *Law Reform (Miscellaneous Provisions) Act 1946* (NSW), the provisions of which section have, to all intents and purposes, been reproduced – at all material times – in this State in Pt IV of the *Wrongs Act 1958*. The critical question for the High Court was whether the statutory provisions also affected the rule that only one sum of damages may be awarded in an action brought against two or more joint tortfeasors. It was necessary for the court to determine this question in the context of a case where a jury had awarded exemplary damages against one joint tortfeasor but not against the other. Drawing upon the decision of the Judicial Committee in *Wah Tat Bank Ltd v Chan*, (citation omitted) the High Court concluded that the former rule had been abolished 'in its entirety' by the statutory provisions and that it was now open to a court to award exemplary damages against individual joint tortfeasors who merited punishment, notwithstanding that this would mean entering different judgments for different sums against such tortfeasors. Gibbs CJ, with whose reasons on this point Mason, Murphy and Wilson JJ agreed, said: (citation omitted)

> Once it is accepted that more than one judgment may be given against joint tortfeasors for damages caused by a joint tort, whether damages are given in the same or in different proceedings, there can remain no foundation for the rule that only one sum can be awarded by the different judgments. The reason for the rule was that there was only one cause of action against the joint tortfeasors, but that is no longer the position—the statute has abolished, 'in its entirety' the old common law principle that a person who suffers damage by a joint tort has only one cause of action which merges in the first judgment recovered in respect of it ... It seems to me impossible now to hold that there is any principle that would prevent a plaintiff from recovering different sums from different tortfeasors if he brings separate actions against them, provided that some are liable for exemplary damages, and others are not, and the same must be true if the joint tortfeasors are all sued in the one action. This result does away with the injustice to which the old law led ... The abolition of the old rule does not mean that the fears of Lord Reid will be realized and that the less guilty tortfeasor will be required to pay exemplary damages which he ought not to pay. With the very greatest of respect to that most distinguished of judges, it does not seem to me in the least impracticable to give separate judgments against two defendants, where one is liable for exemplary damages and the other is not ...

...

[451 [27]] It is apparent from the statements made by the High Court in the *XL Petroleum* case, above, that the old common law rule that there could only be one cause of action and one sum of damages against joint tortfeasors has been relaxed, at least to the point of permitting different judgments in circumstances which merit awards of exemplary damages against one or more of the joint tortfeasors.

Legislation now also alters the common law rule that concurrent tortfeasors are precluded from making claim for contribution between each other.

Wrongs Act 1958 (Vic) s 23B(1)[6]

Section 23B(1) of the *Wrongs Act 1958* (Vic) allows wrongdoers to recover contribution from any other person liable in respect of the same damage.

23B Entitlement to contribution

(1) Subject to the following provisions of this section, a person liable in respect of any damage suffered by another person may recover contribution from any other person liable in respect of the same damage (whether jointly with the first-mentioned person or otherwise).

...

Legislation also now provides that in determining each wrongdoer's respective contribution towards the plaintiff's damage, the court must consider the proportion of each wrongdoer's responsibility for the damage.

Wrongs Act 1958 (Vic) s 24(2)[7]

Section 24(2) of the *Wrongs Act 1958* (Vic) outlines how the court determines each respective wrongdoer's responsibility for the damage.

24 Recovery of contribution

...

(2) ... in any proceedings for contribution under section 23B the amount of the contribution recoverable from any person shall be such as may be found by the jury or by the court if the trial is without a jury to be just and equitable having regard to the extent of that person's responsibility for the damage; and the jury or the court if the trial is without a jury shall have power to exempt any person from liability to make contribution, or to direct that the contribution to be recovered from any person shall amount to a complete indemnity.

...

6 Equivalent provisions in the other jurisdictions are: *Civil Law (Wrongs) Act 2002* (ACT) s 21(1); *Law Reform (Miscellaneous Provisions) Act 1946* (NSW) s 5(1)(c); *Law Reform (Miscellaneous Provisions) Act 1956* (NT) s 12(4); *Law Reform Act 1995* (Qld) s 6(c); *Law Reform (Contributory Negligence and Apportionment of Liability) Act 2001* (SA) s 6(1); *Wrongs Act 1954* (Tas) s 3(1)(c); *Law Reform (Contributory Negligence and Tortfeasors' Contribution) Act 1947* (WA) s 7(1)(c).

7 Equivalent provisions in the other jurisdictions are: *Civil Law (Wrongs) Act 2002* (ACT) s 21(2), (3)(b) and (c); *Law Reform (Miscellaneous Provisions) Act 1946* (NSW) s 5(2); *Law Reform (Miscellaneous Provisions) Act 1956* (NT) s 13; *Law Reform Act 1995* (Qld) s 7; *Law Reform (Contributory Negligence and Apportionment of Liability) Act 2001* (SA) s 6(5)–(7); *Wrongs Act 1954* (Tas) s 3(2); *Law Reform (Contributory Negligence and Tortfeasors' Contribution) Act 1947* (WA) s 7(2).

The following case demonstrates the application of the above principles regarding contribution between multiple wrongdoers.

Vinidex Tubemakers Pty Ltd v Thiess Contractors Pty Ltd [2000] NSWCA 67

Facts and issues

Rooke was awarded damages against Vinidex Tubemakers Pty Ltd ('Vinidex', the appellant in this appeal) and Thiess Contractors Pty Ltd ('Thiess', the respondent in this appeal) in equal shares for injuries suffered by him as a result of Vinidex and Thiess's negligence. At issue in the appeal was whether the trial judge's finding that Vinidex and Thiess were responsible in equal shares for Rooke's damage was correct at law, on the basis of Vinidex's contention that it was Thiess's servant who was primarily responsible for causing the accident in which Rooke was injured.

Decision

As between multiple wrongdoers, responsibility for the plaintiff's harm is determined by what is just and equitable, having regard to the extent to which each party is responsible for the plaintiff's damage.

Rolfe AJA[8]

> **[29]** Several comments in relation to apportionment should be made immediately. First, the principles relating to the apportionment of liability caused by negligence and appellate deference to the discretion exercised by the tribunal of fact are well established … Secondly, the Court must have regard to what is just and equitable and, in doing so, it must make a comparison of the culpability and of the acts of the parties causing damage and, thus, to the relative blameworthiness and the relevant causal potency of the negligence of each party, and to the whole conduct of each negligent party in relation to the circumstances of the accident by way of comparative examination …

His Honour then outlined the evidence relating to the latter matters, drawing particular attention to the fact that the respondents had expressly requested that the appellants load with 'flat dunnage' as opposed to 'scalloped dunnage', this being the primary cause of the accident:

> **[33]** In the present case the learned trial Judge found, correctly in my respectful opinion, that Vinidex and Thiess were both guilty of negligence, which was causative of Mr Rooke's injuries. Having reached that conclusion his Honour decided that the proper exercise of discretion demanded that each be held equally liable. In my respectful opinion that was not the correct result when one has regard to the particular facts of this case and, in doing so, compares the culpability of each, the importance of the acts of the parties causing the damage, the relative blameworthiness and the relevant causal potency of the negligence of each party.
>
> **[34]** I have set out the matters, which I think are relevant in considering those points. A consideration of them leads me to the view that little blame can be attributed to Vinidex. Certainly, if scalloped dunnage had been used, the likelihood is that Mr Rooke would not

8 Sheller and Fitzgerald JJA in agreement: (Sheller JA, [1]), (Fitzgerald, [2]).

have been injured. Perhaps if there had been more communication from Vinidex suitable machinery would have been available. But those were relatively insignificant omissions when compared with the acts and omissions of Thiess.

...

[36] When one has regard to all the matters to which I have referred in the light of the applicable principles, I am led to the conclusion that an equal division of liability between the parties is so clearly incorrect as to justify this Court's intervention. In my opinion the proper division of responsibility to bring about that which is 'just and equitable having regard to the extent of' the parties' relative responsibilities would be as to eighty per cent to Thiess and twenty per cent to Vinidex.

REVIEW QUESTIONS

(1) To what extent does the decision in *De Reus v Gray* (2003) 9 VR 432 (that different sums of damages can be awarded against joint tortfeasors pursuant to s 24AA of the *Wrongs Act 1958* (Vic)) open the door to less blameworthy tortfeasors potentially being required to pay exemplary damages which they ought not to pay?

(2) Like the appellants in *Vinidex Tubemakers Pty Ltd v Thiess Contractors Pty Ltd* [2000] NSWCA 67, might the wrongdoing police officer De R in *De Reus v Gray* (2003) 9 VR 432 have been able to successfully seek contribution from wrongdoing police officers H and P pursuant to s 24(2) of the *Wrongs Act 1958* (Vic), on the basis that De R had been ordered to pay more in damages to the plaintiff in that case than had H and P?

IV Proportionate liability statutes

Concept	Short explanation	Relevant authorities	Principles text
Proportionate liability statutes	Proportionate liability statutes in all states and territories in Australia alter the common law rules with respect to concurrent wrongdoers. These statutes provide that concurrent wrongdoers are liable only for that proportion of the plaintiff's damage that the court thinks is just, having regard to the wrongdoer's responsibility for causing that damage.	*Wrongs Act 1958* (Vic) s 24AI(1)(a)	Chapter 4: [4.27]–[4.33]
	Proportionate liability statutes apply to 'concurrent wrongdoers', namely those wrongdoers responsible for the same indivisible harm.	*Hunt & Hunt Lawyers v Mitchell Morgan Nominees Pty Ltd* (2013) 247 CLR 613	
	A wrongdoer's responsibility is this context is determined by considering the relative degree of departure from the standard of reasonable conduct and the relative causal potency of the conduct.	*Bathurst Regional Council v Local Government Financial Services Pty Ltd (No 5)* [2012] FCA 1200	

Wrongs Act 1958 (Vic) s 24AI(1)(a)[9]

The relative contributions of concurrent wrongdoers is now determined by legislation, according to which concurrent wrongdoers are liable only for that proportion of the plaintiff's damage that the court thinks is just, having regard to the wrongdoer's responsibility for causing that damage.[10]

24AI Proportionate liability for apportionable claims

(1) In any proceeding involving an apportionable claim –

(a) the liability of a defendant who is a concurrent wrongdoer in relation to that claim is limited to an amount reflecting that proportion of the loss or damage claimed that the court considers just having regard to the extent of the defendant's responsibility for the loss or damage.

...

The following case demonstrates the application of the proportionate liability legislation in a case involving concurrent wrongdoers, namely those wrongdoers responsible for the same indivisible harm.

Hunt & Hunt Lawyers v Mitchell Morgan Nominees Pty Ltd (2013) 247 CLR 613

Facts and issues

Mitchell Morgan Nominees Pty Ltd ('Mitchell', the respondent in this appeal) sought unsuccessfully to recover monies lent to Caradonna secured by a mortgage over a property, due to fraud by Caradonna and Caradonna's solicitor in the signing of the loan and mortgage documents. The trial judge found that the loan agreement and mortgage were unenforceable against Caradonna, and that Mitchell's lawyers, Hunt & Hunt Lawyers ('Hunt & Hunt'), had been negligent in the drafting of the loan agreement and were therefore liable for a portion of Mitchell's losses. The Court of Appeal unanimously overturned the trial judge's decision, finding that Hunt & Hunt were not 'concurrent wrongdoers' along with Caradonna and Caradonna's solicitor, as they were guilty

9 Equivalent provisions in the other jurisdictions are: *Civil Law (Wrongs) Act 2002* (ACT) s 107F(1)(a); *Civil Liability Act 2002* (NSW) s 35(1)(a); *Proportionate Liability Act 2005* (NT) s 13(1)(a); *Civil Liability Act 2003* (Qld) s 31(1)(a); *Law Reform (Contributory Negligence and Apportionment of Liability) Act 2001* (SA) s 8(2); *Civil Liability Act 2002* (Tas) s 43B(1)(a); *Civil Liability Act 2002* (WA) s 5AK(1)(a).

10 The proportionate liability statutes do not apply in cases of personal injury or of wrongful death: *Civil Law (Wrongs) Act 2002* (ACT) s 107B(3)(a); *Civil Liability Act 2002* (NSW) s 34(1)(a); *Proportionate Liability Act 2005* (NT) s 4(3)(a); *Civil Liability Act 2003* (Qld) s 28(3)(a); *Law Reform (Contributory Negligence and Apportionment of Liability) Act 2001* (SA) s 3(2)(a)(i); *Civil Liability Act 2002* (Tas) s 43A(1); *Wrongs Act 1958* (Vic) s 24AG(1); *Civil Liability Act 2002* (WA) s 5AI.

of an independent wrong against Mitchell. Consequently, Hunt & Hunt were wholly responsible for Mitchell's loss. The issue in the appeal to the High Court was whether Hunt & Hunt were 'concurrent wrongdoers' along with Caradonna and Caradonna's solicitor for the purposes of the proportionate liability legislation.

Decision

The High Court found that the damage in this case was Mitchell's inability to recover the moneys advanced, which was caused by Caradonna and Caradonna's solicitor, as well as by the Hunt & Hunt's negligence. Accordingly, Hunt & Hunt were 'concurrent wrongdoers' along with Caradonna and Caradonnas's solicitor for the purposes of the legislation.

French CJ, Hayne and Keifel JJ[11]

> **[622 [4]]** In the *Civil Liability Act 2002* (NSW) s 35(1) in Pt 4 provides that in any proceedings involving an 'apportionable claim':
>
> (a) the liability of a defendant who is a concurrent wrongdoer in relation to that claim is limited to an amount reflecting that proportion of the damage or loss claimed that the court considers just having regard to the extent of the defendant's responsibility for the damage or loss …
>
> …
>
> **[6]** … [T]he definition of a 'concurrent wrongdoer' [in section 34(2) of the *Civil Liability Act 2002* (NSW)] … provides:
>
> In this Part, a concurrent wrongdoer, in relation to a claim, is a person who is one of two or more persons whose acts or omissions (or act or omission) caused, independently of each other or jointly, the damage or loss that is the subject of the claim.
>
> …
>
> **Proportionate liability and Pt 4**
>
> …
>
> **[628 [23]]** Where a defendant is found to be a concurrent wrongdoer, within the meaning of s 34(2) s 35(1)(a) requires the court to determine the proportion of the damage or loss claimed that the defendant should bear, having regard to the extent of the defendant's responsibility for that damage or loss.
>
> …
>
> **[630 [28]]** … The harm [Mitchell Morgan] suffered is that it is unable to recover the sums advanced. That is its loss or damage for the purposes of s 34(2). Mitchell Morgan's plea that it continues to suffer loss and damage is explicable on the basis that it continues to be unable to recover those sums.
>
> …

11 Bell and Gageler JJ dissenting: 652, [100]–[101].

[**634** **[43]**] The proper identification of damage should usually point the way to the acts or omissions which were its cause. Causation is largely a question of fact, to be approached by applying common sense to the facts of the particular case (citation omitted) …

…

[**635** **[45]**] The law's recognition that concurrent and successive tortious acts may each be a cause of a plaintiff's loss or damage is reflected in the proposition that a plaintiff must establish that his or her loss or damage is 'caused or materially contributed to' by a defendant's wrongful conduct (citation omitted). It is enough for liability that a wrongdoer's conduct be one cause (citation omitted). The relevant inquiry is whether the particular contravention was a cause, in the sense that it materially contributed to the loss (citation omitted). Material contribution has been said to require only that the act or omission of a wrongdoer play some part in contributing to the loss (citation omitted).

[46] There can be no doubt, on the findings of the primary judge, that Hunt & Hunt was a wrongdoer whose actions were a cause of Mitchell Morgan's inability to recover the moneys advanced. The question under s 34(2) of the *Civil Liability Act* is whether the fraudsters' acts, independently of Hunt & Hunt, also caused that damage.

…

[48] In determining the question of causation, it is necessary to keep clearly in mind the harm suffered by Mitchell Morgan: its inability to recover the moneys advanced. Merely to then state the obvious facts – that the moneys were advanced under the loan agreement and on the security of the mortgage – is to acknowledge that the harm suffered has more than one cause.

[**636** **[49]**] Because Mitchell Morgan's damage is its inability to recover moneys, it is understandable that attention is focused upon the immediate consequence of Hunt & Hunt's negligence, namely the mortgage's inefficacy as security against the property, as causative of the damage. However, as Hunt & Hunt points out in its submissions, there were two conditions necessary for the mortgage to be completely ineffective: (a) that the loan agreement was void; and (b) that the mortgage document did not itself contain the debt covenant, but did so solely by reference to the loan agreement. Hunt & Hunt was responsible for (b), but the fraudsters were responsible for (a).

…

[51] More generally, it is plain that the fraudsters' conduct induced Mitchell Morgan to enter into the transaction, of which the taking of a mortgage was a foreseeable element. The advance of the moneys by Mitchell Morgan may have been made on the faith of an ineffective security, but Mitchell Morgan would never have had the need to take a mortgage, nor Hunt & Hunt to draw one, had Mitchell Morgan not been induced to enter into the transaction. The advance was also made on the faith of forged documents and the false certification of a solicitor. On any view, the fraudsters' conduct in inducing Mitchell Morgan to enter into the transaction and pay the moneys must be regarded as a material cause of the harm which resulted. The importance of the part the fraudsters' conduct played is reflected in the extent to which the primary judge found them to be responsible for Mitchell Morgan's loss (citation omitted).

…

[638 [58]] So far as concerns Hunt & Hunt, it is clearly appropriate that its negligence be adjudged a cause and that it be held liable for Mitchell Morgan's damage. However, it is not consistent with the policy of Pt 4 that Hunt & Hunt be held wholly responsible for the damage, when regard is had to the part played by the fraudsters' conduct. Consistent with that policy, Mitchell Morgan should not recover from Hunt & Hunt any more than that for which Hunt & Hunt is responsible, as found by the primary judge.

Bathurst Regional Council v Local Government Financial Services Pty Ltd (No 5) [2012] FCA 1200

Facts and issues

In 2006, ABN Amro created a new financial product ('CPDOs'), which was subsequently given an AAA rating by S&P. Local Government Financial Services Pty Ltd ('LGFS') caused its client StateCover to purchase $10 000 000 of the CPDOs, and itself purchased $40 000 000 of the CPDOs to on-sell to councils in New South Wales. In 2008, CPDOs were cashed out in Australia because their net asset value had fallen beyond a pre-determined threshold. As a result of the cashout, StateCover lost over $9 200 000, councils who purchased the notes lost $16 000 000, and LGFS lost $16 000 000. StateCover and the councils sued LGFS, S&P and ABN Amro to recover their losses, and a number of cross-claims were made. At issue in this case was the issue of proportionate liability between LGFS, S&P and ABN Amro for the losses suffered by StateCover, the local councils, and LGFS itself.

Decision

A wrongdoer's responsibility for the purpose of the proportionate liability legislation is determined by considering the relative degree of departure from the standard of reasonable conduct and the relative causal potency of the conduct. The Court found that S&P, ABN Amro and LGFS were all responsible for the losses suffered by StateCover and the local councils. Moreover, S&P and ABN Amro were responsible for the losses suffered by LGFS. In the circumstances, the Court held it was just that LGFS, S&P and ABN Amro should be liable in equal thirds for the losses suffered by StateCover and the local councils. It was further just that S&P and ABN Amro share liability in equal shares for the losses suffered by LGFS.

Jagot J

14.15.6 Discussion – apportionment

[3517] … [I]n assessing the relative shares of the concurrent wrongdoers' responsibility all the circumstances must be taken into account with the two principal factors being, first, the relative causal potency of each wrongdoer's acts and, second, the degree to which each wrongdoer departed from the standard of care required.

[3518] I have found the facts material to this assessment in the reasons dealing with the claims against LGFS, S&P and ABN Amro … What is required is an assessment of all of the circumstances to determine the just or just and equitable proportion of responsibility of each of S&P, ABN Amro and LGFS for the relevant categories of loss (that of LGFS in respect of the StateCover settlement and that of the councils).

...

[3520] I am satisfied that the contraventions of each of S&P, ABN Amro and LGFS were all essential or decisive causes of the losses. If S&P had not contravened its general law and statutory duties in connection with the rating the losses would not have been suffered. If ABN Amro had not contravened its general law and statutory duties in connection with the sale of the notes to LGFS the losses would not have been suffered. If LGFS had not contravened its general law and statutory duties in connection with the sale of the notes to StateCover and the councils the losses would not have been suffered.

[3521] In terms of closeness of connection between the parties, LGFS was in direct contact with StateCover and the councils. LGFS was responsible for ensuring that it made investments for StateCover which complied with StateCover's investment policy and failed in that responsibility. LGFS had developed a long-standing relationship of trust and confidence with councils in New South Wales and exploited that relationship to enable itself to enter the structured product market which it perceived to be in its interest given its falling balance sheet. In so doing LGFS failed to perceive its own conflict of interest and thus failed to perceive that the Rembrandt CPDO notes were an unsuitable investment for councils despite their AAA rating and good return given their grotesque complexity and likely high volatility. I infer that LGFS's unperceived conflict of interest also enabled it to engage in a marketing and sales campaign in respect of the councils which gave rise to numerous examples of misleading and deceptive conduct because it emphasised only the positive aspects of the product (the AAA rating and LGFS's belief that this made the product secure, safe and very low risk) and omitted to deal with the negative aspects. LGFS's misrepresentations had a direct and immediate connection with the loss the councils suffered.

...

[3523] In these circumstances it is apparent that, in their own ways, LGFS, ABN Amro and S&P each conducted themselves in a manner that involved serious breaches of their respective duties of care. Moreover, the breaches of each were causally potent ... Despite this, S&P's conduct in assigning the AAA rating to the Rembrandt 2006–3 notes at a time when it knew many facts and circumstances which would and should have led inexorably to the conclusion that the AAA rating was irrational and unreasonable, and ABN Amro's willingness to deploy that rating when it knew all S&P did and more, remains at the heart of all of the derelictions of duty. The conduct of S&P and ABN Amro enabled LGFS to act as it did in dereliction of its own duties of care to the councils.

...

[3532] Having regard to all of the relevant circumstances I consider that the proportions of the loss in respect of the StateCover settlement and councils' claims which it is just that LGFS, S&P and ABN Amro should be liable for having regard to the extent of their respective responsibility for the loss is equal thirds (33⅓%each). The proportion of LGFS's own loss on the Rembrandt 2006–3 notes which S&P and ABN Amro should be liable for is equal halves (50% each).

REVIEW QUESTIONS

(1) To what extent is the definition of 'concurrent wrongdoers' pursuant to the proportionate liability legislation (such as in s 34(2) of the *Civil Liability Act 2002* (NSW) – discussed in *Hunt & Hunt Lawyers v Mitchell Morgan Nominees Pty Ltd* (2013) 247 CLR 613) – similar to the definition of 'concurrent wrongdoers' at common law, as applied in cases such as *The Koursk* [1924] P 140 and *Mahony v J Kruschich (Demolitions) Pty Ltd* (1985) 156 CLR 522?

(2) A wrongdoer's responsibility for the purpose of the proportionate liability legislation is determined by considering the relative degree of departure from the standard of reasonable conduct and the relative causal potency of the conduct. Do you think the legislation in these terms is drafted too broadly?

V Interplay of the three regimes

Each jurisdiction in Australia has three regimes in cases concerning multiple wrongdoers, namely common law rules, proportionate liability legislation, and contribution legislation. These regimes are inconsistent between jurisdictions, and may raise complex choice of law issues when involving multiple wrongdoers from different jurisdictions. Figure 4.1 sets out a generalised approach to take in cases involving multiple wrongdoers.

REVIEW QUESTIONS

(1) Given the complexity of the interaction between common law rules, contribution statutes and proportionate liability statutes, as well the inconsistency of approach between jurisdictions, is the current state of law justifiable in any way?

(2) Given the interplay of common law rules, proportionate liability statutes and contribution statutes in cases concerning multiple wrongdoers along with inconsistency of approach between jurisdictions, what general approach ought to be taken by lawyers when determining a client's position in relation to such an action?

Figure 4.1 Interplay of the three regimes

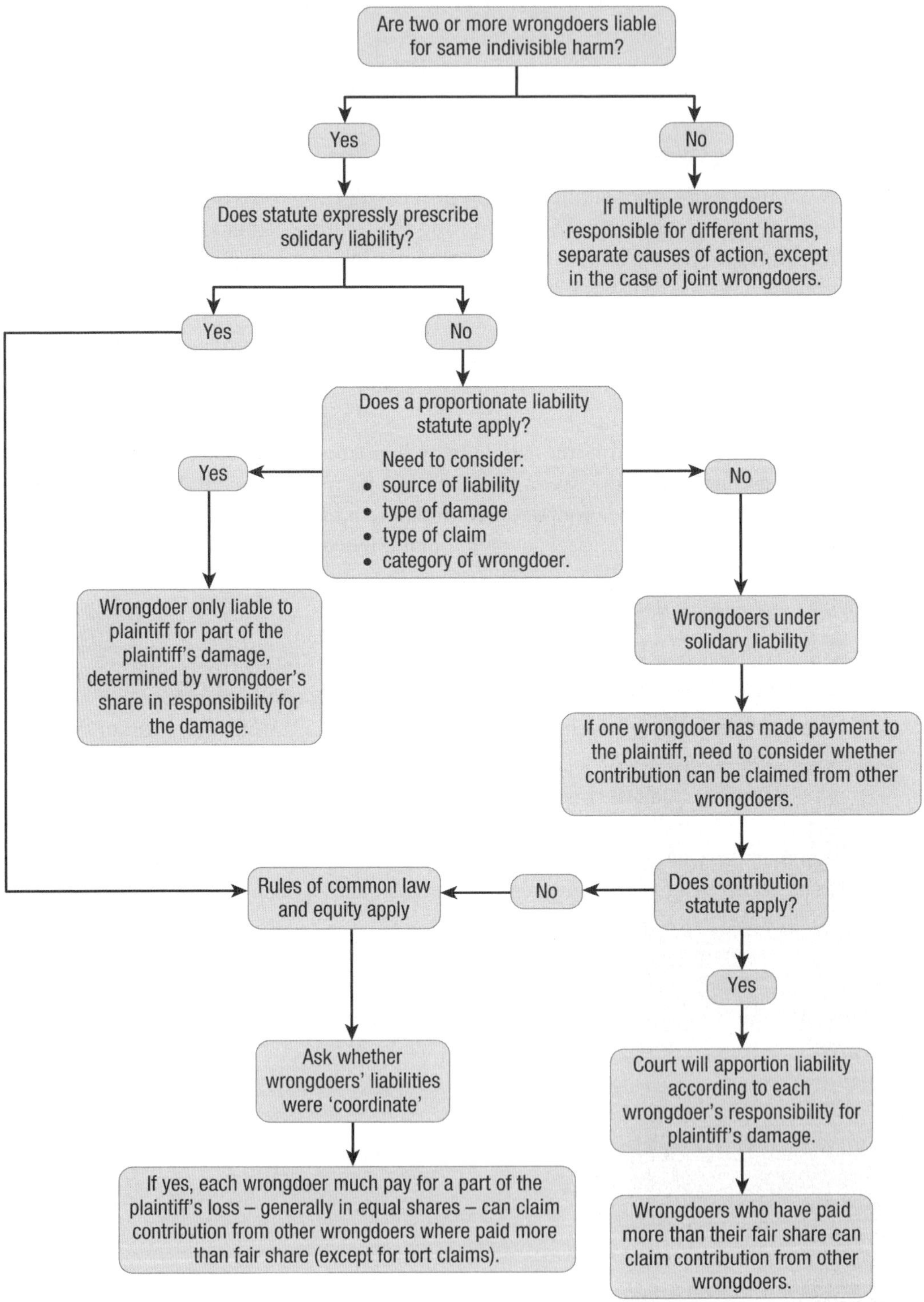

PART 2

COMPENSATION IN SPECIFIC CONTEXTS

5 COMPENSATION FOR BREACH OF CONTRACT

I	Introduction	174
II	Assessment of compensation	174
	A Protection of the plaintiff's expectation interest	176
	B Measure of expectation loss in particular contexts	178
	C The impact of *Clark v Macourt*	190
	D Compensation of reliance loss	190
	E Non-pecuniary loss	193
III	Attribution of responsibility	196
	A Remoteness of damage	197
	B Contributory negligence	203

I Introduction

Damages are the most significant common law remedy for breach of contract. An innocent party to a breached contract is entitled to damages as a right if a compensable loss occurs. This loss must not be too remote and could not have been avoided by mitigation. This chapter commences by discussing the concept of damages as being the primary form of compensation for breach of contract. It then introduces the seminal case on the topic, *Robinson v Harman*,[1] which is followed by the variations on that fundamental concept (including a discussion of the various bases for the assessment of loss). The chapter concludes by discussing the various restrictions on recovery, namely causation, remoteness and contributory negligence.

II Assessment of compensation

The overarching objective of compensation for breach of contract is to put the innocent party in the position they should be in had the contract not been breached. This theme underpins the myriad variations to that basic theme. It is summarised in Figure 5.1.

1 (1848) 154 ER 363.

Figure 5.1 Overview of interests for which compensation for breach of contract is assessed

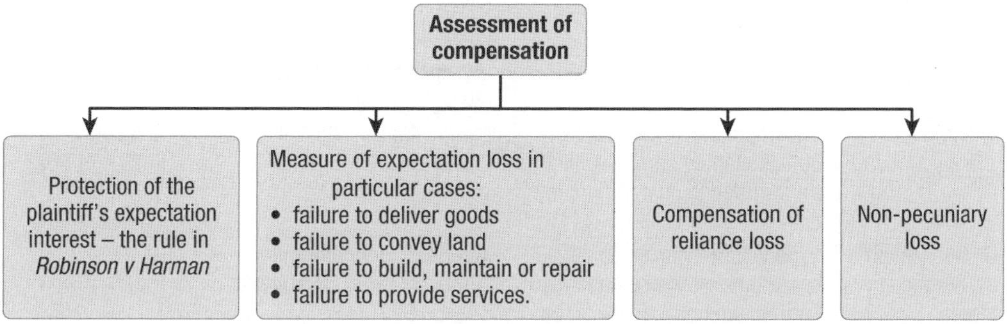

Concept	Short explanation	Relevant authorities	Principles text
Protection of the plaintiff's expectation interest	Expectation damages put the innocent party in the position they would have occupied had the contract not been breached or had been performed.	*Robinson v Harman* (1848) 154 ER 363	Chapter 5: [5.3]–[5.8]
	The right to damages for a disappointed expectation for breach of contract, ie 'the expectation interest'.	Leon Fuller and William Purdue, 'The Reliance Interest in Contract Damages 1' (1936) 46(1) *Yale Law Journal* 52	
Measure of expectation loss in particular contexts	How are contractual damages in a commercial contract to be assessed?	*Commonwealth v Amann Aviation Pty Ltd* (1991) 174 CLR 64	Chapter 5: [5.9]–[5.50]
	Failure to deliver goods as promised.	*Clark v Macourt* (2013) 253 CLR 1 *Sale of Goods Act 1923* (NSW) s 54	
	Failure to convey land as promised.	*Bain v Fothergill* (1874) LR HL 158 *Conveyancing Act 1919* (NSW)	
	Failure to build, maintain or repair property as promised.	*Bellgrove v Eldridge* (1954) 90 CLR 613 *Tabcorp Holdings Ltd v Bowen Investments Pty Ltd* (2009) 236 CLR 272 *Ruxley Electronics and Construction Ltd v Forsyth* [1996] AC 344 *Stone v Chappel* (2017) 128 SASR 165	

Concept	Short explanation	Relevant authorities	Principles text
	Failure to provide other services as promised.	*GEC Marconi Systems Pty Ltd v BHP Information Technology Pty Ltd* (2003) 128 FCR 1 *Zomojo Pty Ltd v Hurd (No 4)* [2014] FCA 441	
The impact of *Clark v Macourt*	The impetus for the view that substitutionary damages might be awarded in an appropriate case.	*Clark v Macourt* (2013) 253 CLR 1	Chapter 5: [5.51]–[5.56]
Compensation of reliance losses	Expenditure incurred as a result of reliance on the defendant's contractual obligations can be recovered.	*McRae v Commonwealth Disposal Commission* (1951) 84 CLR 377	Chapter 5: [5.57]–[5.72]
	The plaintiff is prima facie entitled to damages based on its reliance on the promise of the party in breach (reliance loss).	*Commonwealth v Amann Aviation Pty Ltd* (1991) 174 CLR 64	
Non-pecuniary loss	Subject to some exceptions, contractual damages for non-pecuniary losses are generally irrecoverable. Restrictions to recovery in statute also exist.	*Baltic Shipping Co v Dillon* (1993) 176 CLR 344 *Civil Liability Act 2002* (NSW)	Chapter 5: [5.75]–[5.87]

A Protection of the plaintiff's expectation interest

Compensation for breach of contract is conventionally regarded to mean the obligation on the part of the defendant, so far as money is able, to compensate the plaintiff for the disappointed *expectation* resulting from the defendant's breach. That principle is best known as deriving from *Robinson v Harman*[2] and is often referred to as 'the principle in Robinson and Harman'.

Robinson v Harman (1848) 154 ER 363

Facts and issues

The defendant, Harman, agreed to grant a lease to the plaintiff, Robinson, knowing that he had no title. The primary question was the damages that the plaintiff was entitled to recover. The decision of Parke B is described frequently as the classic statement on the recovery of damages for the expectation interest arising from a breach of contract.

Decision

The damages suffered by reason of the defendant's failure to grant the lease were to be assessed on the basis that they would put the plaintiff in the position they would be in had the contract not been breached.

2 Ibid.

Parke B

> [**365**] ... where a party sustains a loss by reason of a breach of contract, he is, so far as money can do it, to be placed in the same situation, with respect to damages, as if the contract had been performed.

The following extract is from a well-known and frequently quoted article, written jointly by a law professor (Fuller) and a third-year law student (Purdue), who attempt to rationalise the various heads of contractual damages.

Leon Fuller and William Purdue, 'The Reliance Interest in Contract Damages 1' (1936) 46(1) *Yale Law Journal* 52

[**52**] The proposition that legal rules can be understood only with reference to the purposes they serve would today scarcely be regarded as an exciting truth. The notion that law exists as a means to an end has been commonplace for at least half a century.

... In no field is this more true than in that of damages. In the assessment of damages the law tends to be conceived, not as a purposive ordering of human affairs, but as a kind of juristic mensuration. The language of the decisions sounds in terms not of command but of discovery. We *measure* the *extent* of the injury; we *determine* whether it was *caused* by the defendant's act; we *ascertain* whether the plaintiff has included the *same item* of damage twice in his complaint.

...

[**53**] ... it is impossible to separate the law of contract damages from the larger body of motives and policies which constitutes the general law of contracts. It is, unfortunately for the simplicity of our subject, impossible to assume that the purposive and policy-directed element of contract law has been exhausted in the rules which define ·contract and breach. If this were possible the law of contract damages would indeed be simple, and we would have but one measure of recovery for all contracts. Of course this is not the case. What considerations influence the setting up of different measures of recovery for different kinds of contracts? What factors explain the rather numerous exceptions to the normal rule which measures damages by the value of the expectancy? It is clear that these questions cannot be answered without an inquiry into the reasons which underlie (or may underlie) the enforcement of promises generally.

In our own discussion we shall attempt first an analysis of the purposes which may be pursued in awarding contract damages or in 'enforcing' contracts generally; then we shall attempt to inquire to what extent, and under what circumstances, these purposes have found ex pression in the decisions and doctrinal discussions. As the title suggests, the primary emphasis will be on what we call 'the reliance interest' as a possible measure of recovery in suits for breach of contract.

The purposes pursued in awarding contract damages

It is convenient to distinguish three principal purposes which may be pursued in awarding contract damages. These purposes, and the situations in which they become appropriate, may be stated briefly as follows: *First,* the plaintiff has in reliance on the promise of the defendant conferred some value on the defendant. The defendant fails to perform his promise. The court may force the defendant to disgorge the value [**54**] he received from the plaintiff. The object here may be termed the prevention of gain by the defaulting promisor at the expense of the promisee; more briefly, the prevention of unjust enrichment. The interest protected may be called the *restitution interest.* For our present purposes it is quite immaterial how the suit in such a case be classified, whether as contractual or quasi-contractual, whether as a suit to enforce the contract or as a suit based upon a rescission of the contract. These questions relate to the superstructure of the law, not to the basic policies with which we are concerned.

Secondly, the plaintiff has in reliance on the promise of the defendant changed his position. For example, the buyer under a contract for the sale of land has incurred expense in the investigation of the seller's title or has neglected the opportunity to enter other contracts. We may award damages to the plaintiff for the purpose of undoing the harm which his reliance on the defendant's promise has caused him. Our object is to put him in as good a position as he was in before the promise was made. The interest protected in this case may be called the *reliance interest.*

Thirdly, without insisting on reliance by the promisee or enrichment of the promisor, we may seek to give the promisee the value of the expectancy which the promise created. We may in a suit for specific performance actually compel the defendant to render the promised performance to the plaintiff. or. in a suit for damages, we may make the defendant pay the money value of this performance. Here our object is to put the plaintiff in as good a position as he would have occupied had the defendant performed his promise. The interest protected in this case we may call the expectation interest.

B Measure of expectation loss in particular contexts

The overarching principle governing the recovery of expectation loss for 'commercial contracts' is that they are based on the plaintiff's loss of profits arising from the fact of breach. This overarching principle has given rise to numerous variations and modifications in different contractual contexts, such as:

- the failure to deliver goods
- failure to convey land
- failure to build, maintain or repair property and
- failure to provide other services, as promised.

Commonwealth v Amann Aviation Pty Ltd (1991) 174 CLR 64

Facts and issues

Amann Aviation Pty Ltd ('Amann') and the Commonwealth made a contract by which Amann was to conduct aerial coastal surveillance for three years. The Commonwealth repudiated. Evidence was given of the profit that Amann would have made had the contract run the distance. Additionally, evidence was given of Amann's wasted expenditure in preparing to perform the contract. The High Court, in a seminal judgment on the recovery of contractual damages, explored the legal principles underpinning damages for breach of contract generally, including the intersection between reliance and expectation damages. The ultimate issue concerned whether the damages should have been the entirety of its wasted expenditure and whether these should have been reduced to take into account the prospect that the Commonwealth might not have renewed Amann's contract. The extract below addresses concerns the question of how Amann's losses for breach of contract should be assessed.

Decision

Amann was entitled to the loss of its net profit. The High Court explained that this was the amount by which the combination of expenses justifiably incurred by a plaintiff in the discharge of contractual obligations were exceeded by the amount by which gross profits would have been expected to exceed those expenses.

Mason CJ and Dawson J

> [**80**] The general rule at common law, as stated by Parke B. in *Robinson v Harman* (35), is 'that where a party sustains a loss by reason of a breach of contract, he is, so far as money can do it, to be placed in the same situation, with respect to damages, as if the contract had been performed'. This statement of principle has been accepted and applied in Australia.
>
> The award of damages for breach of contract protects a plaintiff's expectation of receiving the defendant's performance. That expectation arises out of or is created by the contract. Hence, damages for breach of contract are often described as 'expectation damages'. The onus of proving damages sustained lies on a plaintiff and the amount of damages awarded will be commensurate with the plaintiff's expectation, objectively determined, rather than subjectively ascertained. That is to say, a plaintiff must prove, on the balance of probabilities, that his or her expectation of a certain outcome, as a result of performance of the contract, had a likelihood of attainment rather than being mere expectation.
>
> [**81**] In the ordinary course of commercial dealings, a party supplying goods or rendering services will enter into a contract with a view to securing a profit, that is to say, that party will expect a certain margin of gain to be achieved in addition to the recouping of any expenses reasonably incurred by it in the discharge of its contractual obligations. It is for this reason that expectation damages are often described as damages for loss of profits. Damages recoverable as lost profits are constituted by the combination of expenses justifiably incurred by a plaintiff in the discharge of contractual obligations and any amount by which gross receipts would have exceeded those expenses. This second amount is the net profit.

1 Failure to deliver goods as promised

Clark v Macourt (2013) 253 CLR 1

Facts and issues

St George Fertility Centre Pty Ltd ('St George') were a provider of assisted reproductive technology services. Clark and St George made a contract, whereby St George agreed to supply 3513 straws of frozen donor sperm to Clark for a price to be calculated by reference to Clark's future income. Of these, Clark expected to be able to use 2500 straws. Macourt guaranteed the performance of St George's obligations.

The majority of the sperm was not usable, as the records were not compliant with the relevant code of practice. Clark acquired substitute, warranty-compliant sperm from an alternative supplier, the costs of which she recovered from patients who received the sperm. St George sued Clark for the balance of the purchase price. Clark sued St George for damages for breach of vendor warranties, guaranteed by Macourt.

The total purchase price for the assets of the company (including sperm samples) had been under $400 000. The agreement did not allocate any particular aspect of the purchase price to sperm and Clark did not charge patients for the St George sperm that was usable, and she accepted she would not have charged for 1996 usable straws (postulated on the basis that she expected to be able to use 2500 straws).

The trial judge awarded damages in an amount representing the cost of buying substitute product. Macourt appealed arguing that any loss suffered by Clark had been mitigated since the loss had been recouped. At issue was whether damages should be measured by reference to the value of the compliant assets.

Decision

Contractual damages are conventionally to place the plaintiff in the position they should be in had the contract been performed. In this case, the Court considered that this was the value of compliant sperm that should have been delivered.

Hayne J

> **[9]** Three different forms of 'loss' might be identified. First, there might be a loss constituted by the amount by which the *promisee* is *worse off* because the promisor did not perform the contract. That amount would include the value of whatever the promisee outlaid in reliance on the promise being fulfilled. Secondly, the loss might be assessed by looking not at the promisee's position but at what the defaulting *promisor gained* by making the promise but not performing it. Thirdly, there is the loss of the value of what the *promisee would have received* if the promise had been performed.
>
> **[10]** Subject to some limitations, none of which was said to be engaged in this case, damages for breach of contract must be measured (15) by reference to the third kind of loss: the loss of the value of what the *promisee would have received* if the promise had been performed.

…

[12] Under the contract which the appellant made, she should have received 1996 more straws of sperm having the warranted qualities than she did receive. The relevant question in the litigation was: what was the value of what the appellant did *not* receive? The answer she proffered in this Court was that it was the amount it would have cost (at the date of the breach of warranty) to acquire 1996 straws of sperm from Xytex. That answer should be accepted.

[13] The answer depends upon determining the content of the unperformed promise. The answer does not depend upon whether the contract can be described as one for the sale of goods or for the sale of a business. How much the appellant paid for the benefit of the promise is not relevant. It does not matter whether the value of what she did not receive was more than the price she had agreed to pay under the contract or (if it could have been determined) the price she had agreed to pay for the stock of sperm. The extent to which the appellant could have turned the performance of the promise to profit would be relevant only if the appellant had claimed for loss of profit. She did not. She sought, and was rightly allowed by the primary judge, the value of what should have been, but was not, delivered under the contract.

Sale of goods legislation in Australia essentially provide that the measure of damages for delivering defective goods – or not delivering goods at all – as promised, is for the loss directly and naturally resulting from the seller's breach. An example is s 54 of the *Sale of Goods Act 1923* (NSW), extracted below. Its content essentially codifies what is commonly described as 'the first limb of remoteness' as set out in the seminal case of *Hadley v Baxendale*.[3] What is commonly described as the 'second limb' of the remoteness test – special damages – are not precluded from recovery by that Act.

Sale of Goods Act 1923 (NSW) s 54

An Act to codify and amend the law relating to the sale of goods.

54 Remedy for breach of warranty

(1) Where there is a breach of warranty by the seller, or where the buyer elects or is compelled to treat any breach of a condition on the part of the seller as a breach of warranty, the buyer is not by reason only of such breach of warranty entitled to reject the goods, but the buyer may:

(a) set up against the seller the breach of warranty in diminution or extinction of the price, or

(b) maintain an action against the seller for damages for the breach of warranty.

(2) The measure of damages for breach of warranty is the estimated loss directly and naturally resulting in the ordinary course of events from the breach of warranty.

3 (1854) 156 ER 145.

(3) In the case of breach of warranty of quality such loss is prima facie the difference between the value of the goods at the time of delivery to the buyer and the value they would have had if they had answered to the warranty.

(4) The fact that the buyer has set up the breach of warranty in diminution or extinction of the price does not prevent the buyer from maintaining an action for the same breach of warranty if the buyer has suffered further damage.

2 Failure to convey land as promised

Bain v Fothergill (1874) LR HL 158

Facts and issues

The House of Lords considered in this case, relevantly, whether upon a contract for the sale of real estate, where the vendor (without their default) is unable to make a good title, the purchaser is by law entitled to recover damages for the loss of their bargain.

Decision

Where the vendor (without their default) is unable to make a good title, the purchaser's damages are confined to the recovery of expenses in investigating the title.

Lord Chelmsford

> **[84]** The rule established by it [*Flureau v Thornhill* [96 ER 635]] is that upon a contract for the purchase of a real estate, if the vendor, without fraud is incapable of making a good title, the purchaser is not entitled to any compensation for the loss of his bargain.

Addressing the question of whether the case fell within an exception to that rule, his Lordship said:

> **[87]** If a person enter, into a contract for the sale of a real estate knowing that he has no title to it, nor any means of acquiring it, the purchaser cannot recover damages beyond the expenses he has incurred by an action for the breach of the contract; he can only obtain other damages by an action for deceit. It is only necessary to add that, in my opinion, if there were any exceptions from the rule in *Flureau v Thornhill* the present case would not fall within any of them, but is within the rule itself. There is no reason to think that the respondents were not acting throughout under a bona fide belief that the lessor's consent might be obtained at any time upon application. They were prevented from performing their contract, not from any wilful act or fraud on their part, but by an unexpected defect in their title, which it was beyond their power to cure. The case falls precisely within the terms of the rule, as stated in *Flureau v Thornhill* and, therefore, in my opinion, the judgment appealed from is right, and ought to be affirmed.

3 Failure to build, maintain or repair property as promised

Bellgrove v Eldridge (1954) 90 CLR 613

Facts and issues

The defendant (Bellgrove), a builder, had breached their contract with the property owner (Eldridge) by substantially departing from the supplied building specifications. The resultant building works were defective in relation to the concrete foundations and the mortar. The question was the measure of damages to be applied, focusing on the idea that the test was whether the damages were necessary and what would be a reasonable course to adopt.

Decision

Damages were awarded based on the cost of demolishing and re-erecting the house in accordance with the specifications.

Dixon CJ, Webb and Taylor JJ

> [**617**] In the present case, the respondent was entitled to have a building erected upon her land in accordance with the contract and the plans and specifications which formed part of it, and her damage is the loss which she has sustained by the failure of the appellant to perform his obligation to her. This loss cannot be measured by comparing the value of the building which has been erected with the value it would have borne if erected in accordance with the contract; her loss can, prima facie, be measured only by ascertaining the amount required to rectify the defects complained of and so give to her the equivalent of a building on her land which is substantially in accordance with the contract. One or two illustrations are sufficient to show that the prima facie rule for assessing damages for a breach of warranty upon the sale of goods has no application to the present case. Departures from the plans and specifications forming part of a contract for the erection of a building may result in the completion of a building which, whilst differing in some particulars from that contracted for, is no less valuable.
>
> For instance, particular rooms in such a building may be finished in one colour instead of quite a different colour as specified. Is the owner in these circumstances without a remedy? In our opinion he is not; he is entitled to the reasonable cost of rectifying the departure or defect so far as that is possible. Subject to a qualification to which we shall refer presently the rule is, we think, correctly stated in *Hudson on Building Contracts*, 7th ed. (1946), p. 343. 'The measure of the damages recoverable by the building owner for the breach of a building contract is, it is submitted, the difference between the contract price of the work or building contracted for and the cost of making the work or building conform to the contract, with the addition, in most cases, of the amount of profits or earnings lost by the breach' … .
>
> [**618**] But the work necessary to remedy defects in a building and so produce conformity with the plans and specifications may, and frequently will, require the removal or

demolition of some part of the structure. And it is obvious that the necessary remedial work may call for the removal or demolition of a more or less substantial part of the building.

The qualification, however, to which this rule is subject is that, not only must the work undertaken be necessary to produce conformity, but that also, it must be a reasonable course to adopt. No one would doubt that where pursuant to a building contract calling for the erection of a house with cement rendered external walls of second-hand bricks, the builder has constructed the walls of new bricks of first quality the owner would not be entitled to the cost of demolishing the walls and re-erecting them in second-hand bricks …

[**619**] As to what remedial work is both 'necessary' and 'reasonable' in any particular case is a question of fact. But the question whether demolition and re-erection is a reasonable method of remedying defects does not arise when defective foundations seriously threaten the stability of a house and when the threat can be removed only by such a course. That work, in such circumstances, is obviously reasonable and in our opinion, may be undertaken at the expense of the builder.

Tabcorp Holdings Ltd v Bowen Investments Pty Ltd (2009) 236 CLR 272

Facts and issues

Tabcorp Holdings (the defendant) leased premises owned by Bowen Investments. A tenant, in breach of covenants in the lease, performed work without consent. The work in question did not significantly affect the value of the property, however, the cost of remediation was significant. The question in this case concerned the measure of damages in the context of an argument that reinstatement or remedial costs were unreasonable and unnecessary. The tenant argued that damages should be assessed on the basis of the reduction in the value of the premises (about $34 000) rather than $1.38 million, which was the cost of the remedial work ($580 000) plus $800 000 (lost rental income).

Decision

Damages were awarded in the amount of $1.38 million.

French CJ, Gummow, Heydon, Crennan and Kiefel JJ

[**286**] The 'ruling principle', confirmed in this Court on numerous occasions, with respect to damages at common law for breach of contract is that stated by Parke B in *Robinson v Harman*:

> The rule of the common law is, that where a party sustains a loss by reason of a breach of contract, he is, so far as money can do it, to be placed in the same situation, with respect to damages, as if the contract had been performed.

…

But as Staughton LJ explained in *Ruxley Electronics Ltd v Forsyth* such a measure of damages seeks only to reflect the financial consequences of a notional transaction whereby the buyer sells the defective goods on the market and purchases the contract goods. The buyer is thus placed in the 'same situation … as if the contract had been performed', with the loss being the difference in market value. However, in cases where the contract is not for the sale of marketable commodities, selling the defective item and purchasing an item corresponding with the contract is not possible. In such cases, diminution in value damages will not restore the innocent party to the 'same situation … as if the contract had been performed'.

[**288**] The Tenant stressed that in *Bellgrove v Eldridge* this Court pointed out that there was a qualification to the rule it stated in regard to damages recoverable by a building owner for the breach of a building contract. 'The qualification … is that, not only must the work undertaken be necessary to produce conformity, but that also, it must be a reasonable course to adopt.' The example which the Court gave of unreasonableness was the following:

> No one would doubt that where pursuant to a building contract calling for the erection of a house with cement rendered external walls of second-hand bricks, the builder has constructed the walls of new bricks of first quality the owner would not be entitled to the cost of demolishing the walls and re-erecting them in second-hand bricks.

That tends to indicate that the test of 'unreasonableness' is only to be satisfied by fairly exceptional circumstances. The example given by the Court aligns closely with what Oliver J said in *Radford v De Froberville*, that is, that the diminution in value measure of damages will only apply where the innocent party is 'merely using a technical breach to secure an uncovenanted profit.' It is also important to note that the 'reasonableness' exception was not found to exist in *Bellgrove v Eldridge*. Nothing in the reasoning in that case suggested that where the reasoning is applied to the present circumstances, the course which the Landlord proposed is unnecessary or unreasonable.

Ruxley Electronics and Construction Ltd v Forsyth [1996] AC 344

Facts and issues

The specifications of a contract between the defendent, Ruxley Electronics & Construction ('Ruxley'), and the plaintiff, Forsyth, for the construction of a swimming pool by the plaintiff were that the pool should have a diving area of a particular depth, namely seven feet and six inches. The completed pool was suitable for diving, albeit not constructed to the contracted specifications. Furthermore, there was no adverse effect on the value of the property. The plaintiff had made a claim for the outstanding balance of the contractual price and the defendant counterclaimed damages for breach of contract (based on the non-conformity with the specifications) and claimed the cost of rebuilding the pool to the specified depth, namely £21 560. At first instance, the trial judge gave judgment to the plaintiff for the outstanding balance but dismissed the counterclaim on the grounds that it was unreasonable. At issue was whether the counterclaim should be allowed on the basis that it would put the defendant in the position they should be in had the contract been performed.

Decision

Where the expenditure was out of all proportion to the benefit to be obtained, the appropriate measure of damages was not the cost of reinstatement but the diminution in the value of the work occasioned by the breach in the light particularly of the lack of intention to carry out the remedial work. The judgment of the trial judge was affirmed.

Lord Jauncey

> [**372**] There is, as Staughton LJ observed, a good deal of authority to the effect that intention may be relevant to a claim for damages based on cost of reinstatement. The clearest decisions on the point are those of Sir Robert Megarry V-C in *Tito v Waddell (No. 2)* and Oliver J in *Radford v De Froberville*. One of the many questions in the former case was whether the plaintiffs could recover the cost of replanting the plots of land in question, or whether the recovery of damages was limited to the difference in the market value of the land by reason of the work not having been done.
>
> . . .
>
> In the present case the judge found as a fact that Mr Forsyth's stated intention of rebuilding the pool would not persist for long after the litigation had been concluded. In these circumstances it would be 'mere pretence' to say that the cost of rebuilding the pool is the loss which he [**373**] has in fact suffered. This is the critical distinction between the present case, and the example given by Staughton LJ of a man who has had his watch stolen. In the latter case, the plaintiff is entitled to recover the value of the watch, because that is the true measure of his loss. He can do what he wants with the damages. But if, as the judge found, Mr Forsyth had no intention of rebuilding the pool, he has lost nothing except the difference in value, if any.
>
> The relevance of intention to the issue of reasonableness is expressly recognised by the respondent in his case. In paragraph 37, Mr Jacob says:
>
>> The respondent accepts that the genuineness of the parties' indicated predilections can be a factor which the court must consider when deciding between alternative measures of damage. Where a plaintiff is contending for a high as opposed to a low cost measure of damages the court must decide whether in the circumstances of the particular case such high cost measure is reasonable. One of the factors that may be relevant is the genuineness of the plaintiff's desire to pursue the course which involves the higher cost. Absence of such desire (indicated by untruths about intention) may undermine the reasonableness of the higher cost measure.
>
> I can only say that I find myself in complete agreement with that approach, in contrast to the approach taken by the majority of the Court of Appeal.

Stone v Chappel (2017) 128 SASR 165

Facts and issues

The defendant, Chappel (a builder) was contracted to construct an apartment for the owner, Stone. Contrary to construction practice, which allowed for a departure of plus or minus 20 millimetres, the ceiling was on average about 48 millimetres too low. The cost of rectification was $331 188. The issue was whether damages based on the cost of rectification should have been awarded.

Decision

Various factors were to be considered, including inter alia the plaintiff's interest in performance, and whether the contractual specification was a matter of functionality or aesthetic. The South Australian Full Court upheld the trial judge's decision to refuse to award damages based on the cost of rectification.

Kourakis CJ

> **[55]** Rectification damages are awarded for a breach of a building contract unless there is good reason to adopt another measure because the award of rectification damages would be manifestly disproportionate to the attaining of the contractual benefit. That rule entrenches rectification costs as the primary measure of damages and emphasises the exceptional nature of any lesser award. In determining whether good reason exists, the authorities suggest that the following are relevant considerations:
>
> (1) the degree of departure from the contractual stipulation;
> (2) the adverse effect of the departure on the functional utility, amenity and aesthetic appearance of the building;
> (3) the reasons, objectively ascertained and commonly known, for which the innocent party made the stipulation which was breached;
> (4) the practical feasibility of rectifying the work, including the effects on third parties of attempting to do so;
> (5) whether or not the innocent party intends to carry out the rectification work;
> (6) the absolute cost of the rectification work and the disproportion between that cost and
>   - the value of the building and contract price;
>   - the diminution in commercial value of the building;
>   - the effect of the departure on the functional utility, amenity and aesthetic appearance of the building;
>
> (7) the nature of the wrongdoer's fault for the defect; and
> (8) the public interest in reducing economic waste.
>
> …
>
> **[61]** The sixth consideration, disproportion, is at the core of the evaluative judgment which must be made.
>
> …

[68] When Mr Chappel executed the contract with the Stones and undertook to provide an apartment with a ceiling height of 2700 mm, he knew that the change in design of the roof meant that the beam was 'too deep' and would need to be modified. Nonetheless, Mr Chappel took no additional precautions to ensure that the building work was carried out in a way which ensured that he would discharge his contractual obligation. Mr Chappel's knowledge must also be imputed to Mr Smallacombe because they were partners. The defendants' reliance on the disproportionate cost of rectification is undermined by their failure to take steps reasonably open to them at the time to avoid the risk of incurring substantial rectification costs.

[69] Be that as it may, against those considerations there is undoubtedly a great disproportion between the cost of the rectification work and the contract price for the unit and its value.

...

[72] If the relevant considerations rested there, I would have been inclined to hold the defendants to their contract and award rectification costs. However, an award of rectification costs in this case must be premised on the performance of building work which, if carried out, would create significant risks of damage to the property of other persons and is likely to result in substantial collateral litigation involving the defendants and other occupants of the building. In fact, despite the earnest evidence of the Stones that they intended to carry out the rectification work, the chances of them doing so are not strong. Indeed, the rectification work is unlikely to be carried out because of its complexity and the risk of damage to the property of others. An attempt to undertake the work will also almost certainly provoke litigation which is likely to delay it, if not obstruct it altogether.

...

[75] For those reasons, I would find that rectification is not a reasonable course and that there is good reason to depart from the ordinary rule in this case.

4 Failure to provide other services as promised

GEC Marconi Systems Pty Ltd v BHP Information Technology Pty Ltd (2003) 128 FCR 1

Facts and issues

Under what were described as 'back-to-back' contracts, security devices were to be supplied by the Commonwealth to BHP Information Technology Pty Ltd ('BHP-IT') which, in turn, was to supply them to GEC Marconi Systems Pty Ltd ('GEC'). The Commonwealth and BHP-IT's failure to supply the devices led to the proceedings in question, with GEC alleging that this justified termination of the head contract and BHP-IT alleging that GEC had repudiated the contract. Having found that GEC had repudiated, at issue was the extent to which BHP-IT was entitled to damages for breach of contract.

Decision

Damages for breach of contract in favour of BHP-IT were assessed on the basis of the cost of substitute goods and services.

Finn J

> **[934]** (1) The general principle governing the measure of damages for breach of contract is that where a party sustains a loss by reason of such a breach that party is, so far as money can do it, to be placed in the same situation with respect to damages as if the contract had been performed: *Robinson v Harman*; *Wenham v Ella*; *Commonwealth v Amann Aviation Pty Ltd*.
>
> **[935]** (2) The usual rule is that damages for breach of contract are assessed as at the date of the breach: *Amann Aviation* at 161–162; Cheshire and Fifoot, *Law of Contract*, para 23.24. '[T]his rule is not universal': *Johnson v Perez*; and if following it would give rise to injustice, the court may fix such other date as is appropriate in the circumstances to give the innocent party the amount in damages which will most fairly compensate that party for the wrong suffered: *Johnson v Agnew* at 400–401; *Johnson v Perez* at 355–356. A common example of another date being fixed is where, after one party fails to provide goods or services, the other party thereafter seeks or proposes to seek substitute performance and claims damages for the cost of so doing: for example, *Radford v De Froberville*; *Cormier Enterprises Ltd v Costello*; *Conquest v Ebbetts*; *Chitty on Contracts*, vol 1, paras 27–014, 27–052.

Zomojo Pty Ltd v Hurd (No 4) [2014] FCA 441

Facts and issues

Zomojo Pty Ltd ('Zomojo') was the employer of Hurd. In breach of the contract of employment, Hurd devoted time to his other businesses. The relevant issue here was whether Zomojo could claim damages based on the value of the time which Hurd had devoted to his other business interests.

Decision

Zomojo was entitled to damages based on Hurd's remuneration for the time not worked.

Jessup J

> **[15]** Limited though they are, the authorities to which I have referred are consistent in holding that, where an employee fails or refuses to work for the full time for which he or she has been contracted, the employer's damages may be measured (at least) by reference to the value of the employee's remuneration in respect of the period of the failure or refusal.

The employer does not, as a general rule, have to establish some loss of production or output, it being presumed that the value to the employer of the employee's work is no less than what the employer was paying for it.

[16] Thus I accept the submission made on behalf of the applicant that its loss consequent on Mr Hurd's failure to devote his full working time to the business of which he was a managing director may be measured by applying to his monthly salary a fraction representing the amount of time that he spent working on his other business.

C The impact of *Clark v Macourt*

The substantive extract of the case is provided on page 180. The effect of *Clark v Macourt might* be that the courts will countenance an award of substitutionary damages where the wrong has not resulted in any actual loss.

D Compensation of reliance loss

The plaintiff might in reliance on the defendant's performance of a contract expend money and incur significant trouble. While the plaintiff can sue for their expectation damages, they have the onus of proving these[4] – and proof could be problematic. This section deals with the circumstances in which a plaintiff is entitled to damages based on the trouble and expense they incurred in reliance on the defendant's performance, reliance loss, including the relationship between reliance loss and expectation losses.

McRae v Commonwealth Disposal Commission (1951) 84 CLR 377

Facts and issues

The parties had entered into a contract for the salvage of an oil tanker which did not exist. In rejecting the argument that there was a common mistake as to the existence of the tanker, the Court held that on a correct construction of the contract, it was an implied term, which the Commonwealth Disposal Commission ('the Commission') had breached, that the tanker existed. The question was whether the plaintiff could recover damages based on their wasted expenditure.

Decision

The plaintiff was entitled to recover its wasted expenditure.

Dixon and Fullagar JJ

[**414**] If we regard the case as a simple and normal case of breach by non-delivery, the plaintiffs have no starting point. The burden of proof is on them, and they cannot establish

4 *Commonwealth v Amann Aviation Pty Ltd* (1991) 174 CLR 64.

> that they have suffered any damage unless they can show that a tanker delivered in performance of the contract would have had some value, and this they cannot show. But when the contract alleged is a contract that there was a tanker in a particular place, and the breach assigned is that there was no tanker there, and the damages claimed are measured by expenditure incurred on the faith of the promise that there was a tanker in that place, the plaintiffs are in a very different position. They have now a starting point. They can say: (1) this expense was incurred; (2) it was incurred because you promised us that there was a tanker; (3) the fact that there was no tanker made it certain that this expense would be wasted. The plaintiffs have in this way a starting point. They make a prima facie case. The fact that the expense was wasted flowed prima facie from the fact that there was no tanker; and the first fact is damage, and the second fact is breach of contract. The burden is now thrown on the Commission of establishing that, if there had been a tanker, the expense incurred would equally have been wasted. This, of course, the Commission cannot establish. The fact is that the impossibility of assessing damages on the basis of a comparison between what was promised and what was delivered arises not because what was promised was valueless but because it is impossible to value a non-existent thing. It is the breach of contract itself which makes it impossible even to undertake an assessment on that basis. It is not impossible, however, to undertake an assessment on another basis, and, in so far as the Commission's breach of contract itself reduces the possibility of an accurate assessment, it is not for the Commission to complain.

Commonwealth v Amann Aviation Pty Ltd (1991) 174 CLR 64

Facts and issues

The fundamental facts are set out on page 178. A question that arose was whether the plaintiff, Amann, was entitled to recover the expenditure incurred in reliance on the contract (the reliance damages). A related issue concerned the recoverability of reliance damages, which are sought where proving loss of profits would have been problematic.

Decision

The plaintiff was entitled to its reliance loss provided they had been reasonably incurred.

Mason CJ and Dawson J

> [**81**] The expression 'damages for loss of profits' should not be understood as carrying with it the implication that no damages are recoverable either in the case of a contract in which no net profit would have been generated or in the case of a contract in which the amount of profit cannot be demonstrated. It would be an invitation to the repudiation of contractual obligations if the law were to deny to an innocent plaintiff the right to recoupment by an award of damages of expenditure justifiably incurred for the purpose of discharging contractual obligations simply on the ground that the contract breached would not have

been or could not be shown to have been profitable. If the performance of a contract would have resulted in a plaintiff, while not making a profit, nevertheless recovering costs incurred in the course of performing contractual obligations, then that plaintiff is entitled to recover damages in an amount equal to those costs in accordance with *Robinson v Harman,* as those costs would have been recovered had the contract been fully performed. Similarly, where it is not possible for a plaintiff to demonstrate whether or to what extent the performance of a contract would have resulted in a profit for the plaintiff, it will be open to a plaintiff to seek to recoup expenses incurred, damages in such a case being described as reliance damages or damages for wasted expenditure.

[**82**] … The amount of wasted expenditure will be the appropriate measure of damages in such a situation because, it having been established that the client would not have entered into the subsequent contract if proper advice had been given, it is not sensible to speak of loss of profits.

…

[**84**] In *Anglia Television Ltd v Reed*, Lord Denning M.R. considered that a plaintiff could claim expenditure thrown away when he has not suffered any loss of profits or if he cannot prove what his profits would have been.

…

[**85**] We do not regard the language of *election* or the notion that *alternative* ways are open to a plaintiff in which to frame a claim for relief as appropriate in a discussion of the measure of damages for breach of contract. In truth, as has been seen, damages for loss of profits and damages for expenditure reasonably incurred are simply two manifestations of the general principle enunciated in *Robinson v Harman.*

…

Naturally, the categories of case in which a plaintiff is likely to make a claim for the recovery of expenditure incurred are those in which the plaintiff has not suffered a loss of profits and those in which it is impossible to assess what would have been the outcome had the contract been performed or those in which that outcome is otherwise uncertain.

…

An award of damages for expenditure reasonably incurred under a contract in which no net profit would have been realized, while placing the plaintiff in the position he or she would have been in had the contract been fully performed, also restores the plaintiff to the position he or she would have been in had the contract not been entered into. In this particular situation it will be noted that there is a coincidence, but no more than a coincidence, between the measure of damages recoverable both in contract and in tort.

…

[**86**] It should be observed that, in a case where it is not possible to predict what position a plaintiff would have been in had the contract been fully performed, as was the case in both *McRae* and *Anglia Television,* it is not possible as a matter of strict logic to assess damages in accordance with the principle in *Robinson v Harman.* But the law considers the just result in such a case is to allow a plaintiff to recover such expenditure as is reasonably incurred in reliance on the defendant's promise.

[**88**] … In the context of the discussion of onus of proof and the presumption relating to recovery of reasonable expenditure incurred which we have described, it is necessary to consider the decision of this Court in *McRae.* There, the plaintiffs recovered as damages

the amount of the agreed purchase price together with the expenditure wasted in reliance on the promise that there was an oil tanker at the locality given, there being no oil tanker anywhere in that locality. The expenditure wasted was incurred by the plaintiffs in taking steps to see whether there was a tanker in the locality given and, if so, whether any and what things should be done to tum her to account.

...

[89] Their Honours pointed out [in *McRae*] that the plaintiffs had a prima facie case for recovery of wasted expenditure because (1) the expense was incurred; (2) it was incurred in reliance on the promise that there was a tanker; and (3) the fact that there was no tanker meant that the expense was wasted. This threw the burden on the defendant 'of establishing that, if there had been a tanker, the expense incurred would equally have been wasted'. But it was impossible to assess damages on the basis of a comparison between what was promised and what was delivered, 'not because what was promised was valueless but because it is impossible to value a non-existent thing'.

Accordingly, *McRae* illustrates the proposition that a plaintiff has a prima facie case for recovery of wasted expenditure once it is established that the expense was incurred in reliance on the promise of the party in breach, there being a failure of performance by that party.

E Non-pecuniary loss

Subject to certain exceptions, one cannot usually get contractual damages for non-pecuniary losses such as mental distress or inconvenience. The situation at common law is summarised in the seminal case, *Baltic Shipping Co v Dillon*.[5] Furthermore, some jurisdictions[6] restrict the right to the recovery of such damages.

1 Restrictions at common law

Baltic Shipping Co v Dillon (1993) 176 CLR 344

Facts and issues

Mrs Dillon, a passenger on a cruise ship, suffered injury when it sank. She sued for damages for breach of contract based on the loss of enjoyment of the cruise. The High Court's judgment addressed the question of the entitlement to damages for non-pecuniary losses in the following seminal judgment.

Decision

While ordinarily contractual damages would not be available for non-pecuniary losses, Mrs Dillon's claim for distress and loss of enjoyment was granted an exception given the nature of her contract with the cruise line.

5 (1993) 176 CLR 344.

6 See, eg, *Civil Liability Act 2002* (NSW).

McHugh J

On the question of whether there was any general rule addressing the unavailability of damages for non-pecuniary losses:

> The general rule relating to damages for distress and disappointment
>
> [**394**] Damages for breach of contract cannot ordinarily be awarded for distress or disappointment arising from that breach.

Deane and Dawson JJ

On the question of the qualifications or exceptions to that general rule:

> [**381**] The many cases in which an award of damages for breach of contract has included compensation for mental distress can be grouped (sometimes a little uncomfortably) into a number of different categories, including breach of promise of marriage, breach of contract causing physical injury and breach of contract directly causing physical inconvenience …

Mason CJ

On the question of the qualifications or exceptions to that general rule:

> [**363**] The approach which has been taken in the more recent English decisions, particularly those decisions which vindicate the last three of the exceptions set forth above, is based on the rule in *Hadley v Baxendale.* Thus, in *Cox v Philips Industries Ltd,* Lawson J concluded that there was:
>
>> no reason in principle why, if a situation arises which within the contemplation of the parties would have given rise to vexation, distress and general disappointment and frustration, the person who is injured by a contractual breach should not be compensated in damages for that breach … .
>
> [**364**] Thus, in *Watts v Morrow,* Bingham LJ denied that the general exclusionary rule was founded on the assumption that the plaintiff's feelings are not foreseeable and asserted that it was founded on considerations of policy. He went on carefully and convincingly to delineate the circumstances in which damages could be awarded, observing:
>
>> But the rule is not absolute. Where the very object of a contract is to provide pleasure, relaxation, peace of mind or freedom from molestation, damages will be awarded if the fruit of the contract is not provided or if the contrary result is procured instead. If the law did not cater for this exceptional category of case it would be defective. A contract to survey the condition of a house for a prospective purchaser does not, however, fall within this exceptional category.
>>
>> In cases not falling within this exceptional category, damages are in my view recoverable for physical inconvenience and discomfort caused by the breach and mental suffering directly related to that inconvenience and discomfort.

On the ultimate question, whether Mrs Dillon was entitled to damages:

> [**366**] In the present case, the contract, which was for what in essence was a 'pleasure cruise', must be characterized as a contract the object of which was to provide for

enjoyment and relaxation. It follows that the respondent was entitled to an award of damages for disappointment and distress and physical inconvenience flowing from that breach of contract. Indeed, an award for disappointment and distress consequential upon physical inconvenience was justified on that account alone.

2 Restrictions under statute

State civil liability legislation has also impacted on the right to recover damages for non-pecuniary losses. An example is the *Civil Liability Act 2002* (NSW). You should read the following extracts closely in conjunction with principles text [5.78]–[5.80].

Civil Liability Act 2002 (NSW) ss 11A, 16, 27–28, 31

The following provisions of the Act restrict the availability of compensation for certain kinds of non-pecuniary loss.

11A Application of Part [here referring to part 1A – 'negligence']

(1) This Part applies to and in respect of an award of personal injury damages, except an award that is excluded from the operation of this Part by section 3B.

(2) This Part applies regardless of whether the claim for the damages is brought in tort, in contract, under statute or otherwise.

(3) A court cannot award damages, or interest on damages, contrary to this Part.

...

16 Determination of damages for non-economic loss

(1) No damages may be awarded for non-economic loss unless the severity of the non-economic loss is at least 15% of a most extreme case.

(2) The maximum amount of damages that may be awarded for non-economic loss is $350 000, but the maximum amount is to be awarded only in a most extreme case.

(3) If the severity of the non-economic loss is equal to or greater than 15% of a most extreme case, the damages for non-economic loss are to be determined in accordance with the following Table ...

...

27 Definitions

In this Part –

consequential mental harm means mental harm that is a consequence of a personal injury of any other kind.

mental harm means impairment of a person's mental condition.

negligence means failure to exercise reasonable care and skill.

personal injury includes –

(a) pre-natal injury, and

(b) impairment of a person's physical or mental condition, and

(c) disease.

pure mental harm means mental harm other than consequential mental harm.

28 Application of Part

(1) This Part (except section 29) applies to any claim for damages for mental harm resulting from negligence, regardless of whether the claim is brought in tort, in contract, under statute or otherwise.

(2) Section 29 applies to a claim for damages in any civil proceedings.

(3) This Part does not apply to civil liability that is excluded from the operation of this Part by section 3B.

...

31 Pure mental harm – liability only for recognised psychiatric illness

There is no liability to pay damages for pure mental harm resulting from negligence unless the harm consists of a recognised psychiatric illness.

REVIEW QUESTIONS

(1) What is the overarching principle for the recovery of damages for breach of contract?

(2) The plaintiff has agreed to sell the defendant what is described as a Chesterfield couch for $150. The couch is actually a fake. However, it is in good condition and is, in fact, actually worth $200. On the other hand, the plaintiff would have had to pay $1200 to buy a genuine Chesterfield couch of precisely the same style on which the fake is based. Assume that by selling a couch that was an imitation, the defendant is in breach of an express term of the contract by failing to deliver to the plaintiff a couch that complied with its description thereunder, namely a genuine Chesterfield.

Discuss the quantum of damages for breach of contract should the plaintiff be successful in an action for breach of contract against the defendant based on nothing more than the principles in *Robinson v Harman*.

(3) How are damages for breach of a commercial contract, which a plaintiff has made in anticipation of making a profit, calculated? Include in your answer an explicit analysis of the principles in *Commonwealth v Amann Aviation Pty Ltd* (1991) 174 CLR 64.

(4) Assuming that a breach of contract is established, who bears the onus of proof and in respect of what facts, in cases respectively of expectation damages and reliance damages?

III Attribution of responsibility

Remoteness is a limiting factor on the plaintiff's right to recover damages for breach of contract. At its loosest, the remoteness is the concept which limits the recoverability of damages to those which can be predicted.

Concept	Short explanation	Relevant authorities	Principles text
Remoteness of damage	Contractual damages to be recoverable must be foreseeable.	Generally: *Alexander v Cambridge Credit Corporation Ltd* (1987) 9 NSWLR 310	Chapter 5: [5.88]–[5.104]
The *Hadley v Baxendale test*	Remoteness is conventionally treated as a two-limbed test.	*Hadley v Baxendale* (1854) 156 ER 145	Chapter 5: [5.89]–[5.03]
The significance of the defendant's knowledge of the plaintiff's circumstances	The 'first' and 'second' limbs of *Hadley v Baxendale* (1854) 156 ER 145.	*Victoria Laundry (Windsor) Ltd v Newman Industries Ltd* [1949] 2 KB 528	Chapter 5: [5.93]–[5.97]
Assumption of responsibility as overriding criterion?	This is a relatively recent judicial development, of giving consideration to the paramountcy of the implied allocation of risk under a contract.	*Transfield Shipping Inc v Mercator Shipping Inc (The Achilleas)* [2009] 1 AC 61	Chapter 5: [5.98]–[5.104]

A Remoteness of damage

Contractual damages to be recoverable must be foreseeable. *Alexander v Cambridge Credit Corporation Ltd*, extracted below, has been selected for the explicit treatment of the proposition that damages that are too remote are irrecoverable.

Alexander v Cambridge Credit Corporation Ltd (1987) 9 NSWLR 310

Facts and issues

Cambridge Credit Corporation Ltd's ('Cambridge Credit') liquidator sued its auditor in relation to the auditor's failure to qualify the company's balance sheet. Had this breach not occurred, the company would have been placed into receivership. The auditors repeated the breach over the next three years. Three years later, the company went into receivership. The liquidator relied on the original breach, seeking damages for the losses suffered in those three years. It was alleged that as a result of that breach the company's debts soared. It was argued that those losses were solely brought about by the federal government's budgetary measures. The case is well known also for its treatment of causation: in relation to remoteness (the subject of the present discussion), the question was whether the losses were foreseeable.

Decision

The damage was too remote and could not be recovered.

McHugh JA

> [**363**] Losses which result from a breach of contract are not compensable if they are too remote. So another question in this case is whether the loss of $145 000 000 was too remote from the breach of contract even if it was causally connected.

...

[**365**] In later cases (eg, *H Parsons (Livestock) Ltd v Uttley, Ingham & Co Ltd*) there has been a tendency to play down the distinction between reasonable foreseeability and reasonable contemplation as semantic only. However, I think that the difference is a real one which results in a significant narrowing of liability. The word 'contemplation' seems to be used in *Koufos* in the sense of 'thoughtful consideration' or perhaps 'having inn view in the future'. It emphasises that, if the parties had thought about the matter, they would really have considered that the result had at least a 'serious possibility' of occurring.

...

[**366**] Cambridge contended that, at the time of the making of the contract in 1970, the parties would have contemplated as a serious possibility that, if in 1971 the auditors failed to perform their contractual duty, damage would occur of such a kind 'as was manifest in the deterioration' of Cambridge's financial position between September 1971 and September 1974. Cambridge argued that there was in contemplation both a serious possibility and a real danger that, if the company was not closed down in 1971 for breaches of the trust deed ratios, the directors would involve the company in further losses of the kind which eventuated. In my opinion this formulation is far too broad.

[**367**] The loss in the present case was caused in 1974 by the inability of Cambridge to meet its commitments as the result of the dramatic slump in land sales and prices and its inability to raise funds. These events were brought about by the severity of the government induced 'credit squeeze'. The claim of causation stretching from 1971 to 1974 was very long … .

It is, of course, unnecessary that the parties should have contemplated that the precise loss or damage would have occurred in the precise way in which it came about. But at least in a general way it was necessary to contemplate the type of damage suffered and the manner of its occurrence.

...

If it is legitimate to look at the loss as a whole, I do not think that it belongs to the kind of loss or damage which the parties would have contemplated as being a serious possibility of occurring. That the loss or damage did not commence to be suffered until 1973 or 1974 is in my opinion of very considerable importance. In 1970 I do not think that the parties would have contemplated as a serious possibility that Cambridge might suffer damage in 1973 or 1974 by reason of events of the kind which then took place.

The decisive consideration, however, is that the economic conditions encountered in 1974 were so different from the 'tightening of economic [**368**] conditions' that the parties might have contemplated in 1970 as to be different in kind.

...

I think that it would never have occurred to either Cambridge or the auditors, if they had directed their minds to the question in 1970, that a breach in 1971 of the kind here in question would bring about dramatic losses of the kind or in the general way that occurred in 1974 or, if it is relevant, the second half of 1973. Applying a phrase, which admittedly in *Koufos* was criticised, I think that the parties would not have thought that the losses in question were 'on the cards'.

1 The *Hadley v Baxendale* test

Remoteness is conventionally treated as a two-limbed test. This is eponymously known as the 'two limbs in *Hadley v Baxendale*'.

Hadley v Baxendale (1854) 156 ER 145

Facts and issues

Baxendale had been contracted to deliver Hadley's broken camshaft of its flour mill to Greenwich, to be used as a model to recast a replacement. In breach, the delivery was delayed. As a result, Hadley's mill was idle – resulting in a loss of profits. The question in this case concerned the extent to which Hadley was entitled to recover his lost profits as damages for breach of contract. This is the seminal case dealing with remoteness of damage in contract.

Decision

Hadley failed in his claim, as his damages were considered too remote.

Alderson B

> [**151**] Now we think the proper rule in such a case as the present is this:- Where two parties have made a contract which one of them bas broken, the damages which the other party ought to receive in respect of such breach of contract should be such as may fairly and reasonably be considered either arising naturally, ie, according to the usual course of things, from such breach of contract itself, or such as may reasonably be supposed to have been in the contemplation of both parties, at the time they made the contract, as the probable result of the breach of it. Now, if the special circumstances under which the contract was actually made were communicated by the plaintiffs to the defendants, and thus known to both parties, the damages resulting from the breach of such a contract, which they would reasonably contemplate, would be the amount of injury which would ordinarily follow from a breach of contract under these special circumstances so known and communicated. But, on the other hand, if these special circumstances were wholly unknown to the party breaking the contract, he, at the most, could only be supposed to have had in his contemplation the amount of injury which would arise generally, and in the great multitude of cases not affected by any special circumstances, from such a breach of contract. For, had the special circumstances been known, the parties might have specially provided for the breach of contract by special terms as to the damages in that case, and of this advantage it would be very unjust to deprive them Now the above principles are those by which we think the jury ought to be guided in estimating the damages arising out of any breach of contract.

2 The significance of the defendant's knowledge of the plaintiff's circumstances

The question of the defendant's knowledge of the plaintiff's circumstances expressly invokes an application of the second limb in *Hadley v Baxendale*. This was explored in the celebrated case of *Victoria Laundry (Windsor) Ltd v Newman Industries*.

Victoria Laundry (Windsor) Ltd v Newman Industries Ltd [1949] 2 KB 528

Facts and issues

By a contract between Victoria Laundry (Windsor) Ltd ('Victoria Laundry') and Newman Industries Ltd ('Newman'), Newman agreed to supply a boiler for Victoria Laundry's dyeing and dry-cleaning business. Delivery was delayed for a significant period of time. Victoria Laundry sought damages for the recovery of profits lost as a result of not having the boiler delivered on time. These included not only the profits for its existing business, but also the profits from a particular, lucrative contract.

Decision

Victoria Laundry succeeded in recovering the ordinary loss of profits but not the loss of profits on the lucrative contract, which were held to be too remote.

Asquith LJ

> [**533**] Seeing that the issue is as to the measure of recoverable damages and the application of the rules in *Hadley v Baxendale*, it is important to inquire what information the defendants possessed at the time when the contract was made as to such matters as the time at which, and the purpose for which, the plaintiffs required the boiler. The defendants knew before and at the time of the contract that the plaintiffs were laundrymen and dyers and required the boiler for purposes of their business as such.
>
> ...
>
> [**536**] He [the trial judge] took the view that the loss of profit claimed was due to special circumstances, and, therefore, recoverable, if at all, only under the second rule in *Hadley v Baxendale*, and not recoverable in the present case because such special circumstances were not at the time of the contract communicated to the defendants.
>
> ...
>
> [**539**] ...
>
> (3) What was at that time reasonably foreseeable depends on the knowledge then possessed by the parties, or, at all events, by the party who later commits the breach.
>
> (4) For this purpose, knowledge 'possessed' is of two kinds—one imputed, the other actual. Everyone, as a reasonable person, is taken to know the 'ordinary course of things' and consequently what loss is liable to result from a breach in that ordinary course. This is the subject-matter of the 'first rule' in in *Hadley v Baxendale,* but to this knowledge, which a contract-breaker is assumed to

possess whether he actually possesses it or not, there may have to be added in a particular case knowledge which he actually possesses of special circumstances outside the 'ordinary course of things' of such a kind that a breach in those special circumstances would be liable to cause more loss. Such a case attracts the operation of the 'second rule' so as to make additional loss also recoverable. In order to make the contract-breaker liable under either rule it is not necessary that he should actually have asked himself what loss is liable to result from a breach.

...

While it is not wholly clear what were the 'special circumstances' on the non-communication of which the learned judge relied, it would seem that they were or included the following:

(a) the [**540**] 'circumstance' that delay in delivering the boiler was going to lead 'necessarily' to loss of profits, but the true criterion is surely not what was bound 'necessarily' to result, but what was likely or liable to do so, and we think that it was amply conveyed to the defendants by what was communicated to them (plus what was patent without express communication) that delay in delivery was likely to lead to 'loss of business';

(b) the 'circumstance' that the plaintiffs needed the boiler 'to extend their business.' It was surely not necessary for the defendants to be specifically informed of this as a precondition of being liable for loss of business. Reasonable persons in the shoes of the defendants must be taken to foresee, without any express intimation, that a laundry which, at a time when there was a famine of laundry facilities, was paying £2000 odd for plant and intended at such a time to put such plant 'into use' immediately, would be likely to suffer in pocket from five months' delay in delivery of the plant in question, whether they intended by means of it to extend their business, or merely to maintain it, or to reduce a loss;

(c) the 'circumstance' that the plaintiffs had the assured expectation of special contracts, which they could only fulfil by securing punctual delivery of the boiler.

Here, no doubt, the learned judge had in mind the particularly lucrative dyeing contracts to which the plaintiffs looked forward and which they mention in para 10 of the statement of claim. We agree that in order that the plaintiffs should recover specifically and as such the profits expected on these contracts, the defendants would have had to know, at the time of their agreement with the plaintiffs, of the prospect and terms of such contracts. We also agree that they did not, in fact, know these things. It does not, however, follow that the plaintiffs are precluded from recovering some general (and perhaps conjectural) sum for loss of business in respect of dyeing contracts to be reasonably expected any more than in respect of laundering contracts to be reasonably expected.

3 Assumption of responsibility as overriding criterion?

There is some authority that the assumption of responsibility for risk is not the overriding criterion for the allocation of loss, arising from the primary decision in *Transfield Shipping Inc v Mercator Shipping Inc (The Achilleas)*.

Transfield Shipping Inc v Mercator Shipping Inc (The Achilleas) [2009] 1 AC 61

Facts and issues

Transfield Shipping Inc ('Transfield'), the appellant, was a charterer of a ship, the *Achilleas*, from its owner, Mercator Shipping Inc ('Mercator'). The ship was chartered with a specific date for redelivery. Prior to that date, Mercator had entered into a follow-on charter with another company, due to commence almost immediately after the redelivery date. The ship was not returned, and damages were claimed on the basis of the difference between the rate originally agreed under the follow-on charter and the reduced rate agreed in the renegotiated with the follow-on charterer. At issue was whether the owner was entitled to damages as claimed or if damages were to be based on market rates.

Decision

On the basis that the charterer had not assumed responsibility for the loss of hire under the follow-on charter, damages were based on the market rates, with Lord Hoffman adopting an 'assumption of responsibility' approach to remoteness.

Lord Hoffman

> [**68**] In their submissions to the House, the owners said that the starting point was that damages were designed to put the innocent party, so far as it is possible, in the position as if the contract had been performed: see *Robinson v Harman*. However, in *Banque Bruxelles Lambert SA v Eagle Star Insurance Co Ltd* (sub nom *South Australia Asset Management Corpn v York Montague Ltd*) I said:
>
> > I think that this was the wrong place to begin. Before one can consider the principle on which one should calculate the damages to which a plaintiff is entitled as compensation for loss, it is necessary to decide for what kind of loss he is entitled to compensation. A correct description of the loss for which the valuer is liable must precede any consideration of the measure of damages. In other words, one must first decide whether the loss for which compensation is sought is of a 'kind' or 'type' for which the contract- breaker ought fairly to be taken to have accepted responsibility.
> >
> > …
>
> [**70**] It is generally accepted that a contracting party will be liable for damages for losses which are unforeseeably large, if loss of that type or kind fell within one or other of the rules in *Hadley v Baxendale*: see, for example, Staughton J in *Transworld Oil Ltd v North Bay Shipping Corpn (The Rio Claro)* and *Jackson v Royal Bank of Scotland plc*. That is generally an inclusive principle: if losses of that type are foreseeable, damages will include compensation for those losses, however large. But the *South Australia* and *Mulvenna* cases show that it may also be an exclusive principle and that a party may not be liable for foreseeable losses because they are not of the type or kind for which he can be treated as having assumed responsibility.

What is the basis for deciding whether loss is of the same type or a different type? It is not a question of Platonist metaphysics. The distinction must rest upon some principle of the law of contract. In my opinion, the only rational basis for the distinction is that it reflects what would reasonably have been regarded by the contracting party as significant for the purposes of the risk he was undertaking. In *Victoria Laundry (Windsor) Ltd v Newman Industries Ltd*, where the plaintiffs claimed for loss of the profits from their laundry business because of late delivery of a boiler, the Court of Appeal did not regard loss of profits from the laundry business 'as a single type of loss. They distinguished losses from particularly lucrative dyeing contracts' as a different type of loss which would only be recoverable if the defendant had sufficient knowledge of them to make it reasonable to attribute to him acceptance of liability for such losses. The vendor of the boilers would have regarded the profits on these contracts as a different and higher form of risk than the general risk of loss of profits by the laundry.

If, therefore, one considers what these parties, contracting against the background of market expectations found by the arbitrators, would reasonably have considered the extent of the liability they were undertaking, I think it is clear that they would have considered losses arising from the loss **[71]** of the following fixture a type or kind of loss for which the charterer was not assuming responsibility. Such a risk would be completely unquantifiable, because although the parties would regard it as likely that the owners would at some time during the currency of the charter enter into a forward fixture, they would have no idea when that would be done or what its length or other terms would be. If it was clear to the owners that the last voyage was bound to overrun and put the following fixture at risk, it was open to them to refuse to undertake it. What this shows is that the purpose of the provision for timely redelivery in the charterparty is to enable the ship to be at the full disposal of the owner from the redelivery date. If the charterer's orders will defeat this right, the owner may reject them. If the orders are accepted and the last voyage overruns, the owner is entitled to be paid for the overrun at the market rate. All this will be known to both parties. It does not require any knowledge of the owner's arrangements for the next charter. That is regarded by the market is being, as the saying goes, res inter alios acta. The findings of the majority arbitrators shows that they considered their decision to be contrary to what would have been the expectations of the parties, but dictated by the rules in *Hadley v Baxendale* as explained in *The Heron II*. But in my opinion these rules are not so inflexible, they are intended to give effect to the presumed intentions of the parties and not to contradict them.

...

In my opinion, the findings of the arbitrators and the commercial background to the agreement are sufficient to make it clear that the charterer cannot reasonably be regarded as having assumed the risk of the owner's loss of profit on the following charter. I would therefore allow the appeal.

B Contributory negligence

Contributory negligence on the part of the plaintiff may diminish or extinguish the liability of the defendant. See the principles text at [5.105]–[5.114] for more details.

REVIEW QUESTIONS

(1) There are said to be two limbs in *Hadley v Baxendale* (1854) 156 ER 145, being limbs of a single rule. Set out in your answer the single rule in the case, then explain what each sub rule/limb cover. Illustrate your understanding of each of the limbs by reference to the reasoning in *Victoria Laundry (Windsor) Ltd v Newman Industries Ltd* [1949] 2 KB 528.

(2) McHugh J said in *Alexander v Cambridge Credit Corporation Ltd* (1987) 9 NSWLR 310: 'there has been a tendency to play down the distinction between reasonable foreseeability and reasonable contemplation as semantic only. However, I think that the difference is a real one … ' (at 365). Was his Honour in favour of narrowing, or broadening, the scope of remoteness and if so in what sense? State also from whose viewpoint the test of 'remoteness' was to be assessed.

(3) As explained in the principles text at [5.102], it is uncertain if the principles in *Transfield Shipping Inc v Mercator Shipping Inc (The Achilleas)* [2009] 1 AC 61 are good law in Australia. If we assume that *Transfield* is considered to be good law in Australia, how would the reasoning in *Transfield* affect the principles in *Hadley v Baxendale* (1854) 156 ER 145?

6 COMPENSATION IN TORT

I	Introduction	205
II	Assessment of compensation	205
	A General principle	207
	B Specific contexts	208
III	Attribution of responsibility	223
	A Remoteness of damage	226
	B Contributory negligence	244

I Introduction

This chapter considers the rules governing claims for compensatory damages in tort. Compensation in tort is generally governed by the same rules that apply to all civil wrongs, although some specific rules apply to torts claims in particular.

II Assessment of compensation

The appropriate measure of compensation for loss caused by wrongful conduct is that which puts the plaintiff into the position they would have been in but for the defendant's wrong. However, what specific order for damages the court should make in any particular case varies according to the type of loss suffered by the plaintiff and the circumstances in which the loss was suffered. The following section considers the appropriate form of damages in relation to a range of losses that a plaintiff may suffer as a result of a defendant's wrongful conduct.

Concept	Short explanation	Relevant authorities	Principles text
General principle	Compensation in tort aims to place the victim 'in the same position as he would have been in if he had not sustained the wrong'.	*Livingstone v Rawyards Coal Co* (1880) 5 App Cas 25	Chapter 6: [6.2]
Specific contexts: damage to reputation – defamation	Damages for defamation are awarded for personal distress and hurt, reparation for harm to reputation, and vindication of reputation.	*Carson v John Fairfax & Sons Ltd* (1993) 178 CLR 44	Chapter 6: [6.4]–[6.11]

Concept	Short explanation	Relevant authorities	Principles text
Specific contexts: damage to land or fixtures	The cost of repair to damaged land or fixtures will be awarded unless it is disproportionate to the diminution of value of the land or fixture.	*Evans v Balog* [1976] 1 NSWLR 36	Chapter 6: [6.12]–[6.20]
	Whether the measure of damages is to be the cost of reinstatement or damages for diminution in value is to be tested by the reasonableness of the plaintiff's desire to reinstate the property.	*Pantalone v Alaouie* (1989) 18 NSWLR 119	
Specific contexts: other wrongful interference with land	Pecuniary loss caused by trespass is compensable.	*Balanced Securities Ltd v Bianco (No 2)* (2010) 27 VR 599	Chapter 6: [6.21]–[6.25]
Specific contexts: damage to goods	Restitution in relation to damaged goods can be made either by repairing the damage and making good the loss of use while the repair is being done, or by replacing the property at once with another of comparable type and condition.	*Jansen v Dewhurst* [1969] VR 421	Chapter 6: [6.26]–[6.32]
Specific contexts: other wrongful interference with goods	In cases of conversion, the plaintiff is entitled to recover no more in damages than they have actually suffered.	*Butler v Egg and Egg Pulp Marketing Board* (1966) 114 CLR 185	Chapter 6: [6.33]–[6.38]
Specific contexts: defective premises or goods	The owner or tenant of a property may have a claim in negligence against a person who is responsible for a latent defect in part of the plaintiff's property where that latent defect leads to the plaintiff suffering loss.	*Pyrenees Shire Council v Day* (1998) 192 CLR 330	Chapter 6: [6.39]–[6.48]
Specific contexts: damage to economic interests – reliance on a misrepresentation	The appropriate measure of damages in an action for deceit where damage is to economic interests is the difference between what the plaintiff has paid and the real market value of the assets acquired.	*Toteff v Antonas* (1952) 87 CLR 647	Chapter 6: [6.49]–[6.54]

A General principle

The following case outlines the general compensatory principle in claims for damages in tort.

Livingstone v Rawyards Coal Co (1880) 5 App Cas 25

Facts and issues

Rawyards Coal Co ('Raywards', the respondents) took coal coming from underground deposits belonging to Livingston (the appellant) and sold it to third parties. This occurred without any fault on their part, innocently believing it to be their own coal when in fact it belonged to Livingston. One of the issues to be determined in this case related to the appropriate measure of damages in tort.

Decision

The House of Lords held that the appropriate measure of damages in tort was the amount that put the plaintiff in the position they would have been in had they not sustained the wrong in question.[1]

Lord Blackburn

> **[39]** I do not think there is any difference of opinion as to its being a general rule that, where any injury is to be compensated by damages, in settling the sum of money to be given for reparation of damages you should as nearly as possible get at that sum of money which will put the party who has been injured, or who has suffered, in the same position as he would have been in if he had not sustained the wrong for which he is now getting his compensation or reparation. That must be qualified by a great many things which may arise such, for instance, as by the consideration whether the damage has been maliciously done, or whether it has been done with full knowledge that the person doing it was doing wrong. There could be no doubt that there you would say that everything would be taken into view that would go most against the wilful wrongdoer – many things which you would properly allow in favour of an innocent mistaken trespasser would be disallowed as against a wilful and intentional trespasser on the ground that he must not qualify his own wrong, and various things of that sort. But in such a case as the present, where it is agreed that the Defenders, without any fault whatever on their part, have innocently, and, being ignorant, with as little negligence or carelessness as possible, taken this coal, believing it to be their own, when in fact it belonged to the Pursuer, then comes the question, – how are we to get at the sum of money which will compensate them?
>
> Now, my Lords, there was a technical rule in the English Courts in these matters. When something that was part of the realty (we are talking of coal in this particular case) is severed from the realty and converted into a chattel, then instantly on its becoming a chattel, it becomes the property of the person who had been the owner of the fee in the land whilst it remained a portion of the land; and then in estimating the damages against a person who

1 Applied in *Butler v Egg and Egg Pulp Marketing Board* (1966) 114 CLR 185, 191; *Nominal Defendant v Gardikiotis* (1996) 186 CLR 49; *Husher v Husher* (1999) 197 CLR 138, 143–4; *Harriton v Stephens* (2006) 226 CLR 52, [81], [264].

had carried away that chattel, it was considered and decided that the owners of the fee was to be paid the value of the chattel at [40] the time when it was converted …

Such was the rule of the Common Law … That was the rule to be applied where it was an innocent person that did the wrong … [I]t was followed in the Court of Chancery, and, so far as I know, it has never been questioned since, that where there is an innocent wrongdoing the point that is to be made out for the damages is, as was expressed in the minutes of the decree: – 'The Defendants to be charged with the fair value of such coal and other minerals at the same rate as if the mines had been purchased by the Defendants at the fair market value of the district;' that I understand to mean as if the mines had been purchased while the minerals were yet part of the soil. That, I apprehend, is what is to be done here, and that is what both the Lord Ordinary and the First Division of the Court of Session have endeavoured to do.

B Specific contexts

1 Damage to reputation: defamation

Damages for defamation are awarded as a single sum, although this sum relates to three particular purposes behind the award. These are:

(1) consolation for personal distress and hurt
(2) reparation for harm done to the person's reputation and
(3) vindication of the person's reputation.

Carson v John Fairfax & Sons Ltd (1993) 178 CLR 44

Facts and issues

Carson (the appellant) was a solicitor whose name appeared in two newspaper articles published by John Fairfax & Sons ('Fairfax', the respondents), which were written by a reporter employed by Fairfax. Carson brought two separate defamation actions against Fairfax and the reporter, and was awarded damages in relation to both actions.

Decision

In deciding whether the damages awarded to Carson at trial were excessive, the High Court commented on the purposes underlying an award of damages for defamation.

Mason CJ, Deane J, Dawson J and Gaudron J

[**60**] … Specific economic loss and exemplary or punitive damages aside, there are three purposes to be served by damages awarded for defamation. The three purposes no doubt overlap considerably in reality and ensure that 'the amount of a verdict is the product of a mixture of inextricable considerations' (citation omitted). The three purposes are

consolation for the personal distress and hurt caused to the appellant by the publication, reparation for the harm done to the appellant's personal and (if relevant) business reputation and vindication of the appellant's reputation (citation omitted). The first two purposes are frequently considered together and constitute consolation for the wrong done to the [**61**] appellant (citation omitted). Vindication looks to the attitude of others to the appellant: the sum awarded must be at least the minimum necessary to signal to the public the vindication of the appellant's reputation. 'The gravity of the libel, the social standing of the parties and the availability of alternative remedies' are all relevant to assessing the quantum of damages necessary to vindicate the appellant (citation omitted).

Brennan J

[**69**] The chief purpose of the law in creating a cause of action for defamation is to provide vindication to counter the injury done to the plaintiff in his or her reputation. Lord Radcliffe said in *Dingle v Associated Newspapers Ltd.* (citation omitted):

> A libel action is fundamentally an action to vindicate a man's reputation on some point as to which he has been falsely defamed, and the damages awarded have to be regarded as the demonstrative mark of that vindication.

The sufficiency of the amount awarded is not to be determined by [**70**] reference solely to circumstances past and present; the amount must be sufficient to vindicate the plaintiff's reputation in the relevant respect in the future.

...

Although damages are awarded to vindicate the plaintiff's reputation, damages are not awarded as compensation for the loss in value of a plaintiff's reputation as though that reputation were itself a tangible asset or a physical attribute which, once damaged, is worth less than it was before (citation omitted). In order to achieve the purpose of vindicating reputation, damages for defamation are quantified by reference, inter alia, to what is needed to achieve that purpose: those damages are not quantified by reference to a depreciation in the value of a plaintiff's reputation. Other heads of damage are compensation for the external consequences produced by the publication of the defamation and 'a solatium' for the plaintiff's internal hurt, that is, for the complex of reactions that the plaintiff has experienced as the result of the publication and its external consequences.

[**71**] The consequences of publication include not only the insult publicly inflicted on the plaintiff but also the effect of the defamation on those to whom it is published (citation omitted), any diminution in the regard in which the plaintiff is held by others, any isolation produced (causing the plaintiff to be 'shunned or avoided' is the traditional formula) and any conduct adverse to the plaintiff engaged in by others because of the publication of the defamatory matter. Damages are awarded also for the plaintiff's injured feelings (citation omittod), including the hurt, anxiety, loss of self-esteem, the sense of indignity and the sense of outrage felt by the plaintiff. Indeed, all those objective consequences and those subjective reactions which flow naturally from the publication of the defamatory matter are relevant factors. Of course, the subjective reactions are often produced by the objective consequences of the publication. The two categories are not cumulative heads of damage but descriptions of kinds of intangible factors which must be taken into account in assessing damages.

2 Damage to land or fixtures

In cases involving damage to land or fixtures, the quantum of damages may be set according to the cost of repair or the diminution of value of the land or the fixture. The following case is an example where the cost of repair was considered to be disproportionate to the loss of value in the damaged land.

Evans v Balog [1976] 1 NSWLR 36

Facts and issues

Balog (the defendant) commenced excavating a site for the purposes of building a dwelling, and the vibrations of the works conducted on the site caused significant damage to Evans's (the plaintiff) home next door. Evans commenced an action against Balog and Balog admitted liability. At issue in the case was the extent of the damages which Evans was entitled to recover.

Decision

The cost of repair to damaged land or fixtures will be awarded unless it is disproportionate to the diminution of value of the land or fixture.

Samuels JA[2]

> [**38**] In their written submissions, counsel for the defendants contended that the measure of damage … was to be established by the cost of effecting reasonable repairs to the premises. Specifically, the defendants disclaimed reliance upon a measure represented by the amount of any diminution in the value of the house occasioned by the damage done by their operations.
>
> His Honour in essence adopted the principle which the defendants asserted, and which the plaintiffs' counsel did not in substance deny. The learned judge, therefore, assessed damages, in relation to the damage to the house, by awarding the plaintiffs the sum reasonably necessary to restore it to the condition in which it had been prior to the defendants' tortious intervention.
>
> The defendants appealed; and their point is that this approach is incorrect, and that the measure to be applied is the extent to which the value of the plaintiffs' house has been diminished by the defendants' wrongful conduct. If this argument is right, then it may follow that … the plaintiffs have suffered no significant damage at all … It founds upon evidence which suggests … that the house, being in an area zoned for high-rise development, the improvements on the land, which should be viewed as a development site only, had no value on the market. The house, therefore, [**39**] had no value in December 1970; hence, of course, its value could not further diminish.
>
> …
>
> One commences, I think, with the general proposition that the measure of damages in tort is: ' … that sum of money which will put the party who has been injured … in the same

2 Moffitt P in agreement (41), Hutley JA in agreement (41).

position as he would have been in if he had not sustained the wrong for which he is now getting his compensation or reparation.'

I have quoted the words of Lord Blackburn in *Livingstone v Rawyards Coal Co*. (citation omitted). I need not multiply citations in support of this principle. But I observe in addition that in *Admiralty Commissioners v SS Susquehanna* (citation omitted) Lord Dunedin said that the purpose of an award of damages is to give the injured party, so far as money can, reparation for the wrongful act. But that object may be achieved in different ways, and a proper assessment is determined by the circumstances of the case and by the overriding requirements of what is reasonable. As Denning LJ, as he then was, said in *Philips v Ward* (citation omitted): 'It all depends on the circumstances of the case: … The general rule is that the injured person is to be fairly compensated for the damage he has sustained, neither more nor less.'

In a case such as the present, involving tortious damage to a building, it cannot be said that the normal measure of damages is the amount of diminution in the value of the land and improvements … The view that an equally admissible measure is the cost of reinstatement and restoration is supported by *Hollebone v Midhurst and Fernhurst Builders Ltd* (citation omitted) and **[40]** *Harbutt's 'Plasticine' Ltd v Wayne Tank and Pump Co Ltd*. (citation omitted) … As the learned author of *McGregor on Damages* says at p. 713 [of *Harbutt*], the case sustains what I take to be the true criterion of the selection between diminution of value and the cost of reinstatement. What he says is this: 'The test which appears to be the appropriate one is the reasonableness of the plaintiffs' desire to reinstate the property; this will be judged in part by the advantages to him of reinstatement in relation to the extra cost to the defendant in having to pay damages for reinstatement rather than damages calculated by the diminution in value of the land.'

Hence, it is sometimes said that a plaintiff may have the cost of restoration provided that it is not disproportionate to the diminution in value. Cf. *Public Trustee v Hormann* (citation omitted). This is merely an alternative way of stating the principle expressed in *McGregor on Damages*.

I turn then to the facts of the present case … The question is whether it was reasonable for the plaintiffs to desire to reinstate their property. In my opinion, there is only one answer. It undoubtedly was. They had, in effect, lost their family home. That is the nature of their damage, and not some diminution in the value of their land. Fair compensation requires that they be given back what they had before; and the only way in which that purpose can be achieved is to award them the sum reasonably necessary to restore their property to the condition in which it was before the defendants effectively destroyed it. This the learned judge did; and, in my opinion, he was right. It is not to the point that the diminution in value basis might on one view produce no damages, while the reinstatement basis produces a substantial sum. The disproportion in question in cases of this kind are not always to be revealed by arithmetical comparison. The cost to a defendant of competing measures is a significant factor. But it is but one ingredient in the calculation of whether the plaintiffs' claim is reasonable or not. There are cases, and this, in my opinion, is one, where the nature of the plaintiffs' loss is such that there is only one mode of fairly repairing it. If that turns out to be more expensive than another, the wrongdoer has no one but himself to blame. That is, I think, sufficient to dispose of the case.

The following case demonstrates the appropriate measure of damages when the plaintiff effects repairs to land or fixtures negligently damaged by the defendant, but where the cost of repairs goes beyond the cost of rectification. In particular, the extract considers when repair will be considered reasonable in these circumstances.

Pantalone v Alaouie (1989) 18 NSWLR 119

Facts and issues

Mr and Mrs Pantalone (the plaintiffs) owned and leased a property which was destroyed as a result of Alaouie's (the defendant) negligent excavation works at an adjoining block of land. The estimated cost of rebuilding the property was $172 000, whereas the difference in value between the land as vacant land and the land with the original building on it was $116 000. At issue in this case was whether the amount of damages the Pantalones were entitled to should be set by reference to the cost of rebuilding or the diminution in the value of the property.

Decision

The measure of damages in relation to tortious damage to buildings is to be tested by the reasonableness of the plaintiff's desire to reinstate the property having regard to the advantages to the plaintiff of reinstatement and the extra cost to the defendant in having to pay damages for reinstatement rather than damages for diminution in value.

Giles J

> [**136**] …
>
> At the time of hearing No 310 was vacant land: the remains of the collapsed building had been wholly removed. The estimated cost of rebuilding as at March 1989 was $172 000, with a total building time including time for council approval of ten to twelve months. The difference in value between No 310 as vacant land and No 310 with the original building standing thereon as at March 1989 was $116 000. The major contest on the Pantalone claim was whether the damages in relation to the building should be assessed on the basis of the cost of rebuilding or on the basis of diminution in the value of No 310.
>
> The general principle in awarding damages in tort is to seek to restore the plaintiff to the position in which he would have been had the wrongful act not been committed: (citations omitted).
>
> A number of decisions have called for the application of that principle in circumstances such as the present.
>
> In *Public Trustee v Hermann*, it was said … that the plaintiff may elect as between damages for loss of market value after the subsidence and damages representing the reasonable cost of restoration to pre-subsidence condition, provided in the latter case that the cost of restoration is not disproportionate to such loss of market value; if it is, then the plaintiff can only recover the loss of market value. Isaacs J considered that a cost of restoration of $14 510 was out of all proportion to the diminution in value of $2000, and held that the plaintiff was not entitled to elect to recover the former figure …

[His honour next considered *Evans v Balog* [1976] 1 NSWLR 36 in which Samuels JA held that a plaintiff may have the cost of restoration provided that it is not disproportionate to the diminution in value, and that on the facts, reinstatement cost was appropriate.]

…

[**137**] In *Parramatta City Council v Lutz*, the plaintiff's house had been destroyed by fire, by reason of the defendant's negligence. The trial judge allowed damages for the replacement value of the house, not the reinstatement cost: the latter was a substantially higher figure than the former. It was held on appeal (by majority consisting of Kirby P and McHugh JA, Mahoney JA dissenting on this point) that the plaintiff should have the reinstatement cost. Kirby P considered that the plaintiff's desire to have her home reinstated was not unreasonable, nor excessive or extravagant. McHugh JA saw nothing unreasonable in her desire, stating … : 'She wants a home, not a sum of money. A sum equivalent to the value of her home will not give her a home.' With a reference to *Evans v Balog*, McHugh JA said … that when the choice is between damages which constitute the value of the property destroyed or the cost of reinstating and restoring that property, and the cost of the restoration exceeds the value of the destroyed property, a plaintiff is entitled to the cost of reinstatement only if it is reasonable to have the property reinstated and restored …

In the present case the Pantalones bought No 310 as an investment …

[**138**] … I apply the test adopted as the true criterion in *Evans v Balog*: how reasonable is the Pantalones' desire to rebuild, judged in part by the advantages to them of rebuilding in relation to the additional cost to the defendants over the diminution in value? …

It is understandable that the Pantalones do not wish to embark upon the search for another investment property, and do not wish to run the risk of choosing wisely. But I do not think that the inconvenience of the search counts for much, as there would also be the inconvenience of seeing to rebuilding … While there is no direct evidence on the point, from occasional reference in the evidence and in particular from the valuation report it seems that the building on No 310 was a fairly typical building, and there is nothing to suggest that it was unable to be replaced by purchase of a like property. And there is no particular reason why the Pantalones should replace their investment property by a property of the same nature – they can replace it by an investment property of a different nature, and I think I can assume that properties would be available in the market to enable them to do so. It seems to me that their understandable desire to rebuild cannot be regarded as reasonable when balanced against the fairly large additional cost of $45 000 which would be imposed upon the defendants if damages were assessed on the basis of rebuilding. I therefore think that the basis of diminution in value should be adopted.

3 Other wrongful interference with land

The following case concerns wrongful interference with land as a result of trespass. It demonstrates, inter alia, that as with damages in negligence, damages in trespass are compensatory and endeavour to restore the plaintiff to the position they would have been in but for the defendant's wrong.

Balanced Securities Ltd v Bianco (No 2) [2010] VSC 201; (2010) 27 VR 599

Facts and issues

Balanced Securities Ltd ('Balanced Securities', the plaintiff) became entitled to possession of a unit in 2003 which was unlawfully occupied by Bianco's (the defendant) tenant until 2010. The issue to be determined in this case was the quantum of the damages payable by Bianco to Balanced Securities as a result of the unlawful occupation of the unit by Bianco's tenant.

Decision

Pecuniary loss caused by trespass is compensable, and damages for trespass are to be treated in no different way to damages in respect of any other form of tort.

Forrest J

> [**4 [11]**] In *Lollis v Loulatzis & Petruccelli*, (citation omitted) Kaye J conducted a scholarly and extensive analysis of the principles associated with an award of damages for trespass. Two of the authorities considered by his Honour merit repetition in the context of this application.
>
> [**5 [12]**] In *Swordheath Properties Ltd v Tabet & Ors* (citation omitted) a leading authority on an allowance for mesne profits, Megaw LJ said:
>
>> It appears to me to be clear, both as a matter of principle and of authority, that in a case of this sort the plaintiff, when he has established that the defendant has remained on as a trespasser in residential property, is entitled, without bringing evidence that he could or would have let the property to someone else in the absence of the trespassing defendant, to have as damages for the trespass the value of the property as it would fairly be calculated; and in the absence of anything special in the particular case it would be the ordinary letting value of the property that would determine the amount of the damages.

It will be noted that his Lordship was not limiting the measure of damages solely to mesne profits, but rather making the observation that this was the usual form of assessment in a trespass case.

> [**5 [13]**] Subsequently in *Inverugie Investments Ltd v Hackett* (citation omitted) the Privy Council said: –
>
>> It is sometimes said that these cases are an exception to the rule that damages in tort are compensatory. But this is not necessarily so. It depends on how widely one defines the 'loss' which the plaintiff has suffered … In *Stoke-On-Trent City Council v W & J Wass Limited* (citation omitted) Nicholls LJ called the underlying principle in these cases the 'user principle'. The plaintiff may not have suffered any actual loss by being deprived of the use of his property. But under the user principle he is entitled to recover a reasonable rent for the wrongful use of his property by the trespasser. Similarly, the trespasser may not have derived any *actual* benefit from

> the use of the property. But under the user principle he is obliged to pay a reasonable rent for the use which he has enjoyed. The principle need not be characterised as exclusively compensatory, or exclusively restitutionary; it combines elements of both.

[5 **[14]**] I should now return to the judgment of Kaye J in *Lollis*. His Honour described the law relating to assessment of damages for trespass as being well settled:

> Damages awarded for trespass to land are sometimes described as 'mesne' profits. The usual measure of such damages is constituted by the value of the market rent for the premises which the trespasser should have paid during the period of the trespasser's occupation of the premises. In order to prove an entitlement to such damages, it is not necessary for the plaintiff to establish that the property has been damaged, or that the plaintiff would have been able, or indeed willing, to lease the premises during the period of [6 **[14]**] the trespass. (Citation omitted).

However, his Honour went on to say as to the principle underpinning such an award:

> Similarly, to the extent to which damages in a case such as this may be compensatory, *it is basic that, in an action for tort, damages are awarded as compensation, in order to restore the plaintiff to the position in which the plaintiff would have been, had the tort not occurred.* (citation omitted) (emphasis added)

[6 **[15]**] There is no suggestion as Kaye J noted, that basic compensatory damages principles are not applicable to a claim in trespass. It must follow, I think, that there is no inherent limitation on a claim for trespass to damages solely in the form of mesne profits.

[6 **[16]**] In light of the above, I think the following can be concluded:

(a) Damages for trespass are to be treated in no different way to damages in respect of any other form of tort. Insofar as such damages are compensatory, they endeavour to restore the plaintiff to the same position which he or she would have been in, but for the wrong.

(b) The usual measure of damages for trespass is by an award of mesne profits, being the value of the market rental for the premises during the period of the trespasser's occupation;

(c) However, given that the damages sought by HGR in this case are compensatory in nature, their evaluation is not limited to mesne profits, but rather, may, be determined by the application of general principles relevant to an award of compensatory damages;

(d) Accordingly, in an appropriate case there may be ways of measuring the loss caused by the trespass other than mesne profits. Damages pursuant to the *Hungerfords* principle are compensatory and, therefore, may be awarded if the facts support such an allowance – that is to say that it is open to HGR to make a claim for the loss of the commercial opportunity to invest the putative [7 **[16]**] funds, realised from the hypothetical mortgagees' sale, in other investments or transactions.

4 Damage to goods

The following case outlines the relevant principles relating to the question of whether, in cases involving wrongful damage to goods, the defendant is required to repair the damage to the relevant piece of property and make good the loss while repair is being effected, or completely replace the relevant piece of property.

Jansen v Dewhurst [1969] VR 421

Facts and issues

Jansen (the applicant) and Dewhurst (the respondent) were involved in a motor vehicle accident caused by Jansen's negligence. Dewhurst claimed $1043.17 in damages from Jansen, which was the sum quoted by a motor vehicle smash repairer to repair Dewhurst's vehicle and restore it to its pre-accident condition. One of the issues in this case related to the appropriate measure of damages in the circumstances.

Decision

The Court found that when property is damaged, restitution can be made to the owner either by repairing the damage and making good the loss of use while the repair is being done, or by replacing the property at once with another of comparable type and condition. Which of these two courses is appropriate will depend on the circumstances and the extent of the damage.

Newton J

[425] ...

The relevant law is set out by Wild, CJ, in *Bartlett v DH Small & Son Ltd*, (citation omitted), at pp. 260–1, in the following terms:

> I think that two principles govern the determination of the proper measure of damages in such a case as this. The first is the well-established rule that the plaintiff is entitled to be put back, so far as money can do it, into the same position as if the damage had not occurred. That is *restitutio in integrum* and it is the basic principle. The second, which is also well known, amounts to a qualification of the principle of restitution. It is that the plaintiff must do what is reasonable to minimise his loss or mitigate the damage.
>
> When a car is damaged in a collision restitution can be made to the owner either by repairing the damage and making good the loss of use while the repair is being done, or by replacing the car at once with another of comparable type and condition. Which of these two courses is appropriate will depend on the circumstances and, in the normal case, mainly on the extent of the damage. If the car is wrecked completely, replacement will no doubt be the only course open. If it is damaged, repair will usually be appropriate. If a car of some age is badly **[426]** damaged, it may be cheaper to make restitution by way of replacement with a car of comparable age and condition than by way of repair. Again, if there is something

> unique about the vehicle as, for example, in the case of a 'vintage car', replacement may be impossible and repair even at very heavy cost may be the only course appropriate. The test of what is appropriate is reasonableness in the particular circumstances, and the reasonableness is a question of fact.
>
> It is on this aspect that the second principle comes into operation. Reasonableness must in my view be considered not only from the point of view of the plaintiff but also from that of the defendant who has to pay.

Subject to two qualifications … I respectfully accept this statement of the law as being correct …

The two qualifications … are … that if the true view in any particular case is that the damages should be primarily based on the cost of replacing the car with another car of comparable age and condition, then, first, an allowance may be made in favour of the plaintiff for the hire of a vehicle during the period while a replacement car is being sought and acquired …, and, secondly, an allowance should be made in favour of the defendant in respect of the value (If any) if(sic) the plaintiff's original car in its damaged condition …

Mr Francis who appeared before me for the respondent submitted that the prima facie measure of damages in the present case was the cost of repairs, and that the onus lay on the applicant to show that cost of replacement was the appropriate measure of damages. I disagree with submission.

In my opinion, in a case such as the present the onus lies on the plaintiff to satisfy the tribunal on the whole of the evidence as to which method of assessing damages is correct (ie, in substance, either cost of repairs or cost of replacement), and also as to the amount of damages to which he is entitled by the application of that method. Of course, in many cases, it would be obvious without any special evidence that one method was appropriate to the exclusion of the other. And there could be cases where either method would be appropriate. But, in my opinion, there is no rule of law that the measure of damages is prima facie the cost of repairs, so that the burden would be on the defendant to show that replacement cost was the appropriate measure in any case where the plaintiff claimed the cost of repairs.

5 Other wrongful interference with goods

Wrongful interference with goods can occur in circumstances where those goods are not damaged. This is demonstrated in the following case, which outlines the relevant principles concerning the appropriate amount of damages in cases of conversion.

Butler v Egg and Egg Pulp Marketing Board (1966) 114 CLR 185

Facts and issues

Butler (the appellant in this appeal and defendant in the originating action) were producers of eggs. As a result of the *Marketing of Primary Products Act 1958* (Vic), property in the eggs produced by Butler was divested from Butler and vested in and became the absolute property of the Egg Pulp

Marketing Board ('the Board', the respondent in this appeal and plaintiff in the originating action) when they came into existence. The rights and interests of Butler in the eggs thereupon were converted into claims for payment in accordance with the legislation. In this case, Butler did not deliver the eggs to the Board, instead selling them to a third party. This act of conversion thereby gave the Board the right to bring a claim against Butler. The issue in this case related to the manner in which the damages should be assessed.

Decision

The Court held that in cases of conversion the plaintiff is entitled to recover no more in damages than they have actually suffered. In the circumstances, the Board was not entitled to the full value of the eggs, but instead was entitled to an amount which represented the difference between the price for which it would have sold the eggs had they been delivered to it by Butler and the amount which in that event it would have had to pay to Butler under the legislation.

Taylor and Owen JJ[3]

> [**190**] ... The Board's contention was that it was entitled to the full value of the eggs converted. The appellants, on the other hand, contended that the Board's loss was represented by the difference between the price for which it would have sold the eggs had they been delivered to it by the appellants and the amount which in that event it would have had to pay to them.
>
> ...
>
> Little J upheld the Board's contention and from his decision this appeal is brought. His Honour's reasons began with the proposition that in an action of conversion the general rule is that the plaintiff is entitled to recover the value of the goods converted. There are, he pointed out, exceptions to that general rule, as where the defendant, as between himself and the plaintiff, has an interest in the thing converted. This exception, he thought, had no application to the present case. The appellants had no interest in the eggs. All that they had were claims for payment which were conditioned upon delivery of the eggs to the Board, a delivery which in fact had not been made. For these reasons his Honour applied what he described as the general rule and held that the Board was entitled to recover the full value of the eggs.
>
> If this be correct, it would mean that the appellants would have to pay to the Board, by way of damages, the amount which the Board would have received had the eggs been delivered to and sold by it. The amount so paid would become part of the Board's funds and as such would be available to meet a proportion of its costs and to provide payments to other producers who were entitled to share in the 'pool' but the appellants would not be entitled to receive any such payments since the eggs had not been delivered by them to the Board. It would follow that the Board would be in a better position financially than would

3 Menzies J in agreement: *Butler v Egg and Egg Pulp Marketing Board* (1966) 114 CLR 185, 192–3.

have been the case had the appellants complied with the Act since it would have received the [**191**] full value of the eggs, would have incurred no expense in handling and disposing of them and be under no obligation to make any payment for them. But such a result would not accord with the general principle upon which compensatory damages are assessed, whether in actions of contract or of tort. That principle is that the injured party should receive compensation in a sum which, so far as money can do so, will put him in the same position as he would have been in if the contract had been performed or the tort had not been committed: *Livingstone v Rawyards Coal Co*. (citation omitted). And this principle is as much applicable to actions of conversion as it is to the case of other actionable wrongs. In most cases of conversion it is, of course, obvious that its application will result in the injured plaintiff recovering the full value of the property converted since that will usually represent the loss that he has sustained by the defendant's wrongful act. Hence the statement which appears so often in the books that the general rule is that the plaintiff in an action of conversion is entitled to recover the full value of the goods converted, but this statement should not be allowed to obscure the broad principle that damages are awarded by way of compensation. If the present case had been one in which the appellants had agreed to sell and deliver the eggs to the Board under a contract which had passed the property in them to the Board and, in breach of their contractual obligation, had failed to deliver the eggs and instead had converted them to their own use, the Board would not have been entitled to recover the full value of the eggs. Its loss would have been represented by the difference between that value and the price which it had agreed to pay and which it would have had to pay had the vendors carried out their contract … (citation omitted). Here there was no such contract. The case is one of compulsory acquisition. It is true that the appellants, by their wrongful act, put it out of their power to make delivery with the result that the Board came under no obligation to pay them but, to adapt the words of Bramwell B in *Chinery v Viall* (citation omitted), it would be singular if the same act which saved the Board the price of the eggs should vest in it a right of action for their full value without deducting the price. The Board's loss must, in our opinion, be determined by considering what sum of money would be required to place it in the same position as it would have been in if the appellants had performed their statutory obligation. Had they done so, the Board would, on the figures agreed upon by the [**192**] parties, have realized £4000 by selling the eggs and out of that sum would have had to pay the appellants £2900. Its loss resulting from the appellants' tortious act is therefore £1100.

6 Defective premises or goods

A plaintiff may be entitled to claim damages from defendant in circumstances where the plaintiff has suffered loss as a result of a latent defect in premises or goods caused by the defendant's wrong. The following case provides an example of this. It concerns the liability of a local council in circumstances where the local council had a discretionary power to act to prevent fires occurring, but did not exercise this power with due care, thus resulting in loss to the plaintiff tenant.

Pyrenees Shire Council v Day (1998) 192 CLR 330

Facts and issues

In this case, a latent defect in a chimney on a leased premises caused a fire to break out after a fire was lit in the fireplace, thereby damaging the premises and an adjoining property. The issue in this case was whether the local authority, Pyrenees Shire Council ('The Shire', the appellant), was under a common law duty of care to the tenants of the property and the neighbouring tenants, as it had previously inspected the chimney and had determined that it was unsafe to use.

Decision

The High Court found that the Shire was under a common law duty of care to the tenants of the property and the neighbouring tenants with respect to the prevention of the fire and the damage resulting from it.

Gummow J

> [**389**]...
>
> The Shire was deemed by par (a) of s 3(2) of the *Local Government Act* to be a municipality and that statute provided for the conduct by municipalities of various activities and the exercise of a range of powers with respect to such things as ... the prevention of fire (Pt XXVI) ... [W]ith particular reference to the fire prevention provisions of Pt XXVI, the exercise of the authority vested by statute in the Shire was a matter of discretion rather than obligation.
>
> What then was the situation occupied by the Shire, or the circumstances in which it was placed, with reference to the condition of the fireplace and chimney at 70 Neill Street at the time of the second fire? In May 1990, the situation occupied in relation to this litigation by the Shire as the arm of local government gave it a significant and special measure of control over the safety from fire of persons and property in Neill Street. Such a situation of control is indicative of a duty of care (citation omitted). The Shire had statutory powers, exercisable from time to time, to pursue the prevention of fire at No 70. This statutory enablement of the Shire 'facilitate[d] the existence of a common law duty of care' (citation omitted), but the touchstone of what I would hold to be its duty was the Shire's measure of control of the situation including its knowledge, not shared by [the subsequent tenants] or by the [neighbouring tenants], that, if the situation were not remedied, the possibility of fire was great and damage to the whole row of shops might ensue (citation omitted). The Shire had a duty of care 'to safeguard others from a grave danger of serious harm', in circumstances where it was 'responsible for its continued existence and [was] aware of the likelihood of others coming into proximity of the danger and [had] the means of preventing it or of averting the danger or of bringing it to their knowledge' (citation omitted).
>
> This is not a case where liability is sought to be imposed upon the [**390**] Shire simply because there was reasonable foreseeability of loss by fire damage if nothing further was done. Apart from [the County Fire Authority, the previous next door tenant and the previous tenant], only Shire officers ... knew of that latent defect in the physical condition of No 70 which presented a significant fire risk to it and neighbouring premises ...

…

The question then is what, as the acceptable minimum, in discharge of its duty of care, should have been done by the Shire before the second fire, bearing in mind the character in which the Shire would have acted and the nature of its duty. At the very least, the Shire was obliged to monitor the failure of [the previous tenants] to carry out the repairs referred to in the letter of 12 August 1988 and to alert the new occupiers of No 70 of the serious but latent danger constituted by the fireplace in the living room. The duty was not discharged. The Shire failed to take steps in the further exercise of its powers which were required by the circumstances …

7 Damage to economic interests: reliance on a misrepresentation

A plaintiff's loss can also be economic in nature, such as when the plaintiff purchases property or goods from a defendant in circumstances where the price paid by the plaintiff to the defendant is higher than the actual value of the property or goods in question. Where the defendant has made misrepresentations to the plaintiff as to the real value of the property or goods, and these are material to the plaintiff's decision to enter into the contract to purchase, the plaintiff may claim damages from the defendant in deceit. The following case concerns the appropriate measure of damages in such cases of deceit.

Toteff v Antonas (1952) 87 CLR 647

Facts and issues

Toteff (the appellant in this appeal and plaintiff in the originating action) purchased a fish-and-chip shop from Antonas (the respondent in this appeal and defendant in the originating action). Toteff was induced to enter into this transaction by Antonas's material and false misrepresentations that the shop made greater profits than it did. The fair value of the business was consequently lower than the amount paid by Toteff. The issue in this case related to the appropriate amount of damages in an action of deceit.

Decision

In an action of deceit, the appropriate measure of damages is the difference between what the plaintiff paid, the sum they were out of pocket, and the real market value of the assets they acquired.

Dixon J

[**650**] I think that … the plaintiff is entitled to recover the full difference between the purchase money he paid for the business as a going concern, including plant and stock as well as goodwill, and the value which he obtained …

In an action of deceit a plaintiff is entitled to recover as damages a sum representing the prejudice or disadvantage he has suffered in consequence of his altering his position under the inducement of the fraudulent misrepresentations made by the defendant. When what he has been induced to do is to make a purchase from the defendant and part with his money to him in payment of the price, then, if the transaction stands and is not disaffirmed or rescinded, what is recoverable is 'the difference between the real value of the property, and the sum which the plaintiff was induced to give for it' per Abbott LCJ *Pearson v Wheeler* (citation omitted). As Sir James Hannen P in *Peek v Derry* (citation omitted) pointed out, the question is how much worse off is the plaintiff than if he had not entered into the transaction. If he had not done so he would have had the purchase money in his pocket. To ascertain his loss you must deduct from the amount he paid the real value of the thing he got ... The measure of damages in an action of deceit consists in the loss or expenditure incurred by the plaintiff in consequence of the inducement on which he [**651**] relied diminished by the corresponding advantage in money or moneys worth obtained by him on the other side: *Potts v Miller* (citation omitted). You look to what he has been induced to part with as the initial step. He is entitled to say that but for the fraud he would never have parted with his money: per Coleridge LCJ, *Twycross v Grant* (citation omitted). But he cannot recover the entire price he has paid unless the thing prove wholly worthless. If the thing has any appreciable value the damages must be reduced pro tanto: per Cockburn LCJ, *Twycross v Grant* (citation omitted). It must not be forgotten that after all deceit is an action on the case for special damage incurred in consequence of the defendant's fraudulent inducement.

...

Williams J

[**654**] The measure of damages is the difference between what the plaintiff paid, the sum he was out of pocket, and the real market value of the assets he acquired. Where the whole value of the assets is their value for use as part of a going concern, the fact that the total purchase money is apportioned between the assets that have been purchased is immaterial. The plaintiff is still out of pocket the difference between what he paid for the whole of those assets as part of a going concern and the real market value of the business: *McConnel v Wright* (citation omitted); *Holmes v Jones* (citation omitted); *Potts v Miller* (citation omitted); *McAllister v Richmond Brewing Co (NSW) Pty Ltd* (citation omitted). In *Holmes v Jones* (citation omitted) O'Connor J said 'where the complaint is that the contract has been induced by a fraudulent misrepresentation, the remedy for that wrong is to put the party, who has been induced to make the contract, as far as possible in the position he would have been in if he had not entered into the contract. To put him into that position he must be recompensed for the damage he has sustained by entering into the contract. In order to ascertain the extent of that damage the whole contract must be looked at' (citation omitted).

Review Questions

(1) What is the primary difference between an award of damages in defamation compared to an award of damages in relation to other torts, such as the torts of negligence, deceit or conversion?

(2) Do you think that the Court's decision in *Parramatta City Council v Lutz* (1988) 12 NSWLR 293 (referred to in *Pantalone v Alaouie* (1989) 18 NSWLR 119) to award damages for restoration of a building destroyed by the defendant's wrong despite the cost of this being significantly greater than the cost of replacement is consistent with the Court's decision in *Pantalone v Alaouie* to order that the cost of restoration in that case was not reasonable?

(3) In *Jansen v Dewhurst* [1969] VR 421, Newton J (at 425) referred to Wild CJ's judgment in *Bartlett v D. H. Small & Son Ltd* [1967] NZLR 260, in which Wild CJ stated that in choosing between repairing damage wrongfully caused to another's goods, or replacing the goods with another of comparable type and condition, a situation may arise where it is reasonable for the court to order that the defendant repair the plaintiff's goods, even in circumstances where this may be at considerable cost to the defendant and at more cost than the cost of replacement. What is the justification for such a position?

III Attribution of responsibility

Responsibility for loss can be attributed in a number of ways in the law of tort. The more culpable the defendant, generally the wider the area of loss for which the defendant can fairly be held responsible. The following section explores the differing tests of remoteness of damage that apply in relation to various torts, including:

- the natural and probable consequences test
- the test of reasonable contemplation and
- the test of reasonable foreseeability.

Also explored in this section are the eggshell skull rule and the principles relating to the issue of contributory negligence.

Concept	Short explanation	Relevant authorities	Principles text
Remoteness of damage: natural and probable consequences	The limitation devices of foresight and remoteness are not applicable to intentional torts.	*Palmer Bruyn & Parker Pty Ltd v Parsons* (2001) 208 CLR 388	Chapter 6: [6.57]–[6.60]
Remoteness of damage: reasonable foreseeability	The appropriate test for remoteness in negligence is the test of reasonable foreseeability.	*Overseas Tankship (UK) Ltd v Morts Dock & Engineering Co Ltd (Wagon Mound No 1)* [1961] AC 388	Chapter 6: [6.61]–[6.78]

Concept	Short explanation	Relevant authorities	Principles text
	A risk must be a real risk in order to be foreseeable to a reasonable person in the position of the defendant. A real risk is one that is not far-fetched.	*Overseas Tankship (UK) Ltd v Miller Steamship Co Pty Ltd (Wagon Mound No 2)* [1967] AC 617	
	A risk which is extremely unlikely to occur may nonetheless still be foreseeable if it is a risk which is not far-fetched or fanciful.	*Wyong Shire Council v Shirt* (1980) 146 CLR 40	
	It is sufficient to found liability that the type or class of injury was foreseeable as a possible consequence of particular conduct.	*Mt Isa Mines Ltd v Pusey* (1970) 125 CLR 383	
	Reasonable foreseeability is the applicable standard in cases of nuisance.	*Sutherland Shire Council v Becker* (2006) 150 LGERA 184	
	Reasonable foreseeability is the applicable test of remoteness in an action for trespass.	*Mayfair Ltd v Pears* [1987] 1 NZLR 459	
Remoteness of damage: reasonable contemplation	For the strict liability tort of conversion, consequential loss must be of a kind that should have been within the contemplation of the defendant as a likely consequence having regard to the defendant's special knowledge or express notice of the fact.	*National Australia Bank Ltd v Nemur Varity Pty Ltd* (2002) 4 VR 252	Chapter 6: [6.79]–[6.82]
Remoteness of damage: eggshell skull	A tortfeasor gets no allowance because of the frailty of their victim.	*Purkess v Crittenden* (1965) 114 CLR 164	Chapter 6: [6.83]–[6.88]
	The defendant takes a plaintiff as they find them, which includes taking into account all of those factors relevant to the plaintiff's wider environment. This includes a range of personal, physical, social and economic factors relevant to the plaintiff.	*Nader v Urban Transport Authority (NSW)* (1985) 2 NSWLR 501	
Contributory negligence: common law	Contributory negligence constitutes a complete defence to an action in negligence at common law.	*Radley v London and North Western Railway Co* (1876) 1 App Cas 754	Chapter 6: [6.89]–[6.90]

Concept	Short explanation	Relevant authorities	Principles text
Contributory negligence: contributory negligence statutes	Legislation in all Australian states and territories now provides that damages may be apportioned between a claimant and any other person in cases where both are responsible for the damage to the claimant.	*Wrongs Act 1958* (Vic)	Chapter 6: [6.91]–[6.92]
Contributory negligence: civil liability statutes	Provisions impacting upon contributory negligence exist in civil liability statutes in all Australian jurisdictions.		Chapter 6: [6.93]–[6.96]
Contributory negligence: the plaintiff's conduct	The standard of care in looking after one's own interests is the same as the standard required in looking after the interests of others.	*Civil Liability Act 2002* (NSW)	Chapter 6: [6.97]–[6.102]
	Contributory negligence is presumed where a claimant's ability to exercise due care and skill is impaired due to intoxication at the time of the accident in question.	*Civil Law (Wrongs) Act 2002* (ACT)	
Contributory negligence: factual causation and scope of the duty	The plaintiff's unreasonable conduct must have been a factual cause of the accident or ensuing loss in order for it to affect the defendant's liability.	*Allan v Fletcher* (2001) 79 SASR 559	Chapter 6: [6.103]–[6.105]
Contributory negligence: apportionable loss	Australian contributory negligence statutes require a reduction of damages according to what the court thinks is 'just and equitable having regard to the claimant's share in the responsibility for the damage'.	*Wrongs Act 1958* (Vic)	Chapter 6: [6.106]
Contributory negligence: apportionment	In considering the extent to which the plaintiff's damages ought to be reduced due to contributory negligence, the courts must consider the degree to which the conduct of both the plaintiff and the defendant departed from the standard of care of a reasonable person.	*Pennington v Norris* (1956) 96 CLR 10	Chapter 6: [6.107]–[6.116]

A Remoteness of damage

The same remoteness of damage test does not apply to all torts. Indeed, three general tests of remoteness of damage have emerged, differing widely with respect to the extent to which the defendant will be considered liable for the plaintiff's harm. These tests are:

(1) the natural and probable consequences test

(2) the reasonable foreseeability test and

(3) the reasonable contemplation test.

Also relevant to the extent of the plaintiff's damages that the defendant will be responsible for is the eggshell skull rule. This section investigates these rules, providing examples of the application of each.

1 The test of natural and probable consequences

A wider test of remoteness of damage applies in cases involving deceit, injurious falsehood and some other torts than applies in relation to torts, such as negligence. This test extends liability to all natural and probable consequences of the defendant's wrong, rather than only the foreseeable consequences of the defendant's wrong. This test extends the scope of the defendant's liability, this being justified on the basis that the commission of the wrong is deliberate rather than due to the inadvertent carelessness of the defendant. The following cases provide examples of when the natural and probable consequences test is the appropriate test of remoteness.

Palmer Bruyn & Parker Pty Ltd v Parsons (2001) 208 CLR 388

Facts and issues

Palmer Bruyn & Parker Pty Ltd ('Palmer', the appellant in this appeal and plaintiff in the originating action) were surveyors who had been engaged by a well-known chain of fast-food restaurants to prepare a development application on its behalf to be submitted to the local council for approval. Palmer sued Parson (the respondent in this appeal and defendant in the originating action), a member of the local council, claiming damages for injurious falsehood. The subject of the claim was a letter sent by Parsons to another member of counsel containing false allegations against Palmer, which was subsequently reported on by a local newspaper. Palmer argued that they had lost the consultancy and all potential future consultancy work with the restaurant as a direct consequence of Parson's intentional falsehood. One of the issues in this case was whether the applicable test of remoteness in such cases entitled the plaintiff to recover all losses that were a natural and probable consequence of the defendant's wrong, or the lesser amount of losses that were a reasonably foreseeable consequence of the defendant's wrong.

Decision

The limitation devices of foresight and remoteness are not applicable to intentional torts as they are in negligence law.

Gummow J

[407] Reasonable foreseeability

...

It was ... said by Mason, Wilson and Dawson JJ in *Gates v City Mutual Life Assurance Society Ltd* (citation omitted) that in an action for [**408**] deceit a plaintiff is entitled 'to all the consequential loss directly flowing from his reliance on the representation, at least if the loss is foreseeable' (footnotes omitted). This has been interpreted in the Federal Court as meaning that a defendant will be liable only for those losses which might reasonably have been foreseen as flowing from the deceit (citation omitted). The contrary view appears to be the law in England. In *Doyle v Olby (Ironmongers) Ltd* (citation omitted), Lord Denning MR said:

> In contract, the damages are limited to what may reasonably be supposed to have been in the contemplation of the parties. In fraud, they are not so limited. The defendant is bound to make reparation for all the actual damages directly flowing from the fraudulent inducement ...
>
> [I]t does not lie in the mouth of the fraudulent person to say that [the damage] could not reasonably have been foreseen.

This passage was approved by the House of Lords in *Smith New Court Securities Ltd v Citibank NA* (citation omitted).

What was said by this Court in ... *Gates* should not be taken as deciding that reasonable foreseeability is a requirement for the recovery of damages in an action for deceit. For the reasons that follow the question left open in those cases should now be answered, in line with *Doyle* and *Smith,* so as to deny the applicability of reasonable foreseeability as a means of limiting liability in the tort of injurious falsehood.

...

[**411**] ...

The point of significance is that, whatever may be its origins, an action in injurious falsehood requires either that the defendant intended to cause the harm or that the harm be the 'natural and probable result' of the publication of the false statement (citation omitted). Where it is established by evidence that the defendant intended to cause the harm that eventuated, and provided the other elements of the tort are satisfied, the defendant will generally be held liable for that harm. Evidence may also be given from which the court may infer the requisite intention. Thus, it is said as a general rule that a man is presumed to intend the natural consequences of his acts (citation omitted). As Pollock said (citation omitted): 'The wrong-doer cannot call on us to perform a nice discrimination of that which is willed by him from that which is only consequential on the strictly wilful wrong.'

...

[**412**] ...

There are more fundamental considerations which tell against the imposition of a limitation on damage based upon the notion of reasonable foreseeability where intention is an element of the tort. In *Smith New Court Securities Ltd v Citibank NA* (citation omitted), Lord Mustill spoke of 'the irrelevance of foreseeability' in a case of fraud. In the same case, Lord

Steyn referred to the policy of the law 'of imposing more extensive liability on intentional wrongdoers than on merely careless defendants' (citation omitted).

[**413**] The tort of injurious falsehood is, in the words of Bowen LJ, 'an action on the case for damage wilfully and intentionally done' (citation omitted). It is difficult to see why a person who 'wilfully and intentionally' causes damage to the plaintiff by maliciously publishing a false statement should be able to escape liability on the basis that a 'reasonable person' would not have foreseen the damage. Such a person is manifestly not a reasonable person. Thus it was said by the High Court of Ontario that (citation omitted) '[t]he limitation devices of foresight and remoteness are not applicable to intentional torts, as they are in negligence law'. To like effect, in *Smith New Court Securities Ltd v Citibank NA* (citation omitted), Lord Steyn stated:

> [I]t is a rational and defensible strategy to impose wider liability on an intentional wrongdoer. As Hart and Honoré, *Causation in the Law* (citation omitted) observed, an innocent plaintiff may, not without reason, call on a morally reprehensible defendant to pay the whole of the loss he caused. The exclusion of heads of loss in the law of negligence, which reflects considerations of legal policy, does not necessarily avail the intentional wrongdoer.

It follows that there is no justification for importing notions found in the law of negligence and nuisance respecting foreseeability into the law of injurious falsehood. It may be, as was said in a New Zealand case, that 'consequences that are direct and natural are generally foreseeable' (citation omitted). However, for the reasons set out above, the notion of reasonable foreseeability is not appropriate in cases of injurious falsehood.

2 The test of reasonable foreseeability

In cases which do not involve deliberate wrongdoing, such as cases of negligence, the court applies the test of reasonable foreseeability as the applicable test of remoteness of damage. This is a narrower test of remoteness than the natural and probable consequences test, limiting the extent of the defendant's liability to the damage to the plaintiff that was reasonably foreseeable. This is justified on the basis that the defendant is less morally culpable in cases of negligence than in cases of intentional torts. The following section considers a number of extracts which demonstrate the development of the principles relating to reasonable foreseeability in relation to remoteness.

Overseas Tankship (UK) Ltd v Morts Dock & Engineering Co Ltd (Wagon Mound No 1) [1961] AC 388

Facts and issues

Overseas Tankship (UK) Ltd ('Overseas Tankship', the appellants in this appeal and defendants in the originating action), charterers of an oil-burning vessel called *The Wagon Mound*, negligently allowed oil to spill into Morts Bay, Balmain, in the Port of Sydney. The oil spread across the bay, which Overseas Tankship made no attempts to clean. Oil which subsequently spread under Morts Dock & Engineering Co Ltd's ('Morts Dock & Engineering', the respondent in this appeal and plaintiff in the originating action) wharf ignited as a result of sparks from welding that was being conducted on the wharf by Morts Dock & Engineering's servants, thereby causing considerable damage to the wharf and two ships being berthed there. One of the issues in this appeal was whether Overseas Tankship were responsible for all losses which were a direct consequence of their negligence, or only those losses which were a reasonably foreseeable consequence of their negligence.

Decision

The appropriate test for remoteness in negligence is the test of reasonable foreseeability.

Privy Council (On appeal from the Supreme Court of New South Wales) (Viscount Simonds)

> [**415**] …
>
> There can be no doubt that the decision of the Court of Appeal in *Polemis* plainly asserts that, if the defendant is guilty of negligence, he is responsible for all the consequences whether [**416**] reasonably foreseeable or not. The generality of the proposition is perhaps qualified by the fact that each of the Lords Justices refers to the outbreak of fire as the direct result of the negligent act. There is thus introduced the conception that the negligent actor is not responsible for consequences which are not 'direct,' whatever that may mean …
>
> …
>
> [**422**] …
>
> Enough has been said to show that the authority of *Polemis* has been severely shaken though lip-service has from time to time been paid to it. In their Lordships' opinion it should no longer be regarded as good law. It is not probable that many cases will for that reason have a different result, though it is hoped that the law will be thereby simplified, and that in some cases, at least, palpable injustice will be avoided. For it does not seem consonant with current ideas of justice or morality that for an act of negligence, however slight or venial, which results in some trivial foreseeable damage the actor should be liable for all consequences however unforeseeable and however grave, so long as they can be said to be 'direct.' It is a principle of civil liability, subject only to qualifications which have no present relevance, that a man must be considered to be responsible for the probable [**423**] consequences of his act. To demand more of him is too harsh a rule, to demand less is to ignore that civilised order requires the observance of a minimum standard of behaviour.
>
> This concept applied to the slowly developing law of negligence has led to a great variety of expressions which can, as it appears to their Lordships, be harmonised with little difficulty with the single exception of the so-called rule in *Polemis*. For, if it is asked why a man should be responsible for the natural or necessary or probable consequences of his act (or any other similar description of them) the answer is that it is not because they are natural or necessary or probable, but because, since they have this quality, it is judged by the standard of the reasonable man that he ought to have foreseen them. Thus it is that over and over again it has happened that in different judgments in the same case, and sometimes in a single judgment, liability for a consequence has been imposed on the

ground that it was reasonably foreseeable or, alternatively, on the ground that it was natural or necessary or probable. The two grounds have been treated as coterminous, and so they largely are. But, where they are not, the question arises to which the wrong answer was given in *Polemis*. For, if some limitation must be imposed upon the consequences for which the negligent actor is to be held responsible – and all are agreed that some limitation there must be – why should that test (reasonable foreseeability) be rejected which, since he is judged by what the reasonable man ought to foresee, corresponds with the common conscience of mankind, and a test (the 'direct' consequence) be substituted which leads to no-where but the never-ending and insoluble problems of causation. 'The lawyer,' said Sir Frederick Pollock, 'cannot afford to adventure himself with philosophers in the logical and metaphysical controversies that beset the idea of cause.' Yet this is just what he has most unfortunately done and must continue to do if the rule in *Polemis* is to prevail …

The nature of the magnitude of risk that is required to have been foreseen by the defendant has been considered extensively by the courts. The following case details the range of considerations the court must have regard to when determining whether the risk of injury to the plaintiff was reasonably foreseeable.

Overseas Tankship (UK) Ltd v Miller Steamship Co Pty Ltd (Wagon Mound No 2) [1967] AC 617

Facts and issues

This case arose out of the same facts in *Overseas Tankship (UK) Ltd v Morts Dock & Engineering Co Ltd (Wagon Mound No 1)*.[4] In this case, Miller Steamship Co Pty Ltd ('Miller Steamship', the respondent in this appeal and plaintiff in the originating action) brought an action in nuisance as well as in negligence against Overseas Tankship. At issue in this case was the magnitude of risk required to be considered foreseeable.

Decision

A risk must be a real risk in order to be foreseeable to a reasonable person in the position of the defendant's. A real risk is one that is not far-fetched.

Privy Council (on appeal from the Supreme Court of New South Wales) (Lord Reid)

[641] …

Before *Bolton v Stone* (citation omitted)] the cases had fallen into two classes: (1) those where, before the event, the risk of its happening would have been regarded as unreal either because the event would have been thought to be physically impossible or because

4 [1961] AC 388.

the possibility of its happening would have been regarded as so fantastic or far-fetched that no reasonable man would have paid any attention to it – 'a mere possibility which would never occur to the mind **[642]** of a reasonable man' (per Lord Dunedin in *Fardon v Harcourt-Rivington* (citation omitted) – or (2) those where there was a real and substantial risk or chance that something like the event which happens might occur, and then the reasonable man would have taken the steps necessary to eliminate the risk.

Bolton v Stone (citation omitted) posed a new problem. There a member of a visiting team drove a cricket ball out of the ground onto an unfrequented adjacent public road and it struck and severely injured a lady who happened to be standing in the road. That it might happen that a ball would be driven onto this road could not have been said to be a fantastic or far-fetched possibility: according to the evidence it had happened about six times in 28 years. And it could not have been said to be a far-fetched or fantastic possibility that such a ball would strike someone in the road: people did pass along the road from time to time. So it could not have been said that, on any ordinary meaning of the words, the fact that a ball might strike a person in the road was not foreseeable or reasonably foreseeable – it was plainly foreseeable. But the chance of its happening in the foreseeable future was infinitesimal. A mathematician given the data could have worked out that it was only likely to happen once in so many thousand years. The House of Lords held that the risk was so small that in the circumstances a reasonable man would have been justified in disregarding it and taking no steps to eliminate it.

But it does not follow that, no matter what the circumstances may be, it is justifiable to neglect a risk of such a small magnitude. A reasonable man would only neglect such a risk if he had some valid reason for doing so, eg, that it would involve considerable expense to eliminate the risk. He would weigh the risk against the difficulty of eliminating it … In their Lordships' judgment *Bolton v Stone* (citation omitted) did not alter the general principle that a person must be regarded as negligent if he does not take steps to eliminate a risk which he knows or ought to know is a real risk and not a mere possibility which would never influence the mind of a reasonable man. What that decision did was to recognise and give effect to the qualification that it is justifiable not to take steps to eliminate a real risk if it is small and if the circumstances are such that a reasonable man, **[643]** careful of the safety of his neighbour, would think it right to neglect it.

In the present case there was no justification whatever for discharging the oil into Sydney Harbour. Not only was it an offence to do so, but it involved considerable loss financially. If the ship's engineer had thought about the matter, there could have been no question of balancing the advantages and disadvantages. From every point of view it was both his duty and his interest to stop the discharge immediately.

It follows that in their Lordships' view the only question is whether a reasonable man having the knowledge and experience to be expected of the chief engineer of the Wagon Mound would have known that there was a real risk of the oil on the water catching fire in some way: if it did, serious damage to ships or other property was not only foreseeable but very likely …

In their Lordships' view a properly qualified and alert chief engineer would have realised there was a real risk here and they do not understand Walsh J to deny that. But he appears to have held that if a real risk can properly be described as remote it must then be held to be not reasonably foreseeable. That is a possible interpretation of some of the authorities. But this is still an open question and on principle their Lordships cannot accept this view. If a real risk is one which would occur to the mind of a reasonable man in the position of the defendant's servant and which he would not brush aside as far-fetched, and if the criterion is to be what that reasonable man would have done in the circumstances, then surely he would not neglect such a risk if action to eliminate it [**644**] presented no difficulty, involved no disadvantage, and required no expense.

In the present case the evidence shows that the discharge of so much oil onto the water must have taken a considerable time, and a vigilant ship's engineer would have noticed the discharge at an early stage. The findings show that he ought to have known that it is possible to ignite this kind of oil on water, and that the ship's engineer probably ought to have known that this had in fact happened before. The most that can be said to justify inaction is that he would have known that this could only happen in very exceptional circumstances. But that does not mean that a reasonable man would dismiss such a risk from his mind and do nothing when it was so easy to prevent it. If it is clear that the reasonable man would have realised or foreseen and prevented the risk, then it must follow that the appellant is liable in damages.

The courts have recognised that accidents may occur in situations where the risk of injury may be extremely unlikely, but which may nonetheless be considered foreseeable. The following case outlined the relevant legal principles relating to the issue of remoteness of damage in such cases.

Wyong Shire Council v Shirt (1980) 146 CLR 40

Facts and issues

Shirt (the respondent in this appeal and plaintiff in the originating action) suffered quadriplegic paralysis after a water-skiing accident in which he struck his head on the lakebed in a shallow area of the lake. Shirt, an inexperienced water skier, believed the area of lake to be sufficiently deep to safely water ski because there was a sign near the area in which he fell facing the shoreline which stated 'Deep Water'. The sign was not intended to indicate that the adjacent area of the lake was safe for water skiing, but was instead intended to warn swimmers that a narrow trench of between six and seven feet was present to allow boats to safely travel from the shore to the main body of the lake. Evidence was led which demonstrated that it was evident to even casual observers that the lake was very shallow, especially near the shore line where the accident occurred. One of the issues in this case was whether the risk that a reasonable person would misinterpret the meaning of the sign, however unlikely, was nonetheless a real and therefore foreseeable risk.

Decision

The High Court held that a risk which is extremely small may nonetheless constitute a foreseeable risk, if it is a risk which is not far-fetched or fanciful. Such a risk, despite the low probability of its occurrence, is nonetheless a real risk and is therefore foreseeable.

Mason J

[**47**] Notwithstanding … Australian support for a narrower version of the foreseeability doctrine as applied to breach of duty, this Court would be well advised to accept that the law upon the point was correctly stated and applied by the Judicial Committee *in The 'Wagon Mound' [No. 2]*. I say this not only because *The 'Wagon Mound' [No. 2]* was a unanimous decision given on appeal from the Supreme Court of New South Wales, but also because there are sound reasons for accepting it as a correct statement of the law.

In essence its correctness depends upon a recognition of the general proposition that foreseeability of the risk of injury and the likelihood of that risk occurring are two different things. I am of course referring to foreseeability in the context of breach of duty, the concept of foreseeability in connexion with the existence of the duty of care involving a more generalized enquiry.

A risk of injury which is quite unlikely to occur, such as that which happened in *Bolton v Stone* (citation omitted), may nevertheless be plainly foreseeable. Consequently, when we speak of a risk of injury as being 'foreseeable' we are not making any statement as to the probability or improbability of its occurrence, save that we are implicitly asserting that the risk is not one that is far-fetched or fanciful. Although it is true to say that in many cases the greater the degree of probability of the occurrence of the risk the more readily it will be perceived to be a risk, it certainly does not follow that a risk which is unlikely to occur is not foreseeable.

In deciding whether there has been a breach of the duty of care the tribunal of fact must first ask itself whether a reasonable man in the defendant's position would have foreseen that his conduct involved a risk of injury to the plaintiff or to a class of persons including the plaintiff. If the answer be in the affirmative, it is then for the tribunal of fact to determine what a reasonable man would do by way of response to the risk. The perception of the reasonable man's response calls for a consideration of the magnitude of the risk and the degree of the probability of its occurrence, along with the expense, difficulty and inconvenience of taking alleviating action and any other conflicting responsibilities which the defendant may [**48**] have. It is only when these matters are balanced out that the tribunal of fact can confidently assert what is the standard of response to be ascribed to the reasonable man placed in the defendant's position.

The considerations to which I have referred indicate that a risk of injury which is remote in the sense that it is extremely unlikely to occur may nevertheless constitute a foreseeable risk. A risk which is not far-fetched or fanciful is real and therefore foreseeable. But, as we have seen, the existence of a foreseeable risk of injury does not in itself dispose of the question of breach of duty. The magnitude of the risk and its degree of probability remain to be considered with other relevant factors.

In some situations, a plaintiff might suffer injury as a result of the defendant's negligence in circumstances where the particular injury suffered by the plaintiff is quite unexpected, notwithstanding that injury of another kind might have been readily predictable. The following case provides such an example, demonstrating that the plaintiff's injury must only have been of a type or class of injury that was foreseeable.

Mt Isa Mines Ltd v Pusey (1970) 125 CLR 383

Facts and issues

Pusey (the respondent in this appeal and plaintiff in the originating action) brought an action for damages for negligently inflicted psychiatric injury against Mount Isa Mines Ltd ('Mt Isa Mines', the appellant in this appeal and defendant in the originating action), his former employer. As a result of the negligence of Mount Isa Mines, a fellow employee of Mount Isa Mines sustained a severe electric shock. Pusey went to the aid of the shocked fellow employee, and thereby witnessed the extreme injuries suffered by him. After subsequently learning that the fellow employee had died, Pusey suffered a severe, although rare, psychiatric injury. At issue in this case was whether Pusey's psychiatric injuries were a foreseeable consequence of Mount Isa Mines' negligence, particularly as Pusey's particular pathological condition was regarded by medical experts as a rare consequence of the shock suffered by him.

Decision

The plaintiff is required to establish that the type of injury they suffered was a reasonably foreseeable consequence of the defendant's conduct, but is not required to show that the particular injury they suffered was foreseeable.

Windeyer J

> [**397**] …
>
> Foreseeability here predicates the foresight of a reasonable man. The reasonable man is not here anyone on the Clapham omnibus. He is a man who notionally stood in the shoes of the defendant and had such knowledge, and capacity for care and foresight, as that defendant actually had and in addition such as a reasonable man in that position is expected to have. He is, in the words of [**398**] Lord Wright in *Bourhill v Young* (citation omitted), 'a reasonable hypothetical observer'. He is not a seer who can foretell future occurrences that are quite unlikely according to the natural and ordinary cause of events. Happenings that were fortuitous, in the sense that no reasonable man would have thought of them as within the range of possible consequences, cannot be said to have been reasonably foreseeable. And knowledge after the event, when it is easy to be wise, cannot shew that the event was foreseeable …
>
> …
>
> [**399**] … A man is culpably negligent if he failed to take measures, reasonably available, to obviate a risk 'which would occur to the mind of a reasonable man in the position of the' defendant 'and which he would not brush aside as far-fetched'. That is how the Privy Council has expressed the matter: *The 'Wagon Mound' [No. 2]* (citation omitted).
>
> …
>
> The contrast which in their judgment their Lordships [in *The 'Wagon Mound' [No. 2]*] spelt out between a mere possibility, a risk which a reasonable man might brush aside as far-fetched, and on the other hand a 'real risk' but one that nevertheless might be 'properly described as remote' may seem elusive and slippery if meticulous attention be fixed on words. The word 'remote' has long had a place in the vocabulary of our law. It has

commonly been used in relation to cause and consequence: a remote cause has been distinguished from the proximate cause: a consequence may be too remote to sound in damages. Sometimes too the phrase 'remote risk' has meant an event which can be seen as a possibility, but one so unlikely to occur, or of such slight gravity of consequence if it should occur, [**400**] that a prudent man might justifiably disregard it. This idea can be expressed by various words … We must always beware lest words used in one case become tyrants over the facts of another case.

…

[**401**] … The question is was it reasonably foreseeable that an accident of that kind, if it occurred, might have consequences for somebody of the kind that it had for the plaintiff … That people in the powerhouse would go promptly to the scene of an accident there was obviously to be expected. If on reaching the upper floor the plaintiff had come in contact with some hot object or an exposed electric cable and been physically harmed by that or by any other abnormal condition created by the detonation, he would have had an indisputable claim to damages …

In *King v Phillips* (citation omitted), Denning LJ, as his Lordship then was, stated what seems to me to be a besetting problem in cases of nervous shock when he said:

> What is the reasoning which admits a cause of action for negligence if the injured person is actually struck, but declines it if he only suffers from shock? I cannot see why the duty of a driver should differ according to the nature of the injury … If he drives negligently with the result that a bystander is injured, then his breach of duty is the same, no matter whether the injury is a wound or is emotional shock. Only the damage is different.

[**402**] However, his Lordship, constrained by the decision of the House of Lords in 1942, said, (citation omitted) ' … there can be no doubt since *Bourhill v Young* (citation omitted) that the test of liability for shock is foreseeability of injury by shock' … Foreseeability does not mean foresight of the particular course of events causing the harm. Nor does it suppose foresight of the particular harm which occurred, but only of some harm of a like kind. That is well established by many cases, including *Chapman v Hearse* (citation omitted), and *Hughes v Lord Advocate* (citation omitted). This comfortable latitudinarian doctrine has, however, the obvious difficulty that it leaves the criterion for classification of kinds or types of harm undefined and at large. The logical problem thus engendered has been noticed by commentators, including Professor Jackson in his learned and critical article 'A Kind of Damage' in *The Australian Law Journal*, vol. 39, pp. 3–16. Lord Wright in *Bourhill v Young* (citation omitted) said:

> The lawyer likes to draw fixed and definite lines and is apt to ask where the thing is to stop. I should reply it should stop where in the particular case the good sense of the jury or of the judge decides.

That perhaps does not reckon with courts of appeal, and varying judicial opinions of where in good sense the proper stopping-place is.

In what way does one test whether a particular harm is of the genus that was foreseeable? We have at least one 'fixed and definite line'. Liability for nervous shock depends on foreseeability of nervous shock. That, not some other form of harm, must have been a foreseeable result of the conduct complained of. The particular pathological condition which the shock produced need not have been foreseeable. It is enough that it is a 'recognizable psychiatric illness'.

[403] ... The plaintiff unquestionably developed a profound psychiatric disability however it be labelled. Perhaps it was latent and aroused by the experience. But, however that may be, the learned trial judge could find – and in my view he quite obviously rightly found – that this condition was a consequence of emotional shock on seeing and aiding the grievously hurt man. The medical witnesses agree that such a chronic pathological condition is a rare consequence of such a shock. But it is not unknown: and reasonable foreseeability is not measured by statistical probability. Moreover, as I have said, the question is not whether shock would be likely to produce this particular illness, but whether there was a real risk that a foreseeable accident such as occurred would cause a man in the powerhouse to suffer a nervous shock having lasting mental consequences.

The reasonable foreseeability test of remoteness applies not only to cases of negligence, but also to cases of nuisance and trespass. The following extracts provide examples of the latter torts.

Sutherland Shire Council v Becker (2006) 150 LGERA 184

Facts and issues

Becker (the respondent in this appeal and plaintiff in the originating action) brought an action in nuisance against the Sutherland Shire Council (the appellant in this appeal and defendant in the originating action), alleging that Sutherland Shire Council's failure to maintain a drainage pipe on a nearby piece of land caused flooding and then a land slip on Becker's property. One of the issues in this case was whether such a claim in nuisance required fault on Sutherland Shire Council's part.

Decision

The Court found that reasonable foreseeability is the applicable standard in cases of nuisance in which the plaintiff alleges a local authority interfered with the plaintiff's private law property rights.

Bryson JA[5]

[224] ...

In oral submissions the respondent's counsel contended that the case in negligence was that the water that escaped from the pipeline caused physical damage and substantial interference to Lot 7 ...

5 Mason J in agreement: 188, [1]. Although finding that the respondent could establish a cause of action in nuisance against the appellant, Giles JA did not specifically comment upon the applicable standard in such cases: see 190, [9].

The respondent's counsel particularly relied on failure to inspect, repair and maintain the pipeline after 1985; the submission was to the effect that events up to then which came to the knowledge of the appellant and Mr Scott's [a site investigation engineer] report [**225**] meant that the appellant should have known of the prospect of the escape of water which it would have been simple to discover by inspection, and should have rectified the open joints and fractures and holes before the escape of water produced slippage …

… *Sedleigh-Denfield* [*v O'Callaghan*] was the occasion for several close examinations of case law relating to flooding risks and the law of nuisance, and observations made by Lord Wright at 904–905 have importance extending well beyond their application to the facts then under consideration. His Lordship said (citation omitted):

> The gist of the present action; however, is the unreasonable and unjustified interference by the defendants in the user of their land with the plaintiff's right to enjoy his property. Negligence, moreover, is not a necessary condition of a claim for nuisance. What is done may be done deliberately, and in good faith, and in a genuine belief that it is justified. Negligence here is not an independent cause of action, but is ancillary to the actual cause of action, which is nuisance …
>
> The liability for a nuisance is not, at least in modern law, a strict or absolute liability. If the defendant, by himself or those for whom he is responsible, has created what constitutes a nuisance, and if it causes damage, the difficulty now being considered does not arise; but he may have taken over the nuisance, ready-made as it were, when he acquired the property, or the nuisance may be due to a latent defect or to the act of a trespasser or stranger. Then he is not liable unless he continued or adopted the nuisance, or, more accurately, did not without undue delay remedy it when he became aware of it, or with ordinary and reasonable care should have become aware of it. This rule seems to be in accordance with good sense and convenience. The responsibility which attaches to the occupier because he has possession and control of the property cannot logically be limited to the mere creation of the nuisance. It should extend to his conduct if, with knowledge, he leaves the nuisance on his land. The same is true if the nuisance was such that, with ordinary care in the management of his property, he should have realised the risk of its existence.
>
> …
>
> if the defendant did not create the nuisance, he must, if he is to be held responsible, have continued it, which I think means simply neglected to remedy it when he became, or should have become, aware of it.

Although there may be some exceptions, fault of some kind is now usually necessary for liability in nuisance; see *The Wagon Mound (No 2)* at 28, and *Montana Hotels Pty Ltd v Fasson Pty Ltd* (citation omitted) at 284 …

[**226**] …

In my opinion whether the appellant is liable depends on whether, when the system became a nuisance, the appellant did not remedy it without undue delay when the appellant became aware of the nuisance, or with ordinary and reasonable care should have become aware of it. Of what was it necessary that the appellant should become aware? There was in my opinion a nuisance when the pipeline and the easement came to be in a defective state so that the escape of water was an unreasonable and unjustified interference with the rights of nearby landowners to enjoy their property. This was not the time when the escape of water caused damage; it was (stating the matter with admitted circularities) the time when with ordinary and reasonable care, the appellant should have become aware of the risk that would happen …

…

[**230**] …

The Trial Judge's conclusion that the appellant should not be found to be negligent in respect of failure to inspect or maintain and repair the stormwater drainage system to ensure that it did not leak was correctly based on there being no evidence as to how frequently the pipeline should have been inspected or the cost of doing so, and should not be disturbed. In the law of nuisance as it operates in this case, negligence is a necessary element: for similar reasons the appellant was not negligent and is not liable in nuisance …

Mayfair Ltd v Pears [1987] 1 NZLR 459

Facts and issues

Pears (the respondent in this appeal and defendant in the originating action) parked his car in Mayfair Ltd's ('Mayfair', the appellant in this appeal and plaintiff in the originating action) building, trespassing on Mayfair's property in the process. Mayfair suffered damage to their building as a result of a fire that started in Pears's car. The Court found that Pears was not negligent in relation to the starting of the fire, and that damage to the building as a result of a fire starting in Pears's car was not foreseeable. The issue in this case was whether in an action for trespass, the defendant was strictly liable for all damage caused by his trespass, or whether the defendant was only liable for damages that were a foreseeable consequence of the defendant's trespass.

Decision

The Court found that the defendant is only liable for damages that are a foreseeable consequence of the defendant's trespass.

McMullin J

[**463**] This case raises a question on the remoteness of damage in a case of trespass to land. Although that tort is centuries old, the extent to which a trespasser is liable for damages is not settled. According to Fleming, *The Law of Torts* (6th ed, 1983) p 37, the prevalent view is that an intentional trespasser is strictly liable for all damage caused by his presence on the land even if it results from conduct which would not have otherwise incurred liability.

Another view is advanced by Dr Glanville Williams in an article 'The Risk Principle' (1961) 77 LQR 179. Consequent upon the refusal of the Judicial Committee in *The Wagon Mound* (citation omitted) to follow the rule that liability attached to the direct but unforeseeable consequences of a wrongful act (*Re Polemis and Furness, Withy & Co* (citation omitted)) Dr Glanville Williams argued that the principle of foreseeability should apply to all torts based on fault, although he acknowledged that *Ellis v Loftus Iron Co* (citation omitted), a livestock trespass case, made the owner of trespassing stock liable even for unforeseeable consequences, a decision which he suggested was out of accord with the rest of the law.

…

Turning to the facts of the present case:

> [**464**] ...
>
> The fire in the respondent's car, causing damage to the appellant's parking building following on the unauthorised parking of the car in that building, cannot be said to have been either foreseeable, or a natural consequence, or a probable consequence, or a direct consequence of the trespass in the sense that it was part of it. Put another way, the trespass was not the proximate cause of the fire in the sense of being the operative or effective cause of the damage to the parking building.
>
> In the end the adoption of an appropriate test is likely to be governed by the weighing of policy considerations. One consideration which would weigh in favour of [the imposition of a test of strict liability] is that trespassers should trespass on the property of others at their peril. There may be cases where it is reasonable that a trespasser should, on this basis, be fairly held liable for quite unexpected damage directly resulting from an intentional trespass. On the other hand it would be unreasonable to adopt a rule that a trespasser should in every case be liable for all damage resulting from his trespass even though he had not been careless. To illustrate: a person may become a trespasser merely by overstaying his licence to occupy a parking place. Should he be liable for all damage consequent upon the overstaying of his vehicle even though his infraction was minimal? And there seems no reason why a passer-by who winds up the window of another's car, necessarily opening the door to do so, in order to save it from the elements, but thereby triggers some electrical fire or explosion, should be liable for his trespass. This last case alone would suggest that there are dangers in adopting an absolute rule that an intentional trespasser should be liable for all the consequences of his acts.
>
> ... The foreseeability test advanced by Dr Glanville Williams and adopted by Casey J [the appeal court judge] has the merit of applying a common test in the determination of the remoteness of damage be the action founded on negligence or trespass. There may, however, be some cases where it is too benevolent to a trespasser. If, in the present case, the foreseeability test were to be applied then [**465**] plainly the respondent could not be held liable for the damage caused by the fire in his vehicle. But, even assuming a rule that a trespasser should be liable for damage which is a direct result of his trespass, the respondent would not be liable for the damage caused by the fire. He did not start the fire, nor was he negligent, and the damage cannot be said to be a direct or natural consequence of his unauthorized parking.

3 The test of reasonable contemplation

Courts have, in some cases, considered the test of reasonable foreseeability to be the appropriate test of remoteness of damage in cases of conversion, particularly in cases of conversion in which the defendant is not knowingly converting the plaintiff's goods. However, the courts have also developed and applied a more restrictive test of remoteness of damage in such cases which limits the defendant's liability to that which was in the contemplation of the defendant as a likely consequence having a regard to the defendant's knowledge of the facts. The following case provides an example of the application of the latter.

National Australia Bank Ltd v Nemur Varity Pty Ltd [2002] VSCA 18; (2002) 4 VR 252

Facts and issues

Nemur Varity Pty Ltd ('Nemur Varity', the respondent in this appeal and plaintiff in the originating action) was an insurance broker who drew a number of cheques payable to an insurer for the payment of insurance premiums on behalf of National Australia Bank Limited's ('NAB', the respondent in this appeal and defendant in the originating action) customers, and sent these to an intermediary purporting to act as an agent of the insurer. The intermediary fraudulently drew cheques to the benefit of a third party, and NAB deposited these funds into the third party's bank account. The third party was also the recipient of a fraudulently obtained electronic transfer of funds. In an action for conversion brought by Nemur Varity against NAB, Nemur Varity claimed damages under a number of heads, including damages for the amounts of the cheques and the electronic transfer. At issue in this case was whether Nemur Varity's claim for damages for loss of profits from a loss of business under the head of consequential loss was too remote a consequence of the wrongful conversion. In particular, the Court had to consider whether the appropriate test for remoteness in an action for conversion was the test of reasonable foreseeability or some more stringent test.

Decision

Some more stringent test of remoteness than reasonable foreseeability is required for the strict liability tort of conversion. Consequential loss must be of a kind that should have been within the contemplation of the defendant as a likely consequence having regard to the defendant's special knowledge or express notice of the fact.

Batt JA[6]

> **[60]** [I]n *Harrisons Group Holdings* (citation omitted) King CJ took reasonable foreseeability as the test of remoteness for conversion … Similarly, in Kuwait Airways the primary judge (Aikens J) had concluded that all three members of the Court of Appeal in *Saleslease Ltd v Davis*, (citation omitted) a conversion case, were considering the question of remoteness by using a foreseeability test and, since counsel conceded that the Court of Appeal in Kuwait Airways was bound by *The Arpad* and *Saleslease*, that court accepted (citation omitted) that that was the test. Their Lordships a little later said: (citation omitted)
>
>> It appears to us that, as the law now stands, in conversion cases a court has to ask whether at the time of the conversion the type of loss that occurred (as opposed to the precise manner in which it occurred) was reasonably foreseeable.
>
> …
>
> **[62]** After much reflection, I am not satisfied that the test for remoteness of damage in conversion is whether the loss claimed is of such a kind as was reasonably foreseeable …

6 Callaway J in agreement: [9]. Although not expressly disagreeing with Batt JA, Phillips JA preferred to rest his decision in this case on the grounds of causation rather than on remoteness: [2].

[63] Nemur Varity, as I understand it, relies on the fact that conversion is a tort of strict liability in its submission, in effect, that this court should hold that no remoteness test is applicable and that all losses flowing naturally and directly from the acts of conversion are recoverable. That view would appear to be supported by the observation of McHugh J in *Burnie Port Authority* about *Cambridge Water Co* ... But that observation depends upon the concept of strict liability having the connotation that the tortfeasor is liable for all damage caused, which ... is not the appropriate connotation. Rather, as it seems to me, conversion may be committed entirely innocently and it is in that sense that liability for it is strict. In virtue of that it is located at the lower or less culpable end of 'the sliding scale from strict liability to intentional wrongdoing' ... However, that is no part of the definition of the tort. (citation omitted) Moreover, the Privy Council in *The Wagon Mound No 2* (citation omitted) declined to discriminate between different cases of the tort there under consideration (nuisance) in determining the test for remoteness. It is implicit in what I have said in this paragraph that I regard the concept of this sliding scale as a useful mechanism to assist in determining the appropriate test for remoteness in a particular tort, given that in tort there are more tests than one.

[64] Thus, some more stringent test of remoteness than reasonable foreseeability is required for the strict liability tort of conversion. The obvious candidate seems to me that stated in *France v Gaudet*, namely, express notice or special knowledge.

...

[69] ... [T]he matters relied on, taken together, are, in my judgment, quite insufficient to constitute special knowledge or express notice sufficient to permit of the recovery of the consequential damages awarded. There must be knowledge on the part of a defendant that in the nature of things inconvenience beyond the loss of the goods must have been occasioned to the plaintiff. The matters relied on did not show directly that loss of business income would occur nor did they show that indirectly, by showing that the chain of events which his Honour found occurred and resulted in loss of business income would occur ... [W]hat was missing from Nemur Varity's proofs here, as it seems to me, was special knowledge on the part of the bank or express notice to it that IIE or ANI was or their respective servants or agents were fraudulent. It is not enough for this test of romoteness that the bank, on reflection, might think that if certain events happened customers of Nemur Varity might be uninsured and, if so, might withdraw their custom from it. What is required is knowledge or express notice of facts, not of a series of possibilities. As regards the ANI cheque, the position is even stronger. The bank had no knowledge or express notice that Nemur Varity would continue to deal with ANI and be duped by it or its associates.

4 The 'eggshell skull' rule

The extent of a defendant's liability may be influenced to a great extent by the particular frailties of the plaintiff. For example, a defendant may by their negligence cause a relatively minor injury which, due to the peculiar sensitivity of the plaintiff, leads to a much more serious injury. The following extracts demonstrate the range of legal principles which apply in such cases.

Purkess v Crittenden (1965) 114 CLR 164

Facts and issues

Purkess (the appellant in this appeal and plaintiff in the originating action) suffered injuries to her spine in an accident which was negligently caused by Crittenden (the respondent in this appeal and defendant in the originating action). There was also evidence that prior to the accident, Purkess was suffering from long-standing degenerative changes in her spine. Crittenden argued that due to these long-standing degenerative changes, Purkess would likely have become similarly disabled at some point in the 10 years following the accident even if the accident had not occurred. At issue in this case was whether Purkess was entitled to be compensated for the full extent of her injuries notwithstanding that she was especially susceptible to such injuries due to her pre-existing condition.

Decision

It will not avail a defendant to show that but for the plaintiff being in some way ailing when they were hurt their injuries would have been less serious than they were. A tortfeasor gets no allowance because of the frailty of their victim.

Windeyer J

> [**170**] …
>
> In a personal injury case the ultimate burden is on the plaintiff to establish the extent of his injuries caused by the conduct of the defendant. If when the tort occurred the plaintiff was suffering from a progressive disease which, even if he had not been tortiously hurt, would certainly and within some reasonably predictable time have disabled him in the same way as the tort did, then the defendant's conduct has merely hastened the inevitable; and damages must be measured accordingly. But a plaintiff, tortiously injured, who suffers thereafter in a way in which he had not previously suffered, may in the absence of any countervailing evidence rely upon the prima facie conclusion that for his disabilities and sufferings the defendant is responsible. It is not incumbent on the plaintiff to lead evidence to displace or discount the inference to which the facts would otherwise give rise. But he must prove his case: and when the whole of the evidence is before the tribunal of fact the burden is on him to establish the measure of his damages. The evidence may not show that the conduct of the defendant did more than accelerate misfortune. But of course, it will not avail a defendant to show that but for the plaintiff being in some way ailing when he was hurt his injuries would have been less serious than they were. A tortfeasor gets no allowance because of the frailty of his victim.
>
> In *Watts v Rake* (citation omitted) there is also a reference by Dixon CJ to another situation, that which arises when it is said that a plaintiff's disabilities should be regarded as the separate consequences of concurrent and independent causes only one of which is the conduct of the defendant. Such cases can no doubt exist. But again a defendant is not relieved of responsibility for the consequences of his conduct because the plaintiff would not have suffered as [**171**] he did unless other contributory factors had existed.

> The ordinary conclusion when a man suffers a hurt is that all the consequences that follow it are attributable to the events that immediately caused it. If it be suggested that this is not so, that some of the apparent consequences are not causally related to it, then some material is required to support that suggestion. It is in this sense and at this stage that a burden of adducing evidence is upon the defendant. This was so clearly stated by the learned Chief Justice in *Watts v Rake* (citation omitted) that I venture to repeat what he said: 'If the disabilities of the plaintiff can be disentangled and one or more traced to causes in which the injuries he sustained through the accident play no part, it is the defendant who should be required to do the disentangling and to exclude the operation of the accident as a contributory cause'. The plaintiff in his own case need do no more than rely upon the conclusion to be drawn from the basic facts that before the accident he was not disabled: that after it he was disabled in a way that could be a consequence of the hurt he sustained. Whether one calls such a conclusion an inference, a presumption of fact or a *presumptio hominis* matters not. It is an inference which any tribunal of fact would ordinarily draw until the defendant had, by evidence elicited in cross-examination or led, provided some material to overcome it – either by proving the contrary or throwing the matter into doubt.

The frailties with which the defendant must be taken to have found the plaintiff include not only those which are purely physical, but also those relating to the plaintiff's wider social and economic environment.

Nader v Urban Transport Authority (NSW) (1985) 2 NSWLR 501

Facts and issues

Nader (the appellant in this appeal and plaintiff in the originating action) suffered physical injuries due to the negligence of Urban Transport Authority (the respondent in this appeal and defendant in the originating action). The injuries suffered by Nader were relatively minor, although led to the development of a much more serious condition known as Ganzer syndrome, a condition causing symptoms similar to extensive brain damage. The Court accepted evidence that the symptoms of Ganzer syndrome were caused and continued by a combination of biological factors, the reaction of Nader's parents, and Nader's parents' failure to obtain appropriate medical treatment. One of the issues in this case was whether Urban Transport Authority's liability to compensate Nader extended to injuries which were partly a consequence of Nader's family environment.

Decision

The defendant takes a plaintiff as they find them, which includes taking into account all of those factors relevant to the plaintiff's wider environment. This includes a range of personal, physical, social and economic factors relevant to the plaintiff.

McHugh JA

[**536**] …

… [I]t is settled law that the defendant must take the plaintiff as he finds him: *Smith v Leech Brain & Co Ltd* (citation omitted); *Beavis v Apthorpe* (citation omitted). The rule of the egg shell skull cases should not be confined to the physical or constitutional characteristics of the particular [**537**] individual. When a defendant takes a plaintiff as he finds him, he does not take him as a naked human being divorced from his environment. Clearly enough taking the plaintiff as you find him involves taking him in at least his social and earning capacity setting. The defendant who is unfortunate enough to run down a millionaire must pay accordingly. In such a case the defendant pays although the capacity which the plaintiff had was unknown or even unknowable. I think that the defendant must take the plaintiff with all his weaknesses, beliefs and reactions as well as his capacities and attributes, physical, social and economic. If the result of an accident is that a ten year old boy reacts to his parents' concern over his injuries and develops an hysterical condition, no reason of justice, morality or entrenched principle appears to me to prevent his recovery of compensation. Not everyone has shared Lord Simonds' view that it is not consonant with current ideas of justice and morality that a defendant should be liable for all the consequences of a trivial act of negligence so long as they are direct (citation omitted). In *Siwek v Lambourn* (citation omitted) Dean J observed that the subsequent erosion of *The Wagon Mound* would appear to have been dictated by a consideration opposed to that quoted, namely, that it is just that the wrongdoer rather than his victim, should bear the loss occasioned by the wrong. Justice to the defendant is fulfilled by the requirement that the plaintiff must belong to the class of persons whom the defendant can reasonably foresee may be injured by his carelessness and by the requirement of a causal connection between the negligence and the plaintiff's condition. In *Walker-Flynn v Princeton Motors Pty Ltd* (citation omitted), the Full Court held that the plaintiff was entitled to recover damages for the distress and disabilities created by her pregnancies resulting from her refusal, as a Roman Catholic, to use contraceptives. Although the case was decided before *The Wagon Mound (No 1)*, it is consistent with that decision since their Honours decided it on the basis that you take the plaintiff as you find him (citation omitted).

Here the plaintiff was a ten year old boy and, in my opinion, the defendant must not only take him as it found him but must take him in the family setting in which he lived …

B Contributory negligence

This section discusses the applicable legal principles in cases where contributory negligence has been alleged by the defendant. This may occur in circumstances where it is alleged that the plaintiff's own actions have contributed to the defendant's wrong, or where it is alleged that the plaintiff's actions have contributed to their loss. The section considers the rules which apply at common law, and also those which have been introduced by statute.

1 Common law

The following case outlines the extent of the defence to an action in negligence constituted by contributory negligence at common law.

Radley v London and North Western Railway Co (1876) 1 App Cas 754

Facts and issues

Radley (the appellant in this appeal and plaintiff in the originating action), a coalmining company, claimed damages in an action against London and North Western Railway Co ('North Western', the respondent in this appeal and defendant in the originating action), a railway company. Radley argued that North Western's servants negligently caused the destruction of Radley's bridge when North Western's servants shunted a number of coal wagons into the bridge. North Western argued that they were not liable for the resulting damage as Radley was contributorily negligent. One of the issues in this case was whether Radley's contributory negligence could constitute a complete defence to their claim in negligence, even in circumstances where North Western's servants could have avoided the harm by the exercise of ordinary care and diligence.

Decision

The Court held that although contributory negligence constitutes a complete defence to an action in negligence at common law, this is not the case where it could be shown that the defendant could have avoided the harm by the exercise of ordinary care and diligence.[7]

Lord Penzance

> **[758]** …
>
> The law in these cases of negligence is … perfectly well settled and beyond dispute.
>
> **[759]** The first proposition is a general one, to this effect, that the Plaintiff in an action for negligence cannot succeed if it is found by the jury that he has himself been guilty of any negligence or want of ordinary care which contributed to cause the accident.
>
> But there is another proposition equally well established, and it is a qualification upon the first, namely, that though the Plaintiff may have been guilty of negligence, and although that negligence may, in fact, have contributed to the accident, yet if the Defendant could in the result, by the exercise of ordinary care and diligence, have avoided the mischief which happened, the Plaintiff's negligence will not excuse him.
>
> This proposition, as one of law, cannot be questioned. It was decided in the case of *Davies v Mann* (citation omitted), supported in that of *Tuff v Warman* (citation omitted) and other cases, and has been universally applied in cases of this character without question.
>
> The only point for consideration, therefore, is whether the learned Judge properly presented it to the mind of the jury.
>
> It seems impossible to say that he did so. At the beginning of his summing-up he laid down the following as the propositions of law which governed the case: It is for the Plaintiffs to satisfy you that this accident happened through the negligence of the Defendants' servants, and as between them and the Defendants, that it was solely through the negligence of the Defendants' servants. They must satisfy you that it was solely by the negligence of

7 See also *Cayzer, Irvine & Co v Carron Co* (1884) 9 App Cas 873, 881; *Wakelin v London and South Western Railway Co* (1887) LR 12 App Cas 41, 45, 47, 51; *Symons v Stacey* (1922) 30 CLR 169.

the Defendants' servants, or, in other words, that there was no negligence on the part of their servants contributing to the accident; so that, if you think that both sides were negligent, so as to contribute to the accident, then the Plaintiffs cannot recover.

This language is perfectly plain and perfectly unqualified, and in case the jurors thought there was any contributory negligence on the part of the Plaintiffs' servants, they could not, without disregarding the direction of the learned Judge, have found in the Plaintiffs' favour, however negligent the Defendants had been, or however easily they might with ordinary care have avoided any accident at all.

The learned Judge then went on to describe to the jury what it was that might properly be considered to constitute negligence, [**760**] first in the conduct of the Defendants, and then in the conduct of the Plaintiffs; and having done this, he again reverted to the governing propositions of law, as follows: 'There seem to be two views. It is for you to say entirely as to both points. But the law is this, the Plaintiff must have satisfied you that this happened by the negligence of the Defendants' servants, and without any contributory negligence of their own; in other words, that it was solely by the negligence of the Defendants' servants. If you think it was, then your verdict will be for the Plaintiffs. If you think it was not solely by the negligence of the Defendants' servants, your verdict must be for the Defendants.'

This, again, is entirely without qualification, and the undoubted meaning of it is, that if there was any contributory negligence on the part of the Plaintiffs, they could in no case recover. Such a statement of the law is contrary to the doctrine established in the case of *Davies v Mann* (citation omitted), and the other cases above alluded to …

It is true that in part of his summing-up the learned Judge pointed attention to the conduct of the engine driver, in determining to force his way by violence through the obstruction, as fit to be considered by the jury on the question of negligence; but he failed to add that if they thought the engine driver might at this stage of the matter by ordinary care have avoided all accident, any previous negligence of the Plaintiffs would not preclude them from recovering.

In point of fact the evidence was strong to shew that this was the immediate cause of the accident, and the jury might well think that ordinary care and diligence on the part of the engine driver would, notwithstanding any previous negligence of the Plaintiffs in leaving the loaded-up truck on the line, have made the accident impossible. This substantial defect of the learned Judge's charge is that that question was never put to the jury.

On this point, therefore, I propose to move that your Lordships should reverse the decision of the Exchequer Chamber, and direct a new trial.

2 Contributory negligence statutes

Legislation which impacts upon a number of matters relevant to the issue of contributory negligence has been enacted by all states and territories. This legislation includes provisions apportioning liability between plaintiffs and defendants, provisions relating to the standard of care the plaintiff is expected to exercise in relation to looking after their own interests, and provisions relating to the plaintiff's ability to exercise due care and skill when the plaintiff is impaired due to intoxication at the time of the accident in question. The following extract provides for the apportionment of damages between plaintiffs and defendants in cases involving contributory negligence.

Wrongs Act 1958 (Vic) s 26(1)[8]

Section 26 of the *Wrongs Act 1958* (Vic) alters the common law rule that a claim in respect of damage is not defeated by reason of the contributory negligence of the claimant, and provides for the apportionment of damages between the claimant and any other person in cases where both are responsible for the damage to the claimant.

26 Liability for contributory negligence

(1) If a person (the claimant) suffers damage as the result partly of the claimant's failure to take reasonable care (contributory negligence) and partly of the wrong of any other person or persons –

(a) except as provided in section 63, a claim in respect of the damage is not defeated by reason of the contributory negligence of the claimant; and

(b) the damages recoverable in respect of the wrong must be reduced to such extent as the court thinks just and equitable having regard to the claimant's share in the responsibility for the damage.

...

3 Civil liability statutes

Provisions impacting upon contributory negligence exist in civil liability statutes in all Australian jurisdictions; however, these are inconsistent between jurisdictions. The provisions in question address issues relating to the plaintiff's conduct, such as the standard of care the plaintiff is expected to exercise in looking after their own interests, and to the relevance of the plaintiff's intoxication or failure to wear a seatbelt.

4 The plaintiff's conduct

Civil liability statutes in a number of Australian jurisdictions contain provisions which relate to the standard of care plaintiffs are expected to exercise in looking after their own interests. The following extract is an example of a provision which provides that the standard of care in looking after one's own interests is the same as the standard required in looking after the interests of others.

8 Equivalent provisions in the other jurisdictions are: *Civil Law (Wrongs) Act 2002* (ACT) s 102; *Law Reform (Miscellaneous Provisions) Act 1965* (NSW) s 9; *Law Reform (Miscellaneous Provisions) Act 1956* (NT) s 16; *Law Reform Act 1995* (Qld) s 10; *Law Reform (Contributory Negligence and Apportionment of Liability) Act 2001* (SA) s 7; *Wrongs Act 1954* (Tas) s 4; *Law Reform (Contributory Negligence and Tortfeasors' Contribution) Act 1947* (WA) s 4.

Civil Liability Act 2002 (NSW) s 5R[9]

The purpose of this legislation is to make the standard of care when considering whether the claimant has been contributorily negligent consistent with the standard of care owed to the claimant by the defendant.

5R Standard of contributory negligence

(1) The principles that are applicable in determining whether a person has been negligent also apply in determining whether the person who suffered harm has been contributorily negligent in failing to take precautions against the risk of that harm.

(2) For that purpose –

(a) the standard of care required of the person who suffered harm is that of a reasonable person in the position of that person, and

(b) the matter is to be determined on the basis of what that person knew or ought to have known at the time.

The following extract is a legislative provision which introduces a statutory presumption of contributory negligence in cases where the plaintiff's ability to exercise due care and skill is impaired due to intoxication at the time of the accident.

Civil Law (Wrongs) Act 2002 (ACT) s 95[10]

The purpose of this legislation is to introduce a statutory presumption of contributory negligence in circumstances where the claimant's ability to exercise due care and skill is impaired due to intoxication.

95 Presumption of contributory negligence – injured person intoxicated

(1) Contributory negligence must be presumed if –

(a) the injured person was –

(i) at least 16 years old at the time of the accident; and

(ii) intoxicated at the time of the accident; and

(b) the defendant claims contributory negligence.

(2) The presumption can be rebutted only if the injured person establishes, on the balance of probabilities, that –

9 Equivalent provisions in the other jurisdictions are: *Civil Liability Act 2003* (Qld) s 23(1) and (2); *Civil Liability Act 1936* (SA) s 44(1) (although no equivalent of *Civil Liability Act 2002* (NSW) s 5R(2)); *Civil Liability Act 2002* (Tas) s 23(1), (2); *Wrongs Act 1958* (Vic) s 62(1), (2); and *Civil Liability Act 2002* (WA) s 5K(1), (2).

10 Equivalent provisions in the other jurisdictions are: *Civil Liability Act 2002* (NSW) s 50(3), (5); *Personal Injuries (Liabilities and Damages) Act 2003* (NT) s 14; *Civil Liability Act 2003* (Qld) s 47(1)–(3); *Civil Liability Act 1936* (SA) s 46(1), (2); *Civil Liability Act 2002* (Tas) s 5(1), (4); *Civil Liability Act 2002* (WA) s 5L.

(a) the intoxication did not contribute to the accident; or

(b) the intoxication was not self-induced.

(3) If the presumption is not rebutted, the damages the injured person would be entitled to, apart from the contributory negligence, must be reduced to the extent that the court considers just and equitable having regard to the injured person's share in the responsibility for the injury.

5 Factual causation and scope of the duty

In cases in which contributory negligence has been alleged, the defendant must establish a sufficient causal connection between the plaintiff's unreasonable conduct and either the defendant's wrong or the plaintiff's loss. The following case outlines the applicable legal principles in relation to the nature of the causal connection the defendant is required to establish, and demonstrates that the plaintiff's unreasonable conduct must have been a factual cause of the accident or ensuing loss.

Allan v Fletcher [2001] SASC 167; (2001) 79 SASR 559

Facts and issues

Allan (the appellant in this appeal and plaintiff in the originating action) sought damages for injuries sustained in a road accident from Fletcher (the respondent in this appeal and defendant in the originating action), the driver of the other vehicle involved in the accident. After a trial the learned trial judge apportioned responsibility for the accident equally between Allan and Fletcher. This was on the basis that Allan's manner of driving had contributed to the accident occurring, and on the basis of expert evidence accepted by the trial judge that Allan's injuries would have been lessened in severity had she been wearing a seatbelt. At issue in this appeal was whether the reduction of damages to the plaintiff by 50 per cent due to Allan's contributory negligence was excessive.

Decision

The Court held that as the evidence demonstrated that the plaintiff's actions had contributed to causing the accident and increasing the severity of the injuries suffered by the plaintiff, it was open to the judge to reduce the plaintiff's damages by the amount decided by the judge.

Martin J[11]

[11] The trial judge referred to the evidence of three orthopaedic surgeons concerning the significance of the plaintiff's failure to wear the seat belt. Her conclusions were as follows:

11 Doyle CJ in agreement: [1]; Williams J in agreement: [2].

> The clear thrust of both the evidence of Mr Lipert and that of Mr Cornish, which I accept, was that the plaintiff's injuries would have been reduced or lessened in severity had she been wearing a seat belt … Accordingly I find that it is appropriate to reduce the award of damages by something more than 15 per cent.
>
> The approach to this question of a reduction to a damages award by reason of contributory negligence, including the failure to wear a seat belt, was discussed at some length by Lander J (with whose judgment Prior and Wicks JJ agreed) in *Barnard v Towill* (citation omitted). Having established that the plaintiff's manner of driving did contribute to the collision, and having further found that her failure to wear a seat belt resulted in her suffering greater injury than she otherwise would have, it is necessary for me to consider both those particulars of contributory negligence as part of an overall assessment. In this connection I have regard to all the evidence bearing on the incident, its causes and its results. Having undertaken this exercise I have determined that it is appropriate to reduce the damages which I shall award to the plaintiff by 50 per cent to reflect her contributory negligence.

[12] Counsel for the plaintiff argued that the trial judge erred in finding that it was appropriate to reduce the award of damages by something more than 15 per cent by reason of the failure to wear the seat belt …

[13] The initial impact between the vehicles propelled the plaintiff's vehicle forward and into a bus shelter on the eastern footpath. That movement involved a small degree of rotation. The secondary impact with the bus shelter was responsible for the plaintiff's major injury.

[14] In essence, counsel for the plaintiff contended that the rear end nature of the initial impact caused the plaintiff's body to move backwards with sufficient force to break the seat. As a consequence, the plaintiff was effectively lying in the rear of the car at the time of the secondary impact which propelled her forward. Counsel argued that in these circumstances the wearing of a seat belt would have had minimal effect and that the plaintiff's damages should only be reduced by the mandatory minimum of 15 per cent.

[15] The difficulty facing the plaintiff's submission is the absence of any expert evidence to support it. Notwithstanding an understandable appeal by counsel to a process of reasoning that he urged accorded with common sense and logic, the scenario he painted amounted to speculation without any foundation in the evidence. A number of different forces were applied to the plaintiff's body and different speculative views based on apparently sound logic could reasonably be propounded. It would be dangerous and inappropriate for this Court to speculate in the manner suggested in the absence of expert evidence to support the conclusions for which counsel contended.

[16] The trial judge relied upon expert evidence in reaching her conclusion. Counsel submitted that her Honour was in error in relying upon the view of Mr Cornish which he argued was a view initially expressed without a full appreciation of the relevant facts. However, when the evidence of Mr Cornish is considered in its entirety, in my opinion it was open to the trial judge to conclude that, given a full appreciation of the facts, Mr Cornish nevertheless maintained his view that the plaintiff's injuries would have been reduced or lessened in severity if she had been wearing a seat belt. It was open to her Honour to accept the thrust of the evidence of Mr Lipert and Mr Cornish in that regard. In those circumstances, it was open to her Honour to conclude that it was appropriate to reduce the award of damages 'by something more than 15 per cent'.

6 Apportionable loss

The following section outlines the relevant principles which apply when the court is determining the extent to which to reduce the plaintiff's damages due to the plaintiff's contributory negligence. The following extract is an example of a legislative provision which exists in the majority of Australian jurisdictions. It provides that the court must reduce the plaintiff's damages according to what the court thinks just and equitable having regard to the claimant's share in the responsibility for the damage.

Wrongs Act 1958 (Vic) s 26(1)(b)[12]

The purpose of this legislation is to require a reduction of damages according to what the court thinks is 'just and equitable having regard to the claimant's share in the responsibility for the damage'.

26 Liability for contributory negligence

(1) If a person (**the claimant**) suffers damage as the result partly of the claimant's failure to take reasonable care (**contributory negligence**) and partly of the wrong of any other person or persons –

...

(b) the damages recoverable in respect of the wrong must be reduced to such extent as the court thinks just and equitable having regard to the claimant's share in the responsibility for the damage.

...

7 Apportionment

Given the wide discretion conferred on the court in relation to the question of what reduction of the plaintiff's damages is just and equitable having regard to the claimant's share in the responsibility for the damage, the courts have been required to further comment upon the matters which ought to be taken into consideration when exercising this discretion. The following case provides an example of the matters which should be taken into consideration by the court when considering this question.

12 Equivalent provisions in the other jurisdictions are: *Civil Law (Wrongs) Act 2002* (ACT) s 102(1)(b); *Law Reform (Miscellaneous Provisions) Act 1965* (NSW) s 9(1)(b); *Law Reform (Miscellaneous Provisions) Act 1956* (NT) s 16(1)(b); *Law Reform Act 1995* (Qld) s 10(1)(b); *Law Reform (Contributory Negligence and Apportionment of Liability) Act 2001* (SA) s 7(2)(b); *Wrongs Act 1954* (Tas) s 4(1). The *Law Reform (Contributory Negligence and Tortfeasors' Contribution) Act 1947* (WA) s 4(1) is worded differently to the above provisions, although it is similar in substance and effect.

Pennington v Norris (1956) 96 CLR 10

Facts and issues

Pennington (the appellant in this appeal and plaintiff in the originating action) was severely injured after being struck by Norris's (the respondent in this appeal and defendant in the originating action) motor vehicle. On the basis of the finding that the parties were equally to blame for the accident, the trial judge reduced Pennington's damages by half. One of the issues in this appeal related to the approach to take in determining to extent to which damages to a plaintiff who has been contributorily negligent ought to be reduced.

Decision

In considering the extent to which the plaintiff's damages ought to be reduced due to contributory negligence, the courts must consider the conduct of both the plaintiff and the defendant, and consider the relative degree to which the actions of each departed from the standard of care of 'a reasonable man'.

Dixon CJ, Webb, Fullager and Kitto JJ

> [**15**] …
>
> It is clear that the Act [referring to the *Tortfeasors and Contributory Negligence Act 1954* (Tas), s 4(1), since superseded by the *Wrongs Act 1954* (Tas), s 4(1)] intends to give a very wide discretion to the judge or jury entrusted with the original task of making the apportionment. Much latitude must be allowed to the original [**16**] tribunal in arriving at a judgment as to what is just and equitable. It is to be expected, therefore, that cases will be rare in which the apportionment made can be successfully challenged: (citations omitted) But, giving full weight to these considerations in the present case, we are unable to avoid the conclusion that, in apportioning the responsibility equally, his Honour must have overlooked certain features of the case, and that the amount by which he reduced the assessed damages cannot really be supported.
>
> The only guide which the statute provides is that it requires regard to be had to 'the claimant's share in the responsibility for the damage' … What has to be done is to arrive at a 'just and equitable' apportionment as between the plaintiff and the defendant of the 'responsibility' for the damage. It seems clear that this must of necessity involve a comparison of culpability. By 'culpability' we do not mean moral blameworthiness but degree of departure from the standard of care of the reasonable man. To institute a comparison in respect of blameworthiness in such a case as the present seems more or less impracticable, because, while the defendant's negligence is a breach of duty owed to other persons and therefore blameworthy, the plaintiff's 'contributory' negligence is not a breach of any duty at all, and it is difficult to impute 'moral' blame to one who is careless merely of his own safety.
>
> Here, in our opinion, the negligence of the defendant was in a high degree more culpable, more gross, than that of the plaintiff. The plaintiff's conduct was *ex hypothesi* careless and unreasonable but, after all, it was the sort of thing that is very commonly done: he simply did not look when a reasonably careful man would have looked. We think too that in

this case the very fact that his conduct did not endanger the defendant or anybody else is a material consideration. The defendant's position was entirely different. The learned judge found only that he was negligent in not keeping a proper look-out, but there were several other important elements in the case ... We think, indeed, that the equal allocation of responsibility by his Honour must have proceeded from an overlooking of these elements. The first matter is his speed. It could not on the evidence have been found to be less than thirty miles per hour. Again, there was a large number of people in the [**17**] vicinity, – the defendant himself says that he noticed 'quite a number of people about'. The hotels, of which there were three in the immediate vicinity, had closed a very short time previously. It was a misty night, and the road was wet. Visibility must have been impaired by these factors, and it was further impaired by mistiness on the inside and outside of the windscreen. To drive at thirty miles per hour in a town at night under these circumstances seems to us to have been to do an obviously dangerous thing, and to have amounted to negligence of far greater culpability than anything that can possibly be attributed to the plaintiff.

Having regard to these factors, and to all the circumstances of the case, we are of opinion that a fair and reasonable allocation of the responsibility for the damage done is to attribute it, as to eighty per cent to the defendant and, as to twenty per cent to the plaintiff.

REVIEW QUESTIONS

(1) In *Palmer Bruyn & Parker Pty Ltd v Parsons* (2001) 208 CLR 388, Gummow J discussed *Smith New Court Securities Ltd v Citibank NA*, in which Lord Mustill spoke of 'the irrelevance of foreseeability' in a case of fraud, and Lord Steyn referred to the policy of the law 'of imposing more extensive liability on intentional wrongdoers than on merely careless defendants'. Do you think this type of distinction between intentional and merely careless wrongdoers is justified and, if so, on what basis?

(2) In *Pennington v Norris* (1956) 96 CLR 10, the defendant struck the plaintiff with his motor vehicle, thereby injuring him. The defendant argued that the plaintiff was contributorily negligence in failing to look when he crossed the road. In this case, the Court found it was just and equitable to apportion responsibility for the accident 80 per cent to the defendant and 20 per cent to the plaintiff on the basis that the negligence of the defendant in driving a motor vehicle carelessly was in a high degree more culpable, more gross, than that of the plaintiff. Do you agree that the factors referred to by the Court in coming to this decision were sufficient to justify this finding?

7 COMPENSATION FOR PERSONAL INJURY AND DEATH

I	Introduction	254
II	The impact of legislation	254
	A Statutory compensation schemes and ancillary regulation of common law damages	255
	B Civil liability statutes	256
III	Meaning of 'personal injury'	257
IV	Loss suffered by an injured person	258
	A Pecuniary loss resulting from needs created by the injury	261
	B Pecuniary loss resulting from the impairment of capacities	267
	C Non-pecuniary loss	275
	D Overlap between different heads of loss	281
V	Benefits arising from an injury	281
VI	Claims based on injury to another person	285
	A Loss of an employee's services	285
	B Loss of consortium	286
VII	Actions on death	288
	A Claim by the estate of the deceased	289
	B Claim by the dependants of the deceased	289

I Introduction

This chapter considers the rules and principles that apply in relation to claims for compensation for personal injury and death resulting from a wrongful act such as a tort, a breach of contract or statutory wrong.

II The impact of legislation

A number of statutory compensation schemes exist in the various Australian jurisdictions and impact greatly upon claims for compensation for personal injury and death. Some of these schemes are considered in this section.

Concept	Short explanation	Relevant authorities	Principles text
Statutory compensation schemes and ancillary regulation of common law damages	A number of statutory compensation schemes exist in the various Australian jurisdictions. Workers' compensation schemes are an example, existing in each of the state and territory jurisdictions in Australia.	*Workers' Compensation and Injury Management Act 1981* (WA)*	Chapter 7: [7.2]–[7.8]

Concept	Short explanation	Relevant authorities	Principles text
Civil liability statutes	Civil liability statutes in each state and territory jurisdiction impact upon the remedies available to claimants in relation to specific causes of action.	*Civil Liability Act 2002* (Tas)[#]	Chapter 7: [7.9]–[7.14]

* Workers' compensation schemes in jurisdictions other than South Australia are *Workers Compensation Act 1951* (ACT); *Workers Compensation Act 1987* (NSW); *Workplace Injury Management and Workers Compensation Act 1998* (NSW); *Return to Work Act 2015* (NT); *Workers' Compensation and Rehabilitation Act 2003* (Qld); *Workers Rehabilitation and Compensation Act 1988* (Tas); *Workplace Injury Rehabilitation and Compensation Act 2013* (Vic); *Return to Work Act 2014* (SA). Such schemes also exist at Commonwealth level: see, eg, *Safety, Rehabilitation and Compensation Act 1988* (Cth); *Seafarers Rehabilitation and Compensation Act 1992* (Cth); *Military Rehabilitation and Compensation Act 2004* (Cth).

[#] Equivalent provisions outlining the specific causes of action to which civil liability legislation in other jurisdictions apply include *Wrongs Act 1958* (Vic) ss 28B, 28C, 28LB, 28LC, 28N; *Civil Liability Act 2002* (WA) ss 3, 6; *Civil Law (Wrongs) Act 2002* (ACT) ss 92, 93; *Civil Liability Act 2002* (NSW) s 11A(2); *Personal Injuries (Liabilities and Damages) Act 2003* (NT) s 4(1); *Civil Liability Act 2003* (Qld) s 50.

A Statutory compensation schemes and ancillary regulation of common law damages

Workers' Compensation and Injury Management Act 1981 (WA) ss 3(a)(i)–(ii), 18(1)–(2)[1]

The purpose of the *Workers' Compensation and Injury Management Act 1981* (WA) (and its equivalents in other jurisdictions) is to establish a no-fault workers' compensation scheme in Western Australia.

3 Purposes

The purposes of this Act are –

(a) to establish a workers' compensation scheme for Western Australia dealing with –

  (i) compensation payable to or in respect of workers who suffer an injury; and

  (ii) the management of workers' injuries in a manner directed at enabling injured workers to return to work; ...

...

1 Workers' compensation schemes in jurisdictions other than South Australia are *Workers Compensation Act 1951* (ACT); *Workers Compensation Act 1987* (NSW); *Workplace Injury Management and Workers Compensation Act 1998* (NSW); *Return to Work Act 2015* (NT); *Workers' Compensation and Rehabilitation Act 2003* (Qld); *Workers Rehabilitation and Compensation Act 1988* (Tas); *Workplace Injury Rehabilitation and Compensation Act 2013* (Vic); *Return to Work Act 2014* (SA). Such schemes also exist at Commonwealth level: see, eg, *Safety, Rehabilitation and Compensation Act 1988* (Cth); *Seafarers Rehabilitation and Compensation Act 1992* (Cth); *Military Rehabilitation and Compensation Act 2004* (Cth).

18 Employers liable to pay compensation for injuries to workers

(1) If an injury of a worker occurs, the employer shall ... be liable to pay compensation in accordance with Schedule 1.

(2) If an injury of a worker occurs and the worker dies, the employer shall ... be liable to pay compensation in accordance with Schedule 1A.

...

B Civil liability statutes

Civil Liability Act 2002 (Tas) ss 3, 3B, 24[2]

Civil liability legislation in each state and territory jurisdiction applies only to those causes of action specified in each piece of legislation.

3 Interpretation

In this Act, unless the contrary intention appears –

...

duty means –

(a) a duty of care in tort; or

(b) a duty of care under contract that is co-extensive with a duty of care in tort; or

(c) another duty under statute or otherwise that is co-extensive with a duty of care referred to in paragraph (a) or (b);

...

3B Civil liability excluded from Act

(1) This Act does not apply to or in respect of civil liability –

(a) in respect of an intentional act that is done with intent to cause injury or death or that is sexual assault or other sexual misconduct; or

(b) relating to an award of damages for personal injury or death where the injury or death concerned resulted from smoking or other use of tobacco products.

(1A) Despite subsection (1), Part 10C applies in respect of an intentional act that is child abuse, within the meaning of section 49J(3).

(2) This Act, except Parts 2, 3, 5 and 5A, Divisions 1, 2, 3, 4 and 7 of Part 6 and Parts 7 and 8, does not apply to or in respect of civil liability relating to an injury to which Part III of the *Motor Accidents (Liabilities and Compensation) Act 1973* applies.

(3) This Act does not apply to civil liability relating to an injury to which Division 2 of Part X of the Workers Rehabilitation and Compensation Act 1988 applies.

(4) This Act does not apply to liability for compensation under *the Workers Rehabilitation and Compensation Act 1988*, the *Asbestos-Related Diseases (Occupational*

2 Equivalent provisions outlining the specific causes of action to which civil liability legislation in other jurisdictions apply include *Wrongs Act 1958* (Vic) ss 28B, 28C, 28LB, 28LC, 28N; *Civil Liability Act 2002* (WA) ss 3, 6; *Civil Law (Wrongs) Act 2002* (ACT) ss 92, 93; *Civil Liability Act 2002* (NSW) s 11A(2); *Personal Injuries (Liabilities and Damages) Act 2003* (NT) s 4(1); *Civil Liability Act 2003* (Qld) s 50.

Exposure) Compensation Act 2011, the *Criminal Injuries Compensation Act 1976* or the *Anti-Discrimination Act 1998* or a scheduled benefit under the *Motor Accidents (Liabilities and Compensation) Act 1973*.

...

24 Application of Part 7

This Part applies in relation to an award of damages for personal injury or death resulting from a breach of duty, except civil liability that is excluded from the operation of this Part by section 3B.

REVIEW QUESTIONS

(1) What are the benefits of regulating claims for damages for workers injured in the course of employment via a statutory workers compensation scheme as opposed to via the common law?

(2) Do you think the various civil liability statutes have improved the law in Australia with respect to claims for personal injury?

III Meaning of 'personal injury'

Concept	Short explanation	Relevant authorities	Principles text
Meaning of 'personal injury'	The civil liability legislation each define the term 'personal injury', and this definition specifies the claims to which each Act applies.	*Civil Liability Act 2002* (NSW)	Chapter 7: [7.15]–[7.20]

Civil Liability Act 2002 (NSW) ss 11, 27, 28(1), 31

The purpose of the provisions defining the term 'personal injury' is to specify the types of claims to which the civil liability legislation applies.

11 Definitions

In this Part –

injury means personal injury and includes the following –

(a) pre-natal injury,

(b) impairment of a person's physical or mental condition,

(c) disease.

personal injury damages means damages that relate to the death of or injury to a person.

Part 3 Mental harm

27 Definitions

In this Part –

consequential mental harm means mental harm that is a consequence of a personal injury of any other kind.

mental harm means impairment of a person's mental condition.

...

personal injury includes –

(a) pre-natal injury, and

(b) impairment of a person's physical or mental condition, and

(c) disease.

pure mental harm means mental harm other than consequential mental harm.

28 Application of Part

(1) This Part (except section 29) applies to any claim for damages for mental harm resulting from negligence, regardless of whether the claim is brought in tort, in contract, under statute or otherwise.

...

31 Pure mental harm – liability only for recognised psychiatric illness

There is no liability to pay damages for pure mental harm resulting from negligence unless the harm consists of a recognised psychiatric illness.

REVIEW QUESTION

The definition of the term 'mental harm' as meaning 'impairment of a person's mental condition' appears to be wider than the common law conception of mental harm, as it may bring within the ambit of the legislation the phenomena of disappointment, distress and inconvenience which seems to go beyond the common law concept of a recognisable psychiatric injury: see, for example, *New South Wales v Ibbett* (2005) 65 NSWLR 168, [124], [211]–[212]. Given that the primary purpose of the civil liability legislation was generally to limit the number of size of claims for personal injury, do you regard this apparent expansion of the concept of personal injury at law as being consistent with the general purpose of the legislation?

IV Loss suffered by an injured person

Concept	Short explanation	Relevant authorities	Principles text
Pecuniary loss resulting from needs created by the injury: medical expenses and cost of institutional care	An injured person can claim compensation for all injury-related medical expenses, including the cost of an ambulance, consultation with a doctor and hospital treatment.	*Blundell v Musgrave* (1956) 96 CLR 73	Chapter 7: [7.22]
Pecuniary loss resulting from needs created by the injury: domestic services provided to the injured person	Loss can be characterised by an incapacity to look after oneself as demonstrated by the need for nursing services.	*Griffiths v Kerkemeyer* (1977) 139 CLR 161	Chapter 7: [7.23]–[7.31]

Concept	Short explanation	Relevant authorities	Principles text
	In a number of Australian jurisdictions, *Griffiths v Kerkemeyer* damages are only available upon the satisfaction of particular requirements.	*Civil Liability Act 2003* (Qld) s 59(1), (2)[a]	
Pecuniary loss resulting from needs created by the injury: increased cost of living at home	When assessing damages relating to housing improvements, the court is required to calculate the reasonable cost of alternative suitable accommodation.	*McNeilly v Imbree* (2007) 47 MVR 536	Chapter 7: [7.32]
Pecuniary loss resulting from needs created by the injury: cost of managing a lump sum award	Damages for the cost of management or investment of lump sum awards of damages are prohibited by statute in South Australia.	*Civil Liability Act 1936* (SA)	Chapter 7: [7.33]–[7.37]
	Expenses associated with obtaining professional assistance to manage a lump sum awarded as damages may be a compensable consequence of the plaintiff's injury, but only where a defendant's negligence has so impaired the plaintiff's intellectual capacity as to put the plaintiff in need of such assistance.	*Gray v Richards* (2014) 253 CLR 660	
Pecuniary loss resulting from the impairment of capacities: loss of earning capacity	An injured plaintiff recovers not merely because their earning capacity has been diminished but because the diminution of their earning capacity is or may be productive of financial loss.	*Graham v Baker* (1961) 106 CLR 340	Chapter 7: [7.38]–[7.49]
	In South Australia, legislation excludes compensation for the first week of incapacity and places a limit on the total amount awarded for pecuniary loss resulting from loss of earning capacity.	*Civil Liability Act 1936* (SA)	
Pecuniary loss resulting from the impairment of capacities: loss of employment-related benefits	As part of a claim for pecuniary loss resulting from impairment of capacities, a plaintiff may claim damages for loss of employment-related benefits, such as the loss of a company car for private purposes.	*Delphin v Martin* [2012] TASSC 13	Chapter 7: [7.50]–[7.51]

Concept	Short explanation	Relevant authorities	Principles text
	Civil liability legislation in some Australian jurisdictions prescribes the amount of lost superannuation benefits as the maximum to be awarded for loss of superannuation benefits.	*Civil Liability Act 2002* (Tas)[b]	
Pecuniary loss resulting from the impairment of capacities: loss of social security benefits	Where a plaintiff was, prior to the accident, in receipt of employment benefits which were likely to have continued after the accident, the plaintiff is in some circumstances entitled to recover the value of those benefits.	*Renehan v Leeuwin Ocean Adventure Foundation Ltd* (2006) 17 NTLR 83	Chapter 7: [7.52]
Pecuniary loss resulting from the impairment of capacities: loss of capacity to do domestic work	The inability to provide domestic services to another as a result of injury does not constitute a separate head of economic loss, but may be compensated as part of loss of amenities.	*CSR Ltd v Eddy* (2005) 226 CLR 1	Chapter 7: [7.53]–[7.55]
	In some Australian jurisdictions, the civil liability statutes provide that, in certain circumstances, the loss of the injured person's capacity to provide gratuitous domestic services can be compensated as a separate head of economic loss rather than as part of non-pecuniary loss.	*Civil Law (Wrongs) Act 2002* (ACT)[c]	
Non-pecuniary loss: pain and suffering	A plaintiff must be able to experience pain and suffering in order to receive compensation for pain and suffering, and as a result, a permanently unconscious plaintiff is not entitled to be compensated under this head for anything other than moderate sums in damages for loss of amenities.	*Skelton v Collins* (1966) 115 CLR 94	Chapter 7: [7.58]
Non-pecuniary loss: loss of amenities	In assessing the amount of damages to be awarded for loss of amenities, the economic situation of the individual, the individual themself, the nature and effects of injuries, family background, responsibilities, past activities and frustrations imposed by reason of the injuries should be taken into account.	*Lawrence v Mathison* (1981) 11 NTR 1	Chapter 7: [7.59]–[7.61]

Concept	Short explanation	Relevant authorities	Principles text
Non-pecuniary loss: loss of expectation of life	Loss of expectation of life is to be assessed objectively, and attracts only a convention sum, moderate in amount.	*Sharman v Evans* (1977) 138 CLR 563	Chapter 7: [7.62]
Non-pecuniary loss: statutory regulation	The Western Australian civil liability legislation imposes particular minimum and maximum thresholds on the amounts that can be awarded for non-pecuniary loss.	*Civil Liability Act 2002* (WA)	
Overlap between different heads of loss	Where the loss of the capacity to provide domestic services is compensated through a separate head of damages, it must not be taken into account in calculating non-pecuniary loss.	*Civil Liability Act 2003* (Qld)[d]	Chapter 7: [7.69]–[7.71]

[a] Equivalent provisions in other Australian jurisdictions include *Competition and Consumer Act 2010* (Cth) s 87W(2); *Civil Liability Act 2002* (NSW) s 15(2); *Personal Injuries (Liabilities and Damages) Act 2003* (NT) s 23(1); *Wrongs Act 1958* (Vic) s 28IA(1). Legislative provisions imposing different requirements on the availability of *Griffiths v Kerkemeyer* damages include *Civil Liability Act 1936* (SA) s 58(1)(a) (damages only available to those who are in a specific relationship with the plaintiff, ie parent, spouse, child, etc); *Civil Liability Act 2002* (WA) ss 12(3), (4), 13 (damages only available to those whose damage meets a specific threshold).

[b] Equivalent provisions in other Australian jurisdictions include *Civil Liability Act 2002* (NSW) s 15C; *Civil Liability Act 2003* (Qld) s 56; *Civil Liability Act 1936* (SA).

[c] Other jurisdictions in which this is the case are New South Wales (see *Civil Liability Act 2002* (NSW) s 15B), Queensland (see *Civil Liability Act 2003* (Qld) ss 59A–59D), Tasmania (see *Civil Liability Act 2002* (Tas) s 28BA(3)), Victoria (see *Wrongs Act 1958* (Vic) ss 28ID, 28IE). The common law position applies in Western Australia, the Northern Territory, South Australia, and under the *Competition and Consumer Act 2010* (Cth).

[d] Civil liability statutes in other Australian jurisdictions which contain similar provisions include *Civil Liability Act 2002* (NSW) s 15B(5)(b); *Wrongs Act 1958* (Vic) s 28ID(3)(b).

A Pecuniary loss resulting from needs created by the injury

This section provides examples of pecuniary losses resulting from needs created by the injury in question which are recoverable.

1 Medical expenses and cost of institutional care

An injured person can claim compensation for all injury-related medical expenses, including the cost of an ambulance, consultation with a doctor and hospital treatment.

Blundell v Musgrave (1956) 96 CLR 73

Facts and issues

Musgrove (the respondent in this appeal and the plaintiff in the originating action), a navy mechanic on leave, was injured after being negligently struck by Blundell's (the appellant in this action and defendant in the originating action) motor vehicle. Musgrove sought and was granted medical treatment for this injury by the Navy Department of the Commonwealth, who subsequently issued Musgrove with a bill for the cost of medical services provided. At trial, the costs of these medical services were included in an amount of special damages the Court ordered Musgrove was entitled to be paid by Blundell. Blundell appealed against this finding on the basis that Musgrove was entitled to free medical attendance pursuant to the *Naval Defence Act 1910* (Cth), and that, given that, the Navy Department had indicated that no action was to be taken to charge Musgrove's pay account until legal liability for the accident had been determined, Musgrove had not actually suffered any loss in relation to these expenses.

Decision

The Court found that Musgrove was entitled to receive damages for the amounts relating to medical treatment costs.

McTiernan, Williams, Webb and Taylor JJ

> [**86**] …
>
> … It is clear that if the charge made against the respondent's account was fictitious and if there never was any intention of exercising the authority given by sub-reg. (7), no part of the amount in question could be recovered by the respondent. But it is equally clear that if the Naval Board had authority to make the charge and took the appropriate steps to impose a liability to pay the amount in question upon the respondent, it is of no consequence that at some later stage they may forgive the whole or some part of the charge. If one may speculate it is probable that if no part of this sum is recovered by the respondent he will not be required to pay it. This will not, however, mean that he was never under a legal liability to pay it and there is no reason why, if the Naval Board, having authority to do so, sees fit to forego part of a lawful claim, the appellant should, in anticipation of that possibility, receive the benefit of it.
>
> The learned trial judge to whom the decision of this issue was committed appears to have taken the view that a decision was made to charge the respondent the sum in question and expressed the view that the probabilities were that that decision would be maintained. But whether it will be maintained or not is of no consequence if, in the first instance, the charge was lawfully made and a liability created. There was ample evidence upon which the learned judge was entitled to reach this conclusion and it is, in our view, the only conclusion reasonably open on the evidence.

Fullager J

> [**92**]
>
> …
>
> In an action for damages for personal injuries caused by negligence, expenditure necessarily or reasonably incurred in connexion with medical, surgical and nursing attention,

> the services of an ambulance and treatment in a hospital, is, of course, recoverable by the plaintiff as part of his damages. It is not necessary for him to prove that he has paid the fees chargeable for the services rendered, but it is, generally speaking, necessary for him to prove that he has incurred a legal obligation to pay those fees. In *Dixon v Bell* (citation omitted) the plaintiff had required the services of a surgeon and also of a physician. At that time a surgeon was entitled to sue for fees for his services, but a physician was not. Lord Ellenborough CJ directed the jury 'that as to the surgeon's bill, they were to consider the amount as paid by the plaintiff, since the surgeon could compel the payment of it as a legal debt, but that the physician's fees could not be taken into the account, since they had not been actually paid, and he could not enforce the payment by action' (citation omitted) … The right to recover depends, of course, on a practical certainty, or at least a high degree of probability, that the payment will have to be made. The existence of a legal liability is strong prima facie evidence that the payment will have to be made. But it is not conclusive evidence. There may be exceptional cases, in which a legal liability exists, but it may be taken as practically certain that the liability will not be enforced. In such cases no amount can be recovered as for a prospective expenditure.

2 Domestic services provided to the injured person

Griffiths v Kerkemeyer (1977) 139 CLR 161

Facts and issues

Kerkemeyer (the respondent in this appeal and plaintiff in the originating action) was seriously injured in a motor vehicle accident caused by the negligence of Griffiths (the appellant in the action and defendant in the originating action). The trial judge allowed a full recovery of damages in respect of past and future nursing services provided gratuitously by friends and family. The issue in this case concerned the correct method to assess loss in cases where the plaintiff requires services but these are provided gratuitously.

Decision

True loss is the loss of capacity which occasions the need for services, quantified by reference to the value or cost of providing those services. This is regardless of whether these services are provided to the injured person gratuitously.

Stephen J[3]

> **[191]** … [I]n *Wilson v McLeay* (citation omitted), Taylor J expressed the view that an injured plaintiff may recover as part of her damages an allowance to permit the reasonable attendance upon her of her parents who lived a great distance away …

3 Gibbs J in agreement, 168–9; Mason J in agreement, 189–94.

Since then it has been held in a succession of cases in England, in particular by the Court of Appeal, that an 'injured plaintiff can recover the value of nursing and other services gratuitously rendered to him by a stranger to the proceedings': ... (citations omitted). In *Cunningham v Harrison* the plaintiff recovered the value of nursing services rendered to him by his wife, there being no legal agreement that he would pay her for what she did. In *Donnelly v Joyce* an infant plaintiff recovered the value of nursing services provided by his mother who gave up her employment to care for him. The Court rejected the argument that in the absence of a legal liability to pay, the reimbursement sought was reimbursement of another person's loss. Megaw L.J., who delivered the judgment of the Court, said (citation omitted):

> The loss is the plaintiff's loss. The question from what source the plaintiff's needs have been met, the question who has paid the money or given the services, the question whether or not the plaintiff is or is not under a legal or moral [**192**] liability to repay, are, so far as the defendant and his liability are concerned, all irrelevant. The plaintiff's loss, to take this present case, is not the expenditure of money to buy the special boots or to pay for the nursing attention. His loss is the existence of the need for those special boots or for those nursing services, the value of which for purposes of damages – for the purpose of the ascertainment of the amount of his loss – is the proper and reasonable cost of supplying those needs.

and went on to say:

> ... it does not matter, for that purpose, whether the plaintiff has a legal liability, absolute or conditional, to repay to the provider what he has received, because of the general law or because of some private agreement between himself and the provider; it does not matter whether he has a moral obligation, however ascertained or defined, so to do. The question of legal liability to reimburse the provider may be very relevant to the question of the legal right of the provider to recover from the plaintiff. That may depend on the nature of the liability imposed by the general law or the particular agreement. But it is not a matter which affects the right of the plaintiff against the wrongdoer.

In *Beck v Farrell* (citation omitted), the Full Court of the Supreme Court of South Australia adopted and applied the recent English decisions and the fomulation(sic) of the relevant principle by the Court of Appeal in *Donnelly v Joyce* (citation omitted). It was correct in so doing, for in my opinion the passages from the judgment of Megaw LJ which I have quoted accurately express the law on the question. The respondent's relevant loss is his incapacity to look after himself as demonstrated by the need for nursing services and this loss is to be quantified by reference to the value or cost of providing those services. The fact that a relative or stranger to the proceedings is or may be prepared to provide the services gratuitously is not a circumstance which accrues to the advantage of the appellant. If a relative or stranger moved by charity or goodwill towards the respondent does him a favour as [**193**] a disabled person then it is only right that the respondent should reap the benefit rather than the wrongdoer whose negligence has occasioned the need for the nursing service to be provided. Enough has been said in the cases which have been decided more recently to indicate that the old view based on the proposition that a plaintiff is not entitled to recover from the defendant the services provided to him unless he can show that he is under a legal liability to pay for them, is no longer acceptable. That view proceeded upon the footing that the relevant loss was the legal liability to pay for the service. It is now recognized that the true loss is the loss of capacity which occasions the need for the service. In consequence the existence of a legal liability to pay is not the dominant consideration …

… In general the value or cost of providing voluntary services will be the standard or market cost of the services.

Civil Liability Act 2003 (Qld) s 59[4]

The purpose of the provisions in question is to limit the availability of *Griffiths v Kerkemeyer* damages to only those cases where the care required is necessary, meets a minimum threshold, and is related only to the injury resulting from the accident which was caused by the defendant's negligence rather than to a pre-existing requirement for such care.

59 Damages for gratuitous services provided to an injured person

(1) Damages for gratuitous services provided to an injured person are not to be awarded unless –
   (a) the services are necessary; and
   (b) the need for the services arises solely out of the injury in relation to which damages are awarded; and
   (c) the services are provided, or are to be provided –
      (i) for at least 6 hours per week; and
      (ii) for at least 6 months.

(2) Damages are not to be awarded for gratuitous services if gratuitous services of the same kind were being provided for the injured person before the breach of duty happened.

(3) In assessing damages for gratuitous services, a court must take into account –
   (a) any offsetting benefit the service provider obtains through providing the services; and
   (b) periods for which the injured person has not required or is not likely to require the services because the injured person has been or is likely to be cared for in a hospital or other institution.

4 Equivalent provisions in other Australian jurisdictions include *Competition and Consumer Act 2010* (Cth) s 87W(2); *Civil Liability Act 2002* (NSW) s 15(2); *Personal Injuries (Liabilities and Damages) Act 2003* (NT) s 23(1); *Wrongs Act 1958* (Vic) s 28IA(1). Legislative provisions imposing different requirements on the availability of *Griffiths v Kerkemeyer* damages include *Civil Liability Act 1936* (SA) s 58(1)(a) (damages only available to those who are in a specific relationship with the plaintiff, ie parent, spouse, child, etc); *Civil Liability Act 2002* (WA) ss 12(3), (4), 13 (damages only available to those whose damage meets a specific threshold).

3 Increased cost of living at home

The defendant is liable to compensate the plaintiff for the loss suffered as a result of his tortious conduct. The plaintiff's needs, resulting from his or her injuries, may include appropriate modifications to his or her home.[5]

4 Cost of managing a lump sum award

Civil Liability Act 1936 (SA) s 57

The purpose of the *Civil Liability Act* (SA) s 57 is to prohibit the availability of damages for the cost of management or investment of lump sum awards of damages in South Australia.

> **57 Exclusion of damages for cost of management or investment**
> Damages are not to be awarded to compensate for the cost of the investment or management of the amount awarded.

Gray v Richards (2014) 253 CLR 660

Facts and issues

Gray (the appellant in this appeal and plaintiff in the originating action) suffered serious brain injuries and significant intellectual impairment as a result of a collision involving Richards' (the respondent in this action and defendant in the originating action) vehicle and the vehicle in which Gray was a passenger. At trial, Gray was awarded a large sum in damages which included a sum for professional services to manage these monies. At issue in this case was whether this amount should include the costs associated with the management of the predicted future income of the managed fund.

Decision

Expenses associated with obtaining professional assistance to manage a lump sum awarded as damages may be a compensable consequence of the plaintiff's injury, but only where a defendant's negligence has so impaired the plaintiff's intellectual capacity as to put the plaintiff in need of such assistance.

French CJ, Hayne, Bell, Gagelar and Keane JJ

> [**665**] In *Todorovic v Waller* (citation omitted), Gibbs CJ and Wilson J summarised the principles which regulate the assessment of damages for personal injuries as follows:
>
> > In the first place, a plaintiff who has been injured by the negligence of the defendant should be awarded such a sum of money as will, as nearly as possible, put him in

5 See, eg, *McNeilly v Imbree* (2007) 47 MVR 536, [165]–[172].

> the same position as if he had not sustained the injuries. Secondly, damages for one cause of action must be recovered once and forever, and (in the absence of any statutory exception) must be awarded as a lump sum; the court cannot order a defendant to make periodic payments to the plaintiff. Thirdly, the court has no concern with the manner in which the plaintiff uses the sum awarded to him; the plaintiff is free to do what he likes with it. Fourthly, the burden lies on the plaintiff to prove the injury or loss for which he seeks damages.

Generally speaking, the third of these principles operates so that a plaintiff does not recover damages for costs he or she might incur in managing a lump sum awarded by way of damages. That is because such costs are not regarded as a loss resulting from the plaintiff's injury. In *Nominal Defendant v Gardikiotis* (citation omitted), Brennan CJ, Dawson, Toohey and Gaudron JJ said:

> it is contrary to common sense to speak of the accident causing a need for assistance in managing the fund constituted by [the] verdict moneys in circumstances where [the plaintiff's] intellectual abilities are not in any way impaired.

To similar effect, McHugh J said (citation omitted) that damages are not recoverable where:

> the plaintiff seeks damages, not for expense necessarily incurred as the result of a disability caused by the defendant's negligence, [**666**] but for an expense arising merely from the size of an award of damages and the exercise of a choice by the plaintiff as to how to invest those damages. The expense of exercising that choice is not the consequence of the plaintiff's injury.

The decisions of this Court in *Nominal Defendant v Gardikiotis* (citation omitted) and *Willett v Futcher* (citation omitted) refined this aspect of the operation of the third principle in *Todorovic v Waller* so that, in a case where a defendant's negligence has so impaired the plaintiff's intellectual capacity as to put the plaintiff in need of assistance in managing the lump sum awarded as damages, expense associated with obtaining that assistance is a compensable consequence of the plaintiff's injury. In such a case, 'the liability for the [management expenses] is a loss flowing directly from the wrong and is recoverable as damages caused by the wrong' (citation omitted); and, in accordance with the first and second of the principles stated in *Todorovic v Waller*, the inclusion of such a component in the lump sum award ensures that the plaintiff receives full restitution for the harm he or she has sustained.

B Pecuniary loss resulting from the impairment of capacities

Where injury impairs the plaintiff's capacities, this can cause the plaintiff to suffer pecuniary loss in a number of distinct ways.

1 Loss of earning capacity

Graham v Baker (1961) 106 CLR 340

Facts and issues

Baker (the respondent in this appeal and plaintiff in the originating action), a fire station officer, was injured as a result of Graham's (the appellant in this appeal and defendant in the originating action) negligence. As a result of the injury, Baker was compulsorily retired approximately three years prior to the date at which he was previously due to retire. The jury at trial gave judgment to Baker for the amount of £12 000. Graham argued on appeal that this amount should be reduced to reflect payments described as 'sick leave payments' made to Baker by his employer for some 178 days following the accident. One of Graham's grounds of appeal was whether the receipt of these payments by Baker should result in Baker's entitlement to damages for loss of earning capacity being reduced.

Decision

An injured plaintiff recovers not merely because their earning capacity has been diminished but because the diminution of their earning capacity is or may be productive of financial loss. In this case, Baker could not be considered to have suffered loss with respect to the amounts paid to him for 'sick leave payments'.

Dixon CJ, Kitto and Taylor JJ

> [**346**]...
>
> So far the matter has been discussed as if the right of a plaintiff whose earning capacity has been diminished by the defendant's negligence is concerned with two separate matters, ie loss of wages up to the time of trial and an estimated future loss because of his diminished earning capacity. It is, we think, necessary to point out that this is not so. A plaintiff's right of action is complete at the time when his injuries are sustained and if it were possible in the ordinary course of things to obtain an assessment of his damages immediately it would be necessary to make an assessment of the probable economic loss which would result from his injuries. But for at least two obvious reasons it has been found convenient to assess an injured plaintiff's loss by reference to the actual loss of wages which occurs up to the time of trial and which can be more [**347**] or less precisely ascertained and then, having regard to the plaintiff's proved condition at the time of trial, to attempt some assessment of his future loss. We mention this matter because it has been suggested that since an injured plaintiff is entitled to recover damages for the impairment of his earning capacity, the fact that a totally incapacitated plaintiff has, during the period of his incapacity, received his ordinary wages is not a matter to be taken into consideration. To be more precise, however, an injured plaintiff recovers not merely because his earning capacity has been diminished but because the diminution of his earning capacity is or may be productive of financial loss. And if, notwithstanding such impairment, both his contract of employment and his right to ordinary wages continue, how can it be said that his impairment has resulted in any loss so far as his earning capacity is concerned? According to Windeyer J in *Paff v Speed* (citation omitted) the answer to this question is clear and the same view has been taken on other occasions. In *McInnes v Crowe* (citation

omitted) McMillan CJ treated 'sick pay' received by the plaintiff in the circumstances of that case as ordinary wages and, after referring to the principle enunciated in *Bradburn v Great Western Railway Co* (citation omitted), he said: 'That principle has no application to the facts of the present case where the plaintiff has not lost the right to her salary, but has merely been relieved of the obligation to work for it' (citation omitted). And in *Receiver for the Metropolitan Police District v Croydon Corporation* (citation omitted) Lord Goddard CJ said: 'The obligation of the defendants here was to compensate the injured men, and to pay them the damage which they had sustained. If a man's employer has agreed to pay him wages, whether he is well or whether he is ill, it seems to me that that affords a benefit in one sense to a defendant, because he does not have to pay the damage which he would have had to pay if that agreement had not been made. That simply means that he does not have to compensate the plaintiff for an injury which he has not suffered. The obligation is, in the words of Earl Jowitt, simply to pay 'such damages as, by reason of his [the defendant's] wrongdoing, the plaintiff has sustained'. Having paid that, his obligation seems to me to be at an end' (citation omitted). The same view was taken by Urquhart J in *Cossitt v CPR* (citation omitted) where, notwithstanding the existing 'custom', he rejected the contention that a plaintiff whilst on sick leave with pay could be said to have suffered a loss of earnings or wages during the relevant period.

Civil Liability Act 1936 (SA) ss 3(1), 54(1)–(2)

The purpose of these provisions of the *Civil Liability Act 1936* (SA) is to preclude claims for pecuniary loss relating to loss sustained during the first week of incapacity, and to set an upper limit on the amount which can be claimed under this head of damages.

3 Interpretation

(1) In this Act, unless the contrary intention appears –

...

prescribed maximum means –

(a) in relation to an injury arising from an accident that occurred during 2002 – $2.2 million; or

(b) in relation to an injury arising from an accident that occurred in a subsequent calendar year – a sum (calculated to the nearest multiple of $10) that bears to $2.2 million the same proportion as the Consumer Price Index for the September quarter of the preceding year bears to the Consumer Price Index for the September quarter 2001;

...

54 Damages for loss of earning capacity

(1) If the injured person was incapacitated for work, damages for loss of earning capacity are not to be awarded in respect of the first week of the incapacity.

(2) Total damages for loss of earning capacity (excluding interest awarded on damages for any past loss) are not to exceed the prescribed maximum.

...

2 Loss of employment-related benefits

Delphin v Martin [2012] TASSC 13

Facts and issues

Delphin (the appellant in this appeal and plaintiff in the originating action) suffered permanent facial nerve damage as a result of dental treatment performed by Martin (the respondent in this appeal and defendant in the originating action). Following the procedure which caused the injury, Delphin further suffered a deterioration in his mental health and subsequently never worked again. In an action for negligence and breach of contract, Delphin sued Martin for failure to provide reasonable care in the provision of dental services, and for failure to warn of the risks associated with the particular treatment provided. One of the issues in this appeal was whether Delphin could claim for the loss of the value of a company car as part of his claim for pecuniary loss resulting from impairment of capacities.

Decision

As part of a claim for pecuniary loss resulting from impairment of capacities, a plaintiff may claim damages for loss of employment-related benefits, such as the loss of a company car.

Blow J

Impairment of earning capacity

...

Past economic loss

[94] If Mr Delphin had remained working for the same employer from 2004 until the present day, I estimate that his net income would have been as follows:

Tax year	Gross	Income tax	Levies	Net
2005	$49 500	$11 022	$743	$37 735
2006	$51 200	$11 220	$768	$39 212
2007	$52 000	$10 950	$780	$40 270
2008	$53 000	$10 500	$795	$41 705
2009	$54 000	$10 200	$810	$42 990
2010	$55 000	$10 350	$825	$43 825
2011	$56 000	$10 350	$840	$44 810
2012	$56 000	$10 350	$870	$44 780

[95] There are some things that I need to explain about the above table:

- The gross figures were suggested by Mr Delphin's counsel, and are based on Mr Cairnduff's evidence.
- The gross income for 2005 represents the gross salary of $48 346 as at the time Mr Delphin ceased work, adjusted upwards to make allowance for the salary review scheduled for January 2005.

- I have assumed that the gross salary would have remained at $56 000 per annum from July 2010 until the present time.
- The levies referred to are the Medicare levy, which applied during all the relevant financial years, and the flood levy, applicable only in the 2012 year. The amount of the flood levy payable by a taxpayer with a gross income of $56 000 is $30.
- The figures for income tax, levies and net income differ from the figures submitted by counsel. The above figures have been calculated on the basis of the rates fixed by the tax legislation.

[96] On the basis of those figures, I calculate that the amount Mr Delphin would have earned if he had stayed in the same job after his date of resignation (10 April 2005) until the present day would be as follows:

Tax year	Net income
2005 (81 days)	$8 374
2006	$39 212
2007	$40 270
2008	41 705
2009	$42 990
2010	$43 825
2011	$44 810
2012 (272 days)	$33 279
Total	$294 465

[97] As I have mentioned, Mr Delphin has done a little busking in recent years. His earnings from that activity have been insignificant. He has undertaken restoration work on a number of cars. Some people can make money doing that, but there is no suggestion that Mr Delphin has done so, or that he is ever likely to do so. He has earned nothing since his resignation in April 2005.

[98] Allowance must be made for the fact that Mr Delphin's remuneration package included the provision of a company car, which he was entitled to use for private purposes without restriction. It is an agreed fact that the value of that benefit was $5000 per annum. The value of that benefit from the commencement of Mr Delphin's retirement on 11 April 2005 until the present day, a period of six years 353 days, is therefore $34 809. It follows that the amount required to compensate him for the loss of his earnings and the loss of the company car for that period totals $329 274. However some allowance should be made for adverse contingencies during that period, particularly the possibilities of unemployment, under-employment, and incapacity due to psychiatric problems. I will deal with superannuation separately. Without taking superannuation into account, I consider that Mr Delphin should recover $265 000 to compensate him for the past impairment of his earning capacity.

Civil Liability Act 2002 (Tas) s 25[6]

The purpose of the *Civil Liability Act 2002* (Tas) s 25 (and its equivalents in other jurisdictions) is to prescribe the amount of lost superannuation benefits as the maximum to be awarded for loss of superannuation benefits.

25 Damages for loss of superannuation entitlements

(1) The maximum amount of damages that may be awarded for economic loss due to the loss of employer superannuation contributions is the relevant percentage of damages payable for the deprivation or impairment of the earning capacity on which the entitlement to those contributions is based.

(2) In this section,

relevant percentage means the percentage of earnings that is the minimum percentage required by law to be paid as employer superannuation contributions.

3 Loss of social security benefits

The value of employment benefits may be claimed by plaintiffs where they were in receipt of such benefits prior to the accident in question and their payment was likely to have continued following the accident.[7]

4 Loss of capacity to do domestic work

CSR Ltd v Eddy (2005) 226 CLR 1

Facts and issues

Eddy (the respondent in this appeal and plaintiff in the originating action) contracted mesothelioma after being negligently exposed to asbestos due to the negligence of CSR (the appellant in this action and defendant in the originating action). Before contracting this disease, Eddy provided domestic assistance in the form of vacuuming and cleaning to his wife, who was suffering from osteoporosis. At issue in this case was whether Eddy was entitled to claim the commercial value of those services.

Decision

The inability to provide domestic services to another as a result of injury does not constitute a separate head of economic loss, but may be compensated as part of loss of amenities.

6 Equivalent provisions in other Australian jurisdictions include *Civil Liability Act 2002* (NSW) s 15C; *Civil Liability Act 2003* (Qld) s 56; *Civil Liability Act 1936* (SA).

7 See, eg, *Renehan v Leeuwin Ocean Adventure Foundation Ltd* (2006) 17 NTLR 83, [203]–[206].

Gleeson CJ, Gummow and Hayden JJ

[12] Special and general damages

...

[**14**] ... [A]s the appellants submitted, *Griffiths v Kerkemeyer* damages are awarded to plaintiffs to compensate them for the cost (whether actually incurred or not) of services rendered to them because [**15**] of their incapacity to render them to themselves, not to compensate them for the cost of services which because of their incapacity they cannot render to others. In each instance there may be a 'need' for services, but it is a different kind of need, and the recipient of the services is different.

The respondent criticised the argument advanced for the appellants by saying that it falsely characterised the plaintiff's reduced capacity to help his wife as causing a loss to his wife, but not to him. That criticism may be fair up to a point, because the reduction in capacity is itself a loss to the plaintiff. But the criticism is not a valid criticism of the proposition that the plaintiff's loss is different from the loss remedied by the rules in *Griffiths v Kerkemeyer*.

It follows that so far as the reasoning in *Sullivan v Gordon* [that an injured plaintiff who loses the ability to care for a disabled relative loses 'something of real value' akin to the loss in a *Griffith v Kirkemeyer* claim] rested on the view that a *Sullivan v Gordon* claim has the same basis as a *Griffiths v Kerkemeyer* claim, it is erroneous (citation omitted). It cannot be said that the *Sullivan v Gordon* problem falls within the rules stated in the *Griffiths v Kerkemeyer* line of cases, or within any proposition logically deducible from those rules.

...

[**31**] The respondent relied on the following factors as reasons not to return to the New South Wales position in *Burnicle v Cutelli*: that it was unjust and inconvenient; that it was out of line with many other common law jurisdictions; and that there had been no statutory repeal of *Sullivan v Gordon*, and some legislative recognition of it. On the [**32**] other hand, there was no contradictor in *Sullivan v Gordon*; it is difficult clearly to formulate the principle on which it rests; it cannot readily be fitted coherently into the general law of tort; and there has in the past been considerable judicial disagreement about it. If *Sullivan v Gordon* were thought to represent a desirable principle, it would be better for that principle to be stated clearly in legislation after reviewing the whole of the relevant field, particularly since to some degree it is not a mere matter of lawyers' law, but raises political issues about the legitimate extent of recovery. These stem from the potential scale of recovery. As increasing numbers of people live to great ages, creating a wider need for care, the question of how far defendants who have tortiously injured the carers of those people should be liable becomes both an important question and a question on which the opinions of citizens may differ sharply. The same is true where a young plaintiff has been caring for a young person (citation omitted), so that very large awards might be made in circumstances where there is no guarantee that the care would have continued.

The respondent's arguments, then, are not necessarily to be rejected for flaws in the policy reasoning on which they rest; they are to be rejected because they rest on policy reasoning which it is more appropriate for legislatures to weigh than for courts.

In these circumstances, if it is desired to confer the rights recognised in *Sullivan v Gordon* on plaintiffs, the correct course to follow is that taken in the Australian Capital Territory and Scotland: to have the problem examined by an agency of law reform, and dealt with by the legislature if the legislature thinks fit (citation omitted).

Conclusion. All the Australian cases supporting *Sullivan v Gordon* as a principle of Australian common law should be overruled (citation omitted).

The common law position outlined in *CSR Ltd v Eddy*[8] applies in the Northern Territory and in Western Australia, and also under the *Competition and Consumer Act 2010* (Cth). In the remaining Australian jurisdictions, the civil liability statutes provide for compensation for loss of capacity provide domestic services.

Civil Law (Wrongs) Act 2002 (ACT) s 100[9]

The purpose of *Civil Law (Wrongs) Act 2002* (ACT) s 100 (and its equivalents in other Australian jurisdictions) is to provide for compensation for loss of capacity to provide domestic services.

100 Damages for loss of capacity to perform domestic services

(1) A person's liability for an injury suffered by someone else because of a wrong includes liability for damages for any resulting impairment or loss of the injured person's capacity to perform domestic services that the injured person might reasonably have been expected to perform for his or her household if the injured person had not been injured.

(2) In an action for the recovery of damages mentioned in subsection (1), it does not matter –

(a) whether the injured person performed the domestic services for the benefit of other members of the household or solely for his or her own benefit; or

(b) that the injured person was not paid to perform the services; or

(c) that the injured person has not been, and will not be, obliged to pay someone else to perform the services; or

(d) that the services have been, or are likely to be, performed (gratuitously or otherwise) by other people (whether members of the household or not).

(3) In this section:

wrong means an act or omission (whether or not an offence) –

(a) that gives rise to a liability in tort; or

(b) that amounts to a breach of a contractual duty of care that is concurrent and coextensive with a duty of care in tort.

8 (2005) 226 CLR 1.

9 Other jurisdictions in which this is the case are New South Wales (see *Civil Liability Act 2002* (NSW) s 15B), Queensland (see *Civil Liability Act 2003* (Qld) ss 59A–59D), Tasmania (see *Civil Liability Act 2002* (Tas) s 28BA(3)), Victoria (see *Wrongs Act 1958* (Vic) ss 28ID, 28IE). The common law position applies in Western Australia, the Northern Territory, South Australia, and under the *Competition and Consumer Act 2010* (Cth).

C Non-pecuniary loss

Non-pecuniary loss resulting from personal injury is generally compensable. This includes pain and suffering, loss of amenities, disfigurement, and loss of expectation of life.

1 Pain and suffering

Skelton v Collins (1966) 115 CLR 94

Facts and issues

Skelton (the appellant in this action and plaintiff in the originating action) was injured in an accident caused by Collins's (the respondent in this action and the defendant in the originating action) negligence, and thereby rendered permanently unconscious as a result of his injuries thereby sustained. Skelton's counsel argued that the damages awarded by the trial judge for pain and suffering were manifestly inadequate, reduced, as they were, by the regard had by the trial judge to the fact that Skelton had remained unconscious since the accident and would continue to remain unconscious for the remainder of his life.

Decision

A plaintiff must be able to experience pain and suffering in order to receive compensation under this head of damages and, as a result, a permanently unconscious plaintiff is not entitled to be compensated under this head for anything other than moderate sums in damages for loss of amenities.

Taylor J

> [**108**] … In *West's Case* [referring to *H West & Son Ltd v Shephard* [1964] AC 326] Lord Reid and Lord Devlin were the dissentients. I quote from the speech of the former: 'There are two views about the true basis for this kind of compensation. One is that the man is simply being compensated for the loss of his leg or the impairment of his digestion. The other is that his real loss is not so much his physical injury as the loss of those opportunities to lead a full and normal life which are now denied to him by his physical condition – for the multitude of deprivations and even petty annoyances which he must tolerate. Unless I am prevented by authority I would think that the ordinary man is, at least after the first few months, far less concerned about his physical injury than about the dislocation of his normal life. So I would think that compensation should be based much less on the nature of the injuries than on the extent of the injured man's consequential difficulties in his daily life … [**109**] … If that is so, then I think it must follow that if a man's injuries make him wholly unconscious so that he suffers none of those daily frustrations or inconveniences, he ought to get less than the man who is every day acutely conscious of what he suffers and what he has lost. I do not say that he should get nothing. This is not a question that can be decided logically. I think that there are two elements, what he has lost and what he must feel about it, and of the two I think the latter is generally the more important to the injured man. To my mind there is something unreal in saying that a man who knows and feels nothing

should get the same as a man who has to live with and put up with his disabilities, merely because they have sustained comparable physical injuries'(citation omitted). Ultimately he added: 'I would consider separately the objective and the subjective element arising from the respondent's injuries … ' (citation omitted). Lord Devlin also thought that in assessing damages for the loss of amenities of life two factors should be taken into consideration, one 'objective' and the other 'subjective'. He said: 'There are two ways in which this loss of enjoyment can be considered. It can be said that from beginning to end it is really all mental suffering. Loss of enjoyment is experienced in the mind and nowhere else. It may start with acute distress at the inability to use a limb in games or exercise as before or just in getting about, and may end with a nagging sense of frustration. If this is the true view, then total unconsciousness as in *Wise v Kaye* (citation omitted) relieves all mental suffering and nothing can be recovered for a deprivation which is not being experienced. [**110**] The other way to look upon the deprivation of a limb is as the loss of a personal asset, something in the nature of property. A limb can be put both to profitable use and to pleasurable use. In so far as it is put to profitable use, the loss is compensated for by calculating loss of earnings and not by assessing mental pain. On the same principle, it can be said, a sum must be assessed for loss of pleasurable use irrespective of whether there is mental suffering or not' (citation omitted) … Finally he concluded: 'What has to be compensated for in this assessment is a total loss of enjoyment of all the faculties, a complete loss of the pleasure of living. When the victim knows his fate, he will suffer from the distress which, except in the most saintly or philosophical, is caused by the prospect of death; and for that clearly he must be compensated. But what if he never knows his fate? It has been decided that he still must have some compensation, which should be moderate … '

…

[**112**] …

I may express my own view shortly upon the point now under consideration for I find the reasons appearing in the speeches of Lord Reid and Lord Devlin compelling … [**113**] … [I]n assessing damages for a loss of the amenities of life resulting from the physical destruction or impairment of some part of the body, I find it impossible to ignore, or, to regard merely as a minimal factor, what has been referred to as the subjective element. The expression 'loss of the amenities of life' is a loose expression but as a head of damages in personal injury cases it is intended to denote a loss of the capacity of the injured person consciously to enjoy life to the full as, apart from his injury, he might have done. It may be said, of course, that a person who is completely incapacitated as a result of his injuries suffers such a loss whether or not his injuries are of such a character to render him insensible to his loss. But, in my view, a proper assessment can be made only upon a comparison of the condition which has been substituted for the victim's previously existing capacity to enjoy life and where the mind is, as it were, willing and the body incapable there is, in my view, a much higher degree of loss than where the victim is completely insensible to his lost capacity. Perhaps, in other words, it may be said that a person who is obliged for the rest of his life to live with his incapacity, fully conscious of the limitations which it imposes upon his enjoyment of life, is entitled to greater compensation than one who, although deprived of his former capacity is spared, by insensibility, from the realization of his loss and the trials and tribulations consequent upon it. In the result I am left with a firm view that the plaintiff's general damages in this case were assessed on a proper basis.

2 Loss of amenities

Lawrence v Mathison (1981) 11 NTR 1

Facts and issues

Lawrence (the plaintiff in this action) was injured in a motor vehicle accident caused by the negligence of Mathison (the defendant), thereby suffering serious injuries to his spine which severely limited his physical capacities. As part of his claim for damages, Lawrence claimed damages for pain and suffering and loss of amenities of life. One of the issues in this case was the extent to which Lawrence was entitled to damages for loss of amenities in relation to his resulting inability to engage in physical pursuits such as riding a bicycle with his children or gardening.

Decision

The Court held that in assessing the amount of damages to be awarded for loss of amenities, the plaintiff's inability to continue to enjoy specific pursuits or hobbies as a result of the injuries they have suffered is a relevant factor.

Muirhead J

> [**9**] … I will assess the plaintiff's damages for loss of amenities on what I understand to be the traditional approach. I take into account the man himself, the nature and effects of his injuries, his family background, his responsibilities, his past activities and the frustrations that will be imposed upon him by reason of his injuries. I do not take into account in any mathematical sense his past, present or future loss of earnings and I have not attempted to evaluate the present value of his future economic loss …
>
> I add two qualifications so there is no confusion. Firstly, if there is evidence that by virtue of his injuries and their consequences a plaintiff is precluded from continuing to enjoy some specific pursuits or hobbies, that fact may be recognized in an assessment of damages for loss of amenities against the background of [the *Motor Accidents (Compensation) Act 1979* (NT)] … If it is proved that the capacity to enjoy amenities previously [**10**] enjoyed is destroyed because funds necessary to provide the amenities are and will not be available by reason of the injury, then damages may be awarded accordingly … Damages for loss of amenities should be designed to compensate for interference with the plaintiff's pre-accident enjoyments or reasonable expectations of enjoyment, in so far as they are proved and capable of assessment at trial …
>
> Secondly, it is proper, in my view, to take into account the loss that may be suffered by reason of the inability to exercise the pre-existing capacities. A man who is proved to paint his house regularly, to make household furniture, to attend to his garden and grow vegetables is entitled to damages which may reflect a loss consequent upon his disablement … I now refer only to activities truly incidental to the plaintiff's life. The man who may prove a pre-accident ability to build his own yacht will not be entitled to damages for loss of amenities assessed upon the cost of having a yacht constructed for him, nor will the artist who paints and sells pictures in his spare time be entitled to damages for loss of amenities calculated upon his financial loss …
>
> …

[**11**] ...

The components relevant to loss of amenities are really the consequences of his pain and suffering and the limitation of mobility. The plaintiff has been an active man, who enjoyed his physical capacities and utilized them. He was interested in spending some of his spare time outside his home. He enjoyed his cycling, which was more than a sport or recreation but a means of travel and a common area of interest with his sons. His sexual relationship with his wife has been impaired to some extent, a situation which causes some stress from time-to-time. I consider the plaintiff and his wife will adapt and cope with this situation. The plaintiff suffers the frustrations, perhaps daily frustrations, of not being able to do the things he used to do. He is comparatively young and his inability to play freely with his children concerns him very much. His earlier capacity to maintain his home and the garden have been limited; he is unlikely to grow vegetables in the future. I do not wish to underestimate the disadvantages his injury has imposed, but I believe at the time the plaintiff gave evidence he had been through a trying and uncertain time recovering from the injury. He had, under difficulty, helped his wife run the business and having sold the business he had assisted the purchaser. The fact that a tremendous work load fell on his wife was a matter which concerned the plaintiff. He is unlikely in the future to play very active sport, but fields of recreation are of course within his limits. The plaintiff lives in a close-knit family and community. He has friends and has many residual capacities. I believe he will accept his limitations and for the rest of his life will make the most of those [**12**] residual capacities. I assess damages for loss of amenities (which includes loss of enjoyment of life) in the sum of $25 000.

3 Loss of expectation of life

Sharman v Evans (1977) 138 CLR 563

Facts and issues

Evans (the respondent in this action and plaintiff in the originating action) was injured in a motor vehicle accident caused by the negligence of Sharman (the appellant in this action and defendant in the originating action). Evans suffered severe injuries, including quadriplegia, and the loss of ability to breathe and speak freely. At trial, Evans was awarded the total sum of $300 547.50 in damages, $6000 of which was for having a shortened life expectancy. One of the issues in this appeal was whether the sum for loss of expectation of life was excessive.

Decision

Loss of expectation of life is to be assessed objectively, and attracts only a moderate sum in damages.

Barwick CJ

[**566**] [A]fter considering the reasons which the trial judge has clearly expressed for making his award of damages, I have been driven to the conclusion that his Honour fell into error ...

...

[568] … [H]is Honour evidently included a substantial sum in his award for the shortening of the life expectancy of the respondent. I am of opinion that this loss calls only for compensation by the inclusion of a nominal sum. Nothing in the case, bearing in mind other items to be the subject of compensation, calls for that nominal sum to exceed the sum of $1260.

Gibbs and Stephen JJ

[584] The last two heads of damages which call for particular mention are those conventionally described as pain, suffering and loss of the enjoyment and amenities of life and damages for shortening of life expectancy. As to the latter it bears no relationship to lost earning capacity during 'lost years' but is rather the loss of a measure of prospective happiness (*Skelton v Collins*, per Taylor J (citation omitted)); it is not compensation for 'the mental distress due to the realization of the loss' (per Kitto J (citation omitted)). That forms instead a part of the general damages for pain and suffering (citation omitted): compare Windeyer J (citation omitted). In the present case a figure 'of the order of' $6000 was allowed for this item in reliance upon the views expressed by Windeyer J in *Skelton v Collins* (citation omitted). If it be correct that compensation under this head is not to take into account the anguish of mind which any appreciation of the loss may cause, that being compensated for under another head, then Windeyer J's suggested maximum figure of $6000, which reflected this very factor, may be thought to have been excessive at the time and to depart from the general standard of the 'conventional sum' which the courts have quite arbitrarily fixed upon ever since *Benham v Gambling* (citation omitted). The amount awarded may properly take into account a fall in the value of money (*Yorkshire Electricity Board v Naylor* (citation omitted)) but is to be no more than a quite conventional sum, very moderate in amount. In our view, despite the fall in the value of money, $6000 departs from previous notions of what is appropriate under this curious and unsatisfactory head of damages. We would have thought that the sum of $2000 is about the amount now appropriate as the conventional award under this head.

4 Statutory regulation

The civil liability statutes in all Australian jurisdictions except the Australian Capital Territory regulate damages for non-pecuniary loss.

Civil Liability Act 2002 (WA) ss 9–10

The purpose of the *Civil Liability Act 2002* (WA) ss 9 and 10 is to impose particular minimum and maximum thresholds on the amounts that can be awarded for non-pecuniary loss in Western Australia.

9 Restrictions on damages for non-pecuniary loss (general damages)

(1) If the amount of non-pecuniary loss is assessed to be not more than Amount A for the year in which the amount is assessed, no damages are to be awarded for non-pecuniary loss.

(2) If the amount of non-pecuniary loss is assessed to be more than Amount A but not more than Amount C for the year in which the amount is assessed, damages for non-pecuniary loss are not to be awarded in an amount that is more than the excess of the amount assessed over Amount A.

(3) If the amount of non-pecuniary loss is assessed to be more than Amount C but less than the sum of Amount A and Amount C for the year in which the amount is assessed, damages for non-pecuniary loss are not to be awarded in an amount that is more than the excess of the amount assessed over the amount calculated as follows –

Amount A – (Amount Assessed – Amount C)

(4) In this section –

Amount A has the meaning given by section 10;

Amount C has the meaning given by section 10;

Non-pecuniary loss means –

(a) pain and suffering; and

(b) loss of amenities of life; and

(c) loss of enjoyment of life; and

(d) curtailment of expectation of life; and

(e) bodily or mental harm.

10 Amount A and Amount C

(1) For the financial year ending on 30 June 2003 –

(a) Amount A is $12 000; and

(b) Amount C is $36 500.

(2) For any other financial year –

(a) Amount A is obtained by varying Amount A for the preceding financial year according to section 4; and

(b) Amount C is obtained by varying Amount C for the preceding financial year according to section 4.

(3) On or before each 1 July after this section commences, the Minister is to publish a notice in the Gazette specifying the amounts that are Amount A and Amount C for the financial year commencing on that 1 July.

(4) Publication under subsection (3) is for public information only and a failure to publish or a delay or error in publication does not affect what is Amount A or Amount C for the year concerned.[10]

10 The amounts gazetted for Amount A and Amount B on 18 June 2021 are $23 000 and $66 500 respectively: see Western Australia, *Western Australian Government Gazette*, No 109, 18 June 2021, 2525 [JU401].

D Overlap between different heads of loss

Double recovery for the same head of loss must be avoided. For example, civil liability statutes in a number of Australian jurisdictions that permit compensation for the loss of the capacity to provide domestic services contain provisions that prohibit double recovery.[11]

REVIEW QUESTIONS

(1) Is the finding in *Gray v Richards* (2014) 253 CLR 660 that only plaintiffs with impaired intellectual capacity may potentially claim damages relating to expenses associated with obtaining professional assistance to manage a lump sum problematic? Ought such damages also be available to plaintiffs who may not be financially sophisticated despite not being intellectually impaired?

(2) Do you agree with the distinction drawn by the High Court in *CSR Ltd v Eddy* (2005) 226 CLR 1 between claims for damages relating to the loss of ability to provide domestic services to another and claims relating to the loss of ability to provide services to oneself?

(3) Do you agree with the High Court's decision in *Sharman v Evans* (1977) 138 CLR 563 that only a very moderate amount should be awarded for loss of expectation of life? Might this be too harsh?

V Benefits arising from an injury

Concept	Short explanation	Relevant authorities	Principles text
An injured person often receives benefits as a result of an injury, which must be deducted from the loss suffered	A wrongdoer's liability to a plaintiff should not be reduced where a benefit is awarded to the plaintiff and the intention underlying the award of the benefit is that it is to be in addition to whatever rights of action or proprietary rights the plaintiff may have.	*National Insurance Co of New Zealand v Espagne* (1961) 105 CLR 569	Chapter 7: [7.72]–[7.79]
	Where an injured person receives a Medicare benefit in relation to a payment they make for professional services, they are obliged by statute to reimburse the Commonwealth.	*Health and Other Services (Compensation) Act 1995* (Cth)	

11 See, eg, *Civil Liability Act 2003* (Qld) ss 59A(1), 59B(1)–(2), 59C(4)(b). Civil liability statutes in other Australian jurisdictions which contain similar provisions include *Civil Liability Act 2002* (NSW) s 15B(5)(b); *Wrongs Act 1958* (Vic) s 28ID(3)(b).

National Insurance Co of New Zealand v Espagne (1961) 105 CLR 569

Facts and issues

Espagne (the respondent in this appeal and plaintiff in the originating action) was severely injured in a motor vehicle accident caused by a driver insured by National Insurance Co of New Zealand ('National Insurance', the appellant in this appeal and defendant in the originating action), and was subsequently awarded damages at trial. One of the issues in this appeal was whether the trial judge ought to have reduced the amount of damages awarded to Espagne on the basis that Espagne was awarded an invalid pension under the *Social Services Act 1947–1957* (Cth) after the accident for total blindness.

Decision

A wrongdoer's liability to a plaintiff should not be reduced where a benefit is awarded to the plaintiff and the intention underlying the award of the benefit is that it is to be in addition to whatever rights of action or proprietary rights the plaintiff may have. In this case, a manifest policy of the Act under which Espagne's pension was awarded was that a blind pensioner was to have their pension in addition to whatever rights of action or proprietary rights they may have. As such, National Insurance's liability should not be reduced as a result of the pension in question being awarded to Espagne.

Windeyer J

> [**599**] … In assessing damages for personal injuries, benefits that a plaintiff has received or is to receive from any source other than the defendant are not to be regarded as mitigating his loss, if: (a) they were received or are to be received by him as a result of a contract he had made before the loss occurred and by the express or implied terms of that contract they were to be provided notwithstanding any rights of action he might have; or (b) they were given or promised to him by way of bounty, to the [**600**] intent that he should enjoy them in addition to and not in diminution of any claim for damages. The first description covers accident insurances and also many forms of pensions and similar benefits provided by employers: in those cases it is immaterial that, by subrogation or otherwise, the contract may require a refund of moneys paid, or an adjustment of future benefits, to be made after the recovery of damages. The second description covers a variety of public charitable aid and some forms of relief given by the State as well as the produce of private benevolence. In both cases the decisive consideration is, not whether the benefit was received in consequence of, or as a result of the injury, but what was its character: and that is determined, in the one case by what under his contract the plaintiff had paid for, and in the other by the intent of the person conferring the benefit. The test is by purpose rather than by cause.
>
> Nevertheless it is not, I think possible, to enunciate an exhaustive rule for all parts of this vexed topic. And the questions that arise can never be determined in the abstract. Each must depend on the terms of the particular contract, pension scheme, charitable

benefaction or statute governing the benefit conferred. In this case it is the *Social Services Act*. Invalid pensions are one of the benefits – in an inexact sense a right – that Australians have. No doubt all such social services go to make up the economic and social conditions in which monetary compensation must be weighed .... I have already said that, in my opinion, invalid pensions granted to persons not permanently blind should be disregarded in assessing damages because they are discretionary and are variable according to the damages recovered. Pensions to permanently blind persons are also, I think, to be disregarded; but for a different reason. That reason is that the manifest policy of the Act, as I read it, is that a blind pensioner is to have his pension in addition to whatever rights of action or proprietary rights he may have. The distinction between blindness and other disability is that the Commonwealth [**601**] when granting a pension undertakes in the one case an obligation that cannot afterwards be diminished if compensation be recovered from the wrongdoer: in the other case it may be. But in neither case is the wrongdoer's liability reduced: for the pension is not given by the Commonwealth to aid him.

Health and Other Services (Compensation) Act 1995 (Cth) ss 3(1), 7(1), (3), 8(1)[12]

The purpose of this legislation is to require those receiving Medicare benefits in relation to a payment they make for professional services to reimburse the Commonwealth for these payments. This is to ensure that a plaintiff does not receive a windfall at the expense of the Commonwealth by receiving compensation for the full payment of professional services to treat an injury as well as a Medicare benefit paid in relation to the payment for those services.

3 Definitions

(1) In this Act, unless the contrary intention appears:

...

reimbursement arrangement means an agreement in writing, an order of a court or compensation authority, or a decision of a person or body, to the effect that the person against whom a claim for compensation is made is liable to pay compensation to reimburse the claimant for expenses as they are incurred by the claimant that:

(a) are incurred in respect of any service or care rendered or provided in the course of treatment of, or as a result of, the claimant's injury; and

(b) are expenses in respect of which an eligible benefit is or may become payable (whether or not the eligible benefit is payable to the claimant).

...

12 The National Disability Insurance Scheme (NDIS) legislation similarly allows the National Disability Insurance Scheme Agency to recover past NDIS amounts where judgment has been given compensating an injured person in relation to which injury NDIS amounts have been paid to the injured person: see *National Disability Insurance Scheme Act 2013* (Cth) s 106.

7 Reimbursement of amounts payable for professional services

(1) This section applies if:

(a) a reimbursement arrangement has been made in respect of an injury to a compensable person; and

(b) the person is entitled, under the reimbursement arrangement, to compensation by way of reimbursement of expenses as those expenses are incurred, being expenses relating to the professional services rendered to the person in the course of treatment of, or as a result of, the injury.

...

(3) If:

(a) Medicare benefit has been paid in respect of a professional service rendered to the person; and

(b) under the reimbursement arrangement, the person is entitled to reimbursement of the whole or any part of the amount payable for the service; the person entitled to the reimbursement is liable to pay to the Commonwealth an amount equal to the Medicare benefit.

...

8 Recovering past payments of Medicare benefit from judgments and settlements

(1) Subject to subsections (2), (3), (6) and (9), if:

(a) an amount of compensation is fixed under a judgment or settlement made in respect of an injury to a compensable person; and

(b) Medicare benefit has already been paid in respect of a professional service rendered to that person in the course of treatment of, or as a result of, the injury; and

(c) a liability has not already arisen under section 7 in respect of that payment of Medicare benefit; there is payable to the Commonwealth an amount equal to the Medicare benefit.

...

REVIEW QUESTIONS

(1) Do you agree with the High Court's decision in *National Insurance Co of New Zealand v Espagne* (1961) 105 CLR 569 that a wrongdoer's liability to a plaintiff should not be reduced even where a government benefit is awarded to the plaintiff and the plaintiff's loss is thereby reduced?

(2) Is it justifiable for the Commonwealth government to seek reimbursement for payments for professional services via the *Health and Other Services (Compensation) Act 1995* (Cth) ss 7, 8 or via the *National Disability Insurance Scheme Act 2013* (Cth) s 106, where an injured person receives a Medicare benefit or an NDIS amount in relation to a payment they make for professional services to treat an injury for which they have received compensation?

VI Claims based on injury to another person

Concept	Short explanation	Relevant authorities	Principles text
Loss of an employee's services	No action for loss of employee's services lies at common law where the employee has been killed.	*Barclay v Penberthy* (2012) 246 CLR 258	Chapter 7: [7.81]–[7.84]
Loss of consortium	Legislation in some Australian jurisdictions extends actions for loss of consortium to all spouses.	*Civil Liability Act 1936* (SA)	Chapter 7: [7.85]–[7.88]
	Legislation in a number of other Australian jurisdictions abolishes actions for loss of consortium entirely.	*Civil Law (Wrongs) Act 2002* (ACT)	

A Loss of an employee's services

Barclay v Penberthy (2012) 246 CLR 258

Facts and issues

This case involved a claim by a company against a pilot, an air charter company, and an aeronautical engineer for economic loss arising out of the death of the company's employees as a result of a plane crash caused by the defendants' negligence. One of the issues in this case was whether an action could be maintained for the loss of an employee's services at common law where the employee has been killed as a result of the defendant's negligence.

Decision

No action for loss of employee's services lies at common law where the employee has been killed.[13]

French CJ, Gummow, Hayne, Crennan, and Bell JJ

> **[279] Issue 1 – the rule in *Baker v Bolton***
> Nautronix seeks special leave to cross-appeal from so much of the decision of the Court of Appeal as held that the rule in *Baker v Bolton*[14] applies in Australia to causes of action in negligence and per quod. Nautronix points to the criticism of the rule expressed in the dictum that the rule makes it 'cheaper to kill than to maim' … .
>
> However, in 1916, in *Admiralty Commissioners v SS Amerika* (citation omitted), the House of Lords declined to disturb the rule in *Baker v Bolton*, however anomalous, as Lord Parker of Waddington put it, 'it may appear to the scientific jurist' (citation omitted). For his part, Lord Sumner emphasised that it was abundantly plain that the rule had received statutory recognition; the preamble to s 1 of *Lord Campbell's Act*, passed in 1846, was a

13 It should be noted that the action *per quod* still survives in relation to key employees who are injured but not killed.

14 This is the common rule that in a civil court the death of a human being cannot be complained of as an injury: see *Baker v Bolton* (1808) 1 Camp 493; 170 ER 1033; *Admiralty Commissioners v Steamship Amerika (Owners)* [1917] AC 38.

response to a particular defect in the existing law, namely the disadvantageous position of widows and children, not to any legislatively perceived defects in the limited rights of masters and employees. Speaking of *Osborn v Gillett*, Lord Sumner referred to 'Bramwell B's intrepid individualism' (citation omitted).

In these reasons reference has been made above (citation omitted) to the provenance in *Lord Campbell's Act* of the Western Australian legislation under which the claims of **[24]** the spouses were brought in the present litigation. *Lord Campbell's Act* has been adopted in all other Australian jurisdictions (citation omitted). However, in its other applications, particularly to the actions in negligence and per quod upon which Nautronix relies in respect of the deaths of Mr Protoolis and Mr Warriner, the rule in *Baker v Bolton* has remained unchanged. One qualification is found in s 58(1)(a) of the *Civil Liability Act 2003* (Qld), which appears to provide that damages (limited as provided in that section) may be awarded for loss of servitium if 'the injured person died as a result of injuries suffered'.

In *Swan v Williams (Demolition) Pty Ltd* (citation omitted) Samuels JA observed that the only continuing influence of the rule in *Baker v Bolton* in New South Wales was to exclude actions at the suit of an employer for damages for loss of services occasioned by the death of an employee. In New South Wales, the *Law Reform (Marital Consortium) Act 1984* (NSW) had abolished liability in tort for loss or impairment of consortium, an action that, at common law in any event, had been denied for loss of consortium to a wife.

The pattern of Australian legislation is a pointer towards the continued existence of the rule in *Baker v Bolton* as a matter of common law (citation omitted). In *Swan* (citation omitted), the New South Wales Court of Appeal rejected submissions that the rule in *Baker v Bolton* should be discarded. Their Honours did say that the decision of this Court in *Woolworths Ltd v Crotty* (citation omitted) was authority for the proposition that the rule in *Baker v Bolton* remained part of the common law in Australia. The better understanding is that the assumption made by both parties in *Crotty* was that the rule did apply unless the term 'wrongful act' in *Lord Campbell's Act*, as was held to be the case, included contractual as well as tortious wrongs.

Any further contraction in the scope of the rule in *Baker v Bolton* is a matter for Australian legislatures.

B Loss of consortium

Civil Liability Act 1936 (SA) s 65(1)[15]

The purpose of the *Civil Liability Act 1936* (SA) s 65 (and its equivalents in other jurisdictions) is to extend actions for loss of consortium to all spouses and domestic partners in South Australia.

65 Spouse or domestic partner may claim for loss or impairment of consortium

(1) If a person causes injury to another by wrongful act, neglect or default, the person will (whether or not the injury results in death) be liable in damages to

15 The *Law Reform Act 1995* (Qld) s 13 similarly extends actions for loss of consortium to all spouses and de facto partners.

the spouse or domestic partner of the injured person for loss or injury suffered by the spouse or domestic partner as a result of the loss or impairment of consortium.[16]

...

Civil Law (Wrongs) Act 2002 (ACT) s 218[17]

The purpose of the *Civil Law (Wrongs) Act 2002* (ACT) s 218, (and its equivalents in other jurisdictions) is to abolish actions for loss of consortium in the Australian Capital Territory.

218 Abolition of action for loss of consortium

If a wife has been injured because of the negligence of a person other than her husband, the person is not liable to the husband for any resulting impairment or loss of consortium.

Review Questions

(1) The common law rule in *Baker v Bolton* (1808) 1 Camp 493; 170 ER 1033 in relation to actions for loss of an injured employee's services (*per quod*) limits such claims to instances where the wrongdoer has injured the plaintiff's employee, and denies such claims where the wrongdoer has killed the plaintiff's employee. Thus, the criticism has been made of this rule that a wrongdoer is in a better position when they have killed another's employee than they would be if they had simply injured the employee. Do you agree with the High Court in *Barclay v Penberthy* (2012) 246 CLR 258 that it is for Australian legislatures to determine whether the rule in *Baker v Bolton* is to be further contracted, or do you regard the High Court has having the authority (and perhaps even the duty) to shape the common law in such a way as to abolish aspects of the common law which have such apparent unjust effects?

(2) Do you regard the extension of claims for loss of consortium to all spouses or the complete abolition of claims for loss of consortium to be the preferred approach?

16 The term 'domestic partner' is defined in the *Family Relationships Act 1975* (SA) s 11A.

17 Other jurisdictions which have abolished claims for loss of consortium include New South Wales (see *Law Reform (Marital Consortium) Act 1984* (NSW) s 3(1)), Tasmania (see *Civil Liability Act 2002* (Tas) s 28D) and Western Australia (see *Law Reform (Miscellaneous Provisions) Act 1941* (WA) s 3).

VII Actions on death

Concept	Short explanation	Relevant authorities	Principles text
Claim by the estate of the deceased	All Australian jurisdictions have now enacted legislative provisions which preserve causes of action which were vested in a person prior to their death for the benefit of their estate.	*Administration and Probate Act 1958* (Vic)	Chapter 7: [7.90]–[7.92]
Claim by the dependants of the deceased	The common law rule preventing a claim for damages being brought by a person against a wrongdoer who has caused loss to that person by wrongfully killing another was abolished in England and Wales by Lord Campbell's Act.	*Fatal Accidents Act 1846* (UK)	Chapter 7: [7.93]–[7.111]
	All Australian jurisdictions have legislation mirroring Lord Campbell's Act.	*Wrongs Act 1958* (Vic)*	
	In cases involving the Australian equivalents of Lord Campbell's Act, dependants are required to show that the death was a foreseeable consequence of the defendant's negligence.	*Lyle v Soc* (2009) 38 WAR 418	
	Legislation in some Australian jurisdictions prohibits a consideration of the prospect of a surviving spouse or domestic partner repartnering after trial in the assessment of material benefits resulting from the death of a person upon whom the plaintiff was dependent.	*Compensation (Fatal Injuries) Act 1974* (NT)	
	The prospect of repartnering warrants a separate discount only where there is evidence that a new relationship has been formed or is proposed and that it will bring financial benefits to the deceased's dependants.	*De Sales v Ingrilli* (2002) 212 CLR 338	
	Benefits that a surviving spouse or domestic partner has received or is likely to receive from a new partner are sometimes deductible.	*Civil Proceedings Act 2011* (Qld)	
	Benefits that a child has received or may receive from any person other than the deceased person, including any financial benefits that the child has received, or may receive, as a result of surviving parent entering into a new relationship, should not be taken into account when assessing damages.	*Civil Proceedings Act 2011* (Qld)	

* Equivalent provisions in the other Australia jurisdictions are: *Civil Law (Wrongs) Act 2002* (ACT) s 24; *Compensation to Relatives Act 1897* (NSW) s 3(1); *Compensation (Fatal Injuries) Act 1974* (NT) s 7(1); *Civil Proceedings Act 2011* (Qld) s 64; *Civil Liability Act 1936* (SA) s 23; *Fatal Accidents Act 1934* (Tas) s 4; *Fatal Accidents Act 1959* (WA) s 4(1).

A Claim by the estate of the deceased

Provisions have been enacted in some Australian jurisdictions which preserve causes of action which were vested in a person prior to their death for the benefit of their estate.[18]

B Claim by the dependants of the deceased

Fatal Accidents Act 1846 (UK)[19]

The purpose of Lord Campbell's Act was to provide a cause of action to families of persons killed by accidents.

Fatal Accidents Act 1846 (9 and 10 Vict., c. 93.)
CAP. XCIII.
An Act for compensating the Families of Persons killed by Accidents.
[26th August 1846]

'WHEREAS no Action at Law is now maintainable against a Person who by his wrongful Act, Neglect, or Default may have caused the Death of another Person, and it is oftentimes right and expedient that the Wrongdoer in such Case should be answerable in Damages for the Injury so caused by him:' Be it therefore enacted by the Queen's most Excellent Majesty, by and with the Advice and Consent of the Lords Spiritual and Temporal, and Commons, in this present Parliament assembled, and by the Authority of the same, That whensoever the Death of a Person shall be caused by wrongful Act, Neglect, or Default, and the Act, Neglect, or Default is such as would (if Death had not ensued) have entitled the Party injured to maintain an Action and recover Damages in respect thereof, then and in every such Case the Person who would have been liable if Death had not ensued shall be liable to an Action for Damages, notwithstanding the Death of the Person injured, and although the Death shall have been caused under such Circumstances as amount in Law to Felony.

An Action to be maintainable against any Person causing Death through Neglect, &c., notwithstanding the Death of the Person injured.

II. Action to be for the Benefit of certain Relations, and shall be brought by and in the Name of Executor or Administrator of the Deceased.
And be it enacted, That every such Action shall be for the Benefit of the Wife, Husband, Parent, and Child of the Person whose Death shall have been so caused, and shall be brought by and in the Name of the Executor or Administrator of the Person deceased; and in every such Action the Jury may give such Damages as they may think proportioned to

18 See, eg, *Administration and Probate Act 1958* (Vic) s 29(1). Equivalent provisions in other Australian jurisdictions include the *Civil Law (Wrongs) Act 2002* (ACT).

19 All Australian jurisdictions have legislation mirroring Lord Campbell's Act, although there are differences between the jurisdictions: see *Civil Law (Wrongs) Act 2002* (ACT) s 24; *Compensation to Relatives Act 1897* (NSW) s 3(1); *Compensation (Fatal Injuries) Act 1974* (NT) s 7(1); *Civil Proceedings Act 2011* (Qld) s 64; *Civil Liability Act 1936* (SA) s 23; *Fatal Accidents Act 1934* (Tas) s 4; *Wrongs Act 1958* (Vic) s 16; *Fatal Accidents Act 1959* (WA) s 4(1).

the Injury resulting from such Death to the Parties respectively for whom and for whose Benefit such Action shall be brought; and the Amount so recovered, after deducting the Costs not recovered from the Defendant, shall be divided amongst the before-mentioned Parties in such Shares as the Jury by their Verdict shall find and direct.

III. Only One Action shall lie, and to be commenced within 12 Months.
Provided always, and be it enacted, That not more than One Action shall lie for and in respect of the same Subject Matter of Complaint; and that every such Action shall be commenced within Twelve Calendar Months after the Death of such deceased Person.

...

All Australian jurisdictions have legislation mirroring Lord Campbell's Act, although there are differences between the jurisdictions.

Wrongs Act 1958 (Vic) ss 16–17[20]

The purpose of the *Wrongs Act 1958* (Vic) s 16 (and its equivalents in other jurisdictions) is to provide a cause of action to families of persons killed by accidents in Victoria.

16 Liability for death caused wrongfully
Whensoever the death of a person is caused by a wrongful act neglect or default and the act neglect or default is such as would (if death had not ensued) have entitled the party injured to maintain an action and recover damages in respect thereof, then and in every such case the person who would have been liable if death had not ensued shall be liable to an action for damages notwithstanding the death of the person injured.

17 Action for death caused wrongfully

(1) Every such action shall be for the benefit of the dependants of the person whose death has been so caused and shall be brought by and in the name of the executor or administrator of the person deceased; and in every such action the jury or the court if the trial is without a jury may give such damages as they or it think proportioned to the injury resulting from such death to the parties respectively for whom and for whose benefit such action is brought; and the amount so recovered after deducting the costs not recovered from the defendant shall be divided amongst the before-mentioned parties in such shares as the jury or court by their or its verdict find and direct.

(2) In subsection (1) the word ***dependants*** means such persons as were wholly mainly or in part dependent on the person deceased at the time of his death or who would but for the incapacity due to the injury which led to the death have been so dependent.

20 Equivalent provisions in the other Australia jurisdictions are *Civil Law (Wrongs) Act 2002* (ACT) s 24; *Compensation to Relatives Act 1897* (NSW) s 3(1); *Compensation (Fatal Injuries) Act 1974* (NT) s 7(1); *Civil Proceedings Act 2011* (Qld) s 64; *Civil Liability Act 1936* (SA) s 23; *Fatal Accidents Act 1934* (Tas) s 4; *Fatal Accidents Act 1959* (WA) s 4(1).

Older cases such as *Haber v Walker*[21] indicated that in an action under the Australian equivalents of Lord Campbell's Act, dependants were only required to establish a causal connection between their injury and the defendant's wrongful act. However, more recent cases have confirmed that dependants are required to show that the death was a foreseeable consequence of the defendant's negligence.

Lyle v Soc (2009) 38 WAR 418

Facts and issues

Soc (the respondent in this appeal and plaintiff in the originating action) made a claim under the *Fatal Accidents Act 1959* (WA) due to the death of his wife as a result of acute combined drug toxicity. Soc's wife had been prescribed powerful analgesics to treat pain in her neck resulting from a motor vehicle accident which was caused by the Lyle's negligence (the appellant in this appeal and defendant in the originating action). One of the issues in this case was whether in a claim under s 4(1) of the *Fatal Accidents Act 1959* (WA), the requirement of reasonable foreseeability must be satisfied.

Decision

In claims under s 4(1) of the *Fatal Accidents Act 1959* (WA), dependants are required to show that the death was a foreseeable consequence of the defendant's negligence.

Steytler P

> [**424**] The trial judge appears to have concluded that, because the Oxycontin was prescribed at least partly in respect of the pain resulting from the injuries sustained in the 1999 accident, for which the appellant was liable, and because the Oxycontin was a material cause of the deceased's death, the appellant's negligence in causing the 1999 accident was a material cause of the deceased's death. A number of factors are missing from this logic.
>
> The first of these is foreseeability. Both parties were content to argue the appeal upon the assumption that the principle of remoteness of damage applies to an action under s 4(1) of the *Fatal Accidents Act*. That section is the equivalent of what is ordinarily referred to as a *Lord Campbell's Act* section (from an 1846 English statute, now the *Fatal Accidents Act 1976* (UK)), which is also mirrored in other Australian jurisdictions.
>
> [**425**] The proposition that the principle of remoteness applies to a *Lord Campbell's Act* action has been controversial (see the helpful article by Associate Professor Douglas Hodgson, 'Suicide and The Law of Intervening Causation' (2008) 16 *Tort Law Rev* 69).
>
> In *Haber v Walker* (citation omitted), the Victorian Full Court dealt with an appeal arising out of an action under s 16 of the *Wrongs Act 1958* (Vic) that had been brought for the benefit of the widow and children of the deceased. The deceased had been injured in a motor vehicle collision caused by the defendant's negligence. His injuries were so severe as to cause him to suffer fits of deep depression resulting, ultimately, in his suicide. The majority (Lowe and Smith JJ) concluded that the plaintiff in a *Lord Campbell's Act* claim was not required to prove that the death by suicide was reasonably foreseeable, but only that the death was a consequence of the defendant's negligence. Hudson J dissented. He considered that the '*Wagon*

21 [1963] VR 339.

Mound' (*Overseas Tankship (UK) Ltd v Morts Dock & Engineering Co Ltd* (citation omitted)) remoteness test of reasonable foreseeability applied and, because the right of action given by the statute was subject to the requirements of the common law, the death must be shown to have been a reasonably foreseeable consequence of the defendant's negligence.

Haber, and other cases touching upon this topic, were considered by the Queensland Court of Appeal in *Lisle v Brice* (citation omitted). That case concerned s 17 of the *Supreme Court Act 1995* (Qld), which is to the same effect as s 4(1) of the Western Australian *Fatal Accidents Act*. The court held that, in a claim for damages for dependency, the requirement of reasonable foreseeability must be satisfied: at [39] per Williams JA; at [9] per Thomas JA; at [1] per McMurdo P Williams JA also said that it seemed clear that the term 'caused' in the statutory provision carried the meaning attributed to that term in other branches of the law (at [24]).

In that case, the deceased had received a minor physical injury in a motor vehicle collision. More than three years later he committed suicide. His widow brought an action for damages. The collision had been reasonably severe, even though the injury (a whiplash-type injury) was relatively minor. However, the deceased developed depression and it was this which led to his suicide. The court accepted that the appellant was liable, having found that the requirements of causation and remoteness had been satisfied. Williams JA (with whom McMurdo P and Thomas JA agreed) accepted that the trial judge had rightly concluded that 'on the day in question it was reasonably foreseeable that negligent driving might result in the train of events which did in fact occur' (at [42]).

Although, in the present case no argument was addressed to the controversy concerning the requirement of reasonable foreseeability (and the controversy was not referred to by the trial judge), it seems to me, with respect, that the preferable approach is that adopted in *Lisle* and that the parties were consequently right to assume that the requirement must be satisfied in the case of a claim under s 4(1) of the *Fatal Accidents Act*.

Compensation (Fatal Injuries) Act 1974 (NT) s 10(4)(h)[22]

The purpose of *Compensation (Fatal Injuries) Act* (NT) s 10(4)(h) (and its equivalents in other jurisdictions) is to prevent the consideration of the prospect of remarriage or entry into a de facto relationship when considering a plaintiff's loss of material benefits as a result of the death of a person upon whom the plaintiff was dependent.

10 Damages

…

(4) In assessing damages in action, no reduction must be made on account of:

…

(h) the marriage or entry into a de facto relationship, or the prospects of doing so, of a surviving spouse or de facto partner or a surviving former spouse or de facto partner.

…

22 Equivalent provisions in other Australian jurisdictions include *Civil Proceedings Act 2011* (Qld) s 67(2), (3); *Wrongs Act 1958* (Vic) s 19(2)–(4).

The law in other Australian jurisdictions is governed by *De Sales v Ingrilli*,[23] which provides that the prospect of repartnering warrants a separate discount only where there is evidence that a new relationship has been formed or is proposed and that it will bring financial benefits to the deceased's dependants; otherwise, it cannot be said whether a new relationship would be to the financial advantage or disadvantage of the deceased's dependants.

De Sales v Ingrilli (2002) 212 CLR 338

Facts and issues

De Sales (the appellant in this appeal and plaintiff in the originating action) brought an action under the *Fatal Accidents Act 1959* (WA) after the death of her husband caused by the negligence of the defendant. The issue in this appeal related to the assessment of damages to be awarded to a surviving spouse under fatal accidents legislation. In particular, the Court was concerned with the question of whether it should take into account the chance of the surviving spouse remarrying and thereby obtaining some financial benefit which offsets or diminishes the claimed loss.

Decision

The Court held that the prospect of repartnering warrants a separate discount only where there is evidence that a new relationship has been formed or is proposed and that it will bring financial benefits to the deceased's dependants.

Gaudron, Gummow and Hayne JJ

> [**366**] It is … wrong to treat the prospect of remarriage or the prospect of forming some new continuing relationship as a separate item for which some identified discount must be made from whatever calculation is made of the present value of future benefits that would have flowed from the deceased to the relatives. Even if the prospects that a surviving spouse would remarry or enter a new continuing relationship could be assessed (and there will be few cases where that would be possible), predicting when that would occur is impossible, and predicting some likely outer limit of time by which it would probably have occurred is only slightly less difficult. But most importantly, it cannot be assumed that any new union will be, or will remain, of financial advantage to any of those for whose benefit the action is brought. That being so, some financially advantageous marriage or relationship must be treated as only one of many possible paths that the future may hold. It is wrong to single it out for special [**367**] and separate allowance. That others in the past have had damages reduced on this account is not reason enough to continue the error.
>
> Nor can the prospect of remarrying or forming a new relationship properly be seen as a matter which, under the general heading of 'the vicissitudes of life', enlarges the

23 (2002) 212 CLR 338.

discount which otherwise must be made from the present value of the benefits which the deceased was providing at death. The assessment of that discount is not easy. It must reflect not only the fact that the future may have been better than the past but also the fact that it may not. It is wrong to fasten upon one of the myriad possible paths that life may take and say that, on account of that possibility, it is right to enlarge the discount that must be made. The discount can be assessed only as a single sum which reflects all of the possibilities.

That is not to say that, if there is evidence at trial that a new relationship has been formed, account may not be taken of evidence revealing whether that brings with it financial advantage or disadvantage. It would be wrong to adopt the rule followed in some American jurisdictions (citation omitted) and require the tribunal of fact to assess the damages without that evidence. If the relationship is reflected in marriage, or if there is relevant legislation creating rights between de facto partners, the property rights of the partners will no doubt loom large in that assessment. Likewise, if there is evidence that a surviving spouse (or de facto spouse) intends, at the time of trial, to establish such a relationship with an identified person, account may be taken of evidence of the probable financial consequences of that relationship. In each case, however, it would be wrong to assume that the financial consequences revealed in evidence will inevitably continue.

Ordinarily, such cases apart, no separate allowance should be made for the possibility, even probability, that a new relationship will be formed. That is because it cannot be said, even on the balance of probabilities, whether, having regard to the whole of the period which must be considered, that relationship would be to the financial advantage or disadvantage of those relatives of the deceased for whose benefit the action is brought. If the period to be considered is very long (as would be the case where the surviving relatives are young) the range of possibilities that must be considered is very large. By contrast, if the period is short (where the surviving relatives are older) the possibilities of death, illness, loss of employment and the like are [**368**] all the higher. No doubt, as was said more than seventy years ago in the United States District Court (citing *The City of Rome* (1930) 48 F 2d 333 at 343):

> If we should enter upon an inquiry as to the relative merits of the new husband as a provider, coupled with his age, employment, condition of health, and other incidental elements concerning him, unavoidably we should embark upon a realm of speculation and be led into a sea of impossible calculations.

But the critical point is not that the inquiry is hard, it is that it is an inquiry which does not lead to a useful answer. In the end, all that can be said is that the future is uncertain. The value of what is lost as a result of the wrongful death must strike a balance of all the gains and losses that have been and may thereafter be suffered. There is no basis for fastening upon some to the exclusion of others.

Civil Proceedings Act 2011 (Qld) s 67

The purpose of s 67 of the *Civil Proceedings Act 2011* (Qld) is to make benefits that a surviving spouse or domestic partner is receiving or has received from a new partner deductible from the damages that they are entitled to receive in relation to a claim for damages due to the death of a spouse or domestic partner.

67 Damages for spouse's benefit

(1) This section applies if, in a proceeding under this part, a court is assessing damages in relation to financial benefits lost by a spouse of the deceased person as a result of the deceased's death.

(2) The court must not take into account any financial benefits that the spouse may receive as a result of a new relationship that the spouse may enter into after the assessment.

(3) Subsection (2) applies even if the spouse intends to enter into a new relationship.

(4) However, if the spouse has entered into a new relationship since the deceased person's death, the court may take into account any financial benefits that the spouse has received, and any financial benefits that the spouse is likely to receive, as a result of the new relationship.

(5) Subsection (4) applies even if the new relationship ends before the assessment.

(6) In considering what financial benefits the spouse is likely to receive as a result of the new relationship, the court must not assume –

(a) that the new relationship will necessarily continue; or

(b) that the spouse will necessarily continue to receive the same financial benefits as a result of the new relationship as the spouse has already received as a result of the new relationship.

(7) In this section –

financial benefits means either or both of the following –

(a) monetary benefits;

(b) other material benefits having a monetary value, including, for example, domestic services.

relationship means –

(a) a marriage; or

(b) a de facto relationship within the meaning of the *Acts Interpretation Act 1954*, schedule 1; or

(c) a civil partnership within the meaning of the *Acts Interpretation Act 1954*, schedule 1.

Similarly, benefits that a child has received or may receive from any person other than the deceased person, including any financial benefits that the child has received, or may receive, as a result of surviving parent entering into a new relationship, should not be taken into account when assessing damages.[24]

24 See, eg, *Civil Proceedings Act 2011* (Qld) s 68(4)(a), (b).

REVIEW QUESTIONS

(1) Do you agree with the findings in cases such as *Lisle v Brice* [2002] 2 Qd R 168 and *Lyle v Soc* (2009) 38 WAR 418 that in claims involving the Australian equivalents of Lord Campbell's Act, dependants are required to show that the death was a foreseeable consequence of the defendant's negligence? Might this be an unnecessary restriction on the claims of dependants of the deceased in such cases?

(2) Do you think the position pursuant to the *Compensation (Fatal Injuries) Act* (NT) s 10(4)(h) (and its equivalents) is preferable to the position at common law pursuant to *De Sales v Ingrilli* (2002) 212 CLR 338 with respect to the relevance of the plaintiff's prospect of remarriage or entry into a de facto relationship when considering a plaintiff's loss of material benefits as a result of the death of a person upon whom the plaintiff was dependent?

(3) Do you think that the position pursuant to the *Civil Proceedings Act 2011* (Qld) s 67 is an improvement on the position pursuant to the *Compensation (Fatal Injuries) Act 1974* (NT) s 10(4)(h) (and its equivalents) and the position pursuant to *De Sales v Ingrilli* (2002) 212 CLR 338?

8 COMPENSATION UNDER THE *AUSTRALIAN CONSUMER LAW*

I	Introduction	297
II	Assessment of compensation	298
	A General principles	299
	B Compensation for misleading or deceptive conduct	301
	C Non-pecuniary loss	306
	D Certainty of loss and recovery for the loss of a chance	309
III	Attribution of responsibility	309
	A The common sense test of causation	311
	B Factual causation	311
	C Scope of liability	313
	D Multiple wrongdoers	319

I Introduction

The *Trade Practices Act 1974* (Cth) greatly affected the law relating to consumer protection. Of its provisions, s 52 (misleading or deceptive conduct) was the most significant. Numerous consumer protection provisions have since been enacted. On January 2011, the *Trade Practices Act* changed its name to the *Competition and Consumer Act 2010* (Cth), and the *Australian Consumer Law* ('ACL') was incorporated as a schedule to that Act. The ACL replaced most of the consumer protection laws throughout Australia at federal, state and territory levels.

Section 18 (misleading or deceptive conduct) of the ACL is the statutory successor to s 52 of the *Trade Practices Act*. The ACL contains specific provisions governing the right to compensation. Of these, the most significant are ss 236, 237 and 238. These sections are worded somewhat differently but the key common concept is that they provide for compensation 'because of' certain proscribed conduct: for example, s 236 entitles an injured person to recover compensation 'because of' the conduct of another person which was in contravention of a provision of chs 2 or 3 (which contains s 18); s 237 enables the injured person to recover compensation if that person has suffered or is likely to suffer loss because of the conduct of a person who was 'engaged in' a contravention of chs 2, 3 or 4 etc.

This chapter focuses on the concept that 'because of' the conduct of the wrongdoer, damage is suffered. Since the conduct of a person which contravenes one or more provisions of the ACL could also make the wrongdoer liable in tort or breach of contract, the extent to which common law principles would apply in the assessment of compensation under the ACL will make up a large part of the discussion.

The jurisprudence created under the s 52 of the 'old' *Trade Practices Act* and associated provisions concerning compensation for misleading or deceptive conduct remains largely applicable to the ACL due to the close similarity in the wording of the respective provisions.

By virtue of s 131A *Competition and Consumer Act 2010* (Cth), the ACL does not apply in respect of financial products. The equivalent provisions of the *Australian Securities and Investments Commission Act 2001* (Cth) ('ASIC Act')[1], which regulate financial services and products, are virtually identical and will not attract dedicated treatment.

II Assessment of compensation

Compensation for breach of the ACL (and equivalent ASIC Act provisions) is assessed for loss suffered 'because of' a contravention of a relevant provision. This is the overarching aspect of the assessment for compensation under the ACL.

Figure 8.1 Assessment of compensation under the ACL

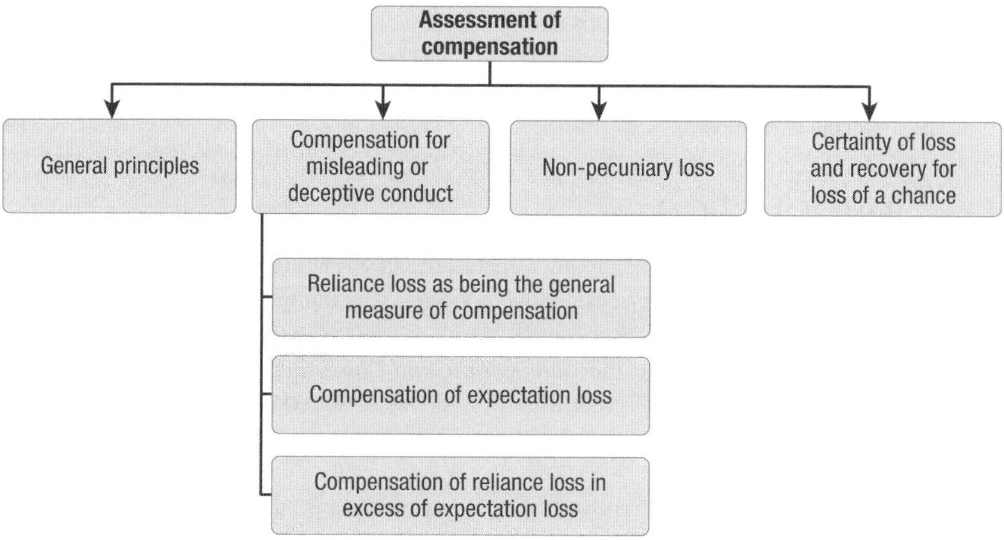

Concept	Short explanation	Relevant authorities	Principles text
General principles	The purpose of compensation is to put the plaintiff in the position they would be in if the contravention had not occurred.	*Wardley Australia Ltd v Western Australia* (1992) 175 CLR 514 *Gates v City Mutual Life Assurance Society Ltd* (1986) 160 CLR 1	Chapter 8: [8.10]–[8.12]
Compensation for misleading or deceptive conduct	Reliance loss is the general measure.	*Gates v City Mutual Life Assurance Society Ltd* (1986) 160 CLR 1 *Marks v GIO Australia Holdings Pty Ltd* (1998) 196 CLR 494	Chapter 8: [8.13]–[8.26]

1 Respectively, s 12DA of the ASIC Act (misleading or deceptive conduct) and s 12CA–12CC (unconscionable conduct).

Concept	Short explanation	Relevant authorities	Principles text
	Compensation of expectation loss.	*Murphy v Overton Investments Pty Ltd* (2004) 216 CLR 388	
	Compensation of reliance loss in excess of expectation loss.	*Henville v Walker* (2001) 206 CLR 459	
Non-pecuniary losses	Compensation is not confined to pecuniary loss.	*New South Wales Lotteries Corporation Pty Ltd v Kuzmanovski* (2011) 195 FCR 234	Chapter 8: [8.27]–[8.30]
Loss of a chance	Compensation may be awarded if as a result of misleading or deceptive conduct the plaintiff is deprived of a commercial opportunity.	*Sellars v Adelaide Petroleum* (1994) 179 CLR 332 (see Chapter 2, page 46 for extract)	Chapter 8: [8.31]; Chapter 2: [2.57]–[2.117]

A General principles

In general, the court will in assessing compensation under the ACL apply the tortuous measure, to place the plaintiff in the position they should be in had the wrong not been committed, not the contractual measure, to put the plaintiff in the position had the contract not been breached.

Wardley Australia Ltd v Western Australia (1992) 175 CLR 514

Facts and issues

As a result of misleading or deceptive conduct, the state granted an indemnity under which it was obliged to make a payment when the loss of the party to be indemnified was ascertained and quantified. The primary issue was whether the cause of action accrued at the time the indemnity was granted, or when it was called on. If the former, then the cause of action was statute barred, conversely with the latter.

Decision

Relief for misleading or deceptive conduct is to place a plaintiff in the same position as if the conduct had not occurred. The state suffered no loss until the indemnity was called on; the proceedings therefore were instituted on time.

Brennan J

> [**534**] The loss or damage for which an amount is recoverable under s 82(1) of the *Trade Practices Act* 1974 (Cth) ('the Act') is loss or damage by conduct that contravenes a provision of Pt IV or Pt V of the Act. It is loss or damage that would not have been suffered if the relevant conduct had not been engaged in. If the relevant conduct is misleading or

deceptive conduct in contravention of s 52 of the Act consisting in false representations of fact, the conduct 'is similar both in character and effect to tortious conduct, particularly fraudulent misrepresentation and negligent misstatement', as Mason, Wilson and Dawson JJ. pointed out in *Gates v City Mutual Life Assurance Society Ltd.* Where economic loss or damage is caused by such conduct, the measure of damages in tort rather than the measure of damages in contract is ordinarily appropriate. Assuming that the amount recoverable under s 82(1) in respect of false representations contravening s 52 is the same as the measure of damages in deceit, the general principle is as Dixon J. defined it in *Toteff v Antonas*:

> In an action of deceit a plaintiff is entitled to recover as damages a sum representing the prejudice or disadvantage he has suffered in consequence of his altering his position under [**535**] the defendant.

In the usual case of deceit, the damages are measured by the difference between the real value of an asset purchased and what the plaintiff paid for it but, as Gibbs J. said in *Gould v Vaggelas*, that rule is 'only a special application of the general principle'. Where a fraudulent misrepresentation induces the purchasing of an asset and payment of a price greater than the value of the asset purchased, the difference between the price and the value of the asset represents 'how much worse off is the plaintiff than if he had not entered into the transaction'. But the rule usually applied cannot be applied when the plaintiff is induced by the misrepresentation to become a surety for another's debt. The surety pays no price and acquires no asset. Where the plaintiff seeks to recover damages for a· loss sustained as a surety, it is necessary to go back to the general principle: what is the prejudice or disadvantage the plaintiff has suffered in consequence of his altering his position under the inducement of the fraudulent misrepresentation? Substituting 'loss or damage' for 'prejudice or disadvantage', that test can be applied, mutatis mutandis, to the assessment of the amount recoverable under s 82(1) when the cause of action arises out of misleading or deceptive conduct consisting in the making of false representations of fact.

The question in this case is not how much worse off is the State than it would have been had the alleged misrepresentation been true, but how much worse off is the State than it would have been had it not relied on the alleged misrepresentation and entered into the transaction. The tortious measure, not the contractual measure, is in question.

...

[**536**] As no cause of action accrues under s 82(1) until the plaintiff 'suffers loss or damage' the question for determination is whether the State suffered the relevant loss or damage when it gave the indemnity.

...

[**538**] The State suffered loss only when it incurred an absolute liability to pay money in discharge of its obligations under the indemnity. That liability arose either when the Bank demanded payment or when the compromise was reached imposing on the State the liability to pay the liquidator $33 million. That is the loss which the respondent claims.

...

B Compensation for misleading or deceptive conduct

Generally, compensation for misleading or deceptive conduct is the reliance loss, to compensate for the loss suffered by reason of the aggrieved party's reliance on the conduct complained of. While the High Court in *Murphy v Overton Investments Pty Ltd*[2] ('*Murphy*') suggested that expectation loss might be recoverable in some cases, most cases suggest that *Murphy* should be confined to its facts and that the appropriate basis for compensation was the tortuous measure.[3]

1 Reliance loss as the general measure of compensation

Gates v City Mutual Life Assurance Society Ltd (1986) 160 CLR 1

Facts and issues

An insurer represented to a proposer for insurance that the total disability clause in a policy entitled him to benefits from his occupation as a builder. The insured suffered an injury which disabled him from occupation as a builder but not from *any* occupation; the clause entitled him to benefits only in the latter event. The question concerned the basis upon which compensation should be assessed; that is, whether on the tortuous or contractual measure.

Decision

Compensation for misleading or deceptive conduct generally should be based on the tortuous, rather than the contractual, measure.

Mason, Wilson and Dawson JJ

> **[14]** The question then is whether it is appropriate to apply the contract measure of damages to the contraventions found to have taken place. [There] is much to be said for the view that the measure of damages in tort is appropriate in most, if not all, Pt V cases, especially those involving misleading or deceptive conduct and the making of false statements. Such conduct is similar both in character and effect to tortious conduct, particularly fraudulent misrepresentation and negligent misstatement.
>
> The disappointed expectations of a person induced by a misrepresentation to believe erroneously that his insurance policy entitles **[15]** him to the payment of benefits on maturity or on the happening of a certain event are sometimes so great as to encourage the thought that compensation on the basis of lost expectations would be appropriate. However, neither authority nor principle offer support for adopting this approach,
>
> ...

2 (2004) 216 CLR 388.

3 See principles text [8.22].

Neither the fact that the representation induces entry into a contract nor the fact that it is a statement of the benefits to which the plaintiff will be entitled under that contract is enough to justify compensation for expectation loss. Just as it is impossible to suppose that there is any difference in the measure of damages in deceit depending upon the nature of the contract into which the plaintiff is induced to enter (*Clark v Urquhart*), so there can be no variation in the measure of damages awarded under the Act for contraventions of ss. 52 and 53(g) depending on the nature of the contract.

Marks v GIO Australia Holdings Pty Ltd (1998) 196 CLR 494

Facts and issues

Borrowers had entered into loan agreements with GIO Australia Holdings Pty Ltd ('GIO'). GIO had represented to borrowers that interest was to be charged at a certain rate, but the contracts stated otherwise. No borrower stated that if the true terms had been known, they would not have borrowed at all or would have entered into alternative arrangements. The question was whether relief should be granted on the grounds of misleading or deceptive conduct.

Decision

Based on the principle that compensation for misleading or deceptive conduct was to place the aggrieved party in the position they would be in had the conduct complained of not occurred, no compensation was recoverable.

Gaudron J

[**502**] When regard is had to the different nature of contractual and tortious liability it is apparent that the so-called 'different measure of damages' in contract and tort is no more than a convenient way of indicating that the wrong involved and, thus, the loss occasioned by a breach of contract is of a different kind from that involved in and [**503**] occasioned by the commission of a tort. The position is explained in *McGregor on Damages*:

> In contract … the wrong consists not in the making but in the breaking of the contract and therefore the plaintiff is entitled to be put into the position he would have been in if the contract had never been broken, or in other words, if the contract had been performed. The plaintiff is entitled to recover damages for the loss of his bargain. In tort, on the other hand, no question of loss of bargain can arise: the plaintiff is not complaining of failure to implement a promise but of failure to leave him alone.

…

[But] there is no basis for thinking that relief under s 82 is to be confined by analogy either with actions in contract or in tort.

…

[There] may be cases where an applicant establishes that, but for the contravention of s 52 of the Act, he or she would not have entered into the contract in question or into any other contract or arrangement of that kind.[4]

...

In this case, the appellants did not assert that, but for the contravention of s 52 of the Act, they would have entered into loan agreements which accorded with their understanding of their arrangement with the GIO. Indeed, there was no evidence that loan facilities of that kind were available. Nor did the appellants establish that, but for the contravention, they would have entered into loan agreements which were more beneficial than those entered into with the GIO.

...

There being no evidence of the kind to which I have referred, the appellants failed to establish that they had suffered any loss or damage and were, thus, not entitled to any remedy under s 82 of the Act.

McHugh, Hayne and Callinan JJ

[**514**] A party that is misled suffers no prejudice or disadvantage unless it is shown that that party could have acted in some other way (or refrained from acting in some way) which would have been of greater benefit or less detriment to it than the course in fact adopted.

...

It is necessary, then, to determine whether the value of what was acquired is less than what was paid. How is value to be assessed? It is to be assessed objectively, not according to what either or both of the parties to the contract believed that it would obtain from the contract. That is, the value of what in fact was acquired is to be identified according to what price freely contracting, fully informed parties would have offered and accepted for it. It is only by comparison with the value assessed in this way that there can be an assessment of whether the party that is misled could have obtained some greater benefit or incurred less detriment. What is important is what that party could have done, not what it might have hoped for or expected. Some examples may serve to illustrate the point.

If a person agrees to pay $50 000 for goods which the vendor falsely represents are worth $100 000 but which are, in fact, worth $50 000, what loss has the purchaser who is misled suffered by agreeing to buy (assuming no more is known)? If a person agrees to pay interest at the rate of 10 per cent for a loan which the lender falsely represents would ordinarily command interest at a rate of 15 per cent but which, in fact, would ordinarily command interest at 12 per cent, what loss has the borrower who is misled suffered by agreeing to borrow (again, assuming no more is known)?

...

4 Or, by parity of reasoning, that they *would* have entered into a separate to contract with a third party that might have yielded a profit. This was the basis for relief in *Sellars v Adelaide Petroleum NL* (1994) 179 CLR 332.

[**515**] The fact that each of the misled parties in the examples given may have thought that it was to obtain some advantage from the transaction is not to the point. The contravening conduct has left the party that was misled no worse off than it was before the contravention occurred.

...

[**516**] It follows, therefore, that the borrowers' concession that, subject to the now immaterial exception of one borrower, the GIO loan at the increased margin was more beneficial to the borrowers than any other loan that was available is critical to the determination of these proceedings.

...

Accordingly, the position of the borrowers is that they were misled into taking a loan which cost them more than was represented to them but which, even so, cost less than any other loan available to them in the market. They suffered and will suffer no loss or damage as a result of the misleading and deceptive conduct of the respondents.

2 Compensation of expectation loss

Murphy v Overton Investments Pty Ltd (2004) 216 CLR 388

Facts and issues

The appellants (Murphy) had bought leasehold interests in a retirement village operated by Overton Investments Pty Ltd ('Overton', the respondent) on the basis inter alia of estimates of outgoings. The estimate was found to be misleading and had understated the outgoings, which Overton then sought to charge. Murphy sought relief. There was no evidence of any difference between the price they paid and the value of the property and no evidence that they were not receiving value for the fees they were paying and thus no reliance loss. The question was whether the applicants were entitled to damages for misleading or deceptive conduct, assessed on the basis that those damages would essentially amount to expectation damages.

Decision

The High Court ordered damages be assessed by reference to the amount which the obligation to meet outgoings was larger than the estimate led them to anticipate. This broadly was tantamount to expectation damages.

Gleeson CJ, McHugh, Gummow, Kirby, Hayne, Callinan and Heydon JJ

[63] [The] damages which the appellants seek to be allowed for past and future outgoings would make good the position they would have been in had the misrepresentation not been made.

...

> **[66]** The appellants had been induced by the respondent's conduct to undertake an obligation which may, but need not, have been more onerous than the respondent's representation led them to believe. When the respondent started to charge all the outgoings it was entitled to charge, the appellants suffered a loss. The amount of that loss was not to be determined, as the majority of the Full Court held, only by comparing the financial position of the appellants according to whether they entered this lease or took some other accommodation. The appellants did not contend that they had suffered loss in that way. The appellants suffered loss because the continuing financial obligations they undertook when they took the lease proved to be larger than they had been led to believe.

The High Court remitted the matter to the trial judge for the assessment of damages on the basis set out.

3 Compensation of reliance loss in excess of expectation loss

Henville v Walker (2001) 206 CLR 459

Facts and issues

Walker made representations that units built on his land could be sold by Henville within about six months for between $250 000 and $280 000. Henville relied on those representations, but also relied upon his own experience to estimate the likely cost of development. Believing the project would be profitable, Henville bought the land and performed significant work. Subsequently the real estate market declined and there were construction delays. Eventually the units were sold by Henville for prices well below the represented amounts.

Henville's loss was thus the cumulative effect of the misleading representations by Walker, his own estimates, and the construction delays. Henville sued Walker for contraventions of s 52 of the *Trade Practices Act* and damages under s 82.

The trial judge estimated Henville's loss as the difference between what Walker represented as the selling prices of the units ($750 000) and their actual sale prices ($545 000) and awarded $205 000 to Henville – essentially the expectation loss. The reliance loss ($320 000) was greater, based on the difference between the total expenditure on the project and what the project realised upon sale ($865 000.00 – $545 000.00). Upon appeal, the Western Australian Full Court held that the necessary connection between the conduct of Walker and the damage suffered by Henville had not been established. Henville appealed to the High Court.

The questions were whether Henville could recover the whole of his reliance loss, since Walker's misleading or deceptive conduct was only one of several causes of it.

Decision

Henville was entitled to recover all his reliance loss in consequence of altering his position.

McHugh J

[132] In this case, the most appropriate approach is to identify what Mr Henville has suffered by way of prejudice or disadvantage in consequence of altering his position by reason of the breach of the Act. The measure of that loss is not determined by reference to what he would have received if Mr Walker's representations had been true.

...

[133] In an action for damages for deceit, the damages are measured by reference to how much worse off the plaintiff is as a result of being fraudulently induced to take the course of action that he or she did. The loss that the plaintiff can recover includes consequential losses flowing directly from the misrepresentation including losses from opportunities forgone.

[134] Here the misrepresentations induced Mr Henville to enter into a contract and to construct units under the belief that the project would produce a substantial profit. If there had been no misrepresentations, Mr Henville would not have embarked on the course that he did and the loss that he suffered would have been avoided. That being so, his loss was a direct result of the misrepresentations and would have been recoverable in an action for damages for deceit.

...

[135] Nor do I see any reason why the principles applicable in an action for deceit at common law should not be applied in the present case. The purposes of the Act include promoting fair trading and protecting consumers from contraventions of the Act. Those purposes are more readily achieved by ensuring that consumers recover the actual losses they have suffered as the result of contraventions of the Act.

C Non-pecuniary loss

Section 236 of the ACL is not confined to pecuniary loss; compensation might be awarded for non-pecuniary loss, for example, distress and disappointment.

New South Wales Lotteries Corporation Pty Ltd v Kuzmanovski [2011] FCAFC 106; (2011) 195 FCR 234

Facts and issues

Mrs Kuzmanovski bought tickets for an instant lottery. There were qualifying terms on the lottery imposed under certain statutory provisions that required the winning ticket to undergo a process of validation. These qualifying terms were not apparent on the face of the ticket; rather, it appeared on its face that the ticket was the winning ticket, which the Kuzmanovskis had believed to be the case.

The Full Federal Court considered that the Kuzmanovskis were bound by the statutory terms and, as the ticket did not satisfy the validation process, no breach of contract had taken place. Two issues remained: if the NSW Lotteries Commission had engaged in misleading or deceptive conduct, and if so whether the Kuzkanovskis were entitled to damages for distress and disappointment.

Decision

The NSW Lotteries Commission had engaged in misleading or deceptive conduct and damages of $20 000.00 were allowed for distress and disappointment.[5]

Siopis, Cowdroy and Tracey JJ

> **[5]** … Mrs Kuzmanovski purchased two $5 Pictionary instant scratchie lottery tickets … as a gift for her husband's birthday. One such ticket is relevant to these proceedings ('the ticket').
>
> …
>
> **[9]** Lotteries declined to recognise the ticket as a winning ticket. Accordingly the Kuzmanovskis commenced proceedings in this Court seeking damages, payment of $100 000, and other orders.
>
> …
>
> **[94]** The primary judge held that Lotteries engaged in conduct in contravention of ss 52 and 53 of the Trade Practices Act in the creation for sale, and sale of, the ticket. …
>
> **[95]** Mr and Mrs Kuzmanovski pleaded that Lotteries made nine representations in trade or commerce, by the play instructions, pictures and content of the ticket. The primary judge found that, even if he was wrong in findings in respect of the contractual argument, Lotteries had, nevertheless, engaged in misleading or deceptive conduct in relation to the making of the following of the pleaded representations, namely, that Lotteries represented that:
>
>> … the governing of the ticket by the Public Lotteries Regulations and Rules is consistent with effect being given to the play instructions in connection with the supply or possible supply of goods [Lotteries] falsely represented that the scratchie ticket had a particular standard, quality and value by reason of the Pictionary game and the $100 000 heading. Whereas the standard of the goods was not determined by the game the quality of the goods was not of a game of chance and the value of $100 000 had no reference to the game but rather whether it was a winning ticket, contrary to s 53(a) of the Trade Practice Act 1974 … .
>
> **[96]** The primary judge accepted Mr Kuzmanovski's evidence that, at the time that he scratched the ticket, he believed that there was nothing in the Lotteries Act or the Rules that was inconsistent with the play instructions. His Honour was of the opinion that such a belief was simply 'commonsense'.
>
> …

5 A successful claim for breach of contract would have resulted in damages of $100 000.

[102] According to Lotteries, the Kuzmanovskis purchased a ticket that stated in plain terms the legal position that existed anyway, namely that it was governed by the Lotteries Act and the Rules. The Kuzmanovskis knew that the ticket was so governed, but simply did not know what the Lotteries Act and the Rules said, and they also chose not to find out.

...

[104] Lotteries' argument is not accepted. Whether a representation is misleading or deceptive is to be determined by reference to the meaning the representation conveyed to the ordinary and reasonable member of the class of consumers to which the representation was addressed: see *Campomar Socieded Limitada v Nike International Ltd.*

[105] Furthermore, it is well settled that s 52 of the Trade Practices Act should be interpreted broadly due to its remedial nature. In *Accounting Systems 2000 (Developments) Pty Ltd v CCH Australia Ltd* (1993) 42 FCR 470, Lockhart and Gummow JJ stated at 503:

> ... the evident purpose and policy underlying Pt V, which includes s 52, recommends a broad construction of its constituent provisions, the legislation being of a remedial character so that it should be construed so as to give the fullest relief which the fair meaning of its language will allow

...

[119] The primary judge accepted that, as the misrepresentation inherent in the ticket became more and more apparent, the sense of disappointment, anger and frustration felt by the Kuzmanovskis increased, especially on the part of Mr Kuzmanovski. Mr Kuzmanovski had planned to use the money for, among other things, financing a trip to Macedonia to visit his ailing grandmother.

[120] While recognising that there were no objective criteria for assessing the value of such injured feelings, his Honour proceeded to assess the damages under the Trade Practices Act at $20 000 ($15 000 for Mr Kuzmanovski and $5000 for Mrs Kuzmanovski).

[121] Lotteries contended that the award was plainly excessive. Lotteries contended that Mr and Mrs Kuzmanovski became aware of the correct position at law the morning after they scratched the ticket. That is, although they stayed up for most of the night with excitement at the thought of winning, the following morning they were informed by the agent for Lotteries that the ticket was in fact not a winning ticket. Regardless of the fact that their disappointment had continued to mount since that time, they had suffered no compensable loss because the day after scratching it they found out the answer to the question of whether they had a winning ticket.

[122] In our view, this contention is not to be accepted. The primary judge found that Lotteries' conduct had caused an initial soaring of the Kuzmanovskis' hopes and dreams and then, when those hopes and dreams were dashed, prolonged feelings of disappointment, anger and frustration arising from a sense of feeling cheated. The primary judge went on to find that that initial feeling of elation by the Kuzmanovskis was the very kind of human emotion played on by the sales pitch of Lotteries.

[123] In our view, Lotteries has not demonstrated that the primary judge erred in principle in the manner in which he approached the question of damages. The assessment of damages for disappointment and injury to feelings is not a precise science. In our view, the primary judge did not err in taking into account the fact that the 'sales pitch' of Lotteries was directed to inducing consumers to believe that with a stroke of luck, they could experience the very elation which the Kuzmanovskis felt when, by reason of the Lotteries' contravening conduct, they believed that their ticket was a winning ticket. Nor, in our view, did the primary judge err in concluding that the deep and lingering sense of disappointment, anger and frustration felt by Mr Kuzmanovski and, to a lesser extent Mrs Kuzmanovski, was a natural human emotional response to Lotteries' contravening conduct. It was, in our view, open to the primary judge to award damages in the sum which he did.

D Certainty of loss and recovery for the loss of a chance

Where misleading or deceptive conduct has caused the plaintiff to lose a commercial opportunity, compensation for the loss of that opportunity might be recoverable. The guiding principles for the recovery of compensation are covered in the seminal case of *Sellars v Adelaide Petroleum NL* ('*Sellars*').[6] The facts and reasoning in *Sellars* are set out in some detail in Chapter 2.

REVIEW QUESTIONS

(1) The balance of authority is that the test for the assessment of damages for misleading or deceptive conduct is to put the plaintiff in the position that they should be in had the conduct not occurred; that is, the tortuous measure. How does the tortuous measure differ from the contractual measure? Illustrate your answer by reference to the reasoning in *Gates v City Mutual Life Assurance Society Ltd* (1986) 160 CLR 1.

(2) In *Marks v GIO Australia Holdings Pty Ltd* (1998) 196 CLR 494, the defendant had engaged in misleading or deceptive conduct. Explain the reasoning whereby the plaintiff nonetheless failed to recover damages.

(3) In *Sellars v Adelaide Petroleum NL* (1994) 179 CLR 332, the plaintiff recovered compensation based on the lost opportunity to enter into commercial arrangements with a third party; that is, a favourable contract. Explain whether those damages are appropriately characterised as based on the tortuous measure, or the contractual measure?

III Attribution of responsibility

Section 236 of the ACL provides that compensation for loss suffered be 'because of' a relevant contravention but provides no further guidance. The present approach is to treat the attribution of responsibility for a loss as a two-tiered approach, *factual causation* and *scope of liability*.

6 (1994) 179 CLR 332.

Figure 8.2 Attribution of responsibility: causation and the scope of liability under the ACL

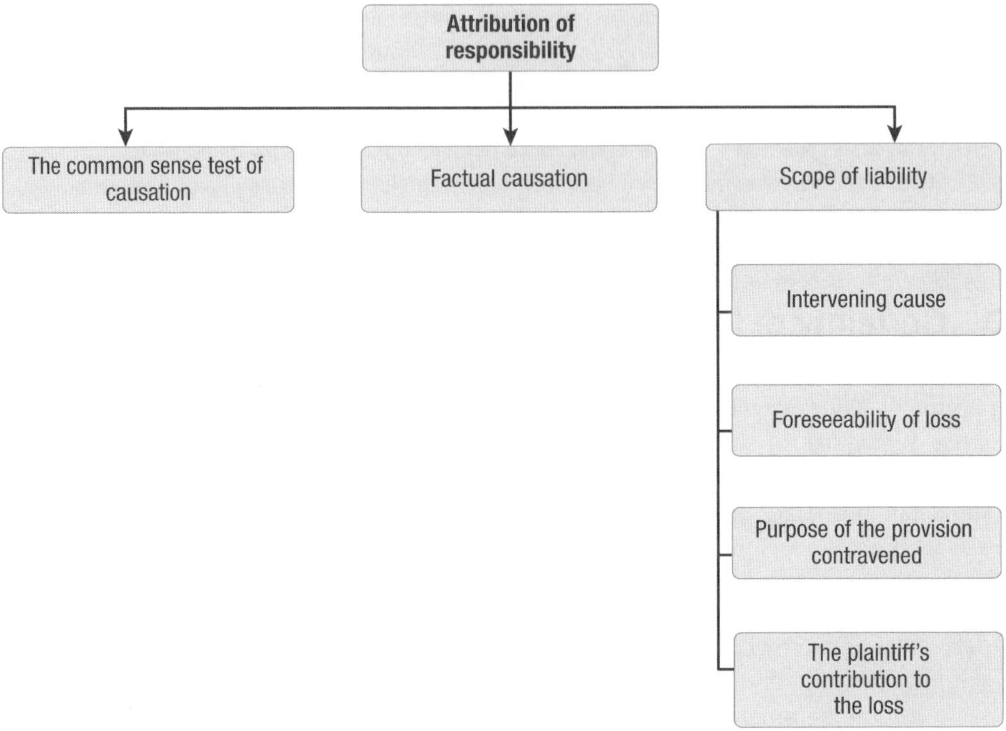

Concept	Short explanation	Relevant authorities	Principles text
The common sense test of causation	Rather than the common sense test of causation, the two-tier test in civil liability legislation should be adopted to determine if the loss has been suffered 'because of' some conduct that contravened the ACL.		Chapter 8: [8.32]–[8.35]
Factual causation	The 'but for' test is generally to be applied; for misleading or deceptive conduct, the defendant's statement need not be the sole or dominant factor in the plaintiff's decision.	*Henville v Walker* (2001) 206 CLR 459	Chapter 8: [8.36]–[8.37]
Scope of liability	Intervening cause.	*Henville v Walker* (2001) 206 CLR 459 *Hay Property Consultants Pty Ltd v Victorian Securities Corporation Ltd* (2010) 29 VR 503	Chapter 8: [8.39]–[8.51]

Concept	Short explanation	Relevant authorities	Principles text
	Foreseeability of the loss.	*Henville v Walker* (2001) 206 CLR 459	
	Purpose of the provision contravened.	*Travel Compensation Fund v Iambree* (2005) 224 CLR 627	
	The plaintiff's contribution to the loss.	*Competition and Consumer Act 2010* (Cth) *Henjo Investments Pty Ltd v Collins Marrickville Pty Ltd (No 2)* (1989) 40 FCR 76	
Multiple wrongdoers	Part VIA of the *Competition and Consumer Act 2010* (Cth) and analogous provisions provide for proportionate liability of concurrent wrongdoer in certain cases of a contravention of s 18 of the ACL.	*Competition and Consumer Act 2010* (Cth)	Chapter 8: [8.52]

A The common sense test of causation

The pivotal words in the ACL concerning compensation are that compensation would be provided 'because of' a relevant contravention. The current jurisprudence concerning the common sense test of causation is that it only applies in the Northern Territory. In all other jurisdictions, the civil liability statutes prescribe the two-step test of 'factual causation' and 'scope of liability'.

B Factual causation

'Factual causation' essentially requires that there be a connection between the defendant's contravention and the loss said to have been suffered. Factual causation is satisfied as if the contravention has materially contributed to the loss even if not its sole cause.

Henville v Walker (2001) 206 CLR 459

Facts and issues

Walker made representations that units built on his land could be sold by Henville within about six months for between $250 000 and $280 000. Henville relied on those representations but also relied upon his own experience to estimate the likely cost of development. Believing the project would be profitable, Henville bought the land and performed significant work. Subsequently the real estate market declined and there were constructions delays. Eventually the units were sold by Henville for prices well below the represented amounts.

Henville's loss was thus the cumulative effect of the misleading representations by Walker, his own estimates, and the construction delays. Henville sued Walker for contraventions of s 52 of the *Trade Practices Act* and damages under s 82.

The relevant issue on the question of *factual causation* was whether the fact that Henville's loss was the cumulative effect of the misleading representations by Walker, Henville's own estimates, and the construction delays, meant that factual causation was not satisfied.

Decision

Though Walker's conduct was not the sole cause of Henville's loss, Henville was entitled to recover damages as it was enough that Walker's conduct was one of several factors in Henville's decision.

McHugh J

[106] If the defendant's breach has 'materially contributed' to the loss or damage suffered, it will be regarded as a cause of the loss or damage, despite other factors or conditions having played an even more significant role in producing the loss or damage. As long as the breach materially contributed to the damage, a causal connection will ordinarily exist even though the breach without more would not have brought about the damage. In exceptional cases, where an abnormal event intervenes between the breach and damage, it may be right as a matter of common-sense to hold that the breach was not a cause of damage. But such cases are exceptional.

[107] Of particular importance to the present case is the long-standing recognition of the possibility that two or more causes may jointly influence a person to undertake a course of conduct. In separate judgments in *Gould v Vaggelas*, Wilson and Brennan JJ emphasised that a representation need not be the sole inducement in sustaining the loss. If 'it plays some part even if only a minor part', in contributing to the course of action taken in that case the formation of a contract – a causal connection will exist.

Hayne J

[156] If the traditional 'but for' test, the test of necessity, is applied to the history I have described, neither the overestimation of the selling price, nor the underestimation of the costs, will be seen as the single cause of the *whole* of the loss that the appellants sustained. It cannot be said of either of these steps that, but for its occurrence, the appellants would not have sustained the amount of loss that they did suffer. Yet it can be said of each step that it was a necessary element of the set of circumstances that, together, were sufficient to bring about the loss that was sustained. Each played its part in the history of the events; each was *a* cause of what happened. Moreover, the two steps were *concurrent* causes of what happened. It cannot be said of either estimate that it was, in any sense, an intervening event.

...

[159] In the present case, the respondents' contravention of the Act can be seen to have caused the appellants' damage because the appellants relied on the respondents' misleading or deceptive conduct in deciding to proceed with the project.

C Scope of liability

'Scope of liability' is the second of the two issues that arises under the civil liability statutes which govern the question of the attribution of responsibility for compensation for contraventions of the ACL in jurisdictions other than the Northern Territory. Even where factual causation is satisfied, the wrong must fall within the 'scope of liability' for compensation to be recoverable. 'Scope of liability' invokes legal causation and raises questions of whether the wrongdoer's liability might be limited. The following matters affecting the scope of the wrongdoer's liability will be covered in this part:

- intervening cause
- foreseeability of the loss
- purpose of the provision contravened and
- the plaintiff's contribution to the loss.

1 Intervening cause

Henville v Walker (2001) 206 CLR 459

Facts and issues

The fundamental facts of this case, as noted on pages 305 and 311, were that Walker made representations that units built on his land could be sold by Henville within about six months for between $250 000 and $280 000. It is particularly noted for the purposes of the present analysis that while Henville relied on those representations, he also relied upon his own experience to estimate the likely cost of development. The present issue concerns the question of whether Henville's own estimate of the cost of development was an intervening cause that broke the chain of causation.

Decision

Henville's reliance on own estimates did not break the chain of causation.

McHugh J

> **[106]** If the defendant's breach has 'materially contributed' to the loss or damage suffered, it will be regarded as a cause of the loss or damage, despite other factors or conditions having played an even more significant role in producing the loss or damage. As long as the breach materially contributed to the damage, a causal connection will ordinarily exist even though the breach without more would not have brought about the damage. In exceptional cases, where an abnormal event intervenes between the breach and damage, it may be right as a matter of common sense to hold that the breach was not a cause of damage. But such cases are exceptional.
>
> **[107]** Of particular importance to the present case is the long-standing recognition of the possibility that two or more causes may jointly influence a person to undertake a

course of conduct). In separate judgments in *Gould v Vaggelas* Wilson and Brennan JJ emphasised that a representation need not be the sole inducement in sustaining the loss. If 'it plays some part even if only a minor part', in contributing to the course of action taken in that case the formation of a contract – a causal connection will exist.

...

[122] ... the Full Court isolated Mr Henville's conduct in relation to the feasibility study in an attempt to identify whether it was the cause of the losses claimed. As this Court pointed out in *Medlin*, in the passage quoted earlier, such an approach is potentially misleading, particularly where the wrongful conduct was itself a direct or indirect contributing cause of the intervening act or decision. Asking itself the wrong question at this point led to an awkward chain of reasoning that was not only out of step with prevailing authority, but also obscured the integral part that Mr Walker's misrepresentations played in the preparation of the feasibility study.

Hay Property Consultants Pty Ltd v Victorian Securities Corporation Ltd [2010] VSCA 247; (2010) 29 VR 503

Facts and issues

Victorian Securities Corporation Ltd ('VSC', the respondent) engaged Hay Property Consultants Pty Ltd ('HPC', the appellants) to value several properties proposed as security for a loan. HPC negligently over-valued the properties and the borrowers defaulted, but before VSC took possession, an unknown third party damaged the properties. The issue was whether HPC was liable for the loss.

Decision

HPC were not liable for the loss in property value resulting from the criminal damage.

Neave JA (Ashley and Hansen JA agreeing)

[85] In Henville and I & L Securities, the decision that the misleading statements of the auditor and accountant caused the customers' loss was consistent with the object of consumer protection.

[86] The loss on resale was not an indivisible loss which was caused by the misleading representations by the valuers, but comprised two separate and distinct types of loss, one of which was attributable to the fact that the properties were damaged by third parties.

...

[88] True ... the lender would not have suffered any loss if it had not made the loan. But the misrepresentations simply initiated a train of events, commencing with the making of the loan, and did not create a legally causal relationship between the loss caused by the damage to the properties and the making of the loan. The criminal damage could have occurred regardless of the valuers' negligent misstatement. …

[89] The purpose and policy of the TPA does not require a negligent valuer to be held liable for loss caused by the criminal acts of third parties, except in circumstances where the original breach increased the risk that those acts would occur.

…

[91] This is an example of an abnormal event intervening between the breach and the damage which breaks the chain of causation between the misleading representation and the loss suffered as the result of the subsequent criminal acts. The dicta in Henville, to which I have referred above, (and also in Australian cases concerning causation at common law) support the view that the valuers should not be held liable for the loss caused by the criminal acts of third parties.

2 Foreseeability of the loss

Henville v Walker (2001) 206 CLR 459

Facts and issues

A more comprehensive outline of the facts is set out on pages 305 and 311. Further distilled for present purposes, relevant facts are Walker made representations that units built on his land could be sold by Henville within about six months for between $250 000 and $280 000. Henville relied on those representations but also relied upon his own experience to estimate the likely cost of development. Believing the project would be profitable, Henville bought the land and performed significant work. Subsequently the real estate market declined and there were constructions delays. Eventually the units were sold by Henville for prices well below the represented amounts. The issue was whether Henville's loss was limited by considerations of foreseeability and contributory negligence.

Decision

Henville's loss was not limited by considerations of foreseeability and contributory negligence.

Gaudron J

[66] It was held in *Marks v GIO Australia Holdings Ltd* that the relief available under s 82(1) of the Act is not to be confined by analogy either with actions in contract or in tort. Rather, the task under that subsection is to ascertain the loss suffered by the contravening conduct and to assess the amount necessary to compensate for that loss. Once that is accepted, it follows, in my view, that considerations of foreseeability and contributory negligence are irrelevant to the exercise required by s 82(l).

3 The purpose of the provision contravened

Travel Compensation Fund v Tambree (2005) 224 CLR 627

Facts and issues

Travel Compensation Fund ('the Fund', the appellant) provided assistance against uninsured losses arising from the conduct of a participating travel agent. An agent, in order to participate, was required to be financially sound. An accountant and auditor ('Tambree', the defendants) prepared a participating agent's accounts in a false and misleading way, knowing they would be furnished to the Fund and relied on to determine if the travel agent was eligible to participate in the Fund. A travel agent while not financially sound, contrary to what was shown on the accounts prepared by the defendants, traded illegally until their business was shut down. The Fund had paid compensation to persons who had suffered loss because of the conduct of the agent. The Fund instituted proceedings for misleading or deceptive conduct against the defendants. The question was whether the travel agent's trading illegally broke the chain of causation with respect to the losses caused by the Fund's obligation to pay compensation during that period.

Decision

Causation was established and not broken as the risk of the travel agent continuing to trade illegally was the reason why the Fund sought protection by requiring audited financial statements.

Callinan J

> **[28]** It is not in doubt that issues of causation commonly involve normative considerations, sometimes referred to by reference to 'values' or 'policy'. …
>
> **[29]** To acknowledge that, in appropriate circumstances, normative considerations have a role to play in judgments about issues of causation is not to invite judges to engage in value judgments at large. The relevant norms must be derived from legal principle. In this case, the primary task of the Court is to apply the legislative norms to be found in the Fair Trading Act, although the outcome is not materially different to applying the common law of negligence.
>
> …
>
> **[31]** This is a case of known reliance, and negligent misrepresentation. The aspect of trade and commerce which attracted the operation of s 42 of the *Fair Trading Act* was the conduct of the business of a travel agent, in a regulatory context that provided for a scheme of compensation for members of the public who suffer loss through failure to account on the part of defaulting agents. That scheme exposed the appellant to claims for compensation, and to the risk of loss by reason of payments made. [The] risk to which the appellant was exposed included the risk of claims for compensation by people who dealt with a travel agent who was no longer a participant in the Fund and was operating

following loss of a licence – perhaps attempting to trade out of financial difficulties. To protect itself against that risk, as well as to protect the public, the appellant required information about the financial position of participating agents. It acted in reliance on that information in making decisions about continuing participation, including decisions as to whether to require further security or additional funding. The first and second respondents participated in the provision of such information, knowing that it was for the purpose of such reliance. The statute prohibited misleading conduct by them. They engaged in misleading conduct by the part they played in the provision of false financial information.

...

[35] The answer to the problem of causation in the present case is to be found, not in a value judgment, but in an accurate identification of the nature of the risk against which the appellant sought protection and of the loss it suffered, considered in the light of the kind of wrongful conduct in which the first and second respondents engaged.

4 The plaintiff's contribution to the loss

Competition and Consumer Act 2010 (Cth) s 137B

This section addresses the question of whether the claimant's entitlement to compensation under sub-s 236(1) of the ACL is liable to be reduced because of the claimant's own conduct (as set out) in that section.

137B Reduction of the amount of loss or damage if the claimant fails to take reasonable care

If:

(a) a person (the ***claimant***) makes a claim under subsection 236(1) of the *Australian Consumer Law* in relation to economic loss, or damage to property, suffered by the claimant because of the conduct of another person; and

(b) the conduct contravened section 18 of the *Australian Consumer Law*; and

(c) the claimant suffered the loss or damage as result:

 (i) partly of the claimant's failure to take reasonable care; and

 (ii) partly of the conduct of the other person; and

(d) the other person did not intend to cause the loss or damage and did not fraudulently cause the loss or damage;

the amount of the loss or damage that the claimant may recover under subsection 236(1) of the Australian Consumer Law is to be reduced to the extent to which a court thinks just and equitable having regard to the claimant's share in the responsibility for the loss or damage.

Henjo Investments Pty Ltd v Collins Marrickville Pty Ltd (No 2) (1989) 40 FCR 76

Facts and issues

Henjo Investments Pty Ltd ('Henjo', the respondent) made false and misleading statements concerning a restaurant business by giving the impression that the number of seats legally permitted was significantly higher than it was. Collins Marrickville Pty Ltd ('Collins', the applicant) relied on these representations by acquiring the business. After Collins took over the business, key employees left, and the method of operation was changed and the business ran at a loss for a significant period. The issue was whether the damages should be discounted on the basis that these factors caused or contributed to the loss.

Decision

Relief for a significant part of the loss was denied on the ground that it was caused by factors not connected with the misleading or deceptive conduct of the defendants.

Burchett J

> [**86**] The evidence revealed that, for about 18 months, the respondent took no steps to endeavour to find an assignee of the lease; that when the respondent did seek a solution, an arrangement was made within about six months for the taking over of the lease by a company (referred to as the Bombay Bicycle Club) which, though the respondent had an involvement in it, was substantially controlled by an apparently successful [**87**] London-based restaurant owner; and that, since 1 July 1988, the respondent has not had to bear any part of the rental. To award $173 999.05 to cover the respondent's expected monthly outgoings for the period 1 January 1987 to 20 May 1990 when it is known that these outgoings ceased on 1 July 1988, and it was not proved, or even alleged, that there was any likelihood they would recommence, seems to me to be wrong.
>
> I understand the proposition that the method of assessment adopted a hypothetical position, which involved the rejection of the respondent's real losses in carrying on the business; and the contention that, having started the calculation hypothetically on 30 June 1986, the court should not switch to a reality which, had the hypothetical situation existed, may never have come about – that is to say, if the respondent had taken the hypothesised action of seeking an assignee promptly after 30 June 1986, some other agreement may very well have been reached long before 1988 which may have precluded any negotiations with the Bombay Bicycle Club. But at least the solution actually found shows that some solution short of the huge losses the trial judge postulated was possible. It is a truism, both of valuation law and of the law of damages, that facts are to be preferred to prophecy. Here, the event should at least be used to correct the prophecy.
>
> ...
>
> [**88**] I reject the appellant's contention that any assessment referable to the future position should have been cut off at 1 July 1988, both because I accept that what is involved is a weighing of the situation as it presented itself to the respondent as at about 30 June

1986, and because the evidence does not reveal the arrangement with the Bombay Bicycle Club to be necessarily a perfect solution for the respondent's problems. But, doing the best I can to make the estimation of the prospects, in the light of the known events, which I think should have been made, I would discount the figure calculated in respect of rental subsidy by approximately 50 per cent. On that basis I would deduct from the damages assessed the sum of $85 000.

D Multiple wrongdoers

The contravention of s 18 of the ACL by concurrent wrongdoers may attract an operation of pt VIA of the *Competition and Consumer Act 2010* (Cth) and analogous provisions, which provide for proportionate liability of concurrent wrongdoers.

REVIEW QUESTIONS

(1) The situation in *Henjo Investments Pty Ltd v Collins Marrickville Pty Ltd (No 2)* (1989) 40 FCR 76 ('*Henjo*') was arguably different to that in *Henville v Walker* (2001) 206 CLR 459 in that in *Henjo*, the trading losses occurred over a significant period, while the losses suffered by Henville were all part of the solitary circumstance, the development and sale of the units. Discuss the arguments for and against the proposition that the losses of the plaintiff should have been discounted such that they should not extend beyond the time at which the plaintiff should have, speaking figuratively cut his losses.

(2) What was the reasoning that underpinned the court's decision to allow the losses claimed by the Fund in *Travel Compensation Fund v Tambree* (2005) 224 CLR 627 and, concomitantly, that the conduct of an agent in financial difficulties did not break the chain of causation? Include in your answer a consideration of the underlying policy of the legislation.

(3) In what way does the statutory cause of action for misleading or deceptive conduct differ from the common law action for misrepresentation in its treatment of foreseeability?

9 EQUITABLE COMPENSATION FOR EQUITABLE WRONGS

I	Introduction		320
II	Assessment of equitable compensation		320
	A	Object of equitable compensation	321
	B	Recoverability of non-pecuniary loss	323
	C	Basic measure of equitable compensation	324
III	Attribution of responsibility		328
	A	Breach of trust	330
	B	Breach of fiduciary duty	340
	C	Breach of an equitable duty of care	348

I Introduction

Common law damages are awarded to compensate the innocent party for the breach of a common law wrong, and equitable compensation is awarded to compensate an innocent party for a purely equitable wrong.

The central concept in Section II, 'Assessment of equitable compensation', is that the object of equitable compensation is to restore the plaintiff to the position they would be in if not for the breach. Section II incorporates a detailed discussion of the application of this central concept to the recoverability of non-pecuniary loss and the basic measure of equitable compensation. The former section explores whether equitable compensation is even available for non-pecuniary loss (embarrassment and distress). The latter section probes the reasoning which establishes that equitable compensation puts the plaintiff into as good a position pecuniarily as before the injury, thereby satisfying the object of equitable compensation.

Section III, 'Attribution of responsibility', segues from the central proposition in Section II, that the basic measure of equitable compensation is to put the plaintiff into as good a position pecuniarily as before the injury thereby satisfying the object of equitable compensation. While constantly keeping this central proposition at the forefront, Section III explores whether the wrongdoer should be visited with the consequences of their conduct in the context of the various equitable wrongs explored – breach of trust; breach of fiduciary duty; and breach of an equitable duty of care.

II Assessment of equitable compensation

The discussion in this section is in three sub-parts:

(1) the object of equitable compensation

(2) the recoverability of non-pecuniary loss and

(3) the basic measure of equitable compensation.

Figure 9.1 The assessment of equitable compensation

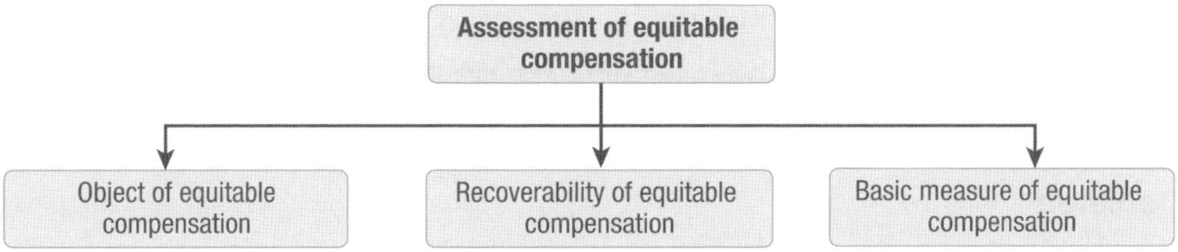

Concept	Short explanation	Relevant authorities	Principles text
Object of equitable compensation	The object of equitable compensation is to restore the plaintiff to the position they would be in if not for the breach.	*O'Halloran v RT Thomas & Family Pty Ltd* (1998) 45 NSWLR 262	Chapter 9: [9.7]–[9.10]
Recoverability of non-pecuniary loss	Equitable compensation can be recoverable for non-pecuniary losses such as for distress.	*Giller v Procopets* (2008) 24 VR 1	Chapter 9: [9.11]–[9.13]
Basic measure of equitable compensation	Equitable compensation compensates a plaintiff by putting them in as good a position pecuniarily as that before the injury.	*Nocton v Lord Ashburton* [1914] AC 932	Chapter 9: [9.14]–[9.16]

A Object of equitable compensation

The fundamental proposition, in cases not involving misappropriation of property, is that the purpose of equitable compensation is to restore persons who have suffered loss to the position they would be in if there had been no breach of an equitable obligation. This proposition is stated explicitly in *O'Halloran v RT Thomas & Family Pty Ltd*.

O'Halloran v RT Thomas & Family Pty Ltd (1998) 45 NSWLR 262

Facts and issues

O'Halloran was an officer of R T Thomas & Family Pty Limited ('Thomas') and Chairman of the Board of Jeffries Industries Ltd ('Jeffries'). Thomas held shares in Jeffries.

Thomas entered into a put and call option with respect to its shares in Jeffries with Bowes & Brown Pty Ltd ('Bowes & Brown'). That agreement was replaced by a new agreement under which there would be an immediate purchase of 225 000 shares in Jeffries for $675 000.

At a time when payment of the $675 000 had not yet been received, a transfer of the shares to Bowes & Brown was registered by O'Halloran in his capacity as managing director of Thomas and chairman of Jeffries. This was held to be in breach of fiduciary obligations owed to Thomas. O'Halloran argued that the mere act of registration of the transfer did not cause loss to Thomas but rather that the events which caused the loss were the failure to rectify the transfer and to resell the shares to Bowes & Brown before the share price decreased in value.

The question was whether O'Halloran's breach caused the loss to Thomas. The case is useful for the unequivocality of the statement of the proposition that the measure of equitable compensation is to restore an aggrieved party to the position it would have been in but for the other's breach.

Decision

A claim for equitable compensation for breach of a fiduciary obligation required a causal link between the breach and the loss. Once satisfied, the measure of compensation was to restore Thomas to the position it would have been in but for O'Halloran's breach.

Spiegelman CJ

> [**272**] It is sufficient to focus on O'Halloran's conduct when, as a director of Thomas, he surrendered possession of the share certificates in Jeffries issued in the name of Thomas, without payment of the purchase price, in order to have the transfer to Bowes & Brown registered so that his, and his allies', control over Jeffries would remain undisturbed. The power he exercised as a director in this regard was a fiduciary power which could not be exercised for an improper purpose … [These] powers were exercised for an improper purpose.
>
> …
>
> [**277**] In *Mulkana Corporation NL (In Liq) v Bank of New South Wales* Powell J reviewed the authorities which used the terminology of trustee in relation to directors and said:
>
> > … while directors are not, properly speaking trustees, but fiduciary agents, the range of duties and obligations to which they are subject or which are imposed upon them, include duties or obligations which place them, in relation to moneys or property which are in their possession, or over which they have control, in a position analogous to, although not identical with, that of trustees. … It is analogous since, just as, in such a case, trustees would be liable to recoup the trust for any loss, directors who misapply, or are parties to the *misapplication* of the funds or other property of the company, are, subject to the court's powers to relieve them from so doing, liable to recoup the company for any loss thereby sustained.
>
> The analogy to which his Honour made reference should encompass the approach to causation for purposes of a claim for equitable compensation
>
> …
>
> [**278**] Applying the test – would loss have occurred if there had been no breach – in this case, compels the conclusion that his Honour's judgment was correct. The act of registration meant that Thomas lost the capacity to deal with the property by way of a sale to a third party. It is of no avail to O'Halloran to say that there was another cause of its failure to make such a sale – namely Thomas' attempt to enforce the contract with Bowes & Brown.

Meagher JA

> [**280**] The company had a valuable asset, O'Halloran neutralised it. Equity will see to it that the value of the asset is restored.

B Recoverability of non-pecuniary loss

The conventional view concerning the recoverability of compensation for non-pecuniary loss for an equitable wrong was that it was irrecoverable. That changed after *Giller v Procopets*,[1] in which the Victorian Court of Appeal held that non-pecuniary loss arising from a breach of confidence, namely for embarrassment and distress, were recoverable for a breach of confidence.

Giller v Procopets (2008) 24 VR 1

Facts and issues

The parties were in a de facto relationship and separated, but continued to be intimate. Procopets (the man) would make videos of their intimacy sessions without Giller's (the woman) consent. Giller initially was unaware of the video-taking, but after she became aware, she continued to be intimate with Procopets. The relationship subsequently terminated and the two separated completely. Procopets threatened Giller that he would reveal the films and videos to her friends and relatives with the intention of harming and embarrassing her, and subsequently did so. Giller sought damages. At issue was whether equitable compensation for Giller's non-pecuniary losses caused by Procopets's breaches of confidence was available. The trial judge found that there was a breach of confidence, but held that equitable compensation was unavailable. Giller appealed.

Decision

Equitable compensation was recoverable for Procopets's breach of confidence.

Neave J

> **[409]** In *Campbell v Mirror Group Newspapers Ltd,* the model, Naomi Campbell, claimed damages for breach of the equitable duty of confidence ... for the distress which she suffered when the defendant newspaper published details of her attendance at Narcotics Anonymous meetings and a photograph of her leaving the premises. The claim succeeded ...
>
> ...
>
> **[417]** In *Cornelius v De Taranto*, a psychiatrist had been consulted by Mrs Cornelius in relation to an employment claim. Without her consent, he sent a copy of his report to her general practitioner and to another consultant psychiatrist. The report expressed the view that she was suffering from a psychiatric condition. The trial judge, Morland J, awarded damages of £3000 to Mrs Cornelius for injury to her feelings caused by the breach of confidence.
>
> ...
>
> **[419]** The Australian position appears to be at large on this issue.
>
> ...
>
> **[423]** Equitable remedies such as injunctions are available to prevent publication of confidential material because of its private nature. It is unnecessary in such applications to

1 (2008) 24 VR 1.

show that, if unrestrained, the breach of confidence will cause financial loss or psychiatric injury. By parity of reasoning, there should be no barrier to the making of an order for equitable compensation to compensate a claimant for the embarrassment or distress she has suffered as the result of a breach of an equitable duty of confidence.

...

[425] Typically, damages have been awarded under Lord Cairns' Act in lieu of an injunction where the defendant has infringed the plaintiff's property rights or has benefited by exploiting commercially valuable information. There is no Australian authority on the issue of whether damages under this head can be awarded to a plaintiff who has suffered distress or embarrassment as a result of the breach of confidence.

...

[428] Damages under Lord Cairns' Act are sui generis, and can be awarded in some circumstances where common law damages are not recoverable. In my view, such damages should be available where the essence of the plaintiff's case is that he or she has been embarrassed by the exposure of private information, rather than that the defendant has profited from the wrongful use of that information. In *Talbot v General Television Corporation Pty Ltd*, Young CJ treated damages under Lord Cairns' Act as compensating the plaintiff for what he or she had lost. It is consistent with that approach to compensate Ms Giller for the mental distress suffered as a result of the defendant's actions.

...

[431] [My] conclusion [is] that damages should be available for breach of confidence occasioning distress, either as equitable compensation or under Lord Cairns' Act.

C Basic measure of equitable compensation

Equitable compensation fundamentally is determined by comparing the plaintiff's actual financial state after the defendant's wrong and the position the plaintiff would have been in without the wrong.[2]

Nocton v Lord Ashburton [1914] AC 932

Facts and issues

Nocton, a solicitor, persuaded his client, Ashburton, to release a charge on property, thereby advancing his own subsequent charge on the same property. At trial, the claim based on deceit was dismissed for want of proof of dishonesty. The issue on appeal was whether relief could be granted in equity in the absence of common law fraud.

2 See *Nocton v Lord Ashburton* [1914] AC 932. Despite the apparent simplicity of this fundamental proposition, the question of assessment for breach of an equitable obligation in truth is often far more complicated, and a careful examination of the cases below must be performed, since the identification of the position that the plaintiff would be in (had there been no breach of an equitable obligation) is itself a multi-nuanced question. The cases discussed below clearly give lie to these difficulties – see, in particular, the discussion of *Target Holdings Ltd v Redferns* [1996]

Decision

As Nocton had breached fiduciary duties, an order for compensation should be made.

Viscount Haldane

[**951**] [In] cases of actual fraud the Courts of Chancery and of Common Law exercised a concurrent jurisdiction from the earliest times …

Operating in personam as a Court of conscience it could order the defendant, not, indeed, in those days, to pay damages as such, but to make restitution, or to compensate the plaintiff by putting him in as good a position pecuniarily as that in which he was before the injury.

But in addition to this concurrent jurisdiction, the Court of Chancery exercised an exclusive jurisdiction in cases which, although classified in that Court as eases of fraud, yet did not necessarily import the element of *dolus malus*. The Court took upon itself to prevent a man from acting against the dictates of conscience as defined by the Court, and to grant injunctions in anticipation of injury, as well as relief where injury had been done. Common instances of this exclusive jurisdiction are cases arising out of breach of duty by persons standing in a fiduciary relation, such as the solicitor to the client.

…

[**953**] Nothing short of proof of a fraudulent [**954**] intention in the strict sense will suffice for an action of deceit

…

But when fraud is referred to in the wider sense in which the books are full of the expression, used in Chancery in describing cases which were within its exclusive jurisdiction, it is a mistake to suppose that an actual intention to cheat must always be proved. A man may misconceive the extent of the obligation which a Court of Equity imposes on him. His fault is that he has violated, however innocently because of his ignorance, an obligation which he must be taken by the Court to have known, and his conduct has in that sense always been called fraudulent, even in such a case as a technical fraud on a power. It was thus that the expression 'constructive fraud' came into existence. …

What it really means in this connection is, not moral fraud in the ordinary sense, but breach of the sort of obligation which is enforced by a Court that from the beginning regarded itself as a Court of conscience.

…

[**956**] When, as in the case before us, a solicitor has had financial transactions with his client, and has handled his money to the extent of using it to pay off a mortgage made to himself, or of getting the client to release from his mortgage a property over which the solicitor by such release has obtained further security for a mortgage of his own, a Court of Equity has always assumed jurisdiction to scrutinize his action. It did not matter that the client would have had a remedy in damages for breach of contract. Courts of Equity had jurisdiction to direct accounts to be taken, and in proper cases to order the solicitor to

AC 421, concerning the exonerating effect of a causally independent non-wrongful event, and the subsequent treatment of the topic, particularly by the High Court in *Youyang Pty Ltd v Minter Ellison Morris Fletcher* (2003) 212 CLR 484.

replace property improperly acquired from the client, or to make compensation if he had lost it by acting in breach of **[957]** a duty which arose out of his confidential relationship to the man who had trusted him. This jurisdiction, which really belonged to the exclusive jurisdiction of the Court of Chancery

...

[958] My Lords, the conclusion at which I have arrived is that this action ought properly to have been treated as one in which the plaintiff had made out a claim for compensation either for loss arising from misrepresentation made in breach of fiduciary duty or for breach of contract to exercise due care and skill.

...

The proper mode of giving relief might have been to order Mr Nocton to restore to the mortgage security what he had procured to be taken out of it, in addition to making good the amount of interest lost by what he did. The measure of damages may not always be the same as in an action of deceit or for negligence. But in this case the question is of form only and is not one which it is necessary to decide.

Agricultural Land Management Ltd v Jackson (No 2) (2014) 48 WAR 1

Facts and issues

The second and third defendants were directors of the plaintiff company, the trustee of a managed investment scheme. In an action for equitable compensation for breach of fiduciary duty relating to the purchase by the plaintiff of certain property, the directors claimed that the duties that they owed were owed to the plaintiff in its own right and that any loss suffered by the plaintiff was in its capacity as trustee and not in its own right. Having determined that the argument was misconceived and that the 'trust' was not a person, and that the duties were owed to the plaintiff as trustee, the question was the basis for the assessment of compensation for the breach.

Decision

The classic 'but for' test of causation applied to the determination of compensation.

Edelman J

[391] The question of the appropriate causal approach in claims for equitable compensation has been the subject of much academic and judicial writing. It is not necessary to embark on that exercise in this case because both counsel in this case proceeded on the basis that the appropriate starting point was to ask whether 'but for' the defendants' breaches Agricultural would have suffered its loss. It is necessary, however, to explain briefly why I am prepared to follow this approach of counsel.

...

[394] Within a 'common sense' approach it has been held that at common law the 'but for' test has an important role to play as a negative criterion. In other words, it is generally necessary, but not always sufficient, for the plaintiff to prove that the plaintiff's loss would not have been suffered but for the defendant's breach of duty.

...

[395] The same negative 'but for' criterion does not apply to all cases where compensation is sought in equity for breach of a fiduciary duty ... [E]quitable claims for substitutive compensation are not concerned with financial loss. It would be nonsense to apply a criterion concerned with whether financial loss would have been suffered but for the breach. Further, in claims for breach of fiduciary duty which are said to be based on a breach of a 'duty' of disclosure a different, and contentious, approach to causation is sometimes applied. But where the claim is not one for substitutive compensation and where there is no plea of failure to disclose some material fact the 'but for' criterion becomes more relevant. Where a claim is brought to recover loss caused by the act of the defendant fiduciary putting himself in a position of conflict then it is very difficult to see why the negative 'but for' criterion should not apply. Why should the defendant fiduciary be required to pay compensation for losses which would have been suffered even if the conflict had not occurred?

[396] This was the approach taken by Ipp J in *Permanent Building Society v Wheeler*, in the context of a claim for equitable compensation for loss caused by a lack of skill and care: 'a court of equity ... should not require an honest but careless trustee to compensate a beneficiary for losses without proof that but for the breach of duty those losses would not have occurred'. The High Court of Australia has also said that for a claim for equitable compensation for loss suffered from breach of fiduciary duty, 'there directly arises a need to specify criteria for a sufficient connection (or 'causation') between breach of duty and ... the loss sustained'. The High Court has subsequently reiterated that the 'basic equitable principle applicable to breach of trust is that the beneficiary is entitled to be compensated for any loss he would not have suffered but for the breach.' And, in a commonly cited and approved passage in McLachlin J's well known minority judgment in *Canson Enterprises Ltd v Boughton & Co,* her Ladyship said that 'it is essential that the losses [from breach of fiduciary duty] made good are only those which, *on a common sense view of causation*, were caused by the breach' (emphasis added). These remarks of McLachlin J were surely intended to refer to the same approach as at common law: it is difficult to see how 'common sense' could be different in common law and equity.

[397] Agricultural sought to prove a causal link between the breaches and its alleged loss by arguing that no reasonable director would have caused Agricultural to enter into the Contract. I accept that if Agricultural had shown this then the negative 'but for' criterion would have been satisfied.... Agricultural has failed to prove that a reasonable director would not have committed a company to the transaction. It has also failed to prove that at the time of the transaction it was not in the best interests of Agricultural to enter it.

REVIEW QUESTIONS

(1) Explain the basis for Neave J's reasoning that Lord Cairns' Act underpinned the grant of relief for emotional distress in *Giller v Procopets* (2008) 24 VR 1.

(2) What is the general approach to the assessment of compensation for a breach of a fiduciary duty?

III Attribution of responsibility

Section II addressed the assessment of equitable compensation, in which the overarching proposition, that the purpose of equitable compensation is to restore persons who have suffered loss to the position they would be in if there had been no breach of an equitable obligation, was explored.

But this overarching proposition is actually multi-nuanced, and the questions of whether the common law test of causation, the conventional 'but for test', should apply, or if the loss should be determined without reference to issues of causation, have arisen frequently. The rules governing attribution of responsibility, which attracts the simpler question of whether the defendant without more is liable for the consequences of the contravention of an equitable obligation, will differ for breach of trust, breach of fiduciary duty, and breach of an equitable duty of care. These are addressed in turn below.

Figure 9.2 The principles relating to the attribution of responsibility when applied to various equitable wrongs

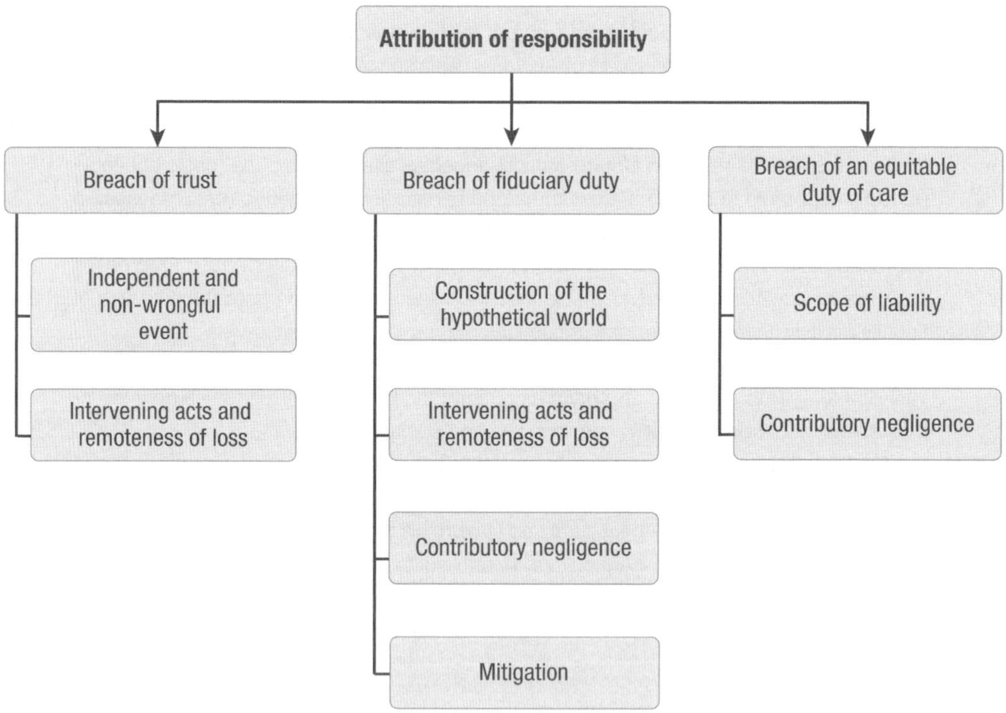

Concept	Short explanation	Relevant authorities	Principles text
Breach of trust: independent non-wrongful event	An independent non-wrongful act that would have inflicted the same loss does not relieve the wrongdoer.	*Re Dawson (Deceased)* [1966] 2 NSWR 211	Chapter 9: [9.18]–[9.38]
	A casually independent non-wrongful event has been held to exonerate the wrongdoer.	*Target Holdings Ltd v Redferns* [1996] AC 421	
	Where the plaintiff's loss can still be attributed to the defendant's breach, then the casually independent non-wrongful event might not exonerate the wrongdoer.	*Youyang Pty Ltd v Minter Ellison Morris Fletcher* (2003) 212 CLR 484	
	Under the concept of substitutive compensation, the fiduciary is required to replenish the trust fund regardless of any loss suffered.	*Agricultural Land Management Ltd v Jackson (No 2)* (2014) 48 WAR 1	
Breach of trust: intervening acts and remoteness of loss	Foreseeability of loss is generally irrelevant – though the loss must still flow from the breach.	*AIB Group (UK) plc v Mark Redler & Co Solicitors* [2015] AC 1503	Chapter 9: [9.39]–[9.42]
Breach of fiduciary duty: construction of the hypothetical world	Where the fiduciary commits a breach of fiduciary duty, they are not relieved from liability even if disclosure would not have altered the constituent's ('beneficiary's') decision.	*Brickenden v London Loan & Savings Co* [1934] 3 DLR 465	Chapter 9: [9.43]–[9.53]
	The *Principle in Brickenden's Case* would operate where a conflict of duty arose, giving rise to compensation for breach of fiduciary duty.	*Commonwealth Bank of Australia v Smith* (1991) 42 FCR 390	
Breach of fiduciary duty: intervening acts and remoteness of loss	One approach to the question of causation is that when a breach of fiduciary duty is shown, there is something akin to a presumption of a causal link to the loss.	*Hodgkinson v Simms* [1994] 3 SCR 377	Chapter 9: [9.54]–[9.61]
	Equitable compensation for breach of fiduciary duty is generally not limited by considerations of foreseeability and remoteness but based on a 'common sense' test of causation must have still caused the loss.	*Canson Enterprises Ltd v Boughton & Co* [1991] 3 SCR 534	

Concept	Short explanation	Relevant authorities	Principles text
Breach of fiduciary duty: contributory negligence	It is unlikely that the plaintiff's contributory negligence would exonerate a breach of fiduciary duty in Australia.	*Pilmer v Duke Group Ltd (in liq)* (2007) 207 CLR 165	Chapter 9: [9.62]–[9.66]
Breach of fiduciary duty: mitigation	The common law view of mitigation is likely to be rejected in Australia, but the principal's failure to take obvious steps to alleviate loss might yet sever the causal link between the breach and the loss.	*Canson Enterprises Ltd v Boughton & Co* [1991] 3 SCR 534	Chapter 9: [9.67]–[9.69]
Breach of an equitable duty of care: scope of liability	On one view, the equitable duty of care is subject to the same limiting factors as with a common law duty of care.	*Permanent Building Society (in liq) v Wheeler* (1994) 11 WAR 187	Chapter 9: [9.70]–[9.76]
	This view has been adopted by the English Court of Appeal.	*Bristol and West Building Society v Mothew* [1998] Ch 1	
Breach of an equitable duty of care: contributory negligence	It is presently unclear if equitable compensation can be reduced by the plaintiff's contributory negligence.	*Youyang Pty Ltd v Minter Ellison Morris Fletcher* (2003) 212 CLR 484	Chapter 9: [9.77]–[9.79]

A Breach of trust

The principles governing the assessment of loss resulting from a breach of trust appear at first blush to be inconsistent. One view is that the defaulting trustee is obliged to effect 'restitution' or 'substitutive compensation'[3] and that in this instance causation is not a consideration.[4] This view has not been universally accepted, with the House of Lords recognising the exonerating effect of a causally independent non-wrongful event.[5] The House of Lords' view, although cited with approval by the High Court of Australia in *Youyang Pty Ltd v Minter Ellison Morris Fletcher*,[6] was distinguished on the facts in that case.

On the other hand, the obligation to effect 'restitution' is said not to apply in the type of case where the default of the trustee leads to their obligation to compensate for the loss caused by a breach of trust. In the latter case, compensation is payable on the basis of

3 It is described as such because it is a substitute for the return of the property – see S Elliott, 'Remoteness Criteria in Equity' (2002) 65(4) *Modern Law Review* 588, 590; S Elliott and C Mitchell, 'Remedies for Dishonest Assistance' (2004) 67(1) *Modern Law Review* 16, 23–4; J Edelman and S Elliott, 'Money Remedies against Trustees' (2004) 18(3) *Tolley's Trust Law International* 116, 116–25; D Hayton, P Matthews and C Mitchell, *Underhill and Hayton: Law Relating to Trusts and Trustees* (LexisNexis, 19th ed, 2016) [87.7]–[87.11]; principles text [9.19].

4 Street J stated that in this circumstance 'considerations of causation … do not readily enter into the matter': *Re Dawson (Deceased)* [1966] 2 NSWR 211, 215.

5 *Target Holdings Ltd v Redferns* [1996] AC 421.

6 (2003) 212 CLR 484.

'reparative compensation' where concepts of factual causation do apply. The fundamental differences between the two types of compensation were specifically addressed by Edelman J (then a judge of the Supreme Court of Western Australia) in *Agricultural Land Management Ltd v Jackson (No 2)*[7] where he explained the respective bases for the 'two different types of "compensation" for breach of trust'.[8]

1 Independent non-wrongful event

Whether an independent non-wrongful event might relieve the wrongdoer is a highly nuanced question. Different approaches have been adopted.

Re Dawson (Deceased) [1966] 2 NSWR 211

Facts and issues

PSD, a trustee of the New Zealand assets of a deceased estate, improperly paid away NZ£4700, which was then lost to the trust estate. At the time there was parity between the Australian and New Zealand currency, but at the time of the proceedings, NZ£4700 was worth A$5829. The issue concerned which value was to be adopted to calculate the estate's loss.

Decision

The trustee was obliged to make good the losses as if no breach had taken place, which then required it to take into account the value of New Zealand currency as against Australian currency as of the date of judgment, which would then have restored the trust to the position it would have been in had no breach occurred.

Street J

> [**214**] The obligation of a defaulting trustee is essentially one of effecting a restitution to the estate. The obligation is of a personal character and its extent is not to be limited by common law principles governing remoteness of damage. In *Caffrey v Darby*, trustees were charged with neglect in failing to recover possession of part of the trust assets. The assets were lost and it was argued by the trustees that the loss was not attributable to their neglect. The Master of the Rolls, in stating his reasons, asked 'will they be relieved from that by the circumstances that the loss has ultimately happened by something that is not a direct and immediate consequence of their negligence?' His [**215**] answer to this question was that, even supposing that 'they could not look to the possibility' of the actual event which occasioned the loss, yet, if they have already been guilty of negligence they must be responsible for any loss in any way to that property; for whatever may be the immediate cause the property would not have been in a situation to sustain that loss if it had not been for their negligence. If they had taken possession of the property it would not have been in

7 (2014) 48 WAR 1.

8 Ibid [334].

> his possession. If the loss had happened by fire, lightning, or any other accident, that would not be an excuse for them, if guilty of previous negligence. That was their fault.
>
> ...
>
> The principles embodied in this approach do not appear to involve any inquiry as to whether the loss was caused by or flowed from the breach. Rather the inquiry in each instance would appear to be whether the loss would have happened if there had been no breach.
>
> ...
>
> Authority for the form of relief being such as to require an actual restoration to the estate or to place it monetarily in the same position as if there had been an actual restoration is not lacking.
>
> ...
>
> [**217**] ... I regard the present defendant as entitled to require the plaintiff to make good to the estate the £4700 taken in 1939 in New Zealand. This was in fact taken in the form of New Zealand currency.

Target Holdings Ltd v Redferns [1996] AC 421

Facts and issues

Redferns, a firm of solicitors, acted for Target Holdings Ltd ('Target'), who was mortgagee for monies to be loaned to Crowngate to buy property. Redferns were instructed to not release the money until the purchase was completed and the mortgage executed. Until then, Redferns were to hold the money on trust for Target. Breaching their instructions, Redferns released £1 490 000 to a company called Panther Ltd. The venture was not successful. Crowngate failed to repay the loan and went into liquidation. Subsequently, Target sold the property for only £50 000.

Target sued Redferns, claiming compensation based on the entire loss on the venture less the sum realised upon sale of the property.

Decision

Target received the security required and it was not entitled to the recovery of the sums claimed.

Lord Browne-Wilkinson

> [**437**] A trustee who wrongly pays away trust money, like a trustee who makes an unauthorised investment, commits a breach of trust and comes under an immediate duty to remedy such breach. If immediate proceedings are brought, the court will make an immediate order requiring restoration to the trust fund of the assets wrongly distributed or, in the case of an unauthorised investment, will order the sale of the unauthorised investment and the payment of compensation for any loss suffered. But the fact that there is an accrued cause of action as soon as the breach is committed does not in my judgment mean that the quantum of the compensation payable is ultimately fixed as at the date when the breach

occurred. The quantum is fixed at the date of judgment at which date, according to the circumstances then pertaining, the compensation is assessed at the figure then necessary to put the trust estate or the beneficiary back into the position it would have been in had there been no breach. I can see no justification for 'stopping the clock' immediately in some cases but not in others: to do so may, as in this case, lead to compensating the trust estate or the beneficiary for a loss which, on the facts known at trial, it has never suffered.

Moreover, in my judgment the distinction is not consistent with the decision in *Re Dawson.* In that case a testator had established separate executors for his New Zealand and his Australian estates. In 1939 the New Zealand estate was under the administration of attorneys for, amongst others, PSD. PSD arranged that NZ£4700 should be withdrawn from the New Zealand estate and paid away to a stranger, X, who in turn was supposed to lend the moneys to an Australian company in which PSD was interested. X absconded with the money. In that case, therefore, the trust money had been paid away to a stranger. Street J. had to decide whether the liability of PSD to compensate the estate was to be satisfied by paying sufficient Australian pounds to buy NZ£4700 at the rate of exchange at the date of breach (when there was parity between the two currencies) or at the date of judgment (when the Australian pound had depreciated against the New Zealand pound). He held that the rate of exchange was to be taken as at the date of judgment. Although, contrary to the present case, this decision favoured the beneficiaries at the expense of the defaulting trustee, the principle is of general application whether operating to the benefit or the detriment of the beneficiaries. The equitable compensation for breach of trust has to be assessed as at the date of judgment and not at an earlier date.

...

[**439**] Equitable compensation for breach of trust is designed to achieve exactly what the word compensation suggests: to make good a loss in fact suffered by the beneficiaries and which, using hindsight and common sense, can be seen to have been caused by the breach.

...

[**440**] ... Target has not demonstrated that it is entitled to any compensation for breach of trust ... Target obtained exactly what it would have obtained had no breach occurred, i.e., a valid security for the sum advanced. ... Target has suffered no compensatable loss.

Youyang Pty Ltd v Minter Ellison Morris Fletcher (2003) 212 CLR 484

Facts and issues

Youyang Pty Ltd ('Youyang') paid $500 000 to Minter Ellison Morris Fletcher ('Minter', a firm of solicitors). Minter received the money as a trustee, with instructions to pay it as a subscription to EC Consolidated Capital Ltd ('ECCCL') and to obtain a bearer deposit certificate to secure the sum paid to ECCCL. Instead, Minter (in breach of trust) paid the money out against a deposit certificate but not a bearer deposit certificate, which did not provide Youyang with security. ECCCL went insolvent and Youyang lost its investment. The question was the extent to which Youyang was entitled to compensation against the solicitors.

Decision

Minter were liable for all Youyang's loss, attributing Youyang's loss to the solicitors' breach of trust.

Gleeson CJ, McHugh, Gummow, Kirby and Hayne JJ

[32] Perhaps the most important duty of a trustee is to obey the terms of the trust. On 24 September 1993 there were several breaches by Minters of the trust obligations it had undertaken to Youyang. First, Minters released the trust moneys as to $256 800 for the purchase from DAL of what was not the requisite certificate of deposit. Secondly, the balance of $221 558.56 remaining after an appropriation by Minters of $21 641.44 was paid out of Minters' trust account to ECCCL in breach of the obligation of Minters not to do so unless the payment to DAL had procured the requisite certificate of deposit. The payment to Minters appears to have been in discharge of indebtedness to the firm by ECCCL. It stands in no better light than the larger sum which ECCCL received. The result is that the whole of the $500 000 was dealt with by Minters in breach of its duties as trustee.

...

[33] The rigour of the rule, as Augustine Birrell QC put it, that it is the duty of a trustee 'to adhere to the terms of his trust in all things great and small, important, and seemingly unimportant'.

...

[43] The essence of Youyang's complaint is shortly identified. It is the misapplication of the moneys held on trust on terms that, in the events that happened, obliged Minters to hold the moneys absolutely for Youyang and at its direction. To adapt what was said by Fry LJ in *Webb v Stenton*, Minters has made itself 'personally liable to pay money to [Youyang] by reason of some breach of trust or default in the performance of [its] duties as trustee'.

[44] This appeal turns upon the significance for the facts of the causal requirement expressed by Fry LJ in the phrase 'by reason of'. That serves to remind, as Mummery LJ recently put it, that '[t]here is no equitable by-pass of the need to establish causation' and that '[i]n questions of causation it is important to focus on the relevant equitable duty' (citation omitted). This raises considerations having an affinity to those which determined the outcome in *Target Holdings*.

Target Holdings

[45] *Target Holdings* concerned the misapplication by the solicitors for a finance company of moneys held by the solicitors on a bare trust for their client. The solicitors had received moneys from their client to be held on trust, subject to any contrary instructions of the client, to pay to or to the order of the proposed mortgagor and borrower from the client; payment out was to occur only when the property in question had been conveyed to the mortgagor and the mortgagor had executed charges in favour of the client. The solicitors acted in breach of trust in paying out the moneys prematurely and before the conditions had been satisfied, and were liable to account. However, ultimately, the property was conveyed to the mortgagor and the charges were duly executed. That was an important circumstance and one that differs from the present case.

...

[46] The litigation in *Target Holdings* arose when it transpired the mortgaged property, on subsequent exercise by the client of its power of sale, was worth far less than the moneys disbursed by the solicitors. The client brought an action claiming restitution of the entire moneys held by the solicitors (£1.525 million).

...

[47] The breach of trust committed by the solicitors in *Target Holdings* left the client in exactly the same position as if there had been no breach; if the instructions had been obeyed, the transaction still would have gone ahead and the client suffered a loss represented by the difference between the amount advanced on security and the amount realised from the security. That loss would have been caused by the fraud of third parties.

[48] The present case is distinguishable from *Target Holdings* in at least two respects. First, Youyang was not the client of Minters, although Minters was trustee of the moneys for it. Secondly, the proposed commercial transaction, involving the provision of security to Youyang, was not after delay, as in *Target Holdings*, completed; the security was never provided and Minters should not have disbursed Youyang's moneys.

...

[51] ... Youyang submits that it would not have suffered the loss of $500 000 but for the breaches of trust by Minters. Youyang's submissions should be accepted.

NOTE

The High Court in *Youyang* did not dissent from the reasoning in *Target Holdings*, whereby Target was not entitled to the losses caused by Crowngate's failed venture. The *Youyang* High Court, however (distinguishing *Target Holdings*), explained that, contrary to the case before them, Target was provided with the security. Subsequently, in *Agricultural Land Management Ltd v Jackson*, Edelman J adopted the concept of *substitutive* compensation and pointed out (in [354]) that *Youyang* had been argued as a case of reparative compensation, and that on the facts, the 'but for' test of causation had not been made out. Edelman J opined also, in [358] of his reasons, that the adoption of the 'but for test' of causation countenanced by the *Youyang* High Court should be seen in the light of those matters (that it had actually been argued as a case of reparative compensation where issues of causation *would* be considered).

Agricultural Land Management Ltd v Jackson (No 2) (2014) 48 WAR 1

Facts and issues

These are set out on page 326. The question discussed below was whether substitutive rather than reparative compensation should be adopted as the basis for compensation.

Decision

The concept of substitutive compensation should be adopted, but on the facts the claim was not made out.

Edelman J

[333] Agricultural has failed to prove that either or both of the promised purchase price or the promised Licence fee under the Contract were at an undervalue in relation to the rights which Agricultural obtained in exchange. Perhaps in anticipation of this difficulty Agricultural framed its case for equitable compensation for breach of fiduciary duty in two different ways. One way focuses upon compensation for loss suffered. The other way permits compensation in the absence of any loss, to restore any unauthorised disposition of assets.

16.1 Two different types of 'compensation' for breach of trust

[334] Historically, the mechanism by which equity courts generally gave effect to monetary remedies against custodial fiduciaries was through orders which followed a process of accounting. The manner in which an account was taken reflected the nature of the ultimate remedy which might be sought. Three different forms of account were (i) the account of administration in common form, (ii) the account on the basis of wilful default, and (iii) the account of profits.

[335] In relation to the account in common form, if the evidence disclosed an unauthorised disbursement then the plaintiff could 'falsify' the unauthorised entry. The falsification would have the effect of creating a deficit between the account and the fund. The custodial fiduciary would be required to replenish the fund to that extent.

[336] When an account in common form was sought, it did not matter whether the dissipation of the asset would have occurred even without the unauthorised act. The analogy for an account in common form is with specific performance or a common law action in debt …

[337] When payment was sought following an account in common form there was a direct analogy with an order for specific performance or payment of a liquidated debt which was due. In each case it is no answer for the defendant to allege that the plaintiff had suffered no loss.

[338] The 'compensation' order following the common account required the defendant to perform his or her duty to maintain the trust fund in an authorised manner. It was not a sufficient response to a disallowance, or falsification, that the disbursement would have been lost even if the trustee had acted properly.

…

[341] As Lord Millett explained in *Libertarian Investments Ltd v Hall*

> Where the defendant is ordered to make good the deficit by the payment of money, the award is sometimes described as the payment of equitable compensation; but it is not compensation for loss but restitutionary or restorative. The amount of the award is measured by the objective value of the property lost determined at the date when the account is taken and with the full benefit of hindsight.'

...

[343] The language of 'restitution' and 'restoration' associated with the common account was used by Street J in *Re Dawson*. One issue in that case was the extent of the liability of a trustee to repay trust funds in New Zealand dollars which had been improperly paid out at a time when the New Zealand dollar was at parity with the Australian dollar. Justice Street held that the trustee was required to restore the trust funds at the higher rate which prevailed at the time of trial. His Honour spoke of 'monetary compensation … paid in lieu of restoring assets'. He explained that the 'form of relief is couched in terms appropriate to require the defaulting trustee to restore to the estate the assets of which he deprived it'. Justice Street also explained that '[c]onsiderations of causation, foreseeability and remoteness do not readily enter into the matter

[344] There is, however, some confusion which has arisen from the statement by Street J that 'if a breach has been committed then the trustee is liable to place the trust estate in the same position as it would have been in if no breach had been committed'. This appears to contemplate a test for causation which examines the situation 'but for' the breach. But, as I have explained, that 'but for' question is irrelevant when the duty is to replenish a distribution of unauthorised trust funds. Like instances of payment of a debt, or of specific performance, it does not matter whether the funds would have been lost in any event.

...

[348] … The historic difference between a claim based upon falsification of a common account and a claim based on surcharge of an account on the basis of wilful default has been concealed in modern cases which generally refer to both as 'equitable compensation'. Even in the leading decision of Street J in *Re Dawson* reference is made to equitable compensation claims which were concerned with loss and which would have historically been treated as based upon wilful default. Those cases are of a fundamentally different character from cases of restoration on a common account. In wilful default claims, the claim is in the nature of a claim based on *breach* by a trustee. And the account taken on the basis of wilful default asks whether loss has been suffered.

[349] Dr Elliott … has suggested the use of the labels 'substitutive compensation' and 'reparative compensation' to differentiate the two types of claim. The former … describes a claim for the substituted value of the asset dissipated without authority: it demands that the trustee perform his or her duty to maintain the assets or fund. The latter, based on the account on the basis of wilful default, describes a claim for reparation for the loss suffered by breach of duty.

...

[354] The appeal to the High Court was argued as a claim for reparation of loss. On appeal to the High Court, senior counsel for the solicitors in breach submitted that the 'issue is whether the required causal connection between breach and loss was established'.

...

[357] The High Court [in *Youyang*] did not reject the 'but for' test which had been applied by the New South Wales Court of Appeal. Instead, the High Court held that the trial judge had not made the causation finding asserted by Handley JA …

[358] This appears to endorse the possibility of a 'but for' causation test which, subject to an evidentiary onus on the defaulting party, requires a plaintiff to prove that the

> unauthorised action would, if requested, have been authorised. But these comments must be understood in the light that
>
> (i) the case was not argued as a substitutive compensation case,
> (ii) the High Court did not need to decide this point …

His Honour held that on the facts Agricultural could not succeed on a claim for substitutive compensation.

2 Intervening acts and remoteness of loss

The fundamental concept is that foreseeability of loss for a breach of trust is not relevant to recovery.

AIB Group (UK) plc v Mark Redler & Co Solicitors [2015] AC 1503

Facts and issues

AIB Group (UK) ('AIB') provided the Sondhis with a business loan of £3.3 million, to be secured by a mortgage over their home, which was valued at £4.25 million. There was a first legal charge on the house in favour of Barclays Bank for £1.5 million. AIB's condition for the remortgage was that Barclays' first charge would be redeemed. Redler ('the Solicitors') acted for both AIB and the Sondhis. At settlement, the Solicitors mistakenly under-calculated the mortgage discharge amount by £300 000.00. Barclays refused to release its first charge unless it was paid in full and AIB had to register as a second mortgage. The Sondhis defaulted, and Barclays repossessed the home, which was sold for £1.2 million, of which AIB received £867 697 – leaving a shortfall of £2.5 million. The trial judge awarded £273 377 by way of equitable compensation. The issue on appeal concerned the basis of AIB's compensation; AIB sought compensation in the full amount of its shortfall, £2.5 million, while the Solicitors argued the amount ordered by the trial judge was the correct amount.

Decision

The applicable concept of compensation was restorative compensation, to 'restore' the trustee to the position it would have been but for the trustee's default; this was the sum awarded by the trial judge.

Lord Toulson

> **[43]** [Counsel] submitted on behalf of the solicitors that the Court of Appeal was right to see the case in terms of causation of loss, and it was also right in concluding that the proper measure of the bank's loss was the difference between its actual financial position and the position in which it would have been if the solicitors had not acted in breach of trust. On the findings of the trial judge, the loss to the bank (excluding interest) was the amount by

which the value of its security was less than it should have been, which was the same as the amount of the overpayment to the borrowers and underpayment to Barclays.

...

[48] In the present case the solicitors ... acted in breach of trust when they released to the borrowers the money advanced by the bank, less a part of the sum required to redeem the Barclays mortgage ...

...

[49] The determination of this appeal involves two essential questions. The more important question in the appeal is whether Lord Browne-Wilkinson s statement in *Target Holdings* of the fundamental principles which guided him in that case should be ... reinterpreted. Depending on the answer to that question, the second is whether the Court of Appeal properly applied the correct principles to the facts of the case.

...

[56] The main criticism advanced against Lord Browne-Wilkinson's approach in *Target Holdings* is that ... he treated equitable compensation in too broad-brush a fashion, muddling claims for restitutive compensation with claims for reparative compensation.

[57] The relevant principle, it is suggested, in a case of unauthorised dissipation of trust funds is that the amount of the award is measured by the objective value of the property lost determined at the date when the account is taken and with the benefit of hindsight, per Lord Millett NPJ in *Libertarian Investments Ltd v Hall.*

[58] This argument has the approval of Edelman J in *Agricultural Land Management Ltd v Jackson (No 2)* ... It is good sense and good law that if a trustee makes an unauthorised disbursement of trust funds, it is no defence to a claim by the beneficiary for the trustee to say that if he had not misapplied the funds they would have been stolen by a stranger. In such a case the actual loss has been caused by the trustee. The hypothetical loss which would otherwise have occurred through the stranger's intervention would have been a differently caused loss, for which that other person would have been liable.

...

[64] The basic right of a beneficiary is to have the trust duly administered in accordance with the provisions of the trust instrument ... Where there has been a breach of that duty, the basic purpose of any remedy will be either to put the beneficiary in the same position as if the breach had not occurred or to vest in the beneficiary any profit which the trustee may have made by reason of the breach ... Placing the beneficiary in the same position as he would have been in but for the breach may involve restoring the value of something lost by the breach or making good financial damage caused by the breach. But a monetary award which reflected neither loss caused nor profit gained by the wrongdoer would be penal.

[65] The purpose of a restitutionary order is to replace a loss to the trust fund which the trustee has brought about. To say that there has been a loss to the trust fund in the present case of £2.5 m by reason of the solicitor's conduct, when most of that sum would have been lost if the solicitors had applied the trust fund in the way that the bank had instructed them to do, is to adopt an artificial and unrealistic view of the facts.

...

[135] The measure of compensation should therefore normally be assessed at the date of trial, with the benefit of hindsight. The foreseeability of loss is generally irrelevant, but the loss must be caused by the breach of trust, in the sense that it must flow directly from it.

NOTE

The differences in the reasoning in *Re Dawson (Deceased); Target Holdings Ltd v Redferns; Youyang Pty Ltd v Minter Ellison Morris Fletcher; Agricultural Land Management Ltd v Jackson (No 2);* and *AIB Group (UK) plc v Mark Redler & Co Solicitors* all give lie to variations in the selection of the bases of equitable compensation, well-illustrated in *AIB Group (UK) plc v Mark Redler & Co Solicitors*, where Lord Toulson described Lord Browne-Wilkinson's reasoning in *Target Holdings* thus:

> The main criticism advanced against Lord Browne-Wilkinson's approach in *Target Holdings* is that … he treated equitable compensation in too broad-brush a fashion, muddling claims for restitutive compensation with claims for reparative compensation.

Clearly, the faultline between restitutive and reparative compensation is troublesome. Table 9.1 clarifies the distinction between the two types of compensation.

Table 9.1 Comparison of restitutive and reparative compensation

	Restitutive compensation	Reparative compensation
Purpose	Also termed 'substitutive' compensation, restitutive compensation serves to replenish the trust fund of funds dissipated by the defaulting trustee, irrespective of the loss suffered – per Edelman J, *Agricultural Land Management*; Lord Toulson, *AIB Group (UK) plc v Mark Redler & Co Solicitors* [2015] AC 1503.	Reparative compensation serves to compensate the innocent party, by giving effect to the trustee's secondary obligation to compensate loss caused by breach of trust – as explained by Edelman J in *Agricultural Land Management*.
Guiding principle	To assess the loss by reference to the objective value of the property lost.	To base the compensation by reference to the loss suffered by reason of the trustee's default.
Relevance of the 'but for' test	By parity of reasoning with payment of a debt, the question of whether 'but for' the breach the loss would have been incurred is not a relevant consideration.	By contrast with restitutive compensation, reparative compensation is a claim for the loss suffered by the breach of the trustee's duty and would attract the classic 'but for' test of causation.

B Breach of fiduciary duty

The topic of 'compensation for breach of fiduciary duty' is addressed in four parts:

(1) 'construction of the hypothetical world' explores the actual world in which defendant's wrong occurred compared to the hypothetical world if the wrong did not occur

(2) 'intervening acts and remoteness of loss' where the clear view is that questions of foreseeability and remoteness do not limit the wrongdoer's liability, but the exonerating effect of intervening acts is more problematic

(3) contributory negligence and

(4) mitigation.

1 Construction of the hypothetical world

This invokes the important question of whether if, hypothetically, the fiduciary had made disclosure, this would have relieved the fiduciary of liability.

Brickenden v London Loan & Savings Co [1934] 3 DLR 465

Facts and issues

Brickenden (a firm of solicitors, the appellant) acted for both the borrower and lender in a loan transaction. Brickenden failed to inform the lender, London Loan & Savings Co ('London Loan'), that part of the loan was to be used to repay loans that Brickenden had granted to the borrower (Mr and Mrs Biggs) secured by mortgages over the same land. Those mortgages were worthless since there were prior mortgages, which exhausted the value of the land, as a consequence of which London Loan received a worthless security. The issue was whether the lender would still have granted the loan had it known that part of the loan would be paid out to repay loans that Brickenden had granted to the borrower – and, if so, if this exonerated Brickenden from the consequences of their breach of fiduciary duty in failing to inform London Loan that part of the loan was to be used to discharge loans granted by Brickenden.

Decision

Brickenden did not argue that the lender would still have granted the loan had it known that part of the loan would be used by Brickenden to repay loans which the solicitor had granted to the borrower. However, in any event, in a famous decision, the Privy Council held that once it was determined that the non-disclosed facts were material, what the lender would have done had it known the non-disclosed facts was immaterial.

Lord Thankerton

> **[3]** The appellant admittedly acted as solicitor for Biggs and his wife in this transaction; … The appellant was thus acting as solicitor to both parties in the matter of the $13 500 loan, and he was personally interested as regards the mortgages for $5000, $2000 and $1200. …The appellant's loans of $2000 and $1200 were not disclosed in either the application or the certificate of title. …
>
> **[4]** Their Lordships are clearly of opinion that the appellant's non-disclosure of these two mortgages was a breach of his duty as solicitor to the Loan Company, particularly in view of his personal interest in them …
>
> **[5]** When a party, holding a fiduciary relationship, commits a breach of his duty by non-disclosure of material facts, which his constituent is entitled to know in connection with the transaction, he cannot be heard to maintain that disclosure would not have altered the decision to proceed with the transaction, because the constituent's action would be solely determined by some other factor, such as the valuation by another party of the property proposed to be mortgaged. Once the Court has determined that the non-disclosed facts were material, speculation as to what course the constituent, on disclosure, would have taken is not relevant.

NOTE

The content of this paragraph has become eponymously known as the '*Principle in Brickenden's Case*' in legal academic commentary.

Commonwealth Bank of Australia v Smith (1991) 42 FCR 390

Facts and issues

The Commonwealth Bank of Australia ('the Bank', the appellant) advised Smith in the purchase of a business while the vendor was a customer of the appellant. The advice was wrong, and Smith suffered loss. It was held that while the Bank may be expected to act in its own interests in ensuring the security of its position, the expectation that it would advise in the customer's interests gave rise to a fiduciary duty. Although the respondent was informed of the Bank's relationship to the vendor, the Bank did not disclose the full extent of its conflict of duty in acting for Smith as well as the vendor. The question then arose whether it was open for the Bank to argue that disclosure would not have altered Smith's decision to continue with the transaction.

Decision

Applying the *Principle in Brickenden's Case*, having determined that the non-disclosure was material, the Bank could not maintain that disclosure would not have altered the decision to continue with the transaction.

Davies, Sheppard and Gummow JJ

> [**392**] The crucial incident of the fiduciary relationship in this case arose from the conflicting interests between the two sets of customers of the bank ... Not only must the fiduciary avoid, without informed consent, placing himself in a position of conflict between duty and personal interest, but he must eschew conflicting engagements.
>
> [**393**] Counsel for the appellants relied strongly on the disclosure which Mr Dungan made. At an early stage he told them of his relationship with the vendor and of the existence of a conflict. In counsel's submission, that was sufficient. The difficulty with that submission is that the matter did not stop there. Mr Dungan did not tell the respondents to go to someone else for advice. On the contrary, he persuaded them not to do so. He did his best to encourage them not to see either an accountant or a hotel broker. He did encourage them to go to the solicitor for the vendor, but with the unfortunate result that the solicitor was in a position of conflict. Had Mr and Mrs Smith sought advice from that solicitor about the merits of the transaction, the solicitor would have been in an impossible position. This is because the acceptance of the double engagement would have placed the solicitor in a dilemma.
>
> ...
>
> The failure of Mr Dungan to act in the manner indicated in that passage leads equity to afford its remedies for breach of duty, including that of compensation

Here the Court set out the *Principle in Brickenden's Case*, reproduced in full on page 353.

2 Intervening acts and remoteness of loss

This section explores the proposition that if a breach of fiduciary duty is established, something akin to a presumption of a causal link to the loss might be established.

Hodgkinson v Simms [1994] 3 SCR 377

Facts and issues

Simms, a tax accountant, had expertise in multi-unit residential buildings ('MURBs'). In 1980, Hodgkinson retained Simms's services in tax planning. Simms recommended four MURB projects to Hodgkinson. Hodgkinson invested in those projects. Simms did not disclose that he was in a financial relationship with the developers. The more MURBs Simms sold, the larger the fees he was paid by the developers. The investments were unsuccessful, and Hodgkinson lost money. The issue was the extent of the liability flowing from Simms's non-disclosure.

Decision

Simms had not adduced 'concrete' evidence that his non-disclosure did not cause Hodgkinson's loss and was found liable for all his losses.

La Forest J

> [**441**] Where the plaintiff has made out a case of non-disclosure and the loss occasioned thereby is established, the onus is on the defendant to prove that the innocent victim would have suffered the same loss regardless of the breach; see *London Loan & Savings Co of Canada v Brickenden*; This Court recently affirmed the same principle with respect to damages at common law in the context of negligent misrepresentation; see *Rainbow Industrial Caterers Ltd v Canadian National Railway Co* [1991] 3 SCR 3 at 14–17 … In *Rainbow*, Sopinka J … had this to say:
>
> > The plaintiff is the innocent victim of a misrepresentation which has induced a change of position. It is just that the plaintiff should be entitled to say 'but for the tortious conduct of the defendant, I would not have changed my position'. A tortfeasor who says, 'Yes, but you would have assumed a position other than the *status quo ante*', and thereby asks a court to find a transaction whose terms are hypothetical and speculative, should bear the burden of displacing the plaintiff's assertion of the *status quo ante*.
>
> [**442**] Further, mere 'speculation' on the part of the defendant will not suffice. In the present case the respondent has adduced no concrete evidence to 'displac[e] the plaintiff's assertion of the *status quo ante*', and this submission must, therefore, be dismissed.
>
> The respondent also argued that even assuming the appellant would not have invested had proper disclosure been made, the non-disclosure was not the proximate cause of the appellant's loss. Rather, he continued, the appellant's loss was caused by the general economic recession that hit the British Columbia real estate market in the early 1980s.

The respondent submits that it is grossly unjust to hold him accountable for losses that, he maintains, have no causal relation to the breach of fiduciary duty he perpetrated on the appellant.

...

[**443**] Contrary to the respondent's submission, this result is not affected by the ratio of this Court's decision in *Canson Enterprises*, *supra*. *Canson* held that a court exercising equitable jurisdiction is not precluded from considering the principles of remoteness, causation, and intervening act where necessary to reach a just and fair result. *Canson* does not, however, signal a retreat from the principle of full restitution; rather it recognizes the fact that a breach of a fiduciary duty can take a variety of forms, and as such a variety of remedial considerations may be appropriate.

...

[**445**] In the present case the duty the respondent breached was directly related to the risk that materialized and in fact caused the appellant's loss. The respondent had been retained specifically to seek out and make independent recommendations of suitable investments for the appellant. This agreement gave the respondent a kind of influence or discretion over the appellant in that, as the trial judge found, he effectively chose the risks to which the appellant would be exposed based on investments which in his expert opinion coincided with the appellant's overall investment objectives.

Canson Enterprises Ltd v Boughton & Co [1991] 3 SCR 534

Facts and issues

The respondents were Boughton & Co ('Boughton', a firm of solicitors), Wollen, Treit, Treit Land Consultants Inc, Pacific Mortgage Corporation Ltd, Wilkins, Sun-Mark Development Corporation ('Sun-Mark') and Peregrine Ventures Inc ('Peregrine').

Canson Enterprises ('Canson') and Peregrine formed a joint venture to purchase and develop a property. The joint venture partners agreed to pay Treit a commission of 15 per cent on resale. Unknown to Canson, but, known to Peregrine, Treit had arranged for an intermediate company, Sun-Mark, to share in the profit from the sale to be shared with Treit. This profit would come about because Sun-Mark had entered an agreement to buy the land from the vendors for $410 000. The purchasers paid $525 000 and the secret profit to Peregrine and Treit was therefore $115 000.

Wollen, a solicitor at Boughton, acted for the purchasers and for Sun-Mark in the purchase and resale of the property, but did not disclose those facts to Canson. Wollen paid the $115 000.00 secret profit to Sun-Mark,

The joint venture was not a success. In addition, due to the negligence of soil engineers engaged by the joint venture partners, extensive damage was caused to the building, causing losses. The soil engineering firm was found liable in negligence, but was unable to pay the damages ordered. The mortgage company from which the joint venture partners borrowed funds foreclosed on the property. Canson suffered a shortfall on the venture of $801 290.00.

Canson sued Wollen and Boughton for the shortfall, alleging that the failure to disclose the secret profits was a breach of fiduciary duty.

The issues included: did the breaches of fiduciary duty cause the losses claimed?

Decision

Per McLachin J, based on a common sense view, the breach of fiduciary duty had not caused the loss resulting from the negligence of the soil engineers. This view has the support of Australian courts.[9]

McLachin J

> **[542]** This case concerns the extent of a solicitor's obligation for breach of fiduciary duty in failing to disclose that a third party was making a secret profit in the plaintiff's purchase of land. More particularly, it raises the question of whether the plaintiff can hold the solicitor liable for loss suffered by the plaintiff due to the negligence of architects and engineers in subsequent construction on the land.
>
> …
>
> **[547]** I come to the central question in this case. What is the ambit of compensation as an equitable remedy? Proceeding in trust, we start from the traditional obligation of a defaulting trustee, which is to effect restitution to the estate. But restitution *in specie* may not always be possible. So equity awards compensation in place of restitution *in specie*, by analogy for breach of fiduciary duty with the ideal of restoring to the estate that which was lost through the breach.
>
> …
>
> **[551]** While foreseeability of loss does not enter into the calculation of compensation for breach of fiduciary duty, liability is not unlimited. Just as restitution *in specie* is limited to the property under the trustee's control, so equitable compensation must be limited to loss flowing from the trustee's acts in relation to the interest he undertook to protect.
>
> …
>
> The need for a link between the equitable breach and the loss for which compensation is awarded is fair and sound in policy
>
> …
>
> **[552]** The requirement that the loss must result from the breach of the relevant equitable duty does not negate the fact that 'causality' in the legal sense as limited by foreseeability at the time of breach does not apply in equity. It is in this sense that I read the statement of Street J. in *Re Dawson*, *supra*, that 'causation, foreseeability and remoteness do not readily enter into the matter' …
>
> Thus while the loss must flow from the breach of fiduciary duty, it need not be reasonably foreseeable at the time of the breach,
>
> …
>
> **[556]** Foreseeability is not a concern in assessing compensation, but it is essential that the losses made good are only those which, on a common-sense view of causation, were caused by the breach.
>
> …

9 See the discussion at principles text, [9.58].

I come finally to the application of these principles to this case. The breach of fiduciary duty is conceded, as is the fact that the plaintiffs would not have bought an interest in the property and the joint venture had there been no breach. This establishes that the breach of fiduciary resulted in the acquisition of this interest. The question is whether, applying a common-sense view of causation, the further losses sustained in the course of construction can be said to have resulted or flowed from the breach of fiduciary duty.

[557] In my view, the answer to this question is no. The construction loss was caused by third parties. There is no link between the breach of fiduciary duty and this loss. The solicitor's duty had come to an end and the plaintiffs had assumed control of the property. This loss was the result, not of the solicitor's breach of duty, but of decisions made by the plaintiffs and those they chose to hire.

3 Contributory negligence

The view in Australia is that, due to the nature of a fiduciary obligation, the plaintiff's contributory negligence should not relieve the fiduciary of liability.

Pilmer v Duke Group Ltd (in liq) (2007) 207 CLR 165

Facts and issues

Duke Group Ltd ('Duke') (formerly called Kia Ora Gold Corp NL) engaged Pilmer (a firm of accountants) to value a target company for a takeover bid. Duke relied on the valuation in the takeover bid. The target company was grossly overvalued. While Pilmer breached contractual obligations, Pilmer was held not to be in a fiduciary relationship with Duke. The issue was whether Duke's contributory negligence limited Pilmer's liability for equitable compensation.

Decision

Contributory negligence would not have limited liability for equitable compensation if Pilmer was in a fiduciary relationship with Duke.

McHugh, Gummow, Hayne and Callinan JJ

[14] The issues were whether the Full Court erred in holding that the appellants owed a fiduciary duty to Kia Ora which they breached; whether, if such a duty existed and was breached, the Full Court erred in its assessment of the amount of equitable compensation; and whether that equitable compensation was properly to be reduced by reason of 'contributing fault' by Kia Ora.

...

[84] The conclusion which follows, that the Full Court erred in finding that the appellants breached a fiduciary duty which they owed to Kia Ora, makes it unnecessary to determine questions (b) and (c). However, the following observations are appropriate.

[85] Various judgments in this Court establish that, in Australia, the measure of compensation in respect of losses sustained by reason of breach of duty by a trustee or other fiduciary is determined by equitable principles and that these do not necessarily reflect the rules for assessment of damages in tort or contract.

...

[86] It is sufficient to say that the decision in *Astley v Austrust Ltd* indicates the severe conceptual difficulties in the path of acceptance of notions of contributory negligence as applicable to diminish awards of equitable compensation for breach of fiduciary duty. *Astley* affirms:

> At common law, contributory negligence consisted in the failure of a plaintiff to take reasonable care for the protection of his or her person or property. Proof of contributory negligence defeated the plaintiff's cause of action in negligence.

Contributory negligence focuses on the conduct of the plaintiff, fiduciary law upon the obligation by the defendant to act in the interests of the plaintiff. Moreover, any question of apportionment with respect to contributory negligence arises from legislation, not the common law. Astley indicates that the particular apportionment legislation of South Australia which was there in question did not touch contractual liability. The reasoning in Astley would suggest, a fortiori, that such legislation did not touch the fiduciary relationship.

NOTE

As noted at principles text [6.63] and [9.64], to the contrary, the New Zealand Court of Appeal in *Mouat v Clark Boyce*[10] and the Canadian Court of Appeal in *Canson Enterprises v Boughton*[11] considered that the unreasonable conduct of the principal might result in a reduction of equitable compensation.

4 Mitigation

While the common law view of causation is likely to be rejected, the failure to take obvious steps to alleviate loss might yet severe the causal link between the breach and loss.

Canson Enterprises Ltd v Boughton & Co [1991] 3 SCR 534

Facts and issues

The essential facts are set out on page 344. The outcome was that the breach of fiduciary duty on the part of Wollen and Boughton did not cause the losses claimed. A related and more nuanced question was whether Canson had failed to mitigate its loss.

10 [1992] 2 NZLR 559.

11 [1991] 3 SCR 534.

Decision

Per McLachlin J,[12] that while common law principles of mitigation did not apply, the principal's failure to take the most obvious steps to alleviate the loss might sever the casual link between the breach and the loss.

McLachin J

> [**553**] … while the plaintiff will not be required to act in as reasonable and pru-[**554**]dent a manner as might be required in negligence or contract, losses stemming from the plaintiff's unreasonable actions will be barred. This is also sound policy in the law of fiduciary duty. In negligence and contract the law limits the actions of the parties who are expected to pursue their own best interest. Each is expected to continue to look after their own interests after a breach or tort, and so a duty of mitigation is imposed. In contrast, the hallmark of fiduciary relationship is that the fiduciary, at least within a certain scope, is expected to pursue the best interest of the client. It may not be fair to allow the fiduciary to complain when the client fails forthwith to shoulder the fiduciary's burden. This approach to mitigation accords with the basic rule of equitable compensation that the injured party will be reimbursed for all losses flowing directly from the breach. When the plaintiff, after due notice and opportunity, fails to take the most obvious steps to alleviate his or her losses, then we may rightly say that the plaintiff has been 'the author of his own misfortune.' At this point the plaintiff's failure to mitigate may become so egregious that it is no longer sensible to say that the losses which followed were caused by the fiduciary's breach. But until that point mitigation will not be required.
>
> …
>
> [**556**] The plaintiff will not be required to mitigate, as the term is used in law, but losses resulting from clearly unreasonable behaviour on the part of the plaintiff will be adjudged to flow from that behaviour, and not from the breach. Where the trustee's breach permits the wrongful or negligent acts of third parties, thus establishing a direct link between the breach and the loss, the resulting loss will be recoverable.

C Breach of an equitable duty of care

Duties of care can arise in equity as in the common law. Two questions are separately addressed in this section:

(1) if the scope of liability for the breach of an equitable duty of care is limited by the same considerations as would apply to a common law duty of care and

(2) if the fiduciary's liability is diminished by the contributory negligence of the beneficiary.

In respect of the first question, Ipp J, in the Full Court of Western Australia in *Permanent Building Society (in liq) v Wheeler*, drew a distinction between cases of a breach of a 'true

12 As stated at principles text [9.69], his Honour's reasoning has been approved in Australia although not specifically in the context of mitigation, so the Australian position is a little uncertain yet.

fiduciary obligation' on the one hand, and a breach of an equitable duty of care on the other.[13] The scope of liability of the wrongdoer for the former would not attract the same considerations as would a common law duty of care, unlike the latter. Ipp J's reasoning was endorsed in *Bristol & West Building Society v Mothew* ('*Bristol*').[14]

Concerning the second question, the *Youyang Pty Ltd v Minter Ellison Morris Fletcher*[15] High Court appeared to doubt the correctness of Millett LJ in *Bristol* (in which His Lordship inferred that compensation for breach of an equitable duty of care would be limited by common law concepts of causation) by reinforcing the rigour of the principle of 'the most important duty of the trustee is to obey the terms of the trust'.[16] While 'contributory negligence' was not explicitly mentioned, the *Youyang* High Court's unfavourable treatment of Millett LJ's acceptance of the proposition that compensation for breach of an equitable duty of care should be limited by the same concepts as would common law concepts of causation (which would include contributory negligence) obliquely suggests that the High Court was averse to that proposition. The second question cannot presently be answered confidently in the absence of more direct Australian authority.

1 Scope of liability

While the situation is not entirely clear beyond doubt, the more probable view is that the equitable duty of care is, like the common law duty of care, subject to the same limiting factors.

Permanent Building Society (in liq) v Wheeler (1994) 11 WAR 187

Facts and issues

Permanent Building Society ('PBS') alleged that several of the respondents made improper use of their position as directors of PBS to gain advantages for others and thereby caused detriment to PBS. Alternatively, they failed to exercise a reasonable degree of care in the discharge of their duties, also said to be a breach of fiduciary duties. The various breaches of duty were alleged to have arisen in connection with the purchase of land referred to as 'the Vickers Hadwa site'. PBS alleged that, as a result, it paid more for the land than it was obliged to pay and claimed compensation of $1.8 million. Having found that some of the respondents were in breach of their equitable duty of care, though not of fiduciary duties, the relevant question here was the extent to which the scope of the defendants' liability for those breaches was limited by common law concepts.

Decision

The equitable duty of care is subject to the same limiting factors as with a common law duty of care. Subsequent decisions have, however, gone both ways.

13 (1994) 11 WAR 187, [246].

14 [1998] Ch 1.

15 (2003) 212 CLR 484.

16 *Youyang Pty Ltd v Minter Ellison Morris Fletcher* (2003) 212 CLR 484, [32].

Ipp J (Seaman J and Malcolm CJ agreeing)

[**239**] We were not referred to, and I have not been able to find any case where equitable compensation has been awarded for the breach by a director of an equitable obligation to exercise care and skill.

...

Taking into account a claim that a beneficiary has against a trustee for breach of the equitable duty to exercise reasonable care and skill, I consider that Hamilton [one of the respondents] owed PBS a duty, both in law and in equity, to exercise reasonable care and skill, and PBS was able to mount a claim against him for breach of the legal duty, and, in the alternative, breach of the equitable duty. For the reasons I have expressed, in my view the equitable duty is not to be equated with or termed a 'fiduciary' duty.

...

[**245**] There are claims for breaches of fiduciary duty where the court does not inquire into aspects of causality. In *Brickenden v London and Loan Savings Company*: [here he set out the *Principle in Brickenden's Case*].

...

[**246**] It is to be stressed, however, that this principle applies where there has been a breach of a true fiduciary obligation, carrying with it, ordinarily, in the words of Southin J in *Girardet Crease & Company:* 'the stench of dishonesty – if not of deceit, then of constructive fraud.' The principle applies because the fiduciary has abused the control of the trust, there is a substantial potential for gain through such wrongdoing, the fiduciary has superior information concerning his or her acts, and there is a need 'to keep persons in a fiduciary capacity up to their duty' (as was said by Lord Dunedin in *Nocton v Lord Ashburton.* These factors do not apply to breach of a duty of care.

...

[**247**] It is also significant, as regards matters of policy, that the tortious duty not to be negligent, and the equitable obligation on the part of a trustee to exercise reasonable care and skill are, in content, the same. There is every reason, in my view, in such circumstances, to apply the maxim that 'equity follows the law'. In this regard the following remarks of La Forest j in *Canson Enterprises Limited v Boughton & Co* are pertinent:

> Where 'the measure of duty is the same', the same rule should apply: see Somers J in *Day v Mead* at p 457. Only when there are different policy objectives should equity engage in its well-known flexibility to achieve a different and fairer result. The foundation of the obligation sought to be enforced, Somers J notes, is the 'trust or confidence' reposed by one and accepted by the other or the assumption to act for the one by that other'. That being so, it would be odd if a different result followed depending solely on the manner in which one framed an identical claim.

...

[**248**] In my opinion, the principles of causation referred to in *Brickendon v London and Loan Savings Company* and in *Green and Clara Pty Ltd v Bestobell Industries Pty Ltd* apply only to breaches of true fiduciary obligations and not to breaches of the equitable obligation on the part of a trustee or director to exercise reasonable skill and care.

...

> Applying the principles laid down in *Re Dawson (deceased)* and *Hill v Rose*,[17] I conclude that PBS failed to prove that, but for the breach by Hamilton of his equitable duty to exercise reasonable care, the loss to PBS would have occurred.

Bristol and West Building Society v Mothew [1998] Ch 1

Facts and issues

Mothew, a solicitor, acted for the purchasers of a property and for the plaintiff Bristol & West Building Society ('B & W'), the prospective lenders. B & W stated that it was prepared to advance the loan on condition that the balance of the purchase price was provided by the purchasers without resort to further borrowing. To this end, Mothew was instructed to report prior to completion any proposal that the purchasers might seek further loan funds to furnish any more security to finance their purchase. Mothew inadvertently reported that the balance of the purchase price was being provided without resort to further borrowing. In truth, the purchasers were arranging for an existing loan to be secured by a second charge on the property. B & W then advanced the loan. When the purchasers defaulted, Bristol enforced its security and the property was sold at a loss. B & W sought to recover all its loss from the transaction.

No damages would be recoverable at common law for Mothew's negligence since B & W would in any event have proceeded with the transaction because the market was buoyant and Mothew's negligence would not have caused the loss. But if Mothew was in breach of fiduciary duties, then in accordance with the *Principle in Brickenden's Case*, he would have been liable for the loss.

The issue then concerned whether Mothew was in breach of fiduciary duties.

Decision

Distinguishing between a breach of an equitable duty of care and a breach of fiduciary duty, the Court found that Mothew was not in breach of fiduciary duties and he was not liable to compensate B & W for its loss.

Millet LJ

> **[17]** I respectfully agree, and endorse the comment of Ipp J. in *Permanent Building Society v Wheeler* (1994)
>
> > It is essential to bear in mind that the existence of a fiduciary relationship does not mean that every duty owed by a fiduciary to the beneficiary is a fiduciary duty. In

17 The reference to *Re Dawson (Deceased)* [1966] 2 NSWR 211 is confusing as it is actually authority for the proposition that considerations of causation, foreseeability and remoteness do not come into the matter and if so this would appear contrary to the propositions primarily advanced by Ipp J. One explanation, explored at principles text [9.72], is that the Court in that case was only talking of factual causation.

> particular, a trustee's duty to exercise reasonable care, though equitable, is not specifically a fiduciary duty …

Ipp J explained, at p. 158:

> The director's duty to exercise care and skill has nothing to do with any position of disadvantage or vulnerability on the part of the company. It is not a duty that stems from the requirements of trust and confidence imposed on a fiduciary …

… Although the remedy which equity makes available for breach of the equitable duty of skill and care is equitable compensation rather than damages, this is merely the product of history and in this context is in my opinion a distinction without a difference. Equitable compensation for breach of the duty of skill and care resembles common law damages in that it is awarded by way of compensation to the plaintiff for his loss. There is no reason in principle why the common law rules of causation, remoteness of damage and measure of damages should not be applied by analogy in such a case. It should not be confused with equitable compensation for breach of fiduciary duty, which may be awarded in lieu of rescission or specific restitution.

…

[18] A fiduciary is someone who has undertaken to act for or on behalf of another in a particular matter in circumstances which give rise to a relationship of trust and confidence. The distinguishing obligation of a fiduciary is the obligation of loyalty. The principal is entitled to the single-minded loyalty of his fiduciary.

…

[22] In my judgment the judge's conclusion that the defendant was in breach of fiduciary duty cannot be supported. It follows that it cannot be sustained as a ground for holding the defendant in breach of a constructive trust of the mortgage money.

2 Contributory negligence

There are conflicting views on whether equitable compensation is reduced by the plaintiff's contributory negligence.

Youyang Pty Ltd v Minter Ellison Morris Fletcher (2003) 212 CLR 484

Facts and issues

The facts of this case are set out on page 333.

Decision

Although 'mitigation' was not specifically in issue nor argued, the High Court appeared to suggest that equitable compensation for breach of an equitable duty of care would not be reduced by contributory negligence.

Gleeson CJ, McHugh, Gummow, Kirby and Hayne JJ

Where the complaint is of maladministration of this kind, then it has been said in the English Court of Appeal in *Bristol and West Building Society v Mothew*:

> Equitable compensation for breach of the duty of skill and care resembles common law damages in that it is awarded by way of compensation to the plaintiff for his loss. There is no reason in principle why the common law rules of causation, remoteness of damage and measure of damages should not be applied by analogy in such a case.

...

[39] [T]here must be a real question whether the unique foundation and goals of equity, which has the institution of the trust at its heart, warrant any assimilation even in this limited way with the measure of compensatory damages in tort and contract. It may be thought strange to decide that the precept that trustees are to be kept by courts of equity up to their duty has an application limited to the observance by trustees of some only of their duties to beneficiaries in dealing with trust funds.

REVIEW QUESTIONS

(1) The *Principle in Brickenden's Case* is as follows:

> When a fiduciary commits a breach of his duty by non-disclosure of material facts, which his constituent is entitled to know in connection with the transaction, he cannot argue that disclosure would not have altered the decision to proceed with the transaction ([1934] 3 DLR 465, [5]).

Given that the breach must at least have caused the loss for which compensation is sought, what is the counter-factual (hypothetical) situation in each of *Brickenden v London Loan & Savings Co* [1934] 3 DLR 465 and *Commonwealth Bank of Australia v Smith* (1991) 42 FCR 390? Which, in your view, was the assumed situation where the breach had not occurred, and which formed the basis of comparison for the purpose of calculating the principle's loss?

(2) Given that the likely position to be taken in Australia is that contributory negligence will not reduce the fiduciary's liability, what if any limitations are there on the grant of equitable compensation in the case of a plaintiff who has been contributorily negligent?

(3) Since a failure to mitigate will not reduce the fiduciary's liability, would this mean that the beneficiary can totally disregard the breach?

PART 3

REMEDIES COMPELLING PERFORMANCE AND RELATED REMEDIES

10 SPECIFIC PERFORMANCE

I	Introduction	356
II	The nature of specific performance	356
III	The relationship between specific performance and injunctions	357
IV	Inadequacy of damages and subject matter of contract	357
	A Inadequacy of damages	358
	B Subject matter of contract	359
V	Other requirements for specific performance	372
	A Personal remedy	372
	B Binding contract	372
VI	Discretionary factors and bars to relief	377
	A General equitable bars to relief	379
	B Bars to relief relevant only to specific performance	383
VII	Specific performance under the *Australian Consumer Law*	394
VIII	Specific restitution or specific delivery of property	395
IX	Debt as a species of specific relief?	397

I Introduction

Specific performance typically enforces a contract, but it can also be invoked to enforce a 'promise' enforceable under principles of estoppel. Equitable remedies like specific performance are discretionary. The inadequacy of damages is a particularly significant consideration in determining if specific performance should be granted, although there is lack of complete consensus on whether the inadequacy of damages is a jurisdictional hurdle or another discretionary factor.

II The nature of specific performance

As suggested by the name, 'specific performance' is a decree directed to a party to 'perform' a contract (ie do the thing they are contracted to do). The particular nuance attracted by the decree, which recurs throughout the chapter, is that ordinarily (ie by default) the remedy for breach of contract is damages and that specific performance would only be granted where damages would be inadequate to compensate the aggrieved party for the breach. (See paragraphs [10.4]–[10.9] of the principles text.)

III The relationship between specific performance and injunctions

Specific performance requires one party to do something. An injunction restrains a party from doing something. They are, however, both equitable remedies, and in many respects the considerations for the grant of the respective remedy will be similar. (We will discuss these concepts throughout this chapter.) Furthermore, the effect of an injunction, while in form *restraining* the party from engaging in the conduct concerned, might in some instances have the practical effect of compelling that party to perform something; in such cases, specific performance again overlaps with injunctions. (See paragraphs [10.10]–[10.19] of the principles text.)

IV Inadequacy of damages and subject matter of contract

Concept	Short explanation	Relevant authorities	Principles text
The inadequacy of damages	Broadly that specific performance may be refused where damages are adequate to compensate the plaintiff.	*Harnett v Yielding* [1803–1813] All ER 704	Chapter 10: [10.19]–[10.26]
Contracts involving land	A contract for the purchase of land is specifically enforceable even where the land is purchased for commercial purposes.	*Pianta v National Finance & Trustees Ltd* (1964) 180 CLR 146	Chapter 10: [10.29]–[10.33]
	Specific performance can be granted of a composite contract involving the sale of land and for the vendor to lend money.	*Loan Investment Corporation of Australasia v Bonner* [1970] NZLR 724	
	Specific performance will not inevitably be granted for a contract for the purchase of generic land.	*Semelhago v Paramadevan* [1996] 2 SCR 415	
Contracts involving shares and stock	Specific performance is more readily ordered for the transfer of shares in a private company than for a publicly listed company.	*Georges v Wieland* [2009] NSWSC 733	Chapter 10: [10.39]–[10.40]
Contracts to loan money	While usually a contract to loan money is not specifically enforceable, specific performance might be ordered if damages are not an adequate remedy.	*Wight v Haberdan Pty Ltd* [1984] 2 NSWLR 280	Chapter 10: [10.41]–[10.42]
Contracts for the benefit of third parties	A contract for the benefit of a third party might be specifically enforceable by a party to the contract.	*Beswick v Beswick* [1968] AC 58	Chapter 10: [10.43]–[10.46]
	Because of principles of privity, a third party to a contract cannot obtain relief.	*Coulls v Bagot's Executor and Trustee Co Ltd* (1967) 119 CLR 460	

Concept	Short explanation	Relevant authorities	Principles text
Contracts involving intellectual property	Contracts involving intellectual property generally are specifically enforceable.	*Cogent v Gibson* (1864) 55 ER 485	Chapter 10: [10.47]
Contracts for services	Specific performance is not usually granted for a contract for services.	*Byrne v Australian Airlines* (1995) 185 CLR 410	Chapter 10: [10.48]–[10.50]

A Inadequacy of damages

Harnett v Yielding,[1] an old case, is introduced here for the broad concept of the inadequacy of damages as being central to specific performance.

Harnett v Yielding [1803–1813] All ER 704

Facts and issues

Harnett (the tenant and the plaintiff) sought specific performance of a promise to renew a long-term lease. At issue was whether the specific performance should be granted if specific performance was adequate to compensate the plaintiff.

Decision

Specific performance was not granted, as it was considered that damages were an adequate remedy.

Lord Redesdale LC

> [**705**] Unquestionably the original foundation of these decrees was simply this: that damages at law would not give the party the compensation to which he was entitled, that is, would not put him in a situation as beneficial to him as if the agreement were specifically performed. On this ground the court, in a variety of cases, has refused to interfere where, from the nature of the case, the damages must necessarily be commensurate to the injury sustained: *Errington v Aynesly*; *Flint v Brandon*. For instance, in agreements for the purchase of stock, it is the same thing to the party where or from whom the stock is purchased, provided he receives the money that will purchase it. These cases show what were the grounds on which courts of equity first interfered, but they have constantly hold that the party who comes into equity for a specific performance roust come with perfect propriety of conduct, otherwise they will leave him to his remedy at law.
>
> …
>
> [**708**] … this bill ought to be dismissed.

1 [1803–1813] All ER 704.

B Subject matter of contract

In determining whether damages are adequate for a thwarted contract, the subject matter of the contract is particularly relevant. There are broad categories that provide guidance whether specific performance might or might not be granted for a contract involving that kind of subject matter. One should, however, go beyond the generalisations and identify the reasoning that led to those outcomes in order to have a better understanding of whether specific performance would be granted in any particular case.

Figure 10.1 The bearing of the nature of the contract, to the availability of specific performance

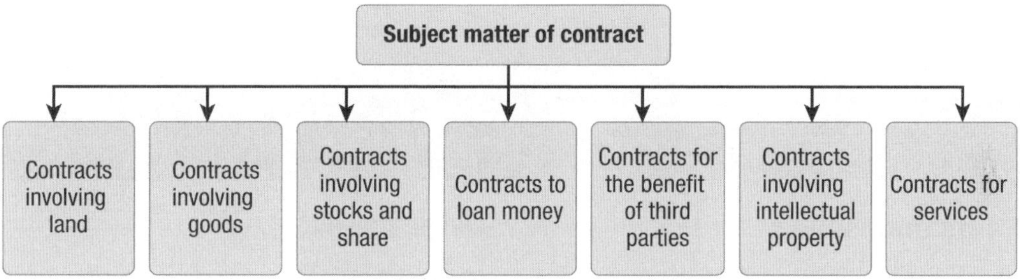

1 Contracts involving land

The traditional view was that someone who bought land did so because of its unique qualities and that damages would be inadequate to compensate the purchaser for its loss; specific performance would then be available to the purchaser. There is, however, a recent movement away from that orthodoxy – since land nowadays is often bought as a generic item of commerce, it cannot be assumed that land is bought because of its unique qualities.

Pianta v National Finance & Trustees Ltd (1964) 180 CLR 146

Facts and issues

National Finance & Trustees Ltd (the respondent) bought the subject land for commercial purposes. The relevant issue was whether the purchaser nonetheless would be entitled to specific performance.

Decision

The respondent was entitled to specific performance.

Barwick CJ

> [**151**] It will be convenient if I say at once that I can discover no reason why a decree for specific performance should not have been made, if there was a binding agreement

> between the appellants and the respondent. If his Honour was right to conclude that an agreement for sale had been made between the parties to this appeal on 26 July, on no view of the facts was the agreement to sell to Chamberlain made on or before 26 July. Nor was there any material before his Honour on which the plaintiff's equity could be found to have lost its priority derived from the time of its creation. There was a faint endeavour made on behalf of the appellants to support the refusal of a decree for specific performance on the ground that, because the respondent was a land developer, damages would be an adequate remedy. But in my opinion this proposition is without foundation in law, even if the respondent had had no other business than that of subdividing and selling land and had made a decision to subdivide and sell the subject land.

Loan Investment Corporation of Australasia v Bonner [1970] NZLR 724

Facts and issues

Bonner (the defendant) sold land to Loan Investment Corporation of Australasia ('Loan Investment', the plaintiff) who wanted to develop it. Bonner also agreed to lend a portion of the purchase price. Bonner repudiated, and Loan Investment sought specific performance of the whole of the contract.

Decision

The majority held that specific performance would not lie. Barwick CJ, dissenting, held that specific performance should be awarded as this was not a composite contract but a whole contract and should be specifically performed because of the special nature of land. Sir Garfield Barwick's dissenting judgment was adopted in *Wight v Haberdan Pty Ltd*[2] and is considered good law in Australia.

Sir Garfield Barwick

> [**741**] None of the reasons [**742**] offered for refusing specific performance in these cases lend colour, in my opinion, to the proposition that equity will never in any circumstances order specific performance of an agreement to lend money; nor, and perhaps this is more significant in this case, to the proposition that equity will not grant specific performance of a contract otherwise specifically enforceable merely because one of its terms calls for a loan of money by one of the parties to the other.
>
> ...
>
> No doubt the general assumption is that damages for breach of a mere promise to lend money adequately compensates the would-be borrower. But, in my opinion, that assumption of fact is not necessarily of universal validity and, again in my opinion, must yield in any case when in fact in the particular circumstances damages would not do justice between the parties. So it seems to me that equity in the more complicated situations of the modern

2 [1984] 2 NSWLR 280.

world may well yet find an occasion when justice can only be done in relation to a contract merely to lend money by ordering its specific performance.

[**744**] … it is said that because the appellant wanted the land as an asset to be sold or to be used as security for the raising of money it had no such peculiar or special value to him as justified specific performance. In my respectful submission this statement misconceives what was said by Sir John Leach in *Adderley v Dixon* and the basis upon which specific performance of contracts for the sale and purchase of land apart from equitable defences is granted almost as of right. Lord Hardwicke in *Buxton v Lister* said:

> As to the cases of contracts for purchase of lands, or things that relate to realties, those are of a permanent nature, and if a person [**745**] agrees to purchase them, it is on a particular liking to the land, and is quite a different thing from matters in the way of trade.

This to my mind gives the key to what Sir John Leach said in *Adderley v Dixon* (supra). The plaintiff by selecting any piece of land for purchase thereby and without more manifests what Lord Hardwicke calls his 'liking to the land' or as Sir John Leach said his 'peculiar and special value' in it.

…

[**748**] It is then said that this agreement is not a 'usual' agreement for the sale and purchase of land. I suppose the form of such agreements which is most commonly seen is that of a single sale and purchase for cash. But whether usual or not, a contract for the sale and purchase of land will be specifically enforced, in my opinion, not because it is a 'usual' contract, but because damages are not an adequate remedy, justice thus requiring specific performance: and if damages are not an adequate remedy for the non-performance of the whole contract, specific performance will not be refused in my opinion simply because what the parties have themselves agreed upon is unusual in the experience of others.

Semelhago v Paramadevan [1996] 2 SCR 415

Facts and issues

Paramedevan (the plaintiff) had agreed to purchase a house and elected to take damages. Specific performance was thus no longer in issue, but *Semelhago* is relevant for its discussion, obiter, of whether specific performance would be granted for the purchase of generic land.

Decision

Specific performance would not invariably be granted in favour of a purchaser of generic land.

Sopinka J

[21] It is no longer appropriate, therefore, to maintain a distinction in the approach to specific performance as between realty and personalty. It cannot be assumed that damages for breach of contract for the purchase and sale of real estate will be an inadequate remedy in all cases. The common law recognized that the distinction might not be valid when the land had no peculiar or special value. In *Adderley v Dixon*, Sir John Leach, VC, stated:

> Courts of Equity decree the specific performance of contracts, not upon any distinction between realty and personalty, but because damages at law may not, in the particular case, afford a complete remedy. Thus a Court of Equity decrees performance of a contract for land, not because of the real nature of the land, but because damages at law, which must be calculated upon the general money value of the land, may not be a complete remedy to the purchaser, to whom the land may have a peculiar and special value.

[22] Courts have tended, however, to simply treat all real estate as being unique and to decree specific performance unless there was some other reason for refusing equitable relief. … Some courts, however, have begun to question the assumption that damages will afford an inadequate remedy for breach of contract for the purchase of land. In *Chaulk v Fairview Construction Ltd* the Newfoundland Court of Appeal after quoting the above passage from *Adderley v Dixon*, stated, at p. 21:

> The question here is whether damages would have afforded Chaulk an adequate remedy, and I have no doubt that they could, and would, have. There was nothing whatever unique or irreplaceable about the houses and lots bargained for. They were merely subdivision lots with houses, all of the same general design, built on them, which the respondent was purchasing for investment or re-sale purposes only. He had sold the first two almost immediately at a profit, and intended to do the same with the remainder. It would be quite different if we were dealing with a house or houses which were of a particular architectural design, or were situated in a particularly desirable location, but this was certainly not the case.

Specific performance should, therefore, not be granted as a matter of course absent evidence that the property is unique to the extent that its substitute would not be readily available.

2 Contracts involving goods

Ordinarily specific performance is not available to a purchaser of goods, because damages would be an adequate remedy, based on the market for those goods. Exceptions include situations where the goods were unique or where, due to the immediate need for those goods, damages would not be regarded as an adequate remedy to the purchaser.

Dougan v Ley (1946) 71 CLR 142

Facts and issues

Ley (the plaintiff) was the purchaser of a taxi and taxi licence from Dougan (the defendant). The issue was whether the contract for the sale of the taxi licence should be specifically performed.

Decision

Damages could not compensate Ley for Dougan's refusal to transfer the licence. Specific performance was therefore ordered for its transfer.

Dixon J

[**149**] The subject matter, it is said, is the sale of a chattel and, in general, a suit for the specific performance of an agreement to sell and deliver chattels will not be entertained. But, when the substance of the matter is considered, the agreement is not of this simple character … The contract is in fact for the transfer of a valuable privilege annexed to a chattel.

[**150**] Though in earlier times the absence of an adequate theory of simple contract had led to the interposition of chancery on wider grounds, by the seventeenth century, if not before, it had come to be 'taken for a good cause of dismission' of a bill 'in most causes, to say that he' the plaintiff 'hath remedy at the common law'. So it became the received doctrine that the foundation of decrees for specific performance was 'that damages at law would not give the party the compensation to which he was entitled; that is, would not put him in a situation as beneficial to him as if the agreement was specifically performed' (per Lord Redesdale, *Harnett v Young*).

…

It was not difficult to say that a purchaser of 'articles of unusual beauty rarity and distinction' was entitled to obtain them in specie (*Falcke v Gray*). Though a less obvious case, it was settled that 'a certain number of railway shares of a particular description, which railway shares are limited in number' and are not to be obtained by going on the share market, are a subject in respect of which a contract of sale will be enforced specifically (*Duncuft v Albrecht*) …

…

In the present case I think that we should have no difficulty in concluding that, because of the limited number of vehicles registered and licensed as taxi-cabs, because of the extent to which the price represents the value of the licence, and because of the essentiality to the purchasers' calling of the chattel and the licence annexed thereto, we should treat the contract as within the scope of the remedy of specific performance.

Howard Perry & Co Ltd v British Railways [1980] 1 WLR 1375

Facts and issues

The British Railways Board (the defendant) supported a strike of steelworkers by refusing to transport steel. The steel could not be stored for long. Howard Perry (the plaintiff) sought permission to transport the steel itself, but was refused. The plaintiff sought an order for specific performance for the delivery up of the steel.

Decision

Specific performance was granted, ordering the board to deliver up the steel.

Sir Robert Megarry VC

[**1378**] [The] steel is the plaintiffs', and they are entitled to possession of it. It lies on the defendants' property, and yet despite demands for it by the plaintiffs the defendants have refused and are refusing either to deliver it in accordance with the terms of the contract between the plaintiffs and the defendants or to allow the plaintiffs, to fetch it for themselves.

...

[**1382**] A principle on which the court has long acted is not to order delivery of goods which are ordinary articles of commerce with no special value or interest, whether to the plaintiff or others, when damages will fully compensate.

...

[**1383**] If a plaintiff can easily replace the goods detained by purchasing their equivalent on the market, then the payment of damages out of which the price of the equivalent may be paid is adequate compensation to the wronged plaintiff, and there is little or no point in making an order for the delivery of the goods. Far better to let the plaintiff fend for himself with the defendant's money.

In normal times, the steel here in dispute might indeed be in this category; but these times are not normal, and at present steel is obtainable on the market only with great difficulty, if at all. If the equivalent of what is detained is unobtainable, how can it be said that damages are an adequate remedy?

...

Damages would be a poor consolation if the failure of supplies forces a trader to lay off staff and disappoint his customers ... and ultimately impels him towards insolvency. On the facts of the present case the perils of the plaintiffs may well not be so great as that at present, but such elements cannot be ignored. In any case, I think that what matters is the adequacy of damages in place of the thing that ought to have been delivered. Under this head I think that my discretion ought to be exercised in favour of making the order that the plaintiffs seek.

Eastern Rolling Mill v Michlovitz, 157 Md 51 (1929)

Facts and issues

Eastern Rolling Mill ('ERM', the defendant) was a seller who sold scrap steel to Michlovitz ('M', the plaintiff) pursuant to long-standing arrangements between them. ERM sought to alter the terms of the arrangement and when M refused, ERM stopped delivering the steel. The issue was whether M was entitled to an order for specific performance of the delivery of steel pursuant to the extant arrangements.

Decision

An order was made for specific performance for ERM to deliver the steel pursuant to the prior arrangements.

Parke J

[**65**] The court as a general rule will refuse to decree specific performance in respect of chattels because damages are a sufficient remedy. This principle does not apply in

all cases of chattels, so there are many exceptions to this rule, because, principally, of the inadequacy of the remedy at law in the particular case, or of the special nature and value of the subject matter of the contract. Pomeroy on *Specific Performance* puts it thus:

> Again, contracts for the delivery of goods will be specifically enforced, when by their terms the deliveries are to be made and the purchase price paid in installments running through a considerable number of years. Such contracts differ from those that are immediately to be executed.' Their profits depending upon future events, cannot be estimated in present damages, which must, of necessity, be almost wholly conjectural. To compel a party to accept damages under such circumstances is to compel him to sell his possible profits at a price depending upon a mere guess.

...

Under the cases, the right to specific performance turns upon whether the plaintiffs can be properly compensated at law. The plaintiffs are entitled to compensatory damages, and if an action at law cannot afford them adequate redress, equity will specifically enforce the contracts.

...

The goods which the parties here had bargained for were not procurable in the neighborhood and, moreover, they possessed a quality and concentrated weight which could not be secured anywhere within the extensive region covered by the 'Philadelphia Market.' In addition, the delivery of the scrap at Baltimore was one of the valuable incidents of the purchase. It follows that the right to these specific goods is a consideration of great importance, and this and the difficulty of securing scrap of the same commercial utility are factors making for the inadequacy of damages.

...

[69] ... the decree [of specific performance] will be affirmed.

3 Contracts involving shares and stock

Specific performance generally is not available for the contract for the sale of shares in publicly listed companies, as their value is readily ascertainable. However, it is more readily granted for a contract for the sale of shares in a private company where damages would not be an adequate remedy.

Georges v Wieland [2009] NSWSC 733

Facts and issues

Under a share purchase agreement, Georges (the plaintiff) agreed to sell shares in a private company to Gnitara Pty Ltd (the fifth defendant). Due to the conduct of the defendants, the value of the shares deteriorated. The shares were untransferred. The issue was whether specific performance would lie for the enforcement of the share purchase agreement.

Decision

Specific performance was granted of the share purchase agreement.

Brereton J

> **[4]** By a Share Sale Agreement, Mr Georges agreed to sell to the fifth defendant Grintara Pty Ltd all the shares in the Company for $150 000, payable as to $37 500 by deposit on signature of the contract, when three shares were to be transferred, and as to the balance on completion, when the remaining nine shares in the Company were to be transferred
>
> ...
>
> **[16]** In these proceedings, three main issues arise. The *first* is Mr Georges' application for enforcement of the Share Sale Agreement, in respect of which the purchase price remains unpaid and the shares remain untransferred ...
>
> ...
>
> **[23]** Though it is an agreement for sale of shares, it has not been suggested that there is any discretionary reason for not granting specific performance as a remedy. Indeed, there are many reasons why, in the context of this case, and despite being a contract for the sale of shares, it should be specifically enforced. The first is that the shares are in a proprietary company, which have since been apparently devalued by the defendants' conduct of and dealings with the Business while the Company was in their control, such that it would likely not be possible to find a replacement purchaser for those shares. The second is that, for the same reason, there would be considerable difficulty in calculating damages.
>
> ...
>
> **[25]** In my view, therefore, notwithstanding that this was an agreement for the sale of shares and notwithstanding that it is effectively a vendor's suit for specific performance, it is one in which the remedy of specific performance is appropriate; the contrary has not been suggested.

Wight v Haberdan Pty Ltd [1984] 2 NSWLR 280

Facts and issues

Wight (the plaintiff), a land developer, agreed to buy land from Haberdan Pty Ltd (the first defendant). The second defendant, Beneficial, agreed to provide mortgage finance to complete the purchase. The first defendant had given a notice to complete the contract of purchase. The plaintiff, while challenging the validity of such notice to complete, also sought specific performance to compel the second defendant to provide finance to complete his purchase.

Decision

Specific performance was granted of the second defendant's obligation to loan money with a pivotal consideration being the complexity of calculating damages.

Kearney J

[**281**] The plaintiff looks to the second defendant (Beneficial) for mortgage finance to complete his purchase.

...

[**289**] … there is no doubt that the general rule is that a contract to lend money cannot be specifically enforced either by the proposed borrower or the proposed lender, and that it is immaterial whether the loan is to be with or without security.

...

The rule is generally accepted to be founded upon the proposition that in the case of such an agreement damages are an adequate remedy.

[**290**] In relation to the question of whether damages are an adequate remedy the true rule requires in my view consideration of the circumstances of the particular case in hand. The test is, in my view, whether by leaving a plaintiff to a remedy in damages justice is done. In other words, the question to be determined is whether such a remedy in damages is adequate to satisfy the demands of justice. In the present instance it is obvious that if the plaintiff is left to pursue common law claims for damages the most complex questions will arise. There will be necessarily difficult questions as to the measure of damages and the remoteness of damages. *Bonner's* case where his Honour says (at 742):

> No doubt the general assumption is that damages for breach of a mere promise to lend money adequately compensates the would-be borrower. But, in my opinion, that assumption of fact is not necessarily of universal validity and, again in my opinion, must yield in any case when in fact in the particular circumstances damages would not do justice between the parties. So it seems to me that equity in the more complicated situations of the modern world may well yet find an occasion when justice can only be done in relation to a contract merely to lend money by ordering its specific performance.

Following his Honour's train of thought, the complications involved in the plaintiff being left to pursue a claim for damages in this instance are so monumental and the prospects of an adequate recovery are so remote as to render such a course an unjust imposition upon the plaintiff.

[**291**] In short, the circumstances create an exception to the general rule, and warrant the conclusion that specific performance ought to be ordered.

4 Contracts to loan money

Axiomatically, because a thwarted contract to loan money can be compensated by damages (a money payment), a contract to loan money is not amenable to specific performance. But in some unusual circumstances, such as discussed in *Loan Investment Corporation of Australasia v Bonner*,[3] where damages are inadequate to compensate the aggrieved party under a thwarted contract for the loan of money. In those circumstances, specific performance might yet be granted. (See paragraphs [10.41]–[10.42] of the principles text.)

3 [1970] NZLR 724.

5 Contracts for the benefit of third parties

The promisee might suffer no damage where the promise benefits a third party, not being the beneficiary of the promised performance. The promisee might yet be entitled to specific performance in that situation (see the reasoning in *Beswick v Beswick*,[4] extracted below). Conversely, however, the third party themselves could not seek specific performance as the principles of privity would preclude them from seeking relief under a contract (see the reasoning in *Coulls v Bagot's Executor and Trustee Co Ltd*[5] extracted below).

Beswick v Beswick [1968] AC 58

Facts and issues

Beswick agreed to transfer his business to his nephew Joseph (the defendant), who agreed to pay an annuity to Beswick's widow when he died. Following Beswick's death, Joseph failed to pay the annuity. Beswick's widow (the plaintiff) sued in her personal capacity and as executrix of the estate. The issue was whether Beswick's widow was entitled to specific performance of the promise to pay the annuity.

Decision

Beswick's widow, as executrix of his estate, was entitled to specific performance of the promise to pay the annuity.

Lord Upjohn

> [**102**] … on the facts of this case damages are nominal for it appears that A [Mr Beswick] died without any assets save and except the agreement which he hoped would keep him and then his widow for their lives. At all events let me assume that damages are nominal. So it is said nominal damages are adequate and the remedy of specific performance ought not to be granted. That is, with all respect, wholly to misunderstand that principle. Equity will grant specific performance when damages are inadequate to meet the justice of the case.
>
> But in any event quantum of damages seldom affects the right to specific performance. If X contracts with Y to buy Blackacre or a rare chattel for a fancy price because the property or chattel has caught his fancy he is entitled to enforce his bargain and it matters not that he could not prove any damage.
>
> In this case the court ought to grant a specific performance order all the more because damages are nominal. C has received all the property; justice demands that he pay the price and this can only be done in the circumstances by equitable relief.

4 [1968] AC 58.

5 (1967) 119 CLR 460.

Coulls v Bagot's Executor and Trustee Co Ltd (1967) 119 CLR 460

Facts and issues

Coulls entered into an agreement with O'Neil Construction Pty Ltd, whereby the company was authorised to pay royalties to Coulls and his wife as joint tenants. Following the death of Coulls, Bagot's Executor and Trustee Co Ltd ('Bagot', the defendant and the executor of his estate) applied to the Court for a determination whether the company was bound to pay the royalties to Coull's widow (the plaintiff) or to the estate.

Decision

The majority of the High Court held that the royalties were payable to the estate and not to Mrs Coulls, as she was not party to the agreement.

McTiernan J

> [**482**] The words of the document including its heading 'Agreement between Arthur Leopold Coulls and O'Neil Construction Proprietary [**483**] Limited' countervail against the inference that Mrs Coulls is a party, sought to be drawn from the fact that she signed it. It seems to me that the third memorandum evidences an agreement between the company and A. L. Coulls on the amount of the royalties and the period of the right to quarry.
>
> I am of opinion that the correct view of the first part of the document is that it is a contract to which the only parties are A L Coulls and the company; and it is implied in the contract that the company is liable to pay to A L Coulls the royalties stipulated by the third and fourth memoranda in the document. Accordingly, I hold that the provisions of the document do not impose on the company a contractual obligation to pay to Mrs Coulls any royalty which accrues due from it after the death of the testator or at all.

Taylor and Owen JJ

> [**486**] We observe first of all that there is nothing whatever in the contract apart from the last paragraph upon which a conclusion could be based that she was a party to the contract.
>
> On the contrary the contract purports expressly to be one made between Arthur Leopold Coulls and O'Neil Construction Pty Ltd. It is the testator alone who engaged to give to the company the sole right to quarry and remove stone from the land described, to grant a 'permanent right of way' along the original council road of 'Watergully' to Perseverance Road and to extend the initial 'period' of ten years for another ten years. On its part the company agrees with the testator to pay royalties at the rates specified.
>
> …
>
> [**487**] We think it is clear that the only person entitled to demand royalties under the contract was the testator and that his wife was not a party to it.

Barwick CJ (dissenting)

[**478**] But as I construe this writing, we have here not a promise by A with B for consideration supplied by B to pay C. It was, in my opinion, a promise by A made to Band C for consideration to pay Band C. In such a case it cannot lie in the mouth of A, in my [**479**] opinion, to question whether the consideration which he received for his promise moved from both Band C or, as between themselves, only from one of them. His promise is not a gratuitous promise as between himself and the promisees as on the view I take of the agreement it was a promise in respect of which there was privity between A on the one hand and Band C on the other. Such a promise, in my opinion, is clearly enforceable in the joint lifetime of Band C: But it is only enforceable if both Band Care parties to the action to enforce it. B, though he only supplied the consideration, could not sue alone. If C were unwilling to join in the action as plaintiff, B no doubt, after suitable tender of costs, could join C as a defendant. And A's promise could be enforced. But the judgment would be for payment to Band C. If B would not join in an action to enforce A's promise, I see no reason why C should not sue joining B as a defendant. Again, in my opinion, A's promise would be enforced and a judgment in favour of Band C would result. In neither of these cases could A successfully deny either privity or consideration. I find nothing in *Dunlop Pneumatic Tyre Co Ltd v Selfridge & Co Ltd* to suggest that he could.

Upon the death of one of the joint promisees the promise remains on foot and remains enforceable but it is still the same promise given to Band C though, because of the death of one and the right of survivorship, the promise is now to pay the survivor. C, it seems to me, being the survivor, may enforce the promise by an action to which both B's estate and C are parties. However, C could not, in any event, in my opinion, be the sole plaintiff against A because A's promise was not made with C alone. Consequently, B's personal representative would need to be either a co-plaintiff or joined as a defendant, though in this case the judgment would be for C alone, the promise with Band C being to pay the survivor of them: see *Attwood v Rattenbury*.

6 Contracts involving intellectual property

Contracts involving intellectual property are generally specifically enforceable due to the unique nature of intellectual property rights.

Cogent v Gibson (1864) 55 ER 485

Facts and issues

Cogent (the plaintiff) agreed to sell a patent right to Gibson (the defendant), which the defendant refused to pay. At issue was whether the plaintiff was entitled to specific performance for the purchase price.

Decision

The plaintiff was entitled to specific performance of the purchase price based on principles of mutuality (discussed on pages 383–6) because the defendant would have been entitled to specific performance of the sale of the patent. The latter issue is the focal point of this extract.

Sir John Romilly MR

> [**558**] I am of the opinion that where there is a valid contract for the sale of a patent, this court will specifically enforce it in a suit by the purchaser and will make the latter execute a conveyance. I am also of the opinion that the opposite is equally true and that the vendor may come into equity

7 Contracts for services

A court will generally not order specific performance of a contract for services as it would be difficult to order parties to maintain a relationship if one party is not willing to do so.

Byrne v Australian Airlines (1995) 185 CLR 410

Facts and issues

Two airport baggage handlers were dismissed by Australian Airlines (the defendant and their employer airline). The primary issue concerned their allegations that, in dismissing them, the airline had failed to observe procedural fairness, and they sought orders for the imposition of a penalty and common law damages. The question of specific performance thus arose only peripherally.

Decision

Specific performance should not be ordered.

Brennan CJ, Dawson and Toohey JJ

> [**428**] … a court will not save in exceptional circumstances order specific performance of a contract of personal service. The possible continuation of the contract of employment after a wrongful dismissal will, therefore, ordinarily be of no real significance as it will for all practical purposes be at an end

REVIEW QUESTIONS

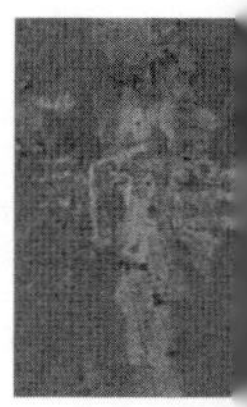

(1) What was recognised in *Harnett v Yielding* [1803–1813] All ER 704 as the 'foundation' of the decree of specific performance?

(2) On that reasoning, would a purchaser of stock be entitled to specific performance of the agreement?

(3) What is the 'original foundation' of the decree of specific performance?

(4) What is the reasoning behind the proposition that specific performance should usually be ordered in favour of a purchaser under a contract for the purchase of land, but not chattels?

(5) Given the general proposition that specific performance would generally be ordered in favour of a purchaser under a thwarted contract for the sale of land, explain the reasoning that it cannot generally be assumed that specific performance would inevitably be granted to a purchaser of land.

(6) Given the general proposition the specific performance would ordinarily not be ordered in favour of a purchaser of chattels, explain the rationes that underpin the cases where specific performance has been granted to a purchaser of chattels.

V Other requirements for specific performance

Specific performance is a personal remedy, rather than the determination of a right as with a common law action for damages. The existence of a binding contract is thus a *sine qua non* of relief by way of specific performance.

Concept	Short explanation	Relevant authorities	Principles text
Personal remedy	Specific performance is a personal remedy not merely a declaration of rights.		Chapter 10: [10.51]–[10.52]
Binding contract	A court will not grant specific performance if nominal consideration only has been furnished.	*Costin v Costin* [1995] ANZ Conv R 289	Chapter 10: [10.53] – [10.70]
	General uncertainty of contract may be a bar to specific performance.	*Joseph v National Magazine Co* [1959] Ch 14	
	Illegality could preclude specific performance.	*REW08 Projects Pty Ltd v PNC Lifestyle Investments Pty Ltd* (2017) 95 NSWLR 458	

A Personal remedy

The concept of specific performance as a personal remedy stems from its equitable origins whereby equity acts in personam. In contrast, a common law judgment is considered a determination of right and not a command to a person.

B Binding contract

As specific performance is a contractual remedy, axiomatically the existence of a binding contract is necessary.

Costin v Costin [1995] ANZ Conv R 289

Fact and issues

Costin Senior was the father of Nicholas Costin (the plaintiff) and Robert Costin (the defendant). Costin Senior, by a signed memorandum of transfer, purported to transfer his one-half interest in real property to Nicholas. The Contract for Sale was rescinded as was the Memorandum of Transfer, and a fresh Memorandum of Transfer for $1 consideration prepared in favour of Nicholas. The discrete issue in the latter transaction was whether the Court would grant specific performance to enforce it.

Decision

The $1.00 consideration expressed to be for the transfer of the interest in the property was nominal consideration only and specific performance was refused to compel the enforce its transfer.

Santow J

> [**290**] It is of course well settled that nominal consideration suffices to support a simple [**291**] contract.
>
> ...
>
> Nonetheless while nominal consideration may support a contract, in the sense of making it binding, the availability of specific performance is typically if not inevitably, negated by the consideration being merely nominal. Thus nominal consideration may go to the proper exercise of the Court's discretion in ordering specific performance, though sometimes subsumed under hardship or unfairness, as I explain below. The language in the cases and the texts tend to confuse whether there is a contract at law with the availability of specific performance and then its unavailability per se with unavailability as a matter of discretion.
>
> ...
>
> [**291**] In the case of purely nominal consideration, equity will look to substance over form. In so doing, it would characterise such a transaction as one of gift, though there may be a contract, when it comes to determining whether specific performance should be allowed. Thus in *Corin v Patton* Deane J said 'In determining whether a party to a transaction has given valuable consideration, equity looks to the substance not mere form.'
>
> ...
>
> In that case itself, there was consideration. But it was what the court treated as 'not valuable consideration' thus implying it was nominal consideration, at best. That was the reciprocal agreement on the part of the intended trustee to act as such and hold [**292**] the property purportedly assigned to the trustee on trust for the purported assignor.
>
> ...
>
> Nominal consideration may still leave a contract at law. But if it be one purporting to assign property and fails to comply with the requirements at law to do so, equity will not treat it as conferring any equitable interest on the purported assignee in its subject matter. Nor will Equity enforce it as a gift, unless the gift be complete so as to bind the conscience of the donor; *Corin v Patton*.

Applying these principles to the present circumstances, it is clear that even if the transfer of 23 June 1989 embodied a contract 'recorded in the transfer itself', such contract, being for nominal consideration, should not be specifically enforced. In equity, the arrangement is to be characterised as one of gift, not sale. It is thus, as a gift, only effective in equity if complete.

Joseph v National Magazine Co [1959] Ch 14

Facts and issues

National Magazine Co (the defendant) had agreed to publish an article by Joseph (the plaintiff). The defendant, in breach of the contract, revised the article. The plaintiff sought specific performance of the contract in terms that the defendant publish the article in its original form. Several versions were produced, but the precise form of the article had never ultimately been agreed upon. The issue was whether the plaintiff was entitled to specific performance.

Decision

The terms of the contract were too uncertain and specific performance was refused.

Harman J

[**20**] It remains to consider what remedy the plaintiff is entitled to have. He claims specific performance, but it is not his wish to have the article of September 18 (the second version) published as it stands but to have it published with the small corrections included the third version, that of September 26, so that there never was an agreed subject-matter for publication.

...

... in this case the exact terms of the article were never agreed on between the parties, and the court would be called on to supervise the editing of the article, whether that of September 18 or 26, by any necessary curtailment or correction of mistakes or possibly grammatical changes which an editor may legitimately make. In my judgment, therefore, this is not an agreement of which specific performance can be ordered by the court.

...

[**21**] There remains the question of damages. As to this, the defendants argue that publicity being all that the plaintiff sought, he could have had all the publicity he wanted if he had agreed to Staal's article going out under his name, and therefore nominal damages only can be awarded. I do not accept this.

...

I see no object in sending the question to inquiry, for I do not think that any evidence would help towards quantifying it. In the absence of a jury, I must do the best I can, and I assess the damages at £200, for which sum there will be judgment for the plaintiff. In addition, he is entitled as special damage to the amount he expended on having the photograph taken, which was 15 guineas.

REW08 Projects Pty Ltd v PNC Lifestyle Investments Pty Ltd [2017] NSWCA 269; (2017) 95 NSWLR 458

Facts and issues

REW08 Projects Pty Ltd ('REWO8', the appellant) was involved in the development of land for subdivision and had entered into a contract to sell a subdivided lot to Lifestyle Investments Pty Ltd ('Lifestyle', the respondent). Several versions of the contract had been prepared to reflect updates to the plans. Following disagreements between the parties, the respondent commenced proceedings in the Equity Division for specific performance of the contract. After the appellant filed a defence alleging that the contract had been entered into 'for the express purpose of avoiding stamp duty' payable on it and was therefore 'void for illegality', Lifestyle paid the full amount of stamp duty to the Office of State Revenue. The question was whether specific performance was available.

Decision

The New South Wales Court of Appeal confirmed the decision to grant specific performance to the respondent.

McFarlan JA

> **[5]** Following disagreements between the parties … the respondent commenced proceedings in the Equity Division for specific performance of the contract dated 13 June 2014, and for other relief. After the appellant filed a defence alleging that the contract had been entered into 'for the express purpose of avoiding stamp duty' payable on it and was therefore 'void for illegality', the respondent paid to the Office of State Revenue the full amount of stamp duty referable to the transactions.
>
> …
>
> **[14]** In *Equuscorp Pty Ltd v Haxton* French CJ, Crennan and Kiefel JJ stated, by reference to earlier decisions, that an agreement may be unenforceable for statutory illegality where:
>
> (i) the making of the agreement or the doing of an act essential to its formation is expressly prohibited absolutely or conditionally by the statute;
>
> (ii) the making of the agreement is impliedly prohibited by statute. A particular case of an implied prohibition arises where the agreement is to do an act the doing of which is prohibited by the statute;
>
> (iii) the agreement is not expressly or impliedly prohibited by a statute but is treated by the courts as unenforceable because it is a 'contract associated with or in the furtherance of illegal purposes'.
>
> In the third category of case, the court acts to uphold the policy of the law, which may make the agreement unenforceable. That policy does not impose the sanction of unenforceability on every agreement associated with or made in furtherance of illegal purposes. The court must discern from the scope and purpose of the

relevant statute 'whether the legislative purpose will be fulfilled without regarding the contract or the trust as void and unenforceable' (ibid).

...

[17] In its pleading the appellant relied on an allegation that the 13 June 2014 contract was 'entered into for the express purpose of avoiding stamp duty'. On appeal however, in light of the primary judge's factual findings of necessity it confined its allegation to one that the purpose of entry into the contract ... was to delay payment of stamp duty. Again, it does not assert that the contract itself was prohibited by statute.

...

[23] These statements and the other authorities to which I refer below identify a number of reasons why the primary judge was correct in finding that the respondent should not be denied an order for specific performance of the subject contract.

[24] First as the primary judge noted, the legislative regime for the payment and collection of stamp duty (in Chapter 11A of the *Duties Act* and Part 5 of the *Taxation Administration Act 1996* (NSW)) does not expressly render an agreement made for the purpose of avoiding duty unenforceable. Rather, s 26 of the *Taxation Administration Act* provides for the imposition of a penalty tax where tax is not paid in accordance with the law, and other sections create various offences relating to the provision of false or misleading information. That the legislature stopped short of providing the sanction of unenforceability is a powerful indication that it did not intend that outcome to eventuate, even by implication. In my view (and that of the primary judge) a finding of unenforceability would not be congruent with the statutory scheme (see *Gnych*). The 'cardinal purpose' of the statutory scheme, as found by the primary judge, is 'to ensure that the proper amount of duty is received by the State in respect of dutiable transactions'.

[27] Fourthly, the supposed illegal purpose 'has not been carried into effect'. Stamp duty has been paid, with interest, and the appellant did not establish that any penalties which were levied remain unpaid.

...

[29] Fifthly, as the primary judge held, to deprive the respondent of the benefit of the ... contract would impose a penalty upon it disproportionate to its assumed wrong, particularly bearing in mind that the respondent has now paid applicable stamp duty and interest.

...

[30] To free the appellant of the obligation to perform the contract for sale of the subject property at a December 2013 price, when it has suffered no loss by reason of the respondent's alleged impropriety, would likely confer a windfall on the appellant. This was a factor that Mason J in *Yango Pastoral Company* found weighed against a finding that the contract was unenforceable.

...

[39] For the reasons I have given, the appeal should be dismissed with costs [the order for specific performance made at first instance was affirmed].

REVIEW QUESTIONS

(1) In *Joseph v National Magazine Co* [1959] Ch 14, the Court declined to award specific performance but was prepared to award damages for breach of contract. Discuss the rationales that would underpin the grant of damages where the breached contract is too uncertain to be enforced by specific performance.

(2) How does the 'policy' of the law impact on the question of whether specific performance would be granted of a contract that did not conform with the provisions of the act?

VI Discretionary factors and bars to relief

Specific performance is an equitable remedy and with equitable remedies relief is *discretionary* and dependent on a consideration of the relevant factors. Some discretionary factors apply generally, others are relevant only to specific performance.

Figure 10.2 Discretionary bars to relief

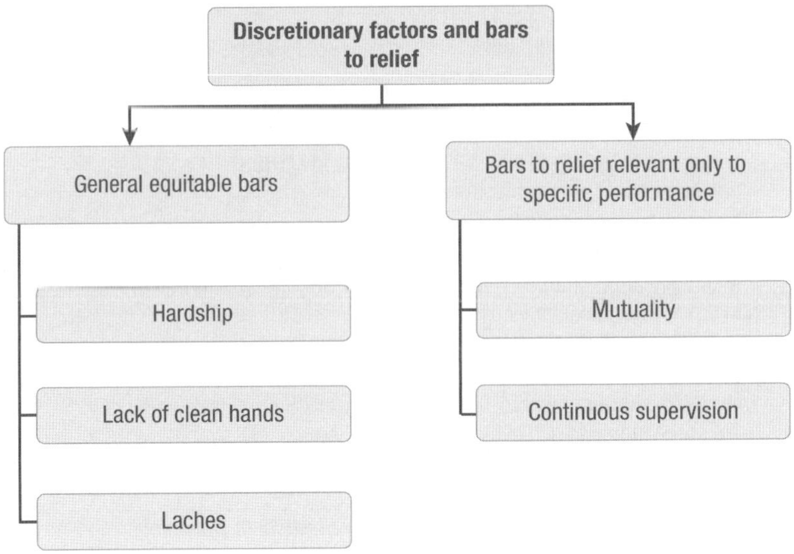

Concept	Short explanation	Relevant authorities	Principles text
General equitable bars	Specific performance might be refused if it caused undue hardship.	*Patel v Ali* [1984] 1 Ch 283	Chapter 10: [10.75]–[10.89]
	A lack of clean hands is a discretionary factor that might preclude relief.	*Summer v Cocks* (1927) 40 CLR 321	
	Laches (delay with acquiescence, causing prejudice) might preclude relief.	*Lindsay Petroleum v Hurd* (1875) LR 5 PC 221	
	A lengthy delay is indicative but not conclusive of acquiescence and prejudice.	*No 68 Ltd v Eastern Services Ltd* [2006] 2 NZLR 43	
Bars to relief relevant only to specific performance	Mutuality: a contract to be amenable to be specifically enforced must be 'mutual'.	Edward Fry and Williams Donaldson Rawlins, *Treatise on the Specific Performance of Contracts* (Stevens and Sons, 1903)	Chapter 10: [10.91]–[10.109]
	Mutuality is adjudged at the time of hearing.	Price v Strange [1977] 3 All ER 371	
	The real basis for mutuality is hardship, in requiring the court to consider whether the defendant would suffer hardship if the plaintiff was unable to be required to carry out their obligations in specie.	*Cannavo v FCD (Holdings) Pty Ltd* [2000] NSWSC 304	
	Continuous supervision and personal service: specific performance usually is not granted where the court would be required to continually supervise performance.	*Ryan v Mutual Tontine Westminster Chambers Association* [1893] 1 Ch 116	
	An obligation to enter a *contract* to provide personal services is specifically enforceable.	*Posner v Scott Lewis* [1997] Ch 25	
	Specific performance is more likely ordered where the defendant is to achieve a definite result by complying with clearly identifiable terms.	*Cooperative Insurance Society Ltd v Argyll Stores (Holdings) Ltd* [1998] AC 1	
	Specific performance may be ordered of obligations that demand supervision if the *practical* effect of the orders sought is not such as to demand constant court supervision.	*Patrick Stevedores Operations No 2 Pty Ltd v Maritime Union of Australia (No 3)* (1998) 195 CLR 1	

A General equitable bars to relief

Certain principles, (discussed in this section) are relevant not only to specific performance, but (generally) to all equitable remedies.

Patel v Ali [1984] 1 Ch 283

Facts and issues

The Alis (the defendants) were joint owners of land who agreed to sell it to Patel (the plaintiff). Before settlement, Mr Ali became bankrupt and went to jail. Mrs Ali was diagnosed with bone cancer and her leg was amputated. The Alis did not want the contract enforced as they wanted to continue to have the support of the local community. The issue was whether specific performance should be ordered.

Decision

Specific performance was refused on the grounds of hardship.

Goulding J

> [**286**] It is not in dispute that, like other equitable relief, the specific performance of contracts is a discretionary remedy; but, in the ordinary case of a sale of land or buildings, the court normally grants it as of course and withholds it only on proof of special facts. The textbooks and reported decisions have long recognised hardship as one ground on which, in a proper case, a purchaser or vendor may be refused specific performance and be left to his right to damages for breach of contract at law. The difficulty is to determine within what limits hardship to a defendant can [**287**] properly be said to justify this exercise of judicial discretion. There is no doubt that, in the majority of cases, the hardship which moves the court to refuse specific performance is either a hardship existing at the date of the contract or a hardship due in some way to the plaintiff. In the present case, neither of those conditions being satisfied, the plaintiffs rely strongly on that principle or practice, which is stated in varying terms in all the well-known textbooks.
>
> …
>
> [**288**] … in the reported cases … hardship successfully relied on has always related to the subject matter of the contract and has not been just a personal hardship of the defendant. Certainly, mere pecuniary difficulties, whether of purchaser or of vendor, afford no excuse from performance of a contract.
>
> …
>
> The important and true principle, in my view, is that only in extraordinary and persuasive circumstances can hardship supply an excuse for resisting performance of a contract for the sale of immovable property. A person of full capacity who sells or buys a house takes the risk of hardship to himself and his dependants, whether arising from existing facts or unexpectedly supervening in the interval before completion. This is where, to my mind, great importance attaches to the immense delay in the present case, not attributable to

the defendant's conduct. Even after issue of the writ, she could not complete, if she had wanted to, without the concurrence of the absent Mr Ahmed. Thus, in a sense, she can say she is being asked to do what she never bargained for, namely to complete the sale after more than four years, after all the unforeseeable changes that such a period entails. I think that in this way she can fairly assert that specific performance would inflict upon her 'a hardship amounting to injustice' to use the phrase employed by James LJ, in a different but comparable context, in *Tamplin v James*. Equitable relief may, in my view, be refused because of an unforeseen change of circumstances not amounting to legal frustration, just as it may on the ground of mistake insufficient to avoid a contract at law.

In the end, I am satisfied that it is within the court's discretion to accede to the defendant's prayer if satisfied that it is just to do so.

Summer v Cocks (1927) 40 CLR 321

Facts and issues

Summers (the plaintiff) had contracted to sell a hotel to Cocks (the defendant). At the time, Summers knew that authorities were planning to revoke the liquor licence but did not tell Cocks. After the contract was signed, the licence was revoked. Cocks refused to settle. Summers sought specific performance. At issue was whether Summers's failure to reveal that the liquor licence was to be revoked amounted to unclean hands, disentitling him from specific performance.

Decision

Summers's failure to reveal that the liquor licence was to be revoked amounted to unclean hands and specific performance was refused.

Isaacs ACJ

[**324**] The vendor 'certainly misled the purchaser as to the attitude of the Board, though without any fraudulent intent, and he did not inform him on 14th January' (should be 12th January) 'that he had received a summons which showed that his licence was not then a perfectly clean one.'

...

Moreover, according to practice, as we were told, though I say nothing as to the correctness of the practice, the compensation paid on delicensing is altogether incommensurate with the value of the property as a hotel. Reviewing the situation as a whole, and seeing that the respondent was in no way chargeable with fault in leading to the result of delicensing, I arrive at the conclusion stated. But this is a case where specific performance could be granted, and should be granted but for the attendant circumstances, which confer discretion on the Court to exclude the application of its jurisdictional power. I adopt the statement of my brother Starke as to the facts and reasoning leading both to the defendant's breach of contract and to the refusal of specific performance.

Starke J

> [**331**] In the present case the Chief Justice found that the omission of Summers to keep the hotel premises in a proper state of repair led to the premises being deprived of their licence. Moreover, he found also that Summers sold the property because he knew that the licence was in some jeopardy, and that he was wanting in candour towards the purchaser. In my opinion it would be unsafe and wrong for us to disturb these findings of the Chief Justice, who saw and heard the witnesses. If they are correct, the Chief Justice acted within the limits of his judicial discretion in refusing specific performance.

Lindsay Petroleum v Hurd (1875) LR 5 PC 221

Facts and issues

Fraud had been established against Hurd (the respondents) in respect of the sale of land, who falsely claimed that one or more of them owned the land and that the offer to sell the land in question represented the true consideration. The question related to the circumstances under which a party who induced another into a contract by their fraud could raise the defence of laches arising by delay. Relevantly here, the respondents could not prove prejudice.

Decision

The defence of laches failed.

Lord Selborne LC

> [**239**] Now the doctrine of laches in courts of equity is not an arbitrary or technical doctrine. Where it would be practically unjust to give a remedy, either because the party has by his con [**240**] duct dono that which might fairly be regarded as equivalent to a waiver of it, or where by his conduct and neglect he has, though perhaps not waiving that remedy, yet put the other party in a situation in which it would not be reasonable to place him if the remedy were afterwards to be asserted in either of these cases, lapse of time and delay are most material. But in every case if an argument against relief which otherwise would be just is founded upon mere delay that delay of course not amounting to a bar by any statute of limitations, the validity of that defence must be tried upon principles substantially equitable. Two circumstances, always important in such case, are the length of the delay and the nature of the acts done during the interval, which might affect either party and cause a balance of justice or injustice in taking the one course or the other, so far as relates to the remedy.
>
> In this case the delay was at all events not of very long duration. because the conveyance to the company was dated about fifteen months before the filing of the bill; the whole purchase-money was not paid before that time; and there is nothing which would justify us in reckoning the currency of time from an earlier period than that conveyance. Neither

were any acts done in the interval, as it appears to us, at all material to the equity between the par ties. There was possession taken, no doubt, but it would be a very novel proposition that mere possession is to be a bar, so as to. raise a counter equity in cases of this description. Nothing appears to have been done beyond the sinking of a single well, by way of trial, upon the ground.

...

The situation of the parties having, therefore, in no substantial way been altered, either by the delay or by anything done during the interval, there is in these circumstances nothing to give special importance to the defence founded on time, even had there been such an allegation of facts in the pleadings as would have been proper, if it was meant seriously to rely upon this as a substantial defence to the suit.

...

[241] In order that the remedy should be lost by !aches or delay, it is, if not universally at all events ordinarily-and certainly when the delay has been only such as in the present case – necessary that there should be sufficient knowledge of the facts constituting the title to relief. What knowledge is there allegation or proof ·of here? Allegation there is none.

...

[242] It appears therefore to their Lordships that the objection of delay entirely fails.

No 68 Ltd v Eastern Services Ltd [2006] 2 NZLR 43

Facts and issues

Eastern Services Ltd ('Eastern Services', the defendant) sold two properties to Maritime Club Ltd ('Maritime'). At the time of sale, there was no vehicular access to the properties. Under the terms of the contract of sale, Eastern Services agreed to provide a registered easement for the purposes of vehicular access. Maritime subsequently sold the properties and assigned the benefit of the contract to No 68 Ltd ('No 68', the plaintiff), who sought specific performance of the obligation to register the easement. By then, nearly 25 years had passed since the making of the original contract. There was no evidence that Eastern Services was prejudiced by the delay.

Decision

Specific performance was ordered of the obligation to provide a registered easement.

McGrath J

[53] ... the crucial question is whether the respondent has an equity which outweighs the appellant's rights. In deciding whether it is unjust for a plaintiff to succeed, the established approach is to consider whether there has been unreasonable delay by the plaintiff and, if so, whether there would be consequential detriment to the defendant if it was required to give effect to the plaintiff's right. The inquiry into detriment is generally directed to the length of delay and the nature and the effect of the acts done during the period in which the plaintiff has delayed asserting rights. Often that inquiry will indicate that there has been prejudice to the defendant as a result of the delay, making it unjust for the Court to order specific performance.

...

[54] In the end, however, a defendant who, like the respondent, is not able to show abandonment of its rights by the plaintiff, and who seeks to invoke laches, must be able to show there are circumstances giving rise to an equity that on balance outweighs the plaintiff's rights. That may be difficult to do in the absence of any significant prejudice. It follows that while a long period of delay will more readily give rise to circumstances from which an inference of prejudice is drawn, it does not follow ... that in those circumstances little by way of prejudice is needed to make it unjust for the plaintiff to succeed.

[56] By way of summary, the defence of laches, deriving as it does from the old maxim 'that equity aids the vigilant, not those who slumber on their rights', bars an action by reason of the staleness of a claim in situations where the limitations legislation does not apply.

...

The application of the defence of laches necessarily turns on the balance of justice or injustice in granting or refusing relief in the circumstances of the particular case, including the time which has elapsed. The relevant inequity, which on balance outweighs the plaintiff's rights, will normally be founded on some change in the condition of property or the relationship of the parties which has occurred over the period of delay. Situations giving rise to laches are never closed, but the vast majority of cases fall into one of two categories: first, a party inappropriately refrains for an excessive period from seeking redress once he or she knows his or her rights have been violated, giving rise to the inference of acquiescence; and secondly, because of a party's unreasonable delay, significant prejudice is caused to the other party.

...

[69] ... There was no evidence of there being any change in the way the respondent used its land over the period since 1980 that could be attributed to its belief the right-of-way was not required.

...

[70] ... It is not possible to identify circumstances linked to the delay which prejudiced the respondent. It follows that the respondent has not been placed in a situation because of the delay which makes it unreasonable or unconscionable to allow the appellant to enforce its rights. In brief, the appellant's contractual rights are not outweighed by the equity of the respondent's position.

B Bars to relief relevant only to specific performance

The doctrine of 'mutuality' as originally formulated by Fry LJ[6] has not stood the test of time well (see, eg, *Price v Strange*).[7] (See the criticisms generally in paragraph [10.92] of the principles text and the more contemporary Australian treatment in *Cannavo v FCD (Holdings) Pty Ltd*.[8])

6 E Fry and WD Rawlins, *Treatise on the Specific Performance of Contracts* (Stevens and Sons, 1903).

7 [1977] 3 All ER 371.

8 [2000] NSWSC 304.

'Continuous supervision and personal services' invokes the proposition that the court will not order specific performance of obligations requiring constant supervision; the corollary is where there is an empirically certain way of measuring the adequacy of performance, specific performance might yet be ordered.

Edward Fry and Williams Donaldson Rawlins, *Treatise on the Specific Performance of Contracts* (Stevens and Sons, 1903)

A contract to be specifically enforceable by the Court must, as a general rule, be mutual, that is to say, such that it might, at the time it was entered into, have been enforced by either of the parties against the other of them. When therefore, whether from personal incapacity to contract, or the nature of the contract, or any other cause, the contract is incapable of enforcing it against the other, though its execution in the latter way might in itself be free from the difficulty attending its execution of the former.

Price v Strange [1977] 3 All ER 371

Facts and issues

By an oral agreement between the two, Strange (the defendant) promised that if Price (the plaintiff) painted the subject's premises, Strange would give him a new lease of the premises. Price's obligation was of personal services and therefore not capable of supervision. This was the case at the time of the making of the contract. Strange tried to argue that based on principles of mutuality, Strange was not bound to give him the lease. By the time of trial, there was no lack of mutuality as Price had finished the work. At issue was the time at which mutuality was to be assessed.

Decision

The time that mutuality should be assessed was the time of hearing. Specific performance was granted in favour of the plaintiff.

Goff LJ

> **[380]** The plaintiff's main case is that the statement in Fry that mutuality has to be determined at the date of the contract is not good law, and that on the contrary the question of mutuality is simply one of the factors, which like hardship, mistake and delay has to be considered in the exercise of a judicial discretion when the court is considering whether or not to order specific performance, and therefore the relevant time is that of the hearing, and he argues if that be the proper rule, then having regard to all the circumstances this is a proper case for an order, especially as the work has now been finished and complete justice can be done by a monetary adjustment ...
>
> ...

Spry formulates the rule thus:

> Although therefore, the authorities on these questions are by no means clear, the view which appears to be most widely supported, and to accord most with equitable principle, is that mutuality, when it is material, need be looked at only as at the time of the making of the proposed order of the court.

...

[381] In my judgment the vendor and purchaser cases show that want of mutuality raises a question of the court's discretion to be exercised according to everything that has happened up to the decree.

...

[383] Surely the defence of want of mutuality should be governed by the state of affairs as seen at the hearing, since one is dealing not with a question affecting the initial validity of the contract, but with whether or not the discretionary remedy of specific performance should be granted. I find support for this view in *Eastern Counties Railway Co v Hawkes*, to which I have already referred, where Lord Campbell said:

> But I am of opinion that whereas, in considering the validity of the agreement, the proper time to regard is the time when it was entered into – as to the specific performance, regard is to be had to the state of things when the bill was filed.

In my judgment, therefore, the proposition in Fry is wrong and the true principle is that one judges the defence of want of mutuality on the facts and circumstances as they exist at the hearing.

Cannavo v FCD (Holdings) Pty Ltd [2000] NSWSC 304

Facts and issues

Cannavo (the plaintiff) sought specific performance of FCD (Holdings) Pty Ltd's ('FCD', the defendant) obligation to transfer to him certain shares in a company formed to exploit an invention. Central to the agreement was that the plaintiff be appointed the managing director of the corporate entity to be formed to exploit the invention. The issue was whether the plaintiff was entitled to an order for specific performance of the obligation to transfer the shares in question given that he could not be ordered to perform his obligations as managing director.

Decision

Specific performance should not be granted in the light of the undue hardship that could be caused to the defendant by reason of the unenforceable obligations on the part of the plaintiff.

Santow J

[62] Given that specific performance would not be allowed in the case of such a contract of personal services more especially where the relationship between the parties had broken down, clearly enough the Plaintiff could not enforce the effectuation of his appointment as managing director insofar as completion of the corporate formalities to bring that about were concerned. Likewise, were the Defendants to seek to enforce the contract against an unwilling Plaintiff, a situation at odds with reality, the Plaintiff could not be compelled to act as managing director for the same reason. I say at odds with reality, because clearly enough the Defendants would not wish to have the Plaintiff be managing director when their relationship has broken down. In those circumstances it would be quite unfair for there to be one fundamental part of the arrangements that could not be specifically enforced in circumstances where specific enforcement were then applied to the remaining parts of the contract and in particular to the acquisition of the twenty- five per cent equity.

[63] That is not to invoke Fry's much criticised statement of the rule requiring mutuality as appears in his 'Specific Performance' 6th Ed at 619: 'A contract to be specifically enforced by the Court must, as a general rule be mutual – that is to say, such that it might, at the time it was entered into, have been enforced by either of the parties against the other of them.'

[64] … The real basis of any notion of mutuality in this context is that it points to the weighing up process that a court necessarily carries out in order to determine whether granting specific performance at the behest of the plaintiff would, by reason of the plaintiff being unable to be required to carry out his obligations in specie, produce such hardship to the defendant that to compel specific performance would be inequitable.

[65] Here, the obligation with respect to appointment of the Plaintiff as managing director is not severable. It then becomes a question of whether enforcement of the contract would be such as to cause undue hardship upon the Defendants. This is in forcing them to accept the Plaintiff not merely as an investor with a twenty-five per cent equity but as a managing director, when this was unacceptable by reason of the breakdown of their personal relations. That hardship is such that it clearly would be unjust to require specific performance.

Ryan v Mutual Tontine Westminster Chambers Association [1893] 1 Ch 116

Facts and issues

Mutual Tontine Westminster Chambers Association (the defendant) rented residential premises to Ryan ('the plaintiff'). The lease contained a term requiring the defendant to provide the services of a resident porter to the plaintiffs; the porter was to be constantly in attendance. The defendant appointed a person who was not qualified and who frequently absented himself. It was not in dispute that the defendant was in breach of contract; the question was whether the plaintiff was entitled to specific performance of the defendant's obligation to provide the services of a porter.

Decision

Specific performance was not granted, as the obligation was one for personal services.

Lord Esher MR

[123] The right of the tenant under the contract is really an entirety, viz., to have a porter employed by whom these services shall be performed; and the breach of the contract substantially is that these services were not performed. [The] contract is that these services shall be performed during the whole term of the tenancy; it is therefore a long-continuing contract, to be performed from day to day, and under which the circumstances of non-performance might vary from day to day. I apprehend, therefore, that the execution of it would require that constant superintendence by the Court, which the Court in such cases ·has always declined to give. Therefore, if the contract is regarded as a whole, there is good ground for saying that it is not one of which the Court could compel specific performance.

Lopes LJ

[124] What was contracted for was not the mere appointment of a porter who might be useless, but the employment of a competent porter who should perform the specified duties. …

But it is a recognised rule that the Court cannot enforce a contract by compelling specific performance, where the execution of the contract requires such watching over and supervision by the Court.

…

Another ground on which the Plaintiff fails, in my opinion, is this: the Court will not compel specific performance when there is another adequate remedy. Here there is such a remedy, viz., by compensation in damages for breach of the contract. The Judge has found … to be adequate damages in respect of the breach of the contract up to the time of action brought.

Kay LJ

[128] Ordinarily the Court will not enforce specific performance of works, such as building works, the prosecution of which the Court cannot superintend; not only on the ground that damages are generally in such cases an adequate remedy, but also on the ground of the inability of the Court to see that the work is carried out.

NOTE

The proposition that the court will not supervise specific performance of a contract for services is probably too wide. The very instance of building work, which Kay LJ took as an example of the type of work that the court would not superintend, would have been considered amenable to an order for specific performance by Lord Hoffman in *Cooperative Insurance Society Ltd v Argyll Stores (Holdings) Ltd.*[9]

9 [1998] AC 1.

Posner v Scott Lewis [1997] Ch 25

Facts and issues

Posner (the plaintiff) rented premises owned by Scott Lewis (the defendant). The lease obliged the defendant to employ a resident porter. The then-resident porter had resigned. At issue was whether the plaintiff was entitled to specific performance of the obligation to employ a resident porter.

Decision

By an order for specific performance, the defendant was ordered to employ a porter.

Mervyn Davies J

> [**32**] … the plaintiffs claim in effect that the defendants are now failing to employ, pursuant to clause 3(11), a resident porter for the purposes specified in clause 3(11), and that the defendants ought to be [**33**] ordered so to employ.
>
> …
>
> I was referred to *Ryan v Mutual Tontine Westminster Chambers Association* a case where the Court of Appeal considered a contract between a landlord and his tenant by which the landlord undertook to employ a porter to perform certain services for the benefit of the tenant. The contract was held to be not specifically enforceable. One ground of the decision was that the execution of the contract would require 'constant superintendence by the court.'
>
> …
>
> [**34**] The plaintiffs submitted that the Ryan case should be distinguished. In short, he said that since the resident porter's functions at Danes Court were already obligations of the lessor to the lessees, there were no duties on the part of the porter towards the tenants that the tenants were seeking to enforce. All that was required was the appointment of a resident porter, whereas in the *Ryan* case the plaintiff was in effect seeking to enforce performance of duties said to be owed by the porter to the plaintiff.
>
> …
>
> In *CH Giles & Co Ltd v Morris* Megarry J. after referring to Ryan's case, said, at p. 318:
>
> …
>
> > [**35**] … the contract of which specific performance has been decreed requires not the performance of personal service or any continuous series of acts, but merely procuring the execution of an agreement which contains a provision for such services or acts.
>
> …
>
> [**36**] Whether or not a specific performance order should be made seems to me to depend on the following considerations:
>
> (a) is there a sufficient definition of what has to be done in order to comply with the order of the court?

(b) Will enforcing compliance involve superintendence by the B court to an unacceptable degree?
(c) What are the respective prejudices or hardships that will be suffered by the parties if the order is made or not made?

As to (a), one may in this case sufficiently define what has to be done by the defendants by ordering the defendants, within say two months, to employ a porter to be resident at Danes Court for the C purpose of carrying out the clause 3(11) duties … As to (b), I do not see that such an order will occasion any protracted superintendence by the court. If the defendants without good cause fail to comply with the order in due time, then the plaintiffs can take appropriate enforcement proceedings against the defendants. As to (c), I see no hardship or prejudice resulting to the defendants from the order. They will simply be performing what they have promised to do.

…

It follows that there should be an order for specific performance.

Cooperative Insurance Society Ltd v Argyll Stores (Holdings) Ltd [1998] AC 1

Facts and issues

With 19 years to run on a lease of premises operated as a supermarket, Argyll Stores (Holdings) Ltd (the defendants and lessees) ceased trading. Cooperative Insurance Society Ltd (the plaintiff and lessor) sought specific performance of the lease.

Decision

As the terms of the lease were not sufficiently precise, specific performance was refused.

Lord Hoffman

[**11**] The principles upon which English judges exercise the discretion to grant specific performance are reasonably well settled and depend upon a number of considerations, mostly of a practical nature, which are of very general application.

…

[**13**] This is a convenient point at which to distinguish between orders which require a defendant to carry on an activity, such as running a business over or more or less extended period of time, and orders which require him to achieve a result. The possibility of repeated applications for rulings on compliance with the order which arises in the former case does not exist to anything like the same extent in the latter. Even if the achievement of the result is a complicated matter which will take some time, the court, if called upon to rule, only has to examine the finished work and say whether it complies with the order. This point was made in the context of relief against forfeiture in *Shiloh Spinners Ltd v Harding*. If it is a

condition of relief that the tenant should have complied with a repairing covenant, difficulty of supervision need not be an objection. As Lord Wilberforce said:

> what the court has to do is to satisfy itself, ex post facto, that the covenanted work has been done, and it has ample machinery, through certificates, or by inquiry, to do precisely this.

This distinction between orders to carry on activities and orders to achieve results explains why the courts have in appropriate circumstances ordered specific performance of building contracts and repairing covenants: see *Wolverhampton Corporation v Emmons* (building contract) and *Jeune v Queens Cross Properties Ltd* (repairing covenant). It by no means follows, however, that even obligations to achieve a result will always be enforced by specific performance. There may be other objections, to some of which I now turn.

One such objection, which applies to orders to achieve a result and a fortiori to orders to carry on an activity, is imprecision in the terms of the order. If the terms of the court's order, reflecting the terms of the obligation, cannot be precisely drawn, the possibility of wasteful litigation over compliance is increased. So is the oppression caused by the defendant having to do things under threat of proceedings for contempt. The less precise the order, the fewer the signposts to the forensic minefield which he has to traverse. The fact that the terms of a contractual obligation are sufficiently definite to escape being void for uncertainty, or to found a claim for damages, or to permit compliance to be made a condition of relief against forfeiture, does not necessarily mean that they will be sufficiently precise to be capable of being specifically enforced. So in *Wolverhampton Corporation v Emmons*, Romer LJ said that the first condition for specific enforcement of a building contract was that:

> the particulars of the work are so far definitely ascertained that the court can sufficiently see what is the exact nature of the work of which it is asked to order the performance.

Patrick Stevedores Operations No 2 Pty Ltd v Maritime Union of Australia (No 3) (1998) 195 CLR 1

Facts and issues

The Full Federal Court granted interlocutory orders restraining employers from terminating the contracts of employment of various employees who were members of the Maritime Union of Australia ('MUA'). At issue was whether the Court should order specific performance under various orders which, it was claimed, amounted to the enforcement of employment obligations. The essence of 'orders 1–5', the relevant orders sought to be specifically enforced was: orders 1 and 4 compelled two of the Patrick Companies to treat the employer companies as the sole supplier of labour under relevant labour supply agreements. Order 2 was directed to the employer companies and bound them to treat the various labour supply agreements as being on foot. Order 3 prevented the completion of a conspiracy to dismiss the employees. Order 5 restrained the employers from doing anything that would result in the termination of the employees.

Decision

Specific performance was ordered.

Brennan, McHugh, Gummow, Kirby and Hayne JJ

> [**46**] We see in the orders no defect which sometimes is expressed as the involvement of the court in 'constant supervision' of continued conduct. Reservations of that nature have been expressed in decisions of this Court. However, questions of degree rather than absolute restrictions upon the scope of curial relief are involved (110). Reference was made in the Federal Court judgments and in submissions to this Court to the speech of Lord Hoffmann in *Cooperative Insurance Society Ltd v Argyll Stores (Holdings) Ltd*. His Lordship affirmed the refusal by the judge at first instance of an order for specific performance of a lease for a term of thirty-five years containing a covenant to keep premises open for retail trade during usual hours of business in the locality. His Lordship's statement that the usual practice was not to grant specific performance to carry on an activity over a period of time was made in response to a submission by the lessor to the effect that the equitable remedy was no longer to be understood as granted in the auxiliary jurisdiction where damages would be an inadequate remedy.
>
> ...
>
> What is significant is the acceptance by the House of Lords that the concept of 'constant supervision by the court' by itself is no longer an effective or useful criterion for refusing a decree of specific [**47**] performance. Rather, Lord Hoffmann placed stress on other propositions. First, a person who is subject to a mandatory order attended by contempt sanction ought to know with precision what is required; and, second, the possibility of 'repeated applications for rulings on compliance' with orders requiring a party 'to carry on an activity, such as running a business over a more or less extended period of time" should be discouraged.
>
> Reference to constant court applications should not be misunderstood. The courts are well accustomed to the exercise of supervisory jurisdiction upon applications by trustees, receivers, provisional liquidators and others with the responsibility for the conduct of administrations. The reservation of liberty to apply to the Federal Court in respect of certain of the orders to be made is in no way out of ordinary in the exercise of equitable jurisdiction.
>
> Further, those orders do not, in form or in substance, require the administrators to carry on business activities in the sense with which the *Argyll* case was concerned. Nor do the undertakings and orders leave those bound by them not knowing what is expected of them. This is not a case, referred to by Isaacs and Rich JJ in *Pakenham Upper Fruit Co Ltd v Crosby*, where the Court 'could never be sure that it was in a position to enforce its order without injustice'.
>
> [**47**] ... No supervision by the Court is required to give practical operation to the legal rights affected by orders 1 to 5, although North J appropriately gave all parties leave to apply: order 10.
>
> ...
>
> [the orders] are confined to the ascertainment and declaration of legal rights and obligations and, when legal rights are in competition, the courts do no more than define which rights take priority over others.

Diagnostic X-Ray Services Pty Ltd v Jewel Food Stores Pty Ltd (2001) 4 VR 632

Facts and issues

Diagnostic X-Ray Services Pty Ltd ('Diagnostic', the plaintiff) owned a shopping centre. The supermarket and adjacent petrol station were leased to Jewel Food Stores Pty Ltd ('Jewel Food', the defendant). Without notice, Jewel Food sold the supermarket business to a third party who sublet those premises. The third party was unprepared to take over the business of the service station. The service station was a strong attraction to tenants of the shopping centre. Jewel Food, finding it unprofitable to run the service station, abandoned it. The issue was whether the plaintiff could specifically enforce the obligations under the lease of the service station including the continuation of its operations.

Decision

Specific performance was granted, with the pivotal reasons being the fact that the petrol station was profitable and that the plaintiff's losses would be impossible to quantify.

Beach J

> **[2]** The defendant was the anchor-tenant of the shopping centre. The petrol station was a strong attraction at the centre and by its presence increased the patronage of the centre, both to the benefit of the defendant and the other tenants who conduct businesses at the centre.
>
> ...
>
> **[7]** The defendant placed great reliance upon the decision of the House of Lords in *Cooperative Insurance Society Ltd v Argyll Stores (Holdings) Ltd*. In *Argyll* the House of Lords held that the settled practice of the court was not to grant a mandatory injunction requiring the carrying on of a business having regard to the difficulty of drawing any such order with sufficient precision to avoid wasteful litigation regarding compliance with it and that the lessee might suffer far greater loss by having to comply with the order than the lessor would suffer from the contract being broken.
>
> **[9]** ... counsel for the plaintiff has pointed to four matters which he contends distinguish this case from Argyll and Ruffy, namely:
>
> 1. In Argyll and Ruffy the supermarkets had become unviable over time and so the decisions to walk away were commercial decisions.
>   There is no evidence that that is so in the present case. ...
>   Further, in this case the petrol station was never a viable business on its own. The defendant always knew that standing alone it would run at a loss. ...
>
> **[11]** ... I have concluded that it is strongly arguable that the facts in this case are so different from the facts in Argyll and Ruffy as to make this case distinguishable, distinguishable

because of the exceptional circumstances which surround the closure of the petrol station. Those circumstances may be enumerated as follows:

...

5. Significant detriment has been caused to the other tenants of the centre as a consequence of the closure of the petrol station. Of the four shopping centres in the Werribee area this is the only shopping centre with a petrol station. On the evidence the very existence of the petrol station at the centre attracted patrons to the centre.

[12] ... The presence of the petrol station attracts them to this shopping centre rather than one of the other three shopping centres. ...

[13] The closure of the petrol station must have a significant financial effect, not only on the plaintiff, but on the tenants of the other businesses at the centre. ...

[14] The actual loss which may be suffered by the plaintiff will be very difficult to quantify. If a tenant finds that his takings drop as a result of the closure of the petrol station, he may take the first opportunity he can to walk away from the centre. Others, whilst prepared to stay, may only do so if they can achieve a reduction in their rental. In either event the plaintiff would suffer loss. ...

The Court ordered the defendant to continue the business of the service station under its lease with the plaintiff.

Review Questions

(1) State broadly the primary factors relevant to the grant of specific performance where there has been a lengthy period of delay from the time of contracting till the time specific performance is sought.

(2) Discuss the approach of the court in *No 68 Ltd v Eastern Services Ltd* [2006] 2 NZLR 43 to delay as a consideration in the grant of specific performance.

(3) Consider the following facts: a confectioner and a movie theatre are parties to a contract. There was a condition in their contract entitling the confectioner to admission to a theatre for the purposes of selling confectionary. That condition was concurrent with conditions governing the time, place and character of the goods supplied. The court considered that the confectioner's obligations were not of a sort that were amenable to specific performance. The confectioner seeks specific performance of the movie theatre's obligations. Based on arguments relating to mutuality, discuss if the confectioner would succeed.

(4) Why is the clarity of an order a significant consideration in the grant of specific performance where the activity is a type that would need the supervision of the court?

VII Specific performance under the *Australian Consumer Law*

Concept	Short explanation	Relevant authorities	Principles text
Specific performance under the *Australian Consumer Law*	Relief under the Act is for the purpose of compensating a person for the misleading or deceptive conduct of the other but not to enforce promises.	*Futuretronics International Pty Ltd v Gadzhis* [1992] 2 VR 217	Chapter 10: [10.110]–10.113]

The question whether specific performance can be granted under the *Australian Consumer Law* or the state fair trading Acts has been considered under the equivalent provisions under the old *Trade Practices Act*. Ormiston J answered the question in the negative in *Futuretronics International Pty Ltd v Gadzhis*.[10]

Futuretronics International Pty Ltd v Gadzhis [1992] 2 VR 217

Facts and issues

Gadzhis (the defendant) had a bid at an auction accepted, but refused to sign the contract. Gadzhis's conduct by bidding represented that the bid was genuine and he intended to be bound, and amounted to misleading or deceptive conduct. The relevant question here was whether specific performance could be granted of the contract.

Decision

Specific performance could not be granted as it was not an appropriate remedy for misleading or deceptive conduct.

Ormiston J

> [**244**] … the plaintiff sought in respect of this misleading conduct that it should have a remedy by enforcing the promise which gave rise to the implied representation. There lay its difficulties, for it appears that this kind of legislation is primarily directed to compensating a party by reason of the fact that he has been misled or deceived. Thus in the leading case on damages under the *Trade Practices Act*, the High Court said the appropriate measure of damages in this type of case, at least, was reliance loss, not expectation loss; in other words the plaintiff is not normally allowed to claim for loss of his bargain: *Gates v City Mutual Life Assurance Society Ltd* (1986) 160 CLR 1. Gibbs CJ saw this resulting from the fact that the Acts referred to in ss 52 and 53 'do not include the breach of a contract.
>
> …

10 [1992] 2 VR 217.

It follows that under both the *Trade Practices Act* and the *Fair Trading Act* the remedies are designed to compensate for misleading or deception, not as a substitute means of enforcing promises.

…

[**245**] Essentially the remedies provided by the *Fair Trading Act* especially those in s 41, are there to restore those affected by misleading or deceptive conduct to the position in which they were before any contraventions of the Act take place.

…

No authority was cited for the proposition that specific performance of the promise could be obtained and the only relevant authority *Milchas Investments Pty Ltd v Larkin* suggests the contrary.

I am not persuaded that there is power to make an order that a promise, especially a promise of this kind, should be specifically performed.

…

An order akin to an order for specific performance would not appropriately compensate for that loss, but would give a different and wider remedy, not contemplated by the Act.

Review question

Explain the jurisprudential objection to the grant of specific performance as relief for conduct that is found to be misleading or deceptive.

VIII Specific restitution or specific delivery of property

Damages is the usual remedy for detinue and conversion. Equity, however, has the power to award specific restitution or specific delivery of the property. As with specific performance, the adequacy of damages is a pivotal consideration.

Concept	Short explanation	Relevant authorities	Principles text
Specific restitution or specific delivery of property	A court might give specific restitution or specific delivery of property, as relief for torts such as detinue or conversion, usually only if damages are inadequate.	*Doulton Potteries Ltd v Bronotte* [1971] 1 NSWLR 591	Chapter 10: [10.117]–[10.118]

Doulton Potteries Ltd v Bronotte [1971] 1 NSWLR 591

Facts and issues

Doulton Potteries Ltd ('Doulton', the plaintiff) owned a die which was needed in the manufacture of pipes. The die was sent to Bronotte (the defendant) for repairs. Bronotte demanded an extortionate amount of money before he would return the die. The issue was whether Doulton was entitled to an order for the return of the die and an injunction to restrain Bronotte from preventing Doulton from having access to the die.

Decision

Specific performance could have been granted but due to a procedural reason (that the order for the return of a chattel could not be justified on an originating summons) the order was not made. Injunctions as sought were, however, ordered.

Hope J

> [**596**] The defendants submitted that the court had no jurisdiction to make the orders and declarations sought, and that if there was jurisdiction, as a matter of discretion I should not make them. It was also submitted that there was no power in the court to make an order for the return of a specific chattel in a suit instituted by originating summons, and that in any event the case was not a suitable one to be dealt with in proceedings so instituted. I rejected the last submission in the exercise of my discretion but I held that an order for the return of a specific chattel is not a form of injunction, mandatory or otherwise, and that consequently there was no jurisdiction … to make the orders sought.
>
> …
>
> I also held that the court would have jurisdiction to make orders with respect to the die if it was established that it was of special value to the plaintiffs in order to carry on their business. I think I should shortly repeat the reasons for coming to this conclusion.
>
> …
>
> [**597**] Although it does not seem to have been frequently used, there is no doubt that the Chancery courts have always had jurisdiction in appropriate circumstances to make an order for the return of a specific chattel.
>
> In *Aristoc Industries Pty Ltd v RA Wenham (Builders) Pty Ltd*, Jacobs J., said:
>
>> In so many circumstances in regard to the sale or dealing with goods does equity decline to interfere that there is, as it were, an inclination to erect into a principle of equity that it will not interfere in relation to chattels except where the chattels are very rare. In my view it should be borne in mind that the rarity of the chattel is one aspect of the general question of inadequacy of damages. If damages at law are an inadequate remedy then there is no principle which will prevent the interference of the Court of Equity simply because the subject-matter is a chattel. I think that this is borne out not only by the general statements which I have last set out, but by the many decisions of the courts.
>
> …

> [**598**] Where specific things, necessary for conducting a particular business, are in the possession of persons who claim a lien upon them, and threaten an immediate sale, this Court had undoubted jurisdiction to interfere by injunction, and prevent irreparable injury to the debtor, by giving him an opportunity of redeeming assets.
>
> ...
>
> ... authorities establish that the jurisdiction of the Court of Equity to intervene in respect of chattels arises, inter alia, where those chattels are of special value to a person in the carrying on of his business, and where its jurisdiction is attracted by the nature of the relevant chattels, the court can give whatever relief be appropriate, including an order for the specific return of the particular chattel.
>
> ...
>
> It is clear that the subject die and flexible core are chattels which have special value to the plaintiffs in the carrying on of their businesses. The plaintiffs originally claimed that this was so because it would take four [**599**] months for them to have the die and flexible core replaced, and their business of manufacturing the plastic pipes I have described would cease until it was replaced.
>
> ...
>
> It is equally clear that damages would be an entirely inadequate remedy for the wrongful detention of the die, and accordingly the jurisdiction of this Court is attracted.
>
> ...
>
> [**600**] I see no reason why I should not make such a declaration where the plaintiffs are entitled to and are granted injunctive relief, and the declaration relates to that relief. Accordingly, when I come to make formal orders I will declare that the sum of $4916.25 is a reasonable price for the second plaintiff to pay to the second defendant in respect of the relevant repairs, and I will order that upon the plaintiffs and each of them undertaking to the Court to pay to the second defendant the sum of $4916.25, and upon the plaintiffs and each of them further undertaking to the Court to pay any safe custody charges payable ... the second defendant be restrained from interfering with the right of the plaintiffs or either of them to have access to the subject die.

REVIEW QUESTION

It was held in *Doulton Potteries Ltd v Bronotte* [1971] 1 NSWLR 591 that specific delivery of a chattel might be ordered where damages were not an adequate remedy for the retention of the chattel. What are the circumstances, recognised in that case, in which this requirement would be satisfied such that specific performance would be ordered?

IX Debt as a species of specific relief?

Some argue that a claim for debt, a sum owing under the terms of a contract, is in some senses 'specific performance'. But a claim from debt differs from specific performance as it is not 'discretionary'. Rather, the prerequisite for the recovery of debt is relatively straightforward and would be satisfied simply by proof that the sum is due.

Concept	Short explanation	Relevant authorities	Principles text
Debt as a species of specific relief	The plaintiff only needs to show that the debt was due in order to recover.	*Young v Queensland Trustees Ltd* (1956) 99 CLR 560	Chapter 10: [10.119]–[10.121]
	Unlike damages the plaintiff is not generally bound to mitigate to recover the debt.	*White and Carter (Councils) v McGregor* [1962] AC 413	

Young v Queensland Trustees Ltd (1956) 99 CLR 560

Facts and issues

Queensland Trustees Ltd (the plaintiff) sued to recover the repayment of loans to Young (the defendant). The questions that the High Court addressed concerned the various onuses of proof that a lender or borrower had to discharge.

Decision

In an action for debt, the defendant must prove any defences to the claim once the plaintiff shows that the debt has not been paid.

Dixon CJ, McTiernan and Taylor JJ

> [**567**] The common law does not and never did conceive of indebtedness in a sum certain for an executed consideration as a mere breach of contract: it is rather the detention of a sum of money …
>
> …
>
> [**569**] A debt recoverable under an *indebitatus* count was not and is not now conceived of simply as a cause of action for breach of duty or obligation. In other words it is a mistake to regard the liability to pay a debt of a kind formerly recoverable in debt or *indebitatus assumpsit* as no more than the result of a breach of contract, a breach which the creditor must affirmatively allege and prove
>
> …
>
> The law was and is that, speaking generally, the [**570**] defendant must allege and prove payment by way of discharge as a defence to an action for indebtedness in respect of an executed consideration.

White and Carter (Councils) Ltd v McGregor [1962] AC 413

Facts and issues

McGregor (the defendant) repudiated its contract with White and Carter (Councils) Ltd ('White and Carter', the plaintiffs) who did not accept the repudiation and continued to perform their obligations under it. White and Carter subsequently sued McGregor for the full contract price. At issue was whether White and Carter had a duty to mitigate.

Decision

White and Carter were entitled to recover the full contract and were not obliged to mitigate.

Lord Reid

> [**427**] The general rule cannot be in doubt. It was settled in Scotland at least as early as 1848 and it has been authoritatively stated time and again in both Scotland and England. If one party to a contract repudiates it in the sense of making it clear to the other party that he refuses or will refuse to carry out his part of the contract, the other party, the innocent party, has an option. He may accept that repudiation and sue for damages for breach of contract, whether or not the time for performance has come; or he may if he chooses disregard or refuse to accept it and then the contract remains in full effect.

Lord Hodson

> [**445**] The true position is that the contract survives and does so not only where specific implement is available. When the assistance of the court is not required the innocent party can choose whether he will accept repudiation and sue for damages for anticipatory breach or await the date of performance by the guilt party. Then, if there is failure in performance, his rights are preserved.
>
> ...
>
> [**446**] The only material obligation which the respondent was bound to fulfil was to pay the sum of money claimed and it is difficult to see how damages should be assessed for breach of this obligation.

Review questions

(1) In what senses is an action for debt similar to, and different from, an action for specific performance?

(2) When can a creditor sue for the recovery of a debt?

11 INJUNCTIONS

I	Introduction	400
II	The rights protected by injunctions and inadequacy of damages	401
	A Inadequacy of damages	403
	B The rights protected by injunctions	404
III	*Quia timet* injunctions	413
IV	Discretionary factors and bars to relief	414
	A General equitable bars to relief	415
	B Bars to injunctions that are equivalent to those in specific performance	419
V	Injunctions under statutes	420
	A Intellectual property	421
	B The *Australian Consumer Law*	422
	C The *Corporations Act 2001* (Cth)	424
	D Other statutory injunctions	426

I Introduction

An injunction, like specific performance, is an equitable remedy. Specific performance compels a plaintiff to perform their contractual obligations, and is granted as final relief at trial, while an injunction extends to a far broader range of circumstances, not limited to breach of contract. Further, an injunction can be granted as interlocutory relief (prior to trial) or as a final injunction at trial and different principles apply to each.

Damages must be inadequate before an injunction for a common law cause of action is granted; conversely there is no need for inadequacy of damages to be shown for injunctions for purely equitable causes of action such as for a breach of fiduciary duty.

Figure 11.1 outlines the broad considerations that must be taken into account depending on whether the injunction is sought at common law, in equity, or under a relevant statute.

Equitable and common law injunctions are subject to bars to relief (hardship, laches, and clean hands). Statutory injunctions are governed by the terms of the statute, not by general equitable principles.

Injunctions can also be classified in accordance to their *effect*. Thus, a prohibitory injunction prevents someone from doing something whereas a mandatory injunction compels them to do something. Table 11.1 broadly outlines the types of injunctions in accordance with their practical effects.

Figure 11.1 Legal, equitable and statutory injunctions

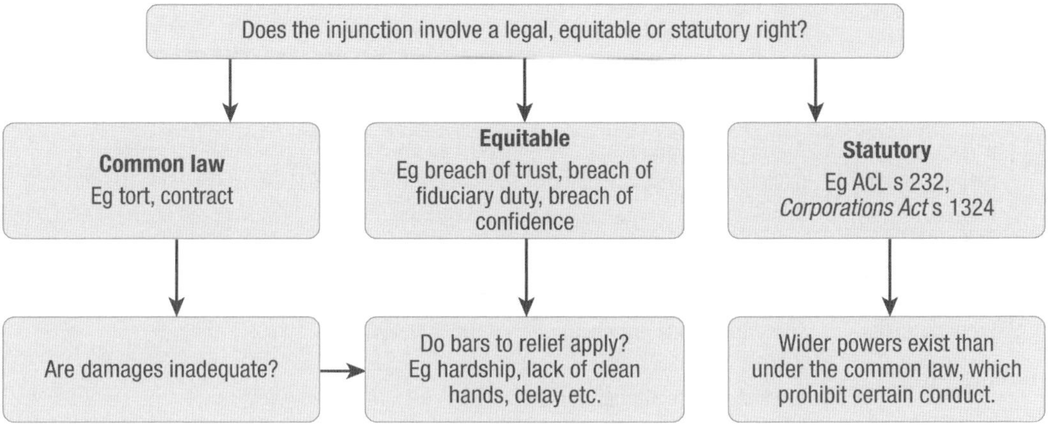

Table 11.1 Injunctions classified by practical effect

Type of injunction	Practical effect
Perpetual	Granted at trial following a final determination of the parties' rights.
Interlocutory	Granted prior to trial.
Prohibitory	*Prevents* the defendant from doing something.
Mandatory	*Compels* the defendant to do a particular thing.
Quia timet	*Prevents* the prospective infringement of a right.

II The rights protected by injunctions and inadequacy of damages

An injunction granted in the court's auxiliary jurisdiction requires it to be shown that damages are inadequate. The remedy shares a common feature with specific performance, but specific performance is final relief whereas an interlocutory injunction can be granted before trial.

The inadequacy of damages (covered more substantially in paragraph [10.20] of the principles text) will be briefly revisited in Part A. Part B, the more substantive, probes the principles applicable to the grant of injunctions in specific situations.

Concept	Short explanation	Relevant authorities	Principles text
Inadequacy of damages	The relevant question whenever an injunction in aid of a common law right is sought is whether it is just that a plaintiff should be confined to damages.	*Evans Marshall & Co Ltd v Bertola SA* [1973] 1 WLR 349	Chapter 11: [11.15]–[11.18]
Injunctions to restrain injury to property rights in land	Courts readily grant injunctions to restrain injury to land.	*Bendal Pty Ltd v Mirvac Project Pty Ltd* (1991) 23 NSWLR 464	Chapter 11: [11.19]–[11.22]
Injunctions to restrain injury to property rights in goods and funds of money	Courts may grant injunctions to restrain injury to goods where the goods are unique or scarce. An injunction might be granted where a claim is made over a particular fund.[a]	*Aristoc Industries Pty Ltd v RA Wenham (Builders) Pty Ltd* [1965] NSWR 581	Chapter 11: [11.23]–[11.24]
Injury to intellectual property	Statutory provisions empower the grant of injunctions to restrain injury for most intellectual property rights.	*Patents Act 1990* (Cth) s 122(1)	Chapter 11: [11.25]
Injury to economic rights	Injunctions may be awarded to restrain injuries to economic rights.	*Erven Warnink BV v J Townend & Sons (Hull) Ltd* [1979] AC 731	Chapter 11: [11.26]– [11.31]
Injury to bodily integrity	Although the jurisdiction does exist to do so, great caution is exercised in granting injunctions to restrain trespasses to the person.	*Parry v Crooks* (1981) 27 SASR 1	Chapter 11: [11.32]–[11.33]
Injury to reputation	Since *Bonnard v Perryman*,[b] Australian courts will rarely restrain defendants from making defamatory statements lest they impinge upon freedom of speech. An injunction will be granted for injury to reputation only in clearcut cases.	*Chappell v TCN Channel Nine Pty Ltd* (1988) 14 NSWLR 153	Chapter 11: [11.34]–[11.35]
Injury to privacy	An injunction does not lie to restrain injury to privacy as there is no general tort of invasion of privacy in Australia.[c] However, injunctions may be awarded to restrain an equitable breach of confidence.	*McKennitt v Ash* [2008] QB 73	Chapter 11: [11.36]

Concept	Short explanation	Relevant authorities	Principles text
Injunctions restraining breaches of negative covenants in a contract	Injunctions for breaches of negative covenants are subject to the same discretionary factors as other injunctions (contrary to the obiter dicta in *Doherty v Allman*[d]).	*Doherty v Allman (1878)* 3 App Cas 709 *JC Williamson Ltd v Lukey* (1931) 45 CLR 282	Chapter 11: [11.37]–[11.39]
Contracts for services	Specific performance of a contract for services will not generally be awarded.[e] However, a court may award an injunction restraining someone from providing unique services for a rival if it does not have the practical effect of being an order for specific performance for services.	*Curro v Beyond Productions Pty Ltd* (1993) 30 NSWLR 337	Chapter 11: [11.40]–[11.44]

[a] *London City Agency (JCD) Ltd v Lee* [1970] Ch 597, 600–1 (Megarry J).
[b] *Bonnard v Perryman* [1891] 2 Ch 269, 284 (Lord Coleridge CJ).
[c] *Australian Broadcasting Corporation v Lenah Game Meats Pty Ltd* (2001) 208 CLR 199.
[d] *Doherty v Allman* (1878) 3 App Cas 709, 719–20.
[e] *JC Williamson Ltd v Lukey* (1931) 45 CLR 282.

A Inadequacy of damages

When an injunction is sought in aid of a common law right, the adequacy of damages is a relevant consideration, and the difficulty in assessing those damages is a factor to be taken into account in this regard (see, eg, *Evans Marshall & Co Ltd v Bertola SA*[1]).

To the contrary, injunctions sought to prevent an equitable wrong do not require a plaintiff to establish the inadequacy of damages.[2]

Evans Marshall & Co Ltd v Bertola SA [1973] 1 WLR 349

Facts and issues

Evans Marshall ('EM', the plaintiff) was a wine merchant. Bertola (the first defendant) was contracted to appoint the plaintiff as its first defendant's exclusive agents for the sale of sherry in England. Bertola alleged that EM's services under that agreement were unsatisfactory and sought to appoint the second defendants as its agent in lieu of the plaintiff. EM alleged that Bertola was in breach of contract and sought an interlocutory injunction to restrain the defendants from selling sherry in England other than through the plaintiff. At first instance, injunctions were refused as it was considered that the prospect of a permanent injunction was not strong. On appeal, while accepting

1 [1973] 1 WLR 349.

2 See, eg, W Gummow, 'The Injunction in Aid of Legal Rights: An Australian Perspective' (1993) 56(1) *Law & Contemporary Problems* 83, 91; see the discussion at principles text, [11.18].

that the fact that there was not a strong prospect of permanent injunctions being granted was a consideration, the question nevertheless was whether it was appropriate to maintain the status quo until trial if damages were not adequate.

Decision

Damages would have been inadequate to compensate the plaintiff for its loss. The appeal was allowed and interlocutory injunctions as sought were granted.

Sachs LJ (The Court of Appeal)

> [**379**] The standard question in relation to the grant of an injunction, 'Are damages an adequate remedy?', might perhaps, in the light of the authorities of recent years, be rewritten: 'Is it just, in all the circumstances, that a plaintiff should be confined to his remedy in damages?'
>
> LSI, by Mr Butler's affidavit,[on behalf of the defendants] chose to emphasise the damage to their [**380**] goodwill and trade reputation that they would suffer if the agency at **will** which they had held for three weeks was unjustifiably disrupted: he emphasised the difficulty of assessing the resulting damage.
>
> These assertions appear a little naive when one looks in comparison at the loss of goodwill, the disruption in trade, and the litigation with sub agents which would be inflicted on the plaintiffs by an unjustified abrupt termination of an agreement with 14 years to run-terminated with the aid of allegations of their having failed to carry out their obligations and of B having made undue profits.
>
> In my judgment damages would not be an adequate remedy in this case …
>
> …
>
> The courts have repeatedly recognised that there can be claims under contracts in which, as here, it is unjust to confine a plaintiff to his damages for their breach. Great difficulty in estimating these damages is one factor that can be and has been taken into account. Another factor is the creation of certain areas of damage which cannot be taken into monetary account in a common law action for breach of contract: loss of goodwill and trade reputation are examples.

B The rights protected by injunctions

1 Injury to property rights in land

Bendal Pty Ltd v Mirvac Project Pty Ltd (1991) 23 NSWLR 464

Facts and issues

Mirvac Project Pty Ltd ('Mirvac', the defendant) performed building work for the second defendant who occupied land next to Bendal Pty Ltd's ('Bendal', the plaintiff) land. The construction method employed used a protective mesh screen which protruded into air space over Bendal's land. Was Bendal was entitled to an injunction to restrain the defendants from trespassing?

Decision

Injunction was granted, given the 'high value' placed on the rights of a landowner.

Bryson J

> [**465**] The first defendant is constructing the office building for the second defendant under a building contract made in 1988.
>
> ...
>
> The building techniques adopted involve some encroachment into space surrounding the second defendant's land ... the objects referred to in the summons as scaffolding (but better described as a screen system) project beyond the real estate boundary.
>
> ...
>
> [**467**] The plaintiff's claim is based on its right as the freehold owner with a registered title to this building and the land on which it stands. The law places very high value on the rights of owners of freehold land to control the use of that land.
>
> ...
>
> [**468**] A recent statement which I regard as appropriate to follow of the law relating to the matter before me was made by Hodgson J in *LJP Investments Pty Ltd v Howard Chia Investments Pty Ltd.*
>
> ...
>
> The plaintiff does not have any operations of its own which have actually been impeded or prevented by the presence of the screens ... Actual events at the plaintiff's building have been very little affected by the presence of the screens and are not likely to be more affected by the continued presence of the screens until the time comes when it suits the defendants to remove them
>
> ...
>
> I think it is quite clear ... that the owner of freehold land has a perfectly legitimate interest to decide who will come on to his land, who will build encroachments there, who will stay off and on what terms he is prepared to give leave and licence whether on payment of money or on no terms whatever.
>
> ...
>
> [**470**] In my view, the defendants' conduct complained of relating to the screen is a continuing trespass and the defendants' own evidence makes it in every way plain that the defendants intend that it should continue and that it is highly probable that it will continue unless restrained by injunction.
>
> ...
>
> [**472**] At the heart of the litigation is a very simple question of using or not using other people's property, and this disqualifies the defendants from any real claim to consideration of hardships which they have incurred.
>
> ...
>
> [**478**] For these reasons, I will grant the plaintiff relief such as it claims.

2 Injury to property rights in goods and funds of money

Aristoc Industries Pty Ltd v RA Wenham (Builders) Pty Ltd [1965] NSWR 581

Facts and issues

Aristoc Industries Pty Ltd ('Aristoc', the plaintiff) agreed to make custom seats to fit a lecture hall that a head contractor was constructing. After the head contractor went into liquidation, RA Wenham (Builders) Pty Ltd ('Wenham', the defendant) was assigned the rights of the main contractor. Title to the seats was retained by Aristoc, because the contract provided ownership only passed upon payment ('delivery *and* payment'). Aristoc sought to restrain Wenham from affixing the seats to the hall or from preventing Aristoc from removing the chairs from the site.

Decision

Aristoc was granted the injunction on terms, given the special value of the seats.

Jacobs J

> [**587**] The defendant relies upon the fact that the subject matter of the dispute is an assembly of chattels which even though they may not be immediately obtainable on the market can be fabricated without great difficulty.
>
> ...
>
> [**588**] It seems to me that there are a number of aspects of the present case which would make damages or any other relief at law an inadequate remedy to the present plaintiff. First, if no injunction is granted it is clear that the materials in question will be affixed to the structure of the building and upon that affixing the property in them will pass with the freehold ... . It would therefore not be possible for the plaintiff to maintain with success at law a claim in detinue to the actual goods since they would have become irrevocably affixed to the freehold.
>
> ...
>
> In the circumstances, it may well be argued that this is of no significance because even if the claim in detinue could not succeed, a claim in trover or conversion could succeed if the property to the goods is in the plaintiff. It is in this regard, in particular, that I think the plaintiff establishes a special value which these goods have to it. It agreed to make up these goods and install them and that agreement was made with a company which is now in liquidation and I think it may reasonably be presumed, in the absence of evidence to the contrary, that no performance of the contract will be obtained in that quarter.
>
> ... These materials have been specially manufactured to fit the Education Centre at the Royal Prince Alfred Hospital and on the market upon which the measure of damages in conversion would have to be found these goods might be of very little value at all. ... It seems to me that the special value that possession of these goods has to the plaintiff, is that it has a real chance of recouping the loss on its contract, not by the measure of damages available at law, but by obtaining a price equal to or not much different from the price under the original contract.

...

I therefore propose to grant the relief claimed but I propose to make it a term of this relief that the plaintiff offer the materials now upon the site to the defendant and to the Crown at the price for those materials which was set out in the quotation made part of the original sub-contract. I make this special condition upon a consideration of the public welfare involved. The building in question is a public building and the time for its completion is long overdue. I have been informed that if these materials are not available the delay will be even greater.

3 Injury to intellectual property

Patents Act 1990 (Cth) s 122(1)

The *Patents Act* provided a system of patent protection in Australia. Section 122(1) contains the statutory power to impose an injunction to restrain the breach of patent.

122 Relief for infringement of patent

(1) The relief which a court may grant for infringement of a patent includes an injunction (subject to such terms, if any, as the court thinks fit) and, at the option of the plaintiff, either damages or an account of profits.

...

4 Injury to economic rights

Erven Warnink BV v J Townend & Sons (Hull) Ltd [1979] AC 731

Facts and issues

Erven Warnink BV ('Warnink', the plaintiffs) were the original producers of a Dutch liqueur sold as 'Advocaat'. J Townend & Sons (Hull) Ltd ('Townend', the defendant) produced a similar drink marketed as 'Keeling's Old English Advocaat'. The plaintiffs sought to restrain Townend from passing off its goods as the plaintiffs'.

Decision

Injunctions were ordered to prevent the tort of passing off because of the character of the plaintiffs' products.

Lord Diplock

[**742**] My Lords, *A G Spalding & Bros v A W Gamage Ltd* and the later cases make it possible to identify five characteristics which must be present in order to create a valid

cause of action for passing off: (1) a misrepresentation (2) made by a trader in the course of trade, (3) to prospective customers of his or ultimate consumers of goods or services supplied by him, (4) which is calculated to injure the business or goodwill of another trader (in the sense that this is a reasonably foreseeable consequence) and (5) which causes actual damage to a business or goodwill of the trader by whom the action is brought or (in a *quia timet* action) will probably do so.

...

[**748**] So, on the findings of fact by Goulding J [the judge at first instance] the type of product that has gained for the name 'advocaat' on the English market the reputation and goodwill of which Keelings are seeking to take advantage by misrepresenting that their own product is of that type, is defined by reference to the nature of its ingredients irrespective of their origin. The class of traders of whose respective businesses the right to describe their products as advocaat forms a valuable part of their goodwill are those who have supplied and are supplying on the English market an egg and spirit drink in broad conformity with an identifiable recipe.

...

I would allow this appeal and restore the injunction granted by Goulding J.

5 Injury to bodily integrity

Parry v Crooks (1981) 27 SASR 1

Facts and issues

Parry (the plaintiff) alleged that Crooks (the defendant, her ex-husband) had trespassed on her property and had threatened to assault and molest her. She sought an injunction to restrain him.

Decision

An injunction to restrain an alleged apprehended assault should be granted with caution.

King CJ

[**6**] The principal question argued before us was whether the Court has power to grant the relief which was refused by Legoe J.

...

Originally Courts of Equity exercised their power to grant injunctions to prevent the commission of future torts only in the case of torts affecting proprietary rights ... . By degrees, following the conferral on the Common Law Courts of power to grant injunctions by the English *Common Law Procedure Act* ... and the *Judicature Act* reforms, the power came to be exercised in relation to other torts. Nevertheless the tort of assault was regarded as unsuited to injunctive relief.

...

It is difficult to see any reason in principle, since the fusion of law and equity, why the power to grant injunctions should not extend to all torts, nor any reasons of policy why the courts should deny to themselves power to grant injunctive relief in proper cases in respect of the commission or apprehended commission of any particular class of tortious acts.

...

Although I am unable to accept the view that there is no jurisdiction in the Court to grant injunctive relief in respect of the tort of assault, I think that the very existence of that view is an indication of some very important considerations which should lead to refusal in the exercise of the Court's discretion of injunctions restraining apprehended future assaults in all but the most exceptional circumstances. The commission of the tort of assault necessarily involves the commission of a criminal offence and while I cannot accede to the argument that the Court is precluded from granting an injunction to restrain an infringement of private rights which also amounts to a crime, I think that such injunctions should be granted with caution

...

[8] It would seem from the above consideration of the relevant principles that the only basis for the injunctions sought which require serious consideration are the prevention of threatened or apprehended assaults and the inherent jurisdiction of the Court to protect children whose welfare is in jeopardy. I think that an injunction should be granted on the first basis in exceptional circumstances only and I cannot discern such circumstances in the present case.

...

... [T]here is no sound basis for the grant of the injunction sought ... .

6 Injury to reputation

Chappell v TCN Channel Nine Pty Ltd (1988) 14 NSWLR 153

Facts and issues

TCN Channel Nine Pty Ltd ('Channel Nine', the defendant) proposed to broadcast a TV segment alleging that Chappell (the plaintiff, a well-known cricketer) had engaged in inappropriate sexual relations. Chappell sought an interlocutory injunction to restrain its showing.

Decision

The defence of justification on the basis of public interest was unsuccessful. The injunctions were granted.

Hunt J

[12] A free and general discussion of public matters is fundamental to a democratic society. It was that factor which led the Full Court of Appeal in *Bonnard v Perryman* to say that the subject matter of an action for defamation is so special as to require exceptional caution

> in exercising the jurisdiction to interfere by injunction before the trial of an action to prevent an anticipated wrong.
>
> …
>
> So far as I am concerned, that independent and overriding principle … will usually continue to be applied in the future to refuse an interlocutory injunction where such an injunction would restrain the discussion in the media of matters of public interest or concern.
>
> …
>
> [**15**] A public figure's private behaviour or character can become a matter of public interest in one of two ways – either because it affects the performance of his public duties (a proposition which I discussed earlier) or because he makes it such a matter himself. If the plaintiff had in fact deliberately put himself forward *to the public* as subscribing to such high standards in his private behaviour, so that he could be taken as having appealed to the public for its judgment on that private behaviour, he cannot then be heard to say that the public does not have the right to pronounce the judgment which he asked of it …
>
> However, an imputation of (say) immorality does not relate to a matter of public interest simply because someone else has in the past asserted that the person now accused of immorality is a moral person. …

At 15–17 his Honour opined that the plaintiff's behaviour was not a matter of public interest as he did not hold himself out as having a reputation for possessing a moral character. Consequently, the injunction as sought was awarded.

7 Injury to privacy

McKennitt v Ash [2008] QB 73

Facts and issues

McKennitt (the plaintiff) was a renowned singer. Her former friend, Ash (the first defendant), intended to publish a book containing intimate details concerning McKennitt. The issue was whether its contents amounted to a breach of confidence entitling McKennitt to injunctions to restrain its publication.

Decision

Disclosure of those details would amount to a breach of confidence and injunctions were granted as sought.

Buxton LJ

> [**8**] I start with some straightforward matters, before going on to issues of more controversy … There is no English domestic law tort of invasion of privacy …
>
> …

Of great importance in the present case, as will be explained further below, the complaint here is of what might be called old-fashioned breach of confidence …

…

[**16**] The judge made substantial findings of fact as to the nature of the relationship between the first claimant and the first defendant, and the expectation of confidence that that created. None of this was challenged on appeal, nor could it have been. Because of the importance of this aspect of the case I set out part of the judge's account:

> It is also clear from a number of quite explicit passages in the book that Ms Ash realised that substantial parts of it, at least, would fall within the scope of a reasonable expectation of privacy or a duty of confidence …

…

[**28**] The first defendant argued that all of the matters set out above were not merely the first claimant s experience, but her own experience as well. That gave her a property in the information that should not be subordinated, or at least should not be readily subordinated, to that of the first claimant.

…

[**31**] … While the first defendant had been involved in some of the matters revealed, and (which is rather different) a spectator of many others, the book, which is what this case is concerned with, is not in any real sense about her at all. The judge made that clear in … the judgment:

> It would appear that the fundamental purpose of the book, which Ms Ash has described on its cover as a must for every Loreena McKennitt fan, was to provide information to her admirers which would not otherwise be available. Much of the content of the book would be of no interest to anyone, I imagine, but for the fact that Ms McKennitt is the central character.
>
> …
>
> It is the central role of Ms McKennitt, and the revelations about her, which provide the main reason for people to acquire the book.

…

[**32**] Those conclusions, which were neither challenged nor could have been, confirm that the matters related in the book were specifically experiences of and the property of the first claimant. The first defendant cannot undermine their confidential nature by the paradox of calling in aid the confidential relationship that gave her access to the information in the first place.

8 Injunctions restraining breaches of negative covenant in a contract

It was stated in *Doherty v Allman*[3] that there was a 'well settled practice' that the court of equity would have no discretion to refuse an injunction to restrain a breach of a negative covenant.[4] That proposition, however, is contrary to propositions set out in more recent

3 (1878) 3 App Cas 709.

4 Ibid 719–20.

authorities, for example *JC Williamson Ltd v Lukey*[5] which suggest that equitable discretions would remain relevant.[6]

9 Contracts for services

Curro v Beyond Productions Pty Ltd (1993) 30 NSWLR 337

Facts and issues

Beyond Productions Pty Ltd ('Beyond', the plaintiff) produced a TV documentary program. In 1991, it contracted with Curro (the defendant) to present the program. The contract was subject to yearly renewal and at the date of judgment (May 1993) had three months to run. The contract provided that Curro would not enter into any agreement which would prevent her from fulfilling her obligations. Curro entered into a contract with a rival TV station in February 1993. Beyond sought an injunction, which was granted by Cole J. Curro appealed to the New South Wales Court of Appeal.

Decision

The injunction was granted as it did not leave Curro with a choice to be idle or be compelled to return to the employment of the plaintiff.

Meagher JA, Handley JA and Cripps JA

> [**345**] A negative promise would not be enforced by injunction if that would have the practical effect of compelling specific performance of a contract of personal service or if it would force the defendant either to perform that contract or remain idle (with overtones of destitution) …
>
> …
>
> In some cases an attempt to obtain an injunction based on *Lumley v* [**347**] *Wagner* has failed. One such decision is *Page One Records Ltd v Britton*. A group of 'musicians' promised not to employ another manager during the four years of their contract with the plaintiff. The court refused to restrain the 'musicians' from continuing a clear breach of this promise. However, there were significant features which distinguish it from *Lumley v Wagner* and other cases in which an injunction has been granted. The injunction sought was for four years which is a long time in this context, and it would have compelled the defendants to re-employ the plaintiff or go out of business.
>
> …
>
> We are of the view that the authorities establish that in a *Lumley v Wagner* case, an injunction will still be granted when the balance of discretionary factors is in the plaintiff's favour. In the present case, to grant the injunction sought is not to order specific performance of the service and services contracts. Miss Curro could comply with the injunctions without resuming work for Beyond. She would not be forced to choose between service with Beyond or idleness. Other employments would be open to her. There is no question of her being destitute.

5 (1931) 45 CLR 282.

6 Ibid 298–300.

In *Page One Records Ltd v Britton*,[7] referred to in *Curro v Beyond Productions Pty Ltd* above, the band 'The Troggs' had hired a manager for a duration of five years, but had a falling out with him a year later. Stamp J held that an injunction should not be granted because:

> the *Troggs* are simple persons, of no business experience, and could not survive without the services of a manager. As a practical matter on the evidence before me, I entertain no doubt that they would be compelled, if the injunction was granted, on the terms that the plaintiffs seek, to continue to employ the first plaintiff as their manager and agent and it is, I think, on this point that this case diverges from *Lumley v Wagner* ...[8]

Review Questions

(1) What principles underpin the willingness to grant injunctions to restrain injuries to property rights in land?

(2) What was the fundamental difference between *Curro v Beyond Productions Pty Ltd* (1993) 30 NSWLR 337, where injunctions were granted, and *Page One Records Ltd v Britton* [1968] 1 WLR 157, where injunctions were refused, to restrain breaches of negative covenants?

III *Quia timet* injunctions

Quia timet means 'be afraid' in Latin. A *quia timet* injunction, therefore, is one that is sought prior to any damage being sustained, but where damage has been threatened.

Concept	Short explanation	Relevant authorities	Principles text
Quia timet injunctions	A *quia timet* injunction is granted in 'fear' that damage might be suffered.	*Proctor v Bayley* (1889) 42 Ch D 390	Chapter 11: [11.45]–[11.48]
	The *imminence* of damage is pivotal for the granting of a *quia timet* injunction which might be granted even before damage has been suffered.	*Barlow v Neville Jeffress Advertising Pty Ltd* (1994) 4 Tas R 391	

It was stated in *Proctor v Bayley*[9] that an injunction could be *preventive*, to prevent the commission of a threatened unlawful act.[10] In *Barlow v Neville Jeffress Advertising Pty Ltd*,[11] a *quia timet* injunction was granted to prevent the defendant from acting in breach of a covenant which he had insisted was unenforceable because he had given no undertakings not to act in breach of it.[12]

7 [1968] 1 WLR 157.

8 Ibid 166.

9 (1889) 42 Ch D 390.

10 Ibid 398.

11 (1994) 4 Tas R 391.

12 Ibid [401].

Review questions

(1) What is the fundamental characteristic of a *quia timet* injunction?

(2) Discuss why a *quia timet* injunction was granted in *Barlow v Neville Jeffress Advertising Pty Ltd* (1994) 4 Tas R 391.

IV Discretionary factors and bars to relief

The grant of an injunction is always subject to the discretion of the court. The discussion below is in two parts: the first analyses general equitable bars and the second discusses bars to injunctions which are equivalent to those in specific performance.

In relation to the second part, an injunction which, by restraining the defendant from doing something, might have the practical effect of specific performance and, in that light, the bars that are equivalent to those in specific performance would equally apply to injunctions.

Concept	Short explanation	Relevant authorities	Principles text
General equitable bars	The general bars to relief are the same in relation to specific performance, and indeed to all equitable remedies.		Chapter 11: [11.50]
Hardship and the public interest	Inconvenience or hardship to the general public is traditionally irrelevant.	*Shelfer v City of London Electric Lighting Co* [1895] 1 Ch 287	Chapter 11: [11.51]–[11.53]
	In some cases, consideration of the public interest might result in the refusal of an injunction to restrain a nuisance.	*Lawrence v Fen Tigers Ltd* [2014] AC 822	
Lack of clean hands	General immorality is no bar to relief: the conduct complained of must relate to the dispute at hand.	*Duchess of Argyll v Duke of Argyll* [1967] Ch 302	Chapter 11: [11.54]–[11.55]
Laches: delay with acquiescence and delay with prejudice	Delay and acquiescence and delay with prejudice are reasons to refuse the award of an injunction. Delay may be matters that would indicate a court might award Lord Cairns Act damages in lieu of an injunction.	*Lindsay Petroleum v Hurd* (1875) LR 5 PC 221 (see Chapter 10, page 381 for extract) *No 68 Ltd v Eastern Services Ltd* [2006] 2 NZLR 43 (see Chapter 10, page 382 for extract)	Chapter 11: [11.56]–[11.57] Chapter 10: [10.86]–[10.89]
Bars to relief that are equivalent to those in specific performance	To the extent that an injunction although negative in form has the effect of a decree of specific performance, the same bars to relief as with specific performance would apply.*	*Page One Records Ltd v Britton* [1968] 1 WLR 157	Chapter 11: [11.58] Chapter 10: [10.90]–[10.109]

* *Page One Records Ltd v Britton* [1968] 1 WLR 157.

A General equitable bars to relief

The cases in sub-part A cover the general bars to relief, namely those which would apply to all forms of equitable remedies, explored here in their specific application to injunctive relief.

1 Hardship and the public interest

Shelfer v City of London Electric Lighting Co [1895] 1 Ch 287

Facts and issues

The Shelfers (the plaintiffs) ran a pub nearby to a building housing electric generators. The building was owned by London Electric Lighting Co (the defendant), which supplied electric lighting to the City of London. Shelfer alleged the engines' vibrations cracked the pub's walls and fixtures and made his wife and daughter unwell. At first instance, Kekewich J awarded damages in lieu of an injunction.

Decision

The Court of Appeal reversed the decision (see below) and granted an injunction.

Lindley LJ

> [**315**] The jurisdiction to give damages instead of an injunction is in words given in all cases ... But in exercising the jurisdiction thus given attention ought to be paid to well settled principles; and ever since *Lord Cairns' Act* was passed the Court of Chancery has repudiated the notion that the Legislature intended to turn that Court into a tribunal for legalizing wrongful acts; or in other words, the Court has always protested against the notion that it ought to allow a wrong to continue simply because the [**316**] wrongdoer is able and willing to pay for the injury he may inflict.
>
> Neither has the circumstance that the wrongdoer is in some sense a public benefactor (eg a gas or water company or sewer authority) ever been considered a sufficient reason for refusing to protect by injunction an individual whose rights are being persistently infringed. Expropriation, even for a money consideration, is only justifiable when Parliament has sanctioned it. Courts of Justice are not like Parliament, which considers whether proposed works will be so beneficial to the public as to justify exceptional legislation, and the deprivation of people of their rights with or without compensation.
>
> ...
>
> Without denying the jurisdiction to award damages instead of an injunction, even in cases of continuing actionable nuisances, such jurisdiction ought not to be exercised in such cases except under very exceptional circumstances.

AL Smith LJ

> [**321**] There is no suggestion of any conduct on the Plaintiff's part depriving him of his *prima facie* right to an injunction.

> Then why is it that Mr Justice Kekewich awarded damages in the place of an injunction?
>
> The learned Judge appears to have thought that, because the Defendants at the trial had consented to abate the nuisance caused by steam, though not that caused by vibration and noise, damages were the proper remedy and adequate to compensate the Plaintiff.
>
> [**322**] It is here that I cannot agree with the learned Judge. Because the Plaintiff does not suffer a money loss, and is only to make arrangements for sleeping somewhere else, he according to the judge is not entitled to stop the continuance of the nuisance, but damages are a very fair compensation.
>
> ...
>
> In such cases the well-known rule is not to accede to the application, but to grant the injunction sought, for the plaintiff's legal right has been invaded, and he is prima facie entitled to an injunction. ...

AL Smith LJ proceeded to outline when damages in lieu of an injunction should be awarded, discussed in Chapter 12 on page 441.

Lawrence v Fen Tigers Ltd [2014] AC 822

Facts and issues

Lawrence (the plaintiff) lived half a mile from a stadium run by Fen Tigers Ltd ('Fen Tigers', the defendants), which regularly held motor races. Lawrence sought an injunction in nuisance to restrain the noise. Fen Tigers argued that their activity had been conducted for over 20 years, and formed part of the character of the locality, particularly as council planning approval had been granted for the conduct of that activity.

Decision

The defendant had created a nuisance, but damages were more appropriate than an injunction, in part because of the public interest in continuation of races.

Lord Neuberger

> [**851**] Where a claimant has established that the defendant's activities constitute a nuisance, prima facie the remedy to which she is entitled ... is an injunction to restrain the defendant from committing such nuisance in the future; of course, the precise form of any injunction will depend very much on the facts of the particular case.
>
> ...

The question which arises is what, if any, principles govern the exercise of the court's jurisdiction to award damages instead of an injunction. The case which is probably most frequently cited on the question is *Shelfer v City of London Electric Lighting Co.*

...

[854] ... The ... problem is the unsatisfactory way in which it seems that the public interest is to be taken into account when considering the issue whether to grant an injunction or award damages ... . Either the public interest is capable of being relevant to the issue or it is not. As part of this ... problem, there is a question as to the extent to which it is relevant that the activity giving rise to the nuisance has the benefit of a planning permission.

...

[855] ... The court's power to award damages in lieu of an injunction involves a classic exercise of discretion, which should not, as a matter of principle, be fettered. And, as a matter of practical fairness, each case is likely to be so fact-sensitive that any firm guidance is likely to do more harm than good. On this aspect, I would adopt the observation of Millett LJ in *Jaggard v Sawyer* where he said:

> Reported cases are merely illustrations of circumstances in which particular judges have exercised their discretion, in some cases by granting an injunction, and in others by awarding damages instead. Since they are all cases on the exercise of a discretion, none of them is a binding authority on how the discretion should be exercised.

...

[856] ... As for the second problem ... of public interest, I find it hard to see how there could be any circumstances in which it arose and could not, as a matter of law, be a relevant factor. Of course, it is very easy to think of circumstances in which it might arise but did not begin to justify the court refusing, or, as the case may be, deciding, to award an injunction if it was otherwise minded to do so. But that is not the point. The fact that a defendant's business may have to shut down if an injunction is granted should, it seems to me, obviously be a relevant fact ... Equally, I do not see why the court should not be entitled to have regard to the fact that many other neighbours in addition to the claimant are badly affected by the nuisance as a factor in favour of granting an injunction.

... In some cases, the grant of planning permission for a particular activity may provide strong support for the contention that the activity is of benefit to the public, which would be relevant to the question of whether or not to grant an injunction. Accordingly, the existence of a planning permission which expressly or inherently authorises carrying on an activity in such a way as cause a nuisance by noise or the like, can be a factor in favour of refusing an injunction and compensating the claimant in damages.

...

[862] ... the order of Judge Seymour QC [to refuse the injunctions] is restored.

2 Lack of clean hands

Duchess of Argyll v Duke of Argyll [1967] Ch 302

Facts and issues

The Duke (the defendant) and the Duchess (the plaintiff) divorced after the Duke alleged that the Duchess had been unfaithful. The Duchess published an account of their marriage in a tabloid newspaper, and the Duke sought to publish his account in a different tabloid newspaper. The Duchess applied for an injunction to restrain his publication. It was accepted that the marital relationship gave rise to an obligation of confidence. The Duke alleged the Duchess did not 'come to the court with clean hands'.

Decision

The Duchess's conduct did not amount to a lack of clean hands; this disentitled her to injunctions because it did not relate to the dispute at hand.

Ungoed-Thomas J

> [**330**] The defendants then submitted that, even if the plaintiff would otherwise be entitled to this injunction which she claims for breach of confidence, nevertheless she ought not to be granted this relief, [**331**] first, on the ground that she herself had broken the mutual obligation of confidence between herself and her husband by some articles by her published in the 'Sunday Mirror' last year; and secondly, by her attitude to the sanctity of marriage as set out in Lord Wheatley's judgment in the divorce proceedings which I have mentioned.
>
> ...
>
> In my view, by far the most serious complaint about anything in the plaintiff's articles is her statement in the article of June 9, 1963, which is exhibited to the plaintiff's affidavit, that her husband had been taking purple hearts or, to give them their medical name, drinamyl tablets.[13] This, in my view, was a serious breach of confidence, nor, rightly, did plaintiff's counsel seek to submit otherwise. The other information in the plaintiff's articles most relied on by the defendants was that the Duke's Castle at Inverary was saved from being closed by assistance from the plaintiff's father and a legacy from a Miss Temple. But even after allowing for the disclosure about the purple hearts the accumulation of the Duke's breaches of most intimate confidences in his articles are, to my mind, of an altogether different order of perfidy. Indeed, the plaintiff's article of June 2, 1963, though not free from objection, yet leaves on my mind a more sympathetic and favourable impression of the Duke than do his own articles.
>
> Lord Wheatley said that by 1960 the plaintiff's attitude to the sanctity of marriage was – and I quote –
>
>> what the moderns might call sophisticated but what in plain language can only be described as wholly immoral.

13 An early form of antidepressant.

...

Should, then the plaintiff be denied the injunction which she would otherwise get because she has herself to an extent broken [**332**] confidence and because she, after the confidences of whose breach she complains, adopted an immoral attitude towards her marriage? A person coming to Equity for relief ... must come with clean hands; but the cleanliness required is to be judged in relation to the relief that is sought.

First, with regard to the plaintiff's articles, for the reasons already indicated I do not consider that the plaintiff's own articles justify the objectionable passages in the Duke's articles or, of themselves, should disentitle the plaintiff to the court's protection.

Secondly, with regard to the plaintiff's immorality, it was, of course, the basis for the divorce and the termination of the marriage. Such behaviour makes the confidential relationship of marriage impossible. However, what it does is to undermine confidence for the future and not betray the confidences of the past. If, on divorce, the innocent party is to be licensed to reveal marriage confidences, is the guilty party to be free to do so too? That would be piling injury on injury to the innocent and would be plainly intolerable.

...

The plaintiff's adultery, repugnant though it be, should not in my view license the husband to broadcast unchecked the most intimate confidences of earlier and happier days.'

3 Laches: delay with acquiescence and delay with prejudice

Delay and acquiescence and delay with prejudice are reasons to refuse the award of an injunction. See the discussion in Chapter 10 in relation to specific performance, and [11.56]–[11.57] of the principles text.

B Bars to injunctions that are equivalent to those in specific performance

This is well illustrated by a consideration of *Page One Records Ltd v Britton*,[14] the facts and reasoning of which are amply set out in the extract of *Curro v Beyond Productions Pty Ltd* on page 412. The crucial aspect of the reasoning there was that the practical effect of an injunction that restrained the musicians from engaging another manager would have had the practical effect of compelling them to specifically perform the agreement with the plaintiff, in effect by re-employing him. This attracted a bar on relief equivalent to that which would have barred specific performance, namely that it would have required constant supervision and was for personal service[15] nor was it of the type that could have achieved a definite result by complying with clearly identifiable terms.[16]

14 [1968] 1 WLR 157.

15 See *Ryan v Mutual Tontine Westminster Chambers Association* [1893] 1 Ch 116 – extracted on page 386.

16 As was the case, eg, with *Cooperative Insurance Society Ltd v Argyll Stores (Holdings) Ltd* [1998] AC 1.

Review questions

(1) Do you think the public interest should be a relevant factor in the grant of an injunction?

(2) If an injunction is not granted for discretionary reasons (eg public interest or delay), what other options does a court have to recognise the plaintiff's interest?

V Injunctions under statutes

Apart from the common law, various statutes also confer the power to grant injunctions. This section introduces the more important statutory provisions, focusing on the interrelationship between the discretions under the statutory power and under the general law.

Concept	Short explanation	Relevant authorities	Principles text
Injunctions under statutes – the general concepts	Where a statute confers the power to grant an injunction, discretions are to be governed by the content of the statute; it should not be assumed that equitable principles apply but rather to look to the policy and content of the statute.	*Cardile v LED Builders Pty Ltd* (1999) 198 CLR 380	Chapter 11: [11.59]–[11.60]
Intellectual property	Injunctions are available under numerous statutes to restrain the breach of intellectual property rights. Despite the statutory power to do so, equity continues to influence the grant of these injunctions.	Eg *Patents Act 1990* (Cth) s 122; *Copyright Act 1968* (Cth) s 115 (2); *Designs Act 2003* (Cth) s 75(1)(a); *Trade Marks Act 1995* (Cth) s 126(1)(a); *Circuit Layouts Act 1989* (Cth) s 27(2), *Plant Breeder's Rights Act 1994* (Cth) s 56(3)	Chapter 11: [11.61]
The *Australian Consumer Law*	The *Australian Consumer Law* confers a power to grant injunctions which is broader than under the general law.	Section 232 (similarly ss 233 and 235) *ICI Australia Operations Pty Ltd v Trade Practices Commission* (1992) 38 FCR 248	Chapter 11: [11.62]–[11.68]
Corporations Act 2001 (Cth)	Section 1324 of the *Corporations Act* contains broad powers to grant injunctions, unconstrained by equitable principles.	*Corporations Act 2001* (Cth) s 1324 *Australian Securities and Investments Commission v Storm Financial Ltd (in liq) (recs and mgrs. apptd) (No 2)* [2011] FCA 858	Chapter 11: [11.69]

The existence of a statutory power to grant injunctions will be governed by the policy under the relevant statute.

Cardile v LED Builders Pty Ltd (1999) 198 CLR 380

Facts and issues

The substantive question in this case was whether a Mareva injunction may be granted against a third party where they had not been shown to have an interest in the fund in question (a power said to be derived from s 37A of the *Conveyancing Act 1919* (NSW)). The extract focuses on the Court's general considerations of the power to grant an injunction under a statute.

Decision

The Court looks at the power in the statute and does not assume that those powers are the same as in equity.

Gaudron, McHugh, Gummow and Callinan JJ

> **[28]** The term 'injunction' is used in numerous statutes to identify a particular species of order, the making of which the law in question provides as part of a new regulatory or other regime, which may be supported by penal provisions. …
>
> These provisions empower courts to give a remedy in many cases where none would have been available in a court of equity in the exercise of its jurisdiction.
>
> …
>
> **[29]** In these situations, the term 'injunction' takes its content from the provisions of the particular statute in question. In other laws, for example Div 2 (ss 43–65) of Pt III of the *Proceeds of Crime Act 1987* (Cth), where the term 'restraining order' is used, remedies having some characteristics of injunctions as understood in courts of equity are given their own particular statutory designation.
>
> …
>
> **[31]** … [I]n England, it is now settled by several decisions of the House of Lords that the power stated in Judicature legislation – that the court may grant an injunction in all cases in which it appears to the court to be just and convenient to do so – does not confer an unlimited power to grant injunctive relief. Regard must still be had to the existence of a legal or equitable right which the injunction protects against invasion or threatened invasion, or other unconscientious conduct or exercise of legal or equitable rights. The situation thus confirmed by these authorities reflects the point made by Ashburner that 'the power of the court to grant an injunction is limited by the nature of the act which it is sought to restrain'.

A Intellectual property

Many intellectual property rights are governed by statute, of which some of the more important are patents, copyright and trademarks, such as *Patents Act 1990* (Cth) s 122; *Copyright Act 1968* (Cth) s 115(2); *Designs Act 2003* (Cth) s 75(1)(a); *Trade Marks Act 1995*

(Cth) s 126(1)(a); *Circuit Layouts Act 1989* (Cth) s 27(2); and *Plant Breeder's Rights Act 1994* (Cth) s 56(3). Equitable principles continue to influence the grant of injunctions under those statutes.[17]

B The *Australian Consumer Law*

The primary provision in the *Australian Consumer Law* ('ACL') conferring the power to grant injunctions is s 232. Note, in particular, the discussion in *ICI Australia Operations Pty Ltd v Trade Practices Commission*[18] (extracted on page 423) concerning the public policy considerations that underpin the statutory power to grant injunctions under that section when compared to the general law, which focuses on the protection of private proprietary rights. Broadly, the power in that section is to grant an injunction to restrain a person from engaging in conduct that would contravene the relevant provisions under that act.

Australian Consumer Law s 232(1)(a), (4)

Australian Consumer Law is a national code, applying to all states and territories, and is set out as a schedule in the *Competition and Consumer Act 2010*. It contains a comprehensive code addressing a broad range of matters that affect the conduct of business in Australia, and the rights of those carrying on business. The power to grant injunctions is significantly broader than under the general law.

232 Injunctions

(1) A court may grant an injunction, in such terms as the court considers appropriate, if the court is satisfied that a person has engaged, or is proposing to engage, in conduct that constitutes or would constitute:

(a) a contravention of a provision of Chapter 2, 3 or 4; …

…

(4) The power of the court to grant an injunction under subsection (1) restraining a person from engaging in conduct may be exercised:

(a) whether or not it appears to the court that the person intends to engage again, or to continue to engage, in conduct of a kind referred to in that subsection; and

(b) whether or not the person has previously engaged in conduct of that kind; and

(c) whether or not there is an imminent danger of substantial damage to any other person if the person engages in conduct of that kind.

…

17 See, eg, the discussion in PW Young, C Croft and ML Smith *On Equity* (Law Book, 2009) [16.180].

18 (1992) 38 FCR 248.

ICI Australia Operations Pty Ltd v Trade Practices Commission (1992) 38 FCR 248

Facts and issues

ICI Ltd appealed against the grant of injunctions restraining it from engaging in retail price maintenance in respect of certain agricultural products, or inducing others to do so. The extract considers the wide powers conferred by the injunctive powers of the (then) *Trade Practices Act 1974* (Cth).

Decision

The appeal was dismissed by the Full Federal Court. The Court noted the wide powers conferred under the *Trade Practices Act* and the focus on the public interest.

Lockhart J

> [**255**] Subsection (2) of s 80 [s 232 Australian Consumer Law] empowers the court to grant an interim injunction 'where in the opinion of the Court it is desirable to do so'. In *World Series Cricket Pty Ltd v Parish* … it was stated by Bowen CJ (at 185) that 'These words confer a judicial discretion of the widest kind upon the Court'; though his Honour then said:
>
> > It is not an arbitrary discretion but one to be exercised judicially in accordance with principle. The principles concerning the grant of interlocutory injunctions were developed in the Court of Chancery, but have been moulded to what is appropriate for different jurisdictions in which interlocutory relief may be obtained.
>
> …
>
> Subsections (4) and (5) of s 80 are novel because they empower the court to grant injunctive relief notwithstanding that the defendant has not previously engaged in the prohibited conduct or does not intend to engage in it again or to continue to engage in it or there is no imminent danger of substantial damage. Yet these are the traditional requirements for equitable injunctive relief.
>
> …
>
> In my opinion subss (4) and (5) are designed to ensure that once the condition precedent to the exercise of injunctive relief has been satisfied (ie contraventions or proposed contraventions of Pt IV or V of the Act), the court should be given the widest possible injunctive powers, devoid of traditional constraints, though the power must be exercised judicially and sensibly.
>
> …
>
> Injunctions are traditionally employed to restrain repetition of conduct. A statutory provision that enables an injunction to be granted to prevent the commission of conduct that has never been done before and is not likely to be done again is a statutory enlargement of traditional equitable principles. But this is because traditional doctrine surrounding the

grant of injunctive relief was developed primarily for the protection of private proprietary rights. Public interest injunctions are different.

...

This does not mean that the traditional [**257**] equitable doctrines are irrelevant. For example, it must be relevant to consider questions of repetition of conduct or whether it has ever occurred before or whether imminent substantial damage is likely: but the absence of any one or more of these elements is not fatal to the grant of an injunction under s 80. That is the effect of subss (4) and (5) (subs (4) in relation to the prevention of conduct and subs (5) in relation to a mandatory injunction). Their presence is not an indication of a new statutory house, rather an old house with some modern extensions.

C The *Corporations Act 2001* (Cth)

Corporations Act 2001 (Cth) s 1324(1), (6)–(8)

The *Corporations Act 2001* is a Federal Act which regulates the conduct of companies in Australia. Its provisions regulate all aspects of the conduct of companies and those associated with companies including the formation of a company, and the duties of directors of companies. Section 1324 of the *Corporations Act 2001* (as with numerous other provisions conferring the statutory power to grant injunctions) is couched in language aimed at restraining persons from engaging in conduct that might constitute a 'contravention' of that Act. Predictably, given the wide-sweeping scope of the Act, the power to grant injunctions is significantly broader than under the general law.

1324 Injunctions

(1) Where a person has engaged, is engaging or is proposing to engage in conduct that constituted, constitutes or would constitute:

(a) a contravention of this Act; etc.

...

the Court may, on the application of ASIC, or of a person whose interests have been, are or would be affected by the conduct, grant an injunction, on such terms as the Court thinks appropriate, restraining the first-mentioned person from engaging in the conduct

...

(6) The power of the Court to grant an injunction restraining a person from engaging in conduct may be exercised:

(a) whether or not it appears to the Court that the person intends to engage again, or to continue to engage, in conduct of that kind; and

(b) whether or not the person has previously engaged in conduct of that kind; and

(c) whether or not there is an imminent danger of substantial damage to any person if the first-mentioned person engages in conduct of that kind.

(7) The power of the Court to grant an injunction requiring a person to do an act or thing may be exercised:

(a) whether or not it appears to the Court that the person intends to refuse or fail again, or to continue to refuse or fail, to do that act or thing; and

(b) whether or not the person has previously refused or failed to do that act or thing; and

(c) whether or not there is an imminent danger of substantial damage to any person if the first-mentioned person refuses or fails to do that act or thing.

(8) Where ASIC applies to the Court for the grant of an injunction under this section, the Court must not require the applicant or any other person, as a condition of granting an interim injunction, to give an undertaking as to damages.

...

Australian Securities and Investments Commission v Storm Financial Ltd (in liq) (recs and mgrs. apptd) (No 2) [2011] FCA 858

Facts and issues

This case was one in a series of actions concerning Storm Financial Ltd ('Storm'), which (prior to being put into liquidation) operated a series of managed investment schemes in a manner alleged to have been in contravention of s 601ED of the *Corporations Act 2001* (Cth). The relief sought by the Australian Securities and Investments Commission ('ASIC') included orders injuncting Storm from operating the managed investment scheme. It was argued, inter alia, that due to the liquidation of Storm, injunctions were futile.

Decision

Given the broad power under the *Corporations Act* to grant injunctions, ASIC had a valid basis for the orders for injunctions.

Reeves J

[49] Mr Gleeson submitted that, so far as these proceedings are now directed to ASIC obtaining an injunction under s 1324 of the Act, they are futile. He submitted this was so because Storm is now in liquidation, all the investment schemes concerned have been wound up and there is therefore no likelihood of any similar conduct occurring in the future. I do not consider this submission can be accepted. There is ample authority to the effect that a statutory provision such as s 1324 is not constrained by the usual equitable principles in relation to the grant of injunctions, including the principle that an injunction should not be issued where there is no likelihood of the conduct in question being repeated in the future. It follows that quite apart from enjoining a repetition of certain conduct, a court may issue an injunction under s 1324 to mark its disapproval of that conduct involved and to deter others from engaging in similar conduct in the future: per Austin J, *Australian Securities and Investments Commission v Parkes* (2001) 38 ACSR 355 at [9] per Austin J and *Australian*

Securities and Investments Commission v Mauer-Swisse Securities Ltd (2002) 42 ACSR 605; [2002] NSWSC 741 at [14]–[16] and [36] per Palmer J.

[50] … I consider ASIC has now made a valid and justiciable claim for relief under s 1324 of the Act …

D Other statutory injunctions

Other statutory injunctions, such as s 12GD of the *Australian Securities and Investments Commission Act 2001* (Cth), generally mirror s 232 of the *Australian Consumer Law* and s 1324 of the *Corporations Act 2001* (Cth) in conferring very broad powers.

REVIEW QUESTIONS

(1) Where an injunction is authorised under a particular statute, to what extent will the general principles of equity be relevant to the grant of the injunction?

(2) Examine sub-ss 232(3) and (4) of the *Australian Consumer Law* and sub-ss 1234(6) and (7) of the *Corporations Act*. What are the common features of these provisions?

12 'EQUITABLE DAMAGES' OR LORD CAIRNS' ACT DAMAGES

I	Introduction	427
II	History	429
III	Advantages of Lord Cairns' Act damages for a plaintiff	429
IV	Jurisdiction to award Lord Cairns' Act damages	430
V	The need for a 'wrongful act' in some Australian jurisdictions	431
	A Australian legislation which mentions 'wrongful act'	432
	B Australian legislation which does not mention 'wrongful act'	432
	C Lord Cairns' Act damages for statutory wrongdoing	434
VI	Factors influencing the exercise of the jurisdiction	436
	A General principles	436
	B The *Shelfer* criteria	441
VII	The basis of assessment	446
	A Timing	446
	B Gain-based relief – 'reasonable fee' awards	446
	C Loss-based relief – compensatory awards of various kinds	448
VIII	Discretionary bars to relief	449
IX	Part 9.5 of the *Corporations Act 2001* (Cth)	449
X	The future of Lord Cairns' Act damages	450

I Introduction

Legislation in all Australian jurisdictions allows courts to award damages in addition to, or in lieu of, specific performance or an injunction.[1] Although these are sometimes called 'equitable damages', to avoid confusion with equitable compensation, they are called 'Lord Cairns' Act damages' in this book and the principles text.

These damages are primarily awarded for proprietary torts such as trespass, and for breaches of negative covenant where no other relief is available. The quantum varies, and the measurement of 'reasonable fee' awards in particular is still controversial.

1 *Supreme Court Act 1933* (ACT) s 34; *Supreme Court Act 1970* (NSW) s 68; *Supreme Court Act 1979* (NT) s 14(1)(b); *Civil Proceedings Act 2011* (Qld) s 8; *Supreme Court Act 1935* (SA) s 30; *Supreme Court Civil Procedure Act 1932* (Tas) s 11(13); *Supreme Court Act 1986* (Vic) s 38; *Supreme Court Act 1935* (WA) s 25(10).

Figure 12.1 How to approach Lord Cairns' Act ('LCA') damages

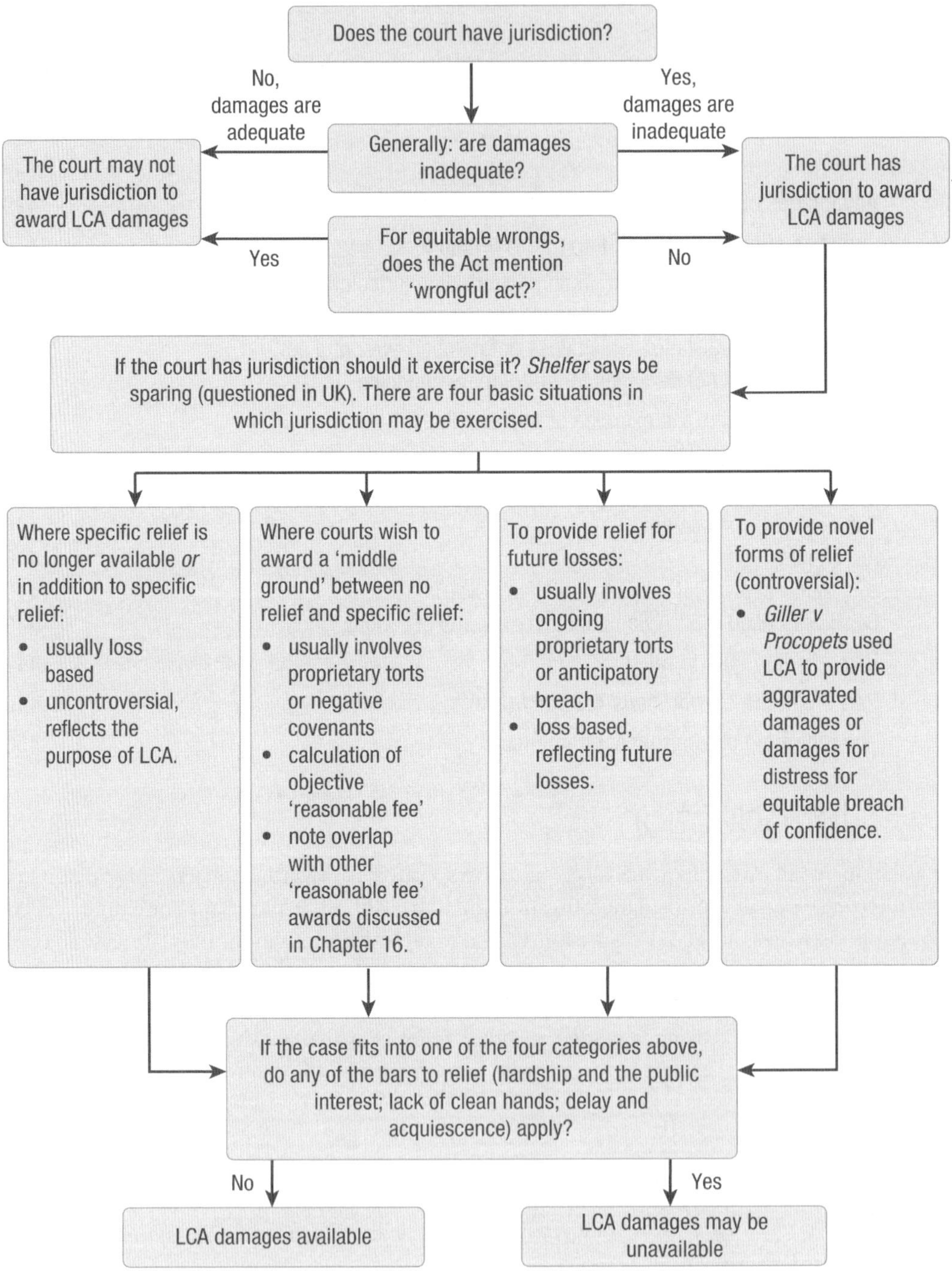

II History

All Australian provisions are based on the English *Chancery Amendment Act 1858*, known as 'Lord Cairns' Act'. This pre-Judicature Act allowed the Courts of Chancery to award damages in lieu if it turned out specific relief was impossible or unavailable for discretionary reasons, or was needed in addition to specific relief. This ensured the plaintiff did not have to start a new action for damages all over again in the common law courts.

Concept	Short explanation	Relevant authorities	Principles text
History of Lord Cairns' Act	The original provisions were designed to prevent circuity of actions in the Courts of Chancery.	*Chancery Amendment Act 1858* (21 & 22 Vict c 27)	Chapter 12: [12.4]–[12.7]

Chancery Amendment Act 1858 (21 & 22 Vict c 27) s 2

The purpose of the original 'Lord Cairns' Act' legislation (excerpted below) was to allow parties who sued in the Court of Chancery to obtain damages from that court, rather than being forced to start all over again in the common law courts.

> 2. In all cases in which the Court of Chancery has jurisdiction to entertain an application for an injunction against a breach of any covenant, contract or agreement, or against the commission or continuance of any wrongful act, or for the specific performance of any covenant, contract or agreement, it shall be lawful for the same court, if it shall think fit, to award damages to the party injured either in addition to or in substitution for such injunction or specific performance, and such damages may be assessed in such manner as the court shall direct.

Some Australian legislation reproduces the original provision, whereas other Australian legislation uses a 'simplified' version.

REVIEW QUESTION

Find the Lord Cairns' Act provision for your jurisdiction and compare it to the provision in the above extract. How does it differ?

III Advantages of Lord Cairns' Act damages for a plaintiff

Concept	Short explanation	Relevant authorities	Principles text
Advantages of Lord Cairns' Act damages	Advantages of Lord Cairns' Act damages to plaintiffs include accessing awards which would otherwise be unavailable.	*Wrotham Park Estate Co Ltd v Parkside Homes Ltd* [1974] 1 WLR 798 (see Chapter 16, page 570 for an extract)	Chapter 12: [12.8]–[12.14]

There are a number of advantages to the Lord Cairns' Act damages:

- Lord Cairns' Act damages can be awarded for common law causes of action (usually proprietary torts or breaches of negative covenant) where common law damages are unavailable or nominal, and the plaintiff is unable to obtain specific relief. More controversially, they may be available for a purely equitable cause of action where traditional equitable compensation is unavailable.[2]
- Common law cannot accommodate future or anticipated losses, and the plaintiff must return to court whenever fresh damage occurs. However, all Australian jurisdictions, except Tasmania,[3] allow for Lord Cairns' Act damages to be awarded for future or ongoing wrongs, as long as a court has jurisdiction to award an injunction or a *quia timet* injunction.
- Lord Cairns' Act damages can also be awarded *in addition* to specific relief. For example, a court may order specific performance of part of a contract, and Lord Cairns' Act damages for the balance of the agreement.[4]
- Lord Cairns' Act has effected 'an actual, though limited, fusion of law and equity'.[5] It has been suggested that Lord Cairns' Act may be a means by which gain-based relief may be awarded for common law wrongs, but this is highly controversial.

REVIEW QUESTION

Do you think courts should use the Lord Cairns' Act as a way of effecting a limited fusion of law and equity?

IV Jurisdiction to award Lord Cairns' Act damages

Concept	Short explanation	Relevant authorities	Principles text
Jurisdiction to award Lord Cairn's Act damages	The court must have jurisdiction to entertain an application for specific relief at the time the action was instituted. The plaintiff must also show normal common law damages are 'inadequate'.	The cases cited in footnotes are authority for the general principle.	Chapter 12: [12.15]–[12.19]

Lord Cairns' Act provisions specify that damages may be awarded where the courts have power to award an injunction or specific performance. Although there is some confusion, it seems that the plaintiff only needs to establish that the court could have awarded specific

2 See, eg, *Giller v Procopets* (2008) 24 VR 1.

3 *Supreme Court Civil Procedure Act 1932* (Tas) s 11(13)(b).

4 *Soames v Edge* (1860) Johns 669, 70 ER 588; *Grant v Dawkins* [1973] 3 All ER 897.

5 JA Jolowicz, 'Damages in Equity – A Study of Lord Cairns' Act' (1975) 34(2) *Cambridge Law Journal* 224, 227.

relief at the time when the suit was instituted.[6] It follows that if specific relief was impossible when the plaintiff commenced proceedings, the court has no jurisdiction to award Lord Cairns' Act damages either.[7]

Some modern authorities hold that 'inadequacy of damages' is a matter of discretion.[8] The better view in this context is that inadequacy of damages constitutes a jurisdictional threshold. Where damages are adequate, the common law measure should prevail.

REVIEW QUESTION

Do you think 'inadequacy of damages' is a useful criterion?

V The need for a 'wrongful act' in some Australian jurisdictions

The original Lord Cairns' Act provision referred to cases where the court could award an injunction 'against the commission or continuance of any *wrongful act*'. There is debate about whether this is confined to common law torts, or includes equitable and statutory wrongs.[9] If the former, Lord Cairns' Act damages should not be granted in relation to statutory wrongdoing or equitable wrongdoing (including breach of fiduciary duty or breach of confidence).

There are two varieties of provision. Some mention 'wrongful act' and some do not.

Concept	Short explanation	Relevant authorities	Principles text
Australian legislation which mentions 'wrongful act'	These provisions may not allow for the grant of damages in lieu of a purely statutory or equitable injunction.	*Supreme Court Act 1970* (NSW) s 68	Chapter 12: [12.23]–[12.24]
Australian legislation which does not mention 'wrongful act'	These provisions may allow for the grant of damages in lieu of a purely statutory or equitable injunction.	*Supreme Court Act 1986* (Vic) s 38	Chapter 12: [12.25]
Lord Cairns' Act damages for statutory wrongdoing	A right to Lord Cairns' Act damages may be found where a statute manifests an intention to create a private cause of action.	*Wentworth v Woollahra Municipal Council* (1982) 149 CLR 672	Chapter 12: [12.26]–[12.27]

6 See, eg, *Isenberg v East India House Estate Co Ltd* (1863) 3 De GJ & S 263, 46 ER 637; *Ferguson v Wilson* (1866) LR 2 Ch App 77, 91–2 (Cairns LJ); *City of London Brewery Co v Tennant* (1873) LR 9 Ch App 212; *Tamplin v James* (1880) 15 Ch D 215; *Sayers v Collyer* (1884) 28 Ch D 103; *JC Williamson Ltd v Lukey* (1931) 45 CLR 282, 295; *McKenna v Richey* [1950] VLR 360; *Dell v Beasley* [1959] NZLR 89; *Bosaid v Andry* [1963] VR 465; *ASA Constructions Pty Ltd v Iwanov* [1975] 1 NSWLR 512; *Hooper v Rogers* [1975] Ch 43; *Edward Street Properties Pty Ltd v Collins* [1977] Qd R 399; *Millstream Pty Ltd v Schultz* [1980] 1 NSWLR 547, 552; *Brooks v Wyatt* (1994) 99 NTR 12, 28–9; *Mills v Ruthol Pty Ltd* (2004) 61 NSWLR 1, 12–13.

7 See, eg, *McMahon v Ambrose* [1987] VR 817.

8 See, eg, *Sky Petroleum Ltd v VIP Petroleum Ltd* [1974] 1 WLR 576; *Verrall v Great Yarmouth Borough Council* [1981] QB 202. See also D Laycock, 'The Death of the Irreparable Injury Rule' (1990) 103(3) *Harvard Law Review* 687; ICF Spry, *The Principles of Equitable Remedies* (Law Book, 9th ed, 2014) 62–3.

9 JD Heydon, MJ Leeming and PG Turner, *Meagher, Gummow and Lehane's Equity: Doctrines and Remedies* (LexisNexis, 5th ed, 2015) [24–020].

A Australian legislation which mentions 'wrongful act'

Legislation in New South Wales, the Northern Territory, South Australia, Tasmania and Western Australia is modelled on the original legislation.[10]

Supreme Court Act 1970 (NSW) s 68

The New South Wales equivalent of Lord Cairns' Act, based on the original legislation, mentions the need for a 'wrongful act'.

> **68 Damages in case for equitable relief**
> Where the Court has power:
> (a) to grant an injunction against the breach of any covenant, contract or agreement, or against the commission or continuance of any wrongful act, or
> (b) to order the specific performance of any covenant, contract or agreement,
> the Court may award damages to the party injured either in addition to or in substitution for the injunction or specific performance.

It has been suggested that these provisions cannot apply to equitable or statutory wrongdoing, as 'wrongful act' was intended originally to only apply to tort.[11] However, in obiter dicta in *Wentworth v Woollahra Municipal Council* (reproduced on page 434) the High Court said that Lord Cairns' Act damages could be awarded for purely equitable wrongs.[12]

B Australian legislation which does not mention 'wrongful act'

Legislation in the Australian Capital Territory, Queensland and Victoria is a simplified version of the original provision and does not refer to 'wrongful act'.[13]

Supreme Court Act 1986 (Vic) s 38

The Victorian equivalent of Lord Cairns' Act does not mention wrongful act.

> **38 Damages in addition to or in place of other remedies**
> If the Court has jurisdiction to entertain an application for an injunction or specific performance, it may award damages in addition to, or in substitution for, an injunction or specific performance.

10 *Supreme Court Act 1970* (NSW) s 68; *Supreme Court Act 1979* (NT) s 14(1)(b); *Supreme Court Act 1935* (SA) s 30; *Supreme Court Civil Procedure Act 1932* (Tas) s 11(13); *Supreme Court Act 1935* (WA) s 25(10).

11 Heydon et al (n 9) [24–090].

12 *Wentworth v Woollahra Municipal Council* (1982) 149 CLR 672, 676 (Gibbs CJ, Mason, Murphy and Brennan JJ).

13 *Supreme Court Act 1933* (ACT) s 34; *Civil Proceedings Act 2011* (Qld) s 8; *Supreme Court Act 1986* (Vic) s 38.

In *Giller v Procopets*,[14] the Victorian Court of Appeal argued that the lack of reference to 'wrongful act' meant that Lord Cairns' Act damages could be awarded in lieu of an injunction for breach of confidence, a purely equitable cause of action.[15]

Giller v Procopets (2008) 24 VR 1

Facts and issues

Procopets (the defendant) and Giller (the plaintiff) lived in a de facto relationship. They broke up, but for a time after that, they still engaged in sexual intercourse. Procopets filmed their sexual activity, at first without Giller's knowledge, but later with her consent. After their relationship deteriorated further, Procopets showed (or attempted to show) the videos to Giller's family and friends. Giller sought damages for the emotional distress resulting from Procopets's breach of confidence. Aggravated damages or damages for distress are generally only available at common law, not as equitable damages.

Decision

Giller was entitled to damages (either aggravated damages or damages for distress) pursuant to the court's inherent equitable jurisdiction. In the alternative, she was entitled to damages in lieu of the injunction she could have obtained to restrain Procopets.

Neave JA (Maxwell P agreeing)

> **[94]** The learned authors of *Meagher, Gummow and Lehane's Equity: Doctrines and Remedies* argue that this provision does not authorise awards of damages in addition to, or in substitution for, injunctions, in aid of purely equitable rights, such as the equitable duty of confidence. They comment that:
>
> > If it does so then it has created a curious situation. For the Act does not make clear in such a case what criteria are to be used beyond those already applied in compensation cases in the exclusive jurisdiction … This suggests that Lord Cairns' Act is to be construed as applicable only to the auxiliary jurisdiction and that the 'wrongful acts' referred to therein are torts and not also breaches of fiduciary duties and equitable obligations.
>
> This view has not, however, been accepted in Victoria. Before the enactment of s 38 of the *Supreme Court Act 1986*, Victorian case law supported the award of damages under s 62(3) of the *Supreme Court Act 1958* (the provision then equivalent to s 2 of *Lord Cairns' Act*) for breach of a right recognised only in equity, such as the equitable duty of confidence.
>
> In *Talbot v General Television Corp Ltd*, Harris J held that an equitable breach of confidence was a 'wrongful act' for this purpose and that the plaintiff was entitled to an award of damages for loss of the chance of profiting from use of the confidential information, in addition

14 (2008) 24 VR 1.

15 Ibid [403] (Neave JA).

to an injunction. Marks J assessed damages on that basis, commenting as he did so that there was 'no authority in the case law regarding the principles on which damages should be awarded for [**95**] the wrongful use of information which is of a purely personal nature'. ...

In *Gas & Fuel Corporation of Victoria v Barba*, Crockett J held that damages could be awarded under s 62(3) to a plaintiff whose equitable easement had been interfered with by the defendant.

The view that damages are payable under *Lord Cairns' Act* for breach of a purely equitable right was also supported in *obiter* of the High Court. In *Wentworth v Woollahra Municipal Council*, the Court said:

> An incidental object of [*Lord Cairns' Act*] was to enable the Court to award damages in lieu of an injunction or specific performance, even in the case of a purely equitable claim.

Although the correctness of *Talbot v General Television Corp Ltd* was doubted by Gummow J in *Concept Television Productions Pty Ltd & Anor v Australian Broadcasting Corporation*, the situation in Victoria has now been placed beyond doubt by the enactment of s 38 of the *Supreme Court Act 1986*. The removal of the reference to a 'wrongful act' (which had appeared in s 62(3) of the *Supreme Court Act 1958*) makes it clear that damages can be awarded for breach of a purely equitable obligation, in addition to, or in substitution for, an injunction.

C Lord Cairns' Act damages for statutory wrongdoing

Lord Cairns' Act damages may be awarded in respect of statutory wrongdoing even if there is no explicit provision in the statute, as long as the statute displays an intention to create private rights.

Wentworth v Woollahra Municipal Council (1982) 149 CLR 672

Facts and issues

Wentworth's (the plaintiff) neighbours erected a house which obstructed her view. She sought an injunction to demolish the house for a breach of the Woollahra Planning Scheme Ordinance. She also sought damages in lieu.

Decision

The High Court denied damages in lieu of an injunction on the basis that the Planning Scheme Ordinance did not intend to create private rights.

Gibbs CJ, Mason, Murphy and Brennan JJ

> [**676**] The main object of the Act was to enable the Court of Chancery to do 'complete justice' between parties by awarding damages in those cases in which it had formerly

refused equitable relief in respect of a legal right and left the plaintiff to sue for damages at common law. An incidental object of the Act was to enable the Court to award damages in lieu of an injunction or specific performance, even in the case of a purely equitable claim. ...

[682] If we are now to declare that s 68 [of the *Supreme Court Act 1970* (NSW)] applies to public as well as to private wrongs, we must ignore the insights which the history of Lord Cairns' Act offers. We know that it was called into existence with the principal object of enabling the Court of Chancery to do justice between the parties by awarding damages for infringement of private rights, whether legal or equitable. Equity's incapacity to award damages for infringement of private rights was the problem which the statute sought to solve. In 1858 it would not have occurred to anyone that, apart from public nuisance, damages might be awarded to an individual on violation of a public right or for non-performance of a public duty. ... Certainly it could not have been supposed in 1858 that Lord Cairns' Act was intended to authorize an award of damages in favour of a plaintiff, who, asserting neither a personal cause of action nor violation of a private right, complained only of the violation of a public right created by statute or the non-performance of a public duty imposed by statute. And there is nothing in the later enactments, including s 68 of the Act, to suggest that they were intended to go beyond the scope of the 1858 statute.

Moreover, the very terms of the section suggest that it is exclusively preoccupied with private rights. The opening words of par (a) and the whole of par (b) deal with private rights. ...

[683] ... We think that the history and the terms of s 68 show that it was not intended to authorize the award of damages for breach of a statutory prohibition which manifests no intention to create a private cause of action for damages.

By contrast, in *Matthews v ACP Publishing Pty Ltd*,[16] Beaumont J awarded Lord Cairns' Act damages for a contravention of s 35(5) of the *Copyright Act 1968* (Cth). The statute provided that where a photograph had been commissioned for a particular purpose, the author could restrain any act which was not in accordance with that purpose. The plaintiff photographer had been commissioned by *Cleo* magazine to photograph a celebrity for the sole purpose of publication on the magazine's cover. The defendant licensed the photograph for publication on another magazine's cover without seeking the plaintiff's consent or providing extra payment. Although s 35(5) did not mention damages, Beaumont J said that it manifested an intention to create a private cause of action and distinguished it from *Wentworth v Woollahra Municipal Council*.[17]

Review question

Do you think that Lord Cairns' Act damages should be available for equitable and statutory wrongdoing?

16 (1998) 87 FCR 152.

17 Ibid 161–2.

VI Factors influencing the exercise of the jurisdiction

Concept	Short explanation	Relevant authorities	Principles text
General principles	There are four categories of case: (1) where specific relief is no longer available or in addition to specific relief (2) 'middle ground' cases (3) relief for future loss and (4) novel forms of relief.	*Bendal Pty Ltd v Mirvac Project Pty Ltd* (1991) 23 NSWLR 464 *Giller v Procopets* (2008) 24 VR 1	Chapter 12: [12.28]–[12.41]
The *Shelfer* criteria	It is unclear whether there is a presumption that an injunction should be awarded. In Australia the matter seems to be discretionary rather than a presumption.	*Shelfer v City of London Electric Lighting Co* [1895] 1 Ch 287 *Lawrence v Fen Tigers Ltd* [2014] AC 822	Chapter 12: [12.43]–[12.46]

A General principles

Lord Cairns' Act damages achieve different aims. There are four different purposes (see Figure 12.1 on page 428).

1 Where specific relief is no longer available or in addition to specific relief

These cases prompted the enactment of Lord Cairns' Act. They generally involve common law torts and breach of contract. In a significant group of cases, the plaintiff was 'too late' to get an injunction, for various reasons.[18] Often damages are based on loss; but sometimes they are also measured as a 'reasonable fee', in which case, the considerations under the 'middle ground' solution apply.

Sometimes Lord Cairns' Act damages are awarded *in addition* to specific relief. In *Grant v Dawkins*,[19] the plaintiff was compensated for mortgages which would have to be discharged for specific performance to be effective.

2 To provide a 'middle ground' solution between no relief and specific relief

When substantial damages are unavailable at common law, Lord Cairns' Act gives the court a 'middle ground' between no relief and specific relief. The cases primarily involve proprietary

18 *Catton v Wyld* (1863) 32 Beav 266, 55 ER 105; *Fritz v Hobson* (1880) 14 Ch D 542; *Davenport v Rylands* (1865) LR 1 Eq 302; *Chapman, Morsons & Co v Guardians of the Auckland Union* (1889) 23 QBD 294; *Johnson v Agnew* [1980] AC 367.

19 *Grant v Dawkins* [1973] 1 WLR 1406.

torts[20] and breaches of negative covenants.[21] Typically the award is measured as a 'reasonable fee'. There are a raft of factors (none of which are determinative) which guide a court in choosing between injunctions and Lord Cairns' Act damages.

Table 12.1 Factors courts take into account when choosing between injunctions or Lord Cairns' Act ('LCA') damages

Injunction more likely	LCA damages more likely
• If injunctions readily awarded for cause of action • If LCA damages effectively licence wrongdoing • If injunction is prohibitory • If D intends to continue with conduct • If D is deliberate • If P has objected to D's conduct	• If injunctions not readily awarded for cause of action • If injunction allows plaintiff to demand an exorbitant fee • If injunction is mandatory • If D does not intend to continue with conduct • If D is not deliberate • If P has not objected to D's conduct

Bendal Pty Ltd v Mirvac Project Pty Ltd (1991) 23 NSWLR 464

Facts and issues

Bendal Pty Ltd ('Bendal', the defendant) deliberately trespassed on Mirvac Project Pty Ltd's ('Mirvac', the plaintiff) property by allowing its building scaffolding to enter the plaintiff's airspace, despite the plaintiff's continuous objections.

Decision

The plaintiff was entitled to an injunction rather than Lord Cairns' Act damages.

Bryson J

> [**677**] I think it is quite clear from the case law to which Hodgson J referred [in *LJP Investments Pty Ltd v Howard Chia Investments Pty Ltd (No 2)* (1989) 24 NSWLR 499] that the owner of freehold land has a perfectly legitimate interest to decide who will come on to his land, who will build encroachments there, who will stay off and on what terms he is prepared to give leave and licence whether on payment of money or on no terms whatever.
>
> There is no power in the court to impose compulsory licences to encroach on real estate or to set the terms on which licences are to be granted. Some judges have endeavoured to mould orders enforcing the rights of freeholders in the direction of licensing or compulsory licensing. Such attempts do not have the approval of courts of appeal. …

20 *Isenberg v East India House Estate Co Ltd* (1863) 3 De GJ & S 263, 46 ER 637; *Colls v Home and Colonial Stores Ltd* [1904] AC 179; *Kine v Jolly* [1905] 1 Ch 480 (aff'd [1907] AC 1); *Ryder v Hall* (1904) 27 NZLR 385; *Wills v May* [1923] 1 Ch 317; *Jaggard v Sawyer* [1995] 1 WLR 269.

21 *Gafford v Graham* (1999) 77 P & CR 73; *Jaggard v Sawyer* [1995] 1 WLR 269; *Lunn Poly Pty Ltd v Liverpool & Lancashire Properties Ltd* [2007] L & TR 6.

Bryson J's statement in *Bendal v Mirvac* can be compared with the statement of Lord Westbury LC in *Isenberg v East India House Estate Co Ltd*:[22]

> This is a case in which the benefit of the recent statute giving power to this Court to assess and ascertain damages is peculiarly felt; and I hold it, therefore, to be the duty of the Court in such a case as the present not, by granting a mandatory injunction, to deliver over the Defendants to the Plaintiff bound hand and foot, in order to be made subject to any extortionate demand that he may by possibility make, but to substitute for such mandatory injunction an inquiry before itself, in order to ascertain the measure of damage that has been actually sustained.

3 To provide relief for future losses

Common law damages can only be awarded for loss which has already accrued before proceedings commence, but Lord Cairns' Act allows awards for losses arising from future or anticipated wrongs. It is not necessary for an injury to have occurred, as Lord Cairns' Act damages may be awarded in lieu of a *quia timet* injunction, as in *Barbagallo v J & F Catelan Pty Ltd*.[23]

4 To provide novel forms of relief

Lord Cairns' Act damages can clearly be awarded in situations where common law damages would not.

The more controversial question is whether they can be awarded in equity where equity would not allow an award.

Giller v Procopets (2008) 24 VR 1

Facts and issues

The facts and issues of this case are outlined on page 323.

Decision

Traditionally, aggravated damages or damages for distress were only awarded for certain torts, and equitable compensation did not allow such awards. However, Giller (the plaintiff) was entitled to aggravated damages or damages for distress pursuant to the court's inherent equitable jurisdiction. In the alternative, she was entitled to damages in lieu of an injunction, notwithstanding the purely equitable origin of breach of confidence.

22 *Isenberg v East India House Estate Co Ltd* (1863) 3 De G & S 263, 273; 46 ER 637, 641.

23 *Barbagallo v J & F Catelan Pty Ltd* [1986] 1 Qd R 245.

Neave JA (Maxwell P agreeing)

The first error of law

[**95**] … [T]he fact that Ms Giller had not sought an injunction to restrain Mr Procopets from showing or distributing the video did not deprive the Court of its power to award damages. That power exists so long as a court has jurisdiction to grant an injunction. In his book on *Equitable Remedies*, Dr Spry says:

> [I]f there is in fact jurisdiction to award an injunction or specific performance, it is probably unnecessary that an injunction or specific performance should have been claimed by the plaintiff, it being sufficient under these circumstances that the plaintiff merely should claim equitable damages.

…

[**96**] In my view, the language of s 38 is quite clear. If the cause of action is such as to give the court *jurisdiction* to grant an injunction, then the power to award damages is enlivened. There is nothing in the section, or in the statutory history, to suggest that the power was intended to be exercisable only where an application for injunction had actually been made.

…

On what basis are 'damages' recoverable?

[**99**] … English authorities assume that 'damages' are recoverable for 'mere distress' not amounting to psychiatric injury, but do not explain whether the basis for such an award is an order for equitable compensation, damages [**100**] under *Lord Cairns' Act*, or on some other basis. Accordingly, it is necessary to decide on what basis 'damages' may be awarded.

I begin by discussing whether equitable principles support the making of an order for equitable compensation to a person who suffers distress or embarrassment as the result of a breach of confidence. I then consider the availability of damages under s 38 of the *Supreme Court Act 1986* as an alternative remedy in these circumstances.

(a) Equitable compensation?

In *Smith Kline & French v Secretary, Department of Community Services and Health*, Gummow J said the conferring of equitable jurisdiction on a court:

> … brings with it, in a case such as the present, the inherent jurisdiction to grant relief by way of monetary compensation for breach of an equitable obligation, whether of trust or confidence.

… [I]njunctions are available to prevent publication of confidential material because of its private nature. It is unnecessary … to show that, if unrestrained, the breach of confidence will cause financial loss or psychiatric injury. By parity of reasoning there should be no barrier to the making of an order for equitable compensation to compensate a claimant for the embarrassment or distress she has suffered as the result of a breach of an equitable duty of confidence which has already occurred. …

… An inability to order equitable compensation to a claimant who has suffered distress would mean that a claimant whose confidence was breached before an injunction could be obtained would have no effective remedy.

(b) Damages under *Lord Cairns' Act*?

[**101**] Typically, damages have been awarded under *Lord Cairns' Act* in lieu of an injunction where the defendant has infringed the plaintiff's property rights or has benefited by exploiting commercially valuable information. There is no Australian authority on the issue of whether damages under this head can be awarded to a plaintiff who has suffered distress or embarrassment as a result of the breach of confidence.

Under the law of negligence, damages are not recoverable for an injury to feelings which is unaccompanied by another recoverable loss (for example, physical injury). …

By contrast, damages for upset and distress can be awarded for torts such as defamation and deceit. …

Damages under *Lord Cairns' Act* are *sui generis*, and can be awarded in some circumstances where common law damages are not recoverable. In my view, such damages should be available where the essence of the plaintiff's case is that he or she has been embarrassed by the exposure of private information, rather than that the defendant has profited from the wrongful use of that information. In *Talbot v General Television Corporation Pty Ltd*, Young CJ treated damages under *Lord Cairns' Act* as compensating the plaintiff for what he or she had lost. It is consistent with that approach to compensate Ms Giller for the mental distress suffered as a result of the defendant's actions.

…

(a) Can a punitive monetary award be made for breach of confidence?

…

[**103**] I am not aware of any authority supporting a punitive monetary award for breach of confidence, nor as damages in lieu of an injunction under s 38 of the *Supreme Court Act 1986*. Further, as the learned trial judge noted, Mr Procopets had already been penalised by the criminal law. In these circumstances, I do not consider it appropriate to make a punitive monetary award for breach of confidence.

(b) Can aggravated damages be awarded for breach of confidence?

[**104**] At common law, aggravated damages may be awarded to compensate a plaintiff 'when the harm done to [him or her] by a wrongful act is aggravated by the manner in which the act was done.' Such damages are compensatory, not punitive. In the *Campbell v Mirror Group Newspapers Ltd,* the monetary award was said to include a component for aggravation as a result of publication of an article which criticised Ms Campbell for initiating proceedings for breach of confidence.

There is academic support for the view that, in a claim for equitable compensation, it is possible to recover for aggravated damage. I can see no reason in principle why this should not be so. Nor is there any reason why damages awarded under s 38 of the *Supreme Court Act 1986*, in lieu of an injunction, could not include a component for aggravation.

Maxwell P and Neave JA awarded Ms Giller $40 000, including $10 000 in aggravated damages. Ashley AJA dissented on quantum and would have awarded her $27 500, including $7500 representing aggravated damages.

B The *Shelfer* criteria

Shelfer v City of London Electric Lighting Co[24] effectively creates a presumption that an injunction should be awarded rather than damages in lieu. AL Smith LJ famously expressed a 'good working rule', as reproduced below.

Shelfer v City of London Electric Lighting Co [1895] 1 Ch 287

Facts and issues

The Shelfers ran a pub nearby to a building housing electric generators. The building was owned by City of London Electric Co (the defendant), which supplied electric lighting to the City of London. Shelfer (the plaintiff) alleged the engines' vibrations cracked the pub's walls and fixtures and made his wife and daughter unwell. At first instance, Kekewich J awarded damages in lieu of an injunction.

Decision

The plaintiff was entitled to an injunction to restrain the nuisance.

Lindley LJ

> [**315–316**] [E]ver since Lord Cairns' Act was passed the Court of Chancery has repudiated the notion that the legislature intended to turn that court into a tribunal for legalising wrongful acts; or in other words, the court has always protested against the notion that it ought to allow a wrong to continue simply because the wrongdoer is able and willing to pay for the injury he may inflict. Neither has the circumstance that the wrongdoer is in some sense a public benefactor (eg, a gas or water company or a sewer authority) ever been considered a sufficient reason for refusing to protect by injunction an individual whose rights are being persistently infringed.

AL Smith LJ

> [**322**] In such cases the well-known rule is not to accede to the application, but to grant the injunction sought, for the plaintiff's legal right has been invaded and he is *prima facie* entitled to an injunction.
>
> There are, however, cases in which this rule may be relaxed and in which damages may be awarded in substitution for an injunction … .

24 *Shelfer v City of London Electric Lighting Co* [1895] 1 Ch 287.

In any instance in which a case for an injunction has been made out, if the plaintiff by his acts or laches has disentitled himself to an injunction the Court may award damages in its place. So again, whether the case be for a mandatory injunction or to restrain a continuing nuisance, the appropriate remedy may be damages in lieu of an injunction, assuming a case for an injunction to be made out.

In my opinion, it may be stated as a good working rule that –

(1) If the injury to the plaintiff's legal rights is small,

(2) And is one which is capable of being estimated in money,

(3) And is one which can be adequately compensated by a small money payment, [**323**]

(4) And the case is one in which it would be oppressive to the defendant to grant an injunction: –

then damages in substitution for an injunction may be given.

There may also be cases in which, though the four abovementioned requirements exist, the defendant by his conduct, as, for instance, hurrying up his buildings so as if possible to avoid an injunction, or otherwise acting with a reckless disregard to the plaintiff's rights, has disentitled himself from asking that damages may be assessed in substitution for an injunction.

Jolowicz has argued that the 'good working rule' should only apply to injunctions where there are no relevant discretionary bars to relief.[25]

The UK Supreme Court recently reformulated and questioned the *Shelfer* criteria.

Lawrence v Fen Tigers Ltd [2014] AC 822

Facts and issues

The Lawrences (a couple) moved into a bungalow near a speed track raceway which had been in operation for over 20 years. They sought an injunction in nuisance to restrain Fen Tigers Ltd (the defendants, the raceway owners) from making noise over certain levels.

Decision

The plaintiff was entitled to damages in lieu of an injunction.

Lord Neuberger (Lords Mance and Carnwath agreeing)

[**30**] It seems to me that there are two problems about the current state of the authorities on this question of the proper approach for a court to adopt on the question whether to award damages instead of an injunction.

25 JA Jolowicz, 'Damages in Equity – A Study of Lord Cairns' Act' (1975) 34(2) *Cambridge Law Journal* 224, 227.

The first is what at best might be described as a tension, and at worst as an inconsistency, between two sets of judicial dicta since *Shelfer*. Observations in *Slack*, *Miller*, *Kennaway*, *Regan*, and *Watson* appear to support the notion that A L Smith LJ's approach in *Shelfer* is generally to be adopted and that it requires an exceptional case before damages should be awarded in lieu of an injunction, whereas the approach adopted in *Colls*, *Kine*, and *Fishenden* seems to support a more open-minded approach, taking into account the conduct of the parties. ...

The second problem is the unsatisfactory way in which it seems that the public interest is to be taken into account when considering the issue whether to grant an injunction or award damages. The notion that it can be relevant where the damages are minimal, but not otherwise ... seems very strange. Either the public interest is capable of being relevant to the issue or it is not. As part of this second problem, there is a question as to the extent to which it is relevant that the activity giving rise to the nuisance has the benefit of a planning permission.

[**31**] So far as the first problem is concerned, the approach to be adopted by a judge when being asked to award damages instead of an injunction should, in my view, be much more flexible ... . It seems to me that (i) an almost mechanical application of A L Smith LJ's four tests, and (ii) an approach which involves damages being awarded only in 'very exceptional circumstances', are each simply wrong in principle, and give rise to a serious risk of going wrong in practice. ...

The court's power to award damages in lieu of an injunction involves a classic exercise of discretion, which should not, as a matter of principle, be fettered, particularly in the very constrained way in which the Court of Appeal has suggested in *Regan* and *Watson*. And, as a matter of practical fairness, each case is likely to be so fact-sensitive that any firm guidance is likely to do more harm than good. ...

... [T]his does not prevent the courts from laying down rules as to what factors can, and cannot, be taken into account by a judge when deciding whether to exercise his discretion to award damages in lieu. Indeed, it is appropriate to give as much guidance as possible so as to ensure that, while the discretion is not fettered, its manner of exercise is as predictable as possible. I would accept that the *prima facie* position is that an injunction should be granted, so the legal burden is on the defendant to show why it should not. And, subject to one possible point, I would cautiously (in the light of the fact that each case turns on its facts) approve the observations of Lord Macnaghten in *Colls* ... where he said:

In some cases, of course, an injunction is necessary – if, for instance, the injury cannot fairly be compensated by money – if the defendant has acted in a high-handed manner – if he has endeavoured to steal a march upon the plaintiff or to evade the jurisdiction of the Court. In all these cases an injunction is necessary, in order to do justice to the plaintiff and as a warning to others. But if there is really a question as to whether the obstruction is legal or not, and if the defendant has acted fairly and not in an unneighbourly spirit, I am disposed to think that the Court ought to incline to damages rather than to an injunction. It is quite true that a man ought not to be compelled to part with his property against his will, or to have the value of his property diminished, without an Act of Parliament. On the other hand, the Court ought to be very careful not to allow an action for the protection of ancient lights to be used as a means of extorting money.

...

[**32**] Where does that leave A L Smith LJ's four tests? ... First, the application of the four tests must not be such as 'to be a fetter on the exercise of the court's discretion'.

Secondly, it would, in the absence of additional relevant circumstances pointing the other way, normally be right to refuse an injunction if those four tests were satisfied. Thirdly, the fact that those tests are not all satisfied does not mean that an injunction should be granted.

As for the second problem, that of public interest, I find it hard to see how there could be any circumstances in which it arose and could not, as a matter of law, be a relevant factor. ... The fact that a defendant's business may have to shut down if an injunction is granted should, it seems to me, obviously be a relevant fact, and it is hard to see why relevance should not extend to the fact that a number of the defendant's employees would lose their livelihood, although in many cases that may well not be sufficient to justify the refusal of an injunction. Equally, I do not see why the court should not be entitled to have regard to the fact that many other neighbours in addition to the claimant are badly affected by the nuisance as a factor in favour of granting an injunction.

It is also right to mention planning permission in this context. In some cases, the grant of planning permission for a particular activity (whether carried on at the claimant's, or the defendant's, premises) may provide strong support for the contention that the activity is of benefit to the public, which would be relevant to the question of whether or not to grant an injunction. ...

In some such cases, the court may well be impressed by a defendant's argument that an injunction would involve a loss to the public or a waste of resources on account of what may be a single claimant, or that the financial implications of an injunction for the defendant would be disproportionate to the damage done to the claimant if she was left to her claim in damages. In many such cases, particularly where an injunction would in practice stop the defendant from pursuing the activities, an injunction may well not be the appropriate remedy.

Lord Sumption (Lord Clark agreeing)

[**37**] What saves, or could save the law from anomaly and incoherence is the court's discretion as to remedies. An injunction is a remedy with significant side-effects beyond the parties and the issues in the proceedings. Most uses of land said to be objectionable cannot be restrained by injunction simply as between the owner of that land and his neighbour. If the use of a site for (say) motocross is restrained by injunction, that prevents the activity as between the defendant and the whole world. Yet it may be a use which is in the interest of very many other people who derive enjoyment or economic benefits from it of precisely the kind with which the planning system is concerned. An injunction prohibiting the activity entirely will operate in practice in exactly the same way as a refusal of planning permission, but without regard to the factors which a planning authority would be bound to take into account. The obvious solution to this problem is to allow the activity to continue but to compensate the claimant financially for the loss of amenity and the diminished value of his property. In a case where planning permission has actually been granted for the use in question, there are particularly strong reasons for adopting this solution. It is what the law normally provides for when a public interest conflicts with a proprietary right.

The main question, as it seems to me, is not whether the judge in deciding on the appropriate remedy should take account of the public interest or, more generally, of interests which are not before the court. He will usually lack the information to do so effectively, and is in danger of stepping outside his main function of deciding the issue between the parties. [**38**] The main question is whether the current principles of law governing the availability of injunctions are consistent with the public interest reflected in the successive and increasingly elaborate legislative schemes of development control which have existed in England since 1947.

The ordinary principle is that the court does not grant an injunction in a case where there is an adequate legal remedy. In particular, it does not do so where damages would be an adequate remedy. Where an injunction is granted, it is usually because the injury to the Claimant is 'irreparable', in the sense that money cannot atone for it. However, this principle has never been consistently followed in cases of nuisance. The leading case is *Shelfer* ... which created a strong presumption in favour of an injunction, to be displaced only in the four narrowly defined categories identified by AL Smith LJ .... The exceptions applied only to cases where the injury to the claimant was small and the grant of an injunction would be oppressive. ...

The courts might have defended the special treatment of nuisance by pointing to the traditional attitude of equity to land as being unique, an approach which is exemplified in its willingness to grant specific performance of contracts for the sale of land. From this, it might have been concluded that paying the claimant enough to buy a comparable property elsewhere where there was no nuisance was not equivalent to letting him use his existing land free of the nuisance. In fact the *Shelfer* principle was based mainly on the court's objection to sanctioning a wrong by allowing the defendant to pay for the right to go on doing it. This seems an unduly moralistic approach to disputes, and if taken at face value would justify the grant of an injunction in all cases, which is plainly not the law. ...

In my view, the decision in *Shelfer* is out of date, and it is unfortunate that it has been followed so recently and so slavishly. It was devised for a time in which England was much less crowded, [**39**] when comparatively few people owned property, when conservation was only beginning to be a public issue, and when there was no general system of statutory development control. The whole jurisprudence in this area will need one day to be reviewed in this court. There is much to be said for the view that damages are ordinarily an adequate remedy for nuisance and that an injunction should not usually be granted in a case where it is likely that conflicting interests are engaged other than the parties' interests. In particular, it may well be that an injunction should as a matter of principle not be granted in a case where a use of land to which objection is taken requires and has received planning permission. However, at this stage, in the absence of argument on these points, I can do no more than identify them as calling for consideration in a case in which they arise.

Australian courts appear to have retained the *Shelfer* criteria.[26] However, they generally apply them in a manner closer to that recommended by the majority in *Lawrence v Fen Tigers Pty Ltd*.[27]

26 *Lord v McMahon* [2015] NSWSC 1619, [170], [183]; *Janney v Steller Works Pty Ltd* (2017) 53 VR 677, [35]–[37] (Riordan J).

27 Heydon et al (n 9) [24–120].

REVIEW QUESTIONS

(1) Do you think the 'middle ground' cases, 'future relief', and 'novel relief cases' are appropriate?

(2) Compare *Bendal Pty Ltd v Mirvac Project Pty Ltd* (1991) 23 NSWLR 464 with *LJP Investments Pty Ltd v Howard Chia Investments Pty Ltd (No 2)* (1989) 24 NSWLR 499 (see Chapter 16). Why did the court choose a different route in that case?

(3) What do you think of the *Shelfer* criteria?

VII The basis of assessment

Concept	Short explanation	Relevant authorities	Principles text
Timing	Lord Cairns' Act may allow for discretion as to date of measurement of damages.	The cases cited in discussion below are authority for the general principle.	Chapter 12: [12.47]–[12.52]
'Reasonable fee' awards	There is conflicting UK authority on whether these are gain-based or compensatory. There is no Australian authority.	*Morris-Garner v One Step (Support) Ltd* [2018] UKSC 20	Chapter 12: [12.53]
Loss-based awards	These are measured according to what the plaintiff has lost, depending upon how the loss is characterised.	The cases cited in footnotes are authority for the general principle.	Chapter 12: [12.54]–[12.60]

A Timing

Megarry J in *Wroth v Tyler* suggested that Lord Cairns' Act damages compensating for loss could be measured as at the date of judgment rather than the date of breach.[28] However, in *Johnson v Agnew*, Lord Wilberforce suggested that the principles governing the calculation of common law damages and Lord Cairns' Act damages should be the same.[29] In *Morris-Garner v One Step (Support) Ltd* (extracted below) Lord Reed doubted the correctness of Lord Wilberforce in *Johnson v Agnew*.[30]

B Gain-based relief – 'reasonable fee' awards

Reasonable fees are awarded primarily in the 'middle ground' cases (particularly in cases of breach of negative covenant and trespass) and reflect an objective pecuniary valuation of the infringement or breach.

28 *Wroth v Tyler* [1974] 1 Ch 30, 57–8.

29 *Johnson v Agnew* [1980] AC 367, 400.

30 *Morris-Garner v One Step (Support) Ltd* [2018] UKSC 20, [47].

In *Morris-Garner v One Step (Support) Ltd*, Lord Reed characterised the award as compensatory,[31] although in *Attorney-General v Blake*, Lord Nicholls had suggested that the Lord Cairns' Act cases were gain-based.[32]

In any event, as discussed in Chapter 16, the categorisation of reasonable fee awards more generally is unsettled.

Morris-Garner v One Step (Support) Ltd [2018] UKSC 20

Facts and issues

Morris-Garner (the plaintiffs) and One Step (Support) Ltd (the defendants) ran a business together, but the defendants sold their share to the plaintiffs. The contract included promises not to use confidential information, and not to set up a rival business for three years without the plaintiffs' consent. The defendants breached this agreement, and the plaintiffs sought a reasonable fee.

Decision

The plaintiffs were entitled only to damages calculated on an ordinary expectation measure. However, among other things, Lord Reed discussed the availability of Lord Cairns' Act damages, as a substitute for an injunction.

Lord Reed (Lady Hale, Lord Wilson and Lord Carnwath agreeing)

> **[43]** … The [Lord Cairns'] Act also enabled the Court of Chancery to award damages 'in substitution for' an injunction: a statutory power to award damages in circumstances in which they could not be awarded at common law. As Millett LJ explained in *Jaggard v Sawyer* … :
>
> > Damages at common law are recoverable only in respect of causes of action which are complete at the date of the writ; damages for future or repeated wrongs must be made the subject of fresh proceedings. Damages in substitution for an injunction, however, relate to the future, not the past. They inevitably extend beyond the damages to which the plaintiff may be entitled at law. In *Leeds Industrial Co-operative Society Ltd v Slack* … the House of Lords confirmed the jurisdiction of the courts to award damages under the Act in respect of an injury which was threatened but had not yet occurred. No such damages could have been awarded at common law.
>
> **[44]** Damages awarded in substitution for an injunction are, as one might expect, a monetary substitute for an injunction. …
>
> **[45]** The power to award damages in substitution for an injunction is dependent on the court's having jurisdiction to grant an injunction, determined as at the commencement

31 Ibid [41]–[47].

32 *A-G v Blake* [2001] 1 AC 268, 281.

of the proceedings. The provision that damages can be awarded 'in substitution for such injunction' might be thought to imply that the court must also have before it an application for an injunction, which it has decided to withhold. The point does not arise for decision in these proceedings, but I would be inclined for that reason to hesitate before endorsing the first part of Lord Walker's principle (5) ...[33]

[46] Like the jurisdiction to grant an injunction, the jurisdiction to grant damages in lieu is equitable in nature, as Millett LJ explained in *Jaggard v Sawyer ...* :

> When the plaintiff claims an injunction and the defendant asks the court to award damages instead, the proper approach for the court to adopt cannot be in doubt. Clearly the plaintiff must first establish a case for equitable relief, not only by proving his legal right and an actual or threatened infringement by the defendant, but also by overcoming all equitable defences such as laches, acquiescence or estoppel.

[47] It follows that it is necessary to treat with care Lord Wilberforce's remark in *Johnson v Agnew ...* that he found in Lord Cairns' Act 'no warrant for the court awarding damages differently from common law damages'. As Millett LJ explained in *Jaggard v Sawyer ...*, all that *Johnson v Agnew* decided was that damages, whether at common law or under the Act, are not invariably to be measured by reference to 'the value of the land ascertained at the date of the breach of contract'. Lord Wilberforce's words should not be read out of context and taken to imply that damages awarded in substitution for an injunction must necessarily be measured in the same way as damages recoverable at common law. That is hardly to be expected, given that the damages are available on a different basis, in different circumstances, and in respect of different types of wrong (past, on the one hand, and future or continuing, on the other).

C Loss-based relief – compensatory awards of various kinds

Compensatory relief is available for the other categories of case discussed: where specific relief was impossible,[34] or in addition to specific relief and loss has been suffered as a result;[35] for future losses (according to anticipated losses);[36] and for novel forms of relief such as aggravated damages for breach of confidence.[37]

33 In *Pell Frischmann Ltd v Bow Valley Iran Ltd* [2011] 1 WLR 2370, [22], Lord Walker said at (5) 'Although damages under Lord Cairns's Act are awarded in lieu of an injunction it is not necessary that an injunction should actually have been claimed in the proceedings, or that there should have been any prospect, on the facts, of it being granted ... .'

34 See, eg, *Catton v Wyld* (1863) 32 Beav 266; 55 ER 105; *Fritz v Hobson* (1880) 14 Ch D 542; *Shiffon Creations (S) Pte Ltd v Tong Lee Co Pte Ltd* [1991] 1 Malayan LJ 65 (SGHCA); *Davenport v Rylands* (1865) LR 1 Eq 302; *Chapman, Morsons & Co v Guardians of the Auckland Union* (1889) 23 QBD 294.

35 See, eg, *Soames v Edge* (1860) Johns 669, 70 ER 588; *Grant v Dawkins* [1973] 1 WLR 1406. Cf *Ryan v Mutual Tontine Westminster Chambers Association* [1893] 1 Ch 116. See Heydon et al (n 9) [24–165].

36 See, eg, *Oakacre Ltd v Claire Cleaners (Holdings) Ltd* [1982] Ch 197; *Leeds Industrial Cooperative Society Ltd v Slack* [1924] AC 851; *Hooper v Rogers* [1975] Ch 43; *Jaggard v Sawyer* [1995] 1 WLR 269, 276–77.

37 See, eg, *Giller v Procopets* (2008) 24 VR 1.

Review questions

(1) What do you think of Lord Reed's judgment in *Morris-Garner*?

(2) Do you prefer a compensatory, restitutionary or other interpretation of Lord Cairns' Act?

VIII Discretionary bars to relief

Concept	Short explanation	Relevant authorities	Principles text
Discretionary bars to relief	Lord Cairns' Act is subject to the ordinary equitable bars to relief.	This is a general principle arising from the equitable nature of Lord Cairns' Act damages.	Chapter 12: [12.61]–[12.64]

Lord Cairns' Act damages are subject to the ordinary equitable bars to relief: hardship, lack of clean hands, and delay and acquiescence. The relevance of the public interest has been discussed in the extract from *Lawrence v Fen Tigers Ltd* [2014] AC 822 on page 416.

All equitable bars to relief must be considered anew in relation to awards of Lord Cairns' Act damages. The fact that an injunction has been precluded for delay and acquiescence, for example, does not mean that Lord Cairns' Act damages are precluded. Indeed, it may be a reason why Lord Cairns' Act damages are appropriate.

Review question

Can you think of an example where a discretionary factor might be a reason why an injunction is inappropriate, but also a reason why Lord Cairns' Act is appropriate?

IX Part 9.5 of the *Corporations Act 2001* (Cth)

Concept	Short explanation	Relevant authorities	Principles text
Part 9.5 of the *Corporations Act 2001* (Cth)	Despite its similarity to Lord Cairns' Act, this does not act as a Lord Cairns' Act provision.	*Corporations Act 2001* (Cth) s 1324(10)	Chapter 12: [12.65]–[12.66]

Corporations Act 2001 (Cth) s 1324(10)

The *Corporations Act 2001* (Cth) contains a subsection which seems to be equivalent to a Lord Cairns' Act style provision in its section dealing with injunctions.

> **1324 Injunctions**
>
> ...
>
> (10) Where the Court has power under this section to grant an injunction restraining a person from engaging in particular conduct, or requiring a person to do a particular act or thing, the Court may, either in addition to or in substitution for the grant of the injunction, order that person to pay damages to any other person.

However, the provision has been interpreted very narrowly, as indicated by *McCracken v Phoenix Constructions (Qld) Pty Ltd*,[38] and has rarely been used. Barnett has recently suggested that it could be used more generously.[39]

Review question

Do you think that s 1324(10) should be interpreted similarly to Lord Cairns' Act provisions?

X The future of Lord Cairns' Act damages

Concept	Short explanation	Relevant authorities	Principles text
The future of Lord Cairns' Act damages	Lord Cairns' Act is still needed for future loss cases, but may not be necessary for the other kinds of award made in this chapter.	The article cited in footnotes by Barnett and Bryan explains this for those interested.	Chapter 12: [12.67]–[12.69]

Bryan and Barnett have argued that, in most cases, Lord Cairns' Act provisions are not needed by the courts.[40] In most states and territories, courts have power to make orders to

38 *McCracken v Phoenix Constructions (Qld) Pty Ltd* [2013] 2 Qd R 27.

39 K Barnett, 'A Reconsideration of Section 1324(10) of the *Corporations Act 2001* (Cth): Damages in Lieu of an Injunction' (2018) 36(4) *Company and Securities Law Journal* 370.

40 K Barnett and M Bryan, 'Lord Cairns's Act: A Study in the Unintended Consequences of Legislation' (2015) 9(2) *Journal of Equity* 150, 154–5.

achieve 'full and complete justice' between the parties. However, it appears that Lord Cairns' Act provisions remain necessary for anticipated losses,[41] because these awards could not be made by a Court of Chancery prior to the judicature Acts.

REVIEW QUESTION

Do you think Lord Cairns' Act provisions are necessary?

41 M Bryan, 'Injunctions and Damages: Taking *Shelfer* off the Shelf' (2016) 28 *Singapore Academy of Law Journal* 921, 927–8.

PART 4

REMEDIES AS VINDICATION

13 SELF-HELP REMEDIES

I	Introduction	454
II	Tort and self-help	454
	A Eviction of trespassers	456
	B Self-defence of property	456
	C Self-defence of the person	458
	D Recaption, replevin and specific restitution	459
	E Abatement of nuisance	462
III	Contract and self-help	464
	A Rescission	465
	B Liquidated damages and penalties	465
	C Debt	474
	D Other stipulated contractual remedies	475

I Introduction

While the focus of this casebook is on remedies that are awarded pursuant to a judicial order, most disputes are settled outside court. Of course, self-help remedies are not remedies in the strict sense of the word, because they do not involve court orders – rather the court gives the plaintiff permission to act in a particular way. It could be said that the plaintiff is vindicating their own rights. However, courts prefer to ensure that 'self-help' is exercised reasonably.

II Tort and self-help

The proprietary torts may allow plaintiffs to undertake self-help, including trespass to land, trespass to goods, trespass to persons and nuisance. Self-help must be reasonable, and not constitute tortious conduct.

Concept	Short explanation	Relevant authorities	Principles text
When trespassers may be evicted	A trespasser may be evicted but only using 'reasonable' force. The trespasser must be asked to leave and given an opportunity to comply before any force is used. However, if a person is drunk and disorderly, it may be unreasonable to evict a person if they are severely injured as a result,* or negligent if the person is incapable of navigating traffic.# The law regarding the right of a landowner to evict an occupier (eg a tenant or a squatter) is more complex, and sometimes it may be an offence to forcibly enter the land.	*Cowell v Rosehill Racecourse Co Ltd* (1937) 56 CLR 605	Chapter 13: [13.9]–[13.14]
Self-defence of one's property must be reasonable	Historically, possessors of land and goods could go to extreme lengths to possess their property. The law shifted with *Bird v Holbrook* (1828) 130 ER 911. It is now an offence in most Australian states to set spring guns, 'man traps' etc. which may cause death or grievous bodily harm.		Chapter 13: [13.15]–[13.17]
	A modern landowner who set a trap would be liable in negligence.	*Hackshaw v Shaw* (1984) 155 CLR 624	
Self-defence of the person in the face of tortious conduct must be reasonable	Extreme acts of force in the face of threats will not be reasonable.	*Fontin v Katapodis* (1962) 108 CLR 177	Chapter 13: [13.18]–[13.20]
Recovery of property must be reasonable	A plaintiff may recover property taken with reasonable force. It is unclear, however, whether the taking of the property must be unlawful from the beginning or not.	*Toyota Finance Australia Ltd v Dennis* (2002) 58 NSWLR 101	Chapter 13: [13.21]–[13.25]
A person who has an action in nuisance may remove the source of the inconvenience through abatement	While a person with nuisance has a right to remove the source of the nuisance However, abatement must be reasonable and must not involve the commission of another tort.	*Traian v Ware* [1957] VR 200	Chapter 13: [13.26]–[13.29]

* *Horkin v North Melbourne Football Club Social Club* [1983] 1 VR 153, 157.

\# *Jordan House v Menow* [1974] 30 DLR (3d) 105. But cf in *Australia CAL No 14 Pty Ltd v Motor Vehicle Accidents Insurance Board* (2009) 239 CLR 290; *Cole v South Tweed Heads Rugby League Football Club Ltd* (2004) 217 CLR 469.

A Eviction of trespassers

Cowell v Rosehill Racecourse Co Ltd (1937) 56 CLR 605

Facts and issues

Cowell sued Rosehill Racecourse Co Ltd ('Racecourse') for assault. The Racecourse argued that Cowell was trespassing on its land and that its employees had requested him to leave, but he had refused to do so, and they had then evicted him using reasonable force. Cowell argued that he had a licence to stay on the land.

Decision

The Court found that the licence to stay on the land was contractual, not proprietary, and could be revoked. The Racecourse's employees were entitled to remove Cowell with reasonable force once he had refused to comply with their request to leave.

Dixon J

> [**630**] A licence which is not coupled with or granted in aid of an interest is revocable at law. It operates as a bare permission to do what would otherwise be an invasion of the licensor's rights. If the permission is terminated, further continuance of the acts it authorized [**631**] becomes wrongful. A licensee does not become a trespasser until he has received notice that the licence is countermanded and until a reasonable time has elapsed in which he may withdraw from the land and remove whatever property he has brought in pursuance of the licence … . But, if he then refuse to leave the premises, he cannot complain of his forcible removal.

B Self-defence of property

Hackshaw v Shaw (1984) 155 CLR 624

Facts and issues

Shaw owned a farm in Korong Vale in Victoria, on which he had a petrol tank used for farm vehicles. For over a year, petrol was regularly stolen from the tank. Shaw and his wife lay in wait near the tank, intending to disable the thief's car and discover the thief's identity. Cox drove up in a car, turned off the headlights and proceeded to fill his car with petrol from the tank. Shaw called for the thief to abandon the car, and fired a rifle twice at the engine of the car. Unbeknown to Shaw, Cox's sixteen-year-old girlfriend, Hackshaw, was cowering hidden in the car. She was hit in the arm by one of the shots. She sued Shaw for trespass to the person and negligence.

Decision

Ordinary principles of negligence applied to this case. Shaw had been negligent in firing the gun at the car (Dawson J dissenting). It was open to find that Hackshaw had been contributorily negligent (Murphy J, dissenting on this point).

Wilson J

> [**639**] One may readily sympathize with the predicament in which the respondent found himself with repeated thefts of his property at night in an isolated area in circumstances where he was left to fend [**640**] for himself. He intended by his actions to scare off the intruder and to obtain evidence on which the police could take action. But clearly, in endeavouring to protect his property and obtain evidence, he went too far. The law cannot condone or excuse such conduct. Even at a time when the law jealously safeguarded the rights of property owners it was recognized, as Erle CJ said in *Potter v Faulkner* that:
>
> > The law of England, in its care for human life, requires consummate caution in the person who deals with dangerous weapons.

Deane J

> [**661**] On balance, it appears to me that their Lordships' judgment in *Cooper* is consistent with the earlier identification in this Court of the duty of an occupier to an actual or potential trespasser as the ordinary common law duty of care.
>
> ...
>
> [**665**] The appellant was on the respondent's land as a trespasser. She came at night as a passenger in an unlit car. The driver was a youth who was in the process of stealing the respondent's petrol when the respondent fired the first shot from his rifle. The appellant was not, on the learned trial judge's direction to the jury which is not [**666**] challenged, implicated in the proposed theft of petrol at least up until the time when the car came to the respondent's property: on her account, she did not even then understand why her companion switched off the car lights and drove onto the property. The second shot was aimed by the respondent at the car for the purpose of immobilizing it. The firing of that second shot at the car obviously involved a significant likelihood of death or injury to anyone in the car. The question whether there was reasonable foreseeability of a real risk of injury to the appellant or to a class of persons of which she was a member turns ultimately on whether it was, in the circumstances in which the respondent was placed, reasonably foreseeable that someone was in the car.
>
> The respondent was neither taken by surprise nor forced to defend himself. He was lying in armed ambush for a petrol thief or petrol thieves whom he expected to come. When the darkened car drove onto his property, there was an obvious possibility that it might contain a passenger as well as a driver. There was an obvious likelihood that any passenger in the car would duck down out of the line of sight when the first rifle shot was fired. Nothing that had occurred up to the time when the first shot was fired had excluded a real risk or likelihood of the presence of a passenger. The appellant claimed that she got out of the car and, when the first shot was fired, got back in it to hide. Even if that evidence

be rejected, there is nothing to suggest that she had huddled down on the front seat before she was frightened by the firing of the first shot. The explanation of why the respondent had not seen her before he fired that first shot is provided by his own evidence: 'I would be about 30 yards away'; 'I couldn't see that clear'; 'It was dark, you know, it wasn't broad daylight'; 'Well I didn't get much time, did I, but there was no one to be seen'; and, perhaps most important, 'I couldn't see the driver in the car, until he got [out]' coupled with the respondent's evidence that, after the driver had got out and while he was at the petrol tank, the respondent had 'concentrate[d] all [his] attention' on the driver and 'did not take [his] eyes off him'. In these circumstances, nothing had occurred to remove the reasonable foreseeability of the presence of a passenger in the car or the reasonable foreseeability of a real risk of injury to any such passenger if a rifle was fired at the car. It follows that the respondent was, in relation to firing the rifle, under a duty to take reasonable care to avoid physical injury to any person who, to paraphrase the jury's finding which is not challenged, might, as he 'should … have known or believed', be in the car.

C Self-defence of the person

Fontin v Katapodis (1962) 108 CLR 177

Facts and issues

Katapodis had purchased pipes at a hardware store. Fontin usually cut glass to sizes suitable for louvres ordered by customers. However, Fontin had assisted Katapodis with his purchase because Katapodis only spoke Greek, and Fontin translated. Katapodis paid cash for the pipes, but the books of the store contained no record of the payment. A few days later, when Katapodis returned to the store, Fontin told the assistant manager that Katapodis had not paid his account, and the assistant manager confronted him. Katapodis found the receipt and showed it to the assistant manager, who apologised profusely. Katapodis then confronted Fontin with the receipt and they began exchanging insults in Greek. Katapodis grabbed the T-square Fontin used to cut glass and hit him on the arm and shoulder. Fontin picked up an off-cut of louvre glass (approximately 38 centimetres x 6 centimetres) and threw it at Katapodis' face. Katapodis raised his hand to stop the glass hitting his face. The glass cut the socket of the thumb and severed the ulna nerve, causing a serious and permanent injury.

Decision

While a person is entitled to defend themself, that defence must be reasonably necessary. This action was found to be unreasonable.

The fact that Katapodis had provoked the fight was not a reason to reduce compensatory damages. His conduct would only be relevant to a reduction of exemplary damages (which had not been awarded in this instance).

McTiernan J

[**181**] It is clear that Fontin had a right to defend himself against being beaten by Katapodis. The question is whether, in the circumstances, it was reasonably necessary for him to throw the piece of glass at Katapodis in order to protect his right of personal safety. The piece of glass which he threw at Katapodis was capable of causing him serious injury. Aimed at the face it is clearly a very dangerous weapon. Apparently, Fontin realized this because he attempted to pitch it so that none of its edges would strike Katapodis. Katapodis had done only trifling harm to Fontin by hitting with the T square. Perhaps, Katapodis may have struck more severe blows if Fontin had not prevented [**182**] him. But to throw the piece of glass at Katapodis as a means of self-defence was out of all reasonable proportion to the emergency confronting Fontin. No other weapon was available to Fontin but instead of throwing the piece of glass at Katapodis he could easily have moved away from him and thus have avoided further blows from the T square. Fontin had no need to stand his ground and it was not reasonably necessary for him to throw at Katapodis the cruel and cutting missile which he did throw. It was somewhat of the nature of a deadly weapon. … [I]n the circumstances, it was not reasonably necessary for Fontin to use it in self-defence, is right.

Owen J (Dixon J agreeing)

[**185**] In my opinion, no good reason has been advanced for disturbing [**186**] either of the findings of fact made by the learned trial judge. He considered that Fontin might have taken steps of a less drastic kind to avoid the plaintiff's attack, for example by moving out from behind the bench to his left. It is true that the fact that a means of escape was open to a person who claims to have been defending himself against attack is not a decisive factor in considering whether he has acted reasonably … and the weight to be attached to such a circumstance will necessarily vary according to the circumstances. In the present case, his Honour thought that the fact that a means of escape was open was a very material matter and, in my opinion, he was right in taking that view. A further fact which, to my mind, is of importance in considering the issue of self-defence is that before the piece of glass was thrown, Fontin had called to Miles [the assistant manager], who was, he said, 'about a yard away', and that Miles was moving to his assistance when the glass was thrown.

D Recaption, replevin and specific restitution

Toyota Finance Australia Ltd v Dennis (2002) 58 NSWLR 101

Facts and issues

Dennis leased a car via a hire purchase arrangement, but he was in arrears, and Toyota Finance Australia Ltd ('Toyota') was entitled to repossess the car. Toweel had been hired to repossess the car. He approached the Dennises, who refused to give him the keys to the car. Toweel grabbed

Mrs Dennis's arm while he attempted to take the car keys. Among other things, Mrs Dennis sued Toweel for assault.

Decision

Recaption is only available if the original taking was unlawful from the beginning (Sheller JA, with whom Meagher JA agreed).

Handley JA (dissenting) held that recaption is available even if the original taking was lawful, as long as possession later became unlawful (applying *Blades v Higgs*).[1]

Sheller JA (Meagher JA agreeing)

> [**131**] Professor Fleming [in *The Law of Torts*, 9th ed (1998)] acknowledged there was some authority for a wider privilege based on the view expressed in *Blades v Higgs* that the plaintiff's wrongful detention against the request of the defendant would be the same violation of the right of property as the taking of the chattels out of the actual possession of the owner. He observed at 101:
>
> > Yet this dictum really begs the question, because it assumes that the privilege inheres to all persons with an immediate right to possession, thereby ignoring the distinction between violation of actual possession [**132**] and a mere right to possession, which determines whether the conduct amounts to trespass or conversion. It is contrary to the early common law and even went beyond the facts of the case whence it originated.
> >
> > Professor Fleming observed that no force was justified until there had been first a demand to yield up possession peaceably, unless perhaps such a request would be futile or dangerous.
>
> ...
>
> [**133**] For the reasons advanced by Professor Fleming, I do not think we should follow *Blades v Higgs* despite the Full Court decision in *Abbott*. With due respect *Blades v Higgs* is not a convincing decision. It is not based on precedent and for no satisfactory reason encourages forcible, perhaps violent, redress where none is required: s 93 of the *Supreme Court Act 1970*; s 83 of the *District Court Act 1973*. It is quite different in kind from the case where a person takes from its owner by a trespass a chattel that that person knows he or she is not entitled to.
>
> ...
>
> In my opinion, Mr Toweel had no right to seek forcibly to seize the vehicle and in the course of doing so, to assault Mrs Dennis. It is to be observed, as Fleming points out, that in three states – Queensland, Western Australia and Tasmania – it is lawful for any person entitled by law to the possession of moveable property to take it from an adverse possessor who does not hold it under a claim of right, and to use such force to overcome resistance as is [**134**] necessary to obtain possession, provided it is not likely to cause death or grievous bodily harm (see s 45 *Tasmanian Criminal Code*; s 276 *Queensland*

1 (1861) 10 CB (NS) 713, 142 ER 634.

Criminal Code; s 253 *Western Australian Criminal Code*). There is no equivalent legislation in New South Wales.

Handley JA (dissenting)

[**111**] Toyota had an immediate right to possession and when Mr Toweel, with its authority, requested delivery up, the result, as Erle CJ held in *Blades v Higgs,* was that Toyota 'in law would have the possession' … so that, as Pollock & Wright accepted [in Frederick Pollock and Robert Samuel Wright, *An Essay on Possession in the Common Law* (1888)] (par 46): 'The use of force could be justified'.

…

[**112**] I cannot, with respect, agree with Sheller JA … that *Blades v Higgs* encourages 'violent redress', or that 'forcible redress' may not be required in cases such as this, or that Erle CJ did not give satisfactory reasons for allowing the reasonable use of force. Erle CJ concluded his judgment by saying (par 18):

> If the owner was compellable by law to seek redress by action for a violation of his right of property, the remedy would be often worse than the mischief, and the law would aggravate the injury instead of redressing it.

… The policy reasons for allowing the use of reasonable force in this context were considered by the Law Reform Committee in para 121 of its 1971 report:

> … the memoranda submitted to us show a wide difference of view as to what the law should be and have involved consideration of the grounds upon which the right of resort to self-help may be said to be based. It may, we think, be said to be justified on the following grounds: first, it avoids the trouble and expense of litigation. Secondly, it avoids the delay normally attendant on legal proceedings, and thus minimises the risk of damage to the owner which may occur as the result of the depreciation, loss or destruction of the chattel … Thirdly it enables the owner to [**113**] recover the chattel itself, which, if the opportunity be lost, he may be unable to trace, and as to which the court may in its discretion refuse an order for specific delivery. Fourthly, it confers upon the owner a more certain remedy than an action for damages, where a judgment in his favour may be wholly or partially unsatisfied.

They then reviewed the policy reasons why resort to self-help should be discouraged and concluded, as already mentioned (par 16–7), that the use of reasonable force, in circumstances such as the present, should be allowed where the person seeking to recover the chattel has acted reasonably.

Mr Toweel told Mrs Dennis that he was there to repossess the vehicle, and asked her to step out of the vehicle. After she refused … he reached for the keys and so took possession of the vehicle for Toyota in accordance with the principles referred to above. Thus when Mrs Dennis acted to prevent Mr Toweel obtaining the keys she was a trespasser who was attempting by force to eject the agent of the lawful owner in possession. …

E Abatement of nuisance

Traian v Ware [1957] VR 200

Facts and issues

The Traians (the plaintiffs) owned land downhill from Ware's (the defendant's) land. The predecessor in title to the Traians had built an earthen embankment to stop the orchard from being flooded by water flowing down from Ware's land when it rained.

During heavy rain, the bank caused water to pool on Ware's higher land, risking flooding his crops. Several times, without asking for permission, Ware or his family members went onto the Traians' land and cut a breach in the bank, causing water to flood into the orchard and ruin their crops and trees.

The Traians sued the Wares for nuisance and trespass, and sought an injunction to restrain the Wares from cutting the embankment. The Wares countersued for a declaration that they were entitled to have the natural flow of surface water, and an injunction to restrain the Traians from maintaining the bank.

Decision

The plaintiffs were obliged to receive the natural flow of the water from the defendant's land. The pooling of water was a nuisance. However, persons who abate a nuisance must give notice of an intention to do so, if it is practicable to do so, because entry onto someone else's land is a trespass. A declaration was awarded in favour of the defendants, but damages were awarded in trespass against them including a sum reflecting their 'unauthorised and high handed' conduct.

Martin J

> **[207]** … [I]t was admitted that both in December 1954 and February 1955 the defendants went upon the plaintiffs' land without giving notice to them, to make a cut in the latter's bank. They seek to justify this on two grounds: First, they say they had a licence from the plaintiff's predecessor in title to cut through the bank whenever they considered such a course necessary for their own protection. Secondly, they assert that, as the bank was an unlawful obstruction, they were entitled to enter upon plaintiffs' property to abate the nuisance it caused.
>
> In view of the evidence of Bayley junior [the predecessor in title] there is no ground for implying a licence such as the defendants suggest they had and I say no more about that.
>
> As regards abatement of a private nuisance, in *Lemmon v Webb*, [1895] AC 1, Lord Davey, at p. 8, said: 'It is true that where a person desires to abate a nuisance, which can only be abated by going on the land of the person from whom the nuisance proceeds, he must usually give notice of his intention to do so … because his act of going upon his neighbour's land is prima facie a trespass … ', and Parke, B, in *Jones v Williams* (1843)

11 M & W 176, at p. 181, speaking for the Court of Exchequer, laid it down: 'It is clear, that if the plaintiff himself was the original wrong-doer, by placing filth upon the locus in quo, it might be removed by the party injured, without any notice to the plaintiff; and so, possibly, if by his default in not performing some obligation incumbent on him, for that is his wrong also; but if the nuisance was levied by another, and the defendant succeeded to the possession of the locus in quo afterwards, the authorities are in favour of the necessity of a notice being given to him to remove, before the party aggrieved can take the law into his own hands.'

Lord Abinger, CB, in the same case (at p. 182), added that notice need not be given where there is such immediate danger to life or health as to render it unsafe to wait, and in this statement the rest of the Court concurred.

If there be a right to abate, the person who has that right need not wait until he has actually suffered damage … .

The law does not favour the remedy of abatement in preference to legal action (*Lagan Navigation Co v Lambeg Bleaching, Dyeing and Finishing Co Ltd*, [1927] AC 226, at pp. 244–5), and requires strong reason to justify it when it involves entering upon the land of another.

The houses of the two parties concerned are close together and there seems to be no reason at all why, both in December 1954 and February 1955, the defendants could not have requested the plaintiffs to permit [**208**] a breach of the bank, or at all events given notice to them of their intention to cut it, and so afforded them an opportunity to plough furrows to lead the water which would come on to their land to a place where it would do no or little damage, as was the case whenever it was breached in the time of Bayley junior. The only reason given by Gerald Ware for cutting the bank in December 1954 without advising plaintiffs of his intention so to do was that they had filled an open gap in it without mentioning their intention to do so to him. I have already found that this alleged action on their part did not take place.

Their action in trespassing on the plaintiffs' property without notice or request to them to abate the danger threatened to their own lands was unauthorised and high handed and I consider they are liable to damages for such trespass as the plaintiffs had not built the bank.

…

[**209**] Gerald Ware was quite conscious of the harm that a breaching of the bank would do, as, in Bayley junior's time, he saw water lying on the orchard and told him he understood the reason why he didn't want the bank to be cut. It is clear that damages for a trespass are not necessarily confined to the pecuniary loss sustained by plaintiffs but may also be awarded for matter of aggravation if the circumstances warrant it … . I consider there should be an enlargement of damages … for the circumstances in which these trespasses were committed … .

As regards the counter-claim, on my understanding of the law the defendants have shown that they are entitled to a declaration as prayed, but, as there is no evidence of any threat by the plaintiffs to obstruct the natural flow in the future and defendants elected to abate the nuisance instead of resorting to the court for redress, I do not consider there should be a decree for the injunction sought by them.

REVIEW QUESTIONS

(1) What is the common thread running through the cases in this section?

(2) In *Toyota Finance Australia Ltd v Dennis* (2002) 58 NSWLR 101, whose approach do you prefer: Sheller JA's or Handley JA's?

III Contract and self-help

Contract law allows more latitude in self-help as contracts arise consensually, and liberal society is generally premised on the idea that we should have freedom of contracting. This extends to remedies.

Concept	Short explanation	Relevant authorities	Principles text
Rescission (where a transaction is reversed) can be seen as a self-help remedy.	Rescission could be seen as a self-help remedy to the extent that parties voluntarily exchange benefits when one party gives notice that they wish to rescind. However, equitable rescission (where adjustments are made) is more likely an act of the court.	*Alati v Kruger* (1955) 94 CLR 216 (see Chapter 18, page 614 for extract)	Chapter 13: [13.35]–[13.36]
The penalties doctrine will only apply to specific kinds of clauses.	At common law, the penalties doctrine will only apply to a payment triggered by breach. In equity, the penalties doctrine applies to collateral stipulations imposing additional detriment.	*Andrews v Australia and New Zealand Banking Group Ltd* (2012) 247 CLR 205	Chapter 13: [13.37]–[13.40]
The test of whether a clause is in fact a penalty depends upon proportionality.	Whether a clause is a penalty in fact depends upon whether it is out of proportion with the the 'legitimate interest' protected by the contract.	*Paciocco v Australia and New Zealand Banking Group Ltd* (2016) 258 CLR 525	Chapter 13: [13.46]–[13.49]
A contracting party may stipulate a remedy such as debt, or termination clauses.	This may be advantageous for parties who wish to ensure that they obtain recovery or have an entitlement to end a contract.		Chapter 13: [13.51]–[13.59]

A Rescission

As noted by Dixon J in *Alati v Kruger*[2] (extracted in Chapter 18 on page 614), rescission is sometimes seen as a self-help remedy. In other words, one party gives notice that they wish to rescind, and the parties voluntarily return to the other what each has received under the contract without the intervention of the court. However, this takes place in the shadow of laws which entitle the rescinding party to go to court and demand rescission in certain circumstances.

Where equitable rescission is awarded, it is harder to argue that the remedy involves self-help, as the court must be involved to make adjustments to what each party returns to the other in order to achieve 'practical justice'.

B Liquidated damages and penalties

The penalties doctrine has been complicated by *Andrews v Australia and New Zealand Banking Group Ltd*,[3] which holds that in Australian law we have both a common law and an equitable doctrine against penalties in contract. There are three questions to be asked in either instance:

(1) Is this a clause to which the penalties doctrine applies?

(2) On the facts is this clause a penalty?

(3) If it is a penalty, what are the consequences?

Table 13.1 lays out a comparison between the two doctrines. The main differences lies in the clauses to which the penalties doctrine applies (broader under equity, not just those triggered by breach) and the consequences (void at common law, voidable in equity).

Table 13.1 Comparison of common law and equitable penalties doctrines

	Common law penalties doctrine	Equitable penalties doctrine
Is this a clause to which the penalties doctrine applies?	Is this payment triggered by breach? If not – penalties doctrine doesn't apply.	Collateral stipulation imposing extra detriment? Penalties doctrine applies. *or* Additional stipulation paying for an extra right? Penalties doctrine does not apply.
On the facts, is this clause a penalty?	Must be extravagant and out of all proportion. Must be in proportion to the legitimate interest.	Must be extravagant and out of all proportion. Must be in proportion to the legitimate interest.
If it is a penalty, what are the consequences?	Void at common law.	Enforceable only to the extent of actual loss.

2 (1955) 94 CLR 216.

3 (2012) 247 CLR 205.

1 Is this a clause to which the penalties doctrine applies?

Andrews v Australia and New Zealand Banking Group Ltd [2012] HCA 30; (2012) 247 CLR 205

Facts and issues

This case was a class action by customers of the Australia and New Zealand Banking Group Ltd ('ANZ') who sought to argue that fees the bank had charged them in relation to transactions made on their accounts were penalties. The representative plaintiffs alleged that certain fees were not genuine pre-estimates of damage and were penalty fees. The five categories of fee were honour fees, dishonour fees, non-payment fees, overlimit fees, and late payment fees.

The trial judge held that the only fees which were capable of being characterised as a penalty were the late payment fees because the other fees were not triggered by breach.[4] The other clauses had been drafted as permissive obligation ('we agree to pay … ') rather than as a fee arising on breach of contract.

The ANZ appealed, and the High Court uplifted the appeal.

Decision

The equitable doctrine of penalties applies beyond breach, to situations where a collateral stipulation imposes an additional detriment. It does not apply where there is an additional stipulation paying for an extra right. A clause which is subject to the equitable penalties doctrine is voidable to the extent it does not reflect actual loss.

French CJ, Gummow, Crennan, Kiefel and Bell JJ

The penalty doctrine

[9] Mason and Deane JJ observed in *Legione v Hateley* that, as the term suggests, a penalty is in the nature of a punishment for non-observance of a contractual stipulation and consists, upon breach, of the imposition of an additional or different liability.

[10] In general terms, a stipulation *prima facie* imposes a penalty on a party ('the first party') if, as a matter of substance, it is collateral (or accessory) to a primary stipulation in favour of a second party and this collateral stipulation, upon the failure of the primary stipulation, imposes upon the first party an additional detriment, the penalty, to the benefit of the second party. In that sense, the collateral or accessory stipulation is described as being in the nature of a security for and *in terrorem* of the satisfaction of the primary stipulation. If compensation can be made to the second party for the prejudice suffered by failure of the primary stipulation, the collateral stipulation and the penalty are enforced only to the extent of that compensation. The first party is relieved to that degree from liability to satisfy the collateral stipulation.

[11] It has been established at least since the decision of Lord Macclesfield in *Peachy v Duke of Somerset* that the penalty doctrine is not engaged if the prejudice or damage

4 Relying on *Interstar Wholesale Finance Pty Ltd v Integral Home Loans Pty Ltd* (2008) 257 ALR 292.

to the interests of the second party by the failure of the primary stipulation is insusceptible of evaluation and assessment in money terms. It is the availability of compensation which generates the 'equity' upon which the court intervenes; without it, the parties are left to their legal rights and obligations. …

[12] It should be noted that the primary stipulation may be the occurrence or non-occurrence of an event which need not be the payment of money. Further, the penalty imposed upon the first party upon failure of the primary stipulation need not be a requirement to pay to the second party a sum of money.

…

[15] The formulation of that distinction between a penalty and a pre-estimate of liquidated damages which was made by Lord Dunedin in *Dunlop Pneumatic Tyre Co Ltd v New Garage and Motor Co Ltd* has been described as a product of centuries of equity jurisprudence. It was recently applied by this Court in *Ringrow Pty Ltd v BP Australia Pty Ltd*. But the present dispute requires attention at an anterior stage of analysis, namely identification of those criteria by which the penalty doctrine is engaged.

The course of the Federal Court litigation

…

[21] The primary judge found that the late payment fee was payable upon breach of contract and therefore was capable of characterisation as a penalty. The ANZ has not sought to appeal against that finding.

[22] However, in respect of the honour, dishonour, non-payment and over limit fees the primary judge held that these were not charged by the ANZ upon breach of contract by the customer, nor was the occurrence of the event upon which the fees were charged (overdrawing the account or credit limit or attempting to do so) an event which the customer had an obligation or responsibility to avoid. Having thus answered in the negative each of the alternative questions, the primary judge held it was unnecessary to answer the question whether these fees were capable of characterisation as a penalty.

…

The Interstar *decision*

[29] In reaching her conclusion respecting the scope of the penalty doctrine, the primary judge, with respect quite properly, followed what had been decided by the New South Wales Court of Appeal in *Interstar Wholesale Finance Pty Ltd v Integral Home Loans Pty Ltd*. In that case the Court of Appeal held that the primary judge (Brereton J) had erred in denying that the doctrine had ceased to be one of equity and now was wholly legal in nature and in concluding that the doctrine was not limited to the failure of stipulations which were breaches of contract.

[30] … The Court of Appeal held that the agreements [in *Interstar*] conferred no accrued rights upon the respondents, so that upon termination there was no forfeiture of accrued property for the collateral purpose of encouraging compliance with the contract and no engagement of the penalty doctrine; further, the character of the provisions was to define entitlement to the commissions.

[31] These holdings would have been sufficient for the Court of Appeal to dispose of the case. However, the Court went on, with reference to observations of Mason and

Wilson JJ in *AMEV-UDC Finance Ltd v Austin* ('*AMEV-UDC*'), to state that '[t]he modern rule against penalties is a rule of law, not equity'. …

[32] The applicants seek in this Court to challenge these statements in *Interstar*. For the reasons which follow that challenge should succeed.

…

Limited scope of the penalty doctrine?

[46] … [W]hile the ANZ maintains that the penalty doctrine has the limited scope, respecting breaches of contract, which in *Interstar* the Court of Appeal identified with *ECGD*, this limitation should not be accepted.

…

[48] In *AMEV-UDC* Gibbs CJ emphasised that this Court was not required to consider the proposition, said to be derived from *ECGD*, that no clause which provided for the payment of money on the happening of a specified event other than a breach of a contractual duty owed by the contemplated payor to the contemplated payee could ever be a penalty.

[49] Brereton J in *Interstar* rejected the submission that liability to pay, forfeit or suffer the retention of money or property which engages the penalty doctrine may never be triggered by the failure in occurrence of an event which is stipulated in a prior agreement between the parties but is not itself the subject of a contractual promise between them. Brereton J pointed to the regard paid by equity to substance rather than merely to form and referred to the grant of relief in the case of penal bonds for non-performance of a condition which was not the subject of any contractual promise. These are significant considerations. They are not displaced by fixing solely upon a breach of contract by the party seeking relief from an alleged penalty.

[50] In *Interstar* the Court of Appeal misunderstood the scope of the penalty doctrine. The question whether in a given case the operation of a stipulation which is not a contractual promise may attract the penalty doctrine is not foreclosed by the rejection in the Court of Appeal of what had been said by Brereton J at first instance.

…

Conclusion

[78] The upshot is that the restrictions upon the penalty doctrine urged by the Court of Appeal in *Interstar* should not be accepted. The primary judge erred in concluding, in effect, that in the absence of contractual breach or an obligation or responsibility on the customer to avoid the occurrence of an event upon which the relevant fees were charged, no question arose as to whether the fees were capable of characterisation as penalties.

[79] Indeed, a further issue appears to have been presented by her Honour's findings set out above. This may be stated as being whether the requirement to pay the fees in question was not enjoyed by the ANZ as security for performance by the customer of its other obligations to the ANZ, or whether the fees were charged by the ANZ, as specified in pre-existing arrangements with the customer, and ANZ, respectively, for the further accommodation provided to the customer by its authorising payments upon instructions by the customer upon which the ANZ otherwise was not obliged to act, or upon refusal of that accommodation.

[80] The operative distinction would be that upon which the majority of the New South Wales Court of Appeal (Jacobs JA and Holmes JA) decided *Metro-Goldwyn-Mayer Pty Ltd* *v Greenham*. Their Honours contrasted a stipulation attracting the penalty doctrine and one giving rise consensually to an additional obligation. This distinction had been identified long before, by Lord St Leonards in *French v Macale*, as follows:

> [I]t appears, that the question for the Court to ascertain is, whether the party is restricted by covenant from doing the particular act, although if he do it a payment is reserved; *or whether according to the true construction of the contract, its meaning is, that the one party shall have a right to do the act, on payment of what is agreed upon as an equivalent*. If a man let meadow land for two guineas an acre, and the contract is, that if the tenant choose to employ it in tillage, he may do so, paying an additional rent of two guineas an acre, no doubt this is a perfectly good and unobjectionable contract; the breaking up the land is not inconsistent with the contract, which provides, that in case the act is done the landlord is to receive an increased rent. (emphasis added)

[81] The English and United States authorities in which the distinction thereafter was applied are collected and discussed in the treatise by Pomeroy, under the heading 'Stipulations not Penalties – Alternative Stipulations'.

[82] In *Metro-Goldwyn-Mayer*, the contract for the hiring of films to exhibitors for public showing conferred the right to one screening only. The exhibitor was obliged to pay for each additional screening a sum equivalent to four times the original fee. The questions of construction of the contract were resolved by Jacobs JA and Holmes JA in such a fashion that the penalty doctrine had no application. Jacobs JA concluded:

> There is no right in the exhibitor to use the film otherwise than on an authorized occasion. If he does so then he must be taken to have exercised an option so to do under the agreement, if the agreement so provides. The agreement provides that he may exercise such an option in one event only, namely, that he pay a hiring fee of four times the usual hiring fee.

[83] But it should be emphasised that the determination, with respect to the relevant exception fees, of live issues of this nature is entirely a matter upon further trial, along with the grounds upon which the applicants submit the penalty doctrine does apply to those fees.

2 On the facts, is this clause a penalty?

Paciocco v Australia and New Zealand Banking Group Ltd [2016] HCA 28; (2016) 258 CLR 525

Facts and issues

This was the follow-up case to *Andrews v Australia and New Zealand Banking Group Ltd* (with a different representative plaintiff) considering (among other things) whether the credit card fees were in fact a penalty.

Decision

The majority (Kiefel J, with whom French CJ agreed on penalties) held that ANZ had a legitimate interest in obtaining performance of the contract, and the fees were not out of proportion with that contract (following the formulation suggested by the UK Supreme Court in *Cavendish Square Holding BV v Makdessi*).[5] Nettle J dissented: he would have applied the test from *Dunlop Pneumatic Tyre Co Ltd v New Garage and Motor Co Ltd* [6] as to whether the sum was disproportionate to the greatest loss which could be suffered by breach.

Gageler J

> **[166]** To accept the appropriateness of framing the inquiry in terms of whether the stipulation in issue is properly characterised as having no purpose other than to punish is to reject the suggestion, which originated with Lord Radcliffe in *Bridge v Campbell Discount Co Ltd*, that the description of a penalty as a threat to be enforced *in terrorem* adds nothing to the requisite analysis. To the contrary, the description captures the essence of the conception to which the whole of the analysis is directed.
>
> **[166]** Framing the inquiry in terms of whether the stipulation in issue is properly characterised as having no purpose other than to punish compels a more tailored inquiry into the commercial circumstances within which the parties entered into the contract containing the stipulation than might be involved in asking, as did the Supreme Court of the United Kingdom in *Cavendish*, whether the stipulation serves a 'legitimate interest'. That is not, of course, to say that the differently framed inquiries might not lead to the same result.
>
> ...
>
> **[172]** Each of those two categories of costs nevertheless represented commercial interests which ANZ had in ensuring that its credit card customers, as a cohort, made minimum monthly payments by the due date. Provisioning costs directly affected recorded profit, and the costs of regulatory capital were a real outgoing. The primary judge was undoubtedly correct in describing provisioning costs and regulatory capital costs as part of the costs of running a bank in Australia. But ANZ was not confined by a principle of law to adopting a pricing strategy for its credit card products which involved cross-subsidisation.
>
> **[173]** The calculations of Mr Inglis showed the commercial interests of ANZ in avoiding those two principal categories of costs to be not grossly disproportionate to the amount of the late payment fee, even if operational costs were ignored.

Keane J

> *ANZ's legitimate interest*
>
> **[271]** It may be accepted immediately that a bank, like any other party to a contract, has no legitimate interest in punishing its customers for their defaults or in threatening them with punishment in order to discipline their behaviour. But a bank has a multi-faceted interest in the timely performance of its customers' obligations as to payment.

5 [2015] 3 WLR 1373.

6 [1915] AC 79.

[272] The legitimate interest of ANZ protected by the late payment fee cannot be apprehended without an understanding of the commercial context in which that interest requires protection. It is an awkward irony of the appellants' case that, in a class action representing many claimants unified in their assertion that this aspect of the contract of adhesion made by each of them with the bank is unenforceable as a penalty, the appellants' focus was upon the individual contract between Mr Paciocco and ANZ.

[273] Lord Dunedin in *Dunlop* recognised that the supposedly penal character of the operation of a contractual term must be understood by reference to the 'inherent circumstances' in which it is to operate. In the present case, those circumstances include the fact that ANZ is a bank engaged in providing financial accommodation by way of bank card facilities to many customers on standard terms. The agreement, common to each customer, to pay the late payment fee required by ANZ was an aspect of ANZ's business which enabled the bank to provide accommodation to each customer. The fixing of risk and reward on each side of each transaction reflected the circumstance that it was one of many transactions and that the very multiplicity of these transactions was a factor bearing upon the pricing of each facility to each of many customers. The circumstance that the value of an increase in credit risk may be difficult to assess is a consideration which tends against an affirmative conclusion that the stipulation is to be characterised as a punishment. That consideration gains added force where the creditor is a bank which, as such, is exposed to the risk that many borrowers may default at one time in circumstances unforeseen at the time of the original arrangements.

[274] One aspect of ANZ's interest is obvious as an ordinary aspect of the business of a bank. Because of the relationship between the financial risks assumed by a lender and the cost of the facility to customers, the economic effect of provisions calculated to secure the protection of the bank by a late payment clause cannot be viewed in isolation from other elements of the cost of the facility to borrowers, such as interest.

Nettle J (dissenting)

Tests for the identification of a penalty

[317] In *Dunlop Pneumatic Tyre Co Ltd v New Garage and Motor Co Ltd*, Lord Dunedin identified four tests (of which the fourth is comprised of four parts) ('the *Dunlop* tests') which his Lordship said may assist in deciding, and in some cases may determine, whether an obligation to pay a sum of money upon a breach of a contract is penal. In substance, those tests are:

(1) whether the contract describes the payment as a penalty or liquidated damages is not decisive;

(2) the essence of a penalty is a payment '*in terrorem*' (which in this context means to deter the offending party from committing the breach), whereas the essence of liquidated damages is a genuine pre-estimate of damage;

(3) the question is one of 'construction' (more accurately, of characterisation) of the terms of the contract having regard to the inherent circumstances of the contract at the time the contract was made;

(4)(a) the agreed sum will be held to be a penalty if it is extravagant and unconscionable in amount in comparison with the greatest loss that could conceivably be proved to have followed from the breach;
(4)(b) the agreed sum may be held to be a penalty where the breach consists only in not paying a sum of money and the stipulated sum is greater than the sum which ought to have been paid;
(4)(c) there is a presumption that a single lump sum is a penalty if it is payable on the occurrence of one or more of several events of which some may occasion serious damage and others do not; and
(4)(d) where the consequences of breach make the precise pre-estimate of damage almost impossible, it is more probable that an agreed sum is a penalty than where the damage is capable of precise estimation.

[318] As Lord Dunedin made plain in *Dunlop*, the *Dunlop* tests are not rules of law and they are not exhaustive. Rather, they represent the distillation of various processes of reasoning that were applied in the several authorities from which the tests were derived and hence are conceived of as likely to prove useful and sometimes determinative in similar cases. Nevertheless, because of the broad range of cases from which the *Dunlop* tests were derived, and consequently the broad spread of cases to which they are capable of application, they have proved to be of widespread and enduring utility. The *Dunlop* tests have been applied by this Court on a number of occasions spanning many years. Recently, in *Ringrow Pty Ltd v BP Australia Pty Ltd*, this Court re-articulated the orthodox application of the *Dunlop* tests, that a penalty is 'out of all proportion' to the 'greatest loss that could conceivably be proved to have followed from the breach'.

...

Are the Dunlop tests adequate in this case?

[322] As will be apparent from the differences between the approach of the primary judge and the reasoning of the Full Court, the outcome of the penalty appeal turns to a large extent on whether this case should be regarded as one of the straightforward kind in which the *Dunlop* tests are 'perfectly adequate' to resolve the issues or whether it should be seen as one of the more complex types of cases referred to in *Cavendish* which necessitate considerations beyond a comparison of the agreed sum and the amount of recoverable damages. In particular, should the Bank be conceived of as having had a legitimate interest in Mr Paciocco's performance of the Monthly Payments obligation which extended beyond its performance or compensation for breach of its performance?

...

[330] ... As the law of penalties has evolved ... it is not concerned with whether an obligation is properly to be conceived of as a punishment as such. It is concerned with whether an obligation to make a payment on breach of a contractual or other principal obligation is of an amount which is grossly disproportionate to the foreseeable consequences of the breach. In effect, the gross disproportion is in itself sufficient to render the obligation 'unconscionable' and therefore unenforceable. Accordingly, in England, and hitherto in this country, the main purpose of the law of penalties has been as a rule of law to prevent a party recovering a sum of money in respect of a breach of contract which bears little or no relationship to the loss actually suffered by that party ... .

[331] For the same reason, the fact that the late payment fee may have been set by reference to what other banks were charging in the context of a competitive banking market is essentially irrelevant. As Lords Neuberger and Sumption observed in *Cavendish*, although the penalty rule originated out of equity's concern to prevent exploitation at a time when credit was scarce and borrowers were particularly vulnerable, the modern rule is substantive, not procedural. It does not normally depend for its operation on establishing that advantage was taken of one party. An obligation to pay a fee does not cease to be penal just because the obligee's competitors impose similar penalties on their customers. Where there is an incentive constituted of an obligation to pay a sum of money conditioned on a breach of contract of which the amount is wholly disproportionate to the greatest costs which would have been conceived of at the time of entry into the contract, the obligation will be regarded as penal unless there be some aspect of the contract which makes it possible to say that the amount of the obligation is not wholly disproportionate to the interest protected by the bargain.

[332] Nor does the fact that the late payment fee may have been set by reference to fees being charged by the Bank's competitors establish that the Bank had an interest in the timeous performance of the Monthly Payments obligation other than its performance or adequate compensation for its breach. Of itself, it suggests no more than that the extent of competition, or more likely lack of it, led the Bank to conclude that the level at which it set the fee was unlikely to result in an unacceptable loss of custom to other banks. That says nothing about whether this fee or those fees were penal in the relevant sense.

[333] In the result, although in some circumstances the test of whether a fee is a penalty may go beyond the quantitative assessment of disproportion between the fee and the greatest loss that could conceivably be proved, and it so may require a qualitative assessment of disproportion between the fee and a more imprecise conception of the interest protected by the bargain, in this case it is not possible to identify any interest to be protected by the bargain other than payment of the amount which was due together with compensation for such costs incurred as a result of late payment as would be recoverable as damages for breach of contract.

[334] That being so, to accept that the Bank was entitled to impose a late payment fee wholly disproportionate to the greatest loss that could conceivably be proved would be in effect to abandon a large part of the existing law relating to penalties. None of the authorities and nothing which was advanced in argument provides an acceptable basis for taking that step. There was and is no reason why the matter should not be determined in accordance with the *Dunlop* tests.

Which Dunlop *tests apply?*

Nettle J decided that test 4(a) and test 4(c) applied:

The greatest recoverable loss that could conceivably be proved

[340] Mr Paciocco further contended that, if test 4(a) of the *Dunlop* tests were applicable, the primary judge was correct to assess the greatest loss that could conceivably be proved to have followed from the breach by reference to what would be recoverable as unliquidated damages. For that reason, it was submitted, the Full Court erred in taking into account forms of projected losses which might be conceived of as bearing some possible relationship to the breach but which at law are regarded as too remote to be recoverable.

[341] That contention should be accepted. As Mason and Wilson JJ observed in *AMEV-UDC*, during the first half-century following *Dunlop* the concept of an agreed sum being extravagant in comparison with the greatest amount of damage that could conceivably have been contemplated by the parties became, in effect, a test of whether the agreed sum was greater than the amount of damages that could be awarded for the breach of contract. That change was 'consistent with an underlying policy of restricting the parties, in case of breach of contract, to the recovery of an amount of damages no greater than that for which the law provides'. Hence, as stated in *Chitty on Contracts*, the word 'damage' in this context means 'net loss' after taking account of the claimant's expected ability to mitigate.

[342] In *AMEV-UDC*, Mason and Wilson JJ posited that it would be in the interests of freedom of contract, and therefore desirable, for the courts to return to the idea that an agreed sum should only be characterised as a penalty if it is 'out of all proportion' to the damage likely to be suffered as a result of the breach. They proposed that the test be one of degree that depends on a number of circumstances including the degree of disproportion between the stipulated sum and the likely loss to be suffered (a factor which they said would be relevant to the oppressiveness of the term to the party required to pay) and the nature of the relationship between the contracting parties (a factor which they said would be relevant to the unconscionability of the party's conduct in seeking to enforce the term). It may be accepted that the law has now reached that stage of development. But, even so, as was stated in *Ringrow*, in assessing the degree of disproportion in typical penalty cases the sum of money stipulated as payable on breach is to be compared with what would be recoverable as unliquidated damages for the breach.

[343] For the reasons already stated, this case is a typical penalty case of the kind referred to in *Ringrow*. In those circumstances, the primary judge was correct to consider whether the late payment fee was out of all proportion to the amount recoverable as unliquidated damages.

C Debt

It is easier for a plaintiff to recover a debt than damages. All that is required to make out debt is that the sum becomes due upon the occurrence of a specific event. The rules of remoteness and mitigation do not apply. Hence, a party may draft their contract to allow them to claim in debt instead of in damages. Moreover, acceleration of a debt is generally not subject to the rule against penalties.[7]

7 *O'Dea v Allstates Leasing System (WA) Pty Ltd* (1983) 152 CLR 359.

D Other stipulated contractual remedies

There are other ways in which parties may stipulate contractual remedies, including by limiting remedies to damages. Termination clauses will also affect the availability of remedies. Further detail can be found in the principles text at [13.54]–[13.59].

REVIEW QUESTIONS

(1) Consider a clause which states:

(a) Yolanda will hire out bicycle to Zachariah on the first Thursday of each month for $10.

(b) If Zachariah uses the bicycle on any other day, he agrees to pay Yolanda $1000.

According to *Andrews v Australia and New Zealand Banking Group Ltd* (2012) 247 CLR 205, is clause (b) a collateral stipulation imposing extra detriment to which the equitable penalties doctrine applies or an additional stipulation paying for an extra right to which the equitable penalties doctrine does not apply?

(2) What is the effect of the majority's 'legitimate interest' test in *Paciocco v Australia and New Zealand Banking Group Ltd* (2016) 258 CLR 525? Will it make it easier or harder to prove that a clause is in fact a penalty?

14 EXEMPLARY DAMAGES AND AGGRAVATED DAMAGES

I	Introduction	476
II	Exemplary damages	476
	A The nature and history of exemplary damages in Australia	480
	B The causes of action for which exemplary damages can be awarded in Australia	488
III	Aggravated damages	494
	A The distinction between exemplary damages and aggravated damages	496
	B Availability of aggravated damages in Australian law	499
IV	'Vindicatory damages'	504

I Introduction

The damages dealt with in this chapter have a vindicatory aspect, in that the court recognises the importance of the plaintiff's rights by making an award.

Exemplary damages explicitly *punish* the defendant for the wrong in question. They are also said to validate the plaintiff's feelings of hurt and anger arising from the contumelious nature of the defendant's wrong.

Aggravated damages aim to compensate the plaintiff for distress caused by the nature of the defendant's breach. They have been said to protect the dignitary interest of the plaintiff, and/or to be a form of damages for distress.

Vindicatory damages are a novel head of damages said to allow for a substantial award of damages in the absence of loss if a right has been violated. It has been argued that they should be extended to breaches of private law rights in some instances. As we will see, the High Court has argued against these awards being a category of their own in Australia.

II Exemplary damages

Exemplary damages have a punitive aim. They are primarily available for torts. It is necessary to make out the 'host' cause of action. They are unavailable if substantial criminal punishment has already been imposed because the punitive aim has already been fulfilled by a different area of law.

Figure 14.1 Exemplary damages

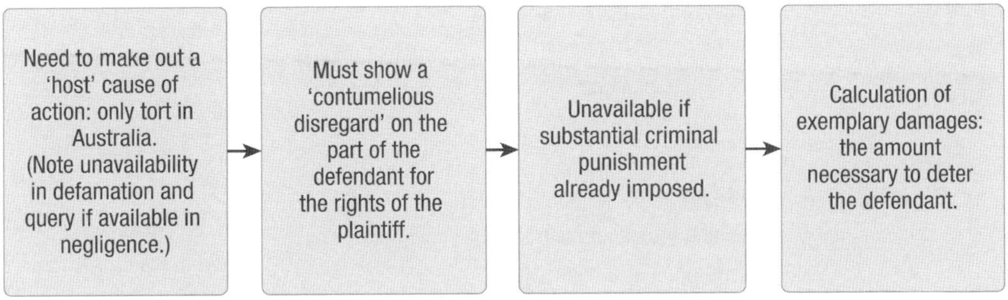

Concept	Short explanation	Relevant authorities	Principles text
Nature and history of exemplary damages in Australia	Exemplary damages are in some senses an anomaly and are primarily available for torts. They are awarded where there has been a contumelious disregard of the plaintiff's rights deserving of punishment.	*Gray v Motor Accident Commission* (1998) 196 CLR 1	Chapter 14: [14.5]–[14.14]
It is necessary to make out the 'host' cause of action before exemplary damages can be awarded	For torts actionable *per se* there is no need to make out factual loss to establish liability, but where damage is the gist of the action, it is necessary to establish actual loss before an award of exemplary damages can be made.	*Fatimi Pty Ltd v Bryant* (2004) 59 NSWLR 678	Chapter 14: [14.15]–[14.17]
Exemplary damages are unavailable if 'substantial punishment' has already been imposed	The majority in *Gray* said that 'substantial punishment' is an absolute bar to the availability of exemplary damages	*Gray v Motor Accident Commission* (1998) 196 CLR 1	Chapter 14: [14.18]–[14.20]
Calculation of exemplary damages	Regard must be had as to what amount is necessary to punish that particular defendant.	*Pollack v Volpato* [1973] 1 NSWLR 653	Chapter 14: [14.21]–[14.25]
Exemplary damages are primarily available for torts in Australia	Historically exemplary damages have been available in tort, and this remains the case in Australia Exemplary damages are available for: • trespass to land[a] • nuisance[b] • trespass to goods[c] • trespass to the person[d] • conversion and detinue[e]	The cases cited in footnotes are authority for the general principle.	Chapter 14: [14.26]–[14.32]

Concept	Short explanation	Relevant authorities	Principles text
	• battery[f] • wrongful arrest involving trespass to land and the person[g] • false imprisonment[h] • malicious prosecution[i] • abuse of process[j] • misfeasance in the public office[k] • inducing breach of contract[l] • interference with contractual relations[m] • deceit[n] • intimidation[o] • conspiracy[p] • negligence, although only if the action was deliberate or reckless?[q] • tort of passing off?[r]		
Some statutes have precluded exemplary damages for some torts	Torts where exemplary damages are precluded by statute: • defamation[s] • claims surviving for the benefit of the estate after the death of a plaintiff[t] • in New South Wales, Queensland and the Northern Territory, claims for certain personal injuries[u] • in New South Wales and Victoria, personal injury in motor vehicle accident cases[v] • in New South Wales and Queensland, common law claims for workers' compensation.[w]	The legislation cited in footnotes are authority for the general principle.	
Exemplary damages are available for some statutory breaches	The statutory power to confer exemplary damages has primarily been available in intellectual property statutes, for 'flagrant' breaches.[x] Some other statutes also confer a power to award exemplary damages.[y]	*Copyright Act 1968* (Cth) s 115(4)	Chapter 14: [14.33]–[14.34]
Exemplary damages are not available for breach of contract in Australia	Exemplary damages are not awarded for breach of contract for historical reasons, and because of the nature of contractual liability.	*Gray v Motor Accident Commission* (1998) 196 CLR 1, [13]	Chapter 14: [14.35]–[14.30]

Concept	Short explanation	Relevant authorities	Principles text
Exemplary damages are not generally available for equitable breaches in Australia	Exemplary damages are not given for equitable breaches for historical reasons, but also because of the nature of equitable liability itself.	*Harris v Digital Pulse Pty Ltd* (2003) 56 NSWLR 298	Chapter 14: [14.41]–[14.48]
Exemplary damages are not generally available for contravention of the *Australian Consumer Law* ('ACL')	The ACL has no explicit provision for exemplary damages. Given the focus of s 236 of the ACL on 'loss or damage' to the claimant, it is unlikely that exemplary damages would be available under that section, as exemplary damages focus on the conduct of the defendant alone.[z]	The case cited in footnotes is authority for the general principle.	Chapter 14: [14.49]–[14.51]

[a] *XL Petroleum (NSW) Pty Ltd v Caltex Oil (Australia) Pty Ltd* (1985) 155 CLR 448; *New South Wales v Ibbett* (2006) 229 CLR 638.

[b] *Commonwealth v Murray* (1988) Aust Torts Reports 80–207; *Willoughby Municipal Council v Halstead* (1916) 22 CLR 352.

[c] *Healing (Sales) Pty Ltd v Inglis Electrix Pty Ltd* (1968) 121 CLR 584.

[d] *Fontin v Katapodis* (1962) 108 CLR 177.

[e] *Cook v Saroukas* (1989) 97 FLR 33.

[f] *Lamb v Cotogno* (1987) 164 CLR 1; *Pearce v Hallett* [1969] SASR 423; *Henry v Thompson* [1989] 2 Qd R 412.

[g] *Adams v Kennedy* (2000) 49 NSWLR 78.

[h] *McFadzean v Construction, Forestry, Mining and Energy Union* [2004] VSC 289; *AW v New South Wales* [2005] NSWSC 543.

[i] *A v New South Wales* (2007) 230 CLR 500; *Coyle v New South Wales* [2006] NSWCA 95.

[j] *Hamer-Mathew v Gulabrai (No 2)* (1995) Aust Torts Reports 81–334.

[k] *Sanders v Snell* (1997) 73 FCR 569, rev'd on other grounds in (1998) 196 CLR 329.

[l] *Whitfield v De Lauret & Co Ltd* (1920) 29 CLR 71.

[m] *Zhu v Sydney Organising Committee for the Olympic Games* [2001] NSWSC 989, *Zhu v Treasurer (NSW)* (2004) 218 CLR 530.

[n] *Musca v Astle Corporation Pty Ltd* (1988) 80 ALR 251 (FCA). Cf *Rookes v Barnard* [1964] AC 1129; *Mafo v Adams* [1970] 1 QB 548; *Cassell & Co Ltd v Broome* [1972] AC 1027, which doubts the availability in England.

[o] *AS v Murray* [2013] NSWSC 733, [23].

[p] *Williams v Hursey* (1959) 103 CLR 30.

[q] *Gray v Motor Accident Commission* (1998) 196 CLR 1 (motor vehicle use); *Midalco Pty Ltd v Rabenalt* [1989] VR 461 (industrial injury); *Amaca Pty Ltd v Banton* (2007) 5 DDCR 314 (industrial injury); *Backwell v AAA* [1997] 1 VR 182 (medical negligence). Cf *Cassell & Co Ltd v Broome* [1972] AC 1027, which doubts availability in England.

[r] *Paramount Pictures Corporation v Hasluck* (2006) 70 IPR 293, [35]; *Flamingo Park Pty Ltd v Dolly Dolly Creations Pty Ltd* (1986) 6 IPR 431, 457.

[s] *Civil Law (Wrongs) Act 2002* (ACT) s 139H; *Defamation Act 2005* (NSW) s 37; *Defamation Act 2006* (NT) s 34; *Defamation Act 2005* (Qld) s 37; *Defamation Act 2005* (SA) s 35; *Defamation Act 2005* (Tas) s 37; *Defamation Act 2005* (Vic) s 37; *Defamation Act 2005* (WA) s 37.

[t] *Civil Law (Wrongs) Act 2002* (ACT) s 16(2); *Law Reform (Miscellaneous Provisions) Act 1944* (NSW) s 2(2)(a)(i); *Succession Act 1981* (Qld) s 66(2)(b); *Survival of Causes of Action Act 1940* (SA) s 3(1)(b); *Administration and Probate Act 1935* (Tas) s 27(3)(a); *Administration and Probate Act 1958* (Vic) s 29(2)(a); *Law Reform (Miscellaneous Provisions) Act 1955* (WA) s 4(2)(a). See also *Hartley Poynton Ltd v Ali* (2005) 11 VR 568.

[u] *Civil Liability Act 2002* (NSW) s 21; *Civil Liability Act 2003* (Qld) s 52; *Personal Injuries (Liabilities and Damages) Act 2003* (NT) s 19.

[v] *Motor Accidents Act 1988* (NSW) s 81A; *Motor Accidents Compensation Act 1999* (NSW); *Transport Accident Act 1986* (Vic) s 93(7).

[w] *Workers Compensation Act 1987* (NSW) s 151R; *Workers' Compensation and Rehabilitation Act 2003* (Qld) s 306B.

[x] *Circuit Layouts Act 1989* (Cth) s 27(4); *Copyright Act 1968* (Cth) s 115(4); *Designs Act 2003* (Cth) s 75(3); *Patents Act 1990* (Cth) s 122(1A); *Trade Marks Act 1995* (Cth) s 126(2).

[y] See, eg, *Public Interest Disclosure Act 2012* (ACT) s 41(3); *Water Act 2000* (Qld) s 788(2)(b); *Environmental Management and Pollution Control Act 1994* (Tas) s 48(5)(g); *Protected Disclosure Act 2012* (Vic) s 47(3); *Electricity Act 1945* (WA) s 50(2).

[z] *Musca v Astle Corporation Pty Ltd* (1988) 80 ALR 251, 262–9 (French J).

A The nature and history of exemplary damages in Australia

Gray v Motor Accident Commission (1998) 196 CLR 1

Facts and issues

In 1988, Bransden deliberately caused personal injury to a group of young Aboriginal men standing on the side of the road, including Gray. In 1991, Bransden was convicted of intentionally causing grievous bodily harm to Gray and sentenced to seven years' imprisonment. In 1993, Gray brought an action in negligence against Bransden, and claimed exemplary damages. The Motor Accident Commission, the compulsory third party insurer of Bransden, was substituted as defendant to the action. The trial judge made a substantial award of compensatory damages in favour of Gray but refused to award exemplary damages. The Full Court of the Supreme Court of South Australia upheld this decision. Gray then appealed to the High Court.

Decision

The Court found that the requisite contumelious disregard for Gray's rights was present. However, the majority (Gleeson CJ, McHugh, Gummow and Hayne JJ) held that if the criminal law has already inflicted 'substantial punishment' on the defendant, this was an absolute bar to an award of exemplary damages. Hence, exemplary damages were unavailable.

Kirby J and Callinan J, in separate judgments, said criminal punishment was not an absolute bar, but a matter of discretion.

Gleeson CJ, McHugh, Gummow and Hayne JJ

The power to award exemplary damages

[**5**] … In Wilkes *v Wood* Pratt LCJ said:

> I have formerly delivered it as my opinion on another occasion, and I still continue of the same mind, that a jury have it in their power to give damages for more than the injury received. Damages are designed not only as a satisfaction to the injured person, but likewise as a punishment to the guilty, to deter from any such proceeding for the future, and as a proof of the detestation of the jury to the action itself.

This Court has long recognised the power to award such damages. …

…

[**6**] Exemplary damages are awarded rarely. They recognise and punish fault, but not every finding of fault warrants their award. Something more must be found. Although they are awarded rarely, they have been awarded in very different kinds of cases: ranging from abuse of governmental power exemplified by *Wilkes v Wood* and its associated cases, through defamation cases of the kind considered in *Uren v John Fairfax & Sons Pty Ltd*], to assault cases such as *Fontin v Katapodis*. And the examples could be multiplied.

In *Butler v Fairclough*, Griffith CJ observed:

> The motive or state of mind of a person who is guilty of a breach of contract is not relevant to the question of damages for the breach, although if the contract itself were fraudulent the question of fraud might be material. A breach of contract may be innocent, even accidental or unconscious. Or it may arise from a wrong view of the obligations created by the contract. Or it may be wilful, and even malicious and committed with the express intention of injuring the other party. But the measure of damages is not affected by any such considerations.

The position is put somewhat differently in *Restatement (Second) of Contracts*:

> Punitive damages are not recoverable for a breach of contract unless the conduct constituting the breach is also a tort for which punitive damages are recoverable.

The reasons underlying the apparent rule excluding an award of [**7**] exemplary damages, even in cases of intentional or malicious breach of contract, were discussed by Judge Friendly in *Thyssen Inc v SS Fortune Star*. That case also is authority that an admiralty court does not award exemplary damages for a deviation or other breach of contract.

Because the kinds of case in which exemplary damages might be awarded are so varied, it may be doubted whether a single formula adequately describes the boundaries of the field in which they may properly be awarded. Nevertheless, the phrase adopted by Knox CJ in *Whitfeld v De Lauret & Co Ltd* of 'conscious wrongdoing in contumelious disregard of another's rights' describes at least the greater part of the relevant field.

In considering whether to award exemplary damages, the first, if not the principal, focus of the inquiry is upon the wrongdoer, not upon the party who was wronged. (The reaction of the party who is wronged to high-handed or deliberate conduct may well be a reason for awarding aggravated damages in further compensation for the wrong done. But it is not ordinarily relevant to whether exemplary damages should be allowed.) The party wronged is entitled to whatever compensatory damages the law allows (including, if appropriate, aggravated damages). By hypothesis then, the party wronged will receive just compensation for the wrong that is suffered. If exemplary damages are awarded, they will be paid in addition to compensatory damages and, in that sense, will be a windfall in the hands of the party who was wronged. Nevertheless, they are awarded at the suit of that party and, although awarded to punish the wrongdoer and deter others from like conduct, they are not exacted by the State or paid to it.

There is an appearance of tension between using civil proceedings to compensate a party who is wronged and using the same proceedings to punish the wrongdoer. But there is a tension only if it is assumed that ' … a sharp cleavage between criminal law on the one hand and the law of torts and contract on the other is a cardinal principle of our legal system'. As Windeyer J points out in *Uren*, the 'roots of tort and crime' are 'greatly intermingled'. And it is not only the roots of tort and crime that are intermingled. The increasing frequency with which civil penalty provisions are enacted, the provisions **[8]** made for criminal injuries compensation, the provisions now made in some jurisdictions for the judge at a criminal trial to order restitution or compensation to a person suffering loss or damage (including pain and suffering) as a result of an offence all deny the existence of any 'sharp cleavage' between the criminal and the civil law. The tension we have mentioned may therefore be more apparent than real.

…

In *Uren* this Court declined to adopt the limitations on the award of exemplary damages stated by the House of Lords in *Rookes v Barnard*. In *Rookes v Barnard* it was held that exemplary damages could be awarded only in three kinds of case: oppressive, arbitrary or unconstitutional acts by government servants; where the defendant's conduct had been calculated to make a profit which might well exceed the compensation payable to the plaintiff; and where expressly authorised by statute. It was said that there are three considerations that should always be borne in mind when awards of exemplary damages are being considered: they can be awarded only if the plaintiff was the victim of the punishable behaviour; the power to award exemplary damages is not only a weapon that can be used in defence of liberty, it is a weapon that can be used against liberty; and the means of the parties, and all matters which aggravate or mitigate the conduct are relevant to the assessment of such damages.

The limitations on the availability of exemplary damages stated in *Rookes v Barnard* have been criticised in England and elsewhere. The United Kingdom Law Commission, in its report *Aggravated, Exemplary and Restitutionary Damages*, concluded that the boundaries set in *Rookes v Barnard* were not 'consistent with either sound principle or sound policy'. It said that its recommendations (for expanding the availability of exemplary damages) were guided by **[9]** five aims which, it may be assumed, the Commission thought were not fulfilled by application of *Rookes v Barnard*:

> First, exemplary damages should be an exceptional remedy, rarely awarded and reserved for the most reprehensible examples of civil wrongdoing which would otherwise go unpunished by the law. Secondly, their availability (and assessment) must be placed on a clear, principled basis. Thirdly, although flexibility is necessary, unnecessary uncertainty as to the availability and assessment of the remedy must be avoided. Fourthly, defendants must not be unfairly prejudiced. Fifthly, the impact on the administration and funding of civil justice should not be adverse.

The last four of those aims are not controversial (although the way in which they are to be implemented may be). The first may excite more debate but it will serve as a useful framework for considering some of the issues that arise in this case.

An exceptional remedy

If, as we have earlier suggested, the remedy is exceptional in the sense that it arises (chiefly, if not exclusively) in cases of conscious wrongdoing in contumelious disregard of the plaintiff's rights, at least two further questions arise: are exemplary damages available where the plaintiff's claim is for damages for negligence rather than some intentional wrong, and is the award of exemplary damages a matter of right or does it depend on the exercise of a discretion informed by some identifiable criteria?

Negligence and exemplary damages

...

... For present purposes it is enough to note two things. First, exemplary damages could not properly be awarded in a case of alleged negligence in which there was no conscious wrongdoing by the defendant. Ordinarily, then, questions of exemplary damages will not arise in most negligence cases be they motor accident or other kinds of case. But there can be cases, framed in negligence, in which the defendant can be shown to have acted consciously in contumelious disregard of the rights of the plaintiff or persons in the position of the plaintiff. Cases of an employer's failure to provide a safe system of work for **[10]** employees in which it is demonstrated that the employer, well knowing of an extreme danger thus created, persisted in employing the unsafe system might, perhaps, be of that latter kind. No doubt other examples can be found.

In many jurisdictions in the United States reckless indifference to the rights of others and other culpable conduct short of malicious intent is sufficient for the issue of an award of exemplary damages to be left to a jury.

Secondly, the present proceeding, although said to have been framed as an action in negligence, appears to have been conducted at trial as if it were a claim in trespass. The allegation made in the appellant's statement of claim, and pursued at trial, was that Bransden drove his vehicle 'deliberately towards [the appellant] without regard for the safety of [the appellant]' and such evidence of the events as was given at trial was all directed to showing Bransden deliberately inflicted injury on the appellant. Whatever may be the true characterisation of the pleading, the case was conducted as one of conscious wrongdoing by the tortfeasor.

A 'discretionary' remedy?

Reported cases usually speak of a 'discretion' to award exemplary damages. Standing alone, such a description, even if followed by the expression 'to be exercised judicially' is of little assistance. At best, it invites attention to what are the criteria that are to inform the exercise of that discretion.

Because exemplary damages are awarded to punish, it is not surprising that their quantification should be treated as a matter for the discretion of the tribunal assessing damages. And for so many years that was a task for the jury, not the judge. Yet there is little to be found in the cases which would identify the proper instructions to a jury for performing this part of its function. Rather, it seems to be treated in a way not very different from what is called the jury's 'constitutional right' to return a verdict of manslaughter notwithstanding proof of the elements of murder. That is, it is treated as if it is a power of the jury that is not to be hedged about by any more precise criterion for its use than the jury's intuitive conclusion that the defendant's conduct was sufficiently reprehensible to warrant punishment. Yet it is clear that there are thought to be limits on the power.

...

Significance of criminal punishment

[**13**] The factor which weighed most heavily with the primary judge in considering whether to award exemplary damages was that Bransden [**14**] had been sentenced to a substantial term of imprisonment for the actions which gave rise to the appellant's claim.

The first aim adopted by the Law Commission spoke of reserving the award of exemplary damages for cases of wrongdoing 'which would otherwise go unpunished by the law'. What significance should be attached to the fact of earlier criminal punishment?

Where, as here, the criminal law has been brought to bear upon the wrongdoer and substantial punishment inflicted, we consider that exemplary damages may not be awarded. We say 'may not' because we consider that the infliction of substantial punishment for what is substantially the same conduct as the conduct which is the subject of the civil proceeding is a bar to the award; the decision is not one that is reached as a matter of discretion dependent upon the facts and circumstances in each particular case.

There are at least two reasons in principle why that is so.

First, the purposes for the awarding of exemplary damages have been wholly met if substantial punishment is exacted by the criminal law. The offender is punished; others are deterred. There is, then, no occasion for their award.

Secondly, considerations of double punishment would otherwise arise. In *R v Hoar*, Gibbs CJ, Mason, Aickin and Brennan JJ said that there is 'a practice, if not a rule of law, that a person should not be twice punished for what is substantially the same act'. That practice or rule would be breached by an award of exemplary damages in the circumstances described.

1 Need to make out the 'host' cause of action

Fatimi Pty Ltd v Bryant (2004) 59 NSWLR 678

Facts and issues

Fatimi Pty Ltd ('Fatimi') obtained judgment against Rylegrove Pty Ltd ('Rylegrove'). When Rylegrove did not pay, Fatimi registered a writ of execution against a block of vacant land, and, in July 1995, sought to wind up Rylegrove. In August 1995, Rylegrove contracted to sell the land to another party on extremely advantageous terms and transferred the land on the same day without receiving the purchase price. The liquidator of Rylegrove set aside the transfer and Rylegrove was wound up.

Fatimi brought an action in the tort of conspiracy against the directors of Rylegrove, a former director, and directors of the purchasing company (all members of the Bryant family). The trial judge found that the defendants had not acted to injure Fatimi, but to benefit shareholders.

Decision

The New South Wales Court of Appeal held that there had been an intention to injure Fatimi, but because it is necessary to prove actual damage for conspiracy, Fatimi failed to make out the tort. It also could not claim exemplary damages.

Giles JA

Exemplary damages

[**690**] It was not in dispute that, if the tort of conspiracy were made out, exemplary damages could be awarded if warranted in the circumstances. Since the tort of conspiracy requires proof of pecuniary loss, Fatimi did not make out the tort.

Where the plaintiff has a complete cause of action without proof of loss, exemplary damages can be awarded. That is illustrated by *Cousins v Wilson* (1994) 1 NZLR 463. The plaintiff sued in trespass. He did not prove loss, but was awarded nominal damages and exemplary damages. …

It is otherwise, however, when proof of loss is an ingredient of the plaintiff's cause of action. In *XL Petroleum (NSW) Pty Ltd v Caltex Oil (Australia) Pty Ltd* … (1985) 155 CLR 448 at 468–9 Brennan J said –

> Exemplary damages are parasitic on compensatory damages, the plaintiff being unable to recover exemplary damages if he is not the [**691**] victim of the behaviour which attracts the exemplary damages: per Lord Devlin in *Rookes v Barnard* … . A single cause of action provides the foundation of a judgment awarding, in an appropriate case, exemplary damages as well as compensatory damages. When a plaintiff's claim for compensatory damages has been satisfied in full, however, he no longer has a cause of action that can support an award of compensatory damages to which an award of exemplary damages can attach.

… If exemplary damages can not be obtained when a plaintiff's claim for compensatory damages has been satisfied in full, despite the single cause of action under which exemplary damages could also be awarded, they equally can not be obtained when the plaintiff's claim for compensatory damages has failed. If there is no host, there can not be a parasite.

…

The point is more fundamental. Whatever be the extent of availability of exemplary damages … the civil law [**692**] is not directed to punishment, deterrence and disapprobation for its own sake. As was said by Lord Reid in *Cassell & Co Ltd v Broome* … (1972) AC 1027 at 1086 … awarding a plaintiff more than compensatory damages is 'highly anomalous' because '[i]t is confusing the function of the civil law which is to compensate with the function of the criminal law which is to inflict deterrent and punitive penalties'. The anomaly is entrenched, and must be accepted. But for a civil law remedy there must be a civil wrong. Tortious and statutory civil wrongs have elements to be made out. Unless they are made out there is no civil wrong and, specific statutory provision aside, the civil law has no business in imposing punishment or in deterring and expressing disapprobation. Deserving punishment or occasioning deterrence and disapprobation is not a civil wrong.

...

As a corollary, a plaintiff who has a cause of action against a defendant can not rely on unrelated outrageous conduct on the defendant's part as a basis for exemplary damages ... In Waddams, *The Law of Damages*, 2nd ed, (1991), para 11.390 the learned author says ...

> ... once the connection between compensation and remedy is lost, as it is by the acceptance of the concept of exemplary damages, there is no strictly logical reason why exemplary damages should not be awarded whenever conduct comes to light which the court considers worthy of punishment. It is irrelevant from the point of view of the purposes of exemplary damages whether they happen to go into the pocket of one plaintiff or another, but this would open the door to actions by informers who had no connection with the conduct complained of. It is submitted, therefore, that the courts are on sound ground in insisting that the punishable conduct must be wrongful vis-à-vis the plaintiff and that the plaintiff cannot attach a complaint of conduct that is not wrongful in this sense to an entirely unrelated cause of action.

...

[693] Principle, supported by this guidance from elsewhere in the common law world, leads to the conclusion that where Fatimi did not make out a cause of action for conspiracy, exemplary damages can not be awarded.

2 Unavailable if criminal punishment already imposed

Exemplary damages are unavailable if 'substantial' criminal punishment has already been imposed, as confirmed in *Gray v Motor Accident Commission*,[1] where the wrongdoer had already been imprisoned for inflicting grievous bodily harm on the plaintiff. This is because the purposes of exemplary damages have already been met by the criminal punishment, and because a person should not be punished twice for the same act.

As discussed in the principles text at [14.19]–[14.20], there is sometimes a question as to whether criminal punishment is sufficiently substantial.

3 Calculation of exemplary damages

Exemplary damages cannot be measured with any certainty; it is only necessary that the sum be sufficient to deter and punish the particular defendant. However, Australian courts exercise moderation in imposing exemplary damages.[2]

1 (1998) 196 CLR 1, [38]–[44], [92]–[98], [142]–[144].

2 See F Maher, 'An Empirical Study of Exemplary Damages in Australia' (2020) 43(2) *Melbourne University Law Review* 694.

Pollack v Volpato [1973] 1 NSWLR 653

Facts and issues

Pollack had a weekly lease at the defendant's premises, where he carried on a hairdressing business. He paid rent weekly in advance. Volpato, the owner, informed Pollack that he intended to demolish the shop to redevelop the site. Volpato did not give Pollack notice to quit, but informed him that he wanted possession on 27 July 1970.

Pollack paid his rent up to 27 July 1970. On 22 July 1970, Volpato and one of his employees entered the shop and demolished a partition, part of which fell and damaged Pollack's bicycle. Pollack retrieved his bicycle, and was injured when the rest of the partition fell on him. Volpato then chopped down the door of the shop with an axe. Pollack carried on his business for the rest of the day. During the afternoon the roof was removed. That evening Pollack vacated the shop.

Decision

Exemplary damages for trespass were awarded. The following extract focuses on Hutley JA's commentary about the assessment of damages.

Hutley JA

> [**656**] There is no tariff or basis for a tariff where a jury is entitled to inflict exemplary damages. Not only is the occasion for the award of such damages rare, but the jury is entitled not only to penalize the defendant for what he did [**657**] but is entitled to make him an example to others. There can be no fixed scale for such deterrents. The need for deterrent action in a provincial city such as Lismore and the extent of the penalty needed to act as a deterrent is peculiarly within the grasp of a jury of its citizens, and the circumstances under which an appellate court can intervene must be rare. The jury has to translate its righteous indignation at the conduct of the defendant into monetary terms appropriate to the local situation, of which this Court is unaware.
>
> However, because a jury's assessment is so free from review it is particularly important that, where a judge rules that it is open to the jury to award punitive or exemplary damages, he should give guidance to the jury as to the basis upon which it is to make the award. I am unable to agree that the jury in this case received adequate guidance, but as no objection was taken to the summing up, this cannot be relied upon by the appellant as a ground for a new trial.
>
> Whereas compensatory damages have to be approached by looking at the situation of the plaintiff in consequence of the wrongful act to which he has been subjected, punitive damages have to be looked at from the side of the defendant. If he is to be punished, it is his proper punishment which provides the basis for the assessment of damages.
>
> ...
>
> Just as, in inflicting a fine, amongst the factors which have to be considered is the capacity to pay of the person ordered to pay it, in my view the means and resources of the defendant are an important consideration for the jury in inflicting punitive damages, eg, if evidence had been given that the defendant was a poor man who, if ordered to pay substantial punitive damages [**658**] would lose his home, and the jury had awarded damages

of this order, a basis for review might have been laid in that the punishment was quite unreasonable. In order to review punitive damages on the ground that they are excessive, in my opinion it is necessary for there to be evidence which would enable the court to assess the impact of the verdict upon the defendant. It must also follow that a plaintiff who is claiming punitive damages can tender evidence of the resources of the defendant.

... In my opinion, while punitive damages remain, courts must assist juries by giving direction as to how the punitive factors have to be weighed, and these principles have to be found in sound principles for the infliction of monetary sanctions in the criminal field; otherwise the punitive or exemplary damages may become a means whereby capricious and harsh penalties are inflicted on persons not able to bear them.

As in this case there is no material which would suggest that the defendant is not well able to meet the verdict and the trespass could have been regarded by the jury as a crude attempt to intimidate the plaintiff and prevent him from insisting on his legal rights, the substantial punitive damages which they awarded should not be reviewed in this court.

B The causes of action for which exemplary damages can be awarded in Australia

1 Exemplary damages available for tort

As Table 14.1 illustrates, exemplary damages are available in Australia primarily for tort, and not for other causes of action. However, there are some torts for which they are unavailable, generally because legislatures have excluded the availability of such awards, or because the tort in question does not involve intentional conduct.

Table 14.1 Causes of action for which exemplary damages are and are not available in Australia

Causes of action for which exemplary damages are available in Australia	Causes of actions for which exemplary damages are *not* available in Australia
Tort • Trespass to land • Nuisance • Trespass to goods • Trespass to the person • Conversion • Detinue • Battery • Wrongful arrest involving trespass to land and the person • False imprisonment • Malicious prosecution • Abuse of process • Misfeasance in the public office	**Tort** • Non-deliberate negligence • Defamation • Claims surviving after the death of the plaintiff • Some states have abolished them for certain personal injuries, personal injuries in motor vehicle accidents, and common law claims for workers' compensation

Causes of action for which exemplary damages are available in Australia	Causes of actions for which exemplary damages are *not* available in Australia
• Inducing breach of contract • Interference with contractual relations • Deceit • Intimidation • Conspiracy • Negligence (at least insofar as it is also deliberate or reckless?)	
Intellectual property breaches (according to statute)	**Breach of contract**
	Equitable breaches, including: • breach of trust • breach of fiduciary duty • breach of contract.
	Claims under the ACL

2 Exemplary damages available for breach of some statutes

Exemplary damages are statutorily provided for some breaches of statute. Intellectual property legislation is an example.

Copyright Act 1968 (Cth) s 115(4)

The *Copyright Act* allows for damages in the nature of exemplary damages.

115 Actions for infringement

...

(4) Where, in an action under this section:

(a) an infringement of copyright is established; and

(b) the court is satisfied that it is proper to do so, having regard to:

(i) the flagrancy of the infringement; and

(ia) the need to deter similar infringements of copyright; and

(ib) the conduct of the defendant after the act constituting the infringement or, if relevant, after the defendant was informed that the defendant had allegedly infringed the plaintiff's copyright; and

(ii) whether the infringement involved the conversion of a work or other subject-matter from hardcopy or analog form into a digital or other electronic machine-readable form; and

(iii) any benefit shown to have accrued to the defendant by reason of the infringement; and

(iv) all other relevant matters;

the court may, in assessing damages for the infringement, award such additional damages as it considers appropriate in the circumstances.

3 Exemplary damages not available for breach of contract

Exemplary damages are not available for breach of contract in Australia, or in most other common law jurisdictions. The exception to this is Canada, which sometimes exceptionally allows exemplary damages for breach of contract. The principles text [14.35]–[14.40] explains the reasoning behind the common law's general disinclination to award exemplary damages for breach of contract.

4 Exemplary damages not available for equitable wrongdoing

Exemplary damages are not available for equitable wrongdoing in Australia, although as the following case extract illustrates, there are diverse opinions on this topic about whether this should always be the case.

Harris v Digital Pulse Pty Ltd (2003) 56 NSWLR 298

Facts and issues

Digital Pulse Pty Ltd ('Digital') was an information technology business providing website design services. The first and second defendants, Harris and Eden, were employees of Digital. Their employment contracts prevented them from competing with Digital during the term of their employment, and they owed fiduciary duties of loyalty to Digital. While still employed at Digital, they diverted work from Digital towards their new business. Later, they incorporated a company called Juice-D (of which they were both directors) which received payments for the work diverted from Digital. Digital sued the defendants and Juice-D in for several causes of actions, including breach of contract and breach of fiduciary duty.

At trlal, Palmer J awarded exemplary damages of $10 000 for breach of fiduciary duty against Harris and Eden, because they had been dishonest, deliberate and cynical, and it appeared that they must have taken more business from Digital, but no one could assess how much because documents had been destroyed.[3] Harris appealed to the New South Wales Court of Appeal.

Decision

Spigelman CJ and Heydon JA held that exemplary damages were unavailable for breach of fiduciary duty. Heydon JA said that equity did not countenance punitive aims, only deterrent aims. Spiegelman CJ said that it might be appropriate to award exemplary damages for some equitable breaches, but not where there was a concurrent breach of contract (for which exemplary damages are also unavailable). Mason P, dissenting, would have upheld the award of exemplary damages.

Spiegelman CJ

Analogy with tort or contract?

[**307**] The argument in this Court proceeded on the basis that in Australia exemplary damages are not recoverable for breach of contract. … [**308**] Whether the common law of Australia should be changed in this regard is a matter for the High Court.

3 *Digital Pulse v Harris* (2002) 166 FLR 421, 449 (NSWSC).

In his judgment, Mason P poses the question of whether the development of equity jurisprudence should proceed by way of analogy with tort or by way of analogy with contract. It is not apparent to me that analogical reasoning at this level of generality is appropriate. Each is a distinct body of law with its own integrity.

...

In his reasons for preferring the tort analogy, in my opinion, Mason P has given insufficient weight to the historical development of the law of tort which was closely connected with the development of criminal law. Many torts constituted crimes and accordingly, civil litigation raised issues of public interest, particularly involving a breach of the peace. In such a context it was entirely appropriate that considerations of punishment and deterrence arose in the context of actions in tort.

As Windeyer J said, in *Uren v John Fairfax & Sons Pty Ltd* (1966) 117 CLR 118 at 149–150:

> Compensation is the dominant remedy if not the purpose of the law of torts today. But fault still has a place in many forms of wrongdoing. And the roots of tort and crime in the law of England are greatly intermingled. Some things that today are seen as anomalies have roots that go deep, too deep for them to be easily uprooted.

As Heydon JA notes, with further references, there was no such historical intermingling between crime and either contract or equity.

To the extent that reasoning by analogy at this level of generality is appropriate, I believe that the contract analogy is more appropriate. Reasoning [**309**] of the highest authority has described the imposition of fiduciary obligations in terms of undertaking and 'agreement', albeit imputed by operation of law. Furthermore, I find the extra judicial writings of Finn J, one of Australia's most significant scholars on fiduciary law, to be persuasive when he identifies an expectation interest on the part of a beneficiary and states it in terms reminiscent of contract law.

...

[**310**] The fiduciary duties in the present case are derived from the existence of the contract of employment. The undertaking or agreement of the employees to act in the interests of the employer, and the employer's 'entitlement to expect' that that will occur— imputed to the relationship by equity—is much closer to a contractual relationship than it is to circumstances creating obligations in tort. If argument by analogy of this kind is appropriate, I prefer the contract analogy.

Where, as here, the essential basis of the fiduciary duties is a contractual relationship this Court should not develop for the first time a remedy which is not available in the law of contract. This analysis does carry with it the corollary that the refusal to develop the law should be confined to cases of the character now before the Court, as identified above. There may be other cases in equity in which a tort analogy is more appropriate.

Heydon JA

Fusion of law and equity?

[**391**] To some extent the language of the trial judge suggested that he viewed the principles of law and of equity as having been fused, or as principles which ought to be fused. ... It is

not the law of New South Wales that law and equity were fused when the judicature system was created by the Supreme *Court Act 1970*, s 57–s 63, and the Law *Reform (Law and Equity) Act 1972*, s 5–s 7. There was no fusion of two systems of principle but of the courts which administer the two systems … .

…

The use of the words 'penal', 'punitive', 'punishment' and 'prophylactic'

[**406**] The theory that the strict rules of equity, particularly those compelling disgorgement of profits, are deterrent and punitive in character rests in part on certain verbal usages by judge and jurist. Thus, in *Phipps v Boardman,* Pearson LJ said:

> … The rule of equity is rigid. The agent who has made a profit from his agency, without having obtained informed consent from his principal, has to account for the whole of the profit. In an ordinary case, where an agent has simply made a secret profit, the rule is so to speak, good for discipline: there is a penal element calculated to deter agents from behaving in that way.

The plaintiff cited cases using the language of punishment, of which the high watermark was *Paul A Davies (Australia) Pty Ltd v Davies.* There are various other cases using the language of punishment which the plaintiff did not cite. The much-cited article by Gareth Jones, 'Unjust Enrichment and the Fiduciary's Duty of Loyalty' (1968) 84 *Law Quarterly Review* 472, says of fiduciary liability, these principles may be penal (at 474); describes the liability as 'penal' (at 478, 486 and 497); speaks of 'a strictly penal rule' (at 490); advocates the need for 'mitigating the liability of the honest and conscientious fiduciary … who is punished as an example to others' (at 497) and whose 'largest punishment' should be a liability to account (at 497); and points to the 'dishonest fiduciary who is punished as a warning to others' (at 501). Jones also says that the authorities 'appear to suggest that a prophylactic, rather than a restitutionary principle', underlies the law relating to fiduciaries (at 474).

These usages must not be misunderstood.

The substantive rules of equity in relation to fiduciaries—the standards which equity requires them to meet—are often high and strict. Honesty is rarely a defence; nor, statute apart, is reasonableness. The height and strictness [**407**] of the standards protect the principals of fiduciaries by nullifying temptation. In that sense they deter fiduciaries from drifting into a position of conflict, or worse.

In like fashion, the existence of the remedy of equitable compensation for unlawfully caused loss and of the remedy of account of profits to capture unlawful gains—the unlawfulness in each case being measured by the high standards referred to—can have a deterrent effect, because it tends to make the unlawful conduct in question futile. … The remedies of equitable compensation and account of profits certainly have a deterrent effect. In the very loose sense of the words as employed by Jones, those remedies may be seen as penal or 'punitive'. But they are not penal or punitive in the sense of exacting any money sanction greater than that which is needed either to give full compensation for loss or full disgorgement of gain.

…

[**409**] The rules that a plaintiff need not show damage and need not show that the fiduciary has taken a profit which the plaintiff could have gained are prophylactic in

the sense that they tend to prevent the disease of temptation in the fiduciary – they preserve or protect the fiduciary from that disease. The temptation might be assisted if the fiduciary had in contemplation the possibility of escaping liability by arguing that the principal was caused no loss, or that the profit made was never available to the principal.

The prevention of or protection from the relevant disease is assisted by the strictness of the standard imposed and the absence of defences justifying departures from it. The rules relating to an account of profits are not restitutionary in the sense that they do not rest on giving back something which the plaintiff once had, or restoring the plaintiff to a state of affairs which the plaintiff once occupied but has lost because of the fiduciary's behaviour, or requiring some damage to the pre-existing position of the principal, or compensating the principal for some loss suffered. They strip the fiduciary of gains whether or not the plaintiff could ever had made the gains in question. No doubt the strictness of the rules, in tending to prevent fiduciary temptation arising and thus tending to protect the principal from fiduciary misconduct, tends to deter fiduciaries from misconduct themselves. But it does not follow that the rules are punitive. ...

...

Conclusion on exemplary damages in equity

[**422**] There is no power in the law of New South Wales to award exemplary damages for equitable wrongs. But a narrower proposition suffices for the purposes of deciding this case. There is no power in the law of New South Wales to award exemplary damages for equitable wrongs of the type involved in the circumstances of this case. No English or Australian authority supports it. There is no convincing reasoning in New Zealand, Canadian or United States authorities. This Court ought not to change the law of New South Wales so as to create power to do so. Nothing in the authorities or the commentaries suggests why it should or why this Court has power to. ...

5 Exemplary damages not available for breaches of the *Australian Consumer Law*

Exemplary damages are not available for breaches of the *Australian Consumer Law* ('ACL') because the statute does not provide for them, and the damages provisions only allow for compensation of 'loss or damage', which focuses on loss to a claimant rather than punishment of a defendant.

Review questions

(1) Is it appropriate for private law to consider punitive aims? Should exemplary damages be abolished?

(2) Should exemplary damages be available for equitable breaches and breach of contract?

(3) Is it problematic that it is impossible to predict the quantum of an award of exemplary damages?

III Aggravated damages

<table>
<tr><th>Concept</th><th>Short explanation</th><th>Relevant authorities</th><th>Principles text</th></tr>
<tr><td>The distinction between exemplary damages and aggravated damages</td><td>Exemplary damages aim to punish the defendant, and aggravated damages aim to compensate the plaintiff for indignity and/or distress. However, the distinction is not always easy to draw as the extract shows.</td><td>Carson v John Fairfax & Sons Ltd (1993) 178 CLR 44</td><td>Chapter 14: [14.57]–[14.64]</td></tr>
<tr><td rowspan="3">Aggravated damages are generally available for tort</td><td>Aggravated damages are generally available for the torts actionable per se.
Aggravated damages are available for:
• assault[a]
• defamation,[b] conspiracy[c]
• false imprisonment[d]
• intimidation[e]
• trespass to land[f]
• interference with contractual relations[g] and
• malicious prosecution.[h]</td><td>The cases cited in footnotes are authority for the general principle.</td><td rowspan="3">Chapter 14: [14.65]–[14.69]</td></tr>
<tr><td>The availability of aggravated damages for fault-based torts is controversial, but it seems that they are available in some cases.
The fault-based torts where they have been awarded are:
• nuisance[i]
• deceit[j]
• injurious falsehood[k] and
• negligence.[l]</td><td>The cases cited in footnotes are authority for the general principle.</td></tr>
<tr><td>Aggravated damages for personal injury claims have been abolished in New South Wales, the Northern Territory and Queensland.[m] They are also unavailable for personal injury in the context of product liability under the Competition and Consumer Act 2010 (Cth).[n]</td><td>The legislation cited in footnotes are authority for the general principle.</td></tr>
<tr><td>Aggravated damages are available for some statutory claims</td><td>Some statutes leave open the possibility of aggravated damages for certain contraventions.[o]
The intellectual property statutes mentioned earlier which allow for 'additional damages' for 'flagrant breaches' also allow for aggravated damages.</td><td>See the example section from the Copyright Act 1968 (Cth) (see page 489 for extract).</td><td>Chapter 14: [14.70]–[14.71]</td></tr>
</table>

Concept	Short explanation	Relevant authorities	Principles text
Aggravated damages are unavailable for breach of contract	While aggravated damages are generally unavailable for breach of contract, it is clear that damages for distress can be recovered for certain kinds of contracts.	*Baltic Shipping Co v Dillon* (1993) 176 CLR 344 (see Chapter 5, page 193 for extract)	Chapter 14: [14.72]–[14.74]
Aggravated damages are generally unavailable for equitable breaches	While aggravated damages are generally unavailable for equitable breaches, exceptions have been made for certain breaches of confidence involving intimate relationships.	*Giller v Procopets* (2008) 24 VR 1	Chapter 14: [14.75]–[14.76]
Aggravated damages are available for contravention of the ACL	Damages for distress or dignitary injury are clearly covered under the loss or damage contemplated by the notion of 'loss or damage' under the ACL.	*New South Wales Lotteries Corporation Pty Ltd v Kuzmanovski* (2011) 195 FCR 234	Chapter 14: [14.77]–[14.78]

[a] *Henry v Thompson* [1989] 2 Qd R 412; *Johnstone v Stewart* [1968] SASR 142; *Pearce v Hallett* [1969] SASR 423.

[b] *Uren v John Fairfax & Sons Pty Ltd* (1966) 117 CLR 118; *Carson v John Fairfax & Sons Ltd* (1993) 178 CLR 44. See *Civil Law (Wrongs) Act 2002* (ACT) s 139F(2); *Defamation Act 2005* (NSW) s 35(2); *Defamation Act 2006* (NT) s 32(2); *Defamation Act 2005* (Qld) s 35(2); *Defamation Act 2005* (SA) s 33(2); *Defamation Act 2005* (Tas) s 35(2); *Defamation Act 2005* (Vic) s 35(2); *Defamation Act 2005* (WA) s 35(2).

[c] *Williams v Hursey* (1959) 103 CLR 30; *Huntley v Thornton* [1957] 1 WLR 321, 350; *Jervois Sulphates (NT) Ltd v Petrocarb Explorations NL* (1974) 5 ALR 1.

[d] *Myers Stores Ltd v Soo* [1991] 2 VR 597; *McFadzean v Construction, Forestry, Mining and Energy Union* [2004] VSC 289.

[e] *Rookes v Barnard* [1964] AC 1129.

[f] *Traian v Ware* [1957] VR 200; *TCN Channel Nine Pty Ltd v Anning* (2002) 54 NSWLR 333, [179].

[g] *Zhu v Sydney Organising Committee for the Olympic Games* [2001] NSWSC 989, *Zhu v Treasurer (NSW)* (2004) 218 CLR 530.

[h] *Commonwealth Life Assurance Society Ltd v Brain* (1935) 53 CLR 343; *A v New South Wales* (2007) 230 CLR 500.

[i] *Willoughby Municipal Council v Halstead* (1916) 22 CLR 352 (court divided 2:2 on availability of aggravated damages for nuisance); *Oldham v Lawson (No 1)* [1976] VR 654, 658–9 (Harris J: damages for distress available for nuisance, but doubted aggravated damages available); *Van Son v Forestry Commission* (1995) 86 LGERA 108 (unnecessary to decide). Aggravated damages were allowed in *Traian v Ware* [1957] VR 200 because of the trespass.

[j] *Archer v Brown* [1985] QB 401; *Mafo v Adams* [1970] 1 QB 548, 554 (Sachs LJ), 558 (Widgery LJ). Both were cited approvingly in *Aldersea v Public Transport Corporation* (2001) 3 VR 499, [44]–[45].

[k] *Joyce v Sengupta* (1993) 1 WLR 337, 350–1; *Khodaparast v Shad* [2000] 1 WLR 618, 630–1; 633; *James v Faddoul* [2007] NSWSC 821 [18] (Price J). Cf *Fielding v Variety Inc* [1967] 2 QB 841, 851, 855; *Bride v KMG Hungerfords* (1991) 109 FLR 256, 281. Equivocal: *Joyce v Sengupta* (1993) 1 WLR 337, 347–8.

[l] *Backwell v AAA* [1997] 1 VR 182. See also *De Reus v Gray* (2003) 9 VR 432, [29].

[m] *Civil Liability Act 2002* (NSW) s 21; *Personal Injuries (Liabilities and Damages) Act 2003* (NT) s 19; *Civil Liability Act 2003* (Qld) s 52.

[n] *Competition and Consumer Act 2010* (Cth) ss 87E, 87ZB.

[o] Eg *Public Interest Disclosure Act 2012* (ACT) s 41(3); *Protected Disclosure Act 2012* (Vic) s 47(3).

A The distinction between exemplary damages and aggravated damages

Carson v John Fairfax & Sons Ltd (1993) 178 CLR 44

Facts and issues

Carson (the plaintiff, a partner at a law firm) brought an action in defamation against John Fairfax & Sons Ltd for an article which had appeared in the *Sydney Morning Herald* about him.

Decision

Exemplary damages for defamation had been abolished in New South Wales under the legislation then in force. At trial, the plaintiff was awarded aggravated damages by a jury, but the amount was so substantial that the defendants appealed. A majority of the New South Wales Court of Appeal held that the award was punitive and excessive. The plaintiff appealed to the High Court. A majority upheld the New South Wales Court of Appeal's judgment. McHugh J's dissenting judgment reflects on the difference between exemplary and aggravated damages.

McHugh J (dissenting)

[101] **Punishment**

Certain parts of the judgment of the learned President indicate that he thought that, because an award of exemplary damages in a defamation action is not permissible in New South Wales, the awards in the present case must be set aside [**102**] because they include a sum by way of punishment. As will appear, I think the verdicts can be sustained as reasonable without any need to assume that they contain damages by way of punishment. But the question whether an award of aggravated damages in New South Wales can include an amount by way of punishment is too important to pass without discussion.

In my opinion, the element of punishment is often a legitimate factor in an award of aggravated damages even in New South Wales where s 46(2) of the [Defamation] Act provides that damages are to be 'recoverable in accordance with the common law, but limited to damages for relevant harm'. A jury which increases its award of damages in a defamation action commits no error if it thinks that the plaintiff cannot be properly compensated for the harm done to him or her unless the damages contain an amount to punish the defendant for the hurt which he or she has inflicted on the plaintiff or to deter the defendant from further defaming the plaintiff. Nor does the jury commit any error if it increases the damages because the conduct of the defendant towards the plaintiff arouses its anger or indignation.

Before turning to the effect of the Act, it is convenient to begin by examining the concept of aggravated damages at common law. Damages in a defamation action are 'the product of a mixture of inextricable considerations'. It can also be said that they are a mixture of conflicting considerations which are the result of defamation being both a tort and a crime. One consideration is the state of mind and the conduct of the defendant which the common law has long regarded as being of great importance on the question of damages even though damage to reputation is the gist of a defamation action.

...

[**104**] … The damage which a defamation produces is ordinarily psychological rather than material. It affects the feelings, sense of security, sense of esteem and self perceptions of the person defamed. As a natural consequence, a defamation excites the anger [**105**] and resentment of the victim and often enough generates a desire for retribution. Judge Posner has pointed out that:

> Part of our biological inheritance is the sense of indignation, and its complement the desire for retribution (by violent means if necessary), that is aroused when someone invades an interest that we value highly … The courts provide a substitute for the costly self-help methods that people would otherwise resort to.

If an award of damages in a defamation action is to fulfil its social purpose, it must be high enough to assuage the hurt, indignation and desire for retribution which the plaintiff feels. Moreover, in many cases, the feelings of a person who has been maliciously defamed will only be assuaged if he or she is satisfied that the award of damages hurts the defendant as much as the defendant has hurt the plaintiff. 'What the plaintiff is really demanding by way of solace to himself' Professor Julius Stone has said 'is that there be inflicted on the defendant pain and humiliation comparable to that which the defendant has inflicted on the plaintiff.' Thus, the anger of the plaintiff is placated only when he or she knows that the defendant has been punished for the wrong. … An award of compensatory damages in such a case will not achieve its restorative effect unless the defendant is made to suffer for the wrong. Furthermore, an award of damages may not properly console the plaintiff who has been the victim of a malicious defamation unless the anguish that that person has suffered is placated by an award which is large enough to deter the defendant from again defaming him or her. Thus, an amount sufficient to deter the defendant from again defaming the plaintiff is in many cases a proper element of aggravated compensatory damages.

…

[**106**] … To say that no element of punishment enters into the assessment of (aggravated) compensatory damages and that the effect of such an award is merely to compensate the plaintiff for the increased harm which that person suffers is to resort to fiction in many cases. In many, perhaps the majority of cases, for example, the plaintiff only becomes aware of the defendant's malice long after publication, perhaps at the trial of the action. Discovery of the malice at that stage may have only a slight effect on the plaintiff's feelings. But in practice the same damages will be awarded because of that malicious conduct as will be awarded if the malice was known to the plaintiff at or about the time of publication. The truth is that, in many cases calling for an award of aggravated damages, the real reason that the defendant is called upon to pay additional damages is that that person has been guilty of malice or some other improper state of mind or conduct. It is not simply because of the effect of the defendant's conduct on the plaintiff. However much judges and jurists may seek to rationalise the right of the jury to increase damages by reason of the conduct of the defendant as being purely compensatory, compensation to the plaintiff is only achieved in many cases of awards of aggravated damages by punishing or deterring the defendant. Eminent judges have accepted that this is so.

In *Broome v Cassell and Co*, Lord Hailsham of St Marylebone LC said:

> The true explanation of *Rookes v Barnard* is to be found in the fact that, where damages for loss of reputation are concerned, or where a simple outrage to the

> individual or to property is concerned, aggravated damages in the sense I have explained can, and should in every case lying outside the categories, take care of the exemplary element, and the jury should neither be encouraged nor allowed to look beyond as generous a solatium as is required for the injuria simply in order to give effect to feelings of indignation. *It is not that the exemplary element is excluded in such cases.* It is precisely because in the nature of things it is, and should be, included in every such case that the jury should neither be encouraged nor allowed to look for it outside the solatium and then to add to [**107**] the sum awarded another sum by way of penalty additional to the solatium. To do so would be to inflict a double penalty for the same offence. (My emphasis.)

Speaking of a case where the defendant has been guilty of contumelious disregard for the plaintiff's rights, Lord Hailsham said that 'so far as regards the law of England, I would say that an adequate award of compensatory damages in such a case must of necessity include, and perhaps more than include, any punitive or exemplary element'. Later the Lord Chancellor said that, when a case was outside the three categories for awarding exemplary damages, laid down in *Rookes v Barnard*, 'the jury must be told to confine the punitive or deterrent element in their thinking within the limits of a fair solatium'.

...

In *Uren v John Fairfax Ltd and Sons*, Windeyer J pointed out that 'in truth a punitive or vindictive element does lurk in many cases in which the damages were aggravated by the defendant's conduct'. In the same case, Taylor J said 'that the same set of circumstances might well justify either an award of exemplary or aggravated damages'. This was in accord with the statement of Lord Devlin in *Rookes v Barnard* that aggravated damages can do most if not all the work which can be done by exemplary damages.

Prior to the decision in *Rookes v Barnard*, no clear line had been drawn between aggravated compensatory damages which could include an amount of damages by way of punishment and exemplary, punitive or vindictive damages which were damages awarded for the sole purpose of punishing the defendant or [**108**] deterring him or her and others. Thus, in *Smith's Newspapers Ltd v Becker*, without mentioning aggravated, punitive, vindictive or exemplary damages, Dixon J said that the 'question what amount awarded to the victim of a public outrage is enough to serve at once as a solatium, vindication and compensation to him and a requital to the wrongdoer can only be solved by an exercise of a discretionary judgment'. What *Rookes v Barnard* and the subsequent cases of *Uren v John Fairfax and Sons Pty Ltd* and *Broome v Cassell and Co* have made clear is that punishment of the defendant can be a factor in an award of aggravated compensatory damages if it is necessary to provide a fair solatium to the plaintiff but that no sum additional to the compensatory damages can be added as a penalty to punish or deter the defendant unless the case is one calling for an award of exemplary damages.

Hence, it should now be regarded as established at common law that, in awarding aggravated damages, the jury can 'inflict an added burden on the defendant proportionate to his conduct' by way of punishment when such an award is necessary to provide a proper consolation for the plaintiff. Moreover, in awarding aggravated damages, the anger or indignation which the jury feels at the way the defendant has treated the plaintiff is a proper reason for making a large rather than a small award to compensate the plaintiff.

B Availability of aggravated damages in Australian law

As outlined in Table 14.2, aggravated damages are generally available for tort, particularly the torts actionable per se, and perhaps some torts where fault is required, but perhaps not for personal injury. Aggravated damages are also available under statute for intellectual property breaches, for contraventions of the ACL and possibly for breach of confidence in the context of an intimate relationship. Insofar as damages for distress are a subspecies of aggravated damages, they may be available in exceptional circumstances for breach of contract where the purpose of the contract was enjoyment, relaxation or freedom from molestation.

Table 14.2 Causes of action for which aggravated damages are and are not available in Australia

Causes of action for which aggravated damages are available in Australia	Causes of actions for which aggravated damages are *not* available in Australia
Tort Clearly available for torts actionable *per se*, including: • trespass to the person • defamation • conspiracy • false imprisonment • intimidation • trespass to land • interference with contractual relations • malicious prosecution. More controversially also available for some torts where fault is required, including: • nuisance • deceit • injurious falsehood • negligence.	**Tort** Unclear whether available for personal injury, and has been abolished by statute in some states
Intellectual property breaches (according to statute)	
Claims under the ACL	
Breach of contract • Damages for distress available in certain circumstances: recall *Dillon v Baltic Shipping*	**Breach of contract** • Generally regarded as unavailable, but damages for distress *are* available for contract in certain circumstances
Equitable breach of confidence? • See *Giller v Procopets*	**Equitable breaches** • Breach of trust • Breach of fiduciary duty • Breach of confidence However, sometimes aggravated damages have been awarded for breaches of confidence in the context of intimate relationships.

1 Aggravated damages available for tort

It is clear that aggravated damages are available for the torts actionable per se, such as trespass, defamation and so forth (as outlined in Table 14.2). Courts have also awarded aggravated damages for torts where fault is required.

It is unclear whether aggravated damages are available for personal injury. In some states, legislation has been passed to make aggravated damages unavailable for personal injury.

2 Aggravated damages available for some statutory causes of action

Aggravated damages are available for intellectual property breaches under the same statutory provisions outlined above.

Aggravated damages have also been found to be available for contraventions of the ACL.

3 Aggravated damages not available for breach of contract

Aggravated damages are generally unavailable for breach of contract. However, where the purpose of a contract is relaxation, enjoyment or freedom from molestation, damages for distress caused by the breach may be available.

4 Aggravated damages not available for equitable wrongdoing

Aggravated damages are generally unavailable for equitable breaches such as breach of trust, breach of fiduciary duty and so forth. An exception may exist for breaches of confidence in the context of intimate relationships, as the extract from the following case illustrates.

Giller v Procopets (2008) 24 VR 1

Facts and issues

Procopets and Giller lived in a de facto relationship. They broke up, but still engaged in sexual intercourse. Procopets filmed their sexual activity, at first without Giller's knowledge, but later with her consent. After their relationship deteriorated further, Procopets showed or attempted to show the videos to Giller's family and friends. Giller sought damages for the emotional distress resulting from Procopets's breach of confidence. Aggravated damages or damages for distress are generally only available at common law, not in equity.

Decision

Giller was entitled to damages (either aggravated damages or damages for distress) pursuant to the court's inherent equitable jurisdiction. In the alternative, she was entitled to damages in lieu of the injunction she could have obtained to restrain Procopets pursuant to Victoria's Lord Cairns' Act provision (s 38 of the *Supreme Court Act 1986* (Vic)).

Neave JA (Maxwell P agreeing)

> **[102]** The notice of appeal sought damages, including aggravated damages, for breach of confidence. In their written submission, counsel for Ms Giller argued that English authority supports the award of damages for breach of confidence which can include an award

for aggravated damages. It was also said that an award for exemplary damages could be made. No authority was cited for the latter proposition. In *Harris v Digital Pulse Pty Ltd*, Spigelman CJ alluded to the importance of using correct terminology in referring to monetary awards. He said:

> 'Damages' are a remedy at common law. The issue before the Court is whether a punitive monetary award can be made in equity. Inexact use of terminology is here, as so often, prone to cause confusion of thought. The use of the word 'damages' with respect to both compensatory damages and exemplary damages obscures the fact that a common law litigant who received an award of the latter has not in fact suffered any [**103**] 'damage' in the relevant respect. The fact that compensatory damages at common law and equitable compensation have a similar justification does not necessarily indicate that a different kind of monetary award at common law, which has come to be referred to as a form of 'damages', can or should be reflected in equity.

[**104**] **(a) Can a punitive monetary award be made for breach of confidence?**

...

I am not aware of any authority supporting a punitive monetary award for breach of confidence, nor as damages in lieu of an injunction under s 38 of the *Supreme Court Act 1986*. Further, as the learned trial judge noted, Mr Procopets had already been penalised by the criminal law. In these circumstances, I do not consider it appropriate to make a punitive monetary award for breach of confidence.

(b) Can aggravated damages be awarded for breach of confidence?

At common law, aggravated damages may be awarded to compensate a plaintiff 'when the harm done to [him or her] by a wrongful act is aggravated by the manner in which the act was done'. Such damages are compensatory, not punitive. In *Campbell v Mirror Group Newspapers Ltd*, the monetary award was said to include a component for aggravation as a result of publication of an article which criticised Ms Campbell for initiating proceedings for breach of confidence.

There is academic support for the view that, in a claim for equitable compensation, it is possible to recover for aggravated damage. I can see no reason in principle why this should not be so. Nor is there any reason why damages awarded under s 38 of the *Supreme Court Act 1986*, in lieu of an injunction, could not include a component for aggravation.

His Honour seems to have regarded Ms Giller's distress as relatively minor. ...

It may be accepted that Ms Giller is a person of some resilience. This does not, in my view, preclude the making of a compensatory award which includes an element for aggravation. The fact that Ms Giller's friends and family knew that she had had a sexual relationship with Mr Procopets was, in my view, irrelevant to an assessment of the impact on her of knowing that others had seen her actually engaging in sexual activity, just as it would be irrelevant where the partners were married and were therefore known 'to have had a sexual relationship over many years'. The showing of the video was inevitably humiliating and distressing. Mr Procopets well knew from his telephone conversations with Ms Giller that she was disturbed and upset by his threats. That, evidently, was his purpose. He is fortunate that she appears not to have suffered any lasting injury. Although Mr Procopets ceased trying to distribute the video after Ms Giller reported him to the police, in mid-1997 he showed it to his new partner Ms Drobitsky.

[**105**] I am satisfied that Mr Procopets breached his duty of confidence with the deliberate purpose of humiliating, embarrassing and distressing Ms Giller, and that his conduct had that effect. I therefore consider it appropriate to include a component for aggravation in the award of compensation.

5 Aggravated damages available for breaches of the *Australian Consumer Law*

New South Wales Lotteries Corporation Pty Ltd v Kuzmanovski (2011) 195 FCR 234

Facts and issues

Mrs Kuzmanovksi bought a 'Pictionary' lottery ticket for her husband's birthday. The terms on the rear of the ticket indicated that if the word matched the picture, the person would win the stipulated sum, as well as stating that it was governed by the terms of the *Public Lotteries Act 1996* (NSW). Mr Kuzmanovski scratched the ticket, and uncovered the word 'Bathe', a picture of a person swimming and $100 000. However, when he went to collect his prize, he was told it was not a winning ticket, and was subject to a verification test. The word intended to match the picture of the person swimming was 'Swim' and the picture for the word 'Bathe' was intended to be a person in a bath. Nonetheless, Mr Kuzmanovski argued that because bathe was a synonym for swim, the picture matched the word, and he was entitled to the prize. New South Wales Lotteries ('Lotteries') argued that the mention of the *Public Lotteries Act 1996* (NSW) incorporated the need for verification into the terms of the ticket.

The trial judge held that the term with regard to verification had not been successfully incorporated, and that Mr Kuzmanovski was entitled to $100 000 as damages for breach of contract. However, he also said that if he was wrong, he would award damages of $20 000 for distress for misleading and deceptive conduct pursuant to s 52 of the *Trade Practices Act 1974* (Cth). Lotteries appealed the trial judge's decision with regard to damages.

Decision

The Full Federal Court upheld the appeal in part, and found that the notice on the back of the ticket as to the Act incorporated the verification requirement. However, they upheld the trial judge's finding that the representation was misleading and deceptive and awarded damages for distress.

Siopis, Cowdroy and Tracey JJ

[**253**] The primary judge concluded that the Kuzmanovskis had suffered loss or damage as a result of Lotteries' misleading conduct. Lotteries submitted no loss or damage was suffered by the Kuzmanovskis, and that the award of damages of $20 000 by his Honour was 'plainly excessive'.

The primary judge found Mr and Mrs Kuzmanovski to be honest witnesses. However, he did not conclude that Mr and Mrs Kuzmanovski were misled into the purchase of the ticket. Rather, the terms of the ticket, once purchased and scratched, misled them as to its inherent characteristics.

The primary judge accepted that, as the misrepresentation inherent in the ticket became more and more apparent, the sense of disappointment, anger and frustration felt by the Kuzmanovskis increased, especially on the part of Mr Kuzmanovski. Mr Kuzmanovski had planned to use the money for, among other things, financing a trip to Macedonia to visit his ailing grandmother.

While recognising that there were no objective criteria for assessing the value of such injured feelings, his Honour proceeded to assess the damages under the *Trade Practices Act* at $20 000 ($15 000 for Mr Kuzmanovski and $5000 for Mrs Kuzmanovski).

Lotteries contended that the award was plainly excessive. Lotteries contended that Mr and Mrs Kuzmanovski became aware of the correct position at law the morning after they scratched the ticket. That is, although they stayed up for most of the night with excitement at the thought of winning, the following morning they were informed by the agent for Lotteries that the ticket was in fact not a winning ticket. Regardless of the fact that their disappointment had continued to mount since that time, they had suffered no compensable loss because the day after scratching it they found out the answer to the question of whether they had a winning ticket.

In our view, this contention is not to be accepted. The primary judge found that Lotteries' conduct had caused an initial soaring of the Kuzmanovskis' hopes and dreams and then, when those hopes and dreams were dashed, prolonged feelings of disappointment, anger and frustration arising from a sense of feeling cheated. The primary judge went on to find that that initial feeling of elation by the Kuzmanovskis was the very kind of human emotion played on by the sales pitch of Lotteries.

In our view, Lotteries has not demonstrated that the primary judge erred in principle in the manner in which he approached the question of damages. The assessment of damages for disappointment and injury to feelings is not a precise science. In our view, the primary judge did not err in taking into account the fact that the 'sales pitch' of Lotteries was directed to inducing consumers to believe that with a stroke of luck, they could experience the very elation which the Kuzmanovskis felt when, by reason of the Lotteries' contravening conduct, they believed that their ticket was a winning ticket. Nor, in our view, did the primary judge err in concluding that the deep and lingering sense of disappointment, anger and frustration felt by Mr Kuzmanovski and, to a lesser **[254]** extent Mrs Kuzmanovski, was a natural human emotional response to Lotteries' contravening conduct. It was, in our view, open to the primary judge to award damages in the sum which he did.

REVIEW QUESTIONS

(1) Do you think the distinction between exemplary and aggravated damages is easy to draw?

(2) Should aggravated damages be available for breach of confidence?

IV 'Vindicatory damages'

Concept	Short explanation	Relevant authorities	Principles text
Vindicatory damages are not available as a separate head of damages in Australia.	Vindicatory damages allow for substantial awards of damages for an infringement of a right in the absence of factual loss. The High Court has decided that Australian law does not recognise this head of damages, and that other remedies are sufficient to vindicate a plaintiff's rights.	*Lewis v Australian Capital Territory* (2020) 271 CLR 192	Chapter 14: [14.79]–[14.82]

Lewis v Australian Capital Territory [2020] HCA 26; (2020) 271 CLR 192

Facts and issues

Lewis was sentenced to a term of 12 months' imprisonment for recklessly or intentionally inflicting actual bodily harm on another. He was sentenced to periodic detention on weekends, but failed to attend four times. He was notified by the Sentence Administration Board ('the Board') of an inquiry. He did not read the notifications he was sent and did not attend the hearing. The Board cancelled Lewis's periodic detention. The statute required the Board to do so once an offender had twice failed to attend periodic detention, and there was no discretion on the part of the Board.[4] The Board decided it had been inquorate during the first inquiry and invited Lewis to a second inquiry, but it was unclear if he received the notifications. Lewis again failed to attend. He was arrested and imprisoned for 82 days. He successfully challenged the cancellation of his periodic detention on the basis that he had been denied procedural fairness by the Board (in separate proceedings) and the Board's decision was invalidated. Lewis was granted bail prior to the hearing of his challenge to the Board's decision and never fully served his initial sentence of periodic detention. He sought damages from the Australian Capital Territory for false imprisonment for 82 days.

The trial judge assessed damages for false imprisonment at $100 000, but awarded only nominal damages because, even if the Board had accorded Lewis procedural fairness, the periodic detention order would have been cancelled and Lewis would have been placed in full-time detention. The Full Court of the Supreme Court of the Australian Capital Territory upheld the trial judge's decision. Lewis appealed to the High Court.

Lewis argued that he was entitled to substantial damages on three bases:

(1) infringement of his right to liberty because he had been falsely imprisoned
(2) 'vindicatory damages' to reflect the infringement of his human right to liberty and
(3) compensatory damages for the non-pecuniary losses he sustained during the 82 days.

4 The legislation, the *Crimes (Sentence Administration) Act 2005* (ACT), is described in detail at [7]–[12] of Kiefel CJ and Keane J's judgment and [53]–[58] of Gordon J's judgment.

Decision

The Court found against Lewis on all three grounds of appeal, holding unanimously that Lewis would have been imprisoned in any case, and accordingly that his rights were best vindicated by an award of nominal damages. The Court further refused to recognise vindicatory rights as a separate head of damage in Australia on the basis that other existing remedies are sufficient to vindicate a plaintiff's rights.

Gordon J (Kiefel CJ and Keane J agreeing)

Vindicatory damages

[104] If substantial compensatory damages are unavailable (as is the position), then Mr Lewis submitted that this Court should recognise that non-compensatory but 'vindicatory' damages are available, as a new head of damages. This submission should also be rejected. There is no need, nor is there any basis in principle, for the Court to recognise a separate head of vindicatory damages. Existing remedies are sufficient.

[105] As was explained in *Lumba*, 'the concept of vindicatory damages has been developed in some Commonwealth countries with written constitutions enshrining certain fundamental rights and principles and containing broadly worded powers to afford constitutional redress'. The aim of the award is not merely compensation, nor is it punishment (though an award may have that effect). The award, not necessarily of substantial size, serves to 'reflect the sense of public outrage, emphasise the importance of [a] constitutional right and the gravity of the breach, and deter further breaches'.

[106] The head of vindicatory damages recognised by some judges in *Lumba* developed from awards of such damages in Privy Council cases where the constitutional context was markedly different. Those cases concerned violations of constitutional rights, in which the relevant constitutions (of countries in the Caribbean) provided for 'redress' or 'relief' with 'such remedy' as the court considers appropriate. It is quite a stretch to say that principles developed in that setting should be recognised as part of the common law of Australia, in circumstances where the common law has adequate means of dealing with the matter already. As Lord Dyson said in *Lumba*, it would be a 'big leap' to carry these principles over from public law in the Caribbean to private common law elsewhere.

[107] Further, there is uncertainty over how vindicatory damages would work. For example, Lord Hope said in *Lumba* that an award of vindicatory damages should take account of 'the underlying facts and circumstances'. But in this case, the circumstances point to the conclusion that only nominal damages are appropriate. Moreover, how could a court meaningfully determine a quantum of damages which is not moored to a compensatory or punitive principle, or to the standard award of nominal damages?

[108] Mr Lewis submitted that this concern is 'overstated' because vindicatory damages would be available 'only where ordinary compensatory damages are not available yet an award of nominal damages is inappropriate having regard to the right that has been infringed'. It is not clear why these are the appropriate bounds of the award. If the right is so important that it warrants some separate vindication, why is that not addressed, as it may be now, by the grant of a declaration or, where appropriate, an award of aggravated or exemplary damages, combined with a compensatory award?

[109] Compensatory or exemplary damages may have a vindicatory effect in some cases. Mr Lewis points to cases in which vindicatory language was used in awarding compensatory damages. For example, as stated above, Gaudron and McHugh JJ said in *Plenty* that '[t]he appellant is entitled to have his right of property vindicated by a substantial award of damages' in an action for trespass to land. Similarly, Mr Lewis submitted that 'a vindicatory purpose is present in the recognised head of non-compensatory exemplary damages'. He cited *New South Wales v Ibbett* in this respect, which quoted the following passage from *Kuddus v Chief Constable of Leicestershire Constabulary*:

> [I]n certain cases the awarding of exemplary damages serves a valuable purpose in restraining the arbitrary and outrageous use of executive power and in vindicating the strength of the law.

These statements do not assist Mr Lewis. The cases explain that vindication is not an alien concept to damages awards. But if a new head of damages were to be recognised, one would expect a very good reason for the law to take that step. In my view, there is no such reason. The 'aim' of vindicatory damages can be and is achieved by existing heads of damages. That last statement necessitates further explanation of exemplary, aggravated and nominal damages.

[110] '[E]xemplary damages may be awarded for conduct of a sufficiently reprehensible kind'. They are appropriate where 'the conduct of the defendant merits punishment' because it 'is wanton, as where it discloses fraud, malice, violence, cruelty, insolence or the like, or, as it is sometimes put, where he [or she] acts in contumelious disregard of the plaintiff's rights'. Exemplary damages 'go beyond compensation and are awarded 'as a punishment to the guilty, to deter from any such proceeding for the future, and as a proof of the detestation of the jury to the action itself''. The award also 'serve[s] to mark the court's condemnation of the defendant's behaviour'. In *Lamb v Cotogno*, the Court noted that the award has a 'punitive aspect', but may also have a compensatory effect in practical terms. In so far as the award is a deterrent, it serves as a deterrent both to the defendant and to others.

[111] Exemplary damages may also have particular significance in restraining executive power. In *Ibbett*, the Court considered exemplary damages for trespass to land and said:

> The common law fixes by various means a line between the interests of the individual in personal freedom of action and the interests of the State in the maintenance of a legally ordered society. An action for trespass to land and an award of exemplary damages has long been a method by which, at the instance of the citizen, the State is called to account by the common law for the misconduct of those acting under or with the authority of the Executive Government. (Footnote omitted.)

The Court went on to say that it is 'well established … that an award of exemplary damages may serve "a valuable purpose in restraining the arbitrary and outrageous use of executive power" and "oppressive, arbitrary or unconstitutional action by the servants of the government"'.

[112] By contrast, aggravated damages are 'compensatory in nature, being awarded for injury to the plaintiff's feelings caused by insult, humiliation and the like'. They are 'a form of general damages, given by way of compensation for injury to the plaintiff, which may be intangible, resulting from the circumstances and manner of the wrongdoing'.

[113] While the same factors may be relevant to both aggravated and exemplary damages, the 'difference is that in the case of aggravated damages the assessment is made from the point of view of the [p]laintiff and in the case of exemplary damages the focus is on the conduct of the [d]efendant'.

[114] The Court has engaged with nominal damages less often. In *Baume v The Commonwealth*, Griffith CJ quoted with approval from the Earl of Halsbury LC in *Owners of Steamship 'Mediana' v Owners, Master and Crew of Lightship 'Comet' (The 'Mediana')*, where his Lordship said:

> 'Nominal damages' is a technical phrase which means that you have negatived anything like real damage, but that you are affirming by your nominal damages that there is an infraction of a legal right which, though it gives you no right to any real damages at all, yet gives you a right to the verdict or judgment because your legal right has been infringed. But the term 'nominal damages' does not mean small damages.

[115] The same passage was quoted by Isaacs J in *Cunningham v Ryan*. There, his Honour said that '[e]very plaintiff who establishes the *liability* of the defendant … is entitled by law to at least *nominal damages*' (emphasis in original). Once a wrongful act is established, the entitlement to nominal damages arises in accordance with *The 'Mediana'*.

[116] Consistently with these statements, McColl JA in the Court of Appeal of the Supreme Court of New South Wales said that nominal damages are 'vindicatory, not compensatory'. Lord Rodger made the same point in *Ashley v Chief Constable of Sussex Police* in the House of Lords, where his Lordship said that 'battery or trespass to the person is actionable without proof that the victim has suffered anything other than the infringement of his right to bodily integrity: the law vindicates that right by awarding nominal damages'.

[117] Thus, different categories of damages have different purposes. Exemplary damages are available (at least) where there has been contumelious disregard of the plaintiff's rights. They serve to punish the defendant and to deter the defendant and others from such behaviour. They mark the court's condemnation of that behaviour. Aggravated damages compensate a plaintiff for the way in which damage was caused. Nominal damages mark the fact that there has been an infraction of a legal right.

[118] Therefore, to the extent that vindicatory damages mark infringement of a right, that is already achieved by nominal damages. Indeed, it is difficult to see what purpose nominal damages would serve if vindicatory damages were recognised as a separate head. Nor is it necessary to award vindicatory damages in order to dissuade the executive from exceeding its powers. Were the executive to do so willingly, or in disregard of a plaintiff's rights, exemplary damages could be awarded to mark the court's disapproval of that conduct and to deter others from repeating it. Similar factors may make an award of aggravated damages appropriate in a case where compensatory damages are awarded.

[119] Two further points should be added to this discussion of remedies. First, as stated earlier, a court can vindicate a right (in the sense of recognising its infringement) by issuing a declaration. A declaration can 'mark in some way the importance of a breach of a public law rule even in a case where it would not be appropriate to award … damages'. That is, a declaration may itself have a vindicatory purpose and effect. And, as has been explained, so too does an award of nominal damages, which can sit alongside the declaration, or finding, of unlawful conduct as part of the appropriate relief.

[120] Second, it is also possible for costs to be awarded on an indemnity basis where appropriate. This ensures that vindication of a right comes at no cost to the plaintiff. With those weapons at hand, there is no good reason to recognise vindicatory damages as a separate head.

[121] As Windeyer J said in *Uren v John Fairfax & Sons Pty Ltd*, 'law has often used its old weapons instead of forging new ones'. There is no need to forge a new weapon here. ...

Edelman J (Gageler J agreeing)

Vindicatory damages

[170] Mr Lewis' submission that he is entitled to substantial damages independently of any consequences to him is not made any more compelling by the addition of the label 'vindicatory damages'. This submission, which amounted to the same point as his submission that substantial damages were available to vindicate a right, but with a different title, was that substantial damages were available not to compensate but to 'vindicate' the plaintiff's right to liberty or 'to recognise the value of the right of every human being not to be imprisoned'.

[171] The association between damages and vindication probably originated in defamation cases. It was once thought to be legitimate for a jury to be directed that since they could not give public reasons to address the consequential damage to the plaintiff's reputation the members of the jury could instead 'give a very big sum, which will indicate what [they] think'. In a subsequent false imprisonment case, where the damages were sought for the consequences to the plaintiff's reputation of the false imprisonment, Slade J described such an award as being made to 'vindicate' a plaintiff by making it 'clear that there was no stain of any kind upon his character'. The suggested reduction of damages where a judge sits without a jury was later rejected in England, but the description of compensatory damages as performing a function of 'vindication' remains. However, the function that it describes is part of the goal of redressing loss.

[172] Damages awards to vindicate a plaintiff's reputation, whether the impaired reputation is consequent upon defamation or false imprisonment, are concerned with loss. They focus upon the consequences of publication upon the plaintiff's reputation including any diminution in the regard with which the plaintiff is held by others and any isolation of the plaintiff. The award 'looks to the attitude of others to the [plaintiff]' and 'must not exceed the amount appropriate to compensate the plaintiff for any relevant harm he or she has suffered'. Hence, putting exemplary damages to one side, if the plaintiff's general reputation was so poor prior to the publication that the statement or implication could do no further injury then this element of 'vindication' would require only nominal damages. The same is true of infringement of a right by an act of assault or false imprisonment where no loss is suffered: 'the law vindicates that right by awarding nominal damages'. And if nominal damages are insufficient to serve the purpose of 'restraining the arbitrary and outrageous use of executive power and in vindicating the strength of the law' then exemplary damages can be awarded. There is no place for a separate species of vindicatory damages.

[173] Mr Lewis also relied upon a line of decisions, primarily from the Privy Council, where substantial damages were said to have been awarded solely to 'vindicate' constitutional rights. Although the award made in each of these cases was expressed to be made as damages 'to uphold, or vindicate, the constitutional right which has been contravened', the awards were not made without regard to the consequences of the breach. Indeed, the justification given for the award of these damages beyond compensation for loss was 'to reflect the sense of public outrage, emphasise the importance of the constitutional right and the gravity of the breach, and deter further breaches'. As Lord Hope observed, giving the reasons of the Privy Council in one of these cases, a declaration on its own might be sufficient to vindicate the right but, where it was not, the award of substantial damages was likely 'in financial terms to cover much the same ground as an award by way of punishment' even if that was not its object. These 'vindicatory damages' are thus 'closely linked ... to punitive and exemplary damages'. In any event, however, neither English law nor Australian law has generally accepted such a vindication principle as establishing a new species of vindicatory damages in the law of torts. And, in the United States, the Supreme Court has held that where there is no proof of actual damage the abstract value of a constitutional right is vindicated by an award of nominal damages only, in accordance with ordinary principles of the law of torts.

[174] An attempt to develop such a new species of damages in English domestic law was made by the appellants in the Supreme Court of the United Kingdom in *R (Lumba) v Secretary of State for the Home Department*. In that case the appellants were two foreign nationals who were detained pending deportation for lengthy periods of time by the blanket application of an unpublished policy. A majority of the House of Lords held that their detention was unlawful and was therefore a false imprisonment. However, six of the nine judges held that only nominal damages should be awarded for the false imprisonment because even without the unlawful application of the unpublished policies it was inevitable that the appellants would have been detained. In a judgment with which the other judges in the majority on this issue agreed, Lord Dyson said:

> The implications of awarding vindicatory damages in the present case would be far reaching. Undesirable uncertainty would result. If they were awarded here, then they could in principle be awarded in any case involving a battery or false imprisonment by an arm of the state. Indeed, why limit it to such torts? And why limit it to torts committed by the state? I see no justification for letting such an unruly horse loose on our law. In my view, the purpose of vindicating a claimant's common law rights is sufficiently met by (i) an award of compensatory damages, including (in the case of strict liability torts) nominal damages where no substantial loss is proved; (ii) where appropriate, a declaration in suitable terms; and (iii) again, where appropriate, an award of exemplary damages.

[175] Even the approach of the minority on this issue in *Lumba* (Lords Hope and Walker and Lady Hale) does not support Mr Lewis. They did not justify a substantial award of vindicatory damages on the basis merely of an infringement of the appellants' rights, irrespective of consequences. Rather, their justifications depended upon considerations that were very closely associated with exemplary damages. Lords Hope and Walker both described the conduct of the officials as 'a serious abuse of power' and 'deplorable', and held that this required damages that were more than nominal. Similarly, Lady Hale would have awarded substantial damages of £500 to recognise the breach by the State and 'to encourage all concerned to avoid anything like it happening again'.

[176] The approach of the majority on this issue in *Lumba* was followed by the Full Court of the Federal Court in *Fernando v The Commonwealth*. It was also addressed by four members of this Court in *CPCF v Minister for Immigration and Border Protection*. In that case, the majority decision in *Lumba* was referred to with approval by Kiefel J and Keane J. In their joint dissenting reasons, Hayne and Bell JJ, who would have held that detention was unlawful, said that nominal damages were 'open' in a case where a form of lawful detention was available and would have been effected but, citing *Lumba*, said that the absence of any 'substantial loss' did not require the conclusion that only nominal damages may be awarded. It is unnecessary to assess the competing views expressed by the parties concerning these obiter dicta passages in this joint judgment, nor to assess the competing views concerning whether the correctness of *Lumba* had been in dispute and the consequential weight of the reasoning on this point generally in *CPCF*. For the reasons above, the decision of the majority on this issue in *Lumba* was correct. …

REVIEW QUESTIONS

(1) Do you think the High Court in *Lewis v Australian Capital Territory* (2020) 271 CLR 192 was right to refuse vindicatory damages to Lewis? Why/why not?

(2) Are there other areas of the law where the courts award damages for infringements of rights in the absence of factual loss?

15 APOLOGIES AND DECLARATORY RELIEF

I	Introduction	511
II	Apologies, declarations and nominal damages	511
	A Apologies	512
	B Declarations, nominal damages and contemptuous damages	516
III	Other vindicatory remedies under the *Australian Consumer Law*	524

I Introduction

In this chapter, we consider other forms of remedies which seek to vindicate the plaintiff's rights by a public statement of those rights, including declarations, awards of nominal damages and apologies. The court may make a public statement of rights (as with declarations) or the defendant themself may be compelled to make the statement (as with apology orders). Below, we first consider apologies, then declarations, nominal damages and contemptuous damages, and then finally other vindicatory awards available under the *Australian Consumer Law* ('ACL').

II Apologies, declarations and nominal damages

Concept	Short explanation	Relevant authorities	Principles text
Apologies	Some civil legislation allows for a defendant to make an apology.	*Wrongs Act 1958* (Vic) ss 14I–14J *Civil Law (Wrongs) Act 2002* (ACT) ss 12–14	Chapter 15: [15.2]–[15.13]
	In defamation law, the lack of an apology can operate in 'mitigation of damages'. Courts are not usually willing to order apologies.	*Defamation Act 2005* (NSW) s 20 *Eatock v Bolt* (2011) 197 FCR 261	
Declarations	A declaratory judgment is an order which conclusively pronounces the existence or non-existence of a right. It is not enforceable, but it is final. Courts have general and specific statutory powers to make such declarations.	*Supreme Court Act 1970* (NSW) s 75 *Competition and Consumer Act 2010* (Cth) s 163A *Corporations Act 2001* (Cth) s 1317E	Chapter 15: [15.14]–[15.32]

Concept	Short explanation	Relevant authorities	Principles text
	Generally to establish an entitlement to a declaration the plaintiff must establish (1) jurisdiction on the part of the court to grant the declaration; (2) standing on the part of the plaintiff to seek the declaration; and (3) that there are no discretionary reasons why a declaration should not be awarded.	*Forster v Jododex Pty Ltd* (1972) 127 CLR 421	
Nominal damages	Common law courts developed nominal damages as an analogue to a declaratory judgment, to signal that the defendant has committed a wrong, but a token amount is awarded to signify that the plaintiff has a right to a verdict in their favour. These awards are only made in relation to wrongs actionable per se.	*The Owners of the Steamship 'Mediana' v The Owners, Master and Crew of the Lightship 'Comet' (The 'Mediana')* [1900] AC 113	Chapter 15: [15.33]–[15.36]
Contemptuous damages	Sometimes the award of a nominal sum is a rebuff for the plaintiff, particularly in defamation (sometimes described as 'contemptuous damages').	*Grobbelaar v News Group Newspapers Ltd* [2002] 1 WLR 3024	Chapter 15: [15.37]–[15.39]

A Apologies

Wrongs Act 1958 (Vic) ss 14I–14J

All Australian states and territories passed legislation allowing for a defendant to make an apology. This is the Victorian version.

14I Definitions

In this Part –

'apology' means an expression of sorrow, regret or sympathy but does not include a clear acknowledgment of fault;

'civil proceeding' includes –

(a) a proceeding before a tribunal; and

(b) a proceeding under an Act regulating the practice or conduct of a profession or occupation; and

(c) a proceeding of a Royal Commission, whether established under the *Inquiries Act 2014* or under the prerogative of the Crown; and

(d) a proceeding of a Board of Inquiry or Formal Review established under the *Inquiries Act 2014*;

'injury' means personal or bodily injury and includes –

(a) pre-natal injury; and

(b) psychological or psychiatric injury; and

(c) disease; and

(d) aggravation, acceleration or recurrence of an injury or disease.

14J Apology not admission of liability

(1) In a civil proceeding where the death or injury of a person is in issue or is relevant to an issue of fact or law, an apology does not constitute –

(a) an admission of liability for the death or injury; or

(b) an admission of unprofessional conduct, carelessness, incompetence or unsatisfactory professional performance, however expressed, for the purposes of any Act regulating the practice or conduct of a profession or occupation.

(2) Subsection (1) applies whether the apology –

(a) is made orally or in writing; or

(b) is made before or after the civil proceeding was in contemplation or commenced.

(3) Nothing in this section affects the admissibility of a statement with respect to a fact in issue or tending to establish a fact in issue.

Civil Law (Wrongs) Act 2002 (ACT) ss 12–14

All Australian states and territories passed legislation allowing for a defendant to make an apology. This is the Australian Capital Territory version.

12 Application – pt 2.3

(1) This part applies to civil liability of any kind.

(2) However, this part does not apply to civil liability for an award of damages or compensation –

(a) for defamation; or

(b) under any of the following:

(i) the *Discrimination Act 1991*;

(ii) the *Workers Compensation Act 1951*.

13 Meaning of apology in pt 2.3

In this part:

'apology' means an oral or written expression of sympathy or regret, or of a general sense of benevolence or compassion, in relation to an incident, whether or not the expression admits or implies fault or liability in relation to the incident.

14 Effect of apology on liability etc.

(1) An apology made by or on behalf of a person in relation to an incident claimed to have been caused by the person –

(a) is not (and must not be taken to be) an express or implied admission of fault or liability by the person in relation to the incident; and

(b) is not relevant to deciding fault or liability in relation to the incident.

(2) Evidence of an apology made by or on behalf of a person in relation to an incident claimed to have been caused by the person is not admissible in any civil proceeding as evidence of the fault or liability of the person in relation to the incident.

Defamation Act 2005 (NSW) s 20

All Australian states and territories passed legislation providing that an apology is not an admission of liability. This is the New South Wales provision.

Section 38 of the *Defamation Act 2005* (NSW) (referred to in s 20(3) below) provides that an apology may lead to a 'mitigation' or lessening of damages.

20 Effect of apology on liability for defamation

(1) An apology made by or on behalf of a person in connection with any defamatory matter alleged to have been published by the person–
  (a) does not constitute an express or implied admission of fault or liability by the person in connection with that matter, and
  (b) is not relevant to the determination of fault or liability in connection with that matter.

(2) Evidence of an apology made by or on behalf of a person in connection with any defamatory matter alleged to have been published by the person is not admissible in any civil proceedings as evidence of the fault or liability of the person in connection with that matter.

(3) Nothing in this section limits the operation of section 38.

The *Racial Discrimination Act 1975* (Cth) and other equal opportunities legislation allows for the court to order a party to make an apology. In the following case, the plaintiffs sought an apology from the defendant, whom they argued had offended, insulted, humiliated or intimidated them on the basis that they were fair-skinned Aboriginal people.

Eatock v Bolt (2011) 197 FCR 261

Facts and issues

Bolt, a newspaper columnist, was alleged to have contravened s 18C of the *Racial Discrimination Act 1975* (Cth), which prohibited acts done because of the race, colour or national or ethnic origin of a person, or some of or all of the people in a group where the act was reasonably likely, in all the circumstances, to offend, insult, humiliate or intimidate another person or a group of people. Bolt had written columns regarding fair-skinned Aboriginal people, including the plaintiffs, one of whom included Eatock. Among other things, the plaintiffs sought an apology order.

Decision

Bolt had contravened s 18C of the *Racial Discrimination Act 1975* (Cth) by writing columns which were likely to 'offend, insult, humiliate or intimidate' fair-skinned Aboriginal people. However, it was not appropriate to order him to apologise. He was instead required to place a corrective notice in the terms ordered by the judge on his website.

Bromberg J

[**365**] There is force in the contention of HWT that an apology should not be compelled by an order of the Court because that compels a person to articulate a sentiment that is not genuinely held. An apology is one means of achieving [**366**] the public vindication of those that have been injured by a contravention of s 18C. The power granted to the Court to require a respondent to redress any loss or damage is a wide power. There are other means by which public vindication may be achieved.

Public vindication is important. It will go some way to redressing the hurt felt by those injured. It will serve to restore the esteem and social standing which has been lost as a consequence of the contravention. It will serve to inform those influenced by the contravening conduct of the wrongdoing involved. It may help to negate the dissemination of racial prejudice.

Whilst I will not order HWT to apologise, in the absence of an appropriate apology, I am minded to make an order which fulfils the purposes which I have identified.

My preliminary view is that a corrective order should be made which would require HWT to publish a notice in the *Herald Sun* in print and online. The terms of the notice would include an introduction which referred to this proceeding and the order requiring its publication and set out the declaration made by the Court. In order to give the publication of the corrective notice a prominence and frequency commensurate with the publication of the Newspaper Articles and to facilitate it being communicated to those likely to have read the Newspaper Articles, I have in mind that the corrective order would require the publication of the notice in the *Herald Sun* newspaper and online, on two separate occasions in a prominent place immediately adjacent to Mr Bolt's regular column.

Courts are generally reluctant to compel parties to make apologies where it appears the apology will not be genuine.

In *Wotton v State of Queensland (No 5)*,[1] Mortimer J declined to order the Commissioner of Police and the State of Queensland to issue an apology in relation to racially discriminatory conduct by officers of the Queensland Police Service when investigating the death of an Aboriginal man in custody. However, she contemplated ordering the Commissioner of Police to explain why an apology should not be awarded. Ultimately, she decided that such an order should not be made until the proceedings were completed.[2] When the class action was subsequently settled, the Queensland government issued an apology in the *Palm Island Voice*, the *Courier Mail* and the *Townsville Bulletin*.[3]

1 (2016) 157 ALD 14.

2 *Wotton v Queensland (No 6)* [2017] FCA 245.

3 E Archibald-Binge, '"Sorry for the Pain You Have Endured": Queensland Government Apologises to Palm Islanders', *NITV News* (28 June 2018) <https://www.sbs.com.au/nitv/article/2018/06/15/sorry-pain-you-have-endured-queensland-government-apologises-palm-islanders>.

B Declarations, nominal damages and contemptuous damages

1 Declarations

A declaratory judgment is an order which conclusively pronounces the existence or non-existence of a right. It is not enforceable, but it is final. Courts have general and specific statutory powers to make such declarations. Figure 15.1 indicates the process the court goes through when deciding to award a declaration.

Figure 15.1 Elements required to make out entitlement to a declaration

Final

- Declarations are final and conclusively pronounce the rights of parties.
- They cannot be made in an interim basis.
- Declarations cannot be followed up with a process of execution (ie they are not enforceable orders of the court).

↓

Jurisdiction

- The jurisdiction to make a declaration is very wide and can only be excluded by clear words in a statute.

↓

Standing

- A plaintiff must have sufficient standing: ie that they have sufficient interest in the subject matter of the dispute.
- Standing is generally uncontroversial for private rights.

↓

Discretion

- The court may choose not to grant a declaration under certain circumstances where:
  - the question is abstract, theoretical or hypothetical
  - there is no uncertainty about the right course of action.

An example of a provision conferring a general power to make a declaration on a court is extracted below.

Supreme Court Act 1970 (NSW) s 75

This legislation generally empowers the Supreme Court of New South Wales to make a declaration in the absence of any other remedy being sought. Other Australian jurisdictions have comparable provisions.

75 Declaratory relief

No proceedings shall be open to objection on the ground that a merely declaratory judgment or order is sought thereby and the Court may make binding declarations of right whether any consequential relief is or could be claimed or not.

In some contexts, legislation empowers courts to make a declaration in specific contexts. Two examples of provisions conferring specific powers to grant injunctions are excerpted below.

Competition and Consumer Act 2010 (Cth) s 163A

This legislation allows a court with jurisdiction to make a declaration in respect of certain contraventions of the *Competition and Consumer Act 2010* (Cth).

163A Declarations and orders

(1) Subject to this section, a person may, in relation to a matter arising under this Act or the consumer data rules, institute a proceeding in a court having jurisdiction to hear and determine proceedings under this section seeking the making of:

  (a) a declaration in relation to the operation or effect of any provision of this Act or the consumer data rules other than the following provisions:

    (i) Part V;

    (ii) Part XIB;

    (iii) Part XIC; or

  (aaa) a declaration in relation to the operation or effect of any provision of the Australian Consumer Law other than Division 1 of Part 3–2 or Part 5–4; or

  (aa) a declaration in relation to the validity of any act or thing done, proposed to be done or purporting to have been done under this Act or the consumer data rules; or

  (b) an order by way of, or in the nature of, prohibition, certiorari or mandamus;

  or both such a declaration and such an order.

(1A) Subsection (1) does not apply in relation to a matter arising under Part IIIAA.

…

Corporations Act 2001 (Cth) s 1317E(1)–(2)

This legislation allows a court with jurisdiction to make a declaration in respect of contraventions of civil penalty provisions within the *Corporations Act 2001* (Cth).

1317E Declaration of contravention of a civil penalty provision

Declaration of contravention

(1) If a Court is satisfied that a person has contravened a civil penalty provision, the Court must make a declaration of contravention.

(2) The declaration must specify the following:

(a) the Court that made the declaration;

(b) the civil penalty provision that was contravened;

(c) the person who contravened the provision;

(d) the conduct that constituted the contravention;

(e) if the contravention is of a corporation/scheme civil penalty provision – the corporation, registered scheme or notified foreign passport fund to which the conduct related;

(f) if the contravention is of subsection 1211B(1) or (2) (complying with the Passport Rules for this jurisdiction) – the passport fund in relation to which the obligation was imposed on the person;

(g) if the contravention is of subsection 670A(4), 727(6), 728(4) or 1309(12) (misleading statements etc.) – the corporation, registered scheme or notified foreign passport fund to which the conduct related.

...

Generally (as illustrated in more detail in Figure 15.1) to establish an entitlement to a declaration the plaintiff must establish:

- jurisdiction on the part of the court to grant the declaration
- standing on the part of the plaintiff to seek the declaration and
- that there are no discretionary reasons why a declaration should not be awarded.

The following case outlines these requirements.

Forster v Jododex Pty Ltd (1972) 127 CLR 421

Facts and issues

A mining company (Jododex Pty Ltd) sought a declaration that it was the holder of a valid mining licence at the relevant time when it applied to renew that licence. The application for renewal was required to be made 'not later than one month before the expiry' of the previous licence.

Decision

A judge sitting in equity of the New South Wales Supreme Court is able to grant declaratory relief on a wide basis pursuant to s 10 of the *Equity Act 1901* (NSW), which mirrors the power given to a judge of the High Court in England by ord 25 r 5 of the *Rules of the Supreme Court 1883* (Eng). Gibbs J's discussion of the principles of declarations is excerpted below. (He disagreed with the majority [McTiernan, Stephen and Mason JJ] that the application had been made within the relevant time).

Gibbs J (dissenting)

> [**435**] The jurisdiction to make a declaration is a very wide one. Indeed, it has been said that, 'under O XXV, r 5, the power of the Court to make a declaration, where it is a question of defining the rights of two parties, is almost unlimited; I might say only limited by its own discretion': *Hanson v Radcliffe Urban District Council* … . However, the jurisdiction may be [**436**] ousted by statute, although the right of a subject to apply to the court for a determination of his rights will not be held to be excluded except by clear words: *Pyx Granite Co Ltd v Ministry of Housing and Local Government*. In the present case it was submitted that the Act reveals an intention that the decision of a warden to grant or refuse an authority to enter should not be subject to review in proceedings for a declaration under s 10 of the *Equity Act*.
>
> With all respect, I find it difficult to see any reason why the Court should have lacked jurisdiction to declare that Jododex held the right which it claimed, namely the right of the holder of an exploration license validly renewed. There is no provision in the Act that gives to any other tribunal exclusive jurisdiction to decide the question whether a person is the holder of a valid exploration license, or that otherwise withdraws the determination of that question from the jurisdiction of the Supreme Court. Section 183 of the Act provides that:
>
> > No proceedings under this Act shall be removable by certiorari or otherwise into the Supreme Court.
>
> That section obviously has no application to the present case, where no proceedings are sought to be removed. It has been held in the Supreme Court of New South Wales that prohibition will not lie against the grant by a warden of an authority to enter upon private lands: *Ex parte Phillips*, followed in *Ex parte Miller*. The reason given was that the warden when so acting is not a court, but prohibition may be directed to bodies other than courts if they perform quasi-judicial functions: *R v Connell*; *Ex parte Hetton Bellbird Collieries Ltd*. However, it is not here necessary to consider whether the actual decision reached in *Ex parte Phillips* was correct. The Supreme Court of New South Wales has also held that when a warden grants or refuses an application for an authority to enter, there are no 'proceedings' within s 168 of the Act and there is consequently no jurisdiction to state a case for the decision of the Supreme Court: *Wake v Murphy*; *Wallamaine Colliery Pty Ltd v Cam & Sons Pty Ltd*; *Keogh v Heffernan*. On the other hand, mandamus will lie to a warden who fails to hear and determine according to law an application for an authority to enter: *Wade v Burns*. However, these decisions, which [**437**] indicate that one procedure is available and another is not to review the decision of a warden who grants or refuses an authority to enter, seem to me to have no relevance to the present question. There is nothing in the provisions considered in those cases that indicates a clear intention to exclude the power of the court to

make a declaratory order. The Act does not provide a specific remedy to which the holder of an exploration license who seeks to establish the rights which it gives him is bound to resort. It was submitted that when s 10 of the *Equity Act* was amended in 1965 the legislature did not intend by those general provisions to alter the effect of the special provisions of the *Mining Act*, which was the subject of considerable authority. The purpose of amending s 10 was to provide a more extensive remedy of a general kind, and there is no possible justification for reading the section as though it contained words excepting from its operation cases arising under the *Mining Act*. Some reliance was placed by the appellant upon *Toowoomba Foundry Pty Ltd v The Commonwealth* where it was held that the decision of an independent tribunal acting under a statute or regulation cannot be challenged in an action claiming only a declaration that the decision is invalid. Since, in the present case, the warden has made no decision, *Toowoomba Foundry Pty Ltd v The Commonwealth* is distinguishable, and it is unnecessary to consider whether that case is consistent with later decisions of the House of Lords, such as *Vine v National Dock Labour Board* and *Pyx Granite Co Ltd v Ministry of Housing and Local Government*. It is true that the purpose of Jododex in seeking a declaration was to forestall a possible contrary decision by the warden, but that does not mean that the validity of any proceeding by the warden is challenged in these proceedings: cf. *Mutual Life and Citizens' Assurance Co Ltd v Attorney-General* (Cth).

It is neither possible nor desirable to fetter the broad discretion given by s 10 by laying down rules as to the manner of its exercise. It does, however, seem to me that the Scottish rules summarized by Lord Dunedin in *Russian Commercial and Industrial Bank v British Bank for Foreign Trade Ltd*, should in general be satisfied before the discretion is exercised in favour of making a declaration:

> The question must be a real and not a theoretical question; the person raising it must have a real interest to raise it; he [**438**] must be able to secure a proper contradictor, that is to say, some one presently existing who has a true interest to oppose the declaration sought.

Beyond that, however, little guidance can be given. As Lord Radcliffe said in *Ibeneweka v Egbuna*:

> After all, it is doubtful if there is more of principle involved than the undoubted truth that the power to grant a declaration should be exercised with a proper sense of responsibility and a full realisation that judicial pronouncements ought not to be issued unless there are circumstances that call for their making. Beyond that there is no legal restriction on the award of a declaration.

In the present case the question whether Jododex held a valid exploration license was in no way hypothetical. Jododex had a real interest to establish the validity of the license and thus ensure that the warden would not grant the authorities to enter which the appellant sought. The appellant had a real interest to contest Jododex's claim which if upheld must result in the refusal of the appellant's applications. If it be assumed, contrary to the decided cases, that Jododex could have obtained prohibition if the warden had wrongly granted the appellant's applications, the existence of the alternative remedy would not require the Court to refuse to make a declaration. In the first place, a declaration would be a more satisfactory remedy than prohibition, being quicker, simpler and attended by less doubts. Even if this were not so, it seems to me, on principle, that a plaintiff should not necessarily be refused one form of relief because another is available in the same court: cf. *Pyx Granite Co Ltd v Ministry of Housing and Local Government*, per Lord Goddard.

The question whether the Court should make a declaration which would have the effect of deciding a question in issue in pending proceedings may often be of some difficulty. It is of course important that the proceedings in the present case were not pending in an ordinary court. However, there were some obvious reasons why a judge should hesitate before intervening when the matter was about to come before the warden. It was, of course, possible that the warden would give effect to the contention that Jododex held a valid exploration license and would therefore refuse to grant any authority to enter to the appellant. The warden might have declined to grant the appellant's applications for some other reason. Moreover, if it were ultimately held that Jododex's contention ought to fail, the proceedings before the [**439**] warden would have been delayed and the appellant would have been put to additional cost and inconvenience. On the other hand, to determine the existence of the right which Jododex sought to establish, it was necessary to ascertain the true meaning and effect of a statutory provision and of an instrument in statutory form. These were pure questions of construction such as would appropriately be decided in the Supreme Court. They were difficult questions, and apparently rights of considerable value depended on the answers to them. When all these conflicting considerations are weighed, it seems to me that it cannot be said that it was not a proper exercise of judicial discretion to proceed to make a declaration in all the circumstances of the case.

2 Nominal damages

Common law courts could not award declarations before the UK Judicature Acts, and hence they developed nominal damages as an analogue to a declaratory judgment in equity.

When the court makes an award of nominal damages, it declares that the defendant has committed a wrong but awards only a token amount to signify that the plaintiff has a right to a verdict in their favour. These awards are made in relation to wrongs actionable per se, such as trespass to land, trespass to the person, defamation, and breach of contract.

The Owners of the Steamship 'Mediana' v The Owners, Master and Crew of the Lightship 'Comet' (The 'Mediana') [1900] AC 113

Facts and issues

The Mersey Docks and Harbour Board ('the Board') had a statutory duty to keep the approaches to the River Mersey lighted. For this purpose, they kept six lightships, four of which were always in use, a fifth kept to replace the lightships as they were repaired, and a sixth (the *Orion*) for emergencies. On 23 April 1898, the steamship *Mediana* collided with the lightship *Comet*, sinking it. The Board used the *Orion* in the *Comet*'s place to keep the approaches to the river lit during the time when the *Comet* was being repaired. The question was whether the Board was entitled to substantial damages for the loss of services of the *Comet*, given that it had a replacement.

Decision

The Board was entitled to recover both the out of pocket expenses caused by the collision and substantial damages for the loss of services of the *Comet*, notwithstanding the fact that the *Orion* had replaced her. The following extract discusses the nature of nominal damages.

Earl of Halsbury LC

> [**116**] And, my Lords, here I wish, with reference to what has been suggested at the bar, to remark upon the difference between damages and nominal damages. 'Nominal damages' is a technical phrase which means that you have negatived anything like real damage, but that you are affirming by your nominal damages that there is an infraction of a legal right which, though it gives you no right to any real damages at all, yet gives you a right to the verdict or judgment because your legal right has been infringed. But the term 'nominal damages' does not mean small damages. The extent to which a person has a right to recover what is called by the compendious phrase damages, but may be also represented as compensation for the use of something that belongs to him, depends upon a variety of circumstances, and it certainly does not in the smallest degree suggest that because they are small they are necessarily nominal damages. Of course the whole region of inquiry into damages is one of extreme difficulty. You very often cannot even lay down any principle upon which you can give damages; nevertheless it is remitted to the jury, or those who stand in place of the jury, to consider what compensation in money shall be given for what is a wrongful act. Take the most familiar and ordinary case: how is anybody to measure pain and suffering in moneys counted? Nobody can suggest that you can by any arithmetical calculation establish what is the exact amount of money which would [**117**] represent such a thing as the pain and suffering which a person has undergone by reason of an accident. In truth, I think it would be very arguable to say that a person would be entitled to no damages for such things. What manly mind cares about pain and suffering that is past? But nevertheless the law recognises that as a topic upon which damages may be given.
>
> Now, in the particular case before us, apart from a circumstance which I will refer to immediately, the broad proposition seems to me to be that by a wrongful act of the defendants the plaintiffs were deprived of their vessel. When I say deprived of their vessel, I will not use the phrase 'the use of the vessel.' What right has a wrongdoer to consider what use you are going to make of your vessel? More than one case has been put to illustrate this: for example, the owner of a horse, or of a chair. Supposing a person took away a chair out of my room and kept it for twelve months, could anybody say you had a right to diminish the damages by shewing that I did not usually sit in that chair, or that there were plenty of other chairs in the room? The proposition so nakedly stated appears to me to be absurd; but a jury have very often a very difficult task to perform in ascertaining what should be the amount of damages of that sort. I know very well that as a matter of common sense what an arbitrator or a jury very often do is to take a perfectly artificial hypothesis and say, 'Well, if you wanted to hire a chair, what would you have to give for it for the period'; and in that way they come to a rough sort of conclusion as to what damages ought to be paid for the unjust and unlawful withdrawal of it from the owner. Here, as I say, the broad principle seems to me to be quite independent of the particular use the plaintiffs were going to make of the thing that was taken, except – and this I think has been the fallacy running through the arguments at the bar – when you are endeavouring to establish the specific

> loss of profit, or of something that you otherwise would have got which the law recognises as special damage. In that case you must shew it, and by precise evidence, so much so that in the old system of pleading you could not recover damages unless you had made a specific allegation in your pleading so [pg118] as to give the persons responsible for making good the loss an opportunity of inquiring into it before they came into court. But when we are speaking of general damages no such principle applies at all, and the jury might give whatever they thought would be the proper equivalent for the unlawful withdrawal of the subject-matter then in question. It seems to me that that broad principle comprehends within it many other things. There is no doubt in many cases a jury would say there really has been no damage at all: 'We will give the plaintiffs a trifling amount' – not nominal damages, be it observed, but a trifling amount; in other cases it would be more serious.

3 Contemptuous damages

In some cases, if the court finds that the wrong caused no loss and awards a nominal sum, the award functions as a rebuff for the plaintiff. This usually occurs in the context of defamation cases. Sometimes these awards are described as 'contemptuous damages'. A case of this nature is extracted below.

Grobbelaar v News Group Newspapers Ltd [2002] 1 WLR 3024

Facts and issues

The former Liverpool Football Club goalkeeper, Bruce Grobbelaar, sued *The Sun* (a newspaper in the stable of News Group Newspapers Ltd) for libel in relation to allegations that he had fixed matches for bribes. While the allegations were technically libellous because Grobbelaar's attempts to match-fix were ultimately unsuccessful, there was nonetheless taped evidence that he had agreed to fix matches.

Decision

At first instance, Grobbelaar was initially awarded £85 000. However, on appeal, the House of Lords slashed his award to £1 and ordered him to pay News Group Newspapers Ltd costs, estimated at £500 000.

Lord Bingham

> **[3036]** … The question then arises whether on that basis the jury's award of damages can be upheld. The jury will have had in mind the newspaper's banner headline on the front page of its first issue devoted to this topic and the similar headline on page 2, quoted in paragraph 5 above. The jury may well have held it against the newspaper that this allegation of match-fixing and attempted match-fixing was persisted in and never withdrawn despite the lack of extraneous evidence to support it. The ambush of the appellant at the airport may have been seen as oppressive, the weight of the newspaper's journalistic onslaught as excessive and the newspaper's attempt to involve the appellant's children as offensive ('How

much of what's been happening have you told the children about? Have they been getting a hard time at school as the result of the allegations against you?'). The jury's generosity towards the appellant is perhaps understandable. But it cannot be supported. The tort of defamation protects those whose reputations have been unlawfully injured. It affords little or no protection to those who have, or deserve to have, no reputation deserving of legal protection. Until 9 November 1994 when the newspaper published its first articles about him, the appellant's public reputation was unblemished. But he had in fact acted in a way in which no decent or honest footballer would act and in a way which could, if not exposed and stamped on, undermine the integrity of a game which earns the loyalty and support of millions. Even if the newspaper had published no more than what, on my interpretation of the jury's verdict, it was entitled to have published, the appellant would have been shown to have acted in a way which any right-thinking person would unequivocally condemn. It would be an affront to justice if a court of law were to award substantial damages to a man shown to have acted in such flagrant breach of his legal and moral obligations.

...

[3037] For the foregoing reasons, I would quash the Court of Appeal's decision and restore the first instance finding in favour of the appellant. I would however quash the jury's award of damages and substitute an award of £1 nominal damages. ...

REVIEW QUESTIONS

(1) Do you think courts should be able to force defendants to make apologies?

(2) What are the advantages and disadvantages of a declaration?

(3) Do you think there is still a place for nominal damages in the law, now that declarations are available for common law causes of action?

III Other vindicatory remedies under the *Australian Consumer Law*

Concept	Short explanation	Relevant authorities	Principles text
Other remedies	Section 246 of the ACL (excerpted below) sets out a range of non-punitive orders that may be sought by a regulator. The orders available in s 246 were discussed by Mortimer J in *Director of Consumer Affairs Victoria v Gibson (No 3)* [2017] FCA 1148. Quasi-punitive orders, such as adverse publishing orders pursuant to s 247 and orders disqualifying persons from managing corporations pursuant to s 248, are also available under the ACL, either where an action has been brought by an individual or by a regulator.	Section 246 of the ACL *Director of Consumer Affairs Victoria v Gibson (No 3)* [2017] FCA 1148	Chapter 15: [15.37]–[15.39]

Vindicatory remedies are remedies which seek to in some way recognise or vindicate the fact that the claimant's rights have been infringed. Of course, in that regard, all remedies could be regarded as vindicatory, but this particular section discusses non-traditional remedies such as ordering defendants to advertise their conduct in the newspaper, or requiring defendants to undertake community service.

Australian Consumer Law s 246

This provision allows a court with jurisdiction to make a range of orders to vindicate the rights of the claimant in relation to contraventions of certain chapters of the ACL, if the regulator seeks such an order.

246 Non-punitive orders

(1) A court may, on application of the regulator, make one or more of the orders mentioned in subsection (2) in relation to a person who has engaged in conduct that:

(a) contravenes a provision of Chapter 2, 3 or 4; or

(b) constitutes an involvement in a contravention of such a provision.

(2) The court may make the following orders in relation to the person who has engaged in the conduct:

(a) an order directing the person to perform a service that is specified in the order, and that relates to the conduct, for the benefit of the community or a section of the community;

(aa) an order requiring the person, at the person's expense, to engage:

(i) another person specified in the order; or

(ii) another person in a class of persons specified in the order;

to perform a service that is specified in the order and that relates to the conduct, for the benefit of the community or a section of the community;

(b) an order for the purpose of ensuring that the person does not engage in the conduct, similar conduct, or related conduct, during the period of the order (which must not be longer than 3 years) including:

(i) an order directing the person to establish a compliance program for employees or other persons involved in the person's business, being a program designed to ensure their awareness of the responsibilities and obligations in relation to such conduct; and

(ii) an order directing the person to establish an education and training program for employees or other persons involved in the person's business, being a program designed to ensure their awareness of the responsibilities and obligations in relation to such conduct; and

(iii) an order directing the person to revise the internal operations of the person's business which led to the person engaging in such conduct;

(c) an order requiring the person to disclose, in the way and to the persons specified in the order, such information as is so specified, being information that the person has possession of or access to;

(d) an order requiring the person to publish, at the person's expense and in the way specified in the order, an advertisement in the terms specified in, or determined in accordance with, the order.

Note: The following are examples of orders that the court may make under subsection (2)(a):

(a) an order requiring a person who has made false representations to make available a training video which explains advertising obligations under this Schedule;

(b) an order requiring a person who has engaged in misleading or deceptive conduct in relation to a product to carry out a community awareness program to address the needs of consumers when purchasing the product.

(2A) An order under subsection (2)(aa) is not enforceable against a person mentioned in subsections (2)(aa)(i) and (ii).

(3) This section does not limit a court's powers under any other provision of this Schedule.

The following case is an example where the regulator sought a vindicatory award under the ACL.

Director of Consumer Affairs Victoria v Gibson (No 3) [2017] FCA 1148

Facts and issues

Gibson, a social media 'influencer', made misleading and deceptive representations in a book and an app (both entitled *The Whole Pantry*). She claimed:

- her special diet had sent her cancer into remission and
- that she was going to donate substantial proportions of her profits to named charities.

In fact, she had never suffered from cancer, and she donated almost none of her substantial profits to the named charities. The Director of Consumer Affairs Victoria sought a publication order pursuant to s 246(d) of the ACL.

Decision

Mortimer J declined to make such an order because there had already been significant adverse publicity regarding the defendant's actions, and Gibson might be forced to commit contempt of court if she could not pay for the advertising. Moreover, the original proposed form of advertisement effectively compelled Gibson to apologise, but Mortimer J found that that would have been inappropriate. Finally, Mortimer J also observed that the Director could have sought for Gibson to perform a service for the benefit of the community pursuant to s 246(2)(a) of the ACL, but noted that such an order was not sought.

Mortimer J

The Director's proposed publication orders

[103] I do not propose to make the publication orders sought by the Director, nor any other kind of publication orders.

[104] As the evidence demonstrates, the cost of this advertising is significant. The cost ranges between approximately $2000 and $40 000, and although it exceeded the sums in the evidence, the Director sought an order for the cost of advertising in the sum of approximately $45 000. There is no evidence at all whether Ms Gibson has the capacity to pay such advertising costs. In orders of this nature there is no principle of general deterrence at work which might lead the Court to discount or ignore the capacity of a respondent to pay.

[105] Here the situation is quite different. If, in fact, Ms Gibson has no capacity to pay for this advertising, then making orders of this kind sets up an inevitable situation of non-compliance. That is inappropriate first because it has the tendency to characterise the Court's orders as ineffectual, and second because it may well expose Ms Gibson to prosecution for contempt, having in a way 'set her up' to contravene the Court's orders. In contrast, pecuniary penalties can be paid by arrangements (such as instalments) which can avoid non-compliance: see, for instance, Middleton J's orders in *Hocking Stuart (No 2)*.

[106] If I had otherwise considered that publication orders were appropriate, it may be that in balancing the question of Ms Gibson's capacity to pay, I may nevertheless have been persuaded it was appropriate to make such orders. However I do not consider the orders will serve the purposes the Director puts forward. There has already been considerable publicity about these proceedings. I consider the public are already well-informed, if they wish to be, about the consequences which have befallen Ms Gibson for engaging in the conduct she did. They will be additionally informed about how seriously the Court has viewed her conduct on publication of these reasons. Those members of the public who are interested will already know her claims were false and will no doubt have followed the exposure of their falsity and of her unconscionable conduct in the print and television media.

[107] The original proposed notice had considerable difficulties, which I raised with counsel during the penalties hearing. First, it compelled Ms Gibson to apologise through the text of the proposed notice. Ms Gibson has had ample opportunity throughout the conduct of this proceeding to apologise and she has chosen not to do so. She could also have arranged for any number of media appearances, during the course of this proceeding, for the purpose of apologising and acknowledging responsibility for her conduct, but she has chosen not to. In a different context, I reviewed the law about compelling a person to apologise: see *Wotton v State of Queensland (No 5)* [2016] FCA 1457 at [1553]–[1584]. Generally, courts see it as inappropriate to compel a person to apologise where they are not prepared to do so voluntarily. Based on my view of the evidence, and her non-participation, I would have concerns about the sincerity of any apology issued by Ms Gibson after these proceedings and because of a court order, and that is another reason no apology should be ordered.

[108] The original proposed notice also sought to compel Ms Gibson to make statements about the inefficacy of the treatments she asserted she underwent for her (supposed) cancer. As I pointed out to counsel for the Director, the Court was not asked to make any findings about the efficacy or otherwise of the treatments publicised by Ms Gibson, including her so-called dietary advice. The proposition that the pursuit of such remedies is hopeless, and that diet and the other 'lifestyle' changes advocated by Ms Gibson have no effect on a person in fact suffering from cancer was no part of the Director's case in this proceeding. It is inappropriate for this subject matter to be dealt with at all in any public notice arising from these proceedings.

[109] In contrast, the amended proposed public notice does no more than describe the proceeding and set out the findings the Court has made. All of that material is available to those members of the public who wish to access it, both through the Court's website, no doubt through the Director's website in due course, and through public legal websites such as AustLII. I am satisfied these matters will also be well-reported when the Court's penalty orders and reasons are published, as were the Court's orders and reasons on liability. No extra or necessary information or words of caution are sounded through the publication of the proposed notice.

[110] Finally, almost all of Ms Gibson's contravening conduct occurred through social media. Those members of the public whom she reached with her representations were those who had access to social media and to technology available on mobile devices. Those persons who might be tempted to engage in similar conduct are also therefore likely to be regular users of social media. I am far from persuaded that those sections of the public will necessarily be any better informed about Ms Gibson's conduct and the Court's views of it by notices published in the print versions of the *Herald Sun* and *The Australian*.

[111] For all of those reasons, I decline to make the publication orders sought by the Director.

...

Some additional observations

[113] There were other non-punitive orders the Director could have sought. As I have already noted, the Director himself could have chosen to publicise the findings on liability and penalty through a court-approved notice, and that would have removed at least some of the concerns identified.

[114] More critically, the Court had available to it the powers in s 246(2)(a): namely, a power to direct a person to 'perform a service that is specified in the order, and that relates to the conduct, for the benefit of the community or a section of the community'.

[115] The Court could have been asked to direct Ms Gibson, for example, to perform a service at one or more of the charitable organisations to which she had promised she and her company would give money. The Court could have been asked to direct her to perform a service at one or more institutions caring for people who really do have cancer. Those would have been orders with tangible features of both specific and general deterrence. Pecuniary penalties may not operate as any real deterrent if people (whether those to whom the orders are directed or those who are the objects of general deterrence) have no capacity to pay, or are willing to do whatever they can to avoid paying, including becoming bankrupt. However, directing a person to give up her or his time, and to perform a service to the community, is an order that can be enforced more readily against any person, irrespective of financial capacity. And, in a case such as this, it is more likely to have brought home to Ms Gibson the impact of her conduct, and its offensiveness to members of the Australian community who really are struggling with cancer and its effects, whether on themselves, their families or their friends. Most Australians are, in one way or another, touched by cancer as a terrible illness.

[116] Perhaps there were good reasons no such orders were sought. It is not possible to know.

[117] The last matter is by way of observation. As I noted at the start of these reasons, by s 134(2)(a) of the *Australian Consumer Law and Fair Trading Act 2012* (Vic), any pecuniary penalty ordered by a court under s 224 of the ACL (Vic) is to be paid into the Victorian Consumer Law Fund. If Ms Gibson were to actually pay the pecuniary penalties imposed (whether by instalments or otherwise), in the Court's respectful opinion, and in the particular circumstances of these contraventions, it may be appropriate for consideration to be given to whether there is a mechanism by which the funds can be donated to some or all of the organisations, and people, which Ms Gibson had promised would receive donations. In that way, some good might still come for the vulnerable people, and the organisations supporting them, which were indirectly drawn into this unconscionable sequence of events.

Review Questions

(1) Do you think it is appropriate for courts to order defendants to, for example, perform civil service obligations or put advertisements in the newspaper? What are the benefits and detriments of such an action?

(2) Do you agree with Mortimer J that it would have been appropriate to order Gibson to perform community service in *Director of Consumer Affairs Victoria v Gibson (No 3)* [2017] FCA 1148?

PART 5

ACCOUNT OF PROFITS AND OTHER GAIN-BASED RELIEF FOR WRONGS

16 DISGORGEMENT OF GAINS AND 'REASONABLE FEE' DAMAGES

I	Introduction	532
II	The distinction between compensation, restitution and disgorgement and the nature of gain-based remedies	533
III	Disgorgement	534
	A Equity and the account of profits	534
	B Election	540
	C Intellectual property and the account of profits	544
	D Torts and 'waiver of tort'	545
	E Breach of contract	549
	F The *Australian Consumer Law*	556
IV	'Reasonable fee' damages	558
	A Introduction and history	559
	B Academic and judicial accounts	559
	C General patterns	561
	D Equity	562
	E Intellectual property	562
	F Tort	563
	G Contract	570
V	Allowances, discretionary factors and bars to relief	581
	A Allowances for skill and effort	581
	B Discretionary factors and bars to relief	584
VI	The future of gain-based relief in Australia	584

I Introduction

This chapter deals with accounts of profits and other forms of gain-based relief. The rationales for accounts of profit have been said to be deterrence and prophylaxis.

The placement of reasonable fee awards in this chapter may be regarded as controversial. 'Reasonable fee' refers to a court-ordered monetary award reflecting what the plaintiff would have asked for to permit the defendant's wrongdoing. They are generally awarded for intellectual property breaches, proprietary torts and breaches of negative covenants. The rationale for these awards is unclear, but Barnett and Harder have argued such awards are gain-based in the principles text at [16.4], so we place them in this chapter.

II The distinction between compensation, restitution and disgorgement and the nature of gain-based remedies

When a defendant commits a wrong, several different factual consequences may occur. Three are set out in Figure 16.1.

Figure 16.1 Compensation, restitution and disgorgement

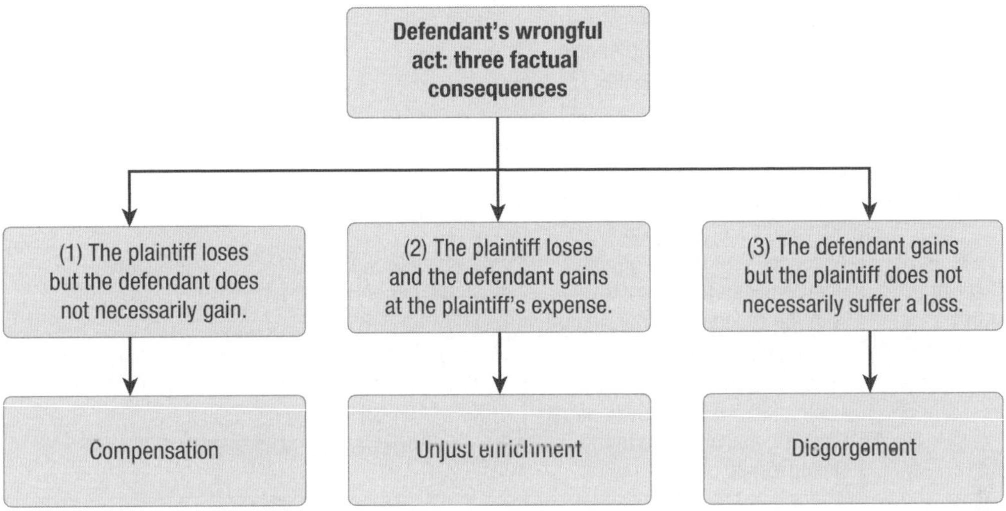

Both possibility (2) and possibility (3) in Figure 16.1 involve gain caused by the defendant's wrong. For this reason, they have often been grouped together as 'restitution'. However, they are importantly different: there is no need for a plaintiff to suffer a loss in order to claim disgorgement. By contrast, for restitution for unjust enrichment, the defendant is generally 'giving back' enrichment (either the value of the enrichment via a personal remedy or the thing itself via a proprietary remedy). This chapter will deal primarily with disgorgement, while personal remedies for unjust enrichment will be dealt with in Chapter 17.

REVIEW QUESTIONS

(1) How would you explain the difference between compensation, restitution for unjust enrichment and disgorgement?

(2) Why do you think it matters whether something is categorised as compensation, restitution for unjust enrichment or disgorgement?

III Disgorgement

Concept	Short explanation	Relevant authorities	Principles text
Equity and the account of profits	The account of profits is available for equitable causes of action including breach of trust, breach of trust and breach of confidence. It is also available in equity's auxiliary jurisdiction for intellectual property breaches.	*Warman International Ltd v Dwyer* (1995) 182 CLR 544	Chapter 16: [16.16]–[16.27]
Election	If there is both profit and loss arising from the same breach the plaintiff must elect between remedies. They must have sufficient information to enable them to make a fair choice.	*Personal Representatives of Tang Man Sit v Capacious Investments Ltd* [1996] AC 514 (Privy Council)	Chapter 16: [16.28]–[16.30]
Intellectual property and the account of profits	Accounts of profits are available for intellectual property breaches, originally through equity's auxiliary jurisdiction, but now primarily by statute.	*Copyright Act 1968* (Cth) s 115(2)	Chapter 16: [16.31]–[16.35]
Torts and 'waiver of tort'	Accounts of profit are generally unavailable in tort in Australia, with the exception of passing off.	*Hospitality Group Pty Ltd v Australian Rugby Union Ltd* (2001) 110 FCR 157	Chapter 16: [16.36]–[16.47]
Breach of contract	Accounts of profit are unavailable for breach of contract in Australia. By contrast, they are now available in the United Kingdom.	*Hospitality Group Pty Ltd v Australian Rugby Union Ltd* (2001) 110 FCR 157 *Attorney-General v Blake* [2001] 1 AC 268	Chapter 16: [16.48]–[16.59]
The *Australian Consumer Law* ('ACL')	Accounts of profit are not listed as an available remedy under the ACL. However, courts have occasionally used the pecuniary penalty provisions to strip profit.*	The case cited in footnotes illustrates the use of pecuniary penalty provisions.	Chapter 16: [16.60]–[16.61]

* *Director of Consumer Affairs Victoria v Gibson (No 3)* [2017] FCA 1148, [95] (Mortimer J).

A Equity and the account of profits

The equitable account of profits is the dominant remedy effecting disgorgement. Because it is equitable, it is awarded primarily in cases of equitable wrongdoing: breach of trust, breach of fiduciary duty and breach of confidence. It is also available for intellectual property breaches and for the tort of passing off.

There are two stages to an account of profits. The first stage simply provides an account of the defendant's financial affairs to the plaintiff, insofar as they relate to their claims. In the second stage the identified profit can be stripped. Importantly, the profits are the defendant's *net* profits, not gross receipts.

Courts have traditionally made allowances for skill and effort. This may be a general allowances or specific allowances reflecting labour and expenditures of money by the defendant. For equitable causes of action, the profit need only be made 'as a result of' the defendant's breach.

Figure 16.2 Accounts of profit for equitable causes of action

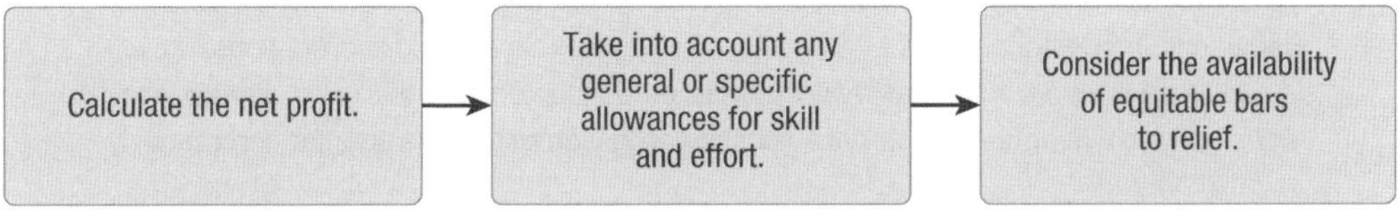

Warman International Ltd v Dwyer (1995) 182 CLR 544

Facts and issues

Warman International Ltd ('Warman') was the Australian distributor for an Italian gearbox manufacturer, Bonfiglioli. Bonfiglioli invited Warman to enter into a joint venture assembling the gearboxes, but Warman declined. Dwyer, the manager of Warman's Queensland branch, told Bonfiglioli that he was considering setting up his own business. He incorporated two companies, BTA Pty Ltd ('BTA') and ETA Pty Ltd ('ETA'), and arranged for Warman's Queensland staff to move to BTA. Dwyer left Warman's employment, and Bonfiglioli terminated its distributorship agreement with Warman. Bonfiglioli then entered into a joint venture with BTA. Warman and his wife owned 50 per cent of the shares in BTA and Bonfiglioli owned the other 50 per cent. BTA assembled Bonfiglioli's products in Australia, and ETA distributed them. Dwyer breached his fiduciary obligations as an employee of Warman by conflicting and profiting. BTA made much more profit than Warman lost as a result of the breach.

Decision

The trial judge awarded Warman an account of profits representing BTA's and ETA's net profits for four years, reduced by an allowance of 50 per cent.

On appeal, the Court of Appeal of Queensland held that a profit-based award was too generous, and awarded Warman equitable compensation for its losses.

The High Court overturned the Court of Appeal's decision. Warman was entitled to an account of profits for Dwyer's breach of fiduciary duty. However, it should encompass only two years' net profit, reduced by an allowance for skill and effort.

Mason CJ, Brennan, Deane, Dawson and Gaudron JJ

> **[556] The consequences of a breach of a fiduciary obligation**
>
> There is no doubt that, before leaving the employment of Warman, Dwyer had made at least a preliminary agreement to set up a joint venture with Bonfiglioli, thus supplanting

Warman. Instead of attempting to enhance the relationship between Bonfiglioli and his employer, Dwyer actively sought to reduce Bonfiglioli's confidence in Warman. So much is plain from the correspondence and from the fact that Dwyer caused BTA and ETA to be incorporated months before he resigned in 1988. It is also plain that Dwyer made arrangements with the other staff of Warman's Queensland branch to the effect that they would leave Warman and become the staff of the new distributing agent if and when his plans came to fruition. Hence, this is a clear case of a fiduciary breaching his obligations.

In *Nocton v Lord Ashburton* Viscount Haldane LC described the three primary remedies consequent upon a breach of a fiduciary obligation between a solicitor and client:

> Courts of Equity had jurisdiction to direct accounts to be taken, and in proper cases to order the solicitor to replace property improperly acquired from the client, or to make compensation if he had lost it by acting in breach of a duty which arose out of his confidential relationship to the man who had trusted him.

Although the Lord Chancellor was addressing the fiduciary relationship which arises between a solicitor and client, his words are of general application. In the present appeal, all three of those remedies are relevant, but, as has been indicated, the primary focus is the remedy of account.

...

[**557**] It has been suggested that the liability of the fiduciary to account for a profit made in breach of the fiduciary duty should be determined by reference to the concept of unjust enrichment, namely, whether the profit is made at the expense of the person to whom the fiduciary duty is owed, and to the honesty and bona fides of the fiduciary. But the authorities in Australia and England deny that the liability of a fiduciary to account depends upon detriment to the plaintiff or the dishonesty and lack of bona fides of the fiduciary. Gibbs J in *Consul Development Pty Ltd v DPC Estates Pty Ltd* stated:

> Where the rule applies, the liability of the person in a fiduciary position does not depend on the fact that the person to whom the duty is owed has suffered injury or loss.

A fiduciary must account for a profit or benefit if it was obtained either (1) when there was a conflict or possible conflict between his fiduciary duty and his personal interest, or (2) by reason of his fiduciary position or by reason of his taking advantage of opportunity or knowledge derived from his fiduciary position. The stringent rule that the fiduciary cannot profit from his trust is said to have two purposes: (1) that the fiduciary must account for what has been acquired at the expense of the trust, and (2) to ensure that fiduciaries generally conduct themselves 'at a level higher than that trodden by the crowd'. The objectives which the rule seeks to achieve are to preclude the fiduciary from being [**558**] swayed by considerations of personal interest and from accordingly misusing the fiduciary position for personal advantage.

Thus, it is no defence that the plaintiff was unwilling, unlikely or unable to make the profits for which an account is taken or that the fiduciary acted honestly and reasonably. So, in *Regal (Hastings) Ltd v Gulliver*, although the directors acted in good faith and in the interests of the company of which they were directors in taking up shares in a subsidiary which the company could not afford to take up, they were held accountable for the profit made on the sale of the shares. And, in *Phipps v Boardman*, the solicitor was held accountable for the profit he made, notwithstanding that he acted bona fide and in the interests of the trust and that the opportunity would not have been availed of but for his skill and knowledge.

The assessment of the profit will often be extremely difficult in practice; accordingly it has been said that '[w]hat will be required on the inquiry … will not be mathematical exactness but only a reasonable approximation'. What is necessary however is to determine as accurately as possible the true measure of the profit or benefit obtained by the fiduciary in breach of his duty.

…

[559] …

Although an account of profits, like other equitable remedies, is said to be discretionary, it is granted or withheld according to settled principles. It will be defeated by equitable defences such as estoppel, laches, acquiescence and delay …

[560] … [T]he basic principle remains that a principal who so elects is entitled to an account of profits, subject to considerations of the kind already mentioned. In the present case, not only was Dwyer actively dishonest, but also Warman commenced proceedings in the Supreme Court of Queensland in October 1988, shortly after Dwyer's departure, so that Dwyer had an opportunity to consider his position and take appropriate action such as the proper purchase of the goodwill of the agency business from Warman. And when the fiduciary is actively dishonest and obtains an identifiable profit from that dishonesty, it is more difficult still to conceive of circumstances in which no account at all should be ordered. …

…

[561] … In the case of a business it may well be inappropriate and inequitable to compel the errant fiduciary to account for the whole of the profit of his conduct of the business or his exploitation of the principal's goodwill over an indefinite period of time. In such a case, it may be appropriate to allow the fiduciary a proportion of the profits, depending upon the particular circumstances. That may well be the case when it appears that a significant proportion of an increase in profits has been generated by the skill, efforts, property and resources of the fiduciary, the capital which he has introduced and the risks he has taken, so long as they are not risks to which the principal's property has been exposed. Then it may be said that the relevant proportion of the increased profits is not the product or consequence of the plaintiff's property but the product of the fiduciary's skill, efforts, property and resources. This is not to say that the liability of a fiduciary to account should be governed by the doctrine of unjust enrichment, though that doctrine may well have a useful part to play; it is simply to say that the stringent rule requiring a fiduciary to account for profits can be carried to extremes and that in cases outside the realm of specific assets, the liability of the fiduciary should not be transformed into a vehicle for the unjust enrichment of the plaintiff.

It is for the defendant to establish that it is inequitable to order an account of the entire profits. If the defendant does not establish that **[562]** that would be so, then the defendant must bear the consequences of mingling the profits attributable to the defendant's breach of fiduciary duty and the profits attributable to those earned by the defendant's efforts and investment, in the same way that a trustee of a mixed fund bears the onus of distinguishing what is his own.

Whether it is appropriate to allow an errant fiduciary a proportion of profits or to make an allowance in respect of skill, expertise and other expenses is a matter of judgment which will depend on the facts of the given case. However, as a general rule, in conformity with the principle that a fiduciary must not profit from a breach of fiduciary duty, a court will not apportion profits in the absence of an antecedent arrangement for profit-sharing but will make allowance for skill, expertise and other expenses.

...

The Court of Appeal's refusal to order an account of profits

...

... As already explained, it is firmly established that the liability of a fiduciary to account for a profit or gain made in breach of fiduciary duty does not depend upon the person to whom that obligation is owed suffering a loss or injury; and it is ordinarily immaterial to the fiduciary's liability to account that the person to whom the fiduciary obligation is owed could not have earned the profit or gain. The [**563**] courts have always insisted on compliance by fiduciaries with strict and rigorous standards with a view to ensuring that they do not expose themselves to a conflict of interest and duty. The point is that a fiduciary is not entitled to make a profit out of, or by reason of, a fiduciary position without the knowledge and assent of the person to whom the fiduciary duty is owed. It follows that, if a profit has been made in breach of fiduciary duty, the person to whom the duty is owed is entitled to an account subject to the considerations discussed above and to the making of any appropriate allowance.

...

[565] The basis for an account of profits

In determining the proper basis for an account of profits, it is of first importance in this, as in other cases, to ascertain precisely what it was that was acquired in consequence of the fiduciary's breach of duty. And, in some situations, it may also be relevant to ascertain what was lost by the plaintiff. The starting point in the present case is that Warman's Bonfiglioli agency business rested on the contract by which Bonfiglioli appointed Warman its exclusive Australian distributor of gearboxes and other components. The contract was terminable by Bonfiglioli on three months' notice to Warman. The local goodwill associated with the Bonfiglioli products distributed by Warman – the local product goodwill – was the property of Bonfiglioli just as the local product goodwill in Australia in *Hospital Products* was that of the United States principal. That, of course, is not to deny the existence in Warman of a goodwill associated with its distribution of Bonfiglioli products. It does not appear that any distinction was drawn at trial between the goodwill of Bonfiglioli and that of Warman or that any attempt was made to identify and value each of them.

But, in light of the fact that the contract was terminable on three months' notice and that Bonfiglioli was dissatisfied with the Australian arrangements and wished to engage in local assembly, it is reasonable to conclude that, in all likelihood, the Warman distributorship would not have endured for much longer in any event. That seems to have been the view of the trial judge from the findings he made. No doubt Dwyer's disloyal machinations played a part in Bonfiglioli's disenchantment with Warman. At the same time, it seems fairly clear that the relationship between Warman and Bonfiglioli was not mutually enthusiastic and that the association was destined to end.

Precisely when it would have ended were it not for Dwyer' s breach of fiduciary obligation is unclear. Earlier in these reasons we set out the findings of the trial judge as they bear on that issue. It seems to us that his Honour, when his findings are properly understood, valued the Bonfiglioli distributorship business in the [**566**] hands of Warman by reference to one year's profits on the basis that, taking account of the various contingencies including the remote possibility that the agency might have continued indefinitely, the distributorship, in all likelihood, would have remained on foot for a further year but no more. That view about what would have happened in the absence of Dwyer's breach of fiduciary obligation was certainly open to his Honour. It should be accepted as correct.

That means that the immediate detriment sustained by Warman by reason of Dwyer's breach of fiduciary obligation, was the loss of an agency (ie, the Bonfiglioli agency) which, on the probabilities, would otherwise have survived for, but only for, a further year. The advantage gained by BTA (and, indirectly, by Dwyer as a shareholder in BTA) from Dwyer's breach of fiduciary duty was not, however, confined to profits or other financial benefits directly attributable to the carrying on of the Bonfiglioli agency during the year following the termination of Warman's distribution agreement. Dwyer's breach of fiduciary duty included, to the knowledge of BTA, the persuasion of employees of Warman to leave Warman and join BTA It was on the basis of the acquisition of the Bonfiglioli agency that the entitlement to assemble the Bonfiglioli products locally was acquired and exploited by BTA In so far as ETA is concerned, the associated distributorship business of that company was likewise established upon the basis of BTA's acquisition of the Bonfiglioli agency. If all of the issued shares in BTA were owned by Dwyer, it might be difficult to reach any conclusion other than that the whole of BTA's assembly and distributorship business had been built upon Dwyer's breach of fiduciary duty. On balance, however, it seems to us that the fact that BTA was half owned by the Bonfiglioli interests precludes that conclusion in the circumstances of this case. As has been mentioned, the local goodwill associated with the Bonfiglioli products had always remained the property of Bonfiglioli. Warman was entitled to exploit that local goodwill only during the period of its distributorship. Warman's agency had not extended at all to the local assembly of the Bonfiglioli products. Realistically, the main basis of BTA's business was what Bonfiglioli had always retained and been entitled to exploit, namely, the local goodwill of the Bonfiglioli products after the termination of Warman's agency and the right to assemble those products locally.

Nonetheless, the fact remains that BTA knowingly benefited from Dwyer's breach of fiduciary duty in the manner and to the extent which has been indicated above. In these circumstances, the appropriate approach is to see BTA's business as built, to the extent of that benefit, upon Dwyer's breach of fiduciary duty but [**567**] otherwise upon Bonfiglioli's ownership of local goodwill and local assembly rights. Similarly, ETA's business, being complementary to BTA's business, can properly be seen as indirectly and correspondingly based upon those foundations.

Once that is accepted, as in our opinion it must be, it seems to us that the appropriate order for an account is an order which is restricted to requiring an account of the profits of BTA's and ETA's business for a limited initial period. The critical question is what is the appropriate duration of that limited initial period. The starting point must be the finding that, were it not for Dwyer's breach of fiduciary duty, Warman's Bonfiglioli distributorship would probably have continued for, but only for, a further period of one year. Clearly, any order against BTA for an account of profits must encompass an account on an appropriate basis for any profits earned by it from the exploitation of the Bonfiglioli agency during that period. Such an order must, however, take account of other advantages knowingly gained by BTA by reason of Dwyer's breach of fiduciary obligation. As has been said, the entitlement to assemble the Bonfiglioli products locally was based upon the Bonfiglioli agency. More important, the acquisition of the services of former Warman employees through Dwyer's breach of fiduciary obligation enabled BTA effectively to take over the limited goodwill of Warman's agency business (as distinct from the local goodwill of the Bonfiglioli products) and to derive benefits from the experience, contacts and know-how of those employees. Those benefits would, at least to some extent, have endured beyond the initial one year period.

As has been indicated, the basis upon which an account of profits should be taken is often extremely difficult to determine in practice. It is so in the present case. Indeed, what is required in the present case is essentially what Lord Wilberforce described as a 'judicial estimation of the available indications'. However, even after making full allowance for the limits of judicial discretion, it appears to us that the learned trial judge's order requiring accounts of four years' profits plus payment of a purchase price for goodwill at the end of that period went beyond what is fair and equitable in the circumstances. It seems to us that, in all the circumstances and in the context of what is said in the following two paragraphs, the adequate and appropriate period in respect of which an account of BTA's profits should be ordered is a total period of two years. An [**568**] account of profits in respect of that period would, in our view, clearly cover the whole of the benefits acquired by BTA through Dwyer's breach of fiduciary duty. It follows from what has been said above that the period of two years is also the appropriate period in respect of which an account of profits should be ordered against ETA.

B Election

As in *Warman International Ltd v Dwyer*[1] (discussed on page 535), sometimes both loss and profit may flow from the breach, but the amounts may differ. The plaintiff must then elect to take the remedy they prefer, and the election is generally binding. In *Warman International Ltd v Dwyer* itself, the plaintiff was given seven days to elect. However, the plaintiff must have sufficient information to enable them to make a fair choice.

Personal Representatives of Tang Man Sit v Capacious Investments Ltd [1996] AC 514 (Privy Council)

Facts and issues

Tang and Kung (through his company Capacious Investments Ltd) entered into a joint venture to construct 22 new houses in Hong Kong. It was agreed that when the houses were completed, Tang would assign 16 houses to Capacious. Kung died, and Tang did not assign the houses. Instead he rented them to elderly people, cramming up to 17 people in houses meant for two or

1 (1995) 182 CLR 544.

three people. Eventually, Capacious became aware and sued Tang's executor (Tang had died). Capacious obtained an account of profits (HK$1.8 million, representing a proportion of the rent received from the houses). However, it became evident that the loss to Capacious was greater than the profit, and was of two kinds:

(1) Head A (the price at which the houses could have been rented) was HK$7.9 million and
(2) Head B (the loss caused to the value of the houses by the wrongful use and occupation) was HK$11 million.

Capacious had obtained summary judgment saying that they were entitled to both profit and loss. Could they get both? And, if not, had Capacious irrevocably elected to receive an account of profits?

Decision

The Privy Council held that Capacious could not make a true choice without all the relevant information. Equitable compensation for the losses under Head A and the account of profits were mutually inconsistent and Capacious would have to elect between the two. However, equitable losses under Head B were available because they did not flow from the same breach (ie loss of use of houses).

Lord Nicholls (for the Privy Council)

> … [T]heir Lordships accept the defendant's submission that there is an inconsistency between an account of profits, whereby for better or worse a plaintiff takes the money the defendant received from the use he made of the property, and an award of damages, representing the financial return the plaintiff would have received for the same period had he been able to use the property. These remedies are alternative, not cumulative. A plaintiff may have one or other, but not both.
>
> …
>
> **Two remedies**
>
> Their Lordships will consider first whether the plaintiff did choose to take the remedy of an account of profits, with the consequence that it [**521**] could no longer pursue a claim for damages so far as this would be inconsistent with an account of profits. This issue lies at the heart of this case. This issue calls for consideration of the principles governing election between remedies.
>
> The law frequently affords an injured person more than one remedy for the wrong he has suffered. Sometimes the two remedies are alternative and inconsistent. The classic example, indeed, is (1) an account of the profits made by a defendant in breach of his fiduciary obligations and (2) damages for the loss suffered by the plaintiff by reason of the same breach. The former is measured by the wrongdoer's gain, the latter by the injured party's loss.
>
> Sometimes the two remedies are cumulative. Cumulative remedies may lie against one person. A person fraudulently induced to enter into a contract may have the contract set aside and also sue for damages. Or there may be cumulative remedies against more than one person. A plaintiff may have a cause of action in negligence against two persons in respect of the same loss.

Alternative remedies

Faced with alternative and inconsistent remedies a plaintiff must choose, or elect, between them. He cannot have both. The basic principle governing when a plaintiff must make his choice is simple and clear. He is required to choose when, but not before, judgment is given in his favour and the judge is asked to make orders against the defendant. A plaintiff is not required to make his choice when he launches his proceedings. He may claim one remedy initially, and then by amendment of his writ and his pleadings abandon that claim in favour of the other. He may claim both remedies, as alternatives. But he must make up his mind when judgment is being entered against the defendant. Court orders are intended to be obeyed. In the nature of things, therefore, the court should not make orders which would afford a plaintiff both of two alternative remedies.

In the ordinary course, by the time the trial is concluded a plaintiff will know which remedy is more advantageous to him. By then, if not before, he will know enough of the facts to assess where his best interests lie. There will be nothing unfair in requiring him to elect at that stage. Occasionally this may not be so. This is more likely to happen when the judgment is a default judgment or a summary judgment than at the conclusion of a trial. A plaintiff may not know how much money the defendant has made from the wrongful use of his property. It may be unreasonable to require the plaintiff to make his choice without further information. To meet this difficulty, the court may make discovery and other orders designed to give the plaintiff the information he needs, and which in fairness he ought to have, before deciding upon his remedy. … The court will take care to ensure that such an order is not oppressive to a defendant.

In the ordinary course the decision made when judgment is entered is made once and for all. That is the normal rule. The order is a final order, [**522**] and the interests of the parties and the public interest alike dictate that there should be finality. The principle, however, is not rigid and unbending. Like all procedural principles, the established principles regarding election between alternative remedies are not fixed and unyielding rules. These principles are the means to an end, not the end in themselves. They are no more than practical applications of a general and overriding principle governing the conduct of legal proceedings, namely, that proceedings should be conducted in a manner which strikes a fair and reasonable balance between the interests of the parties, having proper regard also to the wider public interest in the conduct of court proceedings. …

Cumulative remedies

The procedural principles applicable to cumulative remedies are necessarily different. Faced with alternative and inconsistent remedies a plaintiff must choose between them. Faced with cumulative remedies a plaintiff is not required to choose. He may have both remedies. He may pursue one remedy or the other remedy or both remedies, just as he wishes. It is a matter for him. He may obtain judgment for both remedies and enforce both judgments. When the remedies are against two different people, he may sue both persons. He may do so concurrently, and obtain judgment against both. Damages to the full value of goods which have been converted may be awarded against two persons for successive conversions of the same goods. Or the plaintiff may sue the two persons successively. He may obtain judgment against one, and take steps to enforce the judgment. This does not preclude him from then suing the other. There are limitations to this freedom. ... In the interests of fairness and finality a plaintiff is required to bring forward his whole case against a defendant in one action. Another limitation is that the court has power to ensure that, when fairness so requires, claims against more than one person shall all be tried and decided together. A third limitation is that a plaintiff cannot recover in the aggregate from one or more defendants an amount in excess of his loss. Part satisfaction of a judgment against one person does not operate as a bar to the plaintiff thereafter bringing an action against another who is also liable, but it does operate to reduce the amount recoverable in the second action. However, once a plaintiff has fully recouped his loss, of necessity he cannot thereafter pursue any other remedy he might have and which he might have pursued earlier. Having recouped the whole of his loss, any further proceedings would lack a subject matter. This principle of full satisfaction prevents double recovery.

...

[525] The present case

Their Lordships turn to apply these principles in the present case. As already noted, to some extent at least the remedies claimed by the plaintiff included two alternative and inconsistent remedies. An account of the profits Mr Tang had made from the lettings is an alternative remedy to damages for the loss of use of the houses. However, and this is the unusual feature of the present case, matters went awry at the time of summary judgment on 25 August 1992. The plaintiff should have been required, so far as the two remedies were inconsistent, to choose which it would take. If it chose an account of profits, it could have damages only so far as, on the facts of this case, an award of damages was not inconsistent. In the event, the plaintiff was not required to elect. Instead the order gave the plaintiff both remedies. The judge ordered the defendant to account for the estate's profits and also to pay damages. The latter order was expressed in unqualified terms. The judge can hardly be blamed for this. The point was overlooked by everybody. No discussion seems to have taken place on the form of the order.

What happened thereafter was that the plaintiff proceeded to enforce both remedies ordered by the judge. The defendant produced an account showing receipts in excess of $1.8 million. The plaintiff proceeded to enforce payment by obtaining a charging order. The plaintiff also proceeded with the necessary preparatory steps for an assessment of damages. There is thus no question of the plaintiff having chosen to take an account of profits rather than payment of damages. Nor is there any question of the defendant having paid $1 807 774 in the mistaken belief that the plaintiff had done so.

Subsequently the plaintiff's choice was made abundantly clear. As appeared from the amended particulars of damage served in July 1993, the plaintiff was seeking damages and giving credit for the amounts received in respect of the secret profits. The company sought, and obtained, an assessment of damages on that footing.

In these unusual circumstances it would make no sense to treat receipt of the amount of $1 807 774 as an election by the plaintiff for an account of profits and against damages. To treat receipt of this payment as an election would lack a rational basis, given the terms of the judge's order, and given the continuing steps to proceed with the assessment of damages. It would also be extremely unfair to the plaintiff. It would mean that by accepting payment of one sum due under the court order of 25 August 1992, the plaintiff had unknowingly and inadvertently disabled itself from enforcing payment of a much larger amount due under the same order. That would be unfair, because there is no reason to doubt that, in so far as the two remedies are inconsistent in the present case, the plaintiff, armed first with any further information it required, would have chosen damages had it been required to elect at the time judgment was entered.

The conclusion would be otherwise if in the light of all the circumstances it would be inequitable to permit the plaintiff, after receiving [**526**] the secret profits payment, to proceed with the damages claim even though it gave credit for the amount received. There is no such inequity in this case. The defendant did not make the payment under any misapprehension about the plaintiff's intentions. The belatedness of the plaintiff's choice did not prejudice the defendant.

C Intellectual property and the account of profits

The availability of the account of profits in intellectual property law is largely ruled by legislation.[2] The legislation does not prescribe detailed rules on how the account should be taken, and courts refer to equitable principles to ascertain profits. A sample of such legislation is reproduced below.

Accounts of profits may also be awarded for equitable breaches of confidence,[3] and for the tort of passing off.[4]

Copyright Act 1968 (Cth) s 115(2)

The *Copyright Act 1968* (Cth) is the federal legislation governing copyright law.

115 Actions for infringement

...

(2) Subject to this Act, the relief that a court may grant in an action for an infringement of copyright includes an injunction (subject to such terms, if any, as the court thinks fit) and either damages or an account of profits.

...

In *Colbeam Palmer Ltd v Stock Affiliates Pty Ltd*[5] ('*Colbeam*'), Windeyer J explained how the account of profits works in the context of trademark infringement legislation. In that case, both the plaintiff and the defendant sold painting sets in Australia under the name

2 *Patents Act 1990* (Cth) s 122(1); *Copyright Act 1968* (Cth) s 115(2); *Designs Act 2003* (Cth) s 75(1)(b); *Trade Marks Act 1995* (Cth) s 126(1)(b); *Circuit Layouts Act 1989* (Cth) s 27(2); *Plant Breeder's Rights Act 1994* (Cth) s 56(3).

3 *A-G v Observer Ltd* [1990] 1 AC 109, 262, 266, 286; *Peter Pan Manufacturing Corporation v Corsets Silhouette Ltd* [1964] 1 WLR 96.

4 *My Kinda Town Ltd v Soll* [1983] RPC 15.

5 (1968) 122 CLR 25.

'Craft Master' (one from a US-based company and the other from a UK-based company). He outlined three essential points:

(1) An account of profits is generally ancillary to an injunction. In other words, the plaintiff is generally only entitled to an account if it can be shown that the plaintiff is also entitled to an injunction, although, as the facts of *Colbeam* show, this is not an absolute requirement in trademark litigation. In that case it was enough to show that an injunction *could* have been granted at the commencement of proceedings.[6]

(2) Generally, the plaintiff can only claim profits from the period that the defendant *knowingly* infringed the plaintiff's trademark. This reflects the pre-statutory origin of the account of profits in the auxiliary jurisdiction of equity.[7] This is known as the 'innocent infringement defence'. Note that care must be taken with this defence because it operates differently in statutory contexts in the intellectual property area.

(3) The general equitable discretionary factors operate to some degree. In *Colbeam*, Windeyer J said that he thought delay and acquiescence could operate in the context of considering when the defendant became aware of the infringement.[8]

Windeyer J refused to award all net profits arising from the sale of the US painting sets, and also refused to make an order for delivery of the painting sets.

D Torts and 'waiver of tort'

In some old English cases, plaintiffs used the action for money had and received to effectively strip defendants of the profits made from proprietary torts, often where the defendant sold the plaintiff's property without authority.[9] However, as noted in the principles text, there is no support for an account of profit for tort in Australia as the majority judges in the case below explain.

Hospitality Group Pty Ltd v Australian Rugby Union Ltd (2001) 110 FCR 157

Facts and issues

As a term of admission tickets to rugby matches Australian Rugby Union ('ARU') provided that they were not to be sold at a premium without ARU's written consent. A travel agent, Australian Tours for Sport Pty Ltd ('ATFS'), was a retail licensee of the tickets. The contract between ARU and ATFS stated that ATFS was only to sell the tickets as part of a travel package and could not sell them wholesale. In breach of this agreement, ATFS on-sold the tickets and travel packages to Hospitality Group Pty Ltd ('HG') and ICM (Marketing) Pty Ltd ('ICM'). HG and ICM sold the tickets

6 Ibid 31.

7 Ibid 43.

8 Ibid 33.

9 *Oughton v Seppings* (1830) 1 B & Ad 241, 109 ER 776; *Lamine v Dorrell* (1706) 2 Ld Raym 1216; 92 ER 303.

and packages at a premium and profited. ARU sued HG and ICM, among other things, for the tort of inducing breach of contract, and sought an account of profits.

Decision

Although HG and ICM had induced a breach of contract, the majority (Hill and Finkelstein JJ) held there was no entitlement to an account of profits. Emmett J (dissenting) would have awarded an account of profits for torts in certain circumstances.

Hill and Finkelstein JJ (majority)

> [**196**] Turning to the remedies available to the victim of a tort, those remedies may conveniently (if somewhat inaccurately) be divided into two groups (a) damages; and (b) other remedies. Here, we are not concerned with nonpecuniary remedies, the principal ones being injunction and restitution. So far as pecuniary remedies are concerned, it should be noted that damages may be either compensatory or non-compensatory. In the latter category are contemptuous damages, nominal damages, exemplary damages and restitutionary [**197**] damages. Restitutionary damages may be limited to cases involving the misuse of a plaintiff's property …
>
> Speaking generally, an award of damages is made in order to compensate the plaintiff for his injury. The rule is that the plaintiff is to be placed in the same position as he was before the tort was committed … This is sometimes referred to as the rule of restitutio in integrum. The rule is more easily applied to losses which are capable of calculation in money terms. In areas where the losses are not readily quantifiable, for example where damages are claimed for pain and suffering or in an action for defamation, the court attempts to award 'fair compensation' … .
>
> However described, it is not possible to slot an account of profits into the general framework of remedies that are available in tort, when the account is not awarded to compensate the plaintiff for his actual or presumed loss. That is to say, under presently accepted principles, an injured plaintiff cannot claim a windfall to prevent a wrongdoer profiting from his wrong, except in those cases where exemplary damages are available and it is proper that illicit profits are taken into account in assessing the quantum of the award … .

Emmett J (dissenting)

> [**198**] Whenever one person gains a benefit through the commission of a wrong, the availability of restitution might be determined under one of two distinct approaches. One approach is founded upon concepts of property in the broadest sense. Such concepts would include a spectrum of interests ranging from legal ownership of property, both corporeal and incorporeal, to expectations and opportunities. The essence of such an approach is that a claimant should be entitled to any benefits derived, as a result of wrongdoing, from that which belongs to the claimant. That approach responds to the notion that such benefits belong to the victim of the wrongdoing.
>
> The other approach is based upon the notion of deterrence. Restitution based on notions of deterrence emphasises the injustice and inequity of permitting a wrongdoer to keep gains derived from the wrongdoing, rather than responding on any notion that the

gains belong to the claimant. The forfeiture of profits acquired through the perpetration of wrongdoing, when those profits are not derived from another's property, may be seen as punitive. It may be, therefore, that, like punitive or exemplary damages, deterrent restitution ought generally to be confined to exceptional circumstances ... .

One area where Courts have awarded an account of profits is in the commission of the tort of inducing a breach of contract between master and servant. Where a wrongdoer acquires the benefits of the labour of an employee by reason of inducing that employee to breach his contract of employment with his employer, the employer is entitled to the value of the labour that he has lost. The action is brought for the benefit acquired by the wrongdoer from the service of the employee.

...

[**199**] ... The finding of wrongfully inducing breach of contract that has been made against THG and ICM would satisfy any requirement that they derived profits dishonestly in that sense. The Court has concluded that THG or ICM wrongfully induced both ATFS and the original purchasers of tickets to breach the terms of their contracts with ARU. That required a finding of intent on their part. THG and ICM knowingly put themselves in a position where they stood to derive a benefit that could not have been derived but for the breaches of contract that their conduct induced. If either of THG or ICM has derived profits from the use of the tickets that were acquired as a consequence of the breaches that it induced, it has done so by doing the very thing that it knew ARU was determined to prevent.

The conduct of THG and ICM was a wrongful interference with incorporeal rights of ARU. The choses in action comprising the ATFS contract and the ticket contracts constituted incorporeal property of ARU, insofar as those contracts remained executory and partly performed. True it is that the greater part of the performance remaining at the time of the breaches was performance by ARU. That is to say, ARU was under the obligation to procure access to the stadium for the purposes of watching the matches. Nevertheless, ARU continued to have the benefit of the obligations imposed upon the other parties, since those obligations remained executory and unperformed by them. In other words, ARU had the benefit of promises that the tickets would not be resold at a premium or used for commercial purposes. It also had the benefit of a promise that tickets made available to ATFS would not be sold except as part of a travel package. The effect of the conduct of THG and ICM was that the benefit of those incorporeal rights was lost to ARU.

ARU, by reason of its contract in relation to the stadium, had the capacity to confer on individuals the right of access to the stadium for the purpose of watching the matches. That right was conferred upon the original purchasers of tickets. Under the ATFS contract, ATFS was, in effect, given the capacity to confer such rights, subject to the restrictions contained in cl 3.11. The effect of the wrongful conduct of THG was to appropriate that capacity to itself. It effectively procured that the nominees of its clients were given the right of access, rather than the persons for whom ARU was prepared to procure access.

While the rights of ARU in relation to the stadium may not be property in the same sense that legal ownership of goods or land is property, they are, for present purposes, analogous to rights of ownership. Just as the right to the services of an employee can be characterised as property in the relevant sense, the right to procure access to the stadium can be so characterised. There is no reason in principle why ARU should not be entitled to a restitutionary remedy.

> ARU would have been entitled to injunctions to prevent the breaches of [**200**] contract now complained of, if the proceeding could have been heard in time. It has in fact obtained injunctions to prevent future breach by THG and ICM. That is the type of situation that makes an account of profits a just response to prevent THG and ICM from deriving a benefit from its wrongdoing.
>
> ARU made a decision as to how many tickets it would allocate to the corporate hospitality market. It forwent possible revenue from the corporate hospitality sector in order to advance other legitimate goals that it wished to achieve. It would be difficult to measure the benefit that ARU would have derived from the advancement or achievement of those other goals. Nevertheless, ARU forwent that possible revenue without advancing those other goals. ARU has, therefore, lost the benefit that it would have derived from advancing those goals. At the very least, it has lost the opportunity of advancing those goals. Whatever benefit such advancement may have been to ARU, the opportunity of that benefit has been lost in consequence of the conduct of THG or ICM. Further, by reason of that conduct, THG or ICM may have derived some benefit.
>
> Where the remedy of an account of profits is imposed, the remedy can result in a windfall for the claimant. That is also the consequence of exemplary damages. However, the difference between exemplary damages and an account of profits is that an award of exemplary damages is in the discretion of the court, while an account of profits and forfeiture of the benefit to the claimant is measured by the wrongdoer's gain. A restitutionary remedy, therefore, may be less harsh than the punitive remedy of exemplary damages. Wrongdoers are required to hand over only their profits. Even though the profits may have been to a large extent due to their efforts and investment risk, their capital will remain intact. On the other hand, exemplary damages may be awarded even though the wrongdoer made no gain against which the damages can be offset.
>
> ARU contends that THG made a profit of more than $200 000 by using the tickets in question. There was sufficient material before the learned primary judge to warrant a conclusion that THG had derived some profit. The learned primary judge considered that, if such profits could be retained, whatever they may have been, THG might well decide to 'chance the odds again'. The injunctions ordered by the learned primary judge would, of course, have prohibited such 'chancing'. However, even if there was no basis for concluding that THG would not have acted in contravention of the orders of the Court, the taking of an account to deprive THG of its unjust enrichment may be an appropriate deterrent against future wrongdoing. It may also be regarded as an appropriate punishment for the deliberate interference with ARU's rights. …

As noted in the principles text, there is support for the award of accounts of profit for proprietary torts in the United States.[10] However, these cases should be treated with extreme caution in an Australian context.[11]

10 See principles text [16.43]–[16.45] for a discussion of *Edwards v Lee's Administrator* 96 SW 2d 1028 (Ky Ct App, 1936); *Olwell v Nye & Nissen* 173 P 2d 652 (Wash, 1946).

11 C Rotherham, 'Deterrence as a Justification for Awarding Accounts of Profits' (2012) 32(3) *Oxford Journal of Legal Studies* 537, 539.

E Breach of contract

Accounts of profit are unavailable for breach of contract in Australian law, as the case below illustrates.[12] However, disgorgement for breach of contract is sometimes awarded exceptionally in other jurisdictions including England and Wales,[13] Canada,[14] New Zealand[15] and the United States.[16]

Hospitality Group Pty Ltd v Australian Rugby Union Ltd (2001) 110 FCR 157

Facts and issues

The facts of this case are stated on page 545.

Decision

Hill and Finkelstein JJ in the majority held an account of profits was unavailable for breach of contract. Emmett J in dissent did not consider the issue.

Hill and Finkelstein JJ (majority)

> [**195**] ARU relies on … [*Attorney-General v Blake* [2001] 1 AC 268] to argue that an account of profits is an appropriate remedy that should be awarded in its favour. It should be made quite clear, so that there be no doubt about it, ARU does not seek an account of profits based on some principle of equity such as constructive trust … or in reliance on principles of unjust enrichment. Its claim is founded on the proposition that the remedy is available for breach of contract and in tort …
>
> [**196**] The general rule of the common law was laid down by Baron Parke in *Robinson v Harman* … . Parke B said that the aim of contract damages was to place the plaintiff in the same position he would have occupied had the contract been performed. … In *Tito v Waddell (No 2)*, when considering the appropriate remedy for the failure by the British Phosphate Commissioners to restore Ocean Island following the termination of mining operations, Megarry VC said (at 332):
>
> > … it is fundamental to all questions of damages that they are to compensate the plaintiff for his loss or injury by putting him in the same position he would have been in had he not suffered the wrong. The question is not one of making the defendant

---

12 *Hospitality Group Pty Ltd v Australian Rugby Union Ltd* (2001) 110 FCR 157.

13 *A-G v Blake* [2001] 1 AC 268 ('*Blake*').

14 See L Smith and J Berryman, 'Disgorgement of Profits in Canada' in E Hondius and A Janssen (eds), *Disgorgement of Profits: Gain-Based Remedies throughout the World* (Springer 2015) 281, 289.

15 *A-G (England and Wales) v The Queen* [2002] 2 NZLR 91, [112]–[113] (Tipping J), [146]–[152] (McGrath J).

16 American Law Institute, *Restatement (Third) of Restitution and Unjust Enrichment* (2011) §39 (disgorgement remedy for 'opportunistic' breach of contract); *Kansas v Nebraska*, 135 S Ct 1042 (2015).

> disgorge what he has saved by committing the wrong but one of compensating the plaintiff.
>
> This principle has been accepted as correct by the High Court. … Moreover, as Mason CJ and Dawson J said in *Amann Aviation* at 82:
>
> > The corollary of the principle in Robinson v Harman is that a plaintiff is not entitled, by the award of damages upon breach, to be placed in a superior position to that which he or she would have been in had the contract been performed. …
>
> Whether or not the law of contract is 'seriously defective' (*Attorney-General v Blake* [1998] Ch 439 at 457 per Lord Woolf MR), if the court is unable to award disgorgement damages …, the position in Australia is that the loss recoverable for breach of contract is limited to that laid down in *Robinson v Harman*. That is, the aggrieved party is entitled only to compensation. If he has suffered no loss, he is not entitled to be compensated. In an appropriate case, the aggrieved party may be able to recover (by a claim in restitution) benefits that he has made available to the wrongdoer; for example, he may be able to recover the price paid under an incomplete contract or recover possession of goods sold but not paid for. Presently, however, it would be inconsistent with the current principles laid down by the High Court to confer a windfall on a plaintiff under the guise of damages for breach of contract.

By contrast, the English House of Lords has said that an account of profits may be available in exceptional circumstances.

Attorney-General v Blake [2001] 1 AC 268

Facts and issues

George Blake was employed by the British Secret Intelligence Service. He signed an undertaking pursuant to the *Official Secrets Act 1911* (UK) not to divulge any information gained as a result of his employment, even after his employment ended, without permission from the government. Blake became a 'double-agent' and disclosed information to the Soviet Union. After he was exposed, he was sentenced to 42 years' imprisonment. In 1966, he escaped from prison and fled to Moscow. In 1989, Blake published his autobiography, *No Other Choice*, with Jonathan Cape Ltd, without seeking permission. The British government sought to recover the profits remaining in jurisdiction.

Decision

There was no continuing fiduciary duty or breach of confidence. Nonetheless, the majority decided that the British government was entitled to an account of profits for breach of contract, which was said to be available in exceptional circumstances. Lord Hobhouse dissented.

Lord Nicholls (principal speech)

[275] My Lords, George Blake is a notorious, self-confessed traitor. …

Lord Nicholls discussed the availability of reasonable fee awards and waiver of tort, and the availability of accounts of profit in equity and for intellectual property breaches. He continued:

[281] Damages under Lord Cairns' Act

I must also mention the jurisdiction to award damages under section 2 of the Chancery Amendment Act 1858, commonly known as Lord Cairns' Act. This Act has been repealed but the jurisdiction remains. Section 2 empowered the Court of Chancery at its discretion, in all cases where it had jurisdiction to entertain an application for an injunction or specific performance, to award damages in addition to or in substitution for an injunction or specific performance. Thus section 2 enabled the Court of Chancery, sitting at Lincoln's Inn, to award damages when declining to grant equitable relief rather than … sending suitors across London to the common law courts at Westminster Hall.

Lord Cairns' Act had a further effect. The common law courts' jurisdiction to award damages was confined to loss or injury flowing from a cause of action which had accrued before the writ was issued. Thus in the case of a continuing wrong, such as maintaining overhanging eaves and gutters, damages were limited to the loss suffered up to the commencement of the action … . Lord Cairns' Act liberated the courts from this fetter. In future, if the court declined to grant an injunction, which had the effect in practice of sanctioning the indefinite continuance of a wrong, the court could assess damages to include losses likely to follow from the anticipated future continuance of the wrong as well as losses already suffered. The power to give damages in lieu of an injunction imported the power to give an equivalent for what was lost by the refusal of an injunction … . It is important to note, however, that although the Act had the effect of enabling the court in this regard to award damages in respect of the future as well as the past, the Act did not alter the measure to be employed in assessing damages … . Thus, in the same way as damages at common law for violations of a property right may by measured by reference to the benefits wrongfully obtained by a defendant, so under Lord Cairns' Act damages may include damages measured by reference to the benefits likely to be obtained in future by the defendant. …

The measure of damages awarded in this type of case is often analysed as damages for loss of a bargaining opportunity or … the price payable for the compulsory acquisition of a right. This analysis is correct. The court's refusal to grant an injunction means that in practice the defendant is thereby permitted to perpetuate the wrongful state of affairs he has brought about. But this analysis takes the matter now under discussion no further forward. A property right has value to the extent only that the court will enforce it or award damages for its infringement. The question under discussion is whether the court will award substantial damages for an infringement when no financial loss flows from the infringement and, moreover, in a suitable case will assess the damages by reference to the defendant's profit obtained from the infringement. The cases mentioned above show that the courts habitually do that very thing.

[282] Breach of contract

Against this background I turn to consider the remedies available for breaches of contract. The basic remedy is an award of damages. In the much quoted words of Baron Parke, the rule of the common law is that where a party sustains a loss by reason of a breach of contract, he is, so far as money can do it, to be placed in the same position as if the contract had been performed: *Robinson v Harman* … . Leaving aside the anomalous exception of punitive damages, damages are compensatory. That is axiomatic. It is equally well established that an award of damages, assessed by reference to financial loss, is not always 'adequate' as a remedy for a breach of contract. The law recognises that a party to a contract may have an interest in performance which is not readily measurable in terms of money. On breach the innocent party suffers a loss. He fails to obtain the benefit promised by the other party to the contract. … For him a financially assessed measure of damages is inadequate.

The classic example of this type of case, as every law student knows, is a contract for the sale of land. The buyer of a house may be attracted by features which have little or no impact on the value of the house. An award of damages, based on strictly financial criteria, would fail to recompense a disappointed buyer for this head of loss. The primary response of the law to this type of case is to ensure, if possible, that the contract is performed in accordance with its terms. The court may make orders compelling the party who has committed a breach of contract, or is threatening to do so, to carry out his contractual obligations. To this end the court has wide powers to grant injunctive relief. The court will, for instance, readily make orders for the specific performance of contracts for the sale of land, and sometimes it will do so in respect of contracts for the sale of goods. In *Beswick v Beswick* … the court made an order for the specific performance of a contract to make payments of money to a third party. The law recognised that the innocent party to the breach of contract had a legitimate interest in having the contract performed even though he himself would suffer no financial loss from its breach. Likewise, the court will compel the observance of negative obligations by granting injunctions. This may include a mandatory order to undo an existing breach, as where the court orders the defendant to pull down building works carried out in breach of covenant.

All this is trite law. In practice, these specific remedies go a long way towards providing suitable protection for innocent parties who will suffer loss from breaches of contract which are not adequately remediable by an award of damages. But these remedies are not always available. For instance, confidential information may be published in breach of a non-disclosure agreement before the innocent party has time to apply to the court for urgent relief. Then the breach is irreversible. Further, these specific remedies are discretionary. Contractual obligations vary infinitely. So do the circumstances in which breaches occur, and the circumstances in which remedies are sought. The court may, for instance, decline to grant specific relief on the ground that this would be oppressive.

An instance of this nature occurred in *Wrotham Park Estate Co Ltd v Parkside Homes Ltd* … . **[283]**

Property rights are superior to contractual rights in that, unlike contractual rights, property rights may survive against an indefinite class of persons. However, it is not easy to see why, as between the parties to a contract, a violation of a party's contractual rights should attract a lesser degree of remedy than a violation of his property rights. As Lionel Smith has pointed out in his article *Disgorgement of the profits of Contract: Property, Contract and 'Efficient Breach'* 24 Can. BLJ 121, it is not clear why it should be any more permissible to expropriate personal rights than it is permissible to expropriate property rights.

…

The *Wrotham Park* case, therefore, still shines, rather as a solitary beacon, showing that in contract as well as tort damages are not always narrowly confined to recoupment of financial loss. In a suitable case [**284**] damages for breach of contract may be measured by the benefit gained by the wrongdoer from the breach. The defendant must make a reasonable payment in respect of the benefit he has gained. In the present case the Crown seeks to go further. The claim is for all the profits of Blake's book which the publisher has not yet paid him. This raises the question whether an account of profits can ever be given as a remedy for breach of contract. The researches of counsel have been unable to discover any case where the court has made such an order on a claim for breach of contract. …

There is a light sprinkling of cases where courts have made orders having the same effect as an order for an account of profits, but the courts seem always to have attached a different label. A person who, in breach of contract, sells land twice over must surrender his profits on the second sale to the original buyer. Since courts regularly make orders for the specific performance of contracts for the sale of land, a seller of land is, to an extent, regarded as holding the land on trust for the buyer: *Lake v Bayliss …*

…

These cases illustrate that circumstances do arise when the just response to a breach of contract is that the wrongdoer should not be permitted to retain any profit from the breach. In these cases the courts have reached the desired result by straining existing concepts.

…

My conclusion is that there seems to be no reason, in principle, why the court must in all circumstances rule out an account of profits as a remedy for breach of contract. I prefer to avoid the unhappy expression 'restitutionary damages'. Remedies are the law's response to a wrong (or, more precisely, to a cause of action). When, exceptionally, a just response to a breach of contract so requires, the court should be able [**285**] to grant the discretionary remedy of requiring a defendant to account to the plaintiff for the benefits he has received from his breach of contract. In the same way as a plaintiff's interest in performance of a contract may render it just and equitable for the court to make an order for specific performance or grant an injunction, so the plaintiff's interest in performance may make it just and equitable that the defendant should retain no benefit from his breach of contract.

… The law recognises that damages are not always a sufficient remedy for breach of contract. This is the foundation of the court's jurisdiction to grant the remedies of specific performance and injunction. Even when awarding damages, the law does not adhere slavishly to the concept of compensation for financially measurable loss. When the circumstances require, damages are measured by reference to the benefit obtained by the wrongdoer. This applies to interference with property rights. Recently, the like approach has been adopted to breach of contract. Further, in certain circumstances an account of profits is ordered in preference to an award of damages. Sometimes the injured party is given the choice: either compensatory damages or an account of the wrongdoer's profits. Breach of confidence is an instance of this. If confidential information is wrongfully divulged in breach of a non-disclosure agreement, it would be nothing short of sophistry to say that an account of profits may be ordered in respect of the equitable wrong but not in respect of the breach of contract which governs the relationship between the parties. With the established authorities going thus far, I consider it would be only a modest step for the law to recognise openly that, exceptionally, an account of profits may be the most appropriate remedy for breach of contract.

...

The main argument against the availability of an account of profits as a remedy for breach of contract is that the circumstances where this remedy may be granted will be uncertain. This will have an unsettling effect on commercial contracts where certainty is important. I do not think these fears are well founded. I see no reason why, in practice, the availability of the remedy of an account of profits need disturb settled expectations in the commercial or consumer world. An account of profits will be appropriate only in exceptional circumstances. Normally the remedies of damages, specific performance and injunction, coupled with the characterisation of some contractual obligations as fiduciary, will provide an adequate response to a breach of contract. It will be only in exceptional cases, where those remedies are inadequate, that any question of accounting for profits will arise. No fixed rules can be prescribed. The court will have regard to all the circumstances, including the subject matter of the contract, the purpose of the contractual provision which has been breached, the circumstances in which the breach occurred, the consequences of the breach and the circumstances in which relief is being sought. A useful general guide, although not exhaustive, is whether the plaintiff had a legitimate interest in preventing the defendant's profit-making activity and, hence, in depriving him of his profit.

...

The present case

The present case is exceptional. The context is employment as a member of the security and intelligence services. Secret information is the lifeblood of these services. In the 1950s Blake deliberately committed repeated breaches of his undertaking not to divulge official information gained as a result of his employment. He caused untold and immeasurable damage to the public interest he had committed himself to serve. In 1990 he published his autobiography, a further breach of his express undertaking. By this time the information disclosed was no longer confidential. In the ordinary course of commercial dealings the disclosure of non-confidential information might be regarded as venial. In the present case disclosure was also a criminal offence under the Official Secrets Acts, even though the information was no longer confidential. ...

...

[**287**] When he joined the Secret Intelligence Service Blake expressly agreed in writing that he would not disclose official information, during or after his service, in book form or otherwise. He was employed on that basis. That was the basis on which he acquired official information. The Crown had and has a legitimate interest in preventing Blake profiting from the disclosure of official information, whether classified or not, while a member of the service and thereafter. Neither he, nor any other member of the service, should have a financial incentive to break his undertaking. It is of paramount importance that members of the service should have complete confidence in all their dealings with each other, and that those recruited as informers should have the like confidence. Undermining the willingness of prospective informers to co-operate with the services, or undermining the morale and trust between members of the services when engaged on secret and dangerous

operations, would jeopardise the effectiveness of the service. An absolute rule against disclosure, visible to all, makes good sense.

In considering what would be a just response to a breach of Blake's undertaking the court has to take these considerations into account. The undertaking, if not a fiduciary obligation, was closely akin to a fiduciary obligation, where an account of profits is a standard remedy in the event of breach. Had the information which Blake has now disclosed still been confidential, an account of profits would have been ordered, almost as a matter of course. In the special circumstances of the intelligence services, the same conclusion should follow even though the information is no longer confidential. That would be a just response to the breach. …

As a footnote I observe that a similar conclusion, requiring the contract-breaker to disgorge his profits, was reached in the majority decision of the United States Supreme Court in [**288**] *Snepp v United States* (1980) 444 US 507. The facts were strikingly similar. A former employee of the Central Intelligence Agency, whose conditions of employment included a promise not to divulge any information relating to the agency without pre-publication clearance, published a book about the agency's activities in Vietnam. … The court considered that a remedy which required Snepp 'to disgorge the benefits of his faithlessness', was swift and sure, tailored to deter those who would place sensitive information at risk and, since the remedy reached only funds attributable to the breach, it could not saddle the former agent with exemplary damages out of all proportion to his gain. In order to achieve this result the court 'imposed' a constructive trust on Snepp's profits. In this country, affording the plaintiff the remedy of an account of profits is a different means to the same end.

Lord Hobhouse (dissenting)

[**293**] My Lords,

When he opened this appeal, Mr Clayton, [on behalf of Blake], warned your Lordships against being drawn into making bad law in order to enable an intuitively just decision to be given against a traitor.

…

[296] The concepts of restitution and compensation are not the same though they will on occasions fulfil the same need. Restitution is analogous to property: it concerns wealth or advantage which ought to be returned or transferred by the defendant to the plaintiff. It is a form of specific implement. Its clearest form is an order for the return or transfer of property which belongs in law or in equity to the plaintiff. … Then there are rights recognised in equity such as those which [**297**] arise from a fiduciary relationship. These rights give rise to restitutionary remedies including the remedy of account which, depending on the circumstances, could also derive from a common law relationship such as agency. Then, again, there are the rights now grouped under the heading of the law of restitution or unjust enrichment. These are still truly restitutionary concepts leading to restitutionary remedies. Typically they require the payment of money by the person unjustly enriched to the person at whose expense that enrichment has taken place. In so far as the appropriate remedy is the payment of money or the delivery up of a chattel or goods is concerned the common law could provide it; insofar as it required some other remedy or the recognition of an equitable right, the chancery jurisdiction had to be invoked.

The essential of such rights and their enforcement was the procuring by the courts of the *performance* by the defendant of his obligations. The plaintiff recovers what he is actually entitled to not some monetary substitute for it. If what the plaintiff is entitled to is wealth expressed in monetary terms, the order will be for the payment of money but this does not alter the character of the remedy or of the right being recognised. He gets the money because it was his property or he was in some other way entitled to it. It is still the enforced performance of an obligation. The same is the case where an injunction is granted or a decree of specific performance or the ordering of an account.

It is this class of rights which the Crown is unable to invoke as a result of the judgment of the Vice-Chancellor upheld by the Court of Appeal. There is no obligation of Blake left to perform or which now can be enforced. That time passed with the failure to apply for an injunction in 1989 or 1990. The Crown has no right to an injunction to stop the payment of the royalty to Blake and procure its payment to the Crown instead. The Crown has no right to the royalty and does not now assert one.

The law, including equity, provides extensive and effective remedies for protecting and enforcing property rights. It is no criticism of the law that they are not available now to the Crown. The Crown does not have the substantive rights to support such remedies.

...

While in the recent UK Supreme Court case of *Morris-Garner v One Step (Support) Ltd*,[17] Lord Reed appeared to question Lord Nicholls' interpretation of *Wrotham Park*,[18] it appears that he left intact the rule in *Attorney-General v Blake* that an account of profits may be awarded for breach of contract in exceptional circumstances when other remedies are inadequate.[19]

F The *Australian Consumer Law*

As noted in the principles text, there is no express provision for gain-based relief in the *Australian Consumer Law* ('ACL').[20] However, there seems to be some opportunity for courts to use the pecuniary penalty provisions of the ACL to strip gain from defendants, as effectively occurred in *Director of Consumer Affairs Victoria v Gibson (No 3)*.[21]

REVIEW QUESTIONS

(1) What is the rationale of the account of profits?

(2) Should account of profits be available for common law causes of action and, if so, in what circumstances?

17 [2018] UKSC 20, [72]–[81].

18 *Wrotham Park Estate Co Ltd v Parkside Homes Ltd* [1974] 1 WLR 798.

19 Ibid [35], [82], [95] point (11).

20 *Competition and Consumer Act 2010* (Cth) sch 2.

21 [2017] FCA 1148.

Figure 16.3 Accounts of profit for tort or contract

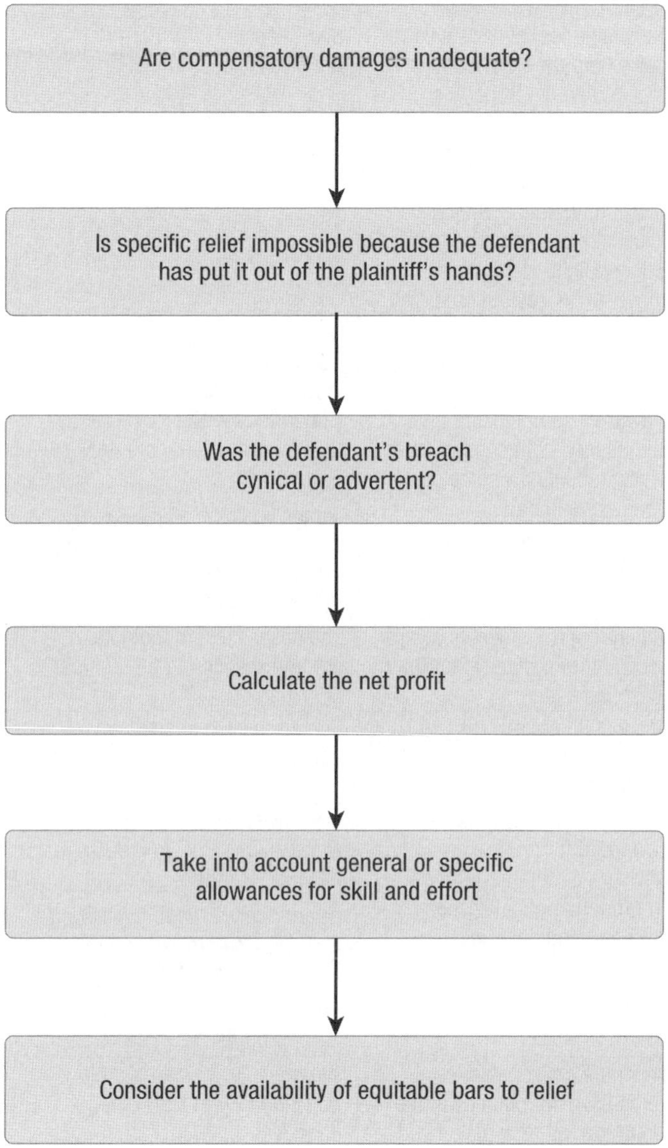

IV 'Reasonable fee' damages

Concept	Short explanation	Relevant authorities	Principles text
Introduction and history	'Reasonable fee' awards involve cases where the defendant has used certain property or infringed certain rights and the plaintiff is paid a 'reasonable fee' (objectively assessed) for that use or infringement. They have traditionally been awarded under multiple heads, including as compensation, restitution, or via Lord Cairns' Act.	See Chapter 12 for Lord Cairns' Act discussion.	Chapter 16: [16.62]–[16.65]
Academic and judicial accounts	There are multiple judicial accounts of reasonable fee awards: compensatory, restitutionary, both compensatory and restitutionary, vindicatory, proprietary and partial disgorgement. The situation of these awards in Australian law is unclear.	Robert J Sharpe and Stephen M Waddams, 'Damages for Lost Opportunity to Bargain' (1982) 2(2) *Oxford Journal of Legal Studies* 290 James Edelman, *Gain-Based Damages: Contract, Tort, Equity and Intellectual Property* (Hart Publishing, 2002)	Chapter 16: [16.66]–[16.77]
Equity	In equity, courts generally award an account of profits rather than a reasonable fee*	The cases cited in footnotes are an exception to the general principle.	Chapter 16: [16.79]–[16.80]
Intellectual property	'Reasonable fee' awards are clearly available for intellectual property infringements.#	See discussion in article in footnote.	Chapter 16: [16.81]–[16.84]
Tort	'Reasonable fee' awards can be awarded for proprietary torts involving a direct interference with property rights (trespass, conversion and detinue).	*LJP Investments Pty Ltd v Howard Chia Pty Ltd* (1990) 24 NSWLR 499 *Strand Electric and Engineering Co Ltd v Brisford Entertainments Ltd* [1952] 2 QB 246 *Morris-Garner v One Step (Support) Ltd* [2018] UKSC 20	Chapter 16: [16.85]–[16.100]
Contract	In Australia, reasonable fee awards have not been awarded in contract, but they have been awarded in the UK.	*Wrotham Park Estate Co Ltd v Parkside Homes Ltd* [1974] 1 WLR 798 *Experience Hendrix LLC v PPX Enterprises Inc* [2003] EWCA Civ 323 *Morris-Garner v One Step (Support) Ltd* [2018] UKSC 20	Chapter 16: [16.101]–[16.109]

* Although cf *Seager v Copydex (No 1)* [1967] 1 WLR 923; *Seager v Copydex (No 2)* [1969] 1 WLR 809.
# David J Brennan, 'The Beautiful Restitutionary Heresy of a Larrikin' (2011) 33(2) *Sydney Law Review* 209, 214.

A Introduction and history

Australian courts may grant 'reasonable fee' awards where defendants have used certain property or infringed certain rights, generally in a tortious manner. 'Reasonable fee' refers to a method of calculating a monetary award. Courts often make these awards when the plaintiff has not suffered a compensable loss in the ordinary sense, yet the situation still calls for damages. They are calculated according to an objective assessment of what a reasonable fee would be for the use of the property or infringement of the right.

Reasonable fee awards may be obtained through several remedial pathways:

- as compensatory damages
- via an action for money had and received through 'waiver of tort' in cases of proprietary torts
- as 'restitutionary damages' or
- under Lord Cairns' Act in lieu of an injunction.

Reasonable fee awards are generally awarded for common law causes of action, particularly for proprietary torts such as trespass to land and for intellectual property infringements. As the principles text describes, there is significant confusion in terminology in this area, as well as disagreement as to the nature of the awards.

B Academic and judicial accounts

Academic and judicial accounts of reasonable fee awards fall into six general camps:

(1) compensatory analyses
(2) restitutionary analyses
(3) compensatory/restitutionary analyses
(4) vindicatory analyses
(5) property or exclusive entitlement analyses and
(6) partial disgorgement analyses.

More detailed versions of all of these accounts can be found in the principles text. For present purposes, compensatory and restitutionary analyses will be considered as those most commonly taken by judges and scholars. Lord Reed of the UK Supreme Court has recently taken a compensatory analysis of 'reasonable fee' awards in *Morris-Garner v One Step (Support) Ltd.*[22]

1 Compensatory analyses

An example of a compensatory analysis is the 'lost opportunity to bargain' analysis is excerpted below. Robert Sharpe is a former academic and judge of the Court of Appeal of Ontario, and Stephen Waddams is a pre-eminent Canadian Remedies scholar.

22 [2018] UKSC 20, [95].

Robert J Sharpe and Stephen M Waddams, 'Damages for Lost Opportunity to Bargain' (1982) 2(2) *Oxford Journal of Legal Studies* 290

[**290**] Where the defendant has profited by his violation of the plaintiff's property right, a damage award based upon the extent of the defendant's gain does reflect something the plaintiff has lost. The defendant's wrongful conduct has deprived the plaintiff of the opportunity to bargain with the defendant, and to set his own price on his consent. The legal position can be explained by saying that the defendant should be prevented from circumventing the bargaining process, and where prevention fails, damages should be awarded to compensate the plaintiff for this lost opportunity.

Injunctive relief is the most effective method of protecting the right to bargain and a brief consideration of injunctions from this point of view is relevant to the [**291**] present enquiry, for, in awarding damages in substitution for an injunction, the courts readily take the view that the award of damages ought, so far as money can do it, to give the plaintiff an equivalent protection. An injunction compels the defendant to refrain from his intended course unless he can persuade the plaintiff to bargain away his right. While some find it odd to conceive of an injunction as a bargaining tool, it has been recognized as such in the case law. …

… [**292**] Where an injunction is refused, the plaintiffs loss of his opportunity to bargain can still be given substantial protection through an award of damages in lieu of the injunction, sometimes called 'equitable damages', and originally made possible by Lord Cairns' Act (Chancery Law Amendment Act, 1858). In such cases, explicit reference has been made to the bargain which might have been made at the outset. … [Footnotes omitted.]

As noted in the principles text at [16.67], some judges have accepted this analysis, but it has been criticised by other judges and by academics.

2 Restitutionary analyses

As noted in the principles text at [16.70]–[16.71], while restitutionary analyses have been made by other scholars and judges, James Edelman's is the most well-known such account. An extract of his argument is excerpted below. James Edelman is a former academic and current Judge of the High Court.

James Edelman, *Gain-Based Damages: Contract, Tort, Equity and Intellectual Property* (Hart Publishing, 2002)

[66] (a) Definition

In the context of the law of wrongs, this book uses the term 'restitutionary damages' to refer to a monetary award which reverses a transfer of value. It is an award which gives back value transferred from a claimant to a defendant as a result of a defendant's wrong and is almost always measured by the objective gain received by the defendant. A simple example can be given. A defendant wrongfully takes £100 of a claimant's money. Ignoring any loss suffered, the claimant may seek to bring an action for restitutionary damages to reverse the wrongful transfer of the £100. This type of action might be pleaded as 'money had and received' for the wrong but it will be referred to in this book as restitutionary damages for the wrong. It reverses the transfer and, in the words of Lord Goff, aims to 'restore the parties to the position they were in before they entered the transaction … [this] is, of course, the function of the law of restitution'. …

…

[67] … Once again, the reference to a transfer of value does not mean that the claimant must have a financial loss to match the transfer of value. In the example of the trespassing tenant, the landlord may not have been able to lease the premises to anyone. This transfer of value has been described as a subtraction from the claimant's *dominium* rather than from his financial wealth. In other words, the generation of value has come from the assets of the claimant even though the claimant may not have suffered any financial loss. …

…

[69] (b) The awards which are restitutionary damages

Historically restitutionary damages awards were made under a number of different names: wayleaves, common counts of indebitatus assumpsit (as well as quantum meruit and quantum valebant awards), mesne profits, reasonable royalties, monetary awards made in the context of rescission, damages in lieu of injunctions or specific performance or even awards simply labelled 'damages' and assessed according to a 'user principle'. Each of these awards, when made for wrongs, operated to reverse wrongful transactions. …

…

[70] (c) Measuring restitutionary damages

In reversing a transfer of value, restitutionary damages focus upon the fact that value has been transferred from a claimant and that value is measured as the objective receipt by the defendant. [Footnotes omitted.]

C General patterns

Courts typically award a 'reasonable fee' for intellectual property breaches, when there has been a breach of negative covenant protecting an interest other than profit-making, or when a proprietary tort has been committed. The plaintiff is awarded a hypothetical reasonable fee reflecting the amount a reasonable plaintiff would have accepted had the defendant sought to be released from the covenant (in contract) or sought permission to use the property (in tort and in intellectual property). The fee is objective. Recent case law from England and Wales[23] and Singapore[24] indicates that reasonable fee awards are understood as

23 *One Step Support Pty Ltd v Morris-Garner* [2018] UKSC 20, [2019] AC 649.

24 *Turf Club Auto Emporium Pte Ltd v Yeo Boong Hua* [2018] SGCA 44.

compensatory in those jurisdictions. Leggatt LJ's judgment in *Marathon Asset Management LLP v Seddon*[25] provides a helpful guide as to how such fees might be calculated:

- If the interest could have been obtained on the market, the reasonable fee should be valued according to market value.
- If it was reasonable to expect the plaintiff to release the covenant or hire out the property, the interest will be valued by the reasonable fee that the plaintiff could have charged.
- If it was not reasonable for the plaintiff to release the covenant or hire out the property, the defendant's gain may be a proxy for the value of the plaintiff's interest.

D Equity

Generally, the account of profits is awarded for breaches of equitable duties. However, reasonable fee awards have been made for breach of confidence in the *Seager v Copydex* cases, where the defendant mistakenly believed it was entitled to use the plaintiff's confidential information. The Court declined to award an injunction or an account of profits, and instead awarded a 'reasonable fee' reflecting the market value of the confidential information.[26] The decision has been criticised in Australia as promoting 'fusion fallacy'.[27]

E Intellectual property

'Reasonable fee' awards are available for intellectual property infringements, as these have been treated similarly to wrongful use of corporeal property. If there is a single use, damages are calculated on the basis of a licence fee,[28] but if there are multiple uses, damages are assessed on a royalty basis.[29] The court must ascertain what a willing licensee would have been prepared to pay and a willing licensor to accept, by reference to the actual characteristics of the parties in dispute.[30] The tort of passing off is included in the stable of intellectual property interests, and hence infringement may give rise to a reasonable fee award.[31] Generally, courts have treated such damages as compensatory. 'Reasonable fee' awards are said to reflect the sales lost as a result of the infringement. The defence of 'innocent infringement' may also be available in this area.

---

25 [2017] EWHC 300 (Comm), [232]–[233], [236].

26 *Seager v Copydex (No 1)* [1967] 1 WLR 923; *Seager v Copydex (No 2)* [1969] 1 WLR 809.

27 JD Heydon, MJ Leeming and PG Turner, *Meagher, Gummow and Lehane's Equity: Doctrines and Remedies* (LexisNexis, 5th ed, 2015) [2–235], [42–190].

28 *Chabot v Davies* [1936] 3 All ER 211, 228.

29 *Lewis Trusts v Bambers Stores* [1982] FSR 281.

30 *General Tire and Rubber Co v Firestone Tyre and Rubber Co Ltd* [1975] 1 WLR 819, 824–6 (Lord Wilberforce).

31 *Winnebago Industries Inc v Knott Investments Pty Ltd (No 4)* (2015) 241 FCR 271.

F Tort

'Reasonable fee' awards are readily made primarily for certain torts which involve a direct interference with property (namely, trespass to land, trespass to goods, detinue and conversion). These have been awarded through several remedial pathways: compensatory damages, the action for money had and received via 'waiver of tort', 'restitutionary damages' and damages in lieu of an injunction pursuant to Lord Cairns' Act. Some Australian cases treat these as compensatory, whereas others treat them as restitutionary. A case where a reasonable fee for trespass is treated as restitutionary is excerpted below.

LJP Investments Pty Ltd v Howard Chia Pty Ltd (1990) 24 NSWLR 499

Facts and issues

The defendant, Howard Chia Pty Ltd ('Chia'), erected on its land scaffolding which extended for 16 metres along the boundary of the plaintiff's LJP Investments Pty Ltd's ('LJP') land and about 1.5 metres into LJP's airspace. Before this, Chia had sought permission from LJP to erect the scaffolding, and LJP had said it would allow the scaffolding to intrude on its land for a lump sum payment of $30 000. Chia deliberately did not comply with these terms. Bryson J first awarded a mandatory injunction for the removal of the scaffolding, but Chia then erected non-trespassing scaffolding. LJP then sought damages for the period Chia had been committing the trespass.

Decision

Hodgson J awarded LJP 'restitutionary damages' in the sum of $37 380 for the period that the trespass occurred.

Hodgson J

> **[507]** It is convenient first to consider the question of what have been called 'restitutory [sic] damages', that is, the damages equal to such sum as Chia should D reasonably pay for the use which it made of LJP's land. Mr Heydon submitted that the measure of damages was simply the market value of what was used. However, in my view, if what is used has peculiar value for a defendant, then damages under this head should reflect that value, rather than the general market value. … I think the plaintiff's damages should not be limited to the general market value of the plaintiff's tenancy, but should reflect the price which the plaintiff and defendant would reasonably have negotiated … .
>
> If I were able to conclude, as Mr Bennett submits, that if Chia had refrained from trespassing, it would in fact have paid the amount LJP was demanding, then I think that would be the correct measure of damages. An inference that this is what would have happened, or alternatively further support for that as the correct measure of damages, could be provided if it appeared that Chia would have incurred comparable expense by alternative measures which were open to it.
>
> …

> **[508]** It is impossible to be certain which course Chia would have taken, if it had refrained from trespassing: Chia's own unlawful act in trespassing, plus the absence of any of Chia's decision-makers from the witness box, have made such a decision highly problematic. I think in these circumstances, the Court is justified in taking the course taken in *Armory v Delamire* … and resolving the question of value against the party whose actions have made an accurate determination so problematic.
>
> For those reasons, in my view, LJP is entitled to $37 380 restitutory damages.

At 509, Hodgson J also said that if he was wrong on the question of restitutionary damages, he would award exemplary damages in a similar quantum because of Chia's contumelious disregard of LJP's rights.

The restitutionary approach to mesne profits has been confirmed as open in Australia by Edelman J in *Hampton v BHP Billiton Minerals Pty Ltd (No 2)*,[32] although he also considered the possibility that such damages could be calculated on a compensatory basis.[33]

In the following case, the Court is split on whether the reasonable fee for interference with proprietary interests in goods is compensatory or restitutionary.

Strand Electric and Engineering Co Ltd v Brisford Entertainments Ltd [1952] 2 QB 246

Facts and issues

The plaintiffs (Strand Electric) loaned portable electric switchboards to a prospective purchaser of a theatre owned by the defendants (Brisford), on the understanding that the prospective purchaser would conclude the sale, and the plaintiffs would manufacture and install permanent switchboards in due course. The sale fell through, and the defendants decided not to proceed with the installation but retained the portable switchboards to make the theatre more saleable. The plaintiffs demanded the return of their property or payment of a hire fee, but the defendants committed the tort of detinue by neither returning the property nor paying a hire fee.

Decision

The plaintiffs were awarded a 'reasonable fee' based on the hiring fee for all the switchboards for that period of time. Romer LJ and Sommervell LJ said in separate judgments that the damages were compensatory, but Denning LJ said they were restitutionary. Romer LJ's and Denning LJ's judgments are excerpted below.

32 [2012] WASC 285, [355]–[359].

33 Ibid [342]–[354].

Denning LJ

[**253**] In assessing damages, whether for a breach of contract or for a tort, the general rule is that the plaintiff recovers the loss he has suffered, no more and no less. This rule is, however, often departed from. Thus in cases where the damage claimed is too remote in law the plaintiff recovers less than his real loss … In other cases the plaintiff may get more than his real loss. …

…

The question in this case is: What is the proper measure of damages for the wrongful detention of goods? Does it fall within the general rule that the plaintiff only recovers for the loss he has suffered or within some other, and if so what, rule? It is strange that there is no authority upon this point in English law; but there is plenty on the analogous case of detention of land. The rule there is that a wrongdoer, who keeps the owner out of his land, must pay a fair rental value for it, even though the owner would not have been able to use it himself or to let it to anyone else. So also a wrongdoer who uses land for his own [**254**] purposes without the owner's consent, as, for instance, for a fair ground, or as a way-leave, must pay a reasonable hire for it, even though he has done no damage to the land at all: *Whitwham v Westminster Brymbo Coal Company*. I see no reason why the same principle should not apply to detention of goods.

If a wrongdoer has made use of goods for his own purposes, then he must pay a reasonable hire for them, even though the owner has in fact suffered no loss. It may be that the owner would not have used the goods himself, or that he had a substitute readily available, which he used without extra cost to himself. Nevertheless the owner is entitled to a reasonable hire. If the wrongdoer had asked the owner for permission to use the goods, the owner would be entitled to ask for a reasonable remuneration as the price of his permission. The wrongdoer cannot be better off because he did not ask permission. He cannot be better off by doing wrong than he would be by doing right. He must therefore pay a reasonable hire. This will cover, of course, the wear and tear which is ordinarily included in a hiring charge; but for any further damage the wrongdoer must pay extra. I do not mean to suggest that an owner who has suffered greater loss will not be able to recover it. Suppose that a man used a car in his business, and owing to its detention he had to hire a substitute at an increased cost, he would clearly be able to recover the cost of the substitute. In such cases the plaintiff recovers his actual loss. I am not concerned with those cases.

I am here concerned with the cases where the owner has in fact suffered no loss, or less loss than is represented by a hiring charge. In such cases if the wrongdoer has in fact used the goods he must pay a reasonable hire for them. Nor do I mean to suggest that a wrongdoer who has merely detained the goods and not used them would have to pay a hiring charge. The damages for detention recoverable against a carrier or a warehouseman have never been measured by a hiring charge. They are measured by the loss actually sustained by the plaintiff, subject, of course, to questions of remoteness. They are like cases of injury to a ship or a car by negligence. If it is put out of action during repair the wrongdoer is only liable for the loss suffered by the plaintiff. … The claim for a hiring charge is therefore not based on the loss to the plaintiff, but on the fact that the defendant has used the goods for his own [**255**] purposes. It is an action against him because he has had the benefit of the goods. It resembles, therefore, an action for restitution rather than an action of tort. But it is unnecessary to place it into any formal category. The plaintiffs are entitled to a hiring charge for the period of detention, and that is all that matters. I can imagine cases where an owner might be entitled to the profits made by a wrongdoer by the use of a chattel, but I do not think this is such a case.

Romer LJ

[**256**] In my judgment the three salient facts on which the assessment of damages in this case depends are, first, that the equipment of the plaintiffs which the defendants detained was profit-earning property; secondly, that the plaintiffs normally hired out the equipment in the course of their business; and, thirdly, that the defendants during the period of wrongful detention applied the property to the furtherance of their own ends. As to the third point, the defendants sought before us to contend that they could not be said to have used the equipment because they did not actively operate the switchboards. This, in my opinion, is immaterial. The judge found that Mrs Pearlberg (who substantially owns the defendant company) refused to return the equipment to the plaintiffs because, without it, the Bedford Theatre could not be let or sold. This finding establishes, in my judgment, that the defendants put the switchboards to the use of making their theatre more attractive and more readily disposable than it would have been without them. This amounts to a use of the equipment by the defendants for their own purposes.

In the light, then, of these three established facts the question is whether Mr Caplan [counsel for the appellant] is right in his proposition that if the use of an article has a recognized hiring value then such value constitutes the measure of damages recoverable by the owner from a defendant who, by wrongful detention, has the use of that article. Although, curiously enough, this question seems never to have come up for decision in our courts, I am of opinion that on principle Mr Caplan's proposition is sound. The fundamental aim in awarding damages is in general to compensate the party aggrieved. The inquiry is: What loss has the plaintiff suffered by reason of the defendants' wrongful act? In determining the answer to this inquiry the question of quantifying the profit or benefit which the defendant has derived from his wrongful act does not arise; for there is no necessary relation between the plaintiffs' loss and the defendants' gain. It follows that in assessing the plaintiffs' loss in the present case one is not troubled by any need to evaluate the actual benefit which resulted to the defendants by having the plaintiffs' equipment at their disposal.

That element then being out of the way, the only substantial reason put forward by the defendants why the plaintiffs should not receive the full hiring value of the equipment during the period of detention is that the plaintiffs might not have been able to find [**257**] a hirer. In my judgment, however, a defendant who has wrongfully detained and profited from the property of someone else cannot avail himself of a hypothesis such as this. It does not lie in the mouth of such a defendant to suggest that the owner might not have found a hirer; for in using the property he showed that he wanted it and he cannot complain if it is assumed against him that he himself would have preferred to become the hirer rather than not have had the use of it at all.

...

It is said, however, on behalf of the defendants, first, that they should not be charged for the use of the equipment during such reasonable time as was necessary for them to satisfy themselves with regard to the plaintiffs' title; and, secondly, that some allowance

> should be made for the possibility that the equipment might have suffered damage, or even destruction, during the period of detention, if it had been restored to the plaintiffs at the [**258**] beginning of that period. I do not think there is anything in either of these points. As to the first, not only is there no evidence that the defendants ever entertained any doubt as to the plaintiffs' title or applied themselves to inquiring into that matter, but the evidence shows, and the learned judge so found, that from first to last the defendants' sole reason for refusing to deliver up the equipment was that they wanted to keep it themselves. Then, as to the possibility of damage to the equipment if the plaintiffs had been given possession of it, this is not a contingency of which, in my judgment, any account should be taken in the present action, although it would have had some relevance if the defendants had been sued for negligence.

In *Bunnings Group Ltd v Chep Australia Ltd*,[34] the New South Wales Court of Appeal applied *Strand Electric*, but discounted the reasonable fee to reflect the true price offered. The plaintiff, Chep, hired out pallets to businesses which used them to deliver goods to the defendant's hardware stores. Over some years, the defendant, Bunnings, accumulated thousands of pallets and used them in its business without returning them or paying for them. The plaintiff requested the return of the pallets in 2002, but the defendants did not return them until 2007. At first instance, the plaintiff successfully made out detinue and conversion, and claimed 'reasonable fee' damages. Allsop P, with whom McFarlan JA agreed, held that the damages were compensatory.[35] The reasonable fee was calculated according to the reduced measure of hire which Chep had offered Bunnings in 2006, not the standard hiring fee. Giles JA agreed with Allsop P, but held that these awards were restitutionary, and that the true measure of the damages was the expense saved by Bunnings, so damages should be measured at the rate which Chep had offered them in 2006.[36]

Lord Reed in the UK Supreme Court has recently suggested that 'user damages' are compensatory.

Morris-Garner v One Step (Support) Ltd [2018] UKSC 20

Facts and issues

The facts of this case are given in Chapter 12 on page 447.

Decision

Lord Reed's speech is the lead speech. For present purposes, the relevant extract deals with his discussion of 'user damages' in tort.

34 (2011) 82 NSWLR 420.

35 Ibid (2011) 82 NSWLR 420, [173].

36 Ibid [194]–[199], [205].

Lord Reed (majority)

(i) User damages in tort

[25] In tort, although damages may in some circumstances be awarded for punitive purposes, the general principle is that damages are compensatory. As Lord Blackburn said in *Livingstone v Rawyards Coal Co* ... :

> I do not think there is any difference of opinion as to its being a general rule that, where any injury is to be compensated by damages, in settling the sum of money to be given for reparation of damages you should as nearly as possible get at that sum of money which will put the party who has been injured, or who has suffered, in the same position as he would have been in if he had not sustained the wrong for which he is now getting his compensation or reparation.

[26] Lord Blackburn's principle can readily be applied in situations where some tangible loss has been sustained: for example, where real property has been damaged or taken by a trespasser (as in the *Livingstone* case itself), or where goods have been converted. Its application is less obvious in situations where there has been an invasion of rights to tangible moveable or immoveable property, but there has been no pecuniary loss or physical damage to the property in question. Nevertheless, where a trespasser has made valuable use of someone else's land, without causing any diminution in its value, the landowner has been held to be entitled to damages measured as what a reasonable person would have paid for the right of user: see, for example, *Whitwham v Westminster Brymbo Coal and Coke Co* .... A similar approach has been adopted in cases of detinue, such as *Strand Electric and Engineering Co Ltd v Brisford Entertainments Ltd* ... . Damages are also available on a similar basis for patent infringement and breaches of other intellectual property rights.

[27] The basis of the award of damages in cases of this kind was considered by Lord Shaw of Dunfermline in *Watson, Laidlaw & Co Ltd v Pott, Cassels & Williamson* ... . The case concerned the sale of machines which infringed the pursuers' patent. The issue in dispute was whether the pursuers were entitled to recover damages for sales which had been made by the defenders in a territory where the pursuers could not themselves have traded, and which, moreover, the defenders would have made even if the machines had not incorporated the infringing part. It was held that they were so entitled. Lord Shaw contrasted the principle underlying the assessment of 'damages in general', whether in contract or in tort, which he described as the principle of 'restoration' as he defined it, with a second principle of 'price or hire', applicable not only to patent cases but 'whenever an abstraction or invasion of property has occurred' ... As he explained, this distinction was relevant to the case before him, since the restoration principle could not support a claim by a patentee relating to a section of trade in which, it was argued, 'he can have sustained no damage, because he would never have sold his patented articles within that section' ... .

[28] Lord Shaw described the second principle as follows, in a passage ... subsequently quoted by Brightman J in *Wrotham Park*:

> ... It is not exactly the principle of restoration, either directly or expressed through compensation, but it is the principle underlying price or hire. It plainly extends – and

> I am inclined to think not infrequently extends – to patent cases. But, indeed, it is not confined to them. For wherever an abstraction or invasion of property has occurred, then, unless such abstraction or invasion were to be sanctioned by law, the law ought to yield a recompense under the category or principle, as I say, either of price or of hire.

He illustrated this by the example of the liveryman's horse … :

> If A, being a liveryman, keeps his horse standing idle in the stable, and B, against his wish or without his knowledge, rides or drives it out, it is no answer to A for B to say: 'Against what loss do you want to be restored? I restore the horse. There is no loss. The horse is none the worse; it is the better for the exercise.'

Lord Shaw also endorsed the view expressed by Fletcher Moulton LJ in *Meters Ltd v Metropolitan Gas Meters Ltd* … that, even if it was not the claimant's practice to grant licences, 'it would be right for the court to consider what would have been the price at which – although no price was actually quoted – could have reasonably been charged for that permission, and estimate the damage in that way'.

[29] The approach adopted in these cases was described by Nicholls LJ in *Stoke-on-Trent City Council v W & J Wass Ltd* … as the 'user principle'. He summarised it as follows … :

> It is an established principle concerning the assessment of damages that a person who has wrongfully used another's property without causing the latter any pecuniary loss may still be liable to that other for more than nominal damages. In general, he is liable to pay, as damages, a reasonable sum for the wrongful use he has made of the other's property. The law has reached this conclusion by giving to the concept of loss or damage in such a case a wider meaning than merely financial loss calculated by comparing the property owner's financial position after the wrongdoing with what it would have been had the wrongdoing never occurred. Furthermore, in such a case it is no answer for the wrongdoer to show that the property owner would probably not have used the property himself had the wrongdoer not done so. …

[30] In these cases, the courts have treated user damages as providing compensation for loss, albeit not loss of a conventional kind. Where property is damaged, the loss suffered can be measured in terms of the cost of repair or the diminution in value, and damages can be assessed accordingly. Where on the other hand an unlawful use is made of property, and the right to control such use is a valuable asset, the owner suffers a loss of a different kind, which calls for a different method of assessing damages. In such circumstances, the person who makes wrongful use of the property prevents the owner from exercising his right to obtain the economic value of the use in question, and should therefore compensate him for the consequent loss. Put shortly, he takes something for nothing, for which the owner was entitled to require payment.

G Contract

As the principles text notes, Australian courts have not presently awarded 'reasonable fees' for breach of negative covenant. Thus all cases extracted below are English ones.

Wrotham Park Estate Co Ltd v Parkside Homes Ltd [1974] 1 WLR 798

Facts and issues

The plaintiffs, Wrotham Park Estate, transferred a certain parcel of land to purchasers, who later transferred it to the defendants, Parkside Homes. Attached to the land was a negative covenant providing that the owner was not permitted to build any houses without submitting plans to the plaintiff and gaining their consent. It became evident during construction of the houses that the defendants did not intend to submit their plans to the plaintiff. The plaintiff did not want to agree to a plan with that many houses. It issued a writ seeking to restrain further building, and a mandatory injunction to pull down the houses already built in breach, but did not seek an interlocutory injunction because it had been advised it would be refused. Meanwhile, the defendants ignored the writ, and completed construction of the properties. Third-party owners moved into the properties.

Decision

Brightman J awarded 5 per cent of the anticipated profits of the development, reflecting a 'reasonable fee' for release of the covenant.

Brightman J

> [**810**] Mr Newsom submitted, and I accept, that it is no answer to a claim for a mandatory injunction that the plaintiffs, having issued proceedings, [**811**] deliberately held their hand and did not seek the assistance of the court for the purpose of preserving the status quo. On the other hand, it is, in my view, equally true that a plaintiff is not entitled 'as of course' to have everything pulled down that was built after the issue of the writ. The erection of the houses, whether one likes it or not, is a fait accompli and the houses are now the homes of people. I accept that this particular fait accompli is reversible and could be undone. But I cannot close my eyes to the fact that the houses now exist. It would, in my opinion, be an unpardonable waste of much needed houses to direct that they now be pulled down and I have never had a moment's doubt during the hearing of this case that such an order ought to be refused. No damage of a financial nature has been done to the plaintiffs by the breach of the lay-out stipulation. The plaintiffs' use of the Wrotham Park Estate has not been and will not be impeded. It is totally unnecessary to demolish the houses in order to preserve the integrity of the restrictive covenants imposed on the rest of area 14. Without hesitation I decline to grant a mandatory injunction. But the fact that these houses will remain does not spell out a charter entitling others to despoil adjacent areas of land in breach of valid restrictions imposed by the conveyances. A developer who tries that course may be in for a rude awakening.

I now consider the question what damages, if any, should be awarded to the plaintiffs. I am able under the jurisdiction which originated with the *Chancery Amendment Act 1858* (Lord Cairns Act) to award damages in substitution for an injunction [against Parkside].

...

[**812**] ... The basic rule in contract is to measure damages by that sum of money which will put the plaintiff in the same position as he would have been in if the contract had not been broken. From that basis, the defendants argue that the damages are nil or purely nominal, because the value of the Wrotham Park Estate as the plaintiffs concede is not diminished by one farthing in consequence of the construction of a road and the erection of 14 houses on the allotment site. If, therefore, the defendants submit, I refuse an injunction I ought to award no damages in lieu. That would seem, on the face of it, a result of questionable fairness on the facts of this case. Had the offending development been the erection of an advertisement hoarding in defiance of protest and writ, I apprehend (assuming my conclusions on other points to be correct) that the court would not have hesitated to grant a mandatory injunction for its removal. If, for social and economic reasons, the court does not see fit in the exercise of its discretion, to order demolition of the 14 houses, is it just that the plaintiffs should receive no compensation and that the defendants should be left in undisturbed possession of the fruits of their wrongdoing? Common sense would seem to demand a negative answer to this question. A comparable problem arose in wayleave cases where the defendant had trespassed by making use of the plaintiff's underground ways to the defendant's profit but without diminishing the value of the plaintiff's property. The plaintiff, in [**813**] such cases, received damages assessed by reference to a reasonable wayleave rent. This principle was considered and extended in *Whitwham v Westminster Brymbo Coal and Coke Co*. ... . For six years the defendant wrongfully tipped colliery waste onto the plaintiff's land. At the trial the defendant was directed to cease tipping and give up possession. The question then arose what damages should be awarded for the wrongful act done to the plaintiff during the period of the defendant's unauthorised user of the land. The official referee found that the diminution in the value of the plaintiff's land was only £200, but that the value of the plaintiff's land to the defendant in 1888 for tipping purposes for six years was some £900. It was held that the proper scale of damages was the higher sum on the ground that a trespasser should not be allowed to make use of another person's land without in some way compensating that other person for the user.

...

The same principle was applied in detinue in *Strand Electric and Engineering Co Ltd v Brisford Entertainments Ltd* ...

The point was further considered in *Penarth Dock Engineering Co Ltd v Pounds* ... by Lord Denning M.R. sitting as a judge of the Queen's Bench Division. The defendant had contracted to buy a floating dock and to remove it from the plaintiff's dock premises. The defendant defaulted in the removal of the purchase. The plaintiff, however, had suffered no damage, since the dock premises had become disused. The plaintiff claimed a mandatory injunction and damages. It was held that the plaintiff was entitled to damages at a rate per week representing a reasonable berthing charge.

The facts of the cases I have mentioned are a long way from the facts of the case before me. Should I, as invited by the plaintiffs, apply a like principle to a case where the defendant Parkside, in defiance of protest and writ, has invaded the plaintiffs' rights in order to reap a financial profit for itself? In *Leeds Industrial Co-operative Society Ltd v Slack* ... Lord Sumner said ... :

> **[815]** ... no money awarded in substitution can be justly awarded, unless it is at any rate designed to be a preferable equivalent for an injunction and therefore an adequate substitute for it, ...

This was said in a dissenting speech but his dissent did not arise in the context of that observation.

In the present case I am faced with the problem what damages ought to be awarded to the plaintiffs in the place of mandatory injunctions which would have restored the plaintiffs' rights. If the plaintiffs are merely given a nominal sum, or no sum, in substitution for injunctions, it seems to me that justice will manifestly not have been done.

As I have said, the general rule would be to measure damages by reference to that sum which would place the plaintiffs in the same position as if the covenant had not been broken. Parkside and the individual purchasers could have avoided breaking the covenant in two ways. One course would have been not to develop the allotment site. The other course would have been for Parkside to have sought from the plaintiffs a relaxation of the covenant. On the facts of this particular case the plaintiffs, rightly conscious of their obligations towards existing resident, would clearly not have granted any relaxation, but for present purposes I must assume that it could have been induced to do so. In my judgment a just substitute for a mandatory injunction would be such a sum of money as might reasonably have been demanded by the plaintiffs from Parkside as a quid pro quo for relaxing the covenant. The plaintiffs submitted that that sum should be a substantial proportion of the development value of the land. This is currently put at no less than £10 000 per plot, ie, £140 000 on the assumption that the plots are undeveloped. Mr Parker gave evidence that a half or a third of the development value was commonly demanded by a landowner whose property stood in the way of a development. I do not agree with that approach to damages in this type of case. I bear in mind the following factors:

(1) The lay-out covenant is not an asset which the estate owner ever contemplated he would have either the opportunity or the desire to turn to account. It has no commercial or even nuisance value. For it cannot he turned to account except to the detriment of the existing residents who are people the estate owner professes to protect.
(2) The breach of covenant which has actually taken place is over a very small area and the impact of this particular breach on the Wrotham Park Estate is insignificant. The validity of the covenant over the rest of area 14 is unaffected.

I think that in a case such as the present a landowner faced with a request from a developer which, it must be assumed, he feels reluctantly obliged to grant, would have first asked the developer what profit he expected to make from his operations. With the benefit of foresight the developer would, in the present case, have said about £50 000 for that is the profit which Parkside concedes it made from the development. I think that the landowner would then reasonably have required a certain percentage of that anticipated profit as a price for the relaxation of the covenant, assuming, as I must, that he feels obliged to relax it. In assessing what would be a fair percentage I think that the court ought, on the particular facts of this case, to act with great moderation. For it is to be borne in mind that the plaintiffs were aware, before the auction look place, that the land was being offered for sale as freehold building land for 13 houses, [**816**] and they knew that they were not going to consent to any such development. They could have informed the Potters Bar Urban District Council of their attitude in advance of the auction, or could have given the like information to Parkside prior to completion of the contract for sale. In either event it seems highly unlikely that Parkside would have parted with its £90 000, at any rate unconditionally. I think that damages must be assessed in such a case on a basis which is fair and, in all the circumstances, in my judgment a sum equal to five per cent. of Parkside's anticipated profit is the most that is fair. I accordingly award the sum of £2500 in substitution for mandatory injunctions. ...

In *Attorney-General v Blake*[37] (see page 550), Lord Nicholls described *Wrotham Park* as shining 'rather as a solitary beacon'[38] for the existence of an explicit gain-based award for breach of contract. However, in *Morris-Garner v One Step (Support) Ltd*[39], Lord Reed appeared to suggest Lord Nicholls was wrong to say *Wrotham Park* was an award of gain-based damages.

Morris-Garner v One Step (Support) Ltd [2018] UKSC 20

Facts and issues

The facts of this case are given in Chapter 12 on page 447.

Decision

Lord Reed's speech is the lead speech. For present purposes, the relevant extract deals with the court's discussions of 'negotiating damages' in contract. In this case, negotiating damages were unavailable because ordinary expectation damages were adequate.

Lord Reed (Lady Hale, Lord Wilson and Lord Carnwath agreeing)

(ii) Common law damages for breach of contract

[31] It is necessary next to consider some basic principles of the law relating to damages for breach of contract: principles which it will be necessary to bear in mind at a later stage of this judgment, when considering the case of *Attorney General v Blake* and its aftermath. Damages in contract serve a different remedial purpose from damages in tort, reflecting

37 [2001] 1 AC 268.

38 Ibid 283.

39 [2018] UKSC 20, [2019] AC 649.

the different nature of the obligation breached by the wrongdoer in each case. The law of tort is concerned with civil wrongs, that is to say with breaches of duties imposed by the law, sometimes generally and sometimes on those who are party to particular relationships or have assumed particular responsibilities, which protect the interests of others in respect of such matters as their bodily integrity, their liberty, their property, their privacy and their reputation. Damages in tort are generally intended to place the claimant as nearly as possible in the same position as he would have been in if the tort had not been committed. The law of contract, on the other hand, gives effect to consensual agreements entered into by particular individuals in their own interests. Remedies granted by the courts are designed to give effect to what was voluntarily undertaken by the parties. Damages in contract are therefore intended to place the claimant in the same position as he would have been in if the contract had been performed.

...

[33] That is not to say that damages in contract will always be different from damages in tort. For example, the damages awarded in cases of medical negligence do not normally depend on whether the claimant was a private patient: the substance of the obligation breached, and the recoverable harm caused, are normally the same whether the cause of action is framed in contract or in tort. Equally, the user principle derived from the property cases discussed earlier is of potential relevance whether the wrongful use of property arises in a contractual or tortious context.

[34] The compensatory nature of damages for breach of contract, and the nature of the loss for which they are designed to compensate, were explained by Lord Diplock in *Photo Production Ltd v Securicor Transport Ltd* ... . As his Lordship stated, a contract is the source of primary legal obligations upon each party to it to procure that whatever he has promised will be done is done. Leaving aside the comparatively rare cases in which the court is able to enforce a primary obligation by decreeing specific performance of it, breaches of primary obligations give rise to 'substituted or secondary obligations' on the part of the party in default. Those secondary obligations of the contract breaker arise by implication of law:

> ... to pay monetary compensation to the other party for the loss sustained by him in consequence of the breach ... ...

[35] Damages for breach of contract are in that sense a substitute for performance. That is why they are generally regarded as an adequate remedy. The courts will not prevent self-interested breaches of contract where the interests of the innocent party can be adequately protected by an award of damages. Nor will the courts award damages designed to deprive the contract breaker of any profit he may have made as a consequence of his failure in performance. Their function is confined to enforcing either the primary obligation to perform, or the contract breaker's secondary obligation to pay damages as a substitute for performance (subject, according to the decision in *Attorney General v Blake,* to a discretion to order an account of profits in exceptional circumstances where the other remedies are inadequate). The damages awarded cannot therefore be affected by whether the breach was deliberate or self-interested.

[37] The quantification of economic loss is often relatively straightforward. There are, however, cases in which its precise measurement is inherently impossible. ... An example

> relevant to the present case is the situation where a breach of contract affects the operation of a business. The court will have to select the method of measuring the loss which is the most apt in the circumstances to secure that the claimant is compensated for the loss which it has sustained. It may, for example, estimate the effect of the breach on the value of the business, or the effect on its profits, or the resultant management costs, or the loss of goodwill … .The assessment of damages in such circumstances often involves what Lord Shaw described in *Watson, Laidlaw …* as 'the exercise of a sound imagination and the practice of the broad axe'.
>
> **[38]** Evidential difficulties in establishing the measure of loss are reflected in the degree of certainty with which the law requires damages to be proved. As is stated in *Chitty*, para 26–015, '[w]here it is clear that the claimant has suffered substantial loss, but the evidence does not enable it to be precisely quantified, the court will assess damages as best it can on the available evidence'. In so far as the defendant may have destroyed or wrongfully prevented or impeded the claimant from adducing relevant evidence, the court can make presumptions in favour of the claimant. The point is illustrated by the case of *Armory v Delamirie …*, where a chimney sweep's boy found a jewel and took it to the defendant's shop to find out what it was. The defendant returned only the empty socket, and was held liable to pay damages to the boy. … Pratt CJ directed the jury 'that, unless the defendant did produce the jewel, and shew it not to be of the finest water, they should presume the strongest against him, and make the value of the best jewels the measure of their damages: which they accordingly did'.

In commenting on *Attorney-General v Blake*,[40] Lord Reed said the following:

> **[71]** Those three disparate types of award (damages for interferences with property, an account of profits made through a breach of fiduciary duty, and damages in substitution for an injunction), each reflecting the characteristics of the obligation which had been breached or the jurisdiction being exercised, formed the stepping stones to the fourth, namely damages for breach of contract. Lord Nicholls began by stating that such damages are compensatory: 'that', he said, 'is axiomatic' … . But 'a party to a contract may have an interest in performance which is not readily measurable in terms of money' … . In such cases, 'a financially assessed measure of damages is inadequate' … . The primary response of the law to this type of case was to provide specific relief, such as an injunction, so as to ensure that the contractual obligation was performed. These specific remedies, it was said, 'go a long way towards providing suitable protection for innocent parties who will suffer loss from breaches of contract which are not adequately remediable by an award of damages' … . But they were not always available.
>
> **[72]** Lord Nicholls then cited *Wrotham Park* as an example of a case in which specific relief had been refused. The judge had been right to apply by analogy the cases concerning interferences with property rights, since 'it is not easy to see why, as between the parties to a contract, a violation of a party's contractual rights should attract a lesser degree of remedy than a violation of his property rights' … . *Wrotham Park* was said … to shine as a solitary beacon, showing:

40 [2001] 1 AC 268.

> … that in contract as well as tort damages are not always narrowly confined to recoupment of financial loss. In a suitable case damages for breach of contract may be measured by the benefit gained by the wrongdoer from the breach. The defendant must make a reasonable payment in respect of the benefit he has gained.

[73] This part of Lord Nicholls' speech is not altogether easy to interpret. A few observations can however be made. First, the fact that 'a party to a contract may have an interest in performance which is not readily measurable in terms of money' … has long been recognised by the law of damages. The law normally responds to inherent difficulties of measurement, and to difficulties arising from a paucity of evidence in a particular case, in the ways discussed at paras 37–38 above. Such difficulties do not justify the abandonment of any attempt to measure loss, and the use of the benefit gained by the wrongdoer as an alternative basis for an award of contractual damages, since that alternative is inconsistent with the logic of contractual damages, as explained at paras 31–35 above.

[74] It is also necessary to recognise that the assessment of a hypothetical release fee is itself a difficult and uncertain exercise. In cases such as *Wrotham Park, Bracewell v Appleby* and *Jaggard v Sawyer*, judges estimated in a rough and ready way the amount which the claimant might fairly and reasonably have demanded as a quid pro quo for the relaxation of the obligation in question. More recently, the practice has developed of instructing forensic accountants to give expert evidence about a hypothetical negotiation between a reasonable person in the position of the claimant and a reasonable person in the position of the defendant. Such imaginary negotiations have become increasingly elaborate, and a host of questions can emerge as to the basis on which they should be hypothesised. …

[75] The artificiality of the exercise can be a further problem. Since the aim is to arrive at an objective valuation, the fact that the claimant might in reality have been unwilling to release the defendant from the obligation is not necessarily a problem, as Brightman J recognised in *Wrotham Park*. But the premise of the hypothetical negotiation – that a reasonable person in the claimant's position would have been willing to release the defendant from the obligation in return for a fee – breaks down in a situation where any reasonable person in the claimant's position would have been unwilling to grant a release, as was found to be the position in *Marathon Asset Management LLP v Seddon …*

[76] Secondly, although it is not clear what Lord Nicholls meant by 'a lesser degree of remedy' …, it is not surprising that damages for breach of contract are generally assessed differently from damages for the invasion of a proprietary right, since the rights and obligations in question are generally of a different character. It is only in circumstances where they are analogous that it would be reasonable to expect some consistency of approach. As has been explained, damages for breach of contract are based on the difference to the claimant between the outcome of performance and non-performance. That is not generally the same as the economic value of the right to performance, considered as an asset (which is not to deny that they may be the same, or similar, in some circumstances). …

[77] Thirdly, as Lord Walker remarked in *Pell Frischmann* at para 48, it is a little surprising that Lord Nicholls should have described *Wrotham Park* as a beacon in relation to common law damages for breach of contract. In the first place, the proceedings were not based on a contractual right: there was no contract between the parties. They were concerned with the invasion of a property right, as Lord Walker observed. Furthermore, *Wrotham Park* was not concerned with common law damages, but with damages awarded in substitution for an injunction. In the circumstances of the case, these were not merely arbitrary matters of legal categorisation, but bore directly on the damages awarded, as has been explained. That is not to say that common law damages for a particular breach of contract are necessarily different from damages for analogous breaches of other types of obligation. As was said earlier, in circumstances where the rights and obligations are analogous, it would be reasonable to expect some consistency of approach.

[78] Fourthly, it is plainly true that 'in contract as well as tort damages are not always narrowly confined to recoupment of financial loss'. However, that proposition does not depend on the *Wrotham Park* line of cases. It is illustrated, in relation to breach of contract, by cases concerned with the award of damages at common law for breaches causing non-economic loss, such as *Ruxley Electronics* … .

[79] Fifthly, since the assessment of damages in the property cases was based on the value of the right to control the use of the property as it had been wrongfully used, there is a sense in which it can be said that the damages in those cases 'may be measured by reference to the benefit gained by the wrongdoer from the breach', provided the 'benefit' is taken to be the objective value of the wrongful use. The same can be said of the *Wrotham Park* line of cases, subject to the same proviso, and subject also to the role of equitable considerations in the making of awards under Lord Cairns' Act. The courts did not, however, adopt a benefits-based approach, but conceived of the awards as compensating for loss.

…

[95] The foregoing discussion leads to the following conclusions:

(1) Damages assessed by reference to the value of the use wrongfully made of property (sometimes termed 'user damages') are readily awarded at common law for the invasion of rights to tangible moveable or immoveable property (by detinue, conversion or trespass). The rationale of such awards is that the person who makes wrongful use of property, where its use is commercially valuable, prevents the owner from exercising a valuable right to control its use, and should therefore compensate him for the loss of the value of the exercise of that right. He takes something for nothing, for which the owner was entitled to require payment.

(2) Damages are also available on a similar basis for patent infringement and breaches of other intellectual property rights.

(3) Damages can be awarded under Lord Cairns' Act in substitution for specific performance or an injunction, where the court had jurisdiction to entertain an application for such relief at the time when the proceedings were commenced. Such damages are a monetary substitute for what is lost by the withholding of such relief.

(4) One possible method of quantifying damages under this head is on the basis of the economic value of the right which the court has declined to enforce, and which it has consequently rendered worthless. Such a valuation can be arrived at by reference to the amount which the claimant might reasonably have demanded as a quid pro quo for the relaxation of the obligation in question. The rationale is that, since the withholding of specific relief has the same practical effect as requiring the claimant to permit the infringement of his

rights, his loss can be measured by reference to the economic value of such permission.

(5) That is not, however, the only approach to assessing damages under Lord Cairns' Act. It is for the court to judge what method of quantification, in the circumstances of the case before it, will give a fair equivalent for what is lost by the refusal of the injunction.

(6) Common law damages for breach of contract are intended to compensate the claimant for loss or damage resulting from the non-performance of the obligation in question. They are therefore normally based on the difference between the effect of performance and non-performance upon the claimant's situation.

(7) Where damages are sought at common law for breach of contract, it is for the claimant to establish that a loss has been incurred, in the sense that he is in a less favourable situation, either economically or in some other respect, than he would have been in if the contract had been performed.

(8) Where the breach of a contractual obligation has caused the claimant to suffer economic loss, that loss should be measured or estimated as accurately and reliably as the nature of the case permits. The law is tolerant of imprecision where the loss is incapable of precise measurement, and there are also a variety of legal principles which can assist the claimant in cases where there is a paucity of evidence.

(9) Where the claimant's interest in the performance of a contract is purely economic, and he cannot establish that any economic loss has resulted from its breach, the normal inference is that he has not suffered any loss. In that event, he cannot be awarded more than nominal damages.

(10) Negotiating damages can be awarded for breach of contract where the loss suffered by the claimant is appropriately measured by reference to the economic value of the right which has been breached, considered as an asset. That may be the position where the breach of contract results in the loss of a valuable asset created or protected by the right which was infringed. The rationale is that the claimant has in substance been deprived of a valuable asset, and his loss can therefore be measured by determining the economic value of the right in question, considered as an asset. The defendant has taken something for nothing, for which the claimant was entitled to require payment.

(11) Common law damages for breach of contract cannot be awarded merely for the purpose of depriving the defendant of profits made as a result of the breach, other than in exceptional circumstances, following *Attorney General v Blake*.

(12) Common law damages for breach of contract are not a matter of discretion. They are claimed as of right, and they are awarded or refused on the basis of legal principle.

The present case

[96] Applying these conclusions to the present case, it is apparent that neither the judge nor the Court of Appeal applied an approach which can now be regarded as correct. The

> judge was mistaken in considering that the claimant had a right to elect how its damages should be assessed. He was mistaken in supposing that the difficulty of quantifying its financial loss, such as it was, justified the abandonment of any attempt to quantify it, and the award instead of a remedy which could not be regarded as compensatory in any meaningful sense.
>
> **[97]** The Court of Appeal was mistaken in treating the deliberate nature of the breach, or the difficulty of establishing precisely the consequent financial loss, or the claimant's interest in preventing the defendants' profit-making activities, as justifying the award of a monetary remedy which was not compensatory. The idea that damages based on a hypothetical release fee are available whenever that is a just response, that being a matter to be decided by the judge on a broad brush basis, is also mistaken. The basis on which damages are awarded cannot be a matter for the discretion of the primary judge.
>
> **[98]** This is a case brought by a commercial entity whose only interest in the defendants' performance of their obligations under the covenants was commercial. Indeed, a restrictive covenant which went beyond what was necessary for the reasonable protection of the claimant's commercial interests would have been unenforceable. The substance of the claimant's case is that it suffered financial loss as a result of the defendants' breach of contract. The effect of the breach of contract was to expose the claimant's business to competition which would otherwise have been avoided. The natural result of that competition was a loss of profits and possibly of goodwill. The loss is difficult to quantify, and some elements of it may be inherently incapable of precise measurement. Nevertheless, it is a familiar type of loss, for which damages are frequently awarded. It is possible to quantify it in a conventional manner … .

Lord Sumption (in the minority) said that he agreed with Lord Reed generally,[41] but he analysed the cases as follows:

- cases where damages are not limited to pecuniary loss, typically where the plaintiff has a proprietary right and an interest which extends beyond financial reparation[42]
- cases where the plaintiff would be entitled to specific relief, and the fee is the price of non-enforcement (as in *Wrotham Park*)[43] and
- cases where there is no right beyond financial reparation or entitlement to specific relief, but the plaintiff has suffered pecuniary loss, and the notional release fee is evidence of that loss.[44]

Lords Reed and Carnwath explicitly disagreed with Lord Sumption's speech.[45]

41 *Morris-Garner v One Step (Support) Ltd* [2018] UKSC 20, [2019] AC 649.

42 Ibid [110].

43 Ibid [112]–[114].

44 Ibid [115]–[125].

45 Ibid [101] (Lord Reed); [132] (Lord Carnwath).

Figure 16.4 Compensatory interpretations of reasonable fee awards for tort or contract

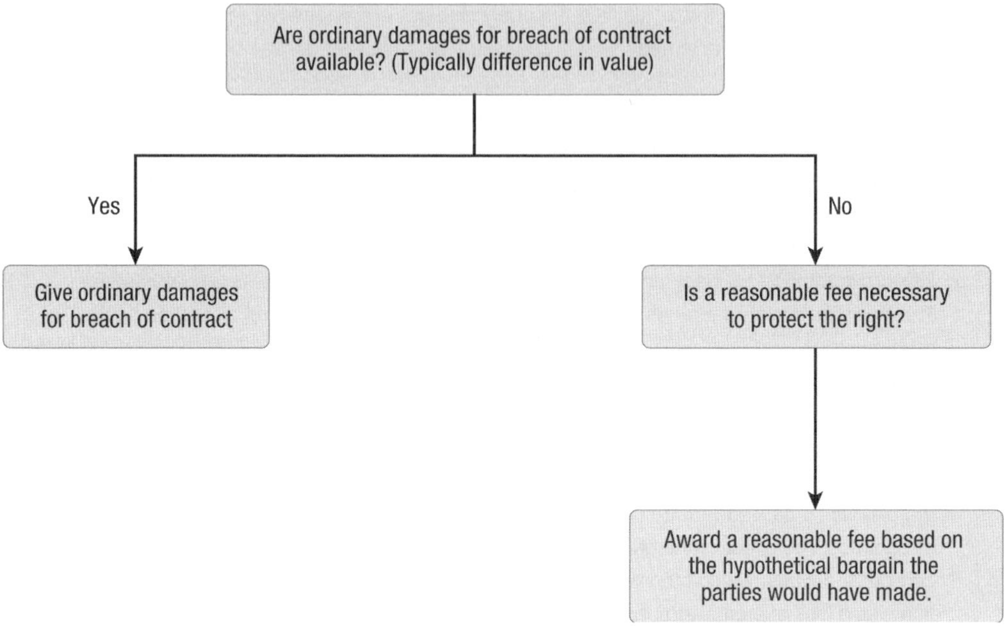

Figure 16.5 Restitutionary interpretations of reasonable fee awards for tort or contract

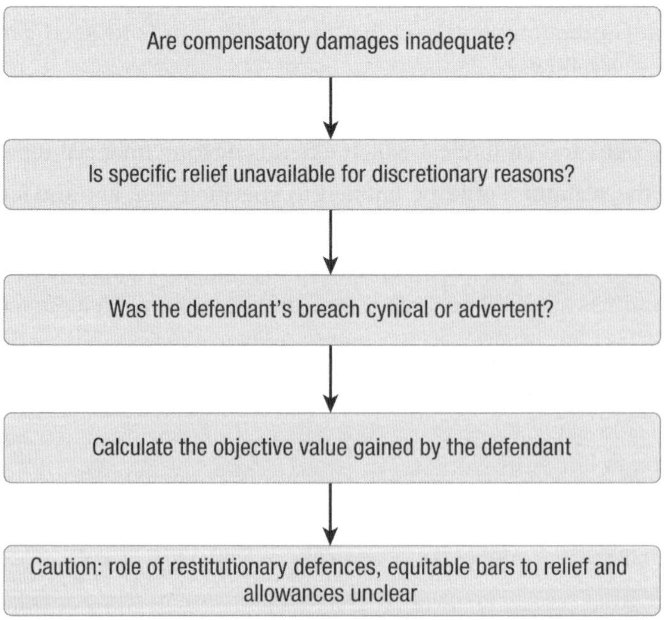

Review Questions

(1) For what causes of action are 'reasonable fee' awards typically given?

(2) How is the 'reasonable fee' calculated?

(3) Is the reasonable fee award compensatory, restitutionary or something else?

V Allowances, discretionary factors and bars to relief

Concept	Short explanation	Relevant authorities	Principles text
Allowances for skill and effort	Breaching fiduciaries may be accorded an allowance for skill and effort.	*Warman International Ltd v Dwyer* (1995) 182 CLR 544 *Dart Industries Inc v Décor Corporation Pty Ltd* (1993) 179 CLR 101, 111	Chapter 16: [16.110]–[16.124]
Discretionary factors and bars to relief	Discretionary factors and bars to relief clearly apply to accounts of profit.* However, it is unclear whether they are relevant to reasonable fee awards.	The case cited in footnotes is an example of the general principle.	Chapter 16: [16.125]–[16.139]

* See, eg, *Re Jarvis (Deceased)* [1958] 1 WLR 815, 820–1 (delay and acquiescence precluding an account of profits).

A Allowances for skill and effort

As *Warman International Ltd v Dwyer* makes clear, breaching fiduciaries may be accorded an allowance for skill and effort, even if the profits are not directly apportioned according to whether they flowed directly from the breach.[46] *Warman International Ltd v Dwyer* is controversial as, while Dwyer's profits were subject to a less generous allowance, he still received an allowance despite his lack of good faith.[47] By contrast, the fact that the fiduciary in *Boardman v Phipps*[48] acted in good faith was used to justify a generous allowance.

Allowances for skill and effort are also possible for defendants who are liable for accounts of profits for intellectual property infringements (as in the case excerpted below). However, the availability will also depend upon the belief in a bona fide right to infringe.

46 (1995) 182 CLR 544, 558–9.

47 Ibid 598.

48 [1967] 2 AC 46.

Dart Industries Inc v Décor Corporation Pty Ltd (1993) 179 CLR 101

Facts and issues

Dart successfully brought an action in infringement of patent against Décor in relation to press button seals of kitchen containers. Dart elected to take an account of profits rather than damages. The question arose as to what costs could be taken into account in an allowance.

Decision

If the infringing product was a 'side line' and the defendant would not have otherwise expended the costs, then it was inappropriate to award an allowance. By contrast, if the defendant forewent the opportunity to manufacture non-infringing products, it would be fair to give some allowance.

Mason CJ, Deane, Dawson and Toohey JJ

> [**112**] Dart's argument, based on incremental costing as the proper method for taking an account of profits of infringing activities, is as follows. The profit should be calculated by taking the gross revenue received from the manufacture and sale of the infringing product and deducting from it [sic] direct costs, such as materials or labour, [**113**] solely due to the manufacture or sale of the infringing product, and also deducting overheads, but only to the extent that they were increased by the manufacture or sale of the infringing product. Otherwise, the defendant would be able to deduct expenditure which it would have incurred in any event. This should not be allowed because if any of the revenue from the sale or manufacture could be set off against general overheads which would have been incurred without the infringing activities, the defendant would profit from the infringing activities. The defendant would gain by reducing the cost of its overheads, but would not have to account to the plaintiff for this gain.
>
> Not only does Dart rely on the passage cited from the judgment of Harvey CJ in Eq. but it maintains that the same principle is to be seen in the judgment of Windeyer J in *Colbeam Palmer Ltd v Stock Affiliates Pty Ltd*. That was a case of infringement of a trade mark in which Windeyer J ordered an account of profits. In doing so, he directed that the cost of selling and delivering the infringing articles be taken into account. But he added:
>
>> This will include any costs directly attributable to such sales and deliveries. But it should not, I think, include any part of the general overhead costs, managerial expenses and so forth of the defendant's business, as it seems that all these would have been incurred in any event in the ordinary course of its business in which as it was put in evidence the painting sets were a 'side line'.
>
> The explanation of the direction given by Windeyer J is that mentioned by him, namely, that the infringing articles were a side line. There appears to have been unused capacity in the defendant's business in the form of overheads which would have been incurred whether or not the infringing articles had been sold and delivered. The sale and delivery of the infringing articles took up that surplus capacity or some of it, and none of the overhead costs

was attributable to the infringing activities because those costs would have been incurred in any event.

But there was no evidence in this case that Décor or Rian had unused or surplus capacity. There was evidence that the infringing canisters were an integral part of one consistent product range produced, marketed and sold according to a common system. From this it might be inferred that, had those companies not been engaged in the manufacture and marketing of the infringing press button seal canisters, their capacity for those activities would have [**114**] been taken up in the manufacture and marketing of alternative products.

Thus the cost of manufacturing and marketing the press button seal canisters may have included the cost of forgoing the profit from the manufacture and marketing of alternative products. The latter cost is called an opportunity cost. 'Opportunity cost' can be defined as 'the value of the alternative foregone by adopting a particular strategy or employing resources in a specific manner … As used in economics, the opportunity cost of any designated alternative is the greatest net benefit lost by taking an alternative.' The practical reality of this concept was recognized in *Schnadig Corp v Gaines Manufacturing Co Inc*, where the Court stated: 'The alternative available uses of the facilities devoted to the infringement must be considered, and these too will vary.'

In calculating an account of profits, the defendant may not deduct the opportunity cost, that is, the profit forgone on the alternative products. But there would be real inequity if a defendant were denied a deduction for the opportunity cost as well as being denied a deduction for the cost of the overheads which sustained the capacity that would have been utilized by an alternative product and that was in fact utilized by the infringing product. If both were denied, the defendant would be in a worse position than if it had made no use of the patented invention. The purpose of an account of profits is not to punish the defendant but to prevent its unjust enrichment.

Where the defendant has forgone the opportunity to manufacture and sell alternative products it will ordinarily be appropriate to attribute to the infringing product a proportion of those general overheads which would have sustained the opportunity. On the other hand, if no opportunity was forgone, and the overheads involved were costs which would have been incurred in any event, then it would not be appropriate to attribute the overheads to the infringing product. Otherwise the defendant would be in a better position than it would have been in if it had not infringed. It is not relevant that the product could not have been manufactured and sold without these overheads. Nor is it relevant that absorption method accounting would attribute a proportion of the overheads to the infringing product. The equitable principle of an account of profits is not to compensate the plaintiff, nor to fix a fair price for the [**115**] infringing product, but to prevent the unjust enrichment of the defendant.

Of course, further possibilities may in some cases be open on the evidence. Overhead costs might have been increased by the manufacture and sale of the infringing product, or overhead costs might have been reduced had the infringing product not been produced. In either case it may be appropriate to attribute the difference in overhead costs to the infringing product.

Apportionment for intellectual property breaches is also used to split profits attributable to the infringement and other profits, as outlined in *Colbeam Palmer Ltd v Stock Affiliates Pty Ltd*.[49]

It is unclear whether an allowance for skill and effort would operate to reduce accounts of profits for breach of contract in Australia, as such awards are not presently available.

B Discretionary factors and bars to relief

As noted in the principles text, there are three relevant bars to relief: hardship, lack of clean hands, and delay and acquiescence. The operation of the bars to relief are described in more detail in the principles text at [16.125]–[16.139]. They incontrovertibly operate in relation to accounts of profit for breach of fiduciary duty.

In relation to intellectual property, delay and acquiescence is the main relevant bar, and there is an interplay with knowledge of the infringement.

It is unclear whether discretionary bars would operate for gain-based relief for tort and breach of contract. It is doubtful whether they operate for reasonable fee awards, although sometimes delay seems to be a reason for reasonable fees to be awarded instead of accounts of profits.

REVIEW QUESTIONS

(1) What do you think the rationale for the allowance for skill and effort is?

(2) What do you think might be the main bar to relief for an account of profits?

VI The future of gain-based relief in Australia

As the principles text notes at [16.140], accounts of profits are incontrovertibly available for equitable breaches and intellectual property breaches. They are subject to allowances for skill and effort and bars to relief. Accounts of profit are presently unavailable for common law causes of action in Australia. The status of reasonable fee awards is radically uncertain. While it is clear they are available for intellectual property breaches, proprietary torts and (in the United Kingdom) breaches of negative covenant, their nature and precise method of operation is unclear.

REVIEW QUESTIONS

(1) Do you think Australian law should allow accounts of profit for tortious breaches and breach of contract?

(2) Do you think reasonable fees should be counted as a form of gain-based relief, or as something else (compensatory or sui generis)? Why does it matter?

49 (1968) 122 CLR 25, 42–3 (Windeyer J).

PART 6

RESTITUTION AND GIVING BACK

17 PERSONAL REMEDIES FOR UNJUST ENRICHMENT

I Introduction 586
II The elements of unjust enrichment 587
III Precise remedies for unjust enrichment 587
A Money claims 588
B Services claims 590
C Goods claims 592
IV Defences to a claim for restitution 592
V The relationship between contract and restitution for unjust enrichment 593

I Introduction

A restitutionary remedy is imposed when a defendant unjustly gains at the plaintiff's expense (whether money, services or goods). The defendant must give back what they gained (or the monetary value thereof). This chapter, following the principles book, will deal with personal restitutionary remedies for subtractive unjust enrichment. The history of unjust enrichment is dealt with by the principles text. The law on this topic must be treated with care in an Australian context. (See the excerpt from *Roxborough v Rothmans of Pall Mall Australia Ltd*[1] in Chapter 1, page 13.)

As Figure 17.1 demonstrates, there are three personal restitutionary remedies for unjust enrichment, all with common law origins. (See principles text [17.20]–[17.22].)

Figure 17.1 The three kinds of personal restitutionary remedies in Australia

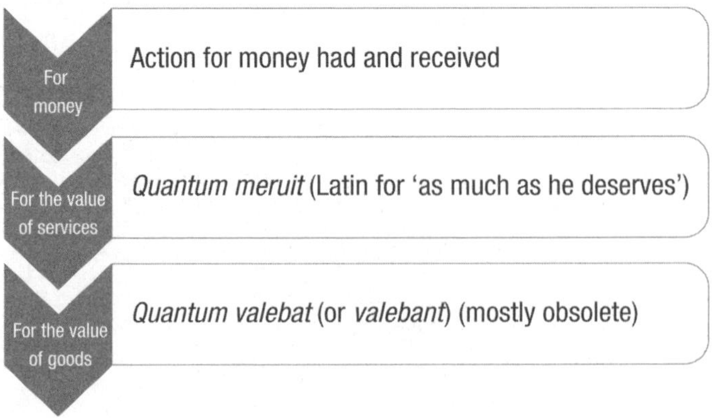

1 (2001) 208 CLR 516.

REVIEW QUESTIONS

(1) Are restitutionary remedies common law or equitable?

(2) Why do you think the *quantum valebat* is mostly obsolete?

II The elements of unjust enrichment

The concept of unjust enrichment is that a person who has been unjustly enriched at the expense of another must make restitution to that other, subject to defences. The High Court has said unjust enrichment is a 'concept' rather than a 'definitive legal principle'.[2]

Concept	Short explanation	Relevant authorities	Principles text
The structure of the 'concept' of unjust enrichment	Typically there are four steps: (1) Identify factor which makes transaction unjust. (2) Identify enrichment of defendant. (3) Identify the way in which the enrichment was at the expense of the plaintiff. (4) Consider defences.	*David Securities Pty Ltd v Commonwealth Bank of Australia* (1992) 175 CLR 353 (see extract on page 589)	Chapter 17: [17.13]–[17.18]

Figure 17.2 illustrates how the concept of unjust enrichment works.

REVIEW QUESTION

Do you think uncertainty about the status of unjust enrichment in Australian law is a problem?

III Precise remedies for unjust enrichment

The remedy for claims in unjust enrichment is restitution of the value of the benefit received by the defendant at the plaintiff's expense, be it money, services or goods. The remedy depends upon the nature of the enrichment received by the defendant.

Concept	Short explanation	Relevant authorities	Principles text
Money claims	When a defendant has 'unjustly' received money at the plaintiff's expense, the plaintiff can bring an action for money had and received.	*David Securities Pty Ltd v Commonwealth Bank of Australia* (1992) 175 CLR 353	Chapter 17: [17.20]–[17.22]

2 Ibid [74] (Gummow J). See also *Mann v Paterson Constructions Pty Ltd* (2019) 267 CLR 560, [212]–[213] (Nettle, Gordon and Edelman JJ), noting that the English Courts have retreated from the rigid application of these categories.

Concept	Short explanation	Relevant authorities	Principles text
Services claims	Where a defendant has 'unjustly' received a service at the plaintiff's expense, the plaintiff can bring an action for *quantum meruit*. However, the defendant may be able to 'subjectively devalue' the benefit.	*Pavey & Matthews Pty Ltd v Paul* (1987) 162 CLR 221	Chapter 17: [17.23]–[17.27]
Goods	Where the defendant has 'unjustly' received goods at the plaintiff's expense, the plaintiff can bring an action for *quantum valebat*.	This cause of action is largely obsolete.	Chapter 17: [17.28]–[17.30]

Figure 17.2 The elements of a claim in unjust enrichment

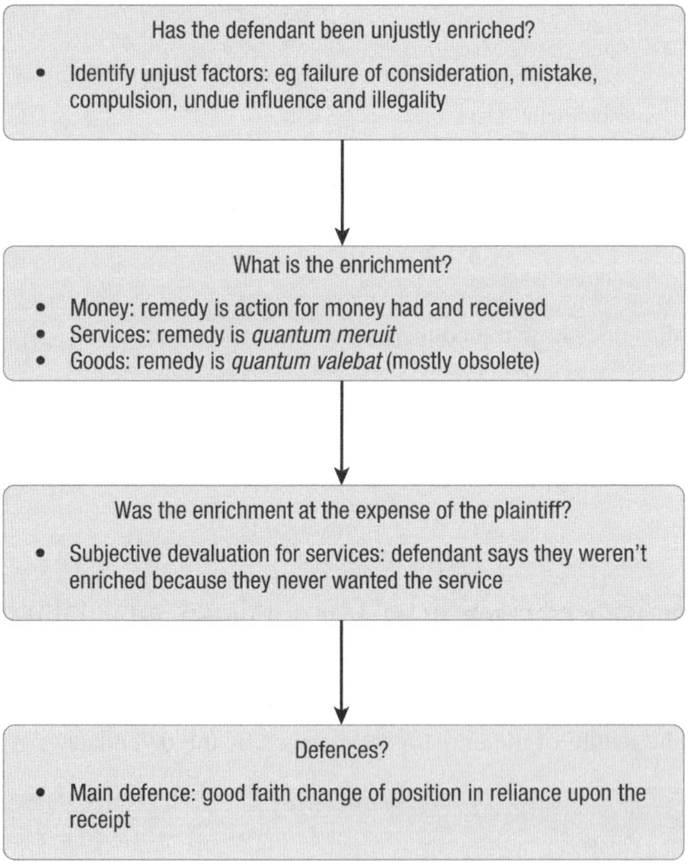

A Money claims

When a defendant has 'unjustly' received money at the plaintiff's expense, the plaintiff can bring an action for money had and received (the cause of action is also the remedy). A defendant is, by default, 'enriched' by receipt of money.

David Securities Pty Ltd v Commonwealth Bank of Australia (1992) 175 CLR 353

Facts and issues

The plaintiffs, David Securities Pty Ltd ('David Securities'), borrowed money from the defendant, the Commonwealth Bank of Australia, under a 'Swiss franc loan agreement'. The interest payable depended upon the relationship between the Australian dollar and the Swiss franc. A clause in the agreement said that any tax payable in respect of interest was payable by the borrower. Then operative s 261 of the *Income Tax Assessment Act 1936* (Cth) rendered the clause void, because borrowers were not to pay tax. The plaintiffs unsuccessfully sued the defendant for losses they sustained because of the loan, and the defendant successfully counter-sued in debt. The plaintiffs sought to set off the debt against the mistakenly paid tax moneys, on the basis that they were entitled to an action for money had and received.

Decision

A majority of the High Court allowed the plaintiff's action for money had and received. The distinction between mistake of fact and law established in *Bilbie v Lumley*[3] was abolished. Brennan J dissented.

Mason CJ, Deane, Toohey, Gaudron and McHugh JJ (majority)

> [**379**] … it is not legitimate to determine whether an enrichment is unjust by reference to some subjective evaluation of what is fair or unconscionable. Instead, recovery depends upon the existence of a qualifying or vitiating factor such as mistake, duress or illegality …
>
> …
>
> As La Forest J. stated in *Air Canada v British Columbia*, the two species of mistake (i.e., fact and law) should be 'considered as factors which can make an enrichment at the plaintiff's expense 'unjust' or 'unjustified'.
>
> The respondent's submission that the appellants must independently prove 'unjustness' over and above the mistake cannot therefore be sustained. The fact that the payment has been caused by a mistake is sufficient to give rise to a prima facie obligation on the part of the respondent to make restitution. Before that prima facie liability is displaced, the respondent must point to circumstances which the law recognizes would make an order for restitution unjust. There can be no restitution in such circumstances because the law will not provide for recovery except when the enrichment is *unjust*. It follows that the recipient of a payment, which is sought to be recovered on the ground of unjust enrichment, is entitled to raise by way of answer any matter or circumstance which shows that his or her receipt (or retention) of the payment is not unjust.
>
> …

3 (1802) 2 East 469; 102 ER 448. See also *York Air Conditioning & Refrigeration (A/asia) Pty Ltd v Commonwealth* (1949) 80 CLR 11.

B Services claims

Where a defendant has 'unjustly' received a service at the plaintiff's expense, the plaintiff can bring an action for *quantum meruit*, reflecting the 'fair value of the benefit provided'. Usually the market value is used to measure the benefit.

Pavey & Matthews Pty Ltd v Paul (1987) 162 CLR 221

Facts and issues

Pavey & Matthews Pty Ltd, the plaintiffs, orally agreed to do building work for the defendant, Paul, at prevailing market rates. When the work was completed, Paul refused to pay the balance of $26 945.50. The oral contract was unenforceable pursuant to s 45 of the *Builders Licensing Act 1971* (NSW).

Decision

A majority of the High Court (Brennan J dissenting) held that Paul would be unjustly enriched at the builders' expense if she was allowed to retain the building work without payment. The plaintiffs received a *quantum meruit* reflecting the reasonable value of their work.

Deane J

> [**263**] There is no apparent reason in justice why a builder who is precluded from enforcing an agreement should also be deprived of the ordinary common law right to bring proceedings on a common indebitatus count to recover fair and reasonable remuneration for work which he has actually done and which has been accepted by the building owner … . Nor, upon a consideration of the words of s 45 in their context in the Act, am I able to identify any legislative intent to deprive the builder of that ordinary common law right. The section does not make an agreement to which it applies illegal or void. Nor do its words disclose any legislative intent to penalise the builder beyond making the agreement itself unenforceable by him against the other party. It may be that the bringing of an action as on a common indebitatus count would conflict with the apparent legislative policy underlying s 45 if the claimant in such an action were entitled as of right to recover the amount which the building owner had agreed to pay under the unenforceable agreement. I am, however, unpersuaded that the bringing by a builder of an action on the common indebitatus count in which he can recover no more than what is fair and reasonable in the circumstances as compensation for the benefit of the work which he has actually done and which has been accepted by the building owner conflicts with any discernible legislative policy. Plainly enough, the survival of the ordinary common law right of the builder to recover, in an action [**263**] founded on restitution or unjust enrichment, reasonable remuneration for work done and accepted under a contract which is unenforceable by him does not frustrate the purpose of the section to provide protection for a building owner. The building owner remains entitled to enforce the contract. He cannot, however, be forced either to comply with its terms or to permit the builder to carry it to completion. All that he can be required to

do is to pay reasonable compensation for work done of which he has received the benefit and for which in justice he is obligated to make such a payment by way of restitution. In relation to such work, he can rely on the contract, if it has not been rescinded, as to the amount of remuneration and the terms of payment. If the agreed remuneration exceeds what is reasonable in the circumstances, he can rely on the unenforceability of the contract with the result that he is liable to pay no more than what is fair and reasonable.

... What the concept of monetary restitution involves is the payment of an amount which constitutes, in all the relevant circumstances, fair and just compensation for the benefit or 'enrichment' actually or constructively accepted. Ordinarily, that will correspond to the fair value of the benefit provided (e.g. remuneration calculated at a reasonable rate for work actually done or the fair market value of materials supplied). In some categories of case, however, it would be to affront rather than satisfy the requirements of good conscience and justice which inspire the concept or principle of restitution or unjust enrichment to determine what constitutes fair and just compensation for a benefit accepted by reference only to what would represent a fair remuneration for the work involved or a fair market value of materials supplied. ... [R]elevant for present purposes is the special category of case where restitution is sought by one party for work which he has executed under a contract which has become unenforceable by reason of his failure to comply with the requirements of a statutory provision which was enacted to protect the other party. In that category of case, it would be contrary to the general notions of restitution or unjust enrichment if what constituted fair and just **[264]** compensation for the benefit accepted by the other party were to be ascertained without regard to any identifiable real detriment sustained by that other party by reason of the failure of the first party to ensure that the requirements of the statutory provision were satisfied. Thus, if it is established on the hearing of the present case that Mrs Paul has sustained an identifiable real detriment by reason of the failure of the builder to ensure that there was a written memorandum of the oral contract which satisfied the requirements of s 45 of the Act, that would be an important factor in determining what constituted fair and just restitution in the circumstances of the case for the work done and materials supplied of which she has accepted the benefit. The mere fact that the reasonable remuneration for the building work done at Mrs Paul's request exceeded Mrs Paul's expectations would not, however, of itself constitute any such identifiable real detriment since it is not necessary for the purposes of s 45 of the Act that a written contract contain either an agreed price for the building work or an estimate of what the cost of it to the building owner will ultimately be.

A defendant may be able to 'subjectively devalue' a benefit. This term means that they were not enriched because they successfully asserted that they never wanted that benefit.[4]

A plaintiff may argue that a defendant should not be permitted to 'subjectively devalue' an enrichment for three reasons:

4 The term 'subjective devaluation' has been disapproved by the Supreme Court of the United Kingdom in *Benedetti v Sawiris* [2014] AC 938. See the discussion in J Edelman and E Bant, *Unjust Enrichment* (Hart, 2nd ed, 2016) 81–4. The term is still used here because it has not been explicitly rejected in Australia yet.

(1) The enrichment is an 'incontrovertible benefit';[5] no reasonable person could argue that the benefit was not wanted.

(2) The defendant objectively chose the benefit.

(3) The defendant chose to retain the benefit despite the fact that they had an opportunity (or duty) to reject it ('free acceptance').

C Goods claims

Where the defendant has 'unjustly' received goods at the plaintiff's expense, the plaintiff can bring an action for *quantum valebat*. As the principles text describes, this action has largely been superseded, but occasionally still arises in construction law cases.

REVIEW QUESTIONS

(1) Is there any reason why Australian law should continue to retain the old common law forms of action such as the *quantum meruit?*

(2) Can you think of any situations where someone might want to 'subjectively devalue' a service?

IV Defences to a claim for restitution

Concept	Short explanation	Relevant authorities	Principles text
Good faith change of position	This is the main defence for unjust enrichment.	See references footnoted below.	Chapter 17: [17.31]–[17.34]

The change of position defence is established if the defendant shows that they have irreversibly changed their position, to their detriment, in good faith in reliance upon the receipt of the benefit.[6] The defendant will not be obliged to make restitution to the extent that the change is irreversible. The rationale of this defence is security of transactions.[7]

As observed in Chapter 18 of the principles text, the adjustments that courts make in ensuring substantial *restitutio in integrum* for equitable rescission have been argued to operate similarly to a change of position defence.[8]

REVIEW QUESTION

Why do you think that the defence of good faith change of position has been developed by courts?

5 *Andrew Shelton & Co Pty Ltd v Alpha Healthcare Ltd* (2002) 5 VR 577, [100]–[104] (Warren J); *Monks v Poynice Pty Ltd* (1987) 11 ACLR 637, 639 (Young J); *Municipality of Peel v Canada* [1992] 3 SCR 762, 794–6 (McLaughlin J).

6 J Edelman and E Bant, *Unjust Enrichment* (Hart, 2nd ed, 2016) 332.

7 Ibid.

8 See principles text [17.33].

V The relationship between contract and restitution for unjust enrichment

Plaintiffs claim a restitutionary remedy, rather than a remedy for breach of contract, generally because the contract is void, unenforceable, discharged by frustration, rescinded, or terminated for breach. Sometimes the contract may be a 'losing contract', where the plaintiff could get more by a restitutionary remedy than she could under the contract.

Concept	Short explanation	Relevant authorities	Principles text
The relationship between contract and restitution for unjust enrichment	Unjust enrichment must not undermine the contractual allocation of risk unduly, but may have operation in relation to uncompleted stages of a contract.	*Mann v Paterson Constructions Pty Ltd* (2019) 267 CLR 560	Chapter 17: [17.35]–[17.47]

Deane J in *Pavey & Matthews Pty Ltd v Paul*[9] suggested that the contract may sometimes operate as a defence to a claim if it is still on foot. Moreover, in these circumstances, the defendant may be able to use the sum agreed on in the contract as evidence of what is fair and reasonable remuneration.[10]

However, in *Roxborough v Rothmans of Pall Mall Australia Ltd*,[11] the contract between the parties remained on foot, yet the High Court allowed the plaintiffs' action for money had and received in relation to mistakenly paid taxes because the portion of the contract which failed was severable from the main contract.[12]

Two questions arise in these cases:

(1) Should courts undermine the contractual allocation of risk between the parties by awarding a restitutionary remedy?

(2) Relatedly, should the measure of restitution should be limited by any 'ceiling' set by the terms of the contract?

As *Lumbers v W Cook Builders Pty Ltd (in liq)* establishes,[13] courts are reluctant to undermine the contractual allocation of risk. In that case, the Lumbers family made an oral contract with W Cook & Sons ('Sons') to build a house. W Cook Builders Pty Ltd ('Builders') was in the same corporate group, but had a different director. Without the Lumbers' knowledge, Builders completed most of the construction of the house. There was no contract between the Lumbers and Builders and the Lumbers were unaware of Builders' existence. Payments for the work were made pursuant to ad hoc requests by Sons' director, and did not reflect the true value of the work or the cost of materials. When Builders

9 (1987) 162 CLR 221.

10 Ibid 257 (Deane J).

11 (2001) 208 CLR 516.

12 Ibid (Gleeson CJ, Gaudron, Gummow, Hayne and Callinan JJ, Kirby J dissenting).

13 (2008) 232 CLR 635.

attempted to obtain a *quantum meruit* for the true value of the work done, the High Court held that a *quantum meruit* award would undermine the contractual allocation of risk. The majority held that, given that there was no 'request' on the part of the Lumbers, there was no entitlement to a *quantum meruit*.[14] Gleeson CJ was prepared to accept that services can be enriching where they are an incontrovertible benefit or where the recipient has freely accepted them, but held that these principles were not relevant in the current case.[15]

Equuscorp Pty Ltd v Haxton establishes that courts are also reluctant to allow restitutionary remedies to undermine statute where a statute precludes a particular kind of contract.[16]

The following case provides further guidance on the relationship between contract and restitutionary remedies.

Mann v Paterson Constructions Pty Ltd (2019) 267 CLR 560

Facts and issues

The Mann family engaged Paterson Constructions Pty Ltd ('Paterson') to construct two double-storey townhouses in Blackburn, Victoria. The contract was said to be prepared in accordance with the *Domestic Building Contracts Act 1995* (Vic) and provided for progress payments to be made at various stipulated stages of completion. The Manns orally requested 42 variations to the townhouses during construction. Paterson carried out the variations, but did not give written notice of owner-initiated variations (as required by the contract and s 38 of the *Domestic Building Contracts Act*). When Unit One was handed over, Paterson told the Manns that the oral variations had resulted in a price increase of $48 000. The Manns refused to pay, and Paterson refused to continue construction until the variation amount was paid. The Manns alleged that Paterson had repudiated the contract and said that they accepted the repudiation. Paterson denied that it repudiated the contract, but said that the Manns' conduct was itself repudiatory, and accepted the repudiation.

Decision

Paterson sought to recover either damages for breach of contract or restitution on the basis of a *quantum meruit* in the Victorian Civil and Administrative Tribunal ('VCAT').[17] VCAT awarded a *quantum meruit* reflecting the fair value of the work. The Supreme Court of Victoria and the Victorian Court of Appeal agreed on appeal that the builder was entitled to a *quantum meruit*. The Manns appealed to the High Court on three bases:

14 Ibid [90].

15 Ibid [51]–[54].

16 (2012) 246 CLR 498.

17 Nettle, Gordon and Edelman JJ criticised the term *quantum meruit* as based on the rejected fiction of quasi-contract and seemed to prefer the term 'restitution as upon a *quantum meruit*': *Mann v Paterson Constructions Pty Ltd* (2019) 267 CLR 560, [150]–[151]. However, this casebook summary uses the term *quantum meruit* for the sake of brevity and clarity.

(1) Paterson should not be entitled to a *quantum meruit*, and should be confined to its contractual claim.
(2) If Paterson could claim a *quantum meruit*, the price specified in the contract operated as a 'cap' on the fair value recovered.
(3) Section 38 of the *Domestic Building Contract Act* precluded a claim for restitution in respect of variations.

As a background to the decision, there had been uncertainty as to whether restitutionary remedies should be allowed for repudiated contracts and whether the contract price should cap the 'fair value' recovered.[18]

The High Court allowed the appeal. There were three different situations for which Paterson had claimed a *quantum meruit*:

(1) work done in respect of the contract for which Paterson had accrued a contractual right to payment at the time of its termination
(2) work done in respect of the contract for which Paterson had not yet accrued any contractual right for payment at the time of termination and
(3) work done in respect of the variation requests.

The High Court held unanimously that a *quantum meruit* was unavailable for the first and third kinds of claim.

A majority of the Court (Gageler J (in a separate judgment) and Nettle, Gordon and Edelman JJ) allowed Paterson to claim a *quantum meruit* in relation to the second kind of claim. While the contractual amount provided a general guide, it was not necessarily determinative as to the fair value.

Kiefel CJ, Bell and Keane JJ dissented and would not have allowed any *quantum meruit* on the basis that it undermined the contractual allocation of risk.

Gageler J

> **Category (3): work for which the Builder has not accrued a contractual right to payment**
>
> [**593**] More difficulty attends the outcome in relation to work done within category (3). Determining the outcome requires this Court to make a choice. Should the Builder be restricted in respect of that work to enforcing the Builder's undoubted entitlement to recover damages for loss occasioned to the Builder in consequence of the termination

18 Generally, courts had held that restitutionary remedies were independent of contractual remedies, even where the contract had been repudiated, and that the contractual amount was not a cap, simply guidance as to the fair value: see *Pavey & Matthews Pty Ltd v Paul* (1987) 162 CLR 221, 257 (Deane J); *Renard Constructions (ME) Pty Ltd v Minister of Public Works* (1992) 26 NSWLR 234, 277–8 (Meagher JA); *Sopov v Kane Constructions Pty Ltd (No 2)* (2009) 24 VR 510, [21]; *Equuscorp Pty Ltd v Haxton* (2012) 246 CLR 498, [29], [101]–[102]. However, in *Sopov v Kane Constructions Pty Ltd (No 2)* (2009) 24 VR 510, the Victorian Court of Appeal indicated at [9]–[11] that if it had not been bound by prior authority, it would have reconsidered this point on the basis that the availability of a *quantum meruit* in such cases proceeded upon the mistaken basis that acceptance of a repudiation operates to rescind the contract ab initio.

of the Contract? Or should the Builder be able to elect to recover instead an amount representing the value of the work by way of restitution on a non-contractual *quantum meruit*?

No decision of this Court is directly in point. ...

Restricting the Builder to recovering damages for breach of contract has the support of some statements made in the House of Lords in *Ranger v Great Western Railway Co* and of a formidable body of recent academic and professional writing. Allowing the Builder to elect to recover an amount representing the value of the work by way of restitution on a non-contractual *quantum meruit* accords with the received understanding of the common law in Australia as repeatedly accepted in intermediate courts of appeal over the last three decades. It also accords with the predominant approach of courts in the United States.

...

[**594**] There are, however, two characteristically scholarly and concise judgments of Jordan CJ, delivered shortly after *McDonald v Dennys Lascelles Ltd* and without reference to *Lodder v Slowey*, which provide a different and more satisfying justification for the received understanding. In *Segur v Franklin*, Jordan CJ noted with reference to *McDonald v Dennys Lascelles Ltd* that it was then 'clearly settled that if one party to a contract repudiates his liabilities under it, [**595**] the other party may treat such repudiation as an invitation to him to regard himself as discharged from the further performance of the contract'. The consequence, he noted, was that the other party 'may accept this invitation and treat the contract as at an end, except for the purposes of an action for damages for breach of contract ... or', he added, 'in a proper case, an action for a *quantum meruit*'. Jordan CJ went on to explain:

> Where a wrongful repudiation has the effect of preventing the other party from becoming entitled to receive remuneration for services already rendered, which remuneration, according to the terms of the contract, he is entitled to receive only if the contract is wholly carried into effect, the innocent party, who has elected to treat the contract as at an end may, instead of suing for damages, maintain an action to recover a *quantum meruit* for the services which he has rendered under the contract before it came to an end. Such an action is not regarded as an action for an unliquidated claim, but an action for a debt or liquidated demand.

Returning to the topic in *Horton v Jones [No 2]*, Jordan CJ re-emphasised that '[a] claim to a *quantum meruit* is in the theory of the law a liquidated claim; and the claimant, if he is successful, is entitled to recover the amount at which he has assessed his claim, unless the jury reduces it'. That is an important statement about the nature of the common law action, to which I will return. Jordan CJ added that there were circumstances in which an action for a *quantum meruit* would lie '[w]here there is or has been an express contract between the parties'. He instanced, with reference to *Segur v Franklin*:

> If one party to an express contract renders to the other some but not all the services which have to be performed in order that he may be entitled to receive the remuneration stipulated for by the contract, and the other by his wrongful repudiation of the contract prevents him from earning the stipulated remuneration, the former may treat the contract as at an end and then sue for a *quantum meruit* for the services actually rendered.

Jordan CJ's explanation of the basis for a claim on a *quantum meruit* for the value of services rendered by the innocent party proceeded expressly on the modern understanding, settled in *McDonald v Dennys Lascelles Ltd*, that termination of a contract on acceptance of repudiation operates only for the future. Unlike the reasoning of the [**596**] New Zealand Court of Appeal in the decision upheld in *Lodder v Slowey*, the reasoning of Jordan CJ did not proceed on the notion that acceptance of repudiation operates to render a contract void from the beginning. The notion had been discarded then, as it remains discarded now.

…

Within the explanation in *Segur v Franklin* and *Horton v Jones [No 2]*, in my opinion, are reasons consistent with *Pavey*'s recognition of 'unjust enrichment' as a 'unifying' (as distinct from 'universal' or 'all-embracing') legal concept as to why the common law should recognise a right to restitution in the particular category of case. Within the same explanation, in my opinion, is also guidance as to what the proper measure of restitution in that category of case should be. For reasons that will become apparent, I am unable to answer the ultimate question, of whether the common law of Australia should continue to recognise a right to restitution in this category of case, without also determining the proper measure of restitution.

The starting point is to appreciate that the category of case is one in which it is the 'very fact' that a contract becomes unenforceable that 'provides the occasion for (and part of the circumstances giving rise to) the imposition by the law of the obligation to make restitution'. The innocent party has rendered services in part performance of the totality of the services necessary to be performed in order for the innocent party to accrue a contractual entitlement to payment in the future. Termination of the contract, consequent upon acceptance by the innocent party of its repudiation by the defaulting [**597**] party, supervenes. The result is that 'as on the one side no further acts of performance can be required, so, on the other side, no liability can be brought into existence [since] it depends upon a further act of performance'. Through acceptance of the wrongful repudiation of the defaulting party, the innocent party is thereby in the present position of having rendered services in part performance of the contract for which that party has not accrued and cannot accrue a contractual entitlement to be paid. The defaulting party is correspondingly in the present position of having had the benefit of the services rendered in part performance of the contract for which that party has not incurred and will not incur any contractual obligation to pay.

To recognise the 'unjustness' of the defaulting party having had the benefit of the services rendered by the innocent party in part performance of the contract in a case of a default amounting to a wrongful repudiation, I do not think it necessary to analogise to any other category of case. Nor do I think it appropriate to attempt to discern and apply some other all-embracing criterion of liability in the common law of restitution. By preferring to maintain a narrow focus, I am adhering to the standard common law judicial technique of deciding no more than what needs to be decided.

…

Nonetheless Gageler J discussed 'failure of consideration':

[**598**] Useful as the concept of total failure of consideration or failure of basis can be, it is important not to surrender to that one concept the hegemonic status steadfastly

denied to the concept of unjust enrichment. The common law method, as Sir Frederick Jordan himself observed extra-judicially, has never purported to be one in which the determination of a particular case has been deduced from supposed 'fundamental principles of justice'. The general principles of the common law are, in his language, 'built up' from the 'collation of decided cases'. They are monitored by reference to how well they fit within the wider body of the law and how well they work in practice; where problems are revealed, they can be revised or even abandoned at the appropriate level within the judicial hierarchy.

Bearing constantly in mind the adage that the life of the common law has been not logic but experience, there is a need to resist the temptation to intellectual gratification that accompanies any quest to portray cases in which the common law recognises an obligation of restitution as the conscious or unconscious application of one Very Big Idea. The need is to avoid the pitfalls of overgeneralisation, just as it is to ensure that considerations that are practically important but theoretically inconvenient are not overlooked or underappreciated.

In the common law of restitution, as in the common law of tort, particular categories of case give rise to their own particular sorts of problem. Once properly identified, the problems that arise in any particular category 'will then become the focus of attention in a judicial evaluation of the factors which tend for or against a conclusion, to be arrived at as a matter of principle'. That is what needs to happen here. The various categories of case in which [**599**] money paid under a contract might or might not be recovered on the ground of a total failure of consideration or failure of basis having resulted from the termination of the contract, upon acceptance of a repudiation or upon the happening of a frustrating event, raise their own problems. So too does the more difficult category of case where it is the defaulting party who seeks to recover the value of services rendered to the innocent party. For present purposes, all of them can be put to one side.

The critical question in the present category of case is why the common law should not treat the innocent party as adequately remunerated for the services rendered to the defaulting party by having an entitlement to maintain an action for damages for breach of the contract in part performance of which the innocent party rendered those services. …

My view is that the answer to that critical question cannot lie in the notion of the contracting parties having arrived at a contractual 'allocation of risk', which the common law of restitution will not disturb. Contracting parties are, of course, at liberty to determine by contract the 'secondary' obligations, which are to arise in the event of breach or termination of the 'primary' obligations they have chosen [**600**] to bind them. Even where the parties have not so determined, it may for some purposes be appropriate to describe obligations that the common law imposes to pay damages for breach of contract as 'secondary' obligations which, in the event of termination by acceptance of a repudiation, are 'substituted' for the primary obligations. However, it would be artificial as a matter of commercial practice and wrong as a matter of legal theory to conceive of contracting parties who have not addressed the consequences of termination in the express or implied terms of their contract as having contracted to limit themselves to the contractual remedy of damages in that event. Parties contract against the background of the gamut of remedies that the legal system makes available to them. The common law gives to them the benefit, and saddles them with the detriment, of what they expressly or impliedly agree in their contract. Outside the scope of what they agree in their contract, the common law gives to them what the common law itself allows them to get.

Nor can I see that the answer is to be found in the notion that overlapping remedies in contract and in restitution are in some way anomalous. Tidiness has never been a feature of a common law system. Overlapping remedies available at the option of an innocent party against another party who is in contractual default are commonplace. Remedies at common law can overlap with those in equity. At common law, causes of action in contract can overlap with causes of action in tort, and the potential for a cause of action in restitution to overlap with a cause of action in damages for breach of contract was recognised in *Baltic Shipping Co v Dillon*.

Rather, I consider that answering the critical question needs to be informed by a weighing of the practical consequences of continuing to allow an innocent party to maintain a non-contractual *quantum meruit* as an alternative to an action for unliquidated damages for breach of contract. To those consequences I now turn.

One practical consequence which flows from a non-contractual *quantum meruit* being 'in the theory of the law' an action for a debt is that the action can have significant procedural advantages to an innocent party over an action for damages for breach of contract under procedural rules in Australian courts. Typically, those advantages include a capacity to obtain default judgment.

[**601**] More importantly, a non-contractual *quantum meruit* has the advantage that proof of the value of services rendered is almost invariably more straightforward than proof of contractual loss. Questions of causation and remoteness play no part. The availability of the action allows the innocent party to choose to adopt the course of quickly and cheaply obtaining judgment for an easily quantifiable liquidated amount instead of embarking on a long and more expensive and more uncertain pursuit of a potentially larger judgment for unliquidated damages. Choice by the innocent party to adopt that course has the flow-on systemic advantage of shortening trial and pre-trial processes.

The practical considerations are not all one way. Against permitting recovery on an action for a non-contractual *quantum meruit* for the value of services rendered under the contract is the prospect of a party recovering more as a result of termination of the contract than would have been due to that party had the contract been performed. If the value of the services rendered is to be determined independently of the contract, as the common law of Australia as declared by intermediate courts of appeal currently stands, recovery in excess of the contract price has the real potential to occur in two main scenarios. One is where the contract has turned out to be under-priced, with the result that the party faces the prospect of making a loss by going on to complete performance. The other is where the contract has been structured to allocate a higher proportion of the overall contract price to work performed at earlier stages for which the party has already accrued a contractual right to payment.

With the potential to recover more from termination than from completion comes the incentive to terminate: to search out and seize upon conduct able to be characterised as a repudiation with a view to making more out of engaging in the ensuing litigation than is available to be made out of completing the contract. Compounding the incentive for one contracting party to find conduct amounting to repudiation is a corresponding incentive for the counter-party to do whatever can be done to avoid it. The result 'is to invert the normal interest of such a party regarding the other's contractual performance':

> While the performing party's objective is to provoke a default, the recipient's goal is to safeguard a favorable bargain – avoiding [**602**] the risk of default by excessive precautions and 'overperformance.' It is difficult to think of a clearer incentive to inefficiency in the contractual relation.

The function of a common law remedy is to remediate an innocent party, not to penalise a defaulting party, and not to distort the incentive of either party to perform the contract. The policy of the common law demands that the problem of distorted contractual incentives be addressed.

In my opinion, the problem is more appropriately addressed by limiting the measure of restitution than by denying the availability of the common law action for restitution. If the measure of the value of the services rendered by the innocent party is capped by reference to the contractually agreed remuneration for those services – the contract price – the distortion is substantially eliminated.

'Upon a *quantum meruit*, usually the value of services is assessed by reference to charges commonly made by others for like services'. That is to say, the amount recovered is usually measured at the market value of the services rendered. Inherent in the nature of the obligation enforced on a *quantum meruit* being to pay only 'reasonable remuneration', however, is that the usual basis of assessment may not yield the appropriate measure of restitution in every case.

...

[**605**] On a non-contractual *quantum meruit* to recover remuneration for services rendered in performance of an unenforceable contract, the general approach has been to treat the contract price as no more than evidence of the value to the owner of the services rendered. The reason is not difficult to discern: were the contractual price automatically to be treated as the measure of the value of the services 'it might be persuasively contended that the action on a quantum meruit was an indirect means of enforcing the [unenforceable] contract'. Deane J nevertheless suggested in *Pavey* that '[t]he defendant will also be entitled to rely on the unenforceable contract, if it has been executed but not rescinded, to limit the amount recoverable by the plaintiff to the contractual amount in a case where that amount is less than what would constitute fair and reasonable remuneration'. How far that suggestion can be taken need not now be considered.

Whatever the position in relation to an unenforceable contract, my view is that the contract price should limit a non-contractual *quantum meruit* to recover remuneration for services rendered in part performance of an enforceable contract that is later terminated so as to preclude future recovery of the contractual amount by an action to enforce the contract. ...

The common law rule should accordingly be that the amount recoverable on a non-contractual *quantum meruit* as remuneration for services rendered in performance of a contract prior to its termination by acceptance of a repudiation cannot exceed that portion of the contract price as is attributable to those services. Issues concerning the identification and appropriate method of apportionment of the contract price are best left to be addressed on a case by case basis if and when they arise.

[**606**] To the extent that they allowed recovery in excess of the contract price for the services rendered, *Renard Constructions (ME) Pty Ltd v Minister for Public Works*, *Iezzi Constructions Pty Ltd v Watkins Pacific (Qld) Pty Ltd* and *Sopov v Kane Constructions Pty Ltd [No 2]* were, in my opinion, wrongly decided.

Qualified to ensure that the amount recovered cannot exceed the portion of the contract price that is attributable to the services rendered, there is no reason to depart from the common law principle of recovery expounded by Jordan CJ in *Segur v Franklin* and *Horton v Jones [No 2]*. The principle is sound in theory and, so qualified, is beneficial in practice.

The preferable outcome, in my opinion, is accordingly that the Builder can recover from the Owners by way of restitution on a non-contractual *quantum meruit* an amount in respect of the work done by the Builder for which the Builder had accrued no contractual right to payment under the Contract at the time of its termination. The amount recoverable is a liquidated amount representing reasonable remuneration for the work. That amount cannot exceed the portion of the overall price set by the Contract that is attributable to the work. …

Nettle, Gordon and Edelman JJ

Recovery of restitution as an alternative to contractual remedies

[**624**] As s 38 has no application to that part of the respondent's claim that was not in respect of variations, it is next necessary to determine whether the respondent was entitled to recover restitution for a cause of action in the category of unjust enrichment (rather than for amounts due under the contract or damages for breach of contract) in relation to those aspects of its claim which were for work and labour done otherwise than in response to requested variations within the meaning of s 38.

…

(i) Restitution upon termination for breach

Where a contract remains 'open' – that is, 'not discharged' – there is generally 'neither occasion nor legal justification for the law to superimpose or impute an obligation or promise to pay a reasonable [**625**] remuneration'. Such an obligation or promise 'would be either inconsistent with the contract or … would duplicate the contractual obligation'. But the position at law for contracts that are 'closed', including, relevantly, those terminated for repudiation, is different.

At least since the decision of Dixon J in *McDonald v Dennys Lascelles Ltd*, it has been accepted that, where a party to a contract elects to accept the other party's repudiation of the contract, both parties are released from contractual obligations which are not yet due for performance, but existing rights and causes of action continue unaffected. Dixon J explained the position thus:

> When a party to a simple contract, upon a breach by the other contracting party of a condition of the contract, elects to treat the contract as no longer binding upon him, the contract is not rescinded as from the beginning. *Both parties are discharged from the further performance of the contract, but rights are not divested or discharged which have already been unconditionally acquired. Rights and obligations which arise from the partial execution of the contract and causes of action which have accrued from its breach alike continue unaffected.* When a contract

> is rescinded because of [**626**] matters which affect its formation, as in the case of fraud, the parties are to be rehabilitated and restored, so far as may be, to the position they occupied before the contract was made. But when a contract, which is not void or voidable at law, or liable to be set aside in equity, is dissolved at the election of one party because the other has not observed an essential condition or has committed a breach going to its root, the contract is determined so far as it is executory only and the party in default is liable for damages for its breach. (emphasis added)

As the law stands in Australia, as it does in England, New Zealand, Canada and the United States, upon termination for repudiation of an uncompleted contract containing an entire obligation (or, as will be seen, divisible stages) for work and labour done, the innocent party may sue either for damages for breach of contract or, at the innocent party's option, for restitution in respect of the value of services rendered under the contract.

The availability of restitution, and the form of restitutionary remedy awarded, will depend on the type of enrichment alleged. Generally speaking, a personal restitutionary remedy will be assessed as money had and received where the alleged enrichment is the receipt of money; it will be assessed as upon a *quantum meruit* where the alleged enrichment is the receipt of services; and it will be assessed as upon a *quantum valebant* where the alleged enrichment is the receipt of goods. Where the alleged enrichment takes more than one form, such as the provision of money and services to a party, the other party [**627**] is entitled to the money paid together with a reasonable sum for the services, subject, of course, to prohibitions against double recovery.

The 'qualifying or vitiating' factor giving rise to a prima facie obligation on the part of the enriched party to make restitution is a total failure of consideration, or a total failure of a severable part of the consideration. In this context, consideration means the matter considered in forming the decision to do the act: 'the state of affairs contemplated as the basis or reason for the payment'. In many cases the relevant basis will be the benefit that is bargained for. In those cases, '[t]he test is whether or not the party claiming total failure of consideration has in fact received any part of the benefit bargained for under the contract or purported contract'.

More specifically, a total failure of consideration for work done exists by reason of the termination of a contract for breach where the basis on which the work was done has failed to materialise or sustain itself, and the total failure of consideration is seen as the occasion and part of the circumstances giving rise to the other party's obligation to make restitution to the extent of the fair value of that work. It is for that reason that no such obligation can arise while the obligation under which the benefit was conferred and accepted remains enforceable, open and capable of performance.

[**628**] Where a contractor is only entitled to receive remuneration if the contract is wholly carried into effect, and the other party's wrongful repudiation of the contract has the effect of preventing the contractor from becoming entitled to receive remuneration for services already rendered, the contractor may, after electing to treat the contract as at an end, maintain an action to recover restitution as upon a *quantum meruit* for those services, instead of suing for damages.

...

(ii) Entire obligations and divisible obligations

It follows from what has been said that, where, under a contract for work and labour, a party is entitled to payment upon completion of *any* part of the work (which is to say that the obligation to complete that work is 'infinitely divisible'), where the contract expressly fixes a price for services, and where the contract is terminated by that party's acceptance of the other party's repudiation of it, the party so **[629]** terminating the contract will have an accrued right to payment under the contract for that part of the work that has been done. There will have been no failure of consideration. Accordingly, that party's remedy in respect of that part of the work that has been done will generally be restricted to a claim for what has accrued due or damages for breach of contract assessed by reference to the contract price less the cost of completing the work.

By contrast, if the obligation to perform work and labour is 'entire', so that nothing is due until all of the work has been completed by the contractor, then, upon termination of the contract by the contractor's acceptance of the other party's repudiation of it, there will be a total failure of consideration. Upon acceptance that the contract is repudiated, either by a renunciation or a manifested unwillingness or inability to perform the contract substantially according to the contract terms, the contractor's right to complete the performance and earn the price will have failed, and thus nothing will be due under the contract for such part of the work as has been completed. In that event, the 'consideration' – in the sense of the condition or the 'basis' for the performance by the contractor – will have failed, and restitution will lie as upon a *quantum meruit* in respect of work and labour done up to the point of termination. In those circumstances, there is a 'qualifying or vitiating' factor, namely, a total failure of consideration, giving rise to a restitutionary remedy in the alternative.

By further contrast, if the obligation to perform work is *divisible into several entire stages*, then, upon termination of the contract for repudiation: (i) the contractor so terminating the contract will have accrued rights under the contract for those stages that have been completed; (ii) there will be a total failure of consideration in respect of the stages that have not been completed, because the **[630]** contractor's right to complete the performance and earn the price will have failed and nothing will be due under the contract in respect of those uncompleted stages; and (iii) restitution will lie as upon a *quantum meruit* in respect of the work and labour done towards completion of the uncompleted stages as an alternative to damages for breach of contract.

The underlying principle concerning restitution of the value of work and labour where the basis for performance has failed is the same as that concerning restitution of money paid where the basis for the payment has failed. …

Generally speaking, a construction contract which is divided into stages, and under which the total contract price is apportioned between the stages by means of specified progress payments payable at the completion of each stage, is viewed as containing divisible obligations of performance. In that event, where at the point of termination of the contract by the builder's acceptance of the principal's repudiation some stages of the contract have been completed, such that progress payments have accrued due in respect of those stages, there will be no total failure of consideration in respect of those stages. The builder will have no right of recovery in restitution in respect of those stages, and the builder's rights in respect of those completed stages will generally be limited to debt for recovery of the amounts accrued due or damages for breach of contract. But if there are any uncompleted stages, there will be a total failure of consideration in respect of those stages due to the failure of the builder's right to complete the performance and earn the price. In that event, there will [**631**] be nothing due under the contract in relation to those stages, and restitution as upon a *quantum meruit* will lie in respect of work and labour done towards completion of those uncompleted stages.

In this matter, it is apparent from the manner in which the Contract expressly provided for stages, and specified that progress payments were payable upon completion of each stage, that the obligation of performance under the Contract was divisible. Accordingly, for the reasons stated, the respondent's right to recovery in respect of the completed stages (other than for variations) was limited to the amount due under the Contract on completion of those stages or damages for breach of contract, and the respondent's right to recovery in respect of the uncompleted stages (other than for variations) was restricted to restitution for work and labour done in respect of those stages or damages for breach of contract.

...

(iii) History of restitutionary relief

...

[**635**] ... For although at the time of *Planché v Colburn* it was considered necessary that an express contract be avoided *ab initio* in order to imply the quasi-contractual obligation which grounded a claim in *indebitatus assumpsit* for work and labour done, it is now recognised that restitutionary obligations are imposed by operation of law in response to circumstances including the retention of a benefit received on a basis which has totally failed to materialise. Of course, as has been observed, it is still the case that no such obligation can arise while the reciprocal obligation for which the benefit was conferred and accepted remains enforceable, open and capable of performance. But circumstances other than the unenforceability or avoidance of a contract *ab initio*, including frustration and termination, may provide the occasion for, and form part of the circumstances giving rise to, an obligation to pay what is reasonable.

The position which arises upon frustration of a contract is therefore instructive. Under the rule in *Taylor v Caldwell* it was once the law that, where an entire obligation to perform work and labour [**636**] became impossible of performance before completion of the work, both parties were excused from further performance of the contract and neither party had any right of recovery in respect of that part of the work which had been completed or moneys paid in anticipation of its completion. That changed with the decision of the House of Lords in *Fibrosa Spolka Akcyjna v Fairbairn Lawson Combe Barbour Ltd*, which recognised that it is not necessary that the contract be 'wiped out altogether' in order to attract restitutionary relief. As Viscount Simon LC stated, where moneys are paid to secure performance of a result, and performance becomes impossible, there is a total failure of consideration in respect of moneys paid because the inducement which brought about the payment is not fulfilled. The same applies to the frustration of a contract for the provision of services. There is a total failure of consideration for the provision of the services where 'the state of affairs contemplated as the basis or reason for the [services] has failed to materialise or, if it did exist, has failed to sustain itself'.

Principle, coherence and authority dictate that the position in relation to a contract terminated for repudiation be the same. Although it was once thought that the innocent party's right to recover reasonable remuneration for the work done up to the point of termination depended on the notion that termination avoided the contract *ab initio* – thereby leaving the way clear to imply a quasi-contractual obligation on the part of the other party to pay reasonable remuneration for that work – now it is recognised that there may be a total failure of consideration for the work so done because, by reason of the termination, the basis on which the work was done has failed to materialise or sustain itself, and that total failure of consideration is seen as the occasion and part of the circumstances giving rise to the other party's obligation to make restitution to the extent of the fair value of that work.

[637] Admittedly, there is a difference between frustration and termination for breach, in that, in the case of frustration, the party who has undertaken work under the contract has no right to damages for breach of contract – there being no breach of contract involved in frustration – and is, therefore, without a remedy other than restitution; whereas, in the case of termination for breach, the innocent party has a right to sue for damages for breach of contract in theory sufficient to put him or her in the position in which he or she would have been if the contract had been performed. On that basis, it has been contended that what applies to frustration cannot or should not be transposed to termination for breach. There is also a great deal of academic writing which is similarly critical of the existence of a non-contractual remedy upon termination.

...

[642] Moreover, as Gummow J was at pains to point out in *Roxborough v Rothmans of Pall Mall Australia Ltd*, ours is not a system in which the theory of unjust enrichment comes first and decisions must then be made to comply with it. It is a common law system of *stare decisis* that develops over time and through which general principle is derived from judicial decisions. Unjust enrichment may be conceived of as a 'unifying legal concept' which serves a 'taxonomical function' that assists in understanding why the law recognises an obligation to make restitution in particular circumstances. But it is in no sense an all-embracing theory of restitutionary rights and remedies pursuant to which existing decisions are to be accepted or rejected by reference to the extent of their compliance with its proportions. Consequently, where a doctrine of the common law has grown up over several centuries – as has the availability of restitutionary relief for work and labour done under a partially completed entire obligation following termination of a contract for breach – and the doctrine remains principled and coherent, widely accepted and applied in kindred jurisdictions, it can hardly be regarded as a sufficient basis to discard it that some of the conceptions which historically informed its gestation have since changed or developed **[643]** over time. Whatever doubts might remain about the theoretical underpinnings of the doctrine by reason of the problematic nature of its origins or subsequent developments in the law of contract, it is too late now for this Court unilaterally to abrogate the coherent rule simply in order to bring about what is said to be a greater sense of theoretical order to the range of common law remedies.

Admittedly, there is cause for concern about the potential for disparity between the amounts recoverable by way of restitution for work done under a contract which is terminated for breach and the amounts recoverable by way of damages for breach of contract. That phenomenon – alarmingly widespread in domestic building disputes of the kind in issue, as it appears – implies a need for development of the law in a manner which better accords to the distribution of risks for which provision has been made by contract. But, as will be explained, that is a problem which may be addressed with less far-reaching measures than abrogation of the rule of recovery and more consistently with the accepted techniques of common law development. ...

The contract price as a limitation on the sum recoverable

Until about the turn of the twentieth century, the measure of restitutionary relief for work and labour done by an innocent party under an entire obligation in a contract terminated for repudiation was truly *quantum meruit* – the amount earned – and thus generally a *pro rata* proportion of the contract price. By 1900, however, a practice seems to have emerged in some American jurisdictions of putting the question of assessment to the jury in the form of what the work and labour done was worth, which directed attention only to its reasonable value rather than the contract price.

[**644**] ... [*Slowey v*] *Lodder* gave rise to the notion, which has held sway since at least the last half of the twentieth century, that the amount recoverable upon a *quantum meruit* is the objective value of the work and labour done, usually measured by reference to the reasonable cost of performing it. Such a method of quantification in effect equates the value of 'the benefit or "enrichment" actually or constructively accepted' by the defendant with the benefit to the hypothetical willing but not anxious purchaser of like services, and that, in turn, with the expenditure by the plaintiff in reliance on the contract. Not infrequently it has resulted in awards of restitution substantially in excess of the contract price. *Sopov v Kane* is one example of the phenomenon, and the amount of restitution awarded by VCAT in this case is another.

[**645**] In some circumstances, it is necessary or appropriate that the benefit of work to the defendant be determined without reference to a contract price. As Dixon J observed in *South Australian Harbors Board v South Australian Gas Co*, identification of 'a fair and reasonable rate of remuneration, in other words a *quantum meruit*', raises a 'question of fact', the answer to which 'depends very much upon the methods of reasoning which are pursued'. Where the claim to *quantum meruit* is founded upon a contract which does not expressly fix a price for services, 'usually' the value of those services will be 'assessed by reference to charges commonly made by others for like services', unless no such standard is available. In such cases, practical necessity justifies the default application of an objective price derived from outside the contract which ordinarily depends on evidence of supply costs and market conditions.

Equally, where the claim is founded on an obligation to pay for services rendered under a contract which is unenforceable, it has been held that '[o]rdinarily' the measure of restitution 'will correspond to the fair value of the benefit provided (e.g., remuneration calculated at a reasonable rate for work actually done or the fair market value of materials supplied)'. Prices stated in the contract are regarded as relevant, but they remain 'evidence only, on the question of amount'. That approach is informed by a legal concern that direct application of the contract price would risk incoherence with the policy of the law rendering the contract unenforceable, although this will always require consideration of that policy. As Mason and Wilson JJ noted in *Pavey & Matthews Pty Ltd v Paul*:

> If the effect of bringing an action on a quantum meruit was simply to enforce the oral contract in some circumstances only, though not in all the circumstances in which an action on the contract would succeed, it might be persuasively contended that the action on a quantum meruit was an indirect means of enforcing the oral contract.

> [646] By contrast, where a contract is enforceable, but terminated for repudiation, there are no reasons of practicality and few in principle to eschew the contract price. It has been said that '[t]he defendant cannot refuse to abide by the contract and at the same time claim its protection' against the innocent plaintiff. But, as has been seen, where a contract is terminated for breach, it continues to apply to acts done up to the point of termination, and it remains the basis on which the work was done. There is, therefore, nothing about the termination of the contract as such that is inconsistent with the assessment of restitution by reference to the contract price for acts done prior to termination. The contract price reflects the parties' agreed allocation of risk. Termination of the contract provides no reason to disrespect that allocation. Granted, there may be difficult questions of apportionment of the contract price, such as where performance of a small part of the entire obligation is the most valuable part of the contractor's work. There may also be difficult questions in identifying the contract price, such as where the expected benefits to the contractor include not only payments of money but also the value of promises or releases. But such difficulties of valuation and apportionment have long been encountered in other areas.

Thus, after a contract has been repudiated, a party may elect between contractual damages or a *quantum meruit* for uncompleted stages and debt for completed stages.

Figure 17.3 The outcome of *Mann v Paterson*

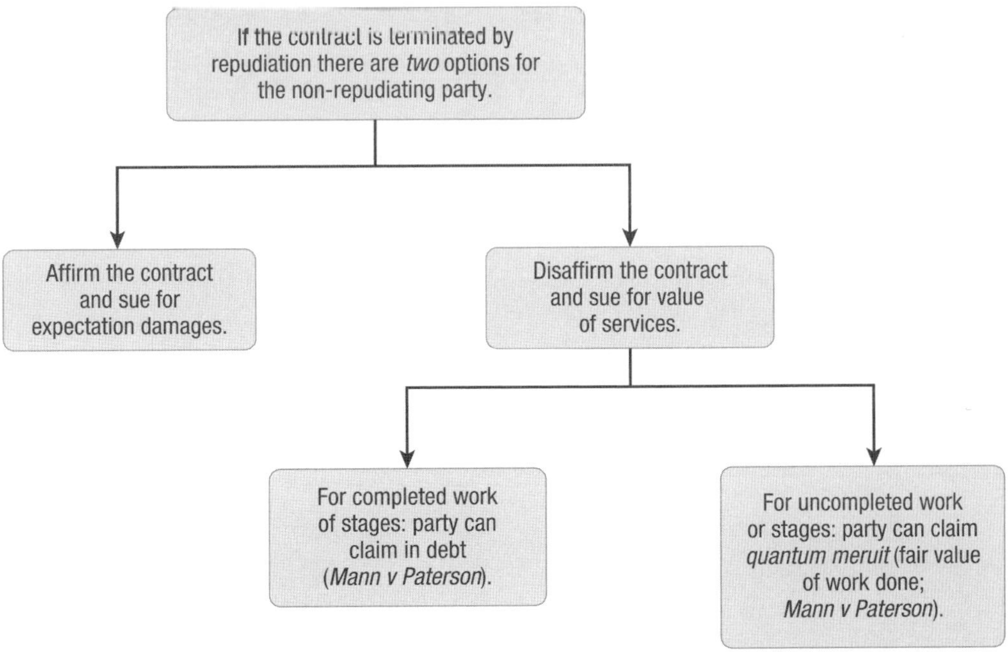

REVIEW QUESTIONS

(1) What has to happen to the contract for a court to allow a restitutionary claim to be brought?

(2) Whose judgment do you prefer in *Mann v Paterson Constructions Pty Ltd* (2019) 267 CLR 560? Why do you prefer this judgment?

18 RESCISSION

I	Introduction	609
	A Legal rescission	611
	B Equitable rescission	611
	C Rescission under the *Australian Consumer Law*	611
II	The requirement of *restitutio in integrum*	612
III	Election	619
	A How to make an election to rescind	620
	B The consequences of an election to rescind	623
	C The reasons behind the election requirement	626
IV	'Partial' rescission	627
V	Bars to rescission	630
	A Impossibility of complete restoration	631
	B Affirmation	633
	C Delay	633
	D Intervening third party rights	636
	E Executed contracts and innocent misrepresentation	639

I Introduction

Concept	Short explanation	Relevant authorities	Principles text
Introduction	Rescission involves the unwinding of a transaction, where both parties to the transaction are restored to their original positions. The extent to which precise restoration is required varies.	*Alati v Kruger* (1955) 94 CLR 216 (see page 614 for extract)	Chapter 18: [18.1]–[18.7]
Legal rescission	Legal rescission only arises in contract for fraud or duress, and requires 'complete *restitutio in integrum*'.	*Clarke v Dickson* (1858) 120 ER 463 (see page 613 for extract)	Chapter 18: [18.8]–[18.10]
Equitable rescission	Equitable rescission applies to contracts, gifts and conveyances, and arises for a broad range of vitiating factors, including misrepresentation, undue influence and breach of fiduciary duty. It requires 'substantial *restitutio in integrum*' and thus the parties need not be restored *precisely* to their previous positions.	*Alati v Kruger* (1955) 94 CLR 216 (see page 614 for extract)	Chapter 18: [18.49]–[18.50]

Concept	Short explanation	Relevant authorities	Principles text
Rescission under the *Australian Consumer Law* ('ACL')	Remedies akin to rescission are available pursuant to s 243 of the ACL, and arise for misleading or deceptive conduct and unconscionable conduct, among other things. Like equitable rescission it requires 'substantial *restitutio in integrum*' but may be even more flexible than equity.	*Australian Consumer Law* s 243(a)–(d)	Chapter 18: [18.16]–[18.18]

Rescission is available to reverse a variety of transactions where one of the parties is subject to a vitiating factor. There are three different kinds of rescission which will be discussed in this chapter:

(1) common law rescission

(2) equitable rescission

(3) 'rescission' under the *Australian Consumer Law* ('ACL').

Table 18.1 Different types of rescission

	Common law rescission	Equitable rescission	Rescission under the ACL s 243(a), (c) and (d)
What does it apply to?	Only to contract	Contracts, gifts and conveyances	All transactions in trade or commerce
Vitiating factors	• Fraud • Duress	• Fraud • Duress • Misrepresentation • Mistake • Undue influence • Unconscionable dealing • Breach of fiduciary duty • An equity pursuant to *Yerkey v Jones* (1939) 63 CLR 649	• Misleading or deceptive conduct (ss 18 and 19) • Unconscionable conduct (ss 20–22A)
Level of *restitutio in integrum* required	Complete	Substantial	Substantial
Effect on title	Election means title immediately returns to original owner	Recipient holds legal title on constructive trust ('CT') for original owner	
Other notes	Only useful in *very* limited circumstances with contracts for goods	Subject to bars to relief	May be subject to defences but unclear whether as restrictive as equity

A Legal rescission

This is only available for contracts, and the relevant vitiating factors are narrow: fraud and duress.

The parties must be restored *precisely* to their pre-transaction position ('complete *restitutio in integrum*'). In *Hunt v Silk*[1] and *Blackburn v Smith*,[2] rescission was barred because the plaintiffs had briefly taken possession of the land the subject of the transaction. It was impossible for the plaintiffs to 'give back' this 'use' of the land, even though they could have returned the legal title.

B Equitable rescission

This is available for contracts, gifts and other conveyances, and the vitiating factors are much broader: not only fraud and duress, but also misrepresentation, mistake, undue influence, unconscionable dealing, breach of fiduciary duty and the *Yerkey v Jones*[3] equity.

The parties need only be restored 'substantially' to their pre-transaction position ('substantial *restitutio in integrum*'). Courts can make adjustments for use of property to an extent.

Equity can impose terms on relief.

Equitable rescission is also subject to equitable bars to relief.

C Rescission under the *Australian Consumer Law*

A remedy akin to rescission may be awarded for breach of certain provisions of the ACL,[4] including ss 18 and 19 (precluding misleading or deceptive conduct) and ss 20–22A (precluding unconscionable conduct). The provisions effecting 'rescission' under the ACL are extracted below.

Australian Consumer Law s 243(a)–(d)

The statute does not describe these remedies as 'rescission' but the effect is similar.

243 Kinds of orders that may be made

(a) Without limiting section 237(1), 238(1) or 239(1), the orders that a court may make under any of those sections against a person (the ***respondent***) include all or any of the following: (a) an order declaring the whole or any part of a contract made between the respondent and a person (the ***injured person***) who suffered, or is likely to suffer, the loss or damage referred to in that section, or of a collateral arrangement relating to such a contract:

1 (1804) 5 East 449; 102 ER 1142.
2 (1848) 2 Ex 782; 154 ER 707.
3 (1939) 63 CLR 649.
4 *Competition and Consumer Act 2010* (Cth) sch 2. For the legislative history, see [8.1] of the principles text.

(i) to be void; and
(ii) if the court thinks fit – to have been void ab initio or void at all times on and after such date as is specified in the order (which may be a date that is before the date on which the order is made);

(b) an order:
(i) varying such a contract or arrangement in such manner as is specified in the order; and
(ii) if the court thinks fit – declaring the contract or arrangement to have had effect as so varied on and after such date as is specified in the order (which may be a date that is before the date on which the order is made);

(c) an order refusing to enforce any or all of the provisions of such a contract or arrangement;

(d) an order directing the respondent to refund money or return property to the injured person;

...

Generally, when making a rescission-style order under these provisions, courts have treated it similarly to equitable rescission.[5] Nevertheless, courts have also warned against unduly confining the statute by analogy to equitable rescission.[6]

II The requirement of *restitutio in integrum*

Concept	Short explanation	Relevant authorities	Principles text
The requirement of *restitutio in integrum*	Common law rescission requires 'complete *restitutio in integrum*'. Equity requires 'substantial *restitutio in integrum*', which allows for greater flexibility, as the court can make financial allowances for things which cannot be returned. However, the party seeking rescission must also give counter-restitution of the benefits they have received under the transaction.	*Clarke v Dickson* (1858) 120 ER 463 *Alati v Kruger* (1955) 94 CLR 216 *Maguire v Makaronis* (1997) 188 CLR 449	Chapter 18: [18.19]–[18.31]

Rescission aims to restore the parties to the position they were in before the contract or gift took place. 'It involves a giving and taking back on both sides.'[7]

5 *Munchies Management Pty Ltd v Belperio* (1988) 58 FCR 274, 288; *Akron Securities Ltd v Iliffe* (1997) 41 NSWLR 353, 367.

6 *Henjo Investments Pty Ltd v Collins Marrickville Pty Ltd* (1988) 39 FCR 546, 565; *Akron Securities Ltd v Iliffe* (1997) 41 NSWLR 353, 366; *Tenji v Henneberry & Associates Pty Ltd* (2000) 98 FCR 324, [14], [114].

7 *Shalson v Russo* [2003] EWHC 1637 (Ch), [2005] Ch 281, [122] (Rimer J).

As noted earlier, common law requires 'complete *restitutio in integrum*' whereas equitable rescission requires only 'substantial *restitutio in integrum*'.

For common law, if the subject matter of the transaction cannot be returned in the same form, rescission is unavailable.

By contrast, for equitable rescission, to the extent that the subject matter of the transaction cannot be returned, or where one party has derived a benefit which has not been paid for, the court will order a financial adjustment reflecting the value of the benefits received.

However, sometimes the situation has changed so greatly that not even equity can effect substantial *restitutio in integrum*, in which case rescission will be unavailable.

Clarke v Dickson (1858) 120 ER 463

Facts and issues

In 1853, Clarke (the plaintiff) bought shares in a mining company from Dickson (the defendant vendors), who were directors of the company. For three years, the plaintiff received dividends (in the form of more shares). The shares were issued on the 'cost book principle' but were later converted into shares in a joint stock corporation. The company failed and was wound up. The plaintiff discovered that the defendants had made fraudulent misrepresentations and sought to rescind the share purchase at common law.

Decision

The Court refused to award rescission because 'complete *restitutio in integrum*' was impossible. The plaintiff was advised to bring a claim in deceit instead.

Erle J

> [**466**] I am of opinion that the nonsuit was right. The plaintiff claims to repudiate the contract under which shares were allotted to him; to give up the shares, and recover back the price. There are several grounds of objection, all falling under the same principle: the plaintiff cannot avoid the contract under which he took the shares, because he cannot restore them in the same state as when he took them. ... After three years working of the mine, and trying to make a profit, he cannot restore the shares as they were before this was done. But, further, he not only had the chance of profit, but dividends were declared, and received by him. They were not received in money, it is true; but the receipt of money's worth has the same effect in law. Then he has also changed the nature of the article: the shares he received were shares in a company on the cost book principle; the plaintiff offers to restore them after he has converted them into shares in a joint stock corporation. Lastly, the offer to restore these shares is not made till after the Company is in the course of being wound up, when all chance of profit is over, and the shares can only be a source of loss. I have looked at this as if no others were concerned but the plaintiff and defendants; but no doubt there may have been liabilities incurred by the plaintiff to third persons, rending it impossible for him to rescind.

Crompton J

[**466**] When once it is settled that a contract induced by fraud is not void, but voidable at the option of the party defrauded, it seems to me to follow that, when that party exercises his option to rescind the contract, he must be in a state to rescind; that is, he must be in such a situation as to be able to put the parties into their original state before the contract. Now here I will assume, what is not clear to me, that the plaintiff bought his shares from the defendants and not from the Company, and that he might at one time have had a right to restore the shares to the defendants if he could, and demand the price from them. But then what did he buy? Shares in a partnership with others. He cannot return those; he has become bound to those others. Still stronger, he has changed their nature: what he now has and offers to restore are shares in a quasi corporation now in the process of being wound up. That is quite enough to decide this case. The plaintiff must rescind in toto or not at all; he cannot both keep the shares and recover the whole price. That is founded on the plainest principles of justice. If he cannot return the article he must keep it, and sue for his real damage in an action on the deceit. Take the case I put in argument, of a butcher buying live cattle, killing them, and even selling the meat to his customers. If the rule of law were as the plaintiff contends, that butcher might, upon discovering a fraud on the part of the grazier who sold him the cattle, rescind the contract and get back the whole price: but how could that be consistently with justice? The true doctrine is, that a party can never repudiate a contract after, by his own act, it has become out of his power to restore the parties to their original condition.

Lord Campbell CJ

[**466**] I will only say that I remain of the opinion which I expressed at the trial. The plaintiff, by his own shewing, cannot rescind the contract and sue for money had and received, but must seek his remedy by a special action for deceit. In that action, if he proves what he states, he will recover, not the original price, but whatever is the real damage sustained.

As the principles text suggests, even if equitable rescission had been sought in *Clarke v Dickson*[8] it may be that the subject matter of the contract had changed too much.

'Substantial *restitutio in integrum*' is required for equitable rescission. A court makes financial adjustments to reflect items which can no longer be restored to both parties.

Alati v Kruger (1955) 94 CLR 216

Facts and issues

Alati (the plaintiff purchaser) sought to rescind the purchase of a fruit business. Kruger (the defendant vendor) had made fraudulent misrepresentations that the business would take an average of £100 per week, but its weekly takings were far less. The vendor knew that a new

8 (1858) 120 ER 463.

supermarket had opened near the business. During the litigation the goodwill of the business had deteriorated, and some of the stock and chattels were lost or sold. The lease no longer existed by the time of the High Court appeal, because just after the trial, the vendor vacated the premises and the landlord repossessed the property.

Decision

The High Court held that substantial *restitutio in integrum* could be effected. The purchaser was required to return stock and chattels still in existence, and the vendor was required to return the purchase price, but a variety of expenses were deducted from it, including the value of chattels and stock not returned and the value of the use of the premises during the lease. The purchase price was not reduced to reflect the deterioration of the business, as this was not the purchaser's fault. It did not matter that the purchaser had vacated the lease; this could be adjusted for.

Dixon CJ, Webb, Kitto and Taylor JJ

> **[223]** If the case had to be decided according to the principles of the common law, it might have been argued that at the date when the respondent issued his writ he was not entitled to rescind the purchase, because he was not then in a position to return to the appellant in specie that which he had received under the contract, in the same plight as that in which he had received it: *Clarke v Dickson*. But it is necessary here to apply the doctrines of equity, and equity has always regarded as valid the disaffirmance of a contract induced by fraud even though precise *restitutio in integrum* is not possible, if the situation is such that, by the exercise of its powers, including the power to take accounts of profits and to direct inquiries as to allowances proper to be made for deterioration, it can do what is practically just between the parties, and by so **[224]** doing restore them substantially to the status quo. It is not that equity asserts a power by its decree to avoid a contract which the defrauded party himself has no right to disaffirm, and to revest property the title to which the party cannot effect. Rescission for misrepresentation is always the act of the party himself. The function of a court in which proceedings for rescission are taken is to adjudicate upon the validity of a purported disaffirmance as an act avoiding the transaction *ab initio*, and, if it is valid, to give effect to it and make appropriate consequential orders. The difference between the legal and the equitable rules on the subject simply was that equity, having means which the common law lacked to ascertain and provide for the adjustments necessary to be made between the parties in cases where a simple handing back of property or repayment of money would not put them in as good a position as before they entered into their transaction, was able to see the possibility of *restitutio in integrum*, and therefore to concede the right of a defrauded party to rescind, in a much wider variety of cases than those which the common law could recognize as admitting of rescission. Of course, a rescission which the common law courts would not accept as valid cannot of its own force revest the legal title to property which had passed, but if a court of equity would treat it as effectual the equitable title to such property revests upon the rescission.
>
> In the present case, what changes affecting the possibility of restitution had occurred in the short period between 16th June when the respondent took possession of the business

and 29th June when he issued the writ? He had had possession of the premises, and although that might have sufficed at common law to preclude rescission: *Blackburn v Smith* ..., it could hardly do so in equity, since a money payment could compensate for any difference there might be between the rental value of the premises and the rent paid by the respondent to the landlords. The title to the term created by the lease had been vested in the respondent by assignment, but that was subject to any right which he had to disaffirm the transaction. The title would revest in equity **[225]** when he elected to rescind, and he was in a position to make a legal re-assignment with the landlords' consent. He had taken over ... about twenty pounds worth of stock, but while of course he could not restore that to the appellant in specie he could pay or allow for its value, and nothing more could in justice be required. The business itself had deteriorated but this would not matter, for, as the trial judge has found, it was not due to any fault on the respondent's part, and even at common law the necessity to return property in its original condition was qualified so as to allow for incidents for which the buyer was not responsible ... . No other change had occurred. The case was therefore typical of the class of cases in which a defrauded purchaser is regarded by a court exercising equitable jurisdiction as entitled to rescind the purchase and obtain a decree, on proper terms, declaring and giving effect to the rescission as an avoidance of the transaction from the beginning.

There remains, however, the question whether the respondent lost his right to such a decree by his conduct in discontinuing the business and leaving the premises before judgment was given in the action. The remedy is discretionary, and if the respondent had acted unconscientiously during the pendency of the action, as by causing the loss of a valuable leasehold and goodwill by discontinuing the business and abandoning the premises without giving the appellant a reasonable opportunity to take them back, no doubt the court might refuse relief. But nothing of that kind happened. The term was, of course, still vested at law in the respondent, and it is not impossible that, despite low takings and actual losses, the business had some residual goodwill. But it is impossible to convict the respondent of any unfairness in the circumstances. The service of the writ had given the appellant clear notice that if the case alleged against him were made out at the trial the business and the lease would be held to have been his all along. He knew from the judge's announcement of his findings that in fact the issues of fact in the case had gone against him. He could have applied for the appointment by the court of a receiver and manager to preserve the property pending the determination of the case, but he made **[226]** no such application. He did not even make any offer to the respondent to take the property back or suggest any *modus vivendi*. He took his chance, contenting himself with such maintenance of the business as the respondent's continuing conduct of it might afford. But the respondent was under no duty to go on indefinitely, working for nothing and incurring losses, especially after the judge had announced findings of fact in his favour. It does not appear from the material before us whether he gave the appellant any specific warning of his intention to give up the business and leave the premises, but, even if he did not, the appellant had ample opportunity to protect his interests, and his inaction is far more likely to have been due to an opinion that neither the lease nor the business was worth worrying about, particularly in view of the competition which the 'super-market' had created, than to any expectation that the respondent would obligingly continue to act as an unpaid manager.

For these reasons the appeal must fail. It is desirable, however, to make one or two variations in the judgment of the Supreme Court, because, as framed, it makes the respondent's right to be repaid his purchase money conditional upon his re-assigning the lease to the appellant and delivering to the appellant all other property the subject of the contract. The lease cannot now be re-assigned, and the other property referred to would include the stock-in-trade which obviously cannot now be returned, and the chattels referred to in the schedule to the contract which now may or may not be available for re-delivery. The judgment should therefore be varied so as to order the plaintiff to return to the defendant Alati such of the chattels mentioned in the schedule to the contract as he is able to return, and to order the defendant to repay to the plaintiff the balance of the purchase money (£700) and interest thereon which shall remain after deducting the value as at the date of the contract of such of the scheduled chattels as the plaintiff cannot return, the value as at that date of the stock-in-trade which the plaintiff received from the defendant under the contract, the damages awarded in the judgment of the Supreme Court, and any amount which ought to be allowed in the defendant's favour in respect of the plaintiff's use of any of the property comprised in the contract.

Fullagar J

[**227**] I agree with the judgment of the majority of the Court, subject to this, that I wish to state very briefly for myself what I conceive to be the position where, as here, a purchaser, who has purported to rescind a contract, remains in possession pending the determination of his right to rescind. …

…

[**228**] The fundamental factor in the situation is, of course, the rule that *restitutio in integrum* is a condition of rescission. It seems to me necessarily to follow from this that a purchaser remaining in possession after giving notice of rescission is under a duty to take reasonable care to preserve the property, so that what he has received from the other party may, so far as reasonably practicable, be restored to that other party. If the property includes the goodwill of a business, then I think that the purchaser in possession must carry on that business and take reasonable care to preserve the goodwill. If he commits a breach of this duty, and deterioration results, one of two consequences may follow according to the circumstances of the particular case. The court may find, having regard to the conduct of the purchaser, that it would not be equitable to decree rescission. Or, while not thinking it proper to refuse a decree, the court may make it a condition of the decree that the purchaser shall compensate the vendor in respect of the deterioration of the property.

I do not think that the purchaser is bound to remain in possession. On the other hand, I think that he would commit a breach of his duty if he simply abandoned the property without notice to the vendor. If he gave reasonable notice to the vendor offering to restore possession of the property to him, I think that the vendor would act at his own risk if he declined to take the opportunity offered to him, and that he could make no claim for compensation if the purchaser then left the property and it were subsequently held that he was entitled to rescind. There the property sold consisted of contributing shares in a company, and, after the purchaser had given notice of rescission, a call was made, of which the vendor had notice. He did not pay the call, and the shares were forfeited. It was held that he had acted at his own risk, and there was a decree for rescission.

It is, of course, in many cases open to either party to apply for an order appointing a receiver or a receiver and manager, but **[229]** often the expense incurred in and by such appointment would be out of proportion to the amount involved.

The application of these principles to the present case, is, I think, a matter of some difficulty. But I think the correct view of the facts is that the defendant failed to establish that any loss had really been suffered through any breach of duty or unreasonable conduct on the part of the plaintiff. One is left with a strong impression that the establishment and development of the 'super-market' were big factors in this case.

Each of the parties to a rescinded transaction has a right to be restored to the position they were in before the transaction was entered into.

If a party seeking rescission has made permanent improvements to the subject matter of the transaction before becoming aware of the right to rescind, they will be entitled to the value of those improvements, as *Brown v Smitt* demonstrates.[9] This is discussed further in the principles text at [18.27].

If the party seeking to rescind the transaction cannot make substantial *restitutio in integrum* in return to the other party, the transaction cannot be set aside, even if the vitiating factor is clearly established. It has been said that the party seeking to rescind must also make 'counter-restitution'.

Maguire v Makaronis (1997) 188 CLR 449

Facts and issues

Mr and Mrs Makaronis took out a short-term loan for $250 000 from their solicitors (Maguire) to purchase a poultry farm. The loan was secured over another property, with an interest rate of 24 per cent, reduced to 22 per cent for prompt payment, which the trial judge found was not unreasonable for 1990. The Makaronises managed one repayment before falling into arrears. When the solicitors sought to repossess the mortgaged property, the Makaronises sought to set aside the mortgage on the basis that the solicitors had breached their fiduciary duty. The Makaronises had poor English and had not realised that the loan was from their solicitors rather than the Commonwealth Bank of Australia.

Decision

Rescission was granted on terms that the Makaronises must pay *all* the money and interest secured by the mortgage before the transaction could be set aside.

9 (1924) 34 CLR 160.

Brennan CJ, Gaudron, McHugh and Gummow JJ

> [**474**] There remains for consideration the submission by the appellants that the majority of the Appeal Division erred in upholding the granting of the remedy of rescission so as to set aside the Mortgage and amend accordingly the registered title of the Radford property, but without calling upon the respondents first to do equity by honouring their contractual obligations to pay the money and interest secured by the Mortgage.
>
> To an extent, the majority appears to have proceeded on the footing ... that the respondents had not taken their advance from the appellants and had not created a relationship of debtor and creditor between them. We have indicated earlier in these reasons that so to conclude would be to depart from the admission on the pleadings and from the documentary and certain of the oral evidence. Moreover, the Mortgage itself, in its terms, both contained covenants by the respondents to pay to the appellants principal and interest, and created the security for that indebtedness. The order made at first instance and upheld by the Full Court that the Mortgage 'be set aside' and the registration thereof be removed from [**475**] the title carries with it the destruction not only of the security but of the covenants therein. ...
>
> Here, given the undisclosed role of the appellants as mortgagee, the breach of duty went to the identity of the parties having the benefit under the Mortgage both of the security and of the covenants to pay money. To set aside the Mortgage purely in its operation as a security, without conditioning that upon repayment, would be to reform the transaction in an impermissible fashion. It would be to strike down the security interest without ensuring repayment of that which was paid in return for it. The respondents would be left with the fruits of the transaction of which they complain, whereas their equity was to have the whole transaction rescinded and, so far as possible, the parties remitted to their original position.
>
> The court said that relief was conditional upon repayment of the principal and interest as allowed from time to time by the Supreme Court of Victoria.

REVIEW QUESTIONS

(1) How are restitutionary remedies similar to rescission (if at all)?

(2) What other actions could the Makaronises have taken in *Maguire v Makaronis* (1997) 188 CLR 449?

III Election

A person entitled to rescind a transaction may affirm or rescind it. If a person chooses to rescind, they must elect to do so. Ordinarily, election occurs when a person gives notice to the other contracting party of their intention to have the transaction set aside. The decision is generally final.

Concept	Short explanation	Relevant authorities	Principles text
How to make an election to rescind	In almost all circumstances, communication must be made by the party seeking to rescind to the other party. However, this is not always the case.	*Car & Universal Finance Co Ltd v Caldwell* [1965] 1 QB 525	Chapter 18: [18.33]–[18.40]
The consequences of an election to rescind	The consequences of an election to rescind are different in common law and equity. At common law, title revests immediately in the party seeking to rescind. In equity, prior to election the party seeking to rescind has a 'mere equity', but after election, the other party holds the legal title on CT for the rescinding party.	*Daly v Sydney Stock Exchange Ltd* (1986) 160 CLR 371	Chapter 18: [18.41]–[18.48]
The reasons behind the election requirement	Election is required to protect innocent defendants and third parties who may deal with the property.	See discussion in principles text.	Chapter 18: [18.49]–[18.50]

A How to make an election to rescind

Generally, an election to rescind will be made where the person entitled to rescind unequivocally communicates to the other party that they choose to disaffirm the transaction. Ways to elect include:

- oral or written statements saying the person does not want to be bound by the contract
- conduct incompatible with the subsisting contract (eg demanding repayment of purchase price)
- filing a writ unequivocally seeking rescission (as in *Alati v Kruger*[10])
- at common law only, recaption of goods sold under a contract, or
- non-performance of a contractual obligation of which the other party is aware.

Usually it is necessary to communicate with the other contracting party, but this is not always possible.

Car & Universal Finance Co Ltd v Caldwell [1965] 1 QB 525

Facts and issues

The defendant, Caldwell, sold his Jaguar car to a rogue, named 'Norris'. Norris sold the car to dealers, Motobella Co Ltd, who had notice of his fraud. Motobella ultimately sold the car to the plaintiff, Car & Universal Finance Co Ltd, a bona fide purchaser for value without notice. If the defendant could show that he rescinded at common law before Motobella sold the car to

10 (1955) 94 CLR 216.

the plaintiff, title would revert to him. Was it sufficient for the defendant to have communicated his intention to rescind to the police and the Automobile Association, and to have asked those authorities to repossess the car?

Decision

Lord Denning had held while it was ordinarily necessary to communicate an intention to rescind to the other party, in a case such as this where the rogue had deliberately absconded, it was sufficient to make it known to the world that the contract was rescinded and to attempt to repossess the car. The English Court of Appeal upheld his conclusion.

Sellers LJ

> [**550**] ... Where a contracting party could be communicated with, and modern facilities make communication practically world-wide and almost immediate, it would be unlikely that a party could be held to have disaffirmed a contract unless he went so far as to communicate his decision so to do. It would be what the other contracting party would normally require and unless communication were made the party's intention to rescind would not have been unequivocally or clearly demonstrated or made manifest. But in circumstances such as the present case, the other contracting party, a fraudulent rogue who would know that the vendor would want his car back as soon as he knew of the fraud, would not expect to be communicated with as a matter of right or requirement, and would deliberately, as here, do all he could to evade any such communication being made to him. In such exceptional contractual circumstances, it does not seem to me appropriate to hold that a party so acting can claim any right to have a decision to rescind communicated to him before the contract is terminated. To hold that he could would involve that the defrauding party, if skilful enough to keep out of the way, could deprive the other party to the contract of his right to rescind, a right to which he was entitled and which [**551**] he would wish to exercise, as the defrauding party would well know or at least confidently suspect. The position has to be viewed, as I see it, between the two contracting parties involved in the particular contract in question. That another innocent party or parties may suffer does not in my view of the matter justify imposing on a defrauded seller an impossible task. He has to establish, clearly and unequivocally, that he terminates the contract and is no longer to be bound by it. If he cannot communicate his decision he may still satisfy a judge or jury that he had made a final and irrevocable decision and ended the contract. I am in agreement with Lord Denning MR who asked 'How is a man in the position of Caldwell ever to be able to rescind the contract when a fraudulent person absconds as Norris did here?' and answered that he can do so '... if he at once, on discovering the fraud, takes all possible steps to regain the goods even though he cannot find the rogue nor communicate with him'.

Upjohn LJ

> [**554**] Where one party to a contract has an option unilaterally to rescind or disaffirm it by reason of the fraud or misrepresentation of the other party, he must elect to do so within a reasonable time, and cannot do so after he has done anything to affirm the contract with knowledge of the facts giving rise to the option to rescind. In principle and

on authority, however, he must, in my judgment, in the ordinary course communicate his intention to rescind to the other party. This must be so because the other party is entitled to treat the contractual nexus as continuing until he is made aware of the intention of the other to exercise his option to rescind. So the intention must be communicated and an uncommunicated intention, for example, by speaking to a third party or making a private note, will be ineffective. ... 'If a party elects to rescind he must within a reasonable time manifest that election by communicating to the other party his intention to rescind the transaction and claim no interest under it. The communication need not be formal provided it is a distinct and positive repudiation of the transaction' ... .

Mr Caplan, for the plaintiffs ... relies strongly on the well-known words of Lord Blackburn in *Scarf v Jardine* to the effect that in general an election must be communicated to the other side ... .

Such in my view must be the general principle. Does it admit of any exception? Mr Caplan concedes that there is one: where the subject-matter of the contract is a transfer of property, then the party entitled to do so may disaffirm the contract by retaking possession of the property. Mr Caplan, however, submits this [**555**] is really a method of communication, though for my part I do not see how that can be true of every case that could be suggested. ... Mr Caplan submits ... that, apart from recaption, there should be a universal rule of law that communication is essential to break the nexus. On the facts of this case, it is clear that Norris intended quite deliberately to disappear and render it impossible for the defendant to communicate with him or to recover the car. While I appreciate Mr Caplan's argument that this point can only arise in cases between the vendor and a third party, I agree with Sellers LJ that this problem must be solved by consideration of the rights between the two contracting parties. Admittedly one of two innocent parties must suffer for the fraud of a third, but that cannot be helped and does not assist to solve the problem. One thing is quite clear – that neither Lord Blackburn nor Lord Hatherley in the cases above mentioned nor the textbook writers had in mind circumstances remotely resembling these. It is indeed strange that there is no authority in point.

If one party, by absconding, deliberately puts it out of the power of the other to communicate his intention to rescind which he knows the other will almost certainly want to do, I do not think he can any longer insist on his right to be made aware of the election to determine the contract. In these circumstances communication is a useless formality. I think that the law must allow the innocent party to exercise his right of rescission otherwise than by communication or repossession. To hold otherwise would be to allow a fraudulent contracting party by his very fraud to prevent the innocent party from exercising his undoubted right. I would hold that in circumstances such as these the innocent party may evince his intention to disaffirm the contract by overt means falling short of communication or repossession.

Davies LJ

[**558**] On the facts of this case Norris must be taken to have known that the defendant might, on ascertaining the fraud, wish to rescind the contract. Norris disappeared; and so did the car. The defendant could, therefore, neither communicate with Norris nor retake the car. It must, therefore, I think, be taken to be implied in the transaction between Norris and the defendant that in the event of the defendant's wishing to rescind he should be

entitled to do so by the best other means possible. *Lex non* **[559]** *cogit ad impossibilia*.[11] It is true that it was conceivably possible that the defendant might decide not to rescind but to sue on the cheque instead; but it is most doubtful whether on the facts of this case such a possibility could have occurred to Norris as a real one. The fact that Norris knew that he was a rogue and that, therefore, the defendant was likely to be after him distinguishes this case from that of an innocent misrepresentor. It would not occur to the latter that the other party to the contract would have any right or desire to rescind, so that there would be no such implication as that which I have suggested arose in the present case.

It was argued that the defendant's action in going to the police and the Automobile Association was not an unequivocal act, since it was open to him to have changed his mind on the next day … . That again, in my opinion, is an unrealistic view of the facts. The defendant was, as I think, declaring to the world: 'I have been swindled and I want my car back.' He was declaring his intention as clearly as if he had seen the car in the street and seized it.

In the result, therefore, I agree with the judgment of Lord Denning MR on this ground …

Although this case has been criticised, it remains good law; but it may be limited to cases of fraud.[12]

B The consequences of an election to rescind

The consequences of election differ between common law and equity.

At common law, election effects an immediate re-vesting of title to the person who seeks to rescind and the other party is left with no title.

In *Car & Universal Finance Ltd v Caldwell*,[13] the election to rescind meant that title to the car immediately re-vested in the defendant. The dealers, Motobella, had no title to pass to the plaintiff after the election to rescind, even though the plaintiff was a bona fide purchaser for value without notice ('BFPV'). (The property law principle of *nemo dat quod non habet* provides that 'no one gives what they do not have').

The effect of an election to rescind in equity is different. Where an executory contract is voidable for a purely equitable ground such as undue influence, breach of fiduciary duty or unconscionable dealing, it is rescinded by notice to the other party and effectively nullified.

Figure 18.1 Ownership of car *before* Caldwell's election

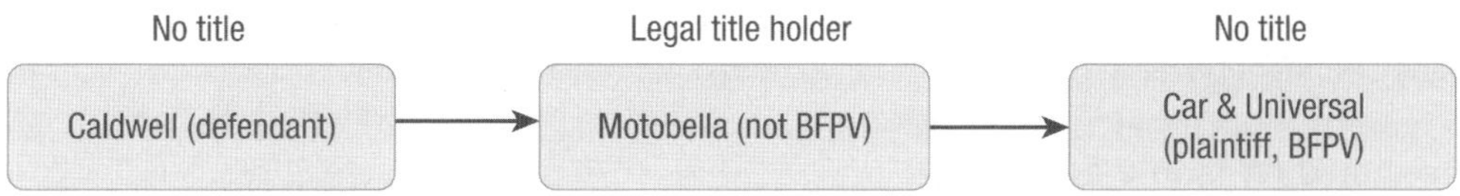

11 'The law does not compel a person to do that which is impossible'.

12 See D O'Sullivan, S Elliott and R Zakrzewski, *The Law of Rescission* (Oxford University Press, 2008) [11.34]–[11.37].

13 [1965] 1 QB 525.

Figure 18.2 Ownership of car *after* Caldwell's election

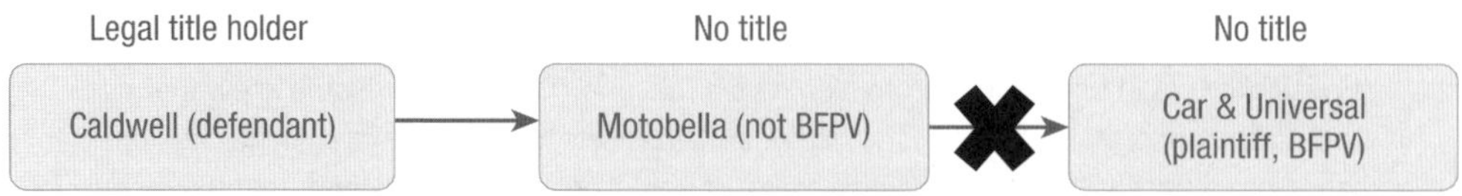

If legal title to an asset has been transferred by a voidable transaction, prior to election the party seeking to rescind has a 'mere equity', an inchoate proprietary right which will be extinguished by a subsequent BFPV of the equitable title without notice.[14] After they have elected to rescind, their mere equity transforms into an equitable title to the property pursuant to a CT.[15] The plaintiff may then seek return of the property pursuant to a court order. Courts sometimes award less intrusive remedies such as a lien, depending upon the circumstances.

Daly v Sydney Stock Exchange Ltd (1986) 160 CLR 371

Facts and issues

An investor, Daly, sought advice from a firm of stockbrokers, Patrick Partners. He was advised to deposit his money with the firm until a good investment could be found, and so he loaned it to the firm. Patrick Partners ceased trading some months later, and was unable to repay the loan. Daly's wife (as assignee) sought compensation from the fidelity fund of the Sydney Stock Exchange. Pursuant to s 97(1)(b) of the then *Securities Industry Act 1975* (NSW), she was required to show that Patrick Partners had held the investment on trust for Daly. She sought to argue that the firm held the investment on constructive trust for her husband.

Decision

While the High Court found that Patrick Partners had breached the fiduciary duty they owed Daly, they declined to find a constructive trust.

The majority did not consider rescission. The minority (Brennan J, with whom Wilson J agreed) considered whether Daly had elected to rescind. It was held that a party seeking to rescind must *elect* before a constructive trust can arise. Daly had not elected to rescind the contract before Patrick Partners became insolvent, and thus he did not have a constructive trust.

Brennan J (Wilson J agreeing)

> [**388**] Menzies J. in *Latec Investments* referred to the view that a plaintiff who was entitled to avoid a contract of sale and to have the conveyance set aside had a mere equity and

14 *Latec Investments Ltd v Hotel Terrigal Pty Ltd* (1965) 113 CLR 265, 277, 284, 290–91.

15 Ibid 277, 290–91.

the competing view that he had an equitable interest in the property from the beginning. He said:

> If there is a difference between the two lines of authority, that difference seems to me to arise from concentration upon different aspects of what follows from a voidable conveyance. Thus, *Phillips v Phillips*, in so far as it says that a person with the right to have a voidable conveyance set aside has but a mere equity, directs attention to the right to have the conveyance set aside as a right to sue which must be successfully exercised as a necessary condition of there being any relation back of the equitable interest established by the suit. *Stump v Gaby* directs attention to the result of the eventual avoidance of the conveyance upon the position ab initio and throughout of the persons by whom and to whom the conveyance of property was made and says that, in the event of a successful suit (which may be maintained by a devisee), the conveyor had an equitable estate capable of devise and that the conveyee holds, and has always held, as trustee.

But where property has been sold and conveyed, the purchaser's beneficial title must be ascertained by reference to the sale so long as it stands; the vendor cannot insist on an equitable interest in the property if he does not choose to enforce his equity to avoid the sale … . Similarly, until the lender elects to avoid the contract of loan, he cannot assert an equitable title to the money lent. He cannot at once leave the contract on foot and deny the borrowers the title to the money which the contract confers. When, as in the present case, a borrower acquires title to money paid to him under and pursuant to a contract of loan, the borrower cannot be made a trustee of the money without his consent so long as the contract stands. There is no analogy between the present case and one in which a constructive trust is imposed on money or other property which is acquired by a fiduciary in breach of his duty but not pursuant to a voidable contract. In such a case there is no question of avoiding the contract before the constructive trust is imposed. A fortiori, there is no analogy between the present case and one where a constructive trust is imposed on money or other property [**390**] which is acquired by a non- fiduciary otherwise than by contract (as, for example, in *Chase Manhattan Bank NA v Israel-British Bank (London) Ltd*).

Although Dr Daly or Mrs Daly was entitled to avoid the contracts of loan for breach of the fiduciary obligation resting on Patrick Partners, there is no evidence that the contracts of loan were avoided. In equity, Patrick Partners' title to the money lent was imperfect from the beginning by reason of their failure to discharge their duty as a fiduciary … and, had the contract of loan been avoided, Mrs Daly's rights as against Patrick Partners might have been determined *as though* the firm had from the beginning held the money lent on a constructive trust for Dr Daly and then for Mrs Daly. But even if that be the true basis on which to measure Mrs Daly's rights as against Patrick Partners and any person into whose hands the borrowed moneys can be traced …, it does not satisfy the statutory criterion of a liability enforceable against the fidelity fund.

… In the absence of evidence of avoidance of the contracts of loan, there is nothing to show that Dr Daly or Mrs Daly has the equitable interest in the moneys lent by Dr Daly to Patrick Partners which might have arisen by relation back. The relationship between Dr Daly and Mrs Daly on the one hand and Patrick Partners on the other was in the beginning and has remained that of creditor and debtor.

If, in *Car & Universal Finance Ltd v Caldwell*,[16] the defendant had rescinded in equity instead of at common law, legal title would have remained with car dealer (with equitable title vesting in the defendant pursuant to a constructive trust). The car dealer would have been able to sell the car to the plaintiff because it would have retained legal title. Car & Universal would have won the case because Caldwell's equitable title under the constructive trust would have been defeated by a BFPV without notice of the legal title.

Figure 18.3 Ownership of car *before* Caldwell's election in a hypothetical scenario involving equitable rescission

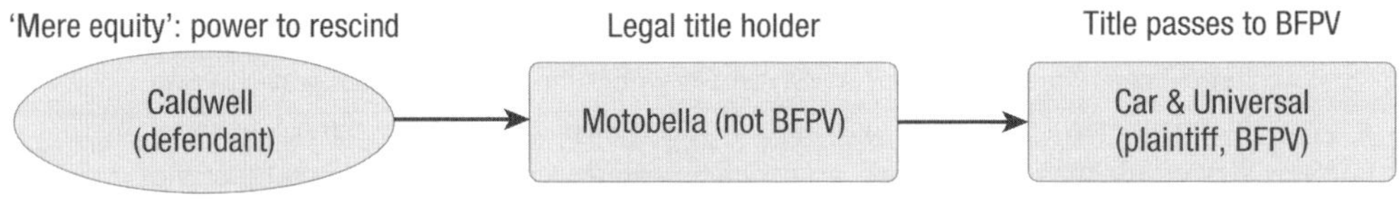

Figure 18.4 Ownership of car *after* Caldwell's election in a hypothetical scenario involving equitable rescission

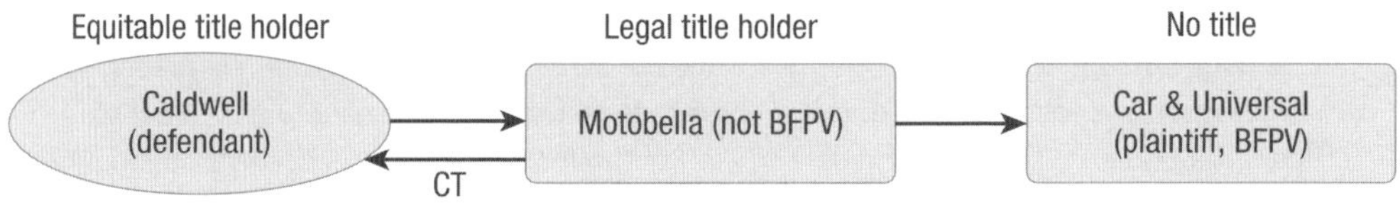

C The reasons behind the election requirement

Election primarily serves to protect the interests of innocent defendants. Courts are less sympathetic towards fraudulent defendants.

Election also protects third parties who might have gained a competing interest in an asset transferred pursuant to a voidable transaction without being aware of the proprietary interest of the party seeking to rescind.

REVIEW QUESTIONS

(1) In what circumstances will common law rescission be advantageous to the party seeking to set a transaction aside?

(2) Why does the strictness of the requirement to communicate an intention to rescind depend upon the good faith the other party?

(3) For equitable rescission, what is the nature of the plaintiff's interest before and after election?

16 [1965] 1 QB 525.

IV 'Partial' rescission

Concept	Short explanation	Relevant authorities	Principles text
Partial rescission	Sometimes Australian courts allow 'partial' rescission, namely an unwinding of only part of the transaction. Does this result in an impermissible remaking of the bargain?	*Vadasz v Pioneer Concrete (SA) Pty Ltd* (1995) 184 CLR 102	Chapter 18: [18.51]–[18.56]

As the principles text notes at [18.51]–[18.56], the traditional position at common law and equity is that rescission must be total. However, the High Court has been prepared to order partial rescission in the following case.

Vadasz v Pioneer Concrete (SA) Pty Ltd (1995) 184 CLR 102

Facts and issues

Vadasz was a director of Vadipile. Pioneer Concrete was owed $200 000 by Vadipile for past concrete supplies and required a personal guarantee from Vadasz before making any further deliveries. Vadasz signed a guarantee of Vadipile's past and future indebtedness to Pioneer Concrete. After the contract had been made, Vadipile incurred further debts of almost $180 000. The trial judge found that Vadasz had been induced to enter the transaction by a misrepresentation by Pioneer Concrete that the guarantee related only to future indebtedness.

Decision

A unanimous High Court left intact that part of the guarantee which related to future indebtedness. The part of the guarantee which related to past indebtedness could be rescinded.

Deane, Dawson, Toohey, Gaudron and McHugh JJ

> [**110**] As has been indicated, the respondent has not sought in this Court to overturn the trial judge's finding that the appellant's execution of the guarantee was induced by misrepresentation. Nor has the respondent sought to attack his conclusion, which was confirmed by the Full Court, that the guarantee should be rescinded at least as regards past indebtedness. The only question on the appeal to this Court is whether the trial judge was entitled to order rescission on a footing which left the appellant liable to the respondent for the debts incurred by Vadipile after the guarantee was signed.
>
> In this context it should be remembered that the trial judge held that the appellant was 'entitled to equitable relief on the ground of the [respondent's] misrepresentation'. And his Honour held that the respondent was entitled in equity (as well as under the *Trade Practices Act*) to enforce the appellant's liability under the guarantee for future indebtedness. Had the appellant sought to rely on the common law, he would not have been entitled to rescission because the contract did not remain completely executory and 'because he was not then in a position to return to the [respondent] in specie that which he had received under the

contract, in the same plight as that in which he had [**111**] received it'. Complete restitution was not and is not possible in the circumstances of the present case … .

Thus we are very much in the realm of equity. Indeed, as we followed the argument, the appellant did not really seek to attack the conclusion of the trial judge and the Full Court that the appropriate relief in the circumstances of the present case is equitable in its nature in the sense that its origins can be traced to the old Court of Chancery. The appellant's case is that the appropriate equitable relief was the unconditional rescission or setting aside of the guarantee in its entirety. …

Where, as in this case, the court has granted equitable relief in the shape of rescission of a contract, the result is to set aside the contract ab initio. While equity followed the law in requiring restitution as a condition of rescission where the contract had been wholly or partly executed, it allowed greater flexibility in the basis upon which restitution and accounting between the parties may be ordered. Thus, equity did not require complete restitution of the position which existed before the contract but allowed its remedies, particularly an order for monetary accounts, to be utilized to achieve practical restitution and justice. …

[**112**] In the present case, the appellant obtained the benefit which he sought as consideration for entering the contract of guarantee, namely, the subsequent supply on credit by the respondent of goods to Vadipile. In those circumstances, a practical restoration of the status quo which existed before the execution of the guarantee and the subsequent supply of goods on credit by the respondent would involve not only a cancellation of the appellant's obligations under the guarantee but either a return of the goods subsequently supplied by the respondent or the actual payment, either by Vadipile or the appellant, of an amount equivalent to the value of the goods which were subsequently supplied in reliance upon the appellant's guarantee of payment of their price.

However, the appellant does not offer to pay the respondent the amount which Vadipile has failed to pay for those subsequently supplied goods. Nor does he offer to submit to terms or conditions which would ensure that the purchase price of those goods, which has not been suggested to exceed their true value, is received by the respondent. As has been said, the appellant seeks to be relieved completely and unconditionally from all liability under the guarantee, leaving the respondent without either its subsequently supplied goods or any payment for them. If such complete and unconditional relief is to be granted, it must be on some basis other than mere entitlement to a practical restoration of the status quo upon rescission or 'disaffirmance' of a contract induced by fraud. The only such basis that comes to mind is equity's general jurisdiction, in setting aside contracts and other dealings on equitable grounds, to ensure the observance of the requirements of good conscience and practical justice. Thus in *O'Sullivan v Management Agency Ltd* an exclusive management agreement made by a young composer was [**113**] set aside by reason of undue influence because of a fiduciary relationship between the parties. The Court of Appeal upheld rescission even though the parties could not be restored to their original position. In their judgments the members of the Court of Appeal pointed out that a contract may be set aside in equity so long as 'the court can achieve practical justice between the parties' and that 'the court will do what is practically just in the individual case' so long as 'it is possible to achieve what is practically just by granting rescission and restitution together with orders for accounts'.

In the present case, the consideration provided by the respondent involved the supply of goods upon credit to Vadipile. Any need for restitution arises by reason of Vadipile's insolvency. The respondent points to the fact that goods were supplied on credit in pursuance of its promise given as consideration for the appellant's guarantee and says in effect: 'I would not have made further deliveries of concrete to Vadipile and risked non-payment if the appellant had not guaranteed payment for those deliveries.' In the way in which the action between the parties was constituted, practical justice is achieved, so the respondent's argument runs, by holding the appellant liable on a money claim for that proportion of Vadipile's debt incurred after the appellant signed the guarantee. As Cussen J noted in *The Bank of Victoria Limited v Mueller*, in the context of insisting that equity shall be done as a condition of setting aside a guarantee: 'This is, of course, something quite different from rectification, although in some cases its effect may be much the same.' …

…

[114] In *Amadio*, Deane J referred to what was said by Cussen J in *Mueller* in support of the proposition:

> Where appropriate, an order will be made which only partly nullifies a transaction liable to be set aside in equity pursuant to the principles of unconscionable dealing … [T]he order will, in an appropriate case, be made conditional upon the party obtaining relief doing equity.

Thus unconscionability works in two ways. In its strict sense, it provides the justification for setting aside a transaction. More loosely, it provides the justification for not setting aside the transaction in its entirety or in doing so subject to conditions, so as to prevent one party obtaining an unwarranted benefit at the expense of the other.

[115] In *Amadio* this Court upheld an order setting aside a mortgage in its entirety where the mortgagors believed they were committing themselves to securing their son's overdraft to a limit of $50 000 and for six months only. The reason for not setting aside the mortgage only to the extent that it involved a liability in excess of $50 000 was that the Amadios would not have entered into the transaction at all, had they known the true financial position of their son. In the present case it cannot be maintained that the appellant would not have entered into the guarantee had it been confined to the future indebtedness of Vadipile. Rather, the evidence is that he would have done so, if not happily, because it was the only way to secure future supplies of concrete for Vadipile. And, by reason of the guarantee of future debts, the respondent supplied concrete to the value of $170 929.32. In giving the guarantee, the appellant, who was one of two directors and one of two shareholders, was fully aware of the financial position of Vadipile. He stood to benefit personally from the operations of the company.

The appellant suggested that to set aside the guarantee in the present case only to the extent of past indebtedness was an invitation to others to misrepresent the terms of a contract because they would be no worse off than if they had revealed the true position. But that suggestion misconceives the ordinary function of civil remedies, including equitable relief. It may, depending upon whether the respondent would in fact have supplied its goods on the basis of the more limited guarantee which the appellant was prepared to give, be true to say that the orders made by the trial judge and upheld by the Full Court disadvantage the respondent only to the extent that it is unable to enjoy the benefit of its misrepresentation and is required to bear its own costs of the trial. Such a result would not, however, be either surprising or inappropriate. The concern of equity, in moulding relief between the parties is to prevent, nullify, or provide compensation for, wrongful injury. If it appears that the other party would not have entered into the contract at all if the true position were known, the contract may be set aside in its entirety as in *Amadio*.

The appellant is 'seeking the assistance of a court of equity and he who seeks equity must do equity'. The Court must look at what is practically just for both parties, not only the appellant. To enforce the guarantee to the extent of future indebtedness is to do no more than hold the appellant to what he was prepared to undertake independently of any misrepresentation. This approach has been taken in several cases. … As Olsson J said in the present case: 'the practical approach adopted by the learned trial judge was clearly justified, if not demanded, by the situation revealed by the evidence.'

As the principles text outlines at [18.53], there has been scholarly criticism of *Vadasz*. This is because it is seen as an impermissible reformulation of the bargain between the parties. The principles text also discusses how and why partial rescission was not applied in *Commercial Bank of Australia Ltd v Amadio*[17] or *Maguire v Makaronis*,[18] but was applied in *Bridgewater v Leahy*.[19]

REVIEW QUESTIONS

(1) Do you think Australian law should allow partial rescission? Why/why not?

(2) How does partial rescission effectively allow courts to remake bargains?

V Bars to rescission

The ordinary equitable bars to relief, such as hardship, apply to equitable rescission. There are some bars which are specific to rescission.

Concept	Short explanation	Relevant authorities	Principles text
Impossibility of complete restoration	Impossibility of counter-restitution by the party seeking rescission can be a complete or partial defence.	*Quek v Beggs* (1990) 5 BPR 11, 761	Chapter 18: [18.59]–[18.61]
Affirmation	If a party affirms a contract, they cannot then disaffirm it.	*Alati v Kruger* (1955) 94 CLR 216 (see extract on page 614)	Chapter 18: [18.62]–[18.66]

17 (1983) 151 CLR 447.

18 (1997) 188 CLR 449.

19 (1998) 194 CLR 457.

Concept	Short explanation	Relevant authorities	Principles text
Delay	'Mere delay' is not a reason to deny rescission. However, if a party delays with acquiescence (related to affirmation) then they may be unable to rescind. Similarly if a party delays such that prejudice is caused to the defendant and/or third parties, then they may be unable to rescind.	*Allcard v Skinner* (1887) 36 Ch D 145	Chapter 18: [18.67]–[18.70]
Intervening third party rights	If a third party who is a bona fide purchaser for value ('BFPV') without notice has received an interest under a contract which is then sought to be rescinded, this may be a partial or total bar to relief. However, there is a possibility of 'pecuniary rescission'.	*Hartigan v International Society for Krishna Consciousness Inc* [2002] NSWSC 810	Chapter 18: [18.71]–[18.77]
Executed contracts and innocent misrepresentation	A contract for the sale of land where the title has already been conveyed or registered cannot be rescinded for innocent misrepresentation. This rule has sometimes also been extended to executed contracts for leases, shares, goods and business.	Sometimes called the rule in *Seddon's case*, referring to *Seddon v Northern Eastern Salt Company* [1905] 1 Ch 326	Chapter 18: [18.78]–[18.80]

A Impossibility of complete restoration

Impossibility of counter-restitution by the party seeking rescission can be a complete or partial defence. It is a complete defence at common law. In equity, it can be a partial defence (as in *Quek v Beggs*,[20] extracted below) or a complete defence (as in *Maguire v Makaronis*[21]).

Quek v Beggs (1990) 5 BPR 11, 761

Facts and issues

Mrs Quek, an eccentric and highly religious woman, made substantial payments to her pastor, Mr Beggs (totalling $247 000) before she died in 1986. She also made gifts of three properties (in Maroubra, Kingswood and Winston Hills) to Mr Beggs and his wife. After Mrs Quek's death, her daughter sought, inter alia, to have the transactions to the Beggs set aside on the basis of undue influence.

Decision

McLelland J found that there was a presumed relationship of undue influence arising from the relationship of spiritual advisor and acolyte, and that the Beggs failed to rebut this presumption.

20 (1990) 5 BPR 11, 761.

21 (1997) 188 CLR 449.

Mrs Quek had given some of the money to the Beggs to refurbish Mr Beggs's mother-in-law's house. McLelland J declined to make a proprietary order against the mother-in-law, or against Mr Beggs in relation to that money. The Beggs were also not required to return the Kingswood property, as they had sold it to finance the defence of the legal action, nor the proceeds of sale or the money they had received from a mortgage over it. The Maroubra and Winston Hills properties and $50 000 were returned to Mrs Quek's estate.

McLelland J

> **[17]** … Since the plaintiff is seeking rescission of the challenged transactions on equitable grounds, it is necessary for the court, in applying equitable principles, to consider and give effect to the requirements of practical justice as between the parties, so as to ensure, so far as possible, that any remedy granted to one party does not involve injustice to the other: see, for example, *O'Sullivan v Management Agency and Music Ltd* … .
>
> One matter which requires consideration in this regard is the circumstance that Mrs Quek gave the money to Mr Beggs for the express purpose of it being applied to the construction and fitting out of the house and facilities on the Bargo property and Mr Beggs expended it for the purpose for which it was given so that the benefit passed to Mrs Crockford [Mr Begg's mother-in-law], the owner of the Bargo property. Mrs Crockford is not a party to the proceedings and no order can be made against her in respect of benefits which she derived from that expenditure.
>
> Accordingly, so far as the gifts of money spent on the Bargo property are concerned, Mr Beggs cannot be restored to the position he would have been in had those gifts never been made. In these circumstances, it appears inequitable that he should be required to restore that money to Mrs Quek's estate. There is an analogy with proceedings to enforce restitution of money payed by one person to another under a fundamental mistake of fact. In such a case 'when the person to whom the payment is directly made receives it as intermediary … [and] … the circumstances are such that the intermediary is to be seen as being himself the initial recipient of the benefit, his prima facie liability will ordinarily be displaced when he has handed the money received on to the person for whom he received it. In such a case he has, in the event, not retained 'the benefit of the windfall' but been 'a mere conduit-pipe'': *Australia and New Zealand Banking Group Ltd v Wespac Banking Corporation* … . In answering the question 'whether the benefit of the payment made under fundamental mistake has been wholly or partly retained by the intermediary or effectively passed on to the third person … the courts will pay regard to the substance rather than to the form of what has occurred' … .
>
> …
>
> **[18]** The Maroubra, Kingswood and Winston Hills properties were all retained by Mr and Mrs Beggs until Mrs Quek's death, and the Maroubra and Winston Hills properties are still held by them unencumbered. They had borrowed about $13 000 from the Commonwealth Bank on the security of a mortgage over the Kingswood property. I infer that this was the amount borrowed by Mr Beggs from the Commonwealth Bank to finance the construction of the swimming pool on the Bargo property. I also infer that Mrs Quek was aware of and approved the construction of the swimming pool from monies derived from her gifts. … In December 1985 Mr and Mrs Beggs contracted to sell the Kingswood property for $50 000,

intending to use the proceeds to make repairs to the Maroubra property. That sale was completed in April 1986, yielding $28 407.09 after discharge of the Commonwealth Bank mortgage, and payment of land tax and expenses of the sale. By that time Mrs Quek had died and, in Mr Beggs' words, 'the claims over her estate had arisen and we were incurring legal expenses'. They decided not to proceed with the work on the Maroubra property, and the nett proceeds of sale of the Kingswood property were applied in payment of legal costs and otherwise for their own purposes.

In my opinion there should be excluded from any liability of Mr and Mrs Beggs to make restitution in respect of the Kingswood property, the amount of the mortgage debt discharged out of the proceeds of its sale. …

McLelland J rejected the Beggs' submission that the defence of laches applied.

B Affirmation

Affirmation involves a choice to leave the contract in question on foot and, potentially, to take action under it. If the party seeking to rescind has affirmed the contract, they will not be entitled to seek to rescind it.

If the plaintiff is still operating under a vitiating factor, a choice cannot be made until *after* the vitiating factor has ceased to apply.[22]

Delay after knowing of the right to rescind may constitute affirmation of the contract.

C Delay

'Mere delay' is not a reason to deny rescission. However, if a party delays with acquiescence (related to affirmation) then they may be unable to rescind, as in *Allcard v Skinner*.[23] Similarly, if a party delays and causes prejudice to the defendant and/or third parties, then they may be unable to rescind.

Allcard v Skinner (1887) 36 Ch D 145

Facts and issues

Miss Allcard, the plaintiff, joined an order of Anglican nuns, under the advice of Mr Nihill. She was required to give her property to her relatives, the poor, or the sisterhood, with the latter strongly encouraged. Three days after joining, Allcard made a will in favour of Miss Skinner, the lady superior of the order. Later, she transferred large sums of money and railway stock to Skinner. Ten years after joining, Allcard left the sisterhood, revoked her will, and became a Catholic nun. Six years after leaving, she sought to rescind the transaction on the basis of Skinner's undue influence.

22 *Hawker Pacific Pty Ltd v Helicopter Charter Pty Ltd* (1991) 22 NSWLR 298, 304–5, 306–8.

23 (1887) 36 Ch D 145.

Decision

There was a presumed relationship of undue influence arising from the relationship of spiritual advisor and acolyte, and the defendant failed to rebut this presumption. However, a majority of the Court of Appeal (Lindley LJ and Bowen LJ) held that Allcard could not rescind because of her delay and acquiescence in bringing her claim.

Cotton LJ (dissenting)

Unlike the other judges, Cotton LJ found that Miss Allcard did not know her rights until long after 1879. He said:

> [**175**] The delay which has occurred since 1879 is, I think, a defence against any claim on behalf of the Plaintiff to the dividends on the stock in the name of the Defendant before the commencement of the action. But in my opinion it is no defence as regards the stock remaining in the hands of the Defendant and the dividends accrued since the commencement of the action. At the time when the Plaintiff left the sisterhood in 1879 that stock was property which the Plaintiff was entitled to claim, as being held by the Defendant in trust for her. The delay in this case does not, in my opinion, amount to evidence that the Plaintiff recognised the gift as her own spontaneous act, and in my opinion it cannot be relied upon as having deprived the Defendant of any evidence in her favour which could have been adduced if the Plaintiff had brought her action shortly after she left the sisterhood. In my opinion the Plaintiff is entitled to a decree for retransfer to her of the stock in question and for payment of the dividends accrued since the commencement of the action.

Lindley LJ

> [**183**] I proceed to consider the second point which arises in this case, namely, whether it is too late for the Plaintiff to invoke the assistance of the Court. More than six years had elapsed between the time when the Plaintiff left the sisterhood and the commencement of the present action. The action is not one of those to which the *Statute of Limitations* in terms applies; nor is that statute pleaded. But this action very closely resembles an action for money had and received where laches and acquiescence are relied upon as a defence: and the question is whether that defence ought to prevail. In my opinion it ought. Taking the statute as a guide … the lapse of six years becomes a very material element for consideration. It is not, however, necessary to decide whether this delay alone would be a sufficient defence to the action. The case by no means rests on mere lapse of time. There is far more than inactivity and delay on the part of the Plaintiff. There is conduct amounting to confirmation of her gift. Gifts liable to be set aside by the Court on the ground of undue influence have always been treated as voidable and not void.
>
> If authority for this proposition be wanted, such authority will be found in *Wright v Vanderplank* and *Mitchell v Homfray*. Moreover, such gifts are voidable on equitable grounds only. A gift intended when made to be absolute and irrevocable, but liable to be set aside by a Court of Justice, not on the ground [**187**] of a change of mind on the part of the donor, but on grounds of public policy based upon the fact that the donor was not sufficiently free relatively to the donee, such a gift is very different from a loan which the borrower knows he is under an obligation to repay, and is also different from a gift expressly made revocable

and never intended to be absolute and unconditional. A gift made in terms absolute and unconditional naturally leads the donee to regard it as his own; and the longer he is left under this impression the more difficult it is justly to deprive him of what he has naturally so regarded. So long as the relation between the donor and the donee which invalidates the gift lasts, so long is it necessary to hold that lapse of time affords no sufficient ground for refusing relief to the donor. But this necessity ceases when the relation itself comes to an end; and if the donor desires to have his gift declared invalid and set aside, he ought, in my opinion, to seek relief within a reasonable time after the removal of the influence under which the gift was made. If he does not the inference is strong, and if the lapse of time is long the inference becomes inevitable and conclusive, that the donor is content not to call the gift in question, or, in other words, that he elects not to avoid it, or, what is the same thing in effect, that he ratifies and confirms it. … A right to have a gift set aside for fraud or undue influence does not cease on the death of the donor but passes to his representatives … . In this particular case the Plaintiff considered when she left the sisterhood what course she should take, and she determined to do nothing, but to leave matters as they were. She insisted on having back her will, but [**188**] she never asked for her money until the end of five years or so after she left the sisterhood. In this state of things I can only come to the conclusion that she deliberately chose not to attempt to avoid her gifts but to acquiesce in them, or, if the expression be preferred, to ratify or confirm them. I regard this as a question of fact, and upon the evidence I can come to no other conclusion than that which I have mentioned. Moreover, by demanding her will and not her money, she made her resolution known to the Defendant.

It was urged that the Plaintiff did not know her rights until shortly before she asked for her money back. But, in the first place, I am not satisfied that the Plaintiff did not know that it was at least questionable whether the Defendant could retain the Plaintiff's money if she insisted on having it back. In the next place, if the Plaintiff did not know her rights, her ignorance was simply the result of her own resolution not to inquire into them. She knew all the facts; she was in communication with her present solicitor in 1880, his remark that 'it was too large a sum to leave behind without asking for it back,' was a clear intimation to her that she ought to ask for her money back, and was a distinct invitation to her to consider her rights. She declined to do so; she preferred not to trouble about it. Under these circumstances it would, in my opinion, be wrong and contrary to sound principle to give her relief on the ground that she did not know what her rights were. Ignorance which is the result of deliberate choice is no ground for equitable relief; nor is it an answer to an equitable defence based on laches and acquiescence. Again, it was urged that the Defendant has not been prejudiced by the delay, and that nothing has been done on the faith that the Plaintiff would not require her money to be returned to her. But I do not think this material. I treat the money as absolutely given to the sisterhood when the Plaintiff determined not to ask for it back, which she did in 1880. But, further, I cannot come to the conclusion that nothing has been done on the faith of the money being the property of the sisterhood. It is contrary to human nature to suppose that the Plaintiff's money was not for years regarded as the money of the sisterhood, and that the sisterhood did not act on that assumption and make their arrangements [**189**] accordingly. … In my judgment, it would not be fair or right to the Defendant to compel her now to restore the money sought to be recovered by this appeal. Nor, in my opinion, would such a result be in conformity with sound, legal, or equitable principles. Upon this ground, therefore, I am of opinion that this appeal ought to be dismissed.

D Intervening third party rights

If the defendant transfers property to an innocent third party before the contract is rescinded, title passes. *Restitutio in integrum* between the original parties is impossible.

The more difficult question is whether the defendant can be ordered to pay for the value of the property even if the defendant has retained neither the property nor the proceeds of sale. This is sometimes known as 'pecuniary rescission'.[24] An example of this is found in *Hartigan v International Society for Krishna Consciousness Inc*.[25]

Hartigan v International Society for Krishna Consciousness Inc [2002] NSWSC 810

Facts and issues

Hartigan (the plaintiff) gifted her family farm and some cattle to the International Society for Krishna Consciousness ('the Society', colloquially known as the 'Hare Krishnas') and joined a community at New Govardhana Farm. The Society sold the plaintiff's property and used the proceeds to pay off debts. The plaintiff later left the Society, and sought to rescind her gift.

Decision

Bryson J of the New South Wales Supreme Court found that there was a presumed relationship of undue influence arising from the relationship of spiritual advisor and acolyte, and that the defendant had failed to rebut the presumption. Although the property had been sold off to a third party, and the Society no longer had the proceeds of sale, it was required to pay back the value of the house (with some pecuniary adjustment for the plaintiff's delay in bringing her claim).

Bryson J

> **[94]** Making the gift was an enormity, quite outside the range of benefactions which a person could be expected to make either according to ordinary community standards of regard for one's own interest or according to the philosophy taught by the Krishna Consciousness Movement. … In my judgment it would be altogether unconscionable for the defendant to rely on the validity of the donation, and a court of equity should set it aside.
>
> …
>
> **[96]** The defendant's contention that equitable relief should be refused on the grounds of hardship was to the following effect. The community at New Govardhana Farm, like each community in the Movement, is expected within the Movement to be self-supporting, and the burden of any remedy awarded to the plaintiff would be treated as the responsibility of the New Govardhana community; the New Govardhana community is not composed on the same individuals now as those who participated in the community in 1988 and

24 See P Birks, 'Unjust Factors and Wrongs: Pecuniary Rescission for Undue Influence' (1997) 5 *Restitution Law Review* 72.

25 [2002] NSWSC 810.

there have been many changes, so that the burden would fall largely on people who did not participate in the advantage of reduction in debt burden which flowed from the gift in 1989. It was contended that the transaction cannot be undone without casting the burden on persons who have ordered their lives on the basis that the farm is free of this burden.

[97] I accept that some element of hardship may well flow to some persons, but I do not regard this as a sufficiently substantial hardship to countervail the claim of justice made by the plaintiff. If the burden falls in the way stated on present members of the community, it will be widely spread. The proceedings have been pending for eight years and the contingency should have been anticipated over that period. The defendant's internal arrangements for allocating burdens to communities should have had the effect that, since 1989 all participants in the New Govardhana community have benefited, to some extent, from the reduction in the debt burden which was made in 1989. In any event, the obligation is an obligation of the defendant, and it is a concern for the defendant how to arrange to meet its obligations, and whether it calls on community members to bear them, on which community members it makes such a call, and generally how it orders its affairs. The defendant has the advantage of owning New Govardhana Farm as equitable owner; and perhaps it has other properties. It has also had the considerable advantage over many years since 1989 that what would otherwise have been its debt burden has been significantly reduced. In my view the remedy should not be refused on the ground of hardship.

[98] It was also contended that proper use has been made of proceeds of sale and that in *Allcard v Skinner* and *Quek v Beggs* relief was withheld in respect of assets which had been applied to proper purposes and were no longer available. In *Allcard v Skinner* the plaintiff accepted the limitation on recovery imposed at first instance and the appeal related only to a small number of items which continued to exist and could be identified. In *Allcard v Skinner* the assets had been consumed over some years on the maintenance of the religious community of which the plaintiff was part and on carrying on its work in which she participated. In *Quek v Beggs* there were similar limitations to recovery in respect of assets which had been applied for proper purposes. The remedies available are not limited to remedies against specific assets; while specific assets will be restored if they still exist and can be identified, personal remedies are available against a donee which itself directly received the property from the donor. … In my view nothing has happened which makes it unjust that the defendant should be required to pay to the plaintiff the amount which it received on sale of the Rosebery Creek Farm. The amount received went immediately to reduce the defendant's debt burden, creating an economic advantage in reduced debt which must be reflected in its overall position now. I see no injustice in restoring the defendant to the relative position of indebtedness which it would have been in if it had not received the proceeds of the sale. In saying this I bring into consideration my view on the award of interest, which I deal with elsewhere.

[99] In relation to hardship, and also in relation of the modification of any remedy awarded the plaintiff by reducing the amount to be awarded, the defendant led a body of evidence in which it endeavoured to quantify disadvantages falling on the defendant from receiving and maintaining cattle which were on the Rosebery Creek Farm at the time of the donation. … Taking over the cattle was part of the whole parcel of receiving the plaintiff, her husband, her children and her farm into the New Govardhana community. As it happened the cows and calves died within about a year, while the Hartigans still lived at New

Govardhana Farm and while Mr Hartigan was still there, not always, it would seem, working in a very effectual manner. Six bullocks however remained on the farm, and are still there at advanced ages. They could not be trained for work although Lagudi gave many hours of attention to trying to train them; his explanation was to the effect that they are Murray Greys and that that breed cannot be trained to draw the plough.

[100] Krishna Consciousness philosophy involves respect for life, reflected in the Regulatory Principle against eating meat, fish and eggs; cattle receive particular care and respect. Religious principle commits the New Govardhana Farm, principally Lagudi, to care for the cattle until they die, and their care involves works of husbandry to maintain fencing, to provide pasture, at times to buy feed, and to provide veterinary medicines, fees for registration and other charges.

[101] The six Murray Grey bulls live on as part of an ever diminishing herd under Lagudi's husbandry and supervision. They require supervision and segregation to impede breeding. The defendant produced calculations of the cost of this exercise, including elements which were shown by cross-examination to have no real force and indeed to be mildly fantastic. In the context of the gift of a farm on which, at the time of the gift, the cattle were pastured, the burden of looking after cattle some of which died while Mr and Mrs Hartigan were still at New Govardhana Farm, while others live on unproductively as part of a much larger herd of largely unproductive bulls under the care of Lagudi, a monk pursuing a life of extreme simplicity, does not appear to me to have any real claim for consideration. The burden can only be a small one and represents the discharge of what are seen as religious obligations to attend to the welfare of the cattle; it is the perception that there are such obligations that gives rise to the need to look after them, and I do not regard it as realistic to treat that need as a burden which should lead to the defendant's obtaining any relief against what otherwise would be its obligations. There have been some burdens of expenditure from time to time for feed and other supplies, but this can be no more than a slight matter when taken with the defendant's having the advantage of being relieved of $83 000 of its obligations to the Westpac Bank under its series of commercial bills. At this point too, I have regard to the view which I take of recovery of interest.

[102] … It was also said that delay by the plaintiff in bringing her claim, and in the conduct of her claim after it commenced in 1994, constitute grounds for refusing relief in terms of confirmation, acquiescence or laches.

[103] There were remarkably long delays. So far as it appears by evidence, the first act by which the plaintiff decided to recall the gift and communicated her decision to the defendant was the issue and service of the statement of claim, which was issued on 9 August 1994 and was served soon afterwards. The plaintiff explained her difficulties by the absence of resources with which to obtain legal representation and meet continuing needs to provide resources to maintain the litigation and by difficulties arising from her living at a distance. Her lack of resources and difficulty in funding the litigation is directly connected with the impoverishing nature of the gift. Defendant's counsel contended that delay had led in various ways to prejudice to the defendant in the conduct of the proceedings. I do not think that any such prejudice has much weight in support of a decision to withhold equitable relief … . The defendant was not in my opinion prejudiced by the lapse of time in dealing with the truly important issues in the litigation.

[104] The delay which has occurred does however have an impact on the remedy which in my view should be awarded to the plaintiff. There is no difficulty in perceiving that the appropriate remedy is to require the defendant to pay to the plaintiff the amount of $83 000 which the defendant received as the price on the sale of Rosebery Creek Farm. On the other hand notwithstanding the economic difficulties which have beset the plaintiff it does not appear to me to be just that she should recover interest in respect of the lengthy period before she brought the proceedings, or in respect of the further lengthy period, from 1994 to 2001, before she brought her claim on for hearing. The interlocutory steps were lengthy and elaborate, and were not conducted expeditiously. In my view then the appropriate dealing with interest is that the plaintiff should recover interest from the commencement of the hearing on 20 November 2001.

E Executed contracts and innocent misrepresentation

As noted in the principles text at [18.78]–[18.80], contracts for the sale of land which have been executed cannot be rescinded for innocent misrepresentation.[26] This rule has been extended to other kinds of contracts of sale, including contracts for goods and shares, but this has been criticised.

The conveyance bar has been statutorily abolished in the Australian Capital Territory,[27] South Australia,[28] England[29] and, in relation to the sale of goods, in New South Wales[30] and Victoria.[31]

REVIEW QUESTIONS

(1) What other remedy does pecuniary rescission start to resemble?

(2) Do you think the result in *Hartigan v International Society for Krishna Consciousness Inc* [2002] NSWSC 810 is fair? Why/why not?

26 *Wilde v Gibson* (1848) 1 HL Cas 605, 9 ER 897; *Svanosio v McNamara* (1956) 96 CLR 186.

27 *Civil Law (Wrongs) Act 2002* (ACT) s 173.

28 *Misrepresentation Act 1971* (SA) s 6.

29 *Misrepresentation Act 1967* (UK) s 1(b).

30 *Sale of Goods Act 1923* (NSW) s 4(2A)(b).

31 *Australian Consumer Law and Fair Trading Act 2012* (Vic) s 24(1).

PART 7

PROPRIETARY REMEDIES

19 PROPRIETARY REMEDIES

I	Introduction	642
II	Proprietary remedies	642
	A Constructive and resulting trusts	643
	B Proprietary powers	648
	C Equitable liens	649
III	Criteria for award of proprietary remedies	650
	A Proprietary remedies and unconscionability	651
	B Proprietary remedies and perfection	651
	C Proprietary remedies and unjust enrichment	652
	D Proprietary remedies and wrongdoing	657
IV	Discretionary factors and bars to relief	663
V	The need for more defined criteria	664

I Introduction

This chapter does not purport to provide an exhaustive account of proprietary remedies. It proves a brief remedial overview of how proprietary remedies work. Because proprietary remedies are enforceable against property rather than a specific person, they are advantageous to plaintiffs in the ways listed below.

II Proprietary remedies

Concept	Short explanation	Relevant authorities	Principles text
Constructive and resulting trusts	Constructive and resulting trusts are the most intrusive of the proprietary remedies, and highly advantageous to the plaintiff for that reason.	*Muschinski v Dodds* (1985) 160 CLR 583	Chapter 19: [19.9]–[19.20]
Proprietary powers	Proprietary powers reflect the complexities of the remedies which arise when the plaintiff makes an election to rescind. Before election the plaintiff has a mere equity; afterwards, the plaintiff may have a constructive trust, but may also have lesser interests.	*Daly v Sydney Stock Exchange Ltd* (1986) 160 CLR 371 (see Chapter 18, page 624 for extract)	Chapter 19: [19.21]–[19.23]
Equitable liens	Equitable liens are the least intrusive of the proprietary remedies because the defendant does not have to give up the property; they may pay the debt secured by the lien using other means.	*Hewett v Court* (1983) 149 CLR 639	Chapter 19: [19.24]–[19.31]

Figure 19.1 Advantages of proprietary remedies for plaintiffs

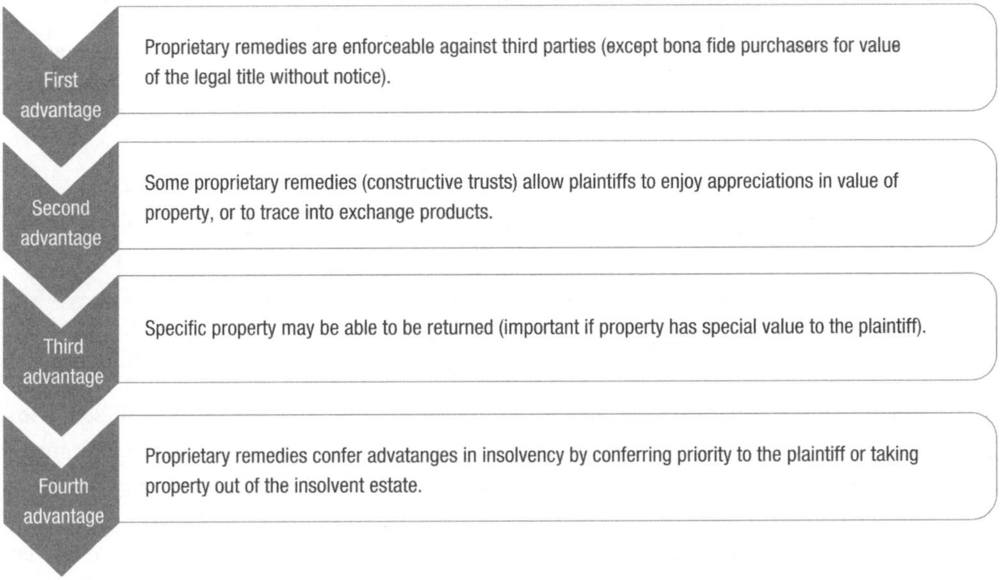

Proprietary remedies are divided in this chapter between constructive or resulting trusts, proprietary powers, and liens, as suggested by Elise Bant.[1]

Constructive trusts are the most intrusive remedy for a defendant, whereas liens are the least. With regard to liens, if the defendant can pay the sum ordered, the court will not seize the property subject to the lien.

Figure 19.2 Proprietary remedies from most intrusive to defendants (CT) to least intrusive to defendants (lien)

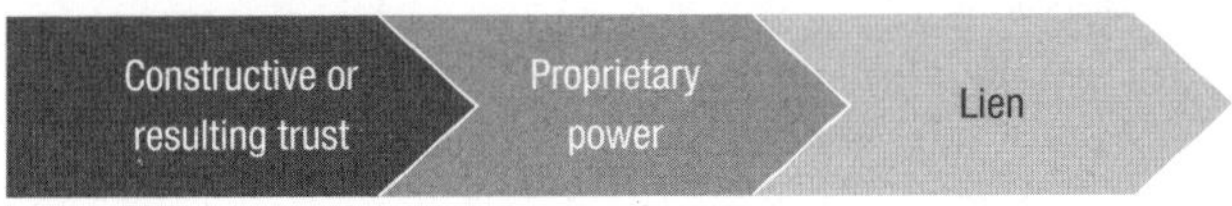

A Constructive and resulting trusts

It is not possible in this chapter to fully canvass all aspects of constructive and resulting trusts, as this would require an entire book. What follows is necessarily a brief sketch of the legal landscape.

1 E Bant, 'Trusts, Powers and Liens: An Exercise in Ground-clearing' (2009) 3 *Journal of Equity* 286.

Constructive trusts and resulting trusts are conventionally regarded as arising 'by operation of law': that is, because a court imposes them on the parties.

Trust rights have been described as 'the most durable and intrusive' equitable proprietary interests.[2] Constructive trusts and resulting trusts are an advantageous remedy for a plaintiff for the following reasons:

- They are enforceable against any third parties (except a bona fide purchaser for value without notice of the legal title).
- They are caveatable under the Torrens land system.[3]
- They encompass any proportionate increase in the value of the property to which they attach.[4]
- They may allow a plaintiff to trace into the hands of third parties.[5]
- If a defendant is bankrupt or insolvent, property subject to a pre-existing trust is unavailable for distribution to creditors, because it belongs in equity to the plaintiff.[6]

There remains doubt regarding the time when a constructive or resulting trust arises. Some constructive trusts arise from the moment that the cause of action arises, as with the common intention constructive trust.[7] Similarly, resulting trusts generally arise at the time when the contribution to the purchase price is made.[8] However, in *Muschinski v Dodds*, Deane J said that 'in a broad sense, the constructive trust is both an institution and a remedy of the law of equity'.[9]

Muschinski v Dodds (1985) 160 CLR 583

Facts and issues

A de facto couple purchased property as tenants in common in equal shares with a plan to develop and use the land for an art and craft business, and to build their home. The council refused permission for the proposed developments. The couple later separated. Ms Muschinski (who had contributed 10/11ths of the purchase price) sought a declaration that Mr Dodds held the property on trust for her absolutely.

2 Ibid 294.

3 *D'Albedyhll v D'Albedyhll* (1885) 3 *NZLR* 391; *George v Biztole Corp Pty Ltd* (VSC, 26 February 1996); *Natuna Pty Ltd v Cook* [2007] NSWSC 121, [201]–[202]; *Deabel v V'Landys* [2002] NSWSC 438, [5].

4 Eg *Foskett v McKeown* [2001] 1 AC 102.

5 Eg Attorney-General for Hong Kong v Reid [1994] 1 AC 324; *Twinsectra Ltd v Yardley* [2002] 2 AC 164; *FHR European Ventures LLP v Mankarious* [2013] 3 WLR 466.

6 *Bankruptcy Act 1966* (Cth) s 116(2)(a).

7 *Parsons v McBain* [2001] FCA 376, (2001) 109 FCR 120, [9]–[13]; *Secretary, Department of Social Security v Agnew* [2000] FCA 59, (2000) 96 FCR 357, [18]–[20].

8 *Calverley v Green* (1984) 155 CLR 242.

9 (1985) 160 CLR 583, 614.

Decision

Ms Muschinski could not establish a resulting trust or a common intention constructive trust. Nonetheless, a majority of the court (Gibbs CJ, Mason and Deane JJ) ordered that the property should be subject to a constructive trust in the proportions 10/11ths for Ms Muschinski and 1/11th for Mr Dodds. Mason J and Deane J decided on the basis that it would be unconscionable for Mr Dodds to only retain the benefit of half the title. The constructive trust was imposed from the date of judgment to lessen the impact on third parties. Gibbs CJ initially decided on the basis that the parties were jointly and severally liable to pay for the purchase price and that Ms Muschinski should be entitled to a lien, but in light of the orders of Deane J, agreed to a constructive trust on those terms. Brennan and Dawson JJ dissented.

Gibbs CJ

> [**598**] In these circumstances it appears that the appellant is entitled to contribution from the respondent to the extent to which she paid more than one-half of the purchase moneys. Further, she would appear to be entitled to an equitable charge upon the respondent's half interest for such an amount … . In determining the amount of the equitable charge, the agreed figures as to the amounts respectively contributed by the parties might well serve as a basis.
>
> …
>
> Since writing the above, I have seen the judgments of the other members of the Court. In the circumstances I agree that the order to be made should be that proposed by my brother Deane.

Deane J

> [**612**] 'The nature and function of the constructive trust have been the subject of considerable discussion throughout the common law world for several decades … [**613**]. At times, disputing factions have tended to polarize the discussion by reference to competing rallying points of 'remedy' and 'institution'. The perceived dichotomy between those two catchwords has, however, largely been the consequence of lack of definition. In a broad sense, the constructive trust is both an institution and a remedy of the law of equity. As a remedy, it can only properly be understood in the context of the history and the persisting distinctness of the principles of equity that enlighten and control the common law. The use or trust of equity, like equity itself, was essentially remedial in its origins. In its basic form it was imposed, as a personal obligation attaching to property, to enforce the equitable principle that a legal owner should not be permitted to use his common law rights as owner to abuse or subvert the intention which underlay his acquisition and possession of those rights. This was consistent with the traditional concern of equity with substance rather than form. In time, the relationships in which the trust was recognized and enforced to protect actual or presumed intention became standardized and were accepted into conveyancing practice (particularly in relation to settlements) and property law as the equitable institutions of the express and implied (including resulting) trust. Like express and implied trusts, the constructive trust developed as a remedial relationship superimposed upon common law rights by order of the Chancery Court. It differs from those other forms of trust, however, in that it arises regardless of intention. For that reason, it was not as well suited to development as a conveyancing device or as an instrument of property law. Indeed, whereas the rationale of the institutions of express and implied trust is now usually identified by reference to

intention, the rationale of the constructive trust must still be found essentially in its remedial function which it has predominantly retained … . The constructive trust shares, however, [**614**] some of the institutionalized features of express and implied trust. It demands the staple ingredients of those trusts: subject matter, trustee, beneficiary (or, conceivably, purpose), and personal obligation attaching to the property … . When established or imposed, it is a relationship governed by a coherent body of traditional and statute law. Viewed in its modern context, the constructive trust can properly be described as a remedial institution which equity imposes regardless of actual or presumed agreement or intention (and subsequently protects) to preclude the retention or assertion of beneficial ownership of property to the extent that such retention or assertion would be contrary to equitable principle.

There is, however, a more limited sense in which there is some superficial plausibility in the notions of 'institution' and 'remedy' as competing characterizations of the constructive trust. If 'institution' is understood as connoting a relationship which arises and exists under the law independently of any order of a court and 'remedy' is defined as referring to the actual establishment of a relationship by such an order, the catchwords of 'institution' and 'remedy' do serve the function of highlighting a conceptual problem that persists about the true nature of a constructive trust. Even in this more limited sense however, any perceived dichotomy between the two notions tends to prove ephemeral upon closer examination. Equity acts consistently and in accordance with principle. The old maxim that equity regards as done that which ought to be done is as applicable to enforce equitable obligations as it is to create them and, notwithstanding that the constructive trust is remedial in both origin and nature, there does not need to have been a curial declaration or order before equity will recognize the prior existence of a constructive trust … . Where an equity court would retrospectively impose a constructive trust by way of equitable remedy, its availability as such a remedy provides the basis for, and governs the content of, its existence inter partes independently of any formal order declaring or enforcing it. In this more limited sense, the constructive trust is also properly seen as both 'remedy' and 'institution'. Indeed, for the student of equity, there can be no true dichotomy between the two notions.

The acknowledgment of the institutional character of the constructive trust does not involve a denial of its continued flexibility as a remedy … . The institutional character of the trust has never completely obliterated its remedial origins even in [**615**] the case of the more traditional forms of express and implied trust. This is a fortiori in the case of constructive trust where, as has been mentioned, the remedial character remains predominant in that the trust itself either represents, or reflects the availability of, equitable relief in the particular circumstances. Indeed, in this country at least, the constructive trust has not outgrown its formative stages as an equitable remedy and should still be seen as constituting an in personam remedy attaching to property which may be moulded and adjusted to give effect to the application and interplay of equitable principles in the circumstances of the particular case. In particular, where competing common law or equitable claims are or may be involved, a declaration of constructive trust by way of remedy can properly be so framed that the consequences of its imposition are operative only from the date of judgment or formal court order or from some other specified date. The fact that the constructive trust remains predominantly remedial does not, however, mean that it represents a medium for the indulgence of idiosyncratic notions of fairness and justice. As an equitable remedy, it is available only when warranted by established equitable principles or by the legitimate processes of legal reasoning, by analogy, induction and deduction, from the starting point of a proper understanding of the conceptual foundation of such principles ... . Viewed as a remedy, the function of the constructive trust is not to render superfluous, but to reflect and enforce, the principles of the law of equity.

Thus it is that there is no place in the law of this country for the notion of 'a constructive trust of a new model' which, '[b]y whatever name it is described, ... is ... imposed by law whenever justice and good conscience' (in the sense of 'fairness' or what 'was fair') 'require it'[10] ... . Under the law of this country ... **[616]** proprietary rights fall to be governed by principles of law and not by some mix of judicial discretion ..., subjective views about which party 'ought to win' ... and 'the formless void of individual moral opinion' ... . Long before Lord Seldon's anachronism identifying the Chancellor's foot as the measure of Chancery relief, undefined notions of 'justice' and what was 'fair' had given way in the law of equity to the rule of ordered principle which is of the essence of any coherent system of rational law. The mere fact that it would be unjust or unfair in a situation of discord for the owner of a legal estate to assert his ownership against another provides, of itself, no mandate for a judicial declaration that the ownership in whole or in part lies, in equity, in that other ... . Such equitable relief by way of constructive trust will only properly be available if applicable principles of the law of equity require that the person in whom the ownership of property is vested should hold it to the use or for the benefit of another. That is not to say that general notions of fairness and justice have become irrelevant to the content and application of equity. They remain relevant to the traditional equitable notion of unconscionable conduct which persists as an operative component of some fundamental rules or principles of modern equity ... .

On whether constructive trusts should be confined to cases of pre-existing fiduciary relationships:

[616] Once its predominantly remedial character is accepted, **[617]** there is no reason to deny the availability of the constructive trust in any case where some principle of the law of equity calls for the imposition upon the legal owner of property, regardless of actual or presumed agreement or intention, of the obligation to hold or apply the property for the benefit of another ... .

...

[618] Nor has it been suggested that there was a true partnership or contractual joint venture between the parties. The case has been approached and argued on the basis that they were not partners and that the overall arrangement between them, while consensual, was a non-contractual one. That does not mean, however, that particular rules applicable to regulate the rights and duties of the parties to a failed partnership or contractual joint venture might not be relevant in the search for some more general or analogous principle applicable in the circumstances of the collapse of the consensual commercial venture and personal relationship in the present case.

Both common law and equity recognize that, where money or other property is paid or applied on the basis of some consensual joint relationship or endeavour which fails without attributable blame, it will often be inappropriate simply to draw a line leaving assets and liabilities to be owned and borne according to where they may prima facie lie, as a matter of law, at the time of the failure.

10 Here, Deane J is referring to the tests suggested by Lord Denning in *Eves v Eves* (1975) 1 WLR 1338 and *Hussey v Palmer* (1972) 1 WLR 1286.

The Australian constructive trust sits on a spectrum somewhere in between the North American constructive trust (which is remedial and discretionary) and the English constructive trust (which is institutional and arises when the cause of action arises). Some constructive trusts, such as the common intention constructive trust, are more institutional in nature, but in other situations constructive trusts are more remedial in nature, and thus subject to the discretion of the court.[11] An advantage of the Australian model is its flexibility, but the institutional-remedial constructive trust has also been criticised as intrinsically incoherent.[12]

The precise criteria and situations in which constructive trusts will be awarded are unclear. They are discussed (to the extent that there is any clarity) in 'Criteria for award of proprietary remedies' on page 650.

B Proprietary powers

A proprietary power is the proprietary interest which may arise when a plaintiff elects to rescind a contract in equity. Equitable rescission may be possible, for example, in cases of misrepresentation (including innocent misrepresentation), duress, undue influence, and breach of fiduciary duty.

The equitable power to rescind is often described as a 'mere equity',[13] which blossoms into a full constructive trust once election occurs.[14] The term 'proprietary power' has not yet gained judicial acceptance,[15] but it is a clearer and more descriptive term. Before the plaintiff exercises their power to elect to rescind, they have only a proprietary interest *in potential* (a 'mere equity'), but once the election to rescind occurs, a fully vested proprietary interest (a constructive trust) comes into being.[16]

The unexercised proprietary power (or 'mere equity') has the following *disadvantages* for a plaintiff, as compared to a constructive trust:

- An unexercised proprietary power is more fragile than a vested trust right.[17] First, as with a constructive trust, it will be defeated by a bona fide purchaser for value without notice

11 See, however, YK Liew, 'Constructive Trusts and Discretion in Australia: Taking Stock' (2021) 44(3) *Melbourne University Law Review* (advance). Liew argues that the only remedial constructive trusts are those imposed for wrongdoing over bribes.

12 P O'Connor, 'Happy Partners or Strange Bedfellows: The Blending of Remedial and Institutional Features in the Evolving Constructive Trust' (1996) 20 *Melbourne University Law Review* 735.

13 *Latec Investments Limited v Hotel Terrigal Pty Ltd* (1965) 113 CLR 265, 277, 290; *Tutt v Doyle* (1997) 42 NSWLR 10, 15.

14 *Daly v Sydney Stock Exchange Ltd* (1986) 160 CLR 371, 388–90 (Brennan J).

15 The term is taken from E Bant (n 1) 286, who builds in turn on B Häcker, *Consequences of Impaired Consent Transfers* (Mohr Siebeck, 2009); B Häcker, 'Proprietary Restitution After Impaired Consent Transfers: A Generalised Power Model' (2009) 68 *Cambridge Law Journal* 324.

16 *Latec Investments Limited v Hotel Terrigal Pty Ltd* (1965) 113 CLR 265, which involved a rationalisation of the lines of authority represented by *Phillips v Phillips* (1861) 4 De G F & J 208; 45 ER 1164 (mere equity) and *Stump v Gaby* (1852) 2 De GM & G 613; 42 ER 1015 (vested equitable interest).

17 R Chambers, *An Introduction to Property Law in Australia* (Law Book Co, 3rd ed, 2013) [24.70], [28.115], [29.145]–[29.155].

of the legal title.[18] However, an unexercised equitable right to rescind is defeated even by a subsequent bona fide purchaser of the equitable estate.[19]

- In Victoria,[20] and possibly in other Australian jurisdictions,[21] an unexercised power to rescind a transfer of property may not be a 'caveatable interest' under the Torrens system.
- It is unclear whether proprietary powers survive the bankruptcy or insolvency of the person who holds the asset that is the subject of the power.[22]

Once the proprietary power has been exercised, it generally blossoms into a fully blown equitable interest in the form of a constructive trust. However, because this interest is associated with rescission, account must be taken of any good faith change of position on the part of the defendant or impact on third parties. Thus, in some circumstances, a court may award a lesser interest such as a lien, or award a constructive trust on terms.

C Equitable liens

Liens exist at both common law and equity. While the common law lien requires the debtor to possess the property which is subject to the lien, the equitable lien does not require possession, and will be imposed by a court on property in the hands of the defendant. The equitable lien is the primary remedy considered here. As Chambers notes, the equitable lien preserves the defendant's freedom of choice as to how they will repay the plaintiff.[23] The defendant may be able to discharge the debt secured by the lien with other funds and retain the asset.

Equitable liens have the following advantages and disadvantages for a plaintiff:

- They give rise to an order for judicial sale of the property the subject of the lien, and act as security. However, they do not encompass any subsequent increase in value of the property.
- They are enforceable against whoever holds legal title to the property to which the lien attaches, unless that person is a bona fide purchaser for value of the legal title without notice of the lien.

---

18 Ibid. Legal rescission is thus more fragile than other legal proprietary rights.

19 *Latec Investments v Hotel Terrigal* (1965) 113 CLR 265. See also *Ruthol Pty Ltd v Mills* [2003] NSWCA 56; (2003) 11 BPR 20,793.

20 *Classic Heights Pty Ltd v Black Hole Enterprises Pty Ltd* [1995] ANZ ConvR 260; *Crampton v French* [1996] ANZ ConvR 156; *Swanston Mortgage Pty Ltd v Trepan Investments Pty Ltd* [1994] 1 VR 672.

21 See *Re Pile's Caveat* [1981] Qd R 81; *Wickham Developments Ltd v Parker* (QCA, 20 June 1995); *Tanzone Pty Ltd v Westpac Banking Corporation* [1999] NSWSC 478; (2000) 9 BPR 17,287; *Global Minerals Australia Pty Ltd v Valerica Pty Ltd* [2000] NSWSC 1143; (2000) 10 BPR 18,463; *Lilex Pty Ltd (Receiver and Manager Appointed) v Smallseeds Pty Ltd* [2011] NSWSC 1426. Cf *Breskvar v Wall* (1971) 126 CLR 376, 409; *Sinclair v Hope Investments Pty Ltd* [1982] 2 NSWLR 870, 875; *Re McKeane's Caveat* [1988] 1 Qd R 524, 525; *Re Cross v National Australia Bank Ltd* [1993] ANZ Conv R 28; *Patmore v Upton* [2004] TASSC 77; (2004) 13 Tas R 95, [61].

22 *Westpac Banking Corp v Markovic* (1985) 82 FLR 7, cf *Re York Street Mezzanine Pty Ltd (in liq)* [2007] FCA 922; (2007) 162 FCR 358. See P Watts, 'Constructive Trusts and Insolvency' (2010) 3 *Journal of Equity* 250, 265–70; E Bant (n 1) 301–3.

23 R Chambers, 'Resulting Trusts in Canada (Part II)' (2002) 16 *Trusts Law International* 138, 143–4.

- They are caveatable interests under the Torrens system.[24]
- They confer true priority on insolvency. In equity, once the debt is satisfied out of the sale of the asset, the remainder of the proceeds of sale go back into the pool of funds available for distribution to creditors.

REVIEW QUESTIONS

(1) What is the difference between a constructive trust and a proprietary power?

(2) What is the difference between a constructive trust and a lien?

(3) Do you think more clarity is required on caveatability of proprietary remedies?

III Criteria for award of proprietary remedies

Unfortunately, the criteria for the award of proprietary remedies are radically unclear. As outlined in Figure 19.3, the first two steps are simply that the defendant must hold property and that the basal cause of action must be made out. Other than that, proprietary remedies can be categorised into those which seek to achieve three basic aims:

(1) perfection (ie where a plaintiff had a reasonable expectation of receiving property and the defendant reneges)

(2) reversal of unjust enrichment and

(3) prevention of wrongdoing.

Figure 19.3 Criteria for award of proprietary remedies

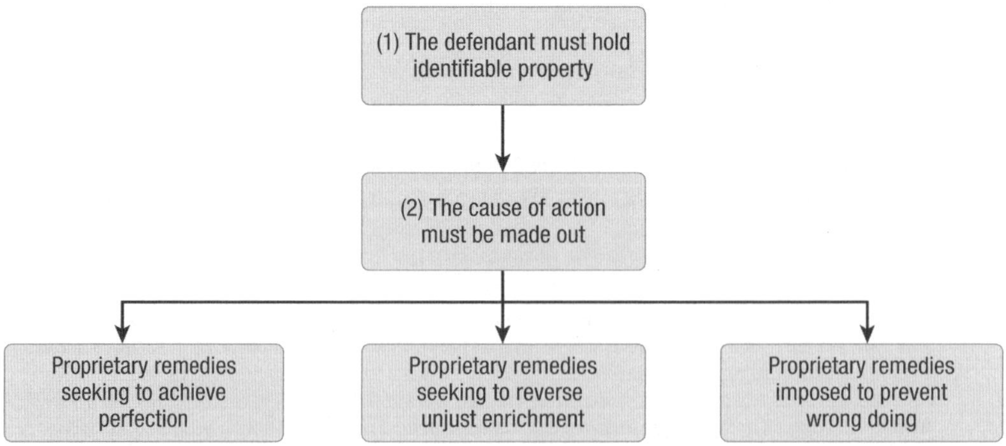

24 *Composite Buyers Ltd v Soong* (1995) 38 NSWLR 286; *Big River Timbers Pty Ltd v Stewart* [1999] NSWCA 34; (1999) 9 BPR 16,605.

Concept	Short explanation	Relevant authorities	Principles text
Proprietary remedies and unconscionability	Unconscionability is not a reason for imposing proprietary remedies except in the broadest sense.		Chapter 19: [19.38]–[19.39]
Proprietary remedies and perfection	Sometimes the reason for imposing a proprietary remedy is the perfection of an imperfect transaction.		Chapter 19: [19.43]
Proprietary remedies and unjust enrichment	Sometimes the reason for imposing a proprietary remedy is the reversal of unjust enrichment.	*Wambo Coal Pty Ltd v Ariff* (2007) 63 ACSR 426	Chapter 19: [19.44]–[19.54]
Proprietary remedies and wrongdoing	Sometimes the reason for imposing a proprietary remedy is the prevention of wrongdoing.	*Grimaldi v Chameleon Mining NL (No 2)* (2012) 200 FCR 296	Chapter 19: [19.56]–[19.64]

A Proprietary remedies and unconscionability

As noted in the principles text, unconscionability is sometimes said to be the rationale for the imposition of proprietary remedies in Australia. However, this is only true in the broadest sense, partly because of the many different meanings of 'unconscionability'. One specific sense of 'unconscionability' is where the plaintiff had an expectation of receiving property and the defendant unfairly defeated this expectation. Only the *Baumgartner*[25] constructive trust operates to prevent this kind of unconscionability.[26]

B Proprietary remedies and perfection

Many proprietary remedies arise to effect 'perfection',[27] where the defendant has chosen to dispose of their property in favour of the plaintiff, the plaintiff had a reasonable expectation, and the defendant reneges or fails to complete the transaction (but there is not necessarily unfairness or moral turpitude in the sense mentioned above).

Proprietary interests arising on this basis include circumstances:

- where a fiduciary obtains property, or an opportunity which ought to have been the beneficiary's, in breach of fiduciary duty[28]
- where a fiduciary misappropriates property from a beneficiary in breach of fiduciary duty[29]

25 *Baumgartner v Baumgartner* (1987) 164 CLR 137.

26 M Bryan and V Vann, *Equity & Trusts in Australia* (Cambridge University Press, 2012) [23.6]. See *Baumgartner v Baumgartner* (1987) 164 CLR 137.

27 G Elias, *Explaining Constructive Trusts* (Clarendon Press, 1990) 4, 10–16.

28 *Keech v Sandford* (1726) Sel Cas T King 61; 25 ER 223; *Chan v Zacharia* (1984) 154 CLR 178; *Boardman v Phipps* [1967] 2 AC 46.

29 *Black v S Freedman & Co* (1910) 12 CLR 105.

- where there was a common intention for the parties to hold the property in a way not reflected in the legal title[30]
- where, in a domestic situation, it would be unconscionable to allow one party to the relationship to claim the benefit of the legal title[31]
- where there is a specifically enforceable contract for the sale of land[32] or unique goods[33]
- involving incomplete gifts[34]
- involving mutual wills[35] and 'secret' trusts[36] and
- involving equitable estoppel, but only where such a remedy would be appropriate.[37]

C Proprietary remedies and unjust enrichment

Other proprietary remedies arise to prevent unjust enrichment (particularly in the context of rescission, but also in other circumstances). They involve the reversal of an impugned transaction.

Circumstances in which scholars have explained the imposition of a proprietary remedy according to an unjust enrichment analysis include:

- where property has been acquired by reason of a mistake[38]
- where a transaction can be set aside because of undue influence or duress[39]
- where a transaction can be set aside because of the unconscionable nature of the bargain[40]
- where there is a failure of consideration (meaning a failure of the purpose of the bargain which has led to the defendant's enrichment)[41] and
- more generally, where there is an 'absence of an intention to benefit' on the part of the plaintiff towards the defendant.

---

30 *Ogilvie v Ryan* [1976] 2 NSWLR 504; *Allan v Snyder* [1977] 2 NSWLR 685; *Kardynal v Dodek* (1977) 5 Fam LR 706; *Hohol v Hohol* [1981] VR 221; *Green v Green* (1989) 17 NSWLR 343; *Parsons v McBain* (2001) 109 FCR 120.

31 *Baumgartner v Baumgartner* (1987) 164 CLR 137.

32 *Lysaght v Edwards* (1876) 2 Ch D 499; *Chang v Registrar of Titles* (1976) 137 CLR 177, 185 (Mason J).

33 *Holroyd v Marshall* (1862) 10 HL Cas 191, 209; 11 ER 999, 1006 (Lord Westbury LC).

34 *Re Rose* [1952] Ch 499; *Corin v Patton* (1990) 169 CLR 540.

35 Eg *Birmingham v Renfrew* (1937) 57 CLR 666, 689–91; *Re Goodchild* [1997] 1 WLR 1216; *University of Manitoba v Sanderson Estate* (1998) 155 DLR (4th) 40; *Olins v Walters* [2009] Ch 212.

36 Eg *Re Boyes* (1884) 26 Ch D 531.

37 *Thorner v Major* [2009] 1 WLR 776. A personal remedy was granted in *Giumelli v Giumelli* (1999) 196 CLR 101.

38 *Chase Manhattan NA v Israel-British Bank (London)* [1981] Ch 105. Cf *Westdeutsche Landesbank Girozentrale v Islington London Borough Council* [1996] AC 669, 715 (Lord Browne-Wilkinson).

39 *Reid v Reid* (New South Wales Supreme Court, Bryson J, 30 November 1998); *Quek v Beggs* (1990) 5 BPR 11,761; *Badman v Drake* [2008] NSWSC 1366. See Bant (n 1) 306–7.

40 *Louth v Diprose* (1992) 175 CLR 621.

41 See, eg, *Muschinski v Dodds* (1985) 160 CLR 583.

The ultimate choice between constructive trust, proprietary power, lien and no remedy is highly fact-specific.

The following case involves a a constructive trust that was imposed in relation to a mistaken payment.

Wambo Coal Pty Ltd v Ariff (2007) 63 ACSR 426

Facts and issues

The plaintiff, Wambo Coal Pty Ltd ('Wambo'), made two mistaken payments to the first defendant, Singleton Earthmoving Pty Ltd ('Singleton'). It had meant to make the payments to a related company. Prior to the mistaken payments, Ariff had been appointed as administrator (and later liquidator) of Singleton. Ariff caused most of the money paid by Wambo to Singleton to be transferred to a company he controlled, to reimburse it for disbursements it had paid (on his behalf) in the liquidation of Singleton. Ariff was notified of the mistake after he had already transferred some of Wambo's money to his company, but continued to transfer money to his company after this.

Decision

The constructive trust was only imposed over that part of the money for which Ariff (and by him, Singleton) knew that it had been mistakenly paid.

White J

> [**435**] Counsel for Wambo submitted that on the basis of the reasoning in *Chase Manhattan Bank NA v Israeli-British bank (London) Ltd* as applied in *Young v Lalic* …, Wambo retained the equitable property in the money it paid by mistake and the recipient of the mistaken payment was subject to a fiduciary obligation to respect that proprietary right. Counsel submitted that Wambo was entitled to recover the amount of the mistaken payment by way of tracing.
>
> In *Chase Manhattan Bank NA v Israel-British Bank (London) Ltd*, the Chase Manhattan Bank paid the same amount of just over US$2 000 000 twice to the defendant's bank account. The second payment was made by mistake due to a clerical error. The defendant was later wound up. As the authorities then stood, Goulding J held that the right of the payer to trace the mistaken second payment depended upon whether the payment into the wrong hands gave rise to a fiduciary relationship … . His Lordship concluded that a person who pays money to another under a factual mistake retains an equitable property in it and the conscience of the other is subjected to a fiduciary duty to respect his proprietary right … . His Lordship held that the payer of money paid under a mistake retains the equitable property in the money paid and is entitled to trace those funds until they are received by a bona fide purchase for value without notice.
>
> In *Westdeutsche Landesbank Girozentrale v Islington London Borough Council* …, Lord Browne-Wilkinson disagreed with this reasoning. His Lordship said … :

> First, it is based on a concept of retaining an equitable property in money where, prior to the payment to the recipient bank, there was no existing equitable interest. Further, I cannot understand how the recipient's 'conscience' can be affected at a time when he [**436**] is not aware of any mistake. Finally, the judge found that the law of England and that of New York were in substance the same. I find this a surprising conclusion since the New York law of constructive trusts has for a long time been influenced by the concept of a remedial constructive trust, whereas hitherto English law has for the most part only recognised an institutional constructive trust …

In *Cashflow Finance Pty Ltd (in liq) v Westpac Banking Corporation* …, Einstein J held that the decision in *Chase Manhattan* had, in effect, been overruled by the House of Lords in *Westdeutsche*. His Honour said that Lord Browne-Wilkinson had authoritatively rejected the proposition that, without more, receipt of money paid under a mistake renders the recipient a trustee and leaves the payee holding an equitable proprietary right in the money. This is also the view of the leading Australian texts … .

In *Westdeutsche* …, both Lord Browne-Wilkinson … and Lord Goff … summarised the law of resulting trusts as applying to the voluntary payment of money as well as to the voluntary transfer of property … . However, Lord Browne-Wilkinson did not suggest that the result in *Chase Manhattan* could be supported on the principle that, in the absence of evidence to the contrary, equity presumes that if A pays money to B without consideration, and in circumstances where there is no presumption of advancement, A does not intend to transfer the beneficial interest in the money to B. Assuming, without deciding, that, at least by analogy to cases where money is paid into a joint account …, the principles of resulting trusts can apply to the payment of money, as well as to payments for the purchase of property, or to transfers of property, those principles do not avail Wambo in this case. First, no argument was advanced on this basis. Secondly, the law of resulting trusts is based upon presumptions as to the transferor's actual intentions. Wambo intended to part with the ownership of the money which it paid. Its mistake was either in thinking that the account into which the money was paid was an account for Quensor trading as Bernie Wood Singleton Earthmoving, or, its mistake was that it owed Singleton Earthmoving for the services for which it had received invoices of $46 130.15. In either case, it did not intend to retain any equitable property in the money paid.

Accordingly, I do not accept that Singleton Earthmoving held the moneys paid into its bank account on trust for Wambo at the time the moneys were received.

In *Westdeutsche* …, Lord Browne-Wilkinson also said (*obiter*) … that:

> Although I do not accept the reasoning of Goulding J, Chase Manhattan may well have been rightly decided. The defendant bank knew of the mistake made by the paying bank within two days of the receipt of the moneys. The judge treated this fact as irrelevant … but in my judgment it may well provide a proper foundation for the decision. Although the mere receipt of the moneys, in ignorance of the mistake, gives rise to no trust, the retention of the moneys after the recipient bank learned of the mistake may well have given rise to a constructive trust …

[**437**] The defendant submitted that this reasoning was unconvincing … and in any event, was *obiter* and did not form part of the law of England and Wales. The reason for the

last proposition is that Lord Browne-Wilkinson said … that although it might be in accordance with principle to impose a remedial constructive trust on the defendant who knowingly retained property of which the plaintiff had been unjustly deprived, it still remained to be decided whether English law should follow the United States and Canada in adopting the remedial constructive trust.

The remedial constructive trust is part of the law of Australia. No such difficulty arises in Australia where the High Court has endorsed the remedial constructive trust in *Muschinski v Dodds* … and *Baumgartner v Baumgartner* … . However, I respectfully doubt whether a trust based on the retention of moneys known to have been paid by mistake would be properly categorised as a remedial constructive trust. Where property is stolen, the property is trust property in the hands of the thief and can be traced into the hands of a third party who receives the property otherwise than as a bona fide purchaser of the legal estate for value without notice. The property is trust property in the hands of the thief because the thief is bound in conscience to hold the property on behalf of its true owner. Whether the trust is characterised as a resulting … or as a constructive trust …, the trust is of an institutional rather than a remedial character. It arises because the conscience of the thief is bound.

In the same way, where property is acquired by fraud and there is a complete failure of consideration, the trust arises immediately on the receipt of the property … . So, in *Neste Oy v Lloyds Bank plc* …, referred to with apparent approval in *Re Goldcorp Exchange Ltd* …, where the payee received payment from its principal of moneys which were not impressed with an express trust, but which were to be used in performance of a contract which the payee knew could not take place, the payee held the payment on trust for the payer from the time of its receipt. The circumstances which created the trust in *Neste Oy* were that the payee knew … that there could be no performance under its contract, so that there was a total failure of consideration for the payment, and the payment could not in conscience be retained. The trust was an institutional trust which attached to the moneys from the time of receipt.

I do not see why, in principle, a constructive trust arising from the retention of moneys known to have been paid by mistake, and for which there was no consideration, would not arise from the time the payee acquired such knowledge, if the moneys paid could still be identified at the time such knowledge was acquired. Such a trust is as much an institutional trust as a trust imposed on property in the hands of the thief.

[**438**] The payments made by Wambo to Singleton Earthmoving were not only made by mistake. They were also made for no consideration. It would be against conscience for Singleton Earthmoving to use the moneys as its own once it knew of Wambo's mistake. Notwithstanding the criticism of this passage from the speech of Lord Browne-Wilkinson in *Meagher, Gummow and Lehane's Equity: Doctrine and Remedies* …, in my view, his Lordship's admittedly obiter statement is consistent with principle. It is consistent with those cases in which a constructive trust is declared over property obtained by fraud where no consideration was provided for the payment … . The recipient's conscience is bound only upon being aware of the mistake. But once the recipient is aware that, by a mistake, he has got something for nothing, a proprietary remedy is appropriate. The fact that the company is insolvent does not affect this conclusion. It would be an unwarranted windfall for the company's creditors to share in the payment … . There is no question in this case of interfering with the statutory scheme for the order of priority of debts recoverable from the company.

> Lord Browne-Wilkinson referred to the constructive trust as arising after the recipient 'learned' of the mistake. The emphasis is on the recipient having actual knowledge of the mistake so that its conscience is bound. A deliberate failure to inquire for fear of knowing that which the payee would rather not know may be equated with knowledge. Where the question is whether money becomes trust property because of the knowledge of the payee that it was paid by mistake and without consideration, as distinct from the question whether a recipient of property already impressed with a trust is bound by the trust, the appropriate question is whether the payee has such knowledge of the mistake as to affect his conscience because he is aware that he is not entitled to deal with the money as if he were the beneficial owner … . I am inclined to think that the appropriate analogy is with the knowledge required to render a third party liable as a constructive trustee under the second limb of *Barnes v Addy*, that is, for knowingly participating in a breach of trust, although not receiving trust property. For the purposes of the second limb of *Barnes v Addy* …, a defendant will be treated as having knowledge of a dishonest and fraudulent design on the part of the trustee or fiduciary if the defendant has (a) actual knowledge, or (b) wilfully shuts his or her eyes to the obvious, or (c) wilfully and recklessly fails to make such inquiries as an honest and reasonable person would make, or (d) has knowledge of circumstances which would indicate the facts to an honest and reasonable person … .

In the instance of rescission for undue influence or unconscionable conduct, where a transaction can be set aside because of undue influence or duress, a variety of remedies have been imposed, including full constructive trusts,[42] proprietary powers,[43] liens,[44] or no remedy at all.[45] Bant and Bryan argue that a proprietary power model can explain these cases. Where the defendant has taken the plaintiff's asset, it remains in the hands of the defendant, it is unique and the plaintiff has elected to seek its return, Bant and Bryan argue that the plaintiff is entitled to 'specific restitution' (a constructive trust).[46] However, where the asset has been exchanged for another asset, the plaintiff should be entitled to the value of the asset secured by a lien.[47] Bant and Bryan argue that equitable discretionary considerations, including hardship, laches and third party considerations, should be taken into account by courts.

As for failure of the purpose of the bargain which has led to the defendant's enrichment, Australian courts have used 'unconscionability'[48] to justify the imposition of a constructive

42 *Reid v Reid* (New South Wales Supreme Court, Bryson J, 30 November 1998).

43 *Quek v Beggs* (1990) 5 BPR 11,761.

44 *Badman v Drake* [2008] NSWSC 1366.

45 *Allcard v Skinner* (1887) 36 Ch D 145.

46 E Bant and M Bryan, 'A Model of Proprietary Remedies' in E Bant and M Bryan (eds), *Principles of Proprietary Remedies* (Thomson Reuters, 2013) [12.160]–[12.180].

47 Ibid [12.190].

48 Unconscionability here means that the plaintiff had a reasonable expectation of receiving property and this has been defeated by the defendant's conduct, as in *Baumgartner v Baumgartner* (1987) 164 CLR 137.

trust. *Muschinski v Dodds*[49] could be understood as the award of a proprietary remedy to prevent unjust enrichment where there has been a failure of consideration.[50] The excerpt above from page 618 of Deane J's judgment supports such an analysis, as does *Roxborough v Rothmans of Pall Mall Australia Ltd*.[51] However, Australian courts have (consistently with *Wambo*[52]) required the recipient to know at the time of the transfer that there was a failure of consideration.[53]

Finally, an 'absence of an intention to benefit' has been said by Robert Chambers to be a reason why courts impose restitutionary proprietary remedies, in particular the resulting trust.[54] However, this has not been accepted by Australian courts.

D Proprietary remedies and wrongdoing

Some proprietary remedies are imposed because of wrongdoing on the part of the defendant, such that the court uses a proprietary remedy to effect disgorgement. This is particularly the case for equitable wrongdoing, especially breach of fiduciary duty. Constructive trusts are readily awarded over an asset obtained in breach of fiduciary duty in two circumstances:

(1) where the fiduciary has misappropriated or stolen property belonging to the beneficiary[55] and

(2) where the fiduciary was under a duty to acquire the property for the beneficiary, if they chose to acquire it at all.[56]

These trusts can be justified according to principles of perfection in cases where the plaintiff had a reasonable expectation of receiving property and this has been defeated by the defendant's conduct. They also have a deterrent, profit-stripping rationale.

The imposition of a constructive trust is more difficult to justify in a third circumstance, namely, where a dishonest fiduciary accepts a bribe. It is axiomatic that an account of profits will at least be awarded to strip the bribe, but it is controversial whether a proprietary remedy should also be used. The High Court has yet to decide the issue. Table 19.1 shows how authority on the issue has changed repeatedly, particularly in England.

---

49 (1985) 160 CLR 583.

50 N Witzleb et al, *Remedies: Commentary and Materials* (Law Book, 6th ed, 2015) [7.35]; J Edelman, 'Australian Challenges for the Law of Unjust Enrichment' (Speech, University of Western Australia Summer School, 24 February 2012) 16–17.

51 (2001) 208 CLR 516, [16] (Gleeson CJ, Gaudron and Hayne JJ), [100]–[104] (Gummow J).

52 *Wambo Coal Pty Ltd v Ariff* (2007) 63 ACSR 426.

53 *Zuecker v Bruggmann (No 3)* [2017] QSC 259, [124] (Bond J); *Re Wan Ze Property Development (Aust) Pty Ltd* (2012) 90 ACSR 593, [51]–[52] (Black J); *Break Fast Investments Pty Ltd v Giannopoulos (No 5)* [2011] NSWSC 1508, [90]–[91] (Black J); *Wambo Coal Pty Ltd v Ariff* (2007) 63 ACSR 429, [40]–[41] (White J).

54 See R Chambers, *Resulting Trusts* (Oxford University Press, 1997).

55 Eg *Black v S Freedman & Co* (1910) 12 CLR 105.

56 Eg *Keech v Sandford* (1726) Sel Cas T King 61, 25 ER 223; *Boardman v Phipps* [1967] 2 AC 46; *Chan v Zacharia* (1984) 154 CLR 178; *Timber Engineering Co Ltd v Anderson* [1980] 2 NSWLR 488.

Table 19.1 Shifting judicial authority on constructive trusts in cases of bribery

Case	Jurisdiction	Should a constructive trust (CT) be awarded?
Lister v Stubbs (1890) 45 Ch D 1	England and Wales	**No**, never. Only a personal remedy
Attorney-General for Hong Kong v Reid [1994] 1 AC 324	New Zealand (Privy Council)	**Yes**, always. The bribe belongs in equity to the beneficiary
Sinclair Investments (UK) Ltd v Versailles Trade Finance Ltd [2012] Ch 453	England and Wales	**No**, never. Only a personal remedy
Grimaldi v Chameleon Mining NL (No 2) (2012) 200 FCR 296	Australia	**Yes, but discretionary** – a lien or lesser remedy may be awarded
FHR v European Ventures LLP v Mankarious [2015] AC 250	England and Wales	**Yes**, always. The bribe belongs in equity to the beneficiary

Grimaldi v Chameleon Mining NL (No 2) (2012) 200 FCR 296

Facts and issues

In a complex set of financial transactions, Grimaldi and Barnes were directors of a company called Chameleon Mining NL. Grimaldi was also the de facto director of a company called Murchison, which was seeking to purchase some profitable iron tenements in a joint venture with another company named Winterfall. Winterfall had promised Grimaldi and Barnes at the outset of their dealings that if Grimaldi and Barnes could assist in ensuring the iron tenement development went ahead, they would receive a 'spotter's fee'.

In breach of their fiduciary duties to Chameleon, Grimaldi and Barnes caused Chameleon to enter into transactions with Murchison. There was no benefit to Chameleon in these transactions, but Murchison benefited considerably. Using those moneys, Murchison and Winterfall purchased the iron tenements. In accordance with the earlier agreement, Winterfall paid Grimaldi and Barnes the 'spotter's fee'. The question was whether this was a 'bribe' to induce Grimaldi and Barnes to breach their fiduciary obligations to Chameleon, and, accordingly, whether it was recoverable.

Decision

The 'spotter's fee' was not a bribe because it was not paid to induce Grimaldi and Barnes to breach their fiduciary obligations. The Court said in obiter that, if the money had been a bribe, it might have awarded a constructive trust, but that lesser awards may be made in some circumstances.

Finn, Stone and Perram JJ

> [**418**] In the second half of the nineteenth century an anomalous limitation was placed upon the reach of the *Keech v Sandford* constructive trust in English law. This was in relation to agents where the property obtained by an agent in breach of fiduciary duty took the form of a *money* bribe or secret commission. The bribed agent was accountable to his principal in

equity for the bribe received, not as a constructive trustee, but as a *debtor* in equity: *Lister & Co v Stubbs* … . The principal could not claim any proprietary interest in the bribe and could not trace into investments made using it. To allow otherwise, Lindley LJ commented in *Lister* … would involve a 'confounding [of] ownership with obligation'. …

[**419**] To exaggerate the *Lister* anomaly – and it has been so described in an Australian decision … a like rule was not applied to property bribes (other than money). In *Eden v Ridsdales Railway Lamp and Lighting Co Ltd* …, for example, a promoter gave 200 shares in the company to a director while questions were still outstanding under a contract between the company and the promoter. In stating a rule said to be 'applicable to all agents', Lord Esher MR commented … :

> In such a case the remedy of the principal is an option either to claim what the agent has received, or to sue for damages. If that which the agent has received is money he must hand it over to his principal, if it is not money, but something else, the principal may insist on having it, or, if he chooses, the value of it.
>
> And in the view of Lindley LJ … :
>
> It would … be contrary to all principles of law and equity to allow the plaintiff to retain the gift … [T]he company has the option of claiming what is given, or its value, ie, the highest value whilst held by the director.

Some number of the property bribe cases such as *Eden* concerned gifts by promoters of shares in the company of which the fiduciary was a director. These could thus be later explained on the narrow ground that the constructive trust of such shares did no more than give back to the company what was its own (notwithstanding that the company could not at that time be a shareholder in itself). However, the matter to be emphasised is that the rule as stated and applied in cases such as *Eden* accords with what has long since been the general understanding in this country of a fiduciary's liability to account for property and profits made in breach of fiduciary duty. *Furs Ltd v Tomkies*, which would seem to have involved a procuration fee (it mattered not to the Court how precisely the benefit derived was categorised), exemplifies this.

The findings in *Lister*, having regard to its facts, seem quite arresting to modern eyes. The facts as described by Lindley LJ were that Lister & Co through their agent bought goods from Varley at market prices and paid for them. Lister & Co became the owner of the goods purchased; the ownership of the money paid was in Varley. Varley had entered into a commission arrangement with Stubbs who ordered the goods and received payments thereunder. The first question posed by Lindley LJ was whether Stubbs could keep the money. And the answer given … : 'Obviously not … he is liable to account for it the moment that he gets it.' This liability, clearly enough, was founded on the then, and now, well accepted proposition that if 'a profit has been made by an agent, without the knowledge of his principal, in the course and execution of his agency … for that profit [he] must … account to [his] principal' … . Stubbs was a 'fiduciary agent' and was accepted to be such in *Lister*. …

[**420**] The second question Lindley LJ addressed was whether the relationship of Stubbs and Lister vis-à-vis the moneys received was that of trustee and beneficiary. For essentially consequentialist reasons relating to the effects which would ensue if the agent were either to become bankrupt or to make traceable investments using the moneys, that

question was answered in the negative, but in a curious way as has been noted. Stubbs could become a trustee prospectively as a result of a later decree of the court, but not simply by virtue of the receipt of the bribe. This, as has been said in *Jacobs'*, 'can hardly be regarded as satisfactory'.

It may be that the exclusion of bribes at this time from the usual operation of what we have called the *Keech v Sandford* principle reflected the idea that a bribe could not be said to be property which the agent could or should have derived, if at all, for his or her principal. That idea had much contemporary significance in cases where agents, partners or directors appropriated opportunities which they should have pursued, if at all, for their principal, etc. … . It was this idea which was embraced – unconvincingly in our view – by the English Court of Appeal in *Sinclair Investments (UK) Ltd v Versailles Trade Finance Ltd* … in its recent re-affirmation of *Lister*; though entitled to an equitable account in respect of any money or asset acquired in breach of fiduciary duty, a beneficiary was not entitled to claim a proprietary interest –

> … unless the asset or money is or has been beneficially the property of the beneficiary or the trustee acquired the asset or money by taking advantage of an opportunity or right which was properly that of the beneficiary … .

English law may have its own reasons for so contriving the limits to proprietary relief. We need not speculate about them. What we would emphasis, though, is that, unlike Australian law, it does not recognise that the constructive trust can be a discretionary remedy … .

We have referred already to the quite different rule affirmed in *Furs Ltd v Tomkies*. Additionally, we would note by way of contrast with the approach taken in *Sinclair Investments*, the observations of Mason J in *Hospital Products* … with which we respectfully agree:

> Any profit or benefit obtained by a fiduciary [in breach of the proscriptions on conflict of duty and interest or on misuse of position] is held by him as a constructive trustee: *Keith Henry & Co Pty Ltd v Stuart Walker & Co Pty Ltd … . Neither principle nor authority provide any support for the proposition that relief by way of constructive trust is available only in the case where a profit or benefit obtained by the fiduciary was one which it was an incident of his duty to obtain for the person to whom he owed the fiduciary duty. Once it is established that the fiduciary is liable to account for a profit or benefit which he has obtained there can be no objection to his being held to account as a constructive trustee of that profit or benefit.* It can make no difference that it was not his duty to obtain the profit or benefit for the person to whom the duty was owed. What is important is that the advantage has accrued to him in breach of his fiduciary duty or by his misuse of his fiduciary position. The consequence is that he must account for it and in equity the appropriate remedy is by means of a constructive trust. (Emphasis added.)

[421] To exclude the bribed fiduciary from the deterrent effect of the constructive trust is, in our view, to make it unavailable in the very situations where deterrence is likely to be the most needed. Bribery at its most naked breeds the crudest form of fiduciary infidelity. To privilege the dishonest fiduciary in this way is to create an incentive which should not be tolerated. This is particularly so in relation to public sector fiduciaries. In combating the corrupt public official, the full range of equity's remedies and techniques (including tracing and following illicit gains) are important instruments of deterrence. The courts in other common law countries have recognised this, as has the decision of the Privy Council in *Attorney-General for Hong Kong v Reid …*

Lister has been a cause of continuing controversy. It was followed in subsequent English Court of Appeal cases in the late nineteenth and early twentieth centuries. Its standing, as noted above, has very recently been reaffirmed in *Sinclair Investments* … . It has not been followed in Singapore primarily because of its inconsistency with the 'property' bribe cases; because it has been overtaken by the developing vigour of the constructive trust in the last quarter of the twentieth century; and because the 'money' bribe exception favours the dishonest fiduciary over the honest one … . The Privy Council in *Reid* on an appeal from New Zealand disapproved both *Lister* and *Metropolitan Bank*. It relocated bribes and secret commissions within the ordinary fiduciary regime: '[a] bribe and the property from time to time representing the bribe are held on a constructive trust for the person injured' … .

In Australia *Lister* has been the subject of long standing criticism by text writers … . It is, in our view, inconsistent with orthodox, twentieth century Australian formulations of the remedial consequences of breach of fiduciary duty exemplified by the observations we have already quoted from *Furs Ltd v Tomkies* and those of Mason J in *Hospital Products* above.

This said, it has been cited approvingly by several judges of the High Court albeit in cases where the particular vice in *Lister* which we have been addressing had not been contested. …

In *Daly* Gibbs CJ commented … that the decision in *Lister* has been criticised as unjust:

> … but the reasons of Lindley LJ appear to me to be impeccable *when applied to* [**422**] *the case in which the person claiming the money has simply made an outright loan* to the defendant. (Emphasis added.)

The Court distinguished *Daly* on the basis that it was not a breach of fiduciary case, but a loan case, and continued:

> [**422**] Whatever may be the reasons for English law's continuing adherence to *Lister*, the weight of High Court decision and expressions of judicial opinion across the twentieth century preordain our rejection of it. … We simply note that in the result Australian law matches that of New Zealand …, Singapore …, United States jurisdictions … and Canada in accepting a proprietary remedy for bribes and secret commissions. … However, Australian law departs from the law as stated in *Reid* in one important respect. *Reid* has the constructive trust arising the moment the bribe is received. In Australia, the constructive trust in this setting is a discretionary remedy.
>
> There are two additional comments we should make. First, to accept that [**423**] money bribes can be captured by a constructive trust does not mean that they necessarily will be in all circumstances. As is well accepted, a constructive trust ought not to be imposed if there are other orders capable of doing full justice: see *John Alexander's Clubs* at [**128**] and the cases there footnoted. Such could be the case, for example, where a bribed fiduciary, having profitably invested the bribe, is then bankrupted and, apart from the investment, is hopelessly insolvent. In such a case a lien on that property may well be sufficient to achieve

> 'practical justice' in the circumstances. This said, a constructive trust is likely to be awarded as of course where the bribe still exists in its original, or in a traceable, form, and no third party issue arises.
>
> Secondly, we have referred to this body of law at some length notwithstanding that we have concluded that the secret commission obtained by Grimaldi and Barnes under the Winterfall/Murchison agreements, was not a secret commission vis-à-vis Chameleon. It was simply an undisclosed personal interest in the making of the advance of the two cheques. We have taken this course both because the parties have made reference to *Sinclair Investments* and to *Reid* and lest it be said that *Lister v Stubbs* ought nonetheless be applied analogically in relation to the commission received by Grimaldi and Barnes.

The Full Federal Court noted the constant changes in English law from one extreme (always a proprietary remedy) to the other (never a proprietary remedy, only a personal remedy). After *Grimaldi* was decided, the English courts again reversed their position in *FHR European Ventures LLP v Mankarious* ('*FHR*').[57] The plaintiffs in *FHR* sought to invest in the hotel industry. They asked Mr Mankarious and his consultancy business, Cedar Capital (the defendants) to act as their agents. The defendants recommended that the plaintiffs should buy a share in the Monte Carlo Grand Hotel ('the Hotel'). Unknown to the plaintiffs, the defendants received a €10 million commission from the Hotel for finding a purchaser. The agreement between the Hotel and the defendants provided that the defendants would disclose the commission to the plaintiffs, but they did not. The property was sold for €211.5 million, and the defendants received €10 million commission. The plaintiffs were entitled to the commission. The question was whether the plaintiffs were entitled simply to a personal remedy (an account of profits) or a more beneficial proprietary remedy (a constructive trust). If the plaintiffs were entitled to a constructive trust, it would be enforceable even in insolvency, and it would allow the plaintiffs to trace into the defendants' accounts and investments. Unusually, Lord Neuberger overruled his own prior decision in the Court of Appeal in *Sinclair Investments (UK) Ltd v Versailles Trade Finance Ltd ('Sinclair Investments')*, where it was held that a proprietary interest should never be awarded over a gain made as an (indirect) result of fiduciary wrongdoing.[58] His Lordship explained his change of opinion in *FHR* by saying:

> Clarity and simplicity are highly desirable qualities in the law. Subtle distinctions are sometimes inevitable, but in the present case, as mentioned above, there is no plainly right answer, and accordingly, in the absence of any other good reason it would seem right to opt for the simple answer.[59]

By contrast in *Sinclair Investments*, Lord Neuberger had said that a bribe to a fiduciary should never be held on constructive trust for a beneficiary:

57 [2015] AC 250.

58 [2012] Ch 453.

59 *FHR European Ventures LLP v Mankarious* [2015] AC 250, [35]. See also Lord Neuberger, 'The Remedial Constructive Trust – Fact or Fiction' (Speech, Banking Services and Financial Law Association Conference, Queenstown, New Zealand, 10 August 2014) [28]–[29], [39].

> [A] bribe paid to a fiduciary could not possibly be said to be an asset which the fiduciary was under a duty to take for the beneficiary. There can thus be said to be a fundamental distinction between (i) a fiduciary enriching himself by depriving a claimant of an asset and (ii) a fiduciary enriching himself by doing a wrong to the claimant.[60]

In *Sinclair Investments*, the defendants were insolvent, and thus the parties who would ultimately be subject to any proprietary interest were the defendants' creditors. Thus, Lord Neuberger noted that deterrence does not operate to justify the imposition of a constructive trust where the fiduciary is insolvent:

> [I]t does not matter to the defaulting fiduciary if he is stripped of his profits because they are beneficially owned by the beneficiary, or because he has to account for those profits to the beneficiary.

But the difference very much matters to the other creditors of the defaulting fiduciary, if they are insolvent. A person with a proprietary claim to assets held in the name of an insolvent person is better off than a secured creditor, and all such assets are unavailable to other creditors.[61]

It is suggested that the Australian discretionary approach is preferable to the English non-discretionary approach.

REVIEW QUESTIONS

(1) Do you think the categorisations of 'perfection', 'unjust enrichment' and 'wrongdoing' work in this chapter?

(2) Do you think knowledge should be relevant to the imposition of a proprietary interest designed to prevent unjust enrichment?

(3) Which approach do you prefer over constructive trusts imposed over bribes made in breach of fiduciary duty?

IV Discretionary factors and bars to relief

Concept	Short explanation	Relevant authorities	Principles text
Discretionary factors and bars to relief	There are no settled principles for how these operate.	The principles text explains the difficulties in this area.	Chapter 19: [19.66]–[19.67]

As the principles text notes at [19.66]–[19.67], discretionary factors and bars to relief *do* operate in relation to proprietary relief, but not in a structured manner. It seems that hardship, impact on third parties and other matters may be relevant.

Where a remedy is granted in response to a right to rescind, the discretionary factors and bars to relief are the same as those discussed with regard to rescission. As noted there, where the bars to relief operate, the court is less likely to award a full constructive trust,

60 [2012] Ch 453, [80].

61 Ibid [53]–[54].

and more likely to award a proprietary power (as in *Quek v Beggs*[62]), a lien (as in *Badman v Drake*[63]) or no relief at all (as in *Allcard v Skinner*[64]).

REVIEW QUESTIONS

(1) Can you identify any situations where discretionary bars to relief have at least arguably operated to curtail relief?

(2) Why do you think the discretionary considerations for proprietary powers are similar to those in rescission?

V The need for more defined criteria

Concept	Short explanation	Relevant authorities	Principles text
The need for more defined criteria	Currently, the criteria for the award of proprietary remedies are unclear.	The principles text explains the lack of clarity.	Chapter 19: [19.68]–[19.69]

Unfortunately, the criteria for when a proprietary remedy will be awarded are unclear. This is not ideal, because it means that litigants find it difficult to predict what remedy will be imposed. The impact of proprietary remedies in insolvency in particular means that greater certainty is needed. All that we can presently do is to analogise from the circumstances where proprietary awards have been made in the past.

REVIEW QUESTIONS

(1) What are the problems in not having clear criteria for the imposition of proprietary remedies?

(2) Do you think you have some idea of the circumstances in which a court will award a proprietary remedy?

62 (1990) 5 BPR 11,761.

63 [2008] NSWSC 1366.

64 (1887) 36 Ch D 145.

PART 8

ENFORCEMENT OF REMEDIES

20 ENFORCEMENT OF REMEDIES

I	Introduction	666
II	Interlocutory injunctions	666
	A Legal, equitable or statutory right	667
	B 'Serious question to be tried' (or a 'prima facie case')	669
	C The balance of convenience	673
	D Mandatory interlocutory injunctions	674
	E *Quia timet* interlocutory injunctions	674
	F Interlocutory injunctions which finally determine the matter	674
	G Undertakings as to damages	676
	H Interim injunctions under statute	676
III	Other pre-judgment remedies	678
	A Arrest of the person	678
	B Freezing orders (Mareva orders)	681
	C Search orders (Anton Piller orders)	684
IV	Post-judgment enforcement	685
	A Enforcement of money remedies	686
	B Enforcement of specific remedies	692

I Introduction

This chapter deals with court orders made prior to final judgment and with enforcement of final judgments. These are matters of civil procedure and are not remedies in the technical sense. They protect the ability of courts to award remedies in two ways. First, if a particular subject matter needs to be protected before judgment, interlocutory remedies can achieve that goal. Second, after final judgment has been handed down, courts must be able to ensure that the defendant does what they were ordered to do, for example by seizing assets to pay for an outstanding judgment debt.

II Interlocutory injunctions

Concept	Short explanation	Relevant authorities	Principles text
Legal, equitable or statutory right	The plaintiff must establish that they have a legal, equitable or statutory right in order to obtain an interlocutory injunction.	*Australian Broadcasting Corporation v Lenah Game Meats Pty Ltd* (2001) 208 CLR 199	Chapter 20: [20.09]
'Prima facie case'	The plaintiff must show that they have a 'prima facie case' in order to obtain an interlocutory injunction.	*Australian Broadcasting Corporation v O'Neill* (2006) 227 CLR 57	Chapter 20: [20.10]–[20.16]

Concept	Short explanation	Relevant authorities	Principles text
The balance of convenience	The plaintiff must show that the balance of convenience favours the grant of an interlocutory injunction.	*Beecham Group Ltd v Bristol Laboratories Pty Ltd* (1968) 118 CLR 618	Chapter 20: [20.17]–[20.30]

Interlocutory injunctions are granted prior to final judgment and generally last until trial or further order. They are usually sought to preserve the status quo, so that final justice can be done. They are discretionary in nature. Ordinarily a plaintiff seeking an injunction must give an 'undertaking as to damages' to ensure that the defendant is compensated for any losses flowing from compliance with the injunction if the plaintiff's claim was ultimately unsuccessful at trial.

There are three questions a court must ask before granting an interlocutory injunction. If the answer to all of those questions is 'yes', the plaintiff will obtain an interlocutory injunction. These are set out in Figure 20.1.

Figure 20.1 Steps to establish an interlocutory injunction

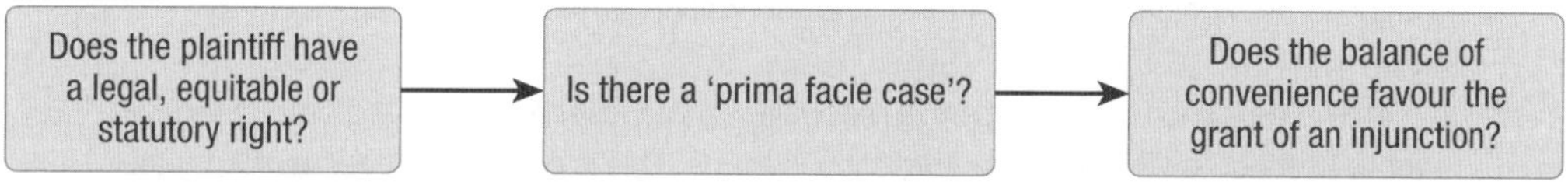

A Legal, equitable or statutory right

A majority of the High Court in *Australian Broadcasting Corporation v Lenah Game Meats Pty Ltd*[1] held that a plaintiff cannot have a 'free-standing' interlocutory injunction simply because it would be just and convenient. It is necessary for the plaintiff to establish some legal, equitable or statutory right supported by the injunction.

Australian Broadcasting Corporation v Lenah Game Meats Pty Ltd (2001) 208 CLR 199

Facts and issues

The Australian Broadcasting Corporation ('ABC') proposed to show a film made by an unknown person who had trespassed on Lenah Game Meats Pty Ltd's ('Lenah's') premises and filmed the processing of possum meat in Lenah's abattoir. The ABC had obtained the film from an animal liberation organisation. Lenah sought an interlocutory injunction to restrain the broadcasting of the film. The ABC was not liable to Lenah for any cause of action: trespass, defamation or breach of confidence.

1 (2001) 208 CLR 199.

Decision

Lenah's application for an interlocutory injunction failed before the trial judge in the Supreme Court of Tasmania. The Full Court of the Supreme Court of Tasmania overturned this decision and allowed an injunction on the basis that it was 'just and convenient'. However, a majority of the High Court reversed the decision of the Full Court, saying that there was no power to grant an interlocutory injunction in a case where no legal or equitable right fell to be determined in the final proceedings. Moreover, there was no possibility of an action for breach of privacy in the present circumstances. Kirby J and Callinan J dissented in separate judgments.

Gleeson CJ

> [**218**] A dispute arose in the course of argument as to 'whether interlocutory injunctive relief to prevent publication can be granted without any underlying cause of action to be tried'. In the context of the present case, this is puzzling. There could be no justification, in principle, for granting an interlocutory injunction here other than to preserve the subject matter of the dispute, and to maintain the status quo pending the determination of the rights of the parties. If the respondent cannot show a sufficient colour of right of the kind sought to be vindicated by final relief, the foundation of the claim for interlocutory relief disappears.
>
> In a context such as the present, a proposition that the respondent has a 'free-standing' right to interlocutory relief is a contradiction in terms. This is demonstrated, not only by the purpose for which interlocutory relief is granted, but by the form of the relief. The Full Court granted the injunction sought 'until further order'. A more usual form of interlocutory injunction would be 'until the hearing of the action or further order', but the effect is the same. If there were a 'free-standing' right to injunctive relief, why would the injunction be limited in time? If there is no serious question to be tried because, upon examination, it appears that the facts alleged by the respondent cannot, as a matter of law, sustain such a right, then there is no subject matter to be preserved. There is then no justice in maintaining the status quo, because that depends upon restraining the appellant from doing something which, by hypothesis, the respondent has no right to prevent.

Gummow and Hayne JJ

> [**239**] Section 10 of the *Supreme Court Civil Procedure Act 1932* (Tas) (the Supreme Court Act) provides for the concurrent administration by the Supreme Court of law and equity, but with the rules of equity to prevail in any conflict or variance between those rules and the rules of the common law (s 11(10)). Sub-section (7) of s 10 provides that the Court shall grant either absolutely or on terms all such remedies as any of the parties may be entitled to in respect of every legal or equitable claim brought forward in the proceeding 'so that, as far as possible, all matters in controversy between the parties may be completely and finally determined, and all multiplicity of legal proceedings concerning any of those matters avoided'.
>
> Section 11 of the Supreme Court Act then deals with miscellaneous matters. Sub-section (12) of s 11 reads: 'A mandamus or an injunction may be granted or a receiver

appointed by an interlocutory order of the Court or a judge thereof in all cases in which it shall appear to the Court or judge to be just and convenient that such order should be made; and any such order may be made either unconditionally or upon such terms and conditions as the Court or judge shall think just; and if, whether before, or at, or after the hearing of any cause or matter, an application is made for an injunction to prevent any threatened or apprehended waste or trespass, the injunction may be granted if the Court or judge thinks fit, whether the person against whom the injunction is sought is or is not in possession under any claim of title or otherwise, or (if out of possession) does or does not claim a right to do the act sought to be restrained under any colour of title, and whether the estates claimed by both or by either of the parties are legal or equitable.' …

[240] Lenah fixes upon the phrase in s 11(12) 'in all cases in which it shall appear to the Court or judge to be just and convenient' as indicating all that has to be shown to enliven the power to award an interlocutory injunction. However, the terms which introduce that phrase, 'injunction' and 'receiver', are legal terms of art. …

Where interlocutory injunctive relief is sought in some special statutory jurisdiction which uses the term 'injunction' to identify a remedy for which it provides, that term takes its colour from the statutory regime in question. …

…

[241] The basic proposition remains that where interlocutory injunctive relief is sought in a Judicature system court, it is necessary to identify the legal (which may be statutory) or equitable rights which are to be determined at trial and in respect of which there is sought final relief which may or may not be injunctive in nature. …

Gummow and Hayne JJ discussed the English law on 'anti-suit' injunctions, the nature of 'unconscionability' and concluded:

[248] The ABC's submission on this branch of the case should be accepted. The conferral upon the Supreme Court by statute of the power to grant interlocutory injunctions in cases in which it appears to the Court to be just or convenient to do so is not at large. Here, the statute did not confer on the Court power to make an order on the application of Lenah other than in protection of some legal or equitable right of Lenah which the Court might enforce by final judgment. …

B 'Serious question to be tried' (or a 'prima facie case')

The Australian test after *Australian Broadcasting Corporation v O'Neill*[2] (excerpted below) appears to be that the plaintiff must have a 'prima facie case' to an injunction (rejecting the previous position that the plaintiff must show a 'serious question to be tried' as first advanced in *American Cynamid Co v Ethicon*[3]).

2 (2006) 227 CLR 57.

3 [1975] AC 396, 407 (Lord Diplock).

Australian Broadcasting Corporation v O'Neill (2006) 227 CLR 57

Facts and issues

The Australian Broadcasting Corporation ('ABC') sought to show a documentary called *The Fisherman*. The program aired suspicions that the plaintiff, O'Neill (a convicted child murderer), was responsible for the notorious unsolved killings of three children. O'Neill sought to restrain the showing of the documentary on the basis that it was defamatory.

Decision

The trial judge and the majority of the Full Court of the Supreme Court of Tasmania awarded the plaintiff an interlocutory injunction. A majority of the High Court said that an injunction was inappropriate because of the value of free speech and the inadequacy of damages. Kirby J and Heydon J dissented in separate judgments. For present purposes, the relevant excerpt involves the 'prima facie case' test proposed by Gummow and Hayne JJ (with which Gleeson CJ and Crennan J agreed). Kirby J issued a strong dissent against Gummow and Hayne JJ's test.

Gummow and Hayne JJ

Interlocutory injunctions

[**81**] The relevant principles in Australia are those explained in *Beecham Group Ltd v Bristol Laboratories Pty Ltd*. This Court … [**82**] said that on such applications the court addresses itself to two main inquiries and continued:

> The first is whether the plaintiff has made out a prima facie case, in the sense that if the evidence remains as it is there is a probability that at the trial of the action the plaintiff will be held entitled to relief … The second inquiry is … whether the inconvenience or injury which the plaintiff would be likely to suffer if an injunction were refused outweighs or is outweighed by the injury which the defendant would suffer if an injunction were granted.

By using the phrase 'prima facie case', their Honours did not mean that the plaintiff must show that it is more probable than not that at trial the plaintiff will succeed; it is sufficient that the plaintiff show a sufficient likelihood of success to justify in the circumstances the preservation of the status quo pending the trial. That this was the sense in which the Court was referring to the notion of a prima facie case is apparent from an observation to that effect made by Kitto J in the course of argument. With reference to the first inquiry, the Court continued, in a statement of central importance for this appeal:

> How strong the probability needs to be depends, no doubt, upon the nature of the rights [the plaintiff] asserts and the practical consequences likely to flow from the order he seeks.

…

Various views have been expressed and assumptions made respecting the relationship between the judgment of this Court in *Beecham* and the speech of Lord Diplock in the subsequent decision, [**83**] *American Cynamid Co v Ethicon Ltd*. It should be noted that both were cases of patent infringement and the outcome on each appeal was the grant of an interlocutory injunction to restrain infringement. Each of the judgments appealed from had placed too high the bar for the obtaining of interlocutory injunctive relief.

Lord Diplock was at pains to dispel the notion, which apparently had persuaded the Court of Appeal to refuse interlocutory relief, that to establish a prima face case of infringement it was necessary for the plaintiff to demonstrate more than a 50 per cent chance of ultimate success. Thus Lord Diplock remarked:

> The purpose sought to be achieved by giving to the court discretion to grant such injunctions would be stultified if the discretion were clogged by a technical rule forbidding its exercise if upon that incomplete untested evidence the court evaluated the chances of the plaintiff's ultimate success in the action at 50 per cent or less, but permitting its exercise if the court evaluated his chances at more than 50 per cent.

In *Beecham*, the primary judge … had refused interlocutory relief on the footing that, while he could not dismiss the possibility that the defendant might not fail at trial, the plaintiff had not made out a strong enough case on the question of infringement. Hence the statement by Kitto J in the course of argument in the Full Court that it was not necessary for the plaintiff to show that it was more probable than not that the plaintiff would succeed at trial.

When *Beecham* and *American Cynamid* are read with an understanding of the issues for determination and an appreciation of the similarity in outcome, much of the assumed disparity in principle between them loses its force. There is then no objection to the use of the phrase 'serious question' if it is understood as conveying the notion that the seriousness of the question, like the strength of the probability referred to in *Beecham*, depends upon the considerations emphasised in *Beecham*.

However, a difference between this Court in *Beecham* and the House of Lords in *American Cynamid* lies in the apparent statement by Lord Diplock that, provided the court is satisfied that the plaintiff's claim is not frivolous or vexatious, then there will be a serious question to be tried and this will be sufficient. The critical statement by his Lordship is '[t]he court no doubt must be satisfied that the claim is not frivolous or vexatious; in other words, that there is a serious question to be tried'. That was followed by a proposition which appears to reverse matters of onus:

> So *unless* the material available to the court at the hearing of the [**84**] application for an interlocutory injunction *fails to disclose* that the plaintiff has any real prospect of succeeding in his claim for a permanent injunction at the trial, the court should go on to consider whether the balance of convenience lies in favour of granting or refusing the interlocutory relief that is sought. (Emphasis added.)

Those statements do not accord with the doctrine in this Court as established by *Beecham* and should not be followed. They obscure the governing consideration that the requisite strength of the probability of ultimate success depends upon the nature of the rights asserted and the practical consequences likely to flow from the interlocutory order sought.

The second of these matters, the reference to practical consequences, is illustrated by the particular considerations which arise where the grant or refusal of an interlocutory injunction in effect would dispose of the action finally in favour of whichever party succeeded on that application. The first consideration mentioned in *Beecham*, the nature of the rights asserted by the plaintiff, redirects attention to the present appeal.

Kirby J (dissenting)

[**102**] In their joint reasons, Gleeson CJ and Crennan J appear to accept the 'flexible rule' for the grant of interlocutory injunctions before the trial of an action for defamation and the applicability to such an action of the general principles governing interlocutory injunctions as stated by this Court in *Beecham*, and appropriately modified in *Australian Coarse Grain Pool Pty Ltd v Barley Marketing Board (Qld)*, *Murphy v Lush*, and *Castlemaine Tooheys Ltd v South Australia*. However, they conclude that the primary judge, and the Full Court, erred in failing to approach the application for the interlocutory injunction with [**103**] 'exceptional caution'. In other words, Gleeson CJ and Crennan J suggest that insufficient weight was given to the public interest in free speech when determining the 'balance of convenience'. They caution against court interference with the 'right of free speech by prior restraint' and state that only Slicer J, dissenting in the Full Court, treated these considerations as 'influential'. In their view, these considerations are decisive. Gleeson CJ and Crennan J also conclude that because of the respondent's already poor reputation only nominal damages might be awarded to him and that this consideration had likewise not been taken into account as a consideration against providing, and upholding, the injunction. These are the errors of principle which are said to authorise the substitution by this Court of contrary orders. I agree with their resolution of the first issue but I disagree with their resolution of the second and third issues.

In their joint reasons, Gummow and Hayne JJ hold that the primary judge conflated the requirement of 'public benefit' in s 15 of the *Defamation Act 1957* with the general question of 'public interest in free speech'. They also hold that his Honour mistook the nature of his discretion and narrowly focused on whether it would be for the 'public benefit' for the plaintiff to face 'trial' or 'conviction' by the media. On the third issue outlined above, Gummow and Hayne JJ record their agreement with the reasons of Gleeson CJ and Crennan J. For the reasons that follow, I do not agree with these assessments.

Relevantly, Gummow and Hayne JJ also argue that the test stated in the phrase 'serious question to be tried', as understood from statements of Lord Diplock in *American Cynamid v Ethicon Ltd*, should not be followed. Rather, that requirement should be read consistently with the 'considerations emphasised in *Beecham*', whereby the 'governing consideration' is that the 'probability of ultimate success depends on the nature of the rights asserted and the practical consequences likely to flow from the interlocutory order sought'. With respect, I do not believe that this formulation is consistent with the approach repeatedly preferred in this Court in determining the threshold question of whether there is a 'serious question to be tried'. It diminishes the right of [**104**] individuals to have serious questions tried on the evidence not pre-judged on limited predictions of success. This is not to deny that the propounded inquiry is relevant in determining whether the *balance of convenience* favours the grant of an interlocutory injunction. As the authorities attest, this is particularly the case when deciding whether to grant an interlocutory injunction to restrain an alleged defamation. But the legal entitlement to an injunction should not be confused with the secondary question of whether convenience favours it being issued.

C The balance of convenience

Five different factors go into deciding whether the balance of convenience favours the grant of an injunction:

(1) Likelihood of success (the higher the plaintiff's likelihood of success the more likely an interlocutory injunction is to be granted).

(2) Irreparable injury, hardship and inadequacy of damages to the plaintiff (the more likely an injury is to be 'irreparable', or damages are to be inadequate or the plaintiff is to suffer hardship, the more likely an interlocutory injunction is to be granted).

(3) Hardship to the defendant and third parties. (The more likely hardship to the defendant will be caused, and where another remedy for the plaintiff is adequate, the less likely an injunction is to be granted. Third party hardship may also be relevant but not determinative.)

(4) Adequacy of undertaking as to damages for the defendant (the more likely an undertaking as to damages is to be adequate for the defendant, the more likely an injunction is to be granted, but the opposite is true if damages will be inadequate).

(5) Delay on the part of the plaintiff (if delay prejudices the defendant, the less likely it is for an injunction to be granted).

Figure 20.2 The balancing process for the award of an interlocutory injunction

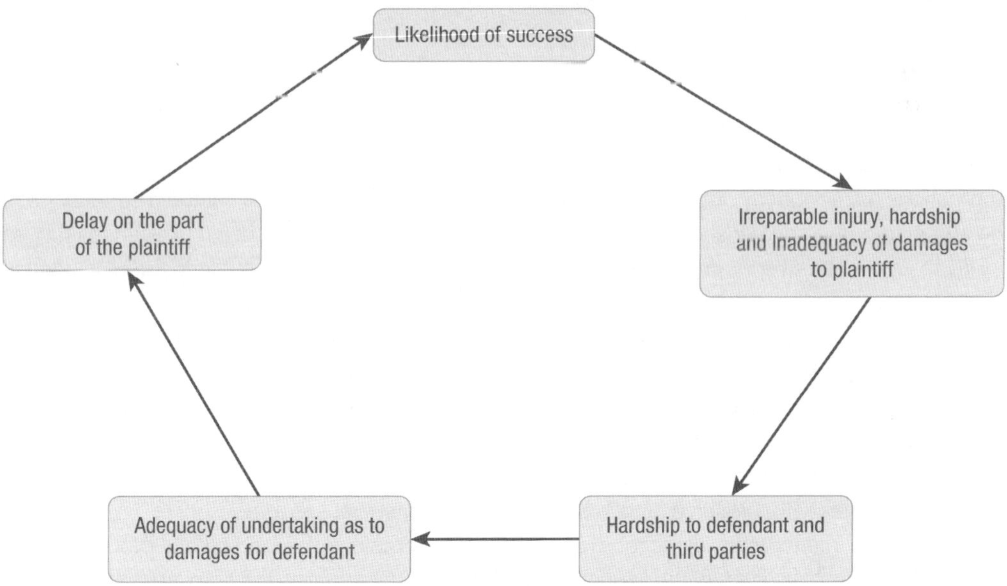

As can be seen, none of these are determinative in and of themselves, and the court has to 'balance' the factors in a given situation.

D Mandatory interlocutory injunctions

As the principles text outlines at [20.31], there is no difference in the test which applies to mandatory interlocutory injunctions as opposed to prohibitory interlocutory injunctions.

E *Quia timet* interlocutory injunctions

A court may award a *quia timet* interlocutory injunction, as long as the risk of injury is not insignificant and illusory, and the balance of convenience favours it. Latin for 'because he fears', *quia timet* injunctions are preventative remedies that restrain conduct before any harm can occur.

F Interlocutory injunctions which finally determine the matter

Sometimes an interlocutory injunction may effectively determine a matter, for example, by preventing a defendant from carrying on a business. Sofronoff's article (excerpted below) discusses when courts should take this into account. At the time of writing the article, Walter Sofronoff was a barrister; from 2017 onwards, he has been the President of the Queensland Court of Appeal.

Walter Sofronoff, 'Interlocutory Injunctions Having Final Effect' (1987) 61(7) *Australian Law Journal* 341

[**341**] In the armoury of litigation tacticians, one of the foremost weapons is the ability in the right circumstances to achieve a decisive result at an early stage of an action by an interlocutory application calculated to paralyse an opponent's business, if not destroy it entirely. Such applications are frequently disguised as remedial measures designed purely for the maintenance of the status quo pending a trial. So, the clever tactician blessed with the right circumstances moves swiftly to have a receiver or provisional liquidator appointed or to obtain an interlocutory injunction to prevent the carrying on of a business or the continuation of employment.

When such an application is successful, it inevitably removes the ground from under the feet of the unfortunate respondent, denying him his income and placing him in the position of having no choice but to begin negotiations from a weak position – this having been, of course, a major consideration in bringing the application.

In this respect legal theory and practice appear to conflict, for the basis of any such application is always the need to preserve and not to destroy rights. Yet, as practitioners know, courts frequently grant interlocutory injunctions restraining, for example, an alleged breach of a restraint of trade clause when the effect of the injunction is not merely to postpone the carrying on of a newly-commenced business said to constitute the breach, but, for all practical purposes, to destroy it altogether. This not only leaves the hapless defendant with no business, but it also leaves him with no reason to continue with the action, the sole remaining purpose of which, from his point of view, is to establish that he did indeed have a right to carry on the business which no longer exists. Moreover, although such relief is granted in some instances on the understanding that money may be an adequate remedy for him, in fact, as a businessman he knows that, unless his loss is likely to be large, he is better off disposing of the action and starting afresh, rather than contesting a sterile suit. Perversely, it is sometimes argued by applicants that this itself shows that the grant of an injunction will cause him no great loss, thereby strengthening the position of the plaintiff on the balance of convenience.

The purpose of this article is to examine whether, in the context of interlocutory injunctions, this all too common and, it is submitted, unjust result accords with received doctrine concerning the principles governing their grant.

...

[348] ...

1. The practice of granting interlocutory relief originally arose to mitigate the risk of injustice to a plaintiff until his rights could be finally determined.
2. The fundamental problem is to weigh the respective risks of injury to plaintiff and defendant caused by the effect of the grant or withholding of relief which at trial may turn out to have been wrongly granted or withheld.
3. The grant of an interlocutory injunction is a remedy that is designed to be temporary.
4. In the usual case the defendant is faced with a mere postponement of the exercise of his rights by the preservation of the status quo, not their eradication.
5. In such cases it is proper to follow the guidelines in American Cynamid, recognising that they do not purport to be rules of law.
6. Such cases require the Court to consider first whether the plaintiff has shown a serious issue to be tried, then to consider the adequacy of damages in each case, and then if necessary to go on to consider other factors relevant to the balance of convenience. If the factors are evenly balanced, then the respective strengths of the parties' cases can be taken into account, but only if there is no credible dispute that one party's case is disproportionately stronger than the others.
7. Where, however, the realities of the case are such that the grant or withholding of relief will have the practical effect of putting an end to the action by granting the successful party all that he seeks, or because the harm caused to the losing party will be complete and for which money cannot constitute any worthwhile recompense, then it is necessary to consider the likelihood that the plaintiff will succeed.
8. In such a case, generally an injunction ought not be granted if the consequence is to deny a defendant an effective right to a trial, if the defendant has put forward a fully arguable case raising a triable issue and if the plaintiff's case is not overwhelming.
9. ... [O]ther factors might clearly point in favour of the grant of an injunction notwithstanding the effective loss by the defendant of his right to a trial, for example, if the risk of injury to the plaintiff is grave.

G Undertakings as to damages

The undertaking as to damages is that if the plaintiff agrees 'to abide by any order which this court may make as to damages, in case this court shall be of opinion that the defendant shall have sustained any, by reason of this order, which the plaintiff ought to pay'.[4]

If the plaintiff fails to make out their case at trial, they will generally be liable to pay damages to the defendant for injuries sustained by reason of the interlocutory injunction.[5] In *European Bank Ltd v Evans*, the High Court observed:

> [T]he undertaking as to damages is given to the court, for enforcement by the court; it is not a contract between parties or some other cause of action upon which one party can sue the other. It is worth repeating the obvious proposition that such an undertaking is not lightly to be given.[6]

Only losses directly flowing from the injunction sound in damages.[7]

H Interim injunctions under statute

'Interim' injunctions (in substance, interlocutory injunctions) are available under statute, including the *Australian Consumer Law* ('ACL')[8] and the *Corporations Act 2001* (Cth).

The ACL provision is extracted below.

Australian Consumer Law s 234

This legislation allows a court to award an 'interim' injunction for contraventions of the ACL.

s 234 Interim injunctions

(1) If an application is made under section 232, the court may, if it considers it is desirable to do so, grant an interim injunction under this subsection pending the determination of the application.

(2) If a responsible Minister or the regulator made the application under section 232, the court must not require the applicant or any other person to give any undertakings as to damages as a condition of granting the interim injunction.

(3) If:

(a) in a case to which subsection (2) does not apply the court would, but for this subsection, require a person to give an undertaking as to damages or costs; and

(b) a responsible Minister gives the undertaking;

the court must accept the undertaking by the responsible Minister and must not require a further undertaking from any other person.

---

4 ICF Spry, *The Principles of Equitable Remedies* (Law Book, 9th ed, 2014) 499.

5 See, generally, ibid 500.

6 (2010) 240 CLR 438, [438]–[439] (French CJ, Gummow, Hayne, Heydon and Kiefel JJ).

7 Ibid [16]–[18]; *Air Express Ltd v Ansett Transport Industries (Operations) Pty Ltd* (1979) 146 CLR 249.

8 *Competition and Consumer Act 2010* (Cth) sch 2.

Where the grant of an interim injunction pursuant to s 234 is sought, adequacy of damages may be a consideration which goes to the balance of convenience.[9]

Corporations Act 2001 (Cth) s 1324(1), (4), (8)

This provision allows a court to award an 'interim' injunction for contravention of the *Corporations Act 2001* (Cth).

s 1324 Injunctions

(1) Where a person has engaged, is engaging or is proposing to engage in conduct that constituted, constitutes or would constitute:

(a) a contravention of this Act; or

(b) attempting to contravene this Act; or

(c) aiding, abetting, counselling or procuring a person to contravene this Act; or

(d) inducing or attempting to induce, whether by threats, promises or otherwise, a person to contravene this Act; or

(e) being in any way, directly or indirectly, knowingly concerned in, or party to, the contravention by a person of this Act; or

(f) conspiring with others to contravene this Act;

the Court may, on the application of ASIC, or of a person whose interests have been, are or would be affected by the conduct, grant an injunction, on such terms as the Court thinks appropriate, restraining the first-mentioned person from engaging in the conduct and, if in the opinion of the Court it is desirable to do so, requiring that person to do any act or thing.

...

(4) Where in the opinion of the Court it is desirable to do so, the Court may grant an interim injunction pending determination of an application under subsection (1)....

(8) Where ASIC applies to the Court for the grant of an injunction under this section, the Court must not require the applicant or any other person, as a condition of granting an interim injunction, to give an undertaking as to damages.

Although courts are not bound to follow equitable principles in granting an interim injunction pursuant to s 1324(4),[10] they have tended to apply similar principles,[11] with due recognition that if the Australian Securities and Investment Commission ('ASIC') is the applicant, then the public interest may be a relevant consideration to be taken into account when assessing the balance of convenience.[12]

9 *Organic Marketing Australia Pty Ltd v Woolworths Ltd* [2011] FCA 279, [22].

10 *Australian Securities and Investments Commission v Parkes* (2001) 38 ACSR 355; *Australian Securities and Investments Commission v Pegasus Leveraged Options Group Pty Ltd* (2002) 41 ACSR 561.

11 Eg *Australian Securities and Investments Commission v Mauer-Swisse Securities Ltd* (2002) 42 ACSR 605; *Australian Securities and Investments Commission v Triton Underwriting Insurance Agency* (2003) 48 ACSR 249, [25].

12 *Australian Securities and Investments Commission v Mauer-Swisse Securities Ltd* (2002) 42 ACSR 605, [36].

REVIEW QUESTIONS

(1) Do you think a court should allow a 'free-standing' interlocutory injunction where it would be 'just and convenient' to award one?

(2) Which test do you prefer, the 'prima facie case' test or the 'serious question to be tried' test?

III Other pre-judgment remedies

A defendant may abscond, or remove property or money from the jurisdiction in order to render any judgment in the plaintiff's favour nugatory. The courts have developed interlocutory remedies to prevent this occurring.

There has been a historical shift from imprisoning the defendant to freezing assets or giving the plaintiff leave to search assets.

Concept	Short explanation	Relevant authorities	Principles text
Arrest of the person	If it appears that a person may abscond from the jurisdiction to avoid paying a plaintiff, the court may imprison the defendant.	*Debtors Act 1870* (Tas) s 5 *Absconding Debtors Act 1978* (NT) ss 5–6	Chapter 20: [20.42]–[20.47]
Freezing orders	If it appears that assets or money may be removed from the jurisdiction, the court may 'freeze' the assets to restrain the defendant from removing them.	*Supreme Court (General Civil Procedure) Rules 2015* (Vic) rr 37A.02–37A.04	Chapter 20: [20.48]–[20.54]
Search orders	If it appears that a defendant may remove or destroy evidence, the court may permit the plaintiff's representatives to enter the defendant's premises, search for evidence and remove it.	*Uniform Civil Procedure Rules 2005* (NSW) rr 25.19–25.20	Chapter 20: [20.55]–[20.57]

A Arrest of the person

Legislation in all states and territories (except New South Wales) allows for the arrest of a person who seeks to abscond from the jurisdiction with an unsatisfied obligation to pay another person.[13] Once arrested, the defendant stays in custody until the court orders otherwise or he gives adequate security.[14] Witzleb, Bant, Degeling and Barker identify two types of legislation concerning pre-judgement arrest remedies: old-style legislation and modern legislation.[15]

13 *Court Procedures Rules 2006* (ACT) rr 2550–2564; *Absconding Debtors Act 1978* (NT); *Civil Proceedings Act 2011* (Qld) s 100; *Enforcement of Judgments Act 1991* (SA); *Debtors Act 1870* (Tas) s 5; *Supreme Court Act 1986* (Vic) ss 86–100, 119; *Supreme Court Act 1935* (WA) ss 63–68; *Restraint of Debtors Act 1984* (WA). Cf *Civil Procedure Act 2005* (NSW) s 124.

14 *Uniform Civil Procedure Rules 1999* (Qld) r 941; *Debtors Act 1870* (Tas) s 5(2); *Supreme Court Act 1935* (WA) ss 63–64; *Supreme Court Act 1986* (Vic) ss 86–100.

15 N Witzleb et al, *Remedies Commentary and Materials* (Law Book, 6th ed, 2015) [12.10].

Old-style legislation (present in Tasmania, Victoria, and Western Australia[16]) requires the applicant to show that the defendant is obliged to pay more than a certain minimum sum,[17] that there is probable cause to believe that the defendant will leave the state, and that the absence of the defendant will materially prejudice or defeat the applicant's cause of action.

Debtors Act 1870 (Tas) s 5

This legislation is 'old-style', in that it sets a minimum sum for which the defendant must be liable before they can be arrested for a failure to pay.

5 Power to arrest defendant about to quit Tasmania

(1) A person shall not be arrested upon mesne process in any action.

(2) Where the plaintiff in any action in the Supreme Court in which, if brought before the commencement of this Act, the defendant would have been liable to arrest, proves at any time before final judgment by evidence on oath, to the satisfaction of a judge, that the plaintiff has good cause of action against the defendant, to the amount of $50 or upwards, and that there is probable cause for believing that the defendant is about to quit Tasmania unless he be apprehended, and that the absence of the defendant from Tasmania will materially prejudice the plaintiff in the prosecution of his action, a judge may in the prescribed manner order such defendant to be arrested and imprisoned for 6 months, unless and until he has sooner given the prescribed security, not exceeding the amount claimed in the action, that he will not go out of Tasmania without the leave of the court or a judge.

(3) Where the action is for a penalty or sum in the nature of a penalty other than a penalty in respect of any contract, it shall not be necessary to prove that the absence of the defendant from Tasmania will materially prejudice the plaintiff in the prosecution of his action, and the security given (instead of being that the defendant will not go out of Tasmania) shall be to the effect that any sum recovered against the defendant in the action shall be paid, or that the defendant shall be rendered to prison.

The modern legislation requires an applicant to show similar evidence to old-style legislation but sets no minimum sum. The Northern Territory legislation requires a liquidated debt.[18] The Northern Territory and Western Australia also permit the court to restrain the transfer or removal of property.[19] The Queensland rules also provide for the making of orders restraining persons from leaving Australia.[20] The South Australian legislation provides

16 *Debtors Act 1870* (Tas) s 5; *Supreme Court Act 1986* (Vic) ss 86–100, 119; *Supreme Court Act 1935* (WA) ss 63–68.

17 *Debtors Act 1870* (Tas) s 5(2) ($50); *Supreme Court Act 1986* (Vic) s 87(a) ($50 000); *Supreme Court Act 1935* (WA) s 63(2)(a) ($100).

18 *Absconding Debtors Act 1978* (NT) s 4(1) (definition of 'debt').

19 *Absconding Debtors Act 1978* (NT) ss 13–15; *Restraint of Debtors Act 1984* (WA) ss 17–19.

20 *Uniform Civil Procedure Rules 1999* (Qld) r 259(2)(c).

its own procedure, and also provides for arrest, imprisonment and contempt proceedings against absconding debtors.[21]

Absconding Debtors Act 1978 (NT) ss 5–6

This legislation is more modern, as it does not contain a minimum sum for which the defendant must be liable before he can be arrested for a failure to pay.

5 Application for warrant

(1) Subject to this Act, a person may, at any time, apply to a Court for a warrant to issue for the arrest of a debtor for the purpose of preventing that debtor from leaving the Territory.

(2) An application under subsection (1) must be:

- (a) in the prescribed form; and
- (b) supported by an affidavit as to all material matters in relation to which the Court is, under section 6(2), required to be satisfied.

6 Issue of warrant

(1) A Court may issue a warrant for which an application has been made under section 5 in accordance with this Part.

(2) A Court must not issue a warrant under subsection (1) unless it is satisfied, after reasonable inquiry, as to all material matters.

(3) A warrant issued under subsection (1) must:

- (a) be in the prescribed form; and
- (b) specify:
  - (i) the amount of the alleged debt; and
  - (ii) the costs, if any, which are claimed by the applicant; and
  - (iii) the name of the person to whom it is addressed; and
- (c) bear such other endorsements as are prescribed.

There is also an equitable writ (the writ of *ne exeat regno*[22]) preventing a person from leaving the jurisdiction where that person owes a debt as a result of breaching an equitable duty. The factors the court considers are similar to those under the statutory provisions above.[23]

Pre-judgment arrest is now very rare, and courts prefer to freeze assets. This legislation is interpreted strictly,[24] and arrest will not be awarded unless departure is imminent.[25] The

21 *Debtors Act 1936* (SA) s 4; *Enforcement of Judgments Act 1991* (SA) s 14.

22 Latin for 'let him not go out of the kingdom'. Sometimes called a writ of *ne exeat colonia* ('let him not go out of the colony') in an Australian context; eg *Glover v Walters* (1950) 80 CLR 172.

23 *Glover v Walters* (1950) 80 CLR 172; *Felton v Callis* [1969] 1 QB 200; *Parsons v Burk* [1971] NZLR 244.

24 *Jira v Burcher* (1960) 78 WN (NSW) 421; *Ingram v Ingram* [1927] VLR 225; *Southern Drug Co Ltd v Lagos* (1980) 24 SASR 590; *QB Investments Pty Ltd v Reed* [1979] Qd R 58; *Felton v Callis* [1969] 1 QB 200.

25 *QB Investments Pty Ltd v Reed* [1979] Qd R 58.

judgment debtor's flight must defeat or materially prejudice the action; it is not enough that it will make enforcement more difficult or expensive.[26]

B Freezing orders (Mareva orders)

Freezing orders are sometimes called 'Mareva orders' because they were developed in *Mareva Compania Naviera SA v International Bulkcarriers SA*.[27] The jurisdictional basis for such orders was initially controversial,[28] but the conditions under which freezing orders may be awarded are now governed by civil procedure rules in all states and territories.[29]

Supreme Court (General Civil Procedure) Rules 2015 (Vic) rr 37A.02–37A.04

An example of a civil procedure rule giving a court a power to make a freezing order.

Order 37A – Freezing orders

...

Reg 37A.02 Freezing order

(1) The Court may make an order (a *freezing order*), upon or without notice to the respondent, for the purpose of preventing the frustration or inhibition of the Court's process by seeking to meet a danger that a judgment or prospective judgment of the Court will be wholly or partly unsatisfied.

(2) A freezing order may be an order restraining a respondent from removing any assets located in or outside Australia or from disposing of, dealing with, or diminishing the value of, those assets.

(3) A freezing order may be in Form 37AA.

(4) In making a freezing order or an ancillary order, the Court shall have regard to the practice note concerning freezing orders.

(5) The affidavits relied on in support of an application for a freezing order or an ancillary order shall, as far as possible, address the following –

  (a) information about the judgment that has been obtained, or if no judgment has been obtained, the following information about the cause of action –

    (i) the basis of the claim for substantive relief;

    (ii) the amount of the claim; and

26 *Moss & Co v Johnston* (1896) 22 VLR 530, 531; *O'Connor v Pitcairn* (1901) 27 VLR 2, 6 (Hood J); *Uniform Civil Procedure Rules 1999* (Qld) r 942.

27 [1975] 2 Lloyd's Rep 509.

28 See L Aitken, 'Note' (1996) 70(2) *Australian Law Journal* 109; *Mercedes-Benz AG v Leiduck* [1996] AC 284.

29 *Federal Court Rules 2011* (Cth) rr 7.31–7.38; *Court Procedures Rules 2006* (ACT) rr 740–745; *Uniform Civil Procedure Rules 2005* (NSW) rr 25.3, 25.10–25.17; *Supreme Court Rules 1987* (NT) ord 37A; *Uniform Civil Procedure Rules 1999* (Qld) rr 260–260G; *Supreme Court Civil Rules 2006* (SA) r 247; *Supreme Court Rules 2000* (Tas) rr 937A–937H; *Supreme Court (General Civil Procedure) Rules 2015* (Vic) ord 37A; *Rules of the Supreme Court 1971* (WA) ord 52A.

(iii) if the application is made without notice to the respondent, the applicant's knowledge of any possible defence;

(b) the nature and value of the respondent's assets, so far as they are known to the applicant, within and outside Australia;

(c) the matters referred to in Rule 37A.05 [which refers to orders against judgment debtors]; and

(d) the identity of any person, other than the respondent, who the applicant believes may be affected by the freezing order and how that person may be affected by it.

Reg 37A.03 Ancillary order

(1) The Court may make an order (an *ancillary order*) ancillary to a freezing order or prospective freezing order as the Court considers appropriate.

(2) Without limiting the generality of paragraph (1), an ancillary order may be made for either or both of the following purposes –

(a) eliciting information relating to assets relevant to the freezing order or prospective freezing order;

(b) determining whether the freezing order should be made.

Reg 37A.04 Respondent need not be party to proceeding

The Court may make a freezing order or an ancillary order against a respondent, whether or not the respondent is a party to a proceeding in which substantive relief is sought against the respondent.

In addition to the uniform legislation, the Northern Territory and Western Australia have legislation which provides for orders against removal of property or its transfer to another person.[30] In Victoria, there is a statutory jurisdiction to make freezing orders additional to the inherent jurisdiction of the court.[31] Section 1323 of the *Corporations Act 2001* (Cth) also gives a power to preserve assets in some circumstances.

Since a freezing order has a drastic effect on the defendant, courts exercise 'a high degree of caution' before awarding one.[32] The plaintiff is always required to offer an undertaking as to damages in support of the application.[33] The order must allow the defendant sufficient funds to conduct a defence,[34] to pay debts and ordinary expenses, and to run a business.[35] The courts have emphasised that the sole purpose of the order is to prevent assets from being dissipated, and not to provide security for the plaintiff's claim.[36] The plaintiff bears the

30 *Absconding Debtors Act 1978* (NT) ss 13–15; *Restraint of Debtors Act 1984* (WA) ss 17–19.

31 *Supreme Court Act 1986* (Vic) s 37(3).

32 *Cardile v LED Builders Pty Ltd* (1999) 198 CLR 380, [50].

33 Ibid [43]; *Frigo v Culhaci* (New South Wales Court of Appeal, Mason P, Sheller JA and Sheppard AJA, 17 July 1998).

34 *Clark Equipment Credit of Australia Ltd v Como Factors Pty Ltd* (1988) 14 NSWLR 552, 569; *Glenwood Management Group Pty Ltd v Mayo* [1991] 2 VR 49.

35 *Clark Equipment Credit of Australia Ltd v Como Factors Pty Ltd* (1988) 14 NSWLR 552.

36 *Jackson v Sterling Industries Ltd* (1987) 162 CLR 612, 621, 625.

onus of establishing the need for the order and the quantum of the amount to be frozen.[37] If loss is suffered as a result of a wrongfully imposed freezing order, damages will be assessed in a similar manner to contract damages, with any losses required to be reasonably foreseeable to the person seeking the freezing order.[38]

The rules provide that the assets the subject of a freezing order can be anywhere in the world.[39] Freezing orders are only granted in support of a foreign judgment or award in exceptional cases.[40]

Courts have been reluctant to formulate rigid rules as to when a freezing order will be awarded against the defendant,[41] but the following guidance can be given:

- The plaintiff must establish that they have an arguable case against the defendant,[42] and that there is a danger that the plaintiff's judgment will be partly or wholly unsatisfied because the defendant is likely to remove certain assets, dispose of them or deal with them so as to diminish their value.[43]
- The plaintiff's evidence as to the possibility of dissipation of assets must be solid and not mere speculation.[44] However, there is no need to show nefarious purposes or an intention to frustrate the court's judgment on the defendant's part, although if such evidence exists, it will be easier to establish that a freezing order should be made.[45]
- The court weighs up the 'balance of convenience', including the hardship to the plaintiff if the freezing order is not awarded balanced against the hardship to the defendant if the freezing order is made.[46] The interests of third parties may be relevant, depending upon the case.[47] Discretionary considerations such as delay may militate against the granting of a freezing order.[48] If it appears that the defendant is not adequately protected against detriment which may arise from imposition of a freezing order, the court will remove the order.[49]

37 *Zhen v Mo* [2008] VSC 300, [24].

38 *Abbey Forwarding Ltd v Hone (No 3)* [2015] Ch 309.

39 Eg *National Australia Bank Ltd v Dessau* [1988] VR 521; *Derby & Co Ltd v Weldon* [1990] Ch 48; *PT Bayan Resources TBK v BCBC Singapore Pte Ltd* (2014) 320 ALR 289.

40 *Rosseel NV v Oriental Commercial Shipping (UK) Ltd* [1990] 1 WLR 1387. Such orders were made in *Babanaft International Co SA v Bassatne* [1990] Ch 13; *Haiti (Republic) v Duvalier* [1990] 1 QB 202.

41 *Jackson v Sterling Industries Ltd* (1987) 162 CLR 612, 621.

42 *Glenwood Management Group Pty Ltd v Mayo* [1991] 2 VR 49, 49.

43 *Federal Court Rules 2011* (Cth) r 7.32(1); *Court Procedures Rules 2006* (ACT) r 741(1), (2); *Uniform Civil Procedure Rules 2005* (NSW) r 25.11(1); *Supreme Court Rules 1987* (NT) r 37A.02(1); *Uniform Civil Procedure Rules 1999* (Qld) r 260A(1); *Supreme Court Civil Rules 2006* (SA) r 247(2)(a); *Supreme Court Rules 2000* (Tas) r 937B (1); *Supreme Court (General Civil Procedure) Rules 2015* (Vic) r 37A.02(1); *Rules of the Supreme Court 1971* (WA) ord 52A r 2(1).

44 *Ninemia Maritime Corporation v Trave Schiffahrtsgesellschaft mbH & Co KG* [1983] WLUK 838 aff'd [1983] 1 WLR 1412.

45 N Witzleb et al, *Remedies Commentary and Materials* (Law Book, 6th ed, 2015) [12.75].

46 *Zhen v Mo* [2008] VSC 300, [27].

47 *Patrick Stevedores Operations No 2 Pty Ltd v Maritime Union of Australia (No 3)* (1998) 195 CLR 1, [66].

48 *Cardile v LED Builders Pty Ltd* (1999) 198 CLR 380, [53].

49 *Frigo v Culhaci* (New South Wales Court of Appeal, Mason P, Sheller JA and Sheppard AJA, 17 July 1998).

C Search orders (Anton Piller orders)

Search orders or 'Anton Piller orders' require a defendant to 'permit' the plaintiff's representatives to enter the defendant's premises to search for evidence, and to remove it from the premises if found. Such orders are primarily (but not solely) made where it is alleged that the defendant has pirated copies of the plaintiff's copyrighted or patented work.[50] A search order is sometimes called an 'Anton Piller order' after the English Court of Appeal case, *Anton Piller KG v Manufacturing Processes Ltd*.[51]

As with freezing orders, the conditions upon which search orders may be awarded are now governed by uniform civil procedure rules in all states and territories.[52] The court must be satisfied that the plaintiff has a strong prima facie case on an accrued cause of action, that the potential or actual loss or damage to the plaintiff will be serious if the order is not made, and that there is sufficient evidence that the defendant possesses material and may destroy it or cause it to be unavailable for use.

Uniform Civil Procedure Rules 2005 (NSW) rr 25.19–25.20

An example of a civil procedure rule giving the court the power to make a search order.

Reg 25.19 Search order

...

The court may make an order (a '**search order**'), in any proceeding or in anticipation of any proceeding in the court, with or without notice to the respondent, for the purpose of securing or preserving evidence and requiring a respondent to permit persons to enter premises for the purpose of securing the preservation of evidence which is or may be relevant to an issue in the proceeding or anticipated proceeding.

Reg 25.20 Requirements for grant of search order

...

The court may make a search order if the court is satisfied that:

(a) an applicant seeking the order has a strong prima facie case on an accrued cause of action, and

(b) the potential or actual loss or damage to the applicant will be serious if the search order is not made, and

(c) there is sufficient evidence in relation to a respondent that:

 (i) the respondent possesses important evidentiary material, and

 (ii) there is a real possibility that the respondent might destroy such material or cause it to be unavailable for use in evidence in a proceeding or anticipated proceeding before the court.

50 PW Young, C Croft and ML Smith, *On Equity* (Law Book, 2009) [4.870].

51 [1976] Ch 55.

52 *Federal Court Rules 2011* (Cth) rr 7.41–7.47; *Court Procedures Rules 2006* (ACT) rr 750–755; *Uniform Civil Procedure Rules 2005* (NSW) rr 25.18–25.24; *Supreme Court Rules 1987* (NT) ord 37B;

The standard search order is drafted carefully, providing for the presence of an independent solicitor and an opportunity for the defendant to obtain legal advice before the order is executed.[53]

REVIEW QUESTIONS

(1) Why do you think a need for freezing orders arose?

(2) Why do you think a need for search orders arose?

IV Post-judgment enforcement

After judgment has been handed down, the defendant may be ordered to pay to the plaintiff a monetary sum or to do a specific thing. If the defendant fails to pay the money or to do the thing specified, courts can ensure compliance with their orders.

The general rule is that common law damages orders are enforced by seizing the judgment debtor's property, whereas orders for specific relief are enforced by means of coercion, including imprisonment for contempt. It is said that this is because 'a common law judgment is a determination of right not a command to the person ... [b]ut a decree in equity has always been a command laid upon the person. So too is a rule absolute at common law'.[54] Because equity is coercive, the ways of enforcing equitable judgments are more likely to be coercive. However, coercion also has a place with regard to some common law judgments.

Concept	Short explanation	Relevant authorities	Principles text
Enforcement of money remedies	Money remedies may be enforced by imprisoning judgment debtors, but more often enforcement is effected by seizing property belonging to the judgment debtor.	*Court Procedures Rules 2006* (ACT) rr 2150, 2154 *Uniform Civil Procedure Rules 1999* (Qld) rr 828–829 *Uniform Civil Procedure Rules 1999* (Qld) rr 855–856 *Uniform Civil Procedure Rules 1999* (Qld) rr 875, 877	Chapter 20: [20.40]–[20.72]
Enforcement of specific remedies	Specific remedies may be enforced against property, particularly in regards to possession of land, but a defendant may also be imprisoned, fined, or have their property sequestered if they refuse to comply.	See principles text for further discussion.	Chapter 20: [20.73]–[20.84]

Uniform Civil Procedure Rules 1999 (Qld) rr 261–261F; *Supreme Court Civil Rules 2006* (SA) r 248; *Supreme Court Rules 2000* (Tas) rr 937I–937O; *Supreme Court (General Civil Procedure) Rules 2015* (Vic) ord 37B; *Rules of the Supreme Court 1971* (WA) ord 52B.

53 Young et al (n 50) [4.870].

54 *Pearson v Arcadia Store, Guyra, Ltd (No 2)* (1935) 53 CLR 587, 590–91.

A Enforcement of money remedies

The history of enforcement of money remedies is outlined in more detail in the principles text at [20.60]–[20.61]. English law allowed for the imprisonment of judgment debtors, and the fact that the defendant could not pay was irrelevant. Gradually the circumstances in which judgment debtors could be imprisoned was reduced.

Powers to arrest and imprison judgment debtors still exist in most Australian states and territories.[55] The New South Wales legislation provides that a judgment or order is not enforceable against a person, but retains the rules regarding contempt of court.[56] The rules in the Australian Capital Territory provide that an enforcement order may only include an arrest and detention warrant in cases of contempt.[57]

In most Australian jurisdictions, there is provision for the court to order that judgment debtors make an instalment payment plan to repay judgment debts.[58]

Court Procedures Rules 2006 (ACT) rr 2150, 2154

This is an example of a civil procedure rule allowing the court to allow instalment payment plans.

Reg 2150 Instalment order – making

(1) The court may make an order (an ***instalment order***) authorising satisfaction of the amount payable under an enforceable money order of the court by instalment payments by the order debtor.

(2) The court may make an instalment order –

- (a) on application by the enforcement debtor when making the money order; or
- (b) on application by the enforcement debtor or someone else under rule 2013 [to stay an enforcement order] … or rule 2051 … [to set aside an enforcement order]; or
- (c) on application by the enforcement debtor under rule 2151 or the enforcement creditor under rule 2153; or
- (d) on the filing in the court of an instalment order agreement under rule 2157; or
- (e) after hearing an application [to amend, suspend or set aside] under rule 2314; or
- (f) after hearing an application under rule 2360 [to amend, suspend or set aside an earnings redirection order].

…

55 *Absconding Debtors Act 1978* (NT); *Civil Proceedings Act 2011* (Qld) s 100; *Enforcement of Judgments Act 1991* (SA) s 5(7); *Debtors Act 1888* (Tas); *Imprisonment of Fraudulent Debtors Act 1958* (Vic); *Judgment Debt Recovery Act 1984* (Vic) s 19; *Restraint of Debtors Act 1984* (WA).

56 *Civil Procedure Act 2005* (NSW) ss 130, 131. See, eg, *Mahaffy v Mahaffy* [2013] NSWSC 245.

57 *Court Procedures Rules 2006* (ACT) rr 2001, 2500.

58 *Court Procedures Rules 2006* (ACT) rr 2150, 2157; *Uniform Civil Procedure Rules 2005* (NSW) pt 37; *Enforcement of Judgments Act 1991* (SA) s 5; *Judgment Debt Recovery Act 1984* (Vic) s 7.

Reg 2154 Instalment order – relevant considerations

(1) In deciding whether to make an instalment order on application by the enforcement creditor or enforcement debtor, the court must have regard to the following matters, as far as they are known to the court:
  - (a) whether the enforcement debtor is employed;
  - (b) the enforcement debtor's means of satisfying the order debt;
  - (c) whether the order debt, including any interest, will be satisfied within a reasonable time;
  - (d) the necessary living expenses of the enforcement debtor and the enforcement debtor's dependants;
  - (e) other liabilities of the enforcement debtor;
  - (f) if the applicant is the enforcement debtor—whether, having regard to the availability of other enforcement means, making the order would be consistent with the public interest in enforcing orders justly, efficiently and quickly.

(2) Subrule (1) does not limit the matters to which the court may have regard.

(3) In deciding the amount and timing of the instalments, the court must be satisfied that the instalment order will not impose unreasonable hardship on the enforcement debtor or any dependant of the enforcement debtor.

(4) However, an enforcement hearing is not necessary before the court makes the instalment order.

The general trend of the law has been to move away from imprisoning defendants towards enforcement against property. All jurisdictions have mechanisms to achieve this.[59] There are three main mechanisms, as illustrated in Figure 20.3.

Figure 20.3 Ways of enforcing against the property of a judgment debtor

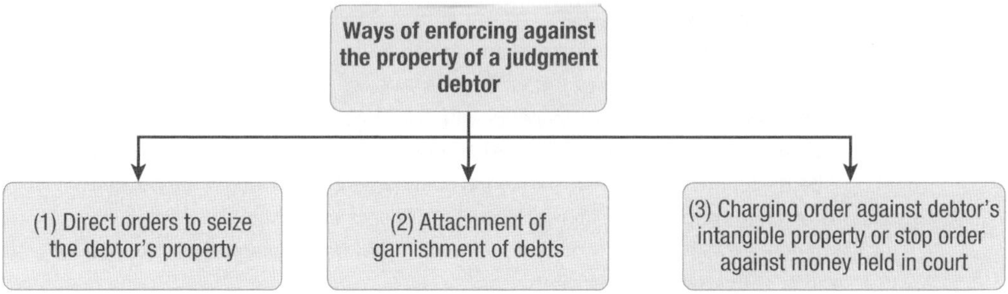

59 *Court Procedures Rules 2006* (ACT) pt 2.18; *Civil Procedure Act 2005* (NSW) pt 8; *Supreme Court Rules 1987* (NT) ords 66–74; *Uniform Civil Procedure Rules 1999* (Qld), ch 19; *Enforcement of Judgments Act 1991* (SA); *Supreme Court Rules 2000* (Tas) pt 35; *Supreme Court (General Civil Procedure) Rules 2015* (Vic) ords 66–74; *Civil Judgments Enforcement Act 2004* (WA).

A direct order of seizure and sale allows the sheriff or court officer to seize almost all types of tangible and intangible property from a judgment debtor sufficient to meet the debt, and to sell it at a public sale. The proceeds of sale are given to the judgment creditor.

Uniform Civil Procedure Rules 1999 (Qld) rr 828–829

Here is an example of a civil procedure rule allowing for a court to order seizure and sale of property to meet a judgment debt.

Reg 828 Seizure of property under enforcement warrant

(1) A court may issue an enforcement warrant authorising an enforcement officer to seize and sell in satisfaction of a money order all real and personal property (other than exempt property) in which the enforcement debtor has a legal or beneficial interest.

...

(2) The registrar must give the enforcement warrant to an enforcement officer to be enforced.

(3) An enforcement officer must –

(a) have the warrant in the enforcement officer's possession when enforcing the warrant; and

(b) show the warrant to any person claiming an interest in the property to be seized.

(4) Actual seizure is not necessary to authorise the sale of real property under an enforcement warrant.

(5) If there is an advertisement of a notice about real property under rule 834, an enforcement officer is taken to have seized the real property for the purposes of these rules.

(6) An enforcement officer must send a copy of the notice by prepaid post to the enforcement debtor at the enforcement debtor's last known address.

Reg 829 Order of selling property

(1) An enforcement officer must seize and sell property –

(a) in the order appearing to the enforcement officer to be best for the prompt enforcement of the warrant without undue expense; and

(b) subject to *paragraph (a)*, in the order appearing to the enforcement officer to be best for minimising hardship to the enforcement debtor and other persons.

(2) However, on the application of an enforcement officer or enforcement creditor, made without notice to an enforcement debtor, the court may order an enforcement officer to seize or sell property in a different order.

(3) An enforcement officer may seize and sell an item of property even though the enforcement officer considers that its value exceeds the amount recoverable, but the enforcement officer must not in that case seize and sell additional items.

There are other provisions setting out how property must be stored, how sales must be occur and so forth.

In some jurisdictions, assets that are essential for life may be exempted from seizure, or the sheriff may choose to seize assets which will impose the least hardship on the debtor.[60] The sheriff has an obligation to get a fair price for the land. In some jurisdictions the market value must be obtained,[61] or the sales procedure must be transparent and fair.[62]

Secondly, a judgment debtor may obtain garnishment and attachment of debts. There must be a judgment for a specific sum of money. Garnishment and attachment is therefore unavailable for judgments for unliquidated damages.[63] First, the creditor obtains a garnishee order *nisi* (*nisi* meaning 'unless'). This orders the third party who owes money to the judgment debtor to pay the money to the judgment creditor or to the court *unless* there is a reason why it should not do so. If there is no reason why the third party should not pay the money, the order is made absolute, and the third party discharges its debt to the judgment debtor. A judgment creditor may seek to garnish the wages of a judgment debtor (so that the wages owing to the judgment debtor are paid to the judgment creditor directly). This is sometimes called an 'attachment of future earnings'.

Uniform Civil Procedure Rules 1999 (Qld) rr 855–856

Here is an example of a civil procedure rule allowing for garnishment of earnings.

Reg 855 General

(1) A court may issue an enforcement warrant authorising redirection to an enforcement creditor of particular earnings of an enforcement debtor from a third person.
Note – The provisions of legislation such as the *Social Security Act 1991* (Cth) contain exemptions for social security payments.

(2) An enforcement warrant redirecting earnings continues in force until
- (a) the total amount specified in the warrant is paid; or
- (b) the warrant is set aside or expires according to its conditions.

Reg 856 Procedure for issue of enforcement warrant redirecting earnings

(1) An enforcement creditor or enforcement debtor may apply to the court for an enforcement warrant authorising the redirection to the enforcement creditor of part of the enforcement debtor's earnings.

(2) Without limiting *subrule (1)*, the application may be made at an enforcement hearing.

60 *Court Procedures Rules 2006* (ACT) rr 2201, 2202; *Uniform Civil Procedure Rules 2005* (NSW) r 39.6(2)(c), (3)(b); *Uniform Civil Procedure Rules 1999* (Qld) r 829(1)(b); *Supreme Court Rules 2000* (Tas) r 906(3)(c); *Civil Judgments Enforcement Regulations 2005* (WA) r 35.

61 *Court Procedures Rules 2006* (ACT) rr 2216(8), 2217; *Uniform Civil Procedure Rules 2005* (NSW) rr 39.7(2), 39.10; *Uniform Civil Procedure Rules 1999* (Qld) r 833; *Supreme Court Civil Rules 2006* (SA) r 320; *Civil Judgments Enforcement Act 2004* (WA) s 66. Cf *Anderson v Liddell* (1968) 117 CLR 36, where a sale for well under the market value was held to be fair.

62 Eg *Court Procedures Rules 2006* (ACT) rr 2218–2221; *Uniform Civil Procedure Rules 2005* (NSW) rr 39.7–39.14. See also *Zhou v Kousal* (2012) 35 VR 419, [124].

63 S Colbran et al, *Civil Procedure: Commentary and Materials* (LexisNexis, 6th ed, 2015) [22.8.3].

(3) In deciding whether to issue an enforcement warrant authorising the redirection to the enforcement creditor of the enforcement debtor's earnings, the court must have regard to the following –
   (a) whether the enforcement debtor is employed and the enforcement debtor's employer has been identified;
   (b) whether the enforcement debtor has sufficient means of satisfying the order after deducting –
      (i) the necessary living expenses of the enforcement debtor and the enforcement debtor's dependants; and
      (ii) any other known liabilities of the enforcement debtor;
   (c) whether the amount of earnings to be redirected would impose unreasonable hardship on the enforcement debtor;
   (d) if the applicant is the enforcement debtor—whether, having regard to the availability of other enforcement means, the issue of the warrant would be consistent with the public interest in enforcing orders efficiently and expeditiously.

In some jurisdictions, a judgment debtor may not be dismissed from employment because of a garnishee order.[64] In other jurisdictions, the judgment debtor must either be able to meet their ordinary living expenses, or must consent to the making of a garnishment order over their wages.[65] At other times, a garnishment order may be refused because the wages are too low[66] or the debt is too small.[67]

In most jurisdictions a judgment debtor may obtain a 'charging order' against intangible property such as stock and shares, or a 'stop order' over money held in court.[68] This is similar to an equitable charge over the assets in question. Like the garnishment procedure, it is a two-stage process involving an initial ex parte application, followed by an order *nisi*. Where stock and shares are concerned, service of the provisional order generally freezes the securities.[69]

---

64 *Court Procedures Rules 2006* (ACT) r 2368; *Magistrates' Court Act 1989* (Vic) s 111(10)–(12); *Enforcement of Judgments Act 1991* (SA) s 6(7).

65 *Enforcement of Judgments Act 1991* (SA) s 6(2).

66 *Uniform Civil Procedure Rules 1999* (Qld) r 856(3).

67 *Uniform Civil Procedure Rules 2005* (NSW) r 39.38(2).

68 *Court Procedures Rules 2006* (ACT) rr 2400–2407, 2420, 2421; *Uniform Civil Procedure Rules 2005* (NSW) rr 39.44–39.45; *Supreme Court Rules 1987* (NT) ords 73–74; *Uniform Civil Procedure Rules 1999* (Qld), ch 19 pts 8–9; *Enforcement of Judgments Act 1991* (SA) s 8; *Supreme Court Rules 2000* (Tas) pt 36 div 1; *Supreme Court (General Civil Procedure) Rules 2015* (Vic) ord 73.

69 *Court Procedures Rules 2006* (ACT) r 2403(1), (2); *Civil Procedure Act 2005* (NSW) s 126; *Supreme Court Rules 1987* (NT) r 73.07; *Uniform Civil Procedure Rules 1999* (Qld) rr 877–878; *Supreme Court Rules 2000* (Tas) r 932(2)(b); *Supreme Court (General Civil Procedure) Rules 2015* (Vic) r 73.07(2).

Uniform Civil Procedure Rules 1999 (Qld) rr 875, 877

The following extract is an example of a civil procedure rule allowing for a court to make a charging order.

Reg 875 Issue of warrant

The court may issue an enforcement warrant imposing a charging order charging all or part of the enforcement debtor's legal or equitable interest in 1 or more of the following –

(a) annuities;
(b) debentures;
(c) stocks;
(d) bonds;
(e) shares;
(f) marketable securities;
(g) interest in a managed investment scheme;
(h) units of—
  (i) shares; or
  (ii) marketable securities.

...

Reg 877 Enforcement debtor dealing with charged property

(1) After being served with an enforcement warrant imposing a charging order, the enforcement debtor must not sell, transfer or otherwise deal with the charged property.

(2) The court may set aside or restrain any sale, transfer or other dealing in contravention of *subrule (1)*, unless to do so would prejudice the rights or interests of a genuine purchaser or chargee without notice.

If the debt sued for is under a credit contract, mortgage or guarantee to which the National Credit Code[70] applies (broadly, a credit contract for personal or investment use rather than commercial use), the judgment debtor under the contract may request postponement of enforcement proceedings or apply to the court for postponement.[71]

If the property cannot be identified or is of an unusual kind, a judgment creditor may seek an equitable order of receivership instead of any of the three procedures above. The receiver obtains the income from the debtor's property and prevents the debtor from using it.[72] It is not used where other procedures are available.

70 *National Consumer Credit Protection Act 2009* (Cth) sch 1.

71 Ibid ss 94–97.

72 S Colbran et al, *Civil Procedure: Commentary and Materials* (LexisNexis, 6th ed, 2015) [22.10.1]–[22.10.3]. See, eg, *Cardile v LED Builders Pty Ltd* (1999) 198 CLR 380.

B Enforcement of specific remedies

Equitable remedies which seek to coerce the defendant into particular behaviour are more likely to be enforced against the person themself. However, they may still be enforced against the property of the person.

In terms of enforcement against property, judgment in relation to property over land can occur in two ways. First, the plaintiff can obtain a writ of possession, according to which the sheriff will enter the land of the defendant and give possession of the land to the plaintiff. This generally occurs where a person has a right to recover possession. For example, if a defendant defaults under a mortgage, the plaintiff will be entitled to recover possession of the land and sell it pursuant to the terms of the mortgage. Secondly, there may be an order for a defendant to give up possession of land (as opposed to a plaintiff recovering possession). This is the second kind of judgment for possession of land. A person is obliged to comply with an order to give up possession. In case of non-compliance, the court will use imprisonment, fines, and sequestration to coerce the defendant into doing so. An order for the delivery up of goods will be enforced in the same way.[73]

In terms of enforcement against the person, if the defendant fails to comply with a coercive order of specific relief, then they have committed contempt of court (sometimes called 'civil contempt' in this context). The breach of the order must be clear and unambiguous, and the order must be capable of being complied with.[74] The defendant must be given time to comply with the order.[75] The standard of proof for establishing contempt of court is beyond reasonable doubt.[76] The court may respond in three different ways: imprisonment, sequestration, or fines to coerce the defendant into complying with its order (see Figure 20.4).

Figure 20.4 Ways of enforcing a coercive remedy against the defendant's person

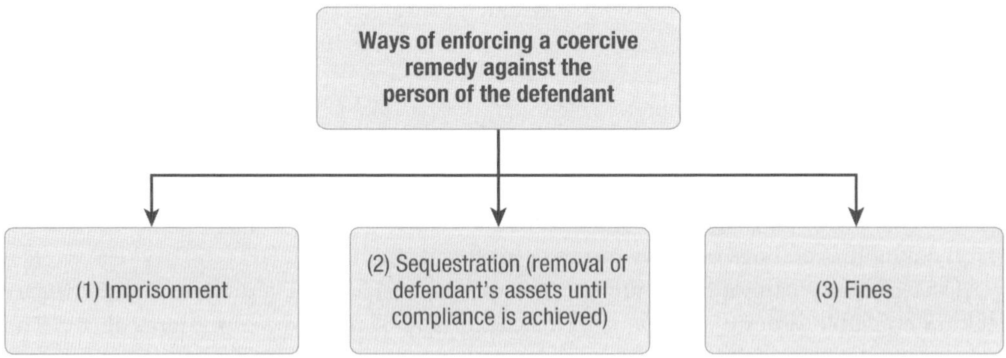

73 *Doulton Potteries Ltd v Bronotte* [1971] 1 NSWLR 591.

74 *Australian Consolidated Press Ltd v Morgan* (1965) 112 CLR 483, 515–16.

75 *High Court Rules 2004* (Cth) r 8.05; *Federal Court Rules 2011* (Cth) r 41.06; *Court Procedures Rules 2006* (ACT) r 2442(1)(b); *Uniform Civil Procedure Rules 2005* (NSW) r 36.5(2); *Supreme Court Rules 1987* (NT) r 66.05; *Uniform Civil Procedure Rules 1999* (Qld) r 904(1)(b); *Supreme Court Civil Rules 2006* (SA) r 225(3); *Supreme Court Rules 2000* (Tas) r 883(1)(b); *Supreme Court (General Civil Procedure) Rules 2015* (Vic) r 66.10; *Rules of the Supreme Court 1971* (WA) ord 42 r 3.

76 *Witham v Holloway* (1995) 183 CLR 525.

As Windeyer J explained in *Australian Consolidated Press Ltd v Morgan*, these measures are not punitive, and:

> *are used primarily to compel obedience rather than to punish disobedience*; for equity acts in personam, and historically the purpose of the processes of the Court of Chancery was to rectify and reform the conscience of the wrongdoer. The jurisdiction was, to use Professor Ashburner's phrase, 'a cathartic jurisdiction'.[77]

Corporations cannot be imprisoned, but a corporation's property may be sequestered,[78] and its officers can be imprisoned if they have been involved in disobedience towards the court's order.[79]

Traditionally, the Court of Chancery could imprison a person in contempt of court for an unfixed period until the defendant 'purged' their contempt. In present day Australia, imprisonment for contempt is usually for a fixed period.[80] It is not lightly ordered. Indeed, the threat of imprisonment associated with non-compliance with an order for specific performance has been given as a reason for specific relief not being more generally available at common law.[81] It highlights the desirability of orders being expressed in a clear manner so that defendants are aware of their precise obligations.[82]

All Australian jurisdictions provide that where a summons has been filed seeking a defendant's committal for contempt of court, and where the person is likely to or has left the jurisdiction, the court may issue a warrant for the defendant's arrest.[83]

REVIEW QUESTIONS

(1) Are you surprised that courts can imprison litigants for a failure to comply with the court's orders? Why/why not?

(2) What do you think of the other responses to a failure to comply with the court's orders (ie fines and sequestration of property)?

---

77 (1965) 112 CLR 483, 498 (emphasis added).

78 *Inland Revenue Commissioners v Hoogstraten* [1985] QB 1077. See *Court Procedures Rules 2006* (ACT) r 2472; *Uniform Civil Procedure Rules 2005* (NSW) r 40.6(2)(c)(ii); *Uniform Civil Procedure Rules 1999* (Qld) r 919; *Supreme Court Rules 2000* (Tas) r 876(3)(c)(ii); *Supreme Court (General Civil Procedure) Rules 2015* (Vic) r 66.05(2)(c)(ii).

79 *Photographic Performance Ltd v Amusement Caterers (Peckham) Ltd* [1964] Ch 195; *Economy Shipping Pty Ltd v ADC Building Pty Ltd* [1971] 1 NSWLR 37.

80 *Court Procedures Rules 2006* (ACT) r 2506; *Supreme Court Rules 1970* (NSW) pt 55 r 13; *Uniform Civil Procedure Rules 1999* (Qld) r 931; *Supreme Court Civil Rules 2006* (SA) r 306; *Supreme Court Rules 2000* (Tas) r 941(2)(d); *Supreme Court (General Civil Procedure) Rules 2015* (Vic) r 75.11(3); *Rules of the Supreme Court 1971* (WA) ord 55 r 7(1). In England, imprisonment for contempt cannot exceed two years: *Contempt of Court Act 1981* (UK) s 14(1).

81 *Cooperative Insurance Society Ltd v Argyll Stores (Holdings) Ltd* [1998] AC 1, 13–14.

82 *Redland Bricks Ltd v Morris* [1970] AC 652, 666.

83 *High Court Rules 2004* (Cth) r 11.02.3; *Federal Court Rules 2011* (Cth) r 42.14; *Court Procedures Rules 2006* (ACT) r 2503; *Supreme Court Rules 1970* (NSW) pt 55 r 10; *Supreme Court Rules 1987* (NT) ord 66 r 75.08; *Uniform Civil Procedure Rules 1999* (Qld) r 927; *Enforcement of Judgments Act 1991* (SA) s 12; *Supreme Court Rules 2000* (Tas) r 942(4); *Supreme Court (General Civil Procedure) Rules 2015* (Vic) rr 75.08, 75.08.1; *Rules of the Supreme Court 1971* (WA) ord 55 r 6.

INDEX

account of profits
  equity and, 534–40
  intellectual property and, 544–5
  stages to, 534
affirmation
  as bar to rescission, 633
aggravated damages, 476
  availability of, 499
    aggravated damages available for some statutory causes of action, 500
    aggravated damages available for the breach of the *Australian Consumer Law*, 502–3
    aggravated damages available for tort, 500
    aggravated damages not available for breach of contract, 500
    aggravated damages not available for equitable wrongdoing, 500–2
  distinction between aggravated damages and exemplary damages, 496–8
Anton Piller orders, 684–5
apologies, 512–15
apportionment, 251–3
assessment of compensation for breach of contract, 174
  compensation for reliance loss, 190–3
  failure to provide other services as promised, 188–90
  impact of *Clark v Macourt*, 190
  measure of expectation loss in particular contexts, 178–9
    failure to build, maintain or repair property as promised, 183–8
    failure to convey land as promised, 182
    failure to deliver goods as promised, 180–2
  non-pecuniary loss. *See* non-pecuniary loss
  protection of the plaintiff's expectation interest, 176–8
assessment of compensation in tort, 205
  general principle, 207–8
  specific contexts
    damage to economic interests by reliance on a misrepresentation, 221–2
    damage to goods, 216–17
    damage to land or fixtures, 210–13
    damage to reputation by defamation, 208–9
    defective premises or goods, 219–21
    other wrongful interference with goods, 217–19
    other wrongful interference with land, 213–15
assessment of compensation under the *Australian Consumer Law*, 298
  attribution of responsibility. *See* attribution of responsibility for compensation under the *Australian Consumer Law*
  certainty of loss and recovery for the loss of a chance, 309
  compensation for misleading or deceptive conduct. *See* compensation for misleading or deceptive conduct
  general principles, 299–300
  non-pecuniary loss, 306–9
assessment of equitable compensation
  basic measure of equitable compensation, 324–7
  object of equitable compensation, 321–2
  recoverability of non-pecuniary loss, 323–4
attribution of responsibility for compensation under the *Australian Consumer Law*, 309
  common sense test of causation, 311
  factual causation, 311–12
  multiple wrongdoers, 319
  scope of liability, 313
    forseeability of the loss, 315
    intervening cause, 313–15
    plaintiff's contribution to the loss, 317–19
    purpose of the provision contravened, 316–17
attribution of responsibility for equitable compensation, 328
  breach of an equitable duty of care, 348–9
  breach of equitable duty of care
    contributory negligence, 352–3
  breach of fiduciary duty, 340
    construction of the hypothetical world, 341–2
    contributory negligence, 346–7
    intervening acts and remoteness of loss, 343–6
    mitigation, 347–8
  breach of trust, 330–1
    independent non-wrongful event, 331–8
    intervening acts and remoteness of loss, 338–40
  scope of liability, 349–52

attribution of responsibility for liability, 88
- causation and. *See* causation

attribution of responsibility for loss, 223
- contributory negligence. *See* contributory negligence
- remoteness of damage. *See* remoteness of damage

Australian Consumer Law
- aggravated damages and, 502–3
- compensation under. *See* compensation under the *Australian Consumer Law*
- disgorgement and, 556
- exemplary damages and, 493
- injunctions under, 422–4
- other vindicatory remedies under, 525–9
- rescission under, 611–12
- specific performance under, 394–5

bars to relief
- affirmation, 633
- discretionary bars to relief, 449
- general equitable bars to relief, 379–83
  - hardship and the public interest, 415–17
  - laches, 419
  - lack of clean hands, 418–19
- relevant only to specific performance, 383–93

betterment discount, 27–31

breach of contract
- aggravated damages not available for breach of contract, 500
- assessment of compensation for. *See* assessment of compensation for breach of contract
- compensation for. *See* compensation for breach of contract
- disgorgement and, 549–56

breach of equitable duty of care
- contributory negligence and, 352–3

breach of fiduciary duty, 340
- construction of the hypothetical world, 341–2
- contributory negligence and, 346–7
- intervening acts and remoteness of loss, 343–6
- mitigation and, 347–8

breach of trust
- attribution of responsibility for equitable compensation for, 330–1
- independent non-wrongful event, 331–8
- intervening acts and remoteness of loss, 338–40

'but for' test, 89, 98–100

causation
- common sense causation in negligence, 92–5
- common sense causation test, 90–2, 311
- duplicative causation, 100–2
- factual causation, 311–12
  - 'but for' test and its application, 89, 98–100
  - causal overdetermination, 100
  - civil liability statutes, 95
  - evidential uncertainty, 104–13
  - overview, 97
- legal concept of, 89–97
- pre-emptive causation, 103
- scope of liability. *See* scope of liability element of causation

clean hands
- lack of, 418–19

common sense causation test, 311

compensation
- assessment of equitable compensation. *See* assessment of equitable compensation
- assessment of under the *Australian Consumer Law*. *See* assessment of compensation under the *Australian Consumer Law*
- attribution of responsibility for equitable compensation. *See* attribution of responsibility for equitable compensation
- benefits flowing from mitigating actions of the plaintiff, 32–7
- certainty of loss and recovery for the loss of a chance, 42
  - balance of probabilities approach, 43
  - consequential loss, 49–51
  - degree of probabilities approach, 43
  - hypothetical conduct of the defendant, 64–8
  - overview of the current law, 43–9
  - personal injury as initial harm, 51–4
  - pure economic loss as initial harm, 54–63
- compensatory principle and the identification of the wrong, 22–4
- interest on compensation awards and compensation for the loss of the use of the money, 83–6
- losses and benefits, 26
  - betterment discount, 27–31
  - cost of repair and diminution in value, 27
  - impact of tax law, 41
  - non-pecuniary loss, 26
  - other benefits arising from the wrong, 37–40
- temporal considerations, 70
  - date of assessment, 71–9
  - determining the present equivalent of future pecuniary loss, 81–3
  - lump sum rule and the 'once and for all' rule, 70–1
  - relevance of inflation, 79–80

compensation for breach of contract, 174
assessment of compensation. *See* assessment of compensation for breach of contract
attribution of responsibility, 196
contributory negligence, 203
remoteness of damage. *See* remoteness of damage
compensation for misleading or deceptive conduct, 301
compensation for expectation loss, 304–5
compensation of reliance loss in excess of expectation loss, 305–6
reliance loss as the general measure of compensation, 301–4
compensation for personal injury and death
actions on death
claim by the dependants of the deceased, 289–95
claim by the estate of the deceased, 289
benefits arising from an injury, 281–4
claims based on injury to another person
loss of an employee's services, 285–6
loss of consortium, 286–7
impact of legislation, 254
civil liability statutes, 256–7
statutory compensation schemes and ancillary regulation of common law damages, 255–6
loss suffered by an injured person. *See* loss suffered by an injured person
meaning of personal injury, 257–8
compensation in tort
assessment of compensation. *See* assessment of compensation in tort
attribution of responsibility. *See* attribution of responsibility for loss
compensation under the *Australian Consumer Law*, 297–8
assessment of. *See* assessment of compensation under the *Australian Consumer Law*
multiple wrongdoers, 319
compensatory awards, 448
compensatory principle, 22
consequential loss, 49–51
contemptuous damages, 523–4
contributory negligence, 244
apportionable loss, 251
apportionment, 251–3
breach of an equitable duty of care and, 352–3
breach of fiduciary duty and, 346–7
civil liability statutes, 247
common law, 244–6
compensation for breach of contract and, 203
contributory negligence statutes, 246–7
factual causation and the scope of the duty, 249–51
plaintiff's conduct, 247–9
Corporations Act 2001 (Cth)
injunctions under, 424–6

damages
aggravated damages. *See* aggravated damages
contemptuous damages, 523–4
equitable damages. *See* Lord Cairns' Act damages
exemplary damages. *See* exemplary damages
Griffiths v Kerkemeyer damages, 265
inadequacy of damages
injunctions, 403–4
specific performance, 358
interlocutory injunctions and, 676
nominal damages, 521–3
reasonable fee damages. *See* reasonable fee damages
vindicatory damages, 476, 504–10
debt
as a species of special relief, 397–9
liquidated damages and penalties and, 474
declarations, 516–21
requirements to establish an entitlement to a declaration, 518
defamation
assessment of compensation for, 208–9
delay
as bar to rescission, 633–5
disgorgement
Australian Consumer Law and, 556
breach of contract, 549–56
election, 540–4
equity and the account of profits, 534–40
intellectual property and the account of profits, 544–5
torts and 'waiver of tort', 545–8
duplicative causation, 100–2

eggshell skull rule, 241–4
enforcement of remedies
interlocutory injunctions. *See* interlocutory injunctions
other pre-judgment remedies, 678
arrest of the person, 678–81
freezing orders, 681–3
search orders, 684–5
post-judgment enforcement, 685
enforcement of specific remedies, 692–3
post-judgment remedies
enforcement of money remedies, 686–91

equitable compensation for equitable wrongs
assessment of equitable compensation. *See* assessment of equitable compensation
attribution of responsibility. *See* attribution of responsibility for equitable compensation
equitable damages.
See Lord Cairns' Act damages
equitable liens, 649–50
exemplary damages, 476
causes of action for award of
exemplary damages available for breach of some statutes, 489
exemplary damages available for tort, 488
exemplary damages not available for breach of contract, 490
exemplary damages not available for breaches of the *Australian Consumer Law*, 493
exemplary damages not available for equitable wrongdoing, 490–3
distinction between aggravated damages and exemplary damages, 496–8
nature and history of in Australia, 480–4
calculation of exemplary damages, 486–8
need to make out the 'host' cause of action, 484–6
unavailable if criminal punishment already imposed, 486

factors influencing the exercise of the jurisdiction of Lord Cairns' Act damages
basis of assessment
compensatory awards, 448
timing, 446
basis of relief
reasonable fee awards, 446–8
Corporations Act 2001 (Cth) pt 9.5, 449–50
discretionary bars to relief, 449
general principles, 436
provide a 'middle ground' solution between no relief and specific relief, 436–8
provide novel forms of relief, 438–41
provide relief for future losses, 438
specific relief no longer available or in addition to specific relief, 436
Shelfer criteria, 441–2
factual causation, 311–12
'but for' test and its application, 89, 98–100
causal overdetermination, 100
duplicative causation, 100–2
pre-emptive causation, 103
civil liability statutes, 95
contributory negligence and, 249–51
evidential uncertainty, 104
inference of factual causation, 104–5
material contribution to the harm, 106–9
material increase in risk, 110–13
overview, 97
fusion fallacy, 12
future pecuniary loss
determining the present equivalent of, 81–3

garnishee order *nisi*, 689, 690
goods
compensation for damage to, 216–17
compensation for failure to deliver as promised, 180–2
compensation for wrongful interference with, 217–19
injury to property rights in, 406–7
specific performance and contracts involving goods, 362–5
Griffiths v Kerkemeyer damages, 265

Hadley v Baxendale test, 199

inflation
relevance of in compensation, 79–80
initial harm
personal injury as, 51–4
pure economic loss as, 54–63
injunctions, 400
bars to injunctions equivalent to those in specific performance, 419
general equitable bars to relief
hardship and the public interest, 415–17
laches, 419
lack of clean hands, 418–19
inadequacy of damages, 403–4
injunctions under statute, 420–1
Australian Consumer Law, 422–4
Corporations Act 2001 (Cth), 424–6
intellectual property, 421–2
other statutory injunctions, 426
interim interlocutory injunctions under statute, 676–7
interlocutory injunctions. *See* interlocutory injunctions
quia timet injunctions, 413, 430
relationship between specific performance, 357
rights protected by injunctions
contracts for services, 412–13
injunctions restraining a breach of negative covenant in a contract, 411–12
injury to bodily integrity, 408–9
injury to economic rights, 407–8
injury to intellectual property, 407
injury to privacy, 410–11

injunctions (*cont.*)
injury to property rights in goods and funds of money, 406–7
injury to property rights in land, 404–5
injury to reputation, 409–10
intellectual property
account of profits and, 544–5
injunctions and, 407
injunctions under statute, 421–2
reasonable fee damages, 562
specific performance and, 370–1
specific performance and contracts involving intellectual property, 370–1
interlocutory injunctions, 667
balance of convenience, 673
interim injunctions under statute, 676–7
interlocutory injunctions which finally determine the matter, 674–5
legal, equitable or statutory rights, 667–9
mandatory interlocutory injunctions, 674
quia timet interlocutory injunctions, 674
'serious question to be tried', 669–72
steps to establish an interlocutory injunction, 667
undertakings as to damages, 676

joint tortfeasors
as multiple wrongdoers, 151
distinction between multiple tortfeasors, 156
liability at common law, 150

laches, 419
land
compensation for damage to, 359–62
compensation for failure to convey as promised, 182
compensation for wrongful interference with, 213–15
injury to property rights in, 404–5
specific performance and contracts involving land, 359–62
liquidated damages and penalties, 465
debt and, 474
does penalty doctrine apply to clause, 466–9
is clause a penalty on the facts, 469–74
other stipulated contractual remedies, 475
Lord Cairns' Act damages
advantages of for a plaintiff, 430
factors influencing the exercise of the jurisdiction of. *See* factors influencing the exercise of the jurisdiction of Lord Cairns' Act damages
for statutory wrongdoing, 434–5
future of, 450–1
history, 429
jurisdiction to award, 430–1
need for a 'wrongful act' in some Australian jurisdictions, 431
Australian legislation mentioning 'wrongful act', 432
Australian legislation not mentioning 'wrongful act', 432–4
loss suffered by an injured person
medical expenses and cost of institutional care, 261–3
non-pecuniary loss, 275
loss of amenities, 277–8
loss of expectation of life, 278–9
pain and suffering, 275–6
statutory regulation, 279–80
overlap between different heads of loss, 281
pecuniary loss resulting from needs created by the injury, 261
cost of managing a lump sum award, 266–7
domestic services to the injured person, 263–5
increased cost of living at home, 266
pecuniary loss resulting from the impairment of capacities, 267
loss of capacity to do domestic work, 272–4
loss of earning capacity, 268–9
loss of employment-related benefits, 270–2
loss of social security benefits, 272

Mareva orders, 681–3
misleading or deceptive conduct
compensation for. *See* compensation for misleading or deceptive conduct
mitigation, 90, 138–47
breach of fiduciary duty and, 347–8
three rules of, 138
multiple wrongdoers, 148
as joint tortfeasors, 151
attribution of responsibility for compensation under the *Australian Consumer Law* and, 319
common law rules, 149–60
contribution claims in equity, 158
contribution statutes, 160–5
interprlay of the three regimes, 171
proportionate liability statutes, 165–70
several concurrent wrongdoers at common law, 154

nemo dat quod non habet, 624
nominal damages, 521–3
non-pecuniary loss, 26, 193
assessment of under the *Australian Consumer Law*, 306–9
recoverability of, 323–4

restrictions at common law, 193–5
restrictions under statute, 195–6
novus actus interveniens, 90, 115
nuisance
abatement of, 462–3

once and for all rule, 70–1

personal injury
as initial harm, 51–4
compensation for. *See* compensation for personal injury and death
meaning of, 257–8
pre-emptive causation, 103
privacy
injury to, 410–11
property
compensation for failure to build, maintain or repair as promised, 183–8
self-defence of, 456–8
proprietary remedies, 643
constructive and resulting trusts, 643–8
criteria for award of, 650
proprietary remedies and unconscionability, 651
discretionary factors and bars to relief, 663–4
equitable liens, 649–50
need for more defined criteria, 664
proprietary powers, 648–9
proprietary remedies and perfection, 651–2
proprietary remedies and unjust enrichment, 652–7
proprietary remedies and wrongdoing, 657–63
pure economic loss
as initial harm, 54–63

quantum meruit, 590, 607
quantum valebat, 592
quia timet injunctions, 413, 430
quia timet interlocutory injunctions, 674

reasonable contemplation test, 239–41
reasonable fee awards, 446–8, 532
introduction and history, 559
reasonable fee damages, 18
academic and judicial accounts, 559
compensatory analyses, 559–60
restitutionary analyses, 560–1
allowances for skill and effort, 581–4
contract, 570–9
discretionary factors and bars to relief, 584
equity, 562
future of, 584
general patterns, 561–2
intellectual property, 562
tort, 563–9
reliance loss
assessment of compensation for, 190–3
remedies
common law and equity divide in Australia, 90–2
fusion of some areas of common law and equitable remedies, 15–18
common law and equity division in Australia
alternative taxonomy of rights and remedies, 13–14
definition, 1–5
distinction between primary and secondary rights, 5–6
dualism view, 9–10
judicial commands and orders and, 6–7
middle ground between monism and dualism, 10–11
monism view, 7–9
enforcement of. *See* enforcement of remedies
functional approach to, 18
proprietary remedies. *See* proprietary remedies
restitutionary remedies, 586
for subtractive unjust enrichment. *See* unjust enrichment
self-help remedies. *See* self-help remedies
vindicatory remedies under the *Australian Consumer Law*, 525–9
remoteness, 90
remoteness of damage, 197–8, 226
assumption of responsibility as overriding criteria, 201–3
eggshell skull rule, 241–4
Hadley v Baxendale test, 199
significance of the defendant's knowledge of the plaintiff's circumstances, 200–1
test of natural and probable consequences, 226–8
test of reasonable forseeability, 228–39
remoteness of damages
test of reasonable contemplation, 239–41
repair
cost of and diminution in value, 27
reputation
injury to, 409–10
rescission, 465
bars to rescission, 630
affirmation, 633
delay, 633–5
executed contracts and innocent misrepresentation, 639
impossibility to complete restoration, 631–3
intervening third party rights, 636–9

rescission (*cont.*)
  election, 619
    consequences of an election to rescind, 623–6
    how to make an election to rescind, 620–3
    reasons behind the election to rescind, 626
  equitable rescission, 611
  legal rescission, 611
  'partial' rescission, 627–30
  requirement of *restitutio in integrum*, 612–19
  rescission under the *Australian Consumer Law*, 611–12
restitutio in integrum, 592, 636
  as requirement of rescission, 612–19
  complete *restitutio in integrum*, 611
  substantial *restitutio in integrum*, 611, 613, 614, 615
restitution, 330
  for unjust enrichment, 533

scope of liability element of causation, 90, 113
  plaintiff's contribution to the loss, 137
    contributory negligence, 137–8
    mitigation, 138–47
  purpose of the duty breached, 135–7
  remoteness of damage, 134–5
  subsequent event
    additional loss intervening events, 115–24
    basic loss casually dependent subsequent event, 133–4
    basic loss casually independent subsequent event, 124–33
    distinction between basic and additional loss, 115
self-help remedies
  contract and self-help
    liquidated damages and penalties. *See* liquidated damages and penalties
    rescission, 465
  tort and self-help, 454
    abatement of nuisance, 462–3
    eviction of trespassers, 456
    recaption, replevin and specific restitution, 459–61
    self-defence of property, 456–8
    self-defence of the person, 458–9
specific performance
  debt as a species of special relief, 397–9
  discretionary factors and bars to relief, 377
    bars to relief relevant only to specific performance, 383–93
    general equitable bars to relief, 379–83
  inadequacy of damages, 358
  nature of, 356
  other requirements for specific performance, 372
    binding contract, 372–6
    personal remedy, 372
  relationship between specific performance and injunctions, 357
  specific restitution or specific delivery of property, 395–7
  subject matter of contract, 359
    contracts for services, 371
    contracts for the benefit of third parties, 368–70
    contracts involving goods, 362–5
    contracts involving intellectual property, 370–1
    contracts involving land, 359–62
    contracts involving shares and stock, 365–7
    contracts to loan money, 367
  under the *Australian Consumer Law*, 394–5

tax law
  compensation and, 41
test of common sense causation, 90–2
test of natural and probable consequences, 226–8
test of reasonable contemplation, 239–41
test of reasonable forseeability, 228–39
tort
  aggravated damages available for, 500
  assessment of compensation in tort. *See* assessment of compensation in tort
  compensation in. *See* compensation in tort
  reasonable fee damages and, 563–9
  and self-help, 454
    abatement of nuisance, 462–3
    eviction of trespassers, 456
    recaption, replevin and specific restitution, 459–61
    self-defence of property, 456–8
    self-defence of the person, 458–9
torts
  'waiver of tort', 545–8
trespassers
  eviction of, 456

unjust enrichment
  defences to a claim for restitution, 592
    change of position defence, 592
  elements of, 587
  precise remedies for, 587
    goods claims, 592
    services claims, 590–2
  precise rememdies for
    money claims, 588–9

proprietary remedies and, 652–7
relationship between contract and restitution for unjust enrichment, 593–607
restitution for, 533

vindicatory damages, 476, 504–10

wrongdoers
multiple wrongdoers. *See* multiple wrongdoers

wrongdoing
aggravated damages not available for equitable wrongdoing, 500–2
Lord Cairns' Act damages for statutory wrongdoing, 434–5
proprietary remedies and, 657–63
wrongs
equitable compensation for. *See* equitable compensation for equitable wrongs